BIOGRAPHICAL DICTIONARY OF INTERNATIONALISTS

BIOGRAPHICAL DICTIONARY OF INTERNATIONALISTS

Edited by WARREN F. KUEHL

GREENWOOD PRESS

WESTPORT, CONNECTICUT
LONDON, ENGLAND

Library of Congress Cataloging in Publication Data
Main entry under title:

Biographical dictionary of internationalists.

    Bibliography: p.
    Includes index.
    1. Internationalists—Biography. I. Kuehl, Warren F.,
1924–
JC361.B56   1983   327.1'7'0922 [B]   82-15416
ISBN 0-313-22129-4 (lib. bdg.)

Library of Congress Catalog Card Number: 82-15416
ISBN: 0-313-22129-4

First published in 1983

Greenwood Press
A division of Congressional Information Service, Inc.
88 Post Road West
Westport, Connecticut 06881

Printed in the United States of America

10 9 8 7 6 5 4 3 2 1

For Their Unstinting
Assistance over the Past
Decade, This Book Is Dedicated to
Helen Frustaci
Pamela Logadich
Susan Shah

CONTENTS

PREFACE

This volume began with the simple idea that a biographical reference directory of internationalists was needed. As the book proceeded, its importance became increasingly evident. It would define the contours of internationalism, provide perspective on the wide variety of approaches and ideas, and offer information on a large number of people who do not appear in standard biographical sources or whose efforts and views as internationalists are slighted in such works. Readers will discover not only prominent activists but also a host of visionaries who sought in their particular ways to translate their dream into reality. Among these are obscure pioneers who explored an idea long before it became commonplace.

What is an internationalist? The concept of organizing the world has taken many forms, and a biographical approach provides ample opportunity to explore them all. The very word *international*, which Jeremy Bentham coined in 1770, reflects the nation-state system, whose evolution began much earlier. The idea of distinct political entities, representing different cultures but related through formal bodies such as a League of Nations or world court, has remained at the core of political internationalist thought. Those seeking to harmonize and reform the nation-state system through universal leagues or courts assume they can do so with the consent of governments. In addition to this worldwide orientation, regional organizations have found their advocates in Europe, the Americas, the Middle East and Africa and Asia. Exponents of more integrated systems in the form of federations or world governments, advanced court systems, collective security arrangements, and networks to resolve disputes peacefully through arbitration, mediation, and conciliation acknowledge the reality of existing nations and seek, in Bentham's term, merely to improve conditions between states.

In contrast, other individuals seek to diminish or transcend nation-states. Such persons are usually described as internationalists even though they operate from a different set of value assumptions. They hope to heighten an awareness of human unity, of spaceship earth. These transnational or community thinkers, with their beliefs in universal brotherhood and world citizenship, frequently propound cultural, intellectual, and economic programs of cooperation that extend beyond or even ignore national boundaries. At various times their goals have seemed distant and idealistic, although their means to reach them can be quite specific and immediate.

Between these two positions one finds an array of notions that can be placed in either camp according to the approaches advanced. International labor movements, for example, have followed the political route through the International Labor Organization, while Socialists have long proclaimed the brotherhood of the worker. Labor unions may operate within the ILO or on a transnational level. The same applies to persons and groups concerned with human rights, health, social problems, intellectual exchange, humanitarian concerns, and business and banking. Indeed, debates over whether corporate enterprises are multinational, transnational, or global reflect such conceptual differences.

Additional problems appear in the way scholars have discussed internationalism and internationalists. Without ground rules, a diverse terminology has appeared, both helpful and confusing. Two of the most useful terms, *community* and *polity* (political), were applied by Sondra Herman. Others have formalized through common use such words as *legalist* and *sanctionist*.[1] The former refers to those who support judicial systems based on principles of international law, while the latter encompasses collective security advocates or those who would imbue their agencies with military and/or economic power. Less satisfying are the words *federalist* and *federationist* because the thinking of persons who fit these categories has ranged from a loose confederation of states to a world government. It was impossible to avoid these terms because contemporaries used them, but readers should be aware that they can have many meanings according to time, organization, programs, concepts, and individuals. Legalists, sanctionists, federalists, and federationists all fall within the polity camp.

The term *liberal internationalist* is also troublesome. It is generally used to describe someone with faith in the ability of a people to change conditions and achieve a stable world based on cooperation rather than force. Since it also embodies a reliance on democratic processes, internationalists with this perspective usually hope that world agencies will be able to correct inequities and extend political democracy. Liberal internationalists seem to be those who attempt to extend the principles of domestic liberalism to the world scene. But the analyses of such individuals raise two conceptual issues. Liberalism has different shades of meaning in various nations and epochs. Also, some authors identify liberal internationalists with Wilsonianism, a term which has been the subject of differing interpretations. The effort to make the world safe for democracy, however sincerely undertaken, has become difficult to distinguish from the attempt to extend the influence of the free market/capitalist/open door system. Some authors have thus lent to Wilsonianism an aura of moral arrogance. Because of its range and diversity, the term *liberal internationalist* has generally been avoided in this volume, except as discussed within the context of a time and place. *Wilsonianism* was impossible to delete; hence, readers must be forewarned to be sensitive to its varied meanings.

Given the range of perspective and definitions, the process of deciding who should be included in a biographical dictionary of internationalists proved challenging. It was decided to have representation from all camps, but certain standards had to be developed. In this selection process, effort was made to have representative figures who:

(A) held important or leadership positions in national or international nongovernmental societies or associations to promote the concept of world organization or cooperation and who played active rather than honorary or minor roles;

(B) held important posts in functional international bodies—courts, bureaus, organizations, commissions, and agencies—and whose roles were those of leadership, significant administrative responsibility, or constructive effort in contrast to general participation as delegates or members;

(C) gained public recognition as originators or exponents of ideas, plans, schemes, or proposals through lectures, writings, or other public effort or who advanced the creation of international bodies by contributing to study or planning groups or commissions;

(D) consistently represented by their lifestyle, attitudes, and beliefs an international community idea of transnational cooperation;

(E) sought actively to promote transnationalism in nonpolitical areas, including economics, business, trade, education, religion, and humanitarian, social, legal, and other international nongovernmental organizations, again, with a positive commitment evident through action, interest, or effort to move beyond national lines.

Activity in more than one of these categories made a person eligible even though the role in a single one may not have been dominant.

Effort was also made to have representative figures from many countries, not an easy task. Internationalist thought flourished in democratic environments; hence, more activity took place in the United States and Great Britain, and the list of subjects reflects this fact. After 1914, leaders became more evident in Europe, Asia, and Latin America. Areas with commonwealth or colonial status saw an emergence of international interest only after they attained a degree of autonomy. The inclusion of only deceased persons eliminated many figures of recent activity from such regions. It also gives the volume a historical dimension because most persons involved in activities since 1945 are still living. An arbitrary decision was also reached to include only individuals alive after 1800. This was done on the assumption that considerable scholarly work exists on the earliest advocates and thinkers.[2]

The list of names began with the editor's files, representing nearly thirty years of research on the history of internationalism, primarily on the period prior to 1945. In addition, an obituary file from the *New York Times* has been maintained since 1958, and volumes of *Obituaries of the Times*, 1950–75, were searched. An initial list of over 1,500 persons emerged, which was checked against published sources to decide on importance. The cards were reviewed by members of the team of editors of a companion

Biographical Dictionary of Modern Peace Leaders, and names, arranged by country, were then examined by other scholars who proposed additions and deletions. Finally, as assignments were made, authors suggested subjects for inclusion or concluded that some individuals did not merit treatment. Despite this elaborate process, the editor assumes full responsibility for any shortcomings of omission.

Some comment should still be made on persons not included who are often associated with an international position or perspective. Leaders of worldwide religious bodies and missionaries do not appear unless they had an ecumenical or special perspective. Persons who spent much of their life in the international arena as colonial administrators, civil servants, diplomats, journalists, scientists, bankers, traders, business leaders, international lawyers, and literary, artistic, and sports figures are not listed unless they clearly related their work to promoting internationalism. Likewise, Socialists and Communists who have proclaimed the virtues of oneness are listed only when their internationalism proved to be based on more than party loyalties. Displaced nationals often become world citizens but still retain their state loyalties as the dominant characteristic of their thinking. They are not included.

In the companion volume of peace leaders other persons concerned with the world will appear. Their focus, however, is usually distinctive from that of the individuals listed as internationalists. The latter often had peace as an end goal, but they did not see it as a paramount objective. Most internationalists believed that the solution to war lay in some type of rethinking related to global awareness, structure, or planning, or to a practical application of theory to problems. Peace workers, while not unsympathetic to such approaches, usually attacked the problem more directly, seeking changes in hearts and minds and focusing on plans to alter basic attitudes. Admittedly, there can be no clear-cut distinctions; hence, one will find a considerable number of cross-references in both volumes to persons in the other book. The general rule followed by the editors was to ask where the subject might prefer to be listed and, if doubt arose, to follow the recommendation of the author of the sketch. Cross-references appear both in major name entries and internally within essays by a symbol. A "+" prior to a person's name indicates an entry in the *Biographical Dictionary of Modern Peace Leaders*; an "*" denotes an essay in the *Biographical Dictionary of Internationalists*.

Each entry follows a set format. An introductory section provides basic information on birth, death, education, and career. All details about each individual's life are not included on the assumption that these can be found in other biographical sources. This is particularly true of titles, honorary degrees, and standard family data regarding wives and children. The authors and the editor have made every effort to provide full information for the pertinent headings, but records do not always contain even dates and places of birth and death. This is especially true for non-U.S. figures because formal record keeping in many countries has not been standardized. Likewise, outside of Canada and the United States, universities are less formal in specifying the name of degrees or even the dates they were awarded. In a few instances, contradictory data on birth and place exist. In such cases, the authors have gone to considerable effort to verify that the facts they provided are the most reliable.

The central part of each sketch concentrates on the subject's work, thought, or activity as an internationalist. Again, other aspects of his or her career are generally available elsewhere. Authors were asked not only to describe the person's involvement but also to interpret, where possible, what motivated the individual and what unique or special features marked his or her efforts.

A bibliography section is divided into three parts. Part A includes works by the subject. No attempt has been made to provide a full list of all writings. The items recorded focus on the international perspective of each author. Part B includes works about the subject or his or her activities in the international sphere plus major biographical sketches and obituary notices. In both A and B, entries are in alphabetical order. A list of abbreviations used can be found in the front of the book. Part C notes the location of personal manuscript collections of the subjects. These are recorded only where they exist in publicly available locations. Papers yet in private or family hands have not been recorded.

A number of appendices have been included to enhance this volume's usefulness as a reference tool. These provide information on the place of birth of each subject, on their major career, and on types of internationalists and a chronology of major events.

While there is considerable emphasis upon this study's utility, it also contains human interest features. There are father–son combinations (Stephen and Laurence Duggan; Hamilton and George C. Holt) husband–wife teams (Edwin D. and Lucia Ames Mead; Hamilton and Elizabeth Wright), and brothers (Nelson and John D. Rockefeller, 3d and Edgar and Paul Mowrer).

Proper acknowledgment must be given in such a cooperative venture to the community of scholars. This volume proves it is real. It is their work, and they are to be thanked for their suggestions, advice, and participation and for the quality of their contributions. Special help came from Calvin D. Davis, Martin D. Dubin, George W. Egerton, Harold Josephson, Richard W. Leopold, David S. Patterson, Solomon Wank, and Swen Welander. Readers will perceive that this book, devoted to internationalists, is in itself an international project, as the list of authors reveals. The network created has resulted in a Society for the Study of Internationalism to maintain contacts and pursue new projects. The History Department and the Center for Peace Studies of the University of Akron provided a supportive environment, and the task would have been impossible without the assistance of

Susan Shah. Her logistical organization and efficient command kept the process moving smoothly. In typing, Dorothy Richards accepted considerable responsibility along with Peg Rexroad, and student assistants Lynette Jefferson, Jeanne Kramer, and Peggy Draine also helped in preparing the manuscript. I am also grateful to Nancy Ferguson and Adulyasak Soonthornrojana for their research help.

Warren F. Kuehl

NOTES

1. Sondra R. Herman, *Eleven Against War: Studies in American Internationalist Thought, 1898-1921* (Stanford, CA, 1969); Warren F. Kuehl, *Seeking World Order: The United States and International Organization to 1920* (Nashville, TN, 1969); and David S. Patterson, *Toward a Warless World: The Travail of the American Peace Movement, 1887-1914* (Bloomington, IN, 1976. A useful dialogue appears in "Internationalism as a Current in the Peace Movement: A Symposium," in *Peace Movements in America*, ed. Charles Chatfield (New York, 1973).

2. Sylvester J. Hemleben, *Plans for World Peace Through Six Centuries* (Chicago, 1943); Elizabeth V. Souleyman, *The Vision of World Peace in Seventeenth and Eighteenth-Century France* (New York, 1941); Elizabeth York, *League of Nations: Ancient, Mediaeval, and Modern* (London, 1919).

ABBREVIATIONS

ABBREVIATIONS FOR FREQUENTLY CITED REFERENCE SOURCES

AHR	*American Historical Review*
AJIL	*American Journal of International Law*
BDAC	*Biographical Directory of the American Congress*
BDUSEB	*Biographical Directory of the United States Executive Branch*
CA	*Contemporary Authors*
CB	*Current Biography*
CWW	*Canadian Who's Who*
DLB	*Dictionary of Labour Biography*
DNB	*Dictionary of National Biography*
DAB	*Dictionary of American Biography*
ICJ Yearbook	*International Court of Justice Yearbook*
IWW	*International Who's Who*
IWWW	*International World Who's Who*
IY	*International Yearbook and Statesmen's Who's Who*
LT	London *Times*
NAW	*Notable American Women*
NCAB	*National Cyclopedia of American Biography*
NYT	*New York Times*
PS	*American Political Science Association Quarterly*
WB	*World Biography*
WW	*Who's Who*
WWA	*Who's Who in America*
WWAJ	*Who's Who in American Jewry*
WWB	*Who's Who in Belgium*
WWBL	*Who's Who in Belgium and Luxemburg*
WWC	*Who's Who in Canada*
WWF	*Who's Who in France*
WWG	*Who's Who in Germany*
WWLA	*Who's Who in Latin America*
WWS	*Who's Who in Spain*
WWUN	*Who's Who in the UN*
WWW	*Who Was Who*
WWWorld	*Who's Who in the World*
WWWA	*Who Was Who in America*
WWWNAA	*Who Was Who Among North American Authors*

OTHER ABBREVIATIONS

UNITED STATES

AL	Alabama
AK	Alaska
AZ	Arizona
AR	Arkansas
CA	California
CO	Colorado
CT	Connecticut
DE	Delaware
FL	Florida
GA	Georgia
HI	Hawaii
ID	Idaho
IL	Illinois
IN	Indiana
IA	Iowa
KS	Kansas
KY	Kentucky
LA	Louisiana
ME	Maine
MD	Maryland
MA	Massachusetts
MI	Michigan
MN	Minnesota
MS	Mississippi
MO	Missouri
MT	Montana
NE	Nebraska
NV	Nevada
NH	New Hampshire
NJ	New Jersey
NM	New Mexico
NY	New York
NC	North Carolina
ND	North Dakota
n.d.	no date
n.p.	no publisher
n.s.	new series
OH	Ohio
OK	Oklahoma
OR	Oregon
PA	Pennsylvania
RI	Rhode Island
SC	South Carolina
SD	South Dakota
TN	Tennessee
TX	Texas
UT	Utah
VT	Vermont
VA	Virginia
WA	Washington
WV	West Virginia
WY	Wyoming

CANADA

AB	Alberta
BC	British Columbia
LB	Labrador
MB	Manitoba
NB	New Brunswick
NF	Newfoundland
NT	Northwest Territories
NS	Nova Scotia
ON	Ontario
PE	Prince Edward Island
PQ	Quebec
SK	Saskatchewan
YT	Yukon Territory

BIOGRAPHICAL DICTIONARY OF INTERNATIONALISTS

A

ABBOTT, Grace (17 November 1878, Grand Island, NB—19 June 1939, Chicago). *Education*: Ph.B., Grand Island Coll., 1898; attended Univ. of Nebraska, 1902–3; M.A., Univ. of Chicago, 1909. *Career*: taught at Grand Island High School, 1899–1907; director, Immigrants' Protective League, 1908–17; director, Massachusetts Immigration Commission, 1914; director, Illinois State Immigrants Commission, 1919–21; chief, Children's Bureau, 1921–34; professor, Univ. of Chicago, 1934–39.

Abbott credited her internationalism to the Garrisonian vision that "our countrymen are all mankind." She felt grateful that immigration had given an opportunity to the United States for world service. As director of the Immigrants' Protective League and resident of Hull House in Chicago, she appreciated the contributions of immigrant communities to American culture and discouraged them from abandoning ethnic traditions in order to assimilate. As a pacifist she feared the resurgence of a virulent "jingoist" nationalism. She knew firsthand how tragically World War I affected immigrants, many of whom had relatives in the warring countries of Europe. She suggested that the immigrant was a more important bond with Europe than commerce and recognized that the days of American isolationism were past. Her concern for the welfare of immigrants and children, as well as her commitment to peace, transcended national boundaries. She participated at the 1915 Women's Congress at The Hague, which led to the Women's International League for Peace and Freedom 1915. She organized the Conference of Oppressed and Dependent Nationalities, which examined U.S. international policy regarding "submerged nationalities." She also planned the International Child Welfare Conference (1918), represented the Children's Bureau in organizing the First International Labor Conference in London (1919); and served as secretary of the Children's Committee of the International Labor Conference in Washington (1919). League of Nations humanitarian work naturally attracted her attention, and she is credited as being the first unofficial U.S. observer designated by the State Department to participate in an "advisory and consultative capacity" with League organizations. In this role, Abbott attended the sessions of the Permanent Advisory Committee on the Traffic in Women and Children (1923), and in 1925 she became a member of the Sub-Committee on Immigration and on Protection of Children. Thereafter, she periodically worked with League bodies, and in 1935 and 1937 she represented the United States officially as a delegate to the International Labor Organization.

BIBLIOGRAPHY:

A. "The Immigrant and American Internationalism," in *The Immigrant and the Community* (New York, 1917).

3

B. Edith Abbott, "Grace Abbott: A Sister's Memories," *Social Service Review* 13 (Sep 1939), 351–407, "Grace Abbott and Hull House," *Social Service Review* 24 (Sep and Dec, 1950), 374–94, 493–518; Helen Cody Baker, "The Abbotts of Nebraska," *Survey Graphic* 25 (Jun 1936), 370–72; DAB supp. 2, 1–2; E. O. Lundberg, "Pathfinders of the Middle Years," *Social Service Review* 21 (Mar 1947), 22–25, NAW 2, 4; NCAB C, 25; H. R. Wright, "Three Against Time: Edith and Grace Abbott and Sophonisba P. Breckinridge," *Social Service Review* 28 (Mar 1954), 41–53. WWWA 1, 2–3.

C. The Abbott papers are in the Univ. of Chicago Library.

Christine C. Kleinegger

ADACHI [ADATCI] Mineichiro (1869, Yamagata, Japan—28 December 1934, Amsterdam). *Education*: graduate, faculty of law, Imperial Univ. of Tokyo, 1892, doctor of law, 1912. *Career*: entered Ministry of Foreign Affairs, 1892; interpreter, Portsmouth Peace Conference; counselor, Paris, 1908–13; minister to Mexico, 1913–15; minister and ambassador to Belgium, 1917–28; member, Japanese delegation at Paris Peace Conference, 1919; member, Japanese delegation, League of Nations, 1919–30; ambassador to France, 1928–30; judge, Permanent Court of International Justice, 1930–34, chief justice, 1931–33.

Adachi's life spanned the entire length of modern Japanese foreign affairs, from the beginning of the Meiji era when the country broke its isolationist tradition to the 1930s when it once again isolated itself from the international community through aggressive expansion in Asia. One continuing theme of Japanese foreign policy during these sixty-odd years was the struggle between particularists on the one hand and internationalists on the other. The former stressed self-centered diplomacy to achieve national security and interests, while the latter were more sensitive to international trends and eager to have their nation play a role in pursuit of transnational objectives. Adachi was one of the small group of men who represented this latter orientation.

Adachi's reputation as an internationalist stems from his activities after 1919. He attended the Paris Peace Conference as a member of the Japanese delegation, serving as head of Japan's specialists' group. After the establishment of the League, he attended almost all its meetings, sometimes serving as chairman of various committees. His skills as a parliamentarian, knowledge of international law, and commitment to the principles of the League were widely recognized. For instance, in 1924 he chaired the League's special subcommittee to study a new protocol for the peaceful resolution of disputes. He faced conflicting pressure, coming, on one side, from pacifists and disarmament advocates and, on the other, from the particularistic orientations of various governments. Adachi also felt limited because his government did not support the protocol, in its original form, which attempted to define aggression. He did his best to have the subcommittee adopt the protocol with the understanding that the League must be involved in all disputes if any country was to be branded an aggressor; in cases where the League abdicated its responsibility, such as conflicts arising out of domestic questions (e.g., immigration policy), it would have no authority to designate the aggressor.

Throughout his term at the League, Adachi seems to have impressed his foreign colleagues as a conscientious and fair-minded man. In 1928, when he was rapporteur for all minority questions discussed at the League, he worked patiently for solutions that the German and Polish representatives were prepared to accept. He was noted for his profound learning and sharp mind. He seems to have commanded the genuine respect of his fellow internationalists. Such esteem led to his selection as a judge on the Permanent Court of International Justice in 1930 and his election as its president in 1931. Had he remained at the League, he might have acted to check his country's military extremism after the Manchurian invasion of 1931. When Japan withdrew from the League in 1933, the government decided he could remain at his post but that he would not be replaced. Adachi felt compelled on 2 December, 1933, to resign as president of the Court while retaining his seat. Thus his death in 1934 put an end to the prewar phase of Japanese internationalism. The Dutch government, in recognition of his services, conducted a state funeral in his honor.

BIBLIOGRAPHY:

B. *Biographical Dictionary of Japanese History* (Tokyo, 1978), 314; NYT 29 Dec 1934, 15; Frank P. Walters, *A History of the League of Nations* (London, 1952).

Akira Iriye

ADAMS, Herbert Baxter (16 April 1850, Shutesbury, MA—30 July 1901, Amherst, MA). *Education*: B.A., Amherst Coll., 1872; Ph.D., Heidelberg Univ., 1876; postgraduate fellow, Johns Hopkins Univ., 1876-78. *Career*: professor, Johns Hopkins Univ., 1878-1901; lecturer, Smith Coll., 1878-81; editor, *Johns Hopkins Studies in Historical and Political Science*, 1882-1901; secretary, American Historical Association, 1884-1900.

Adams's internationalism originated during his postgraduate years as a student of history and political science at Heidelberg. There he studied, among other subjects, international law under his mentor, *J. C. Bluntschli, the Swiss political scientist and international jurist. In Bluntschli's lectures and seminar, Adams absorbed his teacher's profound belief in the evolution of human society in the direction of a world-state.

At Johns Hopkins, Adams planned to translate Bluntschli's *Das moderne Völkerrecht*, but the project never materialized. He did, however, succeed in acquiring his late mentor's extensive private library (1882) for the university. This became the nucleus of the famous Bluntschli Library, where a generation of future historians, political scientists, and journalists labored under Adams's direction. Adams's course in international law, which he taught from 1879 to 1893, owed much to Bluntschli's historicist approach. Beginning with the origin of international life in the ancient and medieval world, Adams traced its development to recent international congresses and tribunals. Adams was a popular teacher, and the course attracted large numbers of graduate and undergraduate students. Among these were such future spokesmen for internationalism as Albert Shaw, *Newton D. Baker, and *Woodrow Wilson. Shaw's reminiscences are pertinent here: "At the university we always studied international law from the standpoint of organizing against war. Woodrow Wilson's League of Nations was forming in his mind at this very time, as I can testify from intimate daily association" ("Recollections of President Gilman [June 10, 1945]," Daniel Coit Gilman Papers, Milton S. Eisenhower Library, Johns Hopkins University, p. 14).

Adams's own internationalism, founded upon a deeply religious worldview and nourished by a paternalistic Anglo-Saxon mystique, was altogether typical of his background and era. Much concerned by such diplomatic tensions as the Venezuela Boundary Crisis (1895) and ambivalent about the results of the Spanish-American War, he intensified his commitment to international arbitration in the late 1890s. A distinguished public speaker, he addressed both academic and popular audiences on this subject. Although Adams liked to quote Tennyson's prophetic verses on "the Parliament of man, the Federation of the world," he did not think the time ripe for a permanent international court of arbitration; he looked rather to special tribunals that include representatives of the interested parties and disinterested referees.

Adams's premature death robbed internationalism of a staunch friend just when it needed articulate advocates. There can be no doubt, however, that his teaching contributed substantially to the better-known internationalism of his more publicized students.

BIBLIOGRAPHY:

A. "Bluntschli's Essay on the Service of Francis Lieber to Political Science and International Law," *International Review* 8 (Jan 1880), 50–55; *Bluntschli's Life-Work* (Baltimore, MD, 1884).

B. *American Masters of Social Science* (New York, 1927), 99–127; DAB 1, 69–70.

C. The Adams papers are in the Milton S. Eisenhower Library and the Archives, Johns Hopkins Univ.

Raymond J. Cunningham

ADDAMS, Jane. See *Biographical Dictionary of Modern Peace Leaders.*

ADDIS, Charles Stewart (23 November 1861, Edinburgh, Scotland—14 December 1945, Frant, Sussex, England). *Education*: Edinburgh Academy. *Career*: with Hongkong & Shanghai Banking Corporation, in China, 1883–1903, London manager, 1905–21, chairman, London Committee, 1921–33; censor, State Bank of Morocco; director, Bank of England,

1918–32; president, Institute of Bankers, 1921–23; manager, British Group, First and Second International Banking Consortium for China; member of British government financial missions to Genoa, 1922, Canada, 1933; delegate on expert committee that drafted the Young Plan, 1929; British director, Reichsbank, 1924–30; director and vice-president, Bank of International Settlements, 1930–32; member, Cunliffe Committee, National Debt Committee, Boxer Indemnity Committee, China Universities Committee; author and lecturer.

As a young employee of the Hongkong & Shanghai Banking Corporation in China in the 1880s, Addis showed an unusual appreciation of Chinese culture. He attempted to explain Chinese beliefs and traditions to his fellow Europeans by writing articles in the Tientsin English-language newspaper, *The Chinese Times*, and in the *Shanghai North China Daily News*. The son of a clergyman of the Free Church of Scotland, the young banker retained the self-discipline and hard work characteristic of Calvinism long after he had abandoned the theological dogma. In his first attempt at public speaking, Addis told the Shanghai Literary & Debating Society in 1890 that the British residents had an obligation to provide education for the Chinese living in the International Settlement. This unpopular view was the first of many that Addis would champion through a long career in which he sought to improve international understanding.

By the late 1890s Addis had gained international prominence as an authority on Chinese finance. Because he feared that continued competition between the various powers for concessions in China would lead ultimately to war and/or the breakup of China, he came to favor a cooperative policy for loans to China. He was instrumental in organizing the International Banking Consortium, which provided the Hukuang Railway Loan of 1911 and the Reorganization Loan of 1913. While Addis never abandoned his belief that the Consortium benefited both China and the lending powers, Chinese leaders always viewed it as the instrument of foreign imperialism. Good arguments can be made for both points of view.

When World War I began in 1914, Addis's knowledge of international exchange and currency led to his appointment to government advisory committees and to the Court of the Bank of England. Through committee testimony, speeches, and articles, Addis sought to convince Allied leaders that a generous policy toward Germany would lead to worldwide economic recovery and permanent peace. He was one of the first fully to appreciate the significance of the United States' emergence from the war as a major creditor nation. Throughout the 1920s he attempted to convince American statesmen and bankers to adopt financial policies suitable to their country's new position. As a British expert at Genoa in 1922, Addis helped devise a plan for Central Bank cooperation that never became viable, largely because the Americans were reluctant to participate.

Addis contributed to international understanding and good will in informal ways as well. He frequently entertained visiting dignitaries from China and Japan in his home, which showed a sense of racial equality all too rare in the early twentieth century. He took leadership roles in such organizations as the Royal Institute of International Affairs and the China Society, frequently chairing the discussions. Throughout the 1920s and 1930s, Addis was regularly consulted by members of the Foreign Office, Treasury, and Cabinet on China policy. He consistently advocated policies of patience and conciliation, adopting these attitudes in his own negotiations. He was a man of large vision, enormous resilience, and great faith.

While some of his contemporaries in the 1930s regarded his belief in the gold standard and free trade as a relic of a bygone era, the final verdict has yet to be reached. Certainly his conviction that international financial cooperation is fundamental to world stability and permanent peace would find few challengers.

BIBLIOGRAPHY:

A. "The Bank of International Settlements," LT 4 Apr 1930; "Bank Reserves and Depreciation," *Economic Journal* 27 (Sep 1917), 414–17; "A British Trade Bank," *Economic Journal* 26 (Dec 1916), 484–91; "The Economics of a War Indemnity," *Nation* 108 (12 Apr 1919), 554–57; "European Policy and Finance in China," *Living Age* 350 (28 Jun 1919), 817–21; "Liberal Economy," *Spectator* 160 (4 Feb 1938), 173–74; "The New Monetary Technique," *Quarterly Review* 269 (Jul 1937), 64–73; "Outlook for International Cooperation in Finance," *Academy of Political Science Proceedings* 14 (Jan 1931), 306–15.

B. Roberta A. Dayer, *Bankers and Diplomats in China 1917–1925: The Anglo-American Relationship* (London, 1981); E.J.S., "Gold and Sir Charles Addis," *Spectator* 132 (19 Jan 1924), 78–80; *Economic Journal* 56 (Sep 1946), 507–10; LT 15 Dec 1945, 6; "Men of Mark: Sir Charles Addis," *Financial News* (17 Dec 1930).

C. The Addis papers are at the Library of the School of Oriental and African Studies, London.

Roberta Allbert Dayer

ADENAUER, Konrad (5 January 1876, Cologne—19 April 1967, Rhöndorf, Germany). *Education*: Univs. of Freiburg, Munich, Bonn. *Career*: practiced law in Cologne; lord mayor of Cologne, 1917–33; member, executive committee, Center party, Weimar Republic; Prussian State Council, 1920–32; various party offices, Christian Democratic Union, 1945–67; president, Parliamentary Council of three Western occupation zones, 1948–49; chancellor, Federal Republic of Germany, 1949–63.

Adenauer was one of the outstanding figures of the European integration movement of the postwar period. Elected lord mayor of Cologne in 1917, he held that post for sixteen years and also played a significant role in German national politics of the Weimar period as a member of the Catholic Center party. In 1933 Adenauer was dismissed from all his positions by the Nazi regime and lived in Germany in political exile. After a brief tenure as mayor of Cologne immediately following World War II, Adenauer became a founder of the Christian Democratic Union (CDU). In 1948 he became president of the Parliamentary Council, which drafted the Basic Law (constitution) of the Federal Repubic of Germany, and in 1949 he was elected the chancellor of the Federal Republic, a post he held until his retirement in 1963.

Adenauer's commitment to international cooperation and, specifically, Western European integration, stemmed from a number of deeply held convictions. He was determined to obviate in the future a German seesaw policy between East and West; and for Adenauer and his supporters in the CDU/Christian Social Union, West German foreign policy goals found meaning and purpose in attempts to establish a European political order that would irrevocably tie German society to the cultural and political forces of Western Europe. This was to be achieved by making Germany an equal and respected partner of the Western powers and by forging a fundamental reconciliation between France and Germany. In the larger context of world politics, and especially for the purpose of meeting the Communist challenge, a united Western Europe was to be anchored to the power of the United States in the framework of an Atlantic alliance. Adenauer's internationalist attitude was not only important for launching European integration efforts, which ultimately culminated in the establishment of the European Community, but it also contributed substantially to the speedy economic and political recovery of the Federal Republic and thus laid the domestic foundations for its political stability.

The creation of international and supranational organizations had a positive and perhaps decisive influence on the process of West Germany's reconstruction. By providing mechanisms for controlling German sovereignty as soon as it was granted (which took place in 1955 as part of the agreement that obliged the Federal Republic to rearm in the context of the North Atlantic Treaty Organization), these organizations made the restoration of sovereignty less risky and less painful for the Western allies, especially France. In turn, Adenauer's continued agitation for political and economic concessions prompted the Allies to set up integrative structures to supervise the Federal Republic. The sovereignty that Adenauer sought for the West German state was thus of a rather special kind. He was willing to relinquish some of its elements, once they were gained, to contractual arrangements that would bind Germany to the West in integrative international structures. As a consequence, the Bonn government could advance its demands for political and legal equality in the name of European integration and the Western alliance, rather than in the name of a discredited German nationalism. It was Adenauer's political genius to combine necessity and choice; and his total commitment to the cause of Western European integration made him one of the founding fathers of the postwar European political and economic order.

BIBLIOGRAPHY:

A. *Memoirs*, 4 vols. (Chicago, 1966–68); *Reden 1917–1967: Eine Auswahl* (Stuttgart, Germany, 1975); *World Indivisible, with Liberty and Justice for All* (New York, 1955).

B. *Biographisches Staatshandbuch* (Bern, 1963), 10–11; *Biographisches Wörterbuch zur Deutschen Geschichte* 1 (Munich, 1973), 19–26; Richard Hiscocks, *The Adenauer Era* (1966; Westport, CT, 1975); *Lexikon der deutschen Geschichte* (Stuttgart, Germany, 1977), 9; NYT 20B Apr 1976, 1; Anneliese Poppinga, *Konrad Adenauer: Geschichtsverständnis, Weltanschauung und politische Praxis* (Stuttgart, Germany, 1975); Terence Prittie, *Konrad Adenauer, 1876–1967* (London, 1972); F. Roy Willis, *France, Germany and the New Europe 1945–1967* (Stanford, CA, 1968).

Wolfram F. Hanrieder

AGÜERO Y BETANCOURT, Aristides de (1865, Cuba—21 June 1933, Geneva). *Education*: lawyer and doctor of science. *Career*: professor, Univ. of Havana, 1890–95, 1899–1904; colonel, Cuban rebel army, 1898–99; Cuban chargé d'affaires, Berlin and Vienna, 1904–10; minister to Argentina, 1910–12, to Norway, 1912–14, to Germany, 1914–17, 1920–24, to Germany and Austria, 1924–33; delegate, League of Nations Assembly, 1920–33; member, League Council, 1920–30.

Agüero's career symbolized Cuba's internationalist commitment in an era when that republic was an American protectorate and its foreign policy sharply circumscribed by Washington's policies in the Caribbean. Like its first president, Don Tomás Estrada Palma, Agüero was a servant of the Spanish Cuban educational system who turned against Spanish rule and joined the rebellion. Unlike other Cuban political figures of the early twentieth century, however, he displayed little interest in the often violent political conflicts of those years and concentrated instead on advancing "Cuban internationalism" in the world community.

In addition to a succession of diplomatic posts in Europe, which earned him the accolade of Cuba's best-known diplomat, he played an important role in League of Nations affairs, where he served as a delegate from its beginning until his death. There he established a reputation for his ability and his commitment to peace and the League's ideals. Nicknamed the Great Elector, he was chosen to be president of the Assembly in 1924; he presided over the Council in 1925, and he participated in the World Disarmament Conference. He was vice-president of the International Labor Organization Conference in 1922 and of the Opium Conference in 1924, and president of a Conference on Transit and Communication in 1926. He was an effective orator who spoke six languages.

In most instances, his stance on issues was from an internationalist perspective, yet in 1924, when a Cuban leader criticized working conditions in that country before the International Labour Conference, Agüero defended his homeland. He also became involved in debates at Geneva over the Monroe Doctrine. At a time of Cuban subservience to American wishes,

Agüero favored a formal League interpretation of the Doctrine when Latin American members, hoping to use the League as a forum for attacking U.S. interventionist policies, pressed the Council for an interpretation of Article XXI of the Covenant. The Council was generally reluctant to antagonize the United States, but neither could it acquiesce in the American argument that the Monroe Doctrine justified intervention. Joining with the Chilean and Colombian delegates, Agüero insisted that Article XXI neither expanded nor enhanced the Monroe Doctrine and that all members of the League had "equal obligations and equal rights."

BIBLIOGRAPHY:

B. Ramiro Guerra, *Cuba en la vida internacional* (Havana, 1933); NYT 22 Jun 1933, 19; Frank P. Walters, *A History of the League of Nations* (London, 1952).

Lester D. Langley

ALBERDI, Juan. See *Biographical Dictionary of Modern Peace Leaders.*

ALESSANDRI, Arturo. See *Biographical Dictionary of Modern Peace Leaders.*

ALFARO, Ricardo Joaquin (20 August 1882, Panama City—23 February 1971, Panama City). *Education*: graduate, Coll. of Balboa, 1900, Univ. of Cartagena, 1904. *Career*: under secretary of foreign affairs, 1905–8; legation in Washington, 1912; U.S. Panama Joint Land Commission, 1915; secretary of justice, 1918–22; minister plenipotentiary to United States, 1922–30, 1933–36; first vice-president of Panama, 1928–30; president, 1931–32; chairman, Panamanian delegation, Pan American Conference, 1928, Pan American Conference on Conciliation and Arbitration, 1929; member, Permanent Court of Arbitration, 1929–41; minister of foreign affairs, 1945–47; head, UN Relief and Rehabilitation Administration mission to Caribbean nations, 1945; judge, International Court of Justice, 1959–64, vice-president, 1961–64; delegate to many conferences of League of Nations, the Inter-American system and the UN.

The career of this diplomat, statesman, lawyer, and jurist contributed significantly to the movement for peace through arbitration and international law. The great interest of his life was the formulation of procedures for the peaceful settlement of international disputes. In 1912 he held a special assignment to work on the resolution of the Costa Rica–Panama boundary dispute, and his skills were recognized in his appointment to the Permanent Court of Arbitration in 1929. His later outstanding performance as arbiter of the Ambatiellos case between Greece and Great Britain in 1956 led to his nomination and election to the World Court. As president of the Juridical Committee of the Assembly of the UN in 1948, he was coauthor of the famed Convention on Genocide. Then he served on the UN's International Law Committee, 1949–53, 1958–59, and sat as its president in 1953.

He served on the Investigation Commission created by the 1943 Santiago Treaty on Prevention of Conflicts, which was able to pave the way for several peaceful settlements of Western Hemisphere disputes.

Alfaro also labored to change the Hay–Bunau Varilla Treaty of 1903 between Panama and the United States. Like all Panamanians he considered it harsh and unfair. It left a U.S. presence so overwhelming that Panamanians considered it to be a form of unabashed colonialism. They continuously agitated for basic changes, and as minister in Washington Alfaro gained the first important revision in the Hull–Alfaro Pact of 1936. Alfaro appreciated the new spirit embodied in the Good Neighbor Policy, and he emerged as one of Latin America's most eloquent supporters of the Allies in World War II. His hopes for world concord had not blinded him to the insidious threat of the Axis powers, and he deplored the tendency of other "peace lovers" to appease. In a memorable address in June 1941, he derided Japanese claims of seeking peace and prosperity for the peoples of East Asia. His remark that two million Chinese had perished in Japan's "tender caresses of steel and fire" and that one-third of the states of the world had been overrun by the Axis was widely quoted. He thus became an exponent of the concept of collective security as one of the best hopes for world order based on law. Yet Alfaro was always an exemplar of human brotherhood and a supporter of humanitarian causes, as many decorations testify. He was a founder of the American Institute of International Law and served for years as its general secretary. He was also the author of many books and articles.

BIBLIOGRAPHY:

A. *Commentary on Pan American Problems* (Cambridge, MA, 1938); *Costa Rica y Panamá; en defense de los que quieren paz y amistad* (Panama, 1927); *Limites entre Panamá y Costa Rica* (Panama, 1913); *Los canales internacionales Panamá* (Panama, 1957); "Manuel Amador Guerrero," *Bulletin of Pan American Union* 67 (Jul 1953), 526–43; *Medio siglo de relaciones entre Panamá y los Estados Unidos* (Panama, 1953).

B. Miles P. DuVal, Jr., *Cadiz to Cathay: The Story of the Long Diplomatic Struggle for the Panama Canal* (Palo Alto, CA, 1940); Lawrence O. Ealy, *The Republic of Panama in World Affairs* (Philadelphia, 1951); Walter LaFeber, *The Panama Canal* (New York, 1978); Sheldon B. Liss, *The Canal: Aspects of United States–Panamanian Relations* (South Bend, IN, 1967); William D. McCain, *The United States and the Republic of Panama* (Durham, NC, 1937); WWLA 1945, 2, 85.

Lawrence O. Ealy

ALOISI, Pompeo (6 November 1875, Rome—15 January 1949, Rome). *Education*: graduate, Naval Academy, Livorno, 1893. *Career*: naval service, 1893–1902; entered diplomatic service by examination, 1902; attached to embassy, Paris, 1902–15; wartime service, 1915–18; head of press office, Italian delegation, Paris Peace Conference, 1919; minister to Denmark, 1920–23; League of Nations commissioner, Memel, 1923; minister to Romania, 1923–25; minister to Albania, 1926–27; ambassador to Tokyo,

1928–29, to Ankara, 1929–32; *capo di gabinetto* of foreign minister (Mussolini) and head of Italian delegation, League of Nations, 1932–36; wartime service as rear admiral, 1940–43.

Most of Aloisi's career was passed in the furtherance of exclusively Italian interests. His wartime exploits in naval counterintelligence won him the title of baron; his promotion to ambassador followed his work in helping transform Albania into a virtual Italian protectorate. Service as League commissioner in Memel, although involving him in preparation of the Memel Statute of 8 March 1924, was a mere hiatus in a conventional diplomatic life. Only after 1932 as Italy's chief delegate to the League of Nations did Aloisi gain standing as an internationalist. Taking up his predecessor's (Dino Grandi) endorsement of disarmament through the League, he became a constant and popular figure at Geneva. A typical sailor in appearance and personality, his bluff honesty won wide approbation. He presided over sessions of the League Council in 1933 and also over the League body that superintended the Saar Plebiscite in 1935. As a result, he was awarded the Grotius Medal by the Dutch Association for the League of Nations.

The Ethiopian Crisis of 1935–36, however, exposed the limits of Aloisi's internationalism. Although privately urging Mussolini to resolve the issue through the League, he stayed at his post and obeyed instructions to voice Fascist Italy's defiance of League recommendations. Moreover, his qualms about the Ethiopian adventure arose less from concern for international probity than for the diplomatic consequences of Italy's breach with Britain and France. Like most Italian career diplomats, he came to distrust Fascist foreign policy after 1936 not out of principle but Realpolitik. He retired from diplomatic service in 1938.

Aloisi's outward collusion with Fascism in the Ethiopian affair damaged his reputation and, after World War II, sparked a move to exclude him from the Italian Senate to which he had been appointed in 1939. In rebuttal, he compiled a short documentary memorial circulated by the Centro Italiano per la Riconciliazione Internazionale, an institution founded by Aloisi as a further token of his internationalism. Aloisi also kept a diary, of which the portion for 1932–36 has been printed. Not written for publication, it constitutes an invaluable day-by-day recapitulation of events in Geneva and Rome but contains little of Aloisi's reflections.

BIBLIOGRAPHY:

A. *Journal: 25 juillet 1932–14 juin 1936*, (Paris, 1957). *La mia attività al servizio della pace: Fatti nuovi e nuovi elementi probatori sottoposto all'esame dell'Alta corte di giustizia* (Rome, 1946).

B. Giuseppe Bruccoleri, ed., *L'opera dei delegati italiani nella Società delle Nazioni*, 4 vols. (Rome, 1935–37); *Dictionnaire diplomatique* 5 (Paris, 1933), 25–26; *Dizionario biografico degli italiani* 2 (Rome, 1960), 518–20; NYT 16 Jan 1949, 68; Mario Toscano, "Il diario di Barone Aloisi," *Rassegna italiana di politica e di cultura* 34, no. 396 (1957), 427–35.

Alan Cassels

ALVAREZ, Alejandro (9 February 1868, Santiago—19 July 1960, Paris). *Education*: LL.B., Univ. of Chile, 1892; LL.D., Univ. of Paris, 1898. *Career*: professor, Univ. of Chile, 1901; legal adviser, Chilean foreign ministry; delegate, League of Nations Assemblies, 1921, 1922; delegate, Fourth, Fifth, and Sixth Pan American Conferences; representative, Barcelona Conference on Communications and Transit, 1921, Conference for the Codification of International Law, The Hague, 1930; member, Permanent Court of Arbitration, 1907–20; judge, International Court of Justice, 1946–55.

Early in his career as a scholar and diplomat, Alvarez was greatly preoccupied with the duty of Latin American jurists to continue a tradition that he termed "American international law." This legal concept clings to the Hispanic classical writings of such figures as Vitoria and Suarez and embraces a history in the Western Hemisphere of keeping international law in stride with contemporary developments in the world. According to Alvarez this philosophy of "American international law" grew in the New World because of its isolation from European power conflicts. Also, the evolution of regional particularism flowed from the Pan American movement, through which legalists of the Western Hemisphere were able to establish rules of international law focusing on topics like the fundamental right and duties of states, domestic jurisdiction, the regime of territorial waters, the right of asylum, and arbitral procedures for territorial disputes. He based the theory of American international law on the synthesis of two separate legal schools present in the Western Hemisphere—the Anglo-Saxon legal system of the United States, and the Roman one of the Latin American nations.

Alvarez explained his theory in writings and at Pan American Conferences, but it was during his term on the World Court that his philosophy of regional particularism in international law became a widespread subject of debate among international lawyers. The universalists attempted to refute the existence of a separate body of law flowing from regionalism. While he wrote about the subject in a 1910 book entitled *Le Droit international amèricain,* it was not until the late 1940s, when he became a member of the Court, that the debate about his theory was brought to the attention of jurists of numerous nationalities.

For newly independent states of Africa and Asia, his support for broad principles of nonintervention and nonaggression had a definite appeal. Perhaps sensing the distaste which many of the politically and economically weak nations had for many of the old international legal rules created during the era of European colonialism, Alvarez began building a theory of the "new international law." The core of this theory is divided into two components: a negative requisite of the limitation of sovereignty of nations; and a positive requirement of the responsible participation of states in constructing a solid international community. Established international law should develop by adapting to the rapid changes in international society. The "new international law" soon became linked with the growing movement in the United Nations toward recognition of global interdependence. Thus, Alvarez's legal ideas prophesied a change commonly referred to as the New International Economic Order. His insights into future developments in international affairs may be seen in over one hundred published articles, judicial opinions, and monographs.

BIBLIOGRAPHY:

A. *La diplomacía de Chile durante emancipación, y la sociedad internacional* (Madrid, 1916); *Le Droit international amèricain* (Paris, 1910); *The Monroe Doctrine: Its Importance in the International Life of States of the New World* (New York, 1924).

B. Luis Durand, *Gente de mi tiempo* (Santiago, 1953); *ICJ Yearbook for 1946-1947*, 43-44; Alan T. Leonhard, "The Legal Thought of the Latin American Judges on the International Court of Justice," dissertation, Duke Univ., 1967; NYT 19 Jul 1960, 29; WWLA 1940, 19-20.

Alan T. Leonhard

AMERASINGHE, Hamilton Shirley   (18 March 1913, Colombo—4 December 1980, New York). *Education*: B.A., London Univ., 1934. *Career*: joined Ceylon Civil Service, 1937; resident manager, Gal Oya Development Board, 1950; counselor, Embassy of Ceylon in Washington, 1953-55; senior civil service posts in Ceylon, 1955-63; high commissioner to India, concurrently ambassador to Nepal and Afghanistan, 1963-67; permanent representative of Sri Lanka to the UN, 1967-78, president, General Assembly, 1976-77; president, UN Conference on the Law of the Sea, 1973-80.

Amerasinghe's association with the United Nations began in 1957, when he served as a member of his country's delegation to the General Assembly, but it became close when he was appointed permanent representative of Sri Lanka to the UN in 1967. He held several important elective posts, including chairman of the Ad Hoc Committee on the Indian Ocean from the time of its establishment, in 1973, and chairman of the Special Committee to Investigate Israeli Practices Affecting the Human Rights of the Population of the Occupied Territories from its creation in 1969. However, he made his most solid contribution to the work of the organization as the acknowledged leader in shaping the international community's attitude toward the law of the sea.

Elected chairman of the UN Ad Hoc Committee on the Peaceful Uses of the Sea-Bed and Ocean Floor Beyond the Limits of National Jurisdiction in 1968, he was the natural choice (1973) as president of the UN Conference on the Law of the Sea. He presided over all the sessions until his death, helping to reconcile widely differing views on such sensitive subjects as free passage of ships through international straits, mining the sea bed, a proposed International Seabed Authority, the continental shelf, access of landlocked states to fisheries in the two hundred–mile economic zone, and protection of the marine environment. The remarkable confidence he earned can be gauged by the unprecedented fact that, even when he ended his term as Sri Lanka's permanent representative, a formula was found to enable him to continue as president of the Law of the Sea Conference. It was expected that the work of the Conference could be completed in 1981, but that was not realized.

BIBLIOGRAPHY:

B. IWW 1979–80, 26; NYT 5 Dec 1980, II–11.

Aamir Ali

AMES, Herbert Brown (27 June 1863, Montreal—31 March 1954, Montreal). *Education*: graduate, Amherst Coll., 1885. *Career*: vice-president and director, Ames, Holden & Co., Montreal, 1885–93; alderman, Montreal, 1898–1906; chairman, Municipal Board of Health, 1900–4; Protestant School Council of Public Instruction, Quebec, 1895–1920; House of Commons for Montreal–St. Antoine, 1904–20, chair, Select Standing Committee on Banking and Commerce, 1915; financial director, Secretariat of League of Nations, 1920–26; Canadian delegate, League Assembly, 1926.

Unhappy in the family firm and preferring a life of public service, Ames left business to become involved in politics. As urban reformer, city alderman, and federal parliamentarian, he applied business management techniques to government affairs. Failing to gain a leadership position in the Conservative party and as his political career was ending, Prime Minister *Robert Borden suggested him to the League of Nations as financial director. From his appointment to the Secretariat, Ames was a vigorous exponent of the League ideals in his contacts and as an early organizer of the League of Nations Society in Canada. Modest monetary advances from the British and French governments initiated League activities, yet the Covenant was "practically silent" on how the League was to be financed. Ames immediately prepared a draft budget of £250,000 and apportioned it among forty-five nations. Letters would be sent to each state by the secretary-general, Ames wrote in 1927, stating the allotted sum and asking an early payment as soon as convenient. These at first arrived slowly owing to the necessity for government approvals. In addition to budgeting for the Secretariat, the Council, and the Assembly, the financial director was to provide for the costs of the International Labor Office and the Permanent Court of International Justice at The Hague. Annual expenditures during the 1920s ran between $4,500,000 and $4,750,000 and eventually were divided among the members according to an estimated ability to pay. Ninety-seven percent of the assessments were annually recovered. If this investment in the peace loomed large, Ames noted that U.S. military expenditures in 1925 were $563,861,346, enough to maintain the League for 125 years. The British government in 1926 paid its apportionment of $495,812 at the same time the Liberian government paid $4,722. Ames negotiated the purchase of the largest building in Geneva, the Hotel National, giving the League its first home and first credit rating. To gain the confidence of its members, the Council appointed a Commission of Control to scrutinize the budget and require an annual audit.

During his six years of service, Ames established a sound financial policy for the League, which gained it the confidence of the world community. A staunch believer in free enterprise, rational organization, and cooperative effort, Ames returned to North America at the beginning of 1927 to lecture in an optimistic vein that the machinery of the League was workable in resolving dangerous disputes such as Fiume, Vilna, and Corfu and in gaining international cooperation on minorities, mandates, disarmament, trade, and transportation.

BIBLIOGRAPHY:

A. *Seven Years with the League of Nations* (Amherst, MA, 1927).

B. *Encyclopedia Canadiana* 1 (Toronto, 1975), 151–52; *Macmillan Dictionary of Canadian Biography* (Toronto, 1978), 14–15; P.F.W. Rutherford, introduction to Ames, *The City Below the Hill* (Toronto, 1972); Richard Veatch, *Canada and the League of Nations* (Toronto, 1978); WWC 1915–16, 296, 1949–50, 148, and 1956–57, 1302.

C. A small collection of Ames papers are in the McGill Univ. Archives.

Terence J. Fay

ANDERSEN, Hendrik Christian (17 April 1872, Bergen, Norway—19 December 1941, Rome). *Education*: studied art and architecture in Boston, Paris, Naples, and Rome. *Career*: sculptor and architect.

Although born in Norway, Andersen came in 1873 to Newport, Rhode Island. Even as a child, he could not understand the divisiveness of life; and as architect, sculptor, and artist, he devoted much of his thought and talent to promoting the ideal of brotherhood through a model world city. While working on a commissioned "Fountain of Life," he began to perceive a world city as the spiritual center of his vision. It would be the seat of a world body and the focus of international banking, publishing, education, religion, the sciences, medicine, and communications.

Fortunately, Andersen inherited considerable wealth, so he could devote himself to this project. In 1912 Andersen, then living in Rome, prepared an elaborately illustrated book with highly detailed plans for his World Centre of Communications. It represented an expenditure on his part of nine years of work and over $150,000, and it embodied the ideas of forty "experts." It included diagrams of streets, buildings and their uses, gardens, and civic and cultural centers. This artistic, creative, and imaginative work attracted many enthusiastic supporters, who thereafter sought to promote his dream even as they may have recognized its impracticality. World War I seemingly destroyed the possibility, but the creation of the League of Nations stimulated Andersen and his devotees to revive the idea. They introduced his plans to the Secretariat, but the League lacked the resources to develop such a grandiose center.

In the 1920s Andersen reprinted his book and offered to come to Washington during the conference on the limitation of armaments (1921–22) to present his views to the assembled dignitaries, and he rebuilt a network to promote the vision. This led to proposals for a site near Brussels as the world capital city to be built with Belgian war debts owed the United States. King Albert of Belgium became a supporter of this project, and King Victor Emmanuel also considered it for Italy. Benito Mussolini also became interested and in 1926 promised an extensive tract of land near Ostia if Andersen could complete his plans and find financial support.

At his death Andersen's studio overlooking the Tiber River was filled with statues he had created for his world center. Andersen's books can still prompt interest in his idealistic image of a world unified by human accomplishments and represented in his universal city.

BIBLIOGRAPHY:

A. *Creation of a World Centre of Communication*, 2 vols. (Rome, 1913–18); *A World-City of Civilization* (Rome, 1921).

B. Helen Hendricks, "Hendrik Christian Andersen," *World Unity Magazine* 8 (Aug 1931), 320–24; NYT 20 Dec 1940, 25; WWWA 1, 22.

Warren F. Kuehl

ANDERSON, Chandler Parsons (5 September 1866, Lakeville, CT—2 August 1936, Washington). *Education*: B.A., Yale Univ., 1877; Harvard Law School, 1888–89. *Career*: attorney, New York, 1891–1936; arbitrator, Cleveland–Hoover administrations; counselor, Department of State, 1905–13; commissioner, Mixed Claims Commission between United States and Germany, Tripartite Claims Commission between United States, Austria, and Hungary, 1923–33.

Serving four secretaries of state opened the doors for Anderson to act as a liaison between the business community and the federal government. As a leading international lawyer, he served American businessmen with investments in Latin America, and he assisted Latin Americans with political ambitions. As their representative to the State Department, he sought to influence U.S. foreign policy. Between 1913 and 1928 Anderson became the chief spokesman for the American business community in Latin America seeking concessions and special privileges from the State Department on behalf of his clients.

Anderson also established a reputation in the field of international relations by working on Anglo–American arbitrations, including the Bering Sea Claims Commission (1896–97); U.S.–Canada questions (1898–99); Alaska Boundary Arbitration (1903); Atlantic Coast Fisheries Arbitration (1910); Fur Seals Conference (1911); and British–American Pecuniary Claims Arbitration (1913–23). He also acted as counsel for the Central American countries of Costa Rica, Guatemala, and Nicaragua in various boundary disputes. When the Mexican Revolution brought a serious threat to U.S.investments in that country, Anderson was eminently qualified to represent Wall Street before the State Department. He found himself and his clients at odds with the *Woodrow Wilson administration concerning the policies pursued with regard to Mexico. Wilson seemed to be more concerned about promoting moral principles and constitutional democracy than protecting American business interests. To Anderson's frustration, Wall Street was not able to alter the course of U.S. foreign policy in Mexico to any measurable degree.

The Harding–Coolidge years witnessed not only problems in U.S.–Mexican relations, but also revolutionary disturbances in Nicaragua, a U.S. quasi-protectorate. Anderson represented both business and political interests in that Central American republic. His activity on behalf of General Emiliano Chamorro's attempt to gain U.S. support for his bid for power in his country approached filibustering. In the end, Anderson was no more successful with such efforts than in his attempts to alter U.S. foreign policy for the sake of Wall Street.

While Anderson revealed a realistic approach toward world conditions, he also showed some idealistic qualities. He attained considerable stature in international law circles as a founder of the American Society of International Law in 1906, and he wrote essays and editorials for its journal on a variety of topics. A wider acceptance and use of arbitration, the evolution of international law, and the development of a public awareness of an interdependent world were all needs he hoped would eventually be fulfilled.

BIBLIOGRAPHY:

A. *Alaska Fur Seals* (Washington, 1906); *Costa Rica–Panama Arbitration* (Washington, 1914); *Inviolability of Private Property Against Confiscation* (New York, 1927); *Mixed Claims Commission Report* (Washington, 1934); *Organization of the World for Peace* (Washington, 1924); *Panama Canal Tolls* (Washington, 1913).

B. Lawrence Dennis, "Nicaragua: In Again, Out Again," *Foreign Affairs* 9 (Apr 1931), 496–600; L. Ethan Ellis, *Frank B. Kellogg and American Foreign Relations, 1925–1929* (New Brunswick, NJ, 1961); Arthur S. Link, *Wilson: The Struggle for Neutrality, 1914–1915* (Princeton, NJ, 1960); NYT 3 Aug 1936, 15.

C. The Anderson papers are in the Manuscript Division, Library of Congress.

Benjamin T. Harrison

ANDREWS, Fannie Fern Phillips (25 September 1867, Margaretville, NS—23 January 1950, Somerville, MA). *Education*: graduate, Salem (Mass.) Normal School, 1884; Harvard Summer School, 1895, 1896; B.A., Radcliffe Coll., 1902, M.A., 1920, Ph.D., 1923. *Career*: schoolteacher, Lynn, MA, 1884–90; social and educational worker, organizer, author, lecturer, 1902–50; founder, secretary, later president, Boston Home and School Association, 1907–18; founder, secretary, American School Peace League (later American School Citizenship League), 1908–50; special collaborator, U.S. Bureau of Education, 1912–21; member, executive committee, and international corresponding secretary, Central Organization for a Durable Peace, 1915–23.

The expanding peace movement prior to World War I saw a notable growth in emphasis on the role of education in the promotion of peace. A key figure in this growth was Andrews, a former schoolteacher and active organizer of educational groups, who was recruited into the movement late in December 1905 by *Lucia Ames Mead. Convinced of the power and responsibility of education to stimulate progress toward a world of peace and justice, Andrews conceived the idea of organizing schoolteachers in an active campaign, and by 1908 she had founded the American School Peace League. As its secretary she vigorously pursued its stated goals of acquainting American teachers with the peace movement, organizing chapters, preparing instructional materials for courses in history and citizenship, and enlisting teachers of all countries in the movement for international cooperation in light of the "new internationalism" ushered in by the First Hague Conference of 1899.

On a trip to Europe in 1910, she promoted the establishment of the School Peace League of Great Britain and Ireland and presented to the Universal Peace Congress meeting in Stockholm a proposed constitution for a School League for International Understanding. Originally conceived as an international teachers organization, this gradually evolved into a plan for an intergovernmental bureau of education; and Andrews was the prime mover behind the first intergovernmental conference on education, scheduled for The Hague in September 1914. Hers was the first such plan officially communicated to governments for consideration; but her historic role was thwarted by the outbreak of the war, which led to cancelation of the conference and a twelve-year delay in the establishment of the International Bureau of Education.

In 1915, as a founding member of the Woman's Peace Party, Andrews served with +Jane Addams as an American member of the International Committee of the International Congress of Women at The Hague and subsequently on the International Committee of Women for Permanent Peace. She also worked for the establishment of the League of Nations as international corresponding secretary of the Central Organization for a Durable Peace and as a member of the League to Enforce Peace. In 1919 Andrews represented the U.S. Bureau of Education at the Paris Peace Conference, where once again she proposed the establishment of an International Bureau of Education, this time within the framework of the League of Nations. Despite favorable reception by the Conference of Allied Societies and a sympathetic hearing by the League of Nations Commission, the plan was not adopted. The International Bureau of Education was created in 1926; and when it was reorganized in 1929 as an intergovernmental body, Andrews was present in Geneva at the signing of its constitution. She was also appointed by *Franklin Roosevelt to serve as a delegate to international conferences on education held by the Bureau in 1934 and 1936.

Andrews made substantial scholarly contributions to the study of international relations in her monograph, *Freedom of the Seas* (1917), her doctoral thesis on the legal aspects of the mandatory system (1923), and her magnum opus, *The Holy Land Under Mandate* (1931), based on extensive field research into the actual operation of the system. The latter was widely regarded as the first comprehensive and impartial view of the whole set of problems facing the Arabs, Jews, and Christians in Palestine under the British Mandate, especially in regard to Zionism and the eventual independence of Palestine.

BIBLIOGRAPHY:

A. With Ella Lyman Cabot and others, *A Course in Citizenship and Patriotism* (Boston, 1914); *The Freedom of the Seas: The Immunity of Private Property at Sea in Time of War* (The Hague, 1917); *The Holy Land Under Mandate* (Boston, 1931); *Memory Pages of My Life* (Boston, 1948); "The Observance of Peace Day in the Schools," *Proceedings of the 76th Annual Meeting of the American Institute of Instruction* (Boston, 1906), 275–82.

B. *Boston Transcript* 27 May 1931, 3; *Bulletin of the International Bureau of Education*, no. 99 (2nd quarter 1951), 73–74; "Dr. Fannie Fern Andrews and the International Conference on Education, Convened for 1914," in P. Rossello, *Forerunners of the International Bureau of Education* (London, 1944), 35–43; Warren F. Kuehl, *Seeking World Order: The United States and International Organization to 1920* (Nashville, TN, 1969); Lucia Ames Mead,. "Fannie Fern Andrews," *World Unity Magazine* 3 (Sep 1929), 403–13; NAW 1, 46–48; NCAB A, 356–57; *New York Evening Post* 23 May 1931, 5; NYT 5 Jul 1931, 1; WWWA 3, 28.

C. The Andrews papers are in the Schlesinger Library, Radcliffe Coll.

Clinton F. Fink

APPONYI, Albert. See *Biographical Dictionary of Modern Peace Leaders.*

ARANHA, Oswaldo Euclides de Sousa (15 February 1892, Algrete, Rio Grande do Sul, Brazil—27 January 1960, Rio de Janeiro). *Education*: graduate, Ecole des Hautes Etudes Sociales, Paris, 1914; Law Faculty, Rio de Janeiro, 1916. *Career*: assistant chief of police, Porto Alegre; mayor, Alegrete, 1926; state legislator, 1927; federal deputy from Rio Grande, 1928; state secretary of interior and exterior, Rio Grande, 1929; leading figure in Revolution of 1930; minister of justice, 1930; minister of finance, 1931; majority leader, Constituent Assembly, 1934; ambassador to United States, 1934–37; foreign minister, 1938–44; delegate to UN, 1946–47, president, General Assembly, 1947, 1957; minister of finance, 1953–54.

Aranha's career paralleled dynamic changes that altered Brazil internally and affected its relations with the world. As minister of finance, he began to move the Brazilian economy out of the British sphere and into the American. He worked to strengthen ties with the United States while ambassador, and, as foreign minister, Aranha was not only the key Brazilian actor in the formation of the wartime alliance with the United States, but he also spearheaded the drive to eliminate Axis influence in Brazil. In June 1942, he was one of several Latin Americans whom *Sumner Welles consulted regarding the future United Nations organization. Welles saw that, with the war's end, "the Western Hemisphere will be immeasurably the strongest entity left on the earth" and that "the American Republics must take the lead jointly when the time comes and must not permit, as they did in 1919, their effective influence to be dissipated and to be largely nullified." (McCann, *Brazilian-American Alliance*, 297.)

Aranha's subsequent career showed his support for that assumption. He favored an inter-American conference similar to the prewar ones to create a united position. Unhappily, in the last two years of the war, Washington lost interest in its Latin American allies, and Aranha came to question U.S. intentions. He took this doubt to the UN after 1945, where he was a voice for the interests of the less powerful nations. He supported African independence and, thanks to his efforts, Brazil sponsored the resolution creating the economic commission for Africa. He defended the neutralist policy of the Afro–Asiatic bloc. Just as he had been concerned earlier in his career with Brazilian economic development, in the UN he became worried over problems of worldwide underdevelopment.

Aranha was convinced that "world peace, security, tranquility, and progress" would benefit Brazil and that his country had a world destiny. He was a man with faith in the future. He had seen his generation transform Brazil, and he believed that the same could be done with the rest of the underdeveloped world.

BIBLIOGRAPHY:

A. *A revolução não se fez pelo poder, fez-se pelo Brasil* (Rio de Janeiro, 1932).

B. Amilcar Alencastre, *Oswaldo Aranha, O mundo Afro-Asiatico e a paz* (Rio de Janeiro, 1961); Frank D. McCann, *The Brazilian–American Alliance, 1937–1945* (Princeton, NJ, 1973); NYT 28 Jan 1960, 31.

C. The Aranha papers are in the Centro de Pesquisa e Documentação da História Contemporânea do Brasil, Fundação Getulio Vargas, Rio de Janeiro.

Frank D. McCann

ARAS, Tevfik Rüştü (11 February 1883, Çanakkale, Turkey—6 January 1972, Istanbul). *Education*: M.D., French Faculty of Medicine, Beirut; studied in Paris. *Career*: gynecologist, Guraba Hospital, Izmir, 1908–9; editor in Chief, *İttihad*, 1908–9; various medical posts, 1909–13; inspector general of public health, Istanbul, 1913–17; member, High Council of Health, 1918–20; deputy, Grand National Assembly, 1920–39; presiding judge, Court of Independence of Çankırı and Kastamonu, 1920–21; head,

Turkish Grand National Assembly delegation to Moscow, 1921–23; acting minister of health, 1923; chairman of Turkish delegation, Greco–Turkish Commission of Exchange of Population, 1923–24; minister of foreign affairs, 1925–38; ambassador to London, 1939–42; Turkish representative on UN Palestine Conciliation Commission, 1950–52.

Trained as a physician, Tevfik Rüştü owed his appointment as foreign minister of Turkey less to any professional qualifications, most of which he acquired in office, than to his early friendship with and loyalty to Mustafa Kemal (Atatürk). Since Kemal set the guidelines of Turkey's foreign policies, often acting as his own foreign minister and brooking little criticism, Tevfik Rüştü served essentially as a trustworthy conduit for his directives and a reliable intermediary between the *gazi* and foreign representatives. Given the complexities Turkey confronted in the interwar years and the necessity of maintaining good relations with nations that were often at odds with one another, Tevfik Rüştü—at once ingratiating, expansive, garrulous, and convivial—was ideally suited to the task. While Tevfik Rüştü fostered good relations with other countries and deflected their criticism, Kemal had ample opportunity to adjust his foreign policies as circumstances demanded.

Tevfik Rüştü believed that Turkey's interests were compatible with and could best be safeguarded by international order. Since Turkey had renounced expansionist and revisionist ventures, he saw international peace as a prerequisite to Turkey's development and continued independence. After Turkey's admission to the League of Nations in 1932, he participated actively in League and later in UN activities, traveling widely and negotiating numerous treaties and agreements to further these objectives. He coauthored the Balkan Pact (1934), the core of which guaranteed each country's territorial integrity and obligated it to consult its allies in the event of threats to peace in the Balkans. He also initiated within the framework of the League a revision of the 1923 Straits Convention, successfully reversing several limitations on Turkey's sovereignty, and in the Montreux Convention of 1936 obtaining control over the International Commission's functions. Turkey's peaceful actions contrasted markedly to Italy's; the outcome reaffirmed Tevfik Rüştü's belief in the League—which he supported in the face of attempts to dilute its effectiveness. He was vice-president of the Naval Commission of the Geneva Disarmament Conference, twice served as president of the Assembly, and presided over other conferences, becoming known in Geneva as "the traveling Turkish agent" because of his extensive personal diplomacy. A pragmatist at heart, he recognized the limitations of international organizations but argued that their deficiencies were exaggerated. The UN Charter, he believed, had to be taken as the source of inspiration for Turkish domestic and foreign policies and could be made to work better only if it were made to function as soon as possible.

BIBLIOGRAPHY:
A. *Görüşlerim* [My views], (Istanbul, 1945); *Görüşlerim: İkinci Kitap* [My views: Book II[, (Istanbul, 1968); *Lozan' in Izlerinde On Yil* [Ten Years in the Steps of Lausanne] (Istanbul, 1935).
B. CB 1942, 27–28; Joseph C. Grew, *Turbulent Era: A Diplomatic Record of Forty Years, 1904–1945*, vol. 2 (Cambridge, MA, 1952); Metin Tamkoç, *The Warrior Diplomats: Guardians of the National Security and Modernization of Turkey* (Salt Lake City, UT: 1976).

Bruce R. Kuniholm

ARCE, José Antonio (15 October 1881, Lobería, Buenos Aires—28 July 1968, Buenos Aires). *Education*: doctor of medical science, 1902; New Faculty of Medicine of Buenos Aires, 1903. *Career*: various posts in medicine; professor, National Univ. of Buenos Aires, 1907–47, rector, 1922–26; delegate, Latin American Medical Congress, Montevideo, 1907, Rio de Janeiro, 1909, Havana, 1922, International Cancer Congress, Madrid, 1933, and International Surgical Congress, Brussels, 1938; Conservative party deputy, 1903–13, Buenos Aires Provincial Chamber of Deputies, national deputy, 1916–20, 1924–28, president, 1912–13, first vice-president, 1934–38; member, Constitutional Convention, Province of Buenos Aires, 1934; ambassador to China, 1945–46; delegate to UN, 1946–49, president, Special General Assembly Session on Palestine Question, 1948.

Arce's position as a leading surgeon and politician helped him improve health and hygiene in Argentina during his life. Appointed ambassador to the Republic of China (1945–46), Arce took $10,000 worth of surgical instruments to present to China as a "token of good will" when he arrived in Shanghai. He became Argentina's first representative to the UN in September 1946. In one of his first speeches, Arce replied to Soviet opposition to the seating of his nation on the grounds that she had remained neutral during World War II by saying, "If the policy of neutrality . . . led us along the wrong road, we have now retraced our steps and that should be enough." (NYT, 29 July 1968, 20) Throughout his career at the UN, Arce supported universal membership in the organization, stating that nations should be admitted if they publicly declared they accepted the obligations set down in the Charter. He was a strong supporter of the powers of the General Assembly. Although the Security Council might make recommendations, Arce argued that the General Assembly should have the ultimate power to decide the question of admission. In this light, he supported the entry of Austria, Spain under Francisco Franco, and Pakistan after its separation from India. He was a leading if unsuccessful advocate of having the Charter amended to abolish the veto held by the five permanent members of the Security Council.

After Arce abruptly resigned his diplomatic post in 1950 for reasons not fully known, he continued his strong advocacy of the UN and the General Assembly. As a private citizen he publicly criticized the Soviet Union for not complying with the Charter, for not trying to resolve Eastern European questions, and for its involvement in the Korean War. He called for a reorganization of the UN, especially the powers of the General Assembly and the Security Council, so that persons in different countries "can freely express their wishes, their aspirations and the purposes that prompted them when trying to form part of the community of nations." (Arce, *Right Now*, 11.)

While most of Arce's writing after his return to Argentina dealt with historical themes, especially the life of former Argentine President Julio Argentino Roca, Arce also published an extensive history of a boundary dispute with Chile in the Straits of Magellan stemming from 1843 in the hope that the foreign ministries of the two nations might arrive at a dignified agreement. That work plus his many writings that sought to extend the effectiveness of the UN made him an important publicist.

BIBLIOGRAPHY:

A. *De Buenos Aires à Shanghai* (Buenos Aires, 1948); *La cuestión de limites con Chile* (Buenos Aires, 1965); *The Malvinas, Our Snatched Little Isles* (Madrid, 1951); *Mi vida: Auto-Recopilación de hechos y comentarios para una posible biografía*, vol. 1 (Madrid, 1957); *Right Now* (Madrid, 1951); *United Nations, Admission of New Members* (Madrid, 1951).

B. CB 1947, 10–12; NYT 29 Jul 1968, 20; *Quién es quién en la Argentina* (Buenos Aires, 1963), 49; *United Nations Bulletin* 45 (1 May 1948), 355; WWLA 1940, 36.

Neale J. Pearson

ARMAND, Louis (17 January 1905, Cruseilles, Haute Savoie, France—30 August 1971, Villiers sur Mer, Calvados, France). *Education*: Ecole Polytechnique, 1924; Ecole des Mines, 1926. *Career*: government mining engineer, Clermont-Ferrand, 1926–34; railway mechanical engineer, 1934–38, chief of matériel research, French National Railways (SNCF), 1938–46, assistant general manager, 1946–49, general manager, 1949–55, president, 1955–57; president, European Atomic Energy Commission (Euratom), 1958–59; president, Lorraine coal mines, 1959–64; executive secretary, International Union of Railways, 1961–71.

Armand was one of the world-class French engineers and administrators of the twentieth century. As he was rising rapidly in the hierarchy of the French National Railways (SNCF) World War II struck. After the French defeat in 1940, Armand began organizing Resistance groups among railwaymen and headed Resistance-Fer, an influential body. Arrested by the Germans in June 1944, he was freed from a death sentence by the liberation of Paris that August.

At the top levels of the SNCF after the war, he presided over their reconstruction. Then he led the way to electrification of major lines on the network and dieselization of the rest. Under his leadership, the SNCF won a world reputation for efficiency and innovation. He used his position with the International Union of Railways to promote their internationalization, with the Trans-Europe Express trains, the European pool of freight cars, and the international adoption of automatic coupling.

A convinced "European," he played a key role in negotiations leading to the Euratom treaty of 1957 and then served as head of the European Atomic Energy Commission at its beginning. He has been credited with originating the word *Euratom*. He ardently supported a railway tunnel from France to England and worked diligently to encourage industrial development in Africa. He served on the Armand–Rueff Committee in 1960 to recommend measures to open up and make more productive the French economic and social system. In the many organizations on which he served and in his writings he urged innovation, looking forward rather than backward, and disdained those, too common about him, who feared the future.

BIBLIOGRAPHY:

A. With M. Drancourt, *Le Pari européen* (Paris, 1968), *Plaidoyer pour l'avenir* (Paris, 1961); *Propos ferroviaires* (Paris, 1970), *Simple propos* (Paris, 1968).

B. CB 1957, 21–23; *Le Monde* 1 Sep 1971, 1; LT 31 Aug 1971, 12; R. Millot, "Notice sur la vie et les travaux de Louis Armand, *Vie sociale* no. 4 (1973), 195–208; NYT 31 Aug 1971, 12.

James M. Laux

ARMSTRONG, Hamilton Fish (7 April 1893, New York—24 April, 1973, New York). *Education*: B.A., Princeton, Univ., 1916. *Career*: *New Republic*, 1916–17; U.S. Army, 1917–19; military attaché to Serbian War Mission in the United States, 1917, to American legation, Belgrade, 1918–19; *New York Evening Post,* 1919–21, special correspondent, Europe, 1921–22; managing editor, *Foreign Affairs*, 1922–28, editor, 1928–71.

For half a century, Armstrong, *Foreign Affairs*, and the Council on Foreign Relations stood as preeminent voices on foreign policy in the United States. From the day the newly founded CFR decided to follow *Isaiah Bowman's dictum to "publish or perish," Armstrong served in an editorial capacity with the quarterly *Foreign Affairs* (1922–73). Under the leadership of *Archibald C. Coolidge and Armstrong, it gained wide recognition as one of the foremost journals of international opinion in the world, and it compiled an enviable record of making the first public pronouncements of ideas soon to be released as policy by the government. Armstrong worked diligently to maintain that reputation, and the journal published articles and essays representative of many viewpoints. Armstrong also served as the executive director of the Council on Foreign Relations from its beginning, and it emerged as one of the most important moderate internationalist bodies formed after World War I. While other organizations worked toward involving the public in foreign policy, the Council remained a selective body which also sought to influence thinking and planning. He also was president from 1944 to 1958. Armstrong moved among the rich and powerful in foreign affairs, and his contacts allowed special entry to important government figures. He was the first American journalist given an audience by Adolf Hitler, and Armstrong proved to be among the first to assess correctly Hitler's nature and his threat to the world.

While as editor Armstrong kept the public stance of *Foreign Affairs* balanced, he held strongly internationalist views. He had played a major role in convincing *Elihu Root to write the lead essay for the first issue, and Armstrong long held Root's published view of the problems of postwar foreign policy. Root had argued that, in democracies, wars stemmed from mistaken beliefs; to prevent such tragedies, the public must be informed to make proper judgments. With proper information, the people would be able to overcome emotion and greed. Autocracies, wrote Root, echoing *Woodrow Wilson, make war for sinister purpose; democracies do not. To Armstrong, those words laid the basis for his journal's stance, and it provided the means for developing a proper foreign policy for nations.

Armstrong came to his internationalism through journalism and contacts with Woodrow Wilson. While a student at Princeton, his nominal Republican leanings had changed during Wilson's campaign for the presidency. During his Princeton years, Armstrong had dined at Wilson's home prior to Wilson's election. As a staff member of the *Daily Princetonian*, Armstrong searched through old issues to discover editorials written by Wilson when the latter was editor; then, after the war came, Armstrong used foreign affairs news to gain appointment to the editorial staff of the campus paper. Later, as a trustee, vice-president (1928–30), and president (1935–37) of the Woodrow Wilson Foundation, he showed his continuing loyalty to Wilsonian ideals. He was introduced to these when as a military attaché en route to Belgrade in 1919 he stopped in Paris, where he watched the delegates gather for the peace settlement. Much of the rest of his life centered on the decisions made there.

Armstrong's Democratic leanings strengthened during the 1920s as he perceived the Republican party overcome by isolationist tendencies. As editor of *Foreign Affairs*, he invited essays from a broad spectrum of individuals, but felt more comfortable with papers that stressed American interdependence. He traveled in Europe, where the decline of monarchies and of democracies alike reinforced his conviction that the United States must act more vigorously in the world to promote the interests of peace. He urged an end to economic nationalism and greater cooperation with other nations. When vigorous action did not come, Armstrong became more pessimistic about the future. The further decline of the goals of internationalism during the Depression and the rising threats to world peace brought by the Fascists intensified Armstrong's pessimism. The continuing failure of the United States to take positive action prompted him to write *Can We Be Neutral?* in 1936, and *Can America Stay Neutral?* in 1939. U.S. entry into World War II saw Armstrong among those internationalists appointed by *Franklin D. Roosevelt to the Advisory Commission on Post-War Problems, and he later became a special assistant to the ambassador to London. In 1945, he served as an advisor to the U.S. delegation at the UN Conference in San Francisco.

Armstrong continued his advocacy of an active U.S. world policy urging immediate implementation of the Marshall Plan and strong support for regional security pacts under Article LI of the United Nations Charter.

BIBLIOGRAPHY:

A. *The Calculated Risk* (New York, 1947); with Allen W. Dulles, *Can America Stay Neutral?* (New York, 1939), *Can We Be Neutral?* (New York, 1936); *Hitler's Reich: The First Phase* (New York, 1933); *Peace and Counterpeace: From Wilson to Hitler: Memoirs of Hamilton Fish Armstrong* (New York, 1971); *When There Is No Peace* (New York, 1939); 49 articles in *Foreign Affairs.*

B. CB 1948, 24–26; *Foreign Affairs* (51 Jul 1973), 651–54; NYT 25 Apr 1973, 46; WWWA 5, 20.

Frank W. Abbott

ARNOLD-FORSTER, William Edward (1886, England—October 1951, England. *Education*: Winchester Coll., 1899–1901; continued privately; Slade School. *Career*: artist, landscape painter, pastellier; served in Navy, World War I; Blockade and Raw Materials Section, Paris Peace Conference; Labor party, secretary to Lord Robert Cecil, 1914–20; secretary to Lord Parmoor and researcher, lecturer, and pamphleteer to Women's International League, National Peace Council, League of Nations Union, Joint Committee of Christian International Organizations, 1920–39; technical adviser and official representative, Geneva, Disarmament Conference (1932); contributor, *Headway, Peace, Peace Year Book, New Statesman and Nation*, and *Manchester Guardian*, 1920–39; researcher, author, administrator, Fabian International Bureau, Transport House, UN Association, UN relief organizations, 1940–51.

In the aftermath of World War I and the formation of the League of Nations, the basic rationale for internationalism found a much more favorable marketplace than it had prior to 1914. In the emerging peace sentiment of the 1920s, internationalists discovered that the theoretical formulations enshrined in the League and its Covenant needed publicists and *philosophes* to get them popularly accepted. Britain became a veritable intellectual bourse. Those who could simplify and popularize the League, who could trade upon its practicality against competing ideologies, and who could demonstrate that internationalism was the security with the greatest and safest return were at a premium. Arnold-Forster became an internationalist-*philosophe* par excellence. An expert on the law of the sea, arbitration, sanctions, and disarmament, he was commissioned by internationalist groups within the peace movement to reduce complex tenets to terms the public could understand. He was very successful. The Disarmament Conference of 1932 witnessed the apogee of his career, when his reports from Geneva were widely distributed in Britain. During 1932–33 he lectured throughout Britain and the United States and addressed a joint session of the Canadian Parliament on disarmament.

While eclectic and unoriginal in his own ideas, he was an innovative communicator whose "holistic" presentations on behalf of the League stressed the connections linking international organization, arbitration, sanctions, security ("collective assurance"), and disarmament. He placed an inordinate faith in his ability to define aggression and in the "immense power" of the League system. Thus he greatly overestimated the deterrent capacity of the League's coercive legal, moral, economic, and political force; and he greatly underestimated the need for the use of armed force. Yet he was noted for asking all of the difficult questions, frequently developing the opponent's case, whether pacifist in debates about sanctions or militarist in confrontations over the efficacy of disarmament. He was also noted for offering answers to difficult questions as in his call for rearming the League after its failure in the Ethiopian affair. His argument, based upon an idealized rationale, led to confusion. For years he had largely laid the failures of the disarmament talks upon the tepid policies of his own government. Thus his subsequent attempt to convince the public to rearm on behalf of the League did not wash.

Arnold-Forster remained convinced that the nationalist preoccupations of Britain and France prevented any peaceful resolution to the crises of the 1930s. From the ruins of World War II he looked back upon the disarmament conference of 1932 as the missed opportunity to prevent that conflict. After World War II he called for England to stand behind the United Nations. He agreed with Clement Atlee that there was nothing wrong with the principles of the League of Nations; its failure was in their application.

Arnold-Forster was a close associate of *Robert Cecil, *Gilbert Murray, and ⁺Norman Angell, but he traveled a greater distance to the left than any of them and remained basically satisfied in that journey. As such, politically, he was much closer to Noel Baker and *Konni Zilliacus. But he was philosophically very close to Liberal Gerald Bailey, the directing secretary of the National Peace Council, who commissioned much of his work.

A "conscientious artist," expert gardener, and early ecologist and environmentalist, Arnold-Foster was an unusual person who combined his interests and vocation. He died shortly after having led an environmental protest against the British Navy and while an exhibition of his pastel landscapes was being shown. He was deemed to have had an inherent genius for understatement, which kept his work from receiving the type of attention it deserved. While a successful publicist for the cause of disarmament and international unity, he maintained a very modest profile; he willingly acquiesced in subordinate roles.

BIBLIOGRAPHY:
A. "Arbitration, Security, Disarmament," in *The Intelligent Man's Way to Prevent War*, ed. Leonard Woolf (London, 1933), 314–455; *The Blockade 1914–1919* (Oxford, 1939); *The Disarmament Conference* (London, 1931); *The First Stage of Disarmament* (Geneva, 1932); *The New Freedom of the Seas* (London, 1942); *Sanc-*

tions of the League of Nations: A Debate (London, 1931); The United Nation's Charter Examined (London, 1946); The Victory of Reason: A Pamphlet on Arbitration (London, 1926).

B. Apollo 54 (Nov 1951), 120; Donald S. Birn, The League of Nations Union, 1918-1945 (Oxford, 1981); Lorna Lloyd and N. A. Sims, British Writing on Disarmament from 1914-1978: A Bibliography (London, 1979); LT, 11 Oct 1951.

Louis R. Bisceglia

ARNOLDSON, Klas. See Biographical Dictionary of Modern Peace Leaders.

ASQUITH, Herbert Henry (12 September 1852, Morely, Yorkshire, England—15 February 1928, Sutton Courtney, Berkshire, England). Education: graduate, Balliol Coll., Oxford Univ., 1874; studied law at Lincoln's Inn, London. Career: barrister, London; member of Parliament, 1886-1918, 1920-24; home secretary, 1892-95; chancellor of the exchequer, 1905-8; prime minister, 1908-16; war secretary, 1914; member, House of Lords, as Earl of Oxford and Asquith, 1925-28.

Asquith, the British prime minister (1908-16) takes his place among the internationalists largely by position rather than inclination. He was a lawyer with the right credentials to rise rapidly in Liberal party leadership circles. The liberal imperialism of Lord Rosebery, Richard Haldane, and *Edward Grey attracted his support, as did prewar arbitration efforts, but his greater interest while chancellor of the exchequer and prime minister before World War I was in domestic affairs, where he was a fiscal conservative.

As prime minister, Asquith's attention was caught up in international policy making when the Agadir crisis of 1911 demanded strong leadership. Before that he allowed Grey broad discretion as foreign secretary. When *David Lloyd George and Winston Churchill shifted from favoring peace at almost any price to outspoken championing of a strong anti-German stance, Asquith had to take notice. From then as long as he held office, Asquith was immersed in international issues.

Asquith's most important act of leadership in foreign policy came with the British decision to enter the war against Germany. He led the Cabinet inexorably to its decision, approving Churchill's plan to put the fleet on a war footing along with France several days before the Cabinet was ready to enter the war. He was masterly in marshaling support for his cause by using Conservative party leaders' enthusiasm for backing France and in taking full advantage of Germany's unprovoked invasion of Belgium to form a broad consensus for war.

Asquith's wartime leadership was marked by hesitation and indecision, so that his place was taken by the younger and more imaginative Lloyd George in late 1916. However, before that, in September 1914, Asquith had spoken out favoring a postwar European partnership, later claiming credit for planting the seed for the League of Nations at that moment. Asquith,

Grey, and Haldane, who were all free from Cabinet responsibility after 1916, were leading backers of a league, and Asquith made the surprising statement in Parliament in late 1917 that Britain's motive for entering the war had been to see that a league of nations was established. When the war ended, he met *Woodrow Wilson and supported the president's plan. Asquith spoke in favor of the League of Nations in and out of Parliament becoming one of the honorary presidents of the League of Nations Union in November 1918. As long as he lived, Asquith remained a strong proponent of the League of Nations.

BIBLIOGRAPHY:

A. *Fifty Years of Parliament*, 2 vols. (London, 1926); *The Genesis of War*, 2 vols. (London, 1923); *Memories and Reflections, 1852-1927*, 2 vols. (London, 1928); *Occasional Addresses, 1893-1916* (London, 1918); *Speeches by the Earl of Oxford and Asquith*, ed. J. B. Herbert (London, 1928).

B. Winston S. Churchill, *Great Contemporaries* (New York, 1937); DNB 1922-30, 29-40; George W. Egerton, *Great Britain and the Creation of the League of Nations* (Chapel Hill, NC: 1978); Roy Jenkins, *Asquith* (London, 1966); Stephen Koss, *Asquith* (London, 1976); LT 16 Feb 1928, 14; McGraw-Hill, *Encyclopedia of World Biography* 1 (New York, 1973), 269-71; NYT 15 Feb 1928, 1; J. A. Spender and Cyril Asquith, *Life of Herbert Henry Asquith, Lord Oxford and Asquith*, 2 vols. (London, 1932); Henry R. Winkler, *The League of Nations Movement in Great Britain, 1914-1919* (New Brunswick, NJ, 1952).

C. The Asquith papers are in the Bodleian Library, Oxford Univ.

Lyle A. McGeoch

ASQUITH, Violet. See Bonham Carter, Violet.

ASSER, Tobias Michael Carel (28 April 1838, Amsterdam—29 July 1913, The Hague). *Education*: Athenaeum Illustre, Amsterdam, 1856; doctor of law, Univ. of Leiden, 1860. *Career*: solicitor, Amsterdam, 1860; professor, Athenaeum Illustro, Amsterdam, 1862-74, Univ. of Amsterdam, 1874-93; member, Council of State, 1893; minister of state, 1904; Nobel Peace Prize, 1911 (shared with Alfred Fried).

The life and works of Asser provide remarkable support for the view that to win fame and public recognition requires above all the possession of those qualities that are in demand in the era in which a person happens to live. Asser's life spanned a period when, in the wake of nineteenth-century Romanticism, nationalism began to assume menacing dimensions. The resulting tendency to attach exaggerated importance to the absolute autonomy of national legal systems coexisted poorly with the simultaneous rapid expansion of international traffic and trade. An escape from this dilemma could not possibly be furnished by theoretical or philosophical contemplations of law. For these Asser, being eminently practical by nature, had no time. A born diplomat and negotiator, gifted with a brilliant, ingenious intellect and a very clear mind, Asser's approach to legal problems was directed entirely to the concrete. To him, the measure of value of legal study was the social relevance of its application. Frequent contacts with *Gustave Rolin-Jaequemyns and John Westlake between 1862 and 1865 led Asser to the discovery of his true vocation: to participate in, preferably to preside over, the "codification" of private international law. In 1869, these three founded the *Revue de droit international et de législation comparée* and became its first board of editors. In 1873 Asser joined Rolin and nine others in founding the Institut de Droit International, still the most prestigious scholarly institution in its field. In 1880 his *Sketch of Private International Law* appeared, and it was soon translated into all the important European languages.

The creation of the *Revue* and the Institute were expressions of the desire for a universal forum for the discussion of international law, in the hope of harmonizing standards so that cases of a private international law character could be resolved despite different national jurisdictions. During the next twenty years, various attempts were made, notably by *Pasquale Mancini, to convene conferences for the purpose of harmonization in the field of private international law. Until 1893 these efforts remained fruitless, but that year, thanks to Asser's perseverance, the long-fostered project was realized with The Hague Conference on Private International Law. As was due to the true architect, Asser was chosen to preside not only in 1893 but also in 1894, 1900, and 1904. Moreover, he chaired the two Conferences on the Law of Exchange of 1910 and 1912.

In later years, Asser became particularly involved in public international law. During both Hague Peace Conferences (1899, 1907), Asser distinguished himself as representative of the host country. After the creation, in 1900, of the Permanent Court of Arbitration, Asser served as arbitrator on several occasions in noted international disputes.

BIBLIOGRAPHY:

A. *Eléments de droit international privé ou du conflit des lois* (Paris, 1884); numerous articles in *Revue de droit international et de législation comparée* (Brussels) especially "Droit international privé et droit uniforme" (12 [1880]); *Le Duché de Limbourg et la Confédération Germanique* (The Hague, 1863); *Les Sociétés anonymes établies à l'étranger* (Brussels, 1863); *Une Législation uniforme sur les lettres de change* (Paris, 1864).

B. Tony Grey, *Champions of Peace* (Birmingham, England, 1976), 109–11; C. C. A. Voskuil, "Tobias Michael Carel Asser (1838–1913)," *Livre du centenaire 1873–1973* (Basel, 1973), 11–31.

Willen G. Zeylstra

ATHERTON, Frank Cooke (1 July 1877, Honolulu—29 May 1945, Honolulu). *Education*: Wesleyan Univ., 1894–96. *Career*: Honolulu businessman and civic leader, 1896–1945.

The proverbial man for all seasons, Atherton achieved notable success as a businessman, philatelist, horticulturist, civic leader, and internationalist. President and subsequently chairman of Castle and Cooke, one of Hawaii's oldest and most important business firms, he was also noted for his collection of Hawaiian stamps, his work with orchids and hibiscus, and his energetic civic involvement.

Of Atherton's various civic undertakings, none was more important than a lifelong commitment to the YMCA. Following the footsteps of his father, who helped organize the YMCA in Hawaii in 1869, Atherton became involved with the group at the turn of the century and was elevated to its presidency shortly thereafter. In this capacity he was instrumental in the formation of Honolulu's racially integrated Nuuanu YMCA in 1917, then one of only two such experiments anywhere in the United States, and became active in the national YMCA's international program.

Impressed by Atherton's forthright manner, national YMCA leaders prevailed upon him in 1922 to direct a long-planned conference on Pacific issues. The famed Institute of Pacific Relations grew out of this decision. In the wake of talks with Asian, European, and North American leaders, Atherton concluded that another conference would likely contribute little to the solution of regional problems but that an independent research and discussion group might. Persuaded by his arguments, the YMCA relinquished control of the project to an international planning committee under the general leadership of Stanford University President *Ray Lyman Wilbur. This committee organized the Institute and arranged its inaugural conference in Honolulu during July 1925. Atherton raised the funds necessary to support this gathering and thereafter served as the group's treasurer until a procedural dispute led him to sever most of his ties in 1935. The Institute, with its remarkable record of conferences, publications, and recommendations, is testimony to his imagination, dedication, and organizational talent.

BIBLIOGRAPHY:

A. "Orchid Growing in Hawaii," *Bulletin: American Orchid Society* 2 (no. 2, 1933), 24–27.

B. Gwenfread E. Allen, *The YMCA in Hawaii: 1869–1969* (Honolulu, 1969); *Honolulu Star Bulletin* 30 May 1945, 1; Paul F. Hooper, *Elusive Destiny: The Internationalist Movement in Modern Hawaii* (Honolulu, 1981); George F. Nellist, ed., *Men of Hawaii*, rev. ed., vol. 5 (Honolulu, 1935), 73–75.

C. The Atherton papers are in the Institute of Pacific Relations Collection, Univ. of Hawaii Archives.

Paul F. Hooper

ATKINSON, Henry Avery (26 August 1877, Merced, CA—24 January 1960, Baltimore, MD). *Education*: B.A., Pacific Methodist Coll., 1897; Garrett Biblical Institute. *Career*: ordained Congregational ministry, 1902; pastor, Albion, IL, 1902–4, Springfield, OH, 1904–8; professor of sociology, Atlanta Theol. Sem., 1904–8; pastor, Atlanta, GA 1908–11; secretary, Social Service Commission of Congregational Churches, 1911–18; general secretary, Church Peace Union, 1918–55.

In December 1917 Atkinson became secretary of the National Committee on the Churches and the Moral Aims of the War, a body initiated by the Church Peace Union (established and endowed by +Andrew Carnegie in February 1914 and later called the Council on Religion and International Affairs). In this post, Atkinson became nationally known as having a primary concern with world peace. One year later, he was named general secretary of the Church Peace Union. In that position he began the international work to which he devoted his life. At the same time, he was appointed secretary of the American Council of the World Alliance for Promoting International Friendship Through the Churches, an affiliate of the Union.

Atkinson traveled abroad extensively, demonstrating special administrative skills. He was not a doctrinaire or absolute pacifist, having supported entry into World War I and having worked late in the 1930s to induce the United States to forgo its neutrality and enter World War II. Yet, as a pacifist in principle, he was considered an ideal leader for the Union, since one of its primary objectives was to educate the clergy and churches in what it called a "peace program."

Under Atkinson's leadership, the Union made many significant contributions in the area of world order, some of them seminal, contributing significantly to later creative advances. The Union conducted a campaign for a speedy ratification of the peace treaty after World War I, embodying the League of Nations Covenant; worked steadily thereafter for the adherence of the United States to the League of Nations and the World Court; developed its affiliate, the International World Alliance so that by 1945 it had chapters in thirty-nine countries; conducted during the first half of the 1940s a continuing series of meetings and conferences across the country on the general theme "Win the War—Win the Peace"; and helped prepare the people of the United States between World War I and 1945 to be a founding member of the United Nations. In all these programs, Atkinson revealed his full personal commitment.

International Peace Through Religion was a daring project of the Union, initiated in 1924 and pursued vigorously by Atkinson. It envisaged a plan to develop a World Religious Congress in behalf of "international friendship and good will." Persons from the various denominations did not meet to discuss or compare religions; the objective was to focus on the goal of world peace "the spiritual force" of their several religious faiths. Representatives of eleven religions attended the preliminary meeting at Geneva, 12–14 September 1928, and twenty countries were represented. A number of planning sessions followed in different places in Europe, and four commissions were created with specific assignments. Commission I issued a book, *Causes of War* (1932). The date for the general conference, however, was regularly set ahead because various factors militated against holding it, specifically the Depression of the 1930s and World War II. The world conference was never held, a genuine disappointment for Atkinson.

Another program that involved Atkinson fared better. In 1921 the Church Peace Union acted as the administrative agency to plan a Universal Christian Conference, which assembled in 1925. Afterward, Atkinson continued to serve as administrative secretary until 1932, and he became involved in several other preliminary meetings, culminating in the creation of the World Council of Churches in 1948.

One of the most influential actions of the Church Peace Union during Atkinson's secretaryship was the development of the Pattern for Peace Through Religion. Catholics, Jews, and Protestants collaborated directly for months in drawing up the statement and then distributing it widely. The Pattern for Peace was translated into Spanish and Portuguese, and British religious leaders commended it. Mass meetings and religious study courses based on the Pattern were arranged.

Participation in the United Nations Conference in San Francisco in 1945 as an unofficial consultant for the Department of State was a capstone to Atkinson's and the Union's efforts for more than three decades to help achieve an organized world. Even then they fully understood their work must go on to help make the UN an effective and universal organization.

BIBLIOGRAPHY:

A. *The Church and the Peoples Play* (Boston, 1915); *Men and Things* (New York, 1918); *Prelude to Peace* (New York, 1937); *Theodore Marburg: The Man and His Work* (New York, 1951).

B. Samuel M. Cavert, *Church Cooperation and Unity in America, 1900–1970* (New York, 1970); DAB supp. 6, 24–25; Charles S. Macfarland, *Pioneers for Peace Through Religion* (New York, 1946); NCAB 44, 178–79; NYT 26 Jan 1960, 30.

C. Extensive Atkinson materials are in the papers of the Council on Religion and International Affairs in the Butler Library, Columbia University.

A. William Loos

ATTOLICO, Bernardo (17 January 1880, Canneto di Bari, Italy—9 February 1942, Rome). *Education*: graduate in law, Univ. of Rome, 1907. *Career*: professor of economics and finance, technical institutes, 1903–7; Commissariat for Emigration, 1907–12; secretary, Royal Commission on Treaties of Commerce, 1914–15; Italian representative on various Allied economic agencies, London, 1915–18; technical adviser, Italian delegation, Paris Peace Conference, 1919; commissioner for Italian economic and financial affairs in the United States, 1919; head, Communications Section, League of Nations Secretariat, 1920, high commissioner for Danzig, 1920, 1921, head, Armaments Section, 1921–22, under secretary-general, 1922–27; ambassador to Brazil, 1927–30; ambassador to the Soviet Union, 1930–35; ambassador to Germany, 1935–40; ambassador to the Vatican, 1940–42.

Attolico's professional destiny was shaped by World War I. His service in London on such Allied agencies as the Wheat Executive, the War Purchases and Finance Council, and above all the Maritime Transport Executive afforded a training and taste for international cooperation. At the war's end he was patronized by *Francesco Nitti, premier (1919–20), who sought vainly to dissuade Italians from a pre-occupation with national war gains in favor of the conciliatory international order propounded by *Woodrow Wilson. Charged by Nitti in 1919 with the care of Italo–American economic affairs, Attolico operated in the ambience of Wilsonianism whose institutional expression was the League of Nations. It was natural for him to move to the new League's Secretariat. There he rejoined forces with his colleagues from the Allied Maritime Transport Executive, the Englishman *Arthur Salter and the Frenchman *Jean Monnet. Occupying various posts, especially as one of the under secretaries-general, Attolico became one of that group of technocrats who, in the absence of guidelines and precedents, set a pattern of vigorous and far-ranging action by the Secretariat, sometimes to the politicians' dismay. In practice, they simply applied on the world stage the habits of executive authority learned in the Allied war effort.

Although a good international civil servant, Attolico was not insulated from the winds of politics. That he was not made permanent Danzig commissioner was due largely to great power rivalries. His recall and appointment to the Italian foreign ministry in 1927 was in order to allow another Italian, Giacomo Paulucci de'Calboli, to ascend to a League under secretaryship. Ironically, Attolico's best-known contributions to international peace stem from his subsequent career as an Italian diplomat. Specifically, he is credited with helping Benito Mussolini dissuade Hitler from war in the Munich crisis in 1938, and with contributing forcibly to Italy's decision for neutrality in 1939. This earned him Nazi opprobrium and recall from Berlin the next year.

Attolico wrote no memoirs, nor have any of his private papers surfaced; he thus remains somewhat enigmatic. The most rounded sketch is that of Magistrati, counselor of his Berlin embassy. Herein, Attolico appears a weary and aloof figure. Not the easiest taskmaster, he was hardest on himself; a legendary professional competence rested on his extraordinary diligence. In truth, he worked himself to an early death while still in diplomatic harness.

BIBLIOGRAPHY:

A. For eleven pamphlets on emigration published from 1909 to 1915, see *Bibliografia per la storia dell'emigrazione italiana in America*, ed. Grazia Dore (Rome, 1956).

B. *Dictionnaire diplomatique* 5 (Paris, n.d.), 47; *Dizionario biografico degli italiani* 4 (Rome, 1962), 556–60; *Enciclopedia italiana* supp. 1938–48 (Rome, 1962), 304–5; Massimo Magistrati, *L'Italia a Berlino, 1937–1939* (Milan, 1956), *Il prologo del dramma: Berlino, 1934–1937* (Milan, 1971).

Alan Cassels

AUSTIN, Warren Robinson (12 November 1877, Highgate Center, VT—25 December 1962, Burlington, VT). *Education*: Ph.B., Univ. of Vermont, 1899. *Career*: attorney, St. Albans and Burlington, VT, 1899–1931; Republican senator, 1931–46; ambassador to the UN, 1946–53.

After a successful legal career in Vermont, Austin was elected senator from that state in 1931. His anti–New Deal stance in domestic affairs and a bipartisan, internationalist position in foreign relations characterized his Senate career. As a member of a small Republican Senate establishment, Austin was a follower on domestic issues, overshadowed by Republican colleagues William E. Borah, *Arthur H. Vandenberg, Jr., Charles L. McNary, and Robert A. Taft. No major piece of legislation bears his name, nor did he significantly provide leadership on major domestic issues. Austin made his name as an internationalist senator. Throughout his law career, he had participated in a number of international legal conferences of the American Bar Association. More significantly, in 1916–17 he worked in China negotiating public works contracts for the American International Corporation. These experiences account for his belief in an American democratic, moralistic, capitalistic mission to the world. He sensed that America should have a flexible foreign policy that incorporated independence without isolation, backed by a strong national defense. Austin's attitude placed him in a tiny minority on the heavily laden isolationist, Republican aisle of the Senate in the 1930s. For example, he voted against the neutrality laws while advocating a buildup in the country's military defenses. After Pearl Harbor, Austin found few congressional Republican followers to his call for planning for the postwar world. But the *Franklin D. Roosevelt administration recognized his bipartisan support, and Austin worked with the State Department on postwar planning. Furthermore, in 1943, he played a key role in directing the Republican party toward accepting a plank favoring an international organization in its 1944 platform. Subsequently, it was not surprising to find him supporting the United Nations Relief and Rehabilitation Administration, the Dumbarton Oaks recommendations, and the 1946 British loan.

As a reward for his bipartisan support, *Harry S Truman appointed Austin as the first ambassador to the UN in 1946. Strongly believing in the UN concept, Austin carried to his post his long-held idealistic premises of how the world organization could improve the conduct of international relations. Nationalistic positions could be brought together at the UN under a system of moral and legal rules where world public opinion could scrutinize each nation's foreign policy. Austin soon found his views isolated from the administration's policy of containment toward the Soviet Union. The government often bypassed its UN Mission in major policy decisions. A weaker individual might have resigned. Austin, however, intellectually accepted the U.S. position by rationalizing containment tactics as a series of short-term alternatives that supported the long-range goals of the UN. By doing this, Austin established a fundamental role for the UN ambassador that has continued. He spoke emphatically for U.S. policy while having little or no influence on policy decisions. The nation's leaders accepted the important relationship between the United States' continued support (albeit rhetorical) for the UN as a part of the country's foreign policy. With Austin's cooperationist outlook, they appreciated his sincerity as the U.S. spokesman in support of the UN.

Throughout his tenure at the world organization, Austin slowly hardened his attitude toward the Soviet Union and its allies. He came to this view because of the continued intransigence of the Soviets coupled with the administration's hard-line stance. The early months of the Korean conflict in 1950 and 1951 capped his conversion to the ranks of the Cold Warriors. After early 1951, he was pessimistic about any agreement with the Communists. Nonetheless, to the end of his career, he never lost faith in the importance of the UN as a peace-keeping organization.

BIBLIOGRAPHY:

B. CB 1944, 18–22; George T. Mazuzan, *Warren R. Austin at the U.N., 1946–1953* (Kent, OH, 1977); NYT 26 Dec 1962, 1; Beverly Smith, "A Yankee Meets the World," *Saturday Evening Post* 219 (24 Aug 1946), 10–12; *Time* 57 (5 Feb 1951), 16–18.

C. The Austin papers are at the Univ. of Vermont.

George T. Mazuzan

AVENOL, Joseph Louis Anne (9 June 1879, Melle, Deux-Sèvres, France— 2 September 1952, Duillier sur Nyon, Switzerland). *Education*: Univ. of Poitiers; LL.D., Univ. of Paris. *Career*: French Ministry of Finance, 1905–23; deputy secretary-general, League of Nations, 1923–33, secretary-general, 1933–40.

Avenol, the League of Nations' second secretary-general, presided over the most tumultuous period in that organization's history. A man of greater sympathy for the spirit of the Covenant might have arrested the precipitous erosion of League authority in the 1930s. Unfortunately, most assessments of Avenol's tenure are justifiably critical.

Trained in economics and finance, he served in various capacities with the French Treasury from 1905 to 1923. During this period, he acquired the right-wing political views that were to mark many of his decisions as secretary-general. Avenol's first association with the League of Nations came in 1923, when he was named deputy secretary-general. It had been expected that *Jean Monnet would continue in that position and succeed *Eric Drummond at the helm, but Monnet withdrew from the Secretariat to pursue other activities. The need for a French financial expert at Geneva led Premier Raymond Poincaré to nominate Avenol. As deputy secretary-general, an important but narrowly specialized position, Avenol was responsible for the coordination of postwar financial reconstruction. His talents were eminently suited to this task.

Although initially opposed to Avenol as his successor in 1932, Drummond was bound by 1919 agreements that the next secretary-general would be French. Besides, Avenol had support from a number of nations opposed to Drummond's tendency to centralize power. The candidate was openly cynical about the League's political activities. He felt, for example, that treaty revision was impossible within the framework of Geneva; he also believed that the potentially contradictory commitments involved in upholding both the Treaty of Versailles and the Convenant could only be rationalized by a moral international agreement linked to disarmament. Thus, when Avenol became secretary-general on 1 July 1933, it was clear that he doubted the League's capacity to deal with the era's most crucial issues.

His first crisis set the tone for his administration. The Sino–Japanese dispute over Manchuria began in 1931, and Japan announced its intention to quit the League before Avenol assumed its directorship. Nevertheless, in contrast to the majority of League delegates, he evinced some sympathy for the Japanese cause, advocating the avoidance of any League political action in Manchuria. Instead he preferred a program of modest technical aid to China. The trend toward ignoring the Covenant's stipulations against aggression reached its logical consequence during the Italo–Ethiopian crisis of 1935–36. Even following Benito Mussolini's attack on Ethiopia, Avenol felt it best to avoid Covenant obligations. His fundamental sympathy for the Italian political system was betrayed by his failure to support even minimal economic sanctions and his championship of lifting sanctions in July 1936. In both Manchuria and Ethiopia, Avenol's actions diminished the role of the secretary-general in dealing with world political issues, thus irrevocably damaging the Geneva institution as a bulwark of collective security.

Avenol's motives may be sought in domestic French politics. His views at this crucial historical juncture coincided with conservative French opinion. He sympathized with Foreign Minister Pierre Laval's policy of forging an Anglo–Franco–Italian bloc against Germany and considered Ethiopia a small price for Italy's adherence to such a coalition. The real danger to France was Germany; the latter's containment required the maintenance of Italian friendship regardless of concessions. The League was sacrificed to this policy.

Politically weakened, the League's future as an international organization lay in the technical field. In this area Avenol made some contribution. One of the League's major weaknesses had been the aloofness of the United States. With the political role of the League truncated, it was hoped that the United States now could be enticed into involvement. In 1938 *Cordell Hull responded to an Assembly request for nonmember nations' views on economic and social questions. Seeing an opportunity for an expanded

American role at Geneva, Avenol established an expert committee and appointed *Stanley M. Bruce, an Australian economics expert, as its chairman. It was charged with examining the League's entire organization for economic and social work and with recommending methods to involve all nations. The Bruce Report, published in August 1939, recommended the secretary-general's proposal to establish a Central Committee for Economic and Social Questions, separate from the political divisions of the League Assembly and open to nonmembers, to exercise control over the specialized, functional agencies. The rump Assembly that met in 1940 approved the Bruce Report and formally established the Central Committee. The war prevented its functioning, but its existence foreshadowed the postwar United Nations Economic and Social Council. It is fitting that Avenol's most important achievement should lie in the financial and technical area of his personal expertise.

As the war progressed and fears mounted about a German invasion of Switzerland, a move developed to relocate the various agencies of the League. In May 1940, Princeton University offered facilities to support the technical services of the League for the duration of the conflict. Avenol, apparently convinced that the Axis would triumph and reconstitute Europe, opposed the Princeton transfer. France's position in the future "new order" might be imperiled if the secretary-general cooperated in moving the international organization, which had opposed the policies of the Fascist leaders. Despite Avenol's objections, the transfer occurred in August 1940. Other functional agencies also moved out of Switzerland.

Avenol resigned on 31 August 1940. It is likely that the new Vichy regime insisted on his resignation because a French secretary-general symbolized a strong attachment to League principles, totally inconsistent with the Pétain–Laval policy of collaboration. There are also indications that Avenol personally was not unfavorably inclined to an Axis victory. His last act as secretary-general was to attempt to shut down the League altogether, an effort undercut by the Supervisory Commission in September 1940. He was replaced by *Seán Lester, who held the position of acting secretary-general until 1946. Avenol's last official act, therefore, was not only to abandon the League but to attempt to destroy even its symbolic value to the international community.

There are no favorable analyses of Avenol's tenure as secretary-general, except for his efforts in fostering the Bruce Report. The role of the secretary-general as a behind-the-scenes advocate of international order vanished under his administration. Mitigating circumstances might be cited as explanation, if not excuse, for his policies. His administration coincided with the rise of Hitler in Germany and the breakdown of European security. It is questionable whether history would have been altered even if Avenol had demanded compliance with Covenant obligations. He was also a Frenchman. The threat to his own nation inherent in the Third Reich undoubtedly contributed to his tendency to view the League as an instrument for appeasing the Nazis and later as a device for guaranteeing France's place in the anticipated "new order." His loyalty to his conception of France was higher than to the League or its principles.

BIBLIOGRAPHY:

A. "The Future of the League of Nations," *International Affairs* 13 (Mar–Apr 1934), 143–53; "The League and China: New Links Between Nanking and Geneva," *Headway* 11 (Jun 1929), 105; *L'Europe silencieuse* (Neuchâtel, Switzerland, 1944).

B. James Barros, *Betrayal from Within: Joseph Avenol, Secretary-General of the League of Nations, 1933–1940* (New Haven, CT, 1969); Raymond B. Fosdick, *The League and the United Nations After Fifty Years: The Six Secretaries-General* (Newtown, CT, 1972); NYT 3 Sep 1952, 29; Arthur W. Rovine, *The First Fifty Years: The Secretary-General in World Politics 1920–1970* (Leiden, Netherlands, 1970), 105–72.

C. The Avenol papers are at the Archives du Ministère des Affaires Étrangères.

William I. Shorrock

AYDELOTTE, Frank (16 October 1880, Sullivan, IN—17 December 1956, Princeton, NJ). *Education*: B.A., Indiana Univ. 1900; A.M., Harvard Univ., 1903; Rhodes scholar, Oxford Univ., 1905–7, B. Litt., 1908. *Career*: instructor, Southwestern Normal School, California, PA, 1900–1901, Indiana Univ., 1901–2, Louisville Male High School, 1903–5; associate professor, Indiana Univ., 1908–15; professor, Massachusetts Institute of Technology, 1915–21; president, Swarthmore Coll., 1921–40; director, Institute for Advanced Study, 1939–47.

A man of boundless energy, Aydelotte's contributions to internationalism took a variety of forms, encompassing the areas of both ideas and of practice. In the aftermath of World War I, Aydelotte through his writings and as American secretary of the Rhodes Trustees (1918–53) and president of the Association of American Rhodes Scholars (1930–56) strongly supported the Oxonian system of education with its emphasis on self-learning, ideas he put into practice as president of Swarthmore College with one of this country's first undergraduate honors programs. As a Rhodes scholar, Aydelotte appreciated the intellectual and social benefits accruing from study abroad and strove constantly to improve the quality of the Rhodes applicants. In addition, from 1925 to 1950 he drafted programs for and served on the Guggenheim Foundation, where he chaired the Educational Advisory Board. Aydelotte also saw the benefit in foreign students having access to the American educational system. He was involved with the fellowship program of the Spellman Foundation and later, more tangentially, with the Commonwealth Fellowship program. The thread running through all these activities was the belief that the road to peace lay not through political alliances but in the greater understanding that would result from these international educational relations.

Aydelotte's internationalist aspirations took more concrete form during the last fifteen years of his life. He had become the director of the Institute for Advanced Study in 1939, and in 1940 he was instrumental in persuading the Institute and Princeton University to invite and provide facilities for the Economic, Financial, and Transit Department of the League of Nations when it was forced to leave Switzerland. Other international and League agencies took up residence in the United States and Canada, but it is clear that without the initial invitation from Princeton and the Institute they would never have been able to survive the war. In addition, although sixty-five years old in 1945, Aydelotte served on a twelve-man Joint Commission on Palestine, organized by the British and U.S. governments, to make recommendations regarding war-dislocated European Jews and Palestine. Its generally moderate proposals were, however, considered unsatisfactory to the British government and viewed as totally unacceptable to either side in Palestine.

While his practical activities are of considerable historical importance, Aydelotte would have been the first to point to his educational efforts as possessing the greater significance. His emphasis on international education helped make it a commonplace feature of colleges and universities.

BIBLIOGRAPHY:

A. *The American Rhodes Scholarships* (Princeton, NJ, 1946); *Breaking the Academic Lock Step* (New York, 1944); *Oxford of Today* (New York, 1922); *The Oxford Stamp* (New York, 1917).

B. *An Adventure in Education: Swarthmore College Under Frank Aydelotte* (New York, 1941); Frances Blanshard, *Frank Aydelotte of Swarthmore* (Middletown, CT, 1970); LT 19 Dec 1956, 10; NYT 18 Dec 1956, 31; WWA 1954, 115–16.

C. The Aydelotte papers are at Swarthmore Coll.

James Ross Macdonald

AZCÁRATE Y FLÓREZ, Pablo de (30 July 1890, Madrid—13 December 1971, Geneva). *Education*: Free Institute of Education, Madrid; Univs. of Madrid, Zaragoza, and Paris; doctorate in law. *Career*: professor of administrative law, Univ. of Santiago de Compostela, 1913, Univ. of Granada, 1915; member of Spanish Parliament, 1918–19; League of Nations Secretariat, 1922–36; Spanish ambassador to the United Kingdom, 1936–39; member, UN Secretariat, 1948–52.

After attending the Free Institute of Education, an important center of humanist and rationalist thought in Spain, and after studying and teaching law, Azcárate became a member in 1922 of the Minorities Section of the League of Nations Secretariat. There he remained eleven years. Of the various posts he held with international organizations over a thirty-year period, this one undoubtedly provided the greatest opportunity for innovation and creativity. First as the principal assistant to the Norwegian, *Erik Colban, the initial director of the Minorities Section, and eventually as director himself from 1930 to 1933, Azcárate played a leading role in developing and administering an entirely new international activity. Racial, linguistic, and religious minorities in fifteen states, primarily in Eastern Europe, were guaranteed equal civil and political rights and the right to maintain their cultural identity by treaties placed under the guarantee of the Council of the League of Nations. Individuals claiming violation of the treaties could petition the Council directly. Azcárate was actively involved in reviewing these petitions, preparing recommendations for action to League Council members, negotiating solutions to the problems raised, and visiting the states concerned for consultation with leaders of both governments and minorities. This was the first significant international organization activity in the field of human rights.

Azcárate's subsequent career included service as one of two deputy secretaries-general of the League of Nations, with responsibility for the internal administrative services of the Secretariat (1933–36), and as the Spanish republic's ambassador in London throughout the Spanish Civil War (1936–39). In 1948 he headed a UN fact-finding mission to Palestine and from 1949 to 1952 was principal secretary of the UN's Palestine Conciliation Commission. After 1952 he lived in retirement in Geneva, writing on Spanish history and politics and on his experiences as an international official.

BIBLIOGRAPHY:

A. *League of Nations and National Minorities: An Experiment* (Washington, 1945); *Mission in Palestine, 1948–1952* (Washington, 1966); *Protection of National Minorities* (New York, 1969).

B. IWW 1971–72, 74; NYT 15 Dec 1971, 38; WW 1972, 128.

Richard Veatch

AZEVEDO, José Philadelpho de Barros (13 March 1894, Rio de Janeiro—7 May 1951, The Hague). *Education*: School of Political Science, Paris; LL.B., Rio de Janeiro, 1914. *Career*: professor, Univ. of Brazil, 1932–41, dean of faculty and vice-rector; president, Institute of Advocates of Brazil, 1936; justice, Brazilian Supreme Court, 1942–46; mayor, Rio de Janeiro, 1945–46; judge, International Court of Justice, 1946–51.

Azevedo's background as a university professor, member of many commissions on the codification and study of international law, judge on the Brazilian Supreme Court, and public official gave him a broad range of competence. While he sat on the International Court of Justice (1946–51), he wrote several separate and dissenting opinions that spelled out his unique legal philosophy. According to him, the judge must confine himself to an objective examination in a particular case and should not engage in political questions that fall under the jurisdiction of the Security Council. Azevedo is best known for his explanation of what is termed the teleological approach to treaty interpretation. In viewing the UN Charter as a treaty, he construed it as a document designed to be a guide to the fulfillment of the principles that it spells out, such as human rights, the peaceful settlement of disputes, and the self-determination of peoples. The member states should treat the Charter as a contract containing an international higher law, similar to the Latin concept *jus naturale*.

In several opinions, Azevedo raised a basic question. What are the purposes of the United Nations, and how has that organization developed or is to develop to fulfill its goal? He used the term *teleological* to mean moving toward certain ends of a continuous process of becoming. In this regard, in cases before the Court regarding the issue of the admission of new members, he was critical of the Security Council for not meeting the obligations of the Charter and becoming entangled in political squabbles. He believed that the principle of universal membership for the international organization was being violated by such disputes. Although he died before his term was to expire in 1954, his separate and dissenting opinions gave him an outstanding reputation as an outspoken jurist committed to a noble set of ideals. He was also regarded as a prominent spokesman for Latin America's contributions to the development of international law.

BIBLIOGRAPHY:

A. *Destinação do immovel* (Rio de Janeiro, 1932); *Valor da transcricas* (Rio de Janeiro, 1942).

B. *ICJ Yearbook 1946–47*, 52; Alan T. Leonhard, "The Legal Thought of the Latin American Judges on the International Court of Justice," dissertation, Duke Univ., 1967; *Encyclopedia Grande Delta Larousse* (Rio de Janeiro, 1972), 656; WWLA 1947, 4, 46–47.

Alan T. Leonhard

B

BADAWI, Abd al-Hamid (13 March 1887, Alexandria, Egypt—5 August 1965, Cairo). *Education*: license in law, Khedival Law Coll., 1908; LL.D., Univ. of Grenoble, 1912, *Career*: assistant prosecutor, Tanta, 1908–9; judge, Court of Appeal, Cairo, 1908–9; professor, Khedival Law Coll., 1912–14; secretary to minister of justice, 1914–19; secretary to prime minister, 1920–22; counselor, Ministry of Public Works for Royal Affairs, 1922–26; president, Royal Affairs Council, 1926–40; minister of finance, 1940–42; member of Senate, 1942–46; minister of foreign affairs, 1945–46; delegate, San Francisco Conference, 1945; judge, International Court of Justice, 1946–65, vice-president, 1955–58.

Badawi was at home both in private and in public international law. He was not a theoretical jurist but a practical legal counselor whose intelligence and profound knowledge assisted him in the interpretation and application of the law in cases and situations that won him a high reputation as a competent jurist.

In the international field, Badawi rendered legal advice to his government as a member of the Egyptian delegation at the Montreux Conference in 1937. He succeeded in the defense of Egypt's position to abolish the Mixed Court (established 1875) of Egyptian and foreign judges to settle disputes between native Egyptians and foreigners in Egypt. After four years of a transitional period, the Court was abolished in 1939.

As foreign minister, Badawi participated in several international conferences and distinguished himself as a spokesman for his country's independence while Egypt was still under British influence under a 1936 treaty granting Britain military bases near Cairo and Suez. At the San Francisco Conference (1945), Badawi often spoke in support of creating a strong UN General Assembly and of giving it veto power over the decisions of the Security Council. He also was a member of the 1945 UN committee that formulated the statute of the International Court of Justice. After election to the ICJ in 1946, he took an active part in its activities and was reelected in 1948 and in 1958. He was named vice-president of the Court in 1955, a position he held until his death. Badawi was an accomplished diplomat, a persuasive speaker, and a great expert in the law. He was also a warm friend and a loyal member of the institutions he served, both national and international.

BIBLIOGRAPHY:
A. "Impact of Foreign Capitulatory Rights on the Egyptian Judiciary and Legislation," in *Golden Jubilee of the Egyptian Mixed Courts* (Cairo, n.d.); *Lectures on Comparative Penal Law* (Cairo, 1914); other papers in Egyptian journals.

B. NYT 6 Aug 1965, 27; Abd al-Razzaq Sanhuri, "Dr. Abd al-Hamid Badawi," *al Qada* 25 (Mar 1966), 1-21.

Majid Khadduri

BAKER, Newton Diehl (3 December 1871, Martinsburg, WV—25 December 1937, Cleveland, OH). *Education*: B.A., Johns Hopkins Univ., 1892; LL.B., Washington and Lee Univ., 1894. *Career*: lawyer, Martinsburg, WV, 1894-99, Cleveland, OH, 1899-1901, 1921-37; private secretary to Postmaster General William L. Wilson, 1896; legal adviser, Cleveland Board of Equalization, 1901-3; city solicitor of Cleveland, 1903-12; mayor of Cleveland, 1912-16; secretary of war, 1916-21.

The cause of international comity had no more persistent advocate following World War I than, paradoxically, the former secretary of war. Baker had sent nearly two million American soldiers into the European war, but, as he readily admitted, he was a pacifist at heart who believed that God had made men for better things than to suffer recurrently the "deadly blight" of war. He thus supported *Woodrow Wilson's fight for U.S. participation in the League of Nations, campaigned vigorously in 1920 for his friend, *James M. Cox, castigated the Republican candidate for his ambiguous stand on the League, and called for U.S. entry as soon as practicable. After returning to the practice of law in Cleveland in 1921, Baker took Wilson's cause as his own for the next decade. In January 1923, when the American Association for International Cooperation and the League of Nations Non-Partisan Committee merged to form the League of Nations Non-Partisan Association, Baker assumed a prominent role as secretary of the Cleveland chapter. In 1924 he fought, as a member of the Resolutions Committee, for a pro-league plank in the platform at the Democratic Convention.

When a majority of members favored delay, he took his minority report favoring immediate entry to the convention floor, where his skillful, passionate plea elicited wild applause. The enthusiasm, however, was not translated into delegate votes. Four years later, at the Democratic Convention in Houston, mindful of the mounting prejudice against the League, Baker shifted his emphasis to the World Court, urging the Resolutions Committee to approve a plank for U.S. entry to that body, including mention of the League only in an accompanying declaration of sympathy and cooperation. This tactic also failed.

As an accomplished orator, Baker was in frequent demand and invariably insisted that his topic be international cooperation. So ardent and persistent was his advocacy of the League that speculation arose that he might be named its secretary-general. He was appointed to the Permanent Court of Arbitration (1928-37). As early as 1926 he proposed the cancelation of war debts as a practical step toward European recovery, and he questioned the efficacy of renouncing war as an instrument of policy by simple declaration as provided in the Kellogg-Briand Pact. He deplored and challenged the growth of isolationist sentiment in the 1930s in writings and radio addresses. When the League proved unable to curb aggression in Europe and the Far East, Baker came again to believe that the democracies must prepare to defend their principles. When Japan moved into Manchuria, he helped promote a petition urging an economic boycott. He still held to his conviction of the irrationality of war as a means of settling international controversies, but as his life drew to its close he believed that the basic principles of civilization were at stake and that action against aggression was probably the only way to preserve them.

Baker was frequently a potential candidate for high political office, particularly in the presidential years 1928 and 1932. Had he had a viable political power base and had he taken these possible candidacies more seriously his courageous battles for Leagues participation might have met with more success. It can hardly be doubted that in spirit he was well represented in San Francisco at the establishment of the United Nations in 1945.

BIBLIOGRAPHY:

A. *Address at the Tomb of Woodrow Wilson in Washington Cathedral, April 13, 1932* (New York, 1932); *Address of Newton D. Baker in Boston, Oct. 8, 1920* (Boston, 1920); "The Debate on the League of Nations," in *Politics: The Citizen's Business*, ed. William A. White (New York, 1924); *Frontiers of Freedom* (New York, 1918); *How Can We Stay out of War?* (Boston, 1935); *The Present International Situation* (Cleveland, OH, 1923); *War in the Modern World* (Boston, 1935).

B. Clarence H. Cramer, *Newton D. Baker: A Biography* (Cleveland, OH, 1961); DAB 22, 17–19; NYT 26 Dec 1937, 1; Hoyt L. Warner, *The Life of Mr. Justice Clarke: A Testament to the Power of Liberal Dissent in America* (Cleveland, OH, 1959); Carl Wittke, "Mr. Justice Clarke—A Supreme Court Judge in Retirement," *Mississippi Valley Historical Review* 36 (Jun 1949), 27–50.

C. The Baker papers are in the Manuscript Division, Library of Congress and at the Western Reserve Historical Society.

David W. Hirst

BAKER, Ray Stannard (17 April 1870, Lansing, MI—12 July 1946, Amherst, MA). *Education*: graduated from Michigan Agricultural Coll. (later Michigan State Univ.), 1889; Univ. of Michigan Law School, 1891. *Career*: reporter and journalist, *Chicago News-Record*, 1892–97, *McClure's*, 1898–1906, *American Magazine*, 1906–15; special envoy to Great Britain for State Department, 1918; head, American Press Bureau, Paris Peace Conference, 1919; biographer and historian, 1920–46.

A leading advocate of *Woodrow Wilson's plan for world peace, Baker in his early years was an unlikely internationalist. Descended from early New England settlers and raised on the Wisconsin frontier, he was unabashedly proud of being a "native American." He early aspired to write the great American novel, while in *McClure's* he celebrated the battles and heroes of America's war against Spain. In *Our New Prosperity* (1900), he proclaimed the nation's arrival among the world's powers. Baker uncovered less happy aspects of national life in his muckraking articles after 1902, but these exposures focused on domestic affairs.

After 1906 an altered vision laid the basis for Baker's wartime conversion to internationalism. Despite widespread recognition, muckraking left him dissatisfied, while mounting evidence of social conflict was frankly frightening. Seeking a new approach he published under the nom de plume David Grayson the first of an immensely popular fictional series of "adventures in contentment." Where the hard-headed reporter had seen the clash of individuals, races, and, eventually, nations, Grayson, a sort of post-Emersonian transcendentalist, described a higher reality in which conflict dissolved and individual nations became "functions of civilization." The Old World powers fought for limited, materialistic ends; America would fight to restore the shattered unity of humankind. True American nationalism was internationalism. Baker's internationalism thus shared the imperatives of his progressivism, not only in proclaiming democracy a worldwide ideal but also in seeking to restore community on a global scale.

A change in political allegiance convinced Baker that Wilson was the authentic prophet of this creed. Although Baker had worked closely with *Theodore Roosevelt until 1906, their relations soured following the president's attack on muckraking and slid downhill until the preparedness issue brought a decisive break in January 1916. Until then, Baker's dealings with Wilson had been cordial but cautious. Although he applauded Wilson's "missionary diplomacy" in Latin America, he continued to have reservations concerning domestic policy. During late 1914 and 1915, he criticized the "empty legalism" of the neutrality policy no less than Roosevelt's militarism and +William Jennings Bryan's pacifism. Turning again to fiction, Baker toyed briefly with the idea of nonresistance while publicly supporting the American League to Limit Armaments. Although his conversion to internationalism preceded his embrace of Wilson, he was thoroughly in the president's camp by mid-1916.

From Baker's departure to Europe in 1918 until the outbreak of World War II, he produced countless memoranda, numerous articles, and some fifteen volumes on behalf of Wilson and internationalism. In *What Wilson Did at Paris* (1919), published serially while approval of the treaty hung in the balance, Baker urged compromise to accommodate the legitimate interests of contending parties. In *Woodrow Wilson and World Settlement* (1922), published when the League's weaknesses were already apparent, he stated the case for internationalism in the more philosophic terms that David Grayson preferred. Critics faulted a resulting tendency to pretend America alone had no "interests," plus his misrepresentation of Wilson's knowledge of the "secret treaties." But a greater number of favorable reviews and a Pulitzer Prize for his multivolume biography of Wilson in

1940 confirmed that Baker had become a leading spokesman for the Wilsonian vision.

BIBLIOGRAPHY:

A. *American Chronicle* (New York, 1945); *Native American* (New York, 1941); *What Wilson Did at Paris* (Garden City, NY 1919); *Woodrow Wilson: Life and Letters*, 8 vols. (Garden City, NY, 1927–39); *Woodrow Wilson and World Settlement*, 3 vols. (Garden City, NY, 1922).

B. Robert C. Bannister, Jr., *Ray Stannard Baker: The Mind and Thought of a Progressive* (New Haven, CT, 1966); David Chalmers, "Ray Stannard Baker's Search for Reform," *Journal of the History of Ideas* 19 (Jun 1958), 422–34; DAB supp. 4, 46–48; NYT 13 Jul 1946, 14; John E. Semonche, *Ray Stannard Baker: A Quest for Democracy in Modern America, 1870–1918* (Chapel Hill, NC, 1969).

C. The Baker papers are in the Manuscript Division, Library of Congress.

Robert C. Bannister

BALCH, Thomas Willing (13 June 1866, Wiesbaden, Germany—9 June 1926, Atlantic City, NJ). *Education*: B.A., Harvard Coll., 1890; LL.B., Univ. of Pennsylvania, 1895. *Career*: attorney, Philadelphia, 1895–1926.

Although born abroad, Balch came from a well-established American line dating from colonial times. Because he was independently wealthy, he could devote considerable time to his interests, one of which was international arbitration. His father, Thomas, had written on this topic, and Balch became a noted publicist, not only for the concept of arbitration but also for the need for careful study to provide a background of issues in dispute. He wrote books on Alsace and Lorraine, on Alaska, and on the *Alabama* case. The latter reflected his belief that knowledge about the historical development of arbitration was important, and he produced a series of books, essays, and pamphlets to document its evolution.

Balch turned inevitably to consider international law and courts as a logical sequence to arbitration. He became interested in Emeric Crucé's plan of 1623, which he reproduced with a lengthy introduction in 1909. Crucé had proposed a world tribunal to hear disputes and uphold its decisions by force. Balch believed that Crucé's recommendations should be implemented. Balch increasingly saw parallels between the evolution of jurisdiction of the U.S. Supreme Court and that of a world tribunal, an idea promoted by other internationalists at the time. Such an approach seemingly lessened both obstacles and objections to what Balch hoped would become a reality. While he contributed essays to international law journals, Balch carefully ignored developments between 1914 and 1920 regarding the league of nations idea. To him, a tribunal alone, endowed with sufficient authority, was all the world needed for peace.

BIBLIOGRAPHY:

A. *The Alabama Arbitration* (Philadelphia, 1900); *the Alasko–Canadian Frontier* (Philadelphia, 1902); *Arbitration as a Term of International Law* (Philadelphia, 1920); "The Arctic and Antarctic Regions and the Law of Nations," AJIL 4 (1910),

265–75; *Emeric Crucé* (Philadelphia, 1900); *La Question des pêcheries . . . de l'Atlantique* (Brussels, 1909); *L'Evolution de l'arbitrage international* (Philadelphia, 1908); ed., *The New Cyneas of Emeric Crucé* (Philadelphia, 1909); *Some Facts About Alsace and Lorraine* (Philadelphia, 1895); *The United States and the Expansion of the Law Between Nations* (Philadelphia, 1915); *A World Court in the Light of the United States Supreme Court* (Philadelphia, 1918).

B. DAB 1, 529–30; WWWA 1, 49.

Warren F. Kuehl

BALFOUR, Arthur James (25 July 1848, Whittingehame, East Lothian, England—19 March 1930, Woking, England). *Education*: Trinity Coll., Cambridge Univ., 1869. *Career*: member of Parliament for Herford, 1874–85, for East Manchester, 1885–1906, for City of London, 1906–22; president, Local Government Board, 1885; secretary for Scotland, 1886; chief secretary for Ireland, 1887–91; leader of Commons and first lord of the treasury, 1891–92, 1895–1902; prime minister, 1902–5; leader, Conservative party, 1902–11; member, Committee on Imperial Defense, 1914; first lord of the admiralty, 1915–16; foreign secretary, 1916–19; lord president of the Council, 1919–22, 1925–29.

Balfour significantly influenced Conservative British politics and international relations for nearly sixty years. His parliamentary career began under the patronage of his uncle, Lord Salisbury, in 1874. As parliamentary private secretary to Salisbury (1878–80), he established important political contacts and obtained valuable experience in international relations at the Congress of Berlin, 1876. He advanced politically by opposing the Gladstone government.

In 1887 Balfour became Irish chief secretary, which was the beginning of what he regarded as the most thrilling and successful periods in his career. Having clearly demonstrated his leadership and ability, he moved to the Conservative leadership in the Commons. After becoming prime minister in 1902, he continued a policy of moving Britain away from its isolation. Balfour and Lord H.C.K. Lansdowne accomplished a diplomatic revolution capped by the Entente Cordiale, 1904. His considerable vision in international relations led to the creation of the Committee on Imperial Defense, which provided invaluable prewar defense planning for Britain. He did not generate a strong national following, and he left office in 1905. Thereafter, he consistently regarded defense issues, foreign affairs, and imperial policy as essentially nonpartisan issues. In 1912 he helped found the Garton Foundation to campaign for world peace.

In 1915, Balfour was named first lord of the admiralty in Herbert H. Asquith's reorganized Cabinet, and under David Lloyd George's government he became minister of foreign affairs, preparing the ground for full cooperation between Britain and the United States. He was largely responsible for securing Cabinet support of Jewish political and territorial claims in Palestine and its subsequent decision, the Balfour Declaration of 1917, gave Balfour great pride as a pro-Zionist.

Balfour took considerable interest in a league of nations as the idea gained in popularity after 1914. He favored a strong organization, one with sufficient force to uphold international law, moved to create the Phillimore Committee to draft a charter for a union, and at the Paris Peace Conference endorsed *Woodrow Wilson's proposals for a moderate settlement and a League of Nations. Thereafter, he spoke in favor of an Atlantic English-speaking federation, lent his name to the League of Nations Union, and headed the British delegation to the League. He chaired the first session of the Council, helping institute procedures, and for the next three years regularly represented Britain. His name, according to *Frank Walters, should be considered among the most important in the League's history. Balfour also attended the Washington Conference on the Limitation of Naval Armaments, and in 1922 he appealed for the cancelation of war debts in the Balfour Note to break the impasse on reparations and loan obligations. In whatever involvement, he sought to present a rational perspective, a position that has led to some criticism that he did not sufficiently support some of the League's efforts in the 1920s. Yet Balfour's Declaration and Note, his leadership at Paris, in the League, and in Washington demonstrate the breadth of his interest, knowledge, and influence in world peace and international accord. He would influence political and policy decisions to the end of his long life and career.

BIBLIOGRAPHY:

A. *Chapters of Autobiography* (London, 1930); *A Defence of Philosophic Doubt* (London, 1920); *The Foundations of Belief: Being Notes Introductory to the Study of Theology* (London, 1895); *Speeches on Zionism* (London, 1928); *Theism and Thought* (London, 1924).

B. Donald S. Birn, *The League of Nations Union, 1918–1945* (Oxford, 1981); Blanche E. C. Dugdale, *Arthur James Balfour*, 2 vols. (New York, 1937); George W. Egerton, *Great Britain and the Creation of the League of Nations* (Chapel Hill, NC, 1978); Alfred M. Gollin, *Balfour's Burden: Arthur Balfour and Imperial Preference* (London, 1965); Denis Judd, *Balfour and the British Empire* (London, 1968); Jon Kimche, *The Balfour Declaration* (London, 1968); Frank P. Walters, *A History of the League of Nations* (London, 1952).

C. The Balfour papers are in the British Library, the Public Record Office in London, and the family home, Whittengehame.

Stephen E. Fritz

BARBOSA, Ruy (5 November 1849, São Salvador, Brazil—1 March 1923, Petropolis, Rio de Janeiro). *Education*: B.A., São Paulo Univ., 1870. *Career*: lawyer, 1870–1923; member, Provisional Assembly, 1878–79; senator, 1891–1923; vice-president and minister of finance, 1889; delegate, Second Hague Peace Conference, 1907; judge, Permanent Court of International Justice, 1922–23; journalist and author.

An almost mythical figure in Brazilian history, Barbosa attracted attention as writer, speaker, linguist, philosopher, and lawyer. By the power of his oratory and his pen and by the sheer force of his personality, he is credited with leading Brazil from the status of colony into the rank of the world powers.

Barbosa made significant contributions to the development of international law, especially in the areas of equality of states, human rights, and relentless opposition to dictatorship. His interest in world affairs stemmed largely from the broadening experience of living in London, Paris, and Buenos Aires while in exile (1893–95) for his criticism of the government.

His first significant international contribution came at the Second Hague Peace Conference of 1907. He had been chosen by the Baron of Rio Branco, *José M. Paranhos, to head the delegation of Brazil, which marked the debut of the Latin American states on the world stage in their own right. Barbosa, in a peerless oration, pointed out at the Conference how the great empires of Europe and later Japan had emerged on the world stage through the gate of war, while the Latin American states came through the gate of peace. In positions taken during the discussions, Barbosa led the Latin American states in establishing their own identities. Their governments instructed their representatives to support Barbosa, and under his leadership they became a formidable bloc favoring law in the outstanding debate that absorbed the Conference, force versus law. Barbosa, as he faced the representatives of heavily armed nations, became known as a fearless David facing Goliath. The prestige of Brazil and other Latin American nations grew as his influence rose.

Barbosa made a constant and brilliant struggle for two principles: equality of all states before international law, and compulsory arbitration of international conflicts. He achieved a notable victory for the former in the predominant voting patterns established at subsequent international organizations. Unfortunately, the very concepts of equality and sovereignty that Barbosa advanced prevented efforts to broaden the arbitration process, and they blocked agreement in 1907 on provision for a court of justice.

Barbosa is noted for additional contributions to the international arena. By organizing the intellectual and spiritual force of Latin America on the world scene, he significantly advanced the concept of Pan Americanism then emerging. He also endorsed the idea of creating a permanent international body based largely on federal principles, using the United States as a model. He hoped the United States would also become a greater force in European and world politics supported by the Latin American nations. He represented Brazil at the Paris Peace Conference, embraced the League of Nations, and agreed to serve as Brazil's first League representative. There he participated vigorously in the debates to create the Permanent Court of International Justice, and he was elected one of its first judges. Unfortunately, he could not attend its first session and was replaced after his death in 1923.

BIBLIOGRAPHY:

A. *Cartas de Ingleterra* (Rio de Janeiro, 1896); *Conceptos modernos del derecho internacional* (Buenos Aires, 1916); *O Brasil em Haya* (Rio de Janeiro, 1909); *Obras completas* (Rio de Janeiro, 1942–).

B. *New International Yearbook* (New York, 1923), 79–80; Calvin D. Davis, *The United States and the Second Hague Peace Conference: American Diplomacy and International Organization, 1899–1914* (Durham, NC, 1976).

Virginia N. Mills

BAROODY, Jamil Murad (8 August 1905, Suq el-Gharb, Lebanon—4 March 1979, New York). *Education*: graduate, American Univ., Beirut, 1929. *Career*: economic and political observer in London for Saudi Arabia, 1929, 1935–39; Lebanese representative at New York World's Fair, 1939–40; lecturer, Princeton Univ., and writer, 1941–45; Saudi Arabian representative to San Francisco Conference and to UN, 1945–79.

Baroody's long career at the UN as Saudi Arabia's spokesman followed minor diplomatic assignments in the 1930s, notably as Arab political and economic adviser in London and as Lebanese representative to the 1939 World's Fair. Although not a citizen of Saudi Arabia, Baroody served the Arabs so successfully in the UN that they retained him as their permanent delegate.

There he established a reputation as a notable and dramatic orator who supported Taiwan in its long effort to prevent the admission of the People's Republic of China, and he championed environmental causes and better pay for UN employees. He became involved in Security Council and General Assembly debates over the Middle East, where he defended the Palestinian cause, opposed Zionism, and sought to terminate wars and resolve territorial questions. In addition to his regular delegation work, Baroody also participated in conferences on the law of the sea (1976, 1977). Because of his colorful personality, Baroody attracted an admiring audience. New York City made him an honorary citizen in 1939, and he was acclaimed at his death for his loyalty to UN objectives and ideals.

BIBLIOGRAPHY:

B. IWW 1978–79, 105–6; NYT 5 Mar 1979, II-11.

Warren F. Kuehl

BARRA, Francisco de la. See *Biographical Dictionary of Modern Peace Leaders*.

BARRETT, John (28 November 1866, Grafton, VT—17 October 1938, Bellows Falls, VT). *Education*: B.A., Dartmouth Coll., 1889. *Career*: instructor, Hopkins Academy, Oakland, CA, 1889; journalist, *San Francisco Chronicle*, 1889, *Astorian* (Oregon), 1890, *Tacoma Daily Ledger*, 1890, *Portland Morning Oregonian*, 1891, *Portland Evening Telegram*, 1891–94; minister to Siam, 1894–98; Spanish-American War correspondent for Hearst publications, 1898–99; publicist for international trade and lecturer for Republican party's Speakers Bureau, 1900–1901; delegate to Second Pan American Conference in Mexico City, 1901–2; commissioner for Asia,

St. Louis World's Fair, 1903; minister to Argentina, 1904, to Panama, 1905, to Colombia, 1906; director-general of the Pan American Union, 1907–20; correspondent for *El Universal* (Mexico City) at the Washington Conference, 1921; consultant and lecturer on Pan American affairs, 1922–37.

Barrett was a significant internationalist who favored a multilateral approach to international problems and generally opposed unilateral intervention. Although he began his diplomatic career in an age of imperialism, he did not seek territorial acquisitions. As an advocate of the Open Door Policy of equal opportunity of trade and protection of territorial sovereignty in Asia, Barrett espoused international cooperation instead of confrontation and exploitation. He believed the United States was fulfilling a civilizing mission by bringing the benefits of modern technology and free enterprise economics to developing peoples. Barrett saw the United States performing an important leadership function in the evolution of a stable and prosperous international socioeconomic world order. In taking this position, Barrett was representative of the progressive era generation of U.S. diplomats who believed in the international development of a modern technical society. To this end, both politically and materially advanced nations and developing states had a symbiotic relationship.

The fruition of Barrett's approach to international relations came during his tenure as director-general of the Pan American Union from 1907 to 1920. Beyond the realm of commercial publicizing, Barrett hoped to make the Union a viable institution in hemispheric diplomacy. He tried to expand its work to include mediation of the Mexican Revolution (1910–13), the Pan Americanization of the Monroe Doctrine, and the establishment of the Pan American Union as a hemispheric league of nations. By gaining the confidence of Latin America, Barrett believed the United States would be in a better position to work for responsible democratic governments and stable societies and economies throughout the hemisphere. Although Barrett found opposition to his internationalist views in the nationalistic Taft and Wilson administrations and in the State Department, many of Barrett's suggestions were adopted in some form in later years. The Good Neighbor Policy, nonintervention, multilateral Pan Americanism, and the restructuring of the Pan American Union into the Organization of American States in 1948 were policies in the tradition of Barrett's earlier internationalist approach to hemispheric diplomacy.

BIBLIOGRAPHY:

A. *Admiral George Dewey* (New York, 1899); *The Call of South America* (New York, 1922); *The Pan American Union and Peace* (Washington, 1911); *Pan Americanism and Its Inspiration in History* (Washington, 1916); *The Panama Canal* (Washington, 1914).

B. *Bulletin of Pan American Union* 72 (Dec 1938), 695–97; DAB 22, 25–26; NCAB 44, 130–31; NYT 18 Oct 1938, 38; Salvatore Prisco, III, *John Barrett: Pro-*

gressive Era Diplomat. A Study of a Commercial Expansionist, 1887–1920. (University, AL, 1973); *Vermonter* (Jan 1939), 7–13; WWWA 1, 61–62.

C. The Barrett papers are in the Manuscript Division, Library of Congress.

Salvatore Prisco, III

BARTHOLDT, Richard (2 November 1855, Schleiz, Thuringia, Germany —19 March 1932, St. Louis, MO). *Education*: gymnasium, Schleiz; studied law in Germany, 1877–78. *Career*: emigrated to United States, 1872; typesetter and printer in Brooklyn, Philadelphia, and St. Louis, MO, reporter on *Brooklyn Freie Presse*, and foreign editor, *New Yorker Staats-Zeitung*, 1872–77, 1878–84; editor-in-chief, *St. Louis Tribune*, 1884–91; member, St. Louis School Board, 1888–92; Republican congressman, 1893–1915.

Throughout his career, Bartholdt sought to bring about closer relations between his native Germany and his adopted country. This effort and the obstacles he encountered as a leader of German-Americans were instrumental in turning his energies toward the cause of international arbitration and world peace. In 1892 he became an articulate voice for the largely German-American population of his St. Louis district. He was a defender of a protective tariff and annexation of the Philippines, while strongly opposing prohibition of alcoholic beverages and attempts to restrict immigration. In later years he spoke regretfully of his vote for war against Spain in 1898.

The First Hague Peace Conference in 1899 and the arbitral tribunal it set up impressed Bartholdt. Afterward he became involved in the work of the Inter-Parliamentary Union (IU), a body of legislators serving in national parliaments who met regularly to promote the cause of international harmony. He persuaded the IU to hold its 1904 meeting in St. Louis to coincide with the international exposition being held there, and a sizable body of world dignitaries attended the conference and toured the United States. Following this success, he formed an American group of the IU and served as its head. Over the next decade, about two hundred U.S. senators and representatives joined the IU, though few expressed more than passing interest in its activities. However, a small corps of American legislators continued to attend its international meetings, and its strongest supporters persisted in believing that it might ultimately become a true world parliament.

In the decade prior to 1914, Bartholdt remained acutely aware of the dangers of a European conflict, as he hoped the United States might play a role in reducing tensions. He recognized, however, that as long as the Franco–Russian alliance was perceived as a threat by Germany, the latter would continue to arm for what he believed was self-defense. His periodic visits with German leaders and their assurances that their intentions were peaceful tended to reinforce his concern over the direction of British diplomacy, particularly the Entente Cordiale with France. He staunchly defended Germany's hold on Alsace–Lorraine. Bartholdt was strongly critical of Russian policies, particularly the backing of Pan-Slavic movements in Central Europe.

Prior to World War I, he participated in numerous international conferences, promoted the idea of periodic Hague conferences, drafted a model arbitration treaty and a plan for a congress of nations, was a strong supporter of *William H. Taft's proposed arbitration treaties, and in a variety of ways sought to strengthen the Hague tribunal. He was a leader in both the American Peace Society and the American Association for International Conciliation. With the outbreak of war in August 1914, Bartholdt became active in the prolonged, often intense debate over U.S. policies toward the belligerents. He became president of the American Independence League, a coalition of mainly German-American and Irish-American groups. The League contended that the United States was showing open partiality to the Entente and complained that critics often had their patriotism impugned by a pro-British press. In March 1915 Bartholdt went on a speaking tour to argue that Britain and her allies rather than the Central Powers were chiefly responsible for the war. In Congress he sponsored one of the bills to place an embargo on munitions shipments to the Entente.

U.S. entry into the war found him increasingly distressed at the nationalist hysteria directed at German-Americans and others critical of the war. Embittered by the Versailles Treaty with its war guilt provisions, he strongly opposed U.S. adherence to the League of Nations. In the 1924 election, Bartholdt broke a long tradition of support for the Republican party by enlisting in Robert La Follette's presidential campaign. During the 1920s he continued to attend meetings of the IU, though no longer a member of Congress. In his memoir, Bartholdt criticized those Anglophilic peace leaders in the United States who over the years had been more devoted to achieving close ties with their ancestral homeland than to pursuing the goal of world peace. This perceptive observation might have applied equally well to him and his native land.

BIBLIOGRAPHY:

A. *From Steerage to Congress: Reminiscences and Reflections* (Philadelphia, 1930).

B. DAB supp. 1, 53–54; Warren F. Kuehl, *Seeking World Order: The United States and International Organization to 1920* (Nashville, TN, 1969); NCAB 25, 120; David S. Patterson, *Toward a Warless World: The Travail of the American Peace Movement, 1887–1914* (Bloomington, IN, 1976); *St. Louis Post Dispatch*, 19 and 20 Mar 1932.

C. The Bartholdt papers are at the Missouri Historical Society.

Michael A. Lutzker

BARTHOU, Louis (25 August 1862, Oloron-Sainte-Marie, Basses-Pyrénées, France—9 October 1934, Marseilles). *Education*: Univ. of Bordeaux; doctor of laws, Univ. of Paris. *Career*: deputy, 1889–1922; senator, 1922–34; minister in several cabinets; prime minister, 1913; foreign minister, October–November 1917; chief delegate, Genoa Conference,

1922; president, Reparations Commission, 1922–26; delegate, Geneva Disarmament Conference, 1932–33; foreign minister, 1934.

Barthou was an internationalist in the sense that he regarded France's need for security as paramount and did everything possible to create a European system that would strengthen her against Germany. Old enough to remember the humiliation of the Franco–Prussian War of 1870–71, Barthou grew up in the patriotic atmosphere of the 1880s, becoming a fervent republican and nationalist. His brilliance as an orator and writer led him into political life, and he remained a member of Parliament for forty-six years. Able and astute, he rose through the system until he reached the premiership in 1913. When war erupted in 1914, Barthou enthusiastically adhered to the Union Sacrée proclaimed by President Raymond Poincaré and worked energetically to defeat the enemy. The death of his only son in battle intensified his hatred of Germany. During the war, Barthou repeatedly denounced the Germans for starting the conflict and demanded that the invader be made to pay for the material losses inflicted upon the Allies.

When the war ended, Barthou was charged with drafting the formal parliamentary report on the Treaty of Versailles negotiated by Georges Clemenceau. He strongly criticized it for failing to provide adequate guarantees against aggression and called for the breakup of the German empire. During the postwar period, Barthou supported a policy of vigilance, seeking to maintain Germany in a state of inferiority vis-à-vis France. As foreign minister in 1934, he confronted the growing menace of Adolf Hitler. Unable to control German rearmament through military conventions and distrustful of the Geneva Disarmament Conference, Barthou worked to establish an eastern Locarno that would secure the boundaries of the Reich while strengthening French ties to the states of Eastern Europe. Barthou visited Poland, Czechoslovakia, Yugoslavia, and Romania in an effort to link their security with that of France. To win over the hesitant Soviet Union, he successfully fought to gain its admission to the League of Nations and a permanent seat on the Council. At the same time, Barthou sought to restrain Germany by reinforcing the three-power guarantee of Austrian independence and by reconciling Italy and Yugoslavia, which had long been at odds. While welcoming King Alexander of Yugoslavia to France, Barthou was mortally wounded by a Croatian nationalist. His death hampered French efforts to create a security zone in Eastern Europe and eliminated a strong, capable statesman from the diplomatic scene. One observer, *Salvador de Madariaga, believed that in his short tenure as foreign secretary in 1934 Barthou was transfigured by his experiences at the League. He had come to see the need for a new style in international relations in which the big powers should cooperate with the smaller ones.

BIBLIOGRAPHY:

A. *Le Traité de paix* (Paris, 1919); *L'Heure du droit: France—Belgique—Serbie* (Paris, 1916); *1914–1915: L'Heure viendra qui tout payera* (Paris, 1915); *Promen-*

ades autour de ma vie: Lettres de la montagne (Paris, 1933); *Sur les routes du droit* (Paris, 1918).

B. Octave Aubert, *Louis Barthou* (Paris, 1935); J. B. Duroselle, *La Décadence, 1932–1939* (Paris, 1979); John R. Jones, Jr., "The Foreign Policy of Louis Barthou, 1933–1934," dissertation, Univ. of North Carolina, 1958; Salvador de Madariaga, *Morning Without Noon: Memoirs* (Westmead, England, 1974).

James Friguglietti

BASDEVANT, Jules (15 April 1877, Anost, France—5 January 1968, Anost). *Education*: Coll. of Autun; LL.D., Univ. of Paris, 1900, Sc.D., 1901. *Career*: lecturer, Univ. of Rennes, 1903–6; professor, Univ. of Grenoble, 1906–14, Univ. of Paris, 1918–46; member, French commission charged with developing the constitution of the League of Nations, 1918; jurisconsul for minister of foreign affairs, 1930; participant, negotiations at League of Nations Assembly and conferences on private international law; French representative, International Court of Justice, 1923–38; delegate, San Francisco Conference, 1945; rapporteur, commission to prepare Statute of International Court of Justice, 1945; judge of the International Court of Justice, 1946–65, president, 1949–52.

Oriented toward public international law by the schoolmate of his father, Louis Renault, Basdevant prepared *Recueil international des traités du XIXième siècle* (1915); then he published *Recueil des traités et conventions entre la France et les puissances étrangères* (1918–22) as three volumes on English and Italian prize court decisions. These works influenced his thinking, in which he placed research on legal reality in the foreground of international life. He believed in recording positive international law by which states would recognize themselves as being obliged. On the basis of this reality, jurists determine the application of the law in concrete cases and explain and clarify it. This is the essence of his *Dictionnaire de la terminologie du droit international* (1960).

Basdevant put forth the idea that the value of law existed with the introduction of ameliorations in the mind, but for him there was a fundamental distinction between stating the law and appraising it. His reflections drew him to ponder fundamental problems, including the idea of a state's sovereignty, its reserved domain, the legal basis of treaties, and international customs. His thought was expressed not only in his teaching but also in his presentation of controversies before the International Court of Justice (notably the *Lotus case*) and as judge in his concurring and dissenting opinions. He participated in the work of the court at a time of decisions that had considerable influence on the evolution of law, including the advisory opinion on the reparation for injuries suffered in the service of the United Nations and the Anglo–Norwegian fisheries case. Attentive to the transformation of international society, the clarity of his thinking on fundamental principles allowed him to focus on international realities. Recognizing that all lawsuits could not be decided by international judges, he defined the conditions under which the Court could intervene usefully and wield its influence on the development of law.

Basdevant's ideas cannot be neatly packaged. His positivism distinguishes itself from that doctrine of state control, where only those rules sanctioned by the state are allowed. While he concentrated on researching the law as effectively applied, he did not limit himself to textual readings but considered law as a social given in international life, reliant upon factual elements and dependent on the psychological, political, and moral environment for its effectiveness. His positivism was at all times tempered by his energetic, pragmatic, realistic, and humanistic faith.

BIBLIOGRAPHY:

A. "La Conclusion et la rédaction des traités et des instrumentes diplomatiques autres que les traités," *Recueil des cours*, 5 (1926), 539-643; "L'Affaire des pêcheries des côtes septentrionales de l'Atlantique entre les Etats-Unis d'Amérique et la Grand Bretagne devant la Cour de la Haye," *Revue générale de droit international public* 19 (1912), 421-582; "La Place et le rôle de la justice internationale dans les relations entre états et à l'égard des organisations internationales," in *Les Affaires étrangères*, ed. Basdevant et al. (Paris, 1959), 331-51; "Hugo Grotius," in *Fondateurs du droit international* (Paris, 1904), 125-267; "Règles générales du droit de la paix," *Recueil des cours* 4 (1936), 475-690.

B. CB 1950, 17-19; NYT 7 Jan 1968, 85.

P. Bastid

BAUER, Charles Christian (17 November 1881, Springfield, OH—15 March 1947, New York). *Education*: high school, Springfield. *Career*: engaged in advertising to 1922; president, Community Councils, New York, 1919-25; secretary, Woodrow Wilson Democracy, 1921-22; executive director, League of Nations Non-Partisan Association, 1922-23, 1925-29, assistant director, 1924; member, Executive Committee, National World Court Committee, 1932-34; director of financial development, National Committee for Mental Hygiene, 1936; member, Executive Committee, American Friends of Czechoslovakia, 1938; executive director, Tax Foundation, 1942-47.

During the 1920s Bauer was an active figure in several organizations with internationalist objectives, contributing skills as an administrator and publicist acquired during an earlier career in advertising. A keen admirer of *Woodrow Wilson, he helped organize the Woodrow Wilson Democracy in the spring of 1921 to perpetuate the former president's principles within the Democratic party. This small partisan body, for which Bauer served as secretary, functioned for a time as a virtual mouthpiece for Wilson's views.

In the late summer of 1922, Bauer assisted in the formation of the League of Nations Non-Partisan Committee, which, after a merger with the American Association for International Cooperation in December 1922, became the League of Nations Non-Partisan Association (LNNA), one of the most prominent internationalist groups of the interwar years. Serving as that organization's executive director until late 1923, Bauer set in motion a nationwide campaign of education and political action aimed at swift approval of U.S. membership in the League of Nations and the World Court. In 1924 he became the LNNA's assistant executive director, helping to establish the American Committee of the Geneva Institute of International Relations to provide guidance, information, and other services to American visitors to the League headquarters in Geneva. By the time he resumed his post as executive director in 1925, the LNNA had lowered its sights, having failed to make the League an issue in the 1924 presidential election.

Bauer remained executive director of the LNNA until 1929. Under his capable but unadventurous guidance, the Association retained League membership as its ultimate goal but emphasized a program of education and limited political activity that included membership in the World Court, cooperation with the League, revision of traditional U.S. neutrality policy, and the negotiation of Locarno-type arbitration treaties. After he resigned as executive director, Bauer retained his connection with the LNNA and assisted several other groups dedicated to a cooperative world order, but he never again attained a position of leadership within an internationalist organization.

BIBLIOGRAPHY:

A. *International Cooperation for Child Welfare* (New York, 1928).

B. Charles DeBenedetti, *Origins of the Modern American Peace Movement, 1915-1929* (Millwood, NY, 1979); Warren F. Kuehl, *Hamilton Holt: Journalist, Internationalist, Educator* (Gainesville, FL, 1960); NYT 16 Mar 1947, 60; WWWA 2, 49.

Robert D. Accinelli

BAXTER, Richard Reeve (14 February 1921, New York—26 September 1980, Boston). *Education*: B.A., Brown Univ., 1942; LL.B., Harvard Law School, 1948; diploma in international law, Cambridge Univ., 1951; LL.M., Georgetown; 1952. *Career*: research associate, Harvard Law School, 1954-55, lecturer, 1955-56, assistant professor, 1956-59, professor, 1959-80; judge, International Court of Justice 1978-80.

Baxter established his reputation in the field of internationalism through his teaching, scholarship, editorship of the *American Journal of International Law* (1970-78), and involvement in professional organizations. Baxter remained unusually broad in his interests at a time of increasing specialization in the field of international law. His writings on international waterways, humanitarian law of war, responsibilities for injuries to aliens, and the relationship between treaty and customary law reflect that diversity. In addition, he was known as an expert on the UN and taught courses on international air law and public international law. He believed in a law that should be enforced.

Baxter revealed little interest in philosophical or theoretical approaches; he became noted for his thorough scholarship, careful reasoning, objective analysis, and total commitment to projects and organizations, especially the American Society of International Law, where he served as president (1974–76), and the International Law Association. He served on the Permanent Court of Arbitration (1968–75), and his nomination and election to the ICJ in 1978 came because of his reputation, his nonideological approach, and his high standards.

BIBLIOGRAPHY:

A. "Armistices and Other Forms of Suspension of Hostilities," *Recueil des cours* 149 (1977), 353–99; ed., *Documents on the St. Lawrence Seaway* (New York, 1960); *The Law of International Waterways* (Cambridge, MA, 1964); with Doris Carroll, *The Panama Canal* (Dobbs Ferry, NY, 1965); with Louis B. Sohn, *Responsibility of States for Injuries to the Economic Interests of Aliens* (Washington, 1961).

B. AJIL 74 (1980), 890–91; *Annual Obituary 1980* (New York, 1981), 575–77; NYT 27 Sep 1980, 16; WWA 1980–81, 212.

Warren F. Kuehl

BECH, Joseph (17 February 1887, Diekirch, Luxemburg—8 March 1975, Luxemburg City). *Education*: Univ. of Fribourg; LL.D., Univ. of Paris, 1912. *Career*: Christian Socialist deputy, 1914–65, president, 1956, 1959, honorary president, 1964–65; minister of viticulture, 1921–59; minister of justice, home affairs, and education, 1921–25; prime minister, 1925–37, 1953–57, in five governments; delegate to League of Nations Assembly, 1926–39, vice-president, 1929; led Council of State, London, 1940–44; chair, delegation to San Francisco Conference, 1945; signer, Benelux Customs Union, 1946; led delegation to UN General Assembly, 1946–49, vice-president, Political and Security Committee, 1946, president, 1947; signer, Brussels Pact, 1948, and its extension, 1949; participated in organizing Council of Europe, 1949, later served on its Council of Ministers; signer, NATO alliance, 1949, sat on its Council, later president; minister of external commerce, 1953–58; signer, European Defense Community agreement, 1954; signer, Treaty of Rome, 1957; member, European Economic Community's Council of Ministers, 1958; Robert Schuman Prize, 1967, also Charlemagne Prize.

A statesman whose international eminence far exceeded his nation's size, Bech was a founding father of European unification. As premier and foreign minister in the interwar era, he regularly led Luxemburg's delegation to the League of Nations and, in an early step toward economic integration, facilitated establishment of the 1926 European Steel Pact in Luxemburg under a Luxemburg president.

In exile during World War II, Bech worked to extend the Belgo-Luxemburg customs union to the Netherlands and indicated that Luxemburg wished to join a future Western security system. After liberation, he strove to create the United Nations, in which he played an early prominent role; the Benelux Union, of which he was a principal architect; and the Brussels Pact, bringing Luxemburg out of its traditional unarmed neutrality to join

Belgium, Britain, France, and the Netherlands in a mutual defense treaty. Benelux was the nucleus for the Common Market; the Brussels Pact, that of NATO. Bech contributed much to the formation and early activities of these larger organizations. In hopes of a United States of Europe, he helped create the Council of Europe and the European Defense Community.

Bech's role in international organization and his efforts toward Western economic and defense arrangements arose partly from recognition that these provided Luxemburg's best hope of peace, prosperity, and security. Simultaneously, he safeguarded his nation's independence, identity, and international rights. After World War II, he gained a Luxemburg voice in the International Ruhr Authority and a share in German reparation of industrial equipment. As the European organizations for which he had worked materialized, he capitalized on the fact that other powers neither envied nor feared the tiniest member to ensure that Euratom and the European Coal and Steel Community were located in Luxemburg, the latter continuing Luxemburg's unique role in the interwar Steel Pact.

From the Steel Pact in 1926 to Euratom in 1958, Bech dominated Luxemburg's foreign policy and personified its progress from a disarmed duchy to an active participant in the New World, Western, and European order he helped to create. With wit and hard work, he persuaded his compatriots and his more powerful partners toward an integrated Europe in which he played a prominent role. In Bech, one of Europe's smallest states produced a European statesman of genuine stature.

BIBLIOGRAPHY:

A. *Luxembourg and the German Invasion, Before and After* (London, 1943).

B. CB 1950, 30–32; IWW 1970–71, 113; LT 10 Mar 1975, 14, 12 Mar 1975, 18, 15 Mar 1975, 16; NYT 10 Mar 1975, 32; WWBL 1962, 42; *WWWorld* 1971–72, 74.

Sally Marks

BEER, George Louis (26 July 1872, New York—15 March 1920, New York). *Education*: graduate, Columbia Coll., 1892; M.A., Columbia Univ., 1893. *Career*: part-time lecturer, Columbia Univ., 1893–97; businessman, 1893–1903; engaged in scholarship, 1903–14; American correspondent of *Round Table* (London), 1915–18; member, the Inquiry, 1917–18, and American Commission to Negotiate Peace, 1918–19.

Beer's parents, of that German-Jewish immigration that had settled in New York during the mid-nineteenth century, provided him with education and *haute culture*. At college and later graduate school, his pronounced interest in history when related to the family's tobacco business may well have influenced his research into the origins and development of the British colonial system, 1578–1765. His four seminal books emphasizing the durability and flexibility of the first British empire established him as a scholar respected in England no less than America.

With the coming of World War I, Beer turned to the international predicament and increasingly to the prerequisites for future peace and national security. He submitted regular articles to the English *Round Table*, a liberal, internationalist journal, which at an early date displayed interest in a postwar association of nations for maintaining the peace. In 1917, some of these earlier articles were recast and expanded to form the nucleus of Beer's *The English-Speaking Peoples*, intended for a generally educated audience. Here he portrayed the grand design of imperial Germany to be the weakening of Anglo-American national societies. Thus America and England must recognize a community of interest in world affairs, one based on a solid historical foundation. Had there been formal recognition of this Anglo-American solidarity at the outset of the twentieth century, "the entire course of history would have been quite different" and indeed American interests bolstered in the process. He anticipated that future world peace would not be achieved until nations willingly sacrificed portions of their sovereign rights and powers in the process of recognizing the interdependence of humankind. Beer insisted that the traditional U.S. posture of isolation in world affairs must be regarded as anachronistic. Americans should recognize the strong bonds existing between their concerns and those of the British Commonwealth. Should the United States revert to its policy of isolation or place its trust in a new league of nations, it would have to rely on military forces greater than if the nation were closely tied to the British Commonwealth.

Beer's background made him a logical choice to direct studies of the many colonial questions that would predictably arise at a peace conference. Chosen for the Inquiry, he compiled numerous reports describing conditions—historical, economic, social—in the German and Turkish colonies. Throughout, his chief concern was with the welfare of the indigenous populations. His panacea for the ills of colonial rule was not international administration, which he believed would be inefficient. Instead, he contributed to the peacemaking by promoting the idea of a mandate system under which a league would assign responsibility over the German-Turkish colonies to one or more of the advanced, allied, or associate victorious nations, which would administer and guide them under the supervision of the international community with the understanding that all countries share equally through economic access. Beer carefully did not apply the mandatory principle indiscriminately. He favored outright annexation of certain German territories in Africa by individual Allied countries. In Paris and later in London during 1919, he served the American Commission to Negotiate Peace both as adviser, chiefly on African affairs, and as member of the Mandates Commission. In a far lesser sense, Beer also made his views known in the controversy over the fate of Fiume and that of Shantung. As an admirer of the British system of government, Beer believed that America's active involvement in world affairs should be in tandem with the British. Just prior to his early death, he had been selected to head the Mandates Section of the League of Nations.

BIBLIOGRAPHY:

A. *African Questions at the Paris Peace Conference: With Papers on Egypt, Mesopotamia, and the Colonial Settlement* (New York, 1923); *The English-Speaking Peoples: Their Future Relations and Joint International Obligations* (New York, 1917).

B. Grace A. Cockroft, "George Louis Beer," in *Some Modern Historians of Britain: Essays in Honor of Robert Livingston Schuyler* (New York, 1951); *George Louis Beer: A Tribute to His Life and Work in the Making of History and the Moulding of Public Opinion* (New York, 1924).

C. The Beer papers are in the Butler Library, Columbia Univ.

Lawrence E. Gelfand

BEERNAERT, Auguste-Marie-François (26 July 1829, Ostend, Belgium—6 October 1912, Lucerne, Switzerland). *Education*: doctor of law, Univ. of Louvain, 1850. *Career*: lawyer in Brussels, 1853–73, 1894–1912; minister of public works, 1873–78; representative to Chamber from Thielt, 1874–1912; president, Federation of Catholic Circles and Associations, 1884; prime minister and minister of finance, 1884–94; minister of state, 1894–1912; president, Chamber, 1895–1900; president, Inter-Parliamentary Council, Inter-Parliamentary Union, 1899–1912; delegate, Hague Peace Conferences of 1899 and 1907; member, Permanent Court of Arbitration, 1900–1912; Nobel Peace Prize, 1909.

Head of the second longest-lived ministry in Belgium's history, Beernaert is noted for revising the franchise clauses of the Belgian Constitution, for his support of the founding of the Congo Free State, and his activity on behalf of European cooperation, the reduction of armaments, and the peaceful settlement of international disputes. A specialist in financial law, Beernaert entered politics as a result of his reputation and his own desire to substitute moderation for the extremism stimulated by the religion and education issue. He joined with Charles Woeste in urging the papacy to take a conciliatory path. As leader of the moderate wing of the Catholic party, Beernaert was concerned for the rights of minorities and campaigned for proportional representation. His lack of success on this point and other reasons stimulated his resignation as prime minister, and thereafter he focused his energies on his international concerns. His ministry showed a substantial record, including a public works program to ease unemployment, child labor laws, free trade legislation, toleration on the school issue, increased recognition of Flemish rights, and constitutional revision. The establishment of nearly universal male suffrage changed Belgium's political structure. In 1899, as president of the Chamber, Beernaert saw proportional representation made law.

Beernaert supported Leopold II's activities in the Congo. The Chambers followed Beernaert's call for recognition of the Congo Free State, for approval of the General Act of the 1885 Berlin Conference, and for granting Leopold permission to serve as sovereign of the Congo Free State. Beernaert persuaded the Chambers to make loans to the new state. He envisaged a civilizing mission in Africa and the suppression of the slave trade. In time he questioned Leopold's policies there, the limitations on free trade, the Fondation de la Couronne, and especially the system of forced labor.

Beernaert strived to improve international law and to bring people together. He worked to promote arbitration as a means of settling disputes and managed to bring about some unification of the laws of the seas. He was a leading spirit behind the European Inter-Parliamentary Union. He chaired its conferences from 1899 until his death; he also presided at the Glasgow Peace Congress of 1901. At the Hague Peace Conferences of 1899 and 1907 Beernaert spoke for limitations on air warfare and helped draft regulations regarding prisoners of war and the rights and obligations of neutrals. He presided over the subcommission in 1907 on land warfare. Beernaert expressed concern about building a world state or federation, a "fearful utopia," yet he clearly saw the need for an improved voluntary system through which nations could resolve their differences. Some of his problems stemmed from a conflict between his personal desires and his political loyalties. King Leopold did not wish any system that would compel him to arbitration over his Congo policy, yet Beernaert sincerely wished to advance judicial processes. This may explain why he opposed suggested plans at the Second Hague Conference regarding changes in the arbitration tribunal and the creation of a court of justice. His contributions were recognized by the Nobel Prize Committee in 1909.

BIBLIOGRAPHY:

A. Beernaert's publications are listed in the *Annuaire de l'Académie Royale de Belgique* (1939), 355–64.

B. *Biographie nationale, Brussels* 33 (Brussels, 1965), 70–106; E. Carton de Wiart, *Auguste Beernaert: Sa vie et son oeuvre* (Ghent, 1913), "Notice sur Auguste Beernaert," *Annuaire de l'Académie Royale de Belgique* (1939), 293–364: Auguste Melot, "Beernaert," *Revue général* (15 Aug 1927), 129–44, (15 Sep 1927), 299–314, 65 (Feb 1932), 147–67.

Jonathan E. Helmreich

BELAÚNDE Y DIÉZ CANCECO, Víctor Andrés (15 December 1883, Arequipa, Peru—14 December 1966, New York). *Education*: LL.D., Univ. of San Marcos, 1908, Ph.D., 1910, Litt.D., 1911. *Career*: secretary, later director, Boundary Archives Division of Peruvian Ministry of Foreign Affairs, 1903–11; professor, San Marcos Univ., 1911–13; chargé d'affaires, Germany, 1914, Bolivia, 1915; minister plenipotentiary, Uruguay, 1919; professor, Columbia, Rice, Virginia Univers. and at Univ. of Miami, 1921–30; member, Peruvian Congress, 1931–33; diplomatic missions to Colombia, 1934–35, to Switzerland, 1936; delegate, League of Nations, 1936, UN, 1949–66, president, General Assembly, 1959–60.

Belaúnde entered the Ministry of Foreign Affairs in 1903, becoming an expert in the field of boundary questions. After two years of teaching at San

Marcos University he returned to the diplomatic service during World War I. When Augusto B. Leguía assumed the presidency, Belaúnde was forced into political exile for his defense of civil rights. For nine years he taught Hispanic American culture at different universities in the United States and returned to Peru in 1930 after Leguía's fall. Belaúnde resumed activities in both academia and public service as a dean at the Catholic University of Peru and as a delegate for Arequipa (1931-33) in the Peruvian Congress.

In 1934 Belaúnde negotiated a border agreement with Colombia and in 1936 headed the Peruvian delegation to the League of Nations, where he represented Latin America on the League's Committee on International Cooperation. He led the Peruvian delegation to the Eighth International Conference of American States in Lima (1938), represented his country at the San Francisco Conference in 1945, and after 1949 sat in every session of the General Assembly of the UN. In 1957 he was appointed foreign minister and two years later was elected president of the General Assembly. There he presided with moderation during intense debates over the Congo and Hungary.

A member of the Peruvian *generación del 900*, Belaúnde belonged to a group of conservative Peruvian intellectuals influenced by Bartolomé Herrera, Peru's great nineteenth-century traditionalist thinker. A profoundly religious man who attended mass every morning before work, his entire *Weltanschauung* came close to neo-Thomism. He was a remarkable orator and an extraordinary educator, and in the United Nations he was widely regarded as without enemies yet firm in his convictions. He gained a reputation there for his espousal of the interests of small states and as a reconciler of regional differences. He helped greatly (1953-55) to find a formula to open up UN membership to emerging nations. Belaúnde was a staunch defender of Hispanic American values and a contributor to the advancement of peace and understanding. His friend Juan Bautista de Lavalle eulogized him by stating that he died with honor.

BIBLIOGRAPHY:

A. *Bolívar and the Political Thought of the Spanish American Revolution* (Baltimore, MD, 1938); *La Conferencia de San Francisco* (Lima, 1945); *La constitución inicial del Peru ante el derecho internacional* (Lima, 1942); *La cuestión de límites peruano-boliviana ante el arbitro agentino* (Lima, 1908); *La realidad nacional* (Paris, 1931); *Memorias*, 3 vols. (Lima, 1960-62); *Nuestra cuestión con Chile* (Lima, 1919).

B. CB 1960, 22-24; *Enciclopedía universal ilustrada europeo-americana* (Madrid, 1931), 2 (app.), 16; *La Prensa* (Lima), 5 Nov 1961, IV-176; NYT, 8 Dec 1957, 88, 15 Dec 1966, 47; OAS Press Release, 1966.

O. Carlos Stoetzer

BELLEGARDE, Dantès (18 May 1877, Port-au-Prince—16 June 1966, Port-au-Prince). *Education*: graduate, Lycée Pétion, 1897. *Career*: teacher, Lycée Pétion, 1898-1904; professor, School of Applied Sciences, 1904-18;

minister of education and agriculture, 1918; ambassador to France, the Vatican, and delegate to League of Nations, 1921–22 and 1930–31; ambassador to United States and Pan American Union–OAS, 1931–33, 1946, and 1957; ambassador to UN, 1951–52.

One of two better-known Haitian social thinkers of this century and the ablest synthesizer of nineteenth-century thought, Bellegarde became the quasi-official ideologue in a period of conservatism in the 1920s and 1930s. He was a historian, educator, and constitutional expert, but he is remembered principally as launching the most prestigious career in Haitian diplomacy of this century.

Fearing U.S. hegemony over Haiti, Bellegarde sought to recapture the European market for Haitian products and developed cultural ties with France, other Latin powers, and the Vatican. In 1920 he became a member of the Permanent Court of Arbitration, then honorary president of the Second Pan-African Conference. W.E.B. Du Bois graced him with the title "international spokesman of the Negroes of the world" (*The Crisis*, Apr 1926, 295). At the League, he argued on behalf of intellectual cooperation, becoming as Jean Piaget recognized in 1955 a precursor of the International Bureau of Education. Bellegarde intervened on behalf of colonized peoples, demanding reforms in the Permanent Mandates Commission. In 1924 he was, at the behest of *Karl Hjalmar Branting, named to the League's Temporary Commission on Slavery and Forced Labor. Under his aegis and that of Nobel Prize winner *Henri LaFontaine, the Twenty-fourth Universal Congress for Peace called for an end to the U.S. occupation of Haiti. In 1925 Bellegarde founded the Haitian League for Human Rights. In 1930 he pronounced the most celebrated speech of his career on U.S. imperialism, seeing "the shadow of a dreadnought behind each Yankee dollar" (NYT 12 Sep 1930). He had warned Haitians in 1907, "God is too far, and the United States too close" (*Pour une Haiti heureuse*, II, 3). International friendship must be based on juridical equality and respect, not on the threat of force.

At the Fourth Pan American Commercial Conference of 1931, he recommended an organism to assist governments in finance, credit, and trade, inserting this in the 1933 Montevideo Conference agenda. He later believed that this idea formed the basis for the OAS Economic and Social Council. In 1938 Bellegarde helped defuse a dangerous crisis between Haiti and the Dominican Republic. At the urging of *James Brown Scott, he attended the Congress of the American Institute of International Law in 1940 and became a founder of the Inter-American Bar Association. In 1941 he was the only black on the Administrative Council of the International Peace Bureau. Following his ambassadorship to the UN, the General Assembly appointed Bellegarde to a three-member commission on the racial situation in South Africa in 1953. The report described the situation as most dangerous to world peace, calling for racial equality.

Dean of Haitian letters, Léon Laleau, summarized well Bellegarde's impact: "He placed audaciously at international gatherings, Race before Nationality, Man before Citizen" (*Conjonction*, no 118, Jul 1972, 89).

BIBLIOGRAPHY:

A. *Au service d'Haiti* (Port-au-Prince, 1962); *Pour une Haiti heureuse*, 2 vols. (Port-au-Prince, 1927–29); *Un Haitien parle* (Port-au-Prince, 1934).

B. Patrick Bellegarde-Smith, "Expression of a Culture in Crisis: Dantès Bellegarde in Haitian Social Thought," dissertation, American Univ., 1977.

C. Some of Bellegarde's papers are at Howard Univ.

Patrick Bellegarde-Smith

BENEŠ, Eduard (28 May 1884, Kožlany, Bohemia—3 September 1948, Sezimovo Ústí, Czechoslovakia). *Education*: J.D., Univ. of Dijon, 1907; Ph.D., Charles Univ., 1908; studied in Paris, London, and Berlin. *Career*: freelance writer and journalist, Paris, 1906–7, Prague, 1908–14; professor, Commercial Academy, Prague, 1909–10; lecturer, Charles Univ., 1912–13, Technological Institute, Prague, 1913–14; joined Thomas G. Masaryk in organizing campaign for Czechoslovak independence, 1914; secretary, underground revolutionary committee, 1914–15; in exile, 1915–18; foreign minister, 1918–35; prime minister, 1921–22; representative to Paris Peace Conference, 1919; president, Council of the League of Nations, on several occasions; rapporteur-general, Disarmament Conference, 1932; president, League Assembly, 1935; president of Czechoslovakia, 1935–38; in exile after 1938; visiting professor, Univ. of Chicago, 1939; formed government-in-exile and recognized as president by Allied powers, 1940–45; president of Czechoslovakia, 1945–48.

Beneš's main premise as the leading politician of his country was that a free Czechoslovakia was possible only in a free Europe, that dictatorship and democracy cannot live side by side in the modern world, that right, not might, must be established in a community where all people are entitled to equal justice and where all nations, big and small, have to coexist in peace on equal terms. The idea of nationalism would give way to a philosophy of humanism through modern democracy. When this vision of the democratization of foreign policy seemed to be losing ground as a result of the spread of Fascism throughout Europe and when independent Czechoslovakia, of which he had been one of the principal builders, crumbled at Munich, Beneš refused to give up his ideal and staked everything on a victory of the democratic world over totalitarianism. He also believed that the common struggle against Fascism would galvanize the democratic forces of the Soviet society and that, after the war, the Soviet Union would adopt democratic rules in both its domestic and foreign policy. The February 1948 coup in Czechoslovakia was the greatest tragedy of his life, greater than the humiliating disaster of Munich.

Beneš sought to advance his ideals as a leader of the League of Nations, where he urged the international community to renounce the use of force as an instrument of national policy, to agree on effective disarmament measures, and to adhere to democratic principles of international conduct based on morality and justice. He especially saw the League as the guarantor of small states and the hope for a stable Europe. In 1924, with the Greek statesman *Nicholas Politis, Beneš initiated and prepared for general approval the Geneva Protocol to prevent aggressive wars by submitting international issues to peaceful negotiation and arbitration, and he was among the chief architects of the system of guarantees created under the Locarno Treaties of 1924–25. In the quest for collective security, he initiated the creation of the Little Entente (a political alliance among Czechoslovakia, Yugoslavia, and Romania) and advocated a comprehensive system of security embracing all European countries. During World War II he prepared the groundwork for a Czechoslovak–Polish federation as a core of a future Central European federation, a plan thwarted by the Soviet Union. On the accession to power of the Communist party, Beneš refused to sign a constitution legitimatizing one-party rule and resigned the presidency in 1948 shortly before his death.

BIBLIOGRAPHY:

A. *Bohemia's Case for Independence* (London, 1917); *Democracy Today and Tomorrow* (New York, 1939); *Memoirs: From Munich to New War and New Victory* (London, 1954); *Mnichovské dny* [The days of Munich] (Prague, 1968; French trans., *Munich*, Paris, 1969); *My War Memoirs* (London, 1928); *Úvahy o slovanství* [Reflections about the destiny of Slavic nations] XIX (Prague, 1947).

B. Pierre Grabitès, *Beneš: Statesman of Central Europe* (London, 1935); Edward B. Hitchcock, *"I Built a Temple for Peace": The Life of Eduard Beneš* (New York, 1940); Godfrey Lias, *Beneš of Czechoslovakia* (London, 1941); Compton Mackenzie, *Dr. Beneš* (London, 1946); Philip Paneth, *Eduard Beneš: A Leader of Democracy* (London, 1945); Joseph S. Roucek, "Eduard Beneš," *World Unity Magazine* 14 (Jun 1934), 136–46; Edward Taborsky, *President Eduard Beneš: Between East and West, 1938–1940* (Stanford, CA, 1981); Paul E. Zinner, "Czechoslovakia: The Diplomacy of Eduard Beneš," in *The Diplomats, 1919–1939*, ed. Gordon A. Craig and Felix Gilbert (Princeton, 1953), 100–122.

C. The Beneš papers are in the Institute for the History of Socialism in Prague.

Vratislav Pechota

BENJAMIN, Robert S. (14 May 1909, New York—22 October 1979, Manhasset, NY). *Education*: Coll. of City of New York, 1924–28; LL.B., Fordham Univ., 1931. *Career*: law practice, 1931–78; vice-president, Pathe Film, 1937–41; president, J. Arthur Rank, 1945–67, United Artists, 1952–69, co-chairman, 1969–74.

Benjamin stands virtually alone in the business community for the length and persistence of his dedication to the United Nations. From the day in October 1952 when he and his wife attended a meeting of the American Association for the United Nations (AAUN) near their home in Great Neck and there met *Eleanor Roosevelt until his death, he never stopped working for UN causes.

The meeting with Roosevelt was fateful. She not only became a close friend, but the inspiration he and his wife derived from her were major elements in their lives and those of their children. Jean Benjamin became president of the Great Neck chapter of the AAUN after that October meeting, and the two of them shared the effort from then on. Less than two years later, upon the recommendation of Roosevelt, President John F. Kennedy appointed him chairman of the United States Committee for the United Nations; a position to which he was reappointed by Kennedy and Lyndon Johnson until 1965.

As early as 1963, Benjamin had written to Kennedy urging that steps be taken to bring about a merger of the United States Committee for the United Nations and the American Association for the United Nations, which had its roots in the pre–World War II League of Nations Association. By then, through Roosevelt, he had developed a close relationship with *Adlai Stevenson. With Kennedy's encouragement, the three of them worked effectively to bring the two rival organizations together in May 1964.

Before then, however, Benjamin had started a chain of events that led directly to the historic visit of +Pope John XXIII to the UN. The Papal Encyclical, *Pacem in Terris*, had made a deep impression on him, and he undertook to have a representative of the Vatican address the annual meeting of the U.S. Committee for the UN. The Vatican's selection of Cardinal Leon-Joseph Suenens, archbishop of Mechlin-Brussels, for this assignment was made for the specific purpose of initiating arrangements for the subsequent visit of the Pope.

Benjamin became the first chairman of the merged organization, the United Nations Association of the United States of America, and at least partly in recognition of that position, Lyndon Johnson appointed him chairman of the National Citizens Commission for International Cooperation Year in 1965, which organized a White House Conference involving nearly 2,000 participants. He continued to occupy a position of top leadership in UNA-USA, either as chairman of the Board of Trustees or of its Board of Governors or cochairman with former UN Ambassador Arthur J. Goldberg and former Chief Justice *Earl Warren.

Official recognition of his work for citizen support of the UN came in the form of a presidential appointment to the U.S. delegation to the UN in 1966 and the award of the Gold United Nations Peace Medal by Secretary General *U Thant in 1971. The partnership of his wife throughout all these endeavors was recognized by President Johnson in 1968 in appointing her as a special adviser to the U.S. delegation to the UN Commission on Human Rights.

Through twenty-seven years of commitment to the UN, Benjamin was active in a wide range of other international organizations. He was, at various times, chairman of the American–Israel Cultural Foundation, cofounder and vice-chairman of the Eleanor Roosevelt Memorial Foundation, director of Near East Emergency Donations, and chairman of the UN Development Corporation. Five months before his death, he established the Robert and Jean Benjamin Fellowship Endowment in International Affairs at Brandeis University.

BIBLIOGRAPHY:

B. NCAB K, 385–88; NYT 23 Oct 1979, II-19.

Porter McKeever

BENTHAM, Jeremy (15 February 1748, London—6 June 1832, Westminster, England). *Education*: B.A., Oxford Univ., 1763, M.A., 1766. *Career*: lawyer; author of plans for constitutional, legal, social, and economic reform; founder, *Westminster Review*, 1824.

Jeremy Bentham, together with philosophers James and John Stuart Mill and two of the most famous lawyers of the period, Sir Samuel Romilly and Lord Henry Brougham, comprised the core of the English Utilitarian Movement. This group of reformers, whose primary purpose was to promote the "greatest happiness of the greatest number," looked to Bentham as their mentor. Actually, Bentham was responsible for coining the term *utilitarian*, and he further enriched the English language through his invention of other words, such as *international, codification, maximize*, and *minimize*. It was through their combined efforts, however, that a new order of society emerged in England that reflected their political and legal thought.

The idea formulated by Bentham and the Utilitarian Movement had potential significance for other nations as well. These included humanizing the penal code, expanding the franchise, reorganizing the workings of the governmental departments, emancipating the colonies, curtailing religious intolerance, and establishing a national system of education, a modern postal system and police force, and a civil service system based on competitive exams. Bentham included some of these ideas in his *Plan for a Universal and Perpetual Peace* (1789) and *Emancipate Your Colonies* (1793). He proposed a European congress, a common court, the emancipation of colonies, the abolition of treaties of alliance, disarmament, and the enforcement of peace and decisions of the court by public opinion and, where necessary, by a combined military force.

Bentham was honored with international acclaim comparatively early in his career. For example, his ideas in support of the French Revolution made such an impact in France that the National Assembly conferred upon him the honorary title of French citizen. It was chiefly through the efforts of the Swiss writer and former clergyman, Etienne Dumont, however, that Bentham attained worldwide recognition. In 1802, Dumont began the enormous thirty-seven-year task of editing Bentham's manuscript material and translating some of it into French. Bentham's writings later appeared in many other languages.

Bentham first gained attention in the United States through the work of Edward Livingston, the distinguished Louisiana jurist. In fact, the first legal codes modeled along the lines of Bentham's philosophy were adopted by the frontier states of the West. He was also probably the only human being to be able to number among his friends both John Quincy Adams and Aaron Burr. It is ironic that Bentham was better known in South America, where many political leaders became his disciples. In his old age, the title "El legislador del mundo" was well deserved.

Reformers all over the world had the utmost respect for Bentham's views because he could provide concrete examples of his theory in action. They could thus see how practical his reforms were, and his ideas remain a challenge in the modern world.

BIBLIOGRAPHY:

A. *Fragment on Government* (London, 1776); *Introduction to the Principles of Morals and Legislation* (Oxford, 1789); *Works*, 11 vols. (New York, 1962).

B. Charles M. Atkinson, *Jeremy Bentham: His Life and Work* (London, 1905); David Baumgardt, *Bentham and the Ethics of Today* (Princeton, NJ, 1952); William L. Davidson, *Political Thought in England: The Utilitarians from Bentham to J. S. Mill* (New York, 1915); Charles Warren Everett, *The Education of Jeremy Bentham* (New York, 1931); Mary P. Mack, *Jeremy Bentham: An Odyssey of Ideas, 1748–92* (London, 1962).

Juanita Montague Duffer

BENTWICH, Norman de Mattos (28 February 1883, London—8 April 1971, London). *Education*: Trinity Coll., Cambridge. *Career*: editor, *Jewish Review*, 1910–13; inspector of courts, Egyptian minister of justice, and lecturer, Cairo Law School, 1912–15; British Army, 1917–18; legal secretary, British Military Administration in Palestine, 1918–20; attorney general of mandate government in Palestine, 1921–31; director, League of Nations Commission for Jewish Refugees from Germany, 1933–36; professor, Hebrew Univ., 1932–51, vice-chairman of its International Board of Governors, 1951–71.

A critical grounding in Jewish thought, harmonized with the Western classics and international law, convinced Bentwich that religious principles were essential for the establishment of one humanity governed by truth and justice. This son of a pioneer English Zionist early came under the influence of Asher Ginzberg (Ahad Ha'am) and Solomon Schechter, twin souls united in an intense conviction to preserve and develop Judaism and the spirit of the Jewish people for the betterment of mankind. The moral order reflected in the Torah and Isaiah's ideal of "nation shall not lift up sword against nation," according to this view, lay at the foundation of Judaism. Reviving this ethos as a conscious national community in its ancient physical center of Palestine, free from historic persecution and the temptation of assimilation, the Children of Israel could again serve as "a light unto the nations" for the triumph of the Kingdom of God on earth.

Bentwich mirrored these regenerative ideals in thought and deed. His earliest works lauded Hellenistic Judaism and championed Philo Judaeus for attempting to diffuse God's ethical word over the world. Exponent of a binationalist commonwealth to resolve the conflict between Arab and Jew in Palestine, the scholar-activist found kindred spirits in Judah Magnes and Henrietta Szold for his appreciation of Jewish nationalism enriched from its prophetic root. His inaugural lectures (1932) as Weizmann Professor of the International Law of Peace at Hebrew University in Jerusalem, published as *The Religious Foundations of Internationalism*, proposed a league of religions to further the cause of universal peace. That seat of higher learning, which claimed much of his subsequent attention, Bentwich envisaged as a most striking instrument to mediate between East and West from its location in the City of Peace. Indefatigable traveler for the cause of Jews and other refugees against the Hitler menace during the 1930s, first as director of the League of Nations High Commission for Refugees from Germany, he was a guiding hand behind the creation of the British Council of Christians and Jews, a legal adviser in the late 1930s to the Ethiopian government, a consultant for Jewish groups seeking an International Bill of Rights, and a United Restitution Organization official to help victims of Nazi atrocities obtain some compensation after World War II. Bentwich still found time to write many distinguished books and articles on these varied experiences.

His belief that public understanding about the emerging world order would more than anything else determine human destiny also led to lucid studies on mandates, the League of Nations, and the UN. The realization of his greatest hopes was not granted this self-styled "wanderer between two worlds," but Bentwich's emphasis that prophetic morality needs inform international relations for the survival of civilization merits emulation more than ever.

BIBLIOGRAPHY:

A. *A Commentary on the Charter of the U.N.* (London, 1950); *England in Palestine* (London, 1932); *From Geneva to San Francisco* (London, 1946); *Fulfillment in the Promised Land* (London, 1938); *Israel Resurgent* (New York, 1960); *Mandate Memories, 1918–1948* (London, 1965); *The Mandate System* (London, 1930); *My 77 Years* (Philadelphia, 1961); *Palestine of the Jews* (London, 1919); *The Refugees From Germany* (London, 1936); *The Religious Foundations of Internationalism* (London, 1933); *Wanderer Between Two Worlds* (London, 1941); *Wanderer in the Promised Land* (New York, 1933); *Wanderer in War* (London, 1946).

B. *Encyclopedia Judaica* 4 (Jerusalem, 1971), 556–57; LT 10 Apr 1971, 14.

C. Bentwich papers are in the Central Zionist Archives, Jerusalem; Institute of Contemporary Jewry, Hebrew Univ., Jerusalem, and in the Middle East Centre, St. Anthony's Coll., Oxford Univ.

Monty N. Penkower

BERENDSEN, Carl August (16 August 1890, Sydney—12 September 1973, Dunedin, New Zealand). *Education*: master of laws, Victoria Univ. Coll.,

Wellington, 1915. *Career*: clerk, Education Department, 1906-16; clerk, Labor Department, 1916-18, chief clerk and deputy registrar of industrial unions, 1918-26; imperial affairs officer, Prime Minister's Department, 1926-35; secretary, External Affairs Department, 1928-43; permanent head, Prime Minister's Department, 1935-43; secretary, War Cabinet, 1939-43; New Zealand high commissioner in Australia, 1943-44; minister to United States, 1944-48, ambassador, 1948-52; New Zealand representative, Far Eastern Commission, 1945-52; New Zealand permanent representative to UN, 1945-52.

Berendsen in the late 1940s was an outspoken opponent of the veto and the rule of Great Power unanimity in the Security Council of the United Nations. So much an evil did he regard this "great and pregnant privilege" that he was reputedly willing to expound his views whenever on his feet in public, even to propose a wedding toast.

A distinguished and highly intelligent civil servant, Berendsen grew convinced of the need for an effective world security organization when he served as New Zealand's chief adviser on international affairs in the 1930s. He had then been profoundly disturbed by the slide into war, hastened, in his view, by the disastrous appeasement of the dictatorships. The need for unity of action against aggression seemed clear, and the answer seemed to lie in effective international arbitration and collective security in which all states could have confidence. Ideally, that world body must have appropriate forces at its disposal, be able to apply effective economic and military sanctions, and be in a position to act without delay or hindrance. Any aggressor must be confronted with the certainty of automatic and overwhelming opposition.

In the Labor government, which took office in December 1935, Berendsen found men who shared his assessment and ideal. At first his role was confined to that of a perceptive, respected, influential adviser. After 1943 he became an increasingly skillful and eloquent exponent of his government's conception of the ideal world order. Although occasionally dogmatic in his views, and prone to see issues in terms of moral absolutes, he was nonetheless renowned for his clarity of vision and aptness of expression, qualities highly regarded by New Zealand leaders.

Berendsen's achievements in promoting the establishment of an effective world organization cannot easily be distinguished from those of the government he served. Nevertheless, he drafted the proposals for the reform and rejuvenation of the ailing League of Nations that New Zealand enthusiastically put forward in 1936. He also played a significant role in the shaping and refining of New Zealand's views on the new world organization at the San Francisco Conference in 1945. As a member of the New Zealand delegation, he ably supported *Peter Fraser, earning a reputation for his passionate yet closely reasoned argument.

For Berendsen, the United Nations that emerged remained faulty, the veto being the most prominent deficiency. Yet he conceded that the UN did represent a major step forward and might eventually evolve in the hoped-for direction. To this end, Berendsen ardently proclaimed the UN and condemned the veto in following years. He especially blamed the Soviet Union's abuse of the veto, its obstruction of the provisions for the pledging of forces to the Security Council, "the very core and kernel of the Charter," and its apparent aggressive designs. He became an implacable opponent of appeasement of "Communist imperialism." While continuing to promote the UN, even during retirement when he lectured in the United States, he came to accept that in present circumstances there could be no early expectation of its reform in the direction of his ideal.

BIBLIOGRAPHY:

B. *Dominion* (Wellington) 15 Jan 1955, 11; *Evening Post* (Wellington) 13 Sep 1973, 6.

Ian C. McGibbon

BERNADOTTE, Folke (2 January 1895, Stockholm—17 September 1948, Jerusalem). *Education*: military school, Karlberg. *Career*: Swedish cavalry officer, 1918–22; manager, Swedish-American pavillion, New York World's Fair, 1939; recruiter of Scandinavian volunteers to aid Finland in Russo–Finnish War, 1939–40; president, Boy Scout Association, 1943; vice-president, Swedish Red Cross, 1943–45, president, 1946–47; UN mediator in Palestine, May–September 1948.

Bernadotte, nephew of King Gustavus V of Sweden, moved from an aristocratic life as an international playboy married to a wealthy American to that of an international mediator in World War II and its aftermath. Swedish neutrality guided Bernadotte into peacemaking roles. For the Red Cross, he traveled to Germany in 1943, negotiating the exchange of British for German prisoners of war. From February to April 1945, Bernadotte worked with SS Chief Heinrich Himmler for the release of primarily Norwegian and Danish concentration camp victims. He claims to have saved 20,000 lives, including 10,000 Jews, while critics say he only tried to steal the credit from others. Between 1945 and 1947 Bernadotte, as president of the Swedish Red Cross, administered refugee relief throughout Central and Eastern Europe.

In November 1947 the United Nations voted to partition British-administered Palestine into two autonomous Arab and Jewish states. The Arabs rejected the UN decision, and Egypt, Transjordan, Syria, and Lebanon sent forces to put down what they termed a Jewish rebellion. The Israelis declared their independence on 14 May 1948, during fighting that resulted in 360,000 Arab refugees. The British withdrew their troops from Palestine and led Western European countries in refusing to recognize the state of Israel. The United States and the Soviet Union, however, conferred immediate recognition, and UN Secretary-General *Trygve Lie sent Bernadotte to Palestine to mediate an Arab–Israeli peace.

Britain wanted to maintain her spheres of influence in Egypt, Transjordan, and Iraq, but Britain was financially dependent on the United States, where the influential Jewish community backed the claims of Israel. The United States pressed Britain to impose an arms embargo on the Arabs, while the British gained a U.S. embargo against Israel. Bernadotte's cease-fire mission, therefore, seemed to have the backing of those governments as the best resolution of an embarrassing situation.

Divisions within the United States, within the UN, and set positions in the Middle East made Bernadotte's mission uncertain. When he left Sweden in May 1948, he observed that his chances were a hundred to one against being able to achieve peace. After forty-five trips between Arab and Jewish cities, Bernadotte gained a first cease-fire from 11 June to 9 July. A second lasted from 18 July until October. He also achieved the demilitarization of Jerusalem and organized United Nations relief for the Palestinian refugees.

Bernadotte concluded that the November 1947 Partition Plan was unworkable geographically, militarily, and ethnically as too generous to the Israelis. In June 1948 he proposed that Jerusalem become an Arab city, but he later suggested internationalization under UN administration. The Jews disagreed. Bernadotte made a second shift, from neutrality on the sovereignty issue to a demand that the Arabs recognize Israel's independence. The majority of both Arabs and Jews rejected Bernadotte as a peacemaker, and the Israeli press and government denounced him as a secret agent of British imperialism. Leaders of the quasi-illegal Jewish Stern Gang assassinated Bernadotte in Jerusalem on September 17. Although the Israeli government moved strongly against the conspirators officially, the leaders soon "escaped."

Just before his death, Bernadotte drafted a report for the United Nations proposing the recognition of Israel, Jerusalem's internationalization, contiguous and ethnically viable territorial frontiers, Arab refugees' right to return home, and unlimited Jewish immigration. But the UN General Assembly did not adopt the plan, and it failed to gain support in the United States.

Bernadotte regarded himself as a man of mercy, not of arms. He placed humanity above nation, race, or religious sect, and he was the first United Nations martyr for peace. His role as an internationalist was thus unique.

BIBLIOGRAPHY:

A. *The Curtain Falls: Last Days of the Third Reich* (New York, 1945); *Instead of Arms: Autobiographical Notes* (New York, 1948); *Progress Report United Nations Mediation*, Gen. Ass. Off. Rec., 3rd ser., supp. 11, (1948); *To Jerusalem* (London, 1951).

B. David Ben-Gurion, *Israel: A Personal History* (New York, 1971); John Glubb, *A Soldier with the Arabs* (New York, 1957); Joseph Heller, "Failure of a Mission: Bernadotte and Palestine, 1948," *Journal of Contemporary History*, 14 (Jul 1979), 515–34; Ralph Hewins, *Count Folke Bernadotte: His Life and Work* (Minneapolis, MN, 1950); Dan Kurzman, *Genesis 1948: The First Arab–Israeli War* (New York,

1970); LT 18 Sep 1948, 6; NYT 18 Sep 1948, 1; John Snetsinger, *Truman, the Jewish Vote and the Creation of Israel* (Stanford, CA, 1974); Hugh Trevor-Roper, "The Strange Case of Himmler's Doctor Felix Kersten and Count Bernadotte," *Commentary* 23, Apr 1957), 356–64.

C. The Bernadotte papers are in the Swedish Foreign Ministry Archives and at Gustavus Adolphus Coll.

Robert H. Whealey

BERNAL, John D. See *Biographical Dictionary of Modern Peace Leaders*.

BERNSTORFF, Johann Heinrich von (14 November 1862, London—6 October 1939, Genf, Switzerland). *Education*: graduate, Ratzeburg Gymnasium, 1881. *Career*: First Guard Field Artillery, 1881–90; military attaché, Constantinople, 1889–90; detached to Foreign Ministry, Berlin, 1890–92; secretary of legation, Belgrade, 1892–94, Dresden, 1894–95, and Saint Petersburg, 1895–97; counselor of legation, Munich, 1897–1902, of embassy, London, 1902–6; consul-general, Cairo, 1906–8; ambassador to United States, 1908–17, to Turkey, 1917–18; member of Reichstag, 1921–28; German representative, League of Nations, member, Preparatory Disarmament Commission, 1926–31.

Born into a family noted for its long and able service to Prussia, Bernstorff was an astute analyst of early twentieth-century international relations. Understanding that Germany's diplomatic freedom was limited by her geographical vulnerability and the perception of other nations that German actions threatened the status quo, he warned his superiors while serving in London that naval competition with England would lead to a conflict Germany was unlikely to win. In Washington when the war began, Bernstorff counseled his government on ways to keep America neutral. Insisting after the Battle of the Marne that intervention by the United States would determine the outcome, Bernstorff argued that the best Germany could hope for was continued U.S. neutrality and a negotiated peace, based on the status quo ante bellum. Unrestricted submarine warfare would not help Germany's military position and would bring the United States into the war against Germany. While chiding his government for its lack of understanding of America as well as for its inability to pursue a single course of diplomatic action, Bernstorff also supported the demands of German reformers at home for a liberalization of the political system. Neither Bernstorff's diplomatic nor domestic advice was heeded in Berlin, but the soundness of his views was borne out by subsequent events.

Summoned from Constantinople in October 1918 to advise the government on peace negotiations, Bernstorff refused several appointments in the Foreign Ministry, fearing his hands would be tied by previous government commitments. Nonetheless, he unofficially advised both the transition government and Ulrich von Brockdorff-Rantzau, the head of the German peace delegation; neither, however, was able to alter significantly the terms of Versailles.

Bernstorff devoted his remaining public years to solidifying the democratic underpinnings of the Weimar Republic and preparing for Germany's reentry into the world community. A charter member of the German Democratic party, he was disappointed by *Gustav Stresemann's support of the German People's party and viewed this political division within the middle class as a major flaw in the system. Despite his disappointment with Stresemann's domestic politics, Bernstorff strongly supported his foreign policy of fulfillment and Western orientation.

President of the German League of Nations Union in the 1920s, Bernstorff viewed the League as an international arena where diplomatic exchange might be made more accessible and effective. He hoped that such a forum would encourage arbitration of international disputes by allaying traditional fears of competing nations. Bernstorff's position on the League Preparatory Disarmament Commission reflected his belief that disarmament was essential for the continued existence of the League and world peace as well as his desire to restore Germany's position in international affairs.

BIBLIOGRAPHY:

A. *Deutschland und Amerika: Erinnerungen aus dem funfjährigen Kriege* (Berlin, 1920); *Memoirs of Count Bernstorff* (New York, 1936); *My Three Years in America* (London, 1920).

B. *Die Grösse Politik der Europäischen Kabinette 1871-1914: Sammlung der Diplomatischen Akten des Auswärtigen Amtes*, vols. 27 (Berlin, 1925), 32 (Berlin, 1926), 39 (Berlin, 1926); Christoph M. Kimmich, *Germany and the League of Nations* (Chicago, 1976); Alice M. Morrissey, *The American Defense of Neutral Rights, 1914-17* (Cambridge, MA, 1939); J. B. Scott, ed., *Diplomatic Correspondence Between the United States and Germany, August 1, 1914-April 6, 1917* (New York, 1918).

Martha Moore Ziegler

BLAINE, Anita Eugenie McCormick (4 July 1866, Manchester, VT—12 February 1954, Chicago). *Education*: private tutors. *Career*: philanthropist, financier, educational reformer.

Throughout her life, Blaine was primarily a philanthropist, although she wrote and published on behalf of the causes she espoused, usually in the form of newspaper advertisements. Her activities began before she was twenty and continued until she died. In the late 1880s, she had founded a mission in Chicago. By the turn of the century, she had focused on promoting several progressive educational experiments. Within a few years, the list of her projects, memberships, and donations reflected an astonishingly active and eclectic social conscience. Blaine promoted such diverse efforts as the Hull House settlement, environmental conservation, women's suffrage, and a plan to institute profit sharing among the workers at International Harvester.

Blaine's interest in international affairs began at an early age. As was usual for Americans of means in the Gilded Age, her family traveled to Europe repeatedly. She received part of her education in France. Her mother, Nettie McCormick, was a devout Presbyterian and often invited churchmen to the household, including missionaries who recounted tales of Asia and Africa and spoke of a Christian duty to uplift foreigners. It was *Woodrow Wilson's leadership that made internationalism a major concern of Blaine. Wilson had first come to Princeton to occupy a chair in government endowed by the McCormick family. His advocacy of idealism and morality so fitted Blaine's conception of a statesman that he became something of a hero to her. She gave faithful support to his foreign policies during World War I and became an enthusiastic exponent of international organization. So important did she deem U.S. membership in the League of Nations that she abandoned her usual habit and became directly involved in political controversy. Blaine was one of the leading proponents of the League in the Midwest, addressing meetings, publishing her views, campaigning for James M. Cox in 1920, and financing numerous activities on behalf of the League.

Her devotion to the cause waned after the electoral debacle of 1920, but it revived with the formation of the League of Nations Non-Partisan Association in 1922. She was a major financial contributor to this group and for a time took charge of organizing a Chicago branch. Her talents in this area were meager, and the local operation languished until she relinquished control and *Clark Eichelberger took charge. Blaine remained, however, the branch's major source of funding and an active participant in its affairs throughout the interwar years while continuing to contribute to the League of Nations Association and to World Court campaigns.

During the 1930s Blaine's intellectual commitment to internationalism deepened. In 1936 she founded and financed the World Citizen's Association, a small discussion group that met to consider world problems from a global perspective. Its members included *Quincy Wright, Louise Wright, and Edwin Embree, and at times *Ray Lyman Wilbur, *Edgar Ansell Mowrer, and *Adlai Stevenson participated. As war threatened Europe anew, Blaine lost faith in the League of Nations but rallied to another hero, *Franklin Roosevelt. She was an ardent and active advocate of aid to the Allies. She belonged to the *William A. White Committee and funded a group of nationwide newspaper advertisements supporting the Lend-Lease bill.

Blaine was well into her seventh decade by Pearl Harbor, but her energy remained vast and her idealism had become decidedly more pronounced. She adopted the cause of the United Nations with all the enthusiasm she had earlier put into the League of Nations, and she applauded the UN as the beginning of true world government. Its success, she felt, was vital to preserve peace and salvage progress in the world. Growing friction between the United States and the Soviet Union after 1945 failed to cool Blaine's desire for international organization. Following Roosevelt's death, her champion became *Henry A. Wallace, who shared her interest in spiritualism. She supported Wallace after his forced resignation from Truman's cabinet in 1946, and in 1948 she provided $800,000—the largest single contribution—to his Progressive party during his campaign for the presidency. She also served as vice-chair of the party in Illinois. In part to provide a continued forum for Wallace's views, Blaine poured over a million dollars into the Foundation for World Government. This abortive effort to promote an advanced concept of world federalism was utterly out of step with the intensifying anti-Communism of the late 1940s. Even fellow internationalists such as Cord Meyer, Jr., and *Ely Culbertson denounced the Foundation as sympathetic to the Soviets. In no sense a Communist, Blaine had grown very remote from the political climate. Yet she never surrendered to popular opinion and contributed vast sums to the *Daily Compass*, a New York City tabloid that was the direct heir of *PM* and the *New York Star* and that served as a forum for the world government movement. Her health and vigor had declined, and she withdrew from public affairs in the final years before her death. Her will set up the New World Foundation, partly to promote projects in international understanding.

BIBLIOGRAPHY:

B. *Chicago Sun-Times* 13 Feb 1954, 29; DAB supp. 5, 60–61; Gilbert Harrison, *A Timeless Affair: The Life of Anita McCormick Blaine* (Chicago, 1979); NCAB 44, 539; NYT 13 Feb 1954, 13; WWWA 3, 80.

C. The Blaine papers are at the State Historical Society of Wisconsin.

James C. Schneider

BLAKESLEE, George Hubbard (27 August 1871, Geneseo, NY—5 May 1954, Worcester, MA). *Education*: A.B., Wesleyan Univ., 1893; M.A., Harvard Univ., 1900, Ph.D., 1903; Johns Hopkins Univ., 1893–94; at Berlin, Leipzig and Oxford Univs., 1901–3. *Career*: instructor to professor, Clark Coll., 1903–14, Clark Univ., 1914–43; visiting Carnegie professor in Pacific-area universities, 1927; professor, Tufts Univ., 1933–43; editor, *Journal of Race Development*, 1919–22, *Journal of International Relations*, 1919–22; consultant and officer, U.S. Department of State, 1931–32, 1942–45; political adviser to chairman, Far Eastern Commission, 1945–52; president, Board of Trustees, World Peace Foundation, 1930–46.

Blakeslee's long professional career brought historical and contemporary world understanding to bear on the peaceful settlement of international problems. He early broadened his professional interests in American history to develop courses, beginning at the graduate level in 1905–6, in "current history" or "contemporary history," after 1920 called "international relations." Under his direction, the Department of History and International Relations at Clark emphasized the uses of the historian's analytic skills to arrive at balanced solutions of contemporary problems arising out of the interactions of nation-states. Grounded in late nineteenth-century evolutionary optimism, Blakeslee's intellectual orientation gave him confidence that, through education and world understanding, Americans could aid in the eventual abolition of war between sovereign states.

Blakeslee's academic concerns and his later service as adviser to international organizations were aspects of the same meliorist orientation. The university could train a new generation of citizens to be more intelligent about international problems, more appreciative of the views of others, and more aware of the international duties of the United States. The same ends were to be sought among scholars and the general public through the organization between 1909 and 1920 of major conferences at Clark on the Far East, Latin America, and the World War, often followed by the publication of the papers, and through Blakeslee's editorship of a pioneer Clark journal as a continuing forum for the scholarly discussion of international problems. Lecturing at other institutions further extended Blakeslee's academic influence; in 1927 he lectured in universities in Australia, New Zealand, China, and Japan under the auspices of the Carnegie Endowment for International Peace.

Clark was one of the earliest universities to award the Ph.D. degree in international relations per se. Several of Blakeslee's graduate students worked on the role of public opinion in U.S. foreign policy formation or became part of the small cadre of Far Eastern experts in university or State Department posts in the 1920s and 1930s. Although in the financially troubled aftermath of World War I Clark had been forced to suspend its series of conferences and close out the *Journal of International Relations*, Blakeslee continued to play a key role in their successor institutions, the conferences of the Williamstown Institute of Politics and the new journal, *Foreign Affairs*.

Blakeslee's service with the Inquiry (1918–19), as adviser to the Washington Conference (1921–22) and as a technical adviser to the Lytton Commission (1932), linked his university-based points of view to real-world diplomacy. As a State Department officer from 1942 through the close of World War II, he assumed major responsibility for developing policies looking toward a peaceful, democratic, economically prosperous, and friendly Japan. After the war, Blakeslee served as political adviser to Frank McCoy, chairman of the Far Eastern Commission. In this capacity, Blakeslee, with his staff and former students, generated the political initiatives guiding U.S. policy in postwar Japan through the administration of Douglas MacArthur.

For forty years Blakeslee served as a trustee or officer of the World Peace Foundation and was also active in the Lake Mohonk Conferences on International Arbitration and the Institute of Pacific Relations. His scholarly, educational, and public activity represents a commitment to the ideal and reality of international cooperation.

BIBLIOGRAPHY:

A. ed., *China and the Far East* (New York, 1910); *The Far Eastern Commission: A Study in International Cooperation, 1945 to 1952* (Washington, 1953); ed., *Japan and Japanese-American Relations* (New York, 1912); ed., *Latin America* (New York, 1914); ed., *Mexico and the Caribbean* (New York, 1920); *The Pacific Area: An International Survey* (Boston, 1929); ed., *Problems and Lessons of the War* (New York, 1916); ed., *Recent Developments in China* (New York, 1913); *The Recent Foreign Policy of the United States: Problems in American Cooperation with Other Powers* (New York, 1925).

B. AHR 60 (Oct 1954), 253–54; NCAB 53, 174–75; ŃYT 6 May 1954, 33; WWWA 3, 81–82.

C. The Blakeslee papers are in the Clark Univ. Archives.

William A. Koelsch

BLISS, Tasker Howard (31 December 1853, Lewisburg, PA—9 November 1930, Washington). *Education*: graduate, U.S. Military Academy, 1875. *Career*: Army officer, 1875–1920, chief of staff, U.S. Army, 1917–18; U.S. permanent military representative, Inter-Allied Supreme War Council, 1918–19; commissioner plenipotentiary, American Commission to Negotiate Peace, Paris Peace Conference, 1919.

Bliss was foremost among a group of American officers who assumed responsible political-military positions during the early years of the twentieth century as the United States accepted an active role in world affairs. A contemplative intellectual, Bliss was the first Army officer to serve on the faculty of the Naval War College. He later became the first president of the the Army War College and in that capacity participated in the development of the general staff system during the tenure of *Elihu Root as secretary of war. Bliss then served as a proconsul in the Philippines. There followed important assignments on the General Staff and service on the Mexican border. In 1917, just after the U.S. intervention in World War I, he became chief of staff, but he served only briefly, for he was soon sent to Europe to represent the United States at the Inter-Allied Supreme War Council. It had been created to coordinate the political-military actions of the Western coalition, and his duty had two consequences. Bliss became fully aware of the devastation wrought by modern warfare, thereafter committing himself to the search for ways of avoiding future sanguinary struggles. Also his distinguished service brought him favorably to the attention of *Woodrow Wilson, who named him one of the nation's five peace commissioners at the Paris Peace Conference.

As a plenipotentiary, Bliss evinced a consuming concern for the elimination of militarism by means of arms limitations, specifically called for in the fourth of the president's Fourteen Points. To create a favorable environment for arms limitations, Bliss concentrated on measures to reestablish a viable balance of power in Europe and in Asia. This preoccupation led him to oppose unduly harsh measures against Germany and schemes of intervention against Bolshevik Russia, both of which he deemed destabilizing in effect. He strongly deprecated territorial concessions to Italy in the Adriatic region and economic ones to Japan in the Shantung peninsula. Like others in the American delegation in Paris, he departed with important reservations about aspects of the peace treaties that appeared to compromise the president's expressed wishes.

Although events in Europe had been disillusioning, the general became an active publicist for internationalist causes during his retirement. He regularly called for membership in the League of Nations and helped found the Council on Foreign Relations, contributing an article to the first issue of *Foreign Affairs*. He became prominent among proponents of some effective limitation on armaments. In 1924, with *David Hunter Miller and *James T. Shotwell, he helped prepare a proposal that stimulated discussion at the Fifth Assembly of the League of Nations toward what became the Geneva Protocol. Increasingly convinced that collective security had not proven effective, he became a strong advocate of judicial methods of maintaining a peaceful world, notably by means of a World Court, and he became a staunch supporter of U.S. membership.

BIBLIOGRAPHY:

A. "The Armistice," AJIL 16 (1922), 509–22; "European Conditions Versus Disarmament," special supp., *Foreign Affairs* 1 (1923) 1–12; *The League of Nations as a Question of Business: An Address by General Tasker H. Bliss* (Philadelphia, 1924); "What Is Disarmament?" *International Conciliation* 220 (1926), 263–79.

B. DAB supp. 1, 88–90; NYT 9 Nov 1930, 18; Frederick Palmer, *Bliss, Peacemaker: The Life and Letters of General Tasker Howard Bliss* (New York, 1934); David F. Trask, "General Tasker Howard Bliss and the 'Sessions of the World,' 1919," *Transactions of the American Philosophical Society*, n.s., 56, 8 (Philadelphia, 1966); *The United States in the Supreme War Council: American War Aims and Inter-Allied Strategy, 1917–1918* (Middletown, CT, 1961).

C. The Bliss papers are in the Manuscript Division, Library of Congress.

David F. Trask

BLOCH, Jean de. See *Biographical Dictionary of Modern Peace Leaders.*

BLUE, Rupert Lee (30 May 1867, Richmond County, NC—12 April 1948, Charleston, SC). *Education*: Univ. of Virginia, 1889–90; M.D., Univ. of Maryland, 1892. *Career*: intern, U.S. Marine Hospital Service, 1892; assistant surgeon, USMHS, 1893–97; passed assistant surgeon, United States Marine Hospital and Public Health Service, 1897–1909; surgeon, USMHPHS, 1909–12; surgeon-general, United States Public Health Service, 1912–20; assistant surgeon-general at large, USPHS, 1920–32.

In his early career, Blue was stationed at a variety of ports for duty in hospital and quarantine work. Familiarity with malaria, yellow fever, plague, cholera, and other epidemic scourges prepared him for his greatest contribution to public health. In 1903 and 1907 he was in charge of operations to control bubonic plague in San Francisco. Blue developed extensive rat extermination drives in 1907 that dramatically halted the epidemic and demonstrated that plague was carried by fleas on rats rather than by human carriers. This work catapulted him to the office of surgeon-general in 1912 and made him the world's authority on plague control measures. In 1910 Blue surveyed sanitary conditions in South America and studied at the London School of Tropical Medicine. He rapidly gained further international renown for methods to control yellow fever and cholera as well as bubonic plague. He also made notable contributions to medical knowledge concerning malaria and typhoid fever.

During World War I, Blue's attentions were primarily devoted to sanitation in U.S. military cantonments; and, although he drafted a proposal for an international program of public health in 1919, he was unable to carry it out. His tenure as surgeon-general expired in 1920, and Secretary of the Treasury Carter Glass was determined that a fellow Virginian should succeed to the post. Given the title assistant surgeon-general at large, Blue directed Public Health Service operations in Europe from 1920 to 1923 and became a familiar figure at numerous international conferences such as the Third Decennial Revision of the International Nomenclature of Diseases. He became a member in 1923 of the League of Nations Advisory Committee on Traffic in Opium and regularly attended its conferences. He was one of the first U.S. citizens to participate in League discussions and thus helped lower official barriers against involvement in international affairs. One of his last contributions concerned the revision of international quarantine laws. The changes were a result of his projection of the possibility of the international transmission of disease by airplane travelers, a farsighted vision in 1928.

Blue's extraordinary contributions to disease control were recognized by many honors, including the presidency of the American Medical Association. In the first hundred years of that body's existence, Blue was the only surgeon-general of the Public Health Service elected to the post.

BIBLIOGRAPHY:

A. *Anti-plague Measures in San Francisco, California, U.S.A.* (Cambridge, MA, 1909); *The Conduct of a Plague Campaign* (Chicago, 1908); *Methods for the Control of Plague with Special Reference to Administrative Details* (Chicago, 1911); *The Underlying Principles of Anti-plague Measures* (San Francisco, 1908).

B. *American Journal of Public Health* 38 (Jun 1948), 909; *American Men of Science* (New York, 1944), 165; Morris Fishbein, *A History of the American Medical Association, 1847–1947* (Philadelphia, 1947); *Journal of the American Medical Association* 137 (29 May 1948), 481; NCAB 40, 136–37; *Newsweek* 26 Apr

1948, 63; *Survey* 84 (May 1948), 173; *Time* 26 Apr 1948, 94; Ralph C. Williams, *A History of the United States Public Health Service, 1798-1950* (Washington, 1951); WWWA 2, 68.

Victoria A. Harden

BLUM, Léon (9 April 1872, Paris—30 March 1950, Jouy-en-Josas, France). *Education*: Ecole Normale Supérieure, 1890–91; law degree, Univ. of Paris, 1894. *Career*: statesman, Socialist leader, and writer; government attorney and jurist, Conseil d'Etat, 1895–1914; drama and literary critic, 1890–1914; editor, *Le Populaire*, 1921–40; deputy, French Chamber of Deputies, 1919–28, 1929–40; premier, June 1936–June 1937, March 1938–April 1938, December 1946–January 1947.

Blum's earliest political writings reflect his lifelong commitment to democratic socialism, internationalism, and peace. A Socialist at an early age, he became actively involved in politics at the time of the Dreyfus affair. After the assassination in 1914 of the Socialist leader Jean Jaurès, Blum gradually succeeded to the leadership of the party, adamantly opposing in 1920 affiliation with the Communist International. Elected to the Chamber of Deputies in 1919, he presided over the Socialist parliamentary delegation and wrote daily editorials for *Le Populaire*, the party newspaper. In the post-1919 years he preached reconciliation with Germany, support for the League of Nations, and general disarmament as the path to peace.

In the 1930s, with the worldwide economic depression, Italian aggression, Hitler's triumph in Germany, and the growth of French antirepublicanism, Blum became the leader in France of a left-liberal coalition known as the Popular Front. After its victory at the polls in 1936, Blum became the first Socialist (and first Jewish) premier of France. Although his government lasted only thirteen months, it introduced a number of memorable labor reforms. In July 1936 Blum was unexpectedly confronted with the Spanish Civil War. Suppressing his personal sympathies for the Spanish Republic, he yielded to pressure from the British and from his French moderate republican political allies and stopped the flow of aid. Concerned that intervention in the Spanish war might lead to a general European conflagration, he arranged for an ill-fated international nonintervention agreement that was quickly violated by the Germans, the Italians, and the Soviet Union. Although a lifelong advocate of universal disarmament, Blum took the necessary steps to provide credits for the rearming of France. Later he worked incessantly for the military strengthening of France, opposing the pacifist, proappeasement forces within his own party.

Refusing to leave France after the military defeat in 1940, Blum was imprisoned and eventually tried in 1942 by the Vichy regime for having weakened France by his reforms and for having contributed to the outbreak of war in 1939, but his defense was so effective that the trial was suspended. Removed in 1943 to Buchenwald, he was rescued in May 1945. While a prisoner, as a continuing testament to his faith in democracy, socialism, and internationalism, he wrote a long, moving, book-length essay published after the war as *A l'échelle humaine* (1945).

After the war Blum continued to write for *Le Populaire*, helped reshape his party, and returned for brief intervals to political life, opposing both Communism and *Charles de Gaulle, whom he criticized as an exemplar of old-fashioned nationalism. Blum championed the movement toward the economic and political integration of Europe, serving with *Edouard Herriot as a member of the permanent committee for the creation of a European federal union. Favoring a strong United Nations, Blum also played an active role in the formation of UNESCO and in the decision to locate the organization in Paris. To the end he remained faithful to his democratic, socialistic, and humanistic ideals, asking why, if the human mind could create poetry, science, and art, it could not create justice, fraternity, and peace.

BIBLIOGRAPHY:

A. *L'Oeuvre de Léon Blum*, 9 vols. (Paris, 1954–72).

B. Joel Colton, *Léon Blum: Humanist in Politics* (New York, 1966); Jean Lacouture, *Léon Blum* (Paris, 1977).

C. The Blum papers are in the Fondation Nationale des Sciences Politiques, Paris.

Joel Colton

BLUNTSCHLI, Johann Caspar (7 March 1808, Zurich—21 October 1881, Karlsruhe, Germany). *Education*: Univ. of Berlin; LL.D., Bonn, 1829. *Career*: professor, Univ. of Zurich, 1833–47; member, Zurich Great Council, 1837–47, president, 1845, member, Zurich Executive Council, 1839–46; professor, Univ. of Munich, 1848–61, Univ. of Heidelberg, 1861–81; at various times member, First or Second Chamber of Baden, 1861–81; cofounder, Institute of International Law, 1873, president, 1875–77.

Born into an old Zurich family, Bluntschli served his town and canton as professor, lawgiver, and political activist. In opposition to the dominant Radicals, he founded a liberal-conservative center party whose initial successes faded during the religio-political conflicts that troubled Switzerland in the 1840s. In 1848 Bluntschli followed his friend, the German philosopher-psychologist Friedrich Rohmer, to Munich, where he assumed a professorship of German private and public law. In 1861 he became professor of constitutional law and political science in Heidelberg. His activities in the political and religious life of the Duchy of Baden led to memberships in the legislative bodies of that state as well as to the presidency of its Evangelical Synod. He became a cofounder of the German Protestant Union (1864) and was active in the brotherhood of Freemasonry.

Shortly after his arrival in Heidelberg, Bluntschli began to turn his scholarly attention to international law. Having written works of lasting value and impact on Zurich, Swiss, and German law, he now published a multivolume *Rechtsbuch* whose first part on "the modern law of warfare among civilized nations" appeared in 1866. The *Rechtsbuch* combined the codification of international law as it existed then with an indication of what kind of new law was necessary and desirable. It established Bluntschli as an authority on the subject and brought him international renown.

In 1873 Bluntschli founded with like-minded scholars the Institute of International Law in Ghent, Belgium. Their goal was to provide a forum for the study of the fundamental principles of international law. The same year he participated as the only German jurist in the Brussels conference that created the International Law Association. During the following years, Bluntschli was one of the most active members of the Institute. He attended its annual conferences in Geneva (1874), The Hague (1875), Zurich (1877), Brussels (1879), and Oxford (1880) and was president (1875-77) and vice-president for four terms. Bluntschli's major works, frequently republished in new and enlarged editions and translated into other European languages, established him as one of the great jurists of the nineteenth century.

BIBLIOGRAPHY:

A. *Das moderne Völkerrecht der zivilisierten Staaten, als Rechtsbuch dargestellt*, 3rd ed., 3 vols. (Nördlingen, Germany, 1878); *Denkwürdiges aus meinem Leben*, ed. R. Seyerlen, 3 vols. (Nördlingen, Germany, 1884), bibliography of 144 titles in vol. 3, 514-24; *Deutsches Staatswörterbuch*, 11 vols. (Stuttgart and Leipzig, Germany, 1857-70); *Die Lehre vom modernen Staat*, 5th ed., 3 vols. (Stuttgart, Germany, 1875-76); *Geschichte des schweizerischen Bundesrechts*, 2 vols. (Zurich, 1846-52).

B. Hans Fritzsche, "Johann Caspar Bluntschli," in *Schweizer Juristen der letzten hundert Jahre* (Zurich, 1945), 134-67; *Historisch-Biographisches Lexikon der Schweiz* 2, 280-81 (Berlin, 1955); *Neue deutsche Biographie* 2, 337-38 (Neuenberg, 1934); Dietrich Schindler, "Jean-Gaspard Bluntschli (1808-1881)," in *Livre du centenaire 1873-1973* (Basel, 1973), 45-60.

Heinz K. Meier

BLYMER, William Hervey (4 March 1865, Mansfield, OH—14 April 1939, Pelham Manor, NY). *Education*: Harvard Law School, 1885-87; Sorbonne and Univ. of Bonn, 1891, 1899. *Career*: lawyer, Mansfield, OH, 1888-90, Paris, 1891-92, New York, 1892-1931.

Blymer's interest in the world flowered as a result of his European visit (1891-92) and the lectures on international law he heard at the Sorbonne. He became an authority on admiralty law and handled numerous cases in that field. He also revealed an early interest in peace, attending the Fourth Universal Peace Congress at Bern in 1892, where he first presented his views on economic sanctions to prevent war. Thereafter, in speeches and pamphlets, Blymer elaborated on this idea, which he believed would lead to a stable world.

In its simplest form, Blymer believed that an imposed economic embargo against aggressors, combined with disarmament and compulsory arbitration, would bring world stability. His "isolation plan" required governments to "embargo economically and diplomatically any nation which refused to arbitrate a dispute." With this approach, Blymer anticipated the basic assumptions of the League to Enforce Peace (1915–21). Unlike the LEP, Blymer would have used force to uphold the decision of any tribunal. Blymer sometimes boasted that *Woodrow Wilson's peace program, including most of the Fourteen Points, embodied suggestions from his plan, but Blymer became a critic of the Covenant of the League of Nations. In structure and operation it could never work, he argued, primarily because its responses against violators of the Covenant were not automatic. He renewed his appeal for the imposition of a universal economic embargo and held to that view even more persistently as he watched the League collapse in the 1930s. Blymer mailed his publications to many other internationalists but rarely affiliated with any groups, preferring to remain singularly independent.

BIBLIOGRAPHY:

A. *The Isolation (or Non-intercourse) Plan with a Proposed Convention* (New York, 1917); *The Isolation Plan with Papers on the Covenant* (Boston, 1921); *Observations on Compulsory Arbitration and Disarmament Under Penalty of Non-Intercourse* (New York, 1905); "Peace Maintenance by Economic Isolation," *World Unity Magazine* 4 (Apr 1929), 40–49.

B. NCAB 28, 70; NYT 16 Apr 1939, III-6.

Warren F. Kuehl

BOLÍVAR, Simón (24 July 1783, Caracas—17 December 1830, near Santa Marta, Colombia). *Education*: private tutors; studied in Madrid. *Career*: planter and businessman, 1807–10; diplomatic mission to England, 1810; member, Venezuelan Congress, 1810–11; leader of independence movement, 1811–24; president of Colombia, 1821–30; Latin American leader, 1826–30.

Bolívar's claim as an internationalist is based largely on his vision of a union of American states during and after the wars of liberation. Yet that aspiration often stumbled upon other realistic positions advanced by Bolívar. For example, he recognized the need for strong governments for the new republics to survive, and he thus criticized the internal application of federalist principles, which were so vital to any cooperative movement among the states externally. While Bolívar had presented his "grandiose idea" of a single New World nation in his Jamaica Letter of 1815, his first concrete effort to translate it into reality came on 7 December 1824, with his invitation to a congress in Panama, which assembled 22 June 1826. Bolívar anticipated that all American governments, including the United States, would send delegates, and he also hoped Great Britain would participate. He saw the Congress as "destined to form a league more extensive, more remarkable, and more powerful than any that has ever existed on the face of the earth." It could formulate common laws, guarantee the existence of states, and maintain peace, while not intruding in the domestic affairs of members. Yet he believed it should aid governments against external attack and "internal anarchic factions." Trade would foster ties of interdependence involving Britain, the United States, and Latin America. The meeting at Panama fell far short of Bolívar's vision. Only delegates from Central America, Greater Colombia, Mexico, and Peru, plus observers from Britain and Holland, attended, and their discussions led to no concrete results. Yet the event has been properly acclaimed as a significant precedent for the future. The areas represented did include three-fourths of the populace of Spanish America.

Bolívar sought to advance unification in other ways. As president of Colombia, he included in his treaties provisions for an international congress, and the Panama Conference also adopted suggestions for another meeting. For whatever reason, Bolívar lost interest in the broader concept and focused thereafter upon a Federation of the Andes to encompass Peru, Bolivia, and Colombia. While this materialized in part with the formation of Greater Colombia, it was neither voluntary nor lasting.

Many interpretations have been advanced that both exaggerate and question Bolívar's importance as an internationalist. It is clear, however, that his plans and efforts have had a continuing ideological impact.

BIBLIOGRAPHY:

A. *Cartas del libertador*, 12 vols. (Caracas and New York, 1929–59); *Selected Writings of Bolívar*, 2 vols. (New York, 1951).

B. Víctor Andrés Belaúnde, *Bolívar and the Political Thought of the Spanish American Revolution* (Baltimore, MD, 1938); Gerhard Masur, *Simón Bolívar* (Albuquerque, NM, 1948); Raimundo Rivas, "Bolivar as Internationalist," *Bulletin of Pan American Union* 64 (Dec 1930), 1266–1311; Arturo Uslar-Pietro, "Bolivar and the Congress of Panama," *UNESCO Courier* 30 (Feb 1977), 28–32; Arthur P. Whitaker, *The Western Hemisphere Idea: Its Rise and Decline* (Ithaca, NY, 1954).

Warren F. Kuehl

BONHAM CARTER, [Helen] Violet (15 April 1887, London—19 February 1969, London). *Education*: privately educated. *Career*: author, Liberal MP adviser, 1951.

The only daughter of *Herbert H. Asquith, prime minister from 1908 to 1916, Violet Asquith married in 1915 Maurice Bonham Carter, her father's principal private secretary. She was defeated in 1945 elections to the House of Commons and entered the House of Lords in 1964 as a life peeress.

She was four when her mother died, and even after her father's remarriage three years later she was his political confidante. When still too small to sit at the dining table, she was placed in a high chair so as not to be excluded from the political discussions. Educated by governesses, she learned German in Dresden and French in Paris. To a remarkable memory she added a felicity of expression and a devastating power of ridicule, which she used widely in constant support of her father after his removal in 1916. A supporter of the National Coalition government in 1931, she remained a zealous advocate of international trade. Later in 1933 she excoriated Franz von Papen for making the deal with Hitler that secured him the chancellorship. She first met Winston Churchill at a dinner party in 1906; later she strongly supported his anti-Nazi stance throughout the 1930s and pressed for his inclusion in government at the outbreak of the war, although she criticized him at times.

From the inception of the League of Nations, Bonham Carter used her formidable talents on its behalf, notably as a member of the executive body of the League of Nations Union until its demise in 1941. Her generous imagination had also been caught by the concept of the organic unity of Europe from the launching by *Richard Coudenhove-Kalergi of the Pan-Europe movement. By the late 1930s she had become an outspoken advocate of collective security. She became a vice-chairperson of the United Europe Movement in 1947, and for the last five years of her life was president of the Royal Institute of International Affairs. She also supported the UN Association. But always she remained what she had become at her father's knee: a passionate Liberal. After World War I her counsel was much sought, not least by Jo Grimond, member of Parliament and leader of the Liberal party, who married her daughter in 1938.

Witty, warm-hearted, and occasionally devastating, Bonham Carter never regarded herself as an orator; others did, and in 1963 she became the first woman to give the Romanes Lecture at Oxford. She chose as her theme "The Impact of Personality on Politics." Starting with her own experience, she ended with a denunciation of "the fallacy of Historic Fatalism." It was typical of her outgoing personality that she did not appreciate that her own life corroborated her belief that throughout time significant figures have overcome adversity by inspiring others.

BIBLIOGRAPHY:

A. *Winston Churchill As I Knew Him* (London, 1965).

B. LT 3 Dec 1962, 12.

Colin Gordon

BONNET, Henri (26 May 1888, Châteauponsac, France—25 October 1978, Paris). *Education*: Ecole Normale Supérieure. *Career*: member, Secretariat, League of Nations, 1920–31; director, International Institute of Intellectual Cooperation, 1931–40; various posts, Free French movement, 1940–44; ambassador to United States, 1944–55.

The title of the announcement of his death in *Le Monde* simply referred to him as "Ambassador of France." Indeed, Bonnet represented his country in Washington for over a decade, but he was much more than a traditional career diplomat. Bonnet was a strong French patriot, yet his professional life always emphasized international dimensions. As early as 1920 he moved to Geneva, where he began his international apprenticeship in the

Secretariat of the League of Nations. Unfortunately, Henri often has been confused with Georges Bonnet, the French foreign minister in 1938–39 who in 1937 also served as ambassador to the United States.

Born in 1888 in a very small town in central France, Bonnet received a traditional classical education, then graduated from the Ecole Normale Supérieure in Paris, where he specialized in history. He taught briefly and fought in World War I, and for a year after he worked as the foreign relations editor for the Radical Socialist daily *L'Ere nouvelle*.

In 1920 Bonnet took a crucial step, which determined his career as an international public servant. He accepted a post in the Secretariat. His eleven years in Geneva significantly stamped his life. Unlike many intellectuals whose concerns were confined by national circumstances, Bonnet was forced to consider problems in a regional or even a worldwide context. He first served in Geneva under the British intellectual *Gilbert Murray. Later Bonnet had no problem working for a German boss. After a brief assignment in the League's Press and Information Section headed by *Pierre Comert, Bonnet became involved in cultural affairs. There observers credited him with creating a model system subsequently copied by other international organizations. He distinguished himself by conscientious hard work while retaining a natural sense of humor and friendly personality.

Bonnet's exemplary record at the League was rewarded by his appointment in 1931 to succeed Julien Luchaire as head of the International Institute of Intellectual Cooperation, which had been established in Paris in 1924 as the executive organ of the League Committee on Intellectual Co-operation. Its major function was to facilitate intellectual exchanges between nations and to encourage collaboration in the arts, letters, sciences, and education. Special emphasis was placed on the need to prepare the young to think in world terms. This was accomplished in part by projects to eliminate national biases in social science textbooks. Bonnet's appointment strengthened and widened the scope of the Institute's work, turning it into the forerunner of UNESCO. The nine years of his directorship marked the apogee of Bonnet's international activities. He traveled all over the world establishing some forty national branches of the Institute and encountered the world's most famous writers, thinkers, and statesmen during the 1930s. His major emphasis lay in the intellectual field, but he also found time to aid various international causes such as disarmament and women's rights.

The purely international phase of Bonnet's life was abruptly closed by World War II. Shortly after the fall of France, he chose to leave and flew to London with *Jean Monnet, the future organizer of the European Common Market. Bonnet came to New York, where he taught at the Ecole Libre des Hautes Etudes, a Francophone branch of the New School for Social Research founded to provide teaching posts for intellectuals fleeing Hitler's Europe. In 1941 he was instrumental in founding France Forever, devoted to rallying French residents of the United States to *Charles de Gaulle and to promoting his cause in the American press. As the vice-president, Bonnet was rewarded by being made a member of its Committee of National Liberation in Algiers. For a year he was in charge of the Information Section and then was named as ambassador to Washington. While in the United States, Bonnet became involved in *Anita Blaine's World Citizens Association. He served on study committees, and his books of this period reflect his belief that a powerful and popularly supported international organization was needed.

Between 1944 and 1955, Bonnet remained a dedicated workhorse, representing his government in the United States. As a respected international statesman, he signed the United Nations Charter for his country in 1945. He participated in negotiations establishing the Marshall Plan and in the discussions leading to the creation of the North Atlantic Treaty Organization and the European Defense Community.

Back in Paris, after 1955, Bonnet remained active in the international field. He served as vice-president of France–Amérique, which promoted friendship between the two nations, and he worked for the French branch of the Children's Emergency Fund. Even in old age, as during his professional career, this highly cultivated, warm-hearted, articulate Frenchman retained an indestructible optimism and faith in international cooperation.

BIBLIOGRAPHY:

A. *International Children's Emergency Fund* (Paris, 1949); *La Société des Nations, son organisation, son oeuvre* (Boulogne-sur-Seine, France, n.d.); *L'Oeuvre de l'Institut International de Co-opération Intellectuelle* (Paris, 1938); *Outlines of the Future: World Organization Emerging from the War* (Chicago, 1942); *The World's Destiny and the United States* (Chicago, 1941).

B. CB 1945, 61–63; *Le Monde* 27 Oct 1978, 7.

Sabine Jessner

BOOTH, Bramwell (8 March, 1856, Halifax, Yorkshire, England—16 June 1929, Hadley Wood, England). *Education*: private and City of London School. *Career*: chief of staff, Salvation Army, 1880–1912, general, 1912–29.

The eldest son of William Booth, who founded the Salvation Army in the slums of London in 1865, Bramwell Booth followed his father's convictions, shared his religious beliefs, and was appointed by him to be his successor in "God's Army." As well as drawing up the rules and regulations incumbent upon Salvationists, he was a prolific writer on Bible studies and social problems; it was through his guidance that the right of the Salvation Army was firmly established legally in the British Isles. In 1885 he obtained some unusual publicity when he was arrested as a result of a technical breach of the law in a campaign for the suppression of criminal vice; tried at the Old Bailey, Booth was discharged, and subsequently the Criminal Law Amendment Act raised the age of consent to sixteen years. A skilled propagandist, Booth promoted foreign missions and the spread of the Army in Europe and the New World. Unlike many denominations of its time, the Army felt no ties to any nation-state. The outbreak of the Great War gave an added dimension to its evangelism and its charitable work, so that by its end it was widely recognized and approved as a skilled and efficient welfare agency.

In all these activities, Booth was supported by his Welsh wife, Florence, who became a Salvation Army worker in 1880, two years before they married. She took charge of the women's social work and found time to produce two sons and five daughters, all of whom subsequently devoted their lives to "the Army." The support of his devoted and united family, as well as his dedication to the aims and ideals of his father, enabled Booth to expand the Salvation Army from a local Christian mission into a worldwide charitable and evangelical movement that commanded and commands respect and admiration.

BIBLIOGRAPHY:

A. *Echoes and Memories* (London, 1925); *These Fifty Years* (London, 1929).

B. Catherine Bramwell-Booth, *Bramwell Booth* (London, 1933); St. John G. Ervine, *God's Soldier*, 2 vols. (London, 1934).

Colin Gordon

BOOTH, Evangeline (25 December 1865, London—17 July 1950, New York). *Education*: tutors and governesses. *Career*: Salvation Army work in England, 1880–96, in Canada, 1896–1904, in the United States, 1904–34, worldwide, 1934–39.

Booth received the rank of sergeant in the Salvation Army when fifteen and became its foreign secretary in 1904, when she left England for the United States. Thereafter, her international activities were intertwined between a sense of public duty and the work of the Salvation Army. She attended an Army World Congress in London in 1914, was U.S. delegate appointed by Warren Harding to the World Conference Against Alcoholism in Denmark in 1923, and in 1934 was elected general of the Salvation Army in charge of all the international movement in ninety countries with eighty-seven different languages.

Booth's contributions internationally often centered around relief and rehabilitation work. After an Armenian massacre in 1896, she led Canadians in providing large sums of money and tons of medical supplies. She organized a Missing Persons' Bureau as part of a worldwide service, aided Japanese victims of a 1923 earthquake, and became a leader in the international crusade against alcohol and the mistreatment of children. During World War I, she revealed a dilemma over what course to follow. After the United States declared war, she announced that the Salvation Army flag was interlocked with those of all peoples and that everyone should be recognized as brothers in all families. She publicly proclaimed that the Salvation Army deplored all war except the ceaseless war against sin and strife and death; yet, she expanded the Army's Naval and Military League to provide for the religious and recreational needs of troops. She organized the National War Board in the United States and gave special recognition to the young women in the Salvation Army who, overseas in their huts, lent money, sewed on buttons, gave advice, held church services, and served hot doughnuts. After she became general in 1934, she directed the Army's work worldwide and traveled extensively to farflung posts. Her basic aim as general was to use the Army to promote better international understanding.

BIBLIOGRAPHY:

A. *Love Is All* (New York, 1908); *Toward a Better World* (Garden City, NY, 1928); with Grace Livingston Hill, *The War Romance of the Salvation Army* (Philadelphia, 1919); *Woman* (New York, 1930).

B. LT 18 Jul 1950, 8; NAW 1, 204–6; NCAB B, 127–29.

Virginia Neel Mills

BORCHARD, Edwin Montefiore (17 October 1884, New York—22 July 1951, Hamden, CT). *Education*: City Coll. of New York, 1898–1902; LL.B., New York Law School, 1905; B.A., Columbia Univ., 1908, Ph.D., 1913. *Career*: law librarian of Congress, 1911–13, 1914–16; assistant solicitor, Department of State, 1913–14; attorney, National City Bank of New York, 1916–17; professor, Yale Law School, 1917–50.

From the time he was hired at Yale University Law School in 1917, Borchard wrote prolifically on many aspects of international law. Among his legal colleagues, he was greatly respected for his expertise in such matters as the diplomatic protection of citizens abroad, declaratory judgments, alien property holdings, and neutrality. To the general public, he was best known for his attacks upon collective security and involvement in both world wars. But if Borchard's general reputation was that of a militant isolationist, he was in one sense a strong internationalist, with his internationalism based upon cooperation through conferences, arbitration, conciliation, and international tribunals, ideas that had developed in the two decades preceding 1914.

Borchard's rise in his profession was almost meteoric, and in his activities he reflected a singular attachment to traditional legal principles. In 1919 he advised the U.S. delegation during the North Atlantic Coast Fisheries Arbitration at The Hague. From 1923 to 1925, he was chief counsel for Peru in the Tacna-Aricna dispute and was appointed by Calvin Coolidge to serve on the Central American Arbitration Tribunal. In 1925 he held the first postwar American lectureship at the University of Berlin. He served on the Pan American Committee of Experts for the Codification of International Law and, in 1930, was technical adviser to the U.S. delegation at The Hague Codification Conference. In 1938 Borchard represented the United States at the Lima Conference on International Codification. From 1924 until his death in 1951, he served on the board of editors of the *American Journal of International Law*.

A disciple of *John Bassett Moore, Borchard considered international law a science and neutrality a legal status. Neutral powers, he maintained, were obliged to treat all belligerents equally, that is, without fear or discrimination. Before World War I, so he argued, international law protected nations from "purposeless" involvement, permitted commercial prosperity, limited the scope of the fighting, and allowed for neutral mediation. Unfortunately, American leaders committed to collective security rode roughshod over generations of codification. Foolish efforts to freeze the status quo and punish aggressors perpetuated continual chaos overseas because they sought to alter well-established principles of international law.

It is hardly surprising that the interventionism of *Woodrow Wilson and *Franklin D. Roosevelt found in Borchard a learned and forceful opponent, one who claimed that he, not their administrations, was the guardian of genuine internationalism. Borchard accused the League of Nations of being an armed alliance, saw the World Court as a political and not a judicial body, and claimed that the Kellogg-Briand Pact really sanctioned war. Rigid Western opposition to Japan in Manchuria, Italy in Ethiopia, and Germany on the European continent, to use a Borchard metaphor, was comparable to sitting on a safety valve. A supporter of the America First Committee, Borchard continued to oppose U.S. diplomacy during World War II and the Cold War. To Borchard, the Pearl Harbor attack resulted from America's intransigent negotiating; the new United Nations would undermine the warmaking powers of Congress; and the Truman Doctrine and Atlantic Pact were commitments to unlimited intervention. When China became Communist in 1949, Borchard blamed the Truman administration for violating traditional canons of neutrality by backing the Nationalists.

Borchard warned against an overreliance upon international courts and law because he believed that nations would never submit questions of vital interest to international authority. Yet many conflicts of the interwar period, he believed, could be eliminated by the cancelation of war debts, tariff reductions, arms limitation, and the redistribution of foreign markets and raw materials. A reliance on traditional international practices would limit U.S. involvement, thereby preserving American peace and prosperity while containing the conflict, and among those early applications was a return to the pre-1914 world of limited international and legal agencies to which nations would voluntarily submit their differences.

BIBLIOGRAPHY:

A. *American Foreign Policy* (Indianapolis, IN, 1946); ed. with Joseph P. Chamberlain and Stephen Duggan, *The Collected Papers of John Bassett Moore*, 7 vols. (New Haven, CT, 1944); *Diplomatic Protection of Citizens Abroad* (New York, 1915); with William P. Lage, *Neutrality for the United States*, rev. ed. (New Haven, CT 1937, 1940).

B. AJIL 45 (1951), 708–9; DAB supp. 5, 81–82; Richard H. Kendall, "Edwin M. Borchard and the Defense of Traditional American Neutrality," dissertation, Yale

Univ., 1964; NYT 23 Jul 1951, 17; WWWA 3, 90; *Yale Law Journal* 60 (Nov 1951), 1071-72.

C. The Borchard papers are at Yale Univ.

Justus D. Doenecke

BORDEN, Robert Laird (26 June 1854, Grand Pré, NS—10 June 1937, Ottawa). *Education*: Acacia Villa Academy; apprenticed in law, 1874-78. *Career*: teacher, Matawan, NJ, 1873-74; lawyer, Halifax, NS, 1878-1905; member of Canadian Parliament, 1896-1921; leader, Conservative party, 1901-20; prime minister, 1911-20; chancellor, McGill Univ., 1918-20, Queen's Univ., 1924-30.

Borden, as Canada's prime minister during World War I, was a major architect of the transition from the British Empire to the Commonwealth of Nations. Seizing the opportunity of membership in the Imperial War Cabinet formed by *David Lloyd George to consult the Dominions on war policy, Borden was the principal author of Resolution IX of the 1917 Imperial War Conference, which declared that the development of constitutional relations within the British Empire "should be based upon a full recognition of the Dominions as autonomous nations of an Imperial Commonwealth" and "should recognize the right of the Dominions and India to an adequate voice in foreign policy and in foreign relations." At subsequent meetings of the Imperial War Cabinet, Borden led the fight for recognition of the right of the Dominions to separate representation at the Paris Peace Conference. Then, at Paris in 1919, Borden's advocacy of "dominion status" was carried to its logical conclusion: separate representation in the League of Nations and International Labor Organization, the right to election to the Councils of both institutions, and separate ratification of the peace treaties. Borden's insistence on the full recognition of dominion status was as significant then in its impact on world thought and the structure of international organization as was the emergence of new states from colonies following World War II.

Sir Robert was an early advocate and firm supporter of the League of Nations, not as a showplace for his nation's newly acquired international status but as an instrument to advance the principles of international law and, along with Anglo-American accord in international relations, as a guarantor of peace. If public opinion did not develop in support of an organization and was not willing to enforce its decisions, he argued in 1917, the existing structure could not survive. After his retirement from public life in 1920, Borden worked to promote support for the League as a member and sometime president of the League of Nations Society in Canada. In 1930 he served as chief Canadian delegate to the Assembly and Canadian representative on the League of Nations Council.

BIBLIOGRAPHY:

A. *Canada in the Commonwealth* (Oxford, 1929); *Canadian Constitutional Studies* (Toronto, 1922); *Letters to Limbo*, ed. H. Borden (Toronto, 1972); *Robert Laird Borden; His Memoirs*, ed. H. Borden, 2 vols. (Toronto, 1938).

B. Robert Craig Brown, *Robert Laird Borden: A Biography, 1854-1937*, 2 vols., (Toronto, 1975-80); *Canadian Directory of Parliament 1867-1967* (Ottawa, 1968), 56-57; *Macmillan Dictionary of Canadian Biography* (Toronto, 1963), 68.

C. The Borden papers are in the Manuscripts Division, Public Archives of Canada.

Robert Craig Brown

BORGESE, Giuseppe Antonio (12 November 1882, Polizzi Generosa, Italy—4 December 1952, Fiesole, Italy). *Education*: Ph.D., Univ. of Florence, 1903. *Career*: professor, Univ. of Rome, 1910-17; literary and foreign editor, *Corriere della sera* (Milan), 1912-31; professor, Univ. of Milan, 1917-25, 1926-31, 1948-52; head, Italian Bureau of Propaganda, 1917-18; professor, Univ. of Chicago, 1936-48.

In the search for a viable form of world government during and after World War II, few intellectuals probed the issues more deeply or attracted greater attention than Borgese. As secretary of the Committee to Frame a World Constitution, a University of Chicago group whose members included *Robert M. Hutchins, Mortimer J. Adler, Stringfellow Barr, and Rexford Tugwell, Borgese was the chief architect of its Preliminary Draft of a World Constitution, which appeared in 1948. The document reflected a conviction, spreading rapidly among leftist intellectuals by 1947, that the United Nations was a half-measure at best. The Draft was discussed in a variety of popular and literary journals in America and was translated into several languages. Borgese and his fellow Chicagoans welcomed serious debate over their proposal, much of it published in *Common Cause*, a monthly magazine Borgese edited throughout its life from 1947 to 1951. The plan that emerged was a complex structure for a world republic, with sovereignty invested in the people, direct popular election of a legislature, a president elected by a regionally apportioned electoral college, a judiciary appointed by the president, and a tribune whose function was to serve as minority spokesman. Without apology Borgese acknowledged the visionary nature of this plan while insisting on its fundamental realism. He referred to the Draft as a sort of midwife to a new international order.

Borgese's internationalist ideas were grounded in his conviction that change was a constant in the universe. An astonishing range of sources, from Eastern religions to Renaissance Italian literature to modern scientific writing, informed his thought. As a university student he had championed the nationalist views of Gabriele d'Annunzio, but he abandoned these long before World War I. During the war he became a fervent Wilsonian and concluded that nationalism represented but a transitory phase of social development. In the modern world it had become an obstacle to human progress. Worse still was the Fascism arising in Italy. Borgese denounced it throughout the 1920s and continued his opposition after emigrating to the United States in 1931. As Europe again plunged into general war, Borgese increasingly focused his energies on the cause of world democracy. To that end he collaborated with Lewis Mumford, Herbert Agar, Thomas Mann, and others in writing *The City of Man* in 1940. Three years later he published *Common Cause*, his greatest popular success. The book was both a warning and an appeal. Borgese believed that following the war the Allied leaders intended to make no fundamental changes in the world order. Without adjustments, he contended, the war would be a meaningless waste. Borgese was deeply influenced by a speech given by the Archbishop of Canterbury in September 1943 which advocated making the public interest as supreme over the elements of land and water as it was over air and light. These ideas were to reappear as a basis of the system outlined in the Chicago Draft.

The key to bringing about world federalism, Borgese believed, was to create a spirit of cooperation among the world's peoples. A workable system would have to reconcile individualism, the desire for personal freedom, with universalism embodying a sense of tolerance and personal responsibility. To help build such a spirit and design such a system was the task to which Borgese devoted the last fifteen years of his life.

BIBLIOGRAPHY:

A. *The City of Man* (New York, 1940); *Common Cause* (New York, 1943); *Foundations of a World Republic* (Chicago, 1953); *Goliath: The March of Fascism* (New York, 1937).

B. CB 1947, 53–55; IWW 1947, 91; NYT 5 Dec 1952, 27; WWA 1946–47, 239–40.

James C. Schneider

BOSS, Charles S., Jr. See *Biographical Dictionary of Modern Peace Leaders.*

BOURGEOIS, Léon Victor Auguste (21 May 1851, Paris—29 September 1925, Château d'Oger, Marne, France). *Education*: doctor of law, Univ. of Paris. *Career*: minor administrative posts, 1876–88; Chamber of Deputies, 1888–1905, president, 1902; Senate, 1905–25, president, 1920–23; various ministerial positions in different Cabinets, 1890–1917; chairman, French delegation to Hague Peace Conferences, 1899 and 1907; member, Permanent Court of Arbitration, 1903–   ; French representative on the League of Nations Commission, 1919; Nobel Peace Prize, 1920.

A man of broad and diverse intellectual interests, Bourgeois had a distinguished career as a statesman, jurist, social reformer, peace advocate, and scholar. Ambitious by disposition, he occupied during his long public service virtually every high office in the Third French Republic except that of the presidency. A believer in social reform, Bourgeois took an active role in efforts to curb tuberculosis and pass needed labor legislation. He instituted reforms both in the universities and in public primary and secondary schools. When Bourgeois had the opportunity to form his own government in November 1895, his program included a retirement system for workers, an income tax, and the separation of church and state. Financial difficulties, however, brought an end to his government before it had been six months in power.

The political, social, and international ideas of Bourgeois had a definite theoretical basis. These views were developed in his famous book *Solidarité* (1897), which appeared in many editions. Elaborating on concepts presented in 1896 in articles in *La Nouvelle Revue*, he emphasized the increasing importance of the idea of solidarity as shown in the family, in the nation, and in the community of sovereign states. Numerous French political theorists commented extensively on these concepts so that solidarist doctrines were well known, and by World War I they had become the dominant social philosophy in France.

During the late nineteenth century Bourgeois found himself increasingly involved in peace movements. He received appointment as first plenipotentiary of the French delegation to the Hague Peace Conference of 1899, and there he presided over the Third Commission, which promoted the establishment of a Permanent Court of Arbitration. Bourgeois became well known for the persuasiveness of his manner and for his sincerity in attempting to devise practical machinery for the maintenance of world peace. After the Permanent Court became a reality, Bourgeois was named early in 1903 as a member. In 1907 he represented France again as that country's chief delegate at the Second Hague Peace Conference, where he served as chairman of the First Commission, which concerned itself with arbitration and the peaceful settlement of disputes. His speeches later appeared in an important publication in Paris in 1910. Early in 1918, Bourgeois headed a commission of inquiry to examine critically the scheme of a league of nations. In the following year, he attended in Paris an international congress that had been convened by various peace organizations interested in the establishment of such a league. Also in 1919, he represented France on the League of Nations Commission presided over by *Woodrow Wilson. There he pleaded eloquently for inclusion in the Covenant of the prewar international peace structure.

The climax of Bourgeois's career occurred in 1920, when he became president of the French Senate, won unanimous election as the first president of the Council of the League of Nations, and was awarded the Nobel Peace Prize. Unfortunately, declining health and approaching blindness prevented him from going to Oslo to receive this coveted award. Quite appropriately, he has been called the "spiritual father" of the League of Nations.

BIBLIOGRAPHY:

A. *L'Oeuvre de la Société des Nations, 1920–1923* (Paris, 1923); *Le Pacte de 1919 et la Société des Nations* (Paris, 1919); *Pour la Société des Nations* (Paris, 1910); *Solidarité*, 7th ed. (Paris, 1912).

B. *Dictionnaire de biographie française* 6 (Paris, 1954), 1475–76; Frederick W. Haberman, ed., *Nobel Lectures Including Presentation Speeches and Laureates' Biographies: Peace, 1901–1925* vol. 1 (Amsterdam, 1972), 303–20; Maurice Hamburger, *Hommes politiques: Léon Bourgeois, 1851–1925* (Paris, 1932); *Hommage à l'apôtre de la solidarité et de la paix: Inauguration du monument élevé à la mémoire de Léon Bourgeois par M. Albert Lebrun, président de la République* (Châlons-sur-Marne, France, 1933); John A. Scott, *Republican Ideas and the Liberal Tradition in France, 1870–1914* (New York, 1966).

C. Bourgeois papers are in the Archives départmentales de la Marne and in the Archives du Ministère des Affaires étrangères.

Bernerd C. Weber

BOURNE, Randolph. See *Biographical Dictionary of Modern Peace Leaders.*

BOWMAN, Isaiah (26 December 1878, Waterloo, ON—6 January 1950, Baltimore, MD). *Education*: graduate, State Normal Coll., Ypsilanti, MI, 1902; B.S., Harvard Univ., 1905; Ph.D., Yale Univ., 1909. *Career*: lecturer, Wesleyan Univ., 1907–9; assistant professor, Yale Univ., 1909–15; director, American Geographical Society, 1915–35; president, Johns Hopkins Univ., 1935–48.

A noted geographer, Bowman was first associated with South America, an area that remained central to his geographical writings. Prior to World War I, he launched a long-term project for a detailed map of South America that is still a significant achievement. Bowman developed broad international applications for geographers under the stimulus of World War I and the unique circumstances that made him, as director of the American Geographical Society, the overseer of the country's best map collection. He became a member of the Inquiry, a body of scholars which investigated geopolitical problems of war for the *Woodrow Wilson administration and which carried on their work at the Society's headquarters in New York City and at the Paris Peace Conference.

Bowman's ability to merge practical considerations with technical geography, a characteristic of his entire career, is illustrated by his influence on the memorandum on U.S. war aims prepared by the Inquiry that Wilson later edited into the Fourteen Points of American peace aims. Bowman became chief territorial specialist and later director of the Inquiry, then he served as a member of the American Polish Commission and the Polish-Ukrainian Armistice Commission (1919). An internationalist perspective continued, although his work as a geographer, organizer, and administrator often transcended it. At the end of the war, Bowman was instrumental in establishing the Council on Foreign Relations. Through its quarterly, *Foreign Affairs*, he and others hoped to orient U.S. foreign policy perspectives along the international lines they felt to be axiomatic. He also wrote an influential geography text, *The New World: Problems in Political Geography* (1921). It helped to break the hold that environmental determinism had on American geography before the war in favor of a pragmatic and objective evaluation of state power.

Many of the economic and political insights later incorporated into the study of geography and international relations were developed after the publication of *The New World*. Bowman used his academic prestige and influence to orient such scholarship toward real problems. Convinced that settlement and frontier life still dominated human experience in many parts of the world, including the United States, Bowman obtained funds for studies of pioneer settlements, which included his own *The Pioneer Fringe* (1931). He perceived the importance of resource competition as a source of conflict between states and of trade as a means of ameliorating tensions and ordering world politics. Democratic values incorporated into diplomacy would reduce the exploitative aspects of international economic relationships that he identified with the old diplomacy. Bowman believed that, once the problems of the Depression and destructive nationalism were solved, the path to a new diplomacy would again be open.

Bowman was appointed president of Johns Hopkins University in 1935, but his influence in geopolitical matters continued to grow. Prior to the outbreak of World War II, he became involved in a comprehensive study of world problems initiated by the Council on Foreign Relations, and *Franklin Roosevelt asked him for a definition of the Western Hemisphere that would justify the administration's protection of British convoys in the North Atlantic. Though gratified by his influence on Roosevelt in this instance, Bowman later expressed regret that the president so often went ahead with ill-considered policies. He was sharply critical of Roosevelt's policy of weakening Germany in the postwar world, generally faulted his Far Eastern policy, and opposed the view that Soviet assistance was necessary for the United States to win the war against Japan.

When the State Department's presidential advisory committee took up and developed the Council on Foreign Relations studies, Bowman accepted the chairmanship of the influential territorial committee, which prepared and reviewed numerous evaluations of geopolitical problems in an effort to inform national policy. That project, with his work at the Dumbarton Oaks Conference, convinced Bowman that the major territorial questions that concerned Europe could be found in a belt facing the Soviet Union. Remembering the dilemmas of state making at the end of World War I, the committee attempted to avoid them by providing an East European Confederation to reduce territorial conflicts and enhance resource development.

This approach became increasingly academic, and in 1944 territorial planning gave way to consideration for an international organization.

Bowman explored that subject at the Dumbarton Oaks Conference and the San Francisco meeting in 1945. He favored orienting the complex of territorial questions toward a consultative rather than a state system. He took grim pride in his conflicts both with the Soviets and with U.S. military representatives, who, he said, favored a strong veto for the great powers in the international organization and, hence, a return to the old diplomacy of the balance of power.

Bowman's continued emphasis on democratic values led him to advise State Department officers and other foreign policy activists that the highest form of patriotism lay in fairness and objective judgment. However, he publicly began in 1946 to issue warnings about the Soviets, and by 1948 he advocated universal military training, which he hoped would include education on international relations to compensate for the lack of attention given that subject in the public schools. After retiring as president of Johns Hopkins, he accepted an appointment as head of the colonial development division of the Economic Cooperation Administration, a part of the Point Four Program.

BIBLIOGRAPHY:

A. "Is an International Society Possible?" in *United Nations World Government*, ed. J. E. Johnsen (New York, 1947), 173–78; *The Pioneer Fringe* (New York, 1931); *South America* (Chicago, 1915); *International Relations* (Chicago, 1930); "The Strategy of Territorial Decisions," *Foreign Affairs* 24 (Jan 1946), 177–94.

B. George F. Carter, "Isaiah Bowman, 1878–1950," *Annals of the American Association of Geographers* 40 (Dec 1950), 335–50; DAB supp. 4, 98–100; NCAB F, 458–59; NYT 7 Jan 1950, 17; Charles Seymour, *Geography, Justice, and Politics at the Paris Peace Conference of 1919* (New York, 1951); John K. Wright, *Geography in the Making: The American Geographical Society, 1851–1951* (New York, 1952).

C. The Bowman papers are in the Johns Hopkins Univ. Library.

Paul P. Abrahams

BOYD-ORR, John (23 September 1880, Kilmaurs, Ayrshire, Scotland—25 June 1971, Brechin, Angus, Scotland). *Education*: M.B., B.Ch., Glasgow Univ., 1912, M.A., M.D., D.Sc. 1914. *Career*: founding director, Nutrition Institute, Aberdeen, 1914; Royal Army Medical Corps, 1914–18; founder, Rowett Research Institute (director), 1922–45, Walter Reid Library on Nutrition, 1923–45, John D. Webster Experimental Farm, 1925–45, Strathcona House for nutrition research scientists, 1930–45, *Nutrition Abstracts and Reviews* (editor), 1930–45; director, Imperial Bureau Animal Nutrition, 1929; member, several British commissions on food, 1932–36; member, League of Nations Commission on Nutrition, 1935; member, War Cabinet Scientific Commission on Food Policy, 1940; head, N. Scotland Coll. of Agriculture; professor, Aberdeen Univ., 1942–45; member of Parliament, 1945–46; president, National Peace Council, 1945; first director-general,

Food and Agricultural Organization, 1945–48; rector, Glasgow Univ., 1945, chancellor, 1946; founder, International Emergency Food Council, 1946; president, World Union of Peace Organizations, 1945; Nobel Peace Prize, 1949; president, World Academy of Science and Art, Jerusalem, 1961.

A pioneer in world nutritional studies on four continents, Boyd-Orr began efforts to achieve peace through international food cooperation at the League of Nations, where his studies led to the establishment of a Committee on Nutrition in 1935. His dynamic advocacy of programs to meet human needs led to his unanimous selection as founding director of the Food and Agricultural Organization in 1945 and of the International Emergency Food Council in 1946. He was credited for averting European famine after World War II, earning him the Nobel Peace Prize for 1949. A prophet ahead of his age, Boyd-Orr was a powerful advocate of the view that nutrition is essential to international peace and unity. He predicted world famine and the collapse of civilization if the recognition of the "common brotherhood of man" did not assure adequate food for all peoples. As a practical administrator, he proposed a world food board to maintain an international granary and lend funds for emergency food purchases and agricultural development. Since this was too ambitious for Cold War politicians, Boyd-Orr became convinced that it would be achieved only through world government. He used his prestige as a scientist to appeal to nations to realize that real peace could be achieved by redirecting research and expenditures from the arms race to human needs for food, health, and housing. As a World Federalist and peace leader, he donated his Nobel award to advance both traditional peace efforts and federalism. He also promoted the strengthening of the UN. His colorful, dynamic, and energetic career did much to apply scientific knowledge to human problems and to promote international awareness and cooperation in the world.

BIBLIOGRAPHY:

A. *Economic and Political Problems of the Atomic Age* (Birmingham, England, 1953); *Feast and Famine* (London, 1957); *As I Recall* (London, 1966); with David Lubbock, *Feeding the People in Wartime* (London, 1940); *Fighting for What?* (London, 1942); *Food: The Foundation of World Unity* (London, 1948); *International Liaison Committee of Organizations for Peace: A New Strategy of Peace* (London, 1950); *The New World Food Proposals* (Ottawa, 1947); *Nutrition in War* (London, 1940); "The Role of Food in Post-War Reconstruction," *International Labour Review* 47 (Mar 1943), 279–96; with G.D.H. Cole, *Welfare and Peace* (London, 1945); with David Lubbock, *The White Man's Dilemma: Food and the Future*, 2nd ed. (New York, 1964).

B. Ritchie Calder, "The Man and His Message," *Survey Graphic* 37 (Mar 1948), 99–104; CB 1946, 440–43; Eva de Vries, *Life and Work of Sir John Boyd Orr* (Wageningen, Netherlands, 1948); Tony Gray, *Champions of Peace* (Birmingham, England, 1976); Gore Hambidge, *The Story of FAO* (New York, 1955); IWW 1970–71, 191; H. D. Kay, *Memoirs of Fellows of the Royal Society*, 18 (1972),

43–81; Leonard S. Kenworthy, *Lord Orr Speaks* (Brooklyn, 1952); NYT 26 Jun 1971, 1; W. H. Waggoner, "To Free the World from Hunger," NYT *Magazine* (19 May 1946), 18; WW 1970, 342.

C. There are Boyd-Orr papers in the FOA Library, Rome and in the National Library of Scotland.

James W. Gould

BRAILSFORD, Henry Noel (25 December 1873, Mirfield, Yorkshire, England—23 March 1958, London). *Education*: B.A., Glasgow Univ., 1894. *Career*: assistant to professor, Glasgow Univ.; and lecturer, Queen Margaret Coll., 1895; leader-writer, *Manchester Guardian, Tribune, Daily News*, and *Nation*; volunteer, Greek Foreign Legion, 1897; relief agent in Macedonia, 1903; joined Independent Labor party, 1907; honorary secretary, Conciliation Committee for Women's Suffrage, 1910–12; member, Carnegie International Commission in the Balkans, 1913; editor, *New Leader*, 1922–26.

Brailsford wrote extensively about international affairs with a special interest in Russia, the Balkans, and the League of Nations. In 1897 he enlisted on the Greek side in an uprising against the Turks and was afterward an advocate of national liberation in the Balkans. He was the leader of a relief mission to Macedonia during the winter of 1903 and a member of the Carnegie International Commission in the Balkans in 1913. He favored national self-determination in Crete and Ireland as well as in the Balkans. He was critical of the foreign policy of *Edward Grey for entering an entente with the tsarist government of Russia and for alienating Germany. Influenced by *J. A. Hobson, Brailsford argued that the motive force of imperial expansion was investment of surplus capital. Armament and imperialism led, in his opinion, to international rivalries—a war of steel and gold.

He hoped that democratic control of foreign policy would lead to the abolition of war and the establishment of international harmony. He expressed this view in his best-known book, *The War of Steel and Gold: A Study of the Armed Peace* (1914). Here he traced European rivalries essentially to economic motives and especially to imperialism. He believed that maintenance of a balance of power did not touch the vital interest of any democracy in Europe. He decried the proliferation of armaments and argued that funds would be better spent on domestic reform. As a Socialist he blamed capitalism, which created the slum and built the *Dreadnought*. In deploring the absence of democratic control of policy and finance, he argued for a European concert and stated that nations should pursue peace rather than imperialistic exploitation. He was disappointed that neither the Socialist call for a general strike nor the appeal of pacifists to reason stopped the outbreak of World War I. In 1914 he joined the Union of Democratic Control and contributed a pamphlet on the origins of the war and another on Turkey. A lasting peace, he was convinced, could come from the establishment of a league of nations. He published a book on that subject in 1917 in an effort to find a peaceful means of settling international disputes.

After the war Brailsford grew pessimistic about the chances of a lasting peace based upon the Paris treaties. As guidelines to the Labor party's international policy, he suggested putting an end to the informal alliance among the victors; canceling all Allied debts to Britain, forgoing Britain's share in the Germany indemnity, offering to share the wealth of colonial mandates, and giving up the unlimited right of blockade—all based on reciprocal concessions that he doubted would be given; reducing the German indemnity to a realistic and honest amount to be paid in kind; and founding an Economic League. As a Socialist, Brailsford doubted that capitalist societies could achieve these goals in 1922. But he continued to hope that "an authoritative federal government might be created for the world" on the basis of a "World Democracy." In *Property or Peace* (1934), he looked forward to a world federation of Socialist republics.

BIBLIOGRAPHY:

A. *After the Peace* (New York, 1922); *A League of Nations* (New York, 1917); *Olives of Endless Age: Being a Study of This Distracted World and Its Need of Unity* (New York, 1928); *Property or Peace* (London, 1934); *The War of Steel and Gold: A Study of the Armed Peace* (London, 1914).

B. DNB 1951–60, 137–39; F. M. Leventhal, "H. N. Brailsford and the Search for a New International Order," in *Edwardian Radicalism 1900–1914*, ed. A.J.A. Morris (London, 1974); LT 24 Mar 1958, 14; Sylvia Straus, introduction to *War of Steel and Gold*, rpt. ed. (New York, 1972).

Marvin Swartz

BRAND, Robert Henry (30 October 1878, Kensington, London—23 August 1963, Firle, Sussex, England). *Education*: graduate, New Coll., Oxford Univ., 1901. *Career*: fellow, All Souls Coll., Oxford Univ., 1901–63, with breaks; served in South Africa, 1902–9 as secretary to Inter-Colonial Council of the Transvaal and Orange River Colony and secretary to the Railway Committee of the Central South African Railway; member, later managing director, Lazard Bros. and Co. Ltd., 1909–60; member, Imperial Munitions Board, Canada, 1915–18; deputy chairman, British War Mission, Washington, 1917–18; financial adviser to chairman, Supreme Economic Council, Paris Peace Conference, 1919; vice-president, International Financial Conference of League of Nations, Brussels, 1920; financial representative of South Africa, Genoa Conference, 1922; member, Expert Committee advising German government on stabilization, 1922; member, Macmillan Committee on Finance and Industry, 1930–31; director, Times Publishing Company, Ltd., 1925–59; head, British Food Mission, Washington, 1941–44; chairman, British Supply Council in North America, 1942, 1945–46; British Treasury representative, Washington, 1944–46; British delegate, Bretton Woods, 1944, and Savannah Conferences, 1946.

Brand was a member of that high-minded species, the banker with international interests and the desire to make the world a safer place. He had two dominant beliefs: first, a profound faith in enlightened British imperialism as a force for good; and second, a strong confidence that international finance was an influence for international cooperation and peace.

Before joining Lazard Bros., the international merchant bankers, in 1909, he had worked for the Colonial Office in South Africa, and he maintained these interests throughout his career. From 1915 to 1919 his work was primarily for the government, first as a key member of the British mission purchasing North American supplies and munitions for the Allies, and then as financial adviser to *Robert Cecil at the Versailles Peace Conference. Brand then decided to concentrate on his banking work, but he nevertheless still found time to act as an adviser or delegate to various European financial conferences in the 1920s and 1930s, himself initiating the League of Nations conference in Brussels in 1920. Much of this work revolved around the German problem in its various forms, and Brand was perhaps ahead of many of his colleagues in deciding by 1933 that Hitler and the Nazis posed a real threat. This stand must have added piquancy to his position as a director of the Times Publishing Company, since the *Times* was the leading appeasement organ of the British press.

Brand spent 1941–46 mainly in Washington. He therefore had the chastening experience of having represented Britain both during World War I, Britain's last period of political and financial dominance, and during World War II, when her economic decline relative to the United States was painfully obvious. Brand was a strong proponent of Anglo–American cooperation. Brand's knowledge of the worlds of finance and economics, of American, European, and Empire politics, and of British politics at the highest level, combined with charm and savoir faire, made him a quietly powerful man. He was one of "the great and the good" in Britain, an example of the man who, while not seen publicly to influence people and events, nevertheless is regularly consulted and used by policy makers domestic and foreign.

BIBLIOGRAPHY:

A. *The Letters of John Dove* (London, 1938); *The Union of South Africa* (London, 1909); *War and National Finance* (London, 1921); *Why I Am not a Socialist* (London, 1923); numerous articles, especially in the *Round Table*.

B. Kathleen Burk, *Britain, America and the Sinews of War 1914-1918* (London, 1983); DNB 1961–70, 130–32; John Kendle, *The Round Table Movement* (Toronto, 1975); LT 24 Aug 1963, 8.

C. The Brand papers are in the Bodleian Library, Oxford Univ.

Kathleen Burk

BRANTING, Karl Hjalmar (23 November 1860, Stockholm—24 February 1925, Stockholm). *Education*: Univ. of Uppsala, 1877–82. *Career*: on staff, *Tiden*, 1883–86; editor, *Socialdemokraten*, 1886–92, 1896–1908, 1911–17;

member of Riksdag, 1896–1925; Swedish delegate, League of Nations Assembly, 1920–24, Council, 1923–25; chairman, International Labor Organization, 1924.

As a student at Uppsala, Branting studied science, but he became increasingly concerned with conditions of the laboring class; he edited the Socialist paper *Tiden* and at age twenty-six became editor of *Socialdemokraten*, with which he remained associated most of his life. In 1889 he was the secretary of the organizational meeting of the Swedish Social Democratic party and guided its program: universal suffrage, a single-chamber Riksdag, freedom of the press, an eight-hour day, public and free schooling, social insurance, pensions, international arbitration, and the elimination of both standing army and state church. He followed Marx only part of the way. He was a pacifist who accepted the necessity of a national defense and favored a citizenry trained like the Swiss in military skills. He succeeded in holding his party to a middle course, and it grew. In 1896 he was elected to the second chamber of the Riksdag on a Stockholm Liberal list, and for six years he was the only Social Democratic member. Cooperation with the Liberals brought victory in the elections of 1917. He was prime minister three times between 1920 and 1925, setting the course for the long period of Social Democratic dominance beginning in 1932.

While domestic concerns dominated Branting's early career, he showed increasing interest in external affairs. He worked for international arbitration and insisted in 1905 that Norway be permitted to leave the Union with Sweden in peace. He presided in 1910 at the Copenhagen Congress of the International, and he belonged to its Executive Council for years. He was influenced by the Socialist movement in Germany but was antagonized by the tendencies there toward militarism. He was sympathetic to the Entente cause in World War I but deplored the Treaty of Versailles and Allied policy toward Russia. Yet the League of Nations became close to his heart, and he helped swing a dubious Sweden into membership.

As a delegate to the Assembly and member of the Council, he worked for the incorporation of the Åaland Islands into Sweden but accepted conscientiously the League Council's decision in favor of Finland. In the League his influence was felt in disputes in the Corfu, Mosul, and the German minority in Poland; he helped prevent military action in the Turkish–Iraq conflict of 1924. Branting felt a special compulsion to push the League toward disarmament talks. He began this effort at the first Assembly in 1920 and served a number of times as chairman of the committee that discussed the reduction of arms. Branting strongly expressed his disappointment when the Assembly in 1923 postponed discussions and acknowledged that talks could not begin until guarantees of security could be arranged. The subject demanded immediate attention. In accord with his pacifist perspective, Branting also opposed League discussions for collective action to guarantee peace. He especially deplored the French occupation of the Ruhr, and he took special interest in the Saar territory to be sure the League responded properly in its oversight of the region.

Branting received the Nobel Peace Prize in 1921. He characterized his own labors for peace as "sound and realistic optimism." His integrity, persistence, personal magnetism, and practical, nondoctrinaire principles won him much success; his idealism was tempered with a strong sense of realism.

BIBLIOGRAPHY:

A. *Social-demokratiens aarhundrede*, 2 vols. (Stockholm, 1911); *Tal och Skrifter i urval*, 11 vols. (Stockholm, 1926–30).

B. Zeth Hoeglund, *Hjalmar Branting*, 2 vols. (Stockholm, 1928–29); S. Shepard Jones, *The Scandinavian States and the League of Nations* (Princeton, NJ, 1939); G. Magnusson, *Hjalmar Branting i naerbild* (Stockholm, 1939); NYT 25 Feb 1925, 19; F. D. Scott, *Sweden: The Nation's History* (Minneapolis, MN, 1977); Herbert Tingsten, *Den svenska Socialdemokratiens idéuveckling*, 2 vols. (Stockholm, 1941), in English as *The Swedish Social Democrats* (Totowa, NJ, 1973); Douglas Verney, *Parliamentary Reform in Sweden, 1866–1921* (Oxford, 1957).

C. The Branting papers are in the Arbetarrörelsens Arkiv, Stockholm.

Franklin D. Scott

BRENT, Charles Henry (9 April 1862, Newcastle, ON—27 March 1929, Lausanne, Switzerland). *Education*: B.A., Trinity Coll., Univ. of Toronto, 1884; ordained deacon, 1886, and priest, 1887, Anglican church, Diocese of Toronto. *Career*: teacher, Trinity Coll. School, Port Hope, ON, 1885–87; organist and curate, St. John's Church, Buffalo, NY, 1887; curate, St. Paul's Cathedral, Buffalo, 1887–89; mission work with Society of St. John the Evangelist (Cowley Fathers), Boston, 1889–91; minister, St. Stephen's Church, Boston, 1891–1901; Episcopal bishop of Philippine Islands, 1901–17; member, Philippine Opium Committee, 1903–4; senior U.S. commissioner, Shanghai Opium Commission, 1908–9; U.S. chief delegate to and president of Hague Opium Conference, 1911–12; senior chaplain, World War I, 1918–19; Episcopal bishop of western New York, 1918–29; leader, World Conference on Faith and Order movement, 1920–29; U.S. delegate, Geneva Opium Conference, 1924–25; president, World Conference on Faith and Order, Lausanne, 1927.

Bishop Brent's internationalism evolved from his dual citizenship as a Canadian and an American, his belief in the benevolence of U.S. imperialism, and his almost intuitive commitment to Christian ecumenism. He was propelled into the arena of international affairs upon his election as the first Episcopal bishop of the Philippines. Preparatory to assuming his duties, he met in Washington with President *Theodore Roosevelt and with the newly appointed civil governor of the islands, *William Howard Taft. Brent's later close relations with these two men contributed to his perception of his role as that of both "citizen and bishop."

Like Roosevelt and Taft, Brent was an ardent defender of the American colonial empire in the Pacific. Throughout his tenure in the Orient, Brent maintained that the Filipinos were incapable of self-government, that if the United States had not accepted them unselfishly they would have been seized by another country. Independence should come to the islanders only after they had developed the habits of political democracy, strengthened by a mature, pervasive Christianity. Believing that Christian unity was necessary to the success of missionary activity, Brent sought to cooperate rather than compete with other Christian groups on the islands and confined his ministry to non-Christian Filipinos such as the Igorots and the Moros and to the resident American community.

No issue accorded better with Brent's perception of the beneficence of U.S. imperial rule in the Orient, the influence of a united Christianity, and his role as citizen-bishop than the campaign against the opium traffic. Following his service on the Philippine Opium Committee, which traveled to several Far Eastern countries and territories in 1903 to investigate the opium problem, Brent, in conjunction with other Christian missionaries in the Philippines and with *Wilbur F. Crafts and Christian and reform groups in the United States, waged a successful campaign between 1903 and 1906 to restrict legal transactions in opium in the islands to medicinal purposes. He did not, however, confine his anti-opium crusade to the Philippines. Believing that transactions in opium were "a social vice . . . a crime" that seriously harmed the Chinese and other Orientals, stigmatized the Western presence in Asia, and hampered Christian missionary endeavors, Brent convinced Roosevelt, Secretary of War Taft, and Secretary of State *Elihu Root in 1906 that the United States should launch an international campaign to help China rid itself of the drug. To assure the cooperation of the British government in such a movement, he then secured the support of the Bishop of China, the Bishop of Canterbury, and other British religious leaders as well as the endorsement in 1907 of a conference at Shanghai of Christian missionaries in the Far East.

At the Shanghai Opium Conference of 1909 and the Hague Opium Conference of 1911–12, Brent's special knowledge, his prestige as a religious leader, and his aggressive but conciliatory personal demeanor invested him with sufficient moral stature to persuade the various delegations to accept the principles that nations had an obligation to help China suppress opium trafficking and consumption by preventing or restricting the shipment of the drug to countries that prohibited or restricted its importation and by attempting to confine transactions in opium to legitimate medical and scientific purposes.

At the Geneva Opium Conference of 1924–25, Brent again took up the cause of China and the Orient. Although bitterly disappointed at the failure of the Geneva conferences to endorse the American position that limitations on opium transactions should begin with the production of raw opium and that opium for smoking should be prohibited entirely, he nevertheless opposed the U.S. government's decision to withdraw from the proceedings.

Two weeks before he died, he wrote President *Herbert Hoover urging that the United States resume leadership of the international anti-opium movement in continuation of the tradition begun at Shanghai and in accordance with America's post–World War I responsibility to be first in a concern for the world.

But Brent's vision of America's world role embraced more than a simple call to altruism. His emphatic support of the concept of a world-state as a supranational manifestation of democracy and brotherhood reflected his belief that "next to the unity of the Church, the unity of nations in some real form is essential to the Kingdom of God throughout mankind." He became involved in ecumenical movements at a missionary conference at Edinburgh in 1911 and played a key role in the Lausanne meeting of 1927, which led to further planning for a permanent body of united Christians. In 1919 he urged President *Woodrow Wilson to include some reference to God in the Covenant of the League of Nations. Although Wilson rejected his suggestion as impractical, Brent steadily maintained during the 1920s that the United States should either join the League or propose a more effective and better one. His contention in 1921 that, because of U.S. position and wealth, it had a duty greater than others to lead in achieving a stable world became a familiar refrain of internationalists in the succeeding decades.

BIBLIOGRAPHY:

A. *The Commonwealth, Its Foundations and Pillars* (New York, 1930); *The Inspiration of Responsibility and Other Papers* (New York, 1915); *Prisoners of Hope* (New York, 1915).

B. DAB 11, 115–17; NYT 28 Mar 1929, 1; Eleanor Slater, *Charles Henry Brent, Everybody's Bishop* (Milwaukee, WI, 1932); WWWA 1, 135; Alexander C. Zabriskie, *Bishop Brent: Crusader for Christian Unity* (Philadelphia, 1948).

C. The Brent papers are in the Manuscript Division, Library of Congress.

Arnold H. Taylor

BRENTANO, Heinrich von (20 January 1904, Offenbach, Germany—14 November 1964, Darmstadt, Germany). *Education*: Univ. of Frankfort/Main, Munich, Grenoble; doctor of laws, Univ. of Giessen, 1930. *Career*: attorney, Darmstadt, 1932–45; member of Hessian Constituent Assembly and Landtag, 1946–49; member, West German Parliamentary Council, 1948–49; member, West German Bundestag, 1949–64; chair, Christian Democratic Union/Christian Social Union delegation in Bundestag, 1949–55, 1961–64; vice-president, Consultative Assembly of Council of Europe, 1950–55; chair, Constitutional Committee of Ad Hoc Assembly of European Coal and Steel Community, 1952–53; foreign minister, West Germany, 1955–61.

Brentano's significance as an internationalist has been somewhat obscured by the fact that throughout his public career he functioned in the shadow of West Germany's first chancellor, *Konrad Adenauer. The son of a Catholic Center party Reichstag deputy of the Weimar era, Brentano was a consistent critic of the Nazis and was imprisoned for a time after the attempt on Hitler's life of 20 July 1944. Like many other opponents of the regime, he became convinced that the achievement of European unity would solidify Germany's place in the postwar world and do much to ensure that such a catastrophe would not recur.

A founding member of the League of German Federalists in 1947, he chaired the committee established by the European Coal and Steel Community (ECSC) in September 1952 to draft a treaty for the creation of a European Political Community. Although the resulting proposal was endorsed by the ECSC's Ad Hoc Assembly, its fate became increasingly enmeshed with that of the European Defense Community. When the latter was rejected by the French in August 1954, the European Political Community became a dead letter, and Brentano's hopes for rapid progress toward the creation of a supranational political and military structure in Western Europe suffered a severe setback.

As foreign minister under Adenauer, Brentano often evinced a deeper distrust of the Soviet Union than did the chancellor and, partly for this reason, was more open to initiatives directed toward the smaller states of Eastern Europe. In 1956, for instance, he was among the first West German leaders to state publicly that under certain conditions his government might recognize Poland's western borders. In general, however, Brentano fully endorsed Adenauer's policies. Indeed, his commitment to integrating the Federal Republic into a united Western Europe, based as it was upon a vision of the West as a bastion against the threat of Communist materialism, may have been stronger than that of the chancellor. When Brentano withdrew from the foreign office in 1961 in the context of difficult negotiations to establish a new coalition government, Adenauer lost one of his most loyal and effective supporters.

BIBLIOGRAPHY:

A. *Germany and Europe* (New York, 1964).

B. Arnulf Baring, *Sehr verehrter Herr Bundeskanzler* (Hamburg, 1974), *Biographisches Wörtenbuch zur deutschen Geschichte* (Munich, 1973), 354; CB 1955, 63–65; Kurt Gelsner, *Heinrich von Brentano* (Munich, 1957); IWW 1963–64, 131; NYT 15 Nov 1964, 86; Maria Stirtz, *Heinrich von Brentano di Tremezzo* (Darmstadt, Germany, 1970); WWG 1964, 213.

C. Brentano papers are in the Bundesarchiv, Coblence.

Kenneth R. Calkins

BRIAND, Aristede Pierre Henri (28 March 1962, Nantes, France—7 March 1932, Paris). *Education*: Licencié ès droit, Univ. of Paris, 1885. *Career*: lawyer and journalist, 1885–1902; member, Chamber of Deputies, 1902–32; member, Council of Ministers, 1906–32, with breaks; president, Council of Ministers, 1909–29, with breaks; Nobel Peace Prize, 1926 (with Gustav Stresemann).

Briand, according to Belgian statesman *Paul Hymans, personally embodied the ideal of friendship and peace. He achieved rapprochement with Germany, was largely responsible for the Locarno Treaties, sponsored the Paris Peace Pact, and formally proposed European union. His actions provoked intense controversy. He appeared to his contemporaries as either a saint or a fool. Although Briand, the statesman, seemed to be moving in the direction of international collaboration, his motives and ultimate objectives remain obscure. He left a vast legacy of speeches and public pronouncements but little evidence that reveals his intentions. His personal papers consist largely of letters written to him.

A man of apparent devotion to high principle, his principles seemed to change with the political wind. His one undying loyalty was to compromise. Briand began his political career on the extreme anarchist left, moved to revolutionary Marxism and then to revisionism, and he became the first Socialist to be expelled from his party for taking political office. A militant advocate of the general strike, he was, as premier, the first to break a strike by conscripting the strikers. The fiercest of anticlericals, he administered the law separating the church and state with such laxity that his death was publicly lamented by the Vatican. He was the preeminent rhetorician of his day, given to long extemporaneous speeches composed of colorful but innocuous platitudes. His real work was done in the corridors, where he negotiated endlessly.

Briand first took the portfolio of foreign affairs in 1916, held it intermittently until 1925, and then applied himself continuously to diplomatic matters until 1932. French security seems to have been his overriding goal. In pursuit of it, he employed great flexibility and imagination. Although not an original thinker, he did have a gift for seizing upon ideas in the air. Although never supported by a stable majority, he was able to maneuver himself into such an unassailable position that he served as foreign minister even under Raymond Poincaré, whose views were almost diametrically opposed.

In October 1921, Briand abruptly abandoned a hard line toward Germany in favor of a program of concessions accompanied by guarantees. His negotiations with Lloyd George for a Guaranty Pact failed, but in 1925 his efforts were rewarded with the Locarno Pacts, which married rapprochement to collective security. Germany recognized its western frontiers as definitive, agreed to an arbitration treaty with France, and joined the League of Nations. The whole arrangement was guaranteed by Great Britain and Italy. Briand proclaimed enthusiastically in Geneva: "Stop the rifles, the machine guns, the cannons! Replace them with conciliation, arbitration and peace!" He refused, however, to renounce France's Polish and Czech alliances. By this time, Briand had formed the habit of regularly attending all Council and Assembly meetings in Geneva. He seems to have found the atmosphere there a welcome refuge from his critics in Paris. He became a firm believer in collective security, believing that the right to be secure was as vital as bread or work. Only through the cooperation of the great powers could it be guaranteed.

Briand had sought since 1922 a means to tie the United States to the emerging European system. In 1927 he made an appeal to the American people for a mutual renunciation of war. Similar notions were in vogue. Both the League Assembly and the Pan American Conference had adopted proposals prohibiting wars of aggression, and Briand had been in touch with *James T. Shotwell and other American internationalists. Briand's appeal was followed by negotiations that led to the Pact of Paris, a multilateral rather than a bilateral renunciation of war.

Now a kind of living monument to peace, Briand next turned to European union. It is not clear what inspired him or what he hoped to achieve, but once again he moved to implement an idea in the air. In 1929 he suggested a federal link among European peoples that would function mostly in the economic field and be compatible with both the League and national sovereignty. The following year he made a formal proposal before the Assembly. There could be, he announced, no economic improvement without political security. Therefore, he called for a European conference with a permanent political committee and a system of arbitration that covered all Europe. Other European governments interpreted the proposal as an attempt to promote French interests, and the project, crowded off the international stage by the Depression, died an obscure death.

Briand's internationalism is easy to deride; nothing he achieved was durable, and his aim seems no more than old-fashioned security fired by a personal ambition he made little effort to hide. Yet no one worked harder or more imaginatively to give the new international system life. His internationalism sprang from the realization that France could not be secure until everyone else was. He may have embraced principle for reasons of *Realpolitik*, but there is little doubt that he became convinced of the justice of his cause.

BIBLIOGRAPHY:

A. *Dans la voie de la paix* (Paris, 1929); *Paroles de paix* (Paris, 1927).

B. *Dictionnaire de biographie française* (Paris, 1956), 7 270–74; *Foreign Policy of France 1914–45* (Boston, 1975); Salvador de Madariaga, *Morning Without Noon: Memoirs* (Westmead, England, 1974); NYT 8 Mar 1932, 1; B. G. Suarez, *Briand, sa vie, son oeuvre*, 6 vols. (Paris, 1939–41).

Douglas W. Houston

BRIDGMAN, Raymond Landon (26 September 1848, South Amherst, MA—20 February 1925, Auburndale, MA). *Education*: B.A., Amherst Coll., 1871; graduate study, Yale Univ., 1874–76. *Career*: reporter, *Boston Daily Advertiser*, 1876–84; owner and editor of several Connecticut and Massachusetts newspapers, 1884–1925.

Bridgman established a reputation as a reporter and authority on Massachusetts politics, producing three books on that topic between 1884 and 1896. At the turn of the century, however, his concerns extended outward. He joined the American Anti-Imperialist League and in two books, *The Master Idea* (1899) and *Loyal Traitors* (1903), criticized American expansion. At the same time, his interest in the idea of world organization appeared in articles in the *Atlantic Monthly* (1903–4), *Arena* (1904), and *New England Magazine* (1904). He combined these with other essays in *World Organization* (1905) and followed with *The First Book of World Law* (1911). In these works, Bridgman revealed a belief held by many of his contemporaries interested in international organization. He sought to document an evolutionary trend bringing nations and people together as revealed by international treaties, meetings, and the creation of societies. Contacts began in nonpolitical areas associated with health, communications, and trade and led inevitably to political gatherings best illustrated by the Hague Peace Conferences of 1899 and 1907 and by an extensive network of arbitration treaties. Indeed, Bridgman saw such periodic assemblies as the basis for a "permanent world legislature," and he envisaged the Permanent Court of Arbitration created at the Hague Conference of 1899 as the beginning of a "world judiciary."

While Bridgman used such examples to support his assertion that an international organization was inevitable, he believed that in form it would eventually be a world government. He argued for a constitution that would contain a "world bill of rights," for a legislature that would actually create laws, for a court that would have clear jurisdiction over national governments, and for a "world executive" in the form of a functioning secretariat to oversee the vast number of boards, bureaus, and commissions that would inevitably evolve.

The doctrine of sovereignty, Bridgman believed, had to give way to the common universal principle of world community. His essays and books sought to convey that message, but Bridgman also worked directly. In 1903 he helped draft a petition in the form of a resolution to the Massachusetts legislature that asked Congress to promote the idea of a "world legislature." It attracted the support of peace groups and public citizens, and in the spring of 1903 both houses unanimously approved a measure asking Congress to authorize a call for periodic international assemblies to discuss common questions and present recommendations to governments. Again, in 1915, Bridgman influenced the Massachusetts Assembly to adopt a resolution favoring a world-state unhindered by national sovereignty.

By the time Bridgman retired from active campaigns during World War I, he had made his mark as a leading propagandist for an international organization in an age when such activity was as yet unusual. While not an original thinker, he revealed a journalist's ability to assimilate ideas and present them in a logical and appealing way. Thus as both writer and activist he stood in the center of a movement and helped direct its flow.

BIBLIOGRAPHY:

A. *The First Book of World Law* (Boston, 1911); *The Passing of the Tariff* (Boston, 1909); *World Organization* (Boston, 1905).

B. Warren F. Kuehl, introduction to *First Book of World Law*, rpt. ed. (New York, 1972), *Seeking World Order: The United States and International Organization to 1920* (Nashville, TN, 1969); WWWA 1, 138.

Warren F. Kuehl

BRIERLY, James Leslie (9 September 1881, Huddersfield, England—20 December 1955, Oxford). *Education*: degrees in classical studies and jurisprudence, 1902–5, Brasenose Coll., Oxford Univ.; called to bar, 1906; *Career*: prize fellow, All Souls Coll., Oxford Univ., 1906; fellow, Trinity Coll., Oxford Univ., 1913; war service, 1914–18; professor, Manchester Univ., 1920–22; Chichele professor of public international law, Oxford Univ., 1922–47; Montague Burton professor of international relations, Edinburgh Univ., 1948–51; editor, *British Year Book of International Law*, 1929–36; member, International Law Commission, 1949–51.

During his lifetime and in the quarter of a century since his death, Brierly has made a considerable impression on the thinking of internationalists through his writings, which are characterized by clarity of expression and precision of thought. His scholarly output was informed by a good deal of experience in public life, and this included acting as adviser to the emperor of Ethiopia during the crisis of 1936. Brierly's interest in international law was not that of a narrow technician; he saw the law as a practical medium for the advancement of peace and the settlement of disputes. Thus, he served as a member of the League of Nations Committee on the Progressive Codification of International Law (1924–27), and he chaired its International Law Committee.

Brierly produced no large treatise, but his publications, including many articles, had wide influence. In particular, *The Law of Nations* (1928), a classical exposition of the law of peace, was translated into four languages. This study, like all of Brierly's writings, attracted many readers outside the ranks of lawyers and was much cited by specialists.

The intellectual style adopted by Brierly did not involve the making of claims to be an innovator, and his general approach to the use of sources of the law was orthodox enough. However, he was not a positivist in the simple sense; for him, the law could play a dynamic role in international relations. Brierly was well aware of the negative effects of the more rigid precepts of positivism and regretted the changes that had undermined the foundations of the law in natural law, which for him was "the most fruitful seed of development."

Outstanding among his particular contributions is the study of "The Basis of Obligation in International Law," which is one of the most useful essays in placing international law in relation to intellectual debate about the nature of law. In many respects, Brierly provides an excellent example of a type of internationalist of the period of the League of Nations, combining liberal values and a strong practical sense.

BIBLIOGRAPHY:

A. *The Basis of Obligation in International Law and Other Papers*, ed. H. Lauterpacht and C.H.M. Waldock (Oxford, 1958); *The Covenant and the Charter* (Cambridge, 1947); *The Law of Nations* (Oxford, 1928; 6th ed., 1963); lectures at Hague Academy, 1928 and 1936, in *Recueil des cours* 23 and 58; *The Outlook for International Law* (Oxford, 1944).

B. *Annuaire de l'Institut de droit international* (1956), 460–65; *British Year Book of International Law* 32 (1955-56) (London, 1958), 1–19; DNB 1951-60, 142–43; LT 22 Dec 1955, 10.

Ian Brownlie

BROWN, Arthur Judson (3 December 1856, Holliston, MA—11 January 1963, New York). *Education*: B.A., Wabash Coll., 1880, M.A., 1884; graduate, Lane Theol. Sem., 1883. *Career*: pastor, Ripon, WI, 1883–84, Oak Park, IL, 1884–88, Portland, OR, 1888–95; secretary, Presbyterian Board of Foreign Missions, 1895-1929.

Even when one hundred years old, Brown wrote succinct and sharply analytical letters on international issues to the editor of the *New York Times*. As an administrator in the Board of Foreign Missions for over thirty years he had traveled widely abroad, especially in Asia. Throughout his life he thought, wrote, and lectured on international questions, with special concentration on Asia and particularly Korea.

A charter trustee of the Church Peace Union (later the Council on Religion and International Affairs), founded and endowed in 1914 by ⁺Andrew Carnegie, Brown gave large amounts of time and energy to the pioneer work of that body. He served on the key committees and asserted leadership in all its activities during the critical early years of the Union when it was charting a new path in education for world peace, a subject the churches had hardly touched before 1914. He was a member of the National Committee on the Churches and the Moral Aims of the War during World War I; worked assiduously with the organization of and participation in the "Win the War—Win the Peace" institutes and conferences during World War II; and took an active part in the development of the interfaith Pattern for Peace, the immensely influential document issued by the Union in 1943.

Perhaps his most outstanding service came while chairman of the American Committee on Religious Rights and Minorities, organized in April 1920 by the Church Peace Union. This distinguished body, dealing with a number of complex and delicate problems left by the terms of the peace treaty, had Roman Catholic, Jewish, and Protestant members. The committee studied and reported on the effectiveness of treaty provisions on minorities in general and religious minorities in particular. Its members traveled widely and brought firsthand information to America about Jews in Poland, the Ukraine, Lithuania, Galicia, and Hungary; and it reported on minority problems in Transylvania, Czechoslovakia, Serbia, Alsace-Lorraine, and Belgium. It found considerable persecution against Jews, Roman Catholics, and Protestants. Major attention focused on the situation in Transylvania, which had been severed from Hungary and ceded to Romania. It became the subject of constant study and action from 1920 to the start of World War II in 1939. Through visits and innumerable protests, the committee fought for the rights of religion and minorities. Part of the record of this vigorous endeavor is contained in two volumes of detailed reports: *The Religious Minorities in Transylvania* (1925), and *Roumania Ten Years After* (1928).

Brown's committee also watched closely the situation in Germany in the early 1930s. It disclosed anti-Semitism there and found evidence that the Evangelical church and other religious bodies were becoming minority problems. In 1934 the committee issued "A Statement Regarding Germany's Treatment of the Jews." Again in 1935 the committee attacked the German persecution of the Jews. Brown served as chairman for seventeen years; then resigned at age eighty. As a charter trustee he had been constantly active in all the work of the Church Peace Union, and he continued his involvement there for twenty-six more years. He was named treasurer in 1936 and faithfully performed his duties until his death.

BIBLIOGRAPHY:

A. *The Chinese Revolution* (New York, 1912); *The Foreign Missionary: An Incarnation of a World Movement* (New York, 1907); *Japan in the World of Today* (New York, 1928); *The Mastery of the Far East* (New York, 1919); *Memoirs of a Centenarian* (New York, 1957); *The New Era in the Philippines* (New York, 1903); *New Forces in Old China* (New York, 1904); *Report on Second Visit to China, Japan and Korea* (New York, 1909); *Russia in Transformation* (New York, 1917); *Unity and Missions: Can a Divided Church Save the World?* (New York, 1915); *The Why and How of Foreign Missions* (New York, 1909).

B. Charles S. Macfarland, *Pioneers for Peace Through Religion* (New York, 1946).

A. William Loos

BRUCE, Stanley Melbourne (15 April 1883, Melbourne—25 August 1967, London). *Education*: graduate, Cambridge Univ., 1908. *Career*: chairman, London board of Paterson, Laing, and Bruce, 1906–14; entered House of Representatives as Nationalist party member for Flinders in Victoria, 1918; leader, Australian delegation to League of Nations Assembly, 1921; treasurer, 1921–23; privy councillor, 1923; prime minister and minister for external affairs, 1923–29; reentered Parliament, 1931; resident minister, London, 1932–33; Australian high commissioner, London, 1933–45; representative, imperial conferences, 1923, 1926, 1937, Ottawa conference, 1932, World Economic Conference, 1933, League of Nations Assembly, 1933–38, Council, 1933–36, president, 1936, British War Cabinet, 1942–45, Pacific War Council, 1942–45; chairman, World Food Council of United Nations

Food and Agriculture Organization, 1947–51; chairman, (British) Finance Corporation for Industry, 1947–57; first chancellor, Australian National Univ., 1951.

Bruce was the first prime minister of Australia to lose his seat while in office, the nation's first viscount, and its first representative at the League of Nations. As one who had fought in the trenches during World War I, he impressed the Assembly with speeches urging disarmament so as to make economic sanctions more effective against aggressors or violators of the Covenant. Like many of his contemporaries, however, his 1920s optimism gave way to 1930s pessimism. Eleven years later he opposed a resolution censuring Japan over her attack on Manchuria on the grounds that it would inhibit the League's task of reconciliation. He later advised Britain that, if it supported sanctions against Italy over its invasion of Ethiopia in 1935, Britain would be bound by principle to support them against Germany for its many violations. He urged Britain, in turn, to urge the League to declare that the nonadherence of the United States and the defection of Japan rendered the League impotent and to announce that it was going to rearm, a move designed to shock a complacent world into a realization that the League had failed. Highly respected in diplomatic circles, he was unanimously accepted as president of the Montreux Conference of 1936, which revised the Treaty of Lausanne to enable Turkey to remilitarize the Straits of Constantinople. In 1936 he was president of a commission to propose changes to the Covenant, but its work was overtaken by events leading to World War II.

In the immediate prewar years, Bruce strongly supported appeasement. He even claimed that the Czechs had not treated the Sudeten Germans fairly and that the Poles had shown little reasonableness in their negotiations with Hitler. After the outbreak of war, he persistently pressed a British government almost solely concerned with winning to declare its war aims and peace terms and to think about the postwar reconstruction of Europe. He also opposed the dismemberment of Germany and continually emphasized the need for progressive universal disarmament coupled with the creation of a small international air force to maintain international law. This would "put teeth" into the ideal the League had striven in vain to achieve. He stressed the need to persuade the United States to commit itself to supporting a future world authority to maintain peace.

Another of Bruce's contributions to world peace and prosperity was his attempt to establish and implement an international policy on food production. From the early 1930s, he strongly opposed the then orthodox policy of restricting food production in the face of surpluses, falling prices, and widespread unemployment. He urged nations to collaborate to produce and distribute sufficient food to abolish hunger, claiming that in so doing they would revive trade and reduce unemployment. In 1934 he supported a League committee report which held that the means taken by most industrial countries to protect their agriculture were harmful both to world trade and to the countries themselves. During the war years, he frequently drew the British government's attention to the need for postwar emergency and permanent food supplies. In 1946 he became independent chairman of a preparatory commission set up by the United Nations Food and Agriculture Organization to create the World Food Council, on which he served as chairman (1947–51). The FAO report of 1946 stressed the need for increased agriculture production, especially in backward countries, so as to increase purchasing power and consumption. Frustrated by national selfishness, Bruce eventually despaired of achieving anything worthwhile and resigned in 1951. In later years he frequently warned that the world's population was increasing faster than its food production, and he drew attention to the interdependence of agriculture and health.

BIBLIOGRAPHY:

B. *The Australian Encyclopaedia* 1 (Sidney, Australia, 1977), 408; Cecil Edwards, *Bruce of Melbourne: Man of Two Worlds* (London, 1965); Alfred Stirling, *Lord Bruce: The London Years* (Melbourne, 1974).

Malcolm Saunders

BRYAN, William Jennings. See *Biographical Dictionary of Modern Peace Leaders.*

BRYCE, James (10 May 1838, Belfast—22 January 1922, Sidmouth, London). *Education*: attended Glasgow Univ.; B.A., Trinity Coll., Oxford Univ., 1862, D.C.L., 1870; fellow, Oriel Coll., Oxford Univ., 1862. *Career*: practiced law until 1882; professor, Oxford Univ., 1870–93; Liberal member of Parliament, 1880–1907; under secretary of state for foreign affairs, 1886; chancellor, Duchy of Lancaster, 1892; president, Board of Trade, 1894–95; chief secretary for Ireland, 1905–7; ambassador to United States, 1907–13.

When Bryce became ambassador to the United States at the age of sixty-nine he already was one of the most distinguished figures in British public life. He enjoyed a worldwide reputation as a classicist, historian, jurist, and man of letters. He was a renowned naturalist, traveler, and mountain climber. As a Liberal of Radical persuasion, he had made the protection of the Armenians, opposition to the Boer War, and Irish home rule central issues during his career in the House of Commons.

Bryce's appointment as ambassador was popular on both sides of the Atlantic. The magnum opus of his literary career had been *The American Commonwealth* (1888), a favorable study of American institutions and society based upon his extensive travel and inquiry in the United States, which gave Bryce a special place in the affections of Americans. Bryce's appointment, nonetheless, was extraordinary because he was not a professional diplomat, yet in Washington Bryce succeeded in eliminating virtually all controversies marring Anglo–American relations. Many of these concerned U.S.–Canada relations. Bryce's knowledge, his friendships with leaders in both countries, and his diplomatic skills helped put Canadian concerns to rest. On 4 April 1908, Bryce and Secretary of State *Elihu Root signed a convention for the arbitration of all Anglo–American disputes not settled by diplomacy, except those concerning national honor or vital interests or involving third parties. Subsequently, they produced a boundary waters convention resolving Great Lakes disputes and establishing an International Joint Commission for future difficulties and a treaty whereby disagreements concerning fishing rights off Newfoundland would be referred to the Permanent Court of Arbitration.

The reconciliation process continued during Taft's presidency. The U.S.–Canadian boundary in Passamaquoddy Bay between Maine and New Brunswick was fixed, and accords were reached for arbitrating U.S.–Canadian pecuniary claims, clarifying navigation rights, resolving claims from ship wrecks, and regulating pelagic sealing in the Bering Sea. In addition, a convention dealt with fishing issues. Bryce experienced only three setbacks. A trade reciprocity agreement was rejected by the Canadians in September 1911; an arbitration treaty omitting the reservations present in the 1908 treaty was amended by the U.S. Senate in March 1912 and discarded by Taft; and the United States passed the Panama Tolls Act in August, 1912, exempting American coastwise shipping, an apparent violation of the 1901 Hay-Pauncefote Treaty. As Bryce's stay in Washington was ending, the newly inaugurated U.S. president, *Woodrow Wilson, pledged to seek repeal of the tolls exemption and did so.

Within the year Europe was at war. Bryce tried to keep Great Britain aloof, but Germany's violation of Belgium's neutrality settled the issue for him. He spoke of the rights of small nations, denounced German militarism, and defended Britain's war effort. Bryce corresponded extensively with Americans and other neutrals, writing often at the suggestion of the Foreign Office to create sympathy for specific British policies, and his widely circulated report on German atrocities did much to win support in the United States for the Allies. In the autumn of 1915 and again in 1916, Bryce also condemned Turkish atrocities against the Armenians.

In considering the future, Bryce took a middle ground, rejecting both a negotiated peace and an economic struggle after the war. He wanted German militarism smashed and a peace marked by national self-determination and the extension of international law. He desired a league of nations to settle all disputes and to limit or reduce arms. While eschewing public discussion of peace terms, Bryce in October 1914 prepared a memorandum for private examination by a few Liberals, who became known as the Bryce Group. Their collective review of Bryce's text evolved into the Proposals for the Avoidance of War. It proposed a league of nations in which all disputes would be referred to arbitration or to conciliation by an independent council. There would be a moratorium on war, forceful sanctions, and provisions for curbing arms and developing international law. The Proposals, circulated privately, influenced British, American, and European thought, and its definition of a "justiciable," or legal, dispute appeared slightly revised in Article XIII of the League of Nations Covenant and then in the Statutes of the Permanent Court of International Justice and of its successor, the International Court of Justice.

A revision of this influential document, published in April 1917 as *Proposals for the Prevention of Future Wars* after U.S. entry into the war, facilitated discussion of a league of nations in Great Britain. Then, in May, Bryce presided over the League of Nations Society's first major public meeting at which the South African general *Jan Christiaan Smuts, a member of the British War Cabinet, and the Archbishop of Canterbury, among others, called for a peace league. Subsequently, Bryce, acting on Smuts's suggestions, urged the appointment of an official Allied, or at least Anglo–American, committee to frame a practical plan. On 8 August 1917, he submitted a petition signed by sixteen prominent clerics and other public figures making this request of the British government. When Wilson refused to cooperate, an official British committee was established under *Lord Phillimore. Bryce was asked to join this committee, but he was chairing a parliamentary commission studying reform of the House of Lords and had to decline. Throughout 1918 Bryce remained one of the major spokesmen for a league of nations. He addressed the issue in the House of Lords on 26 June, inaugurated a new League of Nations Association on 13 September, and in October published his ideas on international organization.

Bryce was concerned about the peace settlement and how it would handle Eastern Europe, the Balkans, Turkey, and the Middle East. He hoped that Turkey would be excluded from Europe and that the United States would accept a League of Nations mandate over Armenia. The peace conference greatly disappointed Bryce. The Covenant was flawed and the peace treaties were illiberal. He particularly deplored American aloofness. After eight years' absence, Bryce returned to the United States in the summer of 1921 to lecture at Williams College. In one of his last public appearances, he praised American idealism, approved of the scheduled Washington Disarmament Conference, appealed for some type of lasting joint action by people concerned with peace, and expressed the hope that the League of Nations, with needed amendments, would ultimately succeed.

BIBLIOGRAPHY:

A. *Essays and Addresses in War Time* (London, 1918); *International Relations, Eight Lectures Delivered in the United States in August 1921* (New York, 1922); *Neutral Nations and the War* (New York, 1914); with others, *Proposals for the Prevention of Future Wars* (London, 1917).

B. DNB 1922–30, 127–35; Martin D. Dubin, "Toward the Concept of Collective Security: The Bryce Group's 'Proposals for the Avoidance of War,' 1914–1917," *In-*

ternational Organization 24 (Spring 1970), 288–318; H.A.L. Fisher, *James Bryce (Viscount Bryce of Dechmont, O.M.)*, 2 vols. (New York, 1927); E. Ions, *James Bryce and American Democracy, 1870–1922* (New York, 1970); LT 23 Jan 1922, 10; K. G. Robbins, "Lord Bryce and the First World War," *Historical Journal* 10, no. 2, 1967, 255–77; J. A. Salter, "Bryce: A Great Victorian," in *Personality in Politics: Studies of Contemporary Statesmen* (London, 1947), 109–12.

C. The Bryce papers are in the Bodleian Library, Oxford Univ.

Martin David Dubin

BUELL, Raymond Leslie (13 July 1896, Chicago—20 February 1946, Montreal). *Education*: B.A., Occidental Coll., 1918; Univ. of Grenoble, 1919; M.A., Princeton Univ., 1920, Ph.D., 1923. *Career*: author, lecturer, publicist, 1920–46; assistant professor, Occidental Coll., 1920–21; instructor to assistant professor, Harvard Univ., 1922–27; research director, Foreign Policy Association, 1927–33, president, 1933–38; staff member, *Fortune*, head, Fortune Round Table, 1939–40, 1941–42; chief research director, Wendell Willkie campaign, 1940; Foreign policy adviser, *Time*, Inc., 1942–46.

In becoming research director of the Foreign Policy Association (FPA) in 1927, Buell formalized his connection with a community of American advocates of international cooperation and a liberal world order. To achieve their objective, they embarked on a campaign to educate the American people in foreign affairs through public discussion, scholarly studies, and analyses of world events.

A prolific scholar, Buell's most influential book, *The Native Problem in Africa* (1928), was written before he joined the FPA. A study of the conditions of Africans under self-government, the mandate system, and colonial rule, it evoked protests even while in manuscript from Belgium, France, and Portugal. Characterizing Firestone Company rubber concessions and loan agreements with Liberia as economic imperialism and as contributing to a forced labor system, the book proved to be disconcerting to the State Department. In 1930, following allegations by Buell and disclosures from other sources regarding labor conditions, the United States, Great Britain, and the League of Nations sent a commission of inquiry to Liberia. Liberia ultimately rejected a resultant League plan to place the country under the League's supervision until the abuses confirmed by the commission had been rectified. Buell initially approved the plan, because it was consistent with his belief that international administration of territories incapable of self-government was preferable to unilateral rule by a single country. Adherence to this principle also contributed to his denunciation in the 1930s of South Africa's racial policies and Italy's conquest of Ethiopia and to his general distaste for European colonialism in Africa.

Buell and his associates in the FPA were especially critical of U.S. imperialism. During the 1920s and 1930s they demanded that the United States grant independence to the Philippines, recognize Mexico's full rights over its oil and other natural resources, and withdraw Marines from Nicaragua and Haiti. In 1935, after a six-month investigation of conditions in Cuba at the request of the Cuban government, a study commission headed by Buell recommended a program of social and economic reform, cessation of U.S. intervention in the island's political affairs, and abrogation of the naval leasehold at Guantanamo Bay.

Deeply disturbed by the rising tide of totalitarianism and aggression in Europe and by Japan's growing assertiveness in Asia in the early 1930s, Buell and other liberal-minded internationalists intensified their demand for greater U.S. cooperation with the League of Nations, U.S. membership in the World Court, and more vigorous action by the United States in concept with other powers to deter aggression. In 1932 Buell urged the United States and the League to impose economic sanctions against Japan. Any international organization that could provide its members with security should be ready to uphold international law with force, he argued. In 1935 Buell recommended a similar course of action against Italy.

By 1936, Buell was firmly opposed to the recently enacted U.S. neutrality legislation, which seemed to inhibit cooperative action with Great Britain and France against aggressors. Nevertheless, he recognized that Japan, Germany, and Italy had legitimate grievances stemming from economic nationalism and the maldistribution among and within nations of the world's material resources. The ultimate solution to the Italian and German problems could be resolved, he declared in 1935, by reallocating raw materials and reviving world trade. Consequently, he supported Secretary of State *Cordell Hull's program of reciprocal trade agreements as conducive to world economic recovery, free trade, and equality of economic opportunity. As late as the eve of Munich, Buell still hoped that appropriate adjustments in world trade patterns coupled with arms reductions and the internationalization of colonial areas could deter Germany.

Munich, however, transformed Buell into an adamant foe of Hitler's designs. In April 1939, in testimony before a Senate committee considering revision of America's neutrality legislation, he advocated a policy of cash-and-carry as a means of helping England and France resist the Axis countries. A year later he suggested that as a last resort the United States consider intervention in the war in Europe on the side of the Allies in order to command a voice in shaping the postwar world.

When the United States finally became a belligerent in December 1941, Buell had already given some attention to impending postwar issues as a staff member of *Fortune* magazine and as a researcher on Wendell Willkie's personal staff. Buell's unsuccessful campaign to become the Republican nominee for membership in Congress from the First Congressional District of Massachusetts in 1942 was waged on a platform of replacing isolationists with internationalists to enable Congress to increase the war effort and begin plans for peace.

Buell, however, was considerably disillusioned by the ensuing peace.

In July 1945 he joined with forty-three other prominent Americans, including *Herbert Hoover, Thomas Dewey, and Alfred Landon, in urging *Harry Truman to use American diplomatic and economic power at the Potsdam Conference to ensure that the Yalta pledge of free and open elections in Poland would be carried out. A few weeks after his death, the *American Mercury* published his article bemoaning the betrayal of Poland, a country that he had long maintained was the key to European peace and stability. He recommended U.S.–British action to stem Soviet imperialism by guaranteeing the Soviet Union against attack, promoting a federalized Europe, or, as a last resort, forming a Western bloc of democratic nations that would force Soviet imperialism to recede peacefully.

BIBLIOGRAPHY:

A. *The Hull Trade Program and the American System* (New York, 1938); *International Co-operation* (New York, 1933); *International Relations* (New York, 1925); *Isolated America* (New York, 1940); *Liberia: A Century of Survival, 1847–1947* (Philadelphia, 1947); *The Native Problem in Africa*, 2 vols. (New York, 1928); *Poland: Key to Europe* (New York, 1939); *The Washington Conference* (New York, 1922).

B. NYT 21 Feb 1946, 21; WWWA 2, 89.

Arnold H. Taylor

BUISSON, Ferdinand. See *Biographical Dictionary of Modern Peace Leaders.*

BUNCHE, Ralph Johnson (7 August 1904, Detroit, MI—9 December 1971, New York). *Education*: B.A., UCLA, 1927; M.A., Harvard Univ., 1928, Ph.D., 1934; Northwestern Univ., Univ. of Chicago, London School of Economics, Univ. of Capetown, 1936–37. *Career*: organized Department of Political Science, Howard Univ., 1929; assistant and associate professor, Howard Univ., 1929–38; researcher with Gunnar Myrdal, 1939–41, culminating in book, *An American Dilemma*; Office of the Coordinator of Information (later Office of Strategic Services), 1941–44; head, Division of Dependent Area Affairs, State Department, 1944–47; adviser to U.S. delegation, San Francisco Conference; director, Trusteeship Division, UN, 1947–55; UN undersecretary-general for special political affairs, 1955–71, in charge of UN peacekeeping operations; Nobel Peace Prize, 1950.

Bunche, a Phi Beta Kappa and star athlete at UCLA, became the first black American Ph.D. in political science, the first black to win the Nobel Peace Prize, and the highest-ranking and most influential American in the UN Secretariat. A modest, soft-spoken man, his achievements resulted from his uncommon determination, integrity, hard work, dedication, and brilliant mind. His most notable accomplishments were in improving race relations, negotiating the Arab–Israeli armistice agreements, and organizing and directing UN peacekeeping operations.

Bunche's positions in the U.S. government and the UN from 1941 to his death precluded his taking any official leadership role in black rights organizations. Nevertheless, his contribution was important. Race relations were his major interest in the 1930s, both as a scholar and as an activist. It led him to become an expert on Africa, which in turn resulted in his appointments at the State Department and the UN. His book, *World View and Race* (1936), was a significant scholarly contribution. His work on *An American Dilemma* with Gunnar Myrdal led to the most widely acclaimed and influential landmark survey of race relations in the United States. He joined the Freedom Marchers in the South during the civil rights struggles of the 1960s. His achievements, his stature, and his total unwillingness to compromise on principle were an inspiration to blacks everywhere.

Bunche's mediation of armistice agreements among Israel, Egypt, Jordan, and Syria in 1948–49 was a masterpiece of diplomacy, made possible by his negotiating skill, iron will, and the respect on all sides for his integrity and impartiality. For this work he was awarded the Nobel Peace Prize in 1950. Peacekeeping, in which Bunche played a key role from 1956 to his death in 1971, is one of the UN's notable unforeseen achievements. Its Charter, in Chapter VII, foresaw the use of major wartime Allied forces as the instrument to deter or defeat any aggression or breach of the peace. The Cold War made such collective coercion or collective security unfeasible. Instead, the UN organized peacekeeping forces that are voluntarily accepted by parties to a conflict as a means of deterring or stopping wars and providing time for a resolution of differences. These forces, lightly armed, are not designed for combat. Instead, their presence as a buffer and observer force gives each party assurance that the other is not violating a truce or armistice. Such units have been used constructively in the Middle East, the Congo, Cyprus, and elsewhere. With Secretaries-General *Dag Hammarskjöld and *U Thant, Bunche was the principal official responsible for designing, organizing, and carrying out such operations. Both Hammarskjöld and U Thant had the utmost confidence in Bunche's ability, integrity, and discretion in handling these delicate operations and in other important political assignments. He was not only the ideal international civil servant; he was also a statesman whose contributions to peace and the effectiveness of the UN were equaled by very few.

BIBLIOGRAPHY:

A. With Gunnar Myrdal, the titular author, *An American Dilemma* (New York, 1941); *The Political Status of the Negro in the Age of FDR* (Chicago, 1972); "The United Nations Is the Only Bridge: How Peace Came to Palestine," *Common Sense* (Aug 1949); "We Can Have Peace in Our Time," *Look* 15 (2 Jan 1951), 44; *A World View of Race* (Washington, 1936).

B. Seymour M. Finger, *Your Man at the UN* (New York, 1980); Jim Haskins, *Ralph Bunche: A Most Reluctant Hero* (New York, 1974); Peggy Mann, *Ralph Bunche, UN Peacemaker* (New York, 1975); Brian Urquhart, *Hammarskjöld* (New York, 1972).

C. The Bunche papers are in the Department of Special Collections, Univ. of California, Los Angeles.

Seymour Maxwell Finger

BURCKHARDT, Carl Jacob (10 September 1891, Basel—4 March 1974, Geneva). *Education*: Univs. of Basel, Zurich, Munich, Göttingen, and Paris; Ph.D., Univ. of Zurich, 1922. *Career*: attaché to Swiss legation, Vienna, 1918–21; professor, Univ. of Zurich, 1928–32; Graduate Institute of International Studies, Geneva, 1932–45; member, International Committee of the Red Cross (ICRC), 1933–45; League of Nations high commissioner, Free City of Danzig, 1937–39; president, ICRC, 1944–48; minister plenipotentiary to France, 1945–49; historian, writer, and essayist.

Burckhardt was a son of the old, illustrious Basel family of the Burckhardts. At the end of World War I, as a junior member of the Swiss legation in Vienna, he witnessed the misery and the sadness that accompanied the transformation of the Habsburg monarchy into the Austrian republic and a number of successor states. In 1923 he went to Asia Minor in the service of the International Committee of the Red Cross to organize the repatriation of Greek colonists in the wake of the Greco–Turkish War. The mission for which Burkhardt is best known, that of high commissioner of the League of Nations for the Free City of Danzig during the late 1930s, was characterized by him as having been the most difficult and unrewarding task of his life. Even though he was unable to keep Adolf Hitler from unleashing the attack on Poland, he did his utmost to uphold and protect the rights of all inhabitants of Danzig, including Jews, as long as he was high commissioner, a fact recognized by all powers concerned.

Before and during World War II, Burckhardt carried out a number of tasks for the ICRC that contributed in various ways toward the alleviation of the immense suffering caused by the war. Whether it was a visit to a German concentration camp, or intervention with Joachim von Ribbentrop on behalf of British prisoners of war, or the routine but mounting chores of the general secretary of the ICRC in Geneva, Burckhardt pursued his objectives with determination, skill, and an unshakable commitment to the humanitarian principles of the Geneva conventions. The Swiss government used his talents and honored him by choosing him to be the country's first minister to the Fourth Republic of postwar France.

Throughout his career Burckhardt wrote. Excerpts from his reports to the ICRC and to League of Nations headquarters about his missions to Asia Minor and Danzig were published as books. His historical research concentrated on France and Europe in the seventeenth century and resulted in a multivolume biography of Cardinal Richelieu. Encounters with writers, poets, musicians, statesmen, officers, and other contemporaries form the subject matter of numerous essays. They are characterized by elegance of style and precision of observation and represent the intellectual and cultural cosmopolitanism of Europe at its best.

BIBLIOGRAPHY:

A. *Gesammelte Werke*, 6 vols. (Bern, 1971), with bibliography, vol. 6, 377–92; *Gestalten und Mächte* (Munich, 1941); *Meine Danziger Mission 1937–39* (Zurich, 1960); *Richelieu*, 4 vols. (Munich, 1961–67).

B. Herbert S. Levine, "The Mediator: Carl J. Burckhardt's Efforts to Avert a Second World War," *Journal of Modern History* 45 (Sep 1973), 439–55; NYT 5 Mar 1974, 36; Hermann Rinn, ed., *Dauer im Wandel: Festschrift zum 70. Geburtstag von Carl J. Burckhardt* (Munich, 1961); Werner Schmid, *Carl J. Burckhardt* (Berlin, 1960); *Schweizerköpfe der Gegenwart* 1 (Zurich, 1945), 14–20.

C. The Burckhardt papers are in the Basle Univ. Library.

Heinz K. Meier

BURRITT, Elihu. See *Biographical Dictionary of Modern Peace Leaders*.

BURTON, Theodore Elijah. See *Biographical Dictionary of Modern Peace Leaders*.

BUSTAMANTE, Antonio Sanchez de (13 April 1865, Havana—24 August 1951, Havana). *Education*: Colegio Belén, Havana; Univ. of Madrid; Univ. of Havana. *Career*: lawyer, Havana, 1884–1951; professor, Univ. of Havana, 1884–1951; member, Cuban Senate, 1902–18; delegate, Second Hague Peace Conference, 1907, Paris Peace Conference, 1919, League of Nations Assembly, president, 1928, many Pan American Congresses, Rio Meeting of Jurists, 1927; member, Permanent Court of Arbitration, 1908–26; judge, Permanent Court of International Justice, 1921–39; dean, Univ. of Havana Law School.

Like many of his generation, Bustamante put his hope for the future in the extension of law in the international sphere. Toward that end, in the early years of the twentieth century, there was a triple thrust; arbitration, codification, adjudication. Bustamante was active in all these areas, and in one he was the acknowledged leader. Even today, work in private law codification begins with the Bustamante Code of Private International Law, adopted in 1928 by the Sixth Pan American Congress in Havana.

A career in law was one of the few choices open to a young man of Bustamante's background and social standing, but he was not content to go through the motions. To the study and practice of law he brought his own individual passion for public service and an astonishing capacity for work. Before he was twenty, he had won the Chair of International Law at the university where he had earned his law degree and where he would one day be dean. By twenty-one, he had published the first of his many works on international law. After that, achievements, publications, and honors followed in an unbroken chain. A measure of the prominence he had attained by 1921 can be found in the request by the secretary of foreign affairs of the Republic of Panama for Bustamante's opinion on four questions regarding

Panama's boundary dispute with the Republic of Costa Rica. Bustamante's legal expertise had become, in effect, a world resource.

The response that Bustamante made to the Panamanian request is a model of forensic logic and learning. He did not address the politics of the question. Local and international pressures that had stimulated controversy for thirty-five years were no concern of his, or of the "scientific" law that he explicated thoroughly, reasonably, and, as it turned out, fruitlessly. The dispute continued another twenty years before being settled, not through law, but through pressures arising out of World War II. The incident evokes an international milieu that is difficult to recapture. In that special world of high endeavor, progress was the environmental norm, to be brought ever nearer to perfection by the power of intellectual effort. Bustamante was one of the leading citizens of that world, and he was at ease with its assumptions. After World War I, he wrote confidently on the "triumphal march" of arbitration and of the universal conscience where the precepts of international law were being permanently engraved. Even the 1930s did not dampen his hopes. In 1936 he wrote that the World Court was going from success to success and that it enjoyed general approval and confidence.

Such a faith may well have been necessary to sustain Bustamante and others of his generation. There can be no question of the magnitude of their efforts and of their accomplishments: the Hague Peace Conferences, the Permanent Court of Arbitration, the League of Nations, the codification of international law, the Permanent Court of International Justice. To all of these, Bustamante devoted his life. Amid later ideological conflicts, his labors of hope reflect a time when international institutions were seen not as weapons for political conflict but as foundation stones for a just and peaceful world.

BIBLIOGRAPHY:

A. *Derecho internacional privado*, 2nd ed., 3 vols. (Havana, 1934); *Derecho internacional público*, 5 vols. (Havana, 1933–37); *Fragmentos immortales* (Havanna, n.d.); *Informe relativo a la Segunda Conferencia Internacional de la Paz en el Haya en 1907*, 2 vols. (Havana, 1908); *Panama–Costa Rica Boundary Controversy* (Panama, 1921); *Proyecto de codigo de derecho internacional privado* (Havana, 1925); *Tratado de derecho internacional privado* (Havana, 1896); *The World Court* (New York, 1926).

B. AJIL 45 (1951), 746–49; *Américas* 3 (Nov 1951), 32; Inter-American Juridical Committee, *Comparative Study of the Bustamante Code, the Montevideo Treaties, and the Restatement of the Law of Conflict of Laws* (Washington, 1954); NYT 26 Aug 1951, 77; William B. Parker, *Cubans of Today* (New York, 1919), 126–29.

Dorothy V. Jones

BUTLER, Harold Beresford (6 October 1883, Reading, England—26 March 1951, Reading). *Education*: Lit. Hum., Eton Coll., Balliol Coll., Oxford Univ., 1905; fellow, All Souls Coll., Oxford Univ., 1905–12. *Career*: civil service, 1907–8; secretary, British delegation, International

Conference on Aerial Navigation, Paris, 1910, acting assistant secretary, 1914; secretary, Foreign Trade Department of Foreign Office, 1916; minister of labor, 1917–19; assistant general-secretary, Labor Commission, Peace Conference, 1919; secretary-general, International Labor Conference, Washington, 1919; deputy director, International Labor Office, 1920–32, director, 1932–38; warden, Nuffield Coll., Oxford Univ., 1939–43; minister to Washington, 1942–46.

If in the history of international organization an example were sought of a somewhat nebulous hope being seized and launched and guided into reality, it might well be that of the personal contribution of Harold Butler to the creation of the International Labor Organization (ILO). In 1918 in the British Ministry of Labor, he and *Edward Phelan produced the first drafts of what was to become the constitution of the ILO, with its unique and novel feature of direct representation of employers and workers with voting rights alongside that of governments. In 1919, following the Paris Peace Conference's approval of the scheme for the ILO that emerged from the Commission on International Labour Legislation, Butler was appointed secretary of the Organizing Committee to prepare the first International Labor Conference. His work reveals Butler's important role in bringing to fruition the hopes and aspirations of those who in many countries believed in the international realization of social justice. As secretary-general of the Conference in Washington, essential responsibility for success or failure rested on Butler. Faced with legal, practical, and political difficulties, Butler led the delegates to the solution of innumerable problems of procedural technique and successful disposal of its agenda. The ILO thus became a going concern. A breakdown at Washington, the first test of the new machinery of international cooperation upon which the hope of peace was founded, would, as Butler later observed, have struck a deadly blow at the League of Nations.

In spite of his appointment only as deputy director and not as director of the new organization, Butler clung to his ideal and made a major contribution to the ensuing vital period of organization. Until 1932 he gave every assistance to the director, *Albert Thomas, in perfecting the practical functioning of the ILO. In particular, he put into practice his own conviction that loyal cooperation and a high standard of performance could be obtained from an international staff composed of officials from a variety of national backgrounds.

The third period of Butler's service to the ILO ran from 1932, when following Thomas's sudden death he became director, to 1938, when he resigned to return to academic life. In those economically and politically troubled years he met the challenges by working for and achieving what has been described as the greatest single reinforcement of the ILO that could then be looked for, namely, the entry of the United States. Butler also contributed to the greater universality of the organization by expanding the membership of its Governing Body to include more non-European countries. He also brought home the wide impact of the ILO's work by instituting technical assistance to member states and by planning regional conferences and international meetings to deal with the problems of specific industries. At the same time, he ensured that the ILO should pay closer attention to economic problems inseparable from social problems. Until his death Butler remained a friend of the ILO and retained his early faith in the realization of social justice through the work of the organization of which he may be said to be a most important founding father.

BIBLIOGRAPHY:

A. *Confident Morning* (London, 1950); "The International Labour Organization," in *The League of Nations Starts* (London 1920); *The Lost Peace: A Personal Impression* (London, 1942); *Peace or Power* (London, 1947); *Problems of Industry in the East* (Geneva, 1938); also director's reports to the International Labor Conference, 1933-38.

B. *International Labour Review* 63 (Apr 1951), 354-63; LT 28 Mar 1951, 6; NYT 28 Mar 1951, 29; Edward Phelan, *Yes and Albert Thomas* (London, 1936); Edward Phelan's memoirs in Archives of the ILO.

Raymond Manning

BUTLER, Nicholas Murray (2 April 1862, Elizabeth, NJ—7 December 1947, New York). *Education*: B.A., Columbia Coll., 1882, M.A., 1883, Ph.D., 1884; Univs. of Berlin and Paris, 1884-85. *Career*: assistant, Columbia Coll., 1885-87; president, New York Coll. for the Training of Teachers, 1887-91; tutor, Columbia, Coll., 1887-89, adjunct professor, 1889-90, professor, dean of the faculty, 1890-95, professor, 1895-1901, president, 1901-45; editor, *Educational Review*, 1891-1920; president, American Association for International Conciliation, 1905-24; director, Division of Intercourse and Education, Carnegie Endowment for International Peace (CEIP), 1911-45; president, CEIP, 1925-45; Nobel Peace Prize, 1931.

Little in Butler's early career suggested a lifetime commitment to internationalism. Trained in philosophy and education at Columbia, Butler at first devoted his extraordinary energies almost exclusively to upgrading the curriculum and transforming Columbia College into a modern university. Though offered the presidencies of other universities as well as of corporations and ambassadorships, Butler refused them all.

Nevertheless, Butler gradually developed an interest in international peace. Paradoxically, the same preoccupation with pedagogical matters that initially constrained his involvement in other causes nourished his interest in internationalism. From the outset, his approach to educational reform was cosmopolitan. Following completion of his graduate training at Columbia, Butler spent a year at the Universities of Berlin and Paris and came away impressed with them as models for Columbia. He also began to make contacts with European leaders, which he cultivated and expanded through correspondence and subsequent trips. During his lifetime, he crossed the Atlantic more than one hundred times.

Butler's contacts with the political and cultural establishments both at home and abroad reflected his preference for enlightened leadership and his distrust of mass public opinion. He liked to think of himself as a "liberal," which he was only in the sense that he fervently believed in the free individual unfettered as much as possible by government interference. He opposed economic nationalism, including high tariffs, as artificial and ultimately harmful to international trade, and following World War I he became a vigorous critic of Prohibition as an unnecessary restriction on personal liberty. Otherwise, Butler revealed little of other liberals' faith in the actual or potential goodness of the ordinary citizen. Butler was also somewhat ambivalent toward the American peace movement. He deplored the reckless speech and extreme sensationalism of debauched journals that had brought on the Spanish-American War, but he shunned organized peace groups, many of which also criticized the war spirit in the nation. Butler in fact considered peace societies too radical and generally avoided a personal commitment to them. "Peace" to Butler was not an ideal but only a means to the achievement of the ideals of justice, liberty, and the proper conduct of a humane and orderly society.

Despite such differences, Butler did reflect one viewpoint held by most peace workers. This was the pre–World War I belief that an evolutionary process had begun that would see war disappear. While it might be inevitable, it needed to be developed and encouraged through education and the building of a juridically based world system to resolve conflicts peacefully.

Butler's approach to achieve these ends was distinctly elitist. He hoped to develop an international elite instructing public opinion on ethical principles, civilized standards, and respect for law. One step in that direction came when he established an American branch of the Association for International Conciliation, which the Frenchman +Baron d'Estournelles de Constant had founded in Europe two years earlier. He also presided over +Alfred K. Smiley's Lake Mohonk Conferences on International Arbitration (1907, 1909–12). His addresses to these select gatherings, published as *The International Mind*, best summarized Butler's assumptions on the nature of man and world politics and the role of the United States in fostering a more stable, orderly world. "The international mind," he then wrote, "is nothing else than that habit of thinking of foreign relations and business, and that habit of dealing with them, which regard the several nations of the civilized world as friendly and cooperating equals in aiding the progress of civilization, in developing commerce and industry and in spreading enlightenment and culture throughout the world" (*The International Mind*, 102).

Butler demonstrated remarkable administrative abilities and enormous energy and influence to achieve this international mind. When *Hamilton Holt asked him to persuade +Andrew Carnegie to establish a peace endowment, Butler proceeded to coordinate efforts. Carnegie had already agreed to finance the American Association for International Conciliation, was on good terms with Butler, and, while others contributed to the philanthropist's decision to provide $10 million for the CEIP in December 1910, Butler's influence was central. Moreover, Butler and *Elihu Root persuaded Carnegie to select trustees of the CEIP who would reflect their perspective on peace. Butler served as director of the Division of Intercourse and Education until 1945 and as the Endowment's president, succeeding Root, from 1925 to 1945.

The Division of Intercourse and Education became an educational agency, issuing pamphlets, organizing conferences, distributing books to "international alcoves" in libraries, and creating international relations clubs, all in support of Butler's goal. It also utilized its financial leverage aggressively to reorganize the peace movement. Specifically, it provided subventions to the American Peace Society and the International Peace Bureau in Bern, Switzerland, for redistribution to their affiliated societies in the United States and abroad. Reflecting his and other trustees' skepticism about peace groups, however, the appropriations were made as much to control as to encourage them. With the outbreak of World War I, Butler's division drastically cut back funds to peace groups. The largest single item in its budget before the war was for the respectable Association for International Conciliation.

Though not a lawyer, Butler also supported plans for a legally organized world. He believed in the Hague Peace Conferences and wanted them to assemble automatically every four or five years to develop international law and peacemaking machinery. He also urged that the Permanent Court of Arbitration, which the First Hague Peace Conference had established in 1899, become a truly judicial body, and he successfully encouraged the Taft administration to use the international prize court as the basis for extending its jurisdiction beyond maritime issues with the creation of a court of arbitral justice. The outbreak of World War I occurred before the realization of this proposal, but Butler continued to promote the establishment of such a court at the end of the war.

Butler readily supported those articles in the League of Nations Covenant providing for the creation of a Permanent Court of International Justice. But because of his belief in limited government, he remained skeptical toward other articles proposing a more authoritative world organization. He had opposed the proposal of the League to Enforce Peace for automatic sanctions against nations refusing to submit their disputes to international conciliation before resorting to battle as historically unsound, simplistic, and likely to involve the United States in wars in which it had little interest. Thus, he similarly objected to collective sanctions provisions in the Covenant. From the outset of the debate over U.S. membership in the League of Nations, Butler took a skeptical position. He had agreed with *Woodrow Wilson on only a few things, and Butler's longtime identification with the Republican party made compromise with the Democratic Wilson even more unlikely. For his part, Wilson had little faith in Butler. *Colonel Edward M. House noted in his diary in mid-1918 that Wilson's derogatory comments about Butler did him "an injustice."

Throughout the 1920s and 1930s, Butler continued his efforts at international understanding. He promoted the United States' membership in the World Court and endorsed limited cooperation with the League of Nations. He was also intimately involved in fostering diplomatic efforts leading to the Kellogg-Briand Pact of 1928, which renounced war as an instrument of national policy. He severely criticized the neutrality acts of the mid-1930s and attacked isolationists. In 1938 he supported the Munich Conference to avert a war that could only result in "the destruction of our civilization," but by 1940 he believed that the use of force against Fascism was justified. Through the CEIP he also encouraged programs of international intellectual cooperation during the interwar years. Butler's persistent commitment to ideals of international understanding brought a reward in 1931 of the Nobel Peace Prize, which he shared with Jane Addams.

BIBLIOGRAPHY:

A. *Across the Busy Years: Recollections and Reflections,* 2 vols. (New York, 1939–40); *The Basis of Durable Peace* (New York, 1917); *The Family of Nations, Its Need and Its Problems: Essays and Addresses by Nicholas Murray Butler* (New York, 1938); *The International Mind: An Argument for the Judicial Settlement of International Disputes* (New York, 1912); *The Path to Peace: Essays and Addresses on Peace and Its Making* (New York, 1930).

B. CB 1940, 130–34; Charles Chatfield, introduction to Butler's *Before the War: Last Voices of Arbitration,* rpt. ed. (New York, 1972); DAB supp. 4, 133–38; Charles DeBenedetti, *Origins of the Modern American Peace Movement, 1915–1929* (Millwood, NY, 1978); Sondra R. Herman, *Eleven Against War: Studies in American Internationalist Thought, 1898–1921* (Stanford, CA, 1969); Warren F. Kuehl, *Seeking World Order: The United States and World Organization to 1920* (Nashville, TN, 1969); Michael A. Lutzker, "The Formation of the Carnegie Endowment for International Peace: A Study of the Establishment-Centered Peace Movement, 1910–1914," in *Building the Organizational Society: Essays on Associational Activities in Modern America,* ed. Jerry Israel (New York, 1972), 143–62; NCAB 34, 1–5; NYT 7 Dec 1947, 1, 8 Dec 1947, 21, 24, 9 Dec 1947, 33, 10 Dec 1947, 38.

C. The Butler and CEIP papers are in the Butler Library, Columbia Univ.

David S. Patterson

BUXTON, Anthony (2 September 1881, Exeter, England—9 August 1970, nr Great Yarmouth, England). *Education*: second class in natural science, Trinity Coll., Cambridge Univ. *Career*: joined Essex Yeomanry, 1905;

served in war, 1914–18; assistant to secretary-general, League of Nations, 1919–31.

Buxton was one of that new group of international civil servants chosen by *Eric Drummond, the first secretary-general of the newborn League of Nations, in 1919. For some time, Buxton served as Drummond's assistant, living in the international headquarters of the League of Nations in Geneva. Information about his role is scanty.

As a decorated war veteran, Buxton clearly saw no contradiction between his own British patriotism and the concept of service to an international organization. Neither during nor after his stint of duty to the League did Buxton trumpet his activities and achievements there. The numerous books he wrote during his lifetime dealt not with international politics but with his two beloved hobbies, hunting and bird watching. Buxton's work as Drummond's assistant appears to have been quiet, unobtrusive, and efficient.

After his resignation from the League in 1931, Buxton did not pursue any noteworthy political or diplomatic activities; it is clear, however, that he remained loyal to the principles of the League. Shortly after his resignation, Buxton, in a newspaper interview, strongly supported the notion that sanctions should be applied by all the nations of the League against Japan for its invasion of Manchuria. The League Covenant, he insisted, had to be applied against any and all violators.

Buxton appears to have been a force for good during his years as Drummond's assistant. In his autobiography, *Robert Cecil, the great leader of pro-League opinion within Great Britain, fondly recalled Buxton's habit of "entertaining foreigners of all sorts who were devoted to him, as indeed were most people." Cecil concluded that Buxton "was in the best sense a great social force for peace" and "one of the institutions of Geneva."

BIBLIOGRAPHY:

A. *Sporting Interludes at Geneva* (London, 1932).

B. Robert Cecil, *A Great Experiment: An Autobiography* (London, 1941); LT 17 Nov 1931, 10, 10 Aug 1970, 8, 17 Aug 1970, 8; WWW 1961–70, 166.

Paul D. Mageli

BUXTON, Charles. See *Biographical Dictionary of Modern Peace Leaders.*

C

CALDWELL, Robert J. (12 May 1875, Louisville, KY—21 December 1951, Winter Park, FL). *Education*: Polytechnic Coll. Inst., Brooklyn, NY. *Career*: cotton merchant and manufacturer, United States and Canada.

As a self-made businessman, Caldwell accumulated sufficient funds to indulge his interests in civic and public affairs. He went to Europe in 1919 as U.S. special industrial commissioner to attend the Paris Peace Conference, and there he became involved in French relief work. The following year as U.S. special economic commissioner to Great Britain, Czechoslovakia, and Belgium, he offered advice on recovery programs. These contacts and events changed his life, and during the next decade he devoted himself almost entirely to advance internationalist goals. He became concerned about the plight of Russian refugees and helped organize a Russian Aid Society and the Russian Refugee Relief Society of America, which enabled over 6,500 persons to enter the United States. He also helped disrupted Poles and increasingly sensed a need for better understanding between people. Joining with his friend, *Hamilton Holt, he helped organize the Armenia–America Society (1921) and the Baltic America Society (1921), and he served as president of the latter. He later supported the France–America Society, the Pilgrims, the English-Speaking Union, and the American Friends of Lithuania. He worked with others to create the Foreign Press Service (1920), designed to present an honest picture of U.S. events to the world through weekly bulletins.

The League of Nations naturally attracted Caldwell. He served on the Executive Committee and Council of the League of Nations Non-Partisan Association to promote U.S. membership after 1922, and he was the first U.S. representative to the Federation of League of Nations Societies in Vienna (1923). He volunteered on a financial mission to Hungary and Czechoslovakia (1923) that resulted in an international loan to Hungary. Further evidence of Caldwell's commitment appeared in the mid-1920s in his unsuccessful plan to underwrite the cost of a statue of *Woodrow Wilson on the grounds of the League of Nations. It was to be inscribed with the names of fifty Americans noted for their friendship toward the League. The Council tentatively accepted his offer, but bureaucratic delays over implementation frustrated Caldwell, who withdrew from the venture. He did present (1928) a statue to Czechoslovakia of *Jan Masaryk.

Caldwell grew discouraged after the 1920s. He suggested to *Herbert Hoover in 1931 the enunciation of a doctrine that the United States would view as unfriendly any violation of the Kellogg-Briand Pact, but that advice was ignored. He supported the Council on Foreign Relations, the International Red Cross, and the Church Peace Union and served on the American Committee of the International Labor Organization, the only affiliation he retained into the UN era.

BIBLIOGRAPHY:

B. NYT 22 Dec 1951, 15; WB 1948, 940; WWWA 3, 132.

Warren F. Kuehl

CALVO, Carlos (12 February 1822, Montevideo—3 May 1906, Paris). *Education*: studied law, Buenos Aires. *Career*: diplomatic agent of Argentina to Uruguay, 1853–58; Paraguayan representative to France and Great Britain, 1860–63; Argentine minister to Berlin, St. Petersburg, and Vienna, 1884–99, to Paris, Brussels, and Holy See, 1899–1905; scholar and publicist.

Calvo moved to Buenos Aires at an early age and always considered himself a citizen of Argentina. He is perhaps the best-known nineteenth-century Latin American international lawyer, and he was a distinguished diplomat and a prolific writer. Calvo's contributions to international law were prodigious. He was a founder of the Institut de Droit International and the author of several major works, most notably his *Le droit international théorique et pratique*, which went through five editions between 1868 and 1896. Calvo's legal philosophy was essentially historical and within the positivist orthodoxy of his time. States were considered fully sovereign and the principal persons or subjects of the law. He defined international law as an aggregation of rules observed by states in relations with each other, and within that framework his contributions of vast detail and depth appeared. One important difference that marks Calvo's approach to international law, however, was his treatment of public and private aspects of the law together rather than as separate fields.

Calvo, often considered more a compiler than an original thinker, became known as a strong defender of the rights and autonomy of the Latin American states, an advocate of arbitration, and the originator of the Calvo Doctrine and Calvo Clause. The Doctrine, while somewhat imprecise, stresses prohibition not only of armed intervention for the collection of private claims or debts, indeed any armed intervention, but also, seemingly, diplomatic intervention as well. Some versions also stress immunity of states from responsibility for injury to aliens resulting from riots and internal turmoil. The Calvo Clause, by contrast, is a statement often incorporated into contracts by which a foreign private contractor agrees to resort only to local legal remedies. Although neither Doctrine nor Clause has been fully accepted in international law, both represent the persistent Latin American resistance to interference with the internal affairs of states. That persistence bore fruit in the more modest Drago Doctrine, which postulated prohibition of force to collect public debts and which has generally been accepted by international law. Calvo supported that doctrine and it is a part of the complex of themes in his own.

BIBLIOGRAPHY:

A. *Annales historiques de la révolution de l'Amérique latine*, 5 vols. (Paris, 1864–75); *Le Droit international théorique et pratique*, 6 vols. (Paris, 1896); *Manuel de droit international public et privé*, 3rd ed. (Paris, 1892); *Recueil complet des traités, conventions, etc., de l'Amérique latine*, 11 vols. (Paris, 1862–69).

B. Percy Bordwell, "Calvo and the Calvo Doctrine," *Green Bag* 18 (Jul 1906), 378–82; Alwyn V. Freeman, "Recent Aspects of the Calvo Doctrine and the Challenge to International Law," AJIL 40 (1946), 121–47; H. B. Jacobini, *A Study of the Philosophy of International Law as Seen in Works of Latin-American Writers* (The Hague, 1954); José Yves Limantour, "Notice sur la vie et les oeuvres de M. Carlos Calvo," *Academie des Sciences Morales et Politiques: Séances et travaux* 172 (1909), 689–718; *Nuevo diccionario biografico argentino* (Buenos Aires, 1969), 56–57; Don Manuel De Peralta, "Carlos Calvo," *Institute of International Law, Annuaire* 21 (1906), 486–91; Donald R. Shea, *The Calvo Clause: A Problem of Inter-American and International Law and Diplomacy* (Minneapolis, MN, 1955).

H. B. Jacobini

CANNON, James, Jr. (13 November 1864, Salisbury, MD—6 September 1944, Chicago). *Education*: B.A., Randolph-Macon Coll., 1884; B.D., Princeton Theol., Sem., 1888; M.A., Coll. of New Jersey (later Princeton Univ.), 1890. *Career*: minister, Methodist Episcopal Church, South, 1888–94; principal, Blackstone Female Institute, 1894–1911, 1914–18; bishop, Methodist Episcopal Church, South, 1918–38; chairman, National Legislative Committee, Anti-Saloon League of America, 1914–44.

As a bishop in the Methodist Episcopal Church, South, and a high-ranking official in the Anti-Saloon League, Cannon faithfully represented the social gospel movement within American Protestantism. To Cannon, the traffic in alcoholic beverages constituted the greatest enemy the Protestant churches faced in their attempt to remake the world according to the teachings of Jesus Christ. Thus his international activities, like his domestic crusade, focused on the control and eventual abolition of the liquor traffic. Appointed an official delegate from the United States to the International Congresses Against Alcoholism in 1913, 1920, 1921, and 1928, he made sure that overseas temperance organizations were familiar with the American method of dealing with the alcohol problem.

When the Eighteenth Amendment, which imposed national prohibition, was ratified in 1919, Cannon and other Anti-Saloon League officials immediately launched a campaign to persuade the world to emulate the United States. At his urging and under the auspices of the Anti-Saloon League, a conference of British, Irish, European, and American temperance workers convened in Paris in April 1919, concurrently with the Peace Conference. As Cannon desired, the meeting requested the proposed League of Nations to prohibit the traffic in distilled liquors in certain of its mandated territories. Eventually the League did so.

The Paris session also resolved to create a new international temperance body. On 7 June 1919 in Washington, temperance advocates from more than fifty countries organized the World League Against Alcoholism. Ostensibly aimed at the "suppression of alcholism," the World League linked national groups, provided literature and speakers for campaigns that sought the passage of temperance and prohibition laws, and collected statistics on alcohol consumption. As chairman of the Executive Committee during the 1920s, Cannon was active in campaigns to enact temperance legislation in Scotland and the Scandinavian countries. The World League also tried to persuade the League of Nations to take additional action against the international liquor traffic.

Much as *Woodrow Wilson had sought to lead the world toward American ideals of democracy and "liberal" capitalism, Cannon sought to persuade other nations to adopt the American method of dealing with the liquor traffic. In the beginning his requests were moderate, but Cannon and other American "drys" wanted a "dry" world. However, the repeal of the Eighteenth Amendment in 1933, accusations against Cannon of improper and illegal conduct, and the Great Depression weakened the authority and financial resources of the World League. In the 1930s it became a paper organization.

If all human institutions were to be made to conform to the teachings of Jesus Christ, Cannon believed, Christian unity was necessary. Thus, just as he sought to end the divisions within American Methodism, he also sought the unification of the world's Christians. He was a delegate to the World Missionary Conference at Edinburgh in 1910, and the Methodist Episcopal Church, South, sent him to the World Conferences of the Faith and Order movement at Lausanne in 1927 and at Edinburgh in 1937. At Lausanne he served as chairman of the Commission on Sacraments. He represented his church at the World Conferences of the Life and Work Movement at Stockholm in 1925 and at Oxford in 1937. At Stockholm, as the American representative to the Commission on Drink, he pressed for resolutions advocating the American method of dealing with intoxicating beverages. Cannon was one of the few American churchmen to participate in all the major ecumenical streams that eventually joined to form the World Council of Churches in 1948. More importantly, he helped link his own denomination, not always in the vanguard, to the twentieth-century ecumenical movement. As bishop, he also became involved in world relief programs.

BIBLIOGRAPHY:

A. *Bishop Cannon's Own Story*, Richard L. Watson, Jr. ed. (Durham, NC, 1955).

B. Ernest H. Cherrington, *The Evolution of Prohibition in the United States*

(Montclair, NJ, 1969); DAB 23, 131–33; Virginius Dabney, *Dry Messiah: The Life of Bishop Cannon* (New York, 1949); NCAB 35, 129–30; NYT 7 Sep 1944, 23.

C. Cannon papers are in the Duke Univ. Library.

G. F. Goodwin

CARNEGIE, Andrew. See *Biographical Dictionary of Modern Peace Leaders.*

CARTER, Edward Clark "Ned" (9 June 1878, Lawrence, MA—9 November 1954, New York). *Education*: B.A., Harvard Coll., 1900. *Career*: graduate secretary, Phillips Brooks House, Harvard Coll., 1900–1902; secretary, YMCA, Calcutta, 1902–8, 1911–17; secretary, North American Student Movement, 1908–11; chief secretary, YMCA, American Expeditionary Force, Paris, 1917–19; foreign secretary, YMCA, London, 1920–22; secretary, The Inquiry, 1923–30, chairman, 1930–33; secretary, American Council, Institute of Pacific Relations (IPR), 1926–33; secretary-general, IPR, 1933–46; executive vice-chairman, American Council, IPR, 1946–48; consultant, UN Economic Commission for Asia and the Far East, 1948; provost, New School for Social Research, 1949–50, director of international studies, 1950–52; president, Russian Relief, 1941–50.

Not a government official, political figure, or writer of any achievement whatsoever, Carter nevertheless played an important role promoting public awareness of international affairs. From the mid-1920s to the mid-1940s, he sought to reduce international tensions and resolve conflicts through the Institute of Pacific Relations, a private organization made up of groups from eleven nations. While chief administrator first of the American Council and then of the international body, he encouraged activity by the IPR in three areas: research on international controversies to suggest alternatives; mediatory discussion by all parties in the spirit of mutual respect; and community education about those issues. For an organization that included groups from China, Japan, the Soviet Union, and Western colonial powers, however, the spirit of mutual respect was not easily preserved during the late 1930s. A rising tide of nationalism, World War II, and the Cold War all made Carter's brand of internationalism, the IPR, and Carter himself targets of public criticism and abuse.

To some extent Carter's difficulties stemmed from the very nature of the IPR. Following the bylaws of the nonpartisan organization, he did try to restrain staff members from voicing their personal bias. But because he believed in freedom of inquiry about controversial subjects, he permitted expression of opinions that opened the organization to bitter criticism. First the IPR and Carter were attacked for bias favoring China against Japan and then for an allegedly pro-Soviet and pro-Chinese Communist bias. Hostile congressional investigations during the Cold War then led to the loss of tax-exempt status, financial support, and scholarly reputation.

Accusations against Carter are difficult to assess because he seldom wrote or spoke for publication. Clearly, during the 1930s he stood as a liberal internationalist who opposed racism, colonialism, and Fascism. He shared a common premise that political conduct generally, including foreign relations, was rooted in underlying economic conditions within nations. He concluded that revolution, Fascism, Communism, aggression, and war all grew out of poverty, backwardness, and injuries to national and racial self-respect. Therefore, he wanted the United States to defend democracy by cooperating in a worldwide effort to improve living standards, promote progress, and eliminate injustice. Anticipating the terrible destructiveness of the coming war, he foresaw the need for a massive program of reconstruction involving large-scale investment by the U.S. government.

No pacifist, Carter argued that, unless the democracies backed their beliefs with force, civilization itself would be eclipsed. Therefore, by 1940 he was defending the draft and backing U.S. aid to Britain, France, and China. Conflict with Germany he regarded as inevitable. What especially aroused his critics was his enthusiastic support of the Soviet Union. A frequent visitor there during the 1930s, he denied that it was a totalitarian state and defended both the purges and the Non-Aggression Pact. Even during the late 1940s, he did not apparently repudiate his Russophilia, which a son warned had been made obsolete by the Soviet threat to free institutions. But he did give up the presidency of Russian Relief before his death.

BIBLIOGRAPHY:

A. "American Foreign Policy and the Peasant and Soldier in Japan," *Annals of the American Academy of Political and Social Science* 168 (Jul 1933), 1–8; "The Hot Spring Conference," *Pacific Affairs* 18 (Mar 1945), 94–96; "Round the Rim of the Pacific," *Survey Graphic* 31 (Nov 1942), 535–38.

B. NCAB 46, 69–70; NYT 19 Nov 1954, 33, 16 Nov 1954, 27; John N. Thomas, *The Institute of Pacific Relations: Asian Scholars and American Politics* (Seattle, WA, 1974); WWWA 3, 142.

C. The Carter papers are at the Univ. of Vermont.

Alan Raucher

CASALS, Pablo Carlos Salvador Defillo de (29 December 1876, Vendrell, Spain—22 October 1973, Hato Rey, Puerto Rico). *Education*: Municipal School of Music, Barcelona, 1887; Royal Conservatory of Music, Madrid, 1894–97. *Career*: Cello debut, Paris, 1899, international tours, from 1900; taught, Paris Normal School of Music, 1914; Prades and Perpignan Festivals, from 1950; Festival Casals, Puerto Rico, 1957–73; recital at United Nations, 1958; president, Puerto Rico Conservatory of Music; Marlboro Festival, from 1961; composer and conductor, symphonies, oratorios, string quartets, songs, motets, sonatas, and solo pieces; founded the Pau Casals Orchestra, Barcelona, 1920; international tours as conductor.

One of the musical giants of the twentieth century, Casals, whose artistic career spanned seventy-five years, was revered for his musical genius and his humanitarian principles. As a young cellist, he evolved a new technique which liberated the performer from the previously accepted yet restrictive hand and arm positions by using innovations in bowing and fingering. He then attempted the remainder of his life to liberate people from moral injustices. Forever empathetic to human suffering, he exemplified by his modest lifestyle and moral convictions those qualities symbolic of universal freedom.

Casals protested the inhumanities of the Bolshevik Revolution in 1917 by refusing to perform in Russia. He effected a similar protest against Nazi Germany and Fascist Italy in the 1930s. As an ardent supporter of the Spanish Republican government, Casals opposed Francisco Franco during the Civil War in Spain. In January 1939, when Franco's victory became imminent, Casals moved to Prades, France, in voluntary banishment, and he devoted himself to aiding Spanish exiles. Disillusioned when the Allied nations recognized Franco's dictatorial government, Casals imposed a personal boycott and refused to perform publicly in those particular countries. He maintained that he could not isolate his human convictions from his integrity as an artist. However, in 1951 he was encouraged to accept a few concert commitments, but he maintained that it represented no change in his ideals.

In 1956 Casals performed in Mexico, and he returned in 1960 to premiere his oratorio *El Pesebre* (*The Manger*). It was dedicated "to those who have struggled and are still struggling for the cause of peace and democracy." He then performed this work at benefit concerts in the major cities of the Western world. Discussing his mission, he said that his first obligation was toward the welfare of his fellow man, and that he would seek to meet that commitment through music, which transcends any barriers of language or politics.

In 1958 Casals performed a cello recital at the United Nations to mark its thirteenth anniversary and to call attention to the perils of nuclear war. To commemorate its twenty-sixth anniversary, the United Nations commissioned Casals to write an *Ode to Peace (Hymn to the United Nations)* which was performed in New York City in October 1971. Casals felt that, although his contribution and efforts for the betterment of man had been small, he had given all he could to an ideal he held sacred. From 1956 until his death, Casals lived in Puerto Rico. As an inspirational figure of international stature, Casals was interviewed and quoted widely.

BIBLIOGRAPHY:

A. *Joys and Sorrows* (New York, 1970).

B. J. Ma Corredor, *Conversations with Casals* (New York, 1958); A. Forsee, *Pablo Casals: Cellist for Freedom* (New York, 1965); *Music Educators Journal* 48, no. 6 (1962), 87; NYT 29 Jan 1956, II-9, 22 Jul 1951, II-5, 4 Mar 1962, II-9, 23 Oct 1973, 52.

C. The Casals archives are in Vendrell, Spain, and Santurce, Puerto Rico.

Olga Llano Kuehl

CASSIN, René-Samuel (5 October 1887, Bayonne, France—20 February 1976, Paris). *Education*: Licencié en droit ès lettres, Facultés, Aix-en-Provence, 1905–8; docteur ès sciences juridiques, politiques et économiques, Faculté de Droit, Paris, 1914. *Career*: World War I, 311th Regiment, wounded in action at Saint-Mihiel; professor of civil law, Univ. of Lille, 1920–29; founder of two veteran groups, L'Union Fédérale des Mutilés et Anciens Combattants and International Confederation of Wounded (CIAMAC), including veterans from both sides; joined French League for the Rights of Man, 1921; agrégé then professor of civil law, Paris, 1919–35; delegate, League of Nations, 1924–38; professor, Hague Academy of International Law, 1930, 1934, 1951; delegate, General Conference on Disarmament, 1932–34; professor, Centre Universitaire Méditerranéen, Nice, and L'Ecole Nationale de la France d'Outre-Mer, 1935–40; arbitrator of labor disputes, 1936–39; active in Alliance Israelite Française; vice-president, Conseil d'Etat, 1944–60; president, Conseil de l'Ecole Nationale d'Administration, 1945; president, Cour Supérieure d'Arbitrage, 1950; president, Provisional Constitutional Committee, 1958–59; member, Conseil Constitutionnel, 1960; president, Centre National des Hautes Etudes de la France d'Outre-Mer, 1960; delegate, UN Commission on War Crimes, 1943–45, UN General Assemblies, 1946–51, and UNESCO, 1945–52, 1958, 1960, 1962; member, Human Rights Commission, 1946–72, vice-president, 1946–55, president, 1955–57; vice-president, European Court of Human Rights, 1959, president, 1965; created International Institute of Human Rights at Strasbourg, 1968; Nobel Peace Prize and UN Human Rights Prize, 1968.

Cassin was a nationalist, internationalist, and regionalist who gained a reputation for being perhaps the world's most eloquent and consistent advocate of peace and universal human rights. Cassin's philosophy grew out of his appreciation of the history of the French Revolution, the Jewish experience, and the fact that he witnessed firsthand the horrors of World War I. A bizarre coincidence saved his life when, after being wounded, he was wheeled into a ward for hopeless cases. His mother was a nurse on duty and persuaded a surgeon to try a seemingly hopeless operation. In addition to teaching law and being active in organizing veteran's organizations, he was France's permanent delegate to the League of Nations and the General Disarmament Conferences. Cassin personally supported peace and human rights then and later more strongly than did the French government. His independence, as when he publicly opposed the Munich Pact as a step toward war, gave him credibility and prestige after his fears materialized. Although sympathetic to victims of war, he believed in resisting evil and never was a pacifist, a position he considered naive. Pacifism was strong among French veterans groups, but Cassin was among those willing to go reluctantly to war again to safeguard civilization against Hitler, whom he first opposed in 1933.

Cassin made a notable contribution to the Resistance, being one of the first to join *Charles de Gaulle in London in June 1940. At their initial meeting, Cassin sized up the general and offered his services, whereupon de Gaulle asked Cassin to draft the accord with Churchill, signed in August. Before agreeing, Cassin asked whether the French forces would be independent and equal to the British or serve under them. When de Gaulle replied, "We are France," Cassin agreed to do it, judging de Gaulle as a man of action. Thereafter Cassin launched a protracted propaganda campaign in English with speeches and 130 BBC broadcasts to stimulate resistance to Nazism and willingness to fight for France. Cassin also injected the notion of human rights into the Atlantic Charter. His appreciation of the dramatic led him in 1941 to conceive the idea of making 18 June a national holiday commemorating de Gaulle's now famous appeal. When he met *Eleanor Roosevelt while she was visiting the Free French in London in 1942, it was the beginning of a respectful friendship and long association that was to bear future results.

Cassin worked three arenas simultaneously in the post–World War II era: the French high court, the Conseil d'Etat, and constitutional committees for what became the Fifth Republic; the UN, where he insisted on the insertion of human rights in the Charter and served initially as a member of the Nuclear Committee that developed the working draft of the Universal Declaration of Human Rights (UDHR) and on the Human Rights Commission; and the European Court of Human Rights.

In creating his quick preliminary working draft of the UDHR in June 1947, Cassin worked from other projects including the Secretariat Outline, which was not merely what its name implies but really a completed draft that had been laboriously prepared by the director of human rights, John P. Humphrey of Canada, and Emile Giraud. Other notable collaborators in this collective effort were Eleanor Roosevelt, Charles Malik, and P. C. Chang, as well as members of the General Assembly. When at the request of the French government in December 1948 Cassin's handwritten draft was displayed at the UN to mark the tenth anniversary of the adoption of the UDHR by the General Assembly, the myth was created that Cassin was the "principal author." During the 1960s he exaggerated the importance of France's role in the UN during the late 1940s and 1950s.

Cassin was proud of his participation on the Human Rights Commission, but he was better as a member than when he chaired because his enthusiasm for his own viewpoint interfered with the objectivity of his rulings, and he tended to lecture people. He, along with others, also advocated the development of enforcement mechanisms, including the creation of a high commissioner for human rights. He criticized Secretary-General *Dag Hammerskjöld's politicization of the UN and attempt to stifle the early momentum that had been achieved by the Human Rights Commission, ECOSOC, and the Third Committee of the General Assembly. What the UN failed to achieve globally was realized on a regional basis by the Council of Europe, in which Cassin eventually became president of the Human Rights Court despite his age and the fact that France had not ratified the European Convention.

In 1968 Cassin received the Nobel Peace Prize because the committee felt his life's work was the extension of human rights both universally and on the European level. He had promoted himself through numerous personal contacts and by preparing extensive biographies and bibliographies in support of his nomination because he wanted the prize money to create the International Institute of Human Rights at Strasbourg. It is certainly true that this childless octagenarian, an "exclusively intellectual man" who had no hobbies, had tirelessly advocated peace and human rights in the UN at a time when human rights opponents abounded. Cassin claimed that the UDHR was the most important moral guide since the Ten Commandments but, unlike them, was the first positive ethical guide developed by organized humanity. Cassin used the occasion of the twentieth anniversary of the UDHR to urge ratification of UN Human Rights Treaties and the European Convention that France was the last original member of the Council of Europe to approve in 1974.

BIBLIOGRAPHY:

A. *Amicorum discipulorumque liber* (Paris, 1969–72); *De l'exception tirée de l'in-exécution dans les rapports synallagmatiques (exception non adimpleti contractus) et de ses relations avec le droit de rétention, la compensation et la résolution* (Paris, 1914); *La Déclaration universelle et la mise en oeuvres des droits de l'homme* (Paris, 1952); *La Pensée et l'action* (Boulogne-sur-Seine, France, 1972); *Les Hommes partis de rien: Le Réveil de la France abattue, 1940–41* (Paris, 1975); *Problèmes de protection internationale des droits de l'homme* (Paris, 1969).

B. *Actualité de la pensée de René Cassin: Actes du colloque* (Paris, 1981); Marc Agi, *De l'idée d'universalité comme fondatrice du concept des droits de l'homme d'après la vie et l'oeuvre de René Cassin* (Antibes, 1980); J. P. Cointet, *La France libre* (Paris, 1975); John P. Humphrey "The Great Adventure" (unpublished memoir covering 1946–66). A. Prost, *Les Anciens Combattants et la société française 1914–1939* (Paris, 1976); Albert Verdoodt, *Naissance et signification de la Déclaration universelle des droits de l'homme* (Louvain-Paris, 1963).

C. The Cassin papers are in the Archives Nationales.

June K. Burton

CATLIN, George (29 July 1896, England—7 February 1979, Lyndhurst, England). *Education*: graduate, New Coll., Oxford Univ.; Ph.D., Cornell Univ., 1924. *Career*: professor, Cornell Univ., 1924–35; McGill Univ., 1959–61; visiting professor and lecturer at several colleges; publicist; activist for Atlantic Union.

One of the leading political theorists of his time, Catlin was initially attracted to the study of politics by the experience of the Great War; thereafter, he devoted his critical efforts to the discovery of the profounder causes of recurring war. In his successive theoretical endeavors Catlin sought to "refound" political science after the example of Thomas Hobbes. It was through the combined inspiration of Hobbes and Alfred Adler that he came to appreciate the centrality of power in politics. After earning his doctorate at Cornell in 1924, Catlin taught there until 1935 and thereafter held academic posts irregularly in hopes of gaining political experience.

Catlin never had his political ambitions realized; his was a life of adventure and excitement punctuated by disappointments. He was forever in search of recognition, almost driven by Faustian compulsion, though checked by his innate shyness. But his talents did not always go unappreciated. While on the faculty of Cornell as a young foreign scholar, he had a hand in the alteration of the U.S. Constitution. He was put in charge of a study of Prohibition by the Rockefeller Foundation in 1926, which prepared the way for the repeal of the Eighteenth Amendment. In 1940, owing to fortuitous circumstance, Catlin found himself briefly advising an American presidential candidate, *Wendell Willkie. In 1943 he had the satisfaction of drafting the International Declaration of Indian Independence.

The Great War did more than kindle the imagination of a would-be political philosopher; it convinced Catlin that the nation-state was obsolete and if mankind was to avert another world catastrophe steps must be taken toward the creation of a world government. Catlin never had much to say about world government as such, however. Instead, he devoted much of his mature life to the defense of a regional integration as a step toward the world ideal. He called it an Atlantic Community, and it was to be made up of the English-speaking nations of the Atlantic. In recognition of his campaign for better Anglo–American relations, Catlin was knighted in 1970.

Although Catlin was not alone to speak of an Atlantic Community, he was probably among the most outspoken and persistent advocates of the idea. Throughout the 1960s and into the 1970s he had the notion that Gaullist France was bent on driving a wedge between the great English-speaking peoples. *George Pompidou's vision of a "European Europe," into which Edward Heath was determined to drag his country, was viewed as a threat to the Atlantic Community and, indeed, as a prelude to the dissolution of the British Commonwealth itself. Catlin denounced Heath as a demagogue and as a betrayer of an ancient British tradition dating back to Cardinal Wolsey, according to which Britain detaches herself from European politics except as a holder of the balance of power.

Catlin's mistrust of the French and his disdain for Francophile British politicians went far beyond the Fifth Republic, however. As he charged Heath with betrayal, so he blamed *Edward Grey for having contributed to the outbreak of World War I at a time when it could have been avoided through an accommodation with Germany. Once the victory had been won, Catlin was appalled, as were many other observers, by the French policy of vengeance and the U.S. and British policy of acquiescence, which, together, seemed to put the continent right back on the course of fratricidal war. During the interwar years Catlin joined *Gilbert Murray, G. P. Gooch, and other eminent men who sought to bring Germany back into the mainstream of European life and, in particular, to do something about Anglo–German reconciliation. After World War II, Catlin joined a small group of men dedicating themselves to the improvement of relations, and through their efforts the Anglo–German Association came into being in 1951, with Catlin as a vice-president.

Having had his own political ambitions rudely dashed, Catlin took much pride in his last years in the successful career of his daughter, Shirley Williams, twice member of a Labor Cabinet. But he did not live to see either the historic foundation of the Social Democratic party under her leadership or her triumphant return to Parliament in 1981.

BIBLIOGRAPHY:

A. *Above All Nations* (London, 1945); *The Anglo-Saxon Tradition* (London, 1938); *The Atlantic Commonwealth* (New York, 1969); *The Atlantic Community* (London, 1959); *For God's Sake, Go! An Autobiography* (Buckinghamshire, England, 1972); *The Grandeur of England and the Atlantic Community* (Oxford, 1966); *Preface to Action* (London, 1934); *Thomas Hobbes as Philosopher, Publicist and Man of Letters* (Oxford, 1922).

B. Sugwon Kang and Francis D. Wormuth, "Sir George Catlin," PS 12 (Fall 1979), 544–45; Francis D. Wormuth, "The Political Science of Sir George Catlin," *Fortuna* 2 (Mar–Jun 1976), 1–11, "The Politics of George Catlin," *Western Political Quarterly* 14 (Sep 1961), 807–11; WW 1979, 428.

Sugwon Kang

CATT, Carrie Chapman. See *Biographical Dictionary of Modern Peace Leaders.*

CAVERT, Samuel McCrea (9 September 1888, Charlton, NY—21 December 1976, Bronxville, NY). *Education*: B.A., Union Coll., 1910; M.A., Columbia Univ., 1914; B.D., Union Theol. Sem., 1915. *Career*: ordained minister in Presbyterian Church, USA, 1915; Army chaplain, 1918–19; secretary, Commission on the War and the Religious Outlook, Federal Council of Churches, 1919–20; associate secretary, Federal Council of Churches, 1920–21, general secretary, 1921–50; general secretary, National Council of Churches, 1950–54; executive secretary, New York Office of World Council of Churches, 1954–58.

The churches and their members learned something of Christian unity across America and the globe when the modern ecumenical movement took form in the twentieth century. Cavert, born on a farm in the midst of a conservative Presbyterianism in upstate New York, had much to do with this development. For thirty-four years he headed the Federal Council and then the National Council of Churches, the conciliar shape of ecumenism in the United States, but a model taken seriously by the churches of the world.

Fresh from seminary, he studied in the Far East and learned the role of missions firsthand. As an executive in the Federal Council, he similarly met the Eastern Orthodox churches, thereby enhancing the unitive cause. When European and American churchmen gathered informally in the 1930s to discuss ecumenical organization, it was Cavert who suggested to William Temple the name, "World Council of Churches." When the WCC was inaugurated in 1948, Cavert had an effective hand in the formation. His own career as an ecclesiastical bureaucrat, however, had been shaped by such leaders as Robert E. Speer and William Adams Brown.

In some respects, Cavert lived as a child of his times. He was a thoroughgoing pacifist after World War I. Yet, in an emphasis upon Christian social action, he believed he could roll up his sleeves to help build the Kingdom of God on earth. This evidenced a kind of American pragmatism, although he mated it to the Protestant evangelicalism of the previous century. Before Hitler's National Socialism seized power in Germany in 1933, Cavert foresaw the approaching holocaust. In the postwar period, he supported relief and reconstruction work, acting as Protestant liaison for the U.S. government in Europe. He spent much of his life building bridges between denominations, nations, and persons. He reconstructed relations between the American and German churches. Through his negotiation, Pastor and Mrs. Martin Niemoeller toured the United States in 1946, when even some prominent Americans believed that "the only good German was a dead one." Because of Cavert's persuasion, Karl Barth finally wrote his letter to American Christians—a tract delineating Barth's social, this-worldly views about the war. Through Cavert's leadership, indeed, he brought the American churches into the WCC.

In the 1930s, Cavert discovered the church in a formal, theological fashion; it was his style of moving into a postliberal age. Along with that transition came one of his key contributions, the conciliar ideal. While he never lost hope for organic church union, Cavert declared that councils of churches could yield further fruit, that the conciliar model had never been genuinely explored. In a word, councils might very well lead to the full unity of churches and therefore to the unity of humankind.

BIBLIOGRAPHY:

A. *The American Churches in the Ecumenical Movement 1900–1968* (New York, 1968); *Church Cooperation and Unity in America: A Historical Review, 1900–1970* (New York, 1970); *The Church Through Half a Century* (New York, 1936); *On the Road to Christian Unity* (New York, 1961).

B. CB 1951, 102–4; NYT 23 Dec 1976, 26; *Religious Leaders of America* 2 (New York, 1941), 26; William J. Schmidt, *Architect of Unity: A Biography of Samuel McCrea Cavert* (New York, 1978); WB 1948, 1036.

William J. Schmidt

CECIL, Edgar Algernon Robert Gascoyne (14 September 1864, London—24 November 1958, Tunbridge Wells, England). *Education*: second class in law, Univ. Coll., Oxford Univ. 1886. *Career*: member of Parliament, 1906–10, 1911–23; House of Lords, 1923–58; chairman, Hertfordshire Quarter Sessions, 1911–20; parliamentary under secretary for foreign affairs, 1915–18; minister of blockade, 1916–18; assistant secretary of state for foreign affairs, 1918–19; lord privy seal, 1923; chancellor, Duchy of Lancaster, 1924–27; Nobel Peace Prize, 1937.

A founder of the League of Nations, Cecil was one of its most dedicated champions. He wrote an authoritative account of its rise and decline, *A Great Experiment* (1941), and in the spring of 1946 presided over its formal demise ("The League is dead; long live the United Nations!"). For his work on behalf of the League, Cecil was awarded the Woodrow Wilson Foundation Peace Prize in 1924 and the Nobel Peace Prize in 1937.

As a son of Lord Salisbury, Cecil was destined to become a distinctive public person and hold important offices of state. But between 1914 and 1918 he embraced an idea that gave an unexpected turn to his public career. In September 1916, he drafted a "Memorandum on Proposals for Diminishing the Occasion of Future Wars," which circulated in the Foreign Office and was placed before the Cabinet. That memorandum, and the report of the Phillimore Committee, appointed at Cecil's insistence in 1918, shaped official thinking in Britain and America and formed the basis for the British draft of the Covenant of the League. As a representative at the Paris Peace Conference, Cecil also helped write the final version of the Covenant.

Cecil had no doubt of the importance of the League as a body of enormous collective strength strictly bound by rules of peace and arbitration and under obligation to prevent by joint action the aggression of any peace breaker. If the collective peace system did not replace jungle attitudes in international relations, he saw no hope. The "Great Experiment" became his obsession. He abandoned a traditional political career and accepted a peerage in 1923 (Viscount Cecil of Chelwood) so that he could devote his time to the promotion of the League.

Cecil became a familiar figure at Geneva between the wars, first as a delegate to the League for South Africa (1920–22). He was responsible for League affairs in the first Baldwin governments (1923, 1924–27), although he resigned because he and the majority of the Cabinet differed on disarmament policy. He became chairman of a committee on League affairs in the Foreign Office and deputy leader of Assembly delegations during the second Labor government, 1929–31. Cecil was also chiefly responsible for the Draft Treaty of Mutual Assistance, an ingenious scheme of disarmament and mutual defense based on a regional group of alliances, which the League Council considered in 1924 but the British government vetoed.

In Great Britain, Cecil was a founder and leader of the League of Nations Union (chairman of the executive committee, 1919–23, and president or joint president, 1923–45), the country's most influential pressure group on foreign affairs. The Union's success in winning the public mind was strikingly apparent in the famous "Peace Ballot" of 1934–35, which Cecil instigated. More than 11.5 million adults voted, with more than 11 million answering "yes" when asked if Britain should remain a member of the League. More than 10 million declared themselves ready to restrain an aggressor by economic action, and nearly 7 million approved the use of military measures should they be necessary.

The Ethiopian War of 1935–36 soon revealed the misleading results of the ballot. Many voters expected the threat of sanctions to deter a peace breaker; they did not show themselves ready to defend the League if it meant war against a major power. Cecil, with Winston Churchill, continued to preach "arms and the Covenant" as the way to secure peace, but the country took other counsel after 1936 and turned to appeasement and limited arming. Cecil never doubted the rightness of his campaign, a conviction reinforced by the message Churchill sent him in 1944 that the war could easily have been prevented if the League of Nations had been used with courage and loyalty by the associated nations. Failure did not embitter Cecil. He was sustained by a positive spirit. In 1941 he wrote on the title page of a copy of his book on the League: "Le jour viendra."

BIBLIOGRAPHY:

A. *All the Way* (London, 1949); *A Great Experiment: An Autobiography* (London, 1941); *The New Outlook* (London, 1919); *Peace and Pacifism* (Oxford, 1938); *The Way of Peace: Essays and Addresses* (London, 1928).

B. Donald S. Birn, *The League of Nations Union, 1918–1945* (Oxford, 1981); Hugh Cecil, "Lord Robert Cecil: A Nineteenth Century Upbringing," *History Today* 25 (Feb. 1975), 118–27; DNB 1951–60, 199–201; George W. Egerton, *Great Britain and the Creation of the League of Nations* (Chapel Hill, NC, 1978); LT 25 Nov 1958, 13; Salvador de Madariaga, *Morning Without Noon: Memoirs* (Westmead, England, 1974); NYT 25 Nov 1958, 33; J. A. Thompson, "Lord Cecil and the Historians," *Historical Journal* 23, no. 3 (1981), 709–15.

C. The Cecil papers are in the British Library.

J. A. Thompson

CHAMBERLAIN, Joseph Perkins (1 October 1873, Cleveland, OH—21 May 1951, New York). *Education*: Harvard Univ. 1894–96; LL.B., Hastings Coll. of Law, 1898; Univs. of Paris, Berlin, and Leipzig, 1898–1900; Ph.D., Columbia Univ., 1923. *Career*: legal practice, San Francisco, 1902–10; lecturer, Univ. of Calif., 1907–8; donor, member, Legislative Drafting Research Fund, 1911–51, director, 1918–51; professor, Columbia Univ., 1923–50.

Chamberlain early established his authority in domestic jurisprudence through his interest in legislative drafting. This led to his personal support of the Legislative Drafting Research Fund at Columbia University in 1911 to help in the writing of laws. He subsequently endowed a professorship of legislation in the Law School and assumed the directorship of the program in 1918. When he completed his doctoral work in 1923 he accepted a professorship in the Political Science Department at Columbia and in 1927 joined the Faculty of Law. He had studied international law in Europe, and during the war he had prepared a study for the Department of State on international rivers. His contacts with his colleague, *James T. Shotwell, thus drew him inevitably into the international area. He helped Shotwell prepare the draft treaty that served as the basis of the Kellogg-Briand Pact.

In the 1920s, Chamberlain also revealed an intense interest in the control of narcotics and slavery. He served on an International Labor Office committee on slavery and forced labor and as a member of the High Commission for Refugees Coming from Germany (1933–35). During World War II he helped thousands of homeless persons resettle in the United States.

Chamberlain's role as an internationalist, however, was not limited to such activities. He commanded respect because of his personality and his logical approach to questions; hence, he was often consulted formally and informally by other internationalists regardless of the topic. His articles reveal an interest in disarmament, neutrality law, and the Manchurian Crisis.

Chamberlain perceived the trend toward world organization as a natural feature of life with the evolution of regulatory agencies, public and private, rules, and courts all moving toward an international society. He believed the trend could be aided by individuals and groups and even by governments through carefully crafted conventions, conferences, and administrative commissions, judicial bodies, and international bureaus and through the careful building of international law.

BIBLIOGRAPHY:

A. "International Organization," *International Conciliation* 385 (Dec 1942), 457–523; *Regime of the International Rivers, Danube and Rhine* (New York, 1923).

B. DAB supp. 5, 107–8; *Foreign Policy Bulletin* 30 (20 Jul 1951), 347; *A History of the School of Law, Columbia University* (New York, 1955); NCAB D, 313–14.

Warren F. Kuehl

CHATTERJEE, Atul Chandra. (24 November 1874, Malda, Lower Bengal —8 September 1955, Bexhill-on-Sea, England). *Education*: B.A., Presidency Coll., Calcutta, 1892; Kings Coll., Cambridge Univ., 1983–95. *Career*: professional diplomat and international civil servant.

Under the Covenant of the League of Nations, self-governing states of the British Dominion gained the full right of membership. Thus, India could send representatives to Geneva to participate in League discussions and serve on its commissions and related bodies. Among these persons, Chatterjee gained the greatest prominence during the interwar years, sitting as a delegate to various League bodies and also working in the Information Section of the Secretariat. He was simple in his taste, a shrewd judge of character, sincere, and direct.

Chatterjee's major interest appeared in his involvement with international labor questions. After intensive debate (1920–22), the Council of the

League agreed to invite India to sit on the Governing Board of the International Labor Organization. Chatterjee became a member of the Board in 1926 and thereafter attained prominence when elected president of the Tenth ILO Conference in 1927 and when chosen in 1932 to chair the Governing Body. He had attended virtually all the ILO conferences from 1919 through 1935, and in holding these prominent positions Chatterjee sought not only to advance India's interests but also to represent fully the concerns and aspirations of the smaller industrial nations. He presided with serenity and impartiality.

Chatterjee became a member of the Permanent Central Opium Board in 1932. His selection reflected confidence in his impartial perspective as well as India's changing role as a producer of raw opium. Well into the 1920s, India had been relatively uncooperative in supporting the League's efforts to limit production and control the traffic in drugs. Chatterjee's appointment represented a significant shift in the policy of the Indian government as well as in public attitudes in India. His impartial position gained him appointment as chair of the Opium Board (1938–46). He also sat as vice-president of the League's Consultative Economic Committee and was a member of the Board of Liquidation (1946–47). Chatterjee long represented India's interests in London, where he held office as high commissioner and other advisory posts.

BIBLIOGRAPHY:

A. *Federalism and Labour Legislation in India* (Montreal, 1944); *The New India* (London, 1948).

B. DNB 1951–60, 212–14; P. P. Pillai, *India and the International Labour Organisation* (Patna, India, 1931); D. N. Verma, *India and the League of Nations* (Patna, India, 1968); WW 1954, 521.

Warren F. Kuehl

CHENG T'ien-hsi [F. T. Cheng] (10 July 1884, Mamoi, near Foochow, China—31 January 1970, Northway, Hampstead, London Garden, England). *Education*: Queens Coll., Hong Kong, 1897–98; LL.B., Cambridge Univ., 1912; LL.D., Univ. of London, 1916. *Career*: law practice, London, 1913–16, Hong Kong, 1917, Shanghai, 1927–32; Ministry of Justice, 1917–19, 1921–24; judge, Supreme Court, 1920; with delegation at Washington Conference, 1921–22; vice-minister of justice, Nanking, 1932–34; cultural mission to England, 1935–36; judge, Permanent Court of International Justice, 1936–45; ambassador to England, 1946–50.

Cheng was the first Chinese student to earn a doctorate in England, writing his dissertation on the "Rules of Private International Law Determining Capacity to Contract." He returned to China, where he translated codes into English while working for the Ministry of Justice. He became involved in the international arena when he attended the Washington Disarmament Conference (1921–22) in an advisory role. He then served on an international judicial commission on extraterritoriality (1926) to investigate whether the Chinese legal system could adapt to the abolishment of extra-territorial jurisdiction. He also participated in conferences on penal law.

Cheng's service on the Permanent Court of International Justice was not notable, largely because of the breakdown of confidence in international law in the late 1930s. He did disclose some independence of thought when he joined neither the majority nor dissenting judges but offered separate opinions. During the war, the Court left The Hague for Switzerland. In 1946 he served on the Board of Liquidation (1945–46) that closed the League of Nations and transferred its assets to the United Nations. He also participated in the shift of the PCIJ to the International Court of Justice. He chose not to return to China after his ambassadorship to England ended in 1950. His international involvements culminated in an appointment to the Permanent Court of Arbitration in 1950 and to a UN panel for inquiry and conciliation. Cheng was noted for his dedication to the principles of law and to those of Confucius and for his public service.

BIBLIOGRAPHY:

A. *East and West: Episodes in a Sixty Years' Journey* (London, 1951); *Reflections at Eighty* (Washington, 1966); *The Rules of Private International Law Determining Capacity to Contract* (London, 1916).

B. IWW 1951, 157; LT 2 Feb 1970, 10; WWW 1961–70, 200.

Warren F. Kuehl

CHERRINGTON, Ben Mark (1 November 1885, Gibbon, NE—2 May 1980, Denver, CO). *Education*: Nebraska Wesleyan Coll., 1904–5; B.A., Univ. of Nebraska, 1911; M.A., Univ. of California, Berkeley, 1917; Ph.D. Columbia Univ. 1934. *Career*: YMCA work, West Coast, 1911–18, national secretary, YMCA 1919–26; director, Foundation for the Advancement of the Social Sciences, Univ. of Denver, 1926–51; Division of Cultural Relations, Department of State, 1938–39; chancellor, Univ. of Denver, 1943–46; Department of State, UNESCO Relations, 1946; director, Regional Office, Institute of International Education, 1951–69.

Cherrington began the first phase of his internationalist career when as a YMCA national secretary he aided +Sherwood Eddy in planning his European seminars. The second phase emerged in 1926, when he became the first director of the newly established Foundation for the Advancement of the Social Sciences at the University of Denver. When Cherrington solicited the opinion of nearly two hundred world leaders as to the worthiest program for that organization, he employed a basic strategy that marked his entire career—copious consultation. It was the result of this compendium of opinion that set the Foundation on the path of the study of world affairs, a decision that was to bring unusual levels of sophistication to the people of heartland Middle America.

That the Foundation became such an effective instrument of adult education in world affairs was the result of Cherrington's deep-seated belief in the cardinal importance of an informed electorate, particularly its lay leadership, this in turn stemming from a nondogmatic, personal, but profound New Testament belief in the ultimate value and victory of the human spirit. These concepts appeared when in 1938 Cherrington accepted *Cordell Hull's invitation to give leadership to a new division of Cultural Relations in the Department of State. An Advisory Board, drawn from the nation's educational and cultural leadership, was immediately appointed, designed not only to secure their expertise in policy making but also to enlist their aid in assuring their constituency that this division had been designed for and would be responsive to the interests of cultural organizations in reciprocal contacts with their international peers.

So strongly did Cherrington believe in the value of "people to people" programs that he proposed to have them removed from the aegis of the State Department, sensing that any program emanating from a source so clearly identified with even enlightened self-interest could be viewed with suspicion by other nationals, curtailing thereby the all-important reciprocal nature of these relationships. He was defeated in this, and was again when, at the close of the war as a member of the Board of Advisers he urged that the program, though kept within State, at least be separated from those responsible for programs of propaganda.

When the concept that was to become UNESCO emerged from the United Nations meeting in San Francisco, Cherrington, an adviser to the U.S. delegation, envisioned enormous possibilities for international reciprocal cultural exchange if the program could be kept free of national political pressures. When asked by State to help organize U.S. participation in UNESCO, the design that emerged had many of the Cherrington hallmarks—a National Commission of one hundred, drawn for the most part from nongovernmental organizations. This group would formulate advisory policy, but it would also maintain a host of channels to the membership of hundreds of lay organizations. Once again Cherrington waged his quiet war to free the Commission from any taint of national political pressure. Again, he was defeated. Before his death, Cherrington witnessed with growing sadness the politicization of UNESCO and its consequent crumbling effectiveness, though by governments largely other than his own. The irony was that the tragedy was in itself a demonstration of the validity of the "Cherrington principle."

By then Cherrington was nearing the close of his third internationalist career as a regional director and continuing adviser to the Institute of International Education. This last devotion, from which he retired at eighty-two, was his final affirmation of a faith that had permeated his work, that the defenses of peace must be built in the minds of people.

BIBLIOGRAPHY:

A. *Inter-American Cultural Relations* (Washington, 1939); *Methods in Education in International Attitudes* (New York, 1934); *The Social Science Foundation of the University of Denver: A Personal Recollection* (Denver, 1973).

B. NYT 6 May 1980, III-12.
C. The Cherrington papers are in the Penrose Library, Univ. of Denver.

Russell Porter

CHISHOLM, George Brock (18 May 1896, Oakville, ON—2 February 1971, Victoria, BC). *Education*: M.D., Univ. of Toronto, 1924; postgraduate medical studies, London, 1924–25, 1933–34, Yale Univ., 1931–33. *Career*: general practice, Oakville, ON, 1925–31; psychiatric practice, Toronto, 1934–40; director-general, Canadian Army Medical Services, 1942–44; deputy minister, Department of National Health and Welfare, Ottawa, 1944–46; general practice, 1954–57; Canadian representative and chairman, Administration and Finance Committee, International Health Conference, New York, 1946; Canadian representative and rapporteur, Technical Preparatory Committee, International Health Conference, Paris, 1946; executive secretary, Interim Commission, World Health Organization, 1946–48, director-general, 1948–53; president, World Federation for Mental Health, 1957–58; vice-president, World Association of World Federalists, 1958.

As a psychiatrist concerned about the world, Chisholm argued that, while great scientific advances had been made, the human species remained socially underdeveloped. People were still operating with outmoded concepts of human relations. Human problems were more often emotional than physical. Such views made Chisholm a controversial figure, a situation he relished. He believed it was absolutely necessary to face reality, and he set about obliging people to do so. He criticized aspects of most moral codes, insisting that true ideals should serve genuine needs. Fantasy and fiction should be set aside. The inclination to gloss over topics people found difficult to discuss was a serious error. The inclination to label certain things as bad or sinful encouraged despising, condemnation, and severe action that was unnecessarily destructive and that bred anxiety and aggression. In the face of biological and atomic warfare, Chisholm argued, many of the wisdoms and accepted practices of the past were invalid. Society had to be restructured. There had to be a rejection of the generally accepted concept of competitive survival and a recognition of the need for cooperative survival.

While Chisholm conceded that war was inherent in human nature, people could be freed from the mass neurosis that led them to fight. The basic human objectives were to survive, to live well, and to reproduce. History recorded the formation and development of survival groups from small primitive units to elaborate states sustained by nationalism. Then technology gave man the capability to annihilate life, and that made nationalism no longer viable. It had to be discarded in favor of internationalism; the only survival unit was the global community. Annihilation was the antithesis of humanity; what was left were the absolute terms of peace.

Health, according to Chisholm was the basis of all human conditions. Without it all other elements of social development would be handicapped. He felt there was a global responsibility for health, that the world has the resources, if managed properly, to give all people the basic requirements of life and that failure to do so was to court disaster. The constitution of the World Health Organization (WHO), although devised by a committee, bears the imprint of Chisholm's work. It embodies the ideals and objectives he sought to establish, that health is "a state of complete physical, mental and social well-being and not merely the absence of disease or infirmity," that it is one of the essential rights of every human being, and that "the health of all people is fundamental to the attainment of peace and security." The WHO thus was directed to harness the resources of many nations to cope with any health problem of whatever scale, and Chisholm, in his administrative positions, planned its first campaign against disease and for maternal and child care and adequate nutrition. While blunt, Chisholm had the ability to organize and to persuade; however, his controversial manner cut short his time in public office.

BIBLIOGRAPHY:

A. *Barriers to World Health* (New York, 1953); *Can People Learn to Learn?* (New York, 1958); "The Individual's Responsibility for World Peace," *Bulletin of the Meninger Clinic* 12 (May 1948), 73–80; "Organization for World Health," *Mental Hygiene* 32 (Jul 1948), 364–71; *Prescription for Survival* (New York, 1957); "Reestablishment of Peacetime Society: The William Alanson White Memorial Lectures, Second Series," *Psychiatry* 9 (Feb 1946), 1–35; "Social Responsibility: The Kurt Lewin Memorial Lecture," *Journal of Social Issues,* supp. series 1 (Dec 1948), 6–13; "This Man Is Dangerous," *Weekend Magazine* 12 (28 Apr 1962), 2–3; "World Health Organization," *British Medical Journal* 1 (6 May 1950), 1021–27.

B. Robert Baker, "Two Billions Call Him Doctor," *Maclean's Magazine* 63 (1 May 1950), 21, 49+; CB 1948, 104–6; CWW 1967–69, 189–90.

C. Chisholm papers are in the Public Archives of Canada.

Ian Casselman

CHOU Ken-sheng [S. R. Chow] (1888, Changsha, Hunan—20 April 1971, Peking). *Education*: M.A., Edinburgh Univ., 1918; LL.D., Univ. of Paris, 1920. *Career*: professor and dean, Univs. of Peiping and Wuhan; member of legislature, Yuan; professor, Nanking Central Univ., 1935–42; president, Wuhan Univ., 1945–50; member, National Asembly, 1946; adviser, Foreign Ministry, 1950; vice-director of proposed law committee, Chinese National People's Congress, 1964.

Chow as a noted professor of the science of law in China was not only engaged in its scientific aspects but also concerned about its relation to peace. In a letter of 1947 he said he had been an advocate of world peace for more than thirty years. Yet the aggression China faced often forced him to abandon that quest. During World War II, he saw China as strategically important in the struggle against Fascism and worked to obtain military supplies. Leaving his family, he went to the United States to seek aid. At the end of 1944, when the U.S. and British governments underestimated the importance of China militarily and lessened their aid, Chow considered this as not only dangerous but a decision that would prolong the war. Chow feared that another destructive conflict could come. He, unlike other Chinese leaders, did not believe that the Soviet Union posed any special threat, and he hoped a more cooperative world would emerge. From 1939, he had participated in annual meetings of the Institute of Pacific Relations, and he had developed a plan for a regional Pacific association of nations. It would have an administrative council, a judicial system, a military staff, and an armed force. Sanctions, both economic and military, should be applied against aggressors. Chow served as adviser to the Chinese delegation at the UN Conference in 1945, participated in meetings of the World Federation of UN Associations, and after 1958 became active in the Chinese People's Committee for World Peace.

BIBLIOGRAPHY:

A. *Le Contrôle parlementaire de la politique étrangère en Angleterre, en France et aux Etats-Unis* (Paris, 1920); *Winning the Peace in the Pacific* (New York, 1944).

B. *Chinese Encyclopedia Yearbook* (Tapei, Taiwan, 1980), 124; *People's Daily* 7 Feb 1979, 4; *Selected letters of Hoo Shih* (Peking, 1980); *Who's Who in China* (Shanghai, 1936), 57; *Who's Who in Communist China* (Kowloon, Hong Kong, 1966), 147–48; Edith Wynner and Georgia Lloyd, *Searchlights on Peace Plans: Choose Your Own Road to World Government* (New York, 1944).

Shong Li-Ling

CHOW Kêng-shêng. See Chou Ken-sheng.

CLARK, Grenville (5 November 1882, New York—12 January 1967, Dublin, N.H). *Education*: B.A., Harvard Coll., 1903; LL.B., Harvard Univ., 1906. *Career*: attorney, New York, 1906–67; founder, Military Training Camps Association, 1915–16; chair, National Emergency Committee for Selective Service, 1940–41; chair, Citizens' Committee for National War Service, 1944–45; member, President and Fellows of Harvard College, 1931–50; chair, Bill of Rights Committee, American Bar Association, 1938–40; a founder of United World Federalists, 1947.

Sometimes called a "statesman incognito" because of the anonymous influence he wielded through his membership in the East Coast Establishment, Clark used his Wall Street and Harvard connections to champion such causes as military preparedness and civil rights before becoming involved in the World Federalist movement during World War II. At the request of Harvard President James B. Conant, Clark first published in the autumn of 1939 a pamphlet calling for a federal union of all democratic countries, proposals similar to Clarence Streit's "Union Now" movement. Although he devoted his main energies to military intervention and War Department consulting over the next few years, Clark in 1944 urged the creation of a postwar international organization with universal membership and sufficient powers to enforce disarmament and prevent war. He criticized the Dumbarton Oaks and San Francisco Conferences for being too respectful of national sovereignty, and Clark's backstage efforts at San Francisco were partly responsible for including Article CIX of the UN Charter and its provision for amendment and Charter review. In August 1945 Clark convoked the Dublin (NH) Conference, which brought together such young World Federalists as Norman Cousins, Alan Cranston, and Cord Meyer, Jr., and called for the transformation of the UN Charter to create a limited world government because of the revolutionary impact of atomic weapons.

Clark took on the dual role of theoretician and backstage activist in his international efforts after 1945. Mostly in collaboration with Louis B. Sohn, he attempted to chart legal and diplomatic scenarios for achieving world government through revision of the UN Charter, disarmament treaties, or the creation of a world development organization. Although Clark always recognized the gap between his goal of world peace under world law and the existing system of national rivalries, he hoped that a crisis, like Cuba in 1962, would convince statesmen that radical change was necessary. He used his contacts to push national policies in the proper direction. Through his cousin Senator Joseph S. Clark and White House adviser John J. McCloy, Clark helped shape disarmament strategy during the Kennedy administration. Through Averell Harriman and Edgar Snow, he nearly gained admission to the People's Republic of China in 1964, where, at age eighty-two, he planned to discuss disarmament with Chinese leaders. He endowed the World Law Fund with $500,000 in the early 1960s, thus launching the continuing World Order Models Project. He was twice nominated for the Nobel Peace Prize before his death in 1967.

BIBLIOGRAPHY:

A. *A Federation of Free Peoples* (New York, 1939); *A Plan for Peace* (New York, 1950); with Louis B. Sohn, *World Peace Through World Law* (Cambridge, MA, 1958; rev. eds., 1960, 1966).

B. J. Garry Clifford, *The Citizen Soldiers: The Plattsburg Training Camp Movement, 1913–1920* (Lexington, KY, 1973); J. Garry Clifford and Norman Cousins, eds., *Memoirs of a Man: Grenville Clark* (New York, 1975); Irving Dilliard, "Grenville Clark: Public Citizen," *American Scholar* 33 (Winter 1963–64), 97–104; NYT 13 Jan 1967, 27.

C. The Clark papers are at Dartmouth Coll.

J. Garry Clifford

CLARKE, John Hessin (18 September 1857, New Lisbon (now Lisbon), OH—22 March 1945, San Diego, CA). *Education*: B.A., Western Reserve Coll., 1877. *Career*: corporation and railroad attorney, Youngstown and Cleveland, OH; Democratic candidate for U.S. Senate, 1903, 1914; editorial writer, *Youngstown Vindicator,* 1889–1929; judge, Federal District

Court of the Northern District of Ohio, 1914–16; associate justice, U.S. Supreme Court, 1916–22; a founder and first president, League of Nations Non-Partisan Association, 1922–28.

Clarke's career as an active internationalist began following his retirement from the Supreme Court in September 1922 at age sixty-five. However, his internationalist sympathies had been of long standing. He had been an advocate of free trade since the 1890s and had backed arbitration treaties and mediation efforts. Not surprisingly, he thus became an early advocate of an association of nations to enforce peace and spoke in behalf of such a commitment by the United States to the American Bar Association in August 1918. A lifelong Democrat and an admirer of *Woodrow Wilson, Clarke readily endorsed the League of Nations Covenant. He refused to accept as final the defeat of "Wilson's League" by the U.S. Senate in 1919–20, or the so-called repudiation by the voters in the election of 1920.

On the Supreme Court he felt restrained by his judicial position and by the partisan nature of the League battle; but once retired he determined to do what he could to revive the League cause in a nonpartisan way. He cooperated in a plan to bring together prominent League supporters, regardless of party, to press for early entry with such modifications, if necessary, of the League Covenant on which all could agree. There was a substantial response to the announcement of his plan from pro-League Republicans as well as Democrats. Assisted by *Hamilton Holt, *Everett Colby, and others who had long been active in organizing pro-League forces, the League of Nations Non-Partisan Association was formed in December 1922 with Clarke as president and *George W. Wickersham as head of the council. However, to attract Wickersham and others and thereby broaden support, Clarke had had to abandon an agreement on specific modifications and to accept a statement innocuous enough not to offend any League partisan.

The new Association began with great promise. It had access to membership lists and other facilities of its immediate predecessors, and growth in membership exceeded expectations. Initially it was well financed by wealthy donors. A man of means, Clarke paid his own travel expenses on speaking tours and contributed substantial sums. Speakers carried the League message into cities and small towns to develop a grass-roots constituency in hopes of forcing the politicians to reopen the issue. In this the Association failed. At the national party conventions of 1924, the Republicans ignored the League of Nations and the Democrats refused to pledge the party to membership, calling instead for a national referendum on the issue. Again in 1928 the Association met the same rebuff, only with a more decisive rejection by both parties. Even U.S. membership in the World Court, which Clarke and the Association supported as second best, eventually failed in the Senate.

Clarke resigned as president in January 1928 and more and more dropped out of its affairs. Although not a strong leader, he had contributed the prestige of his name and his talents as a speaker and had given generously. The failure of the League cause in the 1920s was not the fault of Clarke or his fellow workers. It was the result of factors over which they had little or no control: the sectional and class limitations of their appeal; the deep divisions among partisans over the use of force; and the distractions of more appealing domestic issues. In spite of the failure to achieve their immediate goal, Clarke and his associates did educate the public on the aims and methods of an international organization like the League of Nations, and they kept alive the hope that became manifest in 1945. It is ironic that Clarke died in March 1945, on the eve of the San Francisco Conference, which gave birth to the United Nations.

BIBLIOGRAPHY:

A. *America and World Peace* (New York, 1925); "A Call to Service: The Duty of the Bench and Bar to Aid in Securing a League of Nations to Enforce the Peace of the World," *American Bar Association Journal* 4 (Oct 1918), 568–82; "What I Am Trying to Do," *World's Work* 46 (Oct 1923), 581–84; "Woodrow Wilson, the World Court and the League of Nations," *Congressional Record* 74 (27 Jan 1931), 3268–72.

B. DAB supp. 3, 167–68; NCAB A, 248; Hoyt Landon Warner, *The Life of Mr. Justice Clarke: A Testament to The Power of Liberal Dissent in America* (Cleveland, OH, 1959).

H. Landon Warner

COBDEN, Richard. See *Biographical Dictionary of Modern Peace Leaders.*

COHEN GALLERSTEIN, Benjamin Alberto (18 March 1896, Concepción, Chile—12 March 1960, New York). *Education*: graduate, Univ. of Chile, 1912; M.S., Georgetown Univ., 1927. *Career*: reporter, contributor, and editor, *La Razón, La Mañana,* and *El Mercurio* daily newspapers, Santiago; reporter, *El Sur,* Concepción, 1912–16; secretary, commissions to settle disputes, Tacna–Arica, 1923, 1927, Bolivia–Paraguay, 1929; Guatemala–Honduras, 1931–33; Mixed Claims Commission of Italy, Spain and Germany against Mexico, 1927–32; member, Chilean delegations to Pan American Conferences, 1923, 1928, 1933, 1938; chief interpreter, Pan American Conference on Arbitration and Conciliation, 1929, World Highway and other congresses, 1930–31; faculty, School of Foreign Service, Georgetown Univ., 1927–31; Chilean Legation in Washington, 1923–27; chargé d'affaires and counselor, Mexico, 1932, Washington, 1933; ministry of foreign affairs, Chile, 1936–39; ambassador to Bolivia, 1939–45, to Venezuela, 1946; UN posts, including Preparatory Commission, 1946, assistant secretary-general in charge of Department of Trusteeship and Information for Non-self-governing Territories, 1951–58; delegate to UN, 1958–60.

Cohen represents the dedicated professional who spent much of his life working to advance the machinery of international cooperation. This amiable Chilean, fluent in Spanish, Portuguese, English, and French, and competent in German and Russian, became a perpetual traveling salesman for the ideals of the United Nations after working many years as an interpreter and member of delegations trying to resolve boundary disputes in the Western Hemisphere. In March 1948 he told an interviewer that, while people tended to emphasize the spectacular at the UN, insufficient attention was given to it constructive work and achievements. He could not understand why differing political philosophies could not coexist just as different races and religions did. While the big powers assumed primary responsibility and obtained the so-called special rule of unanimity or veto power in the UN, it was not the machinery of the organization that failed to operate but rather the governments, which did not employ the machinery or the spirit they had agreed upon. It was thus important, Cohen felt, for UN agencies to let the public know what they were doing. That would gain public support and facilitate agreement and compromise.

Cohen sought to expand the publications, radio programs, and promotional facilities of the UN both in New York and major cities around the world so that the press would know more about the organization. That was necessary because of "generally distorted reportage," which he attributed to "special national interests" and the high cost of transmitting and publishing international information.

BIBLIOGRAPHY:

B. CB 1948, 109–11; *New Republic* 114 (11 Apr 1946), 29; *New York Herald Tribune* 15 Apr 1946, 15; NYT 13 Mar 1960, 86; *United Nations Weekly Bulletin* 1 (23 Sep 1946), 19; WWLA 1947, 4, 71–72; WWUN 1951, 89–90.

Neale J. Pearson

COLBAN, Erik Andreas (16 October 1876, Oslo—28 March 1956, Oslo). *Education*: law degree, Univ. of Oslo, 1899. *Career*: deputy judge, Romsdal, Norway, 1899–1900; entered Norwegian ministry of consular affairs, 1903; Norwegian legation, Paris, 1905; vice-consul, Le Havre, 1906; head, Consular Office of Norwegian Foreign Ministry, 1907–8; first secretary, Stockholm legation, 1908–11; chargé d'affaires, Kiev, 1911; consul-general, Rio de Janeiro, 1911–16; foreign ministry, 1916–17; special mission to London, 1917, to London and Paris as adviser on postwar reconstruction, 1918–19; Secretariat of the League of Nations, 1919–30; minister to France, 1930, to Belgium and Luxemburg, 1931–34; minister/ambassador to Great Britain, 1934–46; chair, Preparatory Commission for International Trade Organization and commission chairman of the Havana Conference, 1946–47; personal representative of UN secretary-general on commission dealing with the Kashmir question, 1948–50.

Linguist, jurist, and diplomat, Colban played a major role during the first ten formative years of the League of Nations. As head of the Administrative and Minorities Section, his duties also included the problems of the Saar and of Danzig. Colban directed the negotiations that brought the three new Baltic states into the League, headed the talks leading to the German–Polish Convention that accompanied the partition of Upper Silesia, and arranged for the Greco–Turkish population exchanges in Asia Minor. In his capacity as the League's expert on minorities questions, Colban made frequent visits to the capitals of Eastern Europe to observe conditions, investigate complaints, and confer with government leaders.

Although heading one of the smallest offices of the Secretariat, Colban established an important archive. He also played an activist role as negotiator between the great powers and drafted many of the Council's resolutions pertaining to the areas of his administration. Known for his stern fairness, Colban embodied the spirit of the League's international civil service in the 1920s. As the representative of a small, neutral state, he combined idealism with the practical necessity of maintaining international harmony and the cooperation of great and small powers. His strongest critics in Berlin and Budapest who championed the rights of their ethnic kin could not fault his energy or impartiality but only his penchant for practical compromises. The League's system for discreet, often secret agreements hid Colban's accomplishments as well.

In 1928 Colban moved on briefly to direct the Disarmament Section, just then at the center of world clamor for prompt international control and reduction of armaments. Although he rejoined the Norwegian diplomatic service in 1930, Colban remained an important figure at Geneva, representing his government on the League of Nations Council and at the World Disarmament Conference. Hardy, knowledgeable, and astute, his main contribution was the establishment and implementation of procedures during the interwar period for the international protection of minority rights. However, after his departure, and with the eruption of the violent quarrels of the 1930s, the League system proved inadequate to protect either minorities or their governments. Returning to international service in 1946, Colban tried to help in the settlement of the Kashmir problem.

BIBLIOGRAPHY:

A. *Femti jar* (Oslo, 1952); "La Società della nazioni ed il problema della minoranze," *Nuova Antologia* 242 (16 July 1925), 171–81; "The Minorities Problem," *Norseman* 2 (Sep–Oct 1944), 310–26.

B. Carole K. Fink, "The Weimar Republic as the Defender of Minorities 1919–1933," dissertation, Yale Univ., 1968; IWW 1954, 173; LT 29 Mar 1956, 14; *Norsk Biografisk Leksikon* 3, 51–52; *United Nations Weekly Bulletin* 2 (18 Feb 1947), 140; WWUN 1951, 92; WWW, 1951–60, 226–27.

Carole Fink

COLBY, Bainbridge (22 December 1869, St. Louis, MO—11 April 1950, Bemus Point, NY). *Education*: B.A., Williams Coll., 1890; Columbia Univ., 1890–91; LL.B., New York Law School, 1892. *Career*: admitted to

New York Board and vice-president, U.S. Shipping Board Emergency Fleet, 1917–19; member, American Mission to the Inter-Allied Conference at Paris, 1917; secretary of state, 1920–21; law partner of *Woodrow Wilson, 1921–23.

As a lawyer, Colby served as counsel in a number of noted cases, including the Samuel Clemens (Mark Twain) suit against a publishing house and the reform of the Equitable Life Assurance Society. In 1912 he broke from the Republican party to support *Theodore Roosevelt and the Progressive party. Colby was a candidate for governor of New York in the 1912 Progressive state convention and ran as that party's nominee for U.S. senator in 1914 and in 1916.

Colby made another significant political break in 1916 when he supported Woodrow Wilson for reelection. He formed a committee of Progressives to cooperate with the Democratic National Committee. That action earned him appointment to the U.S. Shipping Board in 1917. President Wilson's confidence in him was reflected in the use of Colby as an intermediary to work with *William Howard Taft and the League to Enforce Peace in 1918. Colby's message was for that organization not to move too rapidly on League issues so as not to embarrass the president. Colby was appointed a member of the American Mission to the Inter-Allied Conference at Paris in November 1917.

After dismissing *Robert Lansing as secretary of state, Wilson surprised most of his advisers in selecting Colby as Lansing's successor. The new secretary of state was almost totally without diplomatic experience. Because of Wilson's impaired state of health, he chose Colby for his loyalty, his idealism, and his ability as a speaker and a writer. Colby furthermore had a reputation as being someone who was in command of the type of information the president wanted. Unlike Wilson's two previous secretaries of state, Colby established a satisfactory working relationship with the president with mutual respect and affection. With the decline of *Edward House's influence, the president tended to rely more on Colby. The State Department played a more important role during his tenure as secretary of state.

Being secretary of state for less than a year, Colby had little opportunity to develop or shape a foreign policy of his own. He did pave the way for the succeeding administration to deal with some major problems. The first was to cooperate with Great Britain in containing Japanese expansionists' plans in Manchuria and Siberia. He did extend American influence through the Mesopotamia Note with the proposition that American oil companies should have equality of treatment and opportunity to oil resources in the Near East. Under Colby, the U.S. government did formulate the policy of nonrecognition of the Communist government in Russia. His most important contribution was the easing of U.S. control of the Caribbean. Colby's Pan American trip in 1920 was widely hailed for the good will established and the stimulus it gave to Pan Americanism. Although briefly on the center stage of American diplomacy, Colby did deal with many important events. Undoubtedly he was handicapped by the incapacity of the president as well as the failure of the United States to join the League of Nations.

BIBLIOGRAPHY:

A. *The Close of Woodrow Wilson's Administration and the Final Years* (New York, 1930).

B. BDUSEB 1774–1977, 67–68; *Encyclopedia Americana* 1979, 218; NYT 12 Apr 1950, 1; Daniel M. Smith, *Aftermath of War: Bainbridge Colby and Wilsonian Diplomacy, 1920–1921* (Philadelphia, 1970), 171; John Spargo, "Bainbridge Colby," in S. F. Bemis, ed., *The American Secretaries of State and Their Diplomacy,* 10 (New York, 1928), 179–218; WWWA 3, 171.

C. The Colby papers are in the Manuscript Division, Library of Congress.

Leon E. Boothe

COLBY, Everett (10 September 1874, Milwaukee, WI—19 June 1943, Montclair, NJ). *Education*: Ph.B., Brown Univ., 1897, M.A., 1906; LL.B., New York Law School, 1900. *Career*: lawyer-broker, New York, 1901– c. 1935; New Jersey House of Assembly, 1903–5; New Jersey Senate, 1906–9; Republican National Committee, various periods, 1916–35.

Interest in international cooperation stemmed naturally, in Colby's case, from his activities as a civic and political reformer in New Jersey. Although born to wealth, he came gradually to devote much of his time and energy to public issues. On the national scene, he supported the candidate of the Progressive party in 1912 but returned to the Republican fold in 1916 to aid *Charles Evans Hughes, fellow alumnus and trustee of Brown University, in the conviction that Hughes could best guide the ship of state through the rocks and shoals of a world at war.

After a wartime assignment with the Food Administration in Washington and overseas service with the Army Tank Corps, Colby became an active member of the League to Enforce Peace. Association with *Hamilton Holt, and later with *John H. Clarke and others, strengthened his growing belief that an association of nations was essential to world order. He wrote articles and spoke widely during 1919 on the meaning of the Covenant of the League of Nations. He remained loyal to his party in 1920 and voted for Warren G. Harding because he believed the Statement of the 31 that support for Harding would result in fuller world cooperation. His ensuing disappointment led him in 1922, on dissolution of the League to Enforce Peace, to become one of the founders of the League of Nations Non-Partisan Committee. When the Committee gave way, early in 1923, to the League of Nations Non-Partisan Association, Colby was named chairman of the Executive Committee. He proved his allegiance to the Association in 1924 by bolting his party to support *John W. Davis, the Democratic candidate. Colby continued to speak out and write on behalf of U.S. entry to the League of Nations for the next decade and was active on the National

World Court Committee. Concerned about the buildup of armaments in Central Europe, he visited Germany in 1934 and, after meeting Hitler, termed him unintelligent but sane. Observing the Soviet experiment at firsthand, he was much impressed and came home to support enthusiastically the United States' recognition of the Soviet regime. Among other causes espoused by Colby was temperance through education, rather than legislation, which he promoted in the 1930s as president of an advisory board of the Council for Moderation.

Although less active in his later years, Colby never ceased his public support of the League of Nations or his opposition to the isolationist sentiment that was growing rapidly among his conservative colleagues. By every test, Colby was in the internationalist camp between the wars, but mainly as a supporter, a follower, and not in the dynamic role that his early maverick years as a reform leader seemed to promise. While at times in the early 1930s he wavered over U.S. membership, he declared in 1935 that he had never lost his faith that the collective security idea as embodied in the League of Nations would ultimately triumph.

BIBLIOGRAPHY:

A. "Charles E. Hughes," *Scribner's Magazine* 83 (May 1928), 553–67; *The League of Nations and Mussolini: Address Delivered Before the Philadelphia Baptist Association, October 12, 1923* (New York, [1924]); *The Political Issues of the Coming Campaign: Address Delivered Before the Brown Union, Brown University, Providence, R.I., Feb. 29, 1916* (n.p., 1916).

B. Ruhl J. Bartlett, *The League to Enforce Peace* (Chapel Hill, NC, 1944); Warren F. Kuehl, *Hamilton Holt: Journalist, Internationalist, Educator* (Gainesville, FL, 1960); *New Jersey's First Citizens and State Guide, 1919–1920* (Paterson, NJ, 1919), 2, 526–27; NYT 20 Jun 1943, 35; Lincoln Steffens, "The Gentleman from Essex," *McClure's*, 26 (Feb 1906), 421–33; H. Landon Warner, *The Life of Mr. Justice Clarke: A Testament to The Power of Liberal Dissent in America* (Cleveland, OH, 1959).

David W. Hirst

COLCORD, Samuel (14 November, 1849, Greenville, IL—23 September 1938, St. Johnland, NY). *Education*: Illinois Coll., 1866–69; *Career*: minister, Brooklyn and New York, 1873–80; realtor, 1880–1918.

Colcord, who became wealthy as a New York City realtor, decided in 1918 to devote his life and fortune to the cause of peace; and he seized upon promoting U.S. membership in the League of Nations as the formula to that end. Thereafter, with singular devotion, he not only campaigned vigorously to convince the American people of the merits of the League but also engaged in public confrontations with those he perceived as its enemies. In the latter role, Colcord was not particularly discriminatory, attacking alike isolationists and those internationalists who advocated moderate or gradual approaches to membership. His long expository letters abound in the collections of almost every public figure who might have had some influence.

He began his campaigns during the treaty fight of 1919–20, when he sought to persuade *Woodrow Wilson and the Senate to compromise on the basis of reservations. He carried the struggle into the election of 1920 where, as a Republican, Colcord supported Warren G. Harding by arguing that the irreconcilables would control the new president if the internationalists abandoned him. When Harding repudiated the League of Nations, Colcord responded with *The Great Deception* (1921), in which he reviewed the election and denounced Harding's contention that the vote had been a mandate against League membership. It was still possible, he argued, for the administration to take constructive steps toward the League.

To carry on the fight, Colcord formed the Committee on Educational Publicity early in 1922 and obtained an illustrious roster of internationalists as sponsors. This nonpartisan agency produced advertising, pamphlets, and original articles to promote peace, to correct false information about the League, and to endorse efforts to advance international cooperation. Colcord personally favored by then any action that would bring greater participation with the League. Since it was largely supported by Colcord, the Committee's work, in a flood of pamphlets and Colcord letters, reflected his special interests. He supported the Washington Conference (1921–22), campaigns for membership on the World Court, and the outlawry of war concept promoted by the Kellogg-Briand Pact. He suggested that it be opened to other countries and acclaimed it as a significant step toward peace.

It is difficult to assess Colcord's significance. There is little evidence that his intense devotion influenced political leaders, and it often alienated other internationalists, who believed in more careful and diplomatic approaches in building support for the League and the World Court. Yet Colcord's massive publicity effort had to have been of some importance in keeping issues and ideas alive in the public mind.

BIBLIOGRAPHY:
A. *The Great Deception* (New York, 1921).
B. NYT 24 Sep 1938, 17.

Warren F. Kuehl

COLORNI, Eugenio (22 April 1909, Milan—30 May 1944, Rome). *Education*: degrees in philosophy and literature, Univ. of Milan, 1933. *Career*: professor Instituto Magistrale, Trieste, Italy; anti-Fascist political activist, journalist.

Belonging to the generation that grew up under Fascism, Colorni was one of the many persons who became disillusioned with the regime in the 1930s. His political opposition was intensified by the Fascist anti-Semitic legislation in 1938, which barred Colorni, a Jew, from professional advancement. Arrested in 1938 for anti-Fascist activity, he spent several months in jail, after which he was confined to the island of Ventotene, a detention center for the regime's opponents. There he came into contact with other dissidents, like Altiero Spinelli and *Ernesto Rossi, who were reflecting on the causes for the interwar international crises and trying to work out a program for a new European order to neutralize the rampant nationalism of the 1920s and 1930s. They found inspiration in *Luigi Einaudi's "Junius" letters, written in 1918, supporting the idea of a United States of Europe, and for them at that time the United States and the U.S. Articles of Confederation and Constitution provided models for the organization of a future European federation.

Transferred to Melfi on the mainland, Colorni contrived to escape and made his way to Rome in May 1943. There he organized a federalist group that published the first issue of the clandestine newspaper, *L'Unità europea: Voce del Movimeto Federalista Europeo.* He also became active in the resistance movement after the armistice in September 1943 as a member of the resurgent Socialist party and editor of its underground newspaper, *Avanti!* On 27 August, 1943, he and others met in Milan and organized the Italian section of the European Federalist Movement. In 1944 Colorni wrote the introduction to a secretly printed pamphlet setting forth the federalist program.

A member of the Executive Committee of the Socialist party, Colorni nonetheless was critical of orthodox Marxism. The European internecine problems and dissensions that had culminated in World War I were far too complex to be explained solely in terms of class warfare. These speculations led him increasingly to see European federation as the sole means of putting an end to the national rivalries and quarrels that had generated two conflicts since 1914.

A few days before the liberation of Rome by the Allies, Colorni, on his way to a meeting of the Executive Committee of the Socialist party, was followed and assassinated by a member of the notorious Koch band, which operated in Nazi-controlled Rome. He was posthumously awarded a gold medal for valor on 25 April 1946.

BIBLIOGRAPHY:

A. Introduction to A. S. [Altiero Spinelli] and E. R. [Ernesto Rossi], *Problemi della federazione europea* (Rome, 1944).

B. Charles F. Delzell, "The European Federalist Movement in Italy: First Phase, 1918-1947," *Journal of Modern History* 32 (Sept 1960), 241-50; *Enciclopedia italiana di scienze, lettere, ed arti, appendix II (1938-1948)* 1 (Rome, 1948); Allessandro Levi, "Eugenio Colorni," *Rivista di filosofia* 38 (Jan-Jun 1947), 142-44.

Emiliana P. Noether

COMERT, Pierre (1880, Montpellier, France—16? March 1964, Paris). *Career*: lecturer, Göttingen Univ., 1907-8; journalist, 1908-16; press officer of French government, 1916-19; director, Information Section, League of Nations, 1919-33; director of information, French Foreign Office, 1933-38; editor, *France,* 1940-48.

Comert, described in his *Times* obituary as "one of the principal pillars of the Secretariat of the League of Nations," entered the League's service because of his journalistic reputation. He had served in Vienna, Berlin, and London and while in the latter post during World War I had made many influential contacts.

The Information Section, which he directed, played an important role in the beginning years of the League. First, the news conveyed in releases to the world was vital to the League's early image and thus its effectiveness. Second, national jealousies made Comert's post especially sensitive. He met both challenges by hiring able experts skilled in languages, even though he had to maintain a quota system in his staff for various nations. Among his outstanding choices were *Salvador de Madariaga, *Henri Bonnet, and *Arthur Sweetser. Comert often played an important role behind the scenes in decisions about how news of events and decisions should be described, and he thus at times influenced the events themselves. He gained a reputation for his efficiency and his shrewdness in judging character.

Comert became a victim of the political situation in 1932 when *Joseph Avenol was suggested as the second secretary-general. Objections about two Frenchmen in significant internal positions led to Comert's resignation late in December 1932. Thereafter, he continued in journalism in the press department in the Quai d'Orsay and after 1940 with *France,* issued first in England by French exiles. He continued to publish *France* in Paris (1944–48) and thereafter served on the staff of *Paris-Match*. His friends noted in his later life a sense of disillusionment in contrast to his earlier League years of selfless idealism.

BIBLIOGRAPHY:

B. LT 17 Mar 1964, 12; Salvador de Madariaga, *Morning Without Noon: Memoirs* (Westmead, England, 1973).

Warren F. Kuehl

COOLIDGE, Archibald Cary (6 March 1866, Boston—14 January 1928, Boston). *Education*: graduate, Harvard Coll., 1887; Ph.D., Univ. of Freiburg, 1892. *Career*: acting secretary, U.S. legation, St. Petersburg, 1890–91; private secretary to U.S. minister, Paris, 1892; secretary, U.S. Legation, Vienna, 1893; with Taft mission to Philippines, 1905–6; delegate, Pan American Scientific Congress, 1908–9; member, the Inquiry, 1917–18; special U.S. agent, Sweden and northern Russia, 1918; staff, American Commission to Negotiate Peace, Paris Peace Conference, 1918–19; chief, special mission in Vienna, 1919; negotiator for American Relief Administration, Soviet Russia, 1921; instructor to professor, Harvard Univ., 1893–1928; librarian-director, Harvard Univ. Libraries, 1910–28; editor, *Foreign Affairs,* 1922–28.

Scion of an old family of Boston Brahmins, Coolidge had cultural and educational advantages afforded to few American youth of the Gilded Age.

At a time when the United States was moving steadily toward the vortex of world affairs, he became increasingly interested in international history. His preparation for a career in teaching and scholarship included an apprenticeship as secretary at several U.S. legations in Europe. Soon after assuming appointment at Harvard, Coolidge began plans for introducing a graduate program in Russian history. This was followed by Coolidge's pioneering in the fields of Middle Eastern and Chinese history, fields that had hitherto not been developed in American higher education. To Coolidge, knowledge of the languages and literature of the respective region was no less important than knowledge of its history.

Coolidge's interest in modern international history, librarianship, and diplomacy led to many innovations. Under his direction, the Harvard Library greatly expanded its collections in international studies, becoming a center for research. He wrote *The United States as a World Power* (1908), which proved to be a widely read study offering numerous implicit suggestions for further research. During World War I, Coolidge directed the Russian and Eastern European Division of the Inquiry. He organized Slavic historians, many of whom had been his former graduate students, and their reports and advice proved valuable during the Paris Peace Conference when national boundaries were being established for the successor states in Eastern and Central Europe. As agent in Stockholm and in northern Russia in 1918, Coolidge transmitted a steady stream of intelligence information to Washington. The next year he became chief of the U.S. mission in Vienna and again provided useful information to the American Commission in Paris.

Coolidge's experience in Europe plus his broad and active interest in international history and politics and his knowledge of national leaders and scholars combined to make him an ideal choice as editor of the new journal, *Foreign Affairs,* started by the Council on Foreign Relations in New York during 1921–22. He merely added this responsibility to his other chores as librarian and teacher. Coolidge sought to create a quarterly that would attract as authors the most important statesmen and scholars, while insisting on the highest possible standards. During his editorship, *Foreign Affairs* became the most important journal of its kind. He invited authors to submit articles on subjects that Coolidge thought important. He would even travel abroad to discuss a manuscript with its author or to solicit articles from highly qualified individuals. At a time when many contemporaries believed that Americans were reverting to some variation of prewar isolation, Coolidge and his fellow internationalists at Harvard, the Council on Foreign Relations, and *Foreign Affairs* were exhibiting a range of knowledge about the world that was previously unknown in American life.

BIBLIOGRAPHY:

A. *Origins of the Triple Alliance: Three Lectures* (New York, 1917); *Ten Years of War and Peace* (Cambridge, MA, 1927); *The United States as a World Power* (New York, 1908).

B. Hamilton Fish Armstrong, *Peace and Counterpeace: From Wilson to Hitler: Memoirs of Hamilton Fish Armstrong* (New York, 1971); Robert F. Byrnes, *Awakening American Education to the World: The Role of Archibald Carey Coolidge, 1866–1928* (Notre Dame, IN, 1982); Harold Jefferson Coolidge and Robert H. Lord, *Archibald Cary Coolidge: Life and Letters* (Boston, 1932).

C. The Archibald Cary Coolidge papers are in the Pusey Library, Harvard Univ. Archives.

Lawrence E. Gelfand

CORDIER, Andrew Wellington (3 March 1901, near Canton, OH—11 July 1975, Manhasset, NY). *Education*: B.A., Manchester Coll., 1922; M.A., Univ. of Chicago, 1923, Ph.D., 1927; postdoctoral study, Geneva Institute of International Studies, 1930–31. *Career*: professor and chairman, Department of History and Political Science, Manchester Coll., 1927–44; Brethren Service Commission, 1939–45; Department of State, 1944–46; technical expert, U.S. delegation, San Francisco Conference 1945; head, General Assembly Section of Preparatory Commission, UN, London, 1945; executive assistant to UN secretary-general, 1946–61, with rank of under secretary; dean, School of International Affairs, Columbia Univ., 1962–72; president, Columbia Univ., 1967–70; chairman, UN Panel on a World University, 1971–73.

Cordier will be remembered as the second-ranking international civil servant who skillfully guided the UN General Assembly from its planning stages through the first fifteen sessions. While the world parliament was in session, he sat at the left hand of the annually chosen president, giving continuity to business and keeping discussion flowing smoothly toward agreement. As executive secretary to the first two secretaries-general with the rank of under secretary, Cordier was charged with the Middle East, an area in almost constant crisis. His most notable accomplishment there was the clearance of the Suez Canal in 1957 known as the Cordier Plan.

Assigned to special peace missions on three continents, he mediated in Korea in 1951 and 1952, Mt. Scopus in 1958, and the Congo in 1960. Characteristic of his low-key diplomatic style was the achievement of a major break in the Cold War hostility of the great powers by bringing Assistant Secretary of State Dean Rusk together with Soviet delegate Yakov Malik in private discussions at the UN. Cordier's approach to such meetings was long-range, directed to establishing a climate in which opponents could work together for the solution of a series of mutual problems.

Cordier shared with Dag Hammarskjöld an altruistic concept of diplomacy and statecraft. Describing the Swedish secretary-general's methods and motivations in *Paths to World Order,* Cordier disclosed that they applied love to international relations. Brought up and ordained a minister in the traditionally absolute pacifist Church of the Brethren, Cordier knew love to be an active force that reached out to reconcile and to heal. Prior to his service with the UN, he was associated with the founding of the Brethren Service Committee (1939) in its international relief and rescue of refugees and homeless victims of World War II. Loyalty to humanity may be narrowly regarded as disloyalty to one's country, but Cordier saw the logic that service to the whole benefits oneself. To him the "highest nationalism" lay in recognizing all of humanity.

Cordier brought other background to his UN responsibilities. Attracted to the seat of the League of Nations where the eminent scholars *William E. Rappard and *Paul Mantoux had begun the first advanced study of international relations, Cordier published a pioneering study of the movement toward European unification. As World War II approached, he made trips into crisis areas to explore major disputes before the League, to Latin America to observe the Chaco War and attempts at mediation, and to Central Europe to examine German irridentist claims to Danzig and Sudetenland.

Always dedicated to the role of education in the creation of international peace, Cordier was also associated with a number of pioneering programs. During World War II he led the Brethren Service Commission's efforts in peace education, which lobbied in Washington and established a college institute of international relations and university relief training units. He moved the Manchester College curriculum in an international direction, attracting such creative teachers as Gladys Muir, who was to begin the first Peace Studies program there in 1948. While at the UN, he used the radio to explain the workings of the organization to the American public. Cordier built the reputation of the Columbia School of International Affairs to one of the leading American graduate programs and inaugurated the annual Dean's Papers of scholarly analyses of foreign policy. After a notably successful pacification of Columbia University during the riots of the late 1960s, he edited the public papers of the first three secretaries-general of the UN. At the end of his life he headed a study group that led to the creation of the first world institution of higher education, the UN University.

BIBLIOGRAPHY:

A. Ed. *Columbia Essays in International Affairs: The Dean's Papers*, 7 vols. (New York, 1966–71); "European Union and the League of Nations," *Geneva Special Studies* 2 (June 1931); ed. with Wilder Foote, *The Quest for Peace. The Dag Hammarskjöld Memorial Lectures* (New York, 1965); ed., with Kenneth Maxwell, *Paths to World Order,* (New York, 1967); ed., with Wilder Foote and Max Harrelson, *Public Papers of the Secretaries-General of the United Nations,* 8 vols. (New York, 1969–78).

B. *Biographic Register of the Department of State* (Washington, D.C., 1945), 62; CB 1950, 100–102; James W. Gould, "Andrew W. Cordier, Model Diplomat," *Bulletin of Peace Studies Institute* 9 (May 1979), 1–4; IWW 1973–74, 346; NYT 13 Jul 1975, I-39, WWUN 1951, 95–96; WWWA 6, 91; WW World 1974–75, 222.

C. The Cordier papers are in the Butler Library, Columbia Univ.

James W. Gould

COSIO VILLEGAS, Daniel (23 July 1898, Mexico City—10 March 1976, Mexico City). *Education*: graduate, Faculty of Law, National Univ. of

Mexico, 1915; Harvard Univ., 1925-26, Univ. of Wisconsin, 1926-27; M.A., Cornell Univ., 1928. *Career*: president, National Student Federation of Mexico, 1921; professor, National Univ. of Mexico, 1920-25; delegate, First Conference on Economical Statistics, Geneva, 1928, Fourth Pan American Commercial Conference, 1931, Fifth Conference, 1935; technical adviser, Seventh Pan American Conference, Montevideo, 1934; financial counselor, Mexican Embassy, United States, 1935-37; counselor, Portugal, 1936-37; chief counselor/director, Banco de Mexico, 1940-46; delegate, Bretton Woods Conference, 1944; special representative to UNESCO, 1957-68, Council president, 1959; founder, *El trimestre económico*, 1934, *Historia mexicana*, 1958, editor, *Foro internacional*, 1960-63; frequent columnist, *Excelsior*; director, Fondo de Cultura Economica, till his death.

A brilliant student leader at the National University, an adviser to Mexico's government officials, the founder and editor of various journals, Cosio Villegas was a man of strong convictions yet critically objective. He possessed a broad range of knowledge and in the 1920s viewed the study of history and the social sciences as a "service to the Mexican people" when his country was trying to build new institutions, new ideologies, and an understanding of its past.

A person of unlimited energy and versatility, he wrote more than three hundred books, essays, and articles. Cosio Villegas was also interested in improving the intellectual quality of Mexican and Latin American government personnel, especially in the area of international relations or foreign service personnel and those working in economic and financial matters. While in Lisbon in 1937, he arranged the transportation of approximately fifty Spanish intellectuals, refugees of the Civil War, to Mexico, where they became the nucleus in 1939 of La Casa de España en Mexico. Later as El Colegio de Mexico, it became a major Latin American research institution that stimulated graduate research and economic diversification.

In 1945 Cosio Villegas examined the work of the Chapultepec Conference, the Bretton Woods Conference, and other international meetings he had attended. He decided the Pan American Union should be transformed into a political institution; otherwise it would be difficult to tie it with any proposed new organization that would be essentially political, a point of view articulated as far back as 1935 by the Colombian *Jesús María Yepes.

Cosio Villegas shared the concern of many Latin Americans in 1945 about the possible economic destabilization after the war if the United States stopped buying essential raw materials or even agricultural products such as coffee. He supported the idea enunciated by the Peruvian delegation to the Chapultepec Conference that a Pan American credit or lending institution be established on the model of the Bank of Reconstruction and Development set up by the Bretton Woods Conference of 1944 to purchase excess exports and foster industrialization. Cosio Villegas also endorsed the idea of continental planning and coordination of economic planning among the hemisphere nations. He felt it unrealistic to accept the U.S. position that private investment would lead to progress and development in the region, where so many government-owned corporations had the best resources in power, intelligence, and money.

While frequently critical of U.S. economic and political policies, he felt that Latin American nations should not ignore the Cold War. They could expect little from the Soviet Union because it did little to share its art, science, and technology with developing countries. He saw the Korean War as part of a Soviet plan to establish Communist parties that would destroy the character and cultures of different nations. Thus he argued that the United States should defend the interests of nations such as Mexico and other Latin American cultures. The preservation of both national and universal values also appeared in Cosio Villegas's directorship of the Fondo de Cultura Económica, a major publishing house for economics, including development.

BIBLIOGRAPHY:

A. *American Extremes* (Austin, TX, 1964); *Lecciones de sociología mexicana*, 3 vols. (Mexico City, 1924–25); *Memorias* (Mexico City, 1976).

B. *AHR* 81 (Oct 1976), 1016–17; *Americas* 33 (Apr 1977), 676–77; *Journal of Inter-American Studies and World Affairs* 18 (May 1976), 192–98; NYT 12 Mar 1976, 36; WWLA 1946, 1, 31–32.

Neale J. Pearson

COUDENHOVE-KALERGI, Richard (16 November 1894, Tokyo—27 July 1972, Schruns, Austria). *Education*: Ph.D., Univ. of Vienna, 1917. *Career:* author and lecturer; founder, Pan-European Union, 1923; founder and executive secretary, European Parliamentary Union, 1947.

Coudenhove-Kalergi devoted his life to propagandizing the idea of a "united states of Europe." For almost fifty years, from 1923 to his death, he raised his voice in Europe and America on behalf of European unity. He never achieved his goal of a politically unified region, but he did live to see the European Economic Community as a fruit of his efforts. Although it was not satisfactory in itself, it was an earnest of a better future. Lonely, quarrelsome, quixotic, he remained an optimist despite repeated setbacks. What sustained him was an invincible belief in the virtues of his goals, an equally powerful conviction of the rightness of his ideas, and an ability to reorder reality intellectually according to his wishes. The latter quality shielded him from a sense of failure that others may have found in his efforts.

The origins of his self-assigned mission stemmed from his unusual background. His father was an Austrian nobleman and diplomat; his mother was an upper-class Japanese. Born in Tokyo, he grew up in Bohemia and was educated in Vienna in the midst of the carnage of World War I. His doctoral dissertation was a book on ethics. He had the temperament, intellect, and means to devote his life to the cause of peace in Europe. The chaos of war in Europe, he believed, could be ended forever if the destructive tendencies of national states could be checked through political unity.

Coudenhove-Kalergi was rarely at a loss for a program. He initially endorsed the League of Nations but soon judged it inadequate. In 1923 he presented his ideas in a book out of which grew his Pan-European Union. As he expressed it, Pan-Europe signified "self-help through the consolidation of Europe into an ad hoc politico-economic federation." [*Pan Europe*, xv] Without any false sense of modesty, he proclaimed that the Pan-European movement began with his Pan-European Union idea. From 1923 until the eve of World War II, he went from country to country addressing statesmen and usually eliciting from them statements that he interpreted as firm support. The mildest of assents was usually sufficient to produce outbursts of euphoria, which were repeatedly expressed either at international congresses he convoked between 1926 and 1943 or in his many books. As war grew closer, his volumes appeared more frequently. He was convinced that imminent peril would push Europeans toward unification. Indeed, in the year the war broke out, Coudenhove-Kalergi produced a volume, *Europe Must Unite*.

After war erupted, Coudenhove-Kalergi moved to New York as a refugee professor at New York University. His enthusiasms and his hopes never flagged. His resolve strengthened as he found new converts seemingly eager to help him reconstruct the stricken Old World. When the war ended, the plight of Europe convinced him more than ever that his dream would be realized. He now had, it seemed, the attention of Europe's leaders. Throughout occupied Europe, national groups emerged in 1945 dedicated to a European federation. His moment of personal triumph came in 1947 when he created the European Parliamentary Union and became its secretary-general. It appeared that not only was Europe ready for conversion, but that America was as well. In a trip to New York and Washington in 1948 as described in his *Kampf um Europa: Aus Meinem Leben* (1949), he had induced the secretary of state as well as powerful congressional leaders to lend America's weight to his proposals. Before he returned to Europe in April, he had established an American Committee for a Free and United Europe, with Senator J. William Fulbright as its president and William C. Bullitt, former ambassador to France, as vice-president. His highpoint was at Interlaken in September 1948, when a comprehensive plan of federal union was introduced and supported by more than five hundred members of European parliaments.

Coudenhove-Kalergi was never able to equal the achievements of 1947–48. It was not simply that the Atlantic alliance usurped federation, or that the Council of Europe was only a mockery of his ideas. Leadership in his movement had passed him by as new advocates emerged. They resented his dominance and disregarded his advice even as they paid homage to his pioneering services. He withdrew his European Parliamentary Union from the Joint International Committee of the Movement for European Unity, remaining outside the umbrella organization he helped to create until 1952.

The schism between his conception of federalism and the looser arrangement sought by the British and others was never resolved in his lifetime. But his energies never flagged. Books continued to pour from his pen. While he was only one of many supporters of European unity in the last two decades of his life, he was made one of the six presidents of honor of the European Movement, along with *Winston Churchill, *Léon Blum, *Paul-Henri Spaak, *Konrad Adenauer, and *Alcide de Gasperi. Alone among that distinguished group he was an international statesman. He was, as Arnold Zurcher has called him, the "prophet" of the united states of Europe.

BIBLIOGRAPHY:

A. *Kampf um Europa: Aus Meinem Leben* (Zurich, 1949); *Pan Europe* (New York, 1926).

B. CB 1948, 113–16; Walter Lipgens, *A History of European Integration, Volume I: 1945–1947* (Oxford, 1982); NYT 29 Jul 1972, 28; Arnold J. Zurcher, *The Struggle to Unite Europe, 1940–1958* (New York, 1958).

Lawrence S. Kaplan

COUDERT, Frederic René (11 February 1871, New York—1 April 1955, New York). *Education*: B.A., Columbia Coll., 1890; LL.B., Columbia Law School, 1891, LL.D., 1894. *Career*: attorney, New York, 1892–1955.

Coudert's father had established a reputation in international law, and the son attended meetings with his father, notably the Bering Sea seal case in Paris in 1893, which led to the conviction on his part that arbitration and a rational approach to world problems could resolve issues without recourse to war. He became an original member of the American Society of International Law (ASIL) in 1907, joined the Institute de Droit International, and established a reputation as a trial lawyer in arguing the Insular Cases before the Supreme Court. As the earth became more complicated, Coudert decided during World War I that an international organization was needed for stability. Yet he remained aloof from the League to Enforce Peace and other groups, and during the treaty fight of 1919–20 he chose not to become involved. During the election of 1920, he believed that a victory for Warren G. Harding would bring changes in the Covenant of the League of Nations that would make it acceptable to the Senate and the people.

When this change did not materialize, a "bitterly disappointed" Coudert shifted ground and became engaged in campaigns to achieve membership in the League. In public statements and speeches, he condemned "League-o-phobia," argued that fears about entanglements abroad were overstated, and insisted that the United States should join even after many other internationalists had abandoned that position. Coudert visited Geneva to see the

League at work and felt ashamed of his country's absence. He thus joined with others in forming the League of Nations Non-Partisan Association, encouraged greater cooperation with League agencies, and endorsed membership in the World Court.

As aggressors marched in the 1930s, Coudert realized the League's ineffectiveness, and he became an increasing advocate of collective security measures. In 1940 he was an original member of the Committee to Defend America by Aiding the Allies. As president of the ASIL (1942–46), Coudert explained his position. International law unfortunately could not be isolated from the world of politics; hence, those who believed in a rule of law had to take positive stands to determine the environment in which justice could prevail. Coudert was a staunch advocate for his views, which he gathered and published in book form in 1954.

BIBLIOGRAPHY:

A. *A Half Century of International Problems: A Lawyer's View* (New York, 1954).

B. AJIL 49 (1955), 548–49; DAB supp. 5, 136–37; NYT 2 Apr 1955, 17.

C. The Coudert papers and his Oral History are at Columbia Univ.

Warren F. Kuehl

COX, James Middleton (31 March 1870, Jacksonburg, OH—15 July 1957, Dayton, OH). *Education*: public school, Jacksonburg. *Career*: founder and publisher, Cox Newspapers; U.S. congressman, 1909–13; governor of Ohio, 1913–14, 1917–21; Democratic candidate for president, 1920; vice-chairman, U.S. delegation, World Monetary Conference, 1933.

Throughout his career Cox advocated cooperation and centralization of power to promote the greater community good. In Congress, Cox supported tariffs to benefit industries with international markets. As governor of Ohio in 1913–14, he presided over a massive expansion of state services and regulatory power, and after returning to office in 1917 he implemented national wartime objectives to promote maximum military efficiency.

With a very limited foreign policy record, Cox emerged in 1920 as a presidential candidate. He had supported *Woodrow Wilson's "peace without victory" objectives and swift ratification of the Versailles Treaty without amendments or reservations. Agreeing with Wilson that Article X, the collective security provision of the League of Nations Covenant, represented the heart of the treaty, Cox also believed the League would help build a stable world economy. In spite of this support, when asked about a potential Cox candidacy, Wilson responded that it would be "a joke" because Cox could not appropriately carry the League issue to the people.

Yet Cox, widely recognized as a domestic reformer not directly associated with the Wilsonians, won the 1920 Democratic presidential nomination behind a phalanx of support from Midwestern and Northeastern urban-based political leaders. Early in the campaign, Cox stressed domestic issues.

As election day approached and defeat appeared likely, Cox shifted his focus to international concerns. While continuing to favor the Versailles Treaty, he abandoned Wilson's demand for an uncompromising position and pledged to support a reservation to the Covenant specifying that the United States had no obligation "to defend or assist" any nation unless Congress approved the action. A concerned Wilson quickly entered the debate by telling a group of internationalists that Article X was a "specific pledge" to resist aggression. With the electorate committed to change, Cox lost by an overwhelming margin to Warren G. Harding, who had pledged to return the country to "normalcy."

As titular head of the Democratic party, Cox continued to espouse a cooperative role for the United States in world affairs. In the summer of 1922, after speaking with several European political leaders, he publicly advocated a scaling down of wartime reparations to revive world prosperity. At the 1924 Democratic Convention, Cox stood among a group of internationalists who wanted to make the League of Nations a central issue in the presidential campaign. In what turned out to be the longest political convention in U.S. history, these internationalists ultimately secured the nomination of *John W. Davis, a Wilsonian committed to U.S. membership in the League. The Davis campaign never overcame the "new era" Republican prosperity, and any hope of League membership ended with the victory of Calvin Coolidge.

In 1932, with the world shaken by economic depression, Cox, Davis, and Alfred E. Smith, the 1928 Democratic party nominee for president, supported the candidacy of *Newton D. Baker in an abortive stop-Roosevelt effort. Following the convention, Cox doubted *Franklin Delano Roosevelt's commitment to cooperation in international affairs. Nevertheless, he campaigned for Roosevelt and later turned down several offers to join the administration. He did serve as vice-chairman of the delegation to the 1933 World Monetary Conference, but Cox's contribution was political. He helped prevent an early breakup of the conference after Roosevelt's decision to devalue the dollar in the midst of the meeting.

Cox then withdrew from the mainstream of politics, but he later used his five-paper newspaper chain to support Roosevelt's activist foreign policy, including repeal of the arms embargo, increased armaments spending, and military aid to England. In 1940 and again in 1944, Cox campaigned for Roosevelt, emphasizing his leadership in world affairs to create a lasting peace.

BIBLIOGRAPHY:

A. *Journey Through My Years* (New York, 1945).

B. James E. Cebula, "James M. Cox, Journalist and Politician," dissertation, Univ. of Cincinnati, 1972; DAB supp. 6, 128–30.

C. The Cox papers are in the Wright State Univ. Library.

James E. Cebula

CRAFTS, Wilbur Fisk (12 January 1850, Fryeburg, ME—27 December 1922, Washington). *Education*: B.A., Wesleyan Univ., CT, 1869, M.A., 1871; B.D., Boston Univ. School of Theology, 1871. *Career*: minister of Methodist churches, in Maine, Massachusetts, and New Hampshire, 1871-77, in Chicago, 1877-79, of a Congregational church, Brooklyn, 1880-83, of a Presbyterian church, New York, 1883-88; moral reform activist, 1868-1922.

The territorial and commercial expansion of the United States into Asia and Latin America during the late nineteenth and early twentieth centuries inspired a number of American reformers to extend their wide-ranging attacks on immoral practices within the United States to similar or related evils in other lands. Because of their involvement in home and foreign missionary activity, religious leaders and organizations were frequently in the vanguard of both spheres of reform activity.

A prolific author of books and tracts on religion and social issues, editor of two reform periodicals, and founder of two reform organizations, Crafts campaigned against most of the presumed social evils of his era: intemperance, prostitution and sexual impurity, obscenity, gambling, horse racing, prize fighting, Sunday work and amusements, divorce, and Mormonism. In the Methodist ministry he early became a leading figure in temperance and Sunday school work. In 1889 he founded the American Sabbath Union. Two years later he became editor of the *Christian Statesman*, a periodical devoted to the "whole wide circle of Christian reforms."

In 1895 Crafts delivered a series of lectures at Princeton Theological Seminary and at Marietta College, later published as *Practical Christian Sociology*. In expounding on the role of religion and the institutional church in the solution of social problems, he maintained that, inasmuch as all vices were interrelated, all reform efforts should be coordinated into "one great reform"—"the Christianizing of Society." Crafts thereupon announced the formation of the National Bureau of Reforms to serve as a "Christian lobby" in behalf of social and moral reforms in the United States. Subsequently, in keeping with his expanded sphere of interest, Crafts renamed his organization the International Reform Bureau.

Although projected as nonsectarian and nonpolitical, virtually all of the Bureau's trustees, officers, and supporters were Protestant ministers and lay men and lay women. Nevertheless, as its superintendent from its founding to his death, Crafts actually ran the organization with the assistance of his wife, Sara J. Timanus Crafts, superintendent of the Sunday School Department of the World's WCTU. With headquarters and residence only a block from the Capitol, he conjoined a vigorous propaganda campaign through the Bureau's journal, *Twentieth Century Quarterly;* and in his books, pamphlets, and public lectures he persistently lobbied in Congress in behalf of moral reform legislation. By 1903 Congress had responded by restricting divorce in the District of Columbia and other territories of the

United States and prohibiting the sale of liquor in military canteens and immigrant stations.

The major international issue to which Crafts devoted his attention was the traffic in opium and alcoholic beverages. Between 1900 and 1906 he led other reformers in persuading the U.S. government to ratify two multilateral treaties restricting or prohibiting the sale of liquor to the people of Africa, to ban, unilaterally, the sale of opium, liquor, and firearms to certain Pacific islanders, to restrict opium transactions in the Philippines to legitimate medical and scientific purposes, and to propose at the 1906 Brussels conference on liquor in Africa a worldwide ban on the sale of liquor and opium to all so-called uncivilized races. Following his attendance at the Brussels conference and one in Paris on the white slave traffic in October 1906, Crafts and his wife embarked the next year on an extended trip that included China, Japan, Korea, the Philippines, and Australia, where he sought to arouse public and official sentiment against opium. During his lifetime Crafts visited some twenty-nine countries in the interest of reform. He also encouraged the study and promotion of world government.

In 1909 the U.S. State Department appointed Crafts chairman of the twelve-member U.S. delegation to the Twelfth International Congress Against Alcoholism, which met in London. Thereafter, Crafts fell out of favor with the State Department. Complaining that he was "somewhat impracticable and radical in his notions of reform along every conceivable line," officials there refused to appoint him to delegations sent to later liquor conferences. Undaunted, Crafts continued to champion prohibition, domestically and internationally, and in his will he stipulated that two-thirds of his estate be used exclusively to continue the propaganda work of the International Reform Bureau.

BIBLIOGRAPHY:

A. *Addresses on the Civil Sabbath* (New York, 1890); *Patriotic Studies* (Washington, 1908); *Practical Christian Sociology* (New York, 1895); *A Primer of Internationalism* (Washington, 1908); with Sara T. Crafts, Mary Leitch, and Margaret Leitch, *Protection of Native Races Against Intoxicants and Opium* (New York, 1900). *World Book of Temperance* (Washington, 1911); *Why Dry* (Washington, 1918).

B. NYT 28 Dec 1922, 17; *Standard Encyclopedia of the Alcohol Problem* 2 (Westerville, OH, 1925), 727–28; *Washington Post* 28 Dec 1922, 9.

Arnold H. Taylor

CRANE, Charles Richard (7 August 1858, Chicago—15 February 1939, Palm Springs, CA). *Education*: Stevens Institute of Technology, Rush Medical School. *Career*: philanthropist; businessman, Crane Brass and Bell Foundry, vice-president, 1894–1912, president, 1912–14; American minister to China, 1909, 1920–21.

When poor health forced Crane to abandon his higher education, he began to travel abroad. He spent much time in Russia, a nation he visited twenty-four times, East Asia, and the Middle East. Crane authored no books, wrote few articles, and delivered few speeches, but his travels established his reputation as an expert on foreign affairs. His great wealth opened the door to public service.

Successive presidents entrusted Crane with major diplomatic assignments. In 1909 *William Taft appointed him minister to China. Before leaving the United States, however, he leaked confidential State Department information to the press. This led to his recall and resignation. The largest contributor to the Democratic party in the 1912 presidential campaign, Crane declined *Woodrow Wilson's offer of the ambassadorship to Russia. In 1915, Wilson appointed him to the commission established under the terms of the American Arbitration Treaty with Russia. Following the March Revolution, he advised Secretary of State *Robert Lansing on Russian affairs. In the summer of 1917, he joined the special diplomatic commission that visited Russia. An unofficial adviser to Wilson at Versailles, Crane served on the Inter-Allied Commission on Mandates in Turkey. In 1920 he again became the U.S. minister to China. During his year in Peking, Crane demonstrated his limits as a diplomat. Taking little interest in the daily affairs of the Legation, he sometimes failed to transmit important information to Washington. He believed he could fulfill his duties by doing what he knew best, traveling in China to meet its people and leaders.

While his diplomatic achievements were limited, his philanthropic endeavors created a lasting legacy. To promote better understanding of Russia, Crane sponsored lectures on Slavic culture at the University of Chicago and provided funds for it to support a professor of Russian language and political institutions. He funded American universities in Istanbul, raised funds for the relief of Albanians and Armenians during the Great War, and rallied the international community in China to provide help during the 1920 famine. After his first visit to Yemen, he sent American engineers to build roads and irrigation systems at his own expense. He endowed the Institute of Current World Affairs, through which selected Americans learned the political, economic, and social problems of other nations in a program of residence and supervised training.

Crane shared friendships with numerous world leaders. Perhaps the most significant was with Thomas Masaryk. Crane introduced the Czech leader to Wilson and advanced the cause of Czech independence.

BIBLIOGRAPHY:

B. Leo J. Bocage, "The Public Career of Charles R. Crane," dissertation, Fordham Univ., 1962; DAB supp. 2, 128–30; "Harvard's Bells, Asia's Crane," *Time* 17 (9 Mar 1931), 16–17.

C. The Crane papers are in the Institute of Current World Affairs.

James R. Roebuck, Jr.

CREMER, William Randal. See *Biographical Dictionary of Modern Peace Leaders.*

CROSBY, Oscar Terry (21 April 1861, Ponchatoula, LA—2 January 1947, Warrentown, PA). *Education*: graduate U.S. Military Academy, 1882. *Career*: resigned Army commission, 1887; head, public utility corporations in District of Columbia, Delaware, Pennsylvania, and New Jersey; director, Commission for the Relief of Belgium, 1915; assistant secretary of the treasury, 1917–18; president, Inter-Allied Council on War Purchases and Finance, 1917–19; U.S. special commissioner of finance in Europe, 1918–19; financial adviser, U.S. Peace Commission, 1919.

Between 1900 and 1937 this rich engineer-businessman was an avid world traveler and explorer who became committed to the cause of international peace. In 1909 he published a plan for an international court that could enforce its decisions with arms, aid members in repelling attacks and rebellions, and repress preparations for attack against any member. The court could conscript an army, abolish or occupy fortifications, and reduce national armies.

Also in 1909, Crosby, *Hamilton Holt, and several others organized the World-Federation League as a subsidiary of the New York Peace Society. In 1910 Crosby became the League's president. Its membership was small, its influence large. Between 1910 and 1914, Crosby, Holt, and their colleagues kept alive ambitions for a world federation while most internationalists focused on arbitration treaties and the slowly evolving but pallid Hague system. Few others were willing (1910–18) to endow a world federation with the armed power and wide responsibility that Crosby demanded, or to allow it to begin life with a judicial-executive–style government but no legislature.

In 1914 Crosby published a pamphlet calling for an "International Court of Decree and Enforcement." In January 1915 he induced Senator John F. Shaforth, Jr., to introduce a congressional resolution that called for such a body and included Crosby's details on organization, powers, and operation. Crosby soon thereafter organized an Armed International Tribunal Association to advance his views, which most World-Federation League members and many other internationalists, including those of the League to Enforce Peace, considered too radical.

In May 1916 Shaforth, at Crosby's prompting, introduced another resolution, which proposed a constitutional amendment to authorize the creation of a peace-enforcing tribunal and to ask the president to open discussions with other nations. The naval appropriations bill of 1916 carried a Crosby-inspired rider that asked the president after the close of the war to call an international conference to create a court of arbitration. In the spring of 1918, Crosby talked with many Allied leaders and *Edward M. House about the creation of a peace-keeping organization.

In 1919 Crosby published a book he had written in 1916, *International War and Its Cures,* too late to affect the Senate's vote on League of Nations membership. It elaborated on his early ideas. His international court would be composed of two judges from each of the major powers, including Ger-

CROWDY, RACHEL ELEANOR   181

many, one from certain lesser states, and one from groups of certain lesser states, for example, Bolivia, Chile, and Peru. Countries with more than 30 million inhabitants could have an additional member for each extra 20 million except for China and non-self-governing colonies. The judges would rule on all issues that threatened peace, regardless of whether or not they were "justiciable." They would appoint an executive who would enforce their decisions. A legislature to develop a law code might follow. The court could conscript its own army and navy from member states, with national forces greatly reduced. The court would not necessarily maintain the status quo but would decide quarrels in the light of existing conditions. Thus boundaries might be altered, rebellions supported, and unfair economic practices stopped. Each nation could maintain nondiscriminatory tariffs, although free trade was best. The Monroe Doctrine must go. If it stayed, Britain, Russia, and Japan could claim one in regions near their territories.

Despite the logic behind Crosby's plan, his vision was too utopian for the times. To Crosby the unarmed League of Nations was virtually useless. In 1932 he again tried unsuccessfully to provide for an armed tribunal through congressional action. From 1933 to 1944 he worked with *David Davies as organizer of a U.S. branch of the New Commonwealth Society, which sought to reconstitute the League of Nations, arm it, and give it a tribunal with wide jurisdiction. Crosby also interested himself in Allied war debts and German reparations, urging compromise.

BIBLIOGRAPHY:

A. *The Armed International Tribunal Association: Its Purposes and Methods* (Washington, 1915); *The Constitution of an International Court of Decree and Enforcement or a Plea for the Poor of all Lands* (Tokyo 1914); *The Constitution of the United States of the World* (Warrenton, VA, 1909); *International War; Its Causes and Its Cure* (New York, 1919).

B. Warren F. Kuehl, *Hamilton Holt: Journalist, Internationalist, Educator* (Gainesville, FL, 1960); *Seeking World Order: The United States and International Organization to 1920* (Nashville, TN, 1969); NYT 9 Apr 1914, 10, 18 Nov 1915, 3, 27 Nov 1915, 14, 9 Nov 1917, 1, 16 Dec 1917, I–3, 21 May 1932, 14, 13 Oct 1932, 18.

C. The Crosby papers are in the Manuscript Division, Library of Congress.

Edward B. Parsons

CROWDY, Rachel Eleanor [Crowdy-Thornhill] (3 March 1884, London—10 October 1964). *Education*: Hyde Park New Coll.; nurse's training, Guy's Hospital, 1908; certificate, Apothecary's Hall, 1910. *Career*: lecturer and demonstrator, National Health Society, 1912–14; Voluntary Aid Detachment in France and Belgium, 1914–19; chief, Social Questions and Opium Traffic Section, League of Nations, 1919–31; member, Royal Commission on Manufacture and Trading in Arms, 1935–36; West Indies Royal Commission, 1938–39; regions' adviser, Ministry of Information, 1939–46.

Although the League of Nations Covenant had established equality between men and women in access to the highest positions of the world organization, Crowdy was the only woman ever to head an administrative section, carrying the title of "chief of the social section," but she never became a director. Crowdy had performed exemplary service as a volunteer nurse on the Western Front in World War I, for which she was decorated in 1919 and accorded the title of Dame. Called by *Eric Drummond to serve the League of Nations, her work breathed life into Article XXIIIc of the Covenant, which announced the interest of the international community in questions relating to drugs, the traffic in women, and child welfare.

In 1921, Crowdy visited Poland during the typhus epidemic. That year she was also instrumental in the establishment of the White Slave Traffic Convention. Her Section, working with the Council's Opium Committee, set out with great energy to curb the lucrative international drug trade. Through the assimilation of extensive data and regular conferences, a series of conventions emerged. One in 1925 strengthened the League's control over illicit traffic; another in 1931 limited drug manufacture. Crowdy also guided the Council's Advisory Committee on Social Questions, which dealt with specific abuses against women and children. This largely humanitarian work proved controversial. British delegate Austen Chamberlain and others expressed concern about specific cases where the League had best not interfere with purely internal affairs of its member states. Crowdy was an outspoken, articulate believer in the League of Nations idea; in her speeches, articles, and interviews, she underscored the importance of Geneva's humanitarian work.

After leaving the League, she served on various royal commissions, traveling to Honolulu and Shanghai in 1930 and 1931 as the British delegate to conferences on Pacific affairs, to the International Red Cross Conference in Tokyo in 1934, to Spain in 1937 during the Civil War, and to the West Indies in 1938–39. During World War II, working for the Ministry of Information, Crowdy visited and reported on conditions in Britain's bombed cities. Crowdy was not only an efficient administrator but also a poet with a lifelong passion for international service. Characterized as gentle but of determined will, she left an indelible impression on her contemporaries as a female of great accomplishment in Geneva.

BIBLIOGRAPHY:

A. "Child Welfare," *Spectator* 140 (28 Apr 1928), 641; "Far Eastern Ferment," *Spectator* 154 (8 Feb 1935), 200–1; "International Aspects of Social Work," *National Conference of Social Work: Proceedings* (1926), 113–18; "The League of Nations: International Position with Regard to Prostitution and the Suppression of Traffic in Women and Children," *Journal of Social Hygiene* 10 (Dec 1924), 549–59.

B. "Dame Crowdy Cites Her Faith in the League," *Trans-Pacific* 22 (8 Nov 1934), 17; IWW 1949, 189; S. Jenkins, "War on Opium," *Far Eastern Survey* 13 (23 Aug 1944), 161–62; Phyllis M. Lovell, "Be Ahead of the World," *Christian Science Monitor Magazine* (3 Jul 1935), 5; LT 12 Oct 1964, 12; Ruth Pennybacker, "Youngest Dame," *Woman Citizen* 11 (Jul 1926), 21–22: WWW 1972, 262.

Carole Fink

CROWE, Eyre Alexander (30 July 1864, Leipzig, Germany—28 April 1925, Swanage, England). *Career*: entered British Foreign Office, 1885, senior clerk, 1906; secretary, British delegation, Hague Peace Conference, 1907; British delegation to London Conference, 1908; British agent in Savarkar arbitration case at The Hague, 1911; assistant under secretary of state for foreign affairs, 1912; director, Contraband Department, 1915; Paris Peace Conference, 1919; permanent under secretary of state for foreign affairs, 1920–25.

Crowe was a leading figure in the pre-1914 generation of permanent officials whose influence on British diplomacy in that era has remained controversial. In the aftermath of World War I, several historians argued that Crowe had acted as an evil genius within the Foreign Office, with his sharp criticisms of Germany and his excessive influence over Foreign Secretary *Edward Grey. That interpretation of Crowe's work no longer prevails, for subsequent research has demonstrated that Crowe influenced Grey much less than originally believed, and the allegations of anti-German prejudice are no longer credible. The suspicion of German foreign policy expressed by Crowe stemmed from a thorough knowledge of modern European history and a belief in the maintenance of British interests around the world but particularly in Europe, and the application of history to foreign policy problems became one of Crowe's trademarks.

Crowe is also remembered as author of perhaps the most famous single British diplomatic document, the Memorandum on the Present State of British Relations with France and Germany, 1 January 1907. Long considered a blueprint for British policy, the Crowe Memorandum was not prophetic but historical. It expressed in classic form the underlying assumptions that animated the official mind of the Victorian Foreign Office, with its emphasis on naval supremacy, free trade, and a balance-of-power relationship between British and the continental states. It is unlikely that the Memorandum provided for action or that specific diplomatic policies were founded on its conclusions. As an internationalist Crowe represented traditional nineteenth-century beliefs in transition. He was a participant in nearly all the major prewar world conferences, and he recognized the growing need for international cooperation. While desirable, however, it could not supersede the dictates of national interest. He still believed during discussions to create a League of Nations that periodic conferences of the prewar type, combined with a balance of power to maintain stability, would best advance international accord. He gave grudging assent to the League, more from a sense of loyalty to government policy than from personal sympathy. As permanent under secretary of state from 1920 to his death, he labored faithfully to expedite policy, although he distrusted the new world of post-Versailles diplomacy.

The enduring significance of Crowe's career derived from the high level of technical skills he brought to the administration of international relations. Though the exact extent of his contribution to the procedural reform of the Foreign Office in the first decade of the twentieth century cannot be measured precisely, Crowe labored effectively to transform the aristocratic atmosphere of Downing Street into a modern department of state. It is upon this foundation that his reputation ultimately has rested.

BIBLIOGRAPHY:

B. Edward T. Corp, "Sir Eyre Crowe and the Administration of the Foreign Office, 1906–1914," *Historical Journal* 22 (1979), 443–54; Richard A. Cosgrove, "The Career of Sir Eyre Crowe: A Reassessment," *Albion* 4 (Winter 1972), 193–205; "The Crowe Memorandum and British Foreign Policy, 1907–1914," *South Atlantic Quarterly* 72 (Autumn 1973), 528–39; Sibyl Eyre Crowe, "Sir Eyre Crowe and the Locarno Pact," *English Historical Review* 87 (Jan 1972), 49–74; George W. Egerton, *Great Britain and the Creation of the League of Nations* (Chapel Hill, NC, 1978); Zara S. Steiner, *The Foreign Office and Foreign Policy, 1898–1914* (Cambridge, 1969).

C. Some of Crowe's papers are in the Public Record Office London.

Richard A. Cosgrove

CULBERTSON, Ely (22 July 1891, Poiana de Verbilao, Romania—27 December 1955, Brattleboro, VT). *Education*: L'Ecole des Sciences Economiques et Politiques, 1913–14; Univ. of Geneva, 1914–15; Sorbonne, Yale Univ., Univ. of Virginia. *Career*: authority on the card game of bridge, inventor of Culbertson System of bidding in contract bridge; founder (1929) and editor, *The Bridge World Magazine;* chair Citizen's Committee for United Nations Reform.

Among those advocates of a federation of the world's nations, Culbertson was a latecomer. However, in 1937, after a brilliant career as an authority on contract bridge, he turned to advocating international peace through world federation. In addition to numerous speeches and appearances before government committees, Culbertson published several works describing his ideas. Most notable was *Total Peace* (1943), which purported to answer the question of how the world could be organized to ensure future peace. In essence, Culbertson's plan was a combination of the United States' federal-state structure, integrated with other plans to meet international needs. He grouped nations into eleven federations, which, including individual states, make up a world federation. Among novel government organs, he included provision for a police force consisting of eleven national contingents and one international one recruited from several states and commanded by the world federalist government. To combat aggression, his body could call into action national contingents to support the internationalist force. Culbertson's *Total Peace* plan thus called for the creation of a collective security system with the United States the architect and balancing power.

With the creation of the UN, Culbertson abandoned the idea of world federation and founded the Citizen's Committee for United Nations Reform. Its chief purpose was to promote the creation of an effective international police force into the UN system. This "Quota Force" or "ABC" Plan called for a revision of the Charter to abolish the veto in matters of aggression and to reorganize the Security Council. As conceived by Culbertson, the latter would be changed to give collective representation to the smaller nations. Atomic energy would be controlled in accordance with the Baruch Proposals, which called for the creation of an International Atomic Development Authority with power to police and inspect in every country. Culbertson further urged the limitation of all other important weapons and the establishment of an efficient but "tyranny-proof" world police force. It would consist of volunteers from smaller member states only, with one-fifth of its strength coming from the five major powers, and their units would serve as reserves to the international contingent. Under this formula, Culbertson claimed, neither the international component nor any of the national forces, because of their size limitations, could become tyrannical. Furthermore, he stated, this system would prevent defiance of the UN force by any one national army.

Culbertson believed the success of his plan lay in the creation of a more perfect balance of power; quotas would be negotiated by national sovereign governments. Moreover, this proposition rested upon the premise that a supernational body could be created for a limited purpose alone, while national sovereighty would remain supreme in all other respects.

By 1950, Culbertson had injected a twist in his "ABC" conception with a proposal that the initial force could begin with the Atlantic Pact nations. After developing unity within, the Atlantic Pact could then be extended into a World Pact, with its own veto-free authority and its own police arm. Once established, the World Pact nations would urge the Soviet Union to join them in revising the UN. Culbertson felt that the World Pact, as designed, would convince the Soviet Union that it could not compete with the organized might of the rest of the world.

Until his death in 1955, Culbertson continued to chair the Citizen's Committee for United Nations Reform. This, coupled with extensive travel, lectures, appearance before congressional committees, and other diverse organizations, led to considerable support for Culbertson's goal, a world of peaceful nations militarily and effectively organized against any aggressor.

BIBLIOGRAPHY:

A. "The ABC Plan for World Peace," *Reader's Digest* 52 (Jun 1948), 82–88; *Must We Fight Russia* (Philadelphia, 1947); *Strange Lives of One Man* (Philadelphia, 1940); *Summary of the World Federation Plan* (New York, 1943); *Total Peace: What Makes Wars and How to Organize Peace* (Garden City, NJ, 1943); "We Can Really Have an Effective U.N. Police Force?" *New American Mercury* 71 (Dec 1950), 679–88; "Why We Need an International Police Force," *Education* 70 (Feb 1950), 379–83.

B. CB 1940, 211–13; Rex Mackey, *The Walk of the Oysters* (Englewood Cliffs, NJ, 1965); *Newsweek* 47 (9 Jan 1956), 49; NYT 28 Dec 1955, 1; *Time* 67 (9 Jan 1956), 84.

C. Culbertson papers are in the Yale Univ. Library and the Syracuse Univ. Library.

Emmett E. Panzella

CUMMING, Hugh Smith (17 August 1869, Hampton, VA—20 December 1948, Washington). *Education*: Baltimore City Coll.; graduate in medicine, Univ. of Virginia, 1893; M.D., Univ. Coll. of Medicine, Richmond, 1894. *Career*: assistant surgeon, U.S. Marine Hospital Service, 1894–99, passed assistant surgeon, U.S. Marine Hospital and Public Health Service, 1899–1911; surgeon, U.S. Public Health Service, 1911–18; assistant surgeon-general, 1918–1920, surgeon-general, 1920–36; director, Pan American Sanitary Bureau, 1920–47.

Throughout his long career in public health, Cumming was faced with three demanding tasks. He was obliged to protect the United States from the foreign introduction of disease; he desired to assist war-dislocated or poor countries in building adequate health programs; and he was compelled to oppose economic and religious interests in a variety of countries that wished to circumvent or subvert health regulations.

To achieve the first, the U.S. Public Health Service completed its quarantine system and inaugurated a preimmigration inspection at U.S. consulates abroad. At the same time, he worked with several international agencies to assist the development of sanitation and immunization programs in other countries. At a time when such programs were incomplete even in the United States, and given the paucity of funds available and the magnitude of the need following World War I, the task was arduous. In addressing his second goal, Cumming was particularly interested in the Pan American Sanitary Bureau, of which he was director for twenty-seven years and to which he devoted all his energies after retiring as surgeon-general in 1936. In 1924 the Pan American Sanitary Code was proposed under his leadership; by 1936, through his tireless work, every republic in the Western Hemisphere had signed the agreement. In addition to extending basic health knowledge in the Americas, Cumming worked to arrange internships and fellowships in the United States for physicians, public health officers, nurses, and sanitary engineers in Latin America.

Cumming served as the president of the Office International d'Hygiene Publique and as a member of the Health Committee and other special bodies of the League of Nations. He actively supported the strong International Sanitary Code proposed in 1926. Unfortunately, that document was rendered ineffectual by the insistence of countries with shipping interests and those where endemic diseases wer : prevalent that individual countries alone be trusted to certify the health of their ports. Religious interests, particularly those in Moslem countries, also resisted quarantine limitations, insisting on free passage across countries for religious pilgrimages. Although not successful in obtaining full international cooperation, Cumming fostered continued negotiations and expanded hygienic techniques in a long effort to raise international health standards. He received a host of awards from governments in Europe and the Americas testifying to his efforts. His work laid the foundation for the later success of the World Health Organization of the United Nations.

BIBLIOGRAPHY:

A. "Immigration Work of the U.S. Bureau of the Public Health Service, U.S. Treasury Department," *Congressional Digest* 2 (Jul 1923), 302; "The International Sanitary Conference," *American Journal of Public Health* 16 (Oct 1926), 975-80; "Situation Abroad as Regards Typhus Fever and Other Epidemic Diseases and the Possibility of Their Importation into the U.S.," *American Journal of Public Health* 12 (Feb 1922), 91-94; *Statement on the Exchange of Medical Personnel and International Cooperation in the Field of Medicine*, Sixth Session of the League Health Committee, (Geneva, 1923).

B. *American Journal of Public Health* 39 (Feb 1949), 225; *American Men of Science* (New York, 1944), 393; *Journal of the American Medical Association* 139 (1 Jan 1949), 46; NCAB E, 279-80; Ralph C. Williams, *The United States Public Health Service, 1798-1950* (Washington, 1951); WWWA 2, 139.

C. Some of the Cumming papers are at the Univ. of Virginia.

Victoria A. Harden

CUMMINGS, Edward (20 April 1861, Colebrook, NH—2 November 1926, Ossipee, NH). *Education*: B.A., Harvard Coll., 1883, M.A., 1885; Harvard Law, Divinity, and Graduate Schools, 1883-85; study in England, Scotland, France, Italy, and Germany, 1888-91. *Career*: instructor, Harvard and Radcliffe Coll., 1885-87; instructor to assistant professor, Harvard Coll., 1891-1900; minister, South Congregational (Unitarian) Church, Boston, 1900-1925.

A brilliant undergraduate student of philosophy, political science, and economics, Cummings left his divinity studies for sociology. In Boston and in Europe he explored labor conditions and found his calling as a practical social worker, lecturer, and philanthropist. At the retirement of Edward Everett Hale, Cummings, ordained as a Unitarian minister, left academia and took up the pulpit. Drawn by Hale into international pacifism, Cummings became trustee of the World Peace Foundation in 1910 and its executive secretary in 1916. His sermons emphasized the practical aspects of the peace movement because world stability meant prosperity and justice in the international arena meant stability. Shattered by the outbreak of World War I and its ensuing violence, Cummings joined those who still hoped that a league of religious leaders would end the carnage and create a just and lasting settlement.

In 1917, his poet son Edward Estlin was interned in the French concentration camp La Ferté-Macé. The father not only offered to replace him as an army chaplain but worked indefatigably through U.S. officials to free his innocent son, even writing directly to *Woodrow Wilson. To alleviate his father's chagrin over a miscarriage of justice, e.e. cummings, in *The Enormous Room,* wrote the history of his imprisonment.

In the summer of 1921, Cummings toured Europe in connection with war relief work of the World Peace Foundation. Returning, he worked vigorously to raise funds for the rehabilitation of Europe and the Near East. Cummings and his organization also supported the humanitarian work of the League of Nations, the International Labor Office, and the establishment of the Permanent Court of International Justice at the Hague. Killed at a railroad crossing in a blinding snowstorm, Cummings in his mid-sixties was an avid American internationalist who grasped the importance of disseminating information from the Old World and of sending help across the Atlantic.

BIBLIOGRAPHY:

A. *The Layman's Answer* (Boston, 1920); articles in *Quarterly Journal of Economics* 1-13.

B. DAB 4, 594-95; Richard S. Kennedy, "Edward Cummings, the Father of the Poet," *Bulletin of the New York Public Library* 70 (1966), 437-49; NYT 3 Nov 1926, 24; WWWA 1, 283.

Carole Fink

CURCHOD, Louis (7 October 1826, Crissier, Switzerland—18 October 1889, Berne, Switzerland). *Education*: graduated as engineer, Ecole Centrale des Arts et Manufactures, Paris, 1849. *Career*: railroad construction engineer; specialist in telegraphy; inspector, in Swiss federal telegraph administration; central director, Swiss telegraph administration; director, Bureau international des Administrations télégraphiques, 1868-89; sometime director-general of the Société du câble transatlantique français; leading participant in international telegraph conferences, 1865-85.

Following his participation in the drafting of the first international telegraph conventions, beginning with Switzerland's neighboring countries and later extending to most European states, Curchod continued throughout his life to devote his outstanding administrative and technical talents to the cause of international communication, in particular as a counsellor and conciliator who succeeded in surmounting conflicting opinions on the most difficult questions. His eminent service and the esteem in which he was held was recognized by numerous national decorations.

Curchod may, indeed, be considered a pioneer of the conception of the international secretariat and of permanent international organizations, involving a limited but early delegation, on the part of national states, of some of their liberty of action to the "International Bureau" progressively established from 1865 to 1872.

Prior to 1865, Napoleon III and Klemens Metternich had in their consultations recognized and foreseen the political importance of the telegraph. In the light of the technological explosion of the industrial era, they were among the first to see the imperative need to set up a body to regulate and standardize internationally the use of this important new method of communication, taking into particular account the fragmentation of Europe into a large number of independent states. Unlike the United States, where telegraphic communication remained in the hands of private enterprise, the European telegraph administrations were governmental. It may well be in part due to studies in Paris during his formative years that Curchod took this prophetic view as his ideal.

The International Bureau, as it was then named, had a difficult and protracted birth. In 1868, as Swiss delegate to a conference in Vienna, Curchod proposed the creation of a permanent bureau to carry on the routine tasks of the Union, under the supervision of the telegraph administration of a member country and headed by a director appointed by the conference. Such appointment was opposed by the French delegate, who considered that, if the bureau and the director were not placed entirely under the direction of a telegraph administration, it would have a position of independence incompatible with the "dignity and liberty" of the telegraph administrations.

Despite arguments against the French view, it was decided simply to mention in the Convention and Regulations that a bureau was to be established under the direction of a telegraph administration chosen by the conference and free to determine its structure. The Swiss Telegraph Administration was chosen, and the conference recommended that Curchod should be its first director.

Curchod achieved a certain amount of independence for the Bureau and the office of director by his own action. After almost a year, he resigned, protesting that the provisions of the Vienna Convention and Regulations did not make adequate provision for the operation of the new Bureau.

As Swiss delegate to the Rome Conference (1871–72), Curchod refrained from supporting proposals which, although strengthening the authority of the director, might have entrusted an auditing of accounts to a non-Swiss telegraph administration. It may be asked if Curchod's reticence was not motivated by a wish to maintain the Bureau under Swiss auspices; in any event, the Bureau was taken from the authority of the Swiss telegraph administration and placed under what was described as the high authority of the chief administration of the Swiss government in order to give it a certain amount of independence. The director of the Bureau was given the right to participate in telegraph conferences. Extra budgetary provision was made to raise the salary of the director. While the Bureau was never given any more independence than was expressed in the Rome Convention and Regulations, the administrative work of the Bureau steadily increased under Curchod's leadership until his death in 1889.

It may be that the subsequent development of the Bureau telegraphique and, in particular, from 1906 the attachment to the Bureau of the newborn Union radiotelegraphique was the long-term consequence of Curchod's persistent but diplomatic pursuit of his aim of making the Bureau an independent organ.

BIBLIOGRAPHY:

B. George A. Codding, Jr. *The International Telecommunication Union: An Experiment in International Cooperation* (Leiden, 1952); *Journal telegraphique,* Berne, 25 October 1889; *Recueil des Genéalogies vaudoises* (III), Lausanne, 1950.

Gilberte Perotin

CZARTORYSKI, Adam Jerzy George (14 January 1770, Warsaw—15 July 1861, Montfermeil, France). *Education*: privately educated, Poland and abroad. *Career*: Russian minister plenipotentiary, Court of Sardinia, 1799–1801; deputy foreign minister, 1802–4; foreign minister, 1804–6; curator, Vilno Univ., 1803–24; member, Senate and State Council, 1805–6; senator and member, Council of Administration, Kingdom of Poland, 1815–31; elected president, Polish Provisional Government, 1830; elected president, Polish National Government, 1831 (29 January–15 August).

Born into nobility, Czartoryski received an extensive education in Poland and abroad, including England. He took part in the war of 1792, but following the disastrous turn of events he went into exile. With the 1795 partition of Poland, the Czartoryski family was threatened with the confiscation of property and land by Russia. The prince was sent to intercede at the Court of St. Petersburg, where he became a virtual hostage. He became fast friends, however, with the future tsar, Alexander I, and until their estrangement was his principal adviser and mentor. Czartoryski thus played a leading role in Russia's foreign and domestic life and as deputy and later foreign minister was one of the outstanding figures in Russia's political life.

At the Conference of Vienna in 1815, Czartoryski acted as spokesman for Polish interests and with Alexander I was responsible for the creation of the Kingdom of Poland. Following the insurrection of 1831, in which he took an active part, the prince went into self-imposed exile. Settling in France, he became the leader of the Polish state in exile, and his Paris residency, the Hôtel Lambert, became the seat of his political offices.

During his career as a Russian statesman, Czartoryski developed his Grand Design, which advocated the organization of Europe into a league of free nations. Although not unique, since it had been considered by others including St. Pierre, Sully, Rousseau, and Kant, the prince tried to reconcile the issues of lasting peace and nationalism. Over the years, he evolved and refined his treatise and presented it as an elaborate historical plan in his *Essai*. Czartoryski believed that a society of states would enable nations to strive for common prosperity and that it could be attained solely through the progress of civilization. Lasting peace could be achieved only through gradual change—by the redrawing of existing frontiers to coincide with natural boundaries or the nationality of the inhabitants and by the adoption of liberal institutions and representative governments. He saw England and

Russia as vital to a real and durable peace, and he viewed their cooperation as essential to a stable Europe.

The prince had a vision of a new Europe composed of national states, joined together into unions or federations and united into a league of nations to safeguard equity and justice in international relations and to act as a system of collective security. Czartoryski did not doubt that most governments would be eager to adhere to a league that would ensure their security. His theory was based on the assumption that all nations have a natural right to an independent existence. If a country is not independent, then its freedom was usurped by an unjust act. Czartoryski opposed the subordination of the rights of nations to the interests of greater powers. No nation should be master of another. However, smaller states could, of their own volition, align themselves with major ones. He believed that all nations are subject to the common laws of mankind and to the principles of justice and equity. The new European order he expounded was far in the future and did not provide an immediate answer to the problems that plagued Europe.

BIBLIOGRAPHY:

A. *Essai sur la diplomatie, par un Philhellène* (Marseilles, 1830; Paris, 1864); *Le Dernier Mot sur le Statut organique imposé à la Pologne* (Paris, 1833); *Mémoires du Prince Czartoryski et sa correspondance avec l'Empéreur Alexandre I*, ed. Charles de Mazade, 2 vols. (Paris, 1887), English edition, ed. Adam Gielgud, 2 vols. (London, 1888).

B. Marian Kukiel, *Czartoryski and European Unity 1770–1861* (Princeton, NJ, 1955); Charles Morley, "Alexander I and Czartoryski," *Slavonic and East European Review* 25, (Apr 1947), 405–26, "Czartoryski's Attempts at a New Foreign Policy Under Alexander I," *American Slavic and East European Review* 12, (no. 4, 1953), 475–85; *Polski słownik biograficzny* 4 (Kraków, 1938), 257–69; *Wielka encyklopedia powszechna PWN* 2 (Warsaw, 1963), 699–700.

Zofia Sywak

D

DAFOE, John Wesley (8 March 1866, Cómbermere, ON—9 January 1944, Winnipeg, MB). *Education*: Arnprior School, near Ottawa. *Career*: reporter for various newspapers, 1882–1900; editor, *Winnipeg Free Press*, 1900–1944.

As editor of the *Winnipeg Free Press,* Dafoe became a strong supporter of collective security through the League of Nations. In 1929 he was appointed as nonnational commissioner under the Treaty for the Advancement of Peace between the United States and Germany, which had been signed in Washington in 1928. In 1936 he was chosen as chairman of the Institute of Pacific Relations for a five-year term. He was a founder of and remained prominent in the Canadian Institute of International Affairs. Dafoe's interest in international affairs, paradoxically, arose out of his Canadian nationalism and his intense desire to detach Canada from the British Empire within the Commonwealth system and to establish the independence of the country. His editorials on this subject led to his choice, in 1919, by *Robert Borden, the Canadian prime minister, as information officer with the Canadian delegation to the Versailles Peace Conference. In fact, he became much more than a press officer and may be described as an unofficial adviser to the delegation.

The breakup of the empire and the withdrawal of the United States into isolationism convinced Dafoe that a strong international organization was essential, and he became a tireless advocate of a League of Nations backed by force if necessary. From the first, he saw Hitler as a "maniac" out to rule the world and appeasement as a sign of weakness that must ultimately lead to disaster. He termed Mussolini's invasion of Ethiopia as a brazen act of military imperialism and repeatedly urged that it be met with international force. Dafoe's paper was one of a very few to see the Munich settlement as utterly calamitous and one which would lead to war. He was, as he put it in a letter, relieved to hear the news of 1 September 1939, and for the five years of life that remained he continued to urge that, following the defeat of Hitler, a truly international order be established.

BIBLIOGRAPHY:

B. Murray Donnelly, *Dafoe of the Free Press* (Toronto, 1968); *Encyclopedia Canadiana* 3 (Toronto, 1970), 189–90; Richard Veatch, *Canada and the League of Nations* (Toronto, 1975); WWWA 2, 142.

C. Dafoe papers are in the Public Archives of Canada and in the Univ. of Manitoba Library.

Murray Donnelly

DANDURAND, Raoul (4 November 1861, Montreal—11 March 1942, Ottawa). *Education*: Coll. of Montreal; LL.B., Laval Univ., 1882. *Career*: Canadian Senate, 1898–1942, speaker, 1905–9, minister without portfolio and government representative, 1921–30, 1935–42, leader, Liberal party, 1930–35; representative to League of Nations, 1924–30, 1937, president of Assembly, 1925.

Few Canadians demonstrated a sustained interest in international affairs before 1939, but Dandurand was one exception. In 1900 he began to participate regularly in the meetings of the Inter-Parliamentary Union, visiting almost all the European capitals and meeting many of the political personalities he was later to work with in Geneva. He was deeply attached to Great Britain and its institutions but no less a great admirer of France, his second mother country, where he associated with a group of influential politicians and intellectuals. Thus when he arrived in Geneva in 1924 as Canada's representative at the League of Nations, he was already known in international circles.

Dandurand was a passionate defender of the League of Nations. It is paradoxical that one of his most-quoted speeches is an explanation of Canada's cautious isolationist attitude to the League: "May I be permitted to add that in this association of mutual insurance against fire the risks assumed by the different states are not equal? We live in a fireproof house, far from inflammable materials. A vast ocean separates us from Europe" (*League of Nations Fifth Assembly Debates* [2 Oct 1924], 222). This statement accurately describes Canadian foreign policy, which avoided involvement in the affairs of other nations. But Dandurand did see the League of Nations as the only body which could avoid war in the future. For him, the League was "a mighty clearinghouse for world grievances," "a tribune from which the human voice can be heard and carried to the four corners of the world" (*Gazette* [Montreal] 9 Nov 1925). Moreover, only the League of Nations could establish a new order based on the three pillars of peace: arbitration, security, and disarmament. In 1924 Dandurand was personally in favor of the Geneva Protocol and recommended without success that Canada adhere to it. In 1925 he was elected president of the Assembly with the support of forty-one out of forty-seven nations. In 1927, although Canada's prime minister was reluctant to be drawn into European conflicts, Dandurand urged and obtained Canada's election to the Council of the League for a three-year term; as Canada's regular representative to the Council, he was concerned with the situation of minority groups in Eastern Europe. In 1929, when he suggested fairer procedures for dealing with the complaints of these minorities, he found himself in the midst of a bitter debate. During the 1930s Dandurand continued to support the League of Nations, insisting to the growing numbers of skeptics that "to abolish it would be to abandon humanity to fatalism and despair." He urged the

United States in particular to take its place at Geneva, convinced that "North America could not escape sharing the fate of Europe if another war convulses it anew" (*Montreal Daily Star* 15 Jun 1935).

Through his political career, Dandurand defended a policy of autonomy vis-à-vis Great Britain. He saw the League of Nations as the ideal vehicle for promoting Canada's new international status; he went out of his way to show that Canada was not bound to a single foreign policy dictated by Great Britain. He regarded his own position as president of the Assembly and Canada's election to a nonpermanent seat on the Council as perfect opportunities to advertise Canada's autonomy to the world. In the context of the interwar years in Canada, Dandurand stands out because of his interest in international affairs. As a result of his participation in the League of Nations, he was one of the first Canadians to be recognized internationally as a diplomat.

BIBLIOGRAPHY:

A. *Les Mémoires du Sénateur Raoul Dandurand (1861–1942)*, ed. Marcel Hamelin (Quebec, 1967).

B. C. P. Stacey, *Canada and the Age of Conflict 2: 1921–1948* (Toronto, 1981); Richard Veatch, *Canada and the League of Nations* (Toronto, 1975).

C. Memoirs of Dandurand are in the Public Archives of Canada.

Marcel Hamelin

DARBY, W. Evans. See *Biographical Dictionary of Modern Peace Leaders.*

DAVIES, Clement Edward (19 February 1884, Llanfyllin, Montgomeryshire, Wales—23 March 1962, London). *Education*: Trinity Hall, Cambridge, degree in law, 1907. *Career*: barrister, 1909–30; government service, World War I; junior counsel to Treasury, 1919–25; king's counsel, 1929; joined board of Unilever, 1930; member of Parliament for Montgomeryshire, 1929–62; leader, Liberal party, 1945–56.

After being called to the bar in 1909, Davies rapidly developed a highly successful commercial practice. At the outbreak of the war, he volunteered for military service in 1914, and he advised the procurator-general on enemy activities in neutral countries and on the high seas, then served in the Board of Trade's department concerned with trading with the enemy. After the war, he returned to the courts, was a junior Treasury counsel, and became king's counsel (i.e. prosecuting barrister) in 1926.

Davies entered Parliament in 1929 as a Liberal. Election year 1929 saw the return of a Labor government and the further decline in the fortunes of the Liberal party; following the formation of the National Government in 1931, he lost favor with some Liberals for giving it his support. In autumn 1939 he became chairman of an action committee in the House of Commons seeking the most effective prosecution of the war, in May 1940 his action was crucial in securing the formation of the Churchill coalition government.

The 1945 general election returned a Labor government under Clement Attlee; Davies became the leader of the handful of Liberal M.P.s returned to the Commons, and he had the unenviable task of holding them together. In 1951, when Churchill offered him the post of minister of education, pressure from Liberal peers ensured his refusal. In the years that followed he became increasingly preoccupied with the ideals of world government. He became involved in Inter-Parliamentary Union conferences and became president (1951) of the World Association of Parliamentarians for World Government, from which body arose the suggestion that he be nominated for the Nobel Peace Prize in 1955. Although unsuccessful, the support he received surprised his sponsors.

He remained leader of the miniscule parliamentary Liberal party until 1956 and an M.P. until his death. Throughout his life a champion of Parliament, he enjoyed public speaking, particularly to students at universities. There especially his zeal for social reform, collective security, and world government found a warm response.

BIBLIOGRAPHY:

B. Lord Boothby, *My Yesterday, Your Tomorrow* (London, 1962); CB 1950, 111–13; LT 24 Mar 1962, 10, 31 Mar 1962, 10; Frank Owen, *Tempestuous Journey* (London, 1954); J. C. Rasmussen, *The Liberty Party* (London, 1965); WWW 1961–70, 282–83.

Colin Gordon

DAVIES, David (11 May 1880, Llandinam, Wales—16 June 1944, Llandinam). *Education*: King's Coll., Cambridge Univ., 1903. *Career*: member of Parliament, 1906–29; major, Royal Welsh Fusiliers, 1914–16; parliamentary private secretary to prime minister, 1916–17; House of Lords, 1932–44.

Davies played a significant role in the interwar peace movement as the chief British exponent of a League of Nations backed by force. As a founder and leader of both the League of Nations Union and the New Commonwealth Society, Davies tried to build public support for collective security. Where most of his fellow internationalists were uncertain about how the League might secure peace and diffident in lobbying for their policies, Davies was outspoken in his advocacy of an international police force.

Davies, born into a rich and influential Welsh family, entered the House of Commons in 1906 as the Liberal member for Montgomeryshire. Uncomfortable as a party politician and as a public speaker, Davies did not establish a great reputation as a parliamentarian. However, as the director of many companies and as a public benefactor, he was an important figure in Welsh society.

When World War I began, Davies saw action in France, then returned to politics in June 1916 to serve as parliamentary private secretary to Prime Minister *David Lloyd George. Davies found it hard to moderate his comments, and after he fought Lloyd George's appointment of the press baron, Lord Northcliffe, to a mission in the United States, Lloyd George dismissed him abruptly in June 1917.

With his brief career in government ended, Davies plunged into what became a lifelong mission to promote international peace. He supported the League of Nations Society, which had been established in 1915 to encourage the creation of an international organization once the war ended. Then in June 1918, along with another coalition Liberal M.P., Charles McCurdy, he established the League of Free Nations Association, which aimed at the formation of a league of allies before the end of the war. The two groups were able to resolve their differences and merge into the League of Nations Union by the end of the year.

Davies was an important leader and the chief financial backer of the group, which attracted over a million members and exercised considerable influence in the years to come. Davies tried, as a member of the Union's Executive Committee and chairman of its Welsh National Council, to commit it to strengthening the League through the creation of an equity tribunal to settle disputes and an international force to uphold its decisions. When this effort failed, Davies founded, in 1932, the New Commonwealth movement to promote his collective security ideas. He attained prominence by his suggestion to combine the air forces of the world into an international police arm. Branches appeared in seventeen countries, and under the presidency of Winston Churchill in Britain it became an important internationalist group.

Davies was able to exert influence in many ways. He spoke in the House of Lords and wrote two books and many pamphlets to advance his ideas. He endowed Britain's first chair in international politics, at Aberystwyth, and acquired control of the National Press Agency, *Review of Reviews*, *Everyman*, and several local newspapers. Yet his ideas never gained the acceptance he hoped for and worked for with such determination.

BIBLIOGRAPHY:

A. *Force* (London, 1934); *The Problem of the Twentieth Century: A Study in International Relationships* (London, 1930).

B. DNB 1941–50, 199–200; LT 17 Jun 1944, 6.

C. The Davies papers are in the National Library of Wales.

Donald S. Birn

DAVIS, Hayne (2 November 1868, near Statesville, NC—5 March 1942, Boston). *Education*: B.A., Univ. of North Carolina, 1888. *Career*: law practice in Knoxville, TN, 1890–1904, New York, 1904–42; secretary, American delegation, Inter-Parliamentary Union, 1905–6; secretary, American Association for International Conciliation, 1907; founder, Peace and Arbitration League, 1908; vice-president, World Narcotic Defense Association, 1932.

Hayne Davis emerged an early American leader in the movement seeking international peace and disarmament through world government which thrived during the pre-World War I era. How he came to his ideas is unknown. As a young lawyer in New York specializing in international law, his writings attracted the attention of *Hamilton Holt, the editor of *The Independent*. He converted Holt to the idea of internationalism, and through *The Independent*, Davis emerged as a major publicist for the internationalist movement. He saw in the chaotic world about him the same forces working, primarily through the Hague Conference of 1899, that had produced the American union from thirteen sovereign states. These ideas, spelled out in his 1903 article in *The Independent*, "The Final Outcome of the Declaration of Independence," and in later ones, predicted the gradual evolution of a world system resembling the United States and including constitutional limitations upon governmental powers. Davis may have been the first to use the term "the United Nations." However, Davis always remained vague and even inconsistent as to the precise powers his world government would hold and those to be reserved to the individual nations. The most unique feature of Davis's internationalism was his strong belief in the need for increased armaments, particularly naval, although at the same time he believed that arbitration agreements between nations could be the foundation of permanent international peace. These ideas he shared with his cousin, Spanish War hero and congressman, *Richmond P. Hobson, with whom he was associated in several organizations. This mixture often brought Davis into conflict with other peace advocates.

An early supporter of the Inter-Parliamentary Union, Davis helped to bring its meeting to America in 1904. He served as secretary to the U.S. delegation in 1905 and 1906 at meetings in Europe, and in 1906 he became secretary of the American Association for International Conciliation, a branch of Conciliation Internationale. In 1907 Davis helped organize the First National Arbitration and Peace Congress in New York. It involved a wide variety of groups and produced much favorable publicity for the ideas then circulating about periodic congresses and arbitration. However, in 1908 Davis was forced out of the American Association for International Conciliation by *Nicholas Murray Butler.

Butler was worried about Davis's identification with the Colombian government, which he represented in its Panama Canal claims, and with his emphasis upon naval armaments. With Hobson, Davis then founded the American Peace and Arbitration League, which called for both arbitration and a larger navy. The new group attracted little support, and Davis appears to have gradually lost interest in internationalism. He failed to campaign for U.S. membership in the League of Nations but later actively endorsed cooperation with it. Davis did take part in one of Hobson's crusades, the World Narcotic Defense Association, and briefly served as vice-president. He also showed interest in a uniform world calendar in the

1930s and in the calling of a third Hague Peace Conference. Concerned that an effective new body be formed after World War II to maintain peace, Davis began a speaking tour in 1941 to promote again the ideal for which he had been a pioneer.

BIBLIOGRAPHY:

A. Ed., *Among the World's Peacemakers* (New York, 1907); "The Development of the Union," *The Independent* 61 (12 May 1904), 1072–76; "The Final Outcome of the Declaration of Independence," *The Independent* 55 (2 July 1903), 1543–47; "National Armament and International Justice," *The Independent* 64 (19 Mar 1908), 633–35; "Taking Our Place in the World," *The Independent* 105 (23 Apr 1921), 426.

B. Warren F. Kuehl, *Seeking World Order: The United States and International Organization to 1920* (Nashville, TN, 1969); Michael A. Lutzker, introduction to Davis, *Among the World's Peacemakers*, rpt. ed. (New York, 1972); WWWA 5, 172.

C. The Davis papers are in the Southern Historical Collection, Chapel Hill.

Walter E. Pittman, Jr.

DAVIS, John William (13 April 1873, Clarksburg, WV—24 March 1955, Charleston, SC). *Education*: A.B., Washington and Lee Coll., 1892; LL.B., Washington and Lee Law School, 1895. *Career*: assistant professor, Washington and Lee Law School, 1896–97; practicing attorney, Clarksburg, WV, 1897–1910; U.S. congressman, 1911–13; solicitor-general of the United States, 1913–18; ambassador to Great Britain, 1918–21; head of New York law firm, 1921–55; Democratic presidential candidate, 1924.

Although Davis's great distinction was as an appellate lawyer, he made a modest contribution to internationalism. While ambassador to the Court of St. James in 1919, he headed the U.S. delegation on the Rhineland Commission and persuaded the French to accept civilian control of the Rhineland. During the presidential campaign of *James M. Cox the following year, Davis spoke eloquently in favor of U.S. membership in the League of Nations. He continued to believe thereafter that the United States had a "duty" to join the League, and he was deeply disappointed when the Democratic National Convention of 1924 rejected *Newton D. Baker's uncompromisingly pro-League platform plank. Nominated for president by that same convention, Davis dutifully muted his own views through the campaign. He did speak forthrightly, however, for U.S. membership on the World Court. Meanwhile he invested himself in the organized peace and international movements through the boards of the Carnegie Endowment for International Peace, the American Foundation, and the League of Nations Association. In addition, he sat almost continuously on various bar associations' committees on international law, and he served as president of the Council on Foreign Relations for twelve years and as a director for many more.

Davis was so disillusioned by the U.S. failure to join the League of Nations that he was initially cautious about supporting the proposed United

Nations during World War II. At the insistence of *John Foster Dulles, he reluctantly agreed in April 1944 to sign the Federal Council of Churches' declaration of support. Then, in November, he joined Philip C. Jessup, *James T. Shotwell, *Quincy Wright, and others in an uncompromising public endorsement of the prospective new organization. In a radio address the following month, Davis attacked the contention of isolationists that it would be unconstitutional to delegate the war-making power to the Security Council. Two months later he again took to the air to call for creation of a permanent United Nations Commission on Human Rights as well as for reduction of trade barriers, stabilization of currency, and the creation of a world bank. Meanwhile he criticized the Nuremberg Trials on the ground that punishment of war criminals should properly be a matter of policy rather than law.

Davis's most important service to internationalism came in 1954, a year before his death. Fearful that the pending Bricker Amendment would make the U.S. procedure for carrying out treaty obligations too cumbersome, he headed a special committee of the Association of the Bar of the City of New York, the only bar association in the country to oppose the amendment. Then, at President Dwight Eisenhower's request, he wrote him a long and apparently influential letter in which he declared, among other things, that adoption of the amendment would measurably increase the difficulty of resolving atomic concerns by general agreement.

BIBLIOGRAPHY:

B. DAB supp. 5, 155–56; William H. Harbaugh, *Lawyer's Lawyer: The Life of John W. Davis* (New York, 1973); NYT 26 Mar 1955, 15.

C. The Davis papers are at Yale Univ.

William H. Harbaugh

DAVIS, Malcolm Waters (18 September 1889, Hartford, CT—14 November 1970, New York). *Education*: B.A., Yale Univ., 1911; M.A., Columbia Univ., 1924. *Career*: journalist, *Springfield* (MA) *Republican*, 1911–13, *New York Evening Post*, 1913–16, 1920–22; U.S. Information Service, 1917–19; managing editor, *Our World Magazine*, 1922–24; executive director, Council on Foreign Relations, 1925–27; editor, Yale University Press, 1927–1931; foundation executive, 1931–51.

Throughout his career, Davis directed most of his efforts to the promotion of world cooperation and the improvement of international relations. He is best known for his long association with the Carnegie Endowment for International Peace (1931–51) and later as consultant. Davis began his career as a journalist, served in World War I in prisoner relief work in Scandinavia and Russia, and was sent by the U.S. Information Service to Russia and Siberia where he crossed overland to Peking in 1918 and then to Vladivostok. During this period, he became proficient in Russian and later translated several works into English. He joined *Herbert Houston in 1922 in developing *Our World Magazine*, an effort to present the American public with international news.

When the Carnegie Endowment in 1931 needed a capable observer in Geneva for the approaching World Disarmament Conference, its leaders chose Davis. From then until 1935, he served as representative of the Endowment in Geneva and as director of the Geneva Research Center. In 1935 he began a twelve-year tenure as associate director of the Carnegie Endowment's European Center in Paris. Beginning in 1941, he also was associate director of the Division of Intercourse and Education in its New York headquarters. He was acting director of the Endowment, 1946–47, and director of publications and research, 1948–51. In 1945 he attended the United Nations Conference in San Francisco. In 1949 he served as chairman of the National Citizens Committee for United Nations Day and the following year was chairman of its Executive Committee.

When he terminated his full-term status with the Carnegie Endowment in 1951, Davis became, for two years, dean of the Free Europe University in Exile and the College of Free Europe in Strasbourg, France. The following year he taught at Wheaton College (Mass.). From 1957 to 1960 he was a consulting editor for *Western World Magazine*. His interest in the foreign-born was demonstrated by his service as a director of and consultant to the American Council for Nationalities Service and as chairman of the American Fund for Czechoslovak Refugees. He was also associate secretary-general of the International League of Red Cross Societies, 1939–40. In all his activities, Davis revealed his strong belief in international intellectual cooperation, what he termed a "league of minds." In 1944 in *Pioneers in World Order*, he wrote, "The quest must go on among peoples for those reconciling truths that underlay differences, for the spiritual unity of common values expressed in rich variety throughout the world."

BIBLIOGRAPHY:

A. "The League of Minds," in *Pioneers in World Order: An American Appraisal of the League of Nations*, ed. Harriet Eager Davis (New York, 1944), 240–49; *Open Gates to Russia* (New York, 1920).

B. Carnegie Endowment for International Peace, *Annual Reports, 1932–51*; Davis's Oral History is at Columbia Univ.; NYT 15 Nov 1970, 82.

A. LeRoy Bennett

DAVIS, Norman Hezekiah (9 August 1878, Normandy, TN—1 July 1944, Washington). *Education*: Vanderbilt Univ., 1897–98; Stanford Univ., 1899–1900. *Career*: businessman and banker, 1902–44; assistant secretary of treasury, 1919–20; under secretary of state, 1920–21; adviser and delegate to international conferences, 1917–37; Red Cross executive, 1938–44.

After attending college and engaging in farming and manufacture, Davis moved to Cuba to take advantage of the newly independent island's expanding economy. In 1905, having mastered Spanish and banking, he founded the Trust Company of Cuba. In this and other enterprises he amassed a considerable fortune and a sound reputation, notwithstanding having been found civilly liable in a fraud action brought by an absent business associate. In addition to financial security, Cuba gave him many of the concepts he carried into later life: optimism, good will, a "business approach" to the problems of the world, and a conviction of the importance of international finance.

When America went to war in 1917, Davis withdrew from Cuba, moved to New York City, and volunteered his services to the government. He soon found a niche in the Treasury Department and started the second phase of his life. Success in negotiating a critical loan from neutral Spain in 1918 established his name. This was the first major achievement of the "unprofessional diplomat," as his friend *John W. Davis described him. Small in stature, quiet and deliberative, patient and persuasive, Davis had a lively sense of humor and a quick intellect. His homely manner of expression made complicated problems seem simple.

After his mission to Spain, Davis went to Paris as a Treasury assistant to *Herbert Hoover, who was negotiating postwar relief policies; then he became financial adviser to the American Commission at the Paris Peace Conference. He was also assigned to the Reparations Commission, where he sought to prevent the imposition of unrealistic war costs upon Germany. His experiences in Paris and his own political convictions made Davis an ardent Wilsonian and a lifelong Democrat. After the Conference he became assistant secretary of the treasury in charge of the Foreign Loan Bureau, where he strongly opposed the cancelation of interallied war debts.

Wilson described Davis as too fine a person to lose from public service and appointed him under secretary of state in 1920. There Davis helped form the policy of nonrecognition of the Soviet government, which had renounced tsarist debts. He advocated a new Pan Americanism in Latin America to replace "dollar diplomacy" and worked to strengthen Anglo–American amity. When the Republicans took office in 1921, Davis refused a request to remain in the State Department. Instead, he accepted an occasional governmental mission and a role as "counselor to the opposition." A strong internationalist, he consistently argued for the League of Nations, the World Court, and reduction of tariffs. He fought, usually unsuccessfully, to have his views embodied in Democratic planks during the interwar years. "America First" was to him the slogan of the backwoodsman. In 1921 he helped organize the Council on Foreign Relations. In 1924 he assisted the League in resolving a dispute over the Baltic port of Memel and also became president of the *Woodrow Wilson Foundation. Later, in 1927, he was named by Calvin Coolidge as a delegate to the Geneva Economic Conference.

Davis's chief preoccupation in the 1930s was disarmament. He believed that mutual security agreements must accompany arms reduction. Hoover sent him to the General Disarmament Conference in Geneva in 1932, and later *Franklin D. Roosevelt elevated him to the chairmanship of the U.S. delegation. This Conference never reached agreement, unfortunately, and lapsed in 1934. He witnessed another futile chapter in disarmament at the London Naval Conference in 1935–36. Davis's other personal concerns focused on the economic nationalism of the early New Deal.

After Japan attacked North China in 1937, Davis led the U.S. delegation to the Brussels Conference, having helped Roosevelt prepare the famed "quarantine" speech. The resulting resurgence of isolationism caused Roosevelt to abandon cooperation at Brussels and to place no obstacle in Japan's path. That same year the Woodrow Wilson Foundation awarded Davis its distinguished medal for "meritorious service to democracy, public welfare, liberal thought, and peace through justice."

In 1938 Roosevelt appointed Davis to head the American Red Cross, a responsibility he undertook with the prophetic observation that he could now "help alleviate human suffering, which cannot be prevented" (*San Francisco Examiner*, 2 May 1938). He presided over the vast wartime expansion of the Red Cross, both as head of the American branch and as chairman of the board of the International Red Cross, and held these posts until his death. He also continued to advise the president on foreign policy and especially on postwar planning that led to the creation of the UN. Although little known to the general public, Davis was respected in government circles both at home and abroad as an executive agent who carried out U.S. foreign policy and a planner who helped shape it.

BIBLIOGRAPHY:

B. DAB supp. 3, 218–19; NYT 2 Jul 1944, 1; Thomas C. Irvin, "Norman Davis and the Quest for Arms Control," dissertation, Ohio State Univ., 1963; H. B. Whiteman, Jr., "Norman H. Davis and the Search for International Peace and Security, 1917–1944," dissertation, Yale Univ., 1958; WWWA 2, 146.

C. The Davis papers are in the Manuscript Division, Library of Congress.

Harold B. Whiteman, Jr.

DAWES, Charles Gates (27 August 1865, Marietta, OH—23 April 1951, Evanston, IL). *Education*: B.A., Marietta Coll., 1884, M.A., 1887; LL.B., Cincinnati Law School, 1886. *Career*: attorney, Lincoln, NE, 1887–95; businessman and banker, Chicago, 1895–1951; comptroller of currency, 1897–1901; director, Bureau of the Budget, 1921–22; U.S. vice-president, 1925–29; ambassador to Great Britain, 1929–32; participant in several international conferences, committees, and League of Nations discussions.

Noted for his political and banking careers, Dawes had an interest in philanthropy, the arts, and anthropology, and wide reading in history equipped him for the internationalist role he played. He served as comptroller of the currency, as purchasing agent for the Expeditionary Force in

World War I, as a member of the Military Board of Allied Supply, and as a participant on the United States Liquidation Commission to dispose of surplus war stocks in France.

Dawes supported the Covenant of the League of Nations. While critical of opponents of the League, he was not oblivious to the problem of U.S. sovereignty in relation to Article X and its principle of collective security. In 1924, as the vice-presidential nominee of the Republican party, he could scarcely have been an active proponent of the Covenant, yet he continued to display a concern for world problems, especially economic ones.

Intergovernmental debts and especially reparations imposed upon the vanquished disturbed the normal international flow of both money and goods. When Germany failed to meet her scheduled payments in 1923, France and Belgium occupied the Ruhr Valley. A German miners' strike plus the inflation of the German mark led to the creation of a Commission of Experts chaired by Dawes and containing representatives from the United States, Britain, Italy, France, and Japan. The resulting Dawes Plan provided for a complex system of payments with a formula on amounts due plus methods for raising funds through assessments against German industry, railroads, the transport system, and the Reich budget. Since the principle of "German capacity to pay" was substituted for the harsher Versailles principle of "payment for all the loss and damage," and since Germany received help through an international loan, she experienced a temporary economic and fiscal revival. For his valuable work, Dawes received the Nobel Peace Prize in 1925.

While vice-president and presiding officer of the Senate, Dawes gave vigorous support to the Kellogg-Briand Pact of 1928 renouncing war as an instrument of national policy. During his ambassadorship to Britain, he tried to improve U.S.–British relations, which had been strained by the abortive negotiations of the Geneva Disarmament Conference of 1927. He participated in the London Naval Conference of 1930, which succeeded in obtaining an Anglo–American–Japanese agreement imposing tonnage quotas on cruisers, destroyers, and submarines. In 1931 he became involved in discussion in Paris to resolve the Japanese attack on Manchuria, and he tried to help in the international economic crisis triggered by the Austro–German banking failure of that year. This last effort clearly confirmed that Dawes, as an internationalist, thought more in economic than in political terms as he sought to broaden interrelationships.

BIBLIOGRAPHY:

B. Harold T. Butler, "Partisan Positions on Isolationism vs. Internationalism (1918–1932)," dissertation, Syracuse Univ., 1963; John M. Carroll, "The Making of the Dawes Plan, 1919–1924," dissertation, Univ. of Kentucky, 1972; Melvyn P. Leffler, *The Elusive Quest: America's Pursuit of European Stability and French Security, 1919–1933* (Chapel Hill, NC, 1979); Gary B. Ostrower, *Collective Insecurity: The United States and the League of Nations during the Early Thirties* (Lewisburg, PA, 1979); Stephen A. Schuker, *The End of French Predominance in Europe: The*

Financial Crisis of 1924 and the Adoption of the Dawes Plan (Chapel Hill, NC, 1976); Bascom N. Timmons, *Portrait of an American: Charles G. Dawes* (New York, 1953).

C. The Dawes papers are in the Northwestern Univ. Library. Some are in the Manuscript Division, Library of Congress.

Harold T. Butler

DE GASPERI, Alcide (3 April 1881, Pieve Tesino, Austria—19 August 1954, Sella di Valsugana, Italy). *Education*: degree in philology, Univ. of Vienna, 1905. *Career*: organized Trentine Popular party, 1906; deputy, Austrian Parliament, 1911–18; as Italian citizen after 1919 entered Sturzo's Italian Popular party, political secretary, 1924–25; deputy, Italian Parliament 1921–26; principal founder, post–World War II Italian Christian Democratic party, secretary, 1953–54; premier, 1945–53.

Both as an activitist in the Catholic movement of the Trentino and as a deputy in the Austrian Parliament, De Gasperi attacked chauvinistic and racial nationalism. He called upon European political parties, and especially those of Catholic inspiration, to develop a sense of internationalism in order to further the cause of both peace and justice.

As a member of the Italian Popular party, De Gasperi supported its endorsement of the League of Nations and all it symbolized in the way of internationalism. The triumph of Mussolini and Fascism and the subsequent expulsion of Popular party deputies from the Italian Parliament stilled De Gasperi's voice from 1926 to 1943. However, when he wrote under a pseudonym for the Vatican journal, *L'Illustrazione Vaticana*, De Gasperi reiterated his longstanding ideals, not the least of which was European unity. He praised the Pan Europe movement of the 1930s as an organic and balanced expression of the common spiritual heritage of European civilization.

As Italian premier, representing the Christian Democratic party and presiding over eight consecutive ministries, De Gasperi consistently gave his support to European unity projects. He was not discouraged by setbacks and in fact was convinced that European unity could be achieved only by pursuing gradualist and flexible approaches. Although the military aspects of NATO displeased him, he favored Italy's entry into the pact; failure to enter would, he feared, jeopardize Italy's relations with her Western European neighbors and thereby retard the progress of European union. He strongly supported the Organization for European Economic Cooperation (OEEC), not only because of the material benefits it would bring to Italy but also because he viewed it as providing the foundation for a European federation. Although the desired integration did not materialize, the OEEC facilitated Italy's entry into the Council of Europe and the European Coal and Steel Community. After 1951 De Gasperi pinned his hopes for European unity on the ECSC. He also supported the Pleven plan for a European

Defense Community, interpreting it as still another link in forging a United States of Europe. In September 1952 he joined *Robert Schuman of France in proposing that an enlarged European Coal and Steel Community Assembly prepare a constitution for a European Political Community. That same month he journeyed to Aachen to receive the Charlemagne Prize for his contributions to the European unity movement. He was very proud of the medal he received there, and he gave his family the following instructions: "Place this decoration, and only this one, on the cushion that will be carried at my funeral." It was done in August 1954.

BIBLIOGRAPHY:

A. *De Gasperi scrive*, ed. Maria Romana Catti De Gasperi, 2 vols. (Brescia, Italy, 1974); *Discorsi politici*, ed. Tommaso Bozza, 2 vols. (Rome, 1956); *I Cattolici dall'opposizione al governo* (Bari, Italy, 1955); *I Cattolici trentini sotto l'Austria*, ed. Gabriele De Rosa, 2 vols. (Rome, 1964).

B. Elisa Carrillo, *Alcide De Gasperi: The Long Apprenticeship* (Notre Dame, IN, 1965); Maria Romana Catti De Gasperi, *De Gasperi uomo solo* (Milan, 1964), *La nostra patria Europe: Il pensiero europeistico di Alcide De Gasperi* (Milan, 1969).

Elisa Carrillo

DE GAULLE, Charles A.J.M. (22 November 1890, Lille, France—9 November 1970, Colombey-les-Deux-Eglises, France). *Education*: Coll. Stanislas, Paris, 1908–9; Saint-Cyr Military Academy, 1910–12. *Career*: officer in French Army, 1914–46; chief, later president, Free French and French Committee of National Liberation, 1940–43; president, Provisional French government, 1944–46; prime minister, June 1958–January 1959; president, 1959–69.

De Gaulle's internationalism is not immediately obvious. A career officer in the French Army after graduation from a military academy, his advancement was slow during the interwar years, notably because the military hierarchy rejected the military theories he presented in his book, *Toward a Career Army*. Recognized in 1940 as the leader of French resistance against the German occupiers, he devoted his efforts during World War II to ensuring the survival of a French government and forces that would be able to reclaim for France its position as a great national power at war's end. In the period 1944–46, as head of the French government, his primary goal was the reestablishment of French national self-esteem by restoration of the economy and of stable political authority. While out of office, between 1946 and 1958, he vigorously denounced all efforts to unify Western Europe, from the formation of the Council of Europe in 1949 to the creation of the Common Market in 1958. Then, as president of France (1958–69), he roused the anger of all supporters of the Common Market in France by his rejection of British membership, his insistence on French veto power in the Council of Ministers, and his determination to reduce the independent powers of the Commission. As the self-proclaimed supporter of a "Europe of the States," de Gaulle appeared the prime opponent of the European integration move-

206 DE GAULLE, CHARLES A.J.M.

ment inspired and organized by such leaders as *Jean Monnet, whose basic premise was that the European nation-states must cede at least part of their sovereignty to a supranational European government. De Gaulle, however, sought to contribute to the effort without in any way compromising his own ideals, both to European integration and indeed to internationalism on a world scale.

First, the Common Market owed to de Gaulle the implementation in parallel in the years 1958–62 of agricultural and industrial integration. Without the threat of a de Gaulle ultimatum, the marathon negotiating sessions which created the Common Agricultural Policy would never have been successfully concluded. Moreover, de Gaulle's realism in insisting that the Community remain restricted in size during its formative years permitted the intermeshing of the economies of the six original members into a union that could, without dislocation, be expanded later to include such varied countries as Britain and Greece. Second, de Gaulle envisaged a united Europe that would embrace both Eastern and Western countries and would, as he said in 1946, extend from the Atlantic to the Urals. Refusing to recognize the inevitable division of Europe by the iron curtain, he constantly sought a reconciliation of non-Communist and Communist countries, spearheaded by a close relationship between France and the Soviet Union. Third, de Gaulle refused to accept the division of the world into warring, ideological blocs. He sought a new multipolar structure of international relations in place of alliance systems dominated by the United States and the Soviet Union. Fourth, he demanded that the industrialized world share more generously its knowledge and wealth with the developing countries. After France's colonial possessions in Africa received their independence (1959–62), de Gaulle insisted that France set an example by granting to them and other Third World countries economic aid that amounted to a higher contribution per capita of the French population than that of any other country. De Gaulle, in short, conceived of an internationalism in which the nation-state would be the constituent unit within a world community of mutually cooperating peoples.

BIBLIOGRAPHY:

A. *Memoirs of Hope: Renewal, 1958–62; Endeavour, 1962–* (New York, 1971); *War Memoirs*, 3 vols. (New York, 1955–60).

B. Edmond Jouve, *Le Général de Gaulle et la construction de l'Europe (1940–1966)* (Paris, 1967); W. W. Kulski, *De Gaulle and the World: The Foreign Policy of the Fifth French Republic* (Syracuse, NY, 1966); Alexander Werth, *De Gaulle: A Political Biography* (Baltimore, MD, 1967); Dorothy White, *Black Africa and de Gaulle: From the French Empire to Independence* (University Park, PA, 1979).

F. Roy Willis

DE LAVALEYE, Emile. See *Biographical Dictionary of Modern Peace Leaders*.

DE VISSCHER, Charles (2 August 1884, Ghent, Belgium—2 January 1973, Brussels). *Education*: Univ. of Ghent; Univ. of Paris, 1908. *Career*: professor, Univ. of Ghent, 1911–30; director, *Revue de droit international et de législation comparée*, 1920–194?; secretary-general, Institut de Droit International, 1925–37, president; member, Permanent Court of Arbitration, 1923–45; lecturer, Academy of International Law, The Hague, 1923, 1925, 1929, 1935; professor, Univ. of Louvain, 1930–73; judge, Permanent Court of International Justice, 1937–46; president, Political Movement for Resistance, 1940–44; minister without portfolio, 1944–45; member, Committee of Jurists to draft statute of the International Court of Justice, 1945; delegate, San Francisco Conference; delegate, General Assembly, 1946; member, International Court of Justice, 1946–52; founding member of council, Royal Institute for International Relations, 1947–73, honorary president, 1947–58.

As a scholar and practitioner of both international law and Belgian foreign policy, de Visscher taught public and private international law and contributed to the conduct and documentation of Belgian diplomacy. The theme of his career, however, unifying his teaching, scholarship, diplomatic activities, international outlook, and juridical accomplishments, was the pursuit of the rule of law in relations between sovereign states.

During World War I, he published a compilation of documents in English highlighting Belgium's unique legal status, whereby her violation in 1914 constituted not only an act of aggression but also a crime against international law. In postwar Belgium, de Visscher became legal adviser to the Foreign Ministry and joined the delegation to the Paris Peace Conference. In both capacities, he worked on the unsuccessful effort to revise the 1839 treaties, which had created both riparian problems and Belgium's distinctive status of guaranteed armed neutrality. At Paris, he also served on the Commission on Ports, Waterways, and Railways.

During the interwar years, de Visscher participated in the League of Nations. He was rapporteur of the commission to amend the Covenant and of one to examine conciliation proceedings. He served on the Committee of Jurists established after the Corfu crisis of 1923 and on the expert committee dealing with codification of international law. He represented Belgium at the first codification conference and served as rapporteur of one of its committees. In addition to joining the Permanent Court of Arbitration, he served as member or president of six permanent League commissions for conciliation between various European states.

At the same time, de Visscher continued his teaching and legal studies, while editing one of Europe's most distinguished journals of international law. He also represented the Romanian, Polish, and Danish governments before the Permanent Court of International Justice in cases concerning international commissions for the Danube and Oder rivers, Polish rights in Danzig, and Eastern Greenland. This last activity was terminated by his election to the Court in 1937.

De Visscher sat upon the Permanent Court of International Justice until its demise in 1946 but passed the war years as leader of the Belgian resistance. After membership in the first postwar cabinet, he represented Belgium at the 1945 Washington deliberations to create a new world court and at the San Francisco Conference to establish the United Nations. His participation in the first UN General Assembly ended with his election to the new International Court of Justice. After serving, 1946–52, de Visscher resumed his scholarly endeavors in Brussels. In addition to his legal studies, he coedited five volumes of interwar Belgian diplomatic documents. His publications, nearly ninety in number, continued until his death.

BIBLIOGRAPHY:

A. *Aspects récents du droit procédural de la Cour Internationale de Justice* (Paris, 1966); *Belgium's Case: A Judicial Enquiry* (New York, 1916); with Fernand van Langenhove, *Documents diplomatiques belges, 1920–1940*, 5 vols. (Brussels, 1964–66); with Paul Fauchille, *La Guerre de 1914: Jurisprudence allemand en matière de prises maritimes*, 2 vols. (Paris, 1922–24); *Théories et réalités en droit international public* (Paris, 1953).

B. Paul Hymans, *Mémoires*, 2 vols. (Brussels, 1958); *ICJ Yearbook 1946–47* (Netherlands, 1947), 48; *Thirteenth Annual Report of the Permanent Court of International Justice* (Leiden, Netherlands, 1937), 26; Hans Wehburg, "Charles de Visscher," *Neue Zürcher Zeitung*, 2 Aug 1954; WB 1948, 1480; WWBL 1962, 322.

Sally Marks

DEAN, Vera Micheles (29 March 1903, St. Petersburg—10 October 1972, New York). *Education*: B.A., Radcliffe Coll., 1925; M.A., Yale Univ., 1926; Ph.D., Radcliffe Coll., 1928. *Career*: researcher, director of research, and editor, Foreign Policy Association, 1928–61.

For over a quarter of a century, Dean worked as research associate and research director for the Foreign Policy Association (FPA), where she established a reputation as an authority on Russia and the Soviet Union. From 1928 to 1961, she played a central role in its publication program, drafting a score of reports on Russia and writing for the FPA Headline series. In 1931 she became an editor for the research staff, and in 1938 she replaced *Raymond Leslie Buell as research director. In opinion essays for the *Foreign Policy Association News Bulletin*, she continually urged the United States to adopt less rigid policies toward the Soviet Union and to forget differences in social and political systems. While hoping for the best, Dean did not fail to recognize the basic antagonisms that existed between the two countries, and during World War II she pleaded for developing forward-looking policies for the postwar period that would ensure broad-based democratic reforms for the world.

In all her works and many lectures, she recommended a greater American understanding of world affairs and a stronger commitment to the ideal of international cooperation. Consistently she argued that Americans must not demand that other nations adopt American institutions and practices.

Rather, the United States should pursue policies which promoted a more peaceful world while recognizing that many nations would retain forms of government which were unacceptable to Americans. Only through such international understanding could real progress occur. Unlike many internationalists of the interwar years, Dean did not embrace pacifism, but rather called for collective action, including force, to maintain a stable world order in which all nations would receive fair treatment.

Dean's hopes for a world in which understanding characterized international relations often made her a controversial figure, and her views caused occasional outbursts directed toward her patriotism. In *Foreign Policy Without Fear*, she responded by asserting that until Americans were free to question foreign policy decisions, "the United States will find it increasingly difficult to inspire confidence in its common sense, its integrity, and its reliability in time of crisis."

In the 1930s Dean began a career as a lecturer, making the college and public affairs circuit. She also accepted visiting appointments to Barnard, Harvard, and Smith Colleges and the University of Rochester. Following her resignation from the FPA in 1961, she became a member of the faculty of New York University's Graduate School of Public Administration.

BIBLIOGRAPHY:

A. *Europe and the United States* (New York, 1950); *Europe in Retreat* (New York, 1939); *Foreign Policy Without Fear* (New York, 1954); *The Four Cornerstones of Peace* (New York, 1946); *The Nature of the Non-Western World* (New York, 1957); *New Governments in Europe* (New York, 1934); *Russia: Menace or Problem* (New York, 1947); *The U.N. Today* (New York, 1965); numerous articles in *Foreign Policy Reports* and *Foreign Policy Association News Bulletin*.

B. CB 1943, 160–62; NAW, *Modern Period*, 182–83; NYT 12 Oct 1972, 46; WWWA 5, 176.

C. The Dean papers are in the Schlesinger Library, Radcliffe Coll.

Frank W. Abbott

DEUTSCH, Eberhard Paul (31 October 1897, Cincinnati, OH—16 January 1980, New Orleans, LA). *Education*: law, Tulane Univ. 1924–25. *Career*: law practice in New Orleans, 1925–80; U.S. Army, 1917–19; General Staff Corps, 1942–46.

During 1945–46 Deutsch served as legal adviser to U.S. High Commissioner Mark W. Clark in the occupation of Austria. He directed the reestablishment of Austrian courts after seven years of Nazi rule and assisted with implementing an ingenious American innovation, the veto in reverse, requiring the veto of all four occupation powers to prevent the passage of Austrian legislation. Between 1956 and 1977 he served in New Orleans as consul-general for the Republic of Austria.

For the American Bar Association he was editor of *The International Lawyer* (1966–74), and he chaired ABA committees on peace and law through the United Nations and law treaties and was a director of the

Foreign Policy Association, the International House, and other international groups. His articles discussed various treaties, law conventions, and the International Court of Justice (ICJ). At the height of U.S. dissent over Vietnam, he staunchly defended the presidential right to conduct military operations abroad during both declared and undeclared wars.

Regarding world justice, Deutsch pointedly traced in his book the shortcomings of the ICJ and its predecessor, focusing on the reluctance of most nations to accept their jurisdiction. Fewer than fifty nations had signed declarations of adherence to jurisdiction of the ICJ, only two unconditionally. He advocated a controversial reconstituting of the Court by providing uniform treatment to all nations through compulsory jurisdiction. This increased power would persuade statesmen to seek greater diplomatic adjustment among themselves to avoid decisions. A two-thirds vote of the entire body could overrule a plea to the jurisdiction of the Court (an answer to the controversial Connally Amendment); judges would enjoy life tenure with voluntary retirement at age seventy, compulsory at seventy-five. Judges retained the power to withdraw from a case. All fifteen must be eligible for their own national judgeships and have reached the age of fifty but not sixty-five.

BIBLIOGRAPHY:

A. *An International Rule of Law* (Charlottesville, VA, 1977); "The President as Commander in Chief," *American Bar Association Journal* 57 (Jan 1971), 27–32.

B. CA 93–96, 122; NYT 18 Jan 1980, II-5; *Who's Who in Finance and Industry, 1979–80* (Chicago, 1979), 167–68.

Donald R. Whitnah

DICKINSON, Edwin DeWitt (19 May 1887, Bradford, IA—26 March, 1961, St. Helena, CA). *Education*: B.A., Carleton Coll., 1909; M.A., Dartmouth Coll., 1911; Ph.D., Harvard Univ., 1918; J.D., Univ. of Michigan, 1919. *Career*: instructor, Dartmouth Coll., 1913–15; assistant professor, Univ. of Illinois, 1915–17; professor, Univ. of Michigan, 1919–33, Univ. of California, 1933–35; professor, Univ. of Pennsylvania, 1948–56; member, Permanent Court of Arbitration, 1951–60.

Noted primarily as a teacher of international law, Dickinson did much to extend education in that field through his posts at three major universities and his publications. He was an authority on the equality of states, and in digests, case books, and many articles he sought to convey the growing complexity of international law and to show the spreading interrelationship of issues. He was convinced that international law was totally indispensable and continually developing. Indeed, the ultimate goal of peace would be attained through law rather than political institutions. Law would bring order and equity.

Dickinson's stature as a legal authority led to service on the board of editors (1924–38) of the AJIL, work with Harvard's Research in International Law, and appointment to the Permanent Court of Arbitration and to the Inter-American Permanent Commission of Investigation and Conciliation (1938). He acted as general counsel for the Mexican American Claims Commission (1943–44) and was president of the American Society of International Law (1952–53). He was an important link in the evolutionary process of moving the study of international law out of the field of political science to a level where it could stand as a separate discipline.

BIBLIOGRAPHY:

A. *Equality of States in International Law* (Cambridge, MA, 1920).

B. AJIL 55 (1961), 637–44; NYT 27 Mar 1961, 31; WWWA 4, 249.

Warren F. Kuehl

DICKINSON, Goldsworthy Lowes (8 June 1862, London—3 August 1932, London). *Education*: B.A., King's Coll., Cambridge Univ., 1884. *Career*: fellow, King's Coll., Cambridge Univ., 1887–93, librarian, 1893–96, lecturer, 1896–1920; lecturer, London School of Economics and Political Science, 1911–20.

A classicist, poet, philosophical writer, and historian, Dickinson was shocked by World War I. He argued for British neutrality, but once the die was cast he turned to considering how future wars might be avoided. He found the cause of conflict in the anarchy of the international system. The avoidance of future wars thus lay in a moderate peace in which Germany would be neither humiliated nor crushed and which provided for national self-determination, arms limitation, and a league of states. Throughout 1914, he described this as a European league which might ultimately control all of the armed forces of its members other than those needed for internal police.

Dickinson and like-minded Liberals agreed that, unless moderate terms were defined during the war, there would be a peace of revenge containing the seeds of yet another war. He presented this idea to *James Bryce, who prepared a memorandum for private discussion. Between November 1914 and February 1915, Bryce's text was examined by a group which transformed it into the Proposals for the Avoidance of War, a scheme for a postwar league of nations. The authors of this document, which was circulated privately in Great Britain and abroad, became known as the Bryce Group. Dickinson credited Quaker lawyer E. Richard Cross with being the group's sparkplug, but it was Dickinson who wrote and revised through successive editions the introductory essay which provided the rationale for the Proposals.

Dickinson corresponded with American league advocates and carried the Proposals to a meeting at The Hague in April 1915 which established the Central Organization for a Durable Peace, which called for a league. In May he joined in establishing the League of Nations Society to disseminate the league idea in Great Britain. Dickinson also participated in Fabian

Society discussions which formulated a design for an "international authority," and he helped frame a statement by the Quakers and the Union for Democratic Control which agreed upon expanded peace machinery. Although he joined the Union of Democratic Control reluctantly, Dickinson became a mainstay of this antiwar organization, speaking and writing on behalf of the democratic control of foreign policy and denouncing militarist conceptions of the peace. He proposed that economic and commercial frictions and colonial jealousies be eliminated by international regulations guaranteeing all states equal access to raw materials.

Dickinson toured the United States early in 1916, lecturing and exchanging views with the leaders of the League to Enforce Peace, whose program had been influenced by the Proposals. In August 1916 Dickinson condemned resolutions adopted by the Allies in June in Paris. These threatened an economic conflict following the war against Germany. In fact, Dickinson favored a European stalemate rather than victory and American mediation to end the war.

The Russian revolution in March 1917 and American entry into the war in April made the movement for a league of nations more acceptable in Great Britain than it had been. The revised Proposals were published in April, and the League of Nations Society held its first large public rally in May. Numerous public figures now openly endorsed the concept. In November Dickinson welcomed Lord Lansdowne's overture for a negotiated peace, but as the war continued his ideas were best represented in the Labor party. In May 1918 he became a member of its International Advisory Committee.

That spring some pro-league Liberals, who regarded the League of Nations Society as compromised by the views on the war held by Dickinson and several of his associates, formed a rival League of Free Nations Association. They wanted the Allies and the United States to create a league of nations immediately, and they proposed that even after the war Germany be excluded until she was chastened and reformed. Dickinson decried these ideas, claiming that only a league formed in the context of a moderate peace with Germany as an initial member could provide a basis for reconciliation. After lengthy negotiations, the two organizations were merged in October 1918 as the League of Nations Union, with *Edward Grey as president.

Dickinson hoped the League of Nations Union would influence the British government in the direction of moderation at the peace conference. He was profoundly disturbed, however, by the Treaty of Versailles, which placed sole guilt for the war upon Germany, levied what he regarded as ruinous reparations, and deprived Germany of all of her colonies under the guise of establishing the mandates system. The harsh and spiteful peace, Dickinson believed, rendered the League of Nations ineffective.

In the postwar era, Dickinson maintained a great interest in the League of Nations. He hoped it might yet override the peace treaties and provide a framework for curtailing armaments. He visited Geneva often, at times as a correspondent for the *Manchester Guardian*. In July 1923 he substituted for his fellow classicist, *Gilbert Murray, at the second session of the League's Committee on Intellectual Co-operation. Dickinson, however, remained disappointed by the aloofness of the United States and the isolation imposed by the Allies on Germany and the Soviet Union. He regretted the failure to disarm, the rejection of the Geneva Protocol, and the misuse of the League as an instrument of great-power diplomacy. He pleaded for a rewriting of the Treaty of Versailles, a strengthening of the League, and a diminution of national sovereignty. Germany's admission to the League in 1926 did little to alter the fundamental defects of the international system.

Late in 1926 Dickinson published his most extensive work on international relations, *The International Anarchy, 1904–1914*. It was to become a minor classic. Its theme, that World War I was the result of international anarchy, had been advanced by him steadily since 1914 in several books. Toward the end of his life, Dickinson retained a spark of optimism, but he had come to realize that the League of Nations nowhere had major support in public opinion. As long as that condition lasted, it would not be reformed, there would be no agreement curbing arms, and the threat of renewed war would loom over civilization.

BIBLIOGRAPHY:

A. *After the War* (London, 1915); *The Autobiography of G. Lowes Dickinson and Other Unpublished Writings*, ed. Dennis Proctor (London, [1973]); *The Choice Before Us* (London, 1917); *Economic War After the War* (London, 1916); *The European Anarchy* (London, 1916); *The International Anarchy, 1904–1914* (New York, [1926]); *War: Its Nature, Cause and Cure* (London, 1923); *The War and the Way Out* (London, 1914).

B. DNB 1931–40, 225–27; Martin D. Dubin, "Toward the Concept of Collective Security: The Bryce Group's 'Proposals for the Avoidance of War,' 1914–1917," *International Organization* 24 (Spring 1970), 288–318; E. M. Forster, *Goldsworthy Lowes Dickinson* (New York, 1934); LT 4 Aug 1932, 12; Keith Robbins, *The Abolition of War: The "Peace Movement" in Britain, 1914–1919* (Cardiff, 1976); Henry R. Winkler, *The League of Nations Movement in Great Britain, 1914–1919* (New Brunswick, NJ, 1952).

C. The Dickinson papers are at King's Coll., Cambridge Univ.

Martin David Dubin

DICKINSON, Willoughby Hyett (9 April 1859, Brownshill, Stroud, Gloucester, England—31 May 1943, Painswick, Gloucester). *Education*: Trinity Coll., Cambridge Univ. *Career*: London County Council, 1889–1907, deputy chairman, 1892–96, chairman, 1900; member of Parliament, 1906–18; president, World Alliance for Promoting Friendship Through the Churches, 1931–43.

Arising out of the liberal and progressive movement of the late nineteenth century, Dickinson led a life of disinterested public service. Early failure at the bar and a sense of guilt stemming from his comfortable upbringing accounts for his interest in public affairs and his broad concern for the human condition. He was also afflicted throughout his life by a diffident nature, a sense of imminent failure and sickness, and the prospect of an early death.

As a member of the London County Council, he devoted his energies to the need for additional housing, the improvement of parks, and the reorganization of greater London into a single administrative unit. During that time, he became involved in the first of his life's great causes, women's suffrage, and he supported several bills while in Parliament before World War I. At the same time, he deprecated the behavior of the militant suffragists and the refusal of the Liberal government to provide adequate facilities for the passage of women's suffrage. During the war, however, women's electoral disabilities were removed by means of an interparty conference (1916–17) in which Dickinson played a leading part.

The greatest cause which consumed Dickinson's energies during the latter part of his life was peace. Again, his views on this subject were an outgrowth of his youthful desire to reform and improve the world. He was also a devout Christian deeply interested in international affairs. Immediately preceding 1914, Dickinson assisted his Quaker friend, Allen Baker, in forming the Associated Councils of Churches in the British and German Empires to foster friendlier relations between the two countries through their respective clergies. In America he helped secure financial assistant from ⁺Andrew Carnegie to found the Church Peace Union. In the early days of August 1914, Dickinson and Baker helped convene an international church conference at Constance, Germany, and escaped the opening conflict only with great difficulty. Their quest for peace, however, survived the war in the World Alliance for Promoting International Friendship Through the Churches, which eventually led to the World Council of Churches.

During the struggle, Dickinson became fully committed to planning an international organization. He was a leader in the Bryce Group, helped organize the League of Nations Society, and served as chairman of its Executive Committee (1915–18). He attended meetings of Europeans in 1918 to develop strategies and served on the British League of Nations Commission at Paris. According to his biographer, the first tentative clauses of the League Covenant were typed from his notes by his secretary at 41 Parliament Street. He was also active in the League of Nations Union and served as vice-president of the latter (1924–28) and as president of the International Federation of League of Nations Societies (1925). He traveled extensively throughout Britain on its behalf and represented Great Britain at Geneva in 1923. Though never an extremist, he was ever an idealist and an advocate and organizer for peace.

BIBLIOGRAPHY:

A. "The Greatest Reform Act," *Contemporary Review* 113 (Mar 1918), 241–49.

B. Donald S. Birn, *The League of Nations Union, 1918–1945* (Oxford, 1981);

George W. Egerton, *Great Britain and the Creation of the League of Nations* (Chapel Hill, NC, 1978); LT 2 Jun 1943, 7; Hope Costley White, *Willoughby Hyett Dickinson, 1859–1943* (Gloucester, England, 1956); Henry R. Winkler, *The League of Nations Movement in Great Britain, 1914–1919* (New Brunswick, NJ, 1952); WW 1941, 844.

C. The Dickinson papers are in the Bodleian Library, Oxford Univ.

John D. Fair

DODD, Norris Edward (20 July 1879, Chickasaw County, IA—23 June 1968, Phoenix, AZ). *Education*: public schools, Nashua, IA; Greenwood and Drew Academy, Chickasaw County, IA. *Career*: pharmacist in Iowa, South Dakota, and Oregon, 1899–1910; farmer, Haines, OR, 1909–68; local and regional agricultural administrator, Agricultural Adjustment Administration, 1933–43; chief, Agricultural Adjustment Administration, 1943–45; director, Field Service Division, Agricultural Production and Marketing Administration, 1945–46; under secretary of agriculture, 1946–48; director-general, Food and Agricultural Organization, 1948–54.

Dodd's career as an agricultural administrator began during World War I, when he served briefly as a regional supervisor for the U.S. Food Administration. In 1933 he returned to public service as a local official in the Agricultural Adjustment Administration (AAA), the New Deal agency established to deal with the problem then afflicting farming in the United States. After other government service, he was unanimously elected in 1948 as director-general of the United Nations Food and Agriculture Organization (FAO).

The first of the permanent organizations of the UN, FAO was officially launched in October 1945 and became a UN agency in December 1946. Its functions included raising the level of nutrition and living standards of peoples, improving production and distribution of agricultural products, enhancing the condition of rural dwellers, and promoting the growth of the world's economy.

Dodd's responsibilities in the U.S. Department of Agriculture had included several that were international in character. As chief of the AAA, he supervised the production of food and fiber to meet the needs of a multinational war effort. Later, Dodd's office cooperated with Mexican authorities to eradicate foot-and-mouth disease in portions of that nation. Dodd headed the delegation of the United States to the International Wheat Council in 1948, frequently advised the FAO during its first years, and served as a representative of the United States at the 1946 and 1947 meetings of the Conference, the governing body of the FAO.

Under the leadership of Dodd, the second individual to serve as director-general, the prestige and role of FAO increased markedly. Membership rose from fifty-eight to more than seventy nations, and by 1953 the budget equaled $6 million, 30 percent of which was contributed by the United

States. Dodd shifted the headquarters from Washington to Rome, opened regional offices in Cairo, Bangkok, and elsewhere, and dispatched experts to assist nations to solve their particular problems. While Dodd was an efficient administrator who commanded respect, he was also concerned about the utilization of agricultural surpluses in those areas of the world that suffered from chronic shortages of foodstuffs.

BIBLIOGRAPHY:

B. R. E. Asher and others, *The United Nations and Economic and Social Cooperation* (Washington, 1957); G. L. Baker and others, *Century of Service: The First 100 Years of the Department of Agriculture* (Washington, 1963); E. P. Chase, *The United Nations in Action* (New York, 1950); Leland M. Goodrich, *The United Nations* (New York, 1959); IY & WWS (Grinstead, England, 1954), 707; NCAB 54, 345; NYT 24 Jun 1968, 37; WWA 1948–49, 657.

C. The Dodd papers are in the Archives of the Hoover Institution on War, Revolution and Peace.

Roy V. Scott

DOYLE, Michael Francis (12 July 1875, Philadelphia—25 March 1960, Philadelphia). *Education*: LL.B., Univ. of Pennsylvania, 1897. *Career*: international lawyer; director, American Czechoslovakia Independence Committee; founder and counsel, Catholic Near East Welfare Association; vice-president, American Peace Society, Catholic Association for International Peace, Mexican Commission Against Religious Persecution.

Doyle's international activities commenced with his appointment in 1914 as special agent of the Department of State to protect the rights of Americans abroad during the war. He visited England, France, Switzerland, Germany, Austria, Holland, and Belgium tending to the safety of citizens. His concern about keeping America out of the war appeared in his communications while acting counsel at Bern and from the embassy in Vienna. *Woodrow Wilson also acknowledged his role in the 1915 American relief effort for Belgium.

Involvement with the Irish cause found Doyle serving in 1916 as a defense lawyer for Sir Roger Casement, who was charged with, convicted of, and subsequently hanged for high treason. He also defended other Irish revolutionary leaders, including Eamon de Valera, later prime minister of Ireland. Doyle was an adviser in drafting the National Constitution of the Irish Free State in 1922.

During the 1920s and 1930s, Doyle signed many treaties for the United States with a number of Latin American nations. As a delegate to the Inter-American Conference at Buenos Aires (1936), he was signatory for treaties supplementing the Good Neighbor Policy on behalf of the United States.

In the interwar years, Doyle created, with *Manley Hudson, the American Committee at the League of Nations in Geneva, and he served as its chairman (1929–39). It welcomed visitors from the United States, issued pro-League literature, and cooperated with other organizations to create a favorable image of the League. Doyle contributed substantial amounts and often spent his summers in Geneva directing the program. He also became involved in the research program of the Geneva Institute of International Relations and served for a time as its chairman.

In 1938 Doyle accepted election to the Permanent Court of Arbitration at The Hague, a post he held until 1951. During these years, he also served as a special counsel to the president of the Philippine Republic, chairman (1945) of the executive committee of the Philippine Foundation, and adviser to the Inter-Parliamentary Union (1957). The American Association for the United Nations received his full support.

Doyle's career was imbued with the concerns of human welfare, human rights, and religious freedom. His strong ties with the Catholic church nurtured these concerns and often directed his actions toward realizing a better state of affairs. His membership in Catholic-sponsored organizations also attests to the bond between the church and Doyle. He arranged in 1933, shortly after Soviet and American ambassadors were exchanged, for a U.S. Roman Catholic priest to go to Moscow to minister to American citizens. He also requested the intervention of Pope Benedict during the Casement trial. As a lay papal chamberlain, Doyle became a member of the Pope's official household, dealing with distinguished visitors at the Pope's private quarters. This post demonstrated the ultimate respect the Vatican held not only for his faith but also for his international commitments.

BIBLIOGRAPHY:
B. NCAB 46, 454–55, A, 524–25; NYT 28 Mar 1960, 29; WWWA 3, 953.

Roy E. Goodman

DRAGO, Luís María (6 May 1859, Buenos Aires—9 June 1921, Buenos Aires). *Education*: doctor of laws, 1882. *Career*: proofreader, *La Nación*, 1875; editor-in-chief, *El Diario* 1881; legislative deputy, Buenos Aires Province, 1882; secretary to civil judge, Chamber of Appeals, 1883; criminal judge, La Plata Province, 1886; attorney-general, La Plata Province, 1890; minister of foreign relations, 1902–3; national deputy, 1906; delegate, Second Hague Peace Conference, 1907; member, tribunal to arbitrate North Atlantic fisheries dispute, 1909; national deputy, 1912.

Drago is best remembered for the Drago Doctrine, which declared that a sovereign nation is obligated to pay its debts but ought not to be forced to do so. In December 1902, Great Britain, Germany, and later Italy imposed a blockade on Venezuela as reprisal for President Cipriano Castro's suspension of payment on the external debt. It was then common practice for foreign investors to participate actively in the internal politics of countries, and they had stimulated much of the indebtedness. Losses during the controversy added 725 ⋅ ⋅w claims, and while Castro authorized a special tribunal composed entirely of Venezuelan nationals to adjudicate these appeals, the foreign creditors insisted that their claims belonged to international public law.

In the weeks that followed the blockade, the United States, which had earlier raised no objection to the "punishment" the British and German governments were planning for Venezuela, became increasingly alarmed over the military and political implications of their action on the Monroe Doctrine. Drago's advancement of the idea that the public debt of a nation should not be cause for intervention emerged as one of crucial importance in the development of hemispheric public law. On 29 December 1902, three weeks after the blockade had been imposed, Drago conveyed his principle to the U.S. government and cleverly connected it with the famous declaration of James Monroe of 1823, which forbade future European territorial expansion in the Western Hemisphere.

Drago failed momentarily in his effort to advance international law in this way and promote the rights of weak, debt-ridden, but sovereign states. Argentina's ruling elements, suspicious of U.S.-Brazilian rapprochment, were more interested in improving U.S.-Argentine relations. *Theodore Roosevelt certainly gave scant credit to Drago when he declared in 1904 that, because of the international dangers created by Latin American foreign indebtedness, the United States would have to become the "policeman" of the Western Hemisphere. Yet Drago's doctrine prevailed. His proposal was widely publicized in the American press, and public leaders in the United States and abroad slowly saw merit in his position. Hence, the United States supported the concept of the Drago Doctrine at the Hague Conference in 1907, where in the form of the Porter Resolution its principles were accepted in modified form. Three decades later, at the Buenos Aires Conference of 1936, the doctrine received general endorsement as a concept, thus enshrining Drago. Although Drago is usually associated with the doctrine that bears his name, he earned wide reputation as an international lawyer and champion of the less powerful states.

BIBLIOGRAPHY:

A. *Colección de fallos en materia civil y comercial* (Buenos Aires, 1886); *La República Argentina y el caso de Venezuela* (Buenos Aires, 1903); *Los hombres de presa* (Buenos Aires, 1882).

B. AJIL 15 (1921), 558–59; Calvin D. Davis, *The United States and the Second Hague Peace Conference, American Diplomacy and International Organization, 1899–1914* (Durham, NC, 1976); *Diccionario histórico argentino* (Buenos Aires, 1953), 213–16; Carlos Saavedra Lamas, *Luís María Drago: Su obra, proyección y trascendencía* (Buenos Aires, 1931).

Lester D. Langley

DRUMMOND, James Eric (17 August 1876, Yorkshire, England—15 December 1951, Rogate, England). *Education*: graduate, Eton, 1900. *Career*: member, British Foreign Office, 1900–17; secretary-general, League of Nations, 1919–33; ambassador to Rome, 1933–39; Liberal politician after 1939.

Drummond, the son of an old Scottish aristocratic family, entered the British Foreign Office in 1900. He was, in succession, private secretary to two undersecretaries, to Prime Minister *Herbert Asquith, and to Foreign Secretary *Arthur Balfour. Drummond accompanied Balfour on his trip to the United States in 1917, and in 1918–19 was attached to the British delegation to the Peace Conference. Here his knowledge of procedure and his grasp of detail won him a high reputation. After the names of various better-known political personalities had been proposed and then dropped, it was Drummond, the career civil servant, who was chosen as the first secretary-general of the League of Nations.

Although the League was weakened by the refusal of the United States to become a member, it did perform many valuable services for peace during Drummond's tenure as secretary-general. Geneva, the headquarters of the League, became the main center for negotiations on that running sore of European international politics, the relationship between France and Germany. The League aided in the financial reconstruction of Austria and Hungary, directed the mandate system in the former German colonies, and carried through a myriad of technical tasks. In 1920–21, the League achieved a permanent solution to the dangerous quarrel between Sweden and Finland over the Åaland Islands; in 1925, the League prevented a border incident between Bulgaria and Greece from turning into an all-out war.

On these and other agenda items, Drummond never pushed a policy of his own, but always helped the governments concerned devise their own solutions to problems. He insisted on the same open impartiality by other staff members, a position eventually embodied in a 1933 oath to place League policy above that of member states. A man of discretion and integrity, he eschewed any dramatic public role, preferring to carry on his most important peacekeeping activity behind the scenes, usually as the informal negotiator or mediator. His contacts with British Foreign Office officials, built up during the years before 1919, proved of great help in winning the cooperation of the British government for the goals of the League.

At times, even Drummond could do little to achieve peace with justice. The Corfu incident of 1923, in which Italy bombarded and occupied a Greek island as retaliation for the murder on Greek soil of Italian members of a boundary delimitation commission, was settled only after Greece paid an enormous indemnity. When the Japanese invaded and occupied the Chinese province of Manchuria in September 1931, Drummond could neither persuade nor coerce them into leaving. The League's effort to bring about a peaceful settlement of the Sino–Japanese dispute was a total failure. In all these frustrating experiences, Drummond revealed a stoic patience in dealing with emotional persons and intransigent governments.

Internal administrative matters occupied much of Drummond's time, especially those related to the budget, to plans for the new headquarters building, and to overseeing an increasing number of committees and commissions. He defended staff members as he generally supported them in their work, and he gained their loyalty and friendship in return. He thus established the groundwork for the concept of an international civil service which has been maintained by the United Nations.

In 1933, Drummond resigned and became ambassador to Italy. Here he tried unsuccessfully to promote good relations between Great Britain and the Fascist regime of Mussolini. After his resignation in 1939, Drummond became involved in politics in Great Britain, entering the House of Lords in 1941 as a representative peer for Scotland; in 1946 he became deputy leader of the Scottish Liberals.

Drummond was probably the best person to be the first secretary-general of the League. He had a knack for administration, he chose talented subordinates, and he delegated authority while still maintaining ultimate control over matters of policy. Thanks in part to his able leadership, the League of Nations enjoyed during his tenure of office many small successes, all of which seemed to reward the hopes that had been placed in the new world organization. That these hopes were not fulfilled was due to circumstances beyond Drummond's control.

BIBLIOGRAPHY:

B. James Barros, *Office Without Power: Secretary-General Sir Eric Drummond, 1919–1933* (Oxford, 1979); DNB 1951–60, 314; Raymond B. Fosdick, *The League and the United Nations after Fifty Years: The Six Secretaries-General* (Newtown, CT, 1972); Salvador de Madariaga, *Morning Without Noon: Memoirs* (Westmead, England, 1974); James A. Salter, *Memoirs of a Public Servant* (London, 1961); Frank P. Walters, *A History of the League of Nations* (London, 1952).

C. A small collection of Drummond papers are in the League of Nations Archives.

Paul D. Mageli

DUFOUR-FERONCE, Albert Freiherr (14 May 1868, London—3 February 1945,). *Education*: Dulwich Coll., London; Commercial Coll., Leipzig. *Career*: businessman, German foreign officer.

Although born and educated in England, Dufour became a successful businessman in Germany. In 1916 his only and adopted son fell in the Second Battle of the Somme. A grieving Dufour retired from business and entered the German Foreign Ministry, where wartime inductions had created many openings. An idealist who dreamed of Anglo–German rapprochement, Dufour secured a post in the German embassy in London in late 1919 as legation counselor. He quickly developed extensive contacts. In 1922 he advanced to senior counselor to the German ambassador to the Court of St. James, where he was assigned a more social than political role. Dufour's wide circle of acquaintances and his excellent relations with his British hosts made him a valued member of the German community in Britain.

In 1926, when it entered the League of Nations, Germany had the right to appoint a number of administrators in the League Secretariat. Among these, the most important was that of an under secretary-general who would direct the International Bureaus and the International Cooperation Section. *Eric Drummond, as secretary-general, suggested Dufour, and within days he was at his post. Dufour's appointment received mixed reviews. The Quai d'Orsay was pleased with a man they considered to be of "great independence" who often seized the initiative. French officials were optimistic that Dufour's insistence on "a more humane and more comprehensive politics" augured well for German diplomacy in the League. Diplomats in Berlin and London were not as sanguine. Perceived as an interloper by many in Berlin, Dufour was not respected by his colleagues in the Wilhelmstrasse. Among the most bitterly disappointed in the Foreign Office in London was British Foreign Minister Austen Chamberlain. Although without question Dufour in his heart supported the League, as his detractors noted he was a political innocent, lacking insight and analytical skill. Thus, Dufour began to question Germany's League policy. While he never allowed his dissatisfaction to become public, clearly he had little effect on the course of either League or German policy. Repeatedly he appealed to his foreign ministers for reassignment. Rebuffed, Dufour remained in Geneva until December 1932, when his contract with the League finally expired. Only six months from retirement, Dufour was put out to pasture briefly as German ambassador to Bulgaria.

BIBLIOGRAPHY:

B. Christoph M. Kimmich, *Germany and the League of Nations* (Chicago, 1976).

Marshall M. Lee

DUGGAN, Laurence (28 May 1905, New York—20 December 1948, New York). *Education*: A.B., Harvard Coll., 1927. *Career*: stockroom clerk and salesman, Harper & Bros., 1927–29; assistant, Institute of International Education, 1929–30; U.S. Department of State, 1930–44; chief, Division of American Republics, 1935–44; assistant diplomatic adviser, UN Relief and Rehabilitation Administration, 1944–45; Latin American consultant, 1945–46; president, Institute of International Education, 1946–48.

Duggan's life was closely bound with U.S. foreign policy toward Latin America, but his views on international relations were neither narrowly political nor regional. As an assistant director of the Institute of International Education, he argued in 1929 that inter-American relations were plagued not so much by political disagreements as by a lack of mutual understanding. His recommendations for increased commercial and cultural contacts between the Americas as a precondition for improved political relationships reflected a social concern that would become a constant in his thinking on foreign policy.

His cultural views were translated into official policy in 1936, when at the Buenos Aires Conference the United States signed a modest agreement on cultural interchange. When this convention failed to live up to expectations, Duggan backed the creation of a Division of Cultural Relations within the State Department. This bureau was viewed not as an agent of American power but as a clearinghouse for the stimulation and coordination of private cultural initiatives with Latin America. It reflected the principle of cultural reciprocity and the expectation that it was eventually to operate on a global basis.

Duggan's universalism was demonstrated by his role in the formulation and execution of the Good Neighbor Policy. As a protege of *Sumner Welles, Duggan helped articulate a conception of the Good Neighbor that was less a realistic response to external pressures than a paradigm for the global application of the principles of law and order and the peaceful pursuit of liberal economic and cultural relationships. Duggan was instrumental in orienting U.S. policy toward the observance of the principles of nonintervention and noninterference in the internal affairs of states. In a number of disputes involving the nationalization of American property, he upheld the principle of compensation while resolutely pursuing negotiated settlements. He accepted the shift of the Good Neighbor posture toward wartime security objectives but always with a view to its integration into a system of global order. Moreover, he continued to feel that security would best be attained by the promotion of economic and educational measures designed to raise standards of living, which would make possible the creation of a world community of free societies. In this respect he thought the Good Neighbor Policy was deficient. In his educational and diplomatic careers, the successful social evolution of nations along liberal lines remained Duggan's basic formula for international harmony. As director of the Institute of International Education, he continued many of the programs developed by his father, *Stephen Duggan, as he focused on expanding its staff and administrative structure in anticipation of an extensive postwar student exchange.

BIBLIOGRAPHY:

A. *The Americas: The Search for Hemisphere Security* (New York, 1949.)

B. Irwin F. Gellman, *Good Neighbor Diplomacy: United States Policies in Latin America, 1933–45* (Baltimore, MD, 1979); Stephen M. Halpern, "The Institute of International Education: A History," dissertation, Columbia Univ., 1969; NCAB 38, 309; Frank Ninkovich, *The Diplomacy of Ideas: United States Foreign Policy and Cultural Relations, 1938–1950* (New York, 1981); Bryce Wood, *The Making of the Good Neighbor Policy* (New York, 1961); WWWA 2, 164.

Frank A. Ninkovich

DUGGAN, Stephen P. (20 December 1870, New York—18 August 1950, Stamford, CT). *Education*: B.S., City Coll. of New York, 1890, M.S., 1896; M.A., Columbia Univ., 1898, Ph.D., 1902. *Career*: instructor to professor, City Coll. of New York, 1896–1928; director, Institute of International Education, 1919–46.

Duggan claimed he was "born interested" in international affairs. The son of immigrants, he discovered cultural diversity on the streets and in the schools of New York City. At Columbia, contacts with *John Bassett Moore and *Nicholas Murray Butler influenced his views and pointed him toward his lifetime effort to reshape U.S. foreign policy and public attitudes toward a cooperative world. After teaching international law and the history of eduction (1896–1928), Duggan resigned to devote full attention to internationalist activities he had undertaken during World War I. Then he had joined Columbia professors *James T. Shotwell and *Joseph Chamberlain in an effort to educate the American public to the complexities of international affairs and America's growing involvement in the world.

Out of a concern for rational policy development, Duggan also joined the Inquiry, that group of social scientists recruited by *Edward M. House to supply information to the U.S. delegation at the Paris Peace Conference. Although a political independent, he became an early supporter of the League of Nations and a member in 1927 of the American Committee on Intellectual Co-Operation that was affiliated with the League. He was also one of the founders of the Foreign Policy Association (1921) and the Council on Foreign Relations (1921), a trustee after 1925 of the World Peace Foundation, and a director of the League of Nations Association.

Most importantly, Duggan became the first director of the Institute of International Education (1919–1946), an agency established at the behest of Butler and the Carnegie Endowment for International Peace to promoting international understanding through educational exchanges. Under Duggan's direction, it became the most active nongovernmental agency in facilitating the formal exchange of students and faculty around the world. Less formally, it worked under Duggan's leadership as a mechanism to support Russian students displaced by the Russian Revolution, to help relocate Nazi-persecuted scholars, and to promote broader U.S.–Latin American cultural exchange. He proved adept in raising funds from a variety of sources so that the program grew in extent and importance. As a scholar, teacher, and administrator, he believed that education provided the most reliable route toward mutual understanding among peoples and thus world peace. He lived his life in accordance with that belief.

BIBLIOGRAPHY:

A. *The Eastern Question: A Study in Diplomacy* (New York, 1902); *The League of Nations: The Principle and the Practice* (Boston, 1919); *A Professor at Large* (New York, 1943).

B. Stephen M. Halpern, "The Institute of International Education: A History," dissertation, Columbia Univ., 1969; NCAB 38, 308–9.

Charles DeBenedetti

DULLES, John Foster (25 February 1888, Washington—24 May 1959, Washington). *Education*: B.A., Princeton Univ., 1908; Sorbonne; LL.B., George Washington Univ., 1911. *Career*: lawyer, member of Sullivan and Cromwell, New York, 1911–53; chair, Commission on a Just and Durable Peace, Federal Council of Churches of America, 1941–47; delegate, San

Francisco Conference, 1945; delegate, UN General Assembly, 1946–48, 1950; Republican senator, 1949; chief negotiator, peace treaty with Japan, 1951; secretary of state, 1953–59.

Dulles's life falls into three well-marked segments. Between 1911 and 1937 he established himself as one of the nation's leading experts in international law. During the second period, 1937–49, he continued his law practice but devoted a large share of his time to the international order concerns of the Federal Council of Churches. From 1949 until his death in 1959 he was a public servant, briefly as U.S. senator from New York, then as adviser to the State Department, and finally as secretary of state.

Dulles's interest in international affairs continued a family tradition, His maternal grandfather, *John Watson Foster, was secretary of state under Benjamin Harrison; his uncle, *Robert Lansing, held that post under *Woodrow Wilson. Through family connections, he became an assistant to *Vance McCormick, chairman of the War Trade Board, during World War I. His assignment was to negotiate agreements with the neutral countries in Europe and make their shipping available to the Allies. This work led to his participation as a member of the U.S. delegation to the Paris Peace Conference, where he served as chief U.S. counsel on reparations and helped draft the clauses of the Treaty of Versailles which dealt with reparations.

During the 1920s Dulles established a solid reputation for international legal skill, carrying a number of assignments on behalf of clients of Sullivan and Cromwell. In 1924 he became special counsel to the American underwriters of the Dawes loan to Germany. In 1927 he represented the Polish government in its monetary stablization problems. On that occasion he worked with *Jean Monnet of France.

Dulles became involved in the Protestant ecumenical world order movement in 1937, when he attended the Oxford Conference sponsored by the Universal Christian Council for Life and Work, a forerunner of the World Council of Churches. The Oxford meeting was a major watershed in churchly world order history, marked by a strong impulse to insert Christian ethical concerns into international relations. An urgent ecumenicity rooted in a subsiding but still powerful missionary movement emerged in its world order manifestation as a modified form of Wilsonian internationalism. Oxford convinced Dulles that the ecumenical church, with a common faith, common hope, and universal scope, linked with Western legal and democratic ideals, was the world's best hope in taming the rampant nationalism of the twentieth century. Acting on that conviction, Dulles was delighted in 1940 to become chairman of the Federal Council of Churches' Commission on a Just and Durable Peace. Under his leadership, it became the most important religious agency in the United States dealing with world order concerns during the 1940s. It also established a reputation for Dulles which led to his participation in the Dumbarton Oaks and San Francisco conferences, which led to the founding of the UN.

In his best published work, *War, Peace and Change,* Dulles reflected his key understandings regarding international order. The goal of statesmen must be peaceful change. Dulles was an avowed disciple of Henri Bergson, who believed that fundamental reality resided in a restless relentless evolutionary flux, fueled by an endemic tension between dynamic and static forces. In international affairs, war was a consequence of the failure of static and dynamic forces to maintain a flexible equilibrium. Disequilibrium in international affairs was generated by two powerful factors. One was the nature of man, where the tension between two contradictory principles, selfishness and gregariousness, frequency erupted in violence. The other was the twentieth-century personified nation-state, whose potency was rooted in man's need to transcend himself.

International order must thus always be open to change, grounded in an ethos of shared values, and regulated by a legal and political consensus. For Dulles the rise of world Communism threatened the emergence of such a world order grounded in Western liberal Christian values and democratic principles. Thus Dulles, and many other internationalist-minded individuals, discovered in the Cold War that their earlier vision of a cooperative global system clashed with realities and forced them to reconsider their views.

BIBLIOGRAPHY:

A. *War or Peace* (New York, 1950); *War, Peace and Change* (New York, 1939).

B. Charles Chatfield, introduction to Dulles, *War, Peace and Change,* rpt. ed. (New York, 1971); DAB supp. 6, 177–80; Herman Finer, *Dulles Over Suez* (Chicago, 1964); Louis L. Gerson, *John Foster Dulles* Vol. 17, in *American Secretaries of State and Their Diplomacy,* eds. Robert H. Ferrell and Samuel F. Bemis (New York, 1967); Townsend Hoopes, *The Devil and John Foster Dulles* (Boston, 1973); Albert N. Keim, "John Foster Dulles and the Federal Council of Churches, 1937–1949," dissertation, Ohio State Univ., 1971; Philip E. Mosely, *Dulles* (New York, 1978); NYT 25 May 1959, 1; Ronald W. Pruessen, *John Foster Dulles: The Root to Power* (New York, 1982).

C. The Dulles papers are at Princeton Univ.

Albert N. Keim

DUNANT, Henri. See *Biographical Dictionary of Modern Peace Leaders.*

DUNN, Frederick Sherwood (10 June 1893, New York—17 March 1962, Philadelphia). *Education*: Litt. B., Princeton Univ., 1914; LL.B., New York Univ. Law School, 1917; Ph.D., Johns Hopkins Univ., 1928. *Career*: admitted to bar, 1917; first lieutenant, U.S. Tank Corps, France, 1917–18; attorney, Washington, 1920–28; attorney, Mixed Claims Commission (U.S.–Mexico), 1923–26; executive secretary, Page School of International Relations, and Creswell lecturer on international law, Johns Hopkins Univ., 1929–35; professor, Yale Univ., 1935–51; director and chair of executive committee, Yale Institute of International Studies, 1940–51; professor and director, Center of International Studies, Princeton Univ., 1951–61.

Dunn's introduction to the realities of the world came because of the Mexican Revolution of 1910, which created a myriad of problems for Americans with investments in Mexico. Property was confiscated, bonds were in default, and during the chronic conditions of the following decade, Americans were injured and some lives lost. By the early 1920s, a degree of stability was restored, and the United States attempted to obtain compensation for claims of its citizens against the Mexican government. Dunn gained firsthand knowledge of the complexity of international dealings when he served as attorney to the Mixed Claims Commission that attempted to settle these differences. Even with the best intentions on both sides, he found the negotiations to be difficult and sometimes impossible. Out of this experience he wrote several works that sought to simplify and regularize the forms of negotiations between nations for the purpose of minimizing the possibility of misunderstanding and discord. His *Practice and Procedure of International Conferences,* written in 1929, soon became a bible for international negotiators. *The Protection of Nationals* in 1932 provided guidelines for the treatment of citizens in foreign nations with the dual purposes of reducing international tensions while ensuring the rights of individuals. In 1933 Dunn wrote *The Diplomatic Protection of Americans in Mexico,* which traced the checkered history of the problems confronted by the United States while attempting to protect its nationals in revolutionary Mexico and pointed out the numerous pitfalls inherent in some of the methods previously employed.

Dunn's publications gained for him a reputation as one deeply concerned with reducing the frequency and seriousness of international crises, confrontations, and conflicts. He was named a trustee of the Carnegie Endowment for International Peace and represented the United States at several conferences of the United Nations Educational, Scientific and Cultural Organization. Unquestionably, his greatest contribution was in his role as a pioneer in teaching international relations and in developing the significant study programs at Johns Hopkins, Yale, and Princeton Universities. There he influenced more than a generation of individuals who would later become international specialists.

BIBLIOGRAPHY:

A. *The Diplomatic Protection of Americans in Mexico* (New York, 1933); *Peaceful Change: A Study of International Procedures* (New York, 1937); *The Practice and Procedure of International Conferences* (Baltimore, MD, 1929); *The Protection of Nationals* (Baltimore, MD, 1932); *War and the Minds of Men* (New York, 1950).

B. NYT 18 Mar 1962, 86; WWWA 1961-70, 270-71.

Stephen D. Bodayla

DURAS, Victor Hugo (6 May 1880, Wilbur, NE—1943, Washington). *Education*: LL.B., Univ. of Nebraska, 1902; LL.M., Columbia Univ.,

1903; D.C.L. and M. Diplomacy, George Washington Univ., 1905. *Career*: law practice, New York and Washington; judge U.S. Court, Panama, 1906; secretary, U.S. delegation, Twentieth International Parliamentary Conference, The Hague, 1913; delegate, International Arbitration and Peace Congress, The Hague, 1913; U.S. vice-consul to Liège, Belgium, 1913–14; vice-consul to Petrograd, 1914–15.

Born of French–Czech parents in a raw prairie village in southeastern Nebraska, Duras attended the public schools of his native Wilbur and his state's university in Lincoln, where he earned a law degree. Instead of hanging out his shingle locally, Duras moved to New York, where he entered a corporate law practice and became keenly interested in the concept of internationalism. A devoted disciple of ⁺Andrew Carnegie (Duras dedicated his major work, *Universal Peace,* to him), he saw the evolutionary move toward a general awareness of genuine brotherhood, which he felt could be institutionalized through organization. Indeed, the world required such a body, because universal peace would come only after international government was established. Similarly, as early as 1909 he advocated the concept of a university of international law.

Like the typical progressive reformer of the early twentieth century, Duras fervently believed that through public education his objectives might be realized. That likely explains why he wrote extensively on the subject of internationalism. While he wrote two books, he turned more frequently to magazines; his essays appeared in such publications as *Americana, Common Cause,* and the *Journal of American History.* But Duras was more than an armchair advocate of his viewpoints. On two occasions, 1908 and 1910, he ran unsuccessfully for Congress from New York on the Republican ticket.

Although this hawk-nosed internationalist viewed the creation of the League of Nations as a turning point in world history, he apparently lost interest in the subject. Perhaps the mere establishment of such a world body was enough, or perhaps he was embittered by the failure of the United States to join. During most of the 1920s he concentrated on his legal practice. By the end of the decade he left the country for France, where he bought a ninth-century castle near Périgueux and enjoyed semiretirement. Duras lived out his life as an eccentric landowner rather than an active internationalist, although he did speak out against Fascism and the Vichy government. The latter forced him to flee to Spain. Later he resided briefly in Portugal before finally returning to America, where he died two years before the formation of the United Nations.

BIBLIOGRAPHY:

A. *La Paix par l'organization international* (Paris, 1910); *Universal Peace* (New York, 1908).

B. WWWA, 6, 122.

H. Roger Grant

DUTTON, Samuel Train (16 October 1849), Hillsboro, NH—28 March 1919, Atlantic City, NJ). *Education*: B.A., Yale Univ., 1873, M.A., 1890. *Career*: school principal, South Norwalk, CT, 1873–78, New Haven, CT, 1878–82; superintendent, New Haven, CT, 1882–90, Brookline, MA, 1890–98, 1899–1900; lecturer, Harvard Univ., 1895–97, Univ. of Chicago, 1897–98, Boston Univ., 1898; professor, Horace Mann School, Teachers Coll., Columbia Univ., 1900–1915.

An eminent educator and prominent religious layman, Dutton in the winter of 1905–6 helped found the Peace Society of the City of New York, in 1910 renamed the New York Peace Society (NYPS), becoming its secretary. That led to service as chairman of the executive committee of the National Arbitration and Peace Congress in New York City in April 1907. Dutton attended the Second Hague Peace Conference, and in September 1907, at the Sixteenth Universal Peace Congress in Munich, he proposed that national councils be formed to coordinate peace societies, to organize national congresses, and to provide representation at future universal peace meetings. His suggestion was approved, and Dutton was elected a member of the Bern Bureau, which administered the universal peace congresses.

With his mild demeanor, persistent work, and managerial skills, Dutton assumed a key role as an organizer, coordinator, and conciliator among American peace workers and internationalists. He participated in a variety of internationalist societies and established ties with those seeking to expand peace sentiment. Thus, Boston publisher *Edwin Ginn early in 1908 enlisted Dutton's help in creating the International School of Peace (1910), renamed the World Peace Foundation. In turn, Dutton joined a small group requesting +Andrew Carnegie, then president of the Peace Society of the City of New York and an intimate friend, to endow peace work on a large scale. He became a trustee of Ginn's foundation, serving for a long time as chairman of its executive committee. When the Carnegie Endowment for International Peace (CEIP) was formed in December 1910, Dutton became one of its agents in the peace movement.

In June 1909 the Lake Mohonk Conference on International Arbitration agreed to consider creating a council to coordinate existing bodies. After considerable delay, a committee to study the idea was formed with Dutton as secretary. Officers of the American Peace Society objected. They asserted that a national organization already existed and proposed removing their headquarters from Boston to Washington. The CEIP, the chief source of its funds, insisted, however, that the American Peace Society be thoroughly reformed. It was restructured, and Dutton became one of its directors (January 1912) responsible for organizing chapters in New York and New Jersey. Nonetheless, Dutton proposed a central headquarters in New York City and a national periodical to federate the separate peace and internationalist organizations. Parochial interests prevented these things from happening.

The CEIP in July 1913 appointed Dutton to an international commission to investigate the causes and conduct of the Balkan wars, where he showed impartiality and integrity. In 1913 he became an associate editor of *The Christian Work,* edited by his son-in-law, *Frederick Lynch. For many years Dutton was a trustee of several overseas educational institutions supported by Christian charities, including the Constantinople College for Women, which he served as treasurer. With the start of World War I, Dutton undertook to raise funds for the relief of non-Moslems in Turkish territories. He was a key figure in the formation in September 1915 of the American Committee for Armenian Relief, which merged with other organizations aiding the distressed in Persia, Syria, and Palestine and eventually adopted the name Near East Relief. He also was engaged in Serbian and Albanian relief activities. Toward the war's end, Dutton developed a plan for the reconstruction of education in Turkey and, at the request of *Edward M. House, devised an abortive scheme for a U.S. protectorate over Armenia.

Dutton devoted much time to promoting U.S. membership in an international organization. He participated in a NYPS committee which in January 1915 proposed that the United States join a postwar peace league. At a World's Court Congress sponsored by the International Peace Forum, of which he had become a director in November 1913, Dutton in May 1915 endorsed the creation of an international judicial tribunal. Then, in June, he attended the founding meeting of the League to Enforce Peace (LEP), whose program for international economic and military sanctions he found repugnant. In opposing this league, Dutton broke with most of his associates in the leadership of the World Peace Foundation and NYPS.

While in September 1915, he agreed to be coopted into the American Commitee of the Netherlands-based Central Organization for a Durable Peace, which favored liberal peace terms and an international organization. Dutton's main propaganda outlet was the World's Court League. It had evolved from the May 1915 congress and enjoyed the backing of key officials in the CEIP. Dutton became its general secretary on 1 October 1916, and with the help of his friend, *Charles H. Levermore, brought the NYPS into alliance with his organization. When toward the end of 1916 it was rumored that *Woodrow Wilson did not favor a coercive peace league, Dutton demanded that the LEP merge with the World's Court League on a common program supporting the president. Unsuccessful discussions regarding such a merger lasted well into 1917.

As the United States approached entry into the war, Dutton advised the American Peace Society to support Wilson. Subsequently, he endorsed the war effort as a moral crusade against militarism and modified his opposition to an international coercive sanction. He attended meetings organized by *Theodore Marburg of the LEP to develop a league of nations constitution. Toward the end of 1918, Dutton invited various peace societies to join the World's Court League in creating a League of Nations Union to promote Wilson's program. The World's Court League and NYPS did form such a body, but Dutton died in March 1919, before the battle began over the League of Nations Covenant.

BIBLIOGRAPHY:

B. J. L. Barton, *Story of Near East Relief (1915–1930): An Interpretation* (New York, 1930); Warren F. Kuehl, *Seeking World Order: The United States and International Organization to 1920* (Nashville, TN, 1969); C. Roland Marchand, *The American Peace Movement and Social Reform 1898–1918* (Princeton, NJ, 1972); David S. Patterson, *Toward a Warless World: The Travail of the American Peace Movement, 1887–1914* (Bloomington, IN, 1976).

B. DAB 8, 556–57; Charles H. Levermore, *Samuel Train Dutton: A Biography* (New York, 1930); NYT 29 Mar 1919, 13; *Record of Yale Graduates 1918–1919,* 916–18; *Teachers College Record* 20 (May 1919), 276–79; WWWA 1, 350.

Martin David Dubin

E

EAGLETON, Clyde (13 May 1891, Sherman, TX—29 January 1958, Tuckahoe, NY). *Education*: B.A., Austin Coll., 1910, M.A., 1911; M.A., Princeton Univ., 1914; B.A. (Rhodes Scholar), Oxford Univ., 1917; Ph.D., Columbia Univ., 1928. *Career*: high school teacher in Texas and Oklahoma, 1911–13; faculty member, Daniel Baker Coll., 1917–18, Univ. of Louisville, 1918–19, Southern Methodist Univ., 1919–23, New York Univ., 1923–56; visiting professor, Univ. of Chicago, 1931, Stanford Univ., 1936–37, Yale Univ., 1938–39, Univ. of Washington, 1957; lecturer, Academy of International Law, The Hague, 1950; assistant secretary, Dumbarton Oaks Conference, 1944; technical expert, San Francisco Conference, 1945; consultant to UN Interim Committee, 1948, and UN International Law Commission, 1949.

For the more than a third of a century that Eagleton was a member of the New York University faculty, he contributed continually to its intellectual life. He was respected for his scholarship, his teaching, his personal qualities, and his powerful advocacy of "international government." In 1948 he founded at the university one of the world's first interdisciplinary programs concerned with the United Nations, the Graduate Program of Studies in United Nations and World Affairs.

As part of that program, he inaugurated a valuable series of volumes, the *Annual Review of United Nations Affairs*. Even earlier, his dissertation, published as *The Responsibility of States in International Law,* had been cited as an important reference work, and his 1932 textbook, *International Government,* ran into three editions. His speeches, remarks, and writings appeared regularly in the *American Journal of International Law,* on whose editorial board he served for twenty years, and his annual reports as chairman of the American Society of International Law's Committee on the Study of Legal Problems of the UN served as primary sources of information.

Eagleton believed that the world possessed opportunities for freedom, comfortable living, and human happiness if people would rise above prejudice and inertia. He was confident that Americans could lead in this crusade for humanity. Yet, while voicing such idealistic visions, Eagleton also viewed conditions realistically. He was an exponent of the idea of collective security before 1941, noting the need for an international government capable of fighting to secure peace. Although shy and retiring, he moved out of his libraries to promote his beliefs. In the 1930s he was active in the League of Nations Association, espoused Clarence Streit's Federal Union program, and promoted David Davies' New Commonwealth proposal in the United States. He served after 1943 in various capacities in the Department of State to help prepare the United States to participate in the UN system, and he later worked as a consultant to several UN bodies. He was also an adviser to foreign rulers, including the Nizam of Hyderabad, and he became a member of the Permanent Conciliation Commission (Denmark-Venezuela) and the Liechtenstein National Group for the International Court of Justice. He served actively on the executive bodies of associations concerned with international affairs, including the Council on Foreign Relations, the Commission to Study the Organization of Peace, the Foreign Policy Association, and the International Law Association-American Branch, of which he was president when he died. He also was a collaborator of the *Revue de droit international et de législation comparée* (Brussels) and expressed his views in letters to the *New York Times*. After his retirement he embarked on a study of the uses of international rivers.

BIBLIOGRAPHY:

A. *Analysis of the Problem of War* (New York, 1937); ed., *Annual Review of United Nations Affairs* (New York, 1949-57); *Attempt to Define Aggression* (New York, 1930); *The Forces That Shape Our Future* (New York, 1945); *International Government* (New York, 1932, 1948, 1957); *International Organization and the Law of Responsibility* (Paris, 1950); *The Responsibility of States in International Law* (New York, 1928); *The United Nations and the United States* (Dallas, TX, 1951).

B. AJIL 52 (1958), 298-300; AJIL *Proceedings* (1958), 254; NYT 31 Jan 1958, 21, 6 Feb 1958, 26; WWWA 3, 247.

Richard N. Swift

EATON, Cyrus Stephen (27 December 1883, Pugwash, NS—9 May 1979, Cleveland, OH). *Education*: B.A., McMaster Univ., 1905. *Career*: industrialist, railroad executive, banker, financier, peace advocate.

Long before detente became fashionable during the late 1960s and early 1970s, Eaton had spent much of his time and money urging a relaxation of tensions between the Communist and capitalist worlds. This was a particularly unusual position for a conservative, profit-oriented, American businessman who had made and lost millions of dollars in rubber, steel, railroads, and utilities. Eaton felt that effective coexistence between East and West could be most easily achieved through commerce; in other words, the more trade there was, the less tension there would be. This seemed a sensible approach to him because the world had entered the nuclear age, in which both superpowers could destroy civilization in a matter of hours.

Originally planning to become a Baptist minister, Eaton was introduced to the world of high finance by John D. Rockefeller, Sr., whom he met in 1901 while visiting his uncle in Cleveland. Eaton soon left the Baptist church and Canada to reside in Ohio, where over the years he made millions of dollars from his interests in utilities, the Cleveland investment banking firm of Otis and Company, Republic Steel Corporation, Goodyear Tire and Rubber Company, Chesapeake and Ohio Railway, Steep Rock Iron Mines

Ltd., and many others. Eaton consistently fought the East Coast financial world because he believed it was impossible to develop leadership in the United States if everything were directed from Wall Street. During the Great Depression he lost his personal fortune but in a few years regained his position.

In sharp contrast to many of his business associates, Eaton preferred to spend his vacations with presidents of universities and other scholars. He would informally invite such intellectuals to visit him in his boyhood home in Pugwash, Nova Scotia. In the 1950s these arrangements became more formalized, resulting in the first Pugwash Conference in July 1957. This assembly brought together the leading nuclear scientists and intellectuals from the East and West to discuss the perils of nuclear weapons. Eaton felt that if American, British, Soviet, and Chinese scholars as well as others could assemble for a few days as private individuals and not representatives of their respective national governments, they could get to know each other as human beings and exchange ideas that would lead to the betterment of all humanity. Pugwash Conferences have continued to meet in various locations throughout the world. Without the prior deliberations of the Pugwash scientists, the 1963 Limited Test Ban Treaty that outlawed atmospheric testing might not have come about.

In addition to hosting the Pugwash meetings, Eaton hoped to promote peace and rapprochement between the Soviet Union and the United States through personal diplomacy. In 1958 he visited the Soviet Union and established a warm relationship with Nikita Khrushchev. In July 1960 the Soviets awarded him the Lenin Peace Prize. These private diplomatic efforts carried the American industrialist throughout the Communist world, including Eastern Europe, Cuba, and Vietnam. On a trip to Hanoi in 1969, Eaton met with representatives of the North Vietnamese and the Vietcong in an effort to end the war. The negotiating terms he brought back were rejected by the Nixon administration but were eventually incorporated into the Paris accords four years later.

Eaton's efforts were not always well received at home. He found it curious that an established capitalist like himself could be called a Communist so often. After he had met briefly with Khrushchev in May 1960 at the Paris airport following the cancelation of the Paris summit talks, Senator Thomas Dodd called for Eaton's prosecution under the Logan Act, which prohibited private citizens from dealing with foreign governments on U.S. policy matters. This attack like the many others never deterred Eaton from seeking a cooperative world in a nuclear age.

BIBLIOGRAPHY:

A. "A Capitalist Looks at Labor," *University of Chicago Law Review* 14 (Apr 1947), 332–36; "The Engineer as Philosopher," *Toronto Daily Star* 5 Aug 1961; "Is the Globe Big Enough for Capitalism and Communism?" *Cleveland Engineering* 51, 3 July 1958, 5–6; "The Third Term 'Tradition,' " *New York Post* 5 Oct 1940.

B. Marcus Gleisser, *The World of Cyrus Eaton* (New York, 1965); E. J. Kahn, Jr., "Profiles: Communists' Capitalist," *New Yorker* 53 (10 and 17 Oct 1977), 50–86, 54–87; NYT 11 May 1979, 1.

Paul E. Masters, Jr.

EDDY, George Sherwood. See *Biographical Dictionary of Modern Peace Leaders.*

EDWARDS MAC-CLURE, Agustín (17 June 1878, Santiago—18 June 1941, Santiago). *Education*: Colegio de los Sagrados Corazones, Valparaiso, and Colegio San Ignacio, Santiago; degree in humanities and philosophy, Univ. of Chile, 1894; postgraduate study, Collège de France, Paris. *Career*: member, Chamber of Deputies, 1900–1910; minister of foreign relations, 1903, 1905, 1909, 1910; delegate, Geneva Conference, 1906; minister plenipotentiary to Italy, Spain, and Switzerland, 1905–6, to Great Britain, 1910–25, to Sweden, 1914–24; vice-president, League of Nations, president of Commission of Finances, 1921, of Assembly, 1922, of Council, 1936; president, Fifth Pan American Conference, 1923; member, Plebescitary Commission on Tacna and Arica, 1925–26; president, Pan American Conference on Education, 1934; president, Chilean delegation, League of Nations, 1937.

Born into a prominent Chilean family, Edwards had the advantages of a sound and varied educational background. Not only did he attend the finest schools in Chile, he also traveled in Europe, first when his father went into exile for political activity and later for a two-year tour following his graduation from the University of Chile. This extended period in Europe, coupled with later trips to the United States, led Edwards to a worldview that went far beyond that of the young men of his social class, who were, for the most part, narrowly nationalistic. When his father died, Edwards inherited the task of directing the prestigious daily newspaper, *El Mercurio de Valparaiso,* which he soon expanded into a three-newspaper empire. As a journalistic entrepreneur he traveled to the United States, where he was again confronted by ideas that contributed to his growing internationalist philosophy.

That outlook was firmly planted when he served as a delegate to the Geneva International Conference of 1906 and as minister to Italy, Spain, and Switzerland. Most Chilean leaders of the era were caught up in an atmosphere of hyperactive nationalism precipitated by the Chilean victory in the War of the Pacific against Peru and Bolivia, but Edwards understood that Chile's progress was dependent upon the rest of the world as well as upon Chile's own initiative, energy, and hard work. He believed that he lived on an interdependent globe in which economic and political issues had to be resolved for the benefit of all nations, or the world would degenerate into bloody and debilitating wars. Because of these convictions, Edwards became a champion of the League of Nations, where he held several key posts. After presiding over the Council during the Ethiopian crisis, he concluded that the League could never be effective on political issues but could be useful in other ways. He increasingly saw the need for more effective machinery, especially for the courts.

Edwards could also be a patriot. When the issue of the final War of the Pacific boundary settlement over the cities of Tacna and Arica arose in 1926, Edwards consented to represent Chile in the negotiations with Peru and Bolivia. There he sought what he regarded as an equitable agreement, as he had done in 1906 and 1909, when he served as Chile's minister of foreign relations; but the U.S. mediator, John J. Pershing, accused Edwards of being a stubborn obstacle. Nevertheless, Edwards was praised by others as an effective diplomat who guided the commission to a reasonable settlement for the nations involved because he was willing to compromise when it became apparent the process might again deteriorate into armed conflict.

BIBLIOGRAPHY:

A. *La América Latina y la Liga de las Naciones* (Santiago, 1931); *La conferencia de Ginebra* (Santiago, 1906); *Mi tierra* (Valparaiso, Chile, 1928); *Observaciones sobre Suecia* (Santiago, 1920).

B. William J. Dennis, *Tacna and Arica: An Account of the Chile–Peru Boundary Dispute and the Arbitrations by the United States* (New Haven, CT, 1931); Francisco Latorre and Manuel Marchant, *Apuntes biográficos de Don Agustín Edwards MacClure* (Santiago, 1943); NYT 19 Jun 1941, 21; WWLA 1940, 166.

Jack Ray Thomas

EICHELBERGER, Clark Mell (29 July 1896, Freeport, IL—26 January 1980, New York). *Education*: Northwestern Univ., 1914–17; Univ. of Chicago, 1919–20. *Career*: Army, 1917–19; lecturer, Radcliffe Chautauqua System, 1922–27; director, Chicago office, League of Nations Non-Partisan Association, 1927–34; national director, League of Nations Association, 1934–45; director, Committee for Concerted Peace Efforts, 1938–39; director, American Union for Concerted Peace Efforts, 1938–40; director, Commission to Study the Organization of Peace, 1939–64, chair, 1964–68, executive director, 1968–74, honorary chair, 1974–80; executive director, Committee to Defend America by Aiding the Allies, 1940–41, chair, 1941; director, United Nations Association, 1943–45; chair, Citizens Council for the United Nations, 1943; chair, Americans United for World Organization, 1944–45; consultant, Subcommittee on Political Problems, Advisory Committee on Post-War Foreign Policy, Department of State, 1942–43; consultant, U.S. delegation to San Francisco Conference, 1945; director, American Association for the United Nations, 1945–64; vice-president, United Nations Association, United States, 1964–74; chair, Drafting Committee, New Dimensions for the UN, 1966.

Throughout a distinguished career at the head of nongovernmental organizations and coalitions in the United States supporting the League of Nations and the United Nations, Eichelberger devoted himself to the ideal of an organized community of nations in which people of all lands could live in "freedom from fear and want." He believed that, in an interdependent world, power politics and selfish foreign economic politics were dangerously anachronistic. Interdependence required an institutionalized world order capable of moving nations toward higher common standards of law and morality, of resolving disputes peacefully and facilitating organized resistance to aggression, of pursuing disarmament, and of promoting economic justice and respect for national self-determination and fundamental human rights. No nation, in his judgment, had a greater responsibility or capacity to provide leadership in creating such a world order than the United States.

A man of action rather than a creative thinker, Eichelberger excelled at the education and mobilization of public opinion. He maintained that public opinion, if strong enough, could determine a nation's foreign policy and that the growth and ultimate success of international organization hinged on popular backing. Through speeches, radio broadcasts, writings, and the diverse activities of the groups he guided, he sought to inform and mold American thinking. He was an engaging and energetic individual as well as an accomplished writer and speaker. A highly skilled lobbyist and publicist, he was equally adept at exercising influence through his network of personal and organizational contacts or by employing the techniques of mass education and persuasion.

Eichelberger first rose to prominence between the world wars as one of a band of dedicated internationalists who labored to steer the United States toward the League of Nations and acceptance of a larger measure of responsibility for preserving peace. As a soldier in France he had developed an enthusiasm for the League which was reinforced by a memorable visit to the fledgling organization in 1923. As a lecturer on national and international affairs in the mid-1920s, he spoke on the League in every state. In 1927 he became the director of the Chicago (later the Midwest) branch of the League of Nations Non-Partisan Association (after 1929 the League of Nations Association). For the next seven years he supervised an energetic program of education and political action in what was reputed to be the geographical heartland of isolationism. In 1934 he became national director of the League of Nations Association, transforming it within a brief span into the country's most dynamic internationalist group and assuming the leadership of the nonpacifist wing of the peace movement. During the mid-1930s, as internationalists and pacifists debated the appropriate response to Fascist aggression and the threat of war, Eichelberger searched for a common ground, while resisting the trend toward political non-entanglement. While domestic and international circumstances as well as its own internal weaknesses limited the effectiveness of the League of Nations Association, the group did keep the internationalist option before the public and provided valuable assistance to the State Department and White House in conflicts with congressional isolationists.

Disturbed by the collapse of the League and by the Fascist challenge to democracy and world order, Eichelberger, in the fall and winter of 1937–38, all but abandoned cooperation with the pacifists and strove instead to construct an internationalist coalition advocating collective security and revitalized peace machinery. Following *Franklin D. Roosevelt's "quarantine" speech of October 1937 (which he may have inspired in a conversation with the president in July), he formed the Committee for Concerted Peace Efforts to propagandize it. In early 1938 he was instrumental in alerting the Roosevelt administration to the perils of the Ludlow amendment, and he successfully marshaled opposition to its passage by Congress. In March 1939 he oversaw the reorganization of the Committee as the American Union for Concerted Peace Efforts, which under his direction spearheaded an abortive attempt to revise the Neutrality Act of 1937 in the direction of collective security.

The outbreak of World War II gave Eichelberger additional incentive and opportunity to persuade the American people and Congress of the tragic folly of shunning the concept of an organized, enforced peace and seeking refuge in a futile and dangerous policy of neutrality. Under the auspices of the newly created Commission to Study the Organization of Peace, the League of Nations Association took the initiative to bring together a group of authorities on international affairs for an intensive examination of the fundamentals of a reformed society of nations to be established at the end of the war. In Eichelberger's view, the long-range objective of a reformed society of nations required in the short run that the United States do everything possible to defeat Nazi Germany. In the period prior to Pearl Harbor, he became one of the country's most active proponents of assistance to Germany's enemies, a major figure in catalyzing interventionist opinion, and a key link to the swelling interventionist movement within the Roosevelt administration. In the spring of 1940 he played a pivotal role in the formation of the influential Committee to Defend America by Aiding the Allies. As its organizing genius, he served as director and after May 1941 as both director and chairman. By mid-1940 he had concluded that American entry into the war would be necessary to defeat Hitler and permit the creation of a new international security system. Although he remained Europe-oriented, he regarded the conflict as part of a global struggle against aggression which also necessitated an end to American appeasement of Japan.

After Pearl Harbor Eichelberger called for a "great crusade" to build a new international order. Probably no private citizen did more in the period which climaxed in the approval of the United Nations Charter by the Senate in July 1945 to guard against the recurrence of *Woodrow Wilson's tragedy with the League. Often working in tandem with the White House or State Department, he directed a series of national coalitions which mobilized popular and congressional support for a new international organization in which the United States would be a fully engaged participant. These coalitions elicited public backing for the so-called $B_2 H_2$ congressional resolution calling on the Allies to form a permanent international security agency, for the Dumbarton Oaks proposals for the United Nations, and for Senate ratification of the Charter. These exceptional educational and publicity campaigns popularized international affairs as never before in the United States, protected against a feared resurgence of isolationism, and guaranteed that the United Nations would become the symbol of American postwar involvement in international politics.

In addition to stimulating and guiding public opinion, Eichelberger contributed to government planning for the postwar period. He collaborated in the preparation of four major reports and a number of pamphlets and statements by the Commission to Study the Organization of Peace. As a member of the Subcommittee on Political Problems of the Department's Advisory Committee on Post-War Foreign Policy, he participated in the drafting of a constitution for a world organization. At the San Francisco Conference he was among the leaders of a group of consultants representing nongovernmental organizations in the United States who acted as semi-official advisers to the U.S. delegation and were responsible for the inclusion of several important provisions in the Charter. A moderate internationalist who rejected proposals for world government or a federation of nations, Eichelberger preferred to build a new international organization on the strengths of the League, while avoiding its weaknesses. Above all, he wanted an organization which could preserve peace, by military force if necessary. He acknowledged the imperfections of the UN Charter but regarded it as an historic achievement deserving of his country's wholehearted endorsement.

The remainder of Eichelberger's career as an association director was dedicated to generating informed opinion in support of the UN. He became a familiar and respected figure at UN headquarters and among advocates of the UN in his own country and abroad. His base of operation was the American Association for the United Nations and its research affiliate, the Commission to Study the Organization of Peace, but he was also active in the World Federation of the United Nations Association.

In spite of a dimming of his short-term expectations, Eichelberger's faith in the UN and in the capacity of the United States for global leadership remained his lodestar after 1945. In the postwar period the same forces which shaped world politics—the Cold War, the beginning of the atomic age, the breakup of the European colonial empires—inevitably affected the character and effectiveness of the UN. While he did not underestimate the deficiencies of the UN or gloss over the fact that it was sometimes neglected, bypassed, or defied, Eichelberger believed that it made the difference between an uneasy peace and a third world war. His unceasing refrain was that all nations must make the UN the foundation of their foreign policies, not merely an instrument to be used or rejected as self-interest dictated. In his writings and associational activities, he underscored the utility, accomplishments, and untapped potential of the UN and recommended measures to strengthen it so as to transform it into a universal society under law. He envisaged a UN which would someday replace power politics and the arms race with collective security, human subjugation and misery with freedom and prosperity, and unbridled national self-assertion with international law. Recognizing that the UN had to adjust to changing circumstances and new problems, he favored a liberal interpretation of the Charter and the extension of the organization's authority to the seabed, outer space, and Antarctica which were beyond the sovereignty of individual nations.

Because practically every dispute before the UN after 1945 was colored by the Cold War, Eichelberger stressed the importance of reducing tension and differences between the United States and the Soviet Union. Although he shared the belief of most Americans that free nations must arrest the spread of Communism and that the Soviet Union's rigidity and obstructionism had handicapped the UN, he consistently urged negotiation and compromise between the two superpowers within the mediating forum of the UN. In spite of the frustrating inconsistency he perceived in U.S. policy towards the UN, he constantly appealed to the American government and people to support a foreign policy whose centerpiece was the UN and whose chief ornament was the nation's moral leadership.

BIBLIOGRAPHY:

A. *Organizing for Peace: A Personal History of the Founding of the United Nations* (New York, 1977); with William T. Stone, *Peaceful Change: The Alternative to War* (New York, 1937); *Proposals for the United Nations Charter* (New York, 1944); *The Time Has Come for Action* (New York, 1944); *UN: The First Fifteen Years* (New York, 1960); *UN: The First Ten Years* (New York, 1955); *UN: The First Twenty Years* (New York, 1965); *UN: The First Twenty-Five Years* (New York, 1970); *The United Nations Charter: What Was Done at San Francisco* (New York, 1945).

B. Robert D. Accinelli, "Militant Internationalists: The League of Nations Association, the Peace Movement, and U.S. Foreign Policy, 1934–38," *Diplomatic History* 4 (Winter 1980), 19–38; Robert A. Divine, *Second Chance: The Triumph of Internationalism in America During World War II* (New York, 1967); Walter Johnson, *The Battle Against Isolation* (Chicago, 1944); Harold Josephson, *James T. Shotwell and the Rise of Internationalism in America* (Rutherford, NJ, 1975); NYT 27 Jan 1980, IV-8; *WWA 1980–81*, 1, 976.

C. The Eichelberger papers are in the New York Public Library.

Robert D. Accinelli

EINAUDI, Luigi (24 March 1874, Carrù (Cuneo), Italy—30 October 1961, Rome). *Education*: Ph.D., Univ. of Turin, 1896. *Career*: professor, Univ. of Turin, 1898–1943; financial and economic correspondent, *La stampa* (Turin), *Il corriere della sera* (Milan), and *The Economist* (London); editor, *Riforma sociale*, 1908–35, *Rivista di storia economica*, 1935–43; governor, Bank of Italy, 1945–48; president, 1948–55.

Through his teaching, journalism, and public service, Einaudi played an important role in Italian life. A firm believer in classical liberal economics, he opposed excessive government interference in and control of economic life. The misery, devastation, and decline in political and economic freedoms brought about by two world wars converted him to the idea of a world federation, and he became one of its staunchest advocates in Italy. In two "letters" of 1918, written under the pseudonym Junius, he advocated the formation of a United States of Europe, modeled on the United States of America and its Constitution, as a step toward the ultimate goal of a United States of the World. While supporting the League of Nations, he felt it did not go far enough in ensuring a future peace, for it did not in any way restrict national sovereignty.

The coming to power in Italy of Fascism, whose nationalist ideology was the antithesis of the federal idea, restricted Einaudi to academic life, but he used the university classroom to oppose the regime covertly. This activity did not escape unobserved, and Einaudi's teachings and writings had come under close government scrutiny by the mid-1930s. After the armistice of Cassibile in September 1943, Einaudi, with other known opponents of Fascism, sought asylum in Switzerland to avoid possible reprisals in the Nazi-dominated Italian Republic of Salò. In Switzerland he joined others working for the creation of a European federation at war's end to replace national divisions, and he wrote on the economic rationale for such a change.

At war's end he returned to Italy to play an important role in the Constituent Assembly elected to draft a charter for an Italian republic. In his speeches and writings, he again strongly supported the European federation idea. He spoke against returning to a Europe of states constantly competing with each other; rather, he favored a Europe where men, ideas, and goods could move freely. To achieve this, nations must be willing to delegate part of their sovereignty to a parliament in which all the peoples of Europe would be represented. Only through a United States of Europe would the threat of another war in that continent almost destroyed by two conflicts in the twentieth century be obviated.

Even as president of Italy, an office that gives the incumbent little real power, Einaudi used his personal prestige to support publicly the various measures, such as the Schuman Plan, the European Defense Community, and its army, which aimed to knit Europe together by stages and lay the foundation for eventual European unity. After his term as president, he returned to teaching and writing.

BIBLIOGRAPHY:

A. With Ferruccio Parri, Piero Calmandrei, Ignazio Silone and Gaetano Salvemini *Europa federata*, (Milan, 1947); with Henri Brugmans and others *Federazione europea*, (Florence, 1948); *I problemi economici della federazione europea* (Lugano, Italy, 1944; Milan, 1945); *La condotta economica e gli effetti sociali della guerra italiana* (Bari, Italy, 1933); *Lettere politiche*, under pseudonym Junius (Bari, Italy, 1920); *Lo scrittoio del presidente (1948–1955)*, pt. 2 (Turin, 1956); *Scritti economici, storici e civili*, ed. Ruggiero Romano (Milan, 1973).

B. Anselmo Bernardino, *Vita di Luigi Einaudi* (Padua, Italy, 1954); Charles F. Delzell, "The European Federalist Movement in Italy: First Phase, 1918-1947," *Journal of Modern History* 32 (Sep 1960), 241-50; *Enciclopedia italiana di scienze, lettere, ed arti* 13 (Milan, 1932), 597, and app. 2 *(1938-1948)* I (A-H) (Rome, 1948), 824; Luigi Firpo, ed., *Bibliografia degli scritti di Luigi Einaudi* (Turin, 1971).

Emiliana P. Noether

EINSTEIN, Albert. See *Biographical Dictionary of Modern Peace Leaders*.

ELIOT, Charles William (20 March 1834, Boston—22 August 1926, Cambridge, MA). *Education*: B.A., Harvard Coll., 1853, M.A., 1856. *Career*: tutor in mathematics, Harvard Coll., 1854, assistant professor, 1858-63; professor, Massachusetts Institute of Technology, 1865-69; president, Harvard Coll. and Univ., 1869-1909.

Eliot believed that international peace was eventually attainable, and from the 1890s he worked to achieve it. He revealed an unusual perspective toward imperialism, seeing certain forms as beneficial to peace. Eliot believed in 1899 that the United States should subdue the Philippine Insurrection and emulate British rule in Asia by keeping the natives in peace, insisting on gradual reforms, and helping them "forward in civilization." As an emissary of good will for the Carnegie Endowment for International Peace, he visited China and Japan in 1911-12. He reported to the Endowment that the current likely causes of war were national distrusts nursed by clashing rivalries for new investments and markets among industrialized nations. The British had stopped most racial and religious warfare in the Asian areas they ruled, and he concluded that the prolongation of Pax Britannica would be a safeguard against nationalistic and economic threats to peace.

In 1900 he declared that America's best stock, its ideals of liberty, and its sense of justice came from England. In 1907 he lauded a decline in the use of violence by free nations and their turn toward the use of nonphysical sanctions. He urged that a reduction in international armaments be made feasible by the advanced nations' adherence to an international tribunal, which was to have a strong armed force to uphold its decisions. Without such an agency to protect her, a nation like Germany could not be expected to reduce her armaments while surrounded by threatening powers. Eventually, he hoped, nations would practice the golden rule and forgive their enemies.

During the 1914–17 period, Eliot supported *Woodrow Wilson's seemingly pro-Allied neutrality policy and adumbrated much of the president's future peace program. He prodded the president through letters to develop a league of nations with an armed force to uphold its decisions, and he presented his views in letters to editors. He backed Wilson's version of a League, despite its omission of a standing armed force, as a step forward. He urged America to create an unpaid citizen army, patterned after that of the Swiss, and thus avoid the growth of militarism through an officers' corps while helping police the Central Powers in the postwar world. After 1918 he again urged an end to the commercial exploitation by strong people over weaker ones and the abandonment of hostile competition in the production and distribution of the world's goods.

During World War I and after, Eliot propagated his views chiefly through public letters and magazine articles. He supported membership in the League during the Senate debates, and in the 1920 election he joined the Pro-League Independents of *Irving Fisher to support *James Cox as the internationalist candidate. In the 1920s critics such as Irving Babbitt lamented the fact that, despite the recent war, many ordinary Americans still believed in an innocent doctrine of progress and inherent human goodness and clung to Eliot's "anachronistic" words.

BIBLIOGRAPHY:

A. *Charles W. Eliot: The Man and His Beliefs*, ed. William A. Neilson, 2 vols. (New York, 1926); *The Road Toward Peace* (Boston, 1915); "Some Roads Towards Peace," Carnegie Endowment for International Peace, Division of Intercourse and Education, Publication no. 1 (Washington, 1914); *Ways to Peace*, ed. Esther E. Lape (New York, 1924); Eliot's addresses in *Report of the Lake Mohonk Conference on International Arbitration* for 1907, 1910, 1915.

B. Irving Babbitt, "President Eliot and American Education," *Forum* 81 (Jan 1929), 1–10; Hugh Hawkins, *Between Harvard and America: The Educational Leadership of Charles W. Eliot* (New York, 1972); Henry James, *Charles W. Eliot: President of Harvard University, 1869–1909*, 2 vols. (Boston, 1930); Warren F. Kuehl, *Seeking World Order: The United States and International Organization to 1920* (Nashville, TN 1969); NYT 23 Aug 1926, 8, 24 Aug 1926, 20, 21, 27 Aug 1926, 16, 29 Aug 1926, VIII-4, 13 Sep 1926, 1.

C. The Eliot papers are in the Harvard Univ. Archives.

Edward B. Parsons

ELIOT, Martha May (7 April 1891, Dorchester, MA—14 February 1978, Cambridge, MA). *Education*: B.A., Radcliffe Coll., 1913; M.D., Johns Hopkins Univ., 1918. *Career*: various hospital posts, 1918–23; instructor to associate professor, Yale Univ., 1921–35, lecturer, 1935–50; attending pediatrician, New Haven Hospital and New Haven Dispensary, 1923–34; director, Child and Maternal Health Division, Children's Bureau, U.S. Department of Labor, 1924–34, assistant chief, Children's Bureau, 1934–41, associate chief, 1941–49, chief, 1951–56; professor and head, Department of Maternal and Child Health, Harvard School of Public Health, 1957–60.

Every human being without distinction of race, religion, political belief, economic, or social condition has the fundamental right to the enjoyment of the highest attainable standards of health according to the constitution of the World Health Organization. Eliot, one of pioneers of international health and the only woman to sign the WHO constitution, used her influence to include child health as a major responsibility of that world body. Believing that the future and destiny of mankind lay in the hands of the young and that what we do for the child can be taken as a criterion for social progress, Eliot spent her active career of over five decades organizing the administrative machinery to make medical care freely available to mothers and children everywhere. The twentieth-century emergence of scientific medicine, along with the prevailing prejudice of America's medical community against women as doctors and medicine as a public responsibility, provided the context in which Eliot worked to realize her goals through the promotion of practical programs.

Denied entrance to Harvard Medical School, where a professor suggested she become a laboratory technician, Eliot obtained her M.D. from Johns Hopkins University and shortly after became first resident pediatrician at Yale. There she studied the prevention, cure, and communitywide treatment of rickets. While working with the U.S. Children's Bureau, she incorporated ideas formulated while working with community health centers into the agency's best-selling pamphlet, *Infant Care*. Experience gained in administering programs under the provisions of the Shepard-Towner Maternity and Infancy Act of the 1920s and the Social Security Act of the 1930s enabled Eliot to extend the general authority of the Children's Bureau to provide care for the wives and babies of servicemen during World War II. The Emergency Maternity and Infant Care Program (EMIC) became America's largest public medical care program to that time.

In 1935 Eliot began working through international organizations when she represented the Children's Bureau at a Child Welfare Conference of the League of Nations. After World War II, she was vice-chair of the U.S. delegation to the International Health Conference in New York (1946), a consultant to the International Children's Emergency Fund (1947), and a delegate to the First World Health Assembly in Geneva (1948). She chaired a 1949 a WHO Expert Committee on Maternal and Child Welfare and that year became assistant director-general of WHO, a post she held until 1951. From 1952 to 1957, she served on the Executive Board of the UN Children's Fund. Apolitical, finding people much the same everywhere, she envisioned a new world growing out of humanity's skill in discovering facts about the physical world and the application of this knowledge through enlightened social philosophy.

BIBLIOGRAPHY:

A. *Civil Defense Measures for the Protection of Children: Report of Observations in Great Britain* (Washington, 1941); "Cultivating Our Human Resources for Health in Tomorrow's World," APHA presidential address, *American Journal of Public Health* 38 (Nov 1948), 1499–1507; *The Effects of Tropical Sunlight on the*

Development of Bones of Children in Puerto Rico (Washington, 1933); "EMIC Program," *Journal of Pediatrics* 25 (Oct 1944), 351–67; *Infant Care* (Washington, 1931); with Edwards A. Park, *Rickets* (Hagerstown, MD, 1937).

B. *American Journal of Public Health* 68 (Jul 1978), 696–700; CB 1948, 184–86; Sandra L. Chaff and others, comps. and eds., *Women in Medicine* (Metuchen, NJ, 1977); IWWW 1949, 621; Andrea Hinding and others, *Women's History Sources* (New York, 1979), 161, 402, 431–32, 735; *Who's Who of American Women 1966–1967* (Chicago, 1966), 343.

C. The Eliot papers are in the Schlesinger Library, Radcliffe Coll. An Oral History is at Columbia Univ.

Mary Van Hulle Jones

EMENY, Brooks (29 July 1901, Salem, OH—12 July 1980, Princeton, NJ). *Education*: B.A., Princeton Univ., 1924; Sorbonne, London School of Economics, Konsular Academie, Vienna, and Univ. of Madrid, 1924–27; Ph.D., Yale Univ., 1934. *Career*: instructor, Yale Univ., 1927–31; faculty, Cleveland Coll., 1935–47; director, Cleveland Council on World Affairs, 1935–47; president, Foreign Policy Association, 1947–53.

Emeny's study at Princeton in political science was followed by his education abroad under a fellowship in international law of the Carnegie Endowment for International Peace. While in Europe he made pilgrimages to the League of Nations to observe it at work, and he attended *Richard Coudenhove-Kalergi's second Pan-Europe Congress, where he heard discussions about a united states of Europe. In his early career he concentrated upon research and writing, producing significant books and articles. He pioneered in the study of global raw materials and is credited with originating the term "have vs. have-not" nations. While Emeny often concentrated on U.S. resource needs, he became increasingly concerned with America's broader relationship toward the world. Thus he readily accepted an invitation in 1935 from *Newton D. Baker to head what was then called the Cleveland Foreign Affairs Council. Emeny had been planning this venture with Baker for over four years, largely because he had grown convinced that an indifferent public had to be knowledgeable about the earth and its problems. His work for the next two decades also reflected his dedication to the idea that community leadership could be important in world affairs and that an educated citizenry could have a constructive impact.

Emeny's directorship was marked by imaginative programming which brought Cleveland into the national and international limelight as an area concerned with global problems. The Council grew from 350 to over 4,000 members, gained impressive financial support, and sponsored programs which reached a broad spectrum of the community through schools, churches, clubs, the press, radio, and adult study groups.

In 1940, *Wendell Willkie asked Emeny to become an adviser on foreign policy during the presidential campaign. At the time, Emeny believed in aid to the European democracies coupled with a clear commitment against military involvement. During the war, he favored a postwar world of cooperation among the great powers tied to an international system that would collectively uphold peace. In cooperation with *Time* magazine, the Cleveland Council in 1947 held an "institute" with many noted international speakers whose views appeared in a "Report to the World." It sought to develop a sense of global responsibility for order and security, and because of extensive publicity it is credited with having considerable impact on subsequent foreign policies.

In 1947, when Emeny became president of the Foreign Policy Association, he did so believing the position would enable him to create a network of council-like groups across the nation. That sense of continuing responsibility to have an informed America ready to assume constructive world leadership reflected Emeny's lifelong ambition. During the Depression, he relinquished his salary to advance the Cleveland Council's programs, and as a popular lecturer he personally reached tens of thousands of listeners with his message of responsible internationalism.

BIBLIOGRAPHY:

A. With Frank H. Simonds, *The Great Powers in World Politics: International Relations and Economic Nationalism* (Cincinnati, OH, 1935); *A History of the Founding of the Cleveland Council on World Affairs* (Cleveland, OH, 1975); *Mainsprings of World Politics* (New York, 1943); *Mainsprings of World Politics* (New York, 1956); with Frank H. Simonds, *The Price of Peace: The Challenge to Economic Nationalism* (New York, 1935); *The Strategy of Raw Materials: A Study of America in Peace and War* (New York, 1935).

B. CB 1947, 194–96; NYT 15 Jul 1980, IV-15.

Warren F. Kuehl

ERICH, Rafael Waldemar (10 June 1879, Turku, Finland—19 February 1946, Helsinki). *Education*: masters in philosophy, Univ. of Helsinki, 1900, in science of law, 1904, doctor of law, 1907. *Career*: professor, Univ. of Helsinki, 1910; specialist in international law, 1921–46; prime minister, 1920–21; delegate, League of Nations, 1926–27; ambassador to Sweden, 1928–36, to Italy, 1936–38; alternate member, International Court of Justice, 1930–37, judge, 1938–45.

During his early years, Erich was active in the so-called passive resistance movement which sought to defend Finland's rights in the face of attempts by imperial Russia to redistrict the autonomy of Finland. During World War I, he joined the independence movement, acting as its representative in Germany and Sweden. After Finland gained its independence in 1917, Erich belonged to a small nucleus of important politicians. He was a Conservative member of Parliament (1919–24). During Erich's time as prime minister, three significant questions dominated Finnish policy: peace with Soviet Russia; Finland's joining the League of Nations; and the handling of the Åaland question so that the League's solution in favor of Finland in June 1921 would result in autonomy for the Åaland Islands and their international guarantee. On presenting the proposal for Finland's joining the League of Nations to the Parliament in May 1920, Prime Minister Erich stated that when a small nation wants admission, it joins trusting that the lesser states can preserve their characteristics, habits, and originality and also make others aware of their existence.

When Erich served as Finland's first permanent representative to the League, he was known for his independent views. His personal expectations for the League and his judicial considerations were paramount to him. This was due to his great authority as an expert on international law and also to his experience. Erich aroused considerable controversy during debate over Germany's entry into the League. In a speech in the Assembly in September 1926, he referred to the military obligations of Article XVI of the Covenant. To facilitate Germany's entry, he claimed, the leading powers had compromised concerning this obligation. This applied especially to Germany's Rapallo treaty (1922) with Soviet Russia. Erich strictly opposed making any exceptions, and his speech not only attracted attention but also caused a strain in relations between Finland and Germany. In an interview, Erich explained his motivation. Small states could not dictate to large ones on how they should fulfill their treaty obligations, but they could do much to see that the charter was not interpreted incorrectly and adversely for the small countries. While Erich's position was in accord with instructions from Helsinki, it nevertheless reflected his high personal regard for the sacredness of the League's principles.

In 1938, when Erich became a member of the International Court of Justice in The Hague, he achieved the highest position accorded a Finnish man of learning until then. He possessed to a great extent the independency and personal integrity expected. Because of the outbreak of World War II, his service was limited. Erich was an internationalist with optimistic views. He believed that the victory of justice represented the best guarantee for the security and existence of small nations.

BIBLIOGRAPHY:

A. *Kansainliiton oikeusjärjestys* (The Law of the League of Nations, Helsinki, 1926); *La Naissance et la reconnaissance des états* (Paris, 1927); *La question des zones démilitarisées* (Paris, 1929); *Probleme der internationalen Organisation* (Breslau, Germany 1914).

Magnus Lemberg

ERLER, Fritz Kurt Gustav (14 July 1913, Berlin—22 February 1967, Pforzheim, Germany). *Education*: Oberrealschule, Königstadt; Berlin School of Administration, 1935. *Career*: administrator, French Occupation Zone, 1946–49; Social Democratic member of Bundestag, 1949–67, Consultative Assembly of Council of Europe (Europa-Rat), 1950–67; associate, Western European Union.

Erler was a key figure in determining the course of the Federal Republic of Germany in the 1950s. Initially overshadowed by Kurt Schumacher, the charismatic leader of the Social Democratic party in the postwar years, Erler became a major foreign policy spokesman for his party in the late 1950s, and he was instrumental in guiding the SDP from its highly doctrinaire stand on foreign policy issues in the early 1950s toward a more pragmatic attitude in the late 1950s and early 1960s.

This approach allowed the SDP to deal with the question of European integration much more constructively. This was not an easy task. Although internationalist-oriented by ideological conviction and historical tradition, the SDP of the 1950s opposed Western European integration, as well as the trans-Atlantic security ties that the *Konrad Adenauer government was establishing with the United States. While the SDP had no intrinsic objections to the idea of European integration and Adenauer's policy of reconciliation with the West, the Socialists believed that the commitments resulting from that policy—rearmament and membership in the Western alliance—were detrimental to the cause of German unity.

Although the SDP echoed the Christian Democratic Union's call for European integration and a rapprochement with France, the party was also apprehensive about the prospect of a Western European community that was limited in membership and exhibited strongly Catholic and conservative overtones. Until the late 1950s, the Socialists' blueprint for a new socioeconomic and political order in Germany was Marxist-reformist and had pronounced antibourgeois and anticlerical overtones. Following the disappointing showing of the SDP in the 1953 and 1957 elections, a more pragmatic wing emerged in the party, made up of younger members like Erler, who hoped to revamp the SDP's orientation and image and change it from a doctrinaire instrument of the "class struggle" into a broad-based party that would appeal to a wider constituency. Erler was a key figure in this process, which allowed the SDP to move closer to the integrationist principles of the government and its NATO-oriented security policies, and which ultimately created the basis for a measure of bipartisanship in foreign policy.

BIBLIOGRAPHY:

A. *Democracy in Germany* (Cambridge, 1965); *Ein Volk sucht Sicherheit: Bemerkungen zur deutschen Sicherheitspolitik* (Frankfurt, 1961); *Politik · für Deutschland: Eine Dokumentation* (Stuttgart, Germany, 1968).

B. *Biographisches Staatshandbuch* (Bern, 1963), 295; *Biographisches Worterbuch zur Deutschen Geschichte* (Munich, 1973), 1, 639; NYT 24 Feb 1967, 35; Harmut Soell, *Fritz Erler: Eine politische Biographie*, 2 vols. (Berlin, 1976).

Wolfram F. Hanrieder

ESTOURNELLES DE CONSTANT, Paul. See *Biographical Dictionary of Modern Peace Leaders.*

EVANS, Alona Elizabeth (27 February 1917, Providence, RI—23 September 1980, Wellesley, MA). *Education*: B.A., Duke Univ., 1940, Ph.D.,

1945. *Career*: War Department, 1942; State Department, 1942–43; instructor, Duke Univ., 1944–45; instructor to professor, Wellesley Coll., 1945–80, chair, Political Science Department, 1959–70, 1972–73.

Evans was unique in establishing a reputation in the field of international law, an area which in both practice and scholarship males have predominated. She succeeded largely because of her studies on extradition and terrorism and her increasing involvement in the American Society of International Law. There she served on committees, sat on the Executive Council, (1956–59, 1965–68), chaired the standing committee on terrorism (1973–80), served on the editorial board of the *American Journal of International Law* (1967–80), and was the first woman to be elected president, in April 1980. She was also the first woman appointed to the State Department Advisory Committee on Historical Diplomatic Documentation. She bridged a gap between the teacher and the involved scholar as she sought to make international law more applicable and understandable.

BIBLIOGRAPHY:

A. With John F. Murphy, ed., *Legal Aspects of International Terrorism* (Lexington, MA, 1978).

B. AJIL 74 (1980), 73–74; NYT 26 Sep 1980, II-6; WWA 1978–79, 986.

Warren F. Kuehl

F

FABELA ALFARO, Isidro (24 June 1882, Atlamcoulco, Mexico—12 Aug 1964, Cuernavaca). *Education*: law degree, National School of Jurisprudence, Cuernavaca, 1908. *Career*: taught at National Institute, 1911–13, Institute of Chihuahua, 1912–13; appointed professor, National School of Jurisprudence, 1921; deputy, Twenty-sixth and Twenty-ninth Union Congresses; secretary of government, state of Chihuahua, 1911–13; secretary of government, state of Sonora, 1913; governor, Mexico, 1942–45.

Fabela's international career is amply illustrated by the many positions he assumed, covering a wide range of activities. His career turned to the direction of foreign service when he was called by Venustiano Carranza, head of the provisional "Constitutionalist" government following the overthrow of Victoriano Huerta, to be secretary of external relations in 1914. He then became diplomatic representative to France, England, Italy, Spain, Argentina, Chile, Uruguay, Brazil, and Germany (1915–20). Entering an even wider arena, he served as a judge on a Mexican-Italian Claims Commission (1929–33) and as Mexican representative to the League of Nations and the International Labor Organization (1937–40). He was elected president of the first Permanent Agricultural Conference at Geneva in 1938 and named a member of the Permanent Court of Arbitration (1938–64). He also represented the Council of the International Labor Organizations at a Labor Conference in Havana in 1940 and headed the Mexican delegation to the Third Caribbean Conference (1940). Based on such an extensive record of involvement, Fabela was elected as a judge of the International Court of Justice (1946–52).

BIBLIOGRAPHY:

A. *Belice: Defensa de los Derechos de México* (Mexico City, 1944); *Intervención* (Mexico City, 1959); *La Sociedad de las Naciones y el Continente Americano ante la Guerra de 1939–1940* (Mexico City, 1940); *Las Doctrinas de Monroe y Drago* (Mexico City, 1957); *Maestros y amigos* (Mexico City, 1962); *Neutralidad: Estudio Histório: La Sociedad Por un mundo libre* (Mexico City, 1943).

B. Mario Colin, *Biographico de Isidro Fabela*, 3rd ed. (Mexico City, 1963); Comité Pro-Monumento al Isidro Fabela, *Homenaje a Isidro Fabela* (Mexico City, 1967); *Enciclopedia de México* 3 (Mexico City, 1968), 1186; Frederico Guillén, *Isidro Fabela: Desensor de España* (Mexico City, 1970); NYT 13 Aug 1964, 29; Manuel López Pérez, *Instantaneos, un foqus al gobierno del Señor Lisc: Isidro Fabela en el Estado de México* (Mexico City, 1958); WWLA, 2, 1946, 38–39.

John Finan and Christian Maisch

FEIS, Herbert (7 June 1893, New York—2 March 1972, Winter Park, FL). *Education*: B.A., Harvard Coll., 1916, Ph.D., 1921. *Career*: instructor,

Harvard Coll., 1920–21; associate professor, Univ. of Kansas, 1922–25; professor and head, Department of Economics, Univ. of Cincinnati, 1926–29; fellow, Council on Foreign Relations, 1930–31; economic adviser to secretary of state, 1931–37; adviser on international economic affairs, 1937–43; special consultant to secretary of war, 1944–46; member, Institute for Advanced Study, Princeton, 1948–50, 1951, 1953, 1958–72; member, Policy Planning Council, Department of State, 1950–51.

Feis was trained in the liberal laissez-faire economic theories of the late nineteenth century but began his career in 1921 in a much different world. The war had severely disrupted the international economic system, sharply reducing European trade and impoverishing many of the participants. Moreover, governments had gone to war willingly, even eagerly, demonstrating that international economic relations could not, as +Norman Angell had implied, of themselves serve to preserve the peace. Trading nations experienced major difficulties after 1918 in reorienting their economies, and classical economic theory provided inadequate guidance on the new complexities and, in fact, appeared to be ignored by statesmen.

Feis saw that conditions had changed as he assumed a leadership role in efforts to secure U.S. entry into the League of Nations and to establish a counterpart international economic system which would support peace by facilitating peaceful participation by all nations in the benefits of international trade. He spent considerable time in Geneva in the 1920s, where he was a periodic adviser to the International Labor Office and worked with Americans there promoting fuller U.S. relations with the League. In that decade, he also published a succession of journal articles and books, intended for his fellow economists and for those who shaped American public opinion and foreign policy, which portrayed how the international economic system actually operated. His successive studies of post–World War I international trade focused increasingly on the interaction among international politics, diplomacy, and economics. His study of the movement of capital, *Europe, the World's Banker, 1870–1914*, led to his appointment as adviser on economic affairs to Secretary of State *Henry L. Stimson. This gave Feis a formal voice in the formulation of policy, which continued under *Cordell Hull. He also influenced opinion makers through articles in *Foreign Affairs* and *Fortune*. At least partially a Keynesian by 1933, Feis favored only moderate governmental intervention in the domestic economy together with cooperation with other governments to establish mechanisms for a revival of world trade.

Though formally only an adviser, Feis contributed much to the administration's move toward open internationalism. He abhorred the rise of Hitler and Fascism and sought to bolster collective security by pushing for U.S. support of the European democracies. As war approached, he pressed with considerable success for the stockpiling of strategic raw materials. When war came, Feis helped avoid tension in U.S.–British relations over questions of rights, and he played important roles in the development of the Lend-Lease program and its later extension to the Soviet Union. He also helped draft what was to become the United Nations Declaration of 1942.

Throughout the war years, he conveyed the message in his writings and speeches that the United States must prepare for a leading role in the postwar years, promoting trade as a vehicle for worldwide reconstruction and reconciliation and supporting an international organization to ensure peace. He counseled against letting differences in the social and economic systems of the United States and Soviet Union affect American willingness to make foreign loans after the war, and he called for the international control of atomic energy.

Feis left the State Department in 1943 and, prompted by the role revisionists' writings had played in American isolation, soon embarked on a series of diplomatic histories of World War II. These meticulous and influential chronicles of U.S.–Soviet relations, which led "from trust to terror," helped shape his wariness of Soviet policy and his advocacy of a U.S. international economic policy that consciously promoted American and Western security as well as his cherished objective of a healthy international economy.

BIBLIOGRAPHY:

A. *The Changing Pattern of International Economic Affairs* (New York, 1940); *Contest Over Japan* (New York, 1967); *Europe, the World's Banker, 1870–1914* (New Haven, CT, 1930); *Foreign Aid and Foreign Policy* (New York, 1964); *From Trust to Terror: The Onset of the Cold War, 1945-1950* (New York, 1970); *1933: Characters in Crisis* (Boston, 1966); *Seen from E. A.: Three International Episodes* (New York, 1946); *The Sinews of Peace* (New York, 1944); "Some Notes on Historical Record-keeping, the Role of Historians, and the Influence of Historical Memories During the Era of the Second World War," in *The Historian and the Diplomat*, Francis L. Loewenheim, ed., (New York, 1967); *The Spanish Story* (New York, 1948).

B. CB 1961, 156–58; Cordell Hull, *The Memoirs of Cordell Hull*, 2 vols. (New York, 1948); NYT 2 Mar 1972, 43.

C. Feis papers are in the Franklin D. Roosevelt Library.

Thomas A. Julian

FELLER, Abraham Howard (24 December 1904, New York—13 November 1952, New York). *Education*: B.A., Columbia Univ., 1925; LL.B., Harvard Law School, 1928; Univ. of Berlin, 1929–30. *Career*: instructor, Harvard Law School, 1931–32, teaching fellow, 1932–34; special assistant U.S. attorney general, 1934–40; federal wartime agencies, 1941–43; general counsel to UN Relief and Rehabilitation Administration, 1943–45; delegate, International Labour Organization Conference, Philadelphia, 1946; special assistant, Department of State, 1945–46; director, Legal Department, UN, 1946–52.

Feller moved into the international arena during World War II, after concentrating on domestic public law and wartime assignments. Yet he had studied international law, served as an assistant during the Austro–German Customs Union case of 1929–32, and published extensively on international questions in the 1930s. His appointment to the UN Relief and Rehabilitation Administration in 1943 finally enabled him to focus his interests. This took him to many world conferences dealing with postwar questions, where he established a reputation for careful work and a willingness to move boldly into uncharted fields. His appointment to the UN, the first American to hold a post, as general counsel and director of the Legal Department, placed him in charge of arranging for the first headquarters offices at Hunter College, Lake Success, and the permanent site in New York City, where he handled the transfers of land donated by *John D. Rockefeller, Jr. Testimony to his accomplishments and abilities appeared in 1952, when *Trygvie Lie named him acting assistant secretary general. The apparent strain of overwork led to his suicide.

BIBLIOGRAPHY:

A. With Manley O. Hudson, ed., *A Collection of the Diplomatic and Consular Laws and Regulations of Various Countries*, 2 vols. (Washington, 1933); *The Mexican Claims Commission, 1923–1934* (New York, 1935); *The United Nations and the World Community* (Boston, 1952).

B. NCAB 39, 557–58; NYT 14 Nov 1952, 1.

Warren F. Kuehl

FENWICK, Charles Ghequiere (26 May 1880, Baltimore, MD—14 April 1973, Washington). *Education*: A.B., Loyola Coll., 1908, M.A., 1909; Ph.D., Johns Hopkins Univ., 1912. *Career*: law clerk, Carnegie Endowment for International Peace, 1911–14; lecturer, Washington Coll. of Law, 1912–14; associate professor to professor, Bryn Mawr Coll., 1915–45; U.S. member, Inter-American Neutrality Committee, 1940–42; U.S. member, Inter-American Juridical Committee, 1942–47; director, Department of International Law and Organization, Pan American Union, Organization of American States, 1948–62, consultant, 1962–73.

Although he never earned a law degree, Fenwick was regarded as one of the distinguished international lawyers of his time. He did not see himself as a promoter or a public relations advocate for international peace and law. He was a careful student and analyst, an architect of the structures underlying international organization, conferences, and law.

Fenwick thus made his principal contribution as a scholar, administrator, and writer. In many carefully reasoned articles he examined concepts of international law, neutrality, collective security, the Kellogg-Briand Pact, and inter-American regional developments. His authoritative textbook on international law, first published in 1924, was used in various editions in undergraduate and graduate work in colleges and universities until his death. Quiet, even self-effacing, he studied carefully and even helped plan institutions of international life and through prescribed study and suggestions helped motivate students to follow that path. Thus while teaching in college and serving the Pan American Union as a director and consultant, he encouraged an international perspective. He also taught by example as a member of the board of editors of the *American Journal of International Law* (1923-73) and by acting as a delegate to the Inter-American Conference for the Maintenance of Peace, Buenos Aires, 1936, and to the Eighth and Ninth International Conferences of American States, Lima, 1938, and Bogotá, 1948. Fenwick also participated actively to influence policy decisions. He prepared confidential reports for the use of the U.S. delegation to the Paris Peace Conference, 1919, and campaigned for membership in the League of Nations (1919-20) and in the World Court throughout the 1920s. In the 1930s, as president of the Catholic Association for International Peace, he argued forcefully against a neutrality policy that could not distinguish right from wrong in the world. He thus joined the ranks of collective security advocates who maintained that force should be used to maintain order.

During his directorship in the Organization of American States, during the last fourteen years of his active career, Fenwick utilized his knowledge, experience, and talents in dealing with leaders of Latin America. A residence in Brazil and his marriage to a Brazilian, Maria José Lynch, in 1942, gave him special opportunities to understand South America, especially Portuguese America.

BIBLIOGRAPHY:

A. *American Neutrality, Trial and Failure* (New York, 1940; reprinted Greenwood Press, Westport, CT, 1974); *Cases on International Law*, 2nd ed., (Chicago, 1951); *Foreign Policy and International Law* (Dobbs Ferry, NY, 1948): *International Law*, 4th ed. (New York, 1965); *The Neutrality Laws of the United States* (Washington, 1913); *The Organization of American States: The Inter-American Regional System* (Washington, 1963).

B. NCAB E, 193-94; NYT 26 Apr 1973, 46; *Washington Post* 26 Apr 1973, B-15; WWA 1942-43, 793, 1950-51, 854; WWWA 5, 229.

Virginia Neel Mills

FERNANDES, Raul (24 October 1879, Valenca, Brazil—6 January 1968, Rio de Janeiro). *Education*: B.S., São Paulo Univ., 1897, law degree, 1898. *Career*: attorney, 1898-1934; member, Brazilian delegation, Second Hague Peace Conference, Brazilian representative, Paris Peace Conference, 1919, Assemblies of League of Nations, 1920-21, 1924-25, Conference on Communications and Transit, Barcelona, 1921; ambassador to Belgium, 1926-27; head, Brazilian delegation, Sixth International American Conference, Havana, 1928; minister of foreign affairs, 1946-51, 1954-55; representative to Paris Peace Conference, 1946, to UN Assembly, 1948.

Fernandes joined the distinguished chief of his Brazilian delegation, *Ruy Barbosa, in projecting for the world at the Second Hague Peace Conference a new image of Brazil and Latin America. He supported the principle of arbitration for international disputes and served on the Commission of Jurists which drafted a plan for a Permanent Court of International Justice. Fernandes was able to continue his effort to develop international law when he attended the first meeting of the League of Nations Assembly in 1920 and was assigned to the Reparations Committee and the Third Commission, which dealt with the organization of the Permanent Court of International Justice.

At the Sixth Assembly he was given credit for devising the optional protocol for the Court which offered a compromise to permit one government to enter arbitration if the other state in the dispute would also agree to do so. In the meantime, he with Brazil supported the ideal of compulsory arbitration among states.

At the Sixth Assembly he also advocated regional agreements on peace and security based on the Protocol of the Court. He endorsed special arbitration treaties in regions in these cases which would be related to the League of Nations. At the Havana Conference in 1928, Fernandes took an unusual posture for a Latin American when he presented Brazil's position on intervention. He did not believe that nonintervention gave a state the right to do anything it pleased; intervention could be justified according to circumstances and as long as it did not encroach on the principle of national independence. There, Fernandes advanced the idea of peacefully resolving conflict when he added a protocol for progressive arbitration which was accepted. Widely respected and admired, both at Geneva and in the Western Hemisphere, Fernandes firmly believed in the peaceful resolution of conflict through established machinery operating under rules of law.

BIBLIOGRAPHY:
A. *A Sociedad das naçoes* (Rio de Janeiro, 1925).
B. NYT 7 Jan 1968, 84; WWLA 1935, 142–43, 1948, 88.

Virginia Neel Mills

FIELD, David Dudley (13 February 1805, Haddam, CT—13 April 1894, New York). *Education*: Williams Coll., 1821–24. *Career*: law student and clerk, Albany, NY, 1825–28; lawyer and law reformer, New York, 1828–88.

Convinced that law was the best means to resolve conflict, a number of nineteenth-century American lawyers sought to end war and provide for better relations among the peoples of the world by promoting the cause and development of international law. Field, who devoted his life to the codification of the Anglo-American common law and to the reform of legal procedure, sought to give definite expression to these beliefs by drafting and circulating a code of international law that would bring a measure of certainty to the nebulous principles comprising the law of nations. At a meeting of the British Social Association in 1866, he proposed that a committee be appointed to sketch the outlines of such a code and to send it to leading jurists and international lawyers for criticism. A committee appointed in response to this plea was unable to act effectively, however, and

Field decided to accomplish this task singlehandedly. In 1872 he completed his comprehensive *Draft Outlines of an International Code* and began to campaign for its acceptance.

Field's code was an ambitious attempt to reform as well as restate the rules of international conduct. It dealt with both wartime and peacetime relationships and covered such diverse topics as extradition, treatment of foreign nationals, international trade and travel, maritime law, international postal service, patents and copyrights, universal standards for weights, measures, and currencies, and arms limitation. The most important provisions of his code prescribed a method for averting war. Each state that ratified Field's code was to reduce simultaneously the size of its military establishment. Field also outlined a three-stage procedure for settling disputes among nations. This system culminated in the selection of an ad hoc world court whose decisions were to be binding. If these measures failed to preserve peace, Field's code set forth rules for the conduct of war that limited the conflict to combatants and outlawed the worst excesses of warfare.

Realizing that he would first have to secure the good opinion of other publicists, international lawyers, and friends of peace to have his code adopted by the nations of the world, Field tried to persuade a wide variety of international groups to endorse his work. He was instrumental in the creation of both the Association for the Reform and Codification of the Law of Nations and the Institute of International Law and became president of the former. While his endeavors within these societies helped further the movements for arbitration and the codification of international law, none of his efforts were completely successful in his lifetime. Although the Association for the Reform and Codification of the Law of Nations used his draft code as a basis for discussion, the organization refused to endorse all of his proposals. The more legalistic and conservative Institute of International Law, preferring gradual reform to codification, rejected Field's entire concept. Some of his contemporaries objected to specific provisions of Field's code, especially those that called for changes in the accepted tenets of international law; other legal scholars disliked the positivistic implications inherent in Field's codification scheme. Field, who had never been greatly concerned with formal jurisprudential theory, might have anticipated such objections. He also failed to enlist the support of the politically powerful members of the American bar, and those governments he hoped would act on his suggestions ignored both the code and his calls for mutual disarmament. In the end, Field's code had little influence on the shaping of international law, but his labors, nonetheless, helped advance study and thinking about the subject.

BIBLIOGRAPHY:

A. *Draft Outlines of an International Code*, 2 vols. (New York, 1872); *Speeches, Arguments, and Miscellaneous Papers of David Dudley Field*, 3 vols. (New York, 1884–90).

B. Herbert W. Briggs, "David Dudley Field and the Codification of International Law (1805–1894)," *Livre du Centenaire 1873–1973* (Basel, 1973), 67–73; DAB 3, 360–62; Daun van Ee, "David Dudley Field and the Reconstruction of the Law," dissertation, Johns Hopkins Univ., 1974; Henry Martyn Field, *The Life of David Dudley Field* (New York, 1898); Kurt H. Nadelmann, "International Law at America's Centennial," AJIL 70 (1976), 519–29.

C. The Field papers are in the Perkins Library, Duke Univ.

Daun van Ee

FILENE, Edward A. (3 September 1860, Salem, MA—26 September 1937, Paris). *Education*: Harvard Univ. *Career*: department store executive, 1901–37; philanthropist.

Filene was often referred to as a notable entrepreneur and philanthropist. His philanthropy, however, was not on an individual charity basis, and his interests led him to view the world broadly. He believed that the profit motive was fundamental in human affairs and that human welfare would be best advanced by assisting people to acquire greater individual economic stability. Beginning with support of local business organizations such as the Boston Chamber of Commerce, his interests and activities expanded to include support for the credit union movement, the establishment of the Twentieth Century Fund, the U.S. Chamber of Commerce, and the International Chamber of Commerce, which he helped found in 1919.

After the outbreak of World War I a group of thoughtful men, largely members of the New York Peace Society, organized a movement for the establishment of a world organization for the preservation of peace through the use of economic and military force if necessary. Filene joined with them in creating the League to Enforce Peace (LEP), and he served as chairman of its Finance Committee and as a vice-chairman of the Executive Committee. The movement gained greater momentum when its general aims were endorsed by President *Woodrow Wilson in May 1916. Filene made the largest individual financial contribution to the League, traveled extensively in the United States speaking in its behalf, and was very influential in securing endorsements of its program from labor groups and business organizations such as the U.S. Chamber of Commerce.

After the United States entered the war, Wilson sought the establishment of an international organization. Filene attended the Peace Conference in Paris, where he represented the LEP. The League to Enforce Peace initially gave its support to the Covenant's provisions for a League and urged American adherence to it. As partisan opposition to membership arose in the Senate, a number of influential members of the LEP either directly or indirectly encouraged a movement to add qualifying reservations. Filene, however, steadfastly supported adherence to the Covenant during the debate in 1919 and the political campaign of 1920. Again, he was the largest single donor during campaigns to educate the public on the question of membership.

After the failure of the United States to adhere to the League of Nations, Filene continued his interests in international affairs. The Twentieth Century Fund supported the work of the International Labor Organization and a study on sanctions, and Filene helped finance and organize peace prize contests, assisted in the invention and development of the "simultaneous translator" widely used in international conferences, spoke widely on world affairs, and was honored by many foreign governments. He died in 1937, before his prophecy had proven true that the failure of the League of Nations would produce depression, protective tariffs, competition in armaments, burdensome taxation, and eventually war.

BIBLIOGRAPHY:

A. *Speaking of Change: Selection of Speeches and Articles* (New York, 1939).

B. Ruhl J. Bartlett, *The League to Enforce Peace* (Chapel Hill, NC, 1936); NCAB 45, 17–19; Edson Leone Whitney, *The American Peace Society* (Washington, 1928).

Ruhl J. Bartlett

FINCH, George Augustus (22 September 1884, Washington—17 July 1957, Washington). *Education*: LL.B., Georgetown Univ., 1907. *Career*: clerk, War Department, 1905; law clerk, Department of State, 1906–11; secretary, American Commission to Liberia, 1909; War Industries Board, 1918; assistant technical adviser, American Commission to Negotiate Peace, 1919; assistant secretary, American Society of International Law, 1909–24, secretary, 1924–43, vice-president, 1943–53, honorary vice-president, 1953–57; assistant editor, *American Journal of International Law*, 1909–24, managing editor, 1924–43, editor-in-chief, 1943–53, honorary editor-in-chief, 1953–57; Carnegie Endowment for International Peace, 1911–57.

International lawyer, legal scholar, and educator, Finch achieved his main prominence through his long tenure as assistant and then successor to *James Brown Scott. In 1906, when Finch was a law clerk at the State Department, he met Scott, who was then the Department's solicitor. Recognizing Finch's legal and organizational skills, Scott asked Finch to serve as his aide, thus beginning a close relationship that spanned over thirty years. Finch helped Scott organize and administer the American Society of International Law and edit the *American Journal of International Law*. When Scott relinquished his positions in 1924, Finch succeeded him as secretary of the ASIL and managing editor of the AJIL. In 1911, when Scott was named secretary and director of the Division of International Law at the newly created Carnegie Endowment for International Peace, he persuaded Finch to leave the State Department to serve as his assistant. At the Endowment, Finch helped Scott found the American Institute of International Law, where Finch served as assistant secretary-general (1927–42), and also establish the Academy of International Law at The Hague. During World War I, Finch assisted Scott at the Joint State–Navy Neutrality Board and in the legal preparations for the Paris Peace Conference. He accompanied Scott to Versailles as a technical legal adviser to the American Commission. When Scott retired from the Endowment in 1940, Finch assumed his mentor's responsibilities.

Finch served as a delegate to numerous international conferences, including the Second, Third and Eighth Pan American Scientific Congresses and as a consultant to the U.S. delegation at San Francisco (1945). A political conservative, Finch testified before several congressional hearings on behalf of the proposed Bricker Amendment to limit presidential power in foreign policy. Finch shared Scott's dedication to education. He taught at the Georgetown University School of Foreign Service and the universities of Michigan, Washington, and McGill and the Washington College of Law. He also lectured at the Academy of International Law at The Hague and delivered numerous speeches.

Through his positions with the Carnegie Endowment and the American Society of International Law, Finch participated in most important events in the movement for international law in the first half of the twentieth century. He was a believer in strict adherence to the rule of law as the only alternative to global chaos. Finch also strongly opposed international Communism, believing it denied the doctrines of Christianity. As a result, especially after 1945, he grew skeptical about negotiations with Communist nations.

BIBLIOGRAPHY:

A. *Sources of Modern International Law* (Washington, 1937).
B. AJIL 51 (1957), 754–57.

Ralph D. Nurnberger

FINLETTER, Thomas Knight (11 November 1893, Philadelphia—24 April 1980, New York). *Education*: B.A., Univ. of Pennsylvania, 1915, LL.B., 1920. *Career*: partner, Coudert Bros. law firm, New York, 1926–41, 1944–48, 1965–70; consultant, San Francisco Conference, 1945; minister to Great Britain, 1948–49; secretary of the Air Force, 1950–53; ambassador to NATO, 1961–65.

In 1917 a generation of young American men marched off to fight the "war to end all wars" and "make the world safe for democracy." That conflict spawned an idea, the League of Nations, for institutionalizing these ideals, which were almost grandiose enough to warrant their sacrifice. When the U.S. Senate failed to approve American participation in *Woodrow Wilson's League, many of the young men who had witnessed firsthand the horrors of modern warfare could not have helped but feel betrayed. Finletter was one of these young men. He had served as an artillery officer and, like many of his generation, was profoundly affected by the experience. When Senate Republicans led their successful fight against the League Covenant, Finletter bolted the Republican party and became a lifelong Democrat. After completing law school, Finletter moved to New York City and began a career as a corporate lawyer. In ensuing years, he was active as a reformer in New York Democratic politics.

While mostly concerned with local politics and his career during this period, Finletter did speak out in support of all proposals calling for U.S. cooperation with the League of Nations. When the threat of war loomed again in Europe in the 1930s, Finletter opposed the neutrality laws. Later he supported *Franklin Roosevelt's cautious steps away from neutrality. In 1940 Finletter became a special assistant to Secretary of State *Cordell Hull and throughout most of World War II served as the coordinator for acquiring strategic materials from neutral nations. Toward the end, he was placed in charge of planning the economic rehabilitation of liberated Europe.

Finletter became active in the movement to establish a new and stronger international security organization when in 1944 he helped form a citizen lobby group, Americans United for World Organization. Americans United was not a mass society, but rather relied on the informal contacts and peer pressure of its elite membership, which included many of the nation's legal, labor, business, academic, and social leaders. It played a leading role in creating public support for a new organization. Americans United was so successful at promoting the United Nations idea that the State Department utilized its apparatus to spearhead its public relations campaign prior to and after the San Francisco Conference. Finletter served as a consultant to the U.S. delegation there.

Finletter was not entirely satisfied with the organization that emerged. It was, he believed, no improvement over the failed League of Nations. Its success, he knew, depended on continued U.S.–Soviet cooperation, and Finletter was not optimistic on that score. He believed that the key to permanent peace lay in total and universal disarmament. Until that could be attained, Finletter recognized, peace could best be served by a militarily strong and watchful United States.

In 1947 Americans United, in which Finletter retained his membership, joined with a number of other organizations interested in revising the UN Charter to provide for an effective peacekeeping force and formed the United World Federalists. At the founding convention in Asheville, NC, Finletter accepted membership on its National Executive Council. UWF's initial policy thrust, however, ran counter to Finletter's thinking. He had concluded that total and universal disarmament would have to precede the establishment of a genuine world government. Most of UWF's leadership, which included *Grenville Clark, Alan Cranston, Norman Cousins, and Cord Meyer, Jr., took the opposite position, that disarmament could not be accomplished without first setting up a genuine government. Given this fundamental difference in viewpoints, Finletter played only a marginal role in formulating UWF policy and strategy. He did, however, continue to support the organization and its general aims.

In light of his acknowledged position on disarmament, Finletter's next endeavor puzzled observers. In 1948 he chaired a presidential commission to study the nation's military policy with respect to air power. Published as *Survival in the Air Age*, it called for a tripling of U.S. air power. Finletter could reconcile the two seemingly contradictory positions. On principle he favored disarmament, but he believed that negotiations had to be conducted from strength. Finletter's air power report led directly to his appointment as the second secretary of the Air Force. Despite criticism from conservative politicians, who opposed his appointment because of his connections with the UWF, which by 1949 was suspected by some conservatives of being Communist-influenced, Finletter refused to resign from the United World Federalists. Even as secretary, he continued to support disarmament and cooperation with the Russians as well as his UWF membership. Finletter resumed his New York law practice in 1953 and in 1958 campaigned unsuccessfully for the Democratic nomination for the Senate, the only elective office he ever sought.

BIBLIOGRAPHY:

A. *Can Representative Government Do the Job?* (New York, 1945); *Foreign Policy: The Next Phase* (New York, 1958); *The Interim Report on the United States' Search for a Substitute for Isolation* (New York, 1968); *Power and Policy: U.S. Foreign Policy and Military Power in the Hydrogen Age* (New York, 1954).

B. CB 1948, 206–8; NYT 25 Apr 1980, II-8; WWA 1979, 833.

C. Finletter papers are at the State Historical Society of Wisconsin.

John F. Bantell

FISHER, Herbert Albert Laurens (21 March 1865, London—18 April 1940, London). *Education*: graduate, New Coll., Oxford Univ., 1888; graduate studies at Univs. of Paris and Göttingen. *Career*: historian and writer, New Coll., Oxford Univ., 1888–1912; vice-chancellor, Univ. of Sheffield, 1912–16; member of Parliament, 1916–26; British Cabinet as president of Board of Education, 1916–22; warden of New Coll., Oxford Univ., 1925–40; member, Royal Commission on Public Services in India, 1912–15; member, British delegation, League of Nations, 1920–22.

Fisher is in the tradition of Englishmen who have moved smoothly from scholarship to public life and back. As a historian of Europe, he was unavoidably an internationalist as well. Before 1912 he wrote widely on British and French history. Then he accepted two assignments, each of which in its own way helped start a new phase in his life. He became an active member of the Royal Commission on the Public Service in India, visiting the Subcontinent twice in that capacity. He was also elected vice-chancellor of the University of Sheffield, taking over as that university's top administrator but not giving his full time to it until early 1914.

In 1916, based on his reputation for imaginative administration, *David Lloyd George asked Fisher to join the Cabinet as president of the Board of Education. Fisher then distinguished himself through his sponsorship of far-reaching and extensive reforms in education, even though the war was still in progress. He also became active in matters of war and peace, visiting France in February 1918 and chairing the Home Affairs Committee, which directed the demobilization of Britain after the war. Along with his entry into the Cabinet, Fisher was elected to Parliament.

Between 1920 and 1922, Fisher was a delegate to the first Assembly of the League of Nations, playing an active role, which encouraged him to write *The International Experiment* (1921). By reputation and inclination he was a logical choice for that honor. As a distinguished historian and successful administrator, his career had already exemplified the qualities needed for British representation in the new international forum. He favored early membership for Germany, but he also believed Germany had been treated fairly at the Paris Peace Conference. In 1923 he traveled to Germany unofficially to ascertain German opinion on reparations. He returned still believing that Germany could pay but seeing there a lack of interest in doing so. Fisher returned to academic life in 1925 and wrote his historical masterpiece, the three-volume *History of Europe* (1935).

BIBLIOGRAPHY:

A. *History of Europe*, 3 vols. (London, 1935); *An International Experiment* (Oxford, 1921); *Political Unions* (Oxford, 1911); *The Republican Tradition in Europe* (London, 1911); *Studies in History and Politics* (London, 1920); *An Unfinished Autobiography* (London, 1940).

B. *AHR* 45 (July 1940), 1009; *Annual Register* 1940, 415–16; DNB 1931–40, 275–78; LT 19 Apr 1940, 9; NYT 18 Apr 1940, 23; David Ogg, *Herbert Fisher, 1865–1940: A Short Biography* (London, 1947); *Proceedings of the British Academy* 26 (1940), 455–65.

C. Fisher papers are in the Bodleian Library, Institute of Economics and Statistics, and New Coll., Oxford Univ.

Lyle A. McGeoch

FISHER, Irving Norton (27 February 1867, Saugerties, NY—29 April 1947, New York). *Education*: B.A., Yale Univ., 1888, Ph.D., 1891. *Career*: economist, Yale Univ., 1890–1935; lectureships at the Univ. of California, 1917–18, London School of Economics and Political Science, 1921–22, Geneva School of International Studies, 1927–28; internationalist speaker and author; chairman, Pro-League Independents, 1920.

Fisher was the product of three major American cultural traditions. In temperament, he was an antebellum New England Romantic reformer driven by the need to do good. In spirit, he was a late nineteenth-century Darwinian, optimistic and confident in the law of progress through competition and racial improvement and driven by a need to sustain the vitality of Anglo-Saxon America. In practice, he was a twentieth-century university-based expert with a logical, precise, empirical mind and a desire to make life more efficient and less wasteful. His internationalism developed at the intersection of these traditions.

Born into a Congregationalist minister's family, he contracted tuberculosis in 1898 and retreated to sanitaria in Colorado and California. He developed through this ordeal a lifelong commitment to the causes of personal and public health. Returning to Yale in 1901, Fisher flung himself into active public life. He wrote studies on economics and mathematics, assumed a prominent role in the eugenics and public health reform movements, and participated in *Theodore Roosevelt's National Conservation Commission, with a special interest in the preservation of the national "vitality." Following the outbreak of World War I, he became active in the prohibitionist movement and proceeded throughout the 1920s to defend the social healthfulness and economic efficiency of the Noble Experiment.

With equal vigor, Fisher also began during World War I to argue the need for a postwar international organization to maintain a cooperative peace. That approach had appealed to him as early as 1890, when he had prepared an essay on the subject. A longtime political nonpartisan, he took part in the formation of the League to Enforce Peace in 1915 and later supported *Woodrow Wilson in his fight for the League of Nations Covenant. When Wilson faltered in 1920, Fisher spearheaded a bipartisan group of Pro-League Independents that sought publicity for the cause, and he traveled the country during the presidential campaign to promote the League and prevent the issue from becoming mired in partisan politics.

The attempt failed, but Fisher did not quit. He became an early member of the League of Nations Non-Partisan Association and one of the country's more vocal pro-League champions in the 1920s. His interest in the League lagged in the 1930s, however, because of the organization's manifest weaknesses and the distraction of his own financial problems. Yet he persisted. Throughout World War II, Fisher spoke of the need for a postwar United Nations and a firm organization. Until his death in 1947, the ideal of world peace through international organization remained paramount in his four-tiered commitment to "the abolition of war, disease, degeneracy, and instability in money."

Fisher's internationalist spirit sprang from that same need to do good, minimize wastefulness, and preserve racial health and public morals that propelled him through associated reform movements. Resolutely independent, he wrote and spoke in support of the need for institutionalizing peace with an enthusiasm that only amplified his determination. "Perhaps I'm a Don Quixote," he once confessed, "but I'm trying to be a Paul Revere."

BIBLIOGRAPHY:

A. *America's Interest in World Peace* (New York, 1924); *League or War?* (New York, 1923).

B. Ruhl J. Bartlett, *The League to Enforce Peace* (Chapel Hill, NC, 1944); MarLynn K. Bohman, "Irving Fisher's System of Thought," dissertation, Univ. of Utah, 1970; Irving N. Fisher, *A Bibliography of the Writings of Irving Fisher* (New Haven, 1961), *My Father, Irving Fisher* (New York, 1956); NCAB 14, 86–87; NYT 30 Apr 1947, 25.

C. The Fisher papers are at Yale Univ.

Charles DeBenedetti

FLEXNER, Abraham (13 November 1866, Louisville, KY—21 September 1959, Falls Church, VA). *Education*: B.A., Johns Hopkins Univ., 1886; M.A., Harvard Univ., 1906; Univ. of Berlin, 1906–7. *Career*: teacher, Louisville High School, 1886–90; headmaster, private school, 1890–1905; expert, Carnegie Endowment for Advancement of Teaching, 1908–12, assistant secretary, 1913–17, secretary, 1917–25; director, Division of Studies and Medical Education, General Education Board, 1925–28; director, Institute for Advanced Study, 1930–39.

Flexner did not wear the traditional internationalist mantle by crusading for world organizations or peace. His support for the League of Nations was neither ardent nor public. Yet his contributions to internationalism were considerable. His comparative studies of social and medical problems enabled reformers, scholars, and teachers on both sides of the Atlantic to share knowledge, while his connection with Rockefeller philanthropies expedited contributions to many international causes. Flexner stood as an example to those who encouraged the exchange of ideas and personnel as a method for further binding the world and promoting peace.

Considered brilliant by some colleagues, the Johns Hopkins–educated Flexner began his career as a teacher and successful preparatory school headmaster. Despite many turns, education remained one of his chief interests. In 1905, at thirty-nine, Flexner abandoned his vocation and enrolled at Harvard to study psychology. Graduate study fueled his interest in higher education, and he produced two critical works, *The American College* and *Medical Education in the United States and Canada*. The latter report and *Medical Education in Europe*, both written for the Carnegie Endowment for the Advancement of Teaching, established Flexner's reputation as an authority on medical education. Flexner's research skills and medical knowledge attracted *John D. Rockefeller, Jr., who appointed him assistant secretary of the General Education Board (GEB), a Rockefeller philanthropy. Shortly thereafter, Rockefeller sent Flexner to Europe to study prostitution for another of the millionaire's projects, the Bureau of Social Hygiene. The soundness of Flexner's study assured the author's place within the Rockefeller organization. Flexner returned to the GEB and helped build a greatly improved medical education system. These efforts carried him to Europe and permitted frequent consultation with Rockefeller on collateral questions. As a semi-official adviser, Flexner helped direct Rockefeller monies to European health projects, medical schools, and the League of Nations.

Flexner's close contact with Europe did not make him an immediate League enthusiast. Yet by the mid-1920s he recognized that Geneva presented the best hope for peace. He thus assisted *Raymond Fosdick, a former League under secretary-general and Rockefeller adviser, in his attempt to convince the philanthropist to build and endow a League library. Flexner, who favored strong, centralized learning centers, argued that it would permit the League to attract to its service high-caliber scholar-administrators and students investigating international problems. Flexner's support was instrumental in Fosdick's success.

Following his 1928 retirement from the GEB, Flexner delivered lectures at Oxford and then returned to the United States to found and serve as first director of the Institute for Advanced Study at Princeton, NJ. For many years he had favored a conceptual research center where eminent scholars could explore their disciplines and teach promising younger students on an informal basis. He envisioned the Institute providing fundamental knowledge to alleviate social and economic maladies. Armed with a handsome endowment and Princeton University's promise to assist, Flexner recruited noted American and foreign scholars, among them +Albert Einstein. When Flexner left the Institute, he thought it represented his belief that the exchange of knowledge should have no barrier.

BIBLIOGRAPHY:

A. *Abraham Flexner: An Autobiography* (New York, 1960); *The American College: A Criticism* (New York, 1908); *I Remember: The Autobiography of Abraham Flexner* (New York, 1940); *Medical Education in Europe* (New York, 1912); *Medical Education in the United States and Canada* (New York, 1910); *Prostitution in Europe* (New York, 1914); *Universities: American, English, German* (New York, 1930).

B. DAB supp. 6, 207–9; Raymond B. Fosdick, *Adventures in Giving: The Story of the General Education Board*; NCAB 52, 320–21; Daryl L. Revoldt, "Raymond B. Fosdick: Reform, Internationalism, and the Rockefeller Foundation," dissertation, Univ. of Akron, 1982.

Daryl L. Revoldt

FOERSTER, Friedrich Wilhelm. See *Biographical Dictionary of Modern Peace Leaders.*

FORSTALL, James Jackson (18 February 1882, New Orleans, LA—29 December 1949, Evanston, IL). *Education*: B.S., Princeton Univ., 1904; LL.B., Northwestern Univ. Law School, 1907. *Career*: attorney in Chicago, 1907–28; investment broker, 1928–49.

Forstall was a quixotic enthusiast who visited Geneva in 1924 and decided to devote himself to international cooperation, especially to support the League of Nations. Because of excellent investments, Forstall had amassed a fortune, and he conferred with *Arthur Sweetser about how he might best apply his money. Sweetser never lacked projects, and Forstall decided to provide Sweetser with funds for whatever would best enhance the League. Sweetser used some for publications on the work of the Assembly and then decided to buy land adjacent to the League's new headquarters to protect it from commercial encroachments. Under the arrangement, the League could acquire the property at its original price whenever it had the money. They first purchased a house, La Pelouse, to be used as the residence of the secretary-general. Then came an extensive acquisition requiring $260,000.

Forstall made the purchase, but before he could complete the transaction he was wiped out by the stock market crash of 1929. At that point, Sweetser persuaded *John D. Rockefeller, Jr., to intercede and cover the commitment. Much of the tract, later acquired by the League, was used as the main entry to its new headquarters.

Forstall told *Eric Drummond that his chief ambition was to serve the movement for international cooperation, and he found other ways to do this. He provided scholarships for the Geneva Institute of International Studies, underwrote the International Club in Geneva, created an International Cooperation Fund, and contributed to the International School in Geneva and the Federation of League of Nations Societies. His enthusiasm for the League never died, even though his grandiose desire to help ended with the Depression.

BIBLIOGRAPHY:

B. *The Book of Chicagoans* (Chicago, 1917), 240; NYT 5 Jul 1929, 8; *Union League Men and Events* 27 (May 1950).

Warren F. Kuehl

FOSDICK, Raymond Blaine (9 June 1883, Buffalo, NY—18 July 1972 Newtown, CT). *Education*: B.A., Princeton Univ., 1905; M.A., 1906; LL.B., New York Law School, 1908. *Career*: assistant corporation counsel, New York City, 1908–10; commissioner of accounts, New York City, 1910–12; comptroller and auditor, Finance Committee, Democratic party, 1912; researcher, Bureau of Social Hygiene, 1913–16; chair, Commission on Training Camp Activities, 1917–18; civilian aide to John J. Pershing, 1919; under secretary-general, League of Nations, 1919–20; law practice, 1920–36; a founder, member, and president, League of Nations Non-Partisan Association, 1923–35; trustee, Rockefeller Foundation, 1921–36, president, 1936–48; member, State Department Far Eastern Study Group, 1949.

Between 1920 and 1950 Fosdick stood as one of America's most notable internationalists, a role for which he had little previous training or experience. Despite involvement in progressive reforms, including a study of European police systems, he failed to develop an interest in foreign affairs until America entered World War I. War Department assignments took him to France, where the slaughter left an indelible impression.

While a student at Princeton, Fosdick had developed an enduring admiration for *Woodrow Wilson, and he eagerly accepted Wilson's vision of a new world order. At the request of *Edward M. House he became an under secretary-general of the League of Nations. Fosdick's tenure proved brief because the United States refused to join the League and he felt obliged to resign, but he had become committed to the principle of international organization. Concerned that in another war the misuse of technology might destroy civilization, he believed that the League with its Assembly in "continuous conference" could resolve crises through diplomacy, sanctions, or collective military action. Fosdick was convinced that the League was only the precursor to an inevitable, more complex international system which would be augmented by a world court and international law. The need to solve issues related to peace, health, communications, and commerce led him to conclude that the nations, like the United States, would eventually adopt a federal system. Fosdick realized that the League was imperfect, but its flaws should not prevent American membership. Thus, he ignored potential difficulties and rejected reservations.

Convinced of the League's importance, Fosdick launched in 1920 a fifteen-year, single-minded fight to bring the United States into the League. He delivered numerous speeches, wrote easily digested articles, and established a news bureau which released features emphasizing the League's accomplishments. In 1922 he helped form the League of Nations Non-Partisan Association and eventually served as its president (1933–35). Retaining close ties with the League of Nations, Fosdick also found financial aid for peace and international causes. He encouraged *John D. Rockefeller, Jr., and his son, *John 3d, to build a new League Library and assist League humanitarian projects. They were also prodded to support the League of Nations Association, World Court campaigns, and the Foreign Policy Association. As a Rockefeller Foundation trustee, Fosdick also encouraged that organization to cooperate with League humanitarian activities; and when he became the Foundation's president, he successfully lobbied for large social science expenditures, arguing that knowledge of international affairs would ultimately promote peace.

Although disappointed by the League's failure to avert World War II, Fosdick enthusiastically supported the United Nations. After his retirement in 1948, he repeatedly suggested that Americans place Communist advances in perspective, understand Third World aspirations, and lend assistance to developing nations. He urged recognition for Communist China and opposed the Vietnam War. He spent his later years seeking to perpetuate Wilson's memory. He chaired the Publications Committee of the Woodrow Wilson Foundation and helped make possible one of Wilson's most enduring monuments, *The Papers of Woodrow Wilson*. He died in 1972 at eighty-nine, just months after publishing a book on the League and the UN in which he repeated his vision of world peace through international organization.

BIBLIOGRAPHY:

A. *Chronicle of a Generation* (New York, 1958); *The League and the United Nations after Fifty Years: The Six Secretaries-General* (Newtown, CT, 1972); *Letters on the League of Nations* (Princeton, NJ, 1966); *The Old Savage in the New Civilization* (Garden City, NY, 1928); *Within Our Power* (New York 1952).

B. CB 1945, 195–97; NCAB 57, 341–43; Daryl L. Revoldt, "Raymond B. Fosdick: Reform, Internationalism, and the Rockefeller Foundation," dissertation, Univ. of Akron, 1981.

C. The Fosdick papers are at Princeton Univ. and the Rockefeller Foundation Archives.

Daryl L. Revoldt

FOSTER, George Eulas (3 September 1847, Apohaqui, NB—30 December 1931, Ottawa). *Education*: B.A., Univ. of New Brunswick, 1868, LL.D., 1894. *Career*: professor, Univ. of New Brunswick, 1872–79; Conservative member, Canada House of Commons, 1882–1900, 1904–21; member, Senate, 1921–31; minister of marine and fisheries, 1885–89; minister of finance, 1889–96; minister of trade and commerce, 1911–21; member, Allied Economic Conference, 1916; member, Canadian delegation, Paris Peace Conference, 1919; head, Canadian delegation, League of Nations Assembly, 1920–21, vice-president, delegate, 1926, 1929; appointed imperial privy councillor, 1916.

Foster rested uneasily in the knowledge that Canada acted with moral irresponsibility in joining the League of Nations. Canadian political leaders sought to demonstrate Canada's nationhood by signing the Versailles Treaty but tried to avoid collective security commitments inherent in Article X of the Covenant. Prime Minister *Robert Borden attacked Article X at Paris in 1919, and his colleague, C. J. Doherty, renewed that attack in 1920 at the First League Assembly in Geneva. Although Foster headed the delegation, he apparently endeavored to dissociate himself from the position Doherty voiced without express Cabinet approval. He caustically alluded to Doherty's action in a 1921 parliamentary address. During House questioning as to whether, under Article X, a country's delegates could commit their nation by their votes, Foster replied that supposedly they voiced their nation's views, not their private opinions; otherwise the Assembly would not be very strong. In the same response, he hailed League progress in constituting a Permanent Court of International Justice. Thus Foster launched a campaign championing support for the League and its agencies, an undertaking which spanned a decade.

Aside from government spokesmen, Foster figured most prominently in parliamentary debate on League of Nations issues. He actively participated in the League of Nations Society of Canada from its founding in 1921 and served as its president (1925–29). In 1926 he represented Canada in the League Assembly and in 1929, at age eighty-two, was once again a delegate. Foster, from 1921 to 1931, annually reviewed League affairs in the Canadian Senate, often presenting the only systematic review of League activities in Parliament. He thereby stimulated some parliamentary discussion, but more frequently he skirted controversial questions and grandiloquently described the League's structure and functions. Occasionally, however, he vigorously advocated specific measures to strengthen the League's security system, as when he voiced support for the Geneva Protocol in 1925 and urged acceptance of the compulsory jurisdiction of the Permanent Court of International Justice in 1927. Few Canadian statesmen in that era dared brave public opinion and call for a more internationalist foreign policy. On this question most Canadian parliamentarians lacked political courage. But Foster recognized that Canada could not isolate itself. He sounded this theme when he urged Canadian adherence to the Geneva Protocol. Its provisions for compulsory arbitration and geographically apportioned military measures reinforced the Covenant. These were "the high notes struck"; and Foster warned that, by refusing to sign, Canada might help fatally weaken an accord which many people regarded as a landmark in the quest for peace. Furthermore, he expressed a sentiment, which recurred in his annual League commentaries, that the League Council's role was misunderstood in Canada and hinted that some of his parliamentary colleagues were so myopic that they preferred not to understand it. He admonished them in graphic terms: Canada could not seize "the bit in her teeth" and ingloriously declare that she refused to support League sanctions out of fear that the Council might later summon her to honor League of Nations obligations. Foster drew from a similar text during an October 1927 speech in Winnipeg, where he put forth a telling case for the League and collective peace.

Foster likewise favored the Kellogg-Briand renunciation of war pact and cast aside charges that it was only a gesture, a toothless agreement, an exercise of pious wish. In 1929 he exhorted his fellow senators to stop "spreading doubt and skepticism" and to "cultivate hope and optimism." As to whether the Pact might have been dangerous for Canadian interests by raising false hopes, Foster remained silent. It enunciated "principle and aspiration." Why, he queried, should we throw a "blur of suspicion and skepticism" upon the good faith of governments so committed? His argument supporting the Pact contained an air of realism despite the rhetoric. Foster recognized that it provided no total final solutions to international problems, but he sincerely believed that the Pact, like the League of Nations, the Geneva Protocol, and the Permanent Court of International Justice, constituted a positive and beneficial concept and that utopian efforts, even when not obtained, were still worth the striving, even though beyond human attainment.

BIBLIOGRAPHY:

A. "Canada and the United States," *North American Review* 216 (Jul 1922), 1–9; *Canadian Addresses* (Toronto, 1914); *Citizenship: The Josiah Wood Lectures* (Sackville, NB, 1927); "The New Internationalism," *Queen's Quarterly* 36 (1929), 369–79.

B. *Canadian Annual Review of Public Affairs* (Toronto, 1921–32); *Canada, Parliamentary Debates* (Commons) 1921, (Senate) 1922–31; John W. Dafoe, "The Political Career of Sir George Foster," *Canadian Historical Review* 15 (Mar 1934), 191–95; *Macmillan Dictionary of Canadian Biography* (Toronto, 1978), 269–70; Sir George E. Foster Papers, vols. 3, 12, 110; Charles P. Stacey, *Canada and the Age of Conflict: A History of Canadian External Policies*, vol. 1, *1867–1921* (Toronto, 1977); *A Standard Dictionary of Canadian Biography: The Canadian Who Was Who* 1 (Toronto, 1934), 195–99; Richard Veatch, *Canada and the League of Nations* (Toronto, 1975); W. Stewart Wallace, *The Memoirs of the Rt. Hon. Sir George Foster* (Toronto, 1933).

C. The Foster papers are in the Public Archives of Canada.

David P. Beatty

FOSTER, John Watson (2 March 1836, Pike County, IN—15 November 1917, Washington). *Education*: graduate, Indiana Univ., 1855; Harvard Law School, one year; read law in a Cincinnati lawyer's office. *Career*: practiced law, Evansville, IN, 1857–61; Union Army, 1861–64; editor, *Evansville Daily Journal*, 1865–69; postmaster, Evansville, IN, 1869–73; chairman, Republican State Central Committee, 1872; minister to Mexico, 1873–80, to Russia, 1881–83, to Spain, 1883–85; special plenipotentiary to negotiate reciprocity treaties with Brazil, Spain, Germany, and Great Britain (for the West Indies), 1891; secretary of state, 1892–93; agent or commissioner in various international settlements, 1893, 1898, 1903; international law practice, Washington, 1881–1917; adviser, Chinese delegation, 1895 peace settlement; represented China at Second Hague Peace Conference, 1907.

Foster became one of the few Americans between the Civil War and World War I to make diplomacy and international relations a full-time career. As diplomat and lawyer, he contributed to the development of those internationalist ideas which emphasized arbitration, permanent tribunals, and the development of law. As a student at Indiana University he was much impressed by Charles Sumner's famous oration, "The True Grandeur of Nations," and ideas for promoting peace thereafter claimed his careful attention. The antislavery movement attracted his interest, and he became involved in the organization of the Republican party. During the Civil War he distinguished himself for bravery. In recognition of his chairmanship of the Indiana Republican State Committee, Ulysses S. Grant in 1873 appointed him minister to Mexico; Rutherford B. Hayes named him minister to Russia in 1880; and Chester Arthur sent him as minister to Spain in 1883. In all three positions Foster handled vexatious problems and learned much about the tensions which disturb peace. But it was while practicing international law in Washington, 1885–89, that he developed his command of legal procedures for settling international claims. This experience qualified him for his prominent role in international arbitration during the next two decades.

From 29 June 1892 to 23 February 1893, Foster served as secretary of state in the Harrison administration. Before assuming that office he had begun preparation of the American case for the Bering Sea Fur Seals Arbitration, and in 1893 he represented the United States during the hearings of the tribunal in London. The ruling went against the United States, but

Foster's reputation as an international lawyer did not suffer. In 1895 he acted as adviser to the Chinese in the negotiation of the treaty of peace ending the Sino–Japanese War. Resuming his law practice, he found his services in demand by many governments. In 1898 William McKinley appointed him to the joint commission to settle Canadian–American disputes, and *Theodore Rooevelt in 1903 named him agent for the American case before the Alaska Boundary Tribunal. He represented China at the Second Hague Peace Conference in 1907.

Foster's last years were especially noteworthy for his promotion of international arbitration and for scholarship. As president of the Lake Mohonk Conference on International Arbitration in 1902, 1903, 1906, and 1908, he staunchly supported the Permanent Court of Arbitration founded by the Hague Peace Conference of 1899, but he warned in 1903 that the Hague arbitration convention and the court could not achieve everything desired primarily because it lacked compulsory arbitration. Although he stressed compulsory arbitration and championed arbitration treaties at every opportunity, it is not likely that he was contemplating anything more than a promise to arbitrate when he urged compulsory arbitration. In 1904 he published *Arbitration and the Hague Court* and in 1906 an essay entitled "Arbitration and Its Procedure" in *The Practice of Diplomacy*, both excellent historical studies, but they offered few ideas about the further development of international institutions for the maintenance of peace.

Foster wrote three additional works of large importance to students of international relations of his time. *A Century of American Diplomacy* was issued in 1900. *American Diplomacy in the Orient* appeared in 1903. These books filled a need for general surveys, and they provided students of later generations with insight into thinking about diplomacy during the era of McKinley and Roosevelt. Foster's most important contribution to the historiography of U.S. diplomacy was his two-volume *Diplomatic Memoirs* (1909).

During his last years Foster's son-in-law, Secretary of State *Robert Lansing, lived with him, allowing the elder statesman to observe the many problems of the *Wilson administration, and he watched as his grandchildren, *John Foster Dulles, Allen W. Dulles, and Eleanor Lansing Dulles, began their remarkable careers in international relations. For them he wrote *War Stories for My Grandchildren*, published privately in 1918. He closed this last book with these words: "There is a certain glamour about warfare which attracts the participant, but it is fictitious and unchristian. I pray God that our country may be delivered from its horrors in the future."

BIBLIOGRAPHY:

A. *American Diplomacy in the Orient* (Boston, 1903); *Arbitration and the Hague Court* (Boston, 1904); *A Century of American Diplomacy: Being a Brief Review of the Foreign Relations of the United States, 1776–1876* (Boston, 1900); *Diplomatic Memoirs*, 2 vols. (Boston, 1909); *The Practice of Diplomacy* (Boston, 1906); *Report of the Lake Mohonk Conference on International Arbitration, 1895–1916*.

B. AJIL 12 (1918), 127–34; William R. Castle, Jr., "John Watson Foster: Secretary of State, June 29, 1892, to February 23, 1893," in *The American Secretaries of State and Their Diplomacy*, ed. Samuel Flagg Bemis, vol. 8 (New York, 1928), 187–223; DAB 5, 551–52; Calvin D. Davis, *The United States and the Second Hague Peace Conference: American Diplomacy and International Organization, 1899–1914* (Durham, NC, 1976); Michael J. Devine, *John W. Foster: Politics and Diplomacy in the Imperial Era 1873–1917* (Athens, OH, 1981).

C. The Foster papers are in the Manuscript Division, Library of Congress.

Calvin D. Davis

FOUCHET, Christian (17 November 1911, Saint-Germain-en-Laye, Switzerland—8 August 1974, Geneva). *Education*: licencié in law and diploma, Ecole des Sciences Politiques. *Career*: before 1939, minor diplomatic posts; joined *Charles de Gaulle on 19 June 1940, and collaborated with him and the Gaullist movement for thirty years.

Because of the importance of several key posts he held under de Gaulle, Fouchet is more important in the history of the Fifth Republic than contemporary works seem to indicate. He served in North Africa in the Fezzan and Libya campaigns, went on missions to the Resistance in France, and after the Liberation in June 1944 served as secretary of the French mission at Moscow. When the Red Army liberated Warsaw, de Gaulle sent Fouchet as representative to the Polish Lublin Committee and later to Warsaw. He served as consul-general in Calcutta, 1945–47. He then became active in French domestic politics as de Gaulle's organizer for the Paris region. After being elected to the National Assembly in 1951, he later became president of the Gaullist party there. With de Gaulle's blessing, he joined the government of Pierre Mendès-France in 1954 as minister of Moroccan and Tunisian affairs. He was not reelected, however, and remained out of the government until August 1958, when de Gaulle's return to power led to his appointment as ambassador to Denmark until 1962.

During the summer of 1960, de Gaulle met *Konrad Adenauer at Rambouillet, where they agreed upon a political followup to the Common Market then being created. The Conference of the Six, held in Paris in February 1961, was the result. From this came the charge for a study commission for a union of states over which Fouchet initially presided. The resulting Fouchet Plan called for regular meetings to compare and harmonize positions, to include education, research, and culture in the discussions, and to study a proposal for a European parliament. After a year, he left this post when the Fouchet Plan was obstructed.

In the 1960s Fouchet was involved in many political movements, holding cabinet posts and assuming various missions. In a 1974 press conference he still advocated European integration. However, it is his 1961 project for a treaty to organize the Six (France, West Germany, Italy, and the Benelux countries) into an open confederation which ranks him among internationalists. Furthermore, his work is indicative of the nature of de Gaulle's internationalism, which preferred a loose confederation over a stronger European union. The three drafts of the Fouchet Plan and the comparative table prepared for use as a working document by the study commission show how close to agreement the Six came before the project was vetoed by Belgium and the Netherlands. Opponents of de Gaulle claim that he sabotaged the union just when it was about to succeed by making unacceptable amendments. Fouchet, however, contends in his memoirs that the Dutch frustrated the plan, which had already been weakened when the British evinced interest in joining the Common Market. The German Federal Republic, he claims, was ready to accept the French amendments. Adenauer and de Gaulle wanted the treaty to attach Germany to the West. While Adenauer certainly wished France to go further toward supranationality, he nevertheless approved the Fouchet Plan unreservedly. If Belgium and the Netherlands had wanted the treaty, they could have done the same. And so, Fouchet claims, a great hope ended, and a magnificent chance was lost. Both he and Adenauer regretted its failure, but Fouchet continued to believe that the idea of the political unification of Europe was irreversible. Hence, at the end of his life he remained a man of vision.

BIBLIOGRAPHY:

A. Fouchet Plan, in C. A. Collard and A. Manin, eds. *Droit international et histoire diplomatique: Documents choisis*, vol. 2 (Paris, 1971), 948-70; *Mémoires d'hier et demain*, 2 vols. (Paris, 1971-74).

B. *Dictionnaire de la politique française* (Paris, 1967), 455; *Le Monde* 13 Aug 1974; *Le Monde hébdomaire* 8 Aug 1974 10; LT 13 Aug 1974, 14; F. Roy Willis, *France, Germany, and the New Europe 1945-1967* (Stanford, CA, 1968).

June K. Burton

FRANÇOIS-PONCET, André (13 June 1887, Provins, Seine-et-Marne, France—8 January 1978, Paris). *Education*: graduate, Ecole Normale Supérieure, 1910. *Career*: professor, Ecole Polytechnique, 1913-14; served in European war, 1914-16; member, Information Service of French Foreign Ministry, 1916-22; founder and director, Société d'Etudes et d'Informations Economiques, 1920-24, and its *Bulletin quotidien*, 1919; deputy, 1924-31; associate delegate, League of Nations, 1930-31; ambassador to Germany, 1931-38, Italy, 1938-40; member, French National Council, 1941; arrested by Gestapo, 1943; liberated by Allies, 1945; French high commissioner to West Germany, 1949-55; ambassador to West Germany, 1955; chair, Standing Committee of International Red Cross Conference, 1949-65; president, French Red Cross, 1955-67.

François-Poncet's career was inextricably connected to Germany. A brilliant student of German life and culture, he earned a professorship of German at the Ecole Polytechnique in Paris on the eve of World War I. During and after the war, he advised the French Foreign Ministry on German matters. François-Poncet's appointment as delegate to the League in 1930 was followed by his ambassadorship to Berlin. His memoirs present a lucid and restrained analysis of the dangers to European peace symbolized by the Nazi movement and an indictment of the myopia of the Western powers in the face of the Third Reich's threat to their existence. A recurring theme in his correspondence with Paris was his insistence that France must seek some understanding with Germany permitting limited rearmament, a policy likely to be more effective than simple verbal condemnations of Versailles Treaty infractions. When Hitler reintroduced conscription in March 1935, François-Poncet called upon France to withdraw its ambassador and seek to isolate Germany through an accord with the Soviet Union, Italy, the Little Entente, and the Baltic states, with or without Great Britain. His championship of a treaty with Italy explains his selection as ambassador to Rome, 1938–40, a final abortive attempt to secure Italian neutrality.

Following the war, François-Poncet served in Germany as diplomatic counselor to French Foreign Minister *Robert Schuman, after which he was designated French high commissioner to West Germany in 1949, a post he held until governmental authority was turned over to the Germans in 1955. During those years of tripartite supervision of the Federal Republic, he energetically argued that Germany must be prepared to join the West ultimately as an equal. It is fitting that his official duties in West Germany ended with the integration of that country into the North Atlantic Treaty Organization and the beginning of arrangements that resulted in its inclusion in the European economic community.

The final years of François-Poncet's career were devoted primarily to the Red Cross. He replaced *Folke Bernadotte, serving for sixteen years as chairman of the Standing Committee of the International Red Cross Conference, its highest ranking official. In this capacity he frequently confronted the intrusion of Cold War politics into international conferences as in Toronto in 1952 and New Delhi in 1957. This frustration led him to propose that future international conferences be restricted to national Red Cross societies only, with government representatives being convened separately if crucial questions concerning the Geneva Conventions were to arise. Such a procedure, it was hoped, would make it difficult for political tensions to block the Red Cross's humanitarian mission.

BIBLIOGRAPHY:

A. *Au Palais farnese* (Paris, 1961); *Carnets d'un captif* (Paris, n.d.); *Ce que pense la jeunesse allemande* (Paris, 1913); *De Versailles à Potsdam* (Paris, 1948); *Discours français* (Paris, 1931); *La France et le problème des réparations* (Paris, n.d.); *Les Affinités électives de Goethe* (Paris, 1910); *Réflexions d'un républicain moderne* (Paris, 1925); *Souvenirs d'une ambassade à Berlin* (Paris, 1946).

B. CB, 1949, 209–11; Franklin L. Ford, "Three Observers in Berlin: Rumbold, Dodd and François-Poncet," in ed. Gordon Craig and Felix Gilbert, *The Diplomats, 1919–1939* (Princeton, NJ, 1953), 437–76; NYT 10 Jan 1978, 36; Roselyn Solo, "André François-Poncet—Ambassador of France," dissertation, Michigan State Univ., 1978.

William I. Shorrock

FRANGULIS, Antoine -F. (8 November 1888, Piraeus, Greece—3 December 1975, Paris?). *Education*: Univs. of Athens, Geneva, Lausanne, Berlin, and Paris; LL.B. *Career*: professional diplomat; delegate, League of Nations, 1920–44; secretary-general, Académie Diplomatique Internationale, 1926–75.

Frangulis, a specialist in international law, became involved in world affairs when he was assigned by Greece to London in 1920 to negotiate a peace treaty with Turkey following World War I. He then served on several commissions (1920–21) to resolve territorial issues related to the frontiers of Greece. These experiences led to his appointment as a delegate from Greece to the first Assembly of the League of Nations in 1920, and thereafter Frangulis appeared regularly at sessions in Geneva. Indeed, he became something of a world citizen, living the rest of his life in European capitals and representing interests far beyond those of his native country.

By the 1930s, Frangulis had established a reputation for impartiality and compassion, largely because of his interest in refugees, his open criticism of Germany's persecution of Jews, and his insistence that the League of Nations could and should assert itself on behalf of human rights. His espousal of individual liberties, as embodied in resolutions in the League's Assembly, can be found in the phraseology of the Charter of the UN. Frangulis also sought to promote a sense of internationalism through the exchange of individuals and the study of foreign relations. He was a joint founder in 1926 of the International Diplomatic Academy in Paris, and he served as its secretary-general for many decades.

BIBLIOGRAPHY:

A. Ed., *Dictionnaire diplomatique* (Paris, 1933); *La Grèce et la crise mondiale*, 2 vols. (Paris, 1926–27); *La Grèce, son statut international, son histoire diplomatique*, 2 vols. (Paris, 1934); *Théorie et pratique des traites internationaux* (Paris, 1934).

B. IWW 1937, 346; WW 1974, 1152–53.

Warren F. Kuehl

FRANK, Louis. See *Biographical Dictionary of Modern Peace Leaders*.

FRASER, Leon (27 November 1889, Boston—8 April 1945, North Granville, NY). *Education*: B.A., Columbia Univ., 1910, M.A., 1911, Litt. B., 1913, Ph.D., 1915. *Career*: reporter, *New York World*, 1913; lecturer, Columbia Univ., 1914–17; U.S. Army, 1917–19; U.S. Veterans Bureau, 1921–22; Coudert Bros. law firm, Paris, 1922–24; general counsel to and Paris representative of agent general for reparations, 1924–27; attended Young Conference, 1929; vice-president and director, Bank of International Settlements, 1930–33, president and chairman of board, 1933–35; vice-president, First National Bank of City of New York, 1935–37; president, 1937–45.

In that optimistic decade, 1919–1929, many Americans regarded the Great War as a terrible aberration, a catastrophe which need never recur.

After the Senate's rejection of membership in the League of Nations in 1920, most American political leaders refused to commit the United States to the enforcement of peace. Yet they promoted international financial stabilization, believing that the resulting prosperity would ease political tensions in Europe as well as enhance American exports. In less overt ways, American leaders encouraged European disarmament and a slow and moderate revision of the peace treaties. The culmination of American efforts to "liquidate the war" and the hatred it spawned came with the establishment in 1929–30 of the first world bank, the Bank for International Settlements (BIS) headquartered in Basel, Switzerland.

Fraser was the first vice-president of the BIS and later its president (1933–35). He came to the BIS after a varied career as newspaper reporter, international lawyer, and legal counsel to the Office of the Agent General for Reparations. There he worked with *S. Parker Gilbert in overseeing the Dawes Plan. As executive of an international bank, Fraser symbolized the power of American finance in Europe and the power of American faith that international economic cooperation was the path to prosperity and peace. Fraser conceived the BIS as an economic institution, an agency that stayed aloof from petty politics. Thus in the 1931 financial crisis the BIS cooperated with national central banks in a vain effort to shore up the international gold standard. As a force for worldwide financial stability, the BIS thus advanced America's broad interest in European order, prosperity, and peace.

Despite this internationalist commitment, Fraser felt a special duty to protect the interests of the United States. Thus in BIS councils he often defended American financial and monetary policy against European criticism. In 1931–32 he worked to minimize foreign attacks on the dollar. Fraser acted as *Herbert Hoover's banking adviser at the time of the Hoover debt moratorium. Finally, he maintained close, secret communication with the State Department, confiding the inner workings of the BIS. Fraser's loyalties were not seriously divided, since Americans had created the BIS to promote international monetary cooperation within the context of America's broadest national interest. Fraser returned to the United States in 1936 and became president of the First National Bank of City of New York. In the 1940s he was an influential figure in wartime finance and in planning the Bretton Woods financial system until, overcome with melancholy after his wife's death, he committed suicide.

BIBLIOGRAPHY:

B. DAB sup 3, 289–90; Eleanor L. Dulles, *The Bank for International Settlements at Work* (New York, 1932); NCAB 56, 416–17; NYT 9 Apr 1945, 1; WWWA 1, 197.

Frank C. Costigliola

FRASER, Peter (28 August 1884, Fearn, Scotland—12 December 1950, Wellington, New Zealand). *Education*: primary education at village school. *Career*: president, Auckland General Laborers' Union, 1911–12; Auckland district secretary, Federation of Labor, 1911–13, member, Executive, 1913–16; national secretary-treasurer, Social Democratic party, 1913–16; member, National Executive, New Zealand Labor party, 1916–50; imprisoned for sedition for opposing conscription, 1916–17; member of Parliament, 1918–50; secretary, Parliamentary Labor party, 1919–35; minister of education, of health, of marine, and of police, 1935–40; acting prime minister, 1939–40; prime minister and minister of external affairs, of police, and in charge of legislative department, 1940–49; minister of island territories, 1943–49; minister of Maori affairs, 1946–49; leader of the opposition, 1949–50.

At the San Francisco Conference in April 1945, Fraser emerged as a vigorous champion of small power rights. With Australia's H. V. Evatt, he stood in the forefront of battles to curb the privileges of the great powers in the Security Council and to expand the role of the General Assembly in the proposed United Nations Organization. Firmly based on principle, his stance derived from a clear vision of an ideal international order.

Well-read, though with little formal education, Fraser was a dour, determined Scot, single-minded but astute in pursuit of his ends. Above all, he was a hard-headed political realist, always willing to grasp the nettle of responsibility. Thus, his views on the international order had evolved with changing circumstances. In the early stages of his political career, his internationalism had taken the traditional working-class form. World War I had been denounced as a betrayal of the brotherhood of workers by the ruling classes of Europe. His opposition to conscription, introduced in New Zealand in 1916, earned him a year's imprisonment for sedition. An opponent of the war, though never a pacifist, he also rejected the peace of Versailles, dismissing the League as the "league of capitalists." However, by the mid-1930s, his views had turned full circle. The League "stood for peace," and the growing challenge from the aggressive dictatorships seemed to demand strenghtening of this once reviled instrument.

Fraser's attitude to the World War II settlement was strongly conditioned by the prewar experience, especially the almost fatal delay of the democracies in resisting aggression. The new peace, he believed, should be founded upon an international organization, having as its core the anti-Fascist coalition, sincerely pledged to resist aggression, to protect the rights of both large and small powers, and to promote economic and social security. The initial proposals for such a body which emerged from discussions at Dumbarton Oaks and Yalta fell short of his conception of the appropriate institution.

With great determination, Fraser set about remedying these faults at San Francisco. Employing all the debating skills acquired in a long parliamentary career and drawing upon the mana acquired as the active wartime leader of a small but cooperative ally, he fought hard to have the Charter amended in the direction of assured and automatic sanctions against future aggressors. On major issues such as the veto, he was unable to move the great powers. Serious defects, he recognized, remained, but better a Charter with defects than none at all.

Fraser did, however, leave his mark. He played an important and constructive part in developing the trusteeship provisions. As chairman of the committee dealing with this matter, his performance provided a fascinating spectacle to interested observers and firmly established him as one of the conference's leading personalities. He was also heavily involved in development of those parts of the Charter relating to economic and social affairs, bringing to these tasks a blend of idealism and realism.

Fraser's hopes of an effective United Nations were not fulfilled. He gave wholehearted support to the new organization, attending both the 1946 and 1948 sessions of the General Assembly, chairing the Social, Humanitarian and Cultural Committee at the former. But in the end he conceded the UN's inability as constituted to provide security in the face of what he viewed as a deliberate Soviet policy of aggression, which seemed to echo prewar Fascist tactics. Ever the realist, he promoted more limited Western efforts to confront the perceived menace, even securing in 1949 the introduction of conscription in New Zealand to this end.

BIBLIOGRAPHY:

B. E. P. Chase, "Peter Fraser at San Francisco," *Political Science* 2 (Mar 1959), 17–24; *The Dominion* (Wellington), 13 Dec 1950, 6, 8; A. D. McIntosh, "Working with Peter Fraser in Wartime: Personal Reminiscences," *New Zealand Journal of History* 10 (Apr 1976), 3–20; James Thorn, *Peter Fraser: New Zealand's Wartime Prime Minister* (London, 1952).

Ian C. McGibbon

FRIED, Alfred Hermann. See *Biographical Dictionary of Modern Peace Leaders.*

FROMAGEOT, Henri-Auguste (10 September 1864, Versailles, France—11 September 1949, Versailles). *Education*: doctor of law, Univ. of Paris, 1891. *Career*: lawyer, 1891–1921; authority on arbitration and judge, Permanent Court of International Justice, 1922–45.

Fromageot, a specialist in maritime law, rendered extraordinary service to world bodies and the French government. In 1895 he went on an unpaid mission to East Asia and the Pacific to study conditions of the merchant marine. Thereafter, he served as secretary of the French delegation to The Hague for the arbitration of the Venezuela case (1903), attended a conference on maritime law at Brussels (1904), represented France at The Hague over perpetual leases in Japan (1902–5), and sat on the committee investigating the Dogger Bank incident (1905). Given such experience, it is understandable that he was chosen as one of the first judges on the Permanent Court of International Justice and that he sat throughout its existence

(1922–45). Representing France, Fromageot served as a *jurisconsulte suppléant* (1912) and *jurisconsulte* (1918) for the Ministry of Foreign Affairs. He performed extraordinary service by preparing and carrying out work related to virtually all of the international conferences France attended after World War I. This was particularly true for the Locarno discussions, which Fromageot attended as France's legal expert. He also represented his country at the League of Nations, where he sat with the Committee of Experts for the Progressive Codification of International Law.

The inventory to his voluminous papers catalogs the numerous proceedings in which he was involved in various capacities. The collection contains information on general questions relating to World War I, such as the Red Cross, prisoners of war, maritime war in 1917, economic affairs in the years 1915–18, and treaties with the Central Powers. He left six cartons on the Permanent Court of International Justice and dozens on individual arbitrations. Yet he remains a rather obscure figure except for his numerous books and the many documents he drafted. He is an excellent example of a quiet practicing internationalist rather than a theoretical or colorful one.

BIBLIOGRAPHY:

A. *Code disciplinaire et pénal pour la marine marchande* (Paris, 1901); *De la faute comme source de la responsibilité en droit privé* (Paris, 1891); *Etude des conflits de lois relatifs aux droits réels sur les navires* (Paris, 1901); *Etude sur les pouvoirs des commissions politiques d'enquête en Angleterre* (Paris, 1893); *L'Arbitrage des baux perpétuels au Japon* (Paris, 1905); *Le Droit de pavillon pour les navires de commerce, loi allemande* (Paris, 1901); *Les Conditions de la nationalité des navires* (Paris, 1903); *Répertoire de la pratique française en matière de droit international public*, ed. Alexandre C. Kiss, 7 vols. (Paris, 1962–72).

B. AJIL 3 (1909), 983–85; *Dictionnaire de biographie française* 14 (Paris, 1976), 1346.

C. The Fromageot papers are in the Archives du Ministère des Affaires etrangères.

June K. Burton

FYFE, David Maxwell (29 May 1900, Edinburgh—27 January 1967, London). *Education*: George Watson's Coll., Univ. of Edinburgh; M.A., Balliol Coll., Oxford Univ. *Career*: barrister, Liverpool, 1922–34; solicitor-general, 1942–45; attorney general, 1945; deputy chief prosecutor, trial of Nazi war criminals, 1945–46; legal committee, Council of Europe, 1949–50; member of Parliament for West Derby division, Liverpool, 1935–54; home secretary, minister for Welsh affairs, 1951–54; lord chancellor, 1954–62; lord rector, St. Andrews Univ., 1955–58.

In the turmoil of the post–World War II reconstruction of Europe, Western European statesmen established the first avowedly political European organization, the Council of Europe. The Council created a Committee of Ministers for cooperation between governments and a Consultative Assembly to serve as a forum for public opinion. The latter had eleven committees to deal with specific issues. Fyfe, who had been deputy chief British prosecutor at the Nuremberg Nazi war crimes trials, served as chairman of the Committee on Legal and Administrative Questions.

At the first session of the Assembly that met in August 1949, Fyfe introduced for debate the subject of human rights—the recognition of which was a condition for membership in the Council. In the general discussion that followed Fyfe's introduction, the members of the Assembly charged Fyfe's Committee with drafting a proposal for an organization within the Council that would provide for the collective guarantee of human rights.

The report of the committee called for a three-point program. A convention was to bind all the Council members to guarantee ten basic human rights, to ensure their allegiance to democracy (with regular free elections using the secret ballot and universal suffrage), and to establish a European Court of Justice and a Commission for Human Rights to implement the convention. On 4 November 1950, these proposals were formally agreed to in the "European Convention for the Protection of Human Rights and Fundamental Freedoms."

This document was the first signed by the members of the Council, and it was the Assembly's and Fyfe's major contribution to the unity movement in Europe. Fyfe also served on the Standing Committee of the Assembly, on the Joint Committee of the Assembly and Foreign Ministers, and as a member of the British delegation to the Assembly. None of his work on these remotely approached the importance of the human rights convention.

After 1950 Fyfe concentrated on domestic issues, but he continued to support British participation in the nascent unity movement. In 1951 Foreign Minister Anthony Eden overruled Fyfe and vetoed British cooperation with an European Defense Community, which effectively killed the idea. Despite this setback, Fyfe maintained his support for closer association with the continental nations. His political career came to an early end when he was mysteriously included in a purge of seven ministers by Prime Minister Harold Macmillan in July 1962.

BIBLIOGRAPHY:

A. *Monopolies* (London, 1948); *Political Adventure* (London, 1964).
B. CB 1951, 223–24; IY 1966, 1117; LT 28 Jan 1967, 10; WWW 1961–70, 630.

Michael D. Smith

G

GARFIELD, Harry Augustus (11 October 1863, Hiram, OH—12 December 1942, Williamstown, MA). *Education*: B.A., Williams Coll., 1885; Columbia Univ. Law School, 1886–87; read law at All Souls Coll., Oxford, Univ., in London at the Inns of Court, 1887–88. *Career*: lawyer, Cleveland, OH, 1888–1903; professor, Western Reserve Univ. Law School, 1892–95; professor, Princeton Univ., 1903–8; president, Williams Coll., 1908–34.

Garfield, the first son of assassinated President James A. Garfield, believed deeply in the power of education to create a better world and in the special responsibility of small, private colleges to train American students for leadership in domestic and international affairs. The outbreak of war in Europe in 1914 interrupted his plans for a summer Institute of Politics at Williams College, where college faculty and graduate students could learn from scholars of international reputation, but he remained convinced of its ultimate importance.

Garfield regarded the European war as a turning point in the history of the United States and of the Western world. It confirmed the destructive force of individualism and competition in modern life. Nations had to accept the new principle of cooperation, and America had a special duty and opportunity to lead the way. Garfield greeted America's final declaration of war with great misgivings, but he accepted *Woodrow Wilson's personal request to head the U.S. Fuel Administration, and he retained his deep interest in foreign affairs. He urged acceptance of the Versailles Treaty despite its imperfections, for he believed, like Wilson, that corrections would come through membership in a League of Nations.

The Treaty went down to defeat, but Garfield kept the faith and joined that little band of internationalists who promoted Wilsonianism in the interwar years. He became involved in the League of Nations Non-Partisan Association, and he revived his proposal for a summer Institute of Politics, but recast it as a forum for leaders in law, government, business, and education. Funded in part by Bernard Baruch, another Wilsonian, and by the Carnegie Corporation, the Institute, inaugurated in 1921, met over the next twelve summers and attracted lecturers from all over the world. The agenda reflected current issues—European reconstruction, disarmament, reparations. It also reflected Garfield's determination to acquaint the Institute's hundreds of members with foreign views. It stood in the vanguard of international education programs being developed in the 1920s. Latin American and Far Eastern affairs received continuous attention, and sessions were also devoted to contemporary problems in Canadian–American and Mexican–American relations.

Garfield served as president of the American Society of International Law in 1923, joined the board of trustees of the World Peace Foundation in 1930, and chaired its Committee on Implementation of the Kellogg Pact. He continued his quest for international cooperation even after the outbreak of war in 1939. Again, he did not advocate U.S. entry but proposed that groups of American citizens meet to consider economic problems underlying the war and bring pressure on Washington to cooperate with foreign governments to revive international trade and establish a stable currency. It was a characteristically optimistic gesture by a man who never lost a passionate belief in the ability of informed men of goodwill to create a cooperative world.

BIBLIOGRAPHY:

A. *Lost Visions* (Boston, 1944).

B. E. Herbert Botsford, *Fifty Years at Williams, Under the Administrations of Presidents Chadbourne, Carter, Hewitt, Hopkins and Garfield* (Williamstown, MA, 1940); Lucretia G. Comer, *Strands from the Weaving: The Life of Harry Garfield* (New York, 1959); DAB supp. 3, 292–94; NYT 13 Dec 1942, 73.

C. The Garfield papers are in the Manuscript Division, Library of Congress.

Robert D. Cuff

GARNER, James Wilford (22 November 1871, Pike County, MS—9 December 1938, Urbana, IL). *Education*: B.S., Mississippi A&M Coll., 1892; Ph.M., Univ. of Chicago, 1900; Ph.D., Columbia Univ., 1902. *Career*: taught elementary school, 1892–96; instructor, Bradley Polytechnic Institute, 1898–1900; lecturer, Columbia Univ., 1902–3; instructor, Univ. of Pennsylvania, 1903–4; professor and head, Department of Political Science, Univ. of Illinois, 1904–38.

Garner was born and grew up on a Mississippi farm, worked his way through college and graduate school, taught at Columbia and at Pennsylvania, and then went to the University of Illinois, where he founded the Department of Political Science and continued as its head until his death in 1938. His graduate training and his earlier teaching covered a wide range of subjects, without any special emphasis on international affairs; and during his first ten years at Illinois he published four books (one in four volumes), edited the *American Journal of Criminal Law and Criminology* (1910–12), and wrote numerous articles for encyclopedias and professional journals, none in the international area. In fact, his developing interest was comparative government, more especially the government of France, and for several years he collected material and wrote articles, intending to do for France what *James Bryce had done for the United States.

It was World War I and events leading to that conflict that turned Garner's attention to international law to such an extent that it became his passion, virtually displacing his other interests, and it brought him recognition as undoubtedly one of the most prolific scholars in that area. He gave his material on France to Lindsay Rogers of Columbia University, turned over his seminars on other subjects to colleagues, and devoted himself to teaching, writing, and speaking on international law. From 1915 until his death he wrote more than sixty articles for the *American Journal of International Law* and many more for other journals and yearbooks, American and foreign. In the same period he published five books in the international area, the most important being the two-volume *International Law and the World War* (1920) and *Prize Law During the World War* (1927). In 1935, as principal reporter, he completed a draft convention on the law of treaties, with bibliography and extended comment on each of thirty-six articles, for the League of Nations Conference for the Codification of International Law. Though not a lawyer, his opinion was requested by the Chinese consul-general in San Francisco and given in two cases before the courts involving Chinese shipping and international law.

Garner's reputation as a scholar of international law led to many honors at home and abroad. He lectured at five British and twelve French universities, the University of Calcutta, the Academy of International Law in The Hague, the Geneva Institute of International Studies, and New York University. He was a charter member of the Institut International de Droit Public, organized in Paris (1927), and served as its president (1935–36). Throughout his career as a teacher and scholar, Garner cultivated a reputation for objectivity and fairness, being particularly careful, in his writings and speeches, to state the views and reasoning with which he himself differed and to note his own views with restraint. He felt so deeply, however, on such developments as the League of Nations, the World Court, neutrality, and related matters that he became openly critical of State Department policies between the world wars. A somewhat dramatic example of this change in Garner's attitude was a paper prepared for a meeting on the Spanish Civil War but which was read by a colleague because Garner died two days before the meeting. It was both a careful review of U.S. neutrality policy and a blistering attack on the State Department's refusal to permit the sale of arms to the Spanish Republican government as a misinterpretation of that historic policy. The paper helped rally support for the Republican cause.

Garner lived a busy and useful life. His scholarly activities brought recognition to the University of Illinois and to his department as among the most distinguished in the country; his seminar on international law attracted students from abroad in increasing numbers. He thus played a significant role in promoting international understanding and goodwill and in creating instrumentalities for peace. He was an internationalist in the best sense.

BIBLIOGRAPHY:

A. "America and the World Community," *Problems of Peace*, series 6 (1931), 236–52; *International Law and the World War*, 2 vols. (New York, 1920); *Recent Developments in International Law* (Calcutta, 1925).

B. DAB supp. 2, 220–21; NCAB 31, 225–26; NYT 10 Dec 1938, 17.

C. The Garner papers are in the Archives of the Univ. of Illinois.

Clarence A. Berdahl

GARNETT, James Clerk Maxwell (13 October 1880, Cambridge—19 March 1958, Seaview, Isle of Wight). *Education*: Trinity Coll., Cambridge Univ. *Career*: legal practice, 1908–12; examiner, Board of Education, 1904–12; principal, Coll. of Technology, and dean, Univ. of Manchester, 1912–20; secretary, League of Nations Union, 1920–38.

Few figures in England in the interwar years showed as much interest in or devotion to the idea of an organized peace than Garnett. He became active in the League of Nations Union (LNU) from its founding and served as its secretary for eighteen years. His paramount role was that of a publicist who sought to stimulate public attitudes favorable to the League of Nations, but he was also instrumental in persuading leading citizens and thinkers to endorse the cause and become involved in the Union.

Contemporaries saw a clear connection between Garnett's Christian beliefs, his devotion to friends killed in World War I, his sense of service, and his conviction that the League of Nations offered a better way. He often defended the League against critics by arguing that they magnified its weaknesses while ignoring its potential. That was implicit in his message to the people of Great Britain as he sought to provide information about the League, its structure, and operation. He produced study manuals designed for schools, churches, and general readers as well as books and articles. He continually argued for fuller world cooperation and remained surprisingly optimistic even in the 1930s as aggressors challenged the League's principles. He resigned as secretary of the LNU in 1938 over disagreements on British foreign policy and his conviction that the Union was being used for political ends. When World War II came, he, like many other internationalists, merely turned to the future. The failure lay not in the concept but in the will; hence, renewed educational efforts were needed. This determined attitude appeared in Garnett's personality, where he displayed a fervor of conviction and certitude which made it difficult for others to work with him. His vision of a heaven on earth achieved through cooperation, world citizenship, and an organized world remained firm until his death.

BIBLIOGRAPHY:

A. With Nowell Smith, *The Dawn of World-Order* (London, 1932); *Education and World Citizenship* (Cambridge, 1921); *A Lasting Peace* (London, 1940); *Organising Peace: An Account of the League of Nations* (London, 1933); *World Loyalty: A Study of the Spiritual Pilgrimage Towards World Order* (London, 1928); *The World We Mean to Make and the Part of Education in Making It* (London, 1943).

B. DNB 1951–60, 392–93; LT 20 Mar 1958, 14; WW 1957, 1103.

Warren F. Kuehl

GAULLE, Charles de. See de Gaulle, Charles A.J.M.

GENTZ, Friedrich von (2 May 1764, Breslau, Germany—9 June 1832, Vienna). *Education*: Univ. of Königsberg, 1783–85. *Career*: secretary, Prussian civil service, 1786–1802; Prussian war councillor, 1783; active in publishing and editing, Berlin, 1793–1802; Austrian court councillor, 1802–32; close adviser to Foreign Minister Prince Metternich, 1810–32; secretary, congresses of Vienna, Aix-la Chappelle, Troppau, Laibach, and Verona.

Gentz's chief contribution, in a long career of public service under both Prussia and Austria, was as a political analyst, writer, and political adviser. He rose from middle-class origins through his bureaucratic career to play a key role in the international politics of the post-Napoleonic era.

Like many of the German intellectuals who had initially greeted the French Revolution as a reform movement, Gentz gradually became disillusioned with both the Revolution and the Enlightenment, which he perceived as its underlying cause. His German translation of Edmund Burke's *Reflections on the French Revolution* (1793), won him favorable attention, financial support, and international recognition. Gentz gradually formulated his highly conservative political principles, favoring legitimate monarchies, which were to be defended against revolutionary movements by a realistic use of power. He rejected as phantasms the ideas of social reform and universal peace espoused by Enlightenment writers. The French Revolution's expansive character endangered the balance of power which had been the basis of European order since the Peace of Westphalia.

Napoleon's assumption of power intensified these French tendencies. In 1802 marital and professional difficulties led Gentz to switch from Prussian to Austrian service, but initially his appointment as an imperial councillor was titular and without meaningful influence on policy. Until 1805 he worked as a publicist who gathered together a circle of those opposing Napoleon as the dominator of Europe; this is reflected in his *Fragments from the Most Recent History of the Balance of Power in Europe* (1806). The defeat of Austria (1805) and Prussia (1806) by Bonaparte made Gentz a temporary exile and unpopular at court. Only after 1809 did he gradually support Metternich in the latter's realistic foreign policy toward Napoleon, and Gentz gained lasting influence as Metternich's adviser. His conservative voice became more influential after the defeat of Napoleon, when he was appointed secretary of the Congress of Vienna. His most important contribution as an internationalist occurred in his efforts to expedite the diplomacy of the Congress, in his influence on Metternich regarding reestablishment of a European order based upon a realistic balance of power, and in a generally conservative tone of politics tempered by expediency. Gentz subsequently continued as secretary of the postwar congresses at Aix-la-Chappelle, Troppau, Laibach, and Verona.

It is difficult to assess Gentz's role, since so much of it was behind the scenes and modified by the ideas of others such as Metternich. He was not rewarded with a title of nobility from the Austrian crown or any extraordinary financial rewards; on the other hand, contemporaries considered his influence extensive and pervasive, a reputation which persisted until his death in 1832. Subsequently, scholars of the twentieth century seeking origins of internationalist trends have cited the congresses of 1814-22 and Gentz's role as important forerunners both of cooperation between states and the concept of sanctions collectively applied to maintain peace. In word and deed, Gentz was an important factor in the limited forms of internationalism of the early nineteenth century.

BIBLIOGRAPHY:

A. *Aus dem Nachlass Varnhagens von Ense: Tagebuecher von Friedrich von Gentz*, 4 vols. (Leipzig, Germany, 1873-74); *Gesamtausgabe der Briefen Friedrichs von Gentz*, 4 vols. (Munich, 1909-13); *Korrespondenz und Schriften*, 5 vols. (Mannheim, Germany, 1838-40); *The Origin and Principles of the American Revolution Compared with the Origin and Principles of the French Revolution* (Philadelphia, 1800); *Staatsschriften und Briefe*, 2 vols. (Munich, 1921).

B. Eugen Guglia, *Friedrich von Gentz* (Vienna, 1901); Golo Mann, *Secretary of Europe: The Life of Friedrich von Gentz, Enemy of Napoleon*, (New Haven, CT, 1946); for a bibliography, see *Mitteilungen des Instituts fuer oesterreichische Geschichtsforschung* 27 (1906), 91-146, 682-84; *Neue deutsche Biographie* 6 (Berlin, 1964), 190-93; Paul F. Reiff, *Friedrich von Gentz: An Opponent of the French Revolution and Napoleon* (Urbana, IL, 1912); Heinrich Ritter von Srbik, *Metternich: der Staatsmann und der Mensch*, 3 vols. (Munich, 1925-54); Paul R. Sweet, *Friedrich von Gentz: Defender of the Old Order* (Madison, WI, 1941).

Roger Wines

GERIG, O. Benjamin (17 January 1894, Smithville, OH—26 February 1976, Venice, FL). *Education*: B.A., Goshen Coll., 1917; A.M., Univ. of Illinois, 1922; fellow, Institut Universitaire des Hautes Etudes Internationales; *doctorat ès sciences politiques*, Univ. of Geneva, 1930. *Career*: ambulance driver in France, 1918; instructor, Univ. of Illinois, 1922-23; assistant professor, Simmons Coll., 1923-28; member, Information and Mandates Sections, League of Nations Secretariat, 1930-39; commissioner-general, League of Nations Pavilion, New York World's Fair, 1939-40; associate professor, Haverford Coll., 1940-42; U.S. Department of State, 1942-61, associate chief, Division of International Security and Organization, 1943-44, technical adviser, Dumbarton Oaks Conference, 1944; deputy secretary-general, U.S. delegation, San Francisco Conference, 1945; chief, Division of Dependent Area Affairs, and associate chief, Division of International Organization Affairs, 1945-49; principal adviser and alternate U.S. delegate, Preparatory Commission for UN, London, 1945; director, Office of Dependent Area Affairs, 1949-61; deputy U.S. representative, Trusteeship Council of the UN, 1947-61; chair, U.S. interdepartmental committee on non–self-governing territories.

A book Gerig completed in 1929, *The Open Door and the Mandates*

System, forecast much of his subsequent career. In the League of Nations Secretariat and later in the State Department, he was largely concerned with the international oversight of non–self-governing territories. In the 1929 study, to which *William E. Rappard contributed an enlightening fore-word, Gerig defined the "open door" as equal economic opportunity. He surveyed the situation of rival colonial powers in the neomercantilist period after 1880, analyzed the working of the open door doctrine at the Paris Peace Conference of 1919, and recommended for the 1930s the open door as a partial solution to the unequal distribution of the markets and resources of the world's undeveloped territories. Extension of the mandate principle to areas other than those formerly held by Germany and the Ottoman Empire would depend, however, on enlightened public opinion in many countries.

In 1941, as Gerig considered a new postwar world, he still assumed that responsible governments would serve, better than before, the interests of both "the world's backward areas" and others in providing equal opportunity. Gerig noted, however, a new insistence that the welfare of the inhabitants take precedence over the economic advantage of metropolitan states, that colonies not be considered to be held in perpetuity, that they be regarded administratively rather than politically or strategically, and that there be some collective international responsibility for their governance until they were able to stand alone. Gerig had practical suggestions for extending the mandates system and creating an international development fund, and as a State Department official (1942–61) he grappled with the theoretical and practical aspects of the colonial and excolonial problem as he sought to apply his 1941 ideas. He was able to do this through his participation in postwar planning, his administrative and operational responsibilities, his involvement in setting up the United Nations machinery, and his detailed negotiations on trusteeship and related issues. While his individual role is difficult to determine, his clear perspective and unique expertise made him an influential figure in shaping U.S. policy toward developing nations. After his retirement, Gerig contributed to a lengthy study of international peace observation, particularly in regard to twelve cases under the League of Nations.

BIBLIOGRAPHY:

A. "An Appraisal of the League of Nations" and "Colonies in an Eventual World Settlement," in Commission to Study the Organization of Peace, *Preliminary Report and Monographs* (New York, 1942), 102–14, 302–8; *International Peace Observation: A History and Forecast*, with David W. Wainhouse and others (Baltimore, MD, 1966), 7–85; "Mandates and Colonies," in Institute of World Organization, *World Organization* (Washington, 1942), 211–30; *The Open Door and the Mandates System* (London, 1930).

B. *American Foreign Policy: Basic Documents, 1950–1955*, 2 vols. (Washington, 1957); *American Foreign Policy: Current Documents, 1956–61*, 6 vols. (Washington, 1959–65); *Biographic Register* of Department of State (Washington, 1959), 268–69;

Foreign Relations of the United States, 1951, vol. 2, *The United Nations: The Western Hemisphere* (Washington, 1979); *Postwar Foreign Policy Preparation, 1939-1945* (Washington, 1950); *Washington Post* 6 Mar 1976, D-4.

Fredrick Aandahl

GIBSON, Hugh Simons (16 August 1883, Los Angeles—12 December 1954, Geneva). *Education*: graduated from Ecole Libre des Sciences Politiques, Paris, 1907. *Career*: entered diplomatic service, 1908; minister to Poland, 1919-24, to Switzerland, 1924-27; chair, U.S. delegation, Preparatory Commission for the General Disarmament Conference, 1926-32; chair, U.S. delegation, and chair, Tripartite Naval Conference, 1927; ambassador to Belgium and minister to Luxemburg, 1927-33, 1937-38; delegate, London Naval Conference, 1930; acting chairman, U.S. delegation, General Disarmament Conference, 1932-33; ambassador to Brazil, 1933-37; delegate, Chaco Peace Conference, 1935; European director, Commission for Polish Relief and Commission for Relief in Belgium, 1940-41; director, Provisional Intergovernmental Committee for the Movement of Migrants from Europe, 1951-52; director, Intergovernmental Committee for European Migration, 1952-54.

An American career diplomat, Gibson combined pronounced loyalty to his own country with a lifetime of service to international efforts to preserve peace and aid victims of war. While never deviating from placing American interests first, he saw those as best served through policies and actions in support of what he frequently called "international collaboration." Gibson, a realist and an optimist, believed that, while there were definite limits on what international diplomacy could accomplish, gradual progress toward peace and understanding were indeed possible.

Gibson was not a theoretician in the field of international affairs. In published writings, private letters, and memoranda, he addressed practical rather than theoretical concerns. His books stressed the mechanics of international relations and diplomacy. They revealed his assumption that international cooperation, not a nationalistic search for advantage, was the key to peace. In *Problems of Lasting Peace*, Gibson joined with *Herbert Hoover in calling for the institution and utilization of international machinery to preserve peace. He believed in the existence of a human "will to peace" that could be mobilized by international instrumentalities.

It was in action more than in words, however, that Gibson was a true internationalist. He was a product of cosmopolitan education, both formal and informal, and moved comfortably in world circles from the beginning of his career. Gibson was secretary of the legation in Belgium when World War I brought havoc to that country. One of the original members of the Commission for Relief in Belgium, he served as a key figure in organizing and coordinating relief efforts. After World War I, as U.S. minister to Switzerland, he became a strong advocate of closer cooperation between the

United States and the League of Nations. In April 1929, *Living Age* credited Gibson with doing more than any other single person to break down American aloofness from League activities and to lay the groundwork for cooperation. This role, in part, led to the major international phase of his career, during which he represented the United States at virtually every disarmament conference from the mid-1920s until 1933. As a negotiator he constantly sought bases for international agreement, preferring identification of areas where accord, however minor, could be reached over belligerent assertions of national interest. For Gibson, international diplomacy was the art of the possible, and he consistently played the role of mediator. If Gibson had a philosophy of international relations, it was meliorism.

Accordingly, he defended the Pact of Paris of 1928, considering it a first step from which further progress could follow. The Pact would, he believed, create the requisite atmosphere in which other forms of international accord could thrive. Among these was disarmament, which Gibson saw as a slow, gradual process. In a speech delivered at Yale University in June 1931, Gibson said he did not expect to see a solution to the problem of armaments in his lifetime, but did expect to see steady progress.

The collapse of the disarmament movement did not diminish Gibson's faith in the wisdom of international collaboration, nor did it end his active career. While serving as ambassador to Brazil in the 1930s, he was also the U.S. delegate to the Chaco Peace Conference in Buenos Aires, called to settle the border dispute between Bolivia and Paraguay. During and after World War II, he returned to the kind of international activity that he had begun during World War I, acting as European director of both the Commission for Polish Relief and the Commission for Relief in Belgium. When he died in 1954, he was head of the Intergovernmental Committee for European Migration. Death came, appropriately, in Geneva, the center of so many international activities. Whether the endeavor involved attempts to prevent wars, to end them, or to ameliorate the conditions caused by them, Gibson spent much of the first half of the twentieth century at the center of efforts to deal with the problem of international conflicts.

BIBLIOGRAPHY:

A. With Herbert Hoover, *The Basis of Lasting Peace* (New York, 1945); *Belgium* (New York, 1939); *A Journal from Our Legation in Belgium* (Garden City, NY, 1917); with Herbert Hoover, *The Problems of Lasting Peace* (Garden City, NY, 1942); *Rio* (Garden City, NY, 1937); *The Road to Foreign Policy* (Garden City, NY, 1944).

B. CB 1953, 217–20; Perrin C. Galpin, ed., *Hugh Gibson, 1883–1954: Extracts from His Letters and Anecdotes from His Friends* (New York, 1956); Ronald E. Swerczek, "The Diplomatic Career of Hugh Gibson, 1908–1938," dissertation, Univ. of Iowa, 1972, "Hugh Gibson and Disarmament: The Diplomacy of Gradualism," in Kenneth Paul Jones, ed., *U.S. Diplomats in Europe, 1919–1941* (Santa Barbara, CA, 1981); WWWA 3, 322.

C. The Gibson papers are in the Archives of the Hoover Institution on War, Revolution and Peace.

Ronald E. Swerczek

GILBERT, Prentiss Bailey (3 October 1883, Rochester, NY—24 February 1939, Berlin). *Education*: Ph.B., Univ. of Rochester, 1906, M.A., 1916; B.A., Yale Univ., 1907. *Career*: U.S. diplomat, 1919–39.

Gilbert died before reaching high rank, but he was an influential teacher of young foreign service officers between the world wars and one of the few American diplomatists admired by the leading journalists of the era. While consul in Geneva, Gilbert became the only American ever to sit with the League Council. He was just sixteen and newly graduated from high school when he accompanied his father on active duty in the Philippines from 1900 to 1902. He suffered the rest of his life from illnesses contracted in the campaign. After attending college, he spent the years 1910–15 wandering around the world. Reentering the Army in 1917, Gilbert ran a military intelligence office in the War Department.

Gilbert was thirty-five when he entered the State Department in March 1919 as director of the Division of Political and Economic Information. Specializing in League matters, he later became assistant director of the influential Division of Western European Affairs from 1925 to 1930. In 1930 Gilbert was selected to head an expanded Geneva consulate. From August 1930 to August 1937, he led successive teams of outstanding young foreign service officers in day-to-day relations with the international organizations clustered in Geneva. Restricted to the rank of consul to placate isolationists, Gilbert developed a major reputation as a reporter, trainer of young talent, and guide to American journalists and other newcomers to Geneva. He received worldwide attention in October 1931, when he sat with the League Council in its first emergency meeting on the Manchurian Crisis. But Secretary of State *Henry Stimson soon curtailed the mission and thus ended the interwar period's closest U.S.–League relationship.

Gilbert and his vice-consuls, including many future ambassadors, continued to cover the League as international violence increased in the 1930s. In August 1937, Gilbert became counselor of the Berlin embassy and, for more than half of the remaining months of his life, chargé. During his first stint as chargé, he attended the Nuremberg rally in the fall of 1937 and vainly attempted to sound out the Nazi leaders about improving relations with Washington. He became chargé for the second extended period when *Franklin Roosevelt in effect recalled Ambassador *Hugh Wilson in the aftermath of Crystal Night, the mid-November 1938 Nazi assault on the Jews. Gilbert's long dispatches and often accurate predictions began to capture the attention of Roosevelt and Secretary of State *Cordell Hull. His increasingly outspoken protests of the Nazi outrages and his clandestine meetings with opponents of the regime sapped his energy. His last communications with Washington prior to his sudden death reflected his anguish over Germany's persecution of the Jews and continuing preparations for war.

BIBLIOGRAPHY:

A. *A Maid of Honor* (play), adapted from Raoul Aurenheimer, *Der Gute König* (1930).

B. *Biographic Register* of the Department of State (Washington, 1937), 191; J. B. Donnelly, "Prentiss Bailey Gilbert and the League of Nations: The Diplomacy of an Observer," in Kenneth Paul Jones, *U.S. Diplomats in Europe, 1919–1941* (Santa Barbara, CA, 1981); NCAB 30, 430–31; NYT 26 Feb 1939, 39; WWWA 1, 454.

C. Gilbert papers are in the Hoover Presidential Library and the Univ. of Rochester Library.

J. B. Donnelly

GILBERT, S. Parker (13 October 1892, Bloomfield, NJ—23 February 1938, New York). *Education*: B.A., Rutgers Coll., 1912, M.A., 1916, LL.B., Harvard Univ., 1915. *Career*: lawyer, 1915–18; member, War Loan Staff, Treasury Department, 1918–20; assistant secretary of the treasury, 1920–21; under secretary of the treasury, 1921–23; agent general for reparation payments, 1924–30; partner, J. P. Morgan & Co., 1931–38.

In the 1920s, a decade when the United States relied on economic unofficial diplomacy and financial issues permeated international politics, Gilbert stood at the nexus of American financial power in Europe. As agent general for reparations under the Dawes Plan, Gilbert supervised the transfer of huge sums of money and oversaw the performance of the German economy. A brilliant financier and indefatigable worker, Gilbert stayed in the Treasury Department during the Republican transition and became, at age twenty-nine, under secretary of the treasury, a post Andrew Mellon created for him.

Although Gilbert severed formal links with the U.S. government before he became agent general, he stayed in close contact with Mellon and State Department and Federal Reserve Bank of New York officials. In addition, Gilbert became an enormously influential figure in European financial politics. Thus he acted as an informal but effective liaison between American and European officials. U.S. political and financial leaders trusted Gilbert because of his abilities and because they realized he reflected America's broad interest in achieving a stable, prosperous, peaceful Europe. Consequently Gilbert saw no basic conflict between his internationalist duties as agent general and his loyalties to the United States. Yet when conflicts did occur, Gilbert, despite occasional tactical differences with Washington and New York, believed his "first duty" was to America.

Unfortunately for Gilbert, America's involvement in the Dawes Plan soon became a contradictory one as a torrent of loans from the United States flooded Germany. Gilbert worried that the dollar inflow financed wasteful socialistic municipal enterprises. Moreover, interest and amortization payments soon competed with reparation payments for Germany's foreign exchange supply, thus undermining the Dawes Plan and Europe's precarious stability. To avert catastrophe, Gilbert in 1927–28 lobbied with European and American political and financial officials for a revision of the Dawes Plan. These efforts were the high point of Gilbert's influence as he shuttled about Europe, moving the French, Germans, and British closer to a revised and he hoped final reparations settlement. In 1928 he was offered the governorship of the Federal Reserve Bank of New York, one of the most important posts in the United States. Gilbert refused and continued his preparatory diplomacy for what became the Young Conference of 1929. He helped establish the Young Plan and the Bank for International Settlements, which took over his reparations duties when the Dawes Plan was replaced in 1930. In 1931, Gilbert became a partner in J. P. Morgan and Company, with which he had developed close personal and professional ties as a treasury official and agent general. His career demonstrated how the United States exercised influence in Europe at a time of supposed isolation.

BIBLIOGRAPHY:

A. *Annual Report of the Agent General for Reparations*, 6 vols. (Berlin, 1925–1930).

B. Frank Costigliola, "The United States and the Reconstruction of Germany in the 1920's," *Business History Review* 50 (Winter 1976), 477–502; DAB supp. 2, 234–35; NYT 24 Feb 1938, 1; Werner Link, *Die Amerikanische Stabilisierungspolitik im Deutschland, 1921–32* (Düsseldorf, Germany, 1970).

Frank C. Costigliola

GILCHRIST, Huntington (16 November 1891, Boston—13 January 1975, Ridgefield, CT). *Education*: B.A., Williams Coll., 1913; M.A., Harvard Univ., 1916; Ph.D., Columbia Univ., 1918. *Career*: instructor, Anglo-American Coll., Foochow, China, and Peking Univ., 1913–15; captain, U.S. Army, 1918–19; League of Nations Secretariat, 1919–28; chemical industry executive, 1928–54; executive officer, UN Relief and Rehabilitation Administration Council, 1943, secretary-general, 1944; executive officer, Commission 2, San Francisco Conference, 1945; executive secretary, Inspection Group, Interim and Full Committees, UN General Assembly; chief, Headquarters Planning Section, UN Secretariat, 1945–46; U.S. delegate, UN Preparatory Commission, London, 1946; director, Industry Division, Economic Cooperation Administration (ECA), Paris, 1949–50; chief, Special Mission for Belgium, Luxembourg, and Belgian Congo, 1950–55; resident representative for Pakistan, UN Technical Assistance Board, Karachi, 1955–57.

Gilchrist spent an active career in the service of international cooperation on four continents. From his sojourn in China before World War I, through his service to the League of Nations, the United Nations, and the U.S. Department of State, to his work in the international chemical business, Gilchrist's work spanned two-thirds of a century. Throughout, he was at the vital level of senior management, the rank which rarely makes headlines but is indispensable to operations and to making policy.

Gilchrist began his international career when he traveled to post-Manchu China to teach and collect information for a doctoral thesis on "The Development of the City in China." When no one on the faculty of Columbia University proved competent to evaluate the work, Gilchrist produced another on government finance in Maine. His financial expertise led him into budgetary matters at Army headquarters in Washington and then into statistical support for John J. Pershing's staff in France.

Gilchrist joined the League of Nations provisional Secretariat as personal assistant to under secretary-general *Raymond Fosdick and was assigned to Paris to maintain liaison with the remnants of the American Commission to Negotiate Peace. In 1920 Gilchrist joined the Administrative Commissions and Minorities Section as chief of its Department on Administrative Commissions, where he handled Secretariat responsibilities for the Saar and Danzig. In 1925 he transferred to the Mandates Section, becoming its principal assistant director and initiating a lifelong interest in the problems of dependency and development.

More important than these formal responsibilities, Gilchrist by his own recollection spent about one-fourth of his time as a kind of minister without portfolio for relations with the United States, becoming unquestionably the second most influential American official, behind *Arthur Sweetser, in formulating and executing the Secretariat's American policy. Gilchrist was not a major League propagandist, nor did he expend much energy on American pro-League organizations, which he considered ineffective; instead, he concentrated on individuals of financial or political influence. He devoted about one-tenth of his time with the League on five trips to the United States, often lobbying government officials to expand American cooperation with Geneva. Included were two urgent visits to Washington, one to secure a conciliatory U.S. response to the Geneva Protocol (1924) and the other to promote the nomination of *Charles E. Hughes to the Permanent Court of International Justice (1928). Gilchrist was never an optimist regarding chances of U.S. membership; in fact, his reports and judgment on the "American question" were the soundest of any American at Geneva.

In 1928, aware that his career in the Secretariat could not advance without U.S. membership and determined to secure the private wealth he deemed necessary to a public career, Gilchrist resigned to join the international chemical firm of Cyanamid. By the time World War II forced him and the company out of Europe, Gilchrist had become managing director of Cyanamid Products, Ltd., in London. He spent the war years as a ranking industry executive in New York, handling relations with the Canadian government on large ordnance construction and operation contracts.

During and after the war, Gilchrist took frequent leaves from Cyanamid to participate in the establishment of the UN family of organizations. He was prominent in the founding of the UN Relief and Rehabilitation Administration, managed staff work on the design of the General Assembly at San Francisco, attended the London meetings of the UN Preparatory Commission as U.S. delegate, and directed the search for a UN headquarters site. His business career came to a practical end in 1949, when he left for five years in Europe with the Marshall Plan organization. His public service closed with his UN service in Karachi, devoted to reestablishing continuity and managerial soundness for scores of projects carried out by over a hundred experts from twenty countries.

Gilchrist remained an active observer and commentator on international affairs during almost two decades of retirement by continuing associations with educational and research bodies. In the 1920s, Gilchrist had helped direct the International School in Geneva, the Geneva Institute of International Relations, and the Williamstown Institute of Politics; in the late 1940s and early 1950s he was vice-chairman of the Brookings Institution Board of Trustees and served four years as chairman of the governing council of the Institute of Pacific Relations, where he defended the organization skillfully against charges that it was soft on communism. In retirement he remained active on the Brookings Board, in the Council on Foreign Relations, and through occasional letters to the *New York Times*, always as a voice raised in support of greater American international collaboration.

BIBLIOGRAPHY:

A. "Colonial Questions at the San Francisco Conference," *American Political Science Review* 39 (Oct 1945), 982–92; "Dependent Peoples and Mandates," in *Pioneers in World Order: An American Appraisal of the League of Nations*, ed. Harriet E. Davis (New York, 1944), 121–55; "The Japanese Islands: Annexation or Trusteeship?" *Foreign Affairs* 22 (Jul 1944), 635–42; ed, *The League of Nations Starts* (London, 1920); "The Operation of the Mandates System," in *Problems of Peace* (London, 1927); "Political Disputes: Dumbarton Oaks and the Experience of the League of Nations," *Proceedings of the Academy of Political Science* 21 (May 1945), 136–46; "Trusteeship and the Colonial System," *Proceedings of the Academy of Political Science* 21 (Jan 1947), 95–109.

B. Waldo H. Heinrichs, Jr. *American Ambassador: Joseph C. Grew and the Development of the United States Diplomatic Tradition* (New York, 1966); WWWA 6, 157–58.

C. The Gilchrist papers are in the Manuscript Division, Library of Congress.

Terry L. Deibel

GILDERSLEEVE, Virginia Crocheron (3 October 1877, New York—7 July 1965, Centerville, MA). *Education*: B.A., Barnard Coll., 1899; M.A., Columbia Univ., 1900, Ph.D., 1908. *Career*: faculty, Barnard Coll., 1900–1911, professor and dean, 1911–45; delegate, San Francisco Conference, 1945.

A longtime, highly respected Barnard College dean, Gildersleeve became an internationalist when World War I aroused her interest in foreign affairs. It convinced her that the tightly interwoven and technically advanced world made peace an imperative. Believing that scholars should be activists, Gildersleeve joined the League to Enforce Peace and ardently supported the League of Nations. Although for thirty years she argued that international organization best promoted world order, she also enthusiastically recommended "grass-roots" contacts among people because personal relationships promoted broader human understanding and peace. Gildersleeve thus chaired the American Association of University Women's Committee on International Relations, served as a founder and president of the International Federation of University Women, brought noted foreign scholars to lecture at Barnard, encouraged student exchange programs, and added an international studies program to Barnard's curriculum.

Gildersleeve, who believed women should participate as equals in life, thought they had special attributes which made them natural peacemakers. She was, however, no pacifist and acknowledged the need for force to counter aggressive nations. When World War II began, she joined the Committee to Defend America by Aiding the Allies. Following Pearl Harbor, she enlisted Barnard students in the war effort and advised the Navy's WAVE program. Although suggesting Germany suffer a "harsh" peace, Gildersleeve urged Americans to eliminate hatred from their thinking. She held membership on the Commission to Study the Organization of Peace and attended the Dumbarton Oaks Conference. Her most notable and personally satisfying accomplishment came in 1945 at the San Francisco Conference, where, as a delegate, she helped draft the preamble to the UN Charter and develop the provisions for the Economic and Social Council. Later she served briefly as an alternate delegate to the General Assembly.

A quest for justice and an appreciation for foreign cultures were at the center of Gildersleeve's value system. On a postwar educational mission to Japan, she questioned the effort to democratize the Japanese political system. Unpopular issues did not give her pause. An amateur archaeologist who admired Middle Eastern and African cultures, she opposed the creation of a Jewish state in Palestine, and in 1948 she chaired a Committee for Justice and Peace in the Holy Land. Following her retirement, she published an autobiography and traveled.

BIBLIOGRAPHY:

A. "Citizen of the World," *Century Magazine* 120 (Jan 1930), 82–87; *Many a Good Crusade* (New York, 1954).

B. CB 1941, 319–40; DAB supp. 7, 288–89; NCAB G, 104–5; NYT 9 Jul 1965, 1; WWWA, 4, 357.

C. The Gildersleeve papers are in the Butler Library, Columbia Univ.

Daryl L. Revoldt

GINN, Edwin (14 February 1838, Orland, ME—21 January 1914, Winchester, MA). *Education*: Westbrook Sem.; B.A., Tufts Coll., 1862.

Career: book agent, 1862–67; founder and publisher, Ginn and Brothers, 1867, later Ginn and Company.

A successful Boston publisher of school and college textbooks, Ginn had an active interest in social reform. During the 1890s he joined the internationalist and peace movements after attending the 1897 Lake Mohonk International Arbitration Conference with his friend *Edwin Mead. Ginn came to oppose what he regarded as an escalating arms race because of the burden excessive weapons placed upon a nation's economy. He condemned war for its human and material destruction and, while convinced that the world's people sought peace, he recognized that the war system had become so thoroughly entrenched that it could not be easily discarded. Jingoistic newspapers and popular histories which glorified war and an arms economy made peace work difficult. Ginn nevertheless believed it was possible for nations to establish a world parliament which would expand international law, create a universal court, and encourage gradual disarmament by forming an international army and navy. Ginn also favored economic sanctions imposed by a world organization against belligerent nations. If such measures failed, collective military force could be employed.

Ginn saw education as essential to make his vision a reality. In 1903 he challenged peace leaders to form a large permanent agency, broaden scope, which would acquire operating funds, employ a professional staff, and develop a systematic educational program. Ginn's suggestion also included the publication of a weekly peace journal. To foster the internationalist spirit, he recommended that the new agency promote international congresses and meetings for postal officials, physicians, businessmen, professors, and students.

Ginn believed that businessmen had a special obligation to assist peace and internationalism, and he acted accordingly. Discovering that the movement lacked inexpensive literature which focused on international affairs, he started in 1905 to publish an International Library. The series featured books and pamphlets such as *Raymond Bridgman's *World Organization* and ⁺Andrew Carnegie's *A League of Peace*. Ginn also began to underwrite the activities of groups such as the International Peace Congress, the American School Peace League, and the Cosmopolitan Clubs. His contributions, however, did little to alleviate his desire for a powerful, well-endowed peace organization. In 1909 Ginn pledged $50,000 a year to a newly created International School of Peace, with a promise to endow it after his death. On 22 December, with Edwin Mead as managing director and with a firm financial base, it became the World Peace Foundation. Its full-time staff executed a wide variety of educational programs and published an exceptional pamphlet series. Ginn lived until 1914, long enough to see the Foundation initiate imaginative programs to advance international organization and conflict resolution, and he provided around $1 million to ensure its continuation.

BIBLIOGRAPHY:

A. *Outline of the Life of Edwin Ginn* (Boston, 1908); *Report of the Lake Mohonk Conference on International Arbitration, 1897–1913.*

B. DAB 4, 317; Arthur N. Holcombe, "Edwin Ginn's Vision of World Peace," *International Organization* 19 (Winter 1965), 1–19; Warren F. Kuehl, *Seeking World Order: The United States and International Organization to 1920* (Nashville, TN, 1969); Denys P. Myers, "Edwin Ginn," *World Unity Magazine* 5 (Oct 1930), 24–30; NCAB 10, 481.

Daryl L. Revoldt

GONDRA, Manuel. See *Biographical Dictionary of Modern Peace Leaders.*

GOODRICH, Carter Lyman (10 May 1897, Plainfield, NJ—8 April 1971, Mexico City). *Education*: B.A., Amherst Coll., 1918; study in England, 1919; Ph.D., Univ. of Chicago, 1921; Amherst memorial fellow in economics, 1921–22, 1923–24. *Career*: instructor, Amherst Coll., 1922–23; assistant professor to full professor, Univ. of Michigan, 1924–31; professor, Columbia Univ., 1931–63; Andrew W. Mellon professor, Univ. of Pittsburgh, 1963–71.

Goodrich's internationalist activities appear a natural and ineluctable outgrowth of his major intellectual interests which encompassed labor economics and economic history, particularly American economic developments in the nineteenth century. His early works, *The Frontier of Control* and *The Miner's Freedom*, illustrated his interest in the first area, as did his later work on migration. But while never fully deserting this interest, he began turning more and more to American economic history, drawing upon it for comparative purposes to aid less developed countries. Thus, in his books on the growth of American railroads and canals, Goodrich attempted to trace a pattern of governmental–private interaction in these two areas, hoping it might prove useful in countries in that stage of development. In addition, Goodrich, as an early proponent of faculty–graduate student seminars in international economic problems and the economic difficulties of underdeveloped countries, established these at Columbia and Pittsburgh.

Goodrich, however, ranged far beyond the confines of academia. He served as U.S. labor commissioner in Geneva (1936–37), and he was the U.S. delegate (1938–46) to the International Labor Office. He simultaneously sat as the U.S. representative to annual ILO conferences, 1937–39, 1941, 1944, and 1945. He also chaired the governing body of the ILO, in which capacity he was instrumental in 1940 in gaining the removal of its records from Geneva to safe haven in Canada. After World War II, Goodrich served in the UN Secretariat for several years, while in 1948–49 he was program director of the UN Scientific Conference on the Conservation and Utilization of Resources.

In 1952–53, as the secretary-general's representative, Goodrich headed a UN technical assistance project to Bolivia, the progenitor of the UN Development Program. In 1955–56 he was chief of the UN's Economic Survey Mission in Vietnam. Finally, in 1959–60, Goodrich returned to Latin America representing Columbia University as director of an exchange program in which Argentinian students studied at Columbia while professors from Columbia and other universities taught at the University of Buenos Aires. Goodrich is a valuable example of a man whose vision extended beyond a narrow specialty and who sought ways through his writings and efforts to apply the lessons of the past to help less developed countries in the present.

BIBLIOGRAPHY:

A. Ed., *Canals and American Economic Development* (New York, 1961); *The Frontier of Control* (New York, 1921); *The Government and the Economy, 1783–1861* (Indianapolis, IN, 1967); *Government Promotion of American Canals and Railroads, 1800–1890* (New York, 1960); "The International Labor Organization," in *Pioneers in World Order: An American Appraisal of the League of Nations*, ed. Harriet E. Davis (New York, 1944), 87–106; *Migration and Economic Opportunity* (Philadelphla, 1936); *The Miner's Freedom: A Study of Working Life in a Changing Industry* (Boston, 1925).

B. NCAB 57, 139–40; NYT 9 Apr 1971, 34; WWA 1970–71, 1207; *Yearbook of the American Philosophical Society* (Philadelphia, 1972), 179.

James Ross Macdonald

GOODRICH, Caspar Frederick (7 January 1847, Philadelphia—26 December 1925, Princeton, NJ). *Education*: U.S. Naval Academy 1861–64. *Career*: U.S. Navy, 1864–1909.

In an era of rapidly increasing arms and growing concern for disarmament, Goodrich was conspicuous as a naval officer who called for arms reduction, as an exponent of Mahanian principles of sea power who cautioned a limited American international role, and as a prophet of brotherhood who believed in immigration restriction and Anglo-Saxon superiority.

Goodrich, who reached the rank of rear admiral, said disarmament would become practical when reason prevailed in international affairs. Until that day, he insisted, force had to exist and therefore had to be controlled. He decried the growth of German militarism and urged a defensive American fleet. He also saw the preservation of world order as a responsibility of the two major English-speaking powers, and he advocated an Anglo–American police force to ensure international harmony. But Goodrich was willing to try other channels. Indeed, Goodrich increasingly saw sanctions as an essential feature of any international organization if it were to preserve peace. Thus he emerged as an advocate of collective military sanctions in an age when that concept was yet unique. While world political leaders were generally hostile to arbitration, he stood out as a proponent of that method of settling disputes. The horrors of World War I failed to dampen his optimism, but rather heightened his sense of the urgency of international cooperation.

BIBLIOGRAPHY:

A. Addresses in *Report of Lake Mohonk Conference on International Arbitration* (Lake Mohonk, NY 1907, 1910); *Closing Address of the President of the War College* (Washington, 1898); "The Conduct of Military and Naval Warfare," in *Problems of Readjustment After the War* (New York, 1915); *Rope Yarns from the Old Navy* (New York, 1931); "Wanted—An International Police," *Living Age* 52 (26 Aug 1911), 543–49.

B. *Nation* 104 (17 May 1917), 606–7; NCAB 13, 76–77; NYT 27 Dec 1925, 28; Clark Reynolds, *Famous American Admirals* (New York, 1978), 140–41; WWWA 1, 468.

C. The Goodrich papers are at the New-York Historical Society.

Kenneth John Blume

GREENE, Jerome Davis (12 October 1874, Yokohama, Japan—28 March 1959, Cambridge, MA). *Education*: B.A., Harvard Coll., 1896; Univ. of Geneva, 1896–97; Harvard Law School, 1897–99. *Career*: staff, Univ. Press of Cambridge, 1899–1901; secretary to president, Harvard Coll., 1901–5; secretary, Harvard Corporation, 1905–10, 1934–43; general manager, Rockefeller Institute for Medical Research, 1910–12; advisor to *John D. Rockefeller, Jr., 1912–17; trustee, secretary, and executive officer, Rockefeller Foundation, 1913–17, trustee, 1928–39; executive secretary, American Shipping Mission, Allied Maritime Transport Council, London, 1917; partner, Lee Higginson and Co., 1918–32; Executive Committee, American Council, Institute of Pacific Relations, 1925–39, trustee, 1927–46, chairman, 1929–32; chairman, Pacific Council, 1929–33; professor, Univ. Coll. of Wales, 1933–34.

The son of Congregationalist missionaries from Massachusetts, Greene was born and raised in Japan. The family has been described as "lower upper middle class," without great wealth but enjoying superior education and social contacts. Through connections with the Rockefellers, Greene emerged by the second decade of the century as one of the early "philanthropoids," or foundation administrators. He joined in the Rockefeller Foundation's health work and served (1913–17) on its International Health Committee. Even after he left to become an investment banker, he remained committed to private humanitarian efforts to improve international understanding and health, especially in Asia. His work for the Rockefellers and his leadership position within the Institute of Pacific Relations after 1925 led Chinese scholar and diplomat Hu Shih to call him the "philosopher-banker."

Although he served internationalism mainly as an administrator and fund-raiser, Greene brought to the cause considerable knowledge of world politics. He had served as U.S. secretary to the Reparations Committee at the Paris Peace Conference. That experience led him to share with many other opponents of isolationism the belief that ignorance was the big problem. He regarded research, public education, and rational discussion as logical remedies to promote the peaceful reconciliation of differences. Accordingly, he supported disarmament and the League of Nations but watched as the peace machinery of the 1930s failed to restrain nations that used force to change an unjust status quo.

During the 1930s, Greene became involved in public controversy because of his statements about Asian affairs. First, after Japan seized Manchuria in 1931, he was accused of being an apologist for the aggressor. The accusation rested upon his statements that behind the Chinese Nationalist rhetoric about democracy lay universal venality and inhuman cruelty. Because he thought that China lacked a national government or real sovereignty over Manchuria and because he believed that international understanding depended on knowledge of all the facts, he wanted Americans to be aware of Japan's position. He warned that a proposed economic boycott was, in fact, not much different from a declaration of war against Japan. Nevertheless, Greene was not an apologist for Japan. Even during the early 1930s he regarded that country as the chief cause of conflict in Asia, pursuing a policy that could only bring disaster.

By the late 1930s, Greene, like his younger brother *Roger, had made clear his support of China, even with its faults. As Rockefeller representative in China from 1914 until the mid-1930s, Roger became chairman of the American Committee for Non-Participation in Japanese Aggression in 1938 and later also associate director of the Committee to Defend America by Aiding the Allies. Jerome Greene shared his brother's views and was ready for the United States to enter the European war by 1940. After the war, the Greene brothers also shared a suspicion that the Soviet Union's record of ruthlessness made tolerance difficult.

BIBLIOGRAPHY:

A. *Idealism and Realism in Efforts Toward Peace* (Aberystwyth, Wales, 1933); *The League: Its Weaknesses and a Possible Remedy* (New York, 1935); *Present Problems of the Orient* (New York, 1932); *The Role of the Banker in International Relations* (Honolulu, 1927); *The United States and the Situation in the Far East* (New York, 1932).

B. DAB supp. 6, 249–50; Warren I. Cohen, *The Chinese Connection: Roger S. Greene, Thomas W. Lamont, George E. Sokolsky and American-East Asian Relations* (New York, 1978); WWWA 3, 344.

C. The Greene papers are in the Harvard Univ. Archives.

Alan Raucher

GREENE, Roger Sherman (29 May 1881, Westborough, MA—27 March 1947, West Palm Beach, FL). *Education*: B.A., Harvard Coll., 1901, M.A., 1902. *Career*: consular service, Brazil, Japan, Siberia, China, 1902–14; officer, Rockefeller Foundation, China Medical Board; medical administrator, Peking Union Medical Coll., 1914–35; lobbyist, New York and Washington, 1938–41.

Greene was the son of Congregationalist missionaries to Meiji, Japan, born while his parents were on furlough in the United States. His early schooling was in Japan, and he spent most of his adult life abroad in the service of the Department of State and the Rockefeller Foundation. He left government work because he felt uncomfortable acting as an agent for particularistic American interests. He desired to serve mankind more broadly conceived. In particular, he was outraged by Washington's insistence that he press inflated American claims against the Chinese government after the Revolution of 1911. His performance as consul-general at Hankow during the uprising had been praised widely by Americans and Chinese alike.

As vice-president of the Rockefeller Foundation and director of the China Medical Board and of the Peking Union Medical College, Greene developed close ties to China's Westernized intellectuals, most notably Hu Shih, the famous philosopher-diplomat. Greene worked with the Chinese on a variety of modernization projects, especially in the field of public health. Throughout these years, he maintained contact with the principal Asian specialists of the Department of State. During the Kuomintang (Nationalist) Revolution of the 1920s, Greene argued against American interference. He insisted that the Chinese were entitled to the freedom Americans had enjoyed in the 1860s, to fight their civil war until one side won a decisive victory and could control the entire country. In 1927–28 he led a group of Americans in Peking, including John Leighton Stuart, who successfully opposed the plan of J.V.A. MacMurray, U.S. minister to China, for multilateral intervention against the revolutionaries. Greene's argument had added weight at the time because his protégé, Nelson T. Johnson, had become the secretary of state's principal adviser on policy toward China.

After the Rockefellers forced his retirement from Peking Union Medical College in 1935, Greene returned to the United States. In the late 1930s he emerged as a leader in organizations formed to work for the support of China and Great Britain against Japan and Germany. From 1938 to 1941 he was chairman of the American Committee for Non-Participation in Japanese Aggression, and he became associate director (1940–41) of *William Allen White's Committee to Defend America by Aiding the Allies. For both organizations he lobbied on behalf of a variety of programs to obtain U.S. aid for China. More than any other private citizen, Greene had the attention of Stanley K. Hornbeck, the Department of State's senior adviser for Far Eastern affairs from 1929 to 1944. Almost alone, Greene kept the Committee to Defend America from restricting its attention to the war in Europe. He retained his credibility with the Atlanticists of that group by accepting the primacy of the campaign to save Great Britain.

Greene spent his life defining a mission that would permit him to serve without commitment to church or flag. He found his place in the effort to alert his countrymen to the menace of Japanese and German imperialism and to the idea that the suffering of Asians and Europeans was something the United States could and should act to alleviate.

BIBLIOGRAPHY:

B. Warren I. Cohen, *The Chinese Connection: Roger S. Greene, Thomas W. Lamont, George E. Sokolsky and American–East Asian Relations* (New York, 1978); DAB supp. 4, 346–47; NYT 29 Mar 1947, 15.

C. The Greene papers are in the Houghton Library, Harvard Univ.

Warren I. Cohen

GREENE, Theodore Ainsworth (12 January 1890, Andover, MA—9 June 1951, Washington, DC). *Education*: B.A., Amherst Coll., 1913, M.A., 1916; B.D., Union Theol. Sem., 1918; M.A., Columbia Univ., 1922. *Career*: assistant pastor, Brick Presbyterian Church, New York, 1918–25; pastor, First Church of Christ (Center Congregational), New Britain, CT, 1925–51.

Although his parish and the administration of the Congregational churches in the United States were his major concerns, Greene began in the 1920s to participate in international, interdenominational movements which sought to unite Christians while permitting them to maintain their separate identities and beliefs. His initial connection with twentieth-century ecumenicism lay in the Life and Work movement. Attending its conferences at Stockholm in 1925 and at Oxford in 1937, he served as associate secretary of the American delegation at Stockholm. The Oxford Conference recommended the establishment of a permanent organization uniting the Christian churches. This goal was achieved in part in Amsterdam in 1948, when most non-Catholic denominations united to form the World Council of Churches. Greene was a member of the joint committee which helped organize American participation. He also served as an alternate delegate of his denomination and chairman of the alternate committee on reconstruction and interchurch aid. He is representative of a host of American clergymen who worked for many decades to create an international, interdenominational organization of Christian churches.

From 1939 to 1951, Greene served on the executive committee of the American branch of the World Alliance for International Friendship Through the Churches, an organization which sought to prevent war by encouraging friendly relations among nations. The American branch during the 1920s and 1930s urged support of the League of Nations. Greene's tenure came during a crucial period. As war approached in Europe in the late 1930s, the American branch, like other church-related peace groups, split. One wing, strongly pacifist, moved to an isolationist position for fear that any association with other nations would mean involvement in the European war. Greene concluded that the triumph of Nazism was worse than war. His wing supported the concept of collective security, urged the revision of American neutrality laws to aid the victims of aggression, and eventually accepted the need for U.S. intervention. After World War II, the American branch strongly supported the United Nations. Like the other churchmen who participated in the World Alliance, Greene gained and helped maintain among his fellow Americans an internationalist perspective in the interwar years.

Greene also participated in efforts to aid the poor and suffering of other countries, but World War II and the human devastation which resulted impressed him and other American Protestant Churchmen with the need to develop a permanent agency to coordinate overseas relief and reconstruction. Some central direction had been achieved during the war, and these tentative steps were confirmed in 1946 with the formation of Church World Service. Greene had served (1944–46) as chairman of World Council Service, one of the agencies Church World Service superseded. He was vice-president of the new organization until 1950. Over the next few years, Church World Service resettled thousands of displaced persons and provided cash, food, clothing, medical supplies, and living accommodations to refugees and disaster victims. Greene, among others, insisted that this relief effort be centered around the congregation. Most of the funds were gained through "One Great Hour of Sharing" held on a Sunday in March, when offerings were taken in local churches. Congregations also contributed food and clothing which Church World Service distributed abroad to the needy through local churches and missions. Each congregation was linked to the larger relief effort, and this emphasis helped to strengthen among American Protestants a sense of responsibility for the world's suffering peoples.

BIBLIOGRAPHY:

A. *What Can Christians Do for Peace?* (Boston, 1934); *Worship Services for Peace and Brotherhood* (Boston, 1940).

B. Harold E. Fey, *Cooperation in Compassion: The Story of Church World Service* (New York, 1966); NCAB 40, 35; NYT 10 Jun 1951, 92; WB 1948, 2064–65; WWWA 3, 345.

C. Greene papers are in the Amherst Coll. Library.

G. F. Goodwin

GREY, Edward (25 April 1862, London—7 September 1933, Fallodon, England). *Education*: Winchester Coll., Balliol Coll., Oxford Univ., 1884. *Career*: Liberal politician; secretary of state for foreign affairs, 1905–16; special ambassador to Washington, 1919.

The harrowing experience of bringing his country into the Great War and serving as wartime foreign secretary for two years converted Grey's prewar liberal imperialism to an enduring internationalism. While foreign secretary, Grey had established links with British liberal intellectuals and Americans who initiated discussion and planning on the project of creating a peace league to prevent future wars. Grey gave his private support to such planning and skillfully used the league idea as a bridge to further Anglo-

American good will and the friendship of *Woodrow Wilson through the period of American neutrality. After his retirement in December 1916, Grey retained his interest in the league project, and late in 1918 he lent the immense prestige of his name to the pro-league movement by agreeing to serve as president of the British League of Nations Union.

Grey's mature reflections on the war and his approach to the creation of a peace organization were set out in *The League of Nations*, a pamphlet written in May 1918 and widely distributed in Britain, the Dominions, and the United States. If modern war and the curse of militarism were not to destroy Western civilization, Grey believed, nations must apply internationally the fundamental political lesson associated with the evolution of national democracies. Anarchy attendant upon the rule of force should be replaced by a regime of law enforced by the collective power of the community. Following the mainstream of internationalist thinking in the Anglo-American pro-league movement, Grey saw the central features of a league to be the obligation to submit all disputes to peaceful discussion and resolution and the agreement to resist by means of economic, and, if needed, military sanctions, any violations of this obligation. For Grey it was vital that heads of governments, following the encouraging lead of Woodrow Wilson, sincerely accept the limitations on sovereignty as well as the definite obligations necessary to the success of any league of nations.

In late 1919, Grey led a special mission to the United States to use his influence with Wilson and other American political leaders to facilitate discreetly the process of treaty ratification. What Grey and other British leaders had dreaded now came true. The American political system deadlocked on the issue of approving the Treaty and forming the League of Nations. Grey's mission proved a failure, as he was excluded from the White House after Wilson's stroke. Privately Grey favored his own government's acceptance of the Lodge reservations if necessary to bring about American participation in the League.

Failing in eyesight and lacking in political ambition, Grey resisted all inducements by *Robert Cecil and others to lead a center party in the early 1920s, built upon dissident factions of Liberals, Conservatives, and Laborites. Preferring the life of a political recluse, Grey nevertheless gave continued support to the cause of the League. He served as president of the League of Nations Union until his death. His memoirs portrayed the League as the necessary path to collective security, disarmament, and peace.

BIBLIOGRAPHY:

A. *The Charm of Birds* (London, 1927); *Fallodon Papers* (London, 1926); *Twenty-Five Years, 1892–1916* (London, 1925).

B. Donald S. Birn, *The League of Nations Union, 1918–1945* (Oxford, 1981); DNB 1931–40, 366–75; George W. Egerton, *Great Britain and the Creation of the League of Nations* (Chapel Hill, NC, 1978); Keith Robbins, *Sir Edward Grey* (London, 1971); WWW 1929–40, 556.

George W. Egerton

GUERRERO, José Gustavo (26 June 1876, San Salvador—26 October 1958, Nice, France). *Education*: LL.D., univs. of San Salvador and Guatemala, 1898. *Career*: governor, San Salvador, 1900–1901; consul, Bordeaux, France, 1902; consul-general, Genoa, Italy, 1903–7; chargé d'affaires, Washington, 1912; president, Tenth Assembly, League of Nations, 1929; judge, Permanent Court of International Justice, 1931–46, president, 1937–46; judge, International Court of Justice, 1946–55.

Guerrero rose rapidly in the diplomatic corps of El Salvador from consul in Bordeaux, France, to minister to Italy, France, and Spain in 1912. As an outspoken supporter of the Pan American movement, he called for a policy of nonintervention by any state in the affairs of another. At the Sixth Pan American Conference in Havana in 1928, he introduced a resolution on nonintervention. In 1946 he participated in a meeting aimed at the creation of a federation of the five Central American states, which gave momentum to the eventual establishment of a Central American Common Market and other institutions fostering unity in that region.

His reputation as an internationalist was earned as a result of his unrelenting service to the League of Nations. His membership on committees dealing with the manufacture of and traffic in arms earned him renown as a strong advocate of arms control. He gained experience in the field of the peaceful settlement of disputes through arbitration and conciliation when he assumed an active role in conflicts among nations on such issues as identity documents for individuals without nationalities, antagonisms among members of the European Commission of the Danube, and the facilitation of rapid communications among League members during crisis. He wrote numerous scholarly works and judicial opinions on questions such as disarmament, the treatment of foreigners, and the codification of international law.

Guerrero was the representative of El Salvador on the Council of the League from 1926 to 1927 and was elected president of the Tenth Assembly in 1929. During his term he became known for a commitment to the ideals of the pacific settlement of global disputes, giving him prominence in international legal circles. After being elected to the Permanent Court of International Justice in 1930, Guerrero served both as vice-president (1931–36) and president (1937–46). During his term he argued in opinions for the development of international law through the use of existing customs and decisions by the Court as sources of new law.

When Germany invaded the Netherlands in 1940, Guerrero and the registrar of the Court moved to Geneva, where they worked to maintain its records and correspondence. This provided the tribunal with an indispensable transition period between the dismemberment of the League during World War II and the creation of the United Nations after the war. In 1946 he was elected as a member and president of the newly created International Court of Justice, making him the only jurist to preside over both agencies.

Once again he argued for the formation of new rules of international law based upon decisions rendered by the Court. Guerrero's more than fifty-year career as an internationalist gave him an outstanding reputation as a statesman and a judge, contributing greatly to the progressive development of international law.

BIBLIOGRAPHY:

A. *La Codification du droit international* (Paris, 1930); *La Responsabilité internationale de l'état* (Paris, 1927); *L'Ordre international* (Neuchâtel, Switzerland 1945).

B. *ICJ Yearbook 1946–47,* 42; NYT 28 Oct 1958, 35; WWLA 1935, 234–35.

Alan T. Leonhard

GULICK, Sidney Lewis (10 April 1860, Ebon, Marshall Islands—20 December 1945, Boise, ID). *Education*: Univ. of California, 1879–80; B.A., Dartmouth Coll., 1883; M.A., Union Theol. Sem., 1886; Andover Theol. Sem., 1895; Oxford Univ., 1895–96; Marburg Univ., 1905–6; Berlin Univ., 1906. *Career*: missionary, American Board to Japan, 1887–1913; professor, Doshisha Univ., Kyoto, 1907–13; lecturer, Imperial Univ., Kyoto, 1907–13; secretary, Federal Council of Churches' Commission on the Orient, 1914–21, American Branch, World Alliance for International Friendship Through the Churches, 1916–19, National Committee for Constructive Immigration Legislation, 1918–24, National Committee on American–Japanese Relations, 1916–27, Commission on International Justice and Goodwill, 1921–34.

Born to a distinguished missionary family, Gulick was raised in Hawaii and educated in the United States and Europe. His life encompassed careers as missionary, scholar-teacher, and administrator. Gulick served as a missionary twenty-six years in Japan. He first undertook traditional tasks, but his love of scholarship led him into the college classroom. He became a scholar of Japanese culture and the conflict between Eastern and Western cultures. His broad humanitarian interests also brought him into contact with the peace movement in Japan and that in turn to groups in the United States seeking to allay tensions between the two countries.

American relations with Japan had been poor since 1906, because of tensions over Japanese expansionism in Asia and the treatment of Japanese immigrants in the United States. When Gulick arrived in California on a medical leave in 1913, he became involved in the immigration issue, studied it deeply, and then sought to convince the fledgling Federal Council of Churches to take up California's "Japanese problem." Hired for a speaking tour on the issue, in 1914 he was appointed secretary to the Federal Council's Commission on Relations with Japan (later widened to the Orient). The post seemed a new "calling"; it opened a career which combined his interest in Japan with a concern for U.S.-Japanese relations and the treatment of Japanese aliens. He became the Council's "Asian specialist," but his interests were always broader. Through his secretaryship, he created a network of Protestant organizations and committees which sought to promote Christian internationalism.

Immigration law reform was a chief concern between 1914 and 1924; he wrote and lectured extensively promoting his quota system plan. His views irked exclusionists and prompted Naval Intelligence to conduct a surreptitious and fruitless investigation attempting to prove him a Japanese agent. Although erroneous, the charges blighted his subsequent career. The passage of the 1924 Immigration Act, which included Oriental exclusion, was a serious setback to Gulick, but he continued to work for that reform.

Other interests involved international issues. His role in the Federal Council of Churches thrust him into campaigns for a world organization, 1916–19, and he joined the Council's delegation to the Paris Peace Conference. He also joined in campaigns for arms limitation, the World Court, and the outlawing of war. Believing internationalism should begin in childhood, he organized a committee on world friendship among children, and he sought to educate adults through a series of brochures on current world problems.

As relations between the United States and Japan deteriorated, Gulick tried to explain Tokyo's policy to an increasingly hostile America. While not a simplistic apologist for Japanese militarism, he believed that if one saw its actions through Japanese eyes one could understand the reasons for expansionism. Retired to Honolulu in 1934, he continued his scholarship and was there when the war he sought to avoid came to Pearl Harbor. The times were such that a voice like his, preaching justice, tolerance, and understanding, could easily be lost in the din of events.

BIBLIOGRAPHY:

A. *The American-Japanese Problem: A Study of the Racial Relations of the East and the West* (New York, 1914); *The East and West: A Study of Their Psychic and Cultural Characteristics* (Rutland, VT, 1962); *Evolution of the Japanese: A Study of Their Characteristics in Relation to the Principles of Social and Psychic Development* (New York, 1905); *Mixing the Races in Hawaii* (Honolulu, 1937); *Toward Understanding Japan: Constructive Proposals for Removing the Menace of War* (New York, 1935); *The White Peril in the Far East: An Interpretation of the Significance of the Russo-Japanese War* (New York, 1905).

B. DAB supp. 3, 322–23; George F. M. Nellist, ed., *Pan-Pacific Who's Who* (Honolulu, 1941), 272–73; NYT 24 Dec 1945, 15; Sandra C. Taylor, "Japan's Missionary to the Americans: Sidney L. Gulick and America's Interwar Relationship with the Japanese," *Diplomatic History* 4 (Fall 1980), 387–408; WWA 1924, 1401.

C. The Gulick papers are in the Houghton Library, Harvard Univ.

Sandra C. Taylor

GUNN, Selskar Michael (25 May 1883, London—2 August 1944, Newtown, CT). *Education*: student, Kensington Park Coll., London, 1896–1900; B.S., Massachusetts Institute of Technology, 1905; C.P.H., Harvard Technology

School of Public Health, 1917. *Career*: bacteriologist, Boston Biochemical Laboratory, 1905-6; assistant bacteriologist, Iowa State Board of Health, 1906-8; health officer, Orange, NJ, 1908-10; instructor to associate professor, MIT, 1910-17; assistant professor, Simmons Coll., 1912-14; secretary, American Public Health Association, 1912-18; managing editor, 1912-14, *American Journal of Public Health*, editor, 1914-18; associate director, Commission for Prevention of Tuberculosis in France, 1917-20; adviser, Ministry of Health, Czechoslovakia, 1920-22; director, Paris office, International Health Board of Rockefeller Foundation, 1922-27; vice-president, Rockefeller Foundation, 1927-41; National Health Council, 1941-42; Office of Foreign Relief and Rehabilitation (later UN Relief and Rehabilitation Administration), 1943-44.

Gunn's professional training at MIT was in public health, and for a time he remained true to his specialty in his career with the Rockefeller Foundation's International Health Division. However, Gunn came eventually to realize that in traditional agricultural societies public health was intimately bound up with political, economic, and social problems that could not be treated by medical methods. Required instead was a holistic approach that would meet total community needs rather than those of health alone. Abandoning a narrow medical orientation, by the end of the 1920s Gunn had moved toward the advocacy of comprehensive social planning. Fortunately, his association with the Rockefeller Foundation during the war gave him an avenue to apply his ideas. As a vice-president, he headed its health work in Europe and after 1932 in China.

Central to his position was the contention that other disciplines, especially the social sciences, were indispensable intellectual tools for effecting rural reconstruction. Although Gunn originally suggested southeastern Europe as a demonstration area, he was given the opportunity to implement his ideas in full only in China. Partly as a result of dissatisfaction with the Foundation's investment in the Peking Union Medical College, and partly because of its newly articulated commitment to the support of applied social science, the trustees were receptive to Gunn's argument that China provided a suitable "laboratory" where experiments could be carried on under controlled conditions. Because the program's emphasis was scientific, the presumption was that success in China could be translated into a formula that possessed global applicability.

In 1935 the Foundation began to support the North China Council for Rural Reconstruction, a body which coordinated the work of Y. C. "Jimmy" Yen's Mass Education Movement with a number of Chinese universities. This organization combined social scientific expertise, a training organization, and the crucial power to nominate civil officials in the demonstration area into a comprehensive experiment of education, research, and application created to span the chasm between a medieval rural society and modern knowledge. It was an experiment in modernization based on the belief that social scientific rationality would become the agent for successful global social reform. It was also part of an ongoing Rockefeller Foundation policy of using science, more exactly the culture of science, as an agent of liberal modernization in China. After a promising start, the Sino–Japanese War disrupted the North China Council and put an end to Gunn's multidisciplinary experiment in sociocultural transformation.

BIBLIOGRAPHY:

B. DAB supp. 3, 323–25; NCAB 34, 319; James C. Thomson, Jr., *While China Faced West: American Reformers in Nationalist China, 1928–1937* (Cambridge, MA, 1969).

C. The Gunn papers are at the Rockefeller Archives Center. An Oral History is at Columbia Univ.

Frank A. Ninkovich

GUSTAVSON, Reuben G. (6 April 1892, Denver, CO—23 February 1974, Bartlesville, OK). *Education*: B.A., Univ. of Denver, 1916, M.S., 1917; Ph.D., Univ. of Chicago, 1925. *Career*: instructor to associate professor, Colorado Coll. of Agriculture, 1917–20; assistant professor to professor, 1920–42; dean and acting president, Univ. of Colorado, 1942–45; vice-president and dean of faculties, Univ. of Chicago, 1945–46; president, Univ. of Nebraska, 1946–53; administrator, Ford Foundation, 1953–59; professor, Univ. of Arizona, 1959–70.

An internationally renowned biochemist and administrator, Gustavson worked while vice-president of the University of Chicago as the liaison official between the atomic energy project and the Department of the Army. Even though he performed this role in the development of the first atomic bomb, he joined with +Albert Einstein as a trustee of the Emergency Committee of Atomic Scientists. Gustavson became committed after 1945 to the idea that the United Nations was the only hope for mankind. He took an active interest in the United Nations Educational, Scientific, and Cultural Organization, serving as a delegate to the UNESCO Mexico City meeting in 1947.

Acting on the UN Charter's declaration that wars start in the minds of men and that it is in the minds of men that peace must be built, Gustavson developed an elaborate array of grass-roots programs in Nebraska. As president of the University of Nebraska, he provided leadership in bringing model UN programs to the campus, and he encouraged the faculty to develop curriculum units on the UN for elementary and secondary students throughout the state. Gustavson was also instrumental in involving Nebraska men and women in international programs. In 1948 he served as general chairman of the Abraham Lincoln Friendship Train, which was a world outreach effort of the Christian Rural Overseas Program sponsored by the Church World Service and the Lutheran World Relief. Gustavson enlisted the support of county and home extension agents, mayors, secretaries of chambers of commerce, and ministers of all faiths in this international project. He also encouraged the sister city approach in which towns of Nebraska adopted European cities devastated by the war. Gustavson ended his career as director of the Ford Foundation's Resources for the Future. It sought through philanthropic work to assist people throughout the world who lacked material and cultural resources. Through somewhat unique processes, Gustavson thus showed for nearly thirty years a true dedication to peace and international cooperation.

BIBLIOGRAPHY:

A. "Contribution of the Physical Sciences to World Citizenship," *North Central Association Quarterly* 22 (Jan 1948), 277–84; "Is War Necessary?" *Nebraska Education Journal* 28 (Nov 1948), 298–99; "Is War the Only Answer?" *Journal of Home Economics* 40 (Sep 1948), 351–52; "Tools for Tomorrow," *American Forest* 62 (Nov 1956), 28–30.

B. John P. McSweeney, "Chancellor Reuben Gustavson, Internationalism and the Nebraska People," *Nebraska History* 57 (Fall 1976), 379–97, "The Chancellorship of Reuben G. Gustavson at the University of Nebraska, 1946–53," dissertation, Univ. of Nebraska, 1971.

John P. McSweeney

GUTT, Camille Adolphe (24 November 1884, Brussels—7 June 1971, Brussels). *Education*: graduate in economics, Free Univ. of Brussels, 1904, LL.D., 1906; licentiate in political and social sciences, Institut Solvay, 1906. *Career*: barrister and journalist, 1906–14; secretary-general, Belgian War Material Purchasing Commission, London, 1916–18; secretary-general, Reparation Commission delegation, 1919–20, assistant delegate, 1924; *chef de cabinet* to minister of finances, 1920–24; deputy to minister of the treasury, 1926; member, Young Reparations Committee, 1929; plenipotentiary, Hoover Moratorium negotiations, 1931; minister of finance, 1934–35, 1939–45, of economic affairs, 1940–45, of national defense, communications, and shipping, 1940–42; member, Bretton Woods Conference, 1944; executive director, International Monetary Fund, 1946, governor, 1946, managing director and chairman of the board, 1946–51.

Gutt devoted the interwar years to his country's financial problems and his post-World War II career to those of the world. His interwar experiences in coping with reparations controversies, Belgium's residue of worthless German paper marks, postwar inflation, and financial crises contributed much to his policies after World War II, including his resistance to another heavy German reparations bill and his commitment to a world monetary system.

In London during World War II, Gutt participated in planning new international monetary arrangements and, with his Dutch counterpart and *Joseph Bech of Luxemburg, created the Benelux Union, cornerstone of later European integration. Upon liberation in 1944, he imposed a drastic monetary reform which eliminated inflation and the proceeds of wartime profiteering, generated rapid Belgian recovery, and served as a model for later reforms in Germany and France. Meanwhile Gutt had played a prominent role in the 1944 Bretton Woods Conference to create the International Monetary Fund and the World Bank. In 1946 he was elected first managing director of the Fund. He set its procedures and often shaped its policies, organizing and reorganizing it into its permanent cast. Economic cooperation was not easy because most Fund directors were nationalists. Gutt struggled to keep the Fund alive, to give it a greater role and more publicity, and to provide the managing director and his international staff some latitude.

Gutt fought for currency stabilization and orderly but flexible procedures for drawing rights and against inflation and gold speculation. In 1948, France defied the Fund to establish multiple discriminatory exchange rates, but Gutt kept others from following suit. His efforts against gold hoarding and toward greater Fund involvement in European agencies under the Marshall Plan failed, but otherwise he broadened the Fund's role and in 1949 facilitated a smooth simultaneous devaluation of sixteen European, Commonwealth, and Middle Eastern currencies. Given the turbulent times, the novelty of the experiment, and the hesitations of his Board, Gutt could not consolidate his accomplishment but laid the basis for his successor to do so. In 1951 he declined extension of his term and returned to private banking, having contributed much to world financial stability and to the creation of a major international agency for that purpose.

BIBLIOGRAPHY:

A. *La Belgique au carrefour* (Paris, 1971); *Pourquoi le franc belge est tombé* (Brussels, 1935); *The Practical Problem of Exchange Rates* (Washington, 1948).

B. CB 1948, 263–66; Léon H. Dupriez, *Monetary Reconstruction in Belgium* (New York, 1947); J. Keith Horsefield, *The International Monetary Fund, 1945–1965*, 3 vols. (Washington, 1969); Paul Hymans, *Mémoires*, 2 vols. (Brussels, 1958); IWW 1970–71, 635; *Le Monde* 9 Jun 1971, 6; LT 9 Jun 1971, 16, 22 Jun 1971, 14; NYT 28 Jun 1971, 30; H. van der Wee and K. Tavernier, *La Banque Nationale de Belgique et l'histoire monetaire entre les deux guerres* (Brussels, 1975); WB 1948, 2106–7; WWBL 1962, 480; *WWWorld* 1971–72, 387.

Sally Marks

H

HACKWORTH, Green Haywood (23 January 1883, Prestonburg, KY—24 June 1973, Washington). *Education*: B.A., Valparaiso Univ., 1905; LL.B., Georgetown Univ. Law School, 1912; graduate studies, George Washington Univ., 1914–15. *Career*: attorney, Department of State, 1916–18, assistant solicitor, 1918–25, solicitor, 1925–31, legal adviser, 1931–46; member, Permanent Court of Arbitration, 1937–46; chairman, UN Commission of Jurists, 1945; adviser, San Francisco Conference, 1945; judge, International Court of Justice, 1946–61, president, 1955–58.

Hackworth spent his legal career in the field of public law and served under five secretaries in his extended tenure at the Department of State. He was legal adviser longer than anyone else to hold that office. His special assignments included service as counsel in all matters coming before the International Joint Commission, Boundary Waters Treaty (Britain–U.S.) of 1909, a member of Special Treaty Missions to Lausanne and Madrid, 1923, and as delegate to the First League of Nations Conference for the Codification of International Law in 1930, to the International Conference of American States, Lima, 1938, and to the Scientific Conference of American States, Washington, 1940. He also participated in the Havana Conference of 1940, the Moscow Conference of 1943, the Dumbarton Oaks meeting in 1944, the Inter-American Conference on Problems of War and Peace in 1945, and the San Francisco Conference. He was senior advisor to the U.S. delegation to the First Session of the UN General Assembly and Security Council in 1946.

Aside from his lengthy service on the International Court of Justice, including his three-year presidency, during which the Court dealt with seventeen controversies and issued eleven advisory opinions, Hackworth's major contribution to international law was his editorship of the eight-volume *Digest of International Law*, an updating and reformulation of the earlier collection by *John Bassett Moore. The Hackworth volumes dealt with all the major legal issues affecting international law and U.S. practice from 1906 to World War II. They included such major categories as the laws of war, belligerency, neutrality, treaties, and pertinent U.S. legislation relating to transnational practice, and they constitute a major source of international law covering the first four decades of the twentieth century.

Hackworth had a special reputation in the Department of State for the clarity and cogency of his memoranda, and he sat in on many of the policy formulation sessions of high-ranking Department officials in the Roosevelt and Truman administrations, particularly on matters relating to U.S. neutrality in the 1930s and U.S. belligerency in the 1940s. He played an influential role in the American contribution to the creation of the UN Charter, and he also aided in the preparation of the Statute of the International Court of Justice.

In the 1930s Hackworth wrote several articles dealing with the legal functions of the Department of State, general principles governing international claims (including the duties and rights of aliens), and various aspects of the 1934 Trade Agreements Act. In 1946 he published an essay on the International Court of Justice and the codification of international law, in which he encouraged the former and supported the latter while warning against overambitious codification undertakings. His dissents on the ICJ argued that the UN Charter was actually a constitution, that the UN has a legal personality and thus can make claims on behalf of its agents, and that the Court in matters of dispute cannot rely upon municipal codes to explain uncertainties in international law.

During his service on the Court, his opinions were viewed as models of legal expression, and he had a knack for consolidating the positions of others into his own majority opinions. Hackworth, on occasion, complained about the comparatively light case load of the Court and worried about its relatively minor role in the settlement of international disputes. He retired in 1961, after an American nominating team had failed to recommend him for another term, largely because of his advanced age.

BIBLIOGRAPHY:

A. *Digest of International Law*, 8 vols. (Washington, 1940–44).

B. AJIL 68 (1974), 91–94; IWW 1973–74, 668; NYT 26 Jun 1973, 48; WWA 1942–43, 972.

C. The Hackworth papers are in the Manuscript Division, Library of Congress.

Robert A. Friedlander

HAEKKERUP, Per Christen (25 December 1915, Ringsted, Denmark—13 March 1979, Stubberup, Denmark). *Education*: graduate, Østre Borgerdyd High School, Copenhagen, 1934; economic studies, Univ. of Copenhagen. *Career*: president, Danish Social Democratic Youth, 1946–52; secretary-general, International Union for Socialist Youth, 1946–54; president, World Association of World Federalists, 1954–56; editor, *Social-Demokraten* (later *Aktuelt*), 1956–62; member of Folketing, 1950–79, Foreign Policy Committee, 1955–62, 1966–71; member, Consultative Assembly of the Council of Europe, 1953–62, 1966–71; minister for foreign affairs, 1962–66; minister for economic and budget affairs, 1971–73; minister for economic affairs, 1975–78; minister for commerce, 1976–77; minister without portfolio, 1978–79.

Born into a politically active family, Haekkerup received his political training in the Social Democratic Youth movement (DSU), of which he became president in 1946. That year he was elected president of the International Union for Socialist Youth and thus assumed responsibility for the reorganization of the international Social Democratic youth movement after the World War II in fierce competition with its Communist rival. These activities gave him crucial experiences in the form of a firm political craftsmanship as well as a practical international outlook.

After entering the Folketing, the Danish parliament, in 1950, Haekkerup continued to concentrate on international issues, becoming president of the World Association of World Federalists in 1954. He also broadened his political base as editor of the party's main paper and, from 1957, as its parliamentary leader.

In 1962 Haekkerup somewhat unexpectedly became minister for foreign affairs, a position in which he thrived. His broad international contacts, his outgoing personality, and a congenial world environment led to unprecedented action. Haekkerup was a firm believer in the official foreign policy line as he found it. Firmly anti-Communist and pro-American, he strongly supported Denmark's membership in NATO and also became a leading exponent of Danish membership in the European Economic Community (EEC). In addition, he staked out new directions. A keen understanding of the manifold problems of the emerging Third World as well as of its potential international clout led him to advocate a progressive, though pragmatic, Third World policy. He firmly opposed apartheid but did not believe in ostracizing the South African regime internationally. At the same time, he conducted an active bilateral diplomacy in Europe as a vocal spokesman for European detente.

For various reasons, one of which may have been his ambivalent relationship with the party leader, Prime Minister *Jens Otto Krag, Haekkerup in 1966 returned to his post as the party's parliamentary leader in order to maintain a fragile coalition with the left-wing Socialist People's party. After the Social Democrats fell from power in 1968, his political career seemed to flag. He failed in his bid to become secretary-general of the Council of Europe, but in 1971 he returned to government to become responsible for domestic economic policy, a position he held with minor interruptions almost until his death. As such he was a pivotal figure in a succession of parliamentary deals and compromises. Haekkerup was very active in the campaign for Denmark's entry into the EEC, but ceased to play any role in the foreign policy field in his later years.

As an internationalist, Haekkerup was a pragmatist rather than a visionary. He believed in a strong United Nations based on law and took firm positions regarding its role. He had a firm and unshaken belief in the necessity of international cooperation, detente, and disarmament, but he never lost sight of what he considered the real power relationships in the world or of the Danish national interest as he saw it.

BIBLIOGRAPHY:

A. *Danmarks udenrigspolitik* [The foreign policy of Denmark] (Copenhagen, 1965).

B. *Aktuelt* 14 Mar 1979, 17; *Dansk Biografisk Leksikon* 6, 650–52; *Information* 14 Mar 1979, 5; LT 20 Feb 1963, 9; NYT 14 Mar 1979, IV-17.

Nikolaj Petersen

HALL-PATCH, Edmund (1896, St. Petersburg—1 June 1975, London). *Education*: Paris. *Career*: Royal Artillery, 1914–18; Reparations Commission; financial adviser to Siamese government; assistant-secretary of the treasury, 1935–44; deputy under secretary of state, 1946–48; chairman, Executive Committee, Organization for European Economic Co-operation (OEEC), 1948), later permanent U.K. representative on OEEC; executive director, International Monetary Fund and International Bank for Reconstruction and Development, 1952–54.

Any account of the life of Hall-Patch risks being regarded as romantic fiction. He was born in St. Petersburg; later his father, an English solicitor, moved to Paris. Bilingually educated, Hall-Patch wished to become a professional musician, despite the opposition of his father. Accordingly, he supported himself by playing in orchestras, writing reviews, and even writing a book (*Deux maîtresses*) under the pen name Henri de Beaurivoire. His realization that his musical talent was insufficient for a professional career coincided with the outbreak of World War I, in which he served in the Royal Artillery.

When peace came he joined the financial section of the Reparations Commission. He rapidly became regarded as a financial expert, so much so that he secured appointment as financial adviser to the Siamese government. Learning Siamese without revealing the fact to his associates, he found Siamese corruption too much to accept and resigned and went to New York. There he sustained an apparently affluent lifestyle by playing the saxophone in a nightclub. Returning to London, he acted as a riding instructor until his luck turned.

He found a number of short-term appointments as financial adviser through the League of Nations before becoming assistant secretary to the treasury in 1935. Almost at once he went to China and divided his energies between that country and Japan until the advent of war there necessitated his return to England. In 1944 he transferred to the Foreign Office, skillfully building the economic side of its work. The end of the war did not immediately bring the realization of how greatly the economic foundations of Europe had been affected. This eventually brought about the Marshall Plan, and British Foreign Secretary Ernest Bevin appointed Hall-Patch to head the British mission to the OEEC, of whose Executive Committee he was also chairman. Despite Cominform-inspired opposition, the economy of Europe was transformed; and when in 1952 the Marshall Plan was terminated, OEEC continued. Hall-Patch then became executive director to the International Monetary Fund and the International Bank for Reconstruction and Development. Resigning from the Foreign Office in 1954, he joined the board of the Standard Bank, of which he was director from 1957 to 1962.

Remarkable as was his career, Hall-Patch cultivated a romantic aura of mystery about his life, neither confirming nor denying the numerous stories which circulated concerning him. He had many friends and though unmarried was extremely fond of children. As a character, he was certainly unique.

BIBLIOGRAPHY:

B. LT 4 Jun 1975, 16; WW 1971, 1328.

Colin Gordon

HAMBRO, Carl Joachim (5 January 1885, Bergen, Norway—15 December 1964, Oslo). *Education*: Ph.B., Univ. of Christiana, 1903, M.A., 1908. *Career*: teacher and school principal, 1905-13; journalist, *Morgenbladet*, 1903-13, editor-in-chief, 1913-21, literary editor, chairman of the board, 1921-40; member of the Storting, 1918-50; chairman, Foreign Affairs Committee, 1924-46, president, 1926-46; chairman, Norwegian Conservative party, 1926-36, 1945-50; delegate, League of Nations, 1926-46, president, Assembly, 1939-46, chair of various committees; delegate to UN, 1945-57, Paris Peace Conference, 1946; president, International Labor Conference, 1947; member, Nobel Prize Committee; president, Norwegian-American Foundation.

Hambro pursued a number of careers. In each of them his achievements were sufficient for an ordinary lifetime. After a start as a schoolteacher, he turned to journalism and soon became editor of the *Morgenbladet*, the chief daily in Norway. In 1921, after he became a member of the Norwegian parliament, the Storting, he resigned as editor but remained with the paper as literary editor and chairman of the board until 1950. In his spare time, he translated the works of such figures as Victor Hugo, Ernest Hemingway, and Sinclair Lewis into Norwegian and wrote a number of works on foreign politics, geography, and immigration history. He held political office continually from 1918 to 1950. When he became Norway's delegate to the League of Nations in 1926, he embarked on a career as a world statesman. Hambro was one of the more prominent figures in Geneva until the war and was active in the early years of the United Nations. Zealous and outspoken, he believed that the "art of living consists in taking sides."

Hambro had originally opposed Norway's entry into the League of Nations, but once he arrived in Geneva he became both an ardent supporter of the organization and one of its most persistent and plainspoken critics. He was the champion of the small powers against the great powers, of the Assembly against the Council, and of the idea that the League must be transformed into a political body rather than a diplomatic congress. He has been described as the self-appointed conscience of the League, always calling the major powers to their responsibilities.

Though his ardor never seems to have dimmed, Hambro's reformism yielded little tangible result. His only success came in 1932, when his agitation in the Assembly resulted in a restructuring of the Secretariat which required that one under secretary be a national of a nonpermanent member state. Until then all five of the top posts in the Secretariat had gone to citizens of the great powers. Hambro was unsuccessful in various efforts to persuade member states to send political figures, rather than professional diplomats, to the League as delegates. He was a fervent partisan of disarmament and in 1927 had charged that, unless some progress were made, renegade nations would destroy human values. He became a strong advocate of U.S. membership in the League, an outspoken opponent of Fascism, and a vocal critic of the Munich agreement. In 1935 he became a convert to Moral Rearmament.

In 1940 Hambro organized the escape of King Haakon to Great Britain and later that year went to the United States, where he stayed until 1945. He remained close to the League of Nations, helping to set up its wartime headquarters in Princeton, New Jersey, and he became increasingly concerned with maintaining maximum continuity between the League and the future world organization. Hambro was a delegate to the San Francisco Conference and then chairman of the League of Nation's Liquidation Committee. In April 1946 he presided over the Assembly at that body's final session in Geneva. Hambro resumed his political career in Norway in 1945. He retired from most of his public offices in 1950 but continued his service as a delegate to the UN until 1957.

BIBLIOGRAPHY:

A. *Crossroads of Conflict* (New York, 1943); *How to Win the Peace* (New York, 1942); *I Saw It Happen in Norway* (New York, 1940).

B. CB 1940, 361–62; LT 16 Dec 1964, 13; NYT 16 Dec 1964, 43; Frank P. Walters, *A History of the League of Nations* (London, 1952); WWWA 4, 398.

Douglas W. Houston

HAMBRO, Edvard Isak (22 August 1911, Oslo—1 February 1977, Paris). *Education*: LL.B., Univ. of Oslo, 1934; doctorate in political science, Univ. of Geneva, 1936. *Career*: Secretariat of League of Nations, 1933–38; director, Section on International Relations, Christian Mikkelsen Institute, Bergen, Norway, 1938–40; liaison officer with British forces in Norway, 1940; visiting lecturer, Northwestern Univ., 1940–41; information worker for Norwegian government in United States, 1941–43; first secretary, Norwegian Foreign Office in London, 1945–46; delegate, San Francisco Conference, 1945; chief, Legal Division, UN Secretariat, London, 1945–46; registrar, International Court of Justice, 1946–53; stipendiat 1953–59 to professor, 1959–66, Norwegian School of Economics and Business Administration, Bergen; visiting professor, Cambridge Univ., 1953–54 and at Univ. of California, Berkeley, 1958; Conservative member of the Storting,

1961–66; ambassador to UN, 1966–71, president, General Assembly, 1970; ambassador to UN and other international bodies in Geneva, 1973–76, to France, 1976–77.

His career and family relationships indicate that Hambro was both thoroughly Norwegian and thoroughly international in activities and outlook. He married the daughter of French and English artists, and his father, *Carl Joachim Hambro, was a notable figure in Norwegian politics and international diplomacy, being president of the Norwegian Storting and of the General Assembly of the League of Nations. His brothers and sisters all became involved in international activities.

Hambro was not only gifted intellectually but was a man of strong convictions and forceful personality. He believed in "optimism tempered with a sense of realism" and realized that without optimism it would be impossible to work in the field of international relations. Law and fairness were the guides to his thinking and conduct, and it was natural that he, as a lawyer and a Norwegian and a judicious person with multilingual abilities, should be selected as a member of various appeals boards, the Council of Europe, the Organization for European Economic Co-operation (OEEC), the Permanent Court of Arbitration, the Permanent Conciliation Commission between Germany and the Netherlands, the Franco-German Arbitral Board for the Saar, and conciliation committees between Finland and the United States, Norway and Spain, and Portugal and Switzerland and as chairman of the UN commission sent to Hong Kong (1954) to report on Chinese refugees. That he could not only conciliate and adjudicate but also act was proved when in 1940, during the Nazi occupation of Norway, he was largely responsible for spiriting the Norwegian gold supply out of Norway to Great Britain; he then became a liaison officer with the British forces in Norway. He was a prolific writer and editor and was in much demand as a speaker.

BIBLIOGRAPHY:

A. *The Case Law of the International Court of Justice*, 7 vols. (Leiden, Netherlands, 1952–74); with Leland Goodrich, *The Charter of the United Nations: A Commentary and Documents* (Boston, 1946), 3rd ed. with Patricia Ann Simons (Boston, 1969); *Folkerettspleie* (Oslo, 1956); *Jurisdiktionsvalg og lovvalg* (Oslo, 1957); *L'Exécution des sentences internationales* (Paris, 1936); *Norge og Folkeforbundet* (Oslo, 1938); *The Problem of Chinese Refugees in Hong Kong* (Leiden, Netherlands, 1955); *The Relations Between International Law and Conflict Law* (Leiden, Netherlands, 1963).

B. *Dictionary of International Biography* (Cambridge, 1976), 391; *Dictionary of Scandinavian Biography* (London, 1972), 153–54; *Hvem er Hvem?* (Oslo, 1964), 224–25; NYT 3 Feb 1977, 36.

Franklin D. Scott

HAMILTON, Alice. See *Biographical Dictionary of Modern Peace Leaders*.

HAMMARSKJÖLD, Dag Hjalmar Agne Carl (29 July 1905, Jonkoping, Sweden—17 September 1961, Ndola, Northern Rhodesia [now Zambia]). *Education*: graduate, Univs. of Uppsala and Stockholm. *Career*: Swedish Civil Service; under secretary, Swedish Ministry of Finance, and chairman of governors, Bank of Sweden, 1936–47; under secretary in charge of economic affairs, Swedish Foreign Office, and Swedish representative to Organization for European Economic Co-operation, 1947–49; secretary-general, Foreign Office, 1949–53; secretary-general, UN, 1953–61.

Hammarskjöld became secretary-general of the UN in its eighth year, when the fortunes and prospects of the world organization were at a low ebb. His predecessor, *Trygve Lie, had resigned because of profound disagreements with the Soviet Union over the United Nations' role in the Korean War and to a lesser extent with the United States over the depredations of McCarthyism in the international Secretariat.

Hammarskjöld immediately set about restoring both the position of the secretary-general and the morale and standing of the international civil service. He was thought, when appointed, to be a nonpolitical, even rather colorless, civil servant, but he soon proved to have formidable powers of intellectual analysis and practical diplomacy as well as a strong sense of vocation. Hammarskjöld was guided in his conduct of the exceedingly complex office of secretary-general by the principles of the Charter and an invincible personal integrity. He was also an experienced administrator and did much to streamline the Secretariat and give new life and meaning to the concept of international civil service.

In responding to a series of international challenges, Hammarskjöld steadily developed the political and diplomatic potential of the office of secretary-general as well as new techniques such as peacekeeping, good offices, and the United Nations "presence" in critical situations. His first major diplomatic success was the release of seventeen U.S. airmen in China. His part in resolving the Suez Crisis of 1956 by intensive diplomacy culminating in the setting-up of the first UN peacekeeping force, UNEF I, also gave impetus to the secretary-generalship as an instrument for crisis management. Later he showed similar effectiveness and ingenuity in dealing with the Lebanese Crisis of 1958. His efforts in Indochina were less successful, and in the Congo he took on, with courage and imagination, a task of unique complexity and political difficulty which gave rise to a major constitutional crisis over the authority of the secretary-general and the role of the UN as an active operational instrument of conflict control. Hammarskjöld was killed in an air crash on a mission to the Congo at the height of this crisis.

In working for the practical development of some kind of supranational authority and executive in times of crisis, and by his extremely active personal role in critical situations, Hammarskjöld eventually aroused considerable opposition, particularly from the Soviet Union and from President *Charles de Gaulle's France. His determined internationalism and independence were evidently regarded as going too fast and too far. But he gave the UN a greatly increased standing in international affairs as a potentially operational organization, and he opened up new possibilities as well as new methods for multilateral diplomacy. He is remembered with great respect for this, as well as for his intellectual gifts, his moral courage, and his great personal integrity.

Hammarskjöld's greatest contribution in the long run may well prove to have been his tireless struggle to give reality to the principles of the Charter in action. In doing this, he pioneered new courses of action for the secretary-general and a new role and status for the international civil service. He was convinced that the successful development of these two institutions lay at the heart of any successful future international order, and he courageously stood for and defended their independence and integrity. It was this attitude and its practical consequences that led to Nikita Khrushchev's demand for Hammarskjöld's resignation. Hammarskjöld's rejection of this challenge received the resounding support of the vast majority of the members of the General Assembly.

If the United Nations becomes progressively a stronger and more effective organization, Hammarskjöld's leadership, ideas, and practical experiments will certainly be a major factor in such a positive development.

BIBLIOGRAPHY:

A. *Markings* (New York, 1964); *Public Papers of the Secretaries-General of the United Nations*, ed. Andrew Cordier and Wilder Foote, vols. 2–5 (New York, 1972–75).

B. L. S. Trachtenberg, "A Bibliographic Essay on Dag Hammarskjöld," in *Dag Hammarskjöld Revisited: The UN Secretary-General as a Force in World Politics*, ed. Robert S. Jordan (Durham, NC, 1982); Brian Urquhart, *Hammarskjöld* (New York, (1972).

C. The Hammarskjöld papers are in the Manuscript Department, Royal Library, Stockholm.

Brian Urquhart

HAMMOND, John Hays (31 March 1855, San Francisco—8 June 1936, Gloucester, MA). *Education*: Ph.B., Sheffield Scientific School of Yale, 1876; graduate, Royal School of Mines, Freiburg, Saxony, 1879. *Career*: mining engineer; mining executive; professor, Yale Univ., 1902–9; active in political and public affairs; chairman, U.S. Coal Commission, 1922–23.

Hammond enjoyed a highly successful career as an international engineering consultant to a number of the world's largest mining syndicates. He worked for a time with Cecil Rhodes in the South African Transvaal. In 1895 he was implicated in what became the Jameson Raid, an attempt by British irregulars encouraged by Rhodes to overthrow the Boer government of Paul Kruger. Hammond was imprisoned under sentence of death for a time and released upon payment of a fine. A mining consultant to the Guggenheim interests in Mexico and Canada, he helped survey through a British firm the natural resource potential of the Ural Mountains for the imperial Russian government.

After 1907 he turned from business to public affairs and took an active part in the election campaign of his friend *William Howard Taft. Although Hammond declined Taft's offer of an ambassadorship to China, he became interested in international affairs, particularly an international court of justice. In 1910 Hammond was one of the founders of the American Society for the Judicial Settlement of International Disputes and served as its president in 1911. He also helped found (1912) and support the International Peace Forum, which published *Peace Forum* to build sentiment for the court idea. Then, in 1915, he became a leader in creating the World's Court League to advance the concept of an international league built upon a judicial system and the codification of law.

Hammond believed that, if the Hague tribunal could evolve into a true judicial court whose decisions would have the authority of international law, the power of world public opinion would provide the backing for its decisions. The legalists were too easily persuaded that the U.S. Supreme Court provided a model that could be applied on an international scale. Their internationalism was somewhat overshadowed by ethnocentrism. When the League to Enforce Peace was organized in 1915, Hammond was a leading participant, despite his reservations about the wisdom of force to back up international decisions. He was also a warm supporter of the military preparedness movement, particularly following the *Lusitania* incident, believing that other countries would be more likely to listen to the United States if it were perceived as militarily powerful.

Following World War I, Hammond favored adherence to the League of Nations provided the reservations enumerated by *Henry Cabot Lodge were accepted. He remained strongly critical of *Woodrow Wilson's inflexible position with regard to the League. Throughout the interwar period Hammond continued to favor U.S. membership in the World Court.

BIBLIOGRAPHY:

A. *The Autobiography of John Hays Hammond*, 2 vols. (New York, 1935).
B. DAB supp. 2, 275–77; NCAB 10, 45–46; NYT 9 Jun 1936, 23.
C. The Hammond papers are at Yale Univ.

                                                    Michael A. Lutzker

HANKEY, Maurice Pascal Alers (1 April 1877, Biarritz, France—25 January 1963, Redhill, England). *Education*: Rugby. *Career*: Royal Marine Artillery, 1895–1901; Naval Intelligence Dept., 1902–6; secretary, Committee of Imperial Defence, 1912–38, War Cabinet, Imperial War Cabinet, 1917–18, Cabinet, 1919–38; minister, War Cabinet, 1939–40.

Hankey's career illustrates well the convergent and digressive themes of imperialism and internationalism in British politics and diplomacy after the

Great War. As the influential secretary of the Committee of Imperial Defence, the War Cabinet, and the Imperial War Cabinet, Hankey's principal concern was the security of the British Empire. A dedicated imperialist, Hankey was initially hostile to early wartime plans for a peace league, arguing that such schemes held out particular dangers for Britain, whose peace-loving population could easily fall prey to the illusions cultivated by social reform enthusiasts and disarmament and antiwar advocates.

As the wartime league of nations movement grew, and with *Woodrow Wilson adding America's support, Hankey came to see the valuable purposes of a new international organization. In early 1918 he submitted his own plan for a peace league to the Phillimore Committee, which had been charged by the British government with studying such schemes. Hankey recommended founding the league on the basis of the existing wartime inter-Allied organs, ranging from the Supreme Council at Versailles down to the smaller economic and technical commissions. After the Allied organizations had been consolidated in wartime, they could be used to conduct eventual peace negotiations with the defeated enemy. In the postwar period, with a stranglehold on the world's economic resources, such a league could compel former neutrals and enemies to join, while promoting peaceful cooperation in social, economic, technical, and humanitarian areas. The principal function of Hankey's league was to promote what he would later call "diplomacy by conference." To this end the great powers would each maintain a permanent representative at Versailles for purposes of constant political and diplomatic exchange. The habits and reserves of cooperation thereby established could be deployed in dealing with international disputes as they arose. Hankey's scheme differed radically from the mainstream of thinking on the league idea in eschewing any reference to obligatory guarantees or sanctions.

After the war, Hankey's enthusiasm for the league project grew as he envisaged for himself a new career as the League's first secretary-general. He went so far as to draft a detailed organizational scheme for the Secretariat which projected to the international plane the same role of discrete and covert influence he enjoyed within British and Allied circles. However, as the drafting of the League Covenant proceeded along the "collective security" line favored by Wilson and *Robert Cecil, Hankey was alienated from the project, and, on the advice of friends, he chose continued service in London over a new career in Geneva. His experience at the Paris Peace Conference left Hankey convinced that the British Empire was worth more than a thousand leagues of nations. For the remainder of his career, Hankey's imperialism and devotion to the security of Britain and the Empire would alienate him from the League as his initial predictions of 1916 seemed to come true with a vengeance during the mid-1930s' quest for collective security.

BIBLIOGRAPHY:

A. *Diplomacy by Conference* (London, 1946); *Government Control in War* (London, 1945); *The Supreme Command, 1914-18* (London, 1961); *The Supreme Control at the Paris Peace Conference, 1919* (London, 1963).

B. George W. Egerton, *Great Britain and the Creation of the League of Nations* (Chapel Hill, NC, 1978); Stephen Roskill, *Hankey: Man of Secrets*, 3 vols. (London, 1970–74).

C. Hankey papers are in Churchill Coll., Cambridge Univ. and in the Public Record Office in London.

George W. Egerton

HANOTAUX, Albert Auguste Gabriel (19 November 1853, Beaurevoir, Aisne, France—11 April 1944, Paris). *Education*: diploma, Ecole des Chartres, 1879. *Career*: foreign ministry official, 1879–86, 1889–94; member, Chamber of Deputies, 1886–89; foreign minister, 1894–95, 1896–98; member, French Academy, 1897; historian, journalist, occasional diplomat; first president, Comité France-Amérique, 1909; member, French Commission for the League of Nations, 1916–19; delegate, League of Nations Assembly, 1920–23, vice-president, 1922–23; member, League Council, 1922–23, president; member, Permanent Court of Arbitration, 1924–30.

For want of a suitable alternative, Hanotaux became foreign minister at forty, remaining nearly four years. He pursued a policy of equilibrium among European powers and aggressive colonial expansion facilitated by the new Franco–Russian alliance. Widely but perhaps wrongly regarded as Germanophile and Anglophobe, Hanotaux enlisted Germany against Britain overseas but not in Europe. He sought Anglo–French entente without French sacrifice, and he resolved all differences save that over Egypt. Ardently nationalistic and opportunistic, Hanotaux expounded France's "civilizing mission" but preferred protectorates to annexation. He consolidated France's fragmented holdings overseas and in the process precipitated the Fashoda crisis of 1898. In the Dreyfus case, which clouded his tenure, Hanotaux opposed trial and equally opposed reopening the case for fear of damage to France's diplomatic and military position.

After 1898, Hanotaux focused on his writing, with volumes on Richelieu, the history of France, and contemporary topics. Then, during World War I, Hanotaux undertook diplomatic good-will missions. In 1916 he openly endorsed a League of Nations and the dismemberment of the Bismarckian Reich. He became active in French groups planning a League of Nations, showing a special concern with mandates. Hanotaux later represented France in the Assembly, where he defended European dominance, and in the Council, where he was involved in plans to stabilize the Austrian economy and where he resisted efforts to punish Italy's 1923 seizure of Corfu. In 1939–40 he endorsed a European economic federation and efforts to use the Pope's moral ascendancy to counter Nazi Germany. Although a strong nationalist, Hanotaux used internationalism to promote France's ends; thus, his service at Geneva came when France briefly defended the League to counter any British effort to supplant it with a new organization where French influence would be reduced.

BIBLIOGRAPHY:

A. *Fachoda* (Paris, 1919); *Histoire du cardinal de Richelieu*, 4 vols. (Paris, 1893–1937), completed by Duc de la Force; *Histoire politique de 1804 à 1926* (Paris, 1929); *La Paix latine* (Paris, 1903); *Le Traité de Versailles* (Paris, 1919); *Mon temps*, 4 vols. (Paris, 1933).

B. Elmer Bendiner, *A Time for Angels* (New York, 1965); *Encyclopaedia Britannica* (Chicago, 1968), 11, 68–69, Alf A. Heggoy, *The African Policies of Gabriel Hanotaux, 1894–1898* (Athens, GA, 1972); Thomas M. Iiams, Jr., *Dreyfus, Diplomatists and the Dual Alliance: Gabriel Hanotaux at the Quai d'Orsay (1894–1898)* (Geneva, 1962); IWW 1937, 438; NYT 12 Apr 1944, 21; Bernadotte E. Schmitt, ed., *Some Historians of Modern Europe* (Chicago, 1942); Frank P. Walters, *A History of the League of Nations* (London, 1952).

C. The Hanotaux papers are at the Archives du Ministere des Affaires étrangère.

Sally Marks

HARRIS, Henry Wilson (21 September 1883, Plymouth, England—11 January 1955, Hove, England). *Education*: Plymouth Coll.; St. John's Coll.; M.A., Cambridge Univ. *Career*: *Daily News*, 1908–23; editor, *Headway* 1919–32; editor, *Spectator*, 1932–53.

Harris, a British journalist, was one of the first private individuals to campaign for the concept of a league of nations. Thus, although not a diplomat, Harris must nonetheless be considered as one of the leading British internationalists of the first half of the twentieth century. The son of a Quaker, Harris joined the staff of the *Daily News*, where he served successfully as news editor, leader writer, and diplomatic correspondent. He became an early admirer of *Woodrow Wilson and gained some repute as the author of a book on Wilson in 1917.

As representative of the *Daily News*, Harris attended international gatherings, including the Paris Peace Conference, which he described in *The Peace in the Making* (1919). From the beginning a staunch advocate of the League of Nations, Harris soon resolved to devote himself wholeheartedly to the cause of peace and international friendship. From 1923 to 1932 he worked on the staff of the League of Nations Union, a British group dedicated to promoting public understanding and support of the new world organization; he edited the organization's journal, *Headway*, and spoke at meetings throughout Great Britain. His earnest propagandizing and his 1925 book describing the League of Nations performed a great service in clarifying public understanding of its goals.

After 1932, Harris, although no longer involved in the struggle for the League, continued to express his own strong and highly individual opinions about politics in his new role as editor of the *Spectator*. In 1945 he was elected to Parliament as a representative of Cambridge University, but his parliamentary career came to an end with the abolition of university seats in 1950. Harris was a man of deep integrity devoted to the common good, a rapid worker, and a voracious reader. His only flaw appears to have been a certain degree of stubbornness and narrowness of outlook, qualities which enabled him to persist in supporting the League of Nations despite its problems.

BIBLIOGRAPHY:

A. *Life So Far* (London, 1954); *The Peace in the Making* (London, 1919); *President Wilson: His Problems and His Policy* (New York, 1917); *Problems of Peace* (Cambridge, 1944); *What the League of Nations Is* (London, 1925).

B. Donald S. Birn, *The League of Nations Union, 1918–1945* (Oxford, 1981); DNB 1951–60, 457–58; LT 13 Jan 1955, 11; NYT 13 Jan 1955, 27.

Paul D. Mageli

HAUSHOFER, Karl Ernst Nikolaus (27 August 1869, Munich—13 March 1946, Bavaria). *Education*: attended military college; doctorate in geography, Univ. of Munich. *Career*: professional soldier; adviser and instructor, Japanese Army, 1908–10; in Far East, 1910–12; served in World War I, rising in rank to general; faculty, Univ. of Munich, 1919–33; director Geopolitical Institute, 1933–45.

Perhaps the most notable exponent of the theory of geopolitics, Haushofer's career and ideas have been questioned because of his close collaboration with Nazi Germany, combined with charges that he helped corrupt geography by using it for political purposes. Haushofer, however, developed his ideas independently during World War I and in the early 1920s. He fully accepted the geopolitical concept of heartland and elaborated on the idea of living space (*lebensraum*). He saw this as vital to any nation's survival as an organic entity which had to grow or die. An enterprising leader, he founded (1924) and edited a journal, *Zeitschrift für Geopolitik*, a Pan-German Academy (1925), and a Geopolitical Institute (1933). Supported by Nazi subventions, Haushofer gathered a noted staff of scholars from many disciplines, and they compiled data on every country and region of the world.

Haushofer developed his heartland theories by elaboration upon five regions of the globe. The most important of these was a Eurasian Union composed of Japan, Russia, and Germany. That vision may have stimulated Hitler's efforts to achieve alliances with Japan and Russia. Haushofer knew Hitler and is credited with introducing Hitler to many theories embodied in *Mein Kampf* and German expansionism. Haushofer argued, however, that such alignments could be viewed as stabilizing influences or tools of peace. He fell from Hitler's favor before the end of World War II. A son was killed by the Gestapo when betrayed by his father, and in 1946 Haushofer and his wife committed suicide.

BIBLIOGRAPHY:

A. *Geopolitik des Pazifschen Ozeans*, rev. ed. (Berlin, 1938); *Weltmeere und Weltmächt* (Berlin, 1937); *Weltpolitik von Heute* (Berlin, 1934).

B. CB 1942, 340–42; NYT 14 Mar 1946, 3; Hans W. Weigert, "The Future in Retrospect: Haushofer and the Pacific," *Foreign Affairs* 20 (Jul 1942), 732–42.

Warren F. Kuehl

HEINDEL, Richard Heathcote (24 August 1912, Hanover, PA—31 July 1979, Harrisburg, PA). *Education*: B.A., Harvard Coll., 1933; M.A. Univ. of Pennsylvania, 1934, Ph.D., 1938. *Career*: instructor to assistant professor, Univ. of Pennsylvania, 1938–46; fellow, Library of Congress, 1940–41; director, American Library, American Embassy, London, 1942–45; chief, Division of Libraries and Institutes, Department of State, 1946–47; professional staff associate, U.S. Senate Foreign Relations Committee, 1947–49; deputy staff director, U.S. National Commission for UNESCO, 1950–54; vice-chancellor, professor, and dean, College of Arts and Sciences, Univ. of Buffalo, 1954–58; president, Wagner Coll., 1958–61; president, Pratt Inst., 1961–67; dean of faculty and professor of international relations, Penn State–Capitol Campus, 1967–78; international affairs editor, *Intellect*, 1974–78.

Heindel was a pioneer in the field of American cultural impact abroad. His *The American Impact on Great Britain* (1940) broke new ground and was followed by other works on America's cultural impact. His subsequent career as a diplomat and educator was devoted to building appropriate international forums for the global appreciation of America's cultural heritage.

Throughout his life Heindel sought to carry out the view expressed in the preface of his book, that it is of vital importance for the United States to understand itself as a major factor in world civilization. During World War II, Heindel was the director of the American Library in London, which served as the principal source of information about the United States for British officials and the press. While in London, he participated in the Conference of Allied Ministers of Education, which laid the groundwork for UNESCO. After the war he helped shape U.S. policy toward UNESCO as deputy director of the U.S. National Commission for UNESCO. In 1946 Heindel, as chief of the Division of Libraries and Institutes at the Department of State, was instrumental in establishing libraries and cultural programs in over seventy U.S. embassies. From 1947 to 1949, as one of two staff associates for the Senate Foreign Relations Committee, he participated in drafting the U.S. Information and Educational Exchange Act (the Fulbright Program).

After leaving government in 1954, Heindel became active in teaching and academic administrative work, yet he found time to write over one hundred articles and reviews, many on America's cultural influence. Toward the end of his career he contributed a monthly column as international affairs editor of *Intellect* and in Harrisburg, PA, promoted community study of world issues and problems.

BIBLIOGRAPHY:

A. *The American Impact on Great Britain* (Philadelphia, 1940); ed., *American Influences Abroad* (New York, 1950); with others, *A Decade of the American Foreign Policy, 1941–49* (Washington, 1950); *The Integration of Federal and Non-Federal Research* (Washington, 1942); *The Present Position of Foreign Area Studies in the United States* (New York, 1950); *War Check List*, 2 vols. (Philadelphia, 1941–42).

B. *American Men and Women of Science* (New York, 1971), 984; NYT 2 Aug 1979, B-9; *Washington Post* 3 Aug 1979, B-6; Victor Weybright, *The Making of a Publisher* (New York, 1966); WWA 1978–79, 1447.

C. Heindel left an extensive collection of papers, a small part of which is at Pennsylvania State University–Capitol Campus.

Ruth V. Noble

HENDERSON, Arthur (13 September 1863, Glasgow—20 October 1935, London). *Education*: St. Mary's school, Newcastle. *Career*: secretary, Labor party, 1911–34; entered Parliament in 1903; War Cabinet, 1916–17; home secretary, 1924; foreign secretary, 1929–31; president, World Disarmament Conference, 1932–35; Nobel Peace Prize, 1934.

Arthur Henderson's two major accomplishments during his lengthy career were that he helped establish the Labor party as a significant force in British politics and that he played a decisive role in converting his party to an acceptance of collective security as a viable policy in maintaining international order. Initially engaged in trade union activity, he placed his considerable talents for administration and organization at the disposal of the fledgling Labor party. He served as its secretary (1911–34) and held a number of other important party posts. He had a distinguished parliamentary career, which included serving briefly in *Lloyd George's War Cabinet, then as home secretary in the first Labor government, and finally as foreign secretary. He was a popular figure in the Labor party, noted for his loyalty, accessibility, and common sense, and members affectionately referred to him as "Uncle Arthur." While nominally a Socialist, he was committed to the tradition of British parliamentary democracy and drew his inspiration more from Wesleyan Methodism and Gladstonian Radicalism than from Marx or Lenin.

Although he supported Britain's effort in World War I, he immediately worked for an honorable peace and reconciliation once the conflict ended. During the 1920s he gained considerable experience in international affairs, traveling extensively, participating in the affairs of the Labor and Socialist International parties, and his regular visits to Geneva helped him master the complex machinery of the League of Nations and brought him in contact with world leaders.

Henderson was increasingly recognized as an expert in international relations within his party, but not until the second Labor government (1929-31) did he become foreign secretary. He made a decided impact upon the Foreign Office, even though his modest education did not provide him with the usual social graces and knowledge of foreign languages. His courageous decisions, mastery over broad outlines of policy, frankness, and willingness to negotiate and compromise played an important role in his success. He soon became one of the most trusted statesmen of Europe and formed a workable friendship with other leaders. He wrestled unsuccessfully, however, with the major diplomatic question of the day: how to reconcile the German demand for equality with the French demand for security. In his deliberations he avoided the anti-French posture and glib condemnations of the Versailles Treaty that were so popular in large circles within the Labor party and Britain and instead showed considerable sympathy for France's special concerns. Although he failed to bring France and Germany together, he was instrumental in making German reparations less burdensome and helped secure an early evacuation of Allied occupation troops from German soil.

Henderson regularly attended League sessions as foreign secretary, served as president of the Council in 1931, and believed that the League provided the way to peace. While concerned with the problem of security, he believed at the same time it was necessary to achieve some measure of disarmament, and he played an important role in laying the groundwork for a world conference on the matter. Although no longer foreign secretary after 1931, his international stature, his reputation for impartiality, and his obvious commitment to the project made him a logical choice to preside over the World Disarmament Conference, and he was unanimously nominated to be its president. For his patient efforts he was awarded the Nobel Peace Prize in 1934.

Along with *Ramsay MacDonald, Henderson helped to give an international outlook to the Labor party, which had been concerned primarily with domestic economic issues. But unlike MacDonald, who had always distrusted the coercive powers given to the League of Nations, Henderson was more optimistic about the nature and future of the new organization. He envisaged the League becoming a sort of superstate, armed with coercive powers of a financial and even military character, the very threat of which would probably deter aggression but could in the final analysis be used to punish an aggressor. MacDonald had not held such views in the early 1920s. However, Henderson's persistent efforts, the defection of MacDonald from the Labor party, and the increasing threat of Fascist aggression during the 1930s, made collective security a more attractive policy. By the time of Henderson's death, the Labor party and much of British public opinion had become converted to a strong League policy. Because of his low-key personality, it is easy to gloss over his contributions to the theory and practice of international relations, but more than one knowledgeable person has suggested that perhaps Henderson has been the most underrated British foreign secretary of the twentieth century.

BIBLIOGRAPHY:

A. *Consolidating World Peace* (Oxford, 1931); *Labour's Foreign Policy* (London, 1933); *Labour's Peace Policy* (London, 1934); *The League of Nations and Labour* (London, 1918); *The Way to Peace* (London, 1935).

B. DLB 1, 161-65; DNB 1931-40, 417-20; Mary Agnes Hamilton, *Arthur Henderson* (London, 1938); LT 21 Oct 1935, 16; NYT 21 Oct 1935, 1; Frank P. Walters, *A History of the League of Nations* (London, 1952).

C. The Henderson papers are in the Public Record Office in London and the Labor party headquarters, London.

David C. Lukowitz

HERRIOT, Edouard (5 July 1872, Troyes, France—26 March 1957, Lyons). *Education*: Lycée Louis-le-Grand; Ecole Normale Supérieure, Paris, 1894; doctorate, Sorbonne, 1905. *Career*: mayor of Lyons, 1905-40, 1945-57; senator, Rhône Department, 1912-19; deputy, Rhône Department, 1919-40, 1945-57; premier, 1924-25, 1926, 1932; president, National Assembly, 1947-53, honorary president, 1953-57; minister, numerous cabinets; leader, Radical Socialist party; statesman and author.

Prepared to teach French literature, Herriot early in his career resigned from the Lycée Ampère in Lyons for politics and was elected mayor of France's second city in 1905. He emerged on the national scene as a senator in 1912 and thereafter combined administrative and legislative careers. He served as an outspoken member of the Radical Socialist party, an organization representing the middle class which stood for a democratic and secular republic, and in 1919 he was elected as its president. Five years later he led a coalition of parties of the left to power and became premier.

Herriot's convictions on French foreign policy were well established by then. He believed in the sanctity of international agreements and therefore advocated enforcement of the Treaty of Versailles. He considered the League of Nations the sole guarantee of world peace. A convinced democrat, Herriot consistently sought a close relationship with Great Britain and the United States as a necessary complement to his domestic political goals. He remained suspicious of Germany, but he optimistically believed that democratic forces within the Weimar Republic could create a new Germany which would be a beneficial force in the society of nations. He was always a proponent of Franco-Russian diplomatic rapprochement, seeing the Soviet Union as a counterbalance to a belligerent Germany.

Premier of France in 1924-25, Herriot acted as his own foreign minister and successfully changed the nationalistic and conservative diplomacy of his predecessor, Raymond Poincaré. The latter had demanded scheduled reparation payments from Germany and had led France in 1923 to occupy the Ruhr, an unwise action which Great Britain strongly opposed. Herriot immediately set out to restore Anglo–French harmony by visiting Prime Minister *Ramsay MacDonald and by initiating the withdrawal of occupation forces from the Ruhr. The new premier also recognized the Soviet Union.

Even more important than the conciliatory foreign policy he inaugurated as French head of state, Herriot's greatest achievement in the international field was his work with the League of Nations. Like so many other advocates of the League, he believed that the imperfections of the Versailles Treaty and other international agreements must be corrected in due course by the world organization. For the League to be just, it also must be strong enough to enforce justice. As foreign minister and head of the French delegation, he addressed the League on 6 September 1924 and proposed the Geneva Protocol. This measure sought to give the world organization the power necessary to guarantee peace by requiring compulsory arbitration of international disputes and by branding as an aggressor any nation which would refuse arbitration. An impressive orator, he gave a bravura performance, speaking without notes or microphone. He coined the phrase "arbitration, security, disarmament," fully aware that these words would remain meaningless abstractions unless they were founded on living realities created by the common will of the member states. The opposition of the Conservative Cabinet in Great Britain to this proposal meant its defeat at the League, but many of Herriot's ideas on arbitration were enshrined in the Locarno treaties signed the following year by seven European nations.

Herriot's stand at Geneva in 1924 represented his most salient contribution to the cause of peace, but he remained active for three more decades in other areas of international life. He of course favored the Locarno agreements, approved of the Kellogg-Briand Pact which renounced war as an instrument of foreign policy, and applauded *Aristede Briand's appeal for a United States of Europe. Indeed, Herriot had been an early supporter of this idea and was an active member of the French Committee for European Cooperation. An intellectual and a prolific author as well as a man of action, Herriott in 1930 published *Europe*, a book which advocated a union within the framework of the League and argued that modern economic evolution required such a multinational federation. His broad perspective also led to involvement on the League's Committee on Intellectual Cooperation, which he chaired.

As premier again in 1932, Herriot insisted during the Depression that France repay her war debts to the United States. He saw this as a moral issue and also as a necessary policy for continued Franco–American friendship. This stand made Herriot the best-known and most popular French statesman in the United States during the 1930s. Undaunted by World War II, Herriot continued after 1945 to promote the Council of Europe. Fearful of a remilitarized Germany, he favored disarmament and opposed the European Defense Community. In recognition of his lifelong commitment to international cooperation, Herriot was made temporary president of the Council of Europe in Strasbourg and addressed its first session on 10 August 1949.

BIBLIOGRAPHY:

A. *Episodes 1940-1944* (Paris, 1950); *Europe* (Paris, 1930), trans. as *The United States of Europe* (London, 1930); *Jadis*, 2 vols. (Paris, 1948, 1952); *La France dans le monde* (Paris, 1933); *Message aux pays libres* (New York, 1942); *Orient* (Paris, 1934); *Le Problème des dettes* (Paris, 1933); *Sanctuaires* (Paris, 1938); *Sous l'olivier* (Paris, 1930).

B. Henri Besseige, *Herriot parmi nous* (Paris, 1960); CB 1946, 252–55; Sabine Jessner, *Edouard Herriot: Patriarch of the Republic* (New York, 1974); Pierre Olivier Lapie, *Herriot* (Paris, 1967); NYT 28 Mar 1957, 31; Michel Soulié, *La Vie politique d'Edouard Herriot* (Paris, 1962).

C. Herriot's papers are in the Municipal Archive in Lyons and in the Archives du Ministere des Affairs étrangère.

Sabine Jessner

HERSHEY, Amos Shartle (11 July 1867, Hershey, PA—12 June 1933, Madison, IN). *Education*: B.A., Harvard Coll., 1892; Ph.D., Heidelberg Univ., 1894; studied law in Paris, 1895. *Career*: faculty, Indiana Univ., assistant professor to professor, 1895–1933, head, Political Science Department, 1914; visiting professor, Harvard Univ., 1920; adviser, American Peace Commission, Paris, 1919.

Hershey was a prominent American scholar in international law during the early twentieth century. His textbook, *The Essentials of International Public Law* (1912), established his reputation as a scholar with sure command of his field, and he won a place in the history of international law by his interpretation of the legal aspects of international developments of his time. When the Russo–Japanese War broke out in February 1904, he immediately began a series of articles, published as a book in 1906, which explained the legal problems of that conflict. The following year, the Second Hague Peace Conference revised the laws of war, adding a new convention requiring a formal declaration prior to the beginning of hostilities and several new ones concerning maritime war. As an important analysis of the legal problems of the recent war, Hershey's book was used during Conference deliberations. Hershey attended as a special reporter for the *New York Evening Post*, and his letters from The Hague constitute a valuable source for the history of the proceedings. Much interested in the unsuccessful efforts to establish a world court, Hershey gave more attention to another abortive court project, the plan for a Permanent International Prize Court, which some proponents saw as a step toward a more universal body.

During World War I, Hershey served on the National Board of Historical Service. With the assistance of fifty collaborators, he and Frank Maloy Anderson of Dartmouth College prepared the *Handbook for the*

Diplomatic History of Europe, Asia, and Africa, 1870–1914, which the American experts used at the Paris Peace Conference. Hershey served there as an adviser in international law, watching with misgivings the struggle to establish a new world order. For a time thereafter, he gave more attention to the legal ideas associated with the Hague Conference than to the League of Nations, translating ⁺Otfried Nippold's *The Development of International Law After the World War*, in which the famed German-born Swiss scholar advocated a world order based on law. As Hershey observed the League of Nations and followed the proceedings of the Locarno Conference, his pessimism about the League disappeared, and he convinced himself that the kind of world order he desired was in fact materializing. Revising his textbook, he republished it as *The Essentials of International Public Law and Organization*, giving almost as much emphasis to the League of Nations as to international law.

While Hershey does not rank as one of the innovators in international law and organization, his scholarship still merits serious attention. Few of his contemporaries were his superiors in the ability to write clear, succinct analyses, and it is doubtful whether any other scholar in international law of the era had a more direct influence upon the actual formulation of new conventions for the laws of war.

BIBLIOGRAPHY:

A. *The Essentials of International Public Law and Organization*, rev. ed. (New York, 1927); ed., with Frank M. Anderson, *Handbook for the Diplomatic History of Europe, Asia, and Africa, 1870–1914* (Washington, 1918); *The International Law and Diplomacy of the Russo-Japanese War* (New York, 1906).

B. Calvin D. Davis, *The United States and the Second Hague Peace Conference: American Diplomacy and International Organization, 1899–1914* (Durham, NC, 1976); *Indiana University Alumni Quarterly* 20 (Jul 1933), 313–16; NYT 13 Jun 1933, 19.

Calvin D. Davis

HIDEYO Noguchi (9 November 1876, Inawashiro, Fukushima Prefecture, Japan—21 May 1928, Accra, Gold Coast). *Education*: M.S., Univ. of Pennsylvania, 1907, M.D., 1911, D.S., 1914. *Career*: lecturer, Takayama Dental School, 1877–79; lecturer, Tokyo Dental School, 1900; research assistant, Carnegie Institute and Staatens Serum Institut (Denmark), 1903–4; fellow, Rockefeller Institute for Medical Research, 1904–28.

Born in extreme poverty in a remote mountain village in northern Japan, handicapped by a childhood accident that left the fingers of his left hand fused together, and with little formal education, Noguchi nonetheless became a world famous bacteriologist. After an operation restored the use of his fingers at age sixteen, Noguchi decided to devote his life helping others as a physician. With the support of a local doctor, he studied intently and passed the Japanese medical examinations in 1897, despite the fact that he had attended neither high school nor college.

Noguchi, drawn toward the study of bacteriology, joined the Infectious Disease Institute in 1898. A year later he was dispatched to China to help combat an outbreak of plague, and in 1900 he went to the United States to study. Arriving without funds and no firm offer of employment, he found a research position at the University of Pennsylvania. In 1904 he joined the staff of the new Rockefeller Institute for Medical Research. Noguchi is credited with making significant contributions to the cure and prevention of syphilis, yellow fever, oroya fever, trachoma, rabies, polio, and Rocky Mountain spotted fever.

Noguchi traveled extensively, lecturing and conducting research. He had a remarkable facility for languages, including English, German, French, Danish, and Spanish. Since he was especially interested in tropical diseases, Noguchi made several trips to Central and South America. In Ecuador he identified the cause of yellow fever and developed a remedy; subsequently, Noguchi was made honorary senior surgeon in the Ecuadorean Army. He received many other honorable titles and degrees from institutions throughout the world. A tireless researcher, Noguchi went to Africa in 1927 to study different strains of yellow fever. There he twice contracted the disease and succumbed to it in 1928.

A self-made man with unconquerable spirit, Noguchi was perhaps Japan's first internationalist, at home in several continents. He worked ceaselessly to improve the lot of his fellow human beings regardless of where they lived, how they looked, or what they thought.

BIBLIOGRAPHY:

A. Noguchi published 186 scientific papers.

B. Noguchi Memorial Association, *Hideyo Noguchi* (Tokyo, 1975).

John Stevens

HILL, David Jayne (10 June 1850, Plainfield, NJ—2 March 1932, Washington). *Education*: graduate, Univ. at Lewisburg, 1874. *Career*: professor, Univ. at Lewisburg, 1874–79, president (renamed Bucknell Univ.), 1879–88; president, Univ. of Rochester, 1888–96; first assistant secretary of state, 1898–1903; minister to Switzerland, 1903–5, to the Netherlands, 1905–8; ambassador to Germany, 1908–11; publicist, 1911–32.

Both as writer and diplomat, Hill was a leading advocate of the world court idea supported by many internationalists early in the twentieth century. International organization, he believed, should rest upon a court of justice, to which nations would be obliged to submit most disputes not settled by diplomacy. As assistant secretary of state, he drafted a plan for such a court in his instructions to the American commission to the Hague Conference of 1899, and he worked to persuade an indifferent administration to send a distinguished delegation to bring about its establishment. Although the Permanent Court of Arbitration that emerged from the conference was not really a court but merely a panel of jurists from which disputants might voluntarily select arbiters, the world for the first time had some form of judicial organization. Hill's plan was again included in the instructions to the American commission to the Second Hague Conference of 1907. As a member of the commission, Hill witnessed the drafting of a treaty for a real court, and then saw the conference stumble to failure over the method of electing judges. German hostility to any permanent judicial machinery had been a major obstacle at both Conferences. While ambassador to Berlin, Hill strove unsuccessfully to overcome German objections to such arrangements. While at that post he also wrote his strongest arguments for a world juristic organization, which were published in English, French, and German.

Ironically, when a world court was finally established in 1920, Hill opposed American participation. He objected to it as a creature of the League of Nations, which he condemned as an instrument of power rather than of law. But his profuse strictures against both organizations revealed more than intense dedication to a strictly legalistic ideal. They were tainted by partisanship and, more fundamentally, contained a paradox not uncommon to other internationalists of his time. Hill genuinely wanted a world court, but there must also be no restraints on the will of the United States. A prolific writer, Hill published some 120 books and articles on international affairs and more than 50 on diverse subjects, including history, literature, and American political issues.

BIBLIOGRAPHY:

A. *American World Policies* (New York, 1920); *A History of Diplomacy in the International Development of Europe*, 3 vols. (New York, 1905-14); *Present Problems in Foreign Policy* (New York, 1919); *The Problem of a World Court* (New York, 1927); *The Rebuilding of Europe* (New York, 1917); *World Organization as Affected by the Nature of the Modern State* (New York, 1911).

B. DAB, supp. 1, 401-2; NYT 3 Mar 1932, 19; Aubrey Parkman, *David Jayne Hill and the Problem of World Peace* (Lewisburg, PA, 1975).

C. The Hill papers are in the Univ. of Rochester Archives.

Aubrey L. Parkman

HITCHCOCK, Gilbert Monell (18 September 1859, Omaha, NE—3 February 1934, Washington). *Education*: graduate, Univ. of Michigan Law School, 1881. *Career*: lawyer, Omaha, NE, 1881-85; newspaperman, editor, *Omaha Daily World*, 1885-89; publisher, *Omaha World-Herald*, 1880-1934; Democratic congressman, 1903-5, 1907-11; senator, 1911-23.

During Hitchcock's early career there was little indication he would espouse the cause of an international organization. As congressman he supported liberal progressive programs, and in the Senate he became sufficiently influential to help shape the legislation of the Wilson administration. *Woodrow Wilson, however, considered him too independent to be a reliable supporter. The Nebraska senator did resent the pressure the president exerted on the Senate through the secret Democratic caucus. He frequently attempted to amend administration bills, but his version rarely prevailed. Still, Hitchcock voted for all significant reform bills during the Wilson administration, and he considered himself "a loyal supporter" of the president.

A strong advocate of strict neutrality in the European war, Hitchcock wanted to give expression to that principle through an arms embargo. He favored peace through negotiation. When Wilson asked the belligerents to state their terms in December 1916, Hitchcock secured senatorial backing for that initiative. Shortly after, he supported the president's call for a League of Nations to maintain peace following the war. His relations with the president had improved during the war.

As acting Democratic minority leader in the Senate, Hitchcock made strenuous efforts to obtain senatorial confirmation of the Treaty of Versailles. He cooperated closely with Wilson, who looked to him to lead the administration forces to secure an acceptable version of the Covenant of the League of Nations. Hitchcock was well aware of the difficulty of achieving the required two-thirds vote. He thus counseled concessions and compromises. Even during the negotiation of the Covenant, he had recommended textual revisions, and Wilson had adopted some changes. With the Treaty before the Senate, he urged Wilson to permit the attachment of sufficiently strong reservations to make confirmation possible. Before Wilson left on his Western speaking trip, which Hitchcock opposed, he entrusted to Hitchcock in confidence four interpretative reservations which the senator could use as a basis for compromise. Hitchcock regretted that the president's concessions did not go far enough, but he generally adhered to the Wilsonian model. He realized the president had the power to pigeonhole the Treaty if the Senate approved an unacceptable version.

The Wilsonian tactics led twice to defeat. Under Hitchcock's leadership, Democratic senators loyal to the president voted against the measure with the Lodge reservations. Hitchcock was convinced that a different course would not have led to ratification. It merely would have worsened adverse political consequences. Later, Hitchcock wondered whether a greater degree of independence on his part would have changed the outcome. He also became convinced that excessive independence on the part of members of Congress tends to impair constructive presidential leadership and endangers the smooth functioning of American democracy. Until his death, Hitchcock's *Omaha World-Herald* remained staunchly internationalist in its outlook.

BIBLIOGRAPHY:

A. Speeches appear in the *Congressional Record*.

B. BDAC 1971, 1124; DAB supp. 1, 410; NCAB 25, 100; NYT 3 Feb 1934, 13; *Omaha World-Herald*, 3 Feb 1934, 1, 4 Feb 1934, 1A; Robert F. Patterson, "Gilbert M. Hitchcock: A Study of Two Careers," dissertation, Univ. of Colorado, 1940; John J. Waldron, "Senator Gilbert M. Hitchcock and the Wilson Administration,

1913–1918, M.A. thesis, Univ. of Nebraska, 1967); Kurt Wimer, "Senator Hitchcock and the League of Nations," *Nebraska History* 44 (Sep 1963), 189–204.

C. The Hitchcock papers are in the Manuscript Division, Library of Congress, and at the Nebraska Historical Society.

Kurt Wimer

HOBHOUSE, Leonard Trelawney (8 September 1864, St. Ive, Cornwall, England—21 June 1929, Alençon, France). *Education*: B.A., Corpus Christi Coll., Oxford Univ., 1887; M.A., Merton Coll., 1890. *Career*: assistant tutor at Corpus Christi Coll., Oxford Univ., 1890, fellow, 1894; writer, *Manchester Guardian*, 1897–1902; political editor, *Tribune* 1904–5; Martin White professor, Univ. of London, 1907–29.

Hobhouse was an important member of the group of British left-wing Liberal and Socialist intellectuals who became critics of the nation-state prior to World War I and who, during the war, were among the originators of the concept of a permanent league of nations, which they anticipated would evolve into a world-state. Hobhouse's contribution to the movement for internationalism in Britain was threefold: his political writings incorporated the idea of a world-state into Liberal political theory; his editorials in the *Manchester Guardian* over a period of nearly twenty years disseminated his internationalist principles to a wider audience; and his studies in sociology developed the theme of a single humanity seeking political expression for its need for unity.

It was not until the Boer War that Hobhouse awakened to the need for a reassertion of the principles of internationalism. In his editorials in the *Manchester Guardian* during the conflict, Hobhouse articulated that paper's view that Britain was violating the principles of international right through its intervention in South Africa. His criticism of government policy was rooted in the notion that there was a fundamental moral law regulating relations between nations which statesmen were obligated to obey. Hobhouse held up William Gladstone's internationalism as a model for statesmen to emulate because it seemed to reconcile the obligations of patriotism with the "sovereign duty to a common humanity."

Even before the outbreak of World War I, Hobhouse considered the doctrine of absolute sovereignty archaic and was urging the transformation of the existing system of independent nation-states into an "international state." He believed that the growing economic interdependence of the world would ultimately be reflected in political institutions. The British Commonwealth seemed an appropriate model upon which an international state might be based; it was a network of self-governing units with an Imperial Council responsible for resolving disputes between members.

When World War I stimulated interest in the creation of an international organization which would resolve differences between nations before they exploded into another world conflict, Hobhouse joined other British internationalists in developing the idea of a league of nations. The inability of prewar systems of arbitration of international disputes to prevent the war led Hobhouse to conclude that there was no guarantee of a permanent peace after the conflict "except in the formation of an international state." Hobhouse envisioned a permanent league of nations emerging out of the wartime alliance of the Entente powers with the neutral states and, eventually, Germany to be included. Its written constitution would prescribe definite functions, including the adjudication of disputes between nations and the power of arms limitation. Hobhouse was deeply disappointed after 1919 with the League of Nations and referred to it as an "imperfect embryo" of the international federation he believed necessary if civilization was to survive.

Hobhouse's approach to sociology also transcended national boundaries, and partly for this reason contemporary sociologists referred to him as an internationalist. Influenced by the Comtean notion of a single humanity seeking to achieve control over the direction of its development, Hobhouse's sociological theories were rooted in the premise that humanity was a unity in the process of becoming a single world community. In his major postwar study in sociology, *Social Development*, Hobhouse concluded that social development must proceed along international lines if progress is to occur.

BIBLIOGRAPHY:

A. *Democracy and Reaction* (London, 1904); *Development and Purpose* (London, 1927); *The Elements of Social Justice* (London, 1922); *The Labour Movement* (London, 1893); *Liberalism* (London, 1911); *The Metaphysical Theory of State* (London, 1918); *Mind in Evolution* (London, 1901, 1915); *Morals in Evolution* (London, 1906); *Social Development* (London, 1924); *Social Evolution and Political Theory* (New York, 1911); *The World in Conflict* (London, 1916).

B. John Hobson and Morris Ginsberg, *L. T. Hobhouse: His Life and Work* (London, 1931); John E. Nordskog, "Leonard T. Hobhouse: Internationalist," *Sociology and Social Research* 14 (Mar-Apr 1930), 373-82; Harold Smith, "World War I and British Left-Wing Intellectuals: The Case of Leonard T. Hobhouse," *Albion* 5 (Winter 1973), 261-73.

Harold L. Smith

HOBSON, John Atkinson (6 July 1858, Derby, Derbyshire, England—1 April 1940, London). *Education*: graduate, Lincoln Coll., Oxford Univ. *Career*: editorial work, *Derbyshire Advertiser*, 1880–87; extension lecturer for Oxford and London Univs., 1887–97; author and journalist, especially for the *Manchester Guardian* and *The Nation*, 1897–1940.

Hobson's seminal work, *Imperialism: A Study*, published in 1902, is the primary basis for his reputation as an internationalist. He linked imperialism and capitalism, using statistics on the growing investment in colonies and the increase in the number and size of those territories. In doing so he set off a debate over imperialism which influenced everything written on the subject since, so no later study of imperialism has been complete without referring to Hobson's contributions. In Britain he was associated with the "New Radicals" and after 1914 with the pacifist Union of Democratic Control, which he helped found and in which he was active throughout his life. His study of imperialism was the basis for Lenin's *Imperialism: The Last Stage of Capitalism*; on the other extreme he was acknowledged by *J. M. Keynes as an important pioneer in economic thought.

Hobson remained on the outside in the British political and academic world. Before his opposition to World War I, he had been one of the radicals who protested the British role in the South African War, the background of which he knew firsthand from his experience there before the war as a correspondent for the *Manchester Guardian*. In 1900 he wrote *The South African War: Its Causes and Effects*, to explain his views. His challenge to other orthodox economic beliefs regarding thrift, underconsumption, and oversaving also kept him beyond the fringes of respectability among British economists so that after 1897 he never again held an academic position.

During and after World War I, Hobson gave considerable thought to the form which a world organization might take. His book, *Towards International Government* (1915), established his credentials as an authority. As early as 1902, in *Imperialism*, he had outlined the basis for a system very like the League's mandates, and he elaborated on that idea, 1915–18. Hobson believed that a union would be effective only if it had the authority of a truly international government including collective force, without being dominated by the big powers, without a requirement for unanimity, and without neglecting economics. Hobson was above all an original thinker who stimulated others to enlarge the scope of man's understanding. He was a humanist in the best sense of the word.

BIBLIOGRAPHY:

A. *Confessions of an Economic Heretic* (London, 1938); *Imperialism: A Study* (London, 1902); *The Industrial System: An Inquiry Into Earned and Unearned Income* (London, 1909); with A. F. Mummery, *The Physiology of Industry*, (London, 1889); *Towards International Government* (London, 1915); *The War in South Africa: Its Causes and Effects* (London, 1900); *Wealth and Life: A Study in Values* (London, 1929).

B. *Annual Register*, 412–13; Cynthia Behrman, introduction to Hobson rpt. ed. *The War in South Africa: Its Causes and Effects* (New York, 1972), 11–15; H. N. Brailsford, *The Life-Work of J. A. Hobson* (London, 1948); DNB 1931–40, 435–36; LT 2 Apr 1940, 10; NYT 2 Apr 1940, 25; Sylvia Strauss, introduction to Hobson, *Towards International Government*, rpt. ed. (New York, 1971), 5–13; Henry R. Winkler, *The League of Nations Movement in Great Britain, 1914–1919* (New Brunswick, NJ, 1952).

C. The Hobson papers are in the Hull Univ. Library and Bodleian Library, Oxford Univ.

Lyle A. McGeoch

HOBSON, Richmond Pearson (13 August 1870, Greensboro, AL—17 March 1937, New York). *Education*: Southern Univ.; graduate, U.S. Naval Academy, 1889. *Career*: naval officer, 1889–1903; congressman, 1907–15; prohibitionist publicist, 1911–23; founder and president, International Narcotics Education Association, 1923–37; founder and president, World Narcotic Defense Association, 1927–37.

Born of traditional Southern plantation aristocracy, Hobson graduated first in his class at Annapolis despite being ostracized by the entire student body because of his overzealous reporting of disciplinary infractions. During the Spanish-American War, young Hobson futilely attempted to trap a Spanish squadron in Santiago Harbor by scuttling the *Merrimac* across the entrance. The heroic episode made Hobson famous and allowed him to begin a career of politics and reform.

Retiring from the Navy in 1903 because of medical disability, Hobson was elected to Congress in 1906 and remained there until defeated in 1914. In Congress he was the most vigorous exponent of increased naval armaments and enjoyed a close, secret rapport with *Theodore Roosevelt, despite being a Southern Democrat. He also became the best-known advocate of the "yellow peril" thesis. He feared that Japan would one day dominate the world. Later he became a leading spokesman for the prohibitionists and was the closest thing to a leader that diffuse movement had. He introduced, futilely, the first prohibition amendment. Hobson was also the Navy's voice on Capitol Hill, fighting tirelessly for naval increases and pioneering such concepts as aviation, research and development, a general staff system, and the national security council.

For all of his ardent militarism, Hobson was deeply concerned with international law and government. He worked closely with his cousin, *Hayne Davis, in organizing the North Carolina Peace Society, which publicized The Hague Conferences as a step toward world organization and the advancement of the peaceful resolution of disputes. Hobson also became a supporter of the Inter-Parliamentary Union and in 1908 founded the Practical Peace League, which balanced arbitration agreements with limited armaments. An indefatigable and respected publicist, he reached much of the nation with his scheme of world government which was a kind of Pax Americana enforced by a strong U.S. Navy.

After leaving Congress in 1915, Hobson made his living as a Chautauqua lecturer and prohibitionist speaker. Growing increasingly concerned with narcotics, he began a new crusade. He founded the International Narcotics Defense Association in 1923, remaining its president until his death. Primarily an antinarcotic propaganda organization, the INDA devoted its efforts to massive educational efforts and to the passage of state enforcement laws. Realizing by 1923 that narcotics was an international problem, Hobson formed and was the president of the World Narcotics Defense Association, which publicized the need to control the international narcotics trade through the League of Nations. Hobson and his followers succeeded after many setbacks in 1935, when both opium production and refining were placed under League control. Honored for what the Pope called his "noble crusade," Hobson did not long outlive the new treaty. He was a "dramatic guerrilla fighter for causes."

BIBLIOGRAPHY:

A. *Alcohol and the Human Race* (New York, 1919); *The Sinking of the Merrimac* (New York, 1899).

B. BDAC (Washington, 1971), 1126; DAB sup. 2, 308–9; NCAB 9, 10–11; Walter E. Pittman, Jr., *Navalist and Progressive: The Life of Richmond P. Hobson* (Manhattan, KS, 1981).

C. The Hobson papers are in the Manuscript Division, Library of Congress.

Walter E. Pittman, Jr.

HOFFMAN, Paul Gray (26 April 1891, Western Springs, IL—8 October 1974, New York). *Education*: Univ. of Chicago, 1908–9. *Career*: automobile salesman; executive, Studebaker Corp., 1909–48.

After one year at the University of Chicago, Hoffman began his career as a used car salesman and within five years was manager of sales for the Los Angeles area for the Studebaker Corporation. Immediately after service in World War I, he purchased the Los Angeles retail branch of the company and was so successful that, at age thirty-four, he was brought to the headquarters at South Bend, Indiana, as vice-president in charge of sales. In 1935 he became president of the corporation and served in that capacity until 1948. Hoffman was also interested in automobile safety and served first as president and then as chairman of the Automotive Safety Foundation (1937–48).

During World War II, Hoffman began twenty years of active service as a member of the Business Advisory Council of the U.S. Department of Commerce and remained an honorary member until his death. In 1942 he helped form, and for six years was chairman of, the privately financed Committee for Economic Development. Also during the war he organized a ten-million-dollar drive for United China Relief. In 1948 *Harry Truman appointed Hoffman as economic cooperation administrator to carry out the Marshall Plan program, and he supervised the spending of ten billion dollars for the economic recovery of Western Europe. Having retired from business, Hoffman served the next two years as president of the Ford Foundation. He then returned to the Studebaker Corporation until 1956.

Restless and unfulfilled in retirement, Hoffman accepted a new challenge at age sixty-eight and for another thirteen years provided inspired and dynamic leadership for the United Nations Special Fund (1959–66) and the United Nations Development Program (1966–72). These agencies provided the major source of multilateral preinvestment aid to poorer countries, and in most years the amounts raised by voluntary contributions from UN member governments exceeded their assessments for the regular budget of the organization. During this thirteen-year period, the agencies directed by Hoffman spent $3.4 billion on 1,430 projects in more than a hundred countries.

On the day Hoffman died the UN General Assembly paid special tribute to his contributions to world cooperation and his efforts to alleviate poverty. His successor as director of the Development Program, Rudolph Peterson, said that he was visionary and pragmatic, a worker for peace and progress. Hoffman's personal philosophy is succinctly summarized in his own statement in *World Without Want* (1962), "Our knowledge and our aspirations have brought within reach the capacity to create, in freedom, a world without want."

BIBLIOGRAPHY:

A. *Peace Can Be Won* (Garden City, NY, 1951); *Seven Roads to Safety* (New York, 1939); *World Without Want* (New York, 1962).

B. CB 1946, 263–67; NYT 9 Oct 1974, 1.

C. Hoffman papers are in the Michigan Historical Collections, Univ. of Michigan.

A. LeRoy Bennett

HOLCOMBE, Arthur Norman (3 November 1884, Winchester, MA—10 December 1977, Cambridge, MA). *Education*: A.B., Harvard Univ., 1906, Ph.D., 1909. *Career*: teacher, Harvard Univ., 1909–55; chair, Committee to Study the Organization of Peace, 1955–64.

A leading scholar, Holcombe first established himself as a student of the American political system and then turned his attention to world politics and global organization. A prolific writer, he spent nearly all his academic career at Harvard, where he served as chair of the Department of Government (1919–33, 1937–42) and taught students who later attained political prominence.

Holcombe's interest in world organization came through an acquaintance with publisher *Edwin Ginn. As a high school student, Holcombe was hired to read to Ginn, whose eyesight was failing. The work led to a lasting friendship with Ginn, who created the World Peace Foundation. Holcombe served as a trustee of Ginn's will, which left a legacy for effective proposals for world peace and international organization. During debates over League of Nations membership, 1919–21, Holcombe suggested revisions to the Covenant that would make it acceptable to the Senate. His intense involvement in international affairs, however, emerged in the 1930s, when he worked with a Harvard program to train Chinese public servants and when he lectured in China. He served as an adviser to Chiang Kai-shek during the 1940s and recorded his experiences in *The Chinese Revolution*. Following World War II, Holcombe became increasingly involved in international affairs as chairman of the Commission to Study the Organization of Peace, overseeing that group's research activities and editing its many reports. His interest in internationalism had become paramount at the time of his retirement, when he promised to devote all of his efforts to enhancing the UN.

Holcombe also presented his views in scholarly works, especially *Dependent Areas in the Post War World* (1941), *Human Rights in the Modern World* (1948), and *A Strategy of Peace in a Changing World* (1967). In the first, published before Pearl Harbor, Holcombe examined the future of League of Nations mandates and the world's colonial areas in the light of the disruption of World War II. Although highly critical of the mandate system, he favored retaining the concept of international control of dependent regions over any revival of colonialism or regional groupings. Holcombe called for new mechanisms of international control, free trade, and more attention to economic development. His ideas closely anticipated the UN trusteeship format adopted after the war, and his early recognition of the importance of the Third World showed considerable perception.

In his book on human rights, Holcombe again anticipated a major issue of subsequent decades. Written prior to the adoption of the UN Declaration of Human Rights, it advanced the major theme that the U.S. political experience might serve as a model. He suggested that UN planners seek to define certain basic rights of all world citizens. He preferred this method to choosing among systems of individual liberties in various nations. Holcombe also argued that the free gathering and disssemination of information must underlie any system of international human rights.

Holcombe's last and perhaps most important internationalist work was *A Strategy of Peace in a Changing World* (1967). Contending that world government was the inevitable alternative to nuclear destruction, this carefully reasoned study sought to suggest a practical mechanism for transforming the UN into an effective world government. There were obstacles, but no insurmountable ones. Again, the U.S. experience provided an example. He advocated a process of transformation that linked increased UN authority with arms control. He also called for the creation of five world political parties, each under the leadership of the five nuclear powers. These could be effective in running a world legislature based on existing power, modified sovereignty, and proportional representation. Eventually he envisioned a legislative branch based directly on population but cautioned that this step would take at least forty years. He stressed the need for patience and diplomacy and expected many sharp political conflicts. He insisted that his plan was one that could be embraced by realistic pacifists.

Although his career was distinguished and his active work in internationalism was considerable, Holcombe's greatest legacies were his ideas, which still stand as challenging models to achieve world order.

BIBLIOGRAPHY:

A. *The Chinese Revolution* (New York, 1933); *Dependent Areas in the Post War World* (Boston, 1941); *Human Rights in the Modern World* (New York, 1948); *A Strategy of Peace in a Changing World* (Cambridge, MA, 1967).

B. *Biographical Directory: American Political Science Association* (Washington, 1973), 216; NYT 14 Dec 1977, IV, 17; PS 12 (Spring 1979), 278–79.

James W. Harper

HOLLAND, George Kenneth (10 May 1907, Los Angeles—9 December 1977, Bronxville, NY). *Education*: B.A., Occidental Coll., 1929; M.A., Princeton Univ., 1931; study at Univ. of Grenoble, 1931, Univ. of Paris 1931–32. *Career*: secretary, International Student Service, 1932–33; director of education, Civilian Conservative Corps Camps, New England area, 1933–35; associate director, American Youth Commission, American Council on Education, 1935–41; chief, Education Section, Office of Inter-American Education Affairs, 1941–42, director, Division of Education, 1942–45; president, Inter-American Educational Foundation, 1945–46; assistant director, Office of International Information and Cultural Affairs, Department of State, 1946–48, director, Office of Educational Exchange, 1949; president, Institute of International Education, 1950–73, president emeritus, 1973–77.

Holland made his contributions to international affairs in both governmental and nongovernmental capacities as an educator, considering education as growth in attitudes, outlook, and appreciation. To promote these goals, he worked mostly with youth in the intercultural field, and he was both an architect of and administrator for the first broad student exchange programs in governmental and private efforts. As an official in the U.S. Department of State, he helped set up the Fulbright scholarship program and plan the administration of the Fulbright Act and served as first executive secretary of the Board of Foreign Scholarships for that program. As head of the Institute of International Education for the larger span of his life, he traveled extensively throughout the world, helping stimulate the exchange of students, scholars, leaders, teachers, and technicians between the United States and the rest of the world, always to promote greater interest and understanding of the need for intercultural interaction among governments and peoples of the world.

In pursuance of the same objectives, Holland served as the first permanent representative of the United States to UNESCO in Paris (1948–50) and as a member of delegations to UNESCO Conferences in London (1945), where its charter was written, in Paris, 1946 and 1949, and in Mexico City (1947), Beirut (1948), and Florence (1950).

Holland is remembered especially in Latin America, where, as an education official from the Department of State during World War II, he worked with what became a pilot program in intercultural education. Brazil, especially, served as a testing ground to build better cultural ties for fuller understanding. Holland was a prime mover in developing this substantial wartime program which flowered afterward.

BIBLIOGRAPHY:

A. *Work Camps for College Students* (Washington, 1941); with George L. Bickel, *Work Camps for College Youth*, (Washington, 1941); *Youth in European Labor Camps* (Washington, 1939); with Frank E. Hill, *Youth in the CCC*, (Washington, 1942).

B. CB 1952, 267–68; *International Institute of Education Press Release* 9 Dec 1977; NYT 10 Dec 1977, 28; WWA 1974–75, 1465.

Virginia Neel Mills

HOLLAND, Thomas Erskine (17 July 1835, Brighton, England—24 May 1926, Oxford). *Education*: B.A., Magdalen Coll., Oxford Univ., 1858. *Career*: professor, Oxford Univ., 1874–1910, fellow, All Souls Coll., Oxford Univ., 1875–1926; president, Institute of International Law, 1913; plenipotentiary, Geneva Conference, 1906.

Holland, English jurist, provided one intellectual path by which Victorian analytic jurisprudence traveled from positivism toward the recognition of international law as a valid system of law. Originally trained in the juristic tradition of John Austin, Holland in his most famous work, *The Elements of Jurisprudence* (1880), reflected the Austinian emphasis on law as a command. By this definition, international law represented a set of rules, not a body of law, because no sovereign existed to enforce international conventions. Without a sovereign body to supervise the supranational order, international law could not gain recognition as a legal system. After the publication of his influential treatise on jurisprudence, Holland turned to a more intensive consideration of the theoretical problems confronting international law. He resolved the problem of validity by defining cosmopolitan elements of law in a fashion that substituted public opinion for a sovereign. Given the rejection of moral opinion as a basis for law by analytic jurisprudence, Holland's justification sacrificed an element of consistency in favor of his work on behalf of peace through international cooperation. The League of Nations enjoyed his support because he hoped that the organization might supply the authority to provide international law with a mechanism of enforcement. Holland died before the collapse of his hopes became fully apparent.

Among his other contributions to international law, Holland made its study a more respectable academic pursuit, rescuing common lawyers from insularity. His work on naval law and neutrality moderated chauvinistic elements in Great Britain when any restriction on naval supremacy caused public concern; at the same time he opposed rules, as in the Declaration of London, which he believed inimical to legitimate British rights. Holland, whose books on international law have fallen into obscurity, deserves greater attention from posterity because his work in sustaining international law has endured.

BIBLIOGRAPHY:

A. *Admiralty Manual of Naval Prize Law* (London, 1888); *The Elements of Jurisprudence* (Oxford, 1880); *Essays Upon the Form of the Law* (London, 1870); *Letters to the Times on War and Neutrality*, 3rd ed. (London, 1921); *Studies in International Law* (London, 1898).

B. J. L. Brierly, "Sir Thomas Erskine Holland," *Law Quarterly Review* 42 (Oct 1926), 475–77; Richard A. Cosgrove, "The Reception of Analytic Jurisprudence: The Victorian Debate on the Separation of Law and Morality, 1860–1900," *Durham University Journal*, 74 (Dec 1981), 47–56. A. Pearce Higgins, "Sir Thomas Erskine Holland," *Law Quarterly Review* 42 (Oct 1926), 471–74; William S. Holdsworth, *Professor Sir Thomas Erskine Holland* (London, 1927); F. H. Lawson, *The Oxford Law School, 1850–1965* (Oxford, 1968).

Richard A. Cosgrove

HOLT, George Chandler (4 November 1907, New York—11 May 1969, New York). *Education*: B.A., Rollins Coll., 1931; Rhodes scholar, 1931–34; B.A., Oxford Univ., 1934, M.A., 1944. *Career*: director of admissions, Rollins Coll., 1936–42; U.S. Navy, 1942–45; director, United World Federalists, Connecticut, 1946–47, president, 1948, executive vice-president, Northeast Branch, 1953–68; executive director, *Grenville Clark Institute for World Law, 1968–69.

The son of noted internationalist *Hamilton Holt, George Holt moved naturally to espouse ideas which would move the world toward greater unity. Unlike his father, who would accept almost any program to advance that goal, Holt focused rather singularly upon federalist concepts which flourished after World War II. His first major involvement came when he administered a Conference on World Government in March 1946 at Rollins College attended by notable educators, writers, atomic scientists, religious, labor, and business leaders, and political figures. It issued an appeal for a world government. This effort took Holt into the World Federalist movement. He led in organizing and amalgamating groups in Connecticut and later New England, and he served on the policy-forming committee which arranged the merger in the spring of 1947 at Asheville, North Carolina, resulting in the United World Federalists.

He continued as an organizer and administrator the rest of his life. In 1948 he was largely responsible for a Connecticut referendum on world government, which voters approved 141,625 to 14,132. He developed dozens of new chapters of the UWF and held various offices in the New England movement, including president of the Connecticut body.

For over a dozen years he wrote a weekly column on world federalism syndicated primarily in the New England region which reached millions of readers. In his essays, he cogently advanced all the logical arguments in favor of world federalism. He also lectured extensively. In 1968 he became executive secretary of the *Grenville Clark Institute for World Law, established in 1966 to advance concepts of peace, justice, and law through world federation.

BIBLIOGRAPHY:

B. NYT 13 May 1969, 47; *Windham County* (CT) *Observer* 14 May 1969, 1.

Warren F. Kuehl

HOLT, Hamilton (19 August 1872, Brooklyn, NY—26 April 1951, Pomfret, CT). *Education*: B.A., Yale Univ., 1894; graduate study, Columbia Univ., 1894–97. *Career*: staff, *The Independent*, 1894–97, managing editor, 1897–1912, editor and owner, 1913–21; lecturer, foundation executive, 1921–25; president, Rollins Coll., 1925–49.

Between 1903 and 1951, no other figure labored more intensely than Holt for some form of organized world. His name is associated with virtually every idea and movement in the United States during that period. From 1903 to 1914 he focused on promoting the general concept of world organization; from 1914 to 1918, he concentrated on the League to Enforce Peace; from 1919 to 1940, he pushed for membership in the League of Nations and the World Court; thereafter, he concentrated on building the United Nations and a more effective world government. While these emerged as the dominant themes of his advocacy, Holt possessed an unusual degree of adaptability which enabled him to endorse virtually any plan, organization, or theory which would advance his dream of peace through international organization.

Holt's conversion to this vision stemmed from advice from his father to become an unquestioned authority on some single subject outside his career as a journalist, and Holt found that field in 1903 when he read an essay by *Hayne Davis which he decided to publish in *The Independent* magazine. Davis argued that the progression to an organized world was inevitable and logical; he applied the analogy of the U.S. experience to show how nations could federate for their own well-being. From that point on, Holt labored with passionate intensity to advance that simple premise. He used his prominent national weekly as a forum, printing his editorials and essays and accepting articles by other exponents. He embarked on extensive lecture tours, weeks in duration, which took him to every section of the nation. While on these rounds, he cleverly built a network of friends in business, academic, and journalistic circles. The latter proved to be especially important in spreading his ideas because editors devoted considerable space to his views.

Holt also associated with any society which he thought could be influenced by his ideas. He became one of the founders of the New York Peace Society (1906), which thereafter led in its advocacy of a world federation; he appeared regularly at the Lake Mohonk Conferences on Arbitration; he was the initial instigator behind the creation of the Carnegie Endowment for International Peace; with others he encouraged *Edwin Ginn to create the World Peace Foundation, and thereafter Holt sat as a director (1911–14); he served as a trustee of the Church Peace Union (1914–51) and became involved in its subsidiary body, the World Alliance for International Friendship Through the Churches. In 1910, with *Oscar Crosby and Walter J. Bartnett, he organized the World Federation League, which succeeded in obtaining passage of a 1910 congressional bill calling for a feasibility study to combine the navies of the world into an international police force and to reduce armaments.

Holt's most significant contribution to internationalist work came when he initiated discussions which resulted in the establishment of the League to Enforce Peace in 1915. This began with his editorial in *The Independent* of 28 September 1914, followed by a series of dinners which he and *Theodore Marburg organized where plans materialized. He served as vice-chairman of its Executive Committee and held other posts as it advanced the idea throughout the United States of a postwar international organization. Holt became intensely involved in discussions over the creation of the League of Nations. Through lectures, editorials in *The Independent*, and personal contacts with political leaders, he sought to influence the nature of the Covenant of the League, and later during debates over U.S. membership he sought an appropriate formula to break the deadlock in the Senate over joining the League. While Holt initially favored attachment with no reservations, his practical approach to problems led him to support a compromise position.

Intensive work followed in the early 1920s. He became active during the election of 1920, even ending his strong attachment to the Republican party because of its failure to endorse League membership. He then became a gadfly, prodding the Harding administration because of its failure to work with the League, and he became the spark which led to the creation of the League of Nations Non-Partisan Association (later the League of Nations Association) late in 1922. In 1921–22 he directed the fund-raising drive for the *Woodrow Wilson Foundation and served as head of the Woodrow Wilson Democracy. This organization sought not only to keep alive the issue of U.S. membership in the League but also to promote Holt as a prospective presidential candidate. He did venture into politics in 1924, when he ran unsuccessfully for the U.S. Senate on the Democratic ticket in a special election in Connecticut. Holt also believed in building an international system outside political channels, largely through the creation of friendship societies. He was one of the organizers of the Japan Society, the American-Scandinavian Society, the Netherlands America Foundation, Friends of Belgium, Friends of Poland, and the Greek-American Club.

Holt's responsibilities as president of Rollins College after 1925 limited his advocacy of League membership, but he never lost his vision of a world organization. He continued to speak on issues, favoring membership in the World Court, opposing the neutrality acts of the 1930s, and supporting aid to democratic governments opposing Fascism (1939–41). As discussions grew during World War II for a new international system, Holt again raised his voice to influence thinking. He had attended the Second Hague Peace Conference in 1907, had been at Paris in 1919, and had appeared at the San Francisco Conference in 1945. His disappointment with the Charter of the UN led him into a circle of constructive critics. He believed it lacked sufficient power to be an effective peacekeeping agency, and he favored revisions to strengthen it. He supported the World Federalist movement of the late 1940s but increasingly moved toward an advocacy of a true world government. He foresaw with telling accuracy what the impact of atomic warheads would be as he argued in favor of an international system to curb this new danger to the survival of humanity.

This same general concern for life underlay almost all Holt's work as a peace leader. He believed that conflict would end with a more organized world. He generally accepted the formula that peace and justice were inextricably combined, but he then went further by arguing that justice would come only through the acceptance of international law and that the latter would come only after the world was organized. He served as president of the Third American Peace Congress (Baltimore, 1911), and he developed an abhorrence against war almost as intense as that of traditional pacifists. This became most evident between 1914 and 1917 as he observed the United States drifting toward war. He helped organize the American Neutral Conference Committee and the American League to Limit Armaments, which fought against what it considered excessive arms appropriations. Again in the 1930s Holt added his views to the peace workers of that decade as he saw a new war approaching. Unlike proponents of nonviolence, however, Holt argued for positive action, even if that meant the use of arms to curb aggressors.

He never tired in his quest for an international organization, despite continual disappointments. The risks were too great and time too short for despair. Persistent advocacy had brought considerable achievement; more work might bring the desired result. He may have been right. Whatever progress the world had seen toward international organization in the first half of the twentieth century owed much to his efforts.

BIBLIOGRAPHY:

A. Holt's major writings appeared in *The Independent*. "A Bibliography of the Writings of Hamilton Holt," Rollins College *Bulletin* (Sep 1959), by Warren F. Kuehl, lists many unsigned items.

B. Sondra Herman, *Eleven Against War: Studies in American Internationalist Thought, 1898–1921*, (Stanford, CA, 1969); David L. Hitchens, "Peace World Order, and the Editorial Philosophy of Hamilton Holt and *The Independent Magazine*," dissertation, Univ. of Georgia, 1968; Warren F. Kuehl, *Hamilton Holt: Journalist, Internationalist, Educator* (Gainesville, FL, 1960), *Seeking World Order: The United States and International Organization to 1920* (Nashville, TN, 1969);

C. Roland Marchand, *The American Peace Movement and Social Reform, 1898–1918* (Princeton, NJ, 1972); NYT 27 Apr 1951, 23; David S. Patterson, *Toward a Warless World: The Travail of the American Peace Movement, 1887–1914* (Bloomington, IN, 1976); WWWA 3, 412.

C. The Holt papers are at Rollins Coll.

Warren F. Kuehl

HOO Chi-Tsai [Victor Hoo] (16 November 1894, Washington—9 June 1972, Yonkers, NY). *Education*: graduate, Ecole Libre des Sciences Politiques, Paris, 1915, Univ. of Paris Law School, 1918. *Career*: chargé d'affaires for China in Berlin, 1924; secretary of the Cabinet, China, 1927, to Ministry of Foreign Affairs, 1928; director, Department of Asiatic Affairs, 1930–31; chargé d'affaires, Switzerland, 1931–33; envoy extraordinary, Bern, 1933–42; vice-minister for foreign affairs, 1942–45; assistant secretary-general, UN, 1946–55, 1962–72; under secretary for conference services, UN, 1955–61; commissioner for technical cooperation, 1962–71.

After his graduation, Hoo joined the Chinese diplomatic service which took him to many international conferences. His first diplomatic assignment was at the Paris Peace Conference, where he acted as an assistant secretary of the Chinese delegation. In the 1920s, as a technical adviser to Chinese delegations, he attended the Washington, Tariff, and Sino-Soviet Conferences. In 1931, after the Japanese attack on Manchuria, he participated in all of the League of Nations sessions discussing the crisis.

Hoo not only devoted himself to diplomatic affairs, he also became involved in international issues, many of them of a moral or humanitarian nature. These included conferences on the Suppression of Traffic in Women and Children at Geneva in 1921, International Labor in 1932, and Refugees in 1933. From May 1932 he represented China advising the League of Nations regarding its treatment of opium and other hazardous medicines. In the Eighteenth Committee Conference on Prohibiting Opium in May 1934, he observed that the problem's resolution lay in practice, not empty talk. He agreed with the American representatives, who wished to utilize the League of Nations to limit the cultivation and production of opium. He put forward his proposal to expel from China those foreigners who violated laws prohibiting opium and to remove international safeguards for foreign steamers and ships smuggling opium along China's coast and inland waters.

While engaged in diplomatic service for China during the war, Hoo became involved in postwar planning as a delegate to conferences at Bretton Woods and Dumbarton Oaks (1944) and San Francisco (1945). Thereafter, he became fully involved in the UN, first as his country's representative and after 1946 as a staff member. His fluency in all five official languages made him especially noteworthy. His initial assignment as assistant secretary-general was in the trusteeship department, where he became involved in early efforts to mediate the Palestine question. In his last post, he supervised aid projects in emerging nations.

BIBLIOGRAPHY:

A. *Les Bases conventionelles des relations modernes entre la Chine et la Russie* (Paris, 1918).

B. *China Diplomatic Annual* bk. 1 (Shanghai, 1935), 117–20, 143–44, bk. 2, 167; NYT 13 Jun 1972, 46; WWWA 5, 346.

Shong Li-ling

HOOVER, Herbert Clark (10 August 1874, West Branch, IA—20 October 1964, New York). *Education*: B.A., Stanford Univ., 1895. *Career*: mining and metallurgical engineer, 1895–1913; war relief administrator, 1914–19; U.S. food administrator, 1917–19; secretary of commerce, 1921–29; president, 1929–33.

Hoover was first introduced to the world when, as a consulting engineer, he traveled in Australia, China, Burma, Russia, and Mexico. His public career began in 1914, when from London he aided thousands of Americans stranded in Europe at the outbreak of World War I, then directed the Commission for Relief in Belgium, and next served as U.S. food administrator. From 1918 to 1922, as head of the American Relief Association, he helped alleviate famine and combat typhus and other diseases in Europe, including the Soviet Union. His world fame as a dedicated and effective humanitarian and public servant propelled him into politics as secretary of commerce and then president. Following World War II, he again headed a Famine Emergency Commission in 1946–47 and then assumed other responsible roles as a public servant.

Hoover early recognized that technological and economic developments had brought an end to America's foreign policy of isolationism, and he developed a view of America's place in the world which sought a balance between nationalism and internationalism. As in his domestic programs, Hoover's foreign policy views sought to combine a kind of Jeffersonian agrarian idealism and individualism with an engineer's recognition that a complex modern world needed expert planning. But effective social coordination in Hoover's view should be done through voluntary associations rather than powerful national or international bureaucracies. He sought a coordinated independence in which world bodies could be useful but not dominant.

How to achieve that balance always troubled Hoover. As an internationalist, he admired *Woodrow Wilson, served on the Executive Committee of the League to Enforce Peace, and initially favored membership in the League of Nations without reservations. But he reluctantly came to accept the reservations to the Treaty of Versailles proposed by *Henry Cabot Lodge as politically necessary. In the election of 1920 he endorsed Warren Harding for president, asserting that a victory for the Republican candidate would result in membership in an effective league. In the 1920s he maintained contacts with leading U.S. internationalists, largely through his secretary, Christian Herter. Yet Hoover also held a nationalistic vision of America as a unique society in which free institutions and an advanced standard of living were best preserved by remaining largely self-sufficient economically, at least within the Western Hemisphere. Hoover did support the concept of an international "open door," but he viewed access to raw materials as more important for the United States than ever-expanding markets. Thus, while promoting international development and trade, he also sought, when necessary, to protect American society through high tariffs, although he modified this position after World War II.

Hoover portrayed himself as advocating a compromise between the beliefs of nationalists and internationalists, and his view of the world did provide an alternative to the isolationism of "irreconcilable" senators and the extensive interventionism—political, economic, and military—of internationalists like Woodrow Wilson, *Franklin Roosevelt, and later presidents.

Although not a believer in total nonresistance, this Quaker president was probably closer to being a pacifist than any other American chief executive. Economic and military force, he believed, only increased suffering and hatred and did not create the basis for lasting peace. That could be maintained only by prosperity and what he called "the club of public opinion." Throughout his public life, Hoover thus worked for the peaceful, noncoercive settlement of international disputes. He favored disarmament and arms limitation, international arbitration, education, and moral suasion in foreign relations, as in the Stimson Doctrine of nonrecognition of territory seized by force and participation in international organizations, as long as they did not intrude upon America's vital interests.

Given his aversion to the use of force, Hoover opposed U.S. entry into World War II. Instead he advocated resistance to economic pressures generated by the Great Depression which he thought were driving the world into war. After the attack on Pearl Harbor, which he believed resulted largely from Roosevelt's economic sanctions against the Japanese, Hoover ended his public criticism. In his most important book on foreign affairs, The Problems of Lasting Peace, written during World War II with diplomat *Hugh Gibson, Hoover emphasized, however, that military victory alone would not ensure lasting peace. He offered fifty proposals, including the separation of the settlement of wartime issues from a general postwar peace conference. He also advocated drastic disarmament and a general ban on future military alliances. During the Cold War, Hoover questioned the stationing of U.S. military forces in Europe, and he disagreed with his friend Douglas MacArthur over expanding the Korean War into North Korea and China. He also opposed the development of nuclear arms. He did not, however, advocate complete abandonment of conventional weapons. Instead, into the 1950s he advocated the protection of the United States through substantial but "defensively oriented" naval and air power. Hoover was willing to extend this "blue-water strategy" to include protection of island nations whose interests he believed coincided with those of the United States. In the Cold War era these included Japan, Taiwan, the Philippines, and possibly Great Britain.

In the great national debates over foreign policy in the late 1930s and the early 1950s, Hoover's views appealed to cautious business and agrarian groups, especially in the Midwest and Far West. Although a vigorous anti-Communist, he refused to accept the bipartisan postwar premise that collective security had to be synonymous with extensive foreign expansion and military intervention. Such a policy, he believed, would transform American society, leading to war and increased state power, and perhaps ultimately to Socialism. In the 1960s and 1970s a number of critics of U.S. foreign policy called attention to Hoover's views. Their reminder showed that the United States, like Hoover, had not yet found the proper balance between national and international paths.

BIBLIOGRAPHY:

A. *Addresses Upon the American Road*, 8 vols. (New York and elsewhere, 1936–61); *America's First Crusade* (New York, 1942); with Hugh Gibson, *The Basis of a Lasting Peace* (New York, 1945); *A Cause to Win: Five Speeches by Herbert Hoover an American Foreign Policy in Relation to Soviet Russia* (New York, 1951); *Memoirs*, 3 vols. (New York, 1951–52); *The Ordeal of Woodrow Wilson* (New York, 1958); with Hugh Gibson, *The Problems of Lasting Peace* (Garden City, NY, 1943); *The Public Papers of the Presidents: Herbert Hoover* 4 vols. (Washington, 1974–77).

B. David Burner, *Herbert Hoover: A Public Life* (New York, 1979); *Chicago Tribune*, 21 Oct 1964, 1–9; Alexander DeConde, *Herbert Hoover's Latin American Policy* (Stanford, CA, 1951); DAB supp. 7, 357–64; Robert H. Ferrell, *American Diplomacy in the Great Depression: Hoover-Stimson Foreign Policy, 1929–1933* (New York, 1957); Lawrence E. Gelfand, ed., *Hoover Hoover: The Great War and Its Aftermath* (Iowa City, IA, 1979); NCAB 56, 295–302; Raymond G. O'Connor, *Perilous Equilibrium: The United States and the London Naval Conference of 1930* (Lawrence, KS, 1962); Joan Hoff Wilson, *Herbert Hoover: Forgotten Progressive* (Boston, 1975).

C. The Hoover papers are in the Hoover Presidential Library and in the Archives of the Hoover Institution on War, Revolution and Peace.

John Whiteclay Chambers II

HOPKINS, Ernest Martin (6 November 1877, Dunbarton, NH—13 August 1964, Hanover, NH). *Education*: B.A., Dartmouth Coll., 1901, M.A., 1908. *Career*: secretary to president of Dartmouth Coll., 1901–5; secretary, Dartmouth Coll., 1905–10; industrial manager in Chicago, Boston, Philadelphia, 1910–16; president, Dartmouth Coll., 1916–45; assistant to secretary of war, 1918; executive director, Office of Production Management, 1941; chair, Americans United for World Organization, 1944–45.

For nearly thirty years as president of Dartmouth College, "Hoppy" Hopkins served as the archetype of the liberal, moderate Republican, internationalist spokesman for higher education. An advocate of military preparedness before World War I, Hopkins supported the League of Nations in 1920 and signed the Statement of the 31 because he believed that Harding, a certain winner, might be influenced in the right direction if Republican internationalists remained loyal to the GOP. As a member of the League of Nations Association and president of the *Woodrow Wilson Foundation, he urged U.S. membership in the World Court and used his influence in New Hampshire Republican politics to boost such internationally inclined spokesmen as *John G. Winant and Robert Bass. Annual trips to Europe to enhance Dartmouth's endowment in the 1920s and 1930s afforded Hopkins an early sensitivity to the potential threat from Nazi Germany. His outspoken opposition to student pacifism after 1936 earned him a national reputation. With the outbreak of war in September 1939, he worked for neutrality revision and urged all aid to the Allies, including intervention. An admirer of *Wendell Willkie, Hopkins supported his presidential candidacy in 1940 and joined eagerly in the ensuing crusade to convert the Republican party to internationalism.

Drawing lessons from World War I, Hopkins warned Americans not to postpone planning for world organization until after the conflict, when weariness and politics would prevail. He called for a postwar commonwealth of all nations, the defeated Axis powers included, served by an international police force and backed by agreed principles of international law. The details of such an organization were less important than an American commitment. Fearing Republican repudiation as in 1919, Hopkins, as chair of Americans United, pressed the national educational campaign in support of the Dumbarton Oaks formula, resigning only when the Senate approved the UN Charter in 1945. Thereafter he urged critics like the world federalists not to be perfectionists. Just as he had instituted the first courses in international politics at Dartmouth before World War II, Hopkins retained a basic faith, even after his retirement, that educated Americans would come to accept their international responsibilities. Never an original thinker, he nonetheless brought respectable establishment credentials to a cause he believed had triumphed.

BIBLIOGRAPHY:

B. NYT 14 Aug 1964, 27; Charles E. Widmayer, *Hopkins of Dartmouth* (Hanover, NH, 1977).

C. Transcribed reminiscences are in the Hopkins papers at Dartmouth Coll.

J. Garry Clifford

HOSKINS, Halford Lancaster (25 March 1891, Carmel, IN—14 September 1967, Washington). *Education*: B.A., Earlham Coll., 1913; Harvard Univ., M.A., 1921, Ph.D., 1924. *Career*: assistant professor, Tufts Univ., 1920–24, professor, 1924–44, head, History Department, 1925–34; organizer, dean, and professor, Fletcher School of Law and Diplomacy, 1933–44; consultant, Department of State, 1942–44; director, School of Advanced International Studies, 1944–49; organizer and director, Middle East Institute, 1947–49; senior specialist in international relations, Legislative Reference Service, Library of Congress, 1949–64; adjunct professor, American Univ., 1957–62, professor, 1963–66.

Scholar, educator, and civil servant, Hoskins was instrumental in the founding of three university schools of international service. The Fletcher School of Law and Diplomacy, which Hoskins helped to organize and served as dean for eleven years, was a joint enterprise of Harvard and Tufts designed to produce an international service elite for American business and government by offering the highest-level professional education to a select group of graduate students. The School for Advanced International Studies, an independent institution, which Hoskins organized and directed for five years, had essentially the same purpose as did American University's School of International Service, which Hoskins helped found in 1957 while he was working for the U.S. government.

Hoskins approached internationalism from a distinctly American perspective. The purpose of education for international service was to enable America to compete. In 1944, when setting forth the objectives of the School for Advanced International Studies, he noted the growing need for selected and skilled personnel for foreign service and found that the exceptionally trained people of other countries revealed a problem. In the postwar period the United States would have to compete with the ablest, and he predicted that one principal condition of success would be cooperation between government and business interests. The tasks required nothing less than uncovering the best people available.

Caught up in the Cold War, Hoskins publicly criticized NATO because it left the Adriatic, Pacific, and Indian oceans vulnerable to Soviet penetration. As a scholar, he wrote in a variety of fields but was gradually drawn by his interest in European imperialism to focus on the Middle East.

BIBLIOGRAPHY:

A. *The Atlantic Pact* (Washington, 1949); *British Routes to India* (New York, 1928); *European Imperialism in Africa* (New York, 1930); *The Middle East: Problem Area of the World* (New York, 1954); *Middle Eastern Oil in United States Foreign Policy* (New York, 1950).

B. NYT 15 Sep 1967, 47; WWA 1966–67, 1006.

Douglas W. Houston

HOSTOS, Eugenio María de (11 January 1839, Mayagüez, Puerto Rico— 11 August 1903, Dominican Republic). *Education*: studied law, Central Univ. of Madrid. *Career*: speaker, writer, and publisher in Europe, the United States, and Latin America, 1866–76; teacher, educational administrator and reformer, and author, Dominican Republic, 1879–88, Chile, 1889–98; activist for Puerto Rican independence, 1898–99; self-imposed exile and educator, Dominican Republic, 1900–1903.

Puerto Ricans celebrate de Hostos's birthday as a national holiday, and a community college in New York City bears his name. His collected works number twenty volumes, yet he remains an enigmatic figure, and many who celebrate his name are unaware of his international perspective. De Hostos gained some prominence as an author and as a leader of campaigns for the independence of Spain's Caribbean possessions, Cuba and Puerto Rico, in the 1860s. Extensive travel provided him with broader perspectives and gave him a universal view of life.

After 1877 he turned to educational reform, teaching and writing on a prolific scale. While a manager of school systems in the Dominican Republic and Chile, he published works on sociology, education, history, and ethics. Had it not been for the Spanish-American War, he would probably never have returned to active politics. When he did, he revealed a more fully developed social philosophy and idealism. His thought reflects Comteian Positivism, Krausism, and Victorianism. In politics he was a liberal republican nationalist. Such analysis, based on comparison and classification, however, tends to obscure the original synthesis and great vision of de Hostos's thoughts.

De Hostos saw the individual human as the essential unit in the evolution of mankind from savagery to civilization. He believed this process stemmed from natural human tendencies toward reason and cooperation. Human nature, he said, gave rise to the basic forms of social organization: the family, the tribe, the clan, the nation, and the family of nations or mankind. De Hostos went beyond such common concepts to propose and predict a federation of all the nations of the New World, which would carry civilization further than the then "decadent" level of European civilization. He considered the still enslaved and impoverished island societies of the Caribbean as the links of cultural interchange and racial fusion between the cultures of North and South America. While de Hostos saw all this as a natural unfolding of a benign human nature toward cooperation, mutual respect, freedom, and racial fusion, the process could be facilitated. He suggested an inter-American university, political independence, and abolition, and these ideals still inform and guide efforts to improve education and intergroup relations in the Caribbean. His views clearly reflect the continued strength of enlightenment philosophy, but de Hostos justified his views on the basis of his observations of real social trends and patterns in the United States, Brazil, and Puerto Rico. He believed he saw where history was heading.

The Spanish-American War interrupted his speculations and also tested his faith. After returning to Puerto Rico in 1898, de Hostos was disturbed at the U.S. occupation and the apparent lack of a policy for satisfying Puerto Rican political aspirations. He formed the League of Patriots, which called for a plebiscite on alternatives, including statehood. In 1900 de Hostos was part of a delegation which met with President William McKinley to press the Puerto Rican status issue. He was so disappointed that he went into self-imposed exile in the Dominican Republic and asked to be buried there rather than in a "colonial Puerto Rico." There he still lies.

BIBLIOGRAPHY:

A. *America: La Lucha por la Libertad*, ed. Manuel Maldonado-Denis (Mexico City, 1980); *Obras*, comp. Camila Henríquez Ureña (Havana, 1976); *Obras completas*, 20 vols. (Havana, 1939); "Prologo," in Pedro Henríquez Ureña, *Antologia* (Madrid, 1952).

B. Juan Bosh, *Hostos: El sembrador* (Piedras, Puerto Rico, 1976); Robert H. Claxton, "Inter-American Relations in the Thought of Eugenio María de Hostos," M.A. thesis, SUNY–Buffalo, 1964; "A Latin American Alternative to Racism: Some Aspects of the Thought of Eugenio María de Hostos," *West Georgia College Studies in Social Sciences* 7 (Jun 1969), 29–39; Juan Antonio Corretjer, *Hostos y Albizu* (Guaynabo, Puerto Rico, 1965); Graciela Mora, *Hostos intimista: Introducción a su diario* (San Juan, 1976); Robert T. Parrish, *A Study of the Personality and Thought of Eugenio María de Hostos* (Madison, WI, 1940); Antonio Salvador Pedreira, *Hostos: Ciudadano de América* (San Juan, 1968).

Raymond T. Multerer

HOUSE, Edward Mandell (26 July 1858, Houston—28 March 1938, New York). *Education*: Cornell Univ., 1877–79. *Career*: businessman and cotton planter; political adviser to Texas governors and President *Woodrow Wilson; member, American Commission to Negotiate Peace, 1918–19.

The son of a wealthy Texas businessman, House had the leisure to pursue his fascination with politics. Throughout his long career, he refused to seek public office and instead chose to guide policy by working through others. During the 1890s he became the political manager and confidant of four Texas governors, but by the turn of the century House tired of life there and sought a larger role in national and international events. He had to wait until 1912, when Woodrow Wilson won the presidency. The two men became intimate friends, closely collaborating in both domestic and foreign affairs. House lacked Wilson's intellectual power and discipline, but he liked people and understood how they worked and how to move them. He also had a strong interest in foreign policy and, due to his travels in Europe in the decade prior to World War I, knew more about the situation there than did any members of Wilson's Cabinet. As a result, with the outbreak of war in August 1914, House quickly became the president's most trusted foreign policy adviser.

From its start, Wilson and House felt a moral duty to end this tragedy of Western civilization. They believed the United States could help fulfill its historic mission and carry out its obligations to mankind by assuming the lead in the search for peace. As Wilson's mind came to grips with the difficulties of mediation, however, he turned to House as his chief emissary to the European capitals. Strongly pro-Allied from the start, House saw no prospect for successful mediation until the belligerents had lost their hope for total victory. Moreover, House wanted American mediation to be based on a previous agreement with the Allies and believed it must be an instrument for achieving moderate Allied success.

Wilson's choice of House gave a strange quality to American attempts to end the war. He was a curious combination of shrewdness and naiveté, driven by the spur of fame to seek a great place in the history of his times and often absorbed in a world of fantasy. House dramatized his wartime missions to Europe, exaggerating their possibilities and his influence on other men. Although his diplomacy had a veneer of realism, he often misjudged British and French leaders and assumed that, in the end, reason, calmness, and idealism would triumph over the baser aims of the Allies.

Prior to U.S. entry into the war, House undertook two missions to Europe. After the first he realized that mediation was premature. As tensions heightened between the United States and Germany, Wilson and House saw the need for further effort. House now viewed the war as a struggle between democracy and autocracy, and he was convinced that American intervention was virtually inevitable. Wilson accepted another mediation attempt, although it is clear that the two men had quite different notions of what was to be achieved. One way or another House wanted to guarantee a limited Allied victory, while Wilson genuinely viewed American mediation as a way in which to end the war. He still believed the United States might keep out and was not willing to use U.S. military power to ensure an Allied triumph. These differences never rose to the surface, for House's second peace mission also failed, and on 6 April 1917, the United States entered the war.

After intervention, House continued as Wilson's closest foreign policy adviser, consulting with the president over his plans for peace and serving as his special emissary. In late October 1917 House traveled to Europe to participate in inter-Allied military discussions and to seek agreement on war aims. A year later, when Germany sought peace on the basis of the Fourteen Points, Wilson again dispatched House to engage in prearmistice negotiations with the Allies. The apparent success of these efforts led Wilson and House to overestimate American influence and to remain convinced that out of the chaos of war a new community of nations would emerge, based on a League of Nations and a sweeping reconstruction of the international order.

In the summer of 1918, Wilson assigned House the responsibility for preparing a constitution for a League which they called a Covenant, and he and the president exchanged drafts in ensuing months. House also sought to maintain contact with American internationalists as that work progressed. As the Paris Peace Conference unfolded, differences between the president and his confidential adviser emerged. House had grown impatient, eager to dominate the discussions and bring about the fulfillment of all his dreams. His arrogance and ambition gradually became apparent to Wilson and to other members of the American Commission to Negotiate Peace as House surrounded himself with sycophants and lost touch with the direction of Wilson's thought. At first during the drafting of the Covenant, House and

Wilson worked together, but a gap became apparent when Wilson returned to the United States in mid-February and House took his place on the Council of Ten. House lacked the president's deep convictions, as well as his distrust of the Allies, and he was far more willing to concede to British, French, and Italian demands. During Wilson's absence he sought, despite the president's clear instructions to the contrary, to speed up the negotiations and, in the process, seriously weakened Wilson's position. In mid-March, when Wilson returned and became aware of House's conduct, he lost confidence in his intimate adviser and ended their friendship. Although House found himself on the sidelines, he still had some influence, and his views helped determine the headquarters of the League of Nations. During the 1920s and 1930s House retained an active interest in national and international affairs, made frequent trips to Europe, energetically supported membership in the League and the World Court, and lobbied behind the scenes to achieve these goals.

BIBLIOGRAPHY:

A. *Philip Dru: Administrator* (New York, 1912); with Charles Seymour, ed., *What Really Happened at Paris* (New York, 1921).

B. DAB 22, 319–21; Inga Floto, *Colonel House in Paris* (Aarhus, Denmark, 1973); Alexander L. and Juliette L. George, *Woodrow Wilson and Colonel House* (New York, 1956); *Handbook of Texas* 1 842; NYT 29 Mar 1938, 1; Charles Seymour, *The Intimate Papers of Colonel House*, 4 vols. (Boston, 1926–28).

C. The House papers are at Yale Univ.

Charles E. Neu

HOUSTON, Herbert Sherman (23 November 1866, Champaign, IL—14 May 1956, New York). *Education*: Ph.B., Univ. of South Dakota, 1888, M.A., 1889; M.A., Univ. of Pennsylvania, 1916. *Career*: city editor, *Sioux City* (IA) *Journal*, 1890–92; desk editor, *Chicago Tribune*, 1892–95; on staff, *Outing Magazine*, 1895–1900; on staff, Doubleday, Page and Co., 1900–1921; president, Associated Advertising Clubs of the World and founder-president of its Better Business Bureau, 1915–17; member, Division of Advertising, Committee on Public Information, 1917–18; member, U.S. Chamber of Commerce committee to study economic results of the war, 1919; publisher, *Our World*, 1921–24; founder-president, Cosmos Newspaper Syndicate, New York, 1924, Cosmos Broadcasting Co., 1933; director, Veterans of Foreign Wars memorial edition, *Pictorial History of World War II*, 1947.

As did many Americans, Houston sought by early 1915 a postwar means to prevent another war. In a January speech, he called for an international agreement to levy a commercial and financial boycott against an offending or warring nation and its nationals. He objected to *Theodore Roosevelt's espousal of an international police force as provocative of war; the armies in Europe were such forces. In June 1915 when the League to Enforce Peace

(LEP) was formed with *William Howard Taft as its president and *A. Lawrence Lowell as chairman of its Executive Committee, Houston became its treasurer and general spokesman as chair of its Committee on Information. The League's platform demanded that both justiciable and other kinds of issues be submitted to one of its agencies. The Executive Committee added that the quarreling parties must await a ruling before resorting to war. If a nation violated one of these conditions, the other members were automatically to take diplomatic and economic action against it. If this pressure failed, the member states could decide independently, according to Lowell, to use military force. In pamphlets he helped write and in speeches he made, Houston accepted the principle of this specific resort to force.

In his 1918 book, *Blocking New Wars*, Houston held that, since modern nations were susceptible to severe damage by an economic boycott, the use of military force against a culprit would probably prove unnecessary. Economic ostracism could be applied more quickly and cheaply than armed force; yet he would permit military action if economic pressure failed. To this point, Houston was a moderate in the mainstream of Americans who in the years 1915–20 called for some sort of a postwar league of nations. Somewhat more radical was his palliative for the widely held belief that economic competition was a major cause of war. The International Chamber of Commerce (ICC), formed before the war, would decide and announce what trade practices were unfair and punishable by a league of nations after a world court found a nation guilty of one or more of them. Houston believed that if the league's members practiced a representative, nonsocialistic style of democracy, this would help bind them together.

As general spokesman for the LEP, Houston defended it, as in January 1917, against Theodore Roosevelt's charge that some League members resembled "discredited pacifists" or were Germany's "dupes." There would be no neutrals in the next war, Houston retorted, and the LEP sought the nation's preservation not only with conventional armaments but by preventing a new conflagration. As World War I drew to a close, Houston announced that the LEP would work to make a league of nations a reality. In February 1919 he lauded the Covenant of the League of Nations, although he conceded that it could undergo modification. He decried senators who attacked it without offering a permanent peace plan of their own. When the League to Enforce Peace's Executive Committee voted in November 1919 to accept the crippling Lodge reservations on American membership, Houston apparently stood with the majority or abstained. Even after the Senate stalemated twice, Houston urged a reversal.

In November 1923, he told the Pen and Brush Club that industry had provided a world engaged in competition and economic struggle and unready spiritually for the challenge. It was up to writers to supply the desperate need to understand this struggle. Houston had decided to respond with *Our World* magazine, a monthly organized in 1922. It sought to explain events, especially to present the activities of the League of Nations. It attracted nearly 20,000 subscribers and had a printing of 40,000 by early 1923. He had raised his flag for the League of Nations, he wrote *Woodrow Wilson, as Houston expanded operations with *Our World Weekly* and the Cosmos Newspaper Syndicate (1924). The former sought subscriptions in schools, and the latter supplied editorials to daily and weekly newspapers with a combined circulation of nearly 5 million readers. Houston poured over $160,000 of his money into the venture and attracted capital from other internationalists, including *Charles R. Crane and *Norman H. Davis. Too rapid an expansion and rising costs, however, forced Houston sadly to abandon the ventures in 1925-26. Thereafter, he continued to show interest in the ICC, the New York World's Fair, and religiously oriented world bodies. In his last years, he became an enthusiastic supporter of the UN.

BIBLIOGRAPHY:

A. *Blocking New Wars* (Garden City, NY, 1918).

B. Ruhl F. Barlett, *The League to Enforce Peace* (Chapel Hill, NC, 1944); NCAB 41, 57; NYT 7 Jan 1915, 7, 19 May 1916, 5, 14 Aug 1916, 8, 30 Sep 1916, 2, 3 Jan 1917, 10, 15 Oct 1918, 3, 17 Feb 1919, 2, 24 Feb 1919, 12, 17 Mar 1919, 2, 11 Oct 1919, 2, 19 Jun 1920, 21, 21 Aug 1920, 3, 17 Oct 1920, 6, 15 Oct 1921, 17, 15 Mar 1922, 17, 16 Nov 1923, 3.

Edward B. Parsons

HSU Mo (22 October 1892, Soochow, China—28 June 1956, The Hague). *Education*: LL.B., Peiyang Univ., Tientsin, 1916; LL.B., and M.A., George Washington Univ., 1922. *Career*: secretary, Chinese delegation, Washington Conference, 1921-22; professor and dean, Faculty of Arts, Nankai Univ., Tientsin, 1922-26; editor-in-chief, *I-Shih-Pao*, 1926-27; judge, Provisional Court of the International Settlement, Shanghai, 1927; various posts in Ministry of Foreign Affairs, Republic of China, including chief, European and American Affairs Department, 1929-32; political vice-minister, 1932-41; ambassador to Australia, 1941-45, to Turkey, 1945-46; judge, International Court of Justice, 1946-56.

For the first fifty years of the twentieth century, China attempted to reassert itself from humiliations imposed by the imperialist powers. It sought to do this by modernizing domestic institutions and by trying to extricate itself from the dominance of foreign powers. The youth of China began to enter new universities at home which offered modern curricula, and they also went abroad for education which could provide leadership in restoring China's national dignity. Hsu Mo followed this path and returned to China. In his posts in the Foreign Ministry, he then worked with a modicum of success to have the "unequal treaties" removed.

After eighteen years in the ministry, this stern and commanding Chinese dignitary came to the conclusion that China's national security and image could only be secured through strong international organizations. As a member of the Chinese delegation to the San Francisco Conference in 1945, he drafted the section of the UN Charter dealing with international disputes. He reached the pinnacle of his career when he was elected unanimously to a judgeship on the International Court of Justice, a post he held until his death.

BIBLIOGRAPHY:

A. Howard L. Boorman, ed., *Biographical Dictionary of the Republic of China*, 2 (New York, 1970) 132–34; IWW 1954, 439; NYT 30 Jun 1956, 17; *Who's Who of Contemporary China: Biographies of Important Personalities of New China* (in Chinese) (Taipeh, 1931).

Raymond M. Lorantas

HUBER, Max (28 December 1874, Zurich—1 January 1960, Zurich). *Education*: study of law, Univs. of Lausanne and Zurich; LL.D., Berlin, 1897. *Career*: professor, Univ. of Zurich, 1902–21; Swiss delegate, Second Hague Peace Conference, 1907; legal adviser, Swiss Federal Council, 1918–22; judge, Permanent Court of International Justice, 1921–30, president, 1925–27, vice-president, 1928–30; member, Permanent Court of Arbitration, 1923–40; member, International Committee of the Red Cross, 1923–47, president, 1928–44, acting president, 1945–47.

Son of an old and wealthy Zurich family, Huber received an education that included training in the industrial and business activities of his relatives and extensive travel around the globe. As a professor at the University of Zurich, Huber paid special attention to the history and ideas that underlay existing political institutions and to the sociological factors at work in the development of law. His interest and competency in comparative constitutional law recommended him to the Swiss government, which began to use his services as a consultant, adviser, and counselor shortly after he had begun teaching.

Huber's participation at the Hague Peace Conference in 1907 gave him insights in the practical workings of international law and diplomacy. Prior to the outbreak of World War I, he advised the Federal Council on neutrality issues and questions of maritime law. At the end of the war, he drafted the Swiss memorandum for the creation of an international peace organization. Unfortunately it had no chance of successfully competing with *Woodrow Wilson's plans. Huber analyzed the political and legal problems that arose for Switzerland in connection with the creation of the League and wrote the position papers with which the Federal Council advocated Swiss membership. The German–Swiss arbitration treaty of 21 June 1921, which became a model for similar treaties, was largely Huber's work.

Huber's achievements and qualifications found international recognition when the second Assembly of the League elected him for a nine-year term as judge to the newly created Permanent Court of International Justice. Huber left a deep and lasting imprint on the Court. He helped establish the scope of the material jurisdiction as well as the procedural norms of the Court, and his formal judgments were designed to advance the codification of international law. His impartiality and good sense led to frequent appointments to arbitration and mediation commissions. Huber declined to be reelected to a second nine-year term. The Court, to his disappointment, was unable to make inroads on the traditional power politics.

The International Committee of the Red Cross (ICRC) provided Huber with another opportunity to use his talents, experience, and expertise. The first German Swiss elected to membership in this venerable Geneva-based organization, he became its fourth president in 1928. Under his inspired leadership the Red Cross idea and ideals steadily expanded to worldwide recognition in the face of mounting international crises. World War II multiplied the tasks of the ICRC, which had already grown considerably during the Ethiopian and Spanish Civil Wars. The ICRC was awarded the Nobel Peace Prize in 1944, during Huber's presidency, for its great humanitarian services.

BIBLIOGRAPHY:

A. *Denkwürdigkeiten 1907-1924*, ed. P. Vogelsanger (Zurich, 1974); *Die soziologischen Grundlagen des Völkerrechts* (Berlin, 1910); *Die Staatensuccession* (Leipzig, Germany, 1897); *Gesammelte Aufsätze*, 4 vols. (Zurich, 1947-57); *Rotes Kreuz, Grundsätze und Probleme* (Zurich, 1941).

B. LT 2 Jan 1960, 10; *Neue deutsche Biographie* 9 (Berlin, 1972), 9, 681-84; NYT 2 Jan 1960, 13; Peter Vogelsanger, *Max Huber: Recht, Politik, Humanität aus Glauben* (Zurich, 1967); *Schweizerköpfe der Gegenwart* (Zurich, 1945), 1, 48-55.

C. The Huber papers are in the Zentralbibliothek, Zurich.

Heinz K. Meier

HUDSON, Manley Ottmer (19 May 1886, St. Peters, MO—13 April 1960, Cambridge, MA). *Education*: B.A., William Jewell Coll., 1906; LL.B., Harvard Law School, 1910, S.J.D., 1917. *Career*: professor, Univ. of Missouri, 1911-16; professor, Harvard Law School, 1919-60; judge, Permanent Court of International Justice, 1935-39; chair, UN International Law Commission, 1948-53.

Few have made as durable a contribution to international law as Hudson, a staunch crusader for peace, who presented challenging perspectives on world affairs. In so doing, he skillfully argued for an effective system of international organization buttressed by a coherent body of international law. At age twenty-five, he organized the Missouri Peace Society and became a proponent of the use of arbitration in the pacific resolution of international disputes. In the years preceding World War I, he promoted peace programs in his native state, participated in national campus discussion groups called polity clubs, and led seminars throughout the United States on international law topics.

He returned to Harvard in 1916 to work under Roscoe Pound, obtained an

S.J.D., accepted a teaching post at Harvard in 1919, and became Bemis professor of international law in 1924. Hudson's formidable talents convinced both *Woodrow Wilson and his adviser, *Edward House, that his services would be invaluable in the organization of America's postwar diplomatic effort. At House's invitation, Hudson joined the Inquiry. This group of technical experts was important in developing plans that would later take shape in the Covenant of the League of Nations and the Statute of the Permanent Court of International Justice (PCIJ). He went to Paris where he served as a legal adviser to the American delegation. There, he made contact with a number of prominent international leaders, including *Eric Drummond, who became secretary-general of the League. In subsequent years, Hudson served as an important link between Drummond and successive Washington administrations in efforts to forge a stronger relationship between the United States and the world organization. He also participated in public campaigns to promote League membership, served parttime on the Secretariat (1919–26), acted as legal adviser at international conferences, joined *Michael F. Doyle in organizing study groups at Geneva, and served on the executive committee of the League of Nations Non-Partisan Association (1922–27). Between 1920 and 1939, he championed the Permanent Court of International Justice (PCIJ), arguing in numerous speeches, articles, and volumes for U.S. participation. He favored Senate acceptance of membership and worked toward this end through intensive efforts with members of the American legal profession.

In October 1936, Hudson became a judge on the PCIJ, a fitting laurel for one who had, in addition to his political activities, published 4 major volumes and 105 articles on its work. Unfortunately for Hudson and the international community, his appointment came at a time when the world was racing toward another disastrous war. The failure of the Versailles settlement, while not evinced in the workings of the Court, did shake the foundations of its parent organization, the League. By 1936 it had suffered dismal setbacks in the areas of disarmament and collective security. In spite of political disruptions, the Court continued to mete out justice with dedication and integrity until World War II, when the Nazi advance forced its members to flee The Hague. Hudson did not leave until after the occupation, negotiating a perilous exit through Italy. He carried with him and kept alive the spirit of the Court.

From 1943 onward, he worked closely with the U.S. legal profession, seeking its support to reconstitute the tribunal, expand its jurisdiction, and improve upon the body of law it might be competent to apply. Of notable importance was his organization of the American Bar Association into regional "working groups." These efforts gave shape to the State Department's position on the Court question when it was discussed at the San Francisco Conference early in 1945. It is also evident that the Statute of the International Court of Justice adopted on 26 June closely followed draft plans outlined in numerous Hudson articles and speeches.

Between 1924 and 1953, Hudson also applied himself to the development of a codified body of international law to serve the nations in the regulation of their affairs. While assigned to the League, he directed the movement to sponsor a series of drafting conferences under its auspices. He was successful in negotiating the Swedish delegation's sponsorship of a measure in September 1924 giving effect to this hope. During the next five years, while a committee of experts appointed by the Assembly determined which law subjects were ripe for codification, Hudson led a major scholarly effort known as the Harvard Research in International Law. Joining with prominent international lawyers, he organized a bank of legal talent to carry through the preparatory work for the first League-sponsored law conference called in 1930. Thereafter, until 1939, the Harvard Research group produced several model conventions. His work with the UN International Law Commission provides yet another example of the breadth of his contribution. In the years following World War II, he cooperated with the General Assembly and the American Bar Association in organizing the Commission and prescribing its responsibilities in the realm of codification.

As chairman of the Bar's Committee on the Progressive Development of International Law, he made a direct appeal to North American lawyers to support codification and the Commission. Additionally, during 1947 he worked closely with the UN Committee on the Progressive Development of International Law and Its Codification, known as the Committee of Seventeen, in supplying this body informed legal opinion. With this encouragement, the Committee approved the draft Statute of the International Law Commission approved by the General Assembly on 21 November 1947. The following year, Hudson was elected to the Commission for a five-year term, becoming that organization's first chairman. Under his direction the group made an ambitious assault on the disorganized field of international law and provided a foundation for the future development of a unified and comprehensible system.

In his later years, though seriously ill, Hudson continued to pursue those ideals he had sought to advance. He continued to write annual reports on the Court for the *American Journal of International Law* and served as president of the American Society of International Law. Acknowledging his preeminence, the Society in 1955 created and awarded him the Manley O. Hudson Medal for a lifetime of service and dedication to the cause of international justice.

BIBLIOGRAPHY:

A. *Bibliography of Manley O. Hudson, 1913-1930*, (Cambridge, MA, 1930); *International Legislation*, vols. 1-9 (Washington, 1931-50); *The Permanent Court of International Justice: A Treatise* (New York, 1943); *The Permanent Court of International Justice and the Question of American Participation* (Cambridge, MA, 1925); *The World Court: A Handbook of the Permanent Court of International Justice* (Boston, 1931); *World Court Reports*, vols. 1-4 (Washington, 1934-43).

B. CB 1944, 312-15; DAB supp. 6, 307-8; James T. Kenny, "The Contributions

of Manley O. Hudson to Modern International Law and Organization," dissertation, Univ. of Denver, 1976, "Manley O. Hudson and the Harvard Research in International Law," *International Lawyer* 11 (Spring 1977), 319–30; NCAB C, 348–49;
NYT 14 Apr 1960, 31.
    C. The Hudson papers are in the Harvard Law School Library.

James T. Kenny

HUGHAN, Jessie Wallace. See *Biographical Dictionary of Modern Peace
Leaders.*

HUGHES, Charles Evans (11 April 1862, Glens Falls, NY—27 August
1948, Washington). *Education*: Colgate Univ., 1876–78; B.A., Brown
Univ., 1881, M.A., 1884; LL.B., Columbia Univ., 1884. *Career*: teacher,
1881–82; professor, Cornell Univ., 1891–93; special lecturer, Cornell Univ.,
1893–95, New York Law School, 1893–1900; legislative counsel to State of
New York, 1905–6; governor, New York, 1907–10; associate justice, U.S.
Supreme Court, 1910–21; Republican presidential candidate, 1916;
secretary of state, 1921–25; private law practice, 1884–91, 1893–1906,
1917–21, 1925–30; member, Permanent Court of Arbitration, 1926–30;
judge, Permanent Court of International Justice, 1928–30; chief justice,
U.S. Supreme Court, 1930–41.
    Hughes began his formal career in international affairs as Warren G.
Harding's secretary of state in 1921, but he had been preparing for this role
throughout an already long and distinguished career in which he had
achieved a solid reputation as an enlightened and progressive, if not liberal,
politician. As the 1916 Republican presidential candidate, Hughes had been
forced to face the issue of America's role in European affairs, including
participation in the war and a postwar league, and it is clear that he did not
endorse the traditional "isolationist" policy. In the election of 1920, he
signed the Statement of the 31, which claimed that a vote for Harding
would advance internationalist principles. But Harding interpreted his victory as a sharp rejection of *Woodrow Wilson's attempt to involve the
United States in the League of Nations. At the same time, a visible influential, and vocal segment of opinion sought actively to change the direction of
U.S. foreign policy from isolationism to internationalism. Harding thus
fluctuated in foreign policy objectives in an effort to please diverse constitu-
encies, until in the end he chose to delegate primary responsibility to his
considerably more able secretary of state. The foreign policy of the Harding–Coolidge administrations (1921–25) is an account of Hughes's efforts
to guide the United States into assuming a role of leadership in the world
appropriate to its new status as a powerful nation.
    Hughes invented creative ways to move the American nation toward a
greater role in international affairs. He had always been sympathetic to

American membership in the League, not so much for collective security reasons but because it might provide an excellent forum for the development of international law and a framework in which it could be exercised. After a period of initial uncertainty, Hughes began sending "unofficial observers" to League meetings at which topics of interest to the United States were to be studied or discussed; these persons reported to Washington what transpired and were permitted to indicate unofficially the position of the U.S. government, although they were not allowed to negotiate. In this way European nations became aware of America's position on common concerns. He also directed that the United States cooperate with League members in nonpolitical areas such as public health, narcotics, child welfare, transport, communications, and contagious diseases. After the World Court was established, Hughes took an extraordinary interest in it, and throughout his Cabinet term and after he repeatedly urged America to join. Although he worked to draw the United States into the Court, the unfortunate circumstances of its connection to the League precluded success. Still, Hughes encouraged extensive communication between his government and the World Court, until finally by 1926 America took a faltering step toward internationalism when the Senate finally voted to join the Court. Even though its reservations prevented membership, Hughes served as a judge (1928–30).

Hughes's most stunning success in international affairs was the Washington Conference of late 1921, which sought an arms limitation agreement among the major world powers and stability in the Far East and the Pacific. At the inaugural session, Hughes made a dramatic proposal to freeze the ratio of naval tonnage among the major powers according to a formula he persuaded all to accept; his idea and agreements on Asia and the Pacific marked the first time that great nations commanding powerful weaponry had agreed to a voluntary reduction and limitation of offensive and defensive forces.

Hughes was not an imaginative person, nor was he a great leader among internationalists, but he was an effective and respected secretary of state. He did not try to force the nation into international obligations. He often noted the futility of trying to assume commitments, such as League membership, where the Senate would not move. Yet he did achieve a degree of cooperation with the League. He recognized a need for the United States to become involved in the reparations question and encouraged the negotiations which resulted in the Dawes Plan (1924). He also favored resolving problems in Latin America peacefully rather than through intervention. In all these efforts, he applied the same dedication to his role in international affairs as he did in his public service as a politician, an administrator, and a jurist.

BIBLIOGRAPHY:

A. *The Pathway of Peace: Representative Addresses Delivered During His Term as Secretary of State* (New York, 1925).

B. DAB supp. 4, 403–8; Betty Glad, *Charles Evans Hughes and the Illusions of Innocence: A Study in American Diplomacy* (Urbana, IL, 1966); Dexter Perkins, *Charles Evans Hughes and American Democratic Statesmanship* (Boston, 1956); Merlo J. Pusey, *Charles Evans Hughes* 2 vols (New York, 1951); Nelson E. Woodward, "Postwar Reconstruction and International Order: A Study of the Diplomacy of Charles Evans Hughes," dissertation, Univ. of Wisconsin, 1970.

C. The Hughes papers are in the Manuscript Division, Library of Congress.

Barbara M. Shaver

HULL, Cordell (2 October 1871, Overton [now Pickett] County, TN—23 July 1955, Bethesda, MD). *Education*: Normal School, Bowling Green, KY, 1886–87; National Normal Univ., Lebanon, OH, 1888–89; LL.B., Cumberland Law School, 1891. *Career*: Tennessee House of Representatives, 1893–97; judge, Fifth Judicial Circuit of Tennessee, 1903–7; Democratic congressman, 1907–21, 1923–31; chairman, Democratic National Committee, 1921–24; senator, 1931–33; secretary of state, 1933–44; Nobel Peace Prize, 1945.

Hull's political career spanned a period when the United States moved toward greater and greater cooperation and involvement in world affairs. He chose an internationalist path and, by example and pronouncements, led the way in instructing Americans to take a broad view of issues. Hull was awarded the Nobel Peace Prize in 1945 and is rightly considered the father of the United Nations.

The starting point for Hull's internationalist philosophy was an economic liberalism which rose naturally from his rural Tennessee surroundings, championing, among other things, a low tariff policy. The outbreak of World War I reinforced Hull's conviction that artificial barriers to commerce contributed to human misery and disorder and were a root cause of war. He never deviated from the cause of dismantling protective tariffs, an action, he said, that would bring an end to economic dislocations and provide the world's people with access to goods and resources. As secretary of state, the matured versions of Hull's outlook led him to make the Good Neighbor Policy and the reciprocal trade agreements program important State Department policies.

In the 1920s Hull's economic liberalism widened. He advocated disarmament coupled with pledges by nations not to interfere in the internal affairs of other states, a program he advanced unsuccessfully in 1933 at the World Disarmament Conference. In the 1930s Hull publicly cited the need to promote international law and order to maintain peace, and he advised nations to pursue policies designed to restore sanity to the world. Yet he refused to become involved in problems, especially in Europe. Privately, he moved closer and closer to a more activist diplomacy, hoping to help construct some foundations of stability. His problem was most clearly visible in the tangled threads of America's East Asian policy. Hull had always opposed what he viewed as Japanese encroachments upon China, and he consistently invoked the Open Door Policy as the solution to deteriorating American–Japanese relations. This was the realm of rhetoric. In practice, Hull tried to modify Japanese policy through sanctions and the diplomacy of deterrence. In the years just prior to American entry into World War II, Hull's internationalism was that of the administration in which he served, pursuing a doctrine of responsibility in world affairs that included opposition to aggression, rearmament, and all aid short of war for nations fighting the Axis powers.

Despite his position as secretary of state, Hull was not at the center of wartime diplomacy; this policy area *Franklin D. Roosevelt kept for himself. Postwar planning was left to Hull. He directed the preparation of the document which became the Declaration of the United Nations, primarily out of an interest in binding the signatories to accept idealistic principles. Hull was a leader in the movement to develop a new organization dedicated to keeping the peace, and he gained Joseph Stalin's assent to the idea at the meeting of foreign ministers in Moscow in 1943. He also worked closely with Senate leaders to assure their support for a more cooperative postwar world. The authority for planning this aspect of U.S. policy remained in Hull's hands, and his efforts laid the groundwork for the United Nations.

BIBLIOGRAPHY:

A. *The Memoirs of Cordell Hull*, 2 vols. (New York, 1948).

B. CB 1940, 412–14; DAB supp. 5, 331–35; Catherine A. Grollman, "Cordell Hull and His Concept of a World Organization," dissertation, Univ. of North Carolina, 1965; Harold Hinton, *Cordell Hull* (Garden City, NY, 1942); *The McGraw-Hill Encyclopedia of World Biography* (New York, 1973), 411–12; NCAB F 16–19; NYT 24 Jul 1955, 1; Julius W. Pratt, *Cordell Hull, 1933–44*, 2 vols. (New York, 1964); Amry Vandenbosch, "Cordell Hull: Father of the United Nations," *World Affairs* 136, (no. 2, 1973), 99–120; WWWA 3, 428.

C. The Hull papers are in the Manuscript Division, Library of Congress.

Jamie W. Moore

HULL, William Isaac. See *Biographical Dictionary of Modern Peace Leaders.*

HUMBER, Robert Lee (30 May 1898, Greenville, NC—10 November 1970, Greenville). *Education*: B.A., Wake Forest Coll., 1918, LL.B., 1921; Rhodes Scholar, Oxford Univ., 1920–23; M.A., Harvard Univ., 1926. *Career*: lawyer, Paris, 1930–40, Greenville, NC, 1940–70; state senator, 1959–63.

The renewal of hostilities in Europe in September 1939 merely confirmed what most observers had long concluded: the collective security concept as embodied in the League of Nations was defective. Most critics took the position that all attempts to abolish war by remedying the supposed weaknesses of the nation-state system were doomed to failure. Some observers, however, viewed the failure of the League as evidence that only by creating a new sovereign layer of government at the international level could war be abolished. Eternal peace would visit the nations only when they gave up the state of anarchy and bowed to the discipline of a genuine world government.

A North Carolina lawyer, Humber held to such a view. He had lived in Paris for business reasons in the interwar years, and he returned to the United States after war broke out in 1939 filled with notions of a European (and world) federation which had become popular among some intellectuals and businessmen. Shortly after his resettling in North Carolina, Humber founded the Movement for World Federation, which sought to promote that idea in the United States. Toward this end, Humber prepared a resolution urging U.S. leadership in establishing a world federation after the war. Introduced in the North Carolina state legislature, Humber's resolution did not provide details on the powers of such a union, but it clearly envisaged an organization with far greater authority than that granted the League of Nations. As early as 1940, Humber convinced the North Carolina lawmakers to adopt his proposal, the first time a major political body went on record favoring participation in a postwar international peacekeeping organization. Yet the widely publicized Humber Resolution had little immediate impact on the nation's foreign policy, although it did reveal the distance Americans had traveled in their understanding of how dependent the United States had become on events overseas. It hardly produced the result Humber desired. He clearly favored something more effective and far reaching than the organization created at San Francisco in 1945. Thus, after operating more or less independently since 1940, Humber joined forces with world government supporters in 1947 to form the United World Federalists (UWF). It emerged as a union of several groups that had supported the creation of the UN but which had become disillusioned by its inability to deal with crises. To remedy the UN's supposed weaknesses, the UWF advocated revising the UN Charter to include many of the powers of the nation-state, especially the authority to raise armies and to tax. In addition, the UWF proposed that representatives to the UN be elected on the basis of weighted representation.

In promoting world government, the UWF utilized a variety of approaches. Its primary one involved a top-level, behind-the-scenes strategy in which its well-connected and influential leaders utilized their contacts to apply pressure on their friends and peers in government. A second line of attack centered on educating the American public to the need for world government. A third involved getting state and national legislatures to endorse the principle. This strategy, if successful, would put pressure on the president to initiate discussions with the other UN members regarding Charter revision. Humber was fully in accord with such tactics.

By late 1948, support for transforming the UN had attained its zenith. The UWF's membership reached 60,000. Dozens of U.S. congressmen and senators supported resolutions favoring the idea, and sixteen state legislatures had passed Humber, or Humber-like, resolutions. Support for world government quickly faded after 1948, however, when the Czech coup in that year, the Soviet development of the atomic bomb, and later, the Korean War heated up the Cold War and made advocacy of a world federation which included the Communists seem impossible if not treasonable. Despite the idea's fall from favor, Humber remained faithful to the world government ideal and the UN. In 1969, the year before his death, he accepted the chairmanship of North Carolina's UN Day celebration.

BIBLIOGRAPHY:

B. NCAB 57, 494–95; NYT 12 Nov 1970, 47; WWWA 5, 356.

John F. Bantell

HURST, Cecil James Barrington (28 October 1870, Sussex County, England—27 March 1963, Horsham, West Sussex, England). *Education*: Trinity Coll., Cambridge Univ., 1888–92). *Career*: called to bar, 1893; bencher of the inn, 1922, treasurer, 1940; assistant legal adviser to Foreign Office, 1902–18, legal adviser, 1918–29; member, Permanent Court of Arbitration, 1929–50; judge, Permanent Court of International Justice, 1929–46, president, 1934–36.

It was Hurst, perhaps better than most, who recognized the implications for national sovereignty in the principle of international law. As a lawyer who fashioned the techniques of his profession to the aims of diplomacy, he had a particular insight into the challenge of multilateral negotiations and an awareness of the extent to which collective security can be subverted by intent as well as circumstances.

He served as legal adviser to the British Foreign Office during the high tide of peacemaking-by-treaty following World War I. His influence on diplomacy in this period is difficult to determine but easy to infer. He worked with *David Hunter Miller in preparing drafts of the League of Nations Covenant, and he served on the committees which wrote the Statute of the Permanent Court of International Justice and the Constitution of the International Labor Organization. At Versailles, the facility with which he translated the decisions of his political masters into the language of the treaty clauses earned him considerable renown. The British delegation was particularly dependent on his skills as arbiter, interpreter, and advocate in the formulation of a legal framework for keeping the peace. Moreover, the skill with which he reconciled the divergent needs of sovereign states with the varying notions of a global diplomacy through law made him a natural, and ultimate, candidate for membership on the PCIJ. Although his close identification with British policy made him a controversial choice, Hurst's wide knowledge of international law and close identification with the objectives of the League proved irresistible.

Hurst also recognized the tension between a nascent nationalism and those states, such as the signatories of the Versailles Treaty, that were prepared to impose a world order largely on their own terms and in their own interests. As such, he paid particular attention at the Conference to promoting recognition of the sovereignty of certain self-governing members of the British Empire. In that sense, he anticipated (and lived to witness) the progressive, and largely administrative, dismantling of the Empire after World War II. A close associate of Austen Chamberlain during the latter's tenure as foreign secretary, he was instrumental in guiding British policy in the 1920s toward a close adherence to the general principles of the League of Nations. In 1929, after a decade as legal adviser to the Foreign Office and some years' experience with the British delegations in Geneva, he observed that compulsory arbitration involved some sacrifice of independence and for Britain that could be greater than for others. Yet it was worth it if the advantages were greater than the disadvantages.

To be sure, Hurst did not lose sight of the pragmatic aspects of peace-making. As editor of *The British Year Book of International Law*, he wrote in 1921 that "the true test as to whether or not a treaty survives the outbreak of war between the parties is to be found in the intention of the parties at the time when the treaty is concluded." Although his interest in League affairs was primarily legal, for that reason he understood the considerable extent to which law could be applied in resolving international disputes. As chairman of the League Commission on War Crimes until his resignation because of ill health in 1945, he provided the foundation upon which the Nuremberg Tribunal ultimately rested, the first attempt to apply a strictly judicial process to the needs of diplomacy.

BIBLIOGRAPHY:

B. LT 28 Mar 1963, 17, 10 Apr 1963, 14; Harold Nicolson, *Peacemaking, 1919* (Boston, 1933); J. W. Wheeler-Bennett and Maurice Fanshawe, *Information on the World Court, 1918–1928* (London, 1929).

Philip Terzian

HUSTON, Howard Riggins (29 July 1892, Sweet Springs, MO—8 June 1955, Truro, MA). *Education*: B.A., Univ. of North Dakota, 1917. *Career*: U.S. Army, 1917–19; secretary, General Staff, American Army in France, 1919; chief, Internal Services Section, League of Nations Secretariat, 1919–30; assistant to president, American Cyanamid Co., 1930–51, vice-president, 1951–55, member, Board of Directors, 1952–55.

Huston was one of a small contingent of Americans, including *Raymond B. Fosdick, *Arthur Sweetser, *Huntington Gilchrist, and *Manley O. Hudson, who pioneered in the establishment of the first global international organization. He grew up in North Dakota and appears to have had some prewar experience in banking and teaching before he enlisted as a private during World War I. He was wounded at Chateau Thierry, participated in the last Allied offensive in the Argonne, then became an aide assigned to AEF headquarters in Tours, France. There Huston was the billet mate of Gilchrist, who recommended him for the job which launched his civilian career in international affairs.

As chief of Internal Services of the League of Nations, Huston prepared for conference, committee, and assembly meetings. The League sent him to the Washington Conference on the Limitation of Armaments (1921–22), but his duties as business manager did not often permit a role in Secretariat political decision making. His occasional reporting on home-leave trips to the United States shows an impressive grasp of the American mentality and discerning judgment. His standing as an authentic American cowboy with a genial and cosmopolitan personality made him a favorite of Secretary-General *Eric Drummond, who included him in his weekly golf foursome. But, like Gilchrist's, Huston's career was limited by the United States' failure to join the League, and he followed his billet mate a second time, out of the League and into the chemical industry with American Cyanamid.

Howard Huston returned to public international service to assist in the founding of the United Nations Internal Services and to consult on its interim facilities. He also served (1948) on the Chemical Industry Committee of the International Labor Office. His early death was the first of the American group at Geneva.

BIBLIOGRAPHY:

B. NYT 10 Jun 1955, 25; WWWA 3, 433–34.

Terry L. Deibel

HUTCHINS, Robert Maynard (17 January 1899, Brooklyn, NY—14 May 1977, Santa Barbara, CA). *Education*: Oberlin Coll., 1915–17; A.B., Yale Univ., 1921; LL.B., Yale Law School, 1925. *Career*: faculty, Lake Placid School, 1921–23, secretary, 1925–27; acting dean, dean, professor, Yale Law School, 1927–29; president, Univ. of Chicago, 1929–45, chancellor, 1945–51; associate director, Ford Foundation, 1951–54; chief executive officer, Fund for the Republic, 1954–74, president, 1975–77; chief executive officer, Center for the Study of Democratic Institutions, 1954–74, president, 1975–77; director, *Encyclopaedia Britannica*, 1954–74.

A tall man with firm jaw and sparse frame, Hutchins was best known for his unorthodox educational philosophy, one that centered on the belief that education must cultivate values based upon a dialog with the greatest thinkers of mankind. As president of the University of Chicago, he abolished football and required a great books course. As president of the Ford Foundation's Fund for the Republic, he fought McCarthyism while initiating studies of American Communism and national security policies. As founder of the Center for the Study of Democratic Institutions, he stimulated dialogs that transcended disciplines and continents.

Hutchins was always involved with issues of international policy. While a student at Oberlin, he had pacifist leanings, and in World War I he served in the Ambulance Corps. When President *Franklin D. Roosevelt's policies threatened intervention in World War II, Hutchins claimed that full-scale participation would destroy the American form of government. He claimed that "Allies" such as Greece, Turkey, and China were dictatorships, that it was difficult to restore prewar boundaries in Europe, and that the administration was conjuring "bogies" and "nightmares" in an effort to create hysteria. He did not join the America First Committee, claiming he was for humanity first, yet he informally advised its leadership on such matters as public opinion polls. In 1945 he oppposed a harsh peace against Germany and Japan, saying one must distinguish between people and leaders.

Hutchins was particularly alarmed by the bombing of Hiroshima and Nagasaki. Yet, he also saw the new weapon as "the good news of damnation," because he believed it would frighten nations to band together and thereby avoid world suicide. He immediately called for controls, claiming that an atomic monopoly was impossible to keep. As atomic storehouses and factories could not be detected, and missiles could be guided from the ground, conventional war was obsolete and nuclear victory impossible.

In 1945 he united with sixteen prominent intellectuals to form the Committee to Frame a World Constitution, in order to draft a constitution for world government. In the spring of 1948 his group, funded by *Anita Blaine, made its report. There should be a convention of nations to institute a powerful world-state based on the realization that "justice" was the basis of peace. It would monopolize all arms as well as possess the right to enter, inspect, and destroy atomic installations anywhere in the world. It would have to act directly upon the individual; otherwise it would merely be a league of sovereigns. Hutchins conceded that the United States, being the richest and most powerful nation on earth, would have to give up many advantages.

Although his proposals received little support, Hutchins revealed his concern in other ways. In 1946, in opposing Truman's pleas for universal military training, he accused the United States of "un-American sabre rattling" and of seeking "peace through intimidation." The United States, he went on, was fomenting a suicidal race in atomic weapons. He organized two worldwide conferences in New York in 1965 and in Geneva in 1967 to promote Pope John XXIII's encyclical Pacem in Terris. In 1967, during the Vietnam War, Hutchins accused the United States of attempting, unsuccessfully, to suppress rising social movements throughout the world. Hutchins tended to be more apt in diagnosing ailments than in finding cures. Yet his utopian approach to world government, which ignored the real world of sovereignty, was firmly within the tradition of internationalist thought.

BIBLIOGRAPHY:

A. *St. Thomas and the World State* (Milwaukee, WI, 1949).

B. CB 1940, 417–19, 1954, 356–58; NYT 16 May 1977, 1; WWA 1976–77, 1547.

Justus D. Doenecke

HUXLEY, Julian Sorell (22 June 1887, London—14 February 1975, London). *Education*: graduate, Oxford Univ., 1909; research in Italy under the Naples Biological Scholarship, 1909–10. *Career*: founder, Department of Biology, Rice Institute, 1912–16; World War I, 1916–17; taught at Oxford Univ. and Kings Coll., 1919–27; director-general, UNESCO, 1946–48; scholar and writer, 1927–75.

Huxley wrote on a wide variety of topics in which he explored the philosophical implications for man of the growing body of scientific fact and the widening application of the scientific method. During World War II, he lectured at home and in the United States on British war aims and concerned himself with problems to be solved when peace came. He served as a member of a commission to make recommendations on higher education in West Africa and then as executive secretary in 1945 of the Preparatory Commission for the United Nations Educational, Scientific, and Cultural Organization. He was then selected as the first director-general of UNESCO in 1946.

Clearly, his major international contribution came as administrator of UNESCO where he was responsible for creating this new international machine and pointing its direction. He turned over to his successor in 1948 a fully working operation with a large number of separate and ambitious projects. Huxley also recruited for UNESCO a staff that was a kaleidoscope of professionals representing nationalities from various areas. UNESCO achieved an intellectual standing under the direction of this great humanistic scientist. Huxley acted upon the Charter's assumption that wars begin in the mind, and he sought to erect fresh barriers against going to war by getting people to know each other culturally.

Huxley's studies lay in a border area between science and moral philosophy. He united aesthetic concern with scientific interest in the matter of nature conservation. He concentrated his energies on man's place in the cosmos and what he should do about it. To Huxley, mankind was in a significant stage of evolution with potential for significant progress. He came to international leadership in the post–World War II era, when men and women were at last being forced to realize that the world was one. His conduct under the continuous sniping of UNESCO critics was of such quality that it gave him incentive and freedom as he worked on international problems without official posts during the latter years of his life.

BIBLIOGRAPHY:

A. *From an Antique Land: Ancient and Modern in the Middle East* (New York, 1955); *Memories*, 2 vols. (London, 1970–73); *UNESCO: Its Purpose and Its Philosophy* (Washington, 1947).

B. CB 1963, 201–4; LT 17 Feb 1975, 14; NYT 16 Feb 1975, 1.

Virginia Neel Mills

HUYSMANS, Camille. See *Biographical Dictionary of Modern Peace Leaders*.

HYDE, Charles Cheney (22 May 1873, Chicago—13 February 1952, New York). *Education*: B.A., Yale Univ., 1895, M.A., 1898; LL.B., Harvard Law School, 1898. *Career*: attorney in Chicago, 1898–1923, Washington, 1920–23; solicitor, Department of State, 1923–25; professor, Northwestern Univ. Law School, 1907–25, Columbia Univ., 1925–45.

A career devoted to international law began with Hyde's studies and continued in Chicago, where he handled cases involving extradition, citizenship, and refugee matters. In 1907 he attended the organizing session of the American Society of International Law (ASIL) and published in 1922 a project he had started in 1905. This was also his two-volume *International Law, Chiefly as Interpreted and Applied by the United States*, which he revised and extended to three volumes in 1945. These works received extensive acclaim for their thoroughness and detail.

They also reflected Hyde's positivist position, in which he searched for practical ways to attain with fairly dependable certainty what was proper. In this way, governments and persons would know what actions to take. While the first edition may have reflected prevailing patterns of thought, Hyde's revision, conducted throughout the interwar years and World War II, sought to provide some assurance of constancy in a world which had largely forsaken established rules of behavior. Obligations and responsibilities were largely eroding. Hyde acknowledged such changes when, as president of the ASIL (1946–49), he encouraged a renewed dedication to international law, which he saw as increasingly passive as precedents were challenged. He also hoped the UN would move vigorously to challenge the disregard of law by the Soviet Union.

Hyde served as counsel (1931–32) for a Guatemalan–Honduras boundary dispute and on the board of editors of the *American Journal of International Law* (1910–52). He published extensively in both legal and popular journals and wrote the sketch of *Charles Evans Hughes, with whom he had worked in the State Department, in a series dealing with American secretaries of state. He was appointed to the Permanent Court of Arbitration in 1951, but died before he could serve. Hyde is revealing of the history of international law as it sought to bridge the gap into a world after 1945 both more and less organized. Machinery without substantive principles or rules would be meaningless, which explains his lifelong quest to establish the reality of international law.

BIBLIOGRAPHY:

A. "Charles Evans Hughes," in Samuel F. Bemis, ed., *The American Secretaries of State and Their Diplomacy* 10 (New York, 1929), 121–401; *International Law, Chiefly as Interpreted and Applied by the United States*, 2nd rev. ed., 3 vols. (Boston, 1945).

B. AJIL 46 (1952), 283–89; DAB supp. 5, 340–41; WWWA 3, 435.

Warren F. Kuehl

HYDE, Herbert Ernest (1890–1959). *Education*: unknown. *Career*: Royal Air Force lieutenant, World War I; otherwise unknown.

A unique plan by Hyde for international government appeared in various forms during and after World War I. In the 1920s Hyde's plan for international government and arms control was praised for its goals but never tried. Still, Hyde remained active in his support of an effective alternative to the arms race and war, urging the acceptance of his plan for an international parliament, law court, and peacekeeping force.

His scheme was both too radical to receive serious consideration and too shallow to serve as the basis for later plans. He would have based representation in an international parliament strictly on size and importance of states. The parliament of the nations would control the production and distribution of all military weapons. The development of new weapons without parliamentary approval was to be a capital offense. The law court he proposed was to decide disputes among nations, and an international army would if necessary enforce those decisions. But Hyde's plan was out of tune with the times. He invariably suggested that Britain "lead the way," as though her nineteenth-century world leadership remained undiminished. He accepted as a foregone conclusion that Asian and African nations would be unready for representative government in the foreseeable future, and he continued to address the bogy of the "yellow peril."

Hyde's first proposal for international government was published in New Zealand during the July crisis of 1914, long before the full impact of the war could have been predicted. After that initial publication of his scheme in a newspaper article and pamphlet, he expanded it into a book in 1916. He continued to push the plan and to participate in the debate over international government through the League of Nations Union. The Third Committee of the League of Nations considered his scheme for armament reduction in 1924 but did not adopt it. After publication of his last book in 1930, he shared his ideas in support of the League of Nations as the instrument of arms control and reduction with the readers of *The Times* through letters to the editor between 1931 and 1936.

BIBLIOGRAPHY:

A. *Dawn of the Age of Appeal to Reason* (Wellington, New Zealand, 1914); *An International Parliament* (London, 1917); *The International Solution* (London, 1917); *The League of Nations and the Peace Conference* (London, 1918); *The Price of National Security* (London, 1930); *The Two Roads: International Government or Militarism* (London, 1916).

B. Henry R. Winkler, *The League of Nations Movement in Great Britain, 1914–1919* (New Brunswick, NJ, 1952).

Lyle A. McGeoch

HYMANS, Paul (23 March 1865, Brussels—8 March 1941, Nice, France). *Education*: Univ. of Brussels. *Career*: professor, Free Univ. of Brussels,

1897–1914; minister to Great Britain, 1915–17; minister of economic affairs, 1917–18; minister of foreign affairs, 1918–20, 1924–25, 1927–35; minister of justice, 1926–27.

Trained as a lawyer and active as a journalist, Hymans became involved in political and foreign affairs during World War I. As minister of foreign affairs, he was an active plenipotentiary at the Paris Peace Conference. In the drafting of the Covenant of the League of Nations, he reacted against the overrepresentation of the great powers in various organs of that projected international body. An excellent administrator and clever diplomat, Hymans was, at Paris and in the League, a spokesman for the small states who even pleaded for the acceptance of Brussels as the permanent League site.

Hymans's prominent role in League of Nations history was based on numerous involvements. He was president of the First Assembly, where he used his organizational skills with a young aide, *Jean Monnet, to establish the bureau destined to become the vehicle for the central direction of all Assembly business. He directed the 1920–21 Conference of Experts at Brussels, which prescribed the specific procedural means that League committees would utilize in Geneva. In what he considered one of his most important contributions, Hymans moved the creation of the Committee on Intellectual Relations almost singlehandedly, with the express purpose of establishing a League instrument for expanding contacts between teachers, artists, scientists, authors, and other intellectual professions. In this area, he stimulated two Belgians, *Paul Otlet and +Henri La Fontaine, to construct the Union of International Associations. These three men were to play a significant part in persuading numerous international organizations to choose Brussels as their central office location. Overall, Hymans wished to make the League a useful instrument for all intellectuals, especially those who worked to create common fronts against the perils of national hatred and prejudice.

The Belgian was involved in the attempted League resolution of many controversial international conflicts, including the reparations, Ruhr, disarmament, and Luxembourg crises in the 1920s. He was the rapporteur on the doomed Special Assembly of the League on Vilna (1920–21) and headed the four rapporteurs' Special Assembly successful proposal concerning Upper Silesia in 1921. In 1932 he chaired a special League committee on the Manchurian question, which preceded the Lytton Commission report and delineated the bases of an armistice at Shanghai.

As a delegate to the League (1920–25, 1927–34), Hymans became identified with the reparations and disarmament issues via his advocacy at the 1924 London Conference of a compromise plan which was later partially integrated into the Locarno Pacts. He was an avid defender of the 1924 Geneva Protocol for the Pacific Settlement of International Disputes until its defeat. His diplomacy in the Dawes Plan was thought by some to be a contributing reason for French acceptance. The international perspective of Hymans was frequently forced to include his primary consideration of smaller states and their roles in decision making. He was, however, truly committed to the idea of conflict resolution through international diplomacy and organs and not, as often cited, simply a follower of the French policy line.

BIBLIOGRAPHY:

A. *Fragments d'histoire, impressions et souvenirs* (Brussels, 1940); *Mémoires* (Brussels, 1958); *Pages libérales* (Brussels, 1936).

B. Sally Marks, *Innocent Abroad: Belgium at the Paris Peace Conference of 1919* (Chapel Hill, NC, 1981); Jane K. Miller, *Belgium Foreign Policy Between the Two Wars* (New York, 1951); NYT 9 Mar 1941, 40; WWW 1941-50, 586.

Pierre-Henri Laurent

I

INMAN, Samuel Guy (24 June 1877, Trinity, TX—19 February 1965, New York). *Education*: B.A., Columbia Univ., 1904, M.A., 1923. *Career*: director of social work, First Church, Disciples of Christ, New York, 1901–4; missionary, Monterrey, Mexico, 1905–7; director, Peoples' Institute, Piedras Negras, Mexico, 1907–15; secretary, Committee on Cooperation with Latin America, 1915–39; founder and editor, *La neuva democracia*, 1920–39; professor, Columbia Univ., 1919–34, Univ. of Pennsylvania, 1937–42, and many other colleges; special adviser to U.S. delegation to Special Inter-American Conference for the Maintenance of Peace, Buenos Aires, 1936; consultant to State Department, San Francisco Conference, 1945; guest of the Argentine government, 1947; member, Secretariat, Ninth Inter-American Conference of American States, Bogotá, 1948; president, Worldover Press, 1944–55; chair, Committee of Inquiry on Internationalization of Jerusalem, 1950; diplomatic mission to Brazil, 1951; lecturer; author of 21 books and over 1,500 pamphlets and articles.

Childhood tragedy in Texas turned Inman to evangelical religion in the mid-1890s. He fell under the influence of a pastor of the Church of the Disciples of Christ, who sparked in him a lifelong drive of Protestant Christian idealism. Joining the Christian Endeavor Society, an interdenominational Protestant youth group, he acquired the experience and zeal which would make him a highly effective Christian worker at home and abroad.

Heightened social concern brought him in 1901 to Manhattan's tenements, where he directed a youth project. Becoming interested in missionary work in Mexico, he developed a new philosophy of Protestant evangelicalism—he would not attack Catholicism as such but apply the techniques of the Social Gospel and attempt to gain the confidence of community leaders. With his bride he established the Peoples' Institute in Coahuila, achieving dramatic results and befriending many future leaders of Mexico, including Venustiano Carranza.

The outbreak of the Mexican Revolution in 1911 raised the question of social justice, threatened investments, and brought foreign intervention. The Institute nurtured the revolutionary cause, and Inman became the advocate of the Mexican people. In 1915 he joined the Protestant ecumenical Committee on Cooperation and, as its secretary, undertook to reform Latin American society. He redirected missionary work along the lines he had developed in Mexico, opposed intervention, and promoted inter-American cooperation.

Inman took up the pen to express dissatisfaction with developing U.S. policy. In 1919 he published the critical but highly acclaimed *Intervention in Mexico*. Inman's testimony before a Senate subcommittee investigating Mexican relations brought a denunciation from Senator A. B. Fall, a spokesman for the oil interests, which threatened Inman's career. In 1924 he published "Imperialistic America" in *Atlantic Monthly* antagonizing State Department officialdom and initiating a controversy with *Leo S. Rowe, director of the Pan American Union. His 1933 work, *América revolucionaria*, became a classic statement of liberal internationalism.

Public affairs claimed more of Inman's attention. He pioneered in cultural cooperation, stressing this approach in numerous teaching assignments, notably at Columbia from 1919 to 1934, and in lectures throughout the hemisphere. He mingled with major Latin American cultural figures and interpreted their work to Americans. His influence peaked in the Good Neighbor era. He met *Cordell Hull prior to the Montevideo Conference in 1933, and he helped liberalize U.S. policy in several inter-American conferences. He held only minor advisory posts because of increasing church opposition. After World War II he interested himself in labor affairs, attacked McCarthyism, became a publisher, and championed Latin America as always.

Although his greatest influence was in reshaping Protestant missionary policy, he also promoted inter-American cooperation and became a major critic of imperialism. He vigorously advanced these goals through his teaching, publications, lectures, and personal contacts. For sixty years he was the unofficial conscience of international friendship.

BIBLIOGRAPHY:

A. *América revolucionaria; Conferencias y ensayos* (Madrid, 1933); *Building an Inter-American Neighborhood* (New York, 1937); *Democracy Versus the Totalitarian State in Latin America* (Philadelphia, 1938); "Imperialistic America," *Atlantic Monthly* 134 (Jul 1924), 107–16; *Intervention in Mexico* (New York, 1919); *Problems in Pan Americanism* (New York, 1921).

B. William J. Castleman, *On This Foundation* (St. Louis, MO, 1966); Colby D. Hall, *Texas Disciples* . . . (Fort Worth, TX, 1953); NYT 21 Feb 1965, 77; Sumner Welles, "Is America Imperialistic?" *Atlantic Monthly*, 134 (Sep 1924), 412–23; Kenneth F. Woods, "Samuel Guy Inman—His Role in the Evolution of Inter-American Cooperation," dissertation, American Univ., 1962; WWA 33, 998.

C. The Inman papers are in the Manuscript Division, Library of Congress.

Lejeune Cummins

IRWIN, William Henry (14 September 1873, Oneida, NY—24 February 1948, New York). *Education*: B.A., Stanford Univ., 1899. *Career*: editorial staff, *San Francisco Wave*, 1899–1900. *San Francisco Chronicle*, 1900–1904; reporter, *New York Sun*, 1904–6; managing editor and editor, *McClure's*, 1906–7; chair, Division of Foreign Service, Committee on Public Information, 1918; free-lance writer, 1900–1948.

The first American correspondent to arrive in Belgium after the German invasion, Irwin covered the war and its aftermath from August 1914 to mid-1920, except for a six-month break in 1918 to organize the Division of Foreign Service of the Committee on Public Information in Washington. Most of his correspondence appeared in the *New York Tribune* and *Satur-*

day Evening Post, in the United States, and in the *Times* and *Daily Mail*, in Great Britain. His dispatches were collected in three books.

In 1920 he returned to New York to crusade for international cooperation to end war and for U.S. participation in the League of Nations. The destruction of lives and property he had witnessed in France and Belgium had impressed upon him the absurdity of war. His hope that the United States could lead the world to permanent peace led to his writing *The Next War*, which foresaw many of the immense destructive forces of World War II. After promoting the League of Nations in *Collier's Weekly*, he wrote *Christ or Mars?*, in which he put his fading faith for lasting peace in Judeo-Christian religious institutions. For several years he also carried his message across the United States in lectures, until his audiences lost interest and he grew disillusioned. The signing of the UN Charter in 1945 left him with a sense of personal triumph.

Until the outbreak of World War II, Irwin also participated in the international writers' organization, PEN, serving as president of the American Center and as a delegate abroad. He was particularly concerned with freedom of information and international copyright.

BIBLIOGRAPHY:

A. *Christ or Mars?* (New York, 1923); *Herbert Hoover: A Reminiscent Biography* (New York, 1928); *The Latin at War* (New York, 1917); *The Making of a Reporter* (New York, 1942); *Men, Women and War* (London, 1915); *Propaganda and the News* (New York, 1936); *The Next War* (New York, 1921); *A Reporter at Armageddon* (New York, 1918).

B. DAB supp. 4, 417–19; *Grassroots Editor* 14 (Jul–Aug 1973), 20–22, 32; Robert V. Hudson, *The Writing Game: A Biography of Will Irwin* (Ames, IA, 1982); *The Independent* 100 (15 Nov 1919), 96; *Journalism History* 2, (Autumn 1975), 84–85, 97; *Journalism Quarterly* 47 (Summer 1970), 263–71; NYT 25 Feb 1948; *Twentieth Century Authors*, first supp. (New York, 1955); WWWA 2, 276.

Robert V. Hudson

ISHII Kikujirō (10 March 1866, Chiba, Japan—26 May 1945, Tokyo). *Education*: graduate, Tokyo Univ., 1890. *Career*: Japanese foreign ministry, 1891–1929; foreign minister, 1915–16; ambassador to France, 1912–15, 1920–27; Privy Council, 1927–45.

For over forty years Ishii was a familiar and respected representative of Japan in major capitals of the world. Though associated with European affairs throughout the greater part of his career, he is remembered most for the 1917 accommodation with the United States which bears his name. The Lansing–Ishii Agreement exemplifies Ishii's lifelong efforts to effect detente between Japan and the powers.

After graduating in law from Tokyo University, the prestigious training school for Japanese government officials, Ishii was assigned by the Foreign Ministry to Paris. In 1896 he became consul at Chemulpo, Korea, and in 1900 as first secretary of the legation in Peking survived the siege by the

Boxers. During the first decade of the century, anti-Japanese discrimination on the North American Pacific Coast was becoming increasingly irritating to Japanese sensibilities. In 1905, not coincidentally in the wake of Japan's victory over the Russian Empire, the San Francisco School Board enacted measures segregating Oriental pupils. In 1907 Ishii was sent by his government to California and British Columbia to investigate the anti-Japanese agitation there. In 1912 he secured his first prominent but brief diplomatic appointment as ambassador to France. Returning to Tokyo in 1915, Ishii assumed the foreign minister portfolio in the second Shigenobu Ōkuma Cabinet.

When the United States entered World War I, Japan sent Ishii as a special envoy to Washington, ostensibly in recognition of the new wartime partnership and to coordinate military operations but in reality to negotiate a mutual understanding of each nation's special interests in the Pacific region. The resulting Lansing–Ishii Agreement in November 1917, eliminated by negotiation on December 27, 1922, acknowledged Japan's "special interests in China" related to contiguous territory, a grudging admission by the United States which provided a holding pattern during the war. At the conferences in Paris and Washington, the American diplomatic offensive against Japanese expansionism would resume in earnest.

Not content to relinquish the issue of racial equality, Ishii campaigned during the Paris Peace Conference for the statement of nondiscrimination which Japan wanted inserted in the League of Nations Covenant. Addressing the Japan Society in New York in March 1919, he pleaded for an end to "race humiliation." His speech was greeted coldly by four Western senators, who publicly vowed to vote against a Covenant containing a racial equality guarantee, and the proposed clause did not appear.

During his second ambassadorship to France, 1920–27, he also served as Japan's chief delegate to the League of Nations. At Geneva he sat as a member of the Council, as president of the Assembly (1923), and as a rapporteur on the Council. Personally modest, patient, and courteous, he spoke not only for Japan's interests but also for those of smaller states, and his opinions usually commanded respect. He also represented Japan at the Geneva Naval Conference (1927) and the London Economic Conference (1933). Retiring from the Foreign Ministry in 1929, he published his diplomatic memoir, *Gaikō Yoroku* [Diplomatic commentaries]. He died in a firebombing of Tokyo.

BIBLIOGRAPHY:

A. *Diplomatic Commentaries*, (Baltimore, MD, 1936); *Gaikō zuisō* [Random thoughts on diplomacy] (Tokyo, 1967); "The Permanent Bases of Japanese Foreign Policy," *Foreign Affairs* 2 (Jan 1933), 220–29.

B. IWW 1937, 516; *Japan Biographical Encyclopedia* (Tokyo, 1958), 404. Frank P. Walters, *A History of the League of Nations* (Oxford, 1952).

Thomas W. Burkman

J

JACKLIN, Seymour (21 August 1882, Graaff-Reinet, South Africa—1971 Pietermaritzburg, South Africa). *Career*: officer, South African Army, World War I; Department of Finance, Pretoria, 1919–25; treasurer, League of Nations, 1926–46; member, South African permanent delegation to UN, 1946–50.

The only South African ever employed in the League Secretariat, Jacklin became treasurer in 1926. As chief financial officer, he supervised the budget, authorized payments, and invested membership contributions. He also advised on all matters involving League expenditures. In 1930 the treasurer's status within the Secretariat was raised, and Jacklin became a full section director and one of the fifteen members of the Secretariat's High Directorate. His long tenure of office is proof of his competence. Although he could have initiated or pressed for partisan expenditure policies, Jacklin remained completely neutral, as all League employees were supposed to be.

Jacklin's task became more difficult after 1929, when a growing number of states failed to pay their subscriptions. The more prosperous members resented the heavy proportion of the League's expenses they bore and constantly pressed for economies. The League's "extravagance" was frequently criticized, but Jacklin succeeded in keeping it solvent and in reducing expenditures. As an ex officio member of the Building Committee and chairman of the Contracts Committee, he was also involved in the financing of the League's large building program in Geneva in the 1930s, now UN headquarters in Europe. Late in 1940, Jacklin moved the Treasury to London via France, Morocco, and New York, with many vital League records on his person. The League's income was greatly reduced during World War II, when few members paid their contributions. However, scaled-down operations could continue because his skillful handling of League finances in former years had resulted in reserves. When the League was terminated in 1946, these were returned to the states which had provided them.

Jacklin did become involved in nonfinancial matters. The failure of League sanctions against Italy in 1936 precipitated a debate on "League reform" in which Jacklin supported proposals for a permanent military force. Though disappointed by the League's ultimate lack of effect in international affairs, Jacklin believed the work of its functional organization to have been of continuing and permanent value. He also acted several times as an unofficial link when the South African government disagreed with the Permanent Mandates Commission on the location of sovereignty in South West Africa (Namibia). In 1929–30 he was instrumental in forestalling a serious confrontation in the League Council on this important issue. When on leave in South Africa Jacklin also tirelessly promoted the League at public meetings and in press interviews. South Africa as a self-governing dominion within the British Commonwealth had been an original member of the League and closely associated with the Permanent Mandates Commission through the South West African mandate. Yet South Africans tended to be isolationist and uninterested in foreign affairs or the League. Jacklin was also known in Britain as a prominent League spokesman and expert. From 1946 to 1950 Jacklin was financial adviser to the South African permanent delegation at the United Nations.

BIBLIOGRAPHY:

B. Felix Morley, *The Society of Nations* (Washington, 1932); *Present Activities of the Secretariat* (Geneva, 1931); E. F. Ranshofen-Wertheimer, *The International Secretariat* (Washington, 1945); Frank P. Walters, *A History of the League of Nations* (London, 1952).

Sara Pienaar

JACOBSSON, Per (5 February 1894, Tanum, Sweden—5 May 1963, London). *Education*: Univ. of Uppsala. *Career*: teacher, 1918–20; staff, Economic and Financial Section, Secretariat, League of Nations, 1920–28; with Industry and Swedish Economic Defense Council, 1928–30; with Bank of International Settlements, 1930–56; managing director, International Monetary Fund, 1956–63.

In the realm of economics, Jacobsson's name is synonymous with service to two major world financial agencies, the Bank of International Settlements (BIS) and the International Monetary Fund (IMF). He began his work in the global arena at the League of Nations where he served (1920–28) on the staff of the Economic and Financial Section. While there, he became involved in several postwar reconstruction programs involving the financial stability of Austria, Hungary, Bulgaria, Greece, and the internationalized City of Danzig. Jacobsson proved to be an efficient administrator with clear views about the postwar world's economy and the wise allocation of financial resources. An essay on postwar economic problems in 1918 and one in 1929 on arms expenditures added to his stature and led to his consideration and appointment in 1930 as economic adviser and in 1931 as head of the Monetary and Economic Department of the BIS. There he oversaw the dissolution of the reparations question, sought to be a stabilizing influence as economies collapsed and nations repudiated their war debts, and tried to advise governments on financial questions, especially on the devaluation of currencies and shifts away from the gold standard. The annual reports of the BIS, which he often wrote, became an essential resource for economists, political leaders, and bankers. He also became involved after World War II in stabilizing currencies in Italy, the Netherlands, Austria, and France. In 1956, Jacobsson succeeded *Ivar Rooth as the managing director of the IMF. It had been established to promote trade and economic growth and development primarily through loans to members. He enlarged its resources and greatly expanded its loan function.

While Jacobsson enjoyed discussing economic theory, he operated with no complex formulas in mind because he was eminently practical in his approaches to the world's economy. He believed in free and relatively uncontrolled exchange of currencies and tight money policies domestically to curb inflation. The latter stood as a threat not only internally, but it also endangered international exchange by affecting the ability to repay loans, and it restricted the development everyone desired. World financial institutions were to help governments technically, provide them with economic advice, encourage free trade, help stabilize currencies, stimulate investments throughout the world, and encourage development through loans and credits from the international banks. There was no magic formula; only persistent and careful effort was needed, and by his work and often personality he proved to be an effective administrator and leader.

BIBLIOGRAPHY:

A. *The Market Economy in the World of To-day* (Philadelphia, 1961); *Monetary Improvements in Europe and Problems of a Return to Convertability* (Cairo, 1950); *Some Monetary Problems: International and National*, ed. E. E. Jucker-Fleetwood (London, 1958).

B. CB 1958, 208–10; IWW 1963–64, 489; LT 6 May 1963, 17; NYT 6 May 1963, 1; *Svenskt Biografiskt Lexicon* 20, 82–86.

Warren F. Kuehl

JAECKH, Ernst (22 February 1875, Urach, Württemberg, Germany—17 August 1959, New York). *Education*: Univs. of Stuttgart, Geneva, Breslau, and Munich; Ph.D., Heidelberg Univ., 1899. *Career*: newspaper editor, *Schwaebische Zeitungs-Korrespondent*, 1899–1902, *Neckar Zeitung*, 1902–12; lecturer and author, 1908–59; adviser to the German government at the international conferences of Versailles, Genoa, Locarno, and Geneva, 1919–31; international director, New Commonwealth Society, and publisher, *The New Commonwealth Quarterly*, 1933–39; consultant on various diplomatic missions to Near East, Middle East, Scandinavia, and Baltic regions, 1934–40; professor, Columbia Univ., 1940–42.

A confidant of twentieth-century statesmen from various nations, Jaeckh was an active political journalist and educator for over five decades. As an early follower of Friedrich Naumann and a pre–World War I National Liberal, he advocated the internal democratization of the German Empire while supporting its external expansion. Until the end of World War I, Jaeckh's public statements and published works emphasized Germany's need for a *"Weltpolitik"* and called for a German *"Mitteleuropa"* stretching from the North Sea to the Persian Gulf. In his view, this Berlin-Baghdad coalition would be built on an economic interdependence with the states of the Balkans and Near East exchanging raw materials for German finished goods. While he had not advocated war as a means to pursue either policy, he implicitly accepted war as a potential consequence of those policies. By agreeing with Alfred von Kiderlen-Waechter's assessment that Germany must support Austria in all situations, he extended that acceptance to include Austrian policy as well. Jaeckh supported Germany's role in the war and provided both propaganda and diplomatic services. Although he applauded *Woodrow Wilson's call for a league of nations in January 1918, Jaeckh was still a moderate annexationist who believed that Germany could achieve both peace and European dominance.

The combat death of his only son on the eve of the Armistice and the German defeat marked Jaeckh's transition from support of German expansionism to a belief in international cooperation and disarmament. Active in the creation of the new German Democratic party and the German League of Nations Union, he hoped his founding of the German Institute of Politics would create a forum where scholars and government officials could exchange ideas and information and hence further peace. Rather than serve Hitler, Jaeckh emigrated to England and later to the United States. In the 1930s he became a strong advocate of the New Commonwealth program of *David Davies and worked to promote its proposals for a league with force to maintain peace. The events of World War II dashed his hope that the dissemination of information would prevent conflict and promote domestic democratization. At that war's end he turned increasingly to collective security as the best means to maintain both world peace and individual rights.

Jaeckh was enthusiastic, prolific, and well meaning, but he was neither impartial nor astute in his analysis of contemporary events. His predictions were shortsighted, and many of his analyses quickly were proven faulty. His assessment of Alfred von Kiderlen-Waechter as a "second Bismarck" who could lead Germany to world power was disputed even before that statesman's death in 1912. His 1910 monograph describing the modernization of Turkey resulting from the 1908 revolution and his publications suggesting how Germany might best control the Near East were as quickly challenged and outmoded. His essays on the "New Germany" of 1926 are filled with unbridled optimism about the new spirit of democracy and stability but devoid of careful analysis of the birth of the Weimar Republic or the problems it faced. It was Germany's misfortune that voices such as Jaeckh's tended to be heard over the more guarded but more carefully reasoned tones of men such as *Johann von Bernstorff.

BIBLIOGRAPHY:

A. *Amerika und Wir 1926–1951* (Stuttgart, Germany, 1951); ed., *Background of the Middle East* (Ithaca, NY, 1952); *Der Goldene Pflug: Lebensernte eines Weltbuergers* (Stuttgart, Germany, 1954); *Der Voelkerbundgedanke in Deutschland Waehrend des Welkrieges* (Berlin, 1929); *Deutschland in Orient nach dem Balkankrieg* (Munich, 1913); *Die Deutsch-Turkische Waffenbruederschaft* (Stuttgart, Germany, 1915); *Die Politik Deutschlands in Voelkerbund* (Berlin, 1932); *Kiderlen-Waechter: Der Staatsmann und Mensch: Briefwechsel und Nachlass*, 2 vols. (Berlin, 1924); *The New Germany* (London, 1927); *The War for Men's Soul* (New York, 1943).

B. Klaus Epstein, *Matthias Erzberger and the Dilemma of German Democracy*

(Princeton, NJ, 1959); Fritz Fischer, *Germany's Aims in the First World War* (New York, 1967), *War of Illusions: German Policies from 1911 to 1914* (New York, 1975).

Martha Moore Ziegler

JENKS, Clarence Wilfred (7 March 1909, Bootle, England—9 October 1973, Rome). *Education*: B.A., Geneva School of International Studies, 1931, M.A., 1936. *Career*: member, Legal Section, International Labor Office, 1931, legal adviser, 1940, assistant director-general, 1948–64, deputy directory-general, 1964–67, principal deputy director-general, 1967–70, director-general, 1970–73; member, ILO delegation at Bretton Woods Conference, 1944, San Francisco, 1945; attended many other conferences, including Copyright, 1952, Peaceful Uses of Atomic Energy, 1955 and 1958, Law of the Sea, 1958 and 1960, Diplomatic Intercourse and Immunities, 1961, Law of Treaties, 1968; professor, Hague Academy of International Law, 1939, 1950, 1955, 1966; Cecil Peace Prize, 1928.

Jenks' contribution to international understanding was twofold and in both fields fundamental. As an international lawyer, he wrote a pioneering work on the legal problems of outer space and in various ways codified and formulated in terms of international law the development of world collaboration and social progress through the work of international institutions. In his own wide and ambitious conception, "the law must protect the common peace, must provide an orderly discipline for the relentlessness of change " (*International Labour Review*, 108 (Dec 1973), 458).

The archetype of the international official, Jenks was the first executive head of an international organization to have risen through the ranks and devoted his entire career to the service of the world community. Before becoming director-general of the International Labor Office, Jenks had been intimately involved in the development of the various activities and policies of the ILO for over four decades. During the war and the immediate postwar period, he worked in close collaboration with *Edward Phelan, who made him one of his principal advisers and who entrusted him with the responsibility of dealing with the fundamental problems facing the ILO. In 1944, when plans were being drawn for the institutional framework for postwar cooperation and the future of the ILO was at stake, Jenks and Phelan contributed to the drafting of the Declaration of Philadelphia, which set out in comprehensive and positive terms the aims and purposes of the ILO and proclaimed, in particular, the principles of freedom of association and nondiscrimination. David Morse, who became director-general in 1948, throughout his twenty-two-year term drew upon the experience and intellect of Jenks in developing many of the ILO's programs and in expanding its sphere of activities.

Jenks was one of the ILO's earliest technical cooperation experts, having undertaken an advisory mission to Venezuela in 1938. He also contributed, especially as a member of the ILO delegation at the San Francisco Conference in 1945, to the establishment and development of a close partnership among the organizations of the UN system, while safeguarding the distinctive identity of the ILO. Before becoming director-general, he had primary responsibility for the ILO's work in the field of labor standards and human rights, and he played a major role in devising the diversified machinery to ensure compliance with the agreed-upon principles. He also played an active part in the development of the ILO's regional activities in Latin America, Asia, and Africa and of its Industrial Committees.

There is no aspect of the ILO's work that does not bear the imprint of Jenks. He was one of the principal architects of the concept of an international civil service and played a leading role in drafting the language concerning the international character of the world public service contained in the UN Charter, which has since been incorporated in the constitutions of all the specialized agencies. He firmly believed in and constantly defended the twin principles on which these provisions are based: that in the performance of their duties international civil servants shall not seek or accept instructions from any government or any other authority external to the Organization and shall refrain from any action which might reflect on their position as international officials; and that each member state shall respect the exclusively international character of the responsibilities of the staff and shall not seek to influence them in the discharge of these responsibilities.

BIBLIOGRAPHY:

A. *The Common Law of Mankind* (New York, 1958); *The Headquarters of International Institutions* (London, 1945); *Human Rights and International Labour Standards* (New York, 1960); *International Immunities* (London, 1961); *The International Protection of Trade Union Freedom* (New York, 1957); *Law, Freedom and Welfare* (New York, 1963); *Law in the World Community* (London, 1967); *A New World of Law?* (Harlow, England, 1969); *The Proper Law of International Organisations* (London, 1962); *The Prospects of International Adjudication* (London, 1964); *Social Justice in the Law of Nations* (London, 1970); *Space Law* (New York, 1965); *The World Beyond the Charter* (London, 1968).

B. *British Year Book of International Law, 1972–1973* (London, 1975), xi–xxx; *International Labour Review*, 108 (Dec 1973), 455–59; LT 11 Oct 1973, 21; NYT 10 Oct 1973, 50.

Raymond Manning

JOAD, Cyril E. M. See *Biographical Dictionary of Modern Peace Leaders*.

JOHN XXIII. See *Biographical Dictionary of Modern Peace Leaders*.

JONG VAN BEEK EN DONK, B. de. See *Biographical Dictionary of Modern Peace Leaders*.

JORDAN, David Starr. See *Biographical Dictionary of Modern Peace Leaders*.

JOUHAUX Léon (1 July 1879, Paris—28 April 1954, Paris). *Education*: Ecole Colbert, Aubervilliers, France, 1891; Ecole Professionnelle Diderot, 1893; Sorbonne and Univ. Populaire at Aubervilliers. *Career*: factory worker; military service in Algiers, 1897–98; joined National Committee, Confédération Générale du Travail (CGT), 1905, secretary-general, 1909–40; member, French delegation, League of Nations, 1925–28; held in house arrest, 1941–43, at Buchenwald and elsewhere, 1943–45; joint secretary-general, CGT, 1945–47; formed non-Communist CGT–Force Ouvrière, president, 1948–54; president, Economic Council of France, 1947–54; Nobel Peace Prize, 1951.

One of the clearest expressions of Jouhaux's view of the international role of organized labor is in his Nobel lecture at Oslo, 11 December 1951. Reviewing his long and sometimes stormy career as a trade union leader, Jouhaux spoke of efforts before 1914 in various countries by himself and others to build effective working-class unity to press for disarmament and the elimination of war. Then he and the CGT had opposed secret treaties and demanded absolute respect for nationalities, arms limitations, and the compulsory arbitration of all conflicts between nations. During the war of 1914–18, in which Jouhaux strongly supported the French cause, he had urged the need for an international labor organization to work for peace through the rational organization of the world, and after the war he became active in founding and fostering the International Labor Organization (ILO). Thereafter he sat regularly as a worker representative to its governing body, where he argued for representations from nonmembers of the League. He led the powerful CGT to support collective security efforts and international economic cooperation, and, until deterred by the rise of Fascism, he continued to advocate disarmament.

In 1936, he joined with the League of Nations Union in England in organizing the French counterpart of the International Peace Campaign, which sought to rally public opinion behind the League. After World War II, Jouhaux served as a French delegate to the UN, and as president of the Economic Council of France (1947–54), he sought to advance discussions on European cooperation. He also worked to further that effort as a president of the European Movement and returned to the Governing Body of the ILO (1945–54).

In his Nobel lecture, Jouhaux did not dwell on the failure of collective security or the League in the 1930s or his own imprisonment by the Nazis but instead described postwar quests for international peace, social justice, and civil liberties. He still defended the two basic and inseparable principles of general disarmament and collective security, called on the free trade union movement to play an essential part in working for them, and reiterated the idea that economic disorder and misery were among the determinative causes of war.

BIBLIOGRAPHY:

A. *A Jean Jaurès: Discours prononcé aux obsèques de Jean Jaurès* (Paris, 1915); *Le Syndicalisme: Ce qu'il est, ce qu'il doit être* (Paris, 1937); "Fifty Years of Trade-Union Activity in Behalf of Peace," in *Nobel Lectures: Peace*, ed. Frederick W. Haberman (Amsterdam, 1972), 3: 10–29, with biography and bibliography, 30–33; *Le Désarmement* (Paris, 1927).

B. Bernard Georges and Denise Tintant, *Léon Jouhaux: Cinquante ans de syndicalisme*, 2 vols. (Paris, 1962); Tony Gray, *Champions of Peace* (Birmingham, England, 1976), 225–27; Lewis L. Lorwin, *The International Labor Movement: History, Politics, Outlook* (New York, 1953); Val R. Lorwin, "The Struggle for Control of the French Trade-Union Movement, 1945–1949," in *Modern France: Problems of the Third and Fourth Republics*, ed., Edward M. Earle (Princeton, NJ, 1951), 200–18; LT 28 Apr 1954, 8; Arno J. Mayer, *Politics and Diplomacy of Peacemaking: Containment and Counterrevolution at Versailles, 1918–1919* (New York, 1967); NYT 29 Apr 1954, 31.

Fredrick Aandahl

JOUVENEL, Henry de (2 April 1875, Paris—4 October 1935, Paris). *Education*: Ecole Stanislas, Paris. *Career*: associate editor, *Le Matin*, 1902–6, editor-in-chief, 1906–26; minister of justice, 1902; French Army, 1914–18; member, General Council, Department of Corrèze, 1920–35; senator and member of the Senate Foreign Affairs Committee, 1921–35; editor, *Revue des vivants*, 1928–35; delegate, League of Nations, various times, 1920–35; high commissioner, French Mandate of Syria and Lebanon, Beirut, 1925–26; ambassador to Rome, 1932.

After serving as an enlisted soldier in World War I, Jouvenel concluded that the highest cause people could serve and the greatest heritage they could leave their children was international peace. Jouvenel, therefore, used the remainder of his career to promote peace and cooperation. He wrote editorials and books espousing these ideals and accepted every opportunity to translate them into action. As a result, Jouvenel participated in several major international events of the interwar period. As a member of the French delegation to the League of Nations, he negotiated the entry of Ethiopia and actively supported Germany's admission because he believed that peace would not be possible until every nation was equally represented in that international body. Similarly, as a French senator, he supported the French left's demand for recognition of the Soviet Union and the right's drive for recognition of the Vatican. At the League, he appended the clause on mutual security to the disarmament agreement of 1922 because he believed that nations would more readily honor such an agreement if their integrity were guaranteed by the community of nations as a whole. As high commissioner of the French Mandate in Syria and Lebanon, Jouvenel concluded treaties and agreements with the countries surrounding the mandate and negotiated continuously with the British to secure the boundaries of the future states.

Jouvenel eschewed the imperialism of the West, arguing instead that all nations were equal and that the West, which had achieved a dominant position because of a technological edge, had a moral obligation to share its technology with the rest of the world. His conviction that differences between nations could best be resolved at conference tables, not on the field of battle, led him in 1932 to represent France in the negotiations for the Four Power Pact with Mussolini. Jouvenel hoped this accord would strengthen the League and prevent Europe from dividing into two armed camps.

Unfortunately, like so many internationalists of the era, Jouvenel saw his work thwarted by the political realities of the time. His successes in the Middle East were overshadowed by the drama surrounding the Locarno Treaties. Without the pressure of world opinion for support, Jouvenel's efforts on behalf of Syrian and Lebanese autonomy were twisted into a means of perpetuating empire. An even greater irony occurred two days before Jouvenel's death, when Mussolini invaded Ethiopia. The nation with which Jouvenel had negotiated the Four Power Pact violated the state he had guided into the League, and the League of Nations did not activate the guarantees of Jouvenel's mutual security clause.

Throughout these fifteen years of political activity on behalf of international cooperation, Jouvenel actively promoted internationalism in editorials and popular writings. His book, *La Paix française, témoignage d'une génération*, is a contemporary analysis of the internationalism of his generation, which having witnessed the collapse of world order in World War I believed that peace and international cooperation were essential to the survival of Western civilization.

BIBLIOGRAPHY:

A. *Huit cents ans de révolution française 897–1789* (Paris, 1932); *La Paix française, témoignage d'une génération* (Paris, 1932); articles in *Revues des vivants* (1926–1935); editorials in *Le Matin* (Paris) and the *Telegraaf* (Amsterdam).

B. Rudolph Binion, *Defeated Leaders* (New York, 1960); René François, "Historique de la mission de M. Henry de Jouvenel en Syrie et au Liban," manuscript, 1926; Joyce Miller, "Henry de Jouvenel and the Syrian Mandate," dissertation, Bryn Mawr Coll., 1970.

Joyce Laverty Miller

K

KEEN, Frank Noel (3 November 1869, London—30 April 1957, London).
Education: Institute of Chartered Accountants, 1892; LL.B., London
Univ., 1897. *Career*: barrister until 1954.

Early training in accounting and the law led Keen to develop an interest in
social questions and ultimately into a broader concern for the future of
mankind. During the first decade of the twentieth century, as a result of his
parliamentary and legal contacts, he compiled and published from acts of
Parliament provisions relating to such subjects as tramway companies and
local authorities; markets, fairs, and slaughter houses; urban police and
sanitation; and local legislation in general.

During the early stages of World War I, Keen became involved with those
ardent spirits organizing the League of Nations Society. In 1917 at the annual meeting of this organization he joined other internationalists in the
Bryce Group to arrive at some specific objectives. But according to the
movement's historian, Henry Winkler, each leader "had a favoured idea,
or a particular emphasis which he considered imperative, but which the
others looked upon with indifference" (*League of Nations Movement in
Great Britain, 1914-1919*).

Such organizational matters, often involving legalistic distinctions, was a
specialty of Keen and probably constituted, through his many books, his
major contribution to the movement. In *The World in Alliance* (1915) he
outlined the challenge of how to prohibit war. Then, drawing from English
constitutional traditions and encouraged by various prewar experiments in
international cooperation, he espoused the establishment of an international parliament, a binding law code, and administrative machinery
capable of enforcement. This body would have the power not only to settle
disputes but also to infringe on national sovereignties and even alter boundaries if necessary to preserve peace. In 1917 Keen described the precise
techniques whereby international law might be developed in *Hammering
Out the Details*. He now envisioned a central international conference as a
legislative organ attended by the most eminent statesmen of the constituent
states. During the interwar period he supported the League of Nations concept and argued continuously in his publications for an expansion of its
powers. Despite its abject failure in the 1930s and another world war, Keen
remained undaunted in his quest for peace. In *The Abolition of War*, written just after his retirement, he warned of the danger of a third world war
fought with nuclear weapons. In the new United Nations he perceived many
of the same organizational weaknesses from which the League had suffered.
Again drawing from English parliamentary practice Keen advocated a
world parliament unencumbered by an unanimity rule or veto powers
among nations. Notwithstanding his detailed plans and sincerity, Keen's ap-

proach was always too mechanical and failed to consider adequately implementation or the passions that lead to war.

BIBLIOGRAPHY:

A. *The Abolition of War* (London, 1955); *A Better League of Nations* (London, 1934); *Crossing the Rubicon* (Birmingham, England, 1939); *The Duties of Nations* (London, 1922); *The Future Development of International Law* (London, 1944); *Hammering Out the Details* (London, 1917); *A League of Nations with Large Powers* (London, 1918); *The Permanent Court of International Justice* (London, 1922); *Real Security Against War* (London, 1929); *Towards International Justice* (London, 1923); *The World in Alliance* (London, 1915); *World Legislation* (London, 1931).

B. LT 2 May 1957, 15; Henry R. Winkler, *The League of Nations Movement in Great Britain, 1914–1919* (New Brunswick, NJ, 1952); WWW 195-60, 604.

C. The Keen papers are at the London School of Economics and Political Science.

John D. Fair

KELLOGG, Frank Billings (22 December 1856, Potsdam, NY—21 December 1937, St. Paul, MN). *Education*: passed Minnesota bar, 1877. *Career*: attorney, Rochester, MN, St. Paul, MN, 1877–1917, 1923; special assistant attorney general of United States, 1906; president, American Bar Association, 1912; Republican senator, 1917–23; ambassador to Great Britain, 1923–25; secretary of state, 1925–29; judge, Permanent Court of International Justice, 1930–35; Nobel Peace Prize, 1929.

During the decade following the Great War, the United States traveled turning and twisting paths toward peace. After briefly considering membership in the League of Nations and adherence to the World Court, testing various disarmament formulae, and negotiating numerous bilateral arbitration and conciliation treaties, the United States in 1928 guided the major states toward a grand scheme to renounce war as national policy. Kellogg played a significant role in each of these diplomatic efforts to abolish "the scourge of war."

World War I was the major turning point in Kellogg's life. After a lengthy and distinguished legal career, in 1917 Kellogg shifted from lawyer to statesman (he disdained the word "politician"), serving as senator, ambassador, and secretary of state. In Kellogg's mind, the Great War became a fiery furnace which tempered the American spirit and stirred the American people with "the patriotism of peace." Additionally, the war helped Kellogg discover his mission in life: to substitute law for force in international relations. European history revealed the folly of depending upon "primitive methods" for keeping peace, like armed alliances, the balance of power, and heavy armaments. The time was right to guarantee security and stability through mutual consideration and the peaceful settlement of disputes. By his own reckoning, Kellogg was neither a dreamer nor an advocate of perfection. Rather he was a man of vision—a cautious optimist—who believed that humankind could attain peace by a gradual movement over time.

In his work for peace, Kellogg was motivated by abhorrence of war and faith in law. A cautious internationalist by philosophy, Kellogg objected to American entanglement with Europe and the implementation of military sanctions against violators of treaties and laws. In place of these traditional methods of keeping peace, Kellogg favored moral sanctions, especially the force of public opinion. In 1918 to support the League of Nations and in 1928 to defend the Pact of Paris—at both ends of his decade for peacekeeping—Kellogg argued that peace could be preserved by an honest public sentiment and the good faith of nations.

Kellogg urged patience in the quest for peace, contending again and again that time could heal wounds and solve problems. Therefore, he advocated a gradual, step-by-step program. That approach appeared in his support of membership in the League of Nations with only mild reservations, and his advocacy of harmony during the Senate's debates revealed that Kellogg was not a blind partisan. Kellogg then promoted disarmament accords as a "practical approach," and he tried to incorporate law into international politics by negotiating nineteen arbitration and thirteen conciliation agreements while secretary of state. Finally, in keeping with his gradualist philosophy, Kellogg took the giant step in the Pact of Paris, by which signatories pledged to renounce war as an instrument of national policy and to settle all disputes by pacific means.

Kellogg viewed the antiwar agreement as a primary first step, a sign and symbol of the major nations moving to be governed by principles of law in their relations with one another. Only educated and honest public sentiment—not military machinery—would enforce the treaty; the same public opinion that had inspired the agreement would guarantee its success. There could be no greater power of enforcement. In his position on sanctions, he clearly rejected emerging collective security principles in favor of prewar internationalist thinking, which endorsed evolutionary and voluntary programs of cooperation. By his own standards, then, the Kellogg-Briand Pact was a fitting climax to his quest for peace.

BIBLIOGRAPHY:

A. "The American Policy in China," *Review of Reviews* 75 (Mar 1927), 269–71; "The Renunciation of War," *Review of Reviews* 78 (Dec 1928), 595–601.

B. David Bryn-Jones, *Frank B. Kellogg: A Biography* (New York, 1937); DAB supp. 2, 355–57; L. Ethan Ellis, *Frank B. Kellogg and American Foreign Relations, 1925–1929* (New Brunswick, NJ, 1961); Robert H. Ferrell, "Frank B. Kellogg," in Robert H. Ferrell and Samuel F. Bemis, eds., *The American Secretaries of State and Their Diplomacy*, Vol. 11 (New York, 1963) 1–136; NYT 22 Dec 1937, 1.

C. The Kellogg papers are in the Minnesota State Historical Society Library.

Stephen J. Kneeshaw

KELLOGG, Paul Underwood. See *Biographical Dictionary of Modern Peace Leaders.*

KELLOR, Frances Alice (20 October 1873, Columbus, OH—4 January 1952, New York). *Education*: LL.B., Cornell Law School, 1897; Univ. of Chicago, 1898–1904; New York Summer School of Philanthropy, 1902. *Career*: sociologist and social reformer, New York and Chicago, 1902–8; New York State Immigration Commission, 1908–10; director, New York State Bureau of Industries and Immigration, 1910–13; vice-chair, Committee for Immigrants in America, 1913–18; director, Inter-Racial Council, 1918–20; arbitration official and author, first vice-president, American Arbitration Association, 1926–52.

A younger contemporary of Jane Addams and ⁺Lillian Wald, Kellor was a major figure in the progressive movement's exposé of the economic exploitation of new European immigrants and Southern black migrants working in Northern cities. A result of her research was *Out of Work* (1904; rev. ed. 1915), one of the first scholarly works on the ethnic and social problems underlying unemployment in the United States. In 1906, with Mary Dreier and Mary White Ovington, she founded the National League for the Protection of Colored Women, which in 1911 joined with three other organizations to create the National Urban League. Her work came to the attention of New York Governor *Charles Evans Hughes and President *Theodore Roosevelt and led to her appointment and eventual leadership of various New York State and federal commissions and bureaus concerned with the problems of the education, training, and employment of immigrants. These assignments enlarged her knowledge and understanding of various national and ethnic groups.

Anti-immigrant sentiment in America during World War I and the isolationist response to the League of Nations deepened Kellor's interest in international problems. After World War I she spent time in Europe studying the economic and diplomatic aspects of the peace settlement. She became a staunch but critical and objective supporter of the League of Nations and the World Court. In *Security Against War* (1924), and *The United States Senate and the International Court* (1925), Kellor advocated the settlement of international disputes through arbitration and cited the bypassing of the World Court as a major reason for the failure of the League of Nations.

As author of the code of practices and procedures of the American Arbitration Association (AAA) she was convinced that successful methods from the field of industrial arbitration could bring efficiency, order, and justice to the resolution of international problems. Although critical of what she viewed as the coercive use of power under the New Deal, the value of her work in arbitration was recognized by both Frances Perkins as labor secretary and *Franklin D. Roosevelt. As a member of the Pan American Union she promoted arbitration and better economic relations between North and South America. In 1944 the Commission to Study the Organization of Peace and the AAA published her major work (with Martin Domke) *Arbitration in International Controversy*. Her efforts led to the decision by eleven national governments to adopt the code and rules of the AAA and to the wider use of arbitration in international commerce. Kellor's writings and public service represents a major pioneering effort in the development of both the theory and practice of international arbitration.

BIBLIOGRAPHY:

A. ed., *Code of Arbitration: Practice and Procedures* (New York, 1931); *Experimental Sociology: Descriptive and Analytical* (New York, 1901); *Security Against War* (New York, 1924); with A. Hatvany, *The United States Senate and the International Court* (New York, 1925).

B. AAA, *Arbitration News* 10 (1953); DAB supp. 5, 380–81; Edward Hartmann, *The Movement to Americanize the Immigrant* (New York, 1948); John Higham, *Strangers in the Land* (New Brunswick, NJ, 1955); Gerd Korman, *Industrialization, Immigrants and Americanizers* (Madison, WI, 1967); William J. Maxwell, "Frances Kellor in the Progressive Era: A Case Study in the Professionalization of Reform" (dissertation, Columbia Univ., 1968); NAW 1, 393–95; NYT 5 Jan 1952, 11; Gilbert Osofsky, *Harlem: The Making of a Ghetto* (New York, 1966); WWWA 3, 468.

William J. Maxwell

KELSEN, Hans (11 October 1881, Prague—19 April 1973, Berkeley, CA). *Education*: doctor of law, Univ. of Vienna, 1906; Univs. of Heidelberg and Berlin. *Career*: assistant professor, Univ. of Vienna, 1911–17, professor, 1919–29; judge and permanent counselor, Austrian Constitutional Court, 1920–29; professor, Univ. of Cologne, 1929–33, Univ. of Geneva, 1933–36, Univ. of Prague, 1936–38, Harvard Law School, 1940–43, Univ. of California, Berkeley, 1943–73; adviser, War Crimes Commission and United Nations.

Perhaps the twentieth century's most brilliant legal philosopher and authority on international law, Kelsen was born of lower middle-class Jewish parents but was well educated and earned a high reputation as a professor and legal scholar. Following the collapse of the Habsburg monarchy at the end of World War I, Kelsen was engaged to draft a republican constitution for the new state of Austria, a document whose basic forms and legal force are still intact. Forced into exile by the Nazis, he moved to the United States in 1940.

Kelsen is best known as author of the positivist "pure theory of law," first presented in his fundamental treatise, *Hauptprobleme der Staatsrechtslehre* (1910), and elaborated in his *Reine Rechtslehre* (1934) and other works. To Kelsen, the philosophy of law was a purely formal discipline whose purpose is to clarify the logical relationships that exist within legal systems between the "basic norm" (*Grundnorm*, or initial hypothesis), which is the foundation of any given system of law, and all positive laws within that system. The basic norm does not entail a moral evaluation of subordinate laws and norms but rather their formal logical consistency in relation to the basic norm itself. In this way Kelsen sought to propose a theory that would be applicable to all systems of law irrespective of the variances of culture and moral belief, and thereby to eliminate the distinction he regarded as fruitless between "positive law" and "natural law." As long as any given law is consistent with its basic norm, it has legal force and should be obeyed.

The "pure theory" logically applied to the international realm. Here Kelsen argued that the force of law derives from the consistency with which its rules conform to the basic norm or norms of the overall system. All legal systems, including those of sovereign nations, are rooted in such norms. There is a hierarchy of values expressed in law embracing the lowliest local statute or custom, the positive laws of sovereign nation-states, and the overarching norms of the law of nations. The binding force of treaties, for example, obtains from a common acceptance of the purposes they serve. Likewise, the subordination of national interest to international custom and order, though not perfect or without conflicting interests, bespeaks the universal recognition of a higher norm. Kelsen believed so strongly in legal solutions to problems that he saw a court with unlimited jurisdiction as the core of any world system. He attracted enthusiastic disciples as well as critics.

BIBLIOGRAPHY:

A. *Allgemeine Staatslehre* (Berlin, 1925); *Das Problem der Souveranität und die Theorie des Völkerrechts* (Tübingen, Germany, 1920); *General Theory of Law and State* (Cambridge, MA, 1946); *Hauptprobleme der Staatsrechtslehre* (Tübingen, Germany, 1910); *The Law of the United Nations* (New York, 1950); *Peace Through Law* (Chapel Hill, NC, 1944); *Principles of International Law* (New York, 1952); A list of over 600 of Kelsen's publications appears in A. J. Merkl and others, eds., *Festschrift für Hans Kelsen zum 90, Geburtstag* (Vienna, 1971), 325-26; and in R. A. Métall, *Hans Kelsen: Leben und Werk* (Vienna, 1969), 122-55; *Pure Theory of Law* (Indianapolis, IN, 1934); *Society and Nature* (Chicago, 1943); *Vom Wesen und Wert der Demokratie* (Tübingen, Germany, 1920).

B. AJIL 67 (1973), 491-501; A list of over 1,100 works dealing with Kelsen and his thought can be found in Métall, *Hans Kelsen*, 162-216. See also Merkl and others, eds., *Festschrift für Hans Kelsen; Neue deutsche Biographie 11* (Berlin, 1977), 479-80; *Neue österreichische Biographie ab 1815 20* (Vienna, 1979) 29-39.

C. The Kelsen papers are at the Hans Kelsen Institut, Vienna.

Richard R. Laurence

KESSLER, Harry Klemens Ulrich (23 May 1868, Paris—2 December 1937, Lyon). *Education*: studied law and art history, Univs. of Bonn and Leipzig, 1888-91. *Career*: coeditor, *Pan*, 1895-1900; curator, Weimar Museum, 1902-6; founder, Cranach Press, Weimar, 1913; officer, German Army, 1914-16; diplomatic officer, Bern, 1916-18; minister to Poland, 1918-21; member, delegation, Genoa Conference, 1922; consul-general, Petrograd, 1922-23; coeditor, *Die Deutsche Nation*, 1923-33; president, Deutsche Friedensgesellschaft; cofounder, *Freien Worts*, 1932; free-lance writer, 1933-37.

It was the *Richtlinien fuer einen wahren Voelkerbund*, published in 1921, that made Kessler a leading spokesman promoting the cause of internationalism. In these guidelines he contended that the League of Nations should deal with human and not just juridicial concerns. It should not be a body composed merely of political entities that were by nature rivals; rather, it should be one which reflected those major economic and humanitarian interests that inherently tended toward internationalism. Groups such as international labor organizations, international trading and raw materials federations, and international banking consortiums should be furnished with power and sanctions against political entities so that in time they would become legally independent of individual states. Kessler asserted, therefore, that a set of rules was necessary rather than an organization and rules which gave the great powers an even greater ascendancy than in the past.

The implementation of his ideas was virtually impossible in a world of nation-states reluctant to yield any sovereignty. Nevertheless, Kessler took the lead in bringing Germany into the League, and he also served as head of the German branch of the League of Nations Union. But by then his attitude about the League was realistic. In a 1923 paper, he allowed that, however close separate states might be, their problems and difficulties required, in addition to good will, permanent accords removed as fully as possible from politics. Kessler concluded that whatever its failings, the League at least was conceived as a lasting agreement. It provided Europe the first real opportunity to solve its basic problems.

During the mid-1920s, Kessler traveled much to proselytize for his cause. Again and again, he returned to his theme that the war had poisoned "the moral atmosphere" of nations; in Germany's case this had been compounded by the injustices of the Treaty of Versailles, especially the incredibly heavy reparations payments. It was not long, however, before Kessler was horrified by the jingoistic nationalism of the Nazis. He viewed Hitler as a serious threat not only to German tranquility but also to world peace. The day of the Reichstag elections, 5 March 1933, Kessler left Germany permanently. Thereafter he devoted himself to writing his memoirs.

BIBLIOGRAPHY:

A. *Germany and Europe* (New Haven, CT, 1923); *In the Twenties: The Diaries of Harry Kessler* (London, 1971); *Krieg und Zusammenbruch* (Weimar, Germany, 1921); *Richtlinien fuer einen wahren Voelkerbund* (Stuttgart, Germany, 1921); *Walther Rathenau: His Life and Work* (New York, 1930).

B. *Der Grosse Brockhaus* 6 (Weisbaden, 1955), 354; *Deutscher Literatur-Lexikon* 2 (Weisbaden, 1955), 1259; NYT 3 Dec 1937, 23; *Kuerschners Deutscher Literatur-Kalendar Nekrolog 1936–1970* (Berlin, 1973), 336; Renate Mueller-Krumbach, *Harry Graf Kessler und die Cranach-Presse in Weimar* (Hamburg, Germany, 1969); *Neu deutsche Biographie* 11 (Berlin, 1977), 545–46.

C. The Kessler papers are in the Deutsches Literaturarchiv.

Werner E. Braatz

KEY, Ellen. See *Biographical Dictionary of Modern Peace Leaders.*

KEYNES, John Maynard (5 June 1883, Cambridge—21 April 1946, Firle, Sussex, England). *Education*: B.A., King's Coll., Cambridge Univ., 1905. *Career*: official, India Office, 1906–8; lecturer, Cambridge Univ., 1908–20; fellow, King's Coll., Cambridge Univ., 1909–46; editor, *Economic Journal*, 1911–45; member, Royal Commission on Indian Finance and Currency, 1913–14; Treasury official, 1915–19; principal representative of Treasury, Paris Peace Conference, 1919; member, Committee on Finance and Industry, 1929–31; member, Economic Advisory Council, 1931–39; adviser, Chancellor of the Exchequer, 1940–46.

Although best known for his theory relating to the management of national economies with the goal of maintaining high levels of employment and output, Keynes's contributions to internationalism as an economist, publicist, and negotiator are as important and as lasting. Many of his contributions lay in the area of promoting a greater understanding of underlying economic forces to enable governments to manage their affairs more effectively and thus increase levels of well-being.

Throughout his career, Keynes attempted to promote international monetary arrangements that would foster trade and accumulation. He was one of the first economists to analyze the workings of the then new gold standard, whereby smaller countries maintained fixed exchange rates by buying and selling foreign balances through an international financial center, thus economizing on the use of gold for monetary purposes. Then, as a publicist and member of a royal commission, he succeeded in shaping a report which recommended changes in India's monetary arrangements to allow the gold exchange standard to operate efficiently. From the late 1920s, he developed the view that the international monetary system would work more effectively if an international institution would supplement national holdings of international reserves and adjust its policies to control the growth of international liquidity. Then came persuasion, most notably in *A Treatise on Money* (1930), again with success, first in the Committee on Economic Information of the Economic Advisory Council, which pressed for the inclusion of his and Hubert Henderson's scheme for an international note issue as one of the British proposals for the 1933 World Economic Conference. The theme appeared again in his *Proposals for an International Clearing Union* (1941–43) which, with a U.S. plan for an international stabilization fund, formed the basis for the International Monetary Fund at Bretton Woods in 1944.

Nor did Keynes's involvement end with currency schemes. Although he substantially modified his earlier unqualified support of free trade in favor of some degree of national self-sufficiency, he remained a powerful advocate of the advantages of liberal multilateral trading arrangements for the post–World War II economy, and he saw his monetary proposals (as well as his scheme for stabilizing the prices of primary products) as an essential prerequisite for freer trade. Also, after both wars he supported deliberate planning for financing postwar reconstruction to restore the world economy. In 1919 his proposals, although adopted by the British government, foundered on American opposition, but during World War II he played a creative role in establishing the UN Relief and Rehabilitation Administration and the International Bank for Reconstruction and Development.

During both wars, Keynes's service as a Treasury official and adviser saw him extensively involved in shaping Britain's external financial policies and negotiating with allies and neutrals. While an articulate defender of Britain's long-term interests, he was ever willing to give ground when persuaded that yielding would favor the more general international interest. Both wars also saw him heavily involved in discussions preceding financial settlements with the former enemies. He always took a moderate position on the postwar treatment of Germany, arguing that an economically strong and vigorous Germany was essential for the prosperity of Europe, and that was the best guarantee of political stability and resistance to Communism. When in May 1919 his advice was ignored as the Allies demanded large reparations from Germany in violation, so he believed, of the original Armistice agreement, Keynes resigned his Treasury position. In the ensuing months he produced his protest, *The Economic Consequences of the Peace* (1919), a brilliant polemical indictment of the immorality, injustice, and unwisdom of the peace treaty. This book, quickly translated into a dozen languages, made Keynes an international figure. It and other hard-hitting studies influenced the attitudes of a generation and created a climate sympathetic toward treaty revision and the appeasement of Germany. It also played a role, undesired by Keynes, in encouraging American isolationism, and he determined to prevent its recurrence through his World War II schemes for postwar international economic cooperation.

BIBLIOGRAPHY:

A. *The Collected Writings of John Maynard Keynes*, 30 vols. (London, 1971–); *The Economic Consequences of the Peace* (London, 1919); *The General Theory of Employment, Interest and Money* (London, 1936); *Indian Currency and Finance* (London, 1913); *The Means to Prosperity* (London, 1933); *Proposals for an International Clearing Union* (London, 1943); *A Revision of the Treaty* (London, 1922); *A Tract on Monetary Reform* (London, 1923); *A Treatise on Money*, 2 vols. (London, 1930).

B. W. M. Keynes, ed., *Essays on John Maynard Keynes* (Cambridge, 1975); R. F. Harrod, *The Life of John Maynard Keynes* (London, 1951); E.A.G. Robinson, "John Maynard Keynes, 1883–1946," *Economic Journal* 57 (Mar 1947), 1–68.

C. The Keynes papers are at King's Coll., Cambridge Univ., the Marshall Library of Economics, Cambridge Univ., and the Public Record Office in London.

D. E. Moggridge

KIMBALL, Chase (20 January 1902, Waterbury, CT—4 June 1977, Milton, MA). *Education*: B.A., Yale Coll., 1925; LL.B., Yale Law School,

1928; M.A., Yale Univ., 1947; Ph.D., Fletcher School of Law and Diplomacy, 1955. *Career*: attorney, 1930–42; war claims arbiter, 1928–30; trust officer, Waterbury, CT, National Bank, 1931–42; U.S. Army, 1942–46; taught at Univ. of Denver, 1947, Boston Univ., 1947–53, Univ. of Hartford, 1959–60, Assumption Coll., 1960–61, Suffolk Univ., 1961–73.

Dedicated volunteers have been the backbone of peace and internationalist efforts. During the 1930s no person in Connecticut was more generous with time, energy, and money in those causes than Kimball. From 1931 until the start of World War II, this wealthy young bachelor devoted evenings, weekends, and vacations almost exclusively to them. He was the largest single contributor to the League of Nations Association in Connecticut, the group's most adroit fund-raiser, and a generous financial backer of many peace organizations, including ones whose programs he disliked. At one time or another, he held office in every major peace society in the state, participated in conferences in and outside of Connecticut, spoke frequently (forty times to church groups in support of the peace ballot during a two-month interval in 1935), conducted for two years a weekly radio program dealing with foreign policy on a Waterbury station, traveled to Europe nine times to study political conditions, and corresponded extensively with almost every major peace figure in the country.

His philosophical position was right of center. A pro-business Republican, Kimball put his faith in international law, which he saw as analogous to the U.S. Constitution, to maintain world order. He believed that law to be effective must have adequate sanctions, and thus he supported the role of the United States as an international policeman. He was an early and vocal advocate of economic sanctions against Italy, Germany, and Japan. The pacifists within the Connecticut peace movement like +Devere Allen, Kimball freely admitted, were persons he abhorred as much as isolationists.

Kimball revealed traits that were a source both of strength and weakness for his causes. Inherited wealth and established family gave him independence and security. From his father, Arthur Kimball, the Mudwump editor of the *Waterbury American*, he learned that a gentleman must participate in public affairs, and experiences at the Taft School and Yale reinforced this sense of noblesse oblige. A devout Congregationalist, he often described his activity in evangelical terms, once referring to himself as an amateur missionary. While producing confidence and commitment, these attitudes made Kimball opinionated and elitist, and his antilabor, anti-Catholic, and anti-immigrant prejudices made it difficult for him to reach the bulk of Connecticut's population.

After military service in World War II, Kimball left Waterbury and the legal profession for an academic career. After earning a Ph.D., he spent twenty-five productive years as a professor of international relations specializing in international organizations. Until his death, he retained his faith that international government provided the only hope of avoiding another major war.

BIBLIOGRAPHY:

B. Herbert Janick, "An Instructive Failure: The Connecticut Peace Movement, 1919-1939," *Peace and Change* 5 (Spring 1978), 12-22.

C. The Kimball papers are at Yale Univ.

Herbert Janick

KING, William Lyon MacKenzie (17 December 1874, Berlin (Kitchener), ON—22 July 1950, Kingsmere, QU). *Education*: B.A., Univ. of Toronto, 1895, LL.B., 1896, M.A., 1897; M.A., Harvard Univ., 1898, Ph.D., 1909. *Career*: deputy minister of labor, 1900-1908; member of Parliament, 1908-48; minister of labor, 1909-11; secretary of state for external affairs, 1921-30, 1935-46; prime minister, 1921-30, 1935-48; member, Council of League of Nations, 1928-36; head, Canadian delegations to Imperial Conferences, 1923, 1926, 1937, San Francisco Conference, 1945, Paris Peace Conference, 1946; delegate, UN General Assembly, 1948.

King was a practical politician, a dedicated liberal with a keenly developed liberal's sense of social and political justice, and a Canadian nationalist. He can be thought of as an internationalist only to the extent that internationalism suited these higher purposes. Yet, much of what he achieved can be considered as internationalism. He was perhaps as influential as anyone in defining the British Commonwealth, and no one worked harder to give it meaning. He led Canada into wholehearted collaboration with Britain in World War II despite domestic political obstacles. He brought Canada into a close economic and military relationship with the United States during the war and continued to foster it afterward.

King's first concern, however, was the independence of his country. The Commonwealth in his mind was always a voluntary association of free states. He had as strong an emotional attachment to the United States as to Great Britain, but he was forever wary and suspicious of U.S. policy. Always alive to the dangers of dominance, he came to feel that the United States was using the United Nations simply as a tool of its own policy, and he became fearful of what seemed to him to be the excessive zeal of his own Bureau of External Affairs in its pursuit of an American connection. One of the strands of his own postwar policy was to use the United States as a device to get Canada international recognition commensurate with her wartime contribution.

Canada under King's leadership was active in the League of Nations and the United Nations, but he seems to have held both bodies in modest regard. He initially expressed favorable opinions but by the 1930s came to doubt the League's usefulness. He opposed any kind of sanctions at Geneva and openly expressed his belief that the League should become simply an organ of conciliation. That position in the 1930s aroused critics who had remained firm in their support. The danger with the United Nations in his view was that its decisions were made by men with great power and no responsibility. Despite his international involvements, he retained his isolationist perspective. In 1947 he echoed in his diary a view he had expressed in 1927, that Canada should be careful about its role in world affairs.

BIBLIOGRAPHY:

A. *Canada at Britain's Side* (Toronto, 1941); *Industry and Humanity* (Boston, 1918).

B. *Encyclopedia Canadiana* 5 (Toronto, 1977), 405–9; J. W. Pickersgill and D. F. Forster, eds. *The MacKenzie King Record*, 4 vols. (Toronto, 1960–70); NYT 23 Jul 1950, C. P. Stacey, *Canada and the Age of Conflict: A History of Canadian External Policies: Volume II, 1921–1948. The Mackenzie King Era* (Toronto, 1981); Richard Veatch, *Canada and the League of Nations* (Toronto, 1975); WWWA 3, 478.

Douglas W. Houston

KIRCHWEY, George Washington. See *Biographical Dictionary of Modern Peace Leaders.*

KIRK, Peter Michael (18 May 1928,—17 April 1977, Essex). *Education*: Oxford Univ. and Univ. of Zurich. *Career*: reporter, editor, and foreign correspondent, *Sunday Times*; member of Parliament, 1955–64, 1965–77; British delegate, Assembly of Council of Europe; parliamentary under secretary of state for the Army, 1963–64; delegate, Council of Europe, 1956–63, 1966–70; sat in Assembly of Western European Union, 1970; parliamentary under secretary of state for the Navy, 1970–72; head, first delegation of British Conservatives to European Parliament, 1973.

Kirk's tireless activity on behalf of Western European unity was, in all likelihood, chiefly responsible for his untimely death from heart failure at the age of forty-eight. A journalist, politician, and member of two Conservative British governments, Kirk was a multitalented individual equally at home making a television documentary or promoting the interests of his constituents. Britain's role in a united Western Europe, however, was his foremost concern. Unlike most members of the Conservative party, Kirk very early recognized the importance of strong European federal institutions. He saw the need for Britain to join the European Economic Community (EEC) when that position was unpopular in his country.

Kirk was an enthusiastic participant in the assemblies of the Council of Europe and the Western European Union. He chaired the General Affairs Committee of the Western European Union (1960–63), the Political Committee of the Council of Europe (1969–70), and the Budget Committee of the Western European Union (1967–69). He maintained his support even though these two forums did not develop into limited decision-making bodies, as Kirk and his fellow "Europeans" originally had hoped. He felt that the EEC's popular assembly, the European Parliament, offered the best means to provide some democratic control over Community decision making, which was dominated by the EEC member governments. His reputation as a "European" and his fluency in several languages made him a natural appointee to the European Parliament when Britain joined the EEC in January 1973.

The addition of the Conservatives to the Community's Assembly generated much publicity. It was anticipated that, as members of the British Parliament, the new delegation would suggest ways to make the EEC body more than the talking shop it had been for two decades. Since its creation as the Common Assembly of the European Coal and Steel Community in 1952, the Parliament had tried unsuccessfully to get the EEC governments to agree to allow it some budgetary and legislative powers and to hold elections to select its membership.

In his maiden speech before the European Parliament, Kirk caused a stir when he called for procedural reforms to make the EEC body more like its distant British cousin. He was outspokenly critical of the low-key, European style of debate. He subsequently outlined his proposals in the twenty-two-page "Kirk Memorandum"; the report called for rules to cut off debates, a "question time" to enable Parliament members to make EEC Commission members more accountable for their actions, a procedure for holding emergency debates, and a more effective committee structure.

Although some of these innovations were implemented, by 1974 the steam had gone out of the British delegation's drive to mold the European Parliament into what its name implied. Never in favor of strong EEC institutions, Britain and France were opposed to strengthening the Parliament's powers and to holding European elections. Other EEC members also had little enthusiasm for altering the status quo. Despite these setbacks, Kirk continued his strenuous duties as member of both the British and European parliaments. He also continued to criticize the EEC governments for impeding economic and political integration and for usurping what limited power the EEC Commission possessed. For his contribution to the cause of Western European unity, Kirk received a knighthood in 1976. He maintained, despite all obstacles, that European elections would be a reality soon. He surely would have been a candidate when the elections were held in June 1979 had not his early death deprived him of this longed-for achievement.

BIBLIOGRAPHY:

A. With Christopher Soames and John Davies, *Three Views of Europe* (London, 1973.

B. *Cassell's Parliamentary Directory* (London, 1974), 47; European Parliament Debates (Strasburg, Jan 1973); LT 11 Feb 1977, 8, 18 Apr 1977, 1; IWW 1977–78, 897; Paula Scalingi, *The European Parliament: The Three-Decade Search for a United Europe* (Westport, CT, 1980).

Paula Scalingi

KISCH, Cecil Hermann (21 March 1884—20 October 1961, England). *Education*: grad., Trinity Coll., Oxford Univ., 1905, Lit. Hum., 1907. *Career*: General Post Office, 1907; India Office, 1908; private secretary to permanent under secretary of state, 1911, to parliamentary undersecretary of state, 1915, to secretary of state for India, 1917–19; secretary, Financial Department, India Office, 1921–33; deputy director-general, Petroleum Department, 1939–42; assistant under secretary of state for India, 1933–43; deputy under secretary of state for India, 1943–46.

Kisch followed in the footsteps of his father, Hermann Michael, who played a major role in combatting famines in Bengal and Madras and represented India at various international postal congresses in Vienna (1891), Washington (1897), London (1898), Bern (1900), and Rome (1906). Entering government service at twenty-three through the British Post Office, Kisch served primarily at the India Office, where he developed skills as a finance and economic expert. At the Paris Peace Conference, as secretary to the British Indian Currency Commission, Kisch mistakenly set the post-war value of the rupee too high. During his twelve-year tenure in the Finance Department of the India Office, Kisch worked to establish the Reserve Bank for India. He was a member of the Preparatory Committee of Experts that laid the groundwork for the World Economic Conference sponsored by the League of Nations in June 1933. There Kisch represented India.

During the 1930s, Kisch became a leading writer on international finance. Realizing that political internationalism required an economic counterpart, he was especially interested in Central Bank cooperation. In 1937 he was named the British delegate to the international commission regulating the finances of Tangier. In 1937 he became a member of the Supervisory Financial Commission of the League of Nations. During World War II, he oversaw the supplies of petroleum for the British Empire. When the League of Nations expired, Kisch was named vice-chairman of the Board of Liquidation, which wound up its operations. He then served on the United Nations Contributions Commission in 1946–47, which established the new world organization. Finally, in 1949, he worked on the international currency committee set up by the UN to aid the Bank of Greece.

An avid intellectual, with a lifelong interest in India, Kisch served on the governing body and as honorary treasurer of the School of Oriental and African Studies of the University of London. In his retirement, he learned and translated Russian poetry. Despite great personal losses, Kisch was to his contemporaries a bright, vigorous, and effective cosmopolitan. With his knowledge of finance and Asian affairs, he lent breadth, practical background, and vision to his government and to world organizations.

BIBLIOGRAPHY:

A. "Bank for International Settlements," *Spectator* 146 (31 Jan 1931), 139–40; *Central Banks* (London, 1928, 1932, 1934); with others, *The International Gold Problem* (London, 1931); *The Portuguese Note Case* (London, 1932).

B. LT 21 Oct 1961, 12, 24 Oct 1961, 15, 26 Oct 1961, 15; WWW 1961–70, 637.

Carole Fink

KITCHELT, Florence Cross (17 December 1874, Rochester, NY—4 April 1961, Wilberforce, OH). *Education*: graduated from Wells Coll., 1897; *Career*: social worker, Ithaca, NY, 1898–99, New York, 1900–1902, New Haven, CT, 1904–5, Brooklyn, NY, 1905–6, Rochester, NY, 1907–15; suffrage organizer, 1915–20; citizenship director, League of Women Voters, CT, 1920–24; executive director, Connecticut Branch, League of Nations Association, 1924–44; chair, Connecticut Committee for the Equal Rights Amendment, 1944–56.

In 1926 at fifty-two, Kitchelt, near the start of her twenty-year tenure as executive secretary of the Connecticut Branch of the League of Nations Association, placed her third career change in perspective. Peace work, she explained to a reporter, was a natural outgrowth of her experience as a social worker and suffrage organizer. Everything progressed in orderly fashion, she concluded. Kitchelt's self-appraisal was accurate, for in her sixty-year public life, which began as an "unprofessional professional" social worker and closed with her retirement in 1956 from the post of chairperson of the Connecticut Committee for the Equal Rights Amendment, she was consistent in her reform motivation, philosophy, and tactics. Kitchelt's internationalism is best understood as an aspect of her commitment to progressive reform.

A religious zeal (Unitarianism), a sense of social responsibility, pride in her family's ten generations in America, respect for duty, and a desire for independence initially motivated Kitchelt into social work. There she demonstrated a Romantic belief in the possibility of personal regeneration, yet while in Rochester she participated in several strikes of Italian construction workers and in 1911 she married a Socialist. She then moved to her second stage of growth, when she campaigned for women suffrage, and after it was attained she became citizenship director of the fledgling Connecticut League of Women Voters. The summer programs she conducted at Yale and at Trinity attracted national publicity.

Chance rather than design brought Kitchelt into the peace movement. In 1924 veterans of the Woman's Peace Party in the state, many with ties to the suffrage cause, hired Kitchelt as the salaried director of the League of Nations Association. Trips to Geneva in 1925 and 1927 convinced her that the League was an instrument of social betterment that she could support wholeheartedly. For two decades as the only paid, full-time peace organizer in Connecticut, she channeled her vast energies into convincing the influential people of the state that the League was the key to peace and prosperity. Without an automobile and with a salary of less than $3,000 a year, she applied the organizational and publicity techniques perfected in settlement and suffrage work to the new cause. She set up a Speakers Bureau that preached to schoolchildren, women's clubs, and civic associations. She spoke to 109 gatherings in 1928 and 79 the following year. Frequent use of local radio stations enlarged her reach. World Court Committees were organized in five cities. In 1934 the League of Nations Association garnered 26,000 signatures on a peace petition. Starting in 1932 the organization submitted questionnaires to all congressional candidates in Connecticut and distributed charts publicizing their positions on issues of disarmament, the World Court, and neutrality. There is evidence that the "peace vote" contributed to the narrow victories of Congressman Herman Koppleman in 1934 and 1936.

Kitchelt's effectiveness was restricted by philosophical and temperamental limitations. Her enthusiasm for causes often took precedence over organizational tidiness. Her liabilities made it difficult to relate to ethnics and blue-collar workers, who made up the brunt of the population of Connecticut. While she preached the need for unity among state peace leaders, she contributed to a split after 1935, when she sided with the politically and socially conservative element which included Horace Taft and *Chase Kimball in urging economic sanctions against Japan, Italy, and Germany. In 1940 she became the head of the New Haven chapter of the Committee to Defend America by Aiding the Allies.

BIBLIOGRAPHY:

B. Herbert Janick, "An Instructive Failure: The Connecticut Peace Movement, 1919-1939," *Peace and Change* 5 (Spring 1978), 12-22; "Senator Frank Brandegee and the Election of 1920," *Historian* 35 (May 1975), 434-51.

C. The Kitchelt papers are in the Schlesinger Library at Radcliffe Coll., Yale Univ., and the Regional History Collection at Cornell Univ.

Herbert Janick

KRAG, Jens Otto (15 September 1914, Randers, Denmark—22 June 1978, Skiveren, Denmark). *Education*: *cand. polit.*, Univ. of Copenhagen, 1940. *Career*: official in Directorate of Supply, 1940–45; chief of bureau, Economic Council of the Danish Labor Movement, 1945–47; Social Democratic member of Folketing, 1947–73, Foreign Policy Committee, 1968–71; minister for commerce, 1947–50; economic counselor, Danish embassy, Washington, 1950–52; minister for economic affairs and labor, 1953–57; minister for foreign trade, 1957–58; minister for foreign affairs, 1958–62, 1966–67; prime minister, 1962–68, 1971–72; chairman, Social Democratic party, 1962–72; leader of delegation, Commission of the European Community at Washington, 1974–75.

As a young minister for commerce in the first Social Democratic government after World War II, and again as a minister of economic affairs in the mid-1950s, Krag was confronted with the intricate problem of the economic viability of a small, highly developed, and therefore dependent state in an unfavorable international environment. Originally attracted to the idea of a planned economy with active state intervention in foreign trade, he gradually came to see the solution in a broadly conceived European free trade arrangement which included all the main trade partners of Denmark. When Krag took over the newly created Ministry for Foreign Trade in 1957, the formation of the European Economic Community was threatening to create a market split between Denmark's two main partners, Britain and West Germany, and gradually to exclude her main export, agricultural products, from the EEC area. Unwilling for political and economic reasons to part company with Britain and the Nordic countries, but not opposing Denmark joining the EEC per se, Krag became an energetic champion of a large European free-trade area encompassing the EEC and the other OEEC countries. When this project failed in 1958, Krag, then minister of foreign affairs, opted for Danish membership in 1959 in the European Free Trade Association after securing concessions for Danish agricultural exports from the other EFTA partners.

When Britain chose to seek membership in the EEC (1961), Krag strongly advocated that Denmark follow suit, and he remained a staunch supporter of membership until Denmark eventually entered in 1973. In his second period as prime minister (1971–72), he undoubtedly saw it as his government's primary goal, but a difficult one because of the growth of anti-EEC sentiments in the Social Democratic party in the early 1970s. Krag insisted on giving EEC opponents a large degree of "fair play" in the campaign before the referendum on membership, and therefore the heavy yes-vote (63 percent) was a personal triumph for Krag and the peak of his political career. The very next morning, 3 October 1972, he stunned the country by announcing his decision to step down immediately and quit political life.

Krag's efforts on behalf of Denmark's membership in the EEC were widely recognized in Europe. He was respected as a competent and flexible negotiator as well as a firm, but undogmatic believer in European unity. In 1966 he was awarded the Charlemagne Prize and in 1973 the *Robert Schuman Prize. He led the EEC Commission's delegation in Washington (1974–75), a frustrating experience in Krag's not altogether happy years of retirement.

Krag's impact on other aspects of Denmark's foreign policy was smaller. In his EEC policy he never lost sight of the interests of the other Nordic countries; and without ever wavering in his support for NATO, he was also an early endorser of detente and East–West cooperation in Europe. Personally, Krag was reserved and shy. Often called "enigmatic," he rarely gave away his innermost political thoughts. His internationalism was undoubtedly economic in origin, but over the years he also developed a political rationale for his belief that Denmark should involve herself in international politics so as not to become isolated. He never believed in the federalist theories of European integration, but he saw the EEC as the most practical framework for the solution of the economic and political—but not military—problems of Western Europe.

BIBLIOGRAPHY:

A. *Dagbog 1971–72* [Diary 1971–72] (Copenhagen, 1973); *Dogbog ved et aarsskifte* [Diary at a turn of the year] (Copenhagen, 1972); with K. B. Andersen, *Kamp og fornyelse: Socialdemokratiets indsats i dansk politik 1955–71* [Struggle and renewal: The effort of the Social Democratic party in Danish politics 1955–71] (Copenhagen, 1971); *Travl tid god tid* [Busy time good time] (Copenhagen, 1974); *Ung mand fra trediverne* [Young man from the thirties] (Copenhagen, 1969).

B. *Aktuelt* 23 Jun 1978, 10–12; *Berlingske Tidende* 23 Jun 1978, 6; CB 1962, 244–46; Søren Hansen, ed., *Krag—som vi kendte ham* [Krag as we knew him] (Copenhagen, 1978).

Nikolaj Petersen

KRAUS, Karl. See *Biographical Dictionary of Modern Peace Leaders*.

KUHN, Arthur Kline (11 November 1876, Philadelphia—8 July 1954, New York). *Education*: B.A., Columbia Coll., 1895; M.A., 1896, LL.B., 1897, Ph.D., 1912; postgraduate study, Univ. of Zurich, 1904; Ecole de Droit, Paris, 1905. *Career*: lawyer, 1898–1954; teaching staff, Columbia Univ., 1909–11, 1915–17; Univ. of Zurich, 1914, Univ. of Pennsylvania, 1926–30.

Described by one writer as possessing a "global" mind, Kuhn devoted his productive career to the furtherance of international law. His interest in the subject began as a college student, when he entered and won an intercollegiate essay contest sponsored by the American Peace Society. The award induced Kuhn to study political science and law. He opened his own practice in 1898, specializing in international law, but six years later he sought further education in international public law, comparative laws, and the conflict of laws through three years of study in Zurich and Paris. He also joined the International Law Association and translated into English a treatise by the Swiss scholar-lawyer Friedrich Meili. *International Civil and Commercial Law as Founded Upon Theory, Legislation and Practice, Translated and Supplemented with Additions of American and English Law* was well received and helped Kuhn establish his reputation as a legal practitioner and scholar. He resumed private practice, began teaching at Columbia, attended the Lake Mohonk Arbitration Conferences and became an early member of a Lake Mohonk spinoff, the American Society of International Law (ASIL).

Kuhn went overseas after the Armistice as counsel for the Committee of Public Information. In Paris, *Oscar Straus and *Hamilton Holt recruited him as a legal specialist for the Paris representatives of the League to Enforce Peace. During the war, Kuhn had drafted a twenty-four-article plan for an international organization replete with a council, court, and council of ministers. Although he grasped the importance of collective security, he did not consider any league as an end unto itself. Rather, it was a means to sanction and advance international law. Yet Kuhn enthusiastically embraced the League of Nations and worked for ratification of the Treaty of Versailles.

Kuhn devoted the 1920s and 1930s to his private practice, teaching and encouraging professional interchange in international law. At the University of Pennsylvania Law School, he offered a course on World Court jurisprudence and twice (1925, 1928) was lecturer at The Hague's Academy of International Law. He played an active part in the International Law Association and the founding of its American branch, and he served as president of the latter (1926, 1940). He helped organize the American Foreign Law Association, participated in the Williamstown Institute of Politics, (1924, 1926), and advised *Manley Hudson's Harvard Research in International Law project. In addition to publishing four scholarly books, Kuhn served on the board of editors of the *American Journal of International Law*, providing essays ranging from aeronautical law and human rights to nationalization and genocide. In commenting on developments in international law, he criticized the toothless Kellogg-Briand Pact and thought that American neutrality legislation foolishly harmed victims of aggression. During World War II, he gave considerable attention to the protection of individual rights through participation in the Committee on Peace Problems of the American Jewish Committee. Thereafter he followed closely the drafting of the UN Charter and the Universal Declaration of Human Rights.

Kuhn believed that law could provide a basis for peace. Science and technology had inextricably bound the world together. Because human activities and problems knew no borders, only international law could provide a uniform method for regulating human activities. But law was no panacea; political conflicts had to be settled by negotiation, preferably within an international organization where the acrimony might be contained. Just prior to his death, Kuhn published a brief autobiography which conveyed his undiminished faith in law. The proliferation of institutions of international law cheered him, but he expressed concern because nations did not fully utilize them. Kuhn hoped that individuals would recognize that progress had occurred and diligently work to make law supreme, thus creating an "international mind" and contributing to peace.

BIBLIOGRAPHY:

A. *Aerial Navigation in its Relation to International Law* (Lancaster, PA, 1909); *Comparative Commentaries on Private International Law or Conflict of Laws* (New York, 1937); *Comparative Study of the Law of Corporations* (New York, 1912); *Conception du droit international privé aux Etat-Unis* (Paris, 1929); *Effets de commerce en droit international* (Paris, 1926); *Gundzüge de Englisch-Amerikanischen Privat und Prozessrechts* (Zurich, 1915); *Pathways in International Law: A Personal Narrative* (New York, 1953); *Principes du droit anglo-américain* (Paris, 1924).

B. AJIL 48 (1954), 592–97; NCAB F, 189–90; NYT 9 Jul 1954, 17.

Daryl L. Revoldt

L

LA MALFA, Ugo (16 May 1903, Palermo, Italy—26 March 1979, Rome). *Education*: doctorate in diplomatic and consular sciences, Univ. of Palermo. *Career*: member, National Consulta, 1945–46; deputy, Constituent Assembly, 1946–47; parliamentary deputy, 1948–79; member, Council of Europe and European Coal and Steel Community.

A militant anti-Fascist, La Malfa helped found the Action party in 1942. When this broke up in 1946, he helped organize the Republican Democratic party, which united in 1948 with the Italian Republican party (PRI). In 1971, La Malfa became secretary and subsequently president of the latter and was then able to involve the small PRI closely in Italian decision making concerning European integration. He sought to popularize such actions in Italy and make sure they were supported by a forward-looking program of domestic economic reforms.

La Malfa was a strong proponent of the European Economic Community (EEC) and of efforts to convert it into a European political body. A foe of *Charles de Gaulle, he sought to expand the EEC by including Britain and other applicants, and he advocated a popularly elected European Parliament. He often warned against rejecting the supranational approach to integration. He served as an Italian parliamentary member of the Council of Europe and of the European Coal and Steel Community. He was also a vice-governor of the International Monetary Fund. La Malfa was an influential member of eight coalition cabinets with the Christian Democrats after World War II, holding a variety of important economic portfolios. He was in Parliament constantly after 1948. In 1948 he headed an Italian commercial delegation to Moscow. In the years 1951–53, as minister of foreign commerce, he played a major role in completing the liberalization of Italian foreign trade. As budget minister, he took a central part in preparing the national economic plan in 1962. In both trade and budgetary matters, La Malfa always thought in terms of the context of European integration. In the early 1960s, La Malfa helped bring the Socialists into the Christian Democratic-led coalition government—the "opening to the left." When this center–left arrangement bogged down in the 1970s, he became increasingly critical of the coalition government's policies. In February 1979 he sought unsuccessfully to organize a new government in which Communists would also participate. At the time of his death a month later, La Malfa held the post of deputy premier and minister for economic planning in Giulio Andreotti's new coalition government.

BIBLIOGRAPHY:

A. *Intervista sul non-governo*, ed., Alberto Ronchey (Bari, Italy, 1977); *La caporetto economica* (Milan, 1974); *La politica economica in Italia, 1946–62* (Milan, 1963).

B. *Chi è?* (Rome, 1961), 362; *Enciclopedia Europea* 6 (Milan, 1978), 677; IWW 1979–80, 953; NYT 26 Mar 1979, II–13; F. Roy Willis, *Italy Chooses Europe* (New York, 1971).

Charles F. Delzell

LA MOTTE, Ellen Newbold (27 November 1873, Louisville, KY—2 March 1961, Washington). *Education*: graduate, Nurses' Training School, Johns Hopkins Univ. Hospital, 1902. *Career*: staff member, Instructive Visiting Nurses Association, Baltimore, MD, 1905–10; superintendent, Tuberculosis Division, Baltimore Department of Health, 1910–13; field hospital nurse, French Army in Belgium, 1915–16; author of short stories, travel observations, essays, and books, 1914–35; anti-opium crusader, 1919–40.

La Motte's work as a wartime nurse in Belgium and her travels in the Far East during the era of World War I reflected as well as intensified her interest in international affairs. Although not a pacifist, she was nevertheless appalled by the carnage of warfare. *Backwash of War* (1918), her book of sketches of the wounded whom she observed and treated in Belgium, was withdrawn from publication in the United States in 1918 because of governmental disapproval of its antiwar implications. Visits to China and Japan in 1916 and 1917 led her to deplore the division of China into European and Japanese spheres of influence, European exploitation of Oriental laborers, and Western racial and cultural arrogance. Consequently, anti-Western imperialism became the dominant theme of her short stories and travel accounts published between 1919 and 1925 in the *Atlantic Monthly, Century, Harper's,* and *Overland Monthly* and collectively in three books.

La Motte found a political outlet for her anti-imperialistic sentiments in the international crusade against opium. Initiated by the United States in 1909, the anti-opium movement continued between the two world wars under the auspices of the League of Nations. While residing in Europe during the interwar years, La Motte attended every public meeting of the League of Nation's Advisory Committee on the Traffic in Opium. A firm supporter of the League, she nevertheless feared that the Committee was less interested in suppressing opium transactions than in protecting the revenue interests of the "opium bloc." She published two books and numerous articles in such periodicals as the *Nation, Atlantic Monthly*, and *Survey* in which she castigated Great Britain, other Western countries, and Japan for promoting or tolerating opium trafficking and consumption in their Far Eastern territories and spheres of influence while discouraging use of the drug at home. She was not unconcerned with the drug problem in the West, particularly in the United States; but she supported the campaign against opium as mainly an expression of international humanitarianism in the interest of the rights and well-being of non-Western peoples. The public phase of her anti-opium career apparently ended with the outbreak of

World War II. She returned to the United States and spent her later years in private pursuits in Washington.

BIBLIOGRAPHY:

A. *The Backwash of War* (New York, 1916); *Civilization: Tales of the Orient* (New York, 1919); *The Ethics of Opium* (New York, 1924); *The Opium Monopoly* (New York, 1910); *Peking Dust* (New York, 1919); *Snuffs and Butters* (New York, 1925); *The Tuberculosis Nurse* (New York, 1915).

B. NYT 4 Mar 1961, 23; *Washington Post* 4 Mar 1961, C-3; WWWA 4, 551.

C. The La Motte papers are in the Manuscript Division, Library of Congress.

Arnold H. Taylor

LADD, William. See *Biographical Dictionary of Modern Peace Leaders.*

La FONTAINE, Henri. See *Biographical Dictionary of Modern Peace Leaders.*

LAIDLAW, Harriet Burton (16 December 1873, Albany, NY—25 January 1949, New York). *Education*: B.Ph., New York State Normal Coll., 1896, M.Pd., 1897; B.A., Barnard Coll., 1902. *Career*: schoolteacher, 1902–5; suffragette, 1908–20; internationalist, 1920–49; board of directors, Standard & Poor, 1932–49.

Politically independent, middle-class, and the descendant of an old New England family, the strikingly attractive Laidlaw resembled in many ways the prototype progressive reformer turned internationalist. Like fellow suffragettes ⁺Jane Addams, Carrie Chapman Catt, Anne H. Martin, and Alice Paul, she shifted from domestic reform to support peace crusades and the idea of international organization. Beginning as a student in the 1890s, she moved from speaking to organizing the New York State's Woman's Suffrage Movement (1908), and she later served as a member of the National Woman's Suffrage Association and the International Woman's Suffrage Alliance. She also joined in other progressive reforms, especially efforts to end white slavery and child labor.

In 1906 Burton married James Lees Laidlaw, a successful investment banker whose firm had extensive international dealings, and her husband was later one of the founders of Standard & Poor. He too was active in civic and philanthropic affairs and became prominent in the Foreign Policy Association during the 1920s. Her husband's extensive international interests and the coming of World War I prompted Laidlaw to redirect her attention to foreign affairs. She became a committed internationalist, a founder of the League of Nations Non-Partisan Association in 1922, and a persistent supporter of the League of Nations. She chaired the Woman's Pro-League Council, which campaigned (1921–22) to secure U.S. entry into the world body.

Laidlaw continued her pro-League activities in the 1920s by writing favorable articles. A consistent theme appeared in her belief that a majority of Americans favored U.S. entry. She spoke regularly and served as an officer of the League of Nations Non-Partisan Association. In the 1930s she supported the Loyalists during the Spanish Civil War. With the revival of internationalism during World War II, she again campaigned until her death, serving as an officer in the American Association for the United Nations and as a regular participant in UN Week observances. When her husband died, Laidlaw became the first female member of the board of directors of Standard & Poor.

BIBLIOGRAPHY:

A. "Democracy Begins at Home," *League of Nations Herald* 1 (1 Jun 1924), 1, 3; "Great World Drama," *League of Nations News* 3 (Jul 1926), 5–8; *James Lees Laidlaw* (New York, 1933); *Organizing to Win* (New York, 1914); "Whose Representatives," *Woman Citizen* 10 (30 May 1925), 15.

B. NAW 2, 358–59; NCAB, 38, 21–22; NYT 26 Jan 1949, 32.

James W. Harper

LAMMASCH, Heinrich (21 May 1853, Seitenstetten, Austria—6 January 1920, Salzburg). *Education*: doctor of laws, Univ. of Vienna, 1876. *Career*: lecturer, Univ. of Vienna, 1879–82; associate professor, Univ. of Innsbruck, 1882–89; professor, Univ. of Vienna, 1889–1914; member, House of Lords, 1899–1918; prime minister, 27 October–11 November, 1918; head, Austrian delegation, International Sugar Conference, Brussels, 1903; legal adviser, Austro-Hungarian delegation, Hague Conferences, 1899 and 1907; member, Permanent Court of Arbitration, 1899–1914.

Lammasch, a devout Roman Catholic, monarchist, and moderate conservative in domestic politics, was a renowned and innovative advocate of international law. His interest stemmed from his writings on international criminal law, which earned him election to the Institute of International Law in 1887. After serving as legal adviser to the Austro-Hungarian delegation at the First Hague Peace Conference, where he played a role in creating the Permanent Court of Arbitration, Lammasch published seminal works on the theory, history, and practice of arbitration. As a judge in four cases, in three of which he served as president, Lammasch went beyond theory to perfecting arbitral procedures, defining legal jurisdiction, and demonstrating the efficacy of arbitration. He argued for the precedence of the decisions of international tribunals over those on the same subjects by national courts and parliaments.

Unlike many bourgeois internationalists, Lammasch was very sympathetic to the pacifist movement, whose moral principles accorded with those of his active Christian conscience. His contacts with pacifists at the First and Second Hague Conferences strengthened his beliefs, and he established close ties to leading peace advocates. He enthusiastically supported the growing pacifist movement without formally associating with its organizations. At the same time, he eschewed what he viewed as radical "utopian pacifist" demands for the cessation of armaments and the abolition of war because they flew in the face of historical experience and frightened statesmen and diplomats of the old school.

Lammasch accepted the reality of national sovereignty and argued that nation-states would give up war and power politics only when they realized it was in their interest to do so. He advocated a close and intimate cooperation of states which should bind themselves through commissions of inquiry, tribunals of arbitration, and courts of justice. To that end, Lammasch, as vice-president of the commission on arbitration at the Second Hague Peace Conference, championed a universal treaty of stipulated arbitration, which would oblige signers to submit to arbitration specified issues not resolved through diplomacy which did not involve vital interests or national honor. Such a treaty would not prevent war, but much would be gained in a legal and moral sense. Agreements for obligatory arbitration would constitute recognition that arbitration was a normal method of settlement after diplomacy had failed. The proposed universal treaty failed at the Conference because of a unanimity rule. Undaunted, he continued to plead his cause and looked forward to its acceptance at a third Hague assembly scheduled for 1915.

Despite his rejection of "utopian pacifist" beliefs, Lammasch, fusing his Christian faith with evolutionary ideas, held war to be an antiquated institution which, like body organs whose functions had been taken over by others, was becoming rudimentary. The existence of the arbitral court and the over one hundred cases submitted to it by 1914 attested to the rational and moral capacity of states for self-limitation. With the extension of the court's functions, war would die out. The outbreak of conflict in 1914 dealt a severe blow to this evolutionary view of international law. He was saved from despair by his belief in mankind's capacity for rational and moral development and his firm Christian faith.

Lammasch criticized Austria-Hungary's declaration of war, but he accepted it as a defensive measure. He never succumbed to hysteria, however, and he sought to end the war on the basis of a just and lasting peace. The Austro-Hungarian General Staff ordered his arrest as a "defeatist" at the outbreak of the war, but Emperor Franz Joseph prevented its implementation. Lammasch lent his prestige to antiwar and peace activities in neutral European countries, while at home he used his unique position of being both close to the peace movement and a political insider to wage a two-front peace campaign. He headed the efforts of Para Pacem, the Austrian Association for International Understanding, and sought to persuade the emperor to conclude a separate peace on the basis of Wilsonian principles. He even engaged in quasi-official negotiations to that end with a confidant of President *Woodrow Wilson, George D. Herron, in Switzerland. Lammasch courageously delivered three speeches in the Austrian House of Lords in 1917–18 in which he condemned the militaristic "spirit of Potsdam" and its annexationist objectives as obstacles to peace. He called for a federal reorganization of Austria along lines of national autonomy, a peace of mutual understanding without annexations, and a commitment to future disarmament and the pursuit of international differences through international courts rather than war. Such efforts failed and led to Lammasch's isolation in the House. As the last imperial Austrian minister, he painfully presided over the peaceful dissolution of the Habsburg state. In his last public role as legal adviser to the Austrian delegation to the peace conference at St. Germain in 1919, he championed the idea of permanent neutrality for the new Austrian republic. He withdrew before the sessions ended because of ill health and what he perceived as a betrayal of Wilsonian principles by the Allies.

In works published abroad during the war, Lammasch affirmed his belief in the existence of indestructible moral ties between nations rooted in natural law which could not be dissolved. Far from undermining international law, the war proved its necessity. It would lead to the strengthening and enlarging of ideas embodied in prewar law as a way of preventing future conflicts. He was an early and avid supporter of the Covenant and founded the Austrian League of Nations Association. In his last book, published posthumously, he warned that the choice for humanity lay between suicide or a league.

BIBLIOGRAPHY:

A. "Compulsory Arbitration at the Second Hague Conference," AJIL 4 (1910), 83–94; *Das Völkerrecht nach dem Krieg* (Christiania (Oslo), 1917), 1–5; *Der Völkerbund zur Bewahrung des Friedens* (Olten, Switzerland, 1919); *Die Lehre von Schiedsgerichtsbarkeit in ihrem ganzen Umfange* (Stuttgart, Germany, 1914); *Die Rechtskraft internationaler Schiedssprüche* (Christiania (Oslo), 1913); *Europas elfte Stünde* (Munich, 1919); *Le Maintien de la paix* (Geneva, 1918); "Unjustifiable War and the Means to Avoid It," AJIL 10 (1916), 689–705; *Völkermord oder Völkerbund* (The Hague, 1920); *Woodrow Wilson's Friedensplan* (Leipzig, Germany, 1919).

B. AJIL 14 (1920) 609–13; Heinrich Benedikt, *Die Friedensaktion der Meinlgruppe 1917/1918* (Graz, Austria, 1965); *Encyclopaedia Britannica* 15 (Chicago), 14th ed. 628; Marga Lammasch and Hans Sperl, eds., *Heinrich Lammasch: Seine Aufzeichnungen, sein Wirken und seine Politik* (Vienna, 1922); Richard Laurence, "The Peace Movement in Austria, 1867-1914," in *Doves and Diplomats*, ed. Solomon Wank (Westport, CT, 1978), 21–41; *Neue Osterreichische Biographie* 1 (Vienna, 1923), 44–54; *New Encyclopaedia Britannica Micropaedia* 6 (Chicago), 15th ed. 10; NYT 29 Jan 1920, 17; *Osterreichisches Biographisches Lexikon, 1815–1950* 4 (Graz, Austria, 1957), 415–16; Stephan Verosta, *Theorie und Realitat von Bundnissen: Heinrich Lammasch, Karl Renner und der Zweibund, 1897–1914* (Vienna, 1971).

Solomon Wank

LAMONT, Thomas William (30 September 1870, Claverack, NY—2 February 1948, Boca Grande, FL). *Education*: B.A., Harvard Coll., 1892. *Career*: reporter, *New York Tribune*, 1893-94; organized Lamont, Corliss

& Co., 1894; secretary, treasurer, and vice-president, Bankers Trust Company, 1903-9; vice-president, First National Bank, 1909-11; partner, J. P. Morgan & Co., 1911-48, chairman of the board, 1943-48; owner, *New York Evening Post*, 1918-22; adviser to American Commission to Negotiate Peace, 1919; chair, American Group, International Consortium for Assistance of China, 1920; International Committee of Bankers, Mexico, 1921; alternate delegate, Commission of Experts on German Reparations (Young Plan), 1929; delegate, World Economic Conference, London, 1933.

No American during the interwar period better represented the link between finance and foreign policy than Lamont. The son of a Methodist minister, Lamont exemplified the Protestant work ethic in action. After some newspaper work and success in saving failing companies, he moved into New York banking circles, where he rose quickly in J. P. Morgan & Co. After 1922, Lamont's influence in the firm became second only to that of Morgan. When Morgan died in 1943, Lamont was elected chairman of the board. Lamont never held elective office or expressed original ideas. His prominence stemmed from his position as the most public member of America's financial community. He advised presidents and served on over a dozen major missions.

Although a lifelong Republican, Lamont firmly endorsed Wilsonian internationalism. He stressed a global ideal of cooperative capitalism, believing that nationalism led inexorably to war and economic dislocation. Although he supported American participation in both world wars, he generally opposed the use of force. Diplomacy for Lamont usually meant economic diplomacy; indeed he viewed international finance as a surrogate for a League of Nations weakened by U.S. abstention. Following World War I, he played a central role in recreating the international banking consortium in China, in paving the way for both American recognition of postrevolutionary Mexico and the repayment of Mexican debts, and in efforts to stabilize the major European currencies. He was instrumental in negotiating the Dawes and Young Plans. His characteristic moderation expressed itself in his opposition to such things as the hard line taken by American oil companies in Mexico and the uncompromising policy of French nationalists who wanted to block German economic reconstruction.

Lamont was not always consistent. In Asia, he felt special sympathy for Japan, which he viewed as an Asian outpost of capitalist orderliness. He also exaggerated the influence of moderate Japanese businessmen. Consequently, he opposed League and U.S. measures aimed against Japan during the Manchurian Crisis. Not until Tokyo signed the Tripartite Pact in 1940 did Lamont endorse the use of economic sanctions to block Japanese expansion. Across the Atlantic, his admiration for British institutions and his close ties to the London financial community predisposed him to Anglo-American cooperation. Long suspicious of German militarism, he quickly grasped the nature of Nazism. He argued that U.S. neutrality legislation would make war more, not less, likely during the mid-1930's, and he supported extensive aid to Britain after 1939. Not even ideology would discourage his advocacy of U.S.-Soviet cooperation after Pearl Harbor.

Contemporary writers frequently overestimated his influence. He failed to prevent Mexico from creating a central bank, for instance, or to stem the general trend toward protectionism. Nevertheless, his successes were many, a tribute to his shrewd diplomatic instincts, his penchant for quiet negotiation, his pragmatism, and his impeccable discretion. Moreover, he was free of the racism so common during his era; Latin Americans and Asians trusted him in ways that paid handsomely. Most importantly, he capitalized on his leadership within the financial world. He thereby gained access to foreign offices whether of the public or private variety. He was as much statesman as banker, an internationalist who comfortably operated outside the framework of international organization.

BIBLIOGRAPHY:

A. *Across World Frontiers* (New York, 1951); *America and the Far East* (New York, 1920); *The Far East Threat: A Friendly Caution to Japan* (New York, 1940); *My Boyhood in a Parsonage* (New York, 1946).

B. John Brooks, *Once in Golconda: A True Drama of Wall Street, 1920-1938* (New York, 1969); Vincent P. Carusso, *Investment Banking in America: A History* (New York, 1970); CB 1940, 476-78; Warren I. Cohen, *The Chinese Connection: Roger S. Greene, Thomas W. Lamont, George E. Sokolsky and American-East Asian Relations* (New York, 1978); DAB supp. 4, 469-71; Michael J. Hogan, "Thomas W. Lamont and European Recovery: The Diplomacy of Privatism in a Corporate Age," in Kenneth Paul Jones, ed., *U.S. Diplomats in Europe, 1919-1941* (Santa Barbara, CA 1981); Corliss Lamont, ed. *The Lamont Family* (New York, 1962); NCAB 41, 6-8; NYT 3 Feb 1948, 1.

C. The Lamont papers are in the Baker Library, Harvard Univ.

Gary B. Ostrower

LANGE, Christian Lous (17 September 1869, Stavanger, Norway—11 December 1938, Oslo). *Education*: graduate, Univ. of Christiania, 1893, Ph.D., 1919; studied history and modern languages, Univ. of London and the Sorbonne. *Career*: teacher, historian, political leader, and social worker; secretary, Nobel Committee of Norwegian Storting, 1900–1909; director, Norwegian Nobel Institute, 1904–9; secretary-general, Inter-Parliamentary Union, 1909–33; member, Norwegian delegation to League of Nations, 1920–38, president, Disarmament Commission, 1936; Nobel Peace Prize, 1921, with *K. H. Branting.

Lange's linguistic abilities led him at the age of thirty to assist in preparations for an Inter-Parliamentary conference at Oslo. Here he demonstrated administrative talents that opened the way for a new and wider career. He became a moving force in establishing the Norwegian Nobel Institute, of which he was director, 1904–9. He served as a technical delegate of Norway at The Hague Peace Conference of 1907 and moved to Brussels in 1909 to become secretary-general of the Inter-Parliamentary Union. There, while carrying out his organizing and negotiating duties, he prepared publications on such subjects as compulsory international arbitration, interparliamentary cooperation, and conditions for a durable peace. After Brussels was occupied by the Germans in 1914, Lange moved the IPU office to his home near Oslo, and from there as a regular correspondent of the Carnegie Endowment for International Peace he twice visited the capitals of the warring countries to explore possibilities for settlement.

In 1915 he wrote a book on the European "civil war," and throughout the war years he was active in Scandinavian and other efforts to build a framework for peace, including a plan for "development of the work of The Hague" that envisaged an international juridicial organization. At the request of the Carnegie Endowment, he went in March 1917 to Petrograd and Helsingfors (Helsinki) to report on conditions after the fall of the czar. Lange's report on Russia in the Kerensky period filled nearly two pages of the *New York Times*, 27 May 1917. During this time he was also active in the Central Organization for a Durable Peace, and he completed the first volume, from antiquity to 1648, of his *Histoire de l'internationalisme*, which he described as a history of ideas, not institutions.

Having long urged the need for some form of international organization to keep the peace, Lange became an early and outspoken member of Norway's delegation to the newly formed League of Nations. At Geneva on 15 September 1921, he accused the big powers of the League of working against a majority of nations to block disarmament. The Assembly had recommended positive steps, but the Council was failing to act. Lange took issue with *Arthur J. Balfour, who argued that it was difficult to discuss disarmament before the world was pacifically inclined. Lange insisted that the world could not wait for the millenium, nor could much be accomplished as long as war ministries dominated the disarmament machinery. Not long afterward, Lange, who had been nominated the previous year, was awarded the Nobel Peace Prize for 1921, jointly with *Karl H. Branting of Sweden. At the ceremony in Oslo, 13 December 1921, Lange was described as a great organizer who had striven, with practical skill, unswerving idealism, and unflagging determination, to keep communication open and international cooperation alive. The theme of Lange's Nobel lecture was internationalism, a social and political theory, which he distinguished from pacifism, a moral theory. He saw pacifism as essentially a negative effort against war, while internationalism sought constructive ways socially and politically to build peace. The sovereign state, isolated by protectionism and militarism, had become a lethal danger to human civilization, he said, and it could only be met by constructive reforms inspired by confidence in the unity of people.

In the years that followed, Lange continued to take a leading part in the

League and the Inter-Parliamentary Union, and he also regularly engaged in writing and lecturing. To a compendium edited by Peter Munch, he contributed chapters on preparation of the League during the war, based considerably on his own experiences, and on the League and the problem of armaments. The latter deplored the melancholy status of disarmament. Not long after, the Academy of International Law at The Hague published his history of "la doctrine pacifique," which drew in part on his history of internationalism. Again Lange found that the fundamental problem facing the world was the need to demilitarize and civilize the state to allow people to be free and to master their destiny.

BIBLIOGRAPHY:

A. *Développement de l'oeuvre de la Haye* (The Hague, 1917); "Histoire de la doctrine pacifique et de son influence sur le développement du droit international," in Académie de Droit International, *Receuil des cours, 1926* 3, bk. 13 (1927), 171–426, including a list of Lange's principal writings, 1904–24; *Histoire de l'internationalisme*, vol. 1 (Christiania, 1919), vols. 2 and 3 posthumously completed by August Schou (Oslo, 1954, 1963); "Internationalism," in *Nobel Lectures, Peace* 1 (Amsterdam, 1972), 336–46; *Les Conditions d'une paix durable: Exposé de l'oeuvre de l'Union interparlementaire* (Christiania, 1917); Peter Munch, ed., *Les Origines de l'oeuvre de la Société des Nations*, 2 vols. (Copenhagen, 1923–24), 1: 1–61, 2: 416–52.

B. Oscar J. Falnes, "Christian L. Lange and His Work for Peace," *American-Scandinavian Review* 57 (Sep 1969), 226–74, *Norway and the Nobel Peace Prize* (New York, 1938); S. Shepard Jones, *The Scandinavian States and the League of Nations* (Princeton, NJ, 1939); *Norsk Biografisk Leksikon* 8 (Oslo, 1938) 172–74; NYT 12 Dec 1938, 19.

Fredrick Aandahl

LANSING, Robert (17 October 1864, Watertown, NY—30 October 1928, Washington). *Education*: graduate, Amherst Coll., 1886; read law in his father's office. *Career*: lawyer, Watertown, NY, and Washington; counselor, Department of State, 1914–15; secretary of state, 1915–20.

Lansing's internationalism is an outstanding example of the legalistic approach to the maintenance of peace. His introduction to international circles began in 1890 when he married Eleanor, daughter of *John Watson Foster. When Foster went to London as U.S. agent for the Bering Sea Fur Seals Arbitration (1893), he took Lansing as associate counsel. Lansing represented the United States in connection with the Alaska Boundary Tribunal in 1903, the North Atlantic Coast Fisheries Arbitration in 1909, and the British–American Claims Arbitration, 1912–14. He also served as counsel for a number of foreign governments in claims cases. By 1914 he had won a reputation as one of the leading American experts on arbitration, and it was said he had taken part in more arbitrations than any other American.

Lansing was more than an accomplished lawyer; he was an ardent promoter of the study of international law. At the Lake Mohonk International Arbitration Conference in 1905 he was one of the leaders in founding the American Society of International Law. For the first issues of the *American Journal of International Law* in 1907, Lansing wrote two articles entitled "Notes on Sovereignty in a State" and another essay, "Notes on World Sovereignty," which the AJIL did not publish until 1921. In these and in an article entitled "A Definition of Sovereignty," printed in *Proceedings of the American Political Science Association* (1913–14), Lansing advanced an interpretation of sovereignty which discounted theories about its origins in the will of peoples or hereditary monarchs. "There is," he said, "in a modern political state, as in a primitive community, an irresistible energy which can control all human contact within the state. This irresistible energy is superior physical might which has no limitations other than those inherent in human nature. The supreme coercive physical power I would define as *sovereignty*; the expression of the dominant will of its possessors I would define as law" (*Notes on Sovereignty*, 94). Such a viewpoint could have been troublesome to individuals who were debating whether international law, not having the backing of physical force, should actually be regarded as law. Lansing, nonetheless, believed that it was necessary to make a realistic appraisal of conditions of the time if there was to be progress. In "Notes on World Sovereignty" he declared that realization by civilized people of the interdependence and mutual responsibility of states compelled "the conviction that the entire human race ought to be considered, and in fact is, a single community which awaits the further development of modern civilization to complete its organization and make of all mankind a great, universal political state."

Lansing long aspired to a career as a diplomat, but his loyalty to the Democratic party limited his role to that of a legal expert, except for being a U.S. representative at the International Fur Seal Conference in Washington in 1911. The election of *Woodrow Wilson opened the career he desired. After recommendation by *Elihu Root, Wilson appointed Lansing counselor of the State Department when *John Bassett Moore resigned in April 1914. After the outbreak of World War I, Lansing's responsibilities grew as the Department dealt with the many problems arising from maritime warfare. When Secretary of State *William Jennings Bryan resigned on 8 June 1915, Lansing was named his successor.

Although often overshadowed by the president's confidential adviser, *Edward M. House, Lansing assumed much responsibility for relations with Latin America and the Far East. After the American declaration of war in 1917 he handled major negotiations with Japan and routine negotiations with the Allied powers, but his influence with Wilson declined.

As the war neared its end, Lansing wrote proposals for peace terms, but Wilson took full responsibility for formulating and announcing the American position on such matters. Wilson and House drafted plans for a new international organization, but failed to consult Lansing. At the Peace Conference Wilson and Lansing disagreed almost completely on the League of Nations. Lansing believed that a peace treaty should have been negotiated first and that the framing of the Covenant should have been deferred until the restoration of peace. He also disapproved of guarantees of territorial integrity and political independence and of intentions of giving the great powers preeminent positions on the League Council. At the same time, he deplored Wilson's disregard of the Hague conventions and his reluctance to provide for a Permanent International Court of Justice. The completed Covenant did provide for the later establishment of such a body, and several articles dealt with arbitration and judicial settlement, but Lansing continued to doubt the wisdom and practicality of the proposed organization. Instead of the collective security guarantee in Article X, he urged that each power covenant and guarantee that it would not violate the territorial independence or impair the political independence of other members of the League unless "authorized so to do by a decree of the arbitral tribunal hereinafter referred to or by a three-fourths vote of the International Council of the League of Nations created by this convention." This "negative gurantee," Lansing believed, would have avoided restrictions upon the freedom of action of the United States. It also made a stronger reference to the use of force than the Covenant did, but Lansing gave little consideration to that aspect of his proposal.

Despite questions about the Covenant and doubts about territorial arrangements of the Versailles Treaty, Lansing recommended acceptance; then, when questioned, he admitted doubts. While the president was on his famous Western tour urging popular support for approval, Lansing publicly called for a new or alternative international tribunal. A Hague Permanent Court of Arbitration would, with a body of concise and simple legal principles, do more to avert war than any other formula. When Wilson on 11 February 1920, requested Lansing's resignation, he did so on the grounds that the latter had exceeded authority in calling Cabinet meetings during the president's illness, but he told Lansing that he had felt since Paris that Lansing had accepted his direction and guidance with growing reluctance. Lansing's official career had ended. He returned to the practice of international law but spent much time during his remaining years explaining his difficulties with Wilson.

BIBLIOGRAPHY:

A. *The Big Four and Others of the Peace Conference* (Boston, 1921); *Notes on Sovereignty from the Standpoint of the State and of the World* (Washington, 1921); *The Peace Negotiations: A Personal Narrative* (Boston, 1921); *War Memoirs of Robert Lansing* (Indianapolis, IN, 1935).

B. DAB 10, 609–11; Calvin D. Davis, *The United States and the Second Hague Peace Conference: American Diplomacy and International Organization, 1899–1914* (Durham, NC, 1976); Warren F. Kuehl, *Seeking World Order: The United States and International Organization to 1920* (Nashville, TN, 1969); Julius W. Pratt, "Robert Lansing, Secretary of State, June 23, 1915, to February 13, 1920," in Samuel Flagg Bemis, ed., *The American Secretaries of State and Their Diplomacy*, Vol. 10 (New York, 1929), 47–175; Daniel M. Smith, *Robert Lansing and American Neutrality 1914–1917* (Berkeley, CA 1958), "Robert Lansing, 1915–1920," in *An Uncertain Tradition: American Secretaries of State in the Twentieth Century*, ed. Norman A. Graebner (New York, 1961), 101–27.

C. The Lansing papers are in the Manuscript Division, Library of Congress and at Princeton Univ.

Calvin D. Davis

LAUTERPACHT, Hersch (16 August 1897, Zolkiew, Galicia—8 May 1960, London). *Education*: Lwow Univ.; LL.D., Univ. of Vienna, 1921, Ph.D., 1922; LL.D., London School of Economics, 1925. *Career*: founder and president, World Federation of Jewish Students, ca. 1920; assistant lecturer, London School of Economics, 1927; professor, Hague Academy of International Law, 1930, 1934, 1937, 1947; professor, Cambridge Univ., 1938–55; visiting professor, Wellesley Coll., 1940, Univ. of Colorado, 1948; member, British War Crimes Executive, 1945–46; member, UN International Law Commission, 1951–55; member, Permanent Court of Arbitration, 1957–60; judge, International Court of Justice, 1955–60.

One of the half-dozen most influential international legalists in the common law world, Lauterpacht began his distinguished career as a student of *Hans Kelsen in Vienna. Lauterpacht's rise to legal prominence was rapid after completing his English law training under *Arnold D. McNair, whom Sir Hersch acknowledged as decisively influencing his career. Three times during the 1930s, Lauterpacht delivered the prestigious Hague Academy lectures. He also helped found and edited the invaluable series of *International Law Reports*, of which he was sole editor from 1935 (under the original title of *Annual Digest of Public International Law Cases*) until his death. He also edited and revised the last four editions of *Lassa Oppenheim's seminal *International Law* in two volumes, beginning with the fifth edition in 1935 and continuing through the eighth in 1955. In 1944 he became the editor for a decade of the influential *British Year Book of International Law*. His reputation was further enhanced by his appointment to the Whewell Chair in International Law at Cambridge in 1938. His impact on the International Court of Justice, interestingly, was not as great as anticipated upon his election in 1955.

Lauterpacht, surprisingly, believed that international law was as yet imperfect but moving to become true law, and he frankly conceded its weaknesses. Despite the strong rules and regulations governing war, he viewed war as "an imperfection" in the international legal process. Increasingly enamored of natural law philosophy, and decidedly influenced by the barbarism of World War II and the extermination of his Polish relatives, Lauterpacht played a crucial role in the formulation of the international protection of human rights after 1945.

Lauterpacht believed that the Permanent Court of International Justice in the interwar period had been prevented by the nature of the times from acting as a direct instrumentality of peace. He therefore emphasized the importance of a case-by-case jurisprudence developing in the Court to aid in the creation of a corpus of international legal decision making. His influence has continued beyond his death with the publication of his collected papers.

BIBLIOGRAPHY:

A. *The Development of International Law by the Permanent Court of International Justice* (New York, 1934); *Development of the International Law of the International Court* (London, 1958); *The Function of Law in the International Community* (Oxford, 1933); *International Law and Human Rights* (New York, 1950), ed., *International Law*, 2 vols. (London, 1955); *Private Law Sources and Analogies of International Law* (New York, 1927); *Recognition in International Law* (Cambridge, 1947).

B. AJIL 55, (1961), 97–103; DNB 1951–60, 611–13; Arnold D. McNair, "Hersch Lauterpacht, 1897–1960," *Proceedings of British Academy* 47 (1961), 371–85; NYT 10 May 1960, 37; WWW 1951–60, 640–41; WWWA 4, 558.

C. The Lauterpacht papers are at Trinity Coll., Cambridge Univ.

Robert A. Friedlander

LAVALEYE, Emile L. V. de. See *Biographical Dictionary of Modern Peace Leaders.*

LAYTON, Walter Thomas (15 March 1884, London—14 February 1966, London.) *Education*: B.A., London Univ., 1904; B.A., Cambridge Univ., 1907, M.A., 1911. *Career*: editor-in-chief, *The Economist*, 1928–38; chair, deputy chair, Economist Newspapers, Ltd., 1938–66; editor-in-chief, chair, News Chronicle Ltd., 1930–50; chair, Star Newspapers, Ltd., 1936–50; director, vice-chair Daily News Ltd., 1930–63; director, Reuters International Ltd., 1945–53; civil servant, Ministry of Munitions, 1914–18; director, Economic and Financial Section, League of Nations, 1919–21; British member, Organization Committee, Bank for International Settlements, 1929; director-general of programs, Ministry of Supply, 1940–42; chief adviser on programs and planning, Ministry of Production, 1942–43; head, Joint War Production Staff, 1942–43; vice-president, Consultative Assembly, Council of Europe, 1949–57; deputy leader, Liberal party, House of Lords, 1952–55; delegate to many conferences.

Layton did not devote his life fully to international causes, but his deep involvement in them flowed logically from his position in British society, his liberal ideological predispositions, and an extraordinary personal dedication to service. Layton had many careers: economist, university lecturer, journalist, editor, publisher, and expert administrator in both government and business, with a primary interest in the press. One of his skills was breathing life into moribund newspapers. The second in importance of his several careers was that of organizational trouble-shooter and innovator to business, government, and international bodies.

Already a well-known economist and newspaper editor, he established his reputation as an administrator in the Ministry of Munitions during World War I. In 1917 he ventured into international affairs as a member of both the Milner mission to Russia and the Balfour mission to the United States. The nature of international problems during the 1920s put his particular expertise in demand. He gave freely of it because he believed in the necessity of international collaboration. Thus, he set up the financial structure of the League of Nations, drafted the statutes for the International Bank for Settlements, served on the Reparations Commission, headed the Preparatory Commission for the World Economic Conference, and led a League of Nations economic mission to Austria. He was the preeminent British expert in international finance.

During World War I, Layton occupied key posts in the Ministries of Supply and Production until ill health overtook him. He became a late convert to the idea of United Europe but emerged from retirement as a vigorous propagandist for that cause. He ended his career as vice-president of the Council of Europe, as familiar a figure in Strasbourg as he had been in Geneva.

Layton was deeply attached to the Liberal party, and that loyalty shaped his career. He failed three times in his quest for a seat in Parliament, and his political ambitions had to be satisfied in the House of Lords. The declining fortunes of the Liberals no doubt made Layton more attractive as the reliable and disinterested expert to be sought out in time of emergency.

BIBLIOGRAPHY:

A. *How to Deal with Germany* (London, 1944); *An Introduction to the Study of Prices* (London, 1912); *United Europe: The Way to Achieve It* (London, 1948).

B. LT 15 Feb 1966, 12; NYT 15 Feb 1966, 39; WW 1966–67, 1231; WWWA, 4, 560–61.

Douglas W. Houston

LEACH, Henry Goddard (3 July 1880, Philadelphia—11 November 1970, New York). *Education*: B.A., Princeton Univ., 1903; M.A., Harvard Univ., 1906, Ph.D., 1908. *Career*: instructor, Groton School, 1903–5; Harvard traveling fellow in Scandinavia, 1908–10; instructor, Harvard Coll., 1910–12; executive officer and general secretary, American-Scandinavian Foundation (ASF), 1912–21; managing editor, *American-Scandinavian Review*, 1913–21; curator of Scandinavian history and literature, Harvard Univ. Library, 1921–31; editor, *The Forum* (later *The Forum and Century*), 1923–40; president, ASF, 1926–47; professor of Scandinavian civilization, Univ. of Kansas City, 1947–49.

Leach's notable career in fostering international cultural and intellectual cooperation grew out of a happy combination: his study of medieval languages and literature, especially Old Norse and Early English, and his enthusiastic interest in the life and institutions of modern Scandinavia. While doing research in Copenhagen, he served as secretary and unofficial protocol officer for Maurice F. Egan, the U.S. minister to Denmark. Leach's professional qualifications, uncommon initiative, and open personality brought him into productive contact with the major elements of Nordic society and led in 1912 to his employment by the newly formed American-Scandinavian Foundation (ASF). Through several decades thereafter, Leach was a driving force in this organization, which pioneered in sponsoring international exchange programs, literary and artistic contacts, and scientific and social investigation. Along with his administrative and editorial duties at ASF, Leach managed to keep up his linguistic and academic pursuits, including the writing of his encyclopedic *Scandinavia of the Scandinavians*.

A man of many talents, Leach took his motto from *The Poetic Edda*: "A better burden may no man bear for wanderings wide than wisdom." In 1923, desiring a wider range of activity, he embarked on a new venture, becoming editor of *The Forum*, which he transformed from a journal of discussion to one of controversy. Its columns revealed considerable interest in and sympathy toward the work of the League of Nations. His aim in publishing it was to develop technological patterns of thinking. At various times Leach also served as president of the Poetry Society of America, a member of the New York Judicial Council, a lecturer, a trustee of the Council on Religion and International Affairs, and president of the International Auxiliary Language Association. After being beaten by thugs in Central Park in January 1940, Leach stepped down as editor of *The Forum*, but later he returned to the ASF, where he became deeply engaged in relief and other wartime activities relating to Scandinavia.

Leach's views on a wide variety of subjects are set forth in his regular editorial column in *The Forum*, but his autobiography, *My Last Seventy Years*, though episodic, gives better insight into his personality and attitudes, his love of the outdoors, and his view that true controversy is the highest exercise in human intelligence. Leach's writings show him to have been less a crusader committed to causes and programs than a man of ideas and associations, active in public affairs, working quietly and steadily for international cooperation in education and the peaceful arts.

BIBLIOGRAPHY:

A. *Angevin Britain and Scandinavia* (Cambridge, MA, 1921); "Education Brings Nations Nearer Together," *New York Evening Post* 26 Jun 1920; "Fridtjof Nansen," *American-Scandinavian Review* 49 (Winter 1961), 360–67; *An Interrupted Courtship: An American Saga, 1904–15* (New York, 1963); *My Last Seventy Years* (New York, 1956); "Nansen's Mission and Norway's Need," *The Independent* 92 (24 Nov 1917), 360; "The Next Forty Years," *Forum* 75 (Mar 1926), 414–19; *A Pageant of Old Scandinavia* (Princeton, NJ, 1946); *Scandinavia of the Scandinavians* (London, 1915); "The Scandinavian Situation," *Nation* 105 (20 Dec 1917), 684–85.

B. James Creese, "Henry Goddard Leach," in *Scandinavian Studies: Essays Presented to Dr. Henry Goddard Leach on the Occasion of His Eighty-fifth Birthday*, ed. Carl F. Bayerschmidt and Erik J. Friis (Seattle, WA, 1965), 3-17, which also includes a bibliography of Leach's writings, 445-52; NCAB 56, 559-60; NYT 12 Nov 1970, 44; Lithgow Osborne, "Henry Goddard Leach," *American-Scandinavian Review* 59 (Summer 1971), 117-21.

C. Some Leach papers are in The Southern Historical Collection, Chapel Hill, NC.

Frederick Aandahl

LEFÈVRE, Théodore Joseph Albéric (17 January 1914, Ghent—18 September 1973, Brussels). *Education*: doctor of laws, State Univ. of Ghent, 1937. *Career*: member, resistance movement, 1941-45; member, Chamber of Representatives, Belgian Parliament, 1946-71, Senate, 1971-73; president, Social-Christian party, 1950-61; minister of state, 1958-73; prime minister of a Catholic-Socialist government, 1961-65; minister in charge of science policy and programming, 1968-71; secretary of state in charge of science policy, 1972.

Known for his national political achievements, Lefèvre also had an impact in the international political arena, especially as one of the chief architects of a unified space program. In his capacity as president of the European Space Conference (Brussels), 1972-73, he participated in the negotiations among the French, Germans, and British on the construction of a European launcher and in discussions as to whether to participate in the post-Apollo program. The two problems were solved in a positive way.

Space travel was not his only scientific interest. In 1967 he served as one of four experts who, under a mandate from the Organization for Economic Cooperation and Development, studied and reported on U.S. science policy. Lefèvre successfully contributed to the interaction between science and technology on the one hand and politics on the other.

Not only a convinced European and antinationalist, he strongly favored Christian Democracy in Western Europe, which he tried to reanimate when he entered Parliament in 1946. As the successor of August De Schrijver, he became the international president of the Nouvelles Equipes Internationales on 22 April 1960, the International Union of Christian Democrats, serving to 1965. During this period, Lefèvre sought better understanding between the Christian Democratic parties. One achievement was a meeting he organized in February 1963. There, six leaders of the Christian Democratic parties of "the Europe of the 6" issued a "Call for Europe" following the failure of the "Fouchet Committee" ("Union of European People"). Men like *Konrad Adenauer, *Alcide de Gasperi and *Robert Schuman were his friends, and he liked to talk about the influence which Christian Democracy played in the unification process of Europe. He had participated in this movement from its beginning, and he served as a member of the Assembly of the European Coal and Steel Community (ECSC) 1952-58 and as a member of the Constitutional Commission (1952) of which *Paul-Henri Spaak became the president.

In 1955, *Jean Monnet created his Action Committee for the United States of Europe, also called the Jean Monnet Committee, of which Lefèvre became a member. Apart from the Committee's goal of European unification, Monnet proposed the creation of an "atomic community" which led to the creation of Euratom (1957). In 1967, Lefèvre became the president of the Belgian Section of the "European Movement," which had been created in 1948 as a master organization for the different groups active in the field of European unification. He also served as a member of the Assembly of the Council of Europe (1950–58) and of the Western European Union (WEU) (1954–58). In 1965 he was a delegate to the United Nations. As premier from 1961–65, his attention was also drawn to the developing countries. After the bad experience Belgium had with its colonies, Lefèvre tried to reestablish relationships with the Third World through economic aid.

BIBLIOGRAPHY:

A. *Amerika en wij: Speurtochten naar onze toekomst* (Lier, Belgium, 1968); "De Europese Integratie," in *Teksten en Dokumenten*, no. 155 (Brussels, 1962); *La Science d'aujourd'hui pour la société de demain* (Brussels, 1971); "Où en est l'Europe?" in *Textes et documents*, no. 241 (Brussels, 1968), "Waar staat Europa?" in *Teksten en Dokumenten*, no. 241 (Brussels, 1968); *Wetenschap vandaag voor de maatschappij van morgen* (Tielt, Belgium, 1970); "Whither Europe?" in *Memo from Belgium* (Brussels, 1968), 106.

B. A. Breyne, "Théo Lefèvre beminde zijn zending," *Spectator* 39 (29 Sep 1973), 10–11; CB 1943, 457–58, 1962, 248–50; L. Beyer De Ryke, *Théo Lefèvre* (Brussels, 1967); IWW 1973–74, 975; LT 19 Sep 1973, 21; NYT 19 Sep 1973, 50; J. Piens, "Théo Lefèvre: Une Certaine Grandeur d'âme," *Revue générale* (Aug–Sep 1977), 1–10; L. Rens and others, *Théo Lefèvre, Minister van Staat* (Antwerp, Belgium, 1968); J. Sterck, "Over Théo Lefèvre," *Spectator* 39 (29 Sep 1973), 6–11; P. Van Molle, *Het Belgisch Parlement 1894–1972* (Antwerp, Belgium, 1972), 217–18; WWB 389.

Marc Riga

LEHMAN, Herbert Henry (28 March 1878, New York—5 December 1963, New York). *Education*: B.A., Williams Coll., 1899. *Career*: businessman, New York, 1899–1908; partner, Lehman Brothers, 1908–29; lieutenant governor of New York, 1929–33; governor, 1933–42; director, Office of Foreign Relief and Rehabilitation Operations, Department of State, 1942–43; director-general, United Nations Relief and Rehabilitation Administration, 1943–46; senator, 1949–57.

Lehman's major international contribution came late in his life, but his earlier experiences in banking, politics, and philanthropy prepared him to lead the first UN organization. The son of a founder of the investment banking firm of Lehman Brothers, he grew up in luxury that permitted travel in Europe. He inherited his parents' dislike of their native Germany and their affinity for England. This bias shaped Lehman's typical American brand of internationalism. In World War I, he supported immediate U.S. intervention on behalf of the Allies. In 1917 he applied for and received an army commission, but to his dismay he was assigned to Washington. After the war he turned his attention to international relief, helping to lead the Joint Distribution Committee (JDC), a private effort by American Jews to relieve destitution among coreligionists, especially in Eastern Europe. During the period 1921-24, Lehman headed a JDC Committee which undertook the economic rehabilitation of Jewish communities ravaged by the war. Throughout the 1930s, he was preoccupied by domestic politics. With the outbreak of World War II in Europe, he private spoke in favor of U.S. intervention on the side of Great Britain. Publicly he endorsed all possible aid short of war.

In December 1942 *Franklin Roosevelt appointed Lehman as director of the Office of Foreign Relief and Rehabilitation, a new State Department agency designed to aid liberated countries until an international effort was organized. On 9 November 1943, representatives of forty-four nations signed an agreement creating the United Nations Relief and Rehabilitation Administration (UNRRA). Its Council elected Lehman director-general, and he dedicated himself to acting on behalf of all member governments to create an organization that transcended national interests. He also set a high standard of selflessness by serving without pay.

UNRRA was established as a temporary agency to provide basic necessities to war victims in countries invaded by the enemy. It required building a staff (eventually numbering some 20,000), raising funds (ultimately $3.8 billion) and securing supplies (totaling 24 million tons from thirty-one nations). UNRRA ultimately provided relief to sixteen countries and initiated the rehabilitation of industry and agriculture. Lehman proved especially effective in winning congressional approval of appropriations for UNRRA. He also generated favorable publicity for the agency when it aroused postwar suspicions. Even as relations between the United States and the Soviet Union deteriorated, Lehman sought to avoid political considerations by dispensing relief to countries, including the Soviet Union, primarily on the basis of need. Discouraged by America's growing reaction against international cooperation and physically exhausted, Lehman resigned from UNRRA on 12 March 1946. He soon reentered domestic politics, becoming a senator and a supporter of *Harry Truman's Cold War policies.

BIBLIOGRAPHY:

B. CB 1955, 352-54; DAB supp. 7, 466-68; *International Hebrew Heritage Library* 8, 115-18; Allan Nevins, *Herbert H. Lehman and His Era* (New York, 1963); NYT 6 Dec 1963, 1; *Universal Jewish Encyclopedia* 6 (New York, 1942), 592-95; George Woodbridge, *UNRRA: The History of the United Nations Relief and Rehabilitation Administration*, 3 vols. (New York, 1950); WWWA 4, 565-66.

C. The Lehman papers are in the School of International Affairs, Columbia Univ.

Robert P. Ingalls

LEIPER, Henry Smith (17 September 1891, Belmar, NJ—22 January 1975, Hightstown, NJ). *Education*: B.A., Amherst Coll., 1913; B.D., Union

Theol. Sem., 1917; M.A., Columbia Univ., 1917. *Career*: ordained minister in Presbyterian Church, USA, 1915; transferred to Congregational church, 1920; missionary in China, 1918–22; associate secretary, Congregational Commission on Missions, 1923–30; executive secretary, Commission on Relations with Churches Abroad, Federal Council of Churches, 1930–45, Provisional Committee, World Council of Churches, 1938–48; associate general secretary, World Council of Churches, 1948–52; executive secretary, Missions Council, Congregational Christian Churches, 1952–59.

American Christians in the first two thirds of the twentieth century discovered that the church was much more than their local congregation. This discovery of the universal lay at the heart of Leiper's career. Reared in Indian territory and the parsonage, he grew to embrace the worldwide fellowship of Christians, which he nurtured by his various global contacts through more than forty years in the ecumenical movement. Born a Presbyterian, he left it for the less constricting Congregational church. Influenced by American revivals and the student missionary conferences at Northfield, Leiper prepared for service in China, where he worked briefly until his wife's ill health forced his return.

Although in the 1920s he played a variety of mission-centered roles as executive and editor, he continued to travel extensively. This "genius for making contacts" qualified him for leadership of the Federal Council's Commission on Relations with Churches Abroad. In essence, Leiper was a key American in the new Life and Work movement which flowed into the organizing of the World Council of Churches in the late 1930s. As associate general secretary of the WCC with responsibilities on the American side, he headed its New York office. His many secretaryships, in fact, indicated a servanthood motif. Moreover, Leiper believed that the unity of the worldwide church would contribute to world peace.

Highly articulate in his writing and speaking, Leiper brought ecumenism down to the level of the average church member. In turn, he represented the American churches at the enthronement of William Temple, Archbishop of Canterbury, and at the Four hundredth Anniversary of the Augsburg Confession. In the last analysis, his was the contribution of interpretation and support. In his office as associate general secretary, he directly raised millions of dollars for the nascent World Council, without which it would have foundered. That practical bent established him as one of America's foremost church leaders.

BIBLIOGRAPHY:

A. *Blind Spots* (New York, 1929); ed., *Christianity Today* (New York, 1947); *Christ's Way and the World's* (New York, 1936); *The Ghost of Caesar Walks* (New York, 1935); *World Chaos or World Christianity* (New York, 1937).

B. CB 1948, 374–76; IWW 1972–73, 969; NYT 23 Jan 1975, 36; *Religious Leaders of America* 2 (1941–42), 678; WB (1948), 2738–39.

William J. Schmidt

LEMMONIER, Charles. See *Biographical Dictionary of Modern Peace Leaders.*

LESTER, Seán (John Ernest) (27 September 1888, Woodburn, Carricksfergus, County Antrim, Ireland—13 June 1959, County Galway, Ireland). *Education*: Methodist Coll., Belfast. *Career*: journalist, Belfast, 1909–22; publicity officer, Department of External Affairs, 1922–29; Irish representative, League of Nations, 1929–33; high commissioner to Danzig, 1933–37; deputy secretary-general, League of Nations, 1937–40, acting secretary-general, 1940–46.

Once in Geneva, Lester showed considerable interest in League affairs. As a Council member, he chaired the committee which resolved the Leticia boundary dispute of Colombia and Peru, and he became involved in efforts to settle the Chaco controversy between Bolivia and Peru. In both instances, he revealed administrative tact coupled with patient and courteous determination. He became the League's high commissioner to the Free City of Danzig in 1933, which had been internationalized because of its diverse population and conflicting territorial claims. It was a time of tension, when the emerging Nazis sought to create conditions favorable to their control of the area. Lester sought to protect various national minorities and the Jewish population despite threats from Nazi factions and to counter German charges of administrative ineptitude by the League. Lester undoubtedly welcomed the opportunity to return to Geneva in 1937 when he was named as the League's deputy secretary-general.

There Lester worked under *Joseph Avenol in an uncomfortable relationship. He did not agree with Avenol's efforts to seek accommodations with the Germans and to subordinate the League's interests to those of France. They clashed openly over Avenol's decision after the defeat of France in 1940 to transfer the League's records and assets to Vichy, a dispute which led to Avenol's resignation and Lester's installation as acting secretary-general. In that post, Lester worked under trying conditions. Payments from most members stopped, and the major sections had been transferred to safe ground in England, Canada, and the United States. Moreover, the annual meetings of the Assembly and Council could not be held because of transit problems; thus, Lester had to preside with little direction. Even the Supervisory Commission could meet only sporadically. The Swiss, always sensitive regarding their neutrality, became increasingly uncooperative toward the potentially dangerous international body on their soil. Lester also had the unrewarding duty of presiding over the demise of the League and the transfer of its assets to the United Nations. When that project ended, he retired to Ireland. The final Assembly of the League in Geneva in April 1946 bestowed upon him the title of the third secretary-general, retroactive to 1940.

BIBLIOGRAPHY:

B. James Barros, *Betrayal from Within: Joseph Avenol, Secretary-General of the League of Nations, 1933–1940* (New Haven, CT, 1969); *Dictionary of Irish Biography* (Dublin, 1978), 183; DNB 1951–60, 624–25; Raymond B. Fosdick, *The League and the United Nations after Fifty Years: The Six Secretaries-General* (Newton, CT, 1972); IWW 1955, 563; Frank P. Walters, *A History of the League of Nations* (London, 1952).

Warren F. Kuehl

LEVERMORE, Charles Herbert (15 October 1856, Mansfield, CT—20 October 1927, Berkeley, CA). *Education*: B.A., Yale Univ., 1879; Ph.D., Johns Hopkins Univ., 1886. *Career*: teacher, 1879–83, 1885–86; instructor, Univ. of California, 1886–87; assistant to full professor, Massachusetts Institute of Technology, 1888–93; principal, Adelphi Acad., 1893–1909; a founder and first president, Adelphi Coll., 1896–1912; a director, World Peace Foundation, 1913–17; secretary, New York Peace Society, 1917–27, World's Court League and League of Nations Union, 1919–27; American Peace Award, 1924.

Levermore wrote several books of history and three on songs and hymns, but he is remembered as a publicist, a committed peace worker, and an internationalist. His involvement began with his attendance at Lake Mohonk Arbitration Conferences; and after he left his presidency of Adelphi College, he accepted a post with the World Peace Foundation in 1913 in Boston as director of its college and university bureau. Then he served as its acting director (1915–17). In 1915 he also helped organize the American Branch of the Central Organization for a Durable Peace, which sought to study peace needs at the end of World War I. He returned to New York City in 1917 when he became secretary of the New York Peace Society (NYPS). Once a center of internationalist thought, it had moved from endorsing a politically organized postwar league to one emphasizing a court.

Levermore's commitment to a legally oriented international structure appeared in 1919, when he accepted the position of secretary of the World's Court League (WCL), a body which called for a judicially focused organization. It contrasted markedly with the League to Enforce Peace program because it renounced sanctions as part of its operational structure. Levermore also edited its journal, the *World Court Magazine*, and kept in touch with other groups of similar outlook.

This background explains why Levermore did not campaign extensively for U.S. membership in the League of Nations under the Covenant; he preferred a less-developed body. He did join with others in 1919 in creating the League of Nations Union through a merger of the NYPS and the WCL and became its secretary. It endorsed membership without commitment to details and thus did not directly confront the issues.

Yet Levermore did approve of the League and U.S. affiliation under proper safeguards, as his work in ensuing years demonstrated. He sat on the executive committee of the Pro-League Independents during the election of 1920, and he prepared annual volumes on the League of Nations which emphasized its constructive work. He helped organize the American Association for International Cooperation in 1922, served as its secretary, and late that year led in negotiations which resulted in the creation of the League of Nations Non-Partisan Association early in 1923. He then became a vice-president of the new body.

Levermore's paramount claim to fame rests with his 1924 "winning plan" of the American Peace Award, offered by Edward W. Bok for "the best practicable plan by which the United States may cooperate with other nations to achieve and preserve the peace of the world." The $100,000 prize attracted hundreds of thousands of responses, and 22,165 proposals were screened by an illustrious jury. Through a national referendum conducted in newspapers, the "Winning Plan" (submitted anonymously) attracted 608,090 favorable votes. At an elaborate dinner in Philadelphia, *John W. Davis conferred a check of $50,000 on Levermore. (The second half of the prize would be given when the plan was implemented.) In accepting, Levermore noted that it represented "a crown and a challenge" and a demand for continuing service toward greater cooperation and peace with justice.

The plan reflected many years of thought and involvement by Levermore plus the political reality of the time in which Republican administrations would not move vigorously along international paths. Levermore admitted that in drafting it he kept continually in mind the word "practical." Thus he cleverly straddled the question of U.S. membership in the League, but in doing so he revealed his own preferences. He called for entry into the Permanent Court of International Justice and cooperation with the League under clearly stated ground rules. Levermore also sought to bridge the gap between supporters of prewar efforts associated with The Hague conferences and those who endorsed the League. The latter, he argued, had moved gradually to support the foundations created, 1899–1907. Programs to foster cooperation and interdependence and to develop international law should move ahead, merging ideas and organs of both prewar and postwar workers. Levermore used the prize money to visit and study conditions in Europe, the Middle East, and North Africa; he was on his way to the Orient on a similar mission when he died.

BIBLIOGRAPHY:

A. *Samuel Train Dutton* (New York, 1922); "The Winning Plan," *International Conciliation* 195 (Feb 1924), 9–19; *Yearbook of the League of Nations* (Brooklyn, NY, 1921–23). Many of Levermore's publications can be found in the World Peace Foundation Pamphlet Series.

B. DAB 11, 199–200; Charles DeBenedetti, "The $100,000 American Peace Award of 1924," *Pennsylvania Magazine of History and Biography* 98 (Apr 1974), 224–49; *Literary Digest* 80 (23 Feb 1924), 50–57; NCAB 33, 137–38.

C. Some Levermore papers are in the Swarthmore Coll. Peace Collection.

Warren F. Kuehl

LEVINSON, Salmon Oliver. See *Biographical Dictionary of Modern Peace Leaders.*

LIE, Trygve Halvdan (16 June 1896, Oslo—30 December 1968, Geilo, Norway). *Education*: graduate, School of Law, Univ. of Oslo, 1919. *Career*: assistant, Trade Union Federation of Norway, 1922–35; minister of justice, 1935–39; member of Parliament, 1935; minister of trade, industry, shipping, and fisheries, 1939–40; in exile in England, acting foreign minister, later foreign minister in government-in-exile, 1940–45; led Norwegian delegation to San Francisco Conference, 1945; foreign minister, 1945–46; first secretary-general of the UN, 1946–53; governor of Oslo and of Akershus Province, 1955.

The creation of the United Nations in 1945 was motivated by a far more fundamental and lasting concept concerning the world than a passing wartime alliance of great powers. The founders hoped to create a universal organization through which the international community could over time develop adequate means for ordering the conduct of states in accordance with the principles of peace and justice. In contrast to the prewar League of Nations, the UN gave its secretary-general rights which went beyond any power previously accorded the head of an international organization, to make decisions which might justly be called political.

Lie was successful in carving out a political role for the office of secretary-general, unheard of for his League of Nations predecessors. He began by establishing the procedural prerogatives of the office and concluded by legitimizing the right of the UN's chief administrative officer to take a position and help decide policy affecting global issues. The development was not planned but rather pragmatic and for the most part generally acceptable to the member states. At the beginning of his tenure, Lie gained support from the contending major powers for his energetic assertion of the secretary-general's right to make any inquiries or investigations he thought necessary to determine whether or not he should bring any situation to the attention of the Security Council under the provisions of the Charter. Using his prerogatives, he interposed himself between the parties, holding that the UN should aim to settle disputes, not enflame them.

Lie's involvement in the resolution of the Palestinian issue at an early stage was the opening round of his movement for mediation, neutrality, and an independent and effective role for the UN. He supported the partition plan for Palestine and was instrumental in *Folke Bernadotte's mediation effort. He worked to get UN personnel into the field for purposes of observation, negotiation, and truce supervision and to act as a buffer between Arab and Israeli forces. On a more general level, Lie sought a consensus among the member states for establishing a military force under the Secretariat with the secretary-general as its commander and with contributions of contingents primarily from small and neutral countries. However, the idea foundered on stiff opposition, particularly from the Soviet Union.

Lie's 1950 Memorandum for Peace Through the United Nations was one of his major contributions to conciliation. It sought to help defuse the antagonisms dividing the big powers and paralyzing the UN. Its ten points included (1) periodic top-level meetings of the Security Council; (2) establishment of an international control system for atomic energy; (3) a new approach to the regulation of armaments; (4) agreement on the armed forces to be made available to the UN; (5) acceptance of the principle of universality, which would allow the People's Republic of China and other states to join the UN; (6) a sound and active program of technical assistance for economic development; (7) a more vigorous use of specialized agencies; (8) continued development of the UN role in the field of human rights; (9) advancement of colonial and dependent peoples toward a place of equality among nations; (10) active use of Charter powers and UN machinery to speed development of international law toward an enforceable world law. The fact that Lie undertook a peace mission to the capitals of big powers to present and discuss the plan, and was given a hearing, was another landmark on the development of the secretary-general's independent political role. The plan was thwarted by the Korean War.

When Lie took the initiative during that event by declaring North Korea an aggressor, he lost the confidence of the Soviet Union. When the question of renewing his term of office arose later in 1950, the Soviet Union vetoed his appointment. The Western majority in the General Assembly insisted on the extension of his term despite the absence of unanimity among the permanent members of the Security Council; however, the Soviet Union would not concede the legality of this approach and ostracized Lie by ignoring his existence and his action. In November 1952 Lie resigned, stating that he was stepping aside in the hope that it would help the UN and serve progress and freedom. It was Lie who described the work of the UN secretary-general as the most impossible task on earth.

BIBLIOGRAPHY:

A. *In the Cause of Peace* (New York, 1954).

B. CB 1946, 342–45; Andrew W. Cordier and Wilder Foote, eds., *Public Papers of the Secretaries-General of the United Nations* 1 (New York, 1969); *New Republic* 114 (25 Mar 1946), 403–4; NYT 31 Dec 1968, 1; NYT *Magazine* 24 Mar 1946, 11, 48–49.

Vratislav Pechota

LIEBER, Francis (18 March 1798, Berlin—2 October 1872, New York). *Career*: publisher, 1829–33; professor, South Carolina Coll., 1835–65, Columbia Coll., 1857–65, Columbia Law School, 1865–72.

A political scientist, Lieber was notable as an internationalist for his codification of the laws of war and his efforts to obtain a private congress of authorities on international law to devise codes. He grew up an ardent nationalist, fighting in the Prussian Army in the Waterloo campaign.

Subsequently he participated in student movements the government considered subversive, and he was imprisoned for his views. In 1821 Lieber went to Greece, hoping to participate in the revolution against the Turks, and, disillusioned, returned to Rome, where the Prussian ambassador and historian, Barthold G. Niebuhr, befriended him and molded his mind. Back in Prussia, Lieber was again imprisoned and upon release made his way first to England, then to the United States.

In America, Lieber received much attention because of his romantic background and wide intellectual interests. He edited the *Encyclopedia Americana* (13 vols., 1829–33), based on the German *Conversations Lexikon*. This publication, like much of Lieber's work, exalted what was American yet it was also significant for its transmission of European ideas to the New World. While he taught in South Carolina, he produced a number of writings, both trivial and significant, including the *Manual of Political Ethics* (2 vols., 1838–39) and *On Civil Liberty and Self-Government* (2 vols., 1853). In these seminal treatises he analyzed the nature of government. He extolled the American system of limited government, contrasted it to the "democratic absolutism" that threatened Europe, and explored the relationship of the citizen and society to the state. Lieber's works significantly influenced the developing fields of political science and sociology in America.

During the Civil War, he was an ardent advocate of the Northern cause and as an adviser to the Union Army moved into the field of international law. In 1862 he prepared *Guerrilla Parties Considered with Reference to the Laws and Usages of War* and in 1863 a code of the laws of war, which the Army promulgated as *General Orders 100: Instructions for the Government of Armies of the United States in the Field*. Not binding upon the troops, it was a guide, backed by precedents in international law dating back as far as the writings of Grotius and Vattel. It remained the standard code for the U.S. Army through the Spanish–American War, and much of its wording has continued in Army manuals. *General Orders 100* served as the basis for a code of the laws of war that a congress of scholars subsequently drafted. That code in turn led to the Hague Conventions of 1899 and 1907.

After the Civil War, Lieber focused his attention upon the interrelationship between nationalism and internationalism, which he summed up in a pamphlet, *Fragments of Political Science on Nationalism and Internationalism* (1868). He posited a future in which strong national states would cooperate as a commonwealth of nations. The basis would be a code of international law, built, as he wrote James A. Garfield, on the rules of good neighborhood and the common law as used by nations. Until his death Lieber was involved in promoting a number of international schemes. He was a proponent of the first conferences on international law in the 1870s and from 1870 to 1872 served with distinction as the umpire of the commission to settle claims arising from the Mexican War. As a graduate student, *Woodrow Wilson praised the concise, clear, and admirable decisions.

BIBLIOGRAPHY:

A. *Manual of Political Ethics*, 2nd ed., 2 vols. (Philadelphia, 1892); *The Miscellaneous Writings of Francis Lieber*, 2 vols. (Philadelphia, 1880); *On Civil Liberty and Self-Government* (Philadelphia, 1875).

B. Frank Freidel, *Francis Lieber: Nineteenth Century Liberal* (Baton Rouge, LA, 1947).

C. Lieber papers are in the Colonial Williamsburg Manuscript Collection, Henry E. Huntington Library, the Johns Hopkins Univ. Library, the Univ. of South Carolina Library, and the Manuscript Division, Library of Congress.

Frank Freidel

LIPPMANN, Walter (23 September 1889, New York—14 December 1974, New York). *Education*: B.A., Harvard Coll., 1910. *Career*: reporter, *Boston Common*, 1910; assistant to Lincoln Steffens, *Everybody's Magazine*, 1910–12; executive secretary to mayor of Schenectady, 1912; associate editor, *New Republic*, 1914–17, 1919–21; assistant to secretary of war, 1917; member, the Inquiry, 1917–18; military intelligence, 1918–19; editorial staff, *New York World*, 1922–23, editor, 1923–31; columnist, *New York Herald Tribune*, 1931–67; columnist, *Newsweek*, 1963–68.

Lippmann's career as journalist, author, and political philosopher coincided with the origin, expansion, and crisis of America's world leadership over almost two-thirds of the twentieth century. Except for short periods in local and national government service, Lippmann's influence was exerted primarily through his writings in the *New Republic*, the *World*, the *Herald Tribune*, and *Newsweek* and through his personal contacts with American and foreign statesmen. The product of and spokesman for the New Liberalism and nationalism of the era of *Alfred Mahan and *Theodore Roosevelt, Lippmann moved from an early Socialism to a restrained political conservatism. He viewed America as an activist, progressive, global power which under strong presidential leadership had a mission to stabilize and purify world politics.

Although Lippmann's views changed over time, there was a constancy to his commitment to reason and order in international affairs. During World War I, he advocated U.S. intervention as the means of securing a just peace. As a member of the Inquiry, he drafted the basis of *Woodrow Wilson's Fourteen Points. Like many internationally-minded liberals, Lippmann opposed the Treaty of Versailles, the League of Nations, and the military struggle against the Bolshevik regime. He argued in his columns that America not sully its crusade for a democratic world order by serving the Allies' imperialist goals. In 1922, Lippmann's *Public Opinion* revealed his disillusionment with the hope of creating an informed citizenry. The power of wartime censorship and propaganda and the postwar emergence of Communism and Fascism convinced him of the urgency of his calling: the specialist analyst of domestic and international affairs probing beyond the transient and sensational and guiding opinion in a responsible direction.

In the interwar period, Lippmann oscillated between more justice for the vanquished and collective security, between disarmament and military preparedness, between isolationism and global politics. Commencing his thirty-six-year column for the Republican *Herald Tribune*, Lippmann would oppose much of the New Deal's domestic program and advocate America's armed neutrality. He moved to Washington in 1938, where he became engrossed in international politics. After Munich, he realized Britain's and France's unwillingness and inability to resist Hitler. The fall of France convinced him that America must join the anti-Nazi coalition. Denouncing his generation, which had been "tried and found wanting," he led those former isolationists who, after 7 December 1941, called for total war and total victory in Europe and in Asia.

A much-chastened Wilsonian, Lippmann in his two wartime books, *U.S. Foreign Policy* and *U.S. War Aims*, rejected world government as he based his internationalism on *Realpolitik*. He advocated the maintenance of the wartime coalition, which after victory would secure the peace not by reliance on world assemblies or the complicity of the vanquished but simply by adjusting their great power interests. In *The Cold War* essays, Lippmann warned against opposing the Soviet Union's natural spheres of influence; and though shocked by the 1948 coup in Czechoslovakia, he insisted on a power balance with Moscow. He subsequently argued against forming NATO and rearming West Germany, and warned against the expansion of the Korean War and America's military involvement in Southeast Asia. Anticipating the East–West struggle in the former colonial world, Lippmann in *The Communist World and Ours* urged American democracy to compete with its Communist adversary; but in the 1960s he denounced Washington's postwar quest for national security that had led to an "imperial role" in Southeast Asia. An elegant and detached analyst, not always consistent, Lippmann reminded six generations of Americans to become involved and committed in the world, to temper their isolationist tendencies, and to curb their crusading excesses.

BIBLIOGRAPHY:

A. *The Cold War* (Boston, 1947); *The Coming Tests with Russia* (Boston, 1961); *The Communist World and Ours* (Boston, 1959); *Drift and Mastery* (New York, 1914); *Essays in the Public Philosophy* (Boston, 1955); *The Good Society* (Boston, 1937); *Isolation and Alliances* (Boston, 1952); *The Phantom Public* (New York, 1925); *A Preface to Morals* (New York, 1929); *A Preface to Politics* (New York, 1913); *Public Opinion* (New York, 1922); *The Stakes of Diplomacy* (New York, 1915); *U.S. Foreign Policy: Shield of the Republic* (Boston, 1943); *U.S. War Aims* (Boston, 1944); *Western Unity and the Common Market* (Boston, 1962).

B. Francine C. Cary, *Influence of War on Walter Lippmann: 1914–1944* (Madison, WI, 1967); Marquis Childs and James Reston, *Walter Lippmann and His Times* (New York, 1959); *Encyclopedia of American Biography* (New York, 1974), 673–75; *Encyclopedia of World Biography* 6 (New York, 1973) 516–17; NYT 15 Dec 1974, 1; Ronald Steel, *Walter Lippmann and the American Century* (Boston, 1980); Anwar Syed, *Walter Lippmann's Philosophy of International Politics* (Philadelphia, 1963).

C. The Lippmann papers are at Yale Univ. There is an Oral History at Columbia Univ.

Carole Fink

LITVINOV, Maksim Maksimovich [born Meer Genokh Moissevich Vallakh, Meyer Wallach in English, many aliases] (17 July 1876, Bielostok, Russian Poland—31 December 1951, Moscow). *Education*: Bielostok Realschule. *Career*: clerical and managerial positions in business firms in the Russian Empire and England, interspersed with periods of imprisonment and full-time revolutionary work, 1898–1917; joined Russian Social Democratic Labor party, 1898; adhered to Bolshevik faction, 1903; first chargé d'affaires of Russian Soviet Republic in London, December 1917—September 1918; entered People's Commissariat for Foreign Affairs (Narkomindel), 1918; deputy commissar of foreign affairs, 1921–30; commisar of foreign affairs, 1930–39; member, Central Committee of the Communist party of the Soviet Union, 1934–41; ambassador to United States, 1941–43, deputy commissar of foreign affairs, 1943–46.

At the highest philosophical level, the Soviet government has consistently stated that genuine, lasting peace can exist only when a classless and, therefore, stateless world society has been achieved. Throughout the period between the world wars, the Communist International, headquartered in Moscow, sought to hasten true peace by encouraging class war in the capitalist world. At the same time, however, the Soviet Foreign Office and especially Litvinov were seeking international peace through conciliation, disarmament, and, after 1933, collective security. Although Litvinov held no illusions that capitalist states could abolish armed conflict, he nonetheless argued that war and its destruction could be averted in the immediate future, especially if the people of Europe brought enough pressure on their war-weakened governments to cooperate with the Soviet Union's initiatives; thus, in his eyes, he addressed not so much the diplomatic community and delegates to the League of Nations as the general population.

A gregarious polyglot, married to an English woman and well acquainted with European middle-class culture, Litvinov combined the political credentials of an Old Bolshevik with the ability to speak eloquently without recourse to a gratingly agitational vocabulary. His common sense and "unrevolutionary" bearing reassured foreigners that the Soviet Union could conduct a normally cooperative foreign policy. Thus, his personality was crucial to whatever small successes he achieved. (Among his personal triumphs were U.S. recognition of the Soviet Union in 1933 and his place as head of the Soviet delegation as it took its seat in the League of Nations in 1934.) His larger efforts to "find a common language" with the Western powers and preserve the security of his country by international agreement rather than by threat, territorial acquisition, or bilateral military pact all ended in failure.

In the late 1920s Litvinov insisted that only total general disarmament could assure peace. Mutual assistance pacts and systems of security that called upon special "guardian" countries were at best useless. With the increasing belligerence of Germany and Japan in the early 1930s, however, he separated the more aggressive capitalist powers from the relatively peaceable ones and called upon the latter to take collective action for collective security. Most of his reputation as an internationalist rests on his speeches of this period, urging the "indivisibility of peace" and demanding that the League of Nations take action against the "violators of international obligations." When his government concluded that the Soviet Union would be more secure through alliance with Germany and additional cushioning territory on the western frontier, Litvinov was retired into obscurity; only the German invasion of 1941 rescued him for a last act, cooperation among nations at war.

BIBLIOGRAPHY:

A. *Against Aggression* (New York, 1939); A biographical sketch is in Georges Haupt and Jean-Jacques Marie, *Makers of the Russian Revolution* (Ithaca, NY, 1974); *The Soviet Union and Peace* (New York, n.d.).

B. Arthur Upham Pope, *Maxim Litvinoff* (New York, 1943); Henry L. Roberts, "Maxim Litvinov," in eds. Gordon A. Craig and Felix Gilbert *The Diplomats, 1919–1939*, (Princeton, NJ, 1953), 344–77; Yojtech Mastny, "The Cassandra in the Foreign Commissariat: Maxim Litvinov and the Cold War," *Foreign Affairs* 34 (Oct 1975), 366–76.

Effie Ambler

LLOYD GEORGE, David (17 January 1863, Manchester—26 March 1945, Criccieth, England). *Education*: Llanystumdwy Church of England School. *Career*: solicitor, 1844; Liberal member of Parliament, Caernarvon Boroughs, 1890–1945; president, Board of Trade, 1905–8; chancellor of the exchequer, 1908–15; minister of munitions, 1915–16; secretary of state for war, 1916; prime minister, 1916–22.

During his fifty-five-year political career, Lloyd George was always a potent figure whose purpose and direction was not easily discerned. His characteristic dynamic force and action obscured the substance of his ideas and accomplishment. His youth and early career were powerfully influenced by his Uncle Richard Lloyd, who cultivated David Lloyd George's radical, Baptist, anticlass establishment ideas. His early interest was in advancing Welsh nationalism and disestablishing the church in Wales, and for more than a decade he was associated almost exclusively with Welsh problems.

The Boer War gave him national attention through his publicly expressed belief that it was unnecessary. His opposition, as a nonconformist, to the Education Bill of 1902 and his emergence as a free-trader enhanced his emerging place in the Liberal party. His tenure at the Board of Trade produced significant legislation, including the Patents Act. As chancellor of the exchequer he developed a close alliance with *Herbert Asquith and emerged as a champion of social reform. Rejection of Lloyd George's "People's Budget" in 1909 by the House of Lords led ultimately to the reform of that body in 1911. The National Insurance Bill of 1911 was the high point of his efforts as a social reformer.

World War I offered new challenges and new political opportunity as minister of munitions, and secretary of state for war, and on 7 December 1916, he became prime minister when his decisive leadership prevailed over the indecisive Asquith. Lloyd George transformed both the Office of Prime Minister and the Cabinet by centralizing authority.

He also saw an opportunity to shape a new England and the world after the war. He endorsed the idea of a league of nations late in 1917 but showed uncertainty in ensuing months about its structure and powers. He left that problem largely to others, especially *Robert Cecil. The Paris Peace Conference thrust him into the world spotlight, and during the next three years he dominated international diplomacy and politics while advancing his ideas on peace. He supported a plan to bring Russian delegates to Paris in 1919 and to include that nation and Germany in the League of Nations. He firmly believed that the wounds of war should be bound quickly with new hope. His Fontainebleau Memorandum was his great appeal for moderation and peace in 1919. He worked tirelessly, 1919–22, to achieve stability through conference diplomacy and believed passionately that the restoration of national economies and international trade were essential to world peace. The Anglo–Russian trade agreement of 1921 was a product of this policy.

In domestic affairs he had to deal with the threat of a general strike, and he continued to move forward with social reform begun years before. Unemployment insurance was applied nationwide. The success of the Washington Naval Conference, which he regarded as leading to international cooperation, was following by diplomatic failure at the Genoa Conference. His Turkish policy and revolt in the Unionist ranks led to his resignation on 19 October 1922. After leaving office, he continued to generate radical ideas on social and economic reform. He also attempted to promote world peace and urged a negotiated peace early in World War II. His later years were spent in political obscurity.

BIBLIOGRAPHY:

A. *Memoirs of the Peace Conference*, 2 vols. (New Haven, CT, 1939); *The Truth About Reparations and War-Debts* (New York, 1932); *The Truth About the Peace Treaties* (London, 1938); *War Memoirs of David Lloyd George, 1914–1918*, 6 vols. (Boston, 1933–37); *We Can Conquer Unemployment* (London, 1929); *Where Are We Going?* (New York, 1923).

B. John Campbell, *Lloyd George: The Goat in the Wilderness* (London, 1977); CB 1944, 419–23; George W. Egerton, *Great Britain and the Creation of the League of Nations* (Chapel Hill, NC, 1978); John Grigg, *Lloyd George: The Peoples Cham-*

pion, 1902–1911 (Berkeley, CA, 1978), *The Young Lloyd George* (London, 1973); Michael Fry, *Lloyd George and Foreign Policy*, 2 vols. (Montreal, 1977); Thomas Jones, *Lloyd George* (Cambridge, 1951); K. O. Morgan, *Consensus and Disunity* (Oxford, 1979).

   C. The Lloyd George papers are in the House of Lords Records Office and the National Library of Wales.

Stephen E. Fritz

LODER, Bernard Cornelis Johannes (13 September 1849, Amsterdam—4 November 1935, The Hague). *Education*: graduate, Leiden Univ., 1873. *Career*: attorney at Rotterdam, 1873–1908; member, Netherlands Supreme Court, 1909–21; judge, Permanent Court of International Justice, 1922–30.

   Loder was one of the leaders of the International Law Association, in which, as in the Institute of International Law (chair in 1925), he played an important role. Loder's interest in the international sphere evolved from his study of the law of the sea. He helped found the International Maritime Commission in 1906, and he represented the Netherlands at conferences in 1905, 1909, 1910, and 1922 to discuss the law of the oceans. However, his name is especially connected with the establishment of the Permanent Court of International Justice, his efforts being instrumental in its having its seat in the Netherlands.

   In March 1919 Loder was sent, with the representatives of other neutral states, as one of the Dutch delegates to the Paris Conference to advise on the Draft Covenant of the League of Nations. In 1920 he presided over deliberations on the drafting of a statute for an international court. These were held in the Peace Palace at The Hague, where the deputies of five neutrals participated—Denmark, the Netherlands, Norway, Sweden, and Switzerland. In the same year, the Council of the League of Nations appointed him a member of the committee of ten international jurists to advise and aid it in its task of submitting to the Assembly plans for the establishment of the Permanent Court of International Justice. In September 1921, on the joint decision of the Council and Assembly, Loder became a judge of the Court, which elected him its first president in February 1922. Loder held this post for three years but served on the Court until 1930.

   Loder had well-defined ideas about the character of the future Court, which he wished to be kept from everything that smacked of arbitration and removed from the domain of national egoism. In a speech to the International Law Association, typical of his views, he outlined the ideal. It should be permanent with power to cite governments and it should not seek to compromise differences but to settle them in accord with justice. To Loder, nothing could substitute for such a process, not even arbitration. Settling disputes that way led only to ambiguity and debate over selecting the arbitrators. The Permanent Court changed all that because no one could question its competency or its judges.

Despite his qualifications about arbitration, Loder did serve as a member of the Permanent Court of Arbitration. He also sat on the Council of the International Institute of Intellectual Co-operation and wrote and spoke extensively on behalf of the peaceful resolution of conflict.

BIBLIOGRAPHY:

A. *Institutions judiciaires et de conciliation* (The Hague, 1917); *La Différence entre l'arbitrage international et la justice internationale* (The Hague, 1923); *The Permanent Court of International Justice* (London, 1920); *Règlement pacifique des conflits internationaux* (The Hague, 1917).

B. *New International Yearbook* (New York, 1935), 408.

Robert C. R. Siekmann

LODGE, Henry Cabot (12 May 1850, Boston—9 November 1924, Cambridge, MA). *Education*: graduate, Harvard Coll., 1871; LL.B., Harvard Law School, 1874; Ph.D., Harvard Univ., 1876. *Career*: assistant editor, *North American Review*, 1873–76; lecturer, Harvard Coll., 1876–79; member, Massachusetts General Court, 1879–81; congressman, 1887–93; senator, 1893–1924, Republican majority leader and chair, Senate Foreign Relations Committee, 1919–24.

For many years Lodge was depicted as the principal villain in the defeat of the League of Nations in the U.S. Senate, and at one time his inclusion in a biographical dictionary of internationalists would have occasioned considerable hue and cry. Later scholars have become cognizant, however, of a great variety of internationalist thought, making it difficult for any one group to monopolize the use of the word "internationalist"; and hence, the inclusion of Lodge seems appropriate.

Intense nationalism and imperialism often obscured Lodge's internationalism. But, like his friend, *Theodore Roosevelt, he regarded an assertive nationalism as a counter to traditional isolationism and a prerequisite for the exercise of international influence. Moreover, Lodge and Roosevelt frequently couched their views on imperialism in terms of the necessity of the United States accepting its international responsibilities. In more concrete ways, the Republican party of Lodge, Root, and Roosevelt forged the rapprochement that led to close cooperation with Britain. Under their leadership, the United States also entered into the innermost councils of the principal powers as at Portsmouth and Algeciras and came, at least temporarily, to recognize that the interests of peace and civilization were best served by a close relationship among all the great powers.

Lodge was an early advocate of the idea of a league of nations (June 1915), but his conception of such an organization was always quite different from that of *Woodrow Wilson. Lodge favored the approach of prewar internationalists who had worked to build a cooperative system to resolve differences, one which would evolve into a functioning organization through periodic congresses. During the war he also thought of the league as an alliance of the "civilized powers" and as a means of resurrecting the Concert of Europe. Gradually he came to see that league advocacy might facilitate his efforts to align the United States with England and France. "Internationalist" is not an easy word to define, but in the early years of World War I and within the context of the Republican party, "internationalists" were those, like Lodge, who were pro-Ally before the events of early 1917 and who recognized that the United States had both a moral and a security interest in an Allied victory, a contention anathema to isolationists, who insisted on unswerving allegiance to a policy of absolute neutrality. It was from the ranks of the latter that all those who became "irreconcilable" rather than reservationists on the League ratification issue were drawn.

Moreover, Lodge cared about the peace settlement in Europe in a way that isolationists never did. He was particularly concerned about its viability and about containing Germany, and he was initially willing to make the United States a guarantor of the European settlement. He endorsed not only the French Guarantee Treaty but also Philander Knox's "new American doctrine," declaring that the domination of Europe by an aggressive military power was also a menace to the safety of the United States. Throughout the ratification struggle, he was willing to see the United States enter the League on the basis of certain reservations, and he continued to regard the League as a means of facilitating ongoing cooperation among the Allies to the end of defending the Versailles settlement. But it is also true that he was determined to change the structure of the League. He did not believe that either the United States or other nations were ready to make an automatic commitment to contribute armed forces to uphold the treaty structure in all cases, and his reservations would definitely have transformed the League into a noncoercive, intermediate international organization, the kind of instrument of collaboration into which the League in actuality evolved.

BIBLIOGRAPHY:

A. *Early Memories* (New York, 1913); *One Hundred Years of Peace* (New York, 1913); *The Senate and the League of Nations* (New York, 1925).

B. DAB 11, 346–49; John A. Garraty, *Henry Cabot Lodge: A Biography* (New York, 1953); John A. S. Grenville and George B. Young, *Politics, Strategy, and American Diplomacy* (New Haven, CT, 1966); Charles S. Groves, *Henry Cabot Lodge: The Statesman* (Boston, 1925); William Lawrence, *Henry Cabot Lodge* (Boston, 1925); NCAB 19, 52–54; William C. Widenor, *Henry Cabot Lodge and the Search for an American Foreign Policy* (Berkeley, CA, 1980).

C. The Lodge papers are at the Massachusetts Historical Society.

William C. Widenor

LOEBE, Paul Gustav Emil (14 December 1875, Liegnitz, Silesia—3 August 1967, Bonn). *Education*: grammar school in Liegnitz; learned the trade of typesetter. *Career*: joined Social Democratic party, 1895; political, then chief editor, *Volkswacht* (party newspaper in Breslau), 1898–1920; member of Silesian Landtag, 1914–20; member and vice-president, Weimar National Assembly, 1919–20; member of Reichstag, 1921, president, 1922–32; chair, Austro-German Anschluss League; vice-president, Paneuropa Union, 1924–33; political editor, *Vorwaerts*, 1932–33; proofreader, Walter de Gruyter & Co., 1935–44; member, Central Committee of the Social Democratic party in the Soviet zone of occupation, 1945; license holder and copublisher, *Der Telegraf*, 1946–67; chair, Berlin Press Association, 1948; member of Parliamentary Council, Bonn, 1948–49; member of West German Bundestag, 1949–53; president, Kuratorium Unteilbares Deutschland, 1954–67.

While president of the Reichstag, Loebe was also active in the cause of international understanding and harmony. As vice-president of the Paneuropa Union, he supported the work of *Richard Coudenhove-Kalergi, its founder and president. Loebe agreed with Coudenhove's notion that the best that could be achieved at that time was the bringing together of the countries of each continent—America, Asia, and Europe—into peaceful unions. As Loebe was much interested in effecting such a union in Europe, he worked closely with Coudenhove writing pamphlets, memoranda, and letters as well as speaking at countless gatherings.

Loebe was also active in the Inter-Parliamentary Union, which promoted the work of international understanding and the compromising of differences between states through the establishment of international courts of arbitration. This organization had its origins in Paris and London at the turn of the century, and it expanded its operations as more and more parliaments joined. With the outbreak of the World War I, the participation of the German representatives ended. When peace returned, Germans once again participated, and the Social Democrats decided to make Loebe the head of the German delegation. In consequence he attended the Union's congresses in Copenhagen, Stockholm, Vienna, Bern, Geneva, Prague, Washington, Ottawa, Berlin, Paris, London, and Bucharest. The Union served the cause of peace through its resolutions supporting cooperation among European states and often exercised at least a suasive influence on governments in the interwar years. The Nazi takeover in Germany in 1933 and the coming of World War II severely hampered its work. By then, Loebe's life in the Third Reich was a most unhappy one. He spent some time in a concentration camp and upon his release worked as proofreader for a Berlin publishing house.

Loebe helped rebuild the Social Democratic party after 1945. He served on the Parliamentary Council that prepared the Basic Law for the Federal Republic and after 1949 sat in the Bundestag as his party's deputy representing Berlin. During his last years, Loebe was president of the Indivisible Germany Group, a semi-official organization promoting German reunification. Loebe was much respected by his contemporaries, and on the occasion of his seventy-fifth birthday, Theodor Heuss, the longtime president of the Federal Republic, called him "the eternal journeyman."

BIBLIOGRAPHY:

A. *Der Weg war lang: Lebenserinnerungen*, 2nd rev. ed. (Berlin, 1954).

B. *Der Grosse Brockhaus* 7 (Weisbaden, 1955), 287; IWW 1949, 545; *Kurzbiographien*, 1948, 147; LT 4 Aug 1967, 10; NYT 4 Aug 1967, 29; Arno Scholz and W. G. Oschilewski, eds., *Ein grosses Vorbild: Paul Loebe zum Gedaechtnis* (Berlin, 1968), *Lebendige Tradition: Paul Loebe zum achtzigsten Geburtstag am 14. Dezember 1955* (Berlin, 1955); Kurt Tucholsky, "A Journeyman with an Umbrella," in *Deutschland, Deutschland ueber alles* (Amherst, MA, 1972); *Wer ist Wer* 12 (Berlin, 1948), 723.

C. The Loebe papers are in the Bundesarchiv, Coblence.

Werner E. Braatz

LOGAN, James Addison, Jr. (11 November 1879, Philadelphia—27 October 1930, Philadelphia). *Education*: Haverford Coll., 1897–98; B.S., Army War Coll., 1912. *Career*: U.S. Army, 1901–22; chief of military mission, U.S. Embassy, Paris, 1912–17; assistant chief of staff, American Expeditionary Force, 1917–18; administrator of American relief, 1919–20; member, American Commission to Negotiate Peace, 1919–20; observer, Reparation Commission, 1920–25; banker, Dillon, Read & Co., 1925–30.

After a distinguished military career, Logan became involved in American peacemaking efforts in Europe when in 1919 *Herbert Hoover, the head of the American Relief Administration, appointed Logan as his principal assistant. Under their leadership, ARA distributed nine million tons of food, clothing, and other supplies to the needy people of war-torn Europe. In the fall of 1919, Logan was transferred to the American Commission to Negotiate Peace, where he joined Albert Rathbone, Roland Boyden, *John Foster Dulles, and other advisers working on the the problem of German reparations. In March 1920 Boyden became chief U.S. observer on the Reparation Commission, with Logan as his assistant.

During the next five years, Logan was one of the most important unofficial diplomats to serve in Europe, where he attempted to reconcile financial problems between France and Germany. Although Boyden initially headed the reparations mission, Logan was often the more influential of the two because he knew most of the leaders in Britain and France on a personal basis and used this advantage to gain interviews and promote U.S. policy. Logan also sought to shape the American position on reparations and war debts. In the fall of 1921, Logan proposed that Washington accept reparation bonds in lieu of cash payment from the Allies to settle 50 percent of the outstanding war debts owed America. By doing this, the United States might force France to moderate her reparation demands on Germany by reducing the French war-related indebtedness and break a dangerous economic cycle. Under this plan, major world currencies could be stabilized, Europe might fully recover from the war, and a real peace might be established. The State Department rejected Logan's proposal because the United States refused to admit any connection between war debts and reparations. In retrospect, Logan's plan was economically sounder than the "business solution" which the Harding–Coolidge administrations supported and implemented beginning with the Dawes Plan of 1924. It is possible that an American intervention in 1921–22, along the lines suggested by Logan, would have prevented the Ruhr Occupation of 1923 and the subsequent disastrous inflation, events which German nationalist leaders exploited a decade later.

Despite personal misgivings concerning official policy, Logan played a leading role in implementing American programs. In June 1922 he helped organize an independent bankers committee in Paris to study the reparations problem and make suggestions for a solution based on business principles. Although this attempt to force a French reduction in reparation demands failed, Logan believed that the discussions served a useful purpose in pointing the way toward an eventual settlement. In November 1923 Logan was instrumental in gaining French acceptance of a proposal to organize an independent expert committee to study the question.

Early in 1924 Logan worked closely with Americans in drafting the Dawes Plan. In August he and *Frank Kellogg, ambassador to Britain, headed the unofficial U.S. delegation which attended the London conference on the ratification of the Dawes Plan. There, Logan played a leading role in winning French acceptance. He received little public recognition or official praise for his efforts. Because of congressional and public pressures demanding nonentanglement in European affairs, the State Department could not risk drawing attention to his achievements. Yet it was unofficial diplomats like Logan who made it possible for the United States to assume some responsibility toward world affairs during the 1920s and contribute toward a solution of war-related problems.

BIBLIOGRAPHY:

B. John M. Carroll, "A Pennsylvanian in Paris: James A. Logan, Jr., Unofficial Diplomat, 1919–1925," *Pennsylvania History* 45 (Jan 1978), 3–18; NYT 28 Oct 1930, 25; WWWA 1, 741.

C. The Logan papers are in the Archives of the Hoover Institution on War, Revolution and Peace.

John M. Carroll

LONG, Breckinridge (16 May 1881, St. Louis, MO—26 September 1958, Laurel, MD). *Education*: B.A., Princeton Univ., 1904; studied law, Washington Univ., St. Louis, 1905–6. *Career*: assistant secretary of state, 1917–20, 1939–44; ambassador to Italy, 1933–36.

Long married into a wealthy family in 1912, and politics thereafter became his major interest. Through his wife's connections and by large contributions and loans to the Democratic National Committee, Long, on 29

January 1917, was appointed third assistant secretary of state. He found the hours long, the assignments diverse, and the responsibilities awesome. He supervised the financial affairs of the State Department and the Far East section. One of his most time-consuming tasks involved preparations for many wartime missions. Long had been a student in *Woodrow Wilson's constitutional law course at Princeton, and Wilson always remained his political and intellectual hero. An enthusiastic supporter of Wilson's internationalist policies, Long thought that U.S. membership in the League of Nations was indispensable for world peace. In June 1920 he resigned to immerse himself in Missouri politics. That year the state Democratic party, shattered over the League issue, nominated Long for the U.S. Senate. But, because of his endorsement of the League treaty without any reservations, the Democratic machine of Senator James A. Reed, a bitter foe of the League, refused to support him, and Long lost the election by more than 120,000 votes.

Throughout the 1920s, Long contributed considerable sums to the Democratic National Committee, while trying to keep the party loyal to Wilsonian principles. With *Franklin Roosevelt's victory in 1932, Long gained the high appointment he had coveted when he became ambassador and minister plenipotentiary to Italy. Long's first days were exciting. His early diplomatic reports noted the political virtues of the corporate state, and he praised Mussolini's imperialist posturing. Within nineteen months, he shifted and cautioned Roosevelt to pass out gas masks to U.S. diplomats in Europe. He soon described Mussolini as determined, deliberate, ruthless, obdurate, and vicious.

Thereafter, his dispatches grew more accurate and perceptive, even predicting the week of the Ethiopian invasion. By then, Long's faith in the League seemed diminished. During 1935, he presented contradictory advice on how to avoid another European war—a united League effort, including military force if necessary, was the subject of one detailed report to Roosevelt, while in another Long argued that only European diplomats working independently of the League could reach accords with Hitler and Mussolini. He opposed any embargo on oil against Italy because of its aggression against Ethiopia.

In the spring of 1936, Long resigned because of ill health. He emerged from semiretirement with the outbreak of World War II, when Roosevelt asked him to become a special assistant secretary of state. After the United States entered the conflict, he sat on several committees to explore postwar settlement, including preparations for the 1944 Dumbarton Oaks meeting. Long was a delegate to that Conference (21 August–7 October), which discussed the draft for a permanent postwar international organization.

Long became involved in a difficult problem when the Visa Section under his supervision had to formulate a policy on refugees. Studies have accused him of insensitivity to the needs of Jewish refugees, but Roosevelt provided little direction, and Long believed his policies were sound. He resigned late in 1944. On 28 July 1945, from the Senate gallery, he watched that body approve membership in the UN. His belief in internationalism had been renewed. Woodrow Wilson's faith had been vindicated. It had motivated his thought for nearly thirty years.

BIBLIOGRAPHY:

A. *The Genesis of the Constitution* (New York, 1925).

B. CB 1943, 454–57; DAB supp. 6, 387–90; Henry L. Feingold, *The Politics of Rescue: The Roosevelt Administration and the Holocaust, 1938–1945* (New Brunswick, NJ, 1970); Saul S. Friedman, *No Haven for the Depressed: United States Policy toward Jewish Refugees, 1933–1945* (Detroit, 1973); Fred L. Israel, ed., *The War Diary of Breckinridge Long* (Lincoln, NE, 1966); Arthur D. Morse, *While Six Million Died* (New York, 1968); James F. Watts, Jr., "The Public Life of Breckinridge Long, 1916–1944," dissertation, Univ. of Missouri, 1964.

Fred L. Israel

LORIMER, James (4 November 1818, Abergaldie, Scotland—4 February 1890, Edinburgh). *Education*: Univs. of Edinburgh, Berlin, Bonn, and Academy of Geneva; passed requisite law classes at Univ. of Edinburgh, 1845. *Career*: author, 1854–90; professor, Univ. of Edinburgh, 1862–90.

During the latter part of the nineteenth century, Lorimer was practically the sole representative of the natural law school of political philosophy and jurisprudence in Great Britain, and he spent much of his career combatting the then dominant philosophies of positivism and utilitarianism as espoused by John Austin and *Jeremy Bentham. In his two major works, *Institutes of Law* and *Institutes of the Law of Nations*, Lorimer viewed positive law as merely declaratory of divinely established fact and considered the rectification of divinely instilled inequalities to be above the province of law. Domestically a vigorous opponent of female suffrage, he argued for a system of plural votes based on wealth, education, age, and social position and strongly defended existing inequalities in property distribution against radical or Socialist attacks.

This belief in natural inequalities led him, in the area of international law, to argue against the equality of states, to defend the principles of intervention and extraterritoriality, and to deny Moslem and Communist states the right to recognition. While his philosophy was nowhere adopted, it nonetheless made some impression, particularly on the Continent, then much more sympathetic to a natural law approach than England.

Lorimer remains of interest not only for his writings with their espousal of Continentally oriented jurisprudential doctrine, but for his elaboration of a theory of universal government, found in *Institutes of the Law of Nations*. Its major threads consist of proportional disarmament, coupled with the creation of an international government consisting of a legislature, judicature, executive, and exchequer, to be dominated by the "six great states—Germany, France, Russia, Austria, Italy, and England." Meeting in

Constantinople (due to the political incapacity of the Turks, he considered that city *res nullius gentis*) or perhaps Geneva, the assembly would consider all international questions, including whether an issue was international or national. In addition, civil wars fell within its jurisdiction, as did claims for accession of territory and changes of frontiers within Europe. The judicial department would possess jurisdiction over all questions of public international law. A bureau and its president could block international legislation, subject to override, and it possessed authority over an international force levied from the members. Despite Lorimer's protestations to the contrary, his scheme was no less utopian than those proposed by Henry the Fourth, the Abbé St. Pierre, Rousseau, Kant, *Bentham, and *Johann Bluntschli, all of whose plans he criticized.

Finally, Lorimer with other leading continental jurists was one of the founders of the Institute of International Law, which was to become one of the most important professional organizations in the field. He published frequently in the Institute's *Proceedings*, constantly asserting the importance of a small country like Scotland remaining in close contact with the great states of Europe. While his philosophical doctrines were, even in his own time, atavistic, through his activity in the Institute and his writings Lorimer brought his students and contemporaries into contact with Continental legal thought at a time when that was largely lacking in Great Britain.

BIBLIOGRAPHY:

A. *Handbook of the Law of Scotland* (Edinburgh, 1862; 6th ed. 1894); *The Institues of Law: A Treatise of the Principles of Jurisprudence* (Edinburgh, 1872); *The Institutes of the Law of Nations*, 2 vols. (Edinburgh, 1883–84); *Political Progress Not Necessarily Democratic* (London, 1857); *Studies National and International* (Edinburgh, 1890), with biographical notes and bibliography.

B. *Annuaire de l'Institut de droit international* (Brussels, 1890); DNB 12, 136–38; Gerald Fitzmaurice, "James Lorimer," in *Livre du Centenaire 1873–1973* (Basel, 1973), 82–89; *Juridical Review* 2, no. 2 (1890), 113–21; LT 15 Feb 1890, 7; Arthur Nussbaum, *A Concise History of the Law of Nations*, rev. ed. (New York, 1954).

James Ross Macdonald

LORWIN, Lewis Levitzki (4 December 1883, near Kiev, Russia—6 June 1970, New York). *Education*: training in Russia, Switzerland, and France; Ph.D., Columbia Univ., 1912. *Career*: economic expert, New York Department of Labor, 1912–16; teaching positions at Columbia Univ., 1914–15, Wellesley Coll., 1916, Univ. of Montana, 1916–19, Beloit Coll., 1920–21; correspondent in Russia for *Chicago Daily News*, 1921–22; research staff, Brookings Institution, 1925–35; economic adviser, International Labor Office, 1935–39; consultant, Temporary National Economic Committee, National Resources Planning Board, Board of Economic Warfare, 1939–42; economic adviser, National Resources Planning Board, 1942–43, Foreign Economic Administration, 1943–45, Office of International Trade,

1945–52, U.S. delegation, UN General Assembly, 1946; member of advisory staff, delegation to Economic and Social Council, 1946–49.

Lorwin was a prominent economist who dealt with international questions all his life. After an early career of teaching, he joined the Brookings Institution in 1925 as a member of the research staff of the Institute of Economics. As the author of numerous books and articles, he became known as a proponent of national and international planning and organization, and from 1935 on served as an economic adviser to a variety of agencies both in the United States and abroad.

Although Lorwin had earlier examined the labor movement in France, his first and major contribution to the study of internationalism came with the publication of *Labor and Internationalism* in 1929. Until this work appeared, there had been no systematic account of the aims, aspirations, and past experiences of the labor movement in its various forms. Drawing on the historical record as well as on his own interviews with leaders around the world, Lorwin described labor's effort to promote internationalism both as an ideal and as a method of organization in current affairs. In his work he assessed the origins of international labor activity in the past century, the forms it took, and the prospects for the future.

In the 1930s Lorwin increasingly stressed the notion of rational planning at both national and international levels as the only way to achieve harmony in the world at large. In 1931 he formed the Economic Planning Discussion Group, which consisted of economists, engineers, legislators, labor leaders, and military officials, who met regularly though informally to consider new approaches to social and industrial activity. From that beginning Lorwin founded the National Economic and Social Planning Association in 1934 to pursue the same goals.

Planning, for Lorwin, was the key to peace and prosperity in the twentieth century. In *Time for Planning*, a group of essays written during the Great Depression and World War II and collected in 1945, he argued that modern industrial problems could not be solved without the rational guidance of economic activity in all phases. World peace required economic cooperation among the nations of the world. Drawing on his experiences with the International Labor Office and with other economic and social agencies, he pointed out how the absence of any international economic-social peace program rendered the League of Nations helpless against aggression and war.

World War II, Lorwin asserted in a number of works, provided another chance to deal with questions of international organization. The prewar international economy was in a state of decline, and there had to be substantial rehabilitation and reconstruction in the years ahead. Examining the trends toward increased industrialization in developing countries and the demands for higher living standards around the globe, Lorwin advanced the notion of a world New Deal to provide the coordination he sought. Different economic systems could coexist within a larger whole as long as certain basic international principles were upheld and cooperative actions endorsed. In the effort to create a new system of world relations, the United States could help provide a sense of direction.

Lorwin remained interested in international affairs after the war. He worked with the United Nations, while continuing to write. In 1953 he examined the international labor movement once again, as he sought to bring his earlier assessments up to date. One of the most productive economic scholars of recent times, Lorwin considered a variety of issues during his long career, but always with careful scholarship in which he translated thought into action and helped advance the cause he embraced.

BIBLIOGRAPHY:

A. *Economic Consequences of the Second World War* (New York, 1941); *International Economic Development: Public Works and Other Problems* (Washington, 1942); *The International Labor Movement* (New York, 1953); *Labor and Internationalism* (New York, 1929); *National Planning in Selected Countries* (Washington, 1941); *Postwar Plans of the United Nations* (New York, 1943); *Time for Planning* (New York, 1945).

B. NYT 7 Jun 1970, 84; *Who Was Who Among North American Authors* 2 (Detroit, 1921–39), 907; *Who Was Who in American History: Arts and Letters* (Chicago, 1975), 299; WWAJ 1938–39, 3, 680: WWWA 5, 440.

C. Lorwin's Oral History is at Columbia Univ.

Allan M. Winkler

LOVEDAY, Alexander (24 October 1888, Williamscote, Oxon, England—19 January 1962, Oxford). *Education*: M.A., Peterhouse Coll., Cambridge Univ., 1914. *Career*: lecturer, Leipzig Institute for Culture and Universal History, 1911–12, Cambridge Univ., 1913–15; with Intelligence Department, War Office, 1915–19; League of Nations Secretariat, 1919–46; member, Institute for Advanced Study, 1946; member, United Nations Nuclear, Economic and Employment Commission, 1946–50; fellow, Nuffield Coll., Oxford Univ., 1940–50, warden, 1950–54.

Loveday was known in the League Secretariat as a fair, firm, and efficient administrator who built both a personal reputation and an institutional reputation that was consistently well respected even when, as a consequence of political developments in Europe, the League itself fell into a state of decline. He was instrumental in organizing the financial and the economic work of the League and while working in the Economic Section became involved in helping several countries reorganize their finances, including Estonia (1924–25), Portugal (1927–28), Austria (1921–24), and Romania (1925–32). He was director of the Financial Section and Economic Intelligence Service from 1931 to 1939. Then, when the League Secretariat was dismantled, he removed his reduced staff and activities to Princeton as the Economic, Financial and Transit Department. From 1939 to February 1946, it produced a series of valuable studies intended to assist in the postwar planning for reconstruction. Finally, he was instrumental in making as smooth as possible the transition of those activities over which he had responsibility from the League to the new United Nations. After his retirement from Nuffield College, he continued to study problems of international organization and staffing, and assisted students at the University. His final book, *Reflections on International Administration*, not only provided an occasion for personal commentary but is also a statement of the principles of the international civil service that he exemplified in his own career.

He had the talent and good sense to select carefully and well the persons with whom he worked. Thus, as is so essential in the professional areas in which he made his mark, the quality of his own work and those of others around him remained consistently high. The statistical, accounting, and economic reports and surveys produced under his supervision set a standard that was emulated when the United Nations and other post–World War II international financial and economic institutions were formed. In fact, two of his colleagues went on to distinction in these areas in their own right. Pierre Quesnay became director of the Bank for International Settlements, and *Per Jacobsson became managing director of the International Monetary Fund.

Loveday never left completely the academic life, which was expressed through a consistent pattern of writing and publications dealing primarily with the unstable economic and social conditions of the interwar period. His concern for the economic well-being of peoples whose lives had been threatened by famine and disasters was first revealed in his book, *History and Economics of Indian Famines*, published in 1914. After World War I and its destruction, he edited a series of his own essays, which appeared as *Britain and World Trade: Quo Vadimus and other Economic Essays* in 1931. Loveday was a passionate believer that, as he put it, Europe will never solve its economic and social problems "by twisting round the precepts of the nineteenth century the red tape of the twentieth." (*Britain and World Trade*, xvi) He believed in individual liberty and argued that the decisions of the consumer should be the major point of assessment as to the efficacy of any set of economic policies. In his opinion the flexibility that would be derived therefrom was preferable to centralized state planning, if the national political system offered such a choice. In 1950 he published a book *The Only Way: A Study of Democracy in Danger*, that afforded him the opportunity to attempt to influence other policy makers to his point of view.

BIBLIOGRAPHY:

A. *Britain and World Trade: Quo Vadimus and other Economic Essays* (London, 1931; Freeport, NY, 1972); with others, *Economic Essays in Honour of Gustav Cassell* (London, 1933); *The History and Economics of Indian Famines* (London, 1914); *The Lessons of Monetary Experience* (London, 1937); *The Only Way: A Study of Democracy in Danger* (London, 1950); *The Other War* (London, 1917); *Reflections on International Administration* (Oxford, 1956; Westport, CT, 1974); *The World's Economic Future* (London, 1938).

B. IWW 1937, 674; LT 22 Jan 1962, 17; NYT 21 Jan 1962, 88; WW 1956, 1708.
C. Some Loveday papers are in the The League of Nations Archives.

Robert S. Jordan

LOWELL, Abbott Lawrence (13 December 1856, Boston—6 January 1943, Boston). *Education*: B.A., Harvard Coll., 1877; LL.B., Harvard Law School, 1880. *Career*: law practice, 1880–97; lecturer to professor, Harvard Univ., 1897–1909, president, 1909–33.

Although noted as an educator, Lowell played a significant role in U.S. internationalist circles, 1915–43. His interest appeared in 1915 when, because of his position and known interests, he was invited to associate himself with a movement to establish an international organization to preserve world peace. This was the League to Enforce Peace (LEP), which derived its immediate impulse from the outbreak of World War I. He became influential in drafting a statement of the League's principles and proposals and in persuading former President *William Howard Taft to join the movement. Taft became president of the LEP and Lowell chairman of the executive committee.

The major premise of the League was stated in its "Warrant from History": "Always peace had been made and kept, when made and kept at all, by the superior power of superior numbers acting in unity for the common good." To this end it was proposed that a league of nations should be created binding its signatories to submit all justiciable questions arising between them, not settled by negotiation, and subject to the limitation of treaties to a judicial tribunal and that other questions should be referred to a Council of Conciliation. The signatories should further agree to "use forthwith both their economic and military forces against any one of their number that goes to war, or commits acts of hostility against another of the signatories" without submitting the question as provided in the agreement. Lowell was largely responsible for the provision on the use of sanctions.

During the next three years, Lowell devoted a very considerable part of his time, talent, money, and energy in promoting the acceptance of the League's principles by the American people. He saw it as the only logical choice in a world that could be torn asunder in war. Significant impetus was given to this effort when the general arms of the League were endorsed by President *Woodrow Wilson in May 1916. When Wilson made the establishment of an organization for the preservation of peace a major war objective, Lowell pledged his full support, which continued after the president secured the adoption of the Covenant of the League of Nations at the Peace Conference. He expressed his views in a series of "Covenanter" articles modeled after the Federalist papers.

Partisan political opposition to the president's peace proposals had appeared in the United States, however, and opposing views surfaced in the Senate when it considered membership in the League. Some senators objected to U.S. involvement in any international organization for the preservation of peace, while others promised the American people a slightly altered but presumably better organization than the Covenant provided. Lowell was willing to accept a compromise version as preferable to nothing. He believed that the reservationists would be dominant in the administration of Warren Harding and placed his trust in their influence and integrity. He signed the Statement of the 31, which told voters that a vote for Harding in 1920 would best promote international cooperation. He was sadly disappointed when Harding betrayed his trust.

Lowell lent his support in the interwar years to pro-League groups and emerged from retirement in the early 1940s to speak on behalf of a new world organization. He lived until 1943, long enough to observe the fruits of the failure of the United States to assist in the establishment of a viable peace system at the end of World War I.

BIBLIOGRAPHY:

A. *Public Opinion in War and Peace* (Cambridge, MA, 1923).

B. Ruhl J. Bartlett, *The League to Enforce Peace* (Chapel Hill, NC, 1944); DAB 3, 468–74; Warren F. Kuehl, *Seeking World Order: The United States and International Organization to 1920* (Nashville, TN, 1969); NCAB A, 31–33; Edward Weeks, *The Lowells and Their Institute* (Boston, 1966); Henry A. Yeomans, *Abbott Lawrence Lowell, 1856–1943* (Cambridge, MA, 1948).

C. The Lowell papers are in the Harvard Univ. Archives.

Ruhl J. Bartlett

LUTHULI, Albert John Mvumbi (1898?, Rhodesia—21 July 1967, Stranger, South Africa). *Education*: graduate, Adams Coll. for Teachers, 1921. *Career*: taught at Adams Coll., 1921–36; secretary, African Teachers' Association, 1928, president, 1933; chief of Abasemakholweni (Groutville), 1936–53; elected to Native Representative Council, 1946; elected president, Natal African National Congress, 1951; elected president, African National Congress in South Africa, 1952; Nobel Peace Prize, 1960.

One of the most outstanding moral leaders of Africa since 1945, as one accolade to Luthuli stated after his death by a train in 1967, and recipient of the Nobel Peace Prize in 1960, he was the best known of black leaders working for majority rule in South Africa. His efforts to achieve African unity place him in the ranks of internationalists, but Luthuli also had a vision of a universal brotherhood.

Luthuli was of humble background. His mother moved from Rhodesia to South Africa after his father's death, and he grew up in a Christian community, Groutville, near Durban. His grandparents had been the first Christian converts in the community. He combined traditional with contemporary influence to leave a shadow described by Chief Gathsha Buthelezi at the unveiling of his tombstone when he observed that his country was not large enough for his stature. He was deposed in 1952 from the chieftainship he had held for sixteen years upon his election to the presidency of the African National Congress. Even though his advocacy of non-violence left him in the conservative ranks of the ANC, he was banned for "treasonous" activities (confinement to his home police district with no participation in public meetings) by the government in 1953 and then arrested in 1956. He was again banned in 1959. As leader of the ANC, he followed the policy established by Alfred Xuma of seeking peaceful change, although he refused to be content with the leavings from the table of white South Africa. He was elected president of the Natal state branch of the ANC in 1951 and its national president a year later upon the arrest of his predecessor, Moroka.

Luthuli's first insight into the problems of his people had come with his election in 1936 to the chieftainship of Groutville. Leading the community of 5,000, he saw for the first time the naked poverty of the people. He organized sugar growers to improve their economic situation, later rallying the people of Umlazi Reservation near Durban against encroachment by urban development. His first trip abroad was to the International Missionary Conference in Madras, 1938. A decade later he came to the United States on a church lecture tour, afterward remembering his experience in the segregated South. He advocated his views impressively at the 1958 All-Africa Peoples' Congress in Accra. His autobiography, *Let My People Go*, concludes: "Somewhere ahead there beckons a civilization, a culture, which will take its place in the parade of God's history beside other great human syntheses, Chinese, Egyptian, Jewish, European. It will not necessarily be all black; but it will be African."

Holding to principles of nonviolence, in 1960 he burned his passbook following the Sharpville Massacre. His nonviolent leadership was known and admired by many though decreasingly observed by his followers. Called an Uncle Tom by some activist colleagues, he was termed a Communist by his government. At the Nobel Prize ceremony he observed that the irony of his award was that it was for peace and brotherhood to a citizen of a country where brotherhood was illegal.

BIBLIOGRAPHY:

A. *Let My People Go* (Johannesburg, 1962).

B. Mary Benson, *Chief Albert Luthuli of South Africa* (London, 1963), *South Africa: Struggle for a Birthright* (London, 1966); Edward Callan, *Albert John Luthuli and South Africa Race Conflict* (Kalamazoo, MI, 1965); CB 1962, 271–73; Rolf Italiander, *Die Friedensmacher* (Kassel, Germany, 1965); Colin and Margaret Legum, *The Bitter Choice: Eight South Africans' Resistance to Tyranny* (London, 1968); NYT 22 Jul 1967, 1.

C. The Luthuli papers are on microfilm in the Center for Research Libraries, Chicago.

Richard A. Fredland

LYNCH, Frederick Henry (21 July 1867, Peace Dale, RI—19 December 1934, New York). *Education*: B.A., Yale Coll., 1894; B.D., Yale Theol. School, 1897. *Career*: assistant minister, New Haven, CT, 1896–98; minister, Lenox, MA, 1898–1903, New York, 1903–8; associate editor, *Christian Work and Evangelist*, 1906–13, editor, 1913–26; secretary, Church Peace Union, 1914–26; president, American Scandinavian Foundation, 1910–18; secretary, World Alliance for International Friendship Through the Churches, 1914–26.

Almost from the outset of his career as a Congregationalist minister, Lynch displayed a strong interest in the role of the clergy in confronting issues of war and peace. He early absorbed the idealism of transcendentalist thinkers from his native New England, and he brought to the early twentieth-century American peace movement an unexamined liberal faith in the ability of men and nations to improve the world. In the pre–World War I years, he wrote a weekly column for *Christian Work* appropriately entitled "The Optimist," whose purpose was "to present the good, and report the bright side of things." Believing in inevitable moral progress, he perceived the peace movement as the great reform of the future. His writings chided the clergy for their neglect of the cause and warned that the churches would lose status in American society if they failed to champion the issue. His international perspective appeared in his endorsement of the Hague Conferences, and in 1908 he was a founder and became the president (1910–18) of the American Scandinavian Society. In 1911 Lynch managed to create a peace and arbitration department of the Federal Council of the Churches of Christ in America, the social gospel agency of the Protestant churches. He also attracted the attention of +Andrew Carnegie who helped subsidize Lynch's peace and internationalist activities and in early 1914, largely because of Lynch's efforts in stimulating clergymen's interest in Europe and the United States, established the Church Peace Union with an endowment of $2 million and made Lynch its secretary. That year Lynch helped found the World Alliance for International Friendship Through the Churches and served as its secretary (1914–26).

The outbreak of war in Europe in 1914 shattered Lynch's illusion of human perfectibility, at least as it applied to Europe, but not his faith in the ability of men to develop a new, more humane world order out of the carnage of the old. Sensitive to the divergent responses of the peace movement to the numerous complex issues arising out of the European maelstrom, Lynch supported several antipreparedness, mediation, and antiwar efforts during U.S. neutrality. From the outset of the war, however, he directed most of his energies into the promotion of an authoritative international organization to prevent war. He had deplored the system of secret diplomacy, entangling alliances, and escalating armaments in Europe before the war and viewed the creation of a new world body as the best hope in curtailing these practices. He was one of a small group of prominent individuals who in 1915 founded the League to Enforce Peace, which quickly emerged as the foremost organization in support of a league of nations at the end of the war, and he became secretary of the American branch of the Central

Organization for a Durable Peace. His editorials in *Christian Work* consistently urged clergymen to work for a new international institution. He also utilized the Church Peace Union to organize speakers' tours and distribute pamphlets in support of this ideal, and he worked closely with two New York leaders of the League to Enforce Peace, *Hamilton Holt and *William H. Short, in coordinating their wide-ranging educational endeavors. Lynch was less interested in the technical details and specific powers of a new world organization than in the moral necessity of creating some kind of association of nations which would command the respect of the major powers and develop into an effective instrument in preventing war. Though a lifelong Republican, Lynch admired *Woodrow Wilson's wartime policies and vigorously endorsed the president's leadership in creating the League of Nations and in urging U.S. membership in the new organization. Lynch's prolific writings and administrative abilities firmly put him in the forefront of American internationalists.

BIBLIOGRAPHY:

A. ed., *The Christian in War Time* (New York, 1917); ed., *The One Great Society: A Book of Recollections* (New York, 1918); *The Peace Problem: The Task of the Twentieth Century* (New York, 1911); *Personal Recollections of Andrew Carnegie* (New York, 1920); ed., *President Wilson and the Moral Aims of the War* (New York, 1918).

B. Warren F. Kuehl, *Seeking World Order: The United States and International Organization to 1920* (Nashville, TN, 1969); Charles S. Macfarland, *Pioneers for Peace Through Religion* (New York, 1946); NYT 21 Dec 1934, 23; David S. Patterson, introduction to Lynch, *Through Europe on the Eve of War; A Record of Personal Experiences; Including an Account of the First World Conference of the Churches for International Peace*, rpt. ed. (New York, 1971); *Toward a Warless World: The Travail of the American Peace Movement, 1887-1914* (Bloomington, IN, 1976); WWWA 1, 756.

C. Lynch papers are in the Manuscript Division, Library of Congress.

David S. Patterson

M

MACADAM, Ivison (18 July 1894, Edinburgh—22 December 1974, Cromer, England). *Education*: Melville Coll., Univ. of Edinburgh; King's Coll., Univ. of London; Christ's Coll., Cambridge Univ., 1914–19. *Career*: City of Edinburgh (Fortress) Royal Engineers, commanding officer, Royal Engineers in Archangel, North Russian Expeditionary Force; secretary and director-general, Royal Institute of International Affairs, 1929–55; assistant director-general and principal assistant secretary, Ministry of Information, 1939–41; founder, president, and trustee, National Union of Students, from 1925.

The second son of a professor at Edinburgh University, Macadam was trained as an engineer. At the outbreak of the Great War he joined the Royal Engineers, seeing service on the western front before being appointed commanding officer of the Royal Engineers in the North Russian Expeditionary Force dispatched to Archangel in the aftermath of the Russian Revolution. For this he secured the first of many honors leading to his knighthood in 1955. His training as an engineer made him an intensely practical man; his experience as a soldier taught him the value of discipline and loyalty. Attracted by the experiments in international organization being developed under the League of Nations after the war, he was led in 1929 to become secretary and director-general of the Royal Institute of International Affairs (Chatham House), which had been established in London ten years earlier. His drive and energy saw the Institute through the troubles of the 1930s, when "appeasement" aroused strong feeling among its academic and political membership. At the outbreak of World War II, he was called to help organize the newly created Ministry of Information. He stayed at Chatham House until 1955, ensuring its development into an internationally recognized center where researchers and practical politicians, soldiers and writers pooled their separate insights. For many years (1947–73), he edited the *Annual Register of World Events*.

While expecting loyalty from his staff, Macadam gave it himself. In this context he worked hard to bring to administrative perfection the National Union of Students and to ensure its dovetailing into the International Union of Students.

BIBLIOGRAPHY:
B. LT 24 Dec 1974, 12, 31 Dec 1974, 14.

Colin Gordon

MACDONALD, James Ramsay (12 October 1866, Lossiemouth, Scotland—9 November 1937, at sea). *Education*: Drainie board school. *Career*: secretary, Labor party, 1906–12, treasurer, 1912–24, leader, 1911–14, 1922–31; member of Parliament, 1906–18, 1922–37; prime minister, 1924, 1929–31, 1931–35.

MacDonald played an important role in the founding and subsequent growth of the British Labor party. A prolific writer, he published many important theoretical tracts on Socialism, helping to steer his party away from Marxist-Leninist principles and keeping it on a course of gradualism and constitutionalism. Throughout his life he evidenced a strong emotional loathing of war and violence. While not an absolute pacifist, he courageously opposed Britain's involvement in World War I and dedicated himself to protecting civil liberties, opposing conscription, and working for an honorably negotiated peace. Taking advantage of the postwar reaction against militarism, secret diplomacy, and the harshness of the Versailles Treaty, he directed his efforts toward creating a new international order. Whether in or out of office, he promoted disarmament, open diplomacy, and reconciliation between Germany and France. While opposed to military pacts and regional alliances, his support for the new League of Nations was conditional and never enthusiastic. Like many pacifists and Socialists of the period, he saw the League as a coalition of victorious powers determined to uphold the status quo, and he was also suspicious of the coercive powers in the Covenant. He preferred to view the League as a world forum for discussion in which arbitration and conciliation rather than collective security would be emphasized.

In 1924 MacDonald became the first Labor prime minister in British history, and he sought to strengthen the League by attending its sessions, the first prime minister to do so. He has been called the most realistic of the idealists and the most idealistic of the realists. He is generally given credit for securing agreement among the great powers on the Dawes Plan, which in turn led to the French evacuation of the Ruhr; his government also recognized the Soviet Union unconditionally. During his second ministry (1929–31), he made a successful trip to the United States, the first prime minister to do so. He secured a modest measure of naval disarmament at the London Conference of 1930; his government signed the General Act and Optional Clause, both embracing the principle of compulsory arbitration; and he presided over an Indian Round Table Conference and also an Imperial Conference. In general, his performance in office gave respectability to the Labor party, and most contemporaries conceded that his handling of foreign policy was skillful and successful.

Much of what he accomplished was due to his considerable qualities of mind and character. Although he possessed only limited education, no one disputed his grasp of international relations. Widely traveled, he was a first-rate chairman at international conferences, where his energy, charm, tact, and endless patience yielded good dividends. He established an excellent rapport with the leaders of several nations, so much so that it could be said he was one of the first to practice "summit diplomacy" in this century.

His final years, marked by bad health and political disappointment, were unhappy. In 1931, during a domestic economic crisis generated by the Great

Depression, he abandoned the Labor party to form a so-called National Government. He was immediately reviled as a "traitor," and in ensuing years his reputation was pilloried by his former associates. Having broken with his Socialist origins, this man of peace and conciliation had to endure the final irony by reluctantly initiating a program of rearmament as Britain had to cope with the increasingly aggressive intentions of the Fascist dictators during the 1930s. But even these final tragedies could not detract from the substantial contributions he made during his career to social democracy and international harmony.

BIBLIOGRAPHY:

A. *The Foreign Policy of the Labour Party* (London, 1923); *National Defence: A Study in Militarism* (London, 1917); *Ramsay MacDonald's Political Writings*, ed. Bernard Barker (New York, 1972).

B. DLB 1, 222–27; DNB 1931–40, 562–70; LT 10 Nov 1937, 19; David Marquand, *Ramsay MacDonald* (London, 1977); NYT 10 Nov 1937, 19.

C. The MacDonald papers are in the Public Record Office in London.

David C. Lukowitz

MACEDO SOARES, José Carlos de (6 October, 1883, São Paulo—26 November, 1968, São Paulo). *Education*: doctorate in law, Univ. of São Paulo, 1905. *Career*: attorney and businessman; secretary of interior, São Paulo, 1930; ambassador to Italy, 1932; chief, Brazilian delegation, Geneva Disarmament Conference, 1932; delegate, Pan American Conference, Buenos Aires, 1936; minister of foreign affairs, 1934–36, 1955–58; minister of justice, 1937; member, Brazilian Commission for Codification of International Law, 1939.

Macedo Soares was distinguished for a variety of activities and contributions to the international community. He wrote and spoke in support of the principles of international law, the peaceful resolution of disputes, and the League of Nations. He filled a number of diplomatic posts abroad, including his representation of Brazil at the Disarmament Conference (1932) and the International Labor Organization (1932). As minister of foreign affairs he sought to resolve long-standing boundary disputes, and in 1936 he prepared and facilitated a solution to the Chaco question, which had caused long strife between Paraguay and Bolivia. During his second term as foreign minister, he negotiated a treaty with Bolivia to reconcile old issues.

Macedo Soares seemed admirably equipped for such roles because he possessed a natural affinity for diplomacy. Latin Americans acclaimed him as a defender and promoter of peace in the Western Hemisphere, and the Brazilian Academy conferred an award on him in 1936 for his clear pacifist and fraternal idealism.

BIBLIOGRAPHY:

A. *Brazil and the League of Nations* (Paris, 1928); *Discursos, Rumos da Diplomacia Brasileira* (Rio de Janeiro, 1937), [speeches as foreign minister].

B. WWLA 1940, 296–97, 1948, 5, 135–36; WWWA 5, 448.

Virginia Neel Mills

MACFARLAND, Charles Stedman (12 December 1866, Boston—26 October 1956, Mountain Lakes, NJ). *Education*: Yale Divinity School, 1897; Ph.D., Yale Univ. 1899. *Career*: T. O. Gardner & Co., Mfrs., Boston and New York, 1885-92; general secretary, YMCA, Melrose, MA, 1892-93; assistant pastor, Maverick Congregational Church, E. Boston, 1893-94; ordained Congregational ministry, 1897; lecturer, Yale Univ., 1908-10; pastor, Malden, MA, 1900-1906, South Norwalk, CT, 1906-11; social service secretary, Federal Council of the Churches of Christ in America, 1911-12, general secretary, 1912-31.

As a church leader, Macfarland indefatigably served the cause of world peace during the early decades of the twentieth century as a "churchman-diplomat." Something of his world connections is suggested by his lectures at the universities of Berlin, Prague, Athens, and Strasbourg and by his decorations from various governments. Among his numerous international assignments were his vice-presidency of the Universal Christian Conference on Life and Work, a forerunner of the World Council of Churches, and his chairmanship of the Huguenot-Walloon-New Netherlands Commission.

In 1911 Macfarland consulted with church leaders in London and Berlin with the immediate purpose of starting the organization of a Three-Nation Conference of churchmen and the longer-range objective of initiating a study of proposals for a cooperative movement of the churches in international affairs. Upon his return, he persuaded the Federal Council of Churches to create a Commission on Peace and Arbitration. From December 1915 to January 1916, Macfarland traveled to Great Britain, France, Holland, Switzerland, and Germany, visiting Germany at the request of *Woodrow Wilson to study the attitude of German church people toward peace.

Macfarland gained a national and international reputation because of his work and his numerous books on church unity and peace. As general secretary of the Federal Council of Churches, he worked closely with the Church Peace Union. The latter, which Macfarland helped establish in 1914, pursued much of its work in its early years through church agencies which already had underway significant programs for world peace with justice. How closely the Union and Federal Council worked together is indicated by the amount of funds disbursed by the Union through the Council from 1914 to 1927, well over a quarter of a million dollars. Both Catholic and Jewish trustees of the Union heartily endorsed this collaboration.

In May 1914 Macfarland became a member of a five-person Church Peace Union committee to prepare for a world conference. It convened at Constance, Germany, 1 August 1914. About ninety delegates attended from twelve nations and thirty confessions, but many failed to arrive because transportation had been disrupted by the war. They were advised to leave Germany, but the Constance Council appointed a Continuation Committee, which then assembled in London. This group, of which Macfarland was a member, instituted an affiliate of the Church Peace Union, the World

Alliance of the Churches for Promoting International Friendship—later the World Alliance for International Friendship Through the Churches. During the war, the Commission on International Justice and Goodwill of the Federal Council of Churches and the American Council of the World Alliance constituted a joint body financed by the Union and housed at the offices of the Federal Council. It did much to carry the idea of a league of nations to American churchgoers.

Macfarland gave dedicated service to the National Committee on the Churches and the Moral Aims of the War during World War I, to the struggle in the interwar years to develop acceptance of the League of Nations by the United States, to many friendship societies, to the Committee on Religious Rights and Minorities, to the movement for International Peace Through Religion, to the Win the War–Win the Peace approach during World War II, to the interfaith Pattern for Peace, and to many other projects. Macfarland was a devoted leader of the burgeoning movement to establish world peace with justice through religion, and he was significantly responsible for its gathering momentum during the first half of the twentieth century.

BIBLIOGRAPHY:

A. *Across the Years* (New York, 1936); *Chaos in Mexico* (New York, 1935); *Christian Unity in the Making* (New York, 1949); *Contemporary Christian Thought* (New York, 1936); *I Was in Prison* (New York, 1939); *The New Church and the New Germany* (New York, 1934); *Pioneers for Peace Through Religion* (New York, 1945); *The Progress of Church Federation, The International Christian Movements, Christian Unity in Practice and Prophecy* (New York, 1933); *Steps Toward the World Council* (New York, 1938).

B. Samuel M. Cavert, *The American Churches in the Ecumenical Movement: 1900–1968* (New York, 1968), *Church Cooperation and Unity in America: A Historical Review, 1900–1970* (New York, 1970); NYT 27 Oct 1956, 21.

A. William Loos

MACKAY, Ronald William Gordon (3 September 1902; Bathurst, N.S.W., Australia—15 January 1960, London). *Education*: LL.B., Univ. of Sydney, 1926, M.A., 1927. *Career*: solicitor, Sydney, 1926–33: founder and chair, Australian Institute of Political Science, 1932–33; solicitor, London, 1934–60; member, House of Commons, 1945–51; leader of British delegation to conference at The Hague, 1948, Interlaken 1948, Brussels 1949; member, British delegation, Consultative Assembly of Council of Europe, Strasbourg, 1949; chair, All-Party Parliament Group for European Union, 1948–51.

Throughout his adult life, Mackay adhered to the view that world peace and social democracy, which went hand in hand, depended on proper forms of government as well as on the good will of people to make them viable. He especially wrote and spoke extensively of the need to overhaul governmental mechanisms if the clash between labor and capital were to be resolved to the benefit of the human race.

In pursuit of this objective, his early activities in Australia were directed toward revising and stabilizing political processes and systems. His decision to gather, in 1932, a group of politically concerned intellectuals and found the Australian Institute of Political Science was prompted by the belief that political progress, which he defined as the development of a democratic governmental system, required open and detached forums. The findings, if properly communicated to the public, would help to raise political debate above crass self-interest, prejudice, and irrationality. He sought to stem the tide of uncivil political behavior which he saw spreading during the 1930s in almost every country.

His lawyer's passion for constitutional and rational solutions to economic and social problems carried over to life in England, where he settled permanently at thirty-one. His first widely read publication, *Federal Europe*, was written on the eve of World War II. It proposed what was to become his life's dedication, the creation of a federation of Western European states. He served as chairman of the English Federal Union Movement, which promoted the ideas of Clarence Streit. After the war, he incorporated into his thesis the argument that this new federal state should be democratic, Socialist, and subservient to neither the Soviet Union nor the United States. He also maintained that the expanded markets which would come from union provided Europe with its one opportunity for mass productivity and industrial efficiency, and hence economic stability and independence. The road to world government lay not by way of the United Nations but through the surrender of national sovereignty to regional units such as a Western European federation.

Having successfully contested the seat of Hull North-West for the Labor party in the 1945 elections, he utilized his new parliamentary position to promote the united and independent Europe concept. Despite strong reservations expressed by the Labor party at its 1948 Scarborough Conference to a United States of Europe that was not Socialist, he continued to press, both within and outside the party, for less than the ideal. He predicted that without the democratic stability and economic prosperity that came from the larger unit, Socialism in an isolated Britain would never endure. A measure of the respect he enjoyed from parliamentary colleagues, despite their disagreement with his commitment to union, is indicated by the many appointments he received to head British delegations on the topic and to participate at such important conferences as the 1948 Strasbourg meeting of the Council of Europe. Defeat in the elections of 1951 and poor health led to his withdrawal from the public arena.

In his career, Mackay consistently pursued the goal of extending the political authority of democratic government over as large an area as possible. Whether dealing with the issue of Australian federation or the unity of Europe, he persisted in a new science of politics suitable for the times, one that advanced the concept of size, so that a balanced agricultural and industrial production could take place. Otherwise the belief that one part of the world could produce food and another not would result in recurring crises. World peace ultimately depended on people's willingness to integrate into ever expanding areas of sovereignty.

BIBLIOGRAPHY:

A. *Britain in Wonderland* (London, 1948), U.S. ed., *You Can't Turn the Clock Back* (Chicago, 1948); *Coupon or Free* (London, 1943); *Federal Europe* (London, 1940), rev. ed., *Peace Aims and the New Order* (London, 1941); *The Much Debated Federal Arbitration Act 1928* (Sydney, 1928); *Western Union in Crisis: Economic Anarchy or Political Union* (Oxford, 1949), rev. ed., *Heads in the Sand* (Oxford, 1950); *Whither Britain?* (Oxford, 1953).

B. *Australian Quarterly* 32 (Mar 1960), 9-12; LT 16 Jan 1960, 10; *Who's Who in Australia* (Melbourne, 1959), 515; NYT 16 Jan 1960, 21; WWW 1951-60. 704-5.

Ralph V. Summy

MADARIAGA Y ROJO, Salvador de (23 July 1886, La Coruña, Galicia, Spain—14 December 1978, Locarno, Switzerland). *Education*: graduate, Coll. Chaptal, Paris; Ecole Polytechnique, 1906-08; graduate, National School of Mines, Paris, 1911. *Career*: technical adviser, Railway Co. of Northern Spain, 1911-16; journalist and critic, London, 1916-21; Secretariat, League of Nations, 1921-22, head, Disarmament Section, 1922-27; King Alphonso Chair of Spanish Studies, Oxford Univ., 1928-31; ambassador to United States, 1931-32, to France, 1932-34; permanent delegate to League of Nations, 1931-36; minister of education and of justice, 1934.

Madariaga established an international reputation as a biographer, philosopher, novelist, critic, poet, satirist, and playwright. He wrote dozens of books, yet he devoted many years to promote peace, notably through the League of Nations. In this work, he defied a long family tradition in which the males had pursued military careers. A technical education led to his appointment to a League of Nations Transit Conference in Barcelona in 1921, which led to his appointment that August to the Information Section of the Secretariat. The following year he became head of the Disarmament Section, a post which threw him into the global limelight when he served as secretary of the Temporary Mixed Commission for Disarmament, as secretary of the Preparatory Commission for a general disarmament conference, and as secretary-general of the International Conference for the Supervision of the Trade in Arms. These positions, which sought to restrict the manufacture of and traffic in weapons and to establish a forum for disarmament talks, proved to be educational and frustrating for Madariaga. His 1929 book on *Disarmament: Obstacles, Results, Prospects* described both his hopes and despairs. Later, as Spain's chief delegate to the Disarmament Conference (1932-34) he occupied a central position in directing the sessions. While Madariaga gained widespread contemporary acclaim for his work in disarmament, he believed nations would not reduce their arms until they felt secure. That would come only after a more complete organization for peace, which could be attained through rational processes and efforts. He thus castigated the outlawry of war movement as misguided and destructive of judicial methods of resolving disputes.

Madariaga served the League in other ways. From 1931 to 1936 he sat as Spain's permanent delegate where he indirectly presided over the Council during debates on the Manchurian Crisis of 1931. In 1935 he chaired the League's Committee of Five, which sought a solution to Italy's attack on Ethiopia. He experienced personal disappointment in 1936, when his confidential proposal for League reforms was printed in Spanish newspapers and led to a press attack and his resignation.

Although he claimed impartiality during the Spanish Civil War, his liberal perspective would not allow him to accept the Francisco Franco regime. His self-imposed exile, his public condemnation of Franco, and his withdrawal from UNESCO work when Spain was admitted in 1952 publicized his opposition.

As early as the 1920s, Madariaga proclaimed the need for a genuine world government based on an inherent sense of unity he believed was real. In this respect, he disliked the word "international" because it stressed the nation-state system. He referred to himself as a premature specimen of a European and described himself and others who had larger interests at heart as world citizens. He often criticized the United States for its absence at Geneva in the interwar years as unjustified and unforgivable in the light of world needs. He saw its absence as contributing significantly to the failure of disarmament talks and the general collapse of the interwar peace structure. In the late 1930s he became involved in a number of world government groups and played a leading role as secretary of World Federation and in *Anita McCormick Blaine's World Citizen's Association.

After World War II, Madariaga became president of the Liberal International and lent his support to the European Movement where through its Cultural Section he aided in creating the European Center of Culture in Geneva and the College of Europe at Bruges, and he sat on their governing boards. As a scholar of world repute, Madariaga also traveled extensively to promote the exchange of ideas, people, and free thought.

BIBLIOGRAPHY:

A. *Americans* (Oxford, 1930); *Anarchy or Hierarchy* (London, 1937); *Disarmament: Obstacles, Results, Prospects* (London, 1929); *Morning Without Noon: Memoirs* (Westmead, England, 1974); *The Price of Peace* (London, 1935); *Spain* (London, 1942); *The World's Design* (London, 1938).

B. CB 1964, 261–69; IWW 1978, 1072; NYT 15 Dec 1978, II-4; WW 1978, 1592; WWS 1963, 535; R. E. Wolseley, "Salvador de Madariaga," *World Unity Magazine*, 10 (Sep 1932), 375–80.

Warren F. Kuehl

MAHAN, Alfred Thayer (27 September 1840, West Point, NY—1 December 1914, Washington). *Education*: Columbia Coll., 1854–56; U.S. Naval Academy, 1856–59. *Career*: U.S. Navy, 1859–96; president, Naval War College, 1886, 1892–93; delegate, First Hague Peace Conference, 1899.

The most prominent spokesman of a new American world outlook developing during the late nineteenth century, Mahan was best known for his theories of sea power and geopolitics. He perceived the world as interconnected by oceans, a single body of water providing access to land masses. As a naval captain, Mahan translated this global reality into practical strategic lessons. A nation's ability to control the seas, he wrote, determines its international strength. A maritime nation therefore needs a large fleet of big ships prepared to fight decisive battles. He suggested that sea power depends upon a nation's geographical position and conformation, territorial extent, size and character of population, and type of government. His understanding of the sea as an avenue of communication and transportation, rather than a barrier, retains its validity in the nuclear age.

That understanding formed the cornerstone of Mahan's geopolitical thinking. He viewed international affairs as a struggle between "haves" and "have nots," and thus global cooperation as desirable but impractical, yet he also comprehended that the actions of one nation affect all others. He knew that world alignments are transitory and that governments base their foreign relations on self-interest and power. The United States and Great Britain, Mahan suggested, were natural partners because of common interests, and he believed that Anglo–American rapprochement was the essential ingredient of a world peace based on Anglo-Saxon hegemony. He also detected common interests uniting Central Europe, and he predicted a war involving all the great powers, with sea powers fighting land powers. He understood the growing significance of Asia and the Pacific, suggesting that Russia was the key to the future of Central Asia and that a Japanese-American Pacific war was likely.

Mahan demonstrated his world view at The Hague in 1899. He cast the only vote against banning poisonous gas projectiles, suggesting they were less cruel than submarines. Claiming armaments prevented warfare, he opposed naval reduction. He also opposed the expansion of wartime neutral rights because warfare should be cruel and unpleasant so that men would strive for peace. He had the United States exempted from compulsory arbitration, explaining that it might conflict with the Monroe Doctrine, that it would prevent governments from settling disputes through compromise or adjustment, and that an international lawmaker had to exist before arbitration could work. Fundamentally, he assumed that only force could maintain peace. His "realism" was praised, but he was basically unsympathetic to the goals of the conference.

Although a believer in national sovereignty, Mahan held that all governments have paternalistic responsibilites toward humankind. His route to universal peace though *Realpolitik* and armaments differed from that of his more idealistic contemporaries but nevertheless exemplified a highly ethical worldview.

BIBLIOGRAPHY:

A. *Armaments and Arbitration* (New York, 1911); *From Sail to Steam* (New York, 1907); *The Influence of Sea Power Upon History* (Boston, 1890); *The Interest of America in International Conditions* (Boston, 1910); *The Interest of America in Sea Power* (Boston, 1897); *Letters and Papers of Alfred Thayer Mahan*, ed. Robert Seager II and Doris D. Maguire, 3 vols. (Annapolis, MD, 1975); *Retrospect and Prospect* (Boston, 1902); *Some Neglected Aspects of War* (Boston, 1907).

B. DAB 12, 206–8; William E. Livezey, *Mahan on Sea Power* (Norman, OK, 1947); W. D. Puleston, *Mahan* (New Haven, CT, 1939); Robert Seager II, *Alfred Thayer Mahan* (Annapolis, MD, 1977).

C. There are Mahan papers in the Manuscript Division, Library of Congress, at the Naval War Coll., and at Duke Univ.

Kenneth John Blume

MAKINO Nobuaki (22 October 1861, Kagoshima, Japan—25 January 1949, Higashi Katsushika-gun, Chiba-ken, Japan). *Education*: graduate, Tokyo Univ., 1879. *Career*: Japanese Foreign Ministry, 1879–1906; governor, Fukui Prefecture, 1891; governor, Ibaraki Prefecture, 1892; vice-minister of education, 1893, minister, 1906; foreign minister, 1913–14; Diplomatic Advisory Council, 1917–18; plenipotentiary, Paris Peace Conference, 1919; imperial household minister, 1921–25; lord keeper privy seal, 1925–35.

Throughout a long and distinguished career as a diplomat and palace adviser, Makino was known as a promoter of moderation and conciliation in Japanese foreign policy. The second son of a Meiji oligarch, Makino was born in the waning years of the Tokugawa Shogunate in the rebellious domain of Satsuma. At twelve he accompanied his father on the Iwakura mission and remained in Philadelphia to attend middle school. His first diplomatic assignment at nineteen was as secretary in the Japanese legation in London. During the critical years of the Russo–Japanese War, he held ministerial posts in Rome and Vienna. Far removed from the heady nationalism of his compatriots, he sensed Japan's essential weakness and immaturity. A protégé of oligarch Hirobumi Itō and close associate of senior statesman Prince Kinmochi Saionji, Makino became identified with the Foreign Ministry's Anglo-American faction, which counseled accommodation with the Western powers.

A cosmopolitan figure, Makino read London and Paris newspapers regularly and was a connoisseur of Western art. His personal friends included famous diplomats and scholars from Europe and North America. A pensive strategist rather than a charismatic figure, he shied away from party politics and political positions and did not shine at the negotiating table, where he often missed opportunities due to lengthy deliberations.

During World War I, Makino embraced Wilsonian ideals and the League of Nations scheme and became openly critical of Japan's aggressive wartime actions in China epitomized by the Twenty-one Demands (1915). Despite the opposition of hardliners, he was selected by the Cabinet of [Satoshi] Hara Kei to attend the Paris Peace Conference. Although Prince Saionji was titular head of the delegation, Makino became Japan's major strategist and spokesman. He served on the commission that drafted the Covenant and led his delegation to embrace the League of Nations and accept its mandate system, both highly controversial issues back home. He failed to win acceptance of a racial equality clause in the Covenant but successfully stood Japan's ground with regard to Japanese retention of former German rights in China.

After 1921 Makino served the emperor as imperial household minister and lord keeper privy seal until retirement in 1935, and he continued to advise the emperor informally thereafter. He was also a member of the Japan League of Nations Association. In 1936 he was a target of an unsuccessful assassination plot by right-wing army officers who feared his liberal influence upon the sovereign. Makino is said to have been grieved by the outbreak of war with the United States. He survived the conflict to see the beginning of Japan's postwar reorientation.

BIBLIOGRAPHY:

A. *Kaikōroku* [Kaikō memoirs] (Tokyo, 1948).

B. Thomas W. Burkman, "Japan, the League of Nations, and the New World Order," dissertation, Univ. of Michigan, 1975; Chihiro Hosoya, "Makino Nobuaki to Berusaiyu kaigi" (Makino Nobuaki and the Versailles Conference), in *Kindai Nihon o tsukutta hyakunin* (One Hundred Builders of Modern Japan), ed. Kazui Ōkochi and Sōichi Oya, 1 (Tokyo, 1965), 245–52.

C. The Makino papers are in the Kensei Shiryōshitsu, National Diet Library.

Thomas W. Burkman

MANCINI, Pasquale Stanislao (17 March 1817, Castel Baronia, Avellino, Italy—26 December 1888, Rome). *Education*: Univ. of Naples. *Career*: professor, Univ. of Turin, 1850; deputy, Subalpine Parliament, 1855; professor, Univ. of Rome, 1872; minister of justice, 1876–78; minister of foreign affairs, 1881–85; minister of state, 1885–88.

Theorist of nationalism and internationalism, Mancini matured in the legal tradition of the Neapolitan Enlightenment, which regarded law as a vehicle of reform. His early legal writing concentrated largely on advocating elimination of the death penalty. His identification with the Italian Risorgimento passed from participation in scientific congresses, often cloaks for political discussion (Naples, 1845; Genoa, 1846), to a brief career as journalist publishing the liberal *Il Riscatto*, and to membership in the Neapolitan Parliament of 1848–49.

Forced into exile like other revolutionaries in 1849, Mancini secured a chair in public and international law at the University at Turin. His inaugural lecture on the principle of nationality reflected Mazzinian influences but clearly recognized the natural and historical conditions from which a nation evolved; moreover, in rejecting "reason of state," Mancini made the state subservient to the nation since the state was created by the nation. Viewing the state as mere agent transformed Mancini's concept of international law, which no longer would hinge upon treaties and diplomacy but upon the principle of nationality. No state could negotiate a valid agreement violating either the integrity of its own nation or that of others. In international law, the principle of nationality was for Mancini what passed for national sovereignty in domestic law. Both manifestations expressed the autonomy and the self-limitation of the nation. In his inaugural lecture at the University of Rome in 1872, he expounded the plebiscite as an example of his principle of nationality in operation.

Following Piedmont's annexation of central and southern Italy, 1859–60, Mancini helped to integrate the laws and the provincial and communal administrations of the various regions, centralizing control under Piedmont. His knowledge of the South helped in thwarting Southern attempts to undo unification. As minister of justice in 1876, his anticlericalism led him to advocate state control of the church, establishing the rule that bishops must apply for *exequatur*.

Mancini's interest in international law became most apparent in the 1870s and 1880s. In his 1872 inaugural lecture in Rome, he urged freedom of international commerce through conventions, a theme he repeated at Constantinople in 1881 at a conference of international lawyers, where he argued the internationalization of the Suez Canal because of its commercial potential.

Mancini believed that Italy's needs and welfare were connected with the Mediterranean world. His earlier stances on the principle of nationality and international law, however, created dilemmas when he became minister of foreign affairs in 1881. In responding to issues regarding the Suez Canal (1882) and the French occupation of Tunis (1881), Mancini advocated a policy in violation of his principle of nationality. Responding to social and economic pressures for colonies, and with British approval, Mancini aided in the Italian government's purchase of Assab (1882), the occupation of Massawa (1885), and the beginning of Italian colonization in the horn of Africa. Perceiving the Red Sea as a "key" to the Mediterranean, Mancini defended the Assab seizure but could never justify the contradictions arising from advocating his principle of nationality and establishing political control over non-Italians without plebiscite.

BIBLIOGRAPHY:

A. *Della nazionalità come fondamento del diritto delle genti* (Turin, 1851); *Diritto internazionale* (Rome, 1873); *Discorsi parlamentari* (Rome, 1896); *Fondamenti della filosofia del diritto e singolarmente intorno alle origini del diritto di punire* (Naples, 1841).

B. Rodolfo De Nova, "Pasquale Stanislao Mancini," *Livre du Centenaire, (1873-1973)* (Basel, 1973), 3-10.

C. The Mancini papers are in The Instituto per la storia del Risorgimento, Rome.

Marion S. Miller

MANDER, Geoffrey Le Mesurier (6 March 1882, Wightwick Manor, Wolverhampton, England—9 September 1962, Wightwick Manor). *Education*: graduate, Trinity Coll., Cambridge Univ. *Career*: director, later chair, Mander Brothers, Limited; member of Parliament, 1929-45; parliamentary private secretary to Archibald Sinclair, secretary of state for air, 1942-45.

Mander, during the tragic years of the 1930s, persistently fought for the cause of a just and stable peace. He made his reputation not as a diplomat but as a representative of the people. The head of a family paint and varnish business, Mander secured election to Parliament in 1929 and thereafter became something of a critic and gadfly regarding British foreign policy. He generally favored international collective responses to problems and believed that aggressors had to be faced firmly. He preached this message "indefatigably and inflexibly." He became a special critic of the appeasement policy pursued by Prime Minister Neville Chamberlain, 1937-40. Chamberlain initially believed that meeting the demands of Hitler would bring lasting peace. According to the Munich agreement of 29 September 1938, France, Germany, Italy, and Great Britain imposed on the small state of Czechoslovakia the cession of the strategic Sudeten region to Germany, in return for a German guarantee of the remainder of Czechoslovakia. Mander bitterly criticized it in the House of Commons and openly called for Chamberlain's resignation. Mander also defended Ethiopia's resistance against Italian aggression in 1935-36.

Mander is outstanding for his strong advocacy of collective security in the 1930s, but he also supported the League of Nations Union, the League itself, and developments leading to the establishment of the United Nations in 1945.

BIBLIOGRAPHY:

A. *We Were Not All Wrong* (London, 1941).

B. LT 10 Sep 1962, 16, 20 Sep 1962, 14; WWW 1962-70, 746.

C. The Mander papers are in the Gladstone Library, London.

Paul D. Mageli

MARBURG, Theodore (10 July 1862, Baltimore, MD—3 March 1946, Vancouver, BC). *Education*: Johns Hopkins Univ., 1880, Oxford Univ., 1892-93, Ecole Libre de Science Politique, 1893-95, Heidelberg Univ., 1901, 1903. *Career*: U.S. minister to Belgium, 1912-14; chief, U.S. delegation, International Federation of League of Nations Societies, 1925-27; publicist, internationalist, civic leader, and philanthropist.

Marburg was a lifelong advocate of international organization and collective security. His father had established a lucrative tobacco business, and his son had sufficient wealth to pursue a life of philanthropy and public service. After extensive university study in Europe, Marburg returned to Baltimore in 1895 and became a leader of the city's reform movement. He was the founder of the Municipal Art League, which directed the city's modern parks movement, and he became an outspoken advocate of municipal efficiency, honest government, and social reform. While remaining active in a variety of Baltimore organizations for the rest of his life, Marburg turned increasingly to the peace movement, which led to his involvement as an internationalist. He founded the Maryland Peace Society, was secretary and chief benefactor of the American Society for the Judicial Settlement of International Disputes, and chairman of the Third American Peace Congress held in Baltimore in 1911. Through his close association with *William Howard Taft, Marburg was appointed minister to Belgium in 1912 and remained there until February 1914. Even before the war he criticized Germany for failing to cooperate in European peace and disarmament talks. When war came in the summer of 1914, Marburg was enraged at Germany's lawless attack on Belgium and urged U.S. entry.

Marburg had known *Hamilton Holt for several years when late in 1914 he joined with Holt in sponsoring a series of dinners that winter which led to the creation of the League to Enforce Peace, with former president Taft as its head. Marburg's extensive correspondence as chairman of the Committee on Foreign Organization, especially with British leaders, resulted in agreement on several significant ideas. Marburg believed a league of nations offered the only practical hope for future world peace.

When Republican party leaders began to question U.S. membership in the League of Nations in 1919–20, Marburg launched a biting attack on *Henry Cabot Lodge and other critical Republicans, charging that their foolish and dishonest opposition was doing incalculable harm. When Warren G. Harding (whom Marburg called Senator Bombast) made his anti-League acceptance speech before the 1920 Republican convention, the Baltimorean abandoned his party and threw his support to Cox and the Democrats. During the campaign he excoriated the Republican leadership. The experience of the World War, he wrote, had taught the Republicans nothing. Their failure to help establish a League of Nations to punish aggressors would, he prophesied, result in another world conflict. He considered America's ultimate rejection of membership a tragic blunder.

Throughout the interwar years, Marburg continued to provide leadership for American supporters of the League. He headed the U.S. delegation to the International Federation of League of Nations Societies conventions in Warsaw (1925), London (1926), and Berlin (1927). He supported the League of Nations Non-Partisan Association while continuing to criticize anti-League Republicans during the 1920s. He faulted the disarmament conferences of the period because something had to provide security before nations would disarm. He also believed it essential that Germany be treated justly. Its military leaders should be tried for violating the rules of war, and it should pay for the direct physical damage it had caused; but the Germans should be allowed enough capital to rebuild their economy. His guiding principle was that international peace required all nations to treat each other justly.

As Germany moved toward dictatorship, Marburg was once again an accurate prophet. He saw the election of Paul von Hindenburg in Germany in 1925 as a resurrection of dangerous forces of militarism which the United States should seek to curb. He opposed the U.S. neutrality acts in the mid-1930s, arguing that any refusal to aid victims of aggression would only encourage aggressors. In 1938, during the Czech crisis, he suggested that if the United States joined with the League members in pledging their armed forces to punish aggressors there would be no new European war. When war came in Europe in 1939, he called for U.S. entry. By this time Marburg was in his late seventies, and he became less active. He did, however, suggest in 1943 the federation of Britain and the United States. As a long-time supporter of the English-Speaking Union, this seemed a natural step. He died while visiting in Vancouver, British Columbia.

BIBLIOGRAPHY:

A. *Development of the League of Nations Idea: Documents and Correspondence of Theodore Marburg* ed. John H. Latané, 2 vols. (New York, 1932); *League of Nations: A Chapter in the History of the Movement* 2 vols. (New York, 1917–18); with H. E. Flack, ed., *Taft Papers on League of Nations* (New York, 1920).

B. Henry Atkinson, *Theodore Marburg: The Man and His Work* (New York, 1951); Ruhl J. Bartlett, *The League to Enforce the Peace* (Chapel Hill, NC, 1944); James B. Crooks, *Progress and Politics: The Rise of Urban Progressivism in Baltimore, 1895–1911* (Baton Rouge, LA, 1968); DAB supp. 4, 550–51; Michael Lutzker, introduction to Marburg, *Expansion* (New York, 1971); NCAB 34, 86–87.

C. A small collection of Marburg papers is in the Manuscript Division, Library of Congress.

Joseph L. Arnold

MARCOARTÚ Y MORALES, Arturo de (birth unknown—1904, Madrid). *Education*: engineering degree. *Career*: chief engineer, C. Spanish Corps; deputy, Cortes, 1871–86; founder and member, International Law Association, 1873–1904; founder and member, Inter-Parliamentary Union, 1889–1904; senator, Cortes, 1886–93.

Shaken by the contrast between nineteenth-century technology and progress and the blood baths which characterized the Crimea, Sedan, and the Spanish revolution and civil war, 1868–74, Marcoartú became an indefatigable spokesman for cooperation among nations. Influenced by admiration for British constitutional gradualism and free trade ideology, Marcoartú was almost the lone Spaniard who sought what he called "the fraternal embrace of nationalities" in the cause of international peace. His vision was a parliament of nations, encompassing both the Americas and Europe, to overcome the nearsightedness of national loyalty.

To achieve this, Marcoartú advocated the codification of international law, compulsory arbitration, neutralization of major waterways and communication links, an international chamber of commerce and clearing bank, and formation of an interparliamentary advisory council which ultimately would have legislative, executive, and judicial arms.

Marcoartú's stance was that of a liberal democrat, decidedly middle-class in orientation. The formation and success of the Socialist International concerned him. If that organization realized its aims, it would, he felt, render asunder the basis on which modern society rested. Thus he urged the educated elite of each nation, in close correspondence, to effect a reform in international relations. The constituency for the new community, however, would not be elitist; it would embrace the civilized peoples of the world. With the spread of democracy and literacy, it was ultimately they to whom questions of war and peace should be referred.

To promote these ideas, Marcoartú spoke regularly before the London Peace Society and the National Association for the Promotion of Social Science in the 1870s. He traveled to Austria, Germany, France, and Italy in 1876 in behalf of disarmament and the limitation of standing armies. Subsequently in 1884–85 he visited America, addressing the peace groups, general audiences, and congressmen. He was a founding member and lifelong supporter of both the International Law Association (1873) and the Inter-Parliamentary Union (1889), the work of which ultimately underlay the 1899 Hague Peace Conference and the Permanent International Court of Arbitration.

Marcoartú was generous not only with his time but with his resources. In 1872 a cash prize he donated stimulated essays on international organization, and in 1876 he underwrote their publication. The engineer and businessman in him proposed—in considerable detail as to route, costs, and specifications—a transoceanic telegraphic cable (1863) to enhance world trade and cooperation.

In Spain, first as a deputy and later senator, his proposals were equally cosmopolitan. He argued in behalf of the Iberian Peninsula as the commercial bridge between Europe and Africa, Europe and the Americas, Europe and the Orient. By the 1890s, his senatorial speeches resulted in Spain's acceptance of the principle of international arbitration and its inclusion in treaties it negotiated. In 1900 and 1901, he was influential in organizing conferences drawing together Spanish-speaking peoples on both sides of the Atlantic for discussion of mutual concerns.

Marcoartú's lifelong involvement in the cause of internationalism summed up that rational optimism and liberal nationalism so characteristic of many *fin de siècle* intellectuals. Equally at home in England, America, and the Continent, fluent in several languages, he popularized peaceful relations and cooperation among nations, proposing specific measures to attain these goals and arguing both their economic and their moral practicality. Although limited by lack of a national peace organization and like-minded colleagues in Spain, his impact was widespread, his zealousness recognized throughout the Atlantic community.

BIBLIOGRAPHY:

A. *Importancia del estrecho hispano-africano en nuestras relaciones con África y con Orient* (Madrid, 1894); *Internationalism* (London, 1876); "The Parliament of Nations," *Advocate of Peace*, n.s. 3 (Nov 1872), 229; *Universal Telegraphic Enterprise, Telegraphic Submarine lines Between Europe and America, and the Atlantic and the Pacific* (New York, 1863).

B. *The Herald of Peace* (1868–1904) and the *Advocate of Peace* (1869–1904) regularly reported on Marcoartú, with a death notice in the latter, 66 (May 1904), 84; A.C.F. Beales, *The History of Peace* (New York, 1931); Antonio Sanchez de Bustamente, *The World Court* (New York, 1925); Merle Curti, *Peace or War: The American Struggle, 1636–1936* (New York, 1936).

Nancy A. Rosenblatt

MARSHALL, George Catlett (31 December 1880, Uniontown, PA—16 October 1959, Washington). *Education*: graduate, Virginia Military Institute, 1901; graduate, Infantry-Cavalry School, Fort Leavenworth, 1907; Army Staff Coll., 1908. *Career*: officer, U.S. Army, 1901–45; chief of staff, 1939–45; mission to China, 1945–46; secretary of state, 1947–49; head, American Red Cross, 1949–50; secretary of defense, 1950–51; Nobel Peace Prize, 1953.

Marshall developed a world perspective as a soldier. His first military service in the Philippine Islands, 1902–3, taught him much about different peoples and cultures. As an officer in World War I, he worked overseas and afterwards visited Western European capitals. From 1924 to 1927, in Tientsin, China, he saw firsthand the fighting between the warlords, the growth of revolutionary ferment, and the increasing Asian hatred of colonial status.

As chief of staff, Marshall had to build U.S. forces, find arms and supplies for allies, help formulate strategy, and attend major conferences. He learned in detail the problems which the war had brought. In a ceremony shortly after his retirement in November 1945, he spoke in the Pentagon courtyard to men and women in uniform of the part they played in bringing military victory and reminded them of their role in rebuilding a ravaged world. "Along with the great problems of maintaining the peace, we must solve the problems of the pittance of food, of clothing and coal and homes." He added: "You are young and vigorous and your services as informed citizens will be necessary to the peace and prosperity of the world" (Speech, 26 November 1945, Marshall Library).

After a frustrating year trying to reconcile opposing forces in China,

Marshall accepted the post of secretary of state. His work involving the negotiating of treaties of peace between the Allies and Germany and Austria convinced him that the Soviet Union was not eager to return the economy of Europe to a normal state, and he realized that a program had to be devised to aid recovery there. On 5 June 1947, Marshall outlined a general proposal directed not against doctrine or country but against desperation, poverty, hunger, and chaos. He opened the possibility of aid to any country willing to cooperate in a program of reconstruction. He suggested that the initiative should come from Europe and be based on cooperative efforts, and the resulting Marshall Plan did much to advance Western European unity. From 1947 to 1949, Marshall participated in the discussions which led to the signing of the North Atlantic Treaty pacts by his successor, and he accepted the suggestion of an adviser that the agreement be placed in the regional framework of the United Nations as outlined in the treaty at Rio de Janeiro. Leaving the post of secretary of state at the beginning of 1949 after a serious operation, Marshall on his recovery became secretary of defense (1950–51) to help strengthen U.S. forces for the Korean War without weakening commitments in Europe.

In Oslo in December 1953, *Carl J. Hambro introduced Marshall as the recipient of the Nobel Peace Prize. He quoted Marshall's position that the law against international murder must be enforced. The enforcing arm, however, should not be a standing army controlled by schemers. The citizen-soldier could prevent any misuse of power. In his remarks, Marshall responded to criticism that the Peace Prize had been given to a soldier. "I know a great deal of the horrors and tragedies of war. . . . The cost of war is constantly spread before me, written nearly in many ledgers whose columns are gravestones." "Perhaps the most important single factor," he declared in offering a formula for peace, "will be a spiritual regeneration to develop good will, faith and understanding among nations. Economic factors will undoubtedly play an important part. Agreements to secure a balance of power, however disagreeable they may seem, must likewise be considered. And with all these there must be wisdom and the will to act on that wisdom" (Oslo speech, 10 December 1953, Marshall Library).

Marshall's military experience had broadened his world view, giving him an understanding and sympathy toward different peoples. The idea of the League of Nations appealed to him, and as secretary of state and secretary of defense he favored support of the United Nations. He often recalled the parochial outlook he had at the turn of the century, when Manila was to him only the name of a kind of rope until the Spanish-American War. His larger view not only allowed him to lead in cooperative military campaigns in three wars, but also enabled him to advance postwar developments in which the United States found itself promoting international cooperation and reconstruction. While committed to his country's defense, he recognized that self-interests required broader perspectives and efforts.

BIBLIOGRAPHY:

A. Larry I. Bland, ed., *The Papers of George Catlett Marshall: Volume I* (Baltimore, 1981).

B. John R. Beal, *Marshall in China* (Garden City, NY, 1970; DAB supp. 6, 428–33; William Frye, *Marshall, Citizen Soldier* (Indianapolis, IN, 1947); Forrest C. Pogue, *George C. Marshall: Education of a General, 1880–1939* (New York, 1963), *George C. Marshall: Ordeal and Hope, 1939–1942* (New York, 1966), *George C. Marshall: Organizer of Victory, 1943–1945* (New York, 1973).

C. The Marshall papers are in the George C. Marshall Research Library.

Forrest C. Pogue

MARTENS, Frederic Frommhold de [Fedor Federovich Martens] (27 August 1845, Pärnu, Livonia, Russia—20 June 1909, Walk, Livonia). *Education*: B.A., St. Petersburg Univ., 1867, M.A., 1869, Ph.D., 1873. *Career*: entered Russian foreign service, 1868; professor, St. Petersburg Univ., 1873–1905; vice-president, Institute of International Law, 1885, 1894; member, Permanent Court of Arbitration, 1902–4.

When de Martens joined the Ministry of Foreign Affairs, the regulation of political affairs through diplomatic conferences had been firmly established among the European powers. Efforts were made in these meetings during the second half of the nineteenth century to improve and codify the existing customary rules of public international law, in particular, those governing the conduct of war. Inspired by *Francis Lieber's code of the rules of warfare, prepared for the U.S. government in 1863, de Martens took a leading role in the movement for the regulation of armed conflict in Europe. As one of the first Russian writers on international law, his scientific works, which dealt largely with the development of international legal principles and the practice of Russia's foreign relations, paved the way for his diplomatic activities in this field. He was closely connected with the comprehensive scheme for peace and disarmament emanating from the Russian tzar and presented at Brussels in 1874. Although the results of this conference, the so-called Brussels Declaration, were never ratified, the Russian initiative marked the beginning of a process to embody the laws of war in multilateral treaties. A year later, the subject was taken up by the Institute of International Law, with the objective of providing governments with a manual to be used by their armies. Together with *J. C. Bluntschli and *T. E. Holland, de Martens served on a committee which refined Gustav Moynier's draft, known as the Oxford Manual, after its adoption by the Institute in Oxford in 1880.

Concurrent with developments in international codification, the last quarter of the nineteenth century showed a growing interest in procedures for the peaceful solution of political and territorial issues. As a result, arbitration clauses in international agreements increased substantially. Between 1891 and 1905, de Martens acted frequently as an international arbitrator. He served as a judge in the Pious Fund case (1902) and the Venezuelan preferential cases (1904). These were the first two issues before the Permanent Court of Arbitration, established by the Hague Peace Conference of 1899.

De Martens was involved in both Hague meetings (1899, 1907). The first of these attempted to crystallize nineteenth-century attitudes toward disarmament, rules and customs of war, and arbitration. The disarmament proposals failed, and only after de Martens' strong appeal was a convention adopted containing the agreed rules of warfare in an annexed code based almost entirely on the Brussels Declaration and the Oxford Manual. The compromise formula in the preamble, which provides that the incomplete code would not derogate from customary international law, has become known as the De Martens Clause. Furthermore, de Martens's proposals for the establishment of an International Commission of Inquiry as a parallel to arbitration were incorporated in the Convention for the Pacific Settlement of International Disputes. In 1904 recourse to such a commission almost certainly avoided war between Great Britain and Russia over the Dogger Bank incident.

Encouraged by this successful use of the procedure, the Second Hague Peace Conference introduced wider powers for the Commission in the revised convention of 1907. The various conventions resulting from both conferences represented a considerable advance in the framework of international law. This development, of which de Martens was one of the major exponents, was abruptly interrupted by World War I, but it is nevertheless a significant contribution to present-day world organization. One symbol of de Martens' generation survived in physical form. This was the Peace Palace at The Hague, which he first suggested in 1900.

BIBLIOGRAPHY:

A. *Collection of Treaties and Conventions Concluded by Russia with Foreign Powers*, 15 vols. (St. Petersburg, 1874–1909); *Consuls and Consular Jurisdiction in the Orient* (St. Petersburg, 1873); *Treatise on International Law*, 2 vols. (St. Petersburg, 1882–83).

B. AJIL 3 (1909), 983–85; Calvin D. Davis, *The United States and the Second Hague Peace Conference: American Diplomacy and International Organization, 1899–1914* (Durham, NC, 1976); *Journal of the Society of Comparative Legislation* 10, no. 21 (1909), 10–12; *Soviet Yearbook of International Law* (Moscow, 1960), 257–60.

J.W.H. Thijssen

MARTIN, Charles Emanuel (11 September 1891, Corsicana, TX—12 January 1977, Seattle, WA). *Education*: B.A., Univ. of California, 1914, M.A., 1915; Ph.D., Columbia Univ., 1918. *Career*: lecturer, Univ. of California, 1919–20; chair, Department of Political Science, Univ. of California, Los Angeles, 1920–25; professor, Univ. of Washington, 1925–62.

In *Life Magazine*'s oft-cited phrase, Martin was an "action intellectual," a scholar as committed to the public arena as to the classroom and the library. With degrees from respected institutions, numerous publications on

American and world affairs, and a distinguished administrative record, he enjoyed a noteworthy reputation in academia. However, he was never content with academic effort alone. Well in advance of most, he recognized the global move toward interdependence and believed the change could come about peacefully only if supported by applied as well as academic activity. This conviction led him to a lifetime of international activism on many fronts.

As a world affairs scholar, he was widely known as an influential writer and teacher. As a consultant to numerous international groups, he was involved with issues extending from immigration and naturalization to Latin American naval policy. As an established mediator, he served in a variety of roles ranging from a labor arbitrator to an international observer during the 1938 Czechoslovakian crisis. As a lecturer on international topics, he was well received by a variety of groups and spoke to audiences throughout North America, Asia, and Europe.

Martin's unceasing involvement is most graphically illustrated by his record of participation in a host of activities concerned with the promotion of international understanding. He was a longtime member of the Council on Foreign Relations and most similarly oriented academic organizations. Additionally, he served as visiting professor in the Orient and Antipodes and at over a dozen U.S. colleges. He was a participant in innumerable international conferences and active in many more specialized groups. He participated in the American Commission on the Organization of Peace, was a trustee of the American Institute of Pacific Relations, and held top posts in the Seattle World Affairs Council. He was president of the American Society of International Law, 1960–61. Martin listed as an avocation the organizing of international relations institutes and his political affiliation as a *Woodrow Wilson Democrat. Fittingly, his last major undertaking in the years following his retirement from the University of Washington was the establishment of an American Studies program at the University of the Philippines. At the time of his death, he had contributed over half a century to an effort to bring greater harmony to both the theory and the practice of international relations.

BIBLIOGRAPHY:

A. *American Government and Citizenship* (New York, 1927); *The Permanent Court of International Justice and the Question of American Adherence* (Stanford, CA, 1932); *The Policy of the United States as Regards Intervention* (New York, 1921); *The Politics of Peace* (Stanford, CA, 1929); ed., *Problems in International Understanding* (Seattle, WA, 1928); *South and Southeast Asia* (Seattle, WA, 1951); *Universalism and Regionalism in International Law and Organization* (Havana, 1959).

B. *Directory of American Scholars* (New York, 1951), 619; *Seattle Times* 13 Jan 1977, E-15; University Archives, Univ. of Hawaii, uncatalogued materials; WW 1976, 1586; WWA 1946–47, 1511, 1950–51, 1749.

Paul F. Hooper

MARTINO, Gaetano (25 November 1900, Messina, Italy—21 July 1967, Rome). *Education*: M.D., Univ. of Rome, 1923; advanced medical and surgical studies, Berlin, Paris, Frankfurt-am-Main, London. *Career*: professor, Univ. of Messina, 1929; director, Medical Sciences Department, Univ. of Asunción, Paraguay, 1930–34; lieutenant colonel in World War II; vice-rector, Univ. of Messina, 1944–57; director, Institute of Human Physiology, Univ. of Rome, 1957–66; rector, Univ. of Rome, 1966–67; Liberal party deputy, Constituent Assembly, 1946–47, Parliament, 1948–67; vice-president, Chamber of Deputies, 1948; minister of public education, 1954; foreign minister, 1954–57; president, Liberal party, 1957–67; president, European Parliament, 1962–64.

A prominent Italian Liberal, Martino was one of the principal architects of the European Economic Community. His "Europeanism" and skill as a diplomat developed from a highly successful early career as a medical professor and university administrator. He launched his political career in the Italian Liberal party (PLI) at the end of World War II and later served as its president. His involvement in politics and parliamentary and cabinet posts was extensive.

A distinguished-looking, soft-spoken scholar who was fluent in several languages and a master of detail, Martino showed as foreign minister (1954–57) the rare political talent of being a good listener as well as a persuasive politician. He guided the intricate negotiations which returned Trieste to Italy with the London Accord of October 1954. A year later, Italy, was admitted to the United Nations, and Martino was the first leader of the Italian delegation to the UN.

When the European Defense Community failed in mid-1954 because of French opposition, Martino helped organize the new West European Union as a substitute. Thus, at a meeting of the foreign ministers in London in September and October 1954, Martino agreed to the admission of West Germany and Italy to the Brussels Pact and of West Germany to NATO. He also agreed to Italian participation in the establishment of an Armaments Control Agency that would supervise the level of arms of the six member states and enforce the ban on German possession of atomic, biological, and chemical weapons.

Martino's force of character enabled him to persuade the six foreign ministers of the European Coal and Steel Community to meet at Messina, the city of his birth, on 1–2 June 1955. Out of that conference emerged plans for the European Economic Community and Euratom. During ensuing negotiations over the structure of EEC, Martino argued cogently in favor of total integration, including agriculture as well as industry, a Community social policy, freedom of movement for labor, a readaptation fund, Community sources of capital, and safeguards for the underdeveloped regions. On 25 March 1957, Martino and Italian President Antonio Segni signed the Treaty of Rome at the Campidoglio in Rome.

Martino served as president of the European Parliament, 1962–64. A staunch Liberal, he saw Europeanism as the "defense of liberty." Its immediate goal was the protection of Western Europe from the advance of the Soviet Union and Communist subversion. He disapproved of a nationalized economy and of *dirigisme*.

BIBLIOGRAPHY:

A. *Elementi di fisiologia umana*, 5th rev. ed. (Milan, 1958); *Foi en l'Europe* (Florence, 1967); *Verso l'avvenire* (Florence, 1963).

B. LT 22 Jul 1967, 12; F. Roy Willis, *Italy Chooses Europe* (New York, 1971).

Charles F. Delzell

MASARYK, Jan (14 September 1886, Prague—10 March 1948, Prague). *Education*: gymnasium, Prague. *Career*: chargé d'affaires, Washington, 1919, London, 1920; minister to Court of St. James, 1925–38; resigned in protest to the Munich dictate, 1938; foreign minister, government-in-exile, 1940–45; foreign minister in reconstituted Cabinet, 1945–48; delegate, San Francisco Conference, 1945; after the February 1948 coup, remained at his post until his mysterious death.

The son of Thomas G. Masaryk, Czech educator and politician, Jan Masaryk worked as a steel laborer in Chicago (1907–13) before returning to Prague and serving in the Austro-Hungarian Army during World War I. He then entered the diplomatic service of the newly independent Czechoslovakia, where he held many posts. Always concerned about his country's precarious status, Masaryk placed little confidence in the League of Nations and pan Slav movements. He believed that Czechoslovakia's destiny lay in a democratically united Europe. During World War II, he resisted the brute rule of the Nazis in occupied Europe. They sought to discourage hopes for a free and democratic existence and to gain acceptance of the domination of the Third Reich as historically inevitable. Human dignity, inalienable rights, and democracy were spurned, and a "new order for the next one thousand years," based on the doctrines of racial inequality and of adherence to the leadership of the strong, was depicted as their only alternative. Through regular broadcasts from London, reaching millions of enslaved people, Masaryk challenged this inhumane ideology, keeping hope alive. His principal weapon was the argument of humanism, expressed in simple words that were filled so overwhelmingly with significance that they became the source of strength for those who had to bear the brunt of the suffering.

During the war, he combined with Eduard Beneš in proposing a postwar world based on a decentralized and disarmed German confederation, with regional federations throughout Europe which would eventually merge into a federation of Europe, including Russia. Masaryk thus recognized the need for equilibrium between the West and the East. His main concern was to build a structure of postwar relationships that would bring together the two worlds on whose crossroads his own country was unhappily situated. He increasingly saw Central Europe as the democratic go-between capable of providing conciliatory assistance should the need arise. The vision of international democracy he shared was functional: the equality of states in the world society had to be attained through cooperation motivated by a strong sense of solidarity and concern for each other's needs. Idealistic as the conception may have appeared, many observers came to recognize it as the only feasible formula for solving the problems of the disparate world.

BIBLIOGRAPHY:

A. *Ani opona ani most* [Neither a curtain nor a bridge] (Prague, 1947); *Speaking to My Country* (London, 1945).

B. Glorney Bolton, *Czech Tragedy* (London, 1955); Robert H. Bruce Lockhart, *Jan Masaryk: Personal Memoir* (New York, 1951); Robert Powell, "Jan Masaryk," *Slavonic and East European Review* 28 (Apr 1950), 332–41; Claire Sterling, *The Masaryk Case* (New York, 1969); Zbynek A. B. Zeman, *The Masaryks: The Making of Czechoslovakia* (London, 1976).

Vratislav Pechota

MAXWELL Fyfe, David. See Fyfe, David Maxwell.

MAY, Herbert Louis (28 July 1877, Philadelphia—1 February 1966, New York). *Education*: Cornell and Columbia Univs. LL.B., New York Law School, 1897. *Career*: lawyer, New York, 1898–1904; general counsel, May Drug Co., Pittsburgh, PA, 1904–22, chairman of board, 1922–28; member, research staff, Foreign Policy Association, 1926–29; member, Permanent Central Opium Board, League of Nations and United Nations, 1928–66; member, Drug Supervisory Body, League of Nations and United Nations, 1933–58.

Although the United States never joined the League of Nations, American officials represented the United States, "unofficially," in "a consultative capacity," as "unofficial observers," and, on occasion, even officially in League committees, in League-sponsored conferences, and in specialized League agencies. Other Americans worked in their private capacities as civil servants of the League. "Nonpolitical" activities such as control of narcotics drew several Americans into the fold, including *Elizabeth Wright, Arthur Woods, Frederic A. Delano, and May. He served the League from 1928 to 1933 as a member of the eight-man Permanent Central Opium Board (PCOB) and the four-man Drug Supervisory Body, creations, respectively, of the Geneva Opium Convention of 1925 and the Drug Limitation Convention of 1931, and two of the three main organs of the League's machinery of international narcotic drug control.

At the time of his appointment to the PCOB, May's credentials as a narcotics expert rested upon his association with his father's drug firm and his study in 1926–27 of the opium problem in the Far East for the Foreign Policy Association. His conclusion that government monopolies of opium transactions were more effective than prohibition in controlling opium trafficking and consumption in the Far East, and that insistence on immediate steps to suppress opium smoking and limit production to strictly medicinal and scientific purposes was at that time unrealistic, was considerably at variance with American policy.

May's service prompted the United States to review its attitude and policy toward the League. In 1928, seeking to avoid contamination by the League, the State Department rejected the Council's invitation to nominate an American to the Board. Consequently, the Foreign Policy Association engineered May's nomination by New Zealand. In 1933, however, the United States seized the opportunity to nominate May and to vote on the nominees in the League Council as a means of assessing U.S. public opinion regarding possible adherence to the Permanent Court of International Justice. Thereafter, the U.S. government did not hesitate to participate in the election process. During World War II the Board and the Drug Supervisory Body conducted their work from the United States.

May's responsibility as a member of the PCOB and the Drug Supervisory Body was to examine statistics of transactions and estimates of needs submitted by governments, to ascertain the quantities, sources, routes, and destinations of drugs in the international traffic, to estimate needs for those countries which failed to provide estimates, and to recommend sanctions in excess of legitimate use. As May observed, the principal defects in this system lay in the absence of effective means to control production of the raw substance from which the various drugs were derived and the lack of a system of international inspection.

In 1946 May suggested that, if the gaps in the machinery of international drug control were remedied, the principles on which the system was based could serve as a model for international control of atomic energy. As in the case of narcotics, control of atomic energy should cover all transactions from production of raw materials to application, be international, be universally applied, be available for legitimate use only, and include substances other than uranium that subsequently might be found to be suitable for production of fissionable material.

May's conceptualization of a system of atomic energy control accorded, retrospectively, with his earlier vision of a future world order based upon political realism. A world of organization designed to maintain peace and prevent war should provide for a hierarchy of responsibilities and decision making consonant with the hierarchical distribution of power among the member states. The big powers should have the "predominant voice" in political questions bearing ultimately upon war and peace. Where the social and economic life of the world community was involved, however, all nations should be heard equally.

BIBLIOGRAPHY:

A. "Narcotic Drug Control," *International Conciliation* 485 (Nov 1952), 489–536. *Narcotic Drugs and Atomic Energy* (New York, 1946); *Survey of Opium*

Smoking in the Far East (New York, 1927); "The Tasks of the Permanent Central Opium Board," *UN Bulletin* 4 (15 Apr 1948), 336-38.

B. Joseph P. Chamberlain, "International Organization and the U.S.," *Foreign Policy Reports* 19 (15 Oct 1943), 208-11; NYT 2 Feb 1966, 35; WWWA 4, 623.

C. May's Oral History is at Columbia Univ.

Arnold H. Taylor

MAYER, René (4 May 1895, Paris—13 December 1972, Paris). *Education*: law degree, Faculté de Droit et de Lettres, Sorbonne, 1920. *Career*: officer, French Army, 1914-18; auditor, Conseil de'Etat, 1920; deputy attorney-general, 1923; *maître des requêtes*, 1926; head, French Armaments Commission, London, and member, Anglo-French Coordinating Committee, 1939; commissioner, Communications and Merchant Marine, National Committee of Liberation, 1943; minister of transport and public works, Provisional Government, 1944; deputy for Constantine, 1946-56; minister of finance and economic affairs, 1947; minister of armed forces, 1948, 1953; president, Council of Ministers, 1953; president, High Authority, European Coal and Steel Community, 1955-57; president and director-general, Eurafrep, S.A., and vice-president, Société Financière de Transports et D'Enter prises Industrielles (SOFINA), 1958-70.

In the fluid and unstable political atmosphere of the Third and Fourth Republics, Mayer followed a distinguished career before World War II propelled him into public service. There he took readily to administrative responsibility, both on the floor of Parliament, in a succession of Cabinets, and as president of the Council of Ministers (January–May 1953). Handsome, quick-witted, and intelligent, he remained visible throughout the Fourth Republic without ever turning into a true leader. According to Jules Moch, he was too much of a businessman to take charge of his divided fellow Radicals, and to radical to weld the "business types" in the chamber into a cohesive force. To other observers, his proselytizing stance on fiscal reform made him at times "the most hated man in France," undoubtedly an exaggeration but a judgment symptomatic of Mayer's inability to turn his gifts to France's salvation from multiple setbacks in the 1950s. It was not surprising that the fall of his government, on 21 May 1953, came after his request for authority to decree 120 billion francs in budget cuts had been rejected.

Mayer subsequently became a "Europeanist," and he became one of the most outspoken advocates of the European Army. While minister of finance, he introduced the Coal and Steel Community agreement to the Assembly, and as prime minister he became involved in negotiations over the European Defense Community accord, which the supporters of *Charles de Gaulle opposed. Given Mayer's clear endorsement, it is understandable that he was appointed in 1955 to succeed *Jean Monnet as president of the High Authority of the European Coal and Steel Community. He guided the organization through the transition that ended with the establishment of the European Economic Community. As an experienced executive and politician he exceeded his predecessor in administrative and political know-how. But beyond his ability to defend the High Authority against public and parliamentary attacks he left no significant imprint on the history of European union either. Hard-core Europeanists never trusted him, perhaps because they suspected that his strong support for unity stemmed from a desire to save France as a power or to help business or banking interests. The establishment of the Fifth Republic in 1958 retired him from national politics, and he withdrew into the world of high finance, where his interesting and inconclusive career had begun.

BIBLIOGRAPHY:

B. Vincent Auriol, *Journal du Septennat 1947-1954*, ed. Jacques Ozouf, esp. vol. 7 (Paris, 1971); CB 1948, 434-36; LT 15 Dec 1972, 16; Herbert Luethy, *France Against Herself* (New York, 1955); Jules Moch, *Une Si Longue Vie* (Paris, 1976); WWF 1971-72, 1109-10.

C. Mayer papers are in the Archives Nationales and in the League of Nations Archives.

Hans A. Schmitt

MCADOO, William Gibbs (31 October 1863, near Marietta, GA—1 February 1941, Washington). *Education*: Univ. of Tennessee, 1879-82; read for the law. *Career*: lawyer, promoter, 1885-1941; president, Hudson and Manhattan Railroad Co., 1906-13; acting campaign manager for *Woodrow Wilson, 1912; secretary of the treasury, 1913-18; director-general of railroads, 1917-19; contender for Democratic presidential nomination, 1920, 1924; Democratic senator, 1933-38; chairman of the board, American President Lines, 1938-41.

McAdoo's views on foreign affairs were not distinguished by depth, consistency, or internationalism in the general meaning of that term. Before entering public life he had taken an active, though limited, interest in the cause of world peace. As secretary of the treasury after 1913, his policies epitomized the Woodrow Wilson administration's curious interbreeding of idealism and tough realism. Generally McAdoo inclined toward a "hard line" in foreign affairs. His first interest was trade. A low-tariff advocate, he wanted to undercut business consolidation by dropping rates to expose U.S. manufacturers to foreign competition. McAdoo adhered to the Wilsonian view that, by expanding markets for American exports, continuous domestic prosperity could be assured.

When Europe went to war in 1914, McAdoo became the administration's leading advocate of an American international economic offensive that would, in particular, give this country dominance in trade with Latin America. This led him to organize the Pan American Financial Conference of 1915, from which grew the quasi-governmental International High Commission to facilitate commercial intercourse. McAdoo was also the prime mover behind 1916 legislation to expand the U.S. Merchant Marine. Ultimately he urged the president toward war with Germany.

McAdoo backed the League of Nations with U.S. membership. In 1919 he joined the Executive Committee of the League to Enforce Peace. Identifying economic tension as the main cause of war, he again called for lower tariffs. He proposed an international educational campaign to undermine intense nationalism, and he espoused complete, universal disarmament. But in the 1930s McAdoo soured on U.S. involvement abroad and opposed what he called any "foreign entanglements," including membership in the League of Nations. Disillusionment stemmed in part from the Allies' failure to settle their war debts. Continuing to insist on repayment, McAdoo proposed that Britain and France hand the United States certain Western Hemisphere possessions, notably in the West Indies. Having earlier espoused the virtual abolition of all navies, by the mid-1930s McAdoo was repudiating the Washington Naval Treaty and backing U.S. fleet expansion. With Europe again at war after 1939, he emerged from his "isolationist" retreat, seeing the new struggle much as he had seen the old, as a question for the United States of markets, prosperity, rights and commerce on the high seas, and honor. His response was the same as before: no backing down even at the cost of war. He died ten months before Pearl Harbor.

BIBLIOGRAPHY:

A. *Crowded Years: The Reminiscences of William G. McAdoo* (Boston, 1931); "The International High Commission and Pan American Cooperation," AJIL 11 (1917), 772–89.

B. John J. Broesamle, *William Gibbs McAdoo: A Passion for Change, 1863–1917* (Port Washington, NY, 1973); DAB supp. 3, 479–82; EAB 1974, 700; Otis L. Graham Jr., *An Encore for Reform: The Old Progressives and the New Deal* (New York, 1967); Mary Synon, *McAdoo, the Man and His Times: A Panorama in Democracy* (Indianapolis, IN, 1924).

C. The McAdoo papers are in the Manuscript Division, Library of Congress, and the Univ. of California Library.

John J. Broesamle

MCCORMICK, Vance Criswell (19 June 1872, Harrisburg, PA—16 June 1946, Cumberland County, PA). *Education*: Ph.B., Yale Univ., 1893, M.A., 1907. *Career*: industrialist in iron and steel industry; publisher and owner, Patriot Co.; member, City Council, Harrisburg, 1900–1902, mayor, 1902–5; chair, Democratic National Campaign Committee, 1916; chair, War Trade Board, 1917–19; member, War Mission to Great Britain and France, 1917; economic adviser to the president, American Commission to Negotiate Peace, Paris, 1919.

McCormick inherited his father's iron and steel mills, but he developed an interest in journalism starting with the purchase of a Harrisburg newspaper in 1902. That same year he was elected mayor of Harrisburg. From his initial involvement in politics, McCormick identified himself with reform. He carried out such changes at the municipal level and later organized the Democratic party in Pennsylvania on progressive principles. In 1911 McCormick was among a small group of strong and faithful supporters who helped develop a *Woodrow Wilson for President campaign. McCormick became a confidant to Wilson. Because of the fear that the Democratic party would split between the progressives and the conservatives, Wilson chose McCormick to be party chairman and to direct his successful 1916 reelection campaign.

When the War Trade Board was organized in October 1917, Wilson selected McCormick as chairman as well as representative of the secretary of state. He also had other assignments working with *Herbert Hoover and others to get food to Italy in 1917. He traveled to France and England in the fall of 1917 as a member of the American Mission to the Allied War Conference. Wilson wrote of his thorough trust in McCormick in selecting him as a member on the Administrative Committee of the Exports Council.

McCormick was to play a significant role in the domestic movement for a League of Nations. He served as a member of the Executive Committee of the League to Enforce Peace (LEP) and supported it with generous contributions. In the 1918 congressional campaigns, McCormick openly talked about the need for America tó approve the League idea. During the fight over the League of Nations after Wilson returned from Paris, McCormick was one of five who at a LEP Executive Committee on November 13, 1919, voted against supporting membership with reservations, which was an endorsement of Wilson's position. McCormick, along with individuals such as *Herbert Hoover and Bernard M. Baruch, was chosen as an economic adviser to the U.S. delegation to the peace conference. When the Supreme War Council established the Supreme Economic Council in February 1919, McCormick was named as president of the Blockade Control Section on the Council. He was also one of four Americans to serve on the Reparations Commission and one of three to serve on the expert commission dealing with reparations. In that regard, he worked closely with Wilson at Paris.

McCormick was unique in that he brought a strong role in domestic politics through his service as national chairman of the Democratic party from 1916 to 1919, and through his involvement with foreign affairs, whether at the War Trade Board, working at Paris, or pushing for a League of Nations. His major contributions were during the administrative years of Woodrow Wilson. McCormick withdrew from public life after Wilson left office.

BIBLIOGRAPHY:

B. NCAB 35, 242-43; NYT 17 Jun 1946, 21; WWWA 2, 357.

C. There are McCormick diaries for 1917-19 in the Archives of the Hoover Institution on War, Revolution and Peace.

Leon E. Boothe

MCCUMBER, Porter James (3 February 1858, Crete, IL—18 May 1933, Washington). *Education*: LL.B., Univ. of Michigan, 1880. *Career*: state's attorney, Richland County, ND, 1897–98; member, territorial House of Representatives, 1885; territorial Senate, 1887; U.S. senator, 1899–1923; member, International Joint Commission, 1925–33.

After moving to North Dakota, McCumber became active in territorial politics. As state's attorney, he developed a reputation for strict enforcement of the prohibition law in North Dakota. With division among the Republicans and the Democrats as to a new U.S. senator, the legislature in 1899 elected McCumber as a compromise candidate, and he won reelection in 1905, 1911, and 1916.

Most of his years in the Senate were spent on events other than foreign affairs. He was, however, to occupy a dramatic place in the domestic fight in the U.S. Senate in 1919–20 over membership in the League of Nations. As an ardent believer in the need for a League of Nations, McCumber never wavered in his thorough support for the concept during the often bitter and acrimonious debate. McCumber was the only Republican on the Foreign Relations Committee who favored the Treaty of Versailles without alteration. His role in the debate was enhanced by his membership on that committee, and when it reported on the Covenant, McCumber issued a separate minority report in which he disagreed with the majority report of the Republicans and the minority position of the Democrats. McCumber felt that major revisions of the League Covenant would invite other powers to add reservations and thus render the League of Nations ineffective.

As the Senate struggle continued, McCumber did shift. In the debate before the first vote on the Treaty of Versailles in November 1919, he appealed to the moderate Democrats and Republicans to compromise their positions and accept mild reservations. He asked the League to Enforce Peace repeatedly not to yield to the strong reservationists. In all of the votes for the League, McCumber was the only Republican who cast his ballot for the treaty in the various alternatives presented. McCumber represented a voice of reason and logic during a time rife with partisanship. Like the other moderates during the League debate, he was not able to rally sufficient political compromise.

McCumber was later to become a sponsor of the Fordney–McCumber Tariff, a measure that reflected a limited understanding of international issues. After his defeat for reelection in 1922, he practiced law in Washington. In 1925 Calvin Coolidge appointed him a member of the International Joint Commission, which was to handle all cases involving the use of boundary waters between Canada and the United States. He served in that capacity until his death.

BIBLIOGRAPHY:
B. BDAC 1774–1971, 1369; DAB supp. 1, 525–26; *Encyclopedia Americana* 18 (Danbury, CT, 1979), 33–34; NCAB 13, 62; NYT 19 May 1933, 17; WWWA 1, 807.
C. A few McCumber papers are in the Regional History Collection at Cornell Univ.

Leon E. Boothe

MCDONALD, James Grover (29 November 1886, Coldwater, OH—26 September 1964, New York). *Education*: B.A., Indiana Univ., 1909, M.A., 1910; attended Harvard Univ., 1911–14. *Career*: chairman of board and president, Foreign Policy Association, 1919–33; high commissioner for refugees coming from Germany, League of Nations, 1933–35; editorial staff, *New York Times*, 1936–38; president, Brooklyn Institute of Arts and Sciences, 1938–42; news analyst, NBC Radio, 1942–44; U.S. special representative and ambassador to Israel, 1948–51.

McDonald, in a varied career, overcame the provincialism of a Midwest birth to play an active role in promoting internationalism. After studying history at Indiana University and Harvard, he moved to New York City, where he joined the staff of the Civil Service Reform Association. Concerned over the coming peace, liberals late in 1918 began to express their views. One organization, the League of Free Nations Association (LFNA), attracted McDonald. In the fight over the approval of the Treaty of Versailles and the Covenant of the League of Nations, liberals split into several groups, some supporting the treaty with its flaws and others opposing the harshness of the terms imposed on Germany. The League of Free Nations Association also divided, with McDonald emerging as leader of the moderate faction favoring acceptance with reservations. Elected first as chairman of the board of directors, he also became the president when Norman Hapgood resigned over the refusal of the Association to support the treaty without reservations.

From 1919 until 1933, McDonald served the LFNA, later the Foreign Policy Association (FPA), in the dual capacity. During those years of trial for internationalism in general, McDonald guided the organization through a struggle to secure U.S. recognition of the revolutionary governments of Mexico and Russia. The LFNA had established those two projects as its major priorities for U.S. policy, and it began active campaigns to bring government acceptance of the policies. Both brought trouble.

In urging recognition of Mexico, McDonald and other members of the LFNA went to Washington to appear before a Senate subcommittee headed by Albert B. Fall. There they charged that the United States planned intervention in Mexico to bring down the popular government and replace it with an oppressive one more friendly to American interest. Unable to substantiate those charges, the LFNA suffered severe abuse from Fall and others. McDonald later defended the Association's actions as helpful in publicizing the possibility of intervention and thus playing a role in preventing it. Criticisms arose because of other positions taken. McDonald, who earlier had been named to a list of unpatriotic American professors during World War I for a pamphlet he wrote on German atrocities, faced a new attack when the LFNA distributed documents relating to U.S. policy toward Russia. The State Department charged that it had released sensitive information for which it had not received clearance. As president of the LFNA,

McDonald had voted to approve the establishment of a Russian committee and had written the foreword to the publication.

In 1922, McDonald guided the LFNA in its transition from an activist organization seeking to influence policy development to an educational organization aimed at promoting greater understanding of foreign affairs. Finding funding limited for active support of specific policies and unsure that such efforts brought success, the LFNA changed its name in 1922 to the Foreign Policy Association and adopted a nonpartisan stance. It began publishing short background studies on international problems aimed at opinion makers, thus hoping to create a broader base of foreign policy knowledge in the country. McDonald initially prepared a number of essays for the *News Bulletin*, but gradually his writing on foreign affairs declined as he became more immersed in administrative activities. He did play a major role in securing radio coverage of biweekly luncheons held by the FPA, which for several years were broadcast nationally by NBC. He also began a series of weekly talks on NBC, entitled "The World Today," which attempted to advance international understanding among the people. The transcripts were published in *Scholastic Magazine* for a brief time.

McDonald promoted disarmament and peace activities. He served as a member of the Steering Committee of the First National Conference on the Cause and Prevention of War and maintained lines of communications between pacifist-minded internationalists and moderate advocates of collective security. Each year, McDonald took time to tour Europe to discuss world affairs. His reputation led in 1933 to the offer that he become the League of Nations high commissioner for refugees coming from Germany. McDonald left the FPA for three frustrating years as high commissioner, a time in which he became concerned for the first time with the problems of Jewish refugees and in which he became an advocate of the establishment of the Jewish state of Palestine.

In 1936 McDonald returned to the United States, serving for two years on the editorial staff of the *New York Times*. During World War II he returned to the airwaves as a news analyst for NBC; then in 1944 he served as chairman of the Committee on Political Refugees. He also developed an interest in the Middle East. He accepted appointment to the Anglo-American Committee of Inquiry on Palestine, where he stood opposed to British desires for the region. Following that service, he headed the U.S. mission to Israel, which led to his appointment, over the opposition of the State Department, as the first ambassador to Israel in 1949. On retirement in 1952, McDonald returned to New York City.

McDonald's career tended more toward the administrative than the philosophic in his commitment to internationalism. Yet, in his writing, particularly in the early years of the LFNA and FPA, McDonald emphasized the need for U.S. recognition of the interrelationships which govern world affairs. An advocate of interdependent cooperation among nations,

McDonald pursued throughout his writing the objective of making Americans both more aware of international affairs and more sensitive to the pecularities of individual nations. He urged a greater understanding of national differences while retaining the knowledge that the world had to act as a single unit in solving its common, complex problems.

BIBLIOGRAPHY:

A. *My Mission to Israel* (New York, 1951); "Refugees," in *Pioneers in World Order: An American Appraisal of the League of Nations*, ed., Harriet E. Davis (New York, 1944), 208–28.

B. CB 1949, 373–75; DAB supp 7, 497–99; NCAB F, 174–75; NYT 17 Apr 1949, 43, 27 Sep 1964, 86; WWWA 4, 635.

C. The McDonald papers are in the School of International Affairs, Columbia Univ.

Frank W. Abbott

MCDOWELL, William Osborne (10 April 1848, Somerset County, NJ—12 March 1927, Newark, NJ). *Education*: public schools. *Career*: businessman and railroad entrepreneur, New York and Newark, NJ, 1869–1927.

A self-made man of wealth, McDowell by the 1890s had developed an interest in promoting nationalistic programs. These included a campaign for funds to complete the foundation for the Statue of Liberty and to celebrate the centennial of George Washington's inaugural, and he led in creating the Sons of the American Revolution. When that body excluded women, McDowell organized the Daughters of the American Revolution and presided at its first meeting.

At the same time, McDowell developed a concern for human welfare that led him on diverse paths. He organized movements to establish a republic in Brazil and a federation in Australia. He also helped develop the Cuban American League before and during the Spanish-American War, calling for Cuban independence. In the 1920s he promoted a congressional resolution endorsing the equality of women and men.

Yet McDowell's pet concern became peace, and he involved himself in it with such conviction that many other peace workers and internationalists considered him crazy. In 1891–92 McDowell organized the Human Freedom League, serving as its president. It sought to advance the ideal of a federation of people based on a worldwide republic. A court was to be empowered to hear disputes and to legislate. McDowell organized a Committee of Three Hundred, which in 1892 held a rally in Independence Hall, Philadelphia, with many notable persons in attendance. In 1903 McDowell, who had been proclaimed "Peacemaker" at the 1892 meeting, designed a world flag and between 1904 and 1907 advanced "The Society of the Who's Who [the intellectual leaders of the world] *Bringing into Existence* The United Nations of the Earth." An accompanying plan called for a well-developed international organization with an executive, a legislative, and a judicial system. McDowell found a medium for his ideas in the *Journal of*

American History, which printed his "First Draft of a Constitution for the United Nations of the World." It listed an elaborate cabinet, gave the government police and regulatory powers, especially over arms manufacturing, and called for a peace tax against each nation's military budget. An international postal system would provide additional revenue.

In 1910, McDowell joined forces with *Richard Bartholdt to merge his ideas with those of the Inter-Parliamentary Union. He succeeded in having a resolution introduced into the U.S. House requesting $600,000 for a world congress in the United States and for "peace propaganda." McDowell proceeded with plans for a gigantic assembly hall in New York City for the 25,000 legislators, judges, and officials who would attend. Similar resolutions also failed to elicit any funds, despite an elaborate campaign by McDowell which gained endorsement of the congress idea from nearly 400 clubs and societies.

McDowell was left out of efforts to promote the league idea between 1914 and 1918, largely because leaders of the League to Enforce Peace and other groups considered him too eccentric. He approved of the Covenant, worried that the Permanent Court of International Justice be properly constituted, sought to have his name presented to the Nobel Peace Committee, and hoped he would be able to visit Geneva, where he could see the "Junior League" at work. The "Senior League" was his plan, not the halfway house that had been created. Shortly before his death at seventy-nine, he was planning a campaign for a world ballot to create a universal and effective international organization.

BIBLIOGRAPHY:

A. "First Draft of a Constitution for the United Nations of the World," *Journal of American History* 2, no. 4 (1908), 537–42.

B. Warren F. Kuehl, *Seeking World Order: The United States and International Organization to 1920* (Nashville, TN, 1969); NCAB 3, 147; NYT 13 Mar 1927 II-11.

C. The McDowell papers are in the New York Public Library and at the New Jersey Historical Society.

Warren F. Kuehl

MCFADYEAN, Andrew (23 April 1887—3 October 1974). *Education*: *litterae humaniores*, Univ. Coll., Oxford Univ., 1909. *Career*: official of British Treasury, 1910–24; secretary, Dawes Committee, 1922–24; commissioner of controlled revenues, Berlin, 1924–30; Liberal party politician.

McFadyean achieved prominence in two types of internationalist activity, first as an expert on German reparations during the 1920s and later as a proponent of European unity after World War II. He began his career in the British Treasury Office, serving as private secretary successively to various ministers, and he went with Stanley Baldwin on a financial mission to the United States in 1917. As the Treasury specialist on reparations, McFadyean established his reputation when he served as secretary of the Reparations Commission (1922–24).

The 1924 report of the Committee on Reparations, headed by *Charles C. Dawes, ended five years of wrangling between France and Germany over the amount of reparations the latter should pay. This report, in the writing of which McFadyean played a major role, recommended the stabilization of the German currency on a gold basis and the definition of the total amount owed by Germany. McFadyean helped influence the terms in the direction of magnaminity. For the next five years, McFadyean served as commissioner of controlled revenues at Berlin. The Young Plan of 1929 represented a further improvement in terms, but the economic slump of 1930 destroyed all hope of Franco-German reconciliation, paving the way for Hitler.

In 1930, McFadyean gave up his old career as a civil servant to pursue a new role as a Liberal party politician. In this new career, he continued to demonstrate his abiding loyalty to the goals of international peace and reconciliation. Between 1930 and 1945, McFadyean served as vice-president of the Royal Institute of International Affairs, was an active member of the Institute of Pacific Relations, and did much work for Palestine and for the Jews of Germany. Following World War II, he was instrumental in the founding (1947) of the Liberal International, an alliance of liberal political groupings in France, Italy, and the Federal Republic of Germany. He held the title of vice-president (1954–67). During these immediate postwar years, McFadyean became a staunch proponent of the causes of the European Common Market and of the United States of Europe. He had been interested in this idea through contacts with *Richard Coudenhove-Kalergi, and he participated in many Pan-European conferences.

BIBLIOGRAPHY:

A. *Reparation Reviewed* (London, 1930).

B. *Annual Register* (1947), 548; LT 3 Oct 1974, 18, 8 Oct 1974, 18; WW 1970, 62.

C. McFadyean papers are in the British Library of Political and Economic Science, London School of Economics.

Paul D. Mageli

MCNAIR, Arnold Duncan (3 April 1885, London—22 May 1975, Cambridge). *Education*: graduate, Caius Coll., Cambridge Univ., 1909. *Career*: solicitor, London, 1909–13; fellow and law lecturer, Cambridge Univ., 1912–16; secretary, Coal Conservation Committee, 1916–18; secretary, Coal Controllers Advisory Board, 1917–19; secretary, Coal Industry (Sankey) Commission, 1919; reader in international law, London Univ., 1926–27; professor, Univ. of Calcutta, 1931, Cambridge Univ., 1935–37, 1945–46; vice-chancellor, Liverpool Univ., 1937–45; member, Permanent Court of Arbitration, The Hague, 1946; judge, International Court of Justice, 1946–55, president, 1952–55; president, Institute of International Law, 1948–50; president, European Court of Human Rights, 1959–65.

McNair began his career as an English solicitor at the age of twenty-one, and his earliest specialty was in the law of contracts. However, following

World War I his interests changed to international law, and his professional stature derived from his prolific studies in these fields. His monograph on the *Legal Effects of War*, written immediately after that conflict, was enlarged and expanded several times after World War II. His study of the *Law of Treaties* (1938) was republished in a new and expanded edition a generation later. A scholar of many talents, he touched upon such diverse subjects as the law of war, air, and treaties, Roman law, the nature of corporations, the Spanish Civil War, merchant marine law, collective security, codification of international law, international legal practice, and human rights.

McNair sought throughout his distinguished career to give a cutting edge to international law, and he championed the causes of codification, precedent, and clearly defined rules, which he termed "hard law." He thus went against the antipositivistic trend of the interwar period, but at the same time he believed that the sphere of law was of necessity a limited one. In fact, he did not shrink from admitting that there were interstate disputes that could not be settled by legal means. As an influential and prominent world jurist, McNair saw the role of international tribunals as one limited to defining and declaring rights and duties rather than creating rights or changing the nature of obligations. In this sense, he could be said to have had an affinity for the narrow tenets of legal positivism.

McNair's last major contribution was made in the field of human rights, particularly from his service and presidency on the European Court of Human Rights. He interpreted the European Convention on Human Rights as a law-making treaty, which had the effect of causing the signatory states to revise or modify their domestic statutes to bring them in harmony with the European Convention. It is interesting to note that, after serving as president of the two major postwar transnational legal tribunals, he believed that a regional approach was more salutary than a global emphasis.

BIBLIOGRAPHY:

A. *Dr. Johnson and the Law* (Cambridge, 1948); ed., *International Law Opinions*, 3 vols. (Cambridge, 1956); *The Law of the Air* (London, 1932); *The Law of Treaties* (Oxford, 1961); *The Legal Effects of War* (Cambridge, 1920, 1944, 1948; with A. D. Watts, 1966); ed., *International Law: A Treatise by L. Oppenheim* (London, 1926, 1928).

B. CB 1955, 396–98; IWW 1973–74, 1063; LT 24 May 1975, 14; WB 1954, 787; 396–98; *Who Was Who Among English and European Authors 1931–1949* 2 (Detroit, 1978), 974.

Robert A. Friedlander

MEAD, Edwin Doak (29 September 1849, Chesterfield, NH—17 August 1937, Brookline, MA). *Education*: British Museum and Cambridge, Oxford, and Leipzig Univs., 1875–79. *Career*: employed by Ticknor & Fields, 1866–75; lecturer and author, 1879–89; editor, *New England Magazine*, 1889–1901; director, World Peace Foundation, 1910–14.

An urban reformer in the New England liberal tradition, Mead commanded respect in Boston's reform community. As editor of the *New England Magazine*, which he helped found in 1889, he criticized industrial America's excesses and campaigned for social justice. He vigorously endorsed municipal socialism, women's suffrage, and the nationalization of railroads. During the 1890s, he became the leader of Boston's anti-imperialists, condemning jingoism over Venezuela, the Spanish-American War, and the U.S. presence in the Philippines. In 1901 he relinquished his editorship and assumed a more active place in the peace movement. He and his wife, *Lucia Ames Mead, formed an effective speaking and writing team that participated in worldwide peace activities.

Influenced by Immanuel Kant and Hugo Grotius, Mead sought to supplant war with international law. He believed that wars seldom resolved problems and only spawned future conflicts. He found them inconsistent with his Christian principles and contrary to the ideals of justice and understanding. War and national defense, he argued, squandered human and material resources. Enlarged weapons inventories and huge armies caused suspicion, precipitated arms races, and reduced security. The militarism which accompanied increased armaments had no place within a republic. Mead used his pen and voice to advance his views. A pamphlet, *Organize the World*, (1898) was widely reprinted and quoted, and he elaborated on that theme many times. Optimistic about the nineteenth century's progress, Mead expressed confidence that in the twentieth century a new world order based upon international law could be established. Heartened by the proliferation of arbitration treaties and the Hague Conferences, he believed that a parliament of man, a global legislature, and a court lay in the near future. Labor and business leaders, women, students, and churches had to be mobilized to achieve this international federation. The United States, with its own federal system and secure borders and distant from European problems, had a "holy call" to lead the movement. The British, Mead suggested, should assist, because of their cultural, religious, and institutional similarities. When international tensions rose, he recommended that the Germans also be included in a Triple Peace League. Seeking to overcome barriers to internationalism, Mead's essays and speeches contained two themes. First, he emphasized that international law and organization were not new or radical ideas but time-honored concepts which had many respected proponents. Second, he stressed that America's founding fathers, rather than turning their backs on the world, had sought methods for peaceful conflict resolution.

Mead's activities extended beyond speaking and writing. He regularly attended the annual Lake Mohonk International Arbitration Conferences and served as an officer in the American and Massachusetts Peace Societies. He participated in the creation of the Carnegie Endowment for International Peace, and in 1910 he assisted Boston publisher *Edwin Ginn in launching the World Peace Foundation. Mead served as its first secretary and as director, administering grants, supervising programs, and editing its International Library Series and pamphlet publications.

He and his wife traveled abroad to several peace conferences (1901, 1903, 1905, 1907, 1908, 1909), and he led in planning the first American Peace Congress in 1907. In 1914, while attending a Church Peace Union meeting in Europe, Mead witnessed the outbreak of World War I. The emotionally trying experience and his concern over a rising militaristic spirit dashed his optimistic hopes and precipitated a severe nervous breakdown in 1915. Though incapacitated for a decade, his interest in peace and internationalism remained strong. Although his subsequent literary output never equaled that of the prewar period, he publicly endorsed the League of Nations and the World Court until his death.

BIBLIOGRAPHY:

A. "Editor's Table," *New England Magazine* (1889–1901); "Immanuel Kant's Internationalism," *Contemporary Review* 107 (Feb 1915), 226–32; *The Principles of the Founders* (Boston, 1903); *Report of the Lake Mohonk Conference on International Arbitration* (1896–1914); World Peace Foundation pamphlets (1910–14).

B. DAB supp. 2, 442–43; Lucia A. Mead, "Edwin D. Mead," *World Unity Magazine* 2 (Aug 1928), 337–43; David S. Patterson, *Toward a Warless World: The Travail of the American Peace Movement, 1887–1914* (Bloomington, IN, 1976).

C. Some Mead papers are in the Swarthmore Coll. Peace Collection and at the Massachusetts Historical Society.

Daryl L. Revoldt

MEAD, Lucia True Ames (5 May 1856, Boscawen, NH—1 November 1936, Boston). *Education*: private and public secondary school. *Career*: lecturer on literature and reform issues, 1888–98; peace activist and publicist, 1898–1936.

Following the Spanish-American War, Lucia Mead assumed a prominent place in the American peace movement. Influenced by the New England reform tradition, she spent her early career appealing for social justice, demanding women's suffrage, and denouncing racial prejudice. In 1898 she married Bostonian *Edwin D. Mead, editor of the *New England Magazine* and an active reformer. He introduced her to the peace movement by taking her to the Lake Mohonk International Arbitration Conferences, and she began to direct her literary and speaking efforts toward peace and disarmament.

Not a doctrinaire pacifist, she espoused the practical peace pathway. She opposed war because it wasted resources, killed society's fittest members, and seldom promoted justice. Conflict, she believed, originated in misunderstanding, and she looked for methods to eliminate such disagreements. A gradualist who defined peace as a condition of organized living among nations, Mead favored international organization. She endorsed arbitration and conciliation treaties and in 1903 recommended that the major powers disarm and establish an international police force. She also proposed that international law be expanded through the Hague Conferences and world congresses and enforced through a world court or sanctions. The millennium need not occur before steps toward limited international organization were taken. Four of five great nations could set the precedent. Yet, as a vehement opponent of imperialism, Mead rejected big-power politics. Given the country's unique heritage and geographic location, she envisaged the United States playing a major role in her quest for justice and understanding. Americans, she contended, had to become internationalists, and she thought schools and mothers had a special obligation to mold global citizens whose first allegiance was to humanity. In numerous speeches and articles she forcefully repeated these themes.

World War I shattered her hope that a more peaceful civilization lay within reach. Filled with despair, she helped +Jane Addams organize the Woman's Peace Party and served as its national secretary. At the same time, she nursed her husband, who was suffering from a nervous breakdown induced by the war. Mead protested against preparedness and condemned the possibility of American intervention. Yet, during the submarine crisis, she endorsed *Woodrow Wilson's proposal to arm merchant vessels. When America entered the conflict, she supported the effort and blamed Germany for the catastrophe, but she also favored a just postwar settlement. She enthusiastically advocated the League of Nations, hoping it would soften the Versailles Treaty, and she spent the 1920s calling in speaking tours and writings for U.S. membership in the League and World Court. She also criticized the government's half-hearted disarmament efforts and the nation's militaristic impulses. Still vigorous at eighty, she died after a fall in the Boston subway.

BIBLIOGRAPHY:

A. *Great Thoughts for Little Thinkers* (New York, 1889); *Law or War* (Garden City, NY, 1928); *Memoirs of a Millionaire* (Boston, 1889); *Patriotism and the New Internationalism* (Boston, 1906); *Swords or Plowshares* (New York, 1912); *To Whom Much Is Given* (New York, 1899).

B. NAW 2, 520–22; NCAB 28, 430; David S. Patterson, introduction to Mead, *Law or War*, rpt. ed. (New York, 1971).

C. Some Mead papers are in the Swarthmore Coll. Peace Collection.

Daryl L. Revoldt

MELLO FRANCO, Afranio de (25 February 1870, Paracatu, Minas Gerais, Brazil—1 January 1943, Rio de Janeiro). *Education*: graduate, Faculty of Law, São Paulo, 1891. *Career*: acting prosecutor, Ouro Preto, Minas Gerais, 1890; prosecutor, Queluz, Minas Gerais, 1891; second secretary of legation, Montevideo, 1896, Brussels, 1897; law practice, Belo Horizonte, Minas Gerais, 1898–43; state legislator, Minas Gerais, 1902–6; federal legislator, 1906–18, 1920–29; secretary of finance, Minas Gerais, 1918; minister of transportation, 1918–19; representative, First International Conference on Labor, 1919; president, Brazilian delegation, Fifth Pan American Conference, Santiago, 1923; president, Brazilian delegation, League of Nations, 1923, permanent ambassador, 1924–26; minister of foreign relations, 1930–33; president, Brazilian delegation, Seventh Pan American Conference, Montevideo, 1933; chair, Commission of Experts to prepare code of Inter-American Law, 1937–38; president, Brazilian delegation, Eighth Inter-American Conference, Lima, 1938; chair, Inter-American Commission of Neutrality, 1940–42; chair, Inter-American Juridicial Commission, 1942.

Mello Franco's life was law. He made his presence felt at the state, national, inter-American, and world levels. A member of the talented elite of turn-of-the-century Minas Gerais, he contributed to that state's tradition of supplying Brazil with skillful diplomats. Willing to disagree with the presidents and foreign ministers he served, he sought to maintain Brazil's reputation for careful diplomacy. At the League of Nations, he established himself as the leading exponent of international law as a defense for small countries. In his view international justice should not distinguish between strong and weak nations; it was the only shield the small countries had against great power imperialism. A proponent of gentlemanly diplomatic style, he refused to read to the League Council the Brazilian government's angry 1926 statement of resignation, substituting instead a milder personal one calculated to preserve the representatives' good will and sympathy.

He played a leading role in the formation of the nonintervention declaration adopted at the 1933 Montevideo Conference and in the settlement of the Chaco War between Bolivia and Paraguay and the Leticia dispute between Colombia and Peru. To these achievements he added the cautious handling of Argentina at the 1938 Lima Conference that preserved Pan American solidarity on the eve of World War II. He left his imprint by acting on his phrase that policy should always seek to attain peace not by force but by peace.

BIBLIOGRAPHY:

B. Stanley E. Hilton, *Brazil and the Great Powers, 1930–1939* (Austin TX, 1975); Alfonso Arinos de Mello Franco, *Um Estadista da República*, 3 vols. (Rio de Janeiro, 1955); NYT 2 Jan 1943, 11; Frank P. Walters, *A History of the League of Nations* (Oxford, 1952).

Frank D. McCann

MEULEN, Jacob ter. See Ter Meulen, Jacob.

MEZES, Sidney E. (23 September 1863, Belmont, CA—10 September 1931, Pasadena, CA). *Education*: B.S., Univ. of California, 1884; B.A., Harvard Coll., 1890, M.A., 1891, Ph.D., 1893. *Career*: taught at Bryn Mawr Coll., 1892–93, Univ. of Chicago, 1893–94, Univ. of Texas, 1894–1902; dean, College of Literature, Science, and Arts, Univ. of Texas, 1902–8, president,

1908–14; president, Coll. of the City of New York, 1914–27; director, the Inquiry, 1917–19.

Mezes had a long career as a philosopher of religion and a university administrator, and there is no evidence that prior to 1917 he had thought extensively about international questions until his friendship with his brother-in-law *Edward M. House gave him a position of responsibility in American wartime diplomacy. House helped advance Mezes' career, and in 1914 House was instrumental in Mezes' appointment as president of the College of the City of New York.

On 2 September 1917, *Woodrow Wilson wrote House, asking him to organize a group of experts to prepare for the postwar peace conference. Far too busy to assume this responsibility himself, House chose his trusted friend as director of the Inquiry. Valuing personal loyalty more than experience or knowledge, House wanted to ensure his control of the new organization and calculated that through it he could expand his influence while diminishing that of the Department of State. Mezes never, however, gained the confidence of the academic experts who staffed the Inquiry, and he was soon overshadowed by powerful figures such as *Isaiah Bowman, *Walter Lippmann, *David Hunter Miller, and *James T. Shotwell. These men regarded Mezes as a weak administrator who was poorly informed on international issues, and tension grew within the group. By the summer of 1918, discontent was so great that many experts threatened to resign, forcing House to work out a compromise that left Mezes largely as a titular leader. The results were unsatisfactory, and the Inquiry remained a poorly run organization, scattering its efforts and never forming a comprehensive vision of the peace settlement. Mezes retained some authority, however, negotiating with Secretary of State *Robert Lansing over how many of the experts should attend the Paris Peace Conference.

In December 1918 twenty-three authorities, including Mezes, traveled to Paris, where they were absorbed into the staff of the American Commission to Negotiate Peace and provided careful analysis of territorial questions. At the Peace Conference, Mezes' official title was director of specialists, and he sought to keep House informed of the views of the Inquiry's scholars, served on a committee to form boundary lines for Germany, and sympathized with Italian territorial claims. But his position remained dependent on his friendship with House, and his role at the conference was a minor one. With the close of the negotiations, Mezes returned to academic life, ending his brief interlude of symbolic prominence in world affairs.

BIBLIOGRAPHY:

A. "The Inquiry," in *What Really Happened at Paris*, ed. Edward M. House and Charles Seymour (New York, 1921).

B. DAB 12, 588–89; Lawrence E. Gelfand, *The Inquiry: American Preparation for peace, 1917–1919* (New Haven, CT, 1963); *Handbook of Texas* 2 (Austin, 1952), 186; NYT 12 Sep 1931, 17.

C. Some Mezes papers are in the Butler Library, Columbia Univ.

Charles E. Neu

MILES, James B. See *Biographical Dictionary of Modern Peace Leaders*.

MILLER, David Hunter (2 January 1875, New York—21 July 1961, Washington). *Education*: LL.B., New York Law School, 1910, LL.M., 1911. *Career*: private law practice, 1911–17, 1919–29; the Inquiry, 1917–18; legal adviser, American Commission to Negotiate Peace, Paris, 1919; counsel to German Republic, 1921; editor-in-chief of treaties, Department of State, 1929–48; chair, U.S. delegation, Conference for Codification of International Law, The Hague, 1930; member, Committee of Archives of the Department of State, 1935–48; delegate, Second General Assembly, Pan American Institute of Geography and History, Washington, 1935.

When U.S. governmental leaders began in 1917 to grapple with the complex problems presented by their involvement in a postwar settlement in Europe, they turned for advice on international law to Miller, who had distinguished himself in that field through his involvement in litigation, his legal writing, and service under the Wilson administration. On the Inquiry, he studied territorial problems that would arise at the peace conference. Later he traveled to Paris with the American Commission to Negotiate Peace as a legal adviser. During the 1918–19 negotiations, Miller's energy and unerring and sound instincts made him a trusted adviser to *Woodrow Wilson, *Edward M. House affirmed that Miller's counsel and involved participation proved of key importance during the negotiations.

Miller and *Cecil J. B. Hurst, the British legal adviser, produced a draft for a league which became the basis of negotiations at the meetings of the League Commission. They jointly prepared the final draft of the Covenant approved first by the Commission and then by the Peace Conference on 28 April 1919.

Miller was involved in a number of Peace Conference issues. He was an informal participant in the Italo-Yugoslav dispute over Fiume and closely advised Wilson and the Chinese on Far Eastern questions. He drafted the Polish Minorities Treaty, which became a model for other such treaties. As a historian of the Peace Conference, Miller also made significant contributions. He kept a diary, privately printed (now available on microfilm) in 1924, limited to forty copies, with nineteen additional volumes of letters and memoranda. This collection became the indispensable source for all later scholars chronicling the Paris discussions, including the compilers of the Department of State's thirteen-volume set produced as part of its *Foreign Relations* series. Miller also published in 1928 a two-volume account, *The Drafting of the Covenant*, judged by League of Nations specialists as essential for the study of its origins.

Although engaged in private law practice (1921–29), Miller participated from time to time in diplomatic efforts to promote world peace. He advised the German government (1921) over drawing the German–Polish border in Upper Silesia. In 1924 Miller joined *James T. Shotwell, *Tasker H. Bliss, and six other American internationalists on an unofficial committee in preparing a draft for a mutual guarantee treaty that aided in formulating the Geneva Protocol. This Anglo-French project, seeking to establish arbitration machinery and providing automatic identification as an aggressor any party which engaged in war without first resorting to arbitration, represented a valiant attempt between the wars to replace traditional power politics with a legal procedure for the resolution of international disputes.

Miller performed a distinctive service contributing toward knowledge of U.S. foreign relations by editing from 1929 until his retirement in 1948, the State Department publication of *U.S. Treaties* in eight volumes covering the years from 1776 to 1863. His position was created by Congress to prepare new texts based on original documents.

Miller also remained an active participant in a variety of world conferences. His involvement in international affairs, spanning three decades, placed him in an influential position at critical junctures as diplomat, counselor, historian, and editor. Even though the pursuit of peace proved ill-fated during those troubled interwar years, Miller diligently pursued that cause by stressing reason, accommodation, and law in international relations.

BIBLIOGRAPHY:

A. *The Drafting of the Covenant*, 2 vols. (New York, 1928); *The Geneva Protocol* (New York, 1925); *My Diary at the Conference at Paris*, 21 vols. (New York, 1924); *The Peace Pact of Paris* (New York, 1928); *San Juan Archipelago: Study of the Joint Occupation of San Juan Island* (Bellow Falls, VT, 1943); ed., *Treaties and Other International Acts of the United States of America, 1776–1863* (Washington, 1931–48).

B. DAB supp. 7, 536–37; John P. Posey, "David Hunter Miller and the Polish Minorities Treaty, 1919," *Southern Quarterly* 8 (Jan 1970), 163–67; "David Hunter Miller and the Far Eastern Question at the Paris Peace Conference, 1919," *ibid.*, 17 (Jul 1969), 373–92; "David Hunter Miller as an Informal Diplomat: The Fiume Question at the Paris Peace Conference, 1919," *Southern Quarterly* 6 (Apr 1967), 251–72; "David Hunter Miller at the Paris Peace Conference, November 1918–May, 1919," dissertation, Univ. of Georgia, 1962.

C. The Miller papers are in the Manuscript Division, Library of Congress.

John P. Posey

MINOR, Raleigh Colston (24 January 1869, Charlottesville, VA—14 June 1923, Charlottesville). *Education*: B.A., Univ. of Virginia, 1887, M.A., 1888, LL.B., 1890. *Career*: law practice, Richmond, VA., 1890–93; assistant to professor, Univ. of Virginia Law School, 1893–1923.

Although a specialist on real property and tax and constitutional law, Minor also developed the field of international law, which he combined with his interest in history. A study on the relationship of states to the federal government led him to speculate on the connection between nations and any international body that might develop. As Minor examined various proposals being advanced during World War I, he decided to write a book, which he called *A Republic of Nations* (1918). To Minor it was useless to create any body without the political capacity to perform. Since the United States provided not only a structural model but also evidence of the expansion of power at the federal level when needed, Minor suggested a constitution modeled after that of the United States. His thirty-eight pages of detailed articles conferred all authority needed for an effective world government, with national states subordinate to it, particularly on territorial, commercial, and political matters, over which most wars began. While he could not have been satisfied with the League of Nations, Minor remained relatively quiet after he produced his work. It stands, however, as one of the fullest expositions presented by internationalists of his generation.

BIBLIOGRAPHY:

A. *A Republic of Nations: A Study of the Organization of a Federal League of Nations* (New York, 1918).

B. NCAB 26, 144–45.

Warren F. Kuehl

MITCHELL, Samuel Chiles (24 December 1864, Coffeeville, MS—20 August 1948, Atlanta, GA). *Education*: M.A., Georgetown Coll. (KY), 1888; Ph.D., Univ. of Chicago, 1899. *Career*: instructor, Georgetown Coll., 1888–89, 1891–95, Mississippi Coll., 1889–91; professor, Richmond Coll., 1895–1908, 1920–45; president, Univ. of South Carolina, 1908–13, Medical Coll. of Virginia, 1913–14, Univ. of Delaware, 1914–20.

After serving as the first professor of history in Richmond College and then as president of three institutions, Mitchell returned in 1920 to the University of Richmond, where he was recognized as a matchless teacher. He especially sought to incite students to think, to express opinions, and to act on their views. Most university classes were canceled 8 December 1941, when many students went to hear Mitchell's reactions to the attack at Pearl Harbor.

One subject lay at the heart of his thinking and teaching. Between the wars Mitchell was an active spokesman, specifically for the League of Nations and broadly for the organization of the world as a community. Even before U.S. intervention in World War I, Mitchell attended Lake Mohonk and other peace congresses, developed a friendship with *Theodore Marburg, and supported *Woodrow Wilson's emerging League of Nations. Mitchell blamed Senators *Henry Cabot Lodge, William E. Borah, and Hiram Johnson for blocking U.S. membership in the League but continued to work for popular American support of the organization. In 1923–24 Mitchell led several Richmond associates in the formation of a society known as Friends of the League. John Stewart Bryan served as president, and Thomas B. McAdams as treasurer. It sought to raise funds to be applied to the League of Nations budget in lieu of the nonmembership of the United

States. It received about $1,500 from Mitchell's group, sending it to the League to be applied to the relief of orphans in the Middle East. Mitchell was unsuccessful, however, in getting the leadership of the League of Nations Non-Partisan Association, which he considered unrepresentative of rank-and-file Americans, to seek broader American financial support for the League.

Mitchell maintained a lifetime interest in organizing the world as a community. In 1939 he led in the formation of the Richmond Committee of Interdemocracy Federal Unionists. Through this group, Mitchell supported the idea, popularized by Clarence K. Streit's *Union Now* (1939), of uniting fifteen North Atlantic democracies. After war again broke out in Europe, Mitchell favored aid to Britain short of war but still looked upon state sovereignty as the chief cause of international anarchy.

Sources of Mitchell's internationalism were his broad contacts and experience in higher education, his wide knowledge of history, and his frequent travels, which in 1935 included a nine-month study tour in Europe. His advocacy of public education in the South during the progressive era, his role as a minor New South prophet, and his dissenting views on race had early made Mitchell one of the South's leading liberals. By 1932, he favored recognition of the Soviet Union, believed isolationism had choked the channels of world trade, and had become an enthusiastic supporter of *Franklin Roosevelt's New Deal. By 1947, Mitchell had declared world socialism inevitable and rebuked *Harry Truman for his Truman Doctrine speech. Still seeking to create popular reactions to world problems, Mitchell urged Virginians to debate Truman's actions in the context of social change. America's part, he believed, was to turn the Greek question over to the United Nations and to set an example of a working democracy by clearing slums and ending lynchings.

BIBLIOGRAPHY:

A. "The Aftermath of Appomattox: A Memoir," mimeo (Atlanta, GA, 1954); "Education in the South Since the War," *History of the Social Life of the South* 10, ed. Mitchell, in *The South in the Building of the Nation* (Richmond, VA, 1909–13).

B. NCAB 14, 88–89; NYT 21 Aug 1948, 15.

C. The Mitchell papers are in the Manuscript Division, Library of Congress, Univ. of South Carolina Library, the Southern Historical Collection, Chapel Hill, and the Univ. of Richmond Library.

Ernest C. Bolt, Jr.

MOFFAT, Jay Pierrepont (18 July 1896, Rye, NY—23 January 1943, Ottawa). *Education*: Harvard Univ., 1915–17. *Career*: private secretary, American Legation, The Hague, 1918; foreign service officer, Warsaw, 1919–21, Tokyo, 1921–23, Constantinople, 1923–25; protocol officer, White House, 1925–27, Bern, 1927–31; chief, Division of Western European Affairs, Department of State, 1931–35; consul-general, Sydney, 1935–37; chief, Division of European Affairs, 1937–40; minister to Canada, 1940–43.

Moffat stood among the key State Department policy advisers during the decade preceding Pearl Harbor. His formal entry into the foreign service in 1919 led him to Warsaw during the Polish–Soviet conflict. His experiences there, including a memorable visit to the front just when the Polish line collapsed, reinforced attitudes that would remain with him for life: deep-rooted anti-Communism, genteel anti-Semitism, nostalgia for the disappearing European aristocracy. His 1927 marriage to Lilla Grew, daughter of the under secretary of state, aided an already flourishing career. After returning in 1931 from Bern, where he had been a delegate to the Preparatory Commission for the World Disarmament Conference, he twice headed the State Department's Western European Division (in 1937, the Western and Eastern European Divisions were merged under Moffat's direction). Here he did his most important work. Moffat eschewed publicity. He was strictly a team player to the degree that his memoirs often fail to delineate his own contributions from those of his close associates. He placed his faith in quiet negotiations among diplomatic professionals.

His cautious nationalism and moderation were perhaps the hallmarks of his work and reflective of many officers of the State Department. He was neither an isolationist, as has been claimed, nor an advocate of appeasement. Nor was he an outspoken friend of internationalism. Even during his work before 1931 at Bern, where he helped oversee U.S.–League of Nations cooperation, he never developed more than a distant sympathy for collective security as represented by the goal of the League. He clearly favored arms limitation efforts, but his contributions in this area were minimal. Immersed in details, he rarely addressed the broad political objectives which guided day-to-day negotiations between 1927 and 1935, and his ideas remained conventional. When President *Herbert Hoover in 1932 proposed a direct plan to break the disarmament deadlock, Moffat, with others in the State Department, tried to discourage him.

Moffat had few illusions about Hitler. His preoccupation with the expansion of Communism, however, combined with his distrust of Great Britain, left him leery of meaningful joint action. He wrote in 1937 that his primary concern was to avoid U.S. involvement in war, and this meant avoiding any common action by the democracies. Yet, he would soon express outrage at the Munich "sellout"; and when *Franklin Roosevelt moved slowly toward a common front after war began in 1939, Moffat dutifully followed. Moffat's anti-Nazi and anti-British sentiments came together in his last years when, as minister to Canada, he used the prospects of U.S.–Canadian cooperation against the Axis to persuade Ottawa to modify the imperial preference system. The use of limited international cooperation to serve nationalistic ends perfectly symbolized his approach throughout the interwar period.

BIBLIOGRAPHY:

A. *The Moffat Papers: Selections from the Diplomatic Journals of Jay Pierrepont Moffat, 1919–1943*, ed. Nancy H. Hooker (Cambridge, MA, 1956).

B. DAB supp. 3, 528-29; NYT 25 Jan 1943, 13; Martin Weil, *A Pretty Good Club: The Founding Fathers of the U.S. Foreign Service* (New York, 1978).

C. The Moffat papers are in the Houghton Library, Harvard Univ.

Gary B. Ostrower

MOLHUYSEN, Philipp Christiaan (20 August 1870, Ermelo, Netherlands—15 July 1944, The Hague). *Education*: Univ. of Leiden, 1896. *Career*: deputy director, Library of Peace Palace, 1913-21; director, Royal Library, The Hague, 1921-37.

Molhuysen grew up in Deventer, where his grandfather had been librarian of the famous Atheneum Library. There he became interested in classical literature and acquired a working knowledge of palaeography. That led to formal study, including considerable time in Italian libraries, notably in Florence. His thesis, "De tribus Homeri Odysseae codicibus antiquissimis," provided information for the first time on the oldest and best manuscript of the Odysseae.

In 1897 he was appointed conservator of the manuscripts in the university library at Leiden, where he published a catalog of the codices of the library in three volumes, and a catalog of printed letters to and from Dutch scholars. Other scholarly works followed. In 1913 he was appointed deputy librarian of the newly opened Peace Palace at The Hague. There he prepared for publication the letters of Hugo Grotius, and in 1919 he published an annotated edition of Grotius's *De Iure Belli ac Pacis*. As deputy director, Molhuysen worked with Alberic Rolin to develop a collection under difficulties. Funding was inadequate for a "world library," and the outbreak of World War I hindered plans. Considerable debate also ensued over the nature and size of the library collection. Molhuysen's chief contribution was the development, with E. R. Oppenheim, of the systematic catalog, first for books and later for articles. This finding aid provided a unique method for locating materials in the specialized fields of peace and international law.

In 1921 he was appointed librarian of the Royal Library in The Hague. There he took the initiative to establish the Central Catalogue, in which are entered the holdings of nearly all Dutch libraries. On his initiative, the Advisory Committee on Library Science was established in 1922, on which all branches of library science are represented and which serves as an advisory body to the government on library policy. On his initiative, an international exchange bureau for science publications was established in 1928 to regulate the exchange of publications between libraries in Holland and those in foreign countries. Molhuysen also stimulated the establishment of public libraries, and he promoted the creation of training courses for functionaries in public libraries.

BIBLIOGRAPHY:

A. *De Iure Belli ac Pacis*, by Hugonis Grotius, ed., (The Hague, 1919).

B. L. Brummel, "Dr. P. C. Molhuysen," *Bibliotheekleven* 29-30 (Sep 1945),

181-88; H. E. Grave, "In memoriam dr. P. C. Molhuysen: integer vitae," *Bibliotheekleven* 29-30 (Sep 1945), 51-52; IWW 1937, 778; A. J. de Mare, *Herinneringen aan dr. P. C. Molhuysen. Feiten en geschriften.* (The Hague, 1948); A. G. Roos, "Herdenking van Philipp Christiaan Molhuysen," *Jaarboek der Koninklijke Nederlandsche Akademie van Wetenschappen, 1944-45* (The Hague, 1945), 161-75.

J. B. van Hall

MOLINARI, Gustave de. See *Biographical Dictionary of Modern Peace Leaders.*

MOLLET, Guy (31 December 1905, Flers, Orne, France—3 October 1975, Arras, Pas de Calais, France). *Education*: Collège de Flers; B.A., lic. litt., and diploma in advanced studies, Univ. of Lille. *Career*: master at boarding school in Le Havre; professor at lycee in Arras, 1923-32; secretary, Fédération de l'Enseignement, Confédération Générale du Travail, 1932-39; interned by Germans, 1940-43, escaped and remained in hiding until the end of German occupation; mayor of Arras, 1945-49; delegate, Constituent Assembly, 1945-46; deputy from Pas de Calais, 1946-56; general secretary, Section Française de l'Internationale Ouvrière (SFIO), 1946-71; minister of state, 1946-47; delegate, Consultative Assembly, Council of Europe, 1949-56, and president, 1954-56; prime minister of France, 1956-57.

The role of the Socialist parties in the development of European unity after World War II was crucial to its success. In France and in Britain this was especially true, since Socialists held the balance of power in both countries immediately after 1945. In Britain the Laborites resisted British participation in any strong European organization until 1970. But in France, under the leadership of Guy Mollet, the SFIO supported not only the Council of Europe in 1949 but the supranational European Coal and Steel Community created one year later. In 1957, Mollet, as prime minister longer than any other French leader of the Fourth Republic, was able to conclude the Treaty of Rome that created the European Common Market.

Joining the French Socialist party early in his career, Mollet had become its general secretary in 1946. Within the party he represented a more radical reformist position than *Léon Blum, but he refused to cooperate with the Communists and broke with them especially over foreign policy.

Although he revealed nationalistic qualities in involving France in the Suez war in July 1956, Mollet was a Europeanist who supported the Schuman Plan. Mollet was upset by the failure of Britain to join and urged that the Council of Europe, to which the British belonged and where he served until 1956, be given a measure of supranational authority. While he supported the economic communities, Mollet refused to accept any kind of political union without Britain and stood with Pierre Mendes France in voting against the European Defense Community and the proposed political authority in 1954. By 1957, however, he had joined Monnet's Action Committee for a United States of Europe and as prime minister in 1957 was ready to push the completion of the Treaty of Rome. Although he continued to urge the inclusion of Britain, Mollet became at this point a strong advocate of progressive European unity. It is better, he declared, to trust that time will correct its imperfections than to reject the whole idea and find oneself faced with a void.

BIBLIOGRAPHY:

A. *Quinze ans après* (Paris, 1973).

B. *Ambassade de France* (Feb 1957); CB 1950, 404–7; *Newsweek* 28 (9 Dec 1946), 45; NYT 2 Feb 1975, 4, 4 Oct 1975, 30; *Témoignes, Guy Mollet* (Paris, 1977); WWF 1965–66, 1968.

Anne Tucker Moore

MONETA, Ernesto Teodore. See *Biographical Dictionary of Modern Peace Leaders*.

MONNET, Jean Omer Marie Gabriel (9 November 1888, Cognac, France—16 March 1979, Houjarray, France). *Education*: Coll. of Cognac, withdrew 1906. *Career*: deputy secretary-general, League of Nations, 1919–23; reorganized Chinese railroads, 1932; member, British Supply Council, 1940; commissioner, French Committee of National Liberation, 1943; director, French Planning Commissariat, 1946–50; president, High Authority of European Coal and Steel Community, 1952–55; president, Action Committee for the United States of Europe, 1955–75.

Monnet's early career prepared him superbly for the enormous contribution he was to make between 1950 and 1975 to the progress of European integration. He gained patience, he said later, from the aging of cognac in the cellars of the Monnet family firm. As salesman in 1906 for the company in Canada, he learned the intricacies of international business. But very early he was taught the interrelationship of politics and business. During World War I, he became coordinator of Anglo–French supplies; and from 1923 he was much in demand by foreign governments from Peking to Bucharest as an economic adviser on matters varying from the rebuilding of the Chinese railroads to the stabilization of the Romanian currency. Perhaps most important of all, as deputy secretary-general of the League of Nations (1919–23) he had shown an extraordinary ability at persuading national governments to seek negotiated solutions to their differences. During World War II he served in London and in 1940 inspired Winston Churchill's proposal for the immediate fusion of France and Britain. In 1943, he had joined *Charles de Gaulle's Free French movement in Algiers and was named head of the commissariat that was to prepare France's first postwar modernization plan.

In 1945, all Western European countries were attempting to solve the economic problems of reconstruction on a national basis, with little attempt to coordinate their planning or to avoid a reversion to the destructive competition of the interwar years. At first, Monnet's goals for France were little different, U.S. aid being channeled to the support of six key sectors Monnet felt to be propulsive to the whole economy. But, aware of the failure of the Organization for European Economic Co-operation to compel its members to integrate their economies and sensitive of the restrictions on growth imposed by planning within a national framework, Monnet conceived the idea of sectoral economic integration. In May 1950 he proposed to French Foreign Minister *Robert Schuman that France and Germany pool their coal and steel industries in an organization, later called the European Coal and Steel Community (ECSC), that would be open to all Western European countries. The brilliance of Monnet's idea lay in its combination of economic and political goals. Free movement of goods, labor, and capital within the coal and steel industries provided a model that was expanded in 1958 in the European Common Market to embrace all sectors of the economy. The new community possessed an executive High Authority, a legislative Common Assembly, and a Court of Justice and was thus the nucleus, in Monnet's words, for the government of a United States of Europe. To ensure that ECSC would in fact achieve his supranational goals, Monnet became its first president (1952–55) and, often to the fury of more conservative business groups, used his position to impel the rapid implementation of the treaty.

His precipitate resignation from the ECSC presidency in 1955 led many to predict the imminent failure of the integration movement. Monnet, however, wearying perhaps of administrative detail, saw that the greatest contribution he, at age sixty-seven, could make to the unification of Europe was to form a unique international pressure group, composed of politicians and trade union leaders, who would ensure the implementation in their own countries of Monnet's views. In 1955 he founded the Action Committee for the United States of Europe. Its members included an impressive number of past and future government heads as well as the most influential non-Communist trade union leaders of the ECSC member countries. In its twenty years of activity, the Action Committee met regularly in Monnet's home to hammer out goals for the coming year. In 1956, the Committee pressed strongly for the creation of a separate European agency for atomic energy, thus contributing to the foundation in 1958 of the European Atomic Energy Community (Euratom); and it put great pressure on the negotiators of the Common Market treaty to stiffen the integrationist aspects of the Community and to strengthen the powers of its Executive Commission. British parliamentary leaders were invited to join the Committee in 1968, thus preparing for its concerted effort to have Britain admitted to the Common Market in 1971. Finally the Committee pressed for closer relations of the Common Market with the Communist countries, suggesting the reunion of West and East Germany within the European Community, closer economic ties with the Soviet Union, and the establishment of official relations between the European Community and China.

The secret of Monnet's lasting influence was not primarily in the official positions that he held but in the vast range of political personalities who fell enthusiastically under his influence. No European had closer ties with leaders in the United States, where his close friends included Dwight D. Eisenhower, *John Foster Dulles, Dean Acheson, and George Ball. In Germany, his friendships in the parliament were so numerous that he was able to ensure the approval of a preamble to the Franco–German Treaty of Friendship in 1963 that ensured that the bilateral relationship engineered by de Gaulle would not infringe upon either the European or the Atlantic Community. But Monnet always held that, if nothing was possible without men, nothing was durable without institutions. Hence he used his influence to ensure that his ideas would be embodied in concrete agencies. As the father of the European Coal and Steel Community, of the European Common Market, and of Euratom, and as one of the originators of the Organization for Economic Cooperation and Development, his place as one of the leading internationalists of the twentieth century is secure. Yet as he concluded in his memoirs, the European Community "is only a stage on the way to the organized world of tomorrow."

BIBLIOGRAPHY:

A. *Les Etats-Unis d'Europe ont commencé: Discours et allocutions, 1952–1954* (Paris, 1954); *Mémoires* (Paris, 1976).

B. Merry and Serge Bromberger, *Jean Monnet and the United States of Europe* (New York, 1969); NYT 17 Mar 1979, 1; "Z," "What Jean Monnet Wrought," *Foreign Affairs* (55 (Apr 1977), 630–35.

C. Monnet papers are in the Centre de recherches européennes in Lausanne.

F. Roy Willis

MOORE, John Bassett (3 December 1860, Smyrna, DE—12 November 1947, New York). *Education*: Univ. of Virginia, 1877–80. *Career*: clerk, Department of State, 1885, third assistant secretary, 1886–91; Hamilton Fish professor of law and diplomacy, Columbia Univ. 1891–1921; assistant secretary of state, 1898–99; secretary and counsel, Paris Peace Commission, 1898–99; delegate, Fourth International Conference of American States, 1910; head, American delegation, International Commission of Jurists, 1912; member, Permanent Court of Arbitration, 1912–38; counselor, Department of State, 1913–14; president, Pan American Society, 1916–21, president, Lake Mohonk Conference on International Arbitration, 1914; delegate, Pan American Financial Conferences, 1915 and 1919; judge, Permanent Court of International Justice, 1921–28, president, Commission of Justice, 1922–23.

Moore was an internationalist whose career spanned the period of U.S. emergence from continental diplomacy to global involvement. He was intimately associated with this transition in official and advisory capacities and in the process became America's foremost international legal scholar and jurist. His contribution to internationalism was twofold: through national and international public service, and through conceptualization and codification of international law.

His service in national policy formulation came through a variety of official posts and advisory roles in the Cleveland, Harrison, McKinley, and *Wilson administrations. When not employed in an official capacity, he was consulted by almost every president and secretary of state from 1891 to 1947. In both his public and private capacity prior to World War I, Moore was an advocate of expanded American commitment to international cooperation and association, and he championed the nation's adherence to the highest standards of international law. He envisaged the attainment of national and international security and prosperity through an expanding web of interlocking legal and economic associations, a system which would create the habit of and vested interest in cooperation and the peaceful resolution of conflict. To this end, he urged, on the inter-American and international levels, the further development of principles and institutions of arbitral and judicial settlement of disputes, as well as the creation of international associations to regularize and codify international law. Throughout, Moore's was a counsel of moderation and practicality, challenging the more chauvinistic and imperialistic expressions of national policy while cautioning against utopian expectations from novel political or legal institutions.

Amid the international anarchy of the World War I era, Moore denounced the sacrifice of the traditional norms of belligerent and neutral conduct to wartime convenience, both at home and abroad. Warning of the future consequences of such opportunism, he challenged both Allied and German perversions of international law. But he was equally severe in criticizing what he considered selective American response to violations of historic neutral rights. Moore's efforts in this regard did not represent an advocacy of either isolation or intervention as national policy, but simply the conviction that any policy should be carried out with scrupulous respect for the relevant international law.

The postwar era saw no abatement of Moore's promotion of traditional forms of international law and association. He vigorously refuted claims that wartime excesses invalidated the entire basis of the international legal system. However, his opinions now placed him outside the mainstream of the internationalist movement, for he also rejected the prevalent arguments which proclaimed the obsolescence of traditional norms of international conduct and saw future justice and order attainable only through a world political authority. Ironically, this led to his condemnation of the League of Nations as originally constituted. He believed that institution fell far short of its potential as a truly international forum, and he deplored its emphasis on political rather than judicial solutions to international problems. Such sentiments even dictated Moore's opposition to U.S. membership in the World Court, that body being associated with the League in a manner which he believed gave League members preferential treatment over non-League members, especially in the realm of advisory opinions.

As international order disintegrated in the 1930s, Moore once again waged a campaign against what he considered the distortion of legal norms by both isolationists and interventionists. He accused the former of abandoning historic neutral rights in the interest of absolute avoidance of war, the latter of cloaking partisan policies in the mantle of traditional neutrality law. As before, Moore's efforts were not on behalf of a particular foreign policy but simply to assure maximum clarity and precision in the use of international law, regardless of the nature of policy.

On the larger world stage, Moore also served the cause of internationalism. His reputation in the field of international law was recognized on a progressively wider sphere as he was appointed a delegate to the Fourth International Conference of American States in 1910, selected to the International Commission of Jurists in 1912, and finally chosen as a member of the Permanent Court of Arbitration in 1912. He attained the summit of his profession when he was appointed the first American judge of the Permanent Court of International Justice in 1921. He served with distinction for seven years, presiding over its International Commission of Jurists to formulate rules concerning the conduct of war.

Moore's official contributions to internationalism were complemented by, and in turn complemented, his scholarly activities in the conceptualization and codification of international law. Familiar with the machinery and personnel of policy formulation, the details of day-to-day negotiation and administration, and the realities of the international scene, Moore possessed practical experience which gave a pragmatic foundation to his conception of international law. His writings and prodigious compilations of legal sources reflected the legal positivist school of American jurisprudence. For Moore, as for other positivists, the core of law consisted of the judicial norms established by the authority and agreement of national states. Yet, characteristically, Moore's was not a rigid positivism which limited the law to textual absolutes. On the contrary, he conceived of statute law as an historical, evolving body of norms emanating from societal needs and conscience, periodically regularized by the courts and developing in consonance with the mood and circumstances of the times. This positivist law, for Moore, possessed a spirit which could only be fully understood through its historical antecedents and context, a spirit which brought the law into conformity with ultimate human values. Convinced of the organic, evolutionary nature of law, the judge took the modest position that its acceptance would have to depend in the final analysis on voluntary official and public opinion rather than arbitrary legislation, novel institutions, or coercive national or international power. He devoted his life to creating such a constituency for international law.

Moore's conception of law also promoted his emphasis on the importance of the historical sources, as well as the texts of statute law. This stimulated his enormous contributions to the codification of international law, a scholarly effort which alone places him in the forefront of America's internationalists. He was introduced to editorial work during his first years in the Department of State, where he assisted Francis Wharton in the completion of his *Revolutionary Diplomatic Correspondence of the United States* 6 vols. (Washington, 1889) and his *Digest of International Law*, 3 vols. (Washington, 1886). Moore's first independent undertaking was the six-volume *History and Digest of the International Arbitrations*, which originated as an outgrowth of his research for the Wharton *Digest*. His own *Digest of International Law*, in eight volumes, was also intended as a revision of Wharton's work, but it was expanded into a far more comprehensive effort, which included not merely a collection of statutes but the historical background and supplementary materials pertinent to the laws. Finally, Moore resigned from the World Court to devote himself to a compilation of *International Adjudications*, designed as the first portion of a comprehensive library of international law including one series on adjudications, one on treaties, and one on state papers. With these monumental collections, Moore hoped to provide the legal and diplomatic foundations for enlightened understanding and formulation of future law and diplomacy.

Over six turbulent decades, Moore tirelessly served the cause of internationalism. For America, he advocated a program of practical internationalism holding the nation to the highest standards of international law and encouraging an expanded role in international institutions commensurate with its new interests and power, while reminding his countrymen of the limitations of any political or judicial solutions to the problems of justice and order. Abroad he gave exceptional service to the world's two premier judicial bodies, was a staunch advocate of international cooperation and conciliation, and provided major sources for the future development of international law.

BIBLIOGRAPHY:

A. *American Diplomacy: Its Spirit and Achievements* (New York, 1905); *The Collected Papers of John Bassett Moore*, 7 vols. (New Haven, CT, 1944); *A Digest of International Law*, 8 vols. (Washington, 1906); *History and Digest of the International Arbitrations to Which the United States Has Been a Party*, 6 vols. (Washington, 1898); *International Ajudications, Ancient and Modern* 6 vols. (New York, 1929–36); *International Law and Some Current Illusions, and Other Essays* (New York, 1924); *Report on Extraterritorial Crime and the Cutting Case* (Washington, 1887); *A Treatise on Extradition and Interstate Rendition*, 2 vols. (Boston, 1891).

B. *American Bar Association Journal* 32 (Sep 1946), 575–82; DAB supp. 4, 597–600; Richard Megargee, "Realism in American Foreign Policy: The Diplomacy of John Bassett Moore," dissertation, Northwestern Univ., 1963; NYT 13 Nov 1947, 27; *Political Science Quarterly* 63 (Mar 1948), 159–60.

C. The Moore papers are in the Manuscript Division, Library of Congress.

Richard Megargee

MORA OTERO, José Antonio (22 November 1897, Montevideo—26 January 1975, Montevideo). *Education*: LL.B., Univ. of Montevideo,

1923, LL.D., 1925. *Career*: Uruguayan foreign service, 1926, secretary of legation, Madrid, 1926–28, Rio de Janeiro, 1928–29, Washington, 1929–30; Ministry of Foreign Affairs, 1933–41; minister to Bolivia, 1942–45; adviser and delegate, Chapultepec and San Francisco Conferences, 1945; delegate, Bogotá Conference, 1948; minister to United States and Organization of American States (OAS), 1946–51; ambassador to the United States, 1951–56; member, Council of OAS, 1946–56, chair, 1954–56, secretary-general, 1956–68; minister of foreign affairs, 1971–72.

The career of Mora illustrates the increasingly important involvement of small nations in international affairs. It was a role forecast in his *Sentido internacional del Uruguay* (1938) and in his *La organización judicial en la Conferencia de San Francisco* (1946). A brilliant career in his country's foreign service led to effective participation in the three wartime consultations of American foreign ministers (Panama, 1939, Havana, 1940, Rio de Janeiro, 1942) and to an even more important role in the San Francisco Conference (1945) and Bogotá Conference (1948) in which the Organization of American States (OAS), already half a century old, received a treaty structure. Thus the Mora career was focused upon international organizations for world peace, their role in respect to democratic government, the peaceful settlement of international disputes, and the protection of individual rights under international law.

An international lawyer and a humanist, Mora labored in the cause of individual human rights. At the Chapultepec, San Francisco, and Bogotá Conferences he helped shape provisions for protecting these rights and supporting democratic government. Named a member of the first UN Commission on Human Rights, he also helped to draft the American Declaration of the Rights and Duties of Man (1948). Appropriately, the OAS Commission on Human Rights was authorized and established while he was secretary-general.

In a 1949 lecture, he proposed an Inter-American Council for Political and Social Research. At the Ninth Inter-American Conference (Caracas, 1954) the Uruguayan delegation strove to engage the OAS in such an endeavor, but secured only (the significant) approval for a survey of public administration in the member states. Other activities in the OAS included successes in 1962 and 1965 regarding the Dominican Republic (supervision of 1962 elections), the First Inter-American Democratic Electoral Seminar (1962), the authorization of an Inter-American Peace Force (1965), mediation in 1965, including the precedent-setting authorization of the secretary-general to act as a mediator, and the naming of experts to organize an election. During these years the OAS also acted under the Rio Treaty to settle several international disputes. The Secretariat of the Organization was also expanded, and the Council increased to include non-American observer nations.

Mora demonstrated his innovative concepts of international organization by introducing scientific principles of public administration into the work of the OAS. He systematized the personnel structure of the Secretariat in accord with principles of public administration. He regularized its personnel, established equitable principles of promotion and compensation, and secured the status of its employees through agreements with host countries.

BIBLIOGRAPHY:

A. *From Panama to Punta del Este: Past Experience and Future Prospects*, (Washington, 1968); *La organización judicial en la Conferencia de San Francisco* (Montevideo, 1946); *The Need for an Inter-American Council for Political and Social Research* (Washington, 1949); *Sentido internacional del Uruguay* (Montevideo, 1938).

B. CB 1956, 447–49; *Washington Post* 12 May 1968, A-22, 28 Jan 1975, A-12; Guillermo de Zéndequi, "José Antonio Mora: A Life at the Service of a Cause," *Américas* 27 (Mar 1975), 25–27; WWLA 5, 245–46; WWWA 6, 291.

Harold Eugene Davis

MOREL, E. D. See *Biographical Dictionary of Modern Peace Leaders*.

MORGAN, Laura Puffer (22 November 1874, Framingham, MA—10 September 1962, Washington). *Education*: B.A., Smith Coll., 1895; M.A., Radcliffe Coll., 1899. *Career*: mathematician, educator, technical expert on arms control and disarmament; editor, *The World Through Washington, 1944–46*.

During World War I, Laura Puffer Morgan worked in war-related organizations, arranging the first Women's Liberty Loan Conference and establishing the National Home for College Women in Government Service. Disillusioned with the terms of peace and convinced that an arms race had been an underlying cause of the war, Morgan turned her attention to the development of world institutions and agreements promoting arms control and international understanding. As a technical analyst and coordinator of organizational efforts, Morgan worked for disarmament and world order. As educator, journalist, and editor, she promulgated transnational values and peace.

Morgan's role as technical analyst represents a unique contribution for her time period, one which predates the Systems Analysis Office by some forty years but is not unlike it. Statistician, instructor, and later adjunct professor of mathematics at the University of Nebraska, Morgan brought a concern for facts, legitimate comparison, budget constraints, costs, and efficiency to her assessment of international defense spending. Her reliable technical reports from the Washington Conference on Limitation and Reduction of Armaments (1921–22), the London Naval Conference (1930), and the Geneva Disarmament Conference (1932–34) were important resources for pacifists and militarists alike. Both groups published her works. Congress and Parliament sought her testimony.

Though not a strict pacifist, Morgan allied herself with the peace movement, working with pacifist Frederick Libby (1922–37) as foreign affairs expert and associate secretary for the National Council for Prevention of War, which coordinated disarmament activities for thirty-two organizations. She presided over the Committee on Permanent Peace for the National Council of Women. As president of the District of Columbia's branch of the American Association of University Women, and vice-president at large, Morgan directed the AAUW's involvement with organizations promoting disarmament and established the International Relations Committee of its International Federation. She chaired the Women's Joint Congressional Committee in Washington and organized and led the Women's World Court Committee, which represented fourteen organizations seeking U.S. adherence to the Court. During her eight years in Geneva (1932–40), she headed the American Inter-Organizational Council.

As an educator, Morgan believed that if accurate information and a world perspective could be shared with the public, broad support for internationalism would emerge. As a member of the District of Columbia's Board of Education in the early 1920s, a period of U.S. isolationism, Morgan promoted the teaching of international ideals. As League of Nations press correspondent (1932–33), she published articles in 2,500 newspapers and 300 weeklies and frequently wrote for *The World Tomorrow* and *The American Teacher*. She established the International Relations Committee within the World Federation of Educational Associations and while on the Governing Board of the Geneva Research Center (1932–40) wrote its monthly *Information Bulletin*, which summarized the activities of the League of Nations and the International Labor Organization. After World war II, Morgan edited *The World Through Washington*, an American University newsletter which described U.S. efforts to establish institutions for peace, and she maintained an active interest in world education until her death.

BIBLIOGRAPHY:

A. *The Background of the London Naval Conference* (Washington, 1930); *The Issues of the General Disarmament Conference* (Washington, 1930); *The Navies at a Glance* (Washington, 1930); *A Possible Technique of Disarmament Control* (Geneva, 1940).

C. The Morgan papers are in the Schlesinger Library, Radcliffe Coll., the Swarthmore Coll. Peace Collection, and the League of Nations Archives.

Rosemary Rainbolt

MORGENTHAU, Hans Joachim (17 February 1904, Coberg, Germany— 19 July 1980, New York). *Education*: Univ. of Berlin; graduate, Univ. of Munich, 1927; LL.D., Univ. of Frankfurt, 1929; Graduate Institute for International Studies, Geneva, 1932. *Career*: attorney, Frankfurt, 1927–30; assistant professor, Univ. of Frankfurt, 1931; acting president, Labor Law

Court, Frankfurt, 1931–33; instructor, Univ. of Geneva, 1932–35; professor, Institute for International and Economic Studies, 1935–36; instructor, Brooklyn Coll., 1937–39; assistant professor, Univ. of Kansas City, 1939–43; associate professor to professor, Univ. of Chicago, 1949–68, director, Center of American Foreign Policy, 1950–68; professor, City Coll. of New York, 1968–74; professor, New School for Social Research, 1974–80; consultant, Department of State, 1949–51, 1961–65, Department of Defense, 1961–65.

Morgenthau was the father of the "realist" approach to international relations in the twentieth century. As such, he was probably the most influential American student of international relations. Although the peak of his intellectual influence occurred in the 1950–65 period, when his opinions coincided with "Cold War" realities, he is also remembered for his activist role in opposing U.S. participation in the Vietnam War. His text, *Politics Among Nations*, went through five editions, and even in the 1970s, when realism was out of vogue, Morgenthau's work was still rated as the most influential in his field, and the text was still widely adopted into the 1980s. Although his activism against Vietnam did not seem to some to square with his own emphasis on power politics, on the supreme importance of effective military force, and on the overriding importance for peace of a balance of power and the old school diplomacy, events in retrospect tended to vindicate his opinion that America would be better off extricating itself from the Southeast Asian conflict.

Morgenthau's views were founded on a careful set of assumptions, categories, and propositions. His international relations theory was constructed on a base-superstructure model, and it thus shared all the strengths and weaknesses of such approaches. At the political base, Morgenthau placed four determining units: human nature (toward which he adopted a classical view); morals and ethics (which views are best expounded by his intellectual colleague, Reinhold Niebuhr); society; and society's three relevant components, nation, state, and government. These together gave rise to four levels of the political superstructure, the first of which comprised the all important (and coequal) determining variables, ideology, interest, and power. These three in turn determine the character of politics and of policy, domestic and foreign. Foreign policy in turn is discussed in terms of several choices, types, and a plentitude of foreign policy means (economic, military, political, and prestige). This edifice enabled Morgenthau to discuss in detail practically any topic of politics and international affairs by reference to a small number of primitive concepts. It is from this simplicity, plus a straightforward yet elegant style of disclosure, that derive the authority and attractiveness of his work. It was power and interest, however, that brought him greatest notice, since it was possible, although inaccurate, to reduce his approach to those two categories. Since Morgenthau nowhere carefully defined power (a deficiency he shared with practically all other students of politics), many later students rejected the whole of his writings. They may have gone too far. Morgenthau is inherently interesting as a student of the uses and limits of morality in politics, as a political theorist in the general sense, and as an international relations theorist whose work can easily be reconciled with that of his "scientific" critics.

BIBLIOGRAPHY:

A. *Dilemmas of Politics* (Chicago, 1958); *In Defense of the National Interest* (New York, 1950); "An Intellectual Autobiography," *Society* 15 (Jan–Feb 1978), 63–68; *Peace, Security, and the United Nations* (Chicago, 1946); *Politics Among Nations: The Struggle for Power and Peace*, 5th ed. (New York, 1972); *Politics in the Twentieth Century*, 3 vols. (Chicago, 1962); *Scientific Man vs. Power Politics* (Chicago, 1946); *Truth and Power* (New York, 1970).

B. CB 1963, 275–77; NYT 20 Jul 1980, 1; WWA 1980–81, 2369.

Thomas W. Robinson

MORRIS, Henry Crittenden (18 April 1868, Chicago—25 July 1948, Ogunquit, ME). *Education*: Univ. of Akron (then Buchtel Coll.), 1883; B.A., Lombard Coll., 1887, M.A., 1890; LL.B., Chicago Coll. of Law, 1889; graduate study, Belgium, France, and Germany. *Career*: lawyer, Chicago and Washington; U.S. consul, Ghent, 1893–98; secretary to Melville W. Fuller in Muskat Dhows arbitration, 1905; president, Chicago Peace Society, 1914–21.

Morris came from a Universalist family, was educated at Universalist colleges, and showed an interest in internationalism from his student days. Independently wealthy, he could devote much time to scholarship and public service. Like many of his generation, he had faith in the destiny of the American national character, which he described as a union of liberalism founded upon conservatism, liberty bounded by law. He saw this philosophy as the way to the future—starting in America, encircling the globe, and replacing the political extremes of Europe.

Morris traveled and studied in Europe and served as U.S. consul at Ghent. Although active in upholding the dignity and rights of the United States and in encouraging trade, this period influenced his thinking on colonization, from the viewpoint of both the colony and the mother country. It led to a two-volume work, *The History of Colonization* (1900). His colonization perspective gained considerable attention following the Spanish-American War, when the U.S. acquired overseas territories and the great debate ensued over the "manifest destiny" of the United States.

In 1905 Morris served as secretary to Supreme Court Chief Justice Melville Fuller in the Muskat Dhows arbitration between Great Britain and France at the Permanent Court of Arbitration at The Hague. Such experiences increased his concern over world conditions, and he became president of the Chicago Peace Society from 1914 to 1921. By this time a recognized international lawyer, he developed a particular interest in arbitration treaties and other plans for establishing and enforcing world peace. He organized mass meetings in cooperation with leading figures in the peace movement, attended national and international meetings, circulated petitions and resolutions, and worked for the cessation of hostilities. He also supported other organizations such as the League to Enforce Peace and the Woman's Peace Party. When the United States joined the war in 1917, opinions differed within the Chicago society as to its role, and Morris could not prevent its collapse or revive it in the 1920s. He became a member of the American Peace Society in 1918 and renewed his membership annually until a year before his death. He also served as a director.

Following his death, Morris left $5,000 outright to the American Society of International Law and over $50,000 to the University of Akron. The income from the latter bequest was to promote interest among students in international relations. He also left his personal library of 20,000 volumes to the university, a collection which reflected his wide-ranging interest in international issues, both historical and contemporary. By these bequests he carried beyond his own lifetime his interest and participation in internationalism and scholarship.

BIBLIOGRAPHY:

A. *The History of Colonization from the Earliest Time to the Present Day*, 2 vols. (New York, 1900).

B. *Akron Beacon Journal* 10 Aug 1948, 21, 18 Dec 1964, 27; *Buchtelite* 25 Feb 1949, 1; Dispatches from U.S. Consuls in Ghent, 1860–1906, T388, rolls 5, 6; NCAB 39, 548–49; NYT 10 Aug 1948, 24; WWWA 2, 384.

C. The Morris papers are at the Chicago Historical Society and in the Univ. of Akron Archives.

Ruth Clinefelter

MORRISON, Charles Clayton. See *Biographical Dictionary of Modern Peace Leaders*.

MORROW, Dwight Whitney (11 January 1873, Huntington, WV—5 October 1931, Englewood, NJ). *Education*: B.A., Amherst Coll., 1895; LL.B., Columbia Law School, 1899. *Career*: attorney, Reed, Simpson, Thacher, and Barnum, New York, 1899–1914; partner, J. P. Morgan and Co., 1914–27; ambassador to Mexico, 1927–30; senator, 1930–31.

Although the greatest achievements of his public life occurred while he was a partner with J. P. Morgan and Co. and ambassador to Mexico, Morrow was a true, albeit somewhat atypical, internationalist. While on leave from Morgan during World War I, Morrow served in Paris and London as an adviser to the Allied Maritime Transportation Council. His duties brought him into regular contact with Europeans who favored the concept of an international body of nations united to preserve the peace. A lifelong Republican, Morrow broke with many party leaders and enthusiastically supported the League of Nations. Yet always the pragmatist, he realized that the treaty with the League of Nations Covenant stood little chance of approval by the Senate. Hence, he labored selflessly to increase its chances for passage in the interest of international peace.

In February and March 1919 Morrow contributed a series of articles to the *New York Evening Post*, later published as *The Society of Free States*, advocating affiliation with the League but insisting that *Woodrow Wilson and Senate opponents of the League must compromise to achieve ratification and membership. He suggested that the League would be neither as good as some proponents argued nor as harmful as opponents feared. Historically, he explained, international cooperation came slowly, but it benefited mankind. He pointed to numerous international law agreements and to postal and sanitation conventions as recent examples.

Proposals before the Paris sessions had tended to go too far too fast and thus were not sufficiently understood by the American people. To rectify these flaws Morrow suggested that as an initial step the treaty should make the United States primarily responsible for execution of the Covenant in the Western Hemisphere, with the European powers responsible in the Eastern. Secondly, he proposed that the Senate should state its understanding of U.S. obligations under the Covenant when it voted on the treaty so that citizens would have no doubts about their nation's commitments.

Morrow wrote privately to *Thomas W. Lamont, a fellow Morgan partner in Paris with the U.S. delegation to the Peace Conference, urging him to try to persuade Wilson to move more slowly. If an idea is right, he observed, one should not wait until everyone understood it. Lamont, however, could not influence Wilson. In articles, books, and private discussions, Morrow articulated many of the arguments later used effectively by *Franklin Roosevelt to persuade Americans that the United Nations was the world's best hope for avoiding future world wars.

In the 1920s Morrow worked with other bankers to stablize the economies of Europe and Cuba. His efforts reflected his belief that economically sound nations contributed to international harmony and debilitated one's fed discord. As ambassador to Mexico, he opposed the special claims of creditor groups seeking compensation for expropriation, arguing that claims should be decided on a fair basis and in an en bloc settlement. This position cost him his friendship with Lamont and other former Morgan partners.

BIBLIOGRAPHY:

A. *The Society of Free States* (New York, 1919).

B. DAB 13, 234–35; Mary M. McBride, *The Story of Dwight W. Morrow* (New York, 1930); NCAB 23, 10–12; Harold G. Nicolson, *Dwight Morrow* (New York, 1935); NYT 6 Oct 1931, 16, 7 Oct 1931, 1.

C. The Morrow papers are at Amherst Coll.

Stephen D. Bodayla

MORTON, Blanche Rosalie Slaughter (28 October 1876, Lynchburg, VA—5 May 1968, Winter Park, FL). *Education*: M.D., Women's Medical Coll. of Pennsylvania, 1897; postgraduate study in Europe and Asia, 1899–1902. *Career*: resident physician, Alumni Hospital and Dispensary, Philadelphia, 1898; gynecologist, Women's Clinic, Washington, 1903–5; private practice, New York 1906–29, Winter Park, FL, 1930–55.

Morton developed a perspective on the world when she went to Europe for extensive graduate work, studying in Vienna, Berlin, Paris, and London (1899–1902). At the suggestion of Sir Victor Horsley, a noted British surgeon, she returned to the United States via India, where for six months she studied the treatment of bubonic plague. She began the practice of medicine in Washington, but after she married George B. Morton she moved to New York. Following his death in 1912, she began to travel frequently, so that by 1955 she could state she had visited every mainland country in the world except Patagonia, Greenland, and Tibet. Although there was an obvious recreational value to these journeys, they always centered upon the study of medicine or her deep-seated social concerns.

In 1916 Morton served in a French Army hospital on the Salonica front and was also a special commissioner of the American Red Cross to the Serbian Army. There she studied emergency medicine, analyzed the organization of hospitals, and evaluated the contributions of women to the war effort. Upon her return to the United States (1917), she was appointed chairperson of the War Service Committee of the Medical Women's National Association and served as the representative for women physicians on the Council of National Defense. Her wartime duties included the relocation of women physicians to replace American male doctors called into service and, later, the recruitment of women physicians to serve in understaffed European hospitals.

During this time, Morton founded and directed the American Women's Hospitals. This organization established and maintained two hospitals in Serbia and two hospitals and twenty dispensaries in France to meet civilian health care needs. Existent medical facilities in those countries had been either destroyed by the war or totally absorbed by the military services. After the war these American Women's Hospitals were phased out, and most of the equipment was shipped to Yugoslavia under the auspices of the Virginia Hospital Fund, which Morton established to care for Eastern European war refugees. The Fund, along with the Serbian Red Cross, set up two hospitals and a tuberculosis camp for children in Serbia. Besides the medical needs of Serbia, Dr. Morton recognized the toll the war had taken on the young leaders of that country, and she founded another organization, the International Serbian Education Committee, to pay for the education of Serbs in American colleges. Under its auspices, sixty-one students studied in the United States. Morton's international interests appeared in other areas. She frequently represented diverse organizations at international meetings. In 1923 she attended the Pan-Pacific Scientific Conference in Australia and a year later was a delegate to a congress of societies to promote the League of Nations. She served two terms as president of Zonta International, an executive women's club founded in 1919 for "the advancement of understanding, good will, and peace through a world fellowship."

Although Morton traveled a great deal, she did not forsake her medical practice at home. Among her contributions to the medical community was the invention of nine surgical instruments and appliances and her chairing of the Public Health Education Committee of the American Medical Association. She was also the first woman appointed to the faculty of the Columbia University Medical School. In 1930 Morton moved to Winter Park, Florida, for health reasons. The change brought a shift in her medical specialty from gynecology and surgery to arthritis and endocrinology, and she found time to write her autobiography, *A Woman Surgeon* (1937), which became a best seller. Her second book, *A Doctor's Holiday in Iran* (1940), detailed the culture, traditions, and geography of that country and paid particular attention to the role of women in that society. Indeed, throughout her career in her involvement in hospitals and programs throughout the world, she did much to establish and advance the position of women as doctors and nurses.

BIBLIOGRAPHY:

A. *A Doctor's Holiday in Iran* (New York, 1940); *A Woman Surgeon* (New York, 1937).

B. *American Women* 1939–40, 639–40; NCAB 6, 268–69; WWWA 5, 516.

C. The Morton papers are in the Hoover Presidential Library.

J. Patrick Wildenberg

MOTT, John Raleigh (25 May 1865, Livingston Manor, NY—31 January 1955, Orlando, FL). *Education*: Upper Iowa Univ., 1881–85; Ph.B., Cornell Univ. 1888. *Career*: student secretary 1888–1915, International Committee of the Student Volunteer Movement, general secretary, 1915–31; general secretary, World's Student Christian Federation, 1895–1920, chair, 1920–28; chair, International Missionary Council, 1928–46.

Aptly described by one biographer as a "provincial Midwesterner" who grew into a "universal" personality, Mott dedicated his life to evangelicalism and world brotherhood. His career began as a history major at Cornell University. With a keen sense of the past, an awareness of current events, a capacity for friendship, a great charisma, and a polished speaking style, he revealed leadership and organizational skills in the university's YMCA chapter.

Influenced by Dwight Moody's emphasis on the importance of foreign missions, Mott as a junior became president of the Cornell YMCA and soon transformed it into the world's largest, most active chapter. Following

MOTT, JOHN RALEIGH   521

graduation, Mott remained with the YMCA. He took a year-long assignment as an intercollegiate evangelical representative and then became senior student secretary. In this capacity, he worked to absorb the Student Volunteer Movement, a Christian missionary agency, and promoted a series of successful quadrennial missionary conventions. During this early period, Mott dreamed of a global Christian student organization, which would be ecumenical, reflect broad Christian principles, and unite members in global citizenship.

His aim to promote Christianity and crush poverty, bigotry, and violence became reality in 1895. Support from *John D. Rockefeller, Jr., and Cyrus McCormick enabled Mott to launch the World's Student Christian Federation. Building the WSCF network carried him repeatedly around the world, and by 1914, having achieved widespread reknown, he declined offers of college presidencies, political appointments, and an ambassadorship to China, preferring to extend Christ's kingdom. He did, however, serve on a 1916 Mexican commission.

A member of the Church Peace Union, Mott considered World War I both un-Christian and a tremendous opportunity. He marshaled the international YMCA organization to assist in the trenches and in prisoner of war camps. As the United States drifted into the conflict, Mott, then the YMCA's national executive, retreated from pacifism, served as a key figure in the National War Work Council, and joined *Elihu Root's Mission to Russia. He also supervised the YMCA's activities with the American Expeditionary Force, and after the Armistice lent support to relief efforts.

During the 1920s and 1930s Mott directed his energy toward world missions and religious cooperation. He joined Rockefeller to launch the still-born Interchurch World Movement, held the chairmanship of the International Mission Council, and helped create the World Council of Churches. During World War II he participated in the Y's program to aid German prisoners, wrote, and lectured. His long effort to join nations, races, and religions was recognized in 1946 with a Nobel Peace Prize, which he shared with +Emily Greene Balch. Mott died disappointed that his endeavors had not fully born fruit but confident that Christian ideals would ultimately prevail.

BIBLIOGRAPHY:

A. *Addresses and Papers of John R. Mott*, 6 vols. (New York, 1946–47); *The Evangelization of the World in This Generation* (New York, 1900); *The Future Leadership of the Church* (New York, 1909); *The Present-Day Summons to the World Mission of Christianity* (Nashville, TN, 1931); *The Students of North America United* (New York, 1903); *The World's Student Christian Federation: Origin, Achievements, Forecast* (New York, 1920).

B. DAB supp. 5, 506–8; *Dictionary of American Religious Biography* (Westport, CT, 1977) 318–19; Galen M. Fisher, *John R. Mott: Architect of Co-operation and Unity* (New York, 1952); C. H. Hopkins, *John R. Mott, 1865–1955: A Biography* (Grand Rapids, MI, 1979); Basil J. Mathews, *John R. Mott: World Citizen* (New

York, 1934); NCAB 44, 346–47; *New Catholic Encyclopedia* 10 (New York, 1967), 43; NYT 1 Feb 1955; 29.

C. The Mott papers are in the Yale Univ. Divinity School Library.

Daryl L. Revoldt

MOTTA, Giuseppe (29 December 1871, Airolo, Switzerland—23 January 1940, Bern). *Education*: Univ. of Fribourg, Munich; LL.D., Univ. of Heidelberg, 1893. *Career*: attorney in Airolo, 1893–1911; member, Swiss National Council, 1908–11; Swiss federal councillor, 1911–40; head, Federal Political Department, 1920–40; president, Swiss Confederation 1915, 1920, 1927, 1932, and 1937; first Swiss delegate, Assembly of League of Nations, 1920–39; president, opening meeting of League, 15 November 1920, honorary president, 1920; president of Assembly, 1924; vice-president of Assembly, 1921–23, 1925–39; member of various League commissions.

Motta was one of the prominent fixtures of the League of Nations during the two decades of its existence. Federal councillor in charge of Swiss foreign affairs, he attended every session of the Assembly as first delegate of the Swiss Confederation. He was a captivating orator; his consummate skills as negotiator were paired with diplomatic tact. Strong ethical-religious principles stemming from his conservative Catholic background underpinned all his activities and put their stamp on them.

Motta's commitment to the League of Nations had been instrumental in generating a narrow majority in favor Switzerland's membership in the League in a hotly contested national referendum. He saw in the League an instrument for peace, international justice, and humanitarianism. Motta deplored the absence of the United States and actively worked for the admission of Germany in the face of emotional French opposition. To him, the League was designed not to maintain the status quo as established by the victorious powers at the end of World War I but to create a community of nations that adhered to principles of peaceful cooperation in the solution of their problems. Motta participated in numerous attempts to strengthen all forms of arbitration and mediation and pushed hard for the submission of conflicts to mandatory international jurisdiction.

As a representative of a small neutral country, Motta had no design on getting involved in the politics of the Council of the League. He focused on the Assembly, and he worked diligently at strengthening that body vis-à-vis the Council. He insisted that deliberations of League commissions be open to public scrutiny. His skills were tested in 1926 as president of the committee created to resolve the impasse over membership in the Council in the wake of the admission of Germany to the League. Eight years later, Motta made world headlines with his fiery speech in which he opposed on moral grounds the admission of the Soviet Union to the League.

During the second half of the 1930s, the ideals of universality and peaceful solution of conflicts receded further and further from the world of reality. As a consequence, Motta took the steps necessary to remove all conditions that might oblige Switzerland to become a participant in League sanctions. Switzerland's return to integral neutrality, as offically recognized by the League on 14 May 1938, is considered to have been Motta's diplomatic masterpiece and his testament to his beloved fatherland. One of Europe's foremost proponents of peace and ardent champion of the League of Nations, Motta had to witness the outbreak of another European war before a stroke removed him from his duties and offices.

BIBLIOGRAPHY:

A. *Testimonia Temporum*, 3 vols. (Bellinzona, Switzerland, 1931–40).

B. Aymon de Mestral, *Le Président Motta* (Lausanne, Switzerland, 1941); NYT 23 Jan 1940, 22; Jean R. de Salis, *Giuseppe Motta: Dreissig Jahre eidgenössische Politik* (Zurich, 1941).

C. The Motta papers are in the Archives fédérales suisse.

Heinz K. Meier

MOWINCKEL, Johan Ludwig (22 October 1870, Bergen, Norway—30 September 1943, New York). *Education*: Germany, England, and France; graduate, Univ. of Oslo, 1889. *Career*: Town Council, Bergen, 1899–1915; member of Storting, 1907–43, president, 1913–21; prime minister and minister of foreign affairs, 1925–27, 1928–31, 1933–35; member, Council of League of Nations, 1930, 1933, president, 1933.

Like many Scandinavian leaders, Mowinckel favored an international organization as a stabilizing influence, especially in Europe. In his hopes and work he was to face disappointment. His interests appeared during World War I when he participated in study groups to determine what course the Scandinavian states should take in a proposed league. They had supported prewar efforts to develop processes for the peaceful resolution of disputes, and this seemed to Mowinckel a logical path to follow. When the Covenant appeared, Mowinckel gave it his support but advised against Norwegian membership because of the absence of the United States, which he saw as essential to its success. Later he commented favorably when the United States began to cooperate in some of the deliberations and bodies at Geneva.

Mowinckel believed so strongly in the machinery of the League that he decided as foreign and prime minister to attend personally the sessions in Geneva. Most of his efforts there were pointed toward two goals. One was to increase the representation of the smaller or "neutral" states in League bodies. He felt not only that they deserved such positions but also that the League would be healthier with their greater participation. His second concern focused on the ever-weakening influence of the League after 1930, when Europe began to rearm. Again and again he warned of the danger of another war and pleaded for greater firmness on the part of the democracies. His voice was not heeded, and after Germany invaded Norway he came to the United States, where he died.

BIBLIOGRAPHY:

A. *The Fight of the Norwegian Church* (New York, 1942); *Hverdagens harmoni* (Oslo, 1935); *Utenrikskommisjonen, 1919–1920.* (Christiania, Norway, 1920–21).

B. S. Shepard Jones, *The Scandinavian States and the League of Nations* (Princeton, NJ, 1939); *Hvem er hvem?* (Oslo, 1934), 341; *Norsk Biografisk Leksikon* 9 (Oslo, 1940), 377–96; NYT 1 Oct 1943, 19.

Warren F. Kuehl

MOWRER, Edgar Ansel (8 March 1892, Bloomington, IL—3 March 1971, Madeira, Portugal). *Education*: B.A., Univ. of Michigan, 1913; Univ. of Chicago; Sorbonne. *Career*: European war correspondent, *Chicago Daily News*, 1914–22, bureau chief in Berlin, 1923–33, in Paris, 1933–41; Washington correspondent, 1940–41; deputy director, Office of Facts and Figures, Office of War Information, 1941–43; commentator, *New York Post*, 1943–48; editor-in-chief for North America, *Western World*, 1957–60.

The fame of Mowrer rests upon his career as foreign correspondent for the *Chicago Daily News*. Writing from Europe between 1915 and 1940, Mowrer was considered one of the ablest journalists of his day and one who spoke ably for collective security. In 1914 he had scooped rivals with accounts of the Battle of Ypres. A year later, while assigned to Rome, he had covered the Italian defeat at Caporetto. His enthusiasm for postwar Italy ended with the March on Rome of Mussolini, whom Mowrer knew personally. In 1923 Mowrer left for Berlin, where he watched the rise of Hitler. While there, he wrote a book on the Nazi revolution, received a Pulitzer Prize for his dispatches, and was elected president of the Foreign Press Association. Stationed in Paris from 1934 to 1940, Mowrer mourned the fall of the government of his friend *Léon Blum, judged the Saar plebiscite of 1935 a farce, and sought to raise sympathy for the Spanish Loyalists. In 1938 he spent a few months in China, after which he claimed that the Japanese could not possibly conquer that nation.

While Mowrer viewed the League with sympathy and at times succumbed to the "spirit of Geneva," he believed that the unsatisfactory terms of the Versailles Treaty and the League's inadequate powers rendered it ineffective when challenged by the dictators. He thus understandably revealed strong anti-Fascist views during World War II. In 1940, with Colonel William J. Donovan, he wrote exposés of fifth-column activities that were widely reprinted. From 1941 to 1943 he was a government broadcaster. When the State Department blocked a pending trip to North Africa because of Mowrer's opposition to the Vichy regime and the Darlan deal, Mowrer resigned. The publisher of the *Chicago Daily News* found Mowrer too impolitic to rehire. Hence Mowrer wrote for the *New York Post* until his support for Chiang Kai-shek made him anathema to its editor. He participated in discussions of the World Citizens Association and in 1943 and 1944 helped launch the Non-Partisan Council to Win the Peace and the Committee for a Democratic Foreign Policy. In these groups, Mowrer favored a collective security arrangement to be enforced by military contingents drawn from member states. Commenting on the Dumbarton Oaks proposals, Mowrer sought to eliminate the veto from the UN Security Council and to grant more power to the General Assembly.

During the Cold War, Mowrer, who was always strongly suspicious of the Soviet Union, moved increasingly to the right. Beginning in 1949 he was a consultant to Radio Free Europe. From 1957 to 1960 he served as editor for *Western World*, a monthly dedicated to strengthening the Atlantic community. He felt the UN was inadequate and became a leading World Federalist until 1951, when he withdrew because he found the group lax concerning Communism in Asia. In a book in 1948, he advocated a voluntary world federation that would keep order by enforcing world law. Two years later, in *Challenge and Decision*, he sought a federation of non-Communist countries, one centering on the weakening of the Soviet Union. Peaceful coexistence, he kept stressing, was the opiate of the West. He said in 1951 that Kremlin efforts to conquer the world should be thwarted by an economic blockade, sabotage, and skilled psychological warfare. To meet the crises of Korea (1950), Hungary (1956), Suez (1956), and Vietnam, Mowrer favored the strongest possible responses.

BIBLIOGRAPHY:

A. *The American World* (New York, 1928); *Challenge and Decision: A Program for the Times of Crisis Ahead* (New York, 1950); *The Dragon Awakes: A Report from China* (New York, 1938); *An End to Make-Believe* (New York, 1968); *Germany Puts the Clock Back* (New York, 1932; rev. ed, 1939); *A Good Time to Be Alive* (New York, 1959); *The Nightmare of American Foreign Policy* (New York, 1948); *Sinon; or the Future of Politics* (London, 1930).

B. CB 1941, 597–600, 1962, 310–12; Lilian T. Mowrer, *Journalist's Wife* (New York, 1937); NYT 4 Mar 1977, IV–12.

C. The Mowrer papers are in the Manuscript Division, Library of Congress.

Justus D. Doenecke

MOWRER, Paul Scott (14 July 1887, Bloomington, IL—4 April 1971, Beaufort, SC). *Education*: Univ. of Michigan, 1906–8. *Career*: reporter, *Chicago Daily News*, 1908, Paris correspondent, 1910–22, director, European news service, 1922–24, general European correspondent, 1924–34, associate editor and chief editorial writer, 1934–36, editor, 1936–44; European editor, *New York Post*, 1945–49.

An early leader in the first generation of professional foreign correspondents, Mowrer, as chief of the *Chicago Daily News* European service, helped train and shape what was widely considered the finest American overseas news service of its time. Like many aspiring writers, Mowrer found work as a journalist; and it was his literary bent rather than an interest in international politics that drew him initially to Europe. Not until he reached Paris did the opportunity to observe political and economic forces leading to World War I attract his interest and challenge his analytical powers. Two assignments to cover developments in Eastern Europe, coupled with wartime service as a member of the Ango-American Press Mission to the French Army, laid the foundations for his shrewd assessment of international affairs. One result was *Balkanized Europe* (1919), in which he contrasted the potential strength and economic interdependence of postwar Europe with the political and nationalistic rivalries which, he argued, would block recovery unless effectively checked. Although the book attracted little public notice, it was respectfully received by specialists and particularly by his fellow correspondents, for whom it served as a model of professional journalism.

During the 1920s Mowrer's influence and reputation grew. He wrote for European as well as American papers, advised public and private leaders on both continents, and supervised the efforts of an outstanding staff of journalists. Believing that European stability and peace depended upon international cooperation through the League of Nations or some other form of federation, Mowrer grew increasingly concerned at the failure of the United States to play a responsible role. He believed that American idealism and moralism blinded the nation to a realistic understanding of its international position and interests. World peace and economic development, he argued, rested upon American participation in maintaining effective mechanisms for balancing and adjusting national interests. These ideas were set forth in *Our Foreign Affairs* (1924). Here, Mowrer analyzed the American isolationist tradition, its sources, and its inappropriateness for a nation engaged in worldwide technological, economic, and security developments. Recognizing the extent of public indifference and reluctance, he urged the formation of elite groups of informed citizens to stimulate discussion, mobilize opinion, and influence policy makers.

In 1928, Mowrer was awarded the first Pulitzer Prize granted to a foreign correspondent. Increasingly disenchanted with the failures of both European and American statesmanship, he accepted in 1933 an offer by *Daily News* publisher Frank Knox to become the paper's managing editor and chief editorial writer. In this capacity he extended his influence and responsibility for a newspaper noted for the quality of its foreign coverage and its internationalist editorial stance. Mowrer left in 1944 to resume overseas reporting as European editor of the *New York Post*. In 1949 he retired to New Hampshire and the pursuit of his literary interests, leaving an example of responsible international journalism seldom equaled. He was named poet laureate of New Hampshire in 1968.

BIBLIOGRAPHY:

A. *Balkanized Europe* (New York, 1919); *The Foreign Relations of the United States* (Chicago, 1927); *The House of Europe* (Boston, 1945); *Our Foreign Affairs* (New York, 1924); *Poems Between Wars* (Chicago, 1941).

B. IWW 1971–72, 1152–53; NYT 7 Apr 1971, 46.

C. The Mowrer papers are in the Newberry Library, Chicago.

Morrell Heald

MUDALIAR, Ariot Ramaswami (14 October 1887, Madras—17 July 1976, Madras). *Education*: graduate, Madras Christian Coll. and Law Coll. *Career*: member, Madras Legislative Council, 1920–26; member, Madras Corporation, mayor, 1928–30; member, Legislative Assembly of India, 1931–34; adviser to secretary of state for India in London; member, Viceroy's Executive Council, 1939–46; member, Imperial War Cabinet, 1942–43; prime minister of Mysore State, 1946–49; leader, Indian delegation, San Francisco Conference, 1945; president, UN Economic and Social Council, 1946–47; chair, UN-ILO Ad Hoc Committee on Forced Labor, 1953; chair, UN International Civil Service Advisory Board; chair, ILO Committee of Experts on the Application of Conventions and Recommendations, 1962–70.

Mudaliar made his first major contribution on the international scene as leader of the Indian delegation to the UN Conference in San Francisco, 1945. India was not yet an independent state but had been a member of the League of Nations. Mudaliar was elected chairman of the committee which drew up the economic and social provisions of the UN Charter. He led the Indian delegation in the first session of the General Assembly, and he was the natural choice as first president of the Economic and Social Council in 1946; he was reelected in 1947. He played an important role in drawing up the 1946 agreement between the UN and the International Labor Organization (ILO), which made it the first specialized agency associated with the UN. This set a pattern followed by other organizations such as FAO, UNESCO, and WHO.

Following allegations of forced labor in certain countries, the UN and ILO established an Ad Hoc Committee on Forced Labor with Mudaliar as chairman. It conducted a worldwide survey and reported in 1953. In a world climate of political acrimony, the independence and impartiality of the Committee was universally recognized.

In 1949, Mudaliar was affiliated with the International Civil Service Advisory Board, which advised the UN family on matters relating to employment. Mudaliar, who chaired its sessions, 1959–68, was a strong advocate of an independent, impartial civil service, and in 1954 he made an important contribution to ICSAB's definition of the standards of conduct for international officials.

In 1959 he became a member of the ILO Committee of Experts on the Application of Conventions and Recommendations, and in 1962 was unanimously elected its chairman. Perhaps the oldest and most respected supervisory body in the UN system, the Committee supervises the application of the ILO's international labor conventions and recommendations. These cover every aspect of labor, including sensitive human rights questions such as freedom of association, forced labor, discrimination in employment, and equal pay. Mudaliar presided with immense authority and wisdom, never compromising its independence or impartiality, always seeking a clear and sensible solution. At its fortieth anniversary meeting (1967), the committee stressed the need for its complete independence, impartiality, and objectivity. In 1971 Mudaliar resigned from the committee for health reasons.

BIBLIOGRAPHY:

B. *Annual Register* (London, 1976), 509–10; IWW 1948, 667.

Aamir Ali

MUNRO, Leslie Knox (26 February 1901, Auckland, New Zealand—13 February 1974, Hamilton, New Zealand). *Education*: master of laws, Auckland Univ. Coll., 1923. *Career*: practicing barrister and solicitor, 1923–41; lecturer, Auckland Univ. Coll., 1925–38; associate editor and editor, *New Zealand Herald*, 1941–51; ambassador to United States and permanent representative at the UN, 1952–58; president, General Assembly, 1957–58; special representative on the Hungarian question, 1958–62; secretary-general, International Commission of Jurists, 1961–63; member of New Zealand Parliament, 1963–72.

Munro's reputation as an internationalist rests on the high offices he held in the United Nations, 1953–58. He began by serving on the Trusteeship Council; then, New Zealand's election to the "Commonwealth seat" on the Security Council in 1954 brought him into the international limelight. Under the rotating system of chairmanship, he presided over the Council on several occasions during New Zealand's two-year term. These activities undoubtedly facilitated his election as chairman of the General Assembly's Political Committee in 1955 and two years later as president of the Assembly.

A lawyer by training, Munro was adept at the procedural tasks of chairmanship and in dealing with complicated documents and points of order. Self-confident and effusive, he enjoyed the duties and prestige of various UN positions. It was as a chairman rather than as a proponent of any particular cause that he made his mark. Munro took to the United Nations no scheme or ideas on resolving the problems besetting it. As editor of the Auckland daily *New Zealand Herald* he had expounded the view, shared by most New Zealanders at the time, that an aggressive Soviet Union lay at the heart of the world's troubles. Cold War influences dominated his thinking on international affairs in 1952, when his consistent support for the governing National party was rewarded by his appointment to the ambassadorship in the United States and the UN post. He was fortunate to arrive at the UN at a time when his country was about to sit on the Security Council, when an anti-Soviet advocate from a small British Commonwealth country was sure to find himself at home in a world body dominated by the anti-Communist Anglo-Americans, and when New Zealand's participation in the Korean action had enhanced its role in the organization.

Munro's career as his country's representative at the UN ended in 1958, the victim of political changes in New Zealand. His international role thereafter was something of an anticlimax. After a term as special UN representative dealing with the insoluble Hungarian question, he became, in July 1961, secretary-general of the International Commission of Jurists at Geneva, a privately organized and funded non-Communist body which sought to investigate abuses of human rights. Tiring of this minor place on the international stage, and perhaps coveting the position of minister of foreign affairs in New Zealand, he determined to enter politics. But, although elected to Parliament in 1963, his hopes were never fulfilled. His 1960 book on the UN revealed both his experiences and his aspirations.

Munro achieved an international prominence emulated by few of his countrymen. Yet, in the lexicon of New Zealand internationalists, he ranks far behind such other exponents of the United Nations as *Peter Fraser and *Carl Berendsen.

BIBLIOGRAPHY:

A. *United Nations: Hope for a Divided World* (New York, 1960).

B. CB 1953, 446-48; LT 14 Feb 1974, 24; *New York Evening Post* 14 Feb 1974, 4; NYT 14 Feb 1974, 44; *New Zealand Herald* 14 Feb 1974, 3.

Ian C. McGibbon

MURAV'EV, Mikhail Nikolaevich (7 April 1845, St. Petersburg—8 June 1900, St. Petersburg). *Education*: Poltava gymasium; Heidelburg Univ. *Career*: Russian Ministry of Foreign Affairs, 1864; series of increasingly important secondary diplomatic posts in a succession of major Western European cities, 1864–92; representative, Russian Red Cross, Balkan war zone, 1877–78; ambassador to Denmark, 1893–96; minister of foreign affairs, 1897–1900.

During his brief tenure as minister of foreign affairs of the Russian Empire, before his sudden death in office of heart failure, Murav'ev established a reputation for cautious and conciliatory policies during a difficult period for the Russian foreign service, when the Emperor +Nicholas II often intervened with sudden and short-lived enthusiasms for dangerous foreign adventures.

Murav'ev is best known, however, as the author of proposals to convene an international conference on arms reduction that became, in fact, the First Hague Peace Conference of 1899. When the Russian minister of war proposed talks with Austria to postpone introduction of new types of very expensive artillery into the Russian and Austrian armies, Murav'ev broadened the scope of the idea to include all European powers and a general reduction of all military budgets. By the time he issued the first conference invitation in August 1898, he had added a proposal for an international court of arbitration. The major powers, although unable to oppose such a plan publicly, refused to consider attending until assured that all political questions would be excluded from discussion. Thus the second invitation, December–January 1898–99, proposed an agenda that included discussion only on regulation of the conduct of war, limitation of armed forces and expenditures for a fixed period, and establishment of a regular system of arbitration. Although the Russians were most concerned to reduce military spending, the accomplishments of the First Hague Peace Conference were confined to establishing nonbinding procedures of arbitration and prohibiting certain types of weapons and military methods. As such, Murav'ev attained considerable prestige as a peace worker and pioneer internationalist.

Yet Murav'ev's proposal was motivated in broad terms by the problems of the Russian Empire as a poor and technologically backward state attempting to maintain great power position in a highly competitive military world of ever more expensive weapons in which sheer size of armies could no longer be decisive. For the immediate diplomatic moment, the proposal raised the prestige of Russia and discouraged suspected anti-Russian maneuvers by Britain in the Far East. Nonetheless, there can be no doubt that both Murav'ev and Nicholas II were also inspired by a great vision of universal peace, with themselves in the role of peacemakers.

BIBLIOGRAPHY:

A. Texts of conference invitations, *Pravitel'stvennyi vestnik* (St. Petersburg) (16/28 Aug 1898, 30 Dec 1898/11 Jan 1899); memoranda, *Krasnyi arkhiv* 50–51 (1932), 64–96; 54–55 (1932), 49–79.

B. Thomas K. Ford, "The Genesis of the First Hague Peace Conference," *Political Science Quarterly* 51 (Sep 1936), 354–68; Dan L. Morrill, "Nicholas II and the Call for the First Hague Conference," *Journal of Modern History* 46 (Jun 1974), 296–313.

Effie Ambler

MURRAY, George Gilbert Aimé (2 January 1866, Sydney—20 May 1957, Oxford). *Education*: first class in *literae humaniores*, St. John's Coll., Oxford Univ., 1887. *Career*: fellow, New Coll., Oxford Univ., 1888; professor, Univ. of Glasgow, 1889–99; Regius professor, Oxford Univ. 1908–36.

A famous Greek scholar, Murray became devoted to the ideals of the League of Nations and the United Nations. He was a delegate to the League for South Africa (1921–23), but his chief activity at Geneva was as a member (1922–39) and chairman for eight years of the Committee of Intellectual Co-Operation, which, as Henri Bergson expressed it, represented "the deeper spirit of the League." In Great Britain, Murray was a founder and longtime officer of the League of Nations Union (chairman of the executive committee, 1923–38, and joint president, 1939–45) and the United Nations Association (joint president, 1945–47, 1949–57, and president, 1947–49).

Murray's obsession with peace began during the years 1914–18. *Edward Grey's speech on 3 August converted him to the rightness of the British decision to enter the conflict, and in a brief study in 1915 Murray argued that Germany's desire for power had to be met with force after conciliation had failed. A week after the outbreak of hostilities, however, he urged fellow Liberals to work against a grabbing or jingo settlement. They should seek to strengthen the Concert of Europe and to reduce armaments by treaty.

Murray fully embraced the ideas written into the League's Covenant in 1919, including the use of sanctions to deter or punish aggressors, and he preached them thereafter with the zeal of a missionary. The League movement soon captured the support of British public opinion, secular and religious, and the League of Nations Union (LNU) became the country's most influential pressure group on foreign affairs. A striking demonstration of the public's faith in the League was given in 1934–35, when more than 11.5 million adults in Great Britain completed the famous Peace Ballot, organized by, among others, the LNU. More than 11 million answered "yes" when asked if Britain should remain a member of the League. More than 10 million declared themselves ready to restrain an aggressor by economic action, and nearly 7 million approved of the use of military measures should they be necessary. Murray saw the Ballot as the greatest enterprise and success with which the Union had ever been associated.

Public confidence in "collective defense" was shattered in 1935–36, however, when the League powers failed to prevent or end the Ethiopian war. Faith in the League waned, and membership in the LNU declined. Murray continued to promote the League but admitted after 1936 that it was no longer the guardian of international right or the final arbiter in international differences. Britain was driven back to a network of countries prepared to live by the rules of the Covenant but ready to defend one another where militarily possible. That, Murray wrote in 1938, was a great, though limited ideal.

In retrospect, Murray admitted that he and his colleagues had overrated the "reasoning element" in the organized and less civilized masses and underrated the immense power of national feelings when seriously aroused. He confessed, too, that the LNU had not fully explained the obligations that came with League membership. Until the mid-1930s, it had emphasized the pacific functions of the League—investigation, arbitration, conciliation—and placed sanctions (except moral) in the background as an almost unthinkable contingency. Not until December of 1936 had the Union passed a resolution admitting the necessity of British rearmament as a "national quota" for collective defense. But the one fatal fact, Murray concluded, was that without America the League was too weak to resist those who rebelled against the rules of peace.

The failure of the League did not embitter Murray. On the contrary, it stimulated him to redouble his efforts on behalf of its ideals. Nor did he think that his work between the wars had been without value. He was persuaded, he wrote in 1955, that the ruling ideas of the League of Nations and the United Nations and of intellectual cooperation were now widely accepted and deeply rooted. He had involved himself in the most important of all causes but one that involved a change that needed at least two generations and perhaps three to realize.

BIBLIOGRAPHY:

A. *Essays and Addresses* (London, 1921); *Faith, War and Policy* (London, 1918); *The Foreign Policy of Sir Edward Grey, 1906-1915* (Oxford, 1915); *From the League to U.N.* (London, 1948); *The League of Nations Movement: Some Recollections of the Early Days* (London, 1955); *The Ordeal of This Generation: The War, the League and the Future* (London, 1929); *The Problem of Foreign Policy: A Consideration of Present Dangers* (London, 1924); *Then and Now: The Changes of the Last Fifty Years* (Oxford, 1935).

B. DNB 1951-60, 757-61; LT 21 May 1957, 13; NYT 21 May 1957, 35; Jean Smith and Arnold Toynbee, eds., *Gilbert Murray: An Unfinished Autobiography* (London, 1960); J.A.K., Thompson and A. J. Toynbee, eds., *Essays in Honour of Gilbert Murray* (London, 1936).

C. The Murray papers are in the Bodleian Library, Oxford Univ.

J. A. Thompson

MYERS, Denys Peter (26 June 1884, Newton, IA—11 February 1972, Washington). *Education*: B.A., Harvard Coll., 1906. *Career*: reporter, *Davenport Democrat*, 1898-1902, *Boston Herald*, 1904-06, *Boston Globe*, 1906, *Christian Science Monitor*, 1908-10; director, World Peace Foundation, 1913-16, corresponding secretary, 1916-27, librarian and research director, 1927-42; research librarian, Fletcher School of Law and Diplomacy, 1933-42; research specialist, Department of State, 1942-53.

Myers established his reputation as an internationalist and peace worker primarily as an administrator and publicist. As such, he oversaw the publication programs of the World Peace Foundation for nearly three decades. Since this was the paramount focus of the WPF, his role was vital in producing its pamphlet series and many special publications. These provided citizens with detailed and authoritative studies of current international issues and problems. Myers prepared many of these, all models of research and, ostensibly, of objectivity. They often summarized ideas and developments with accompanying documents, references, or supporting data. While Myers publicly proclaimed the impartial nature of the publications, he fully appreciated the propagandistic nature of such educational materials. The selection process in itself helped determine what the issues were, and the information imparted invariably favored the League of Nations, the World Court, international law, and the peaceful resolution of conflict.

Myers also became involved in publicity programs outside the WPF, notably *Raymond B. Fosdick's League of Nations News Bureau, which the WPF funded and to which it assigned Myers as an associate director. He also prepared articles for popular journals, including annual summaries of League of Nations activities published by *Current History*, and he began the valuable annual compilations on American foreign relations which the Council on Foreign Relations later prepared. As a member of the American Society of International Law, he wrote extensively for its journal and served as its assistant secretary (1950–62). Many of Myers' studies have stood the test of time and remain valuable sources of information to scholars.

BIBLIOGRAPHY:

A. With S. Shepard Jones, ed., *Annual Documents on American Foreign Relations* (Boston, 1938–41); *Handbook on the League of Nations Since 1920* (Boston, 1930, 1935); *Manual of Collections of Treaties and Collections Relating to Treaties* (New York, 1922); *Origin and Conclusion of the Paris Pact* (Boston, 1929); *The Reparation Settlement* (Boston, 1929); *World Disarmament: Its Problems and Prospects* (Boston, 1932).

B. AJIL 66 (1972), 608; Charles DeBenedetti, introduction to Myers, *Origins and Conclusion of the Paris Pact*, rpt. ed. (New York, 1972); WWA 1941–42, 1622.

Warren F. Kuehl

N

NABUCO, Joaquim. See *Biographical Dictionary of Modern Peace Leaders*.

NANSEN, Fridtjof (10 October 1861, Oslo—13 May 1930, Lysaker, Norway). *Education*: Ph.D., Univ. of Oslo, 1888; research on sealing ship in the Arctic, 1882; study at Pavia and at Naples Biological Station, 1886. *Career*: explorer, zoologist, oceanographer, inventor, artist, diplomat, statesman, and international administrator; Nobel Peace Prize, 1922.

Nansen had two distinguished careers, the first, before World War I, as a scientist and Arctic explorer, and the second, after 1918, as an international statesman and administrator in refugee work. Each career brought him both national and international recognition. Nansen began his explorations of the Arctic when in 1882 he took passage on a sealing ship, the *Viking*. In addition to his duties as a seal hunter, Nansen collected data on wind, weather, ice, the sea, and animal life. That summer he was appointed curator of the zoological collection in the Bergen Museum. After defending his doctoral thesis, he left on an expedition in 1888 to cross Greenland from east to west. All previous attempts had started from the west and failed. Nansen invented and designed his own scientific and travel equipment, and his party of six crossed in less than three months. Nansen spent the next winter studying Eskimo life in Greenland before returning to a hero's welcome.

By studying Arctic currents, Nansen developed a theory that a ship frozen in ice north of Siberia would be carried near the North Pole and, after two or three years, would emerge near Greenland. Nansen supervised the design of a ship, the *Fram*, to withstand the ice and be forced upward as it was frozen. It sailed 24 June 1893, and became frozen into the drifting ice in late September. Eighteen months later, when it seemed that the *Fram* would drift no closer to the Pole than 400 miles, Nansen set off with one companion, by dog sledge and carrying kayaks for their return, to try to reach the Pole. On 7 April 1895, he arrived at the farthest point north reached by any person to that time. He returned by way of Franz Josef Land and reached Norway in August 1896, the same month the *Fram* arrived. The expedition added greatly to world and Arctic scientific data in such diverse areas as geography, meteorology, botany, zoology, magnetism, paleontology, geology, oceanography, astronomy, nutrition, and physics.

Thereafter, Nansen became involved in publishing his findings, lecturing, teaching, and pursuing other research. From 1906 to 1908 he served as Norway's first minister to England. In 1913 he crossed Siberia to Vladivostok. In 1917–18 he was in Washington arranging for food supplies for Norway.

After the war, he devoted most of his career to the League of Nations. He attended the Paris Peace Conference, was president of the Norwegian League of Nations Society, was influential in bringing Norway into the League, and served as Norwegian delegate. In 1920 he undertook, on behalf of the League, the repatriation of war prisoners. He gained the cooperation of the Russian government, in spite of its hostility to the League of Nations. In 1921 and 1922 he was entrusted by the League with the care of Russian, Greek, and Armenian refugees. To finance this work, he created the Nansen Relief Organization independent of the League, and with the help of such groups as the International Red Cross and the American Relief Administration under *Herbert Hoover, he raised and administered funds for millions of people. In recognition of this work he was awarded the Nobel Peace Prize in 1922. Many of Nansen's speeches during the 1920s stressed peace, with the League of Nations as a major instrumentality and the hope it would become the organ and parliament of the "United States of Humanity."

Nansen continued his refugee work as the League's high commissioner until his death in 1930. He worked with the nearly 2 million refugees from the Greco-Turkish War. One of his notable innovations was the issuance of the Nansen International Passport for persons who could claim no citizenship. These carried Nansen's picture and were recognized by fifty-two governments, with the fees used for further refugee work. Nansen served the League without salary and donated most of his Nobel Prize money to refugee projects. Altogether, Nansen repatriated nearly 500,000 prisoners of war from more than thirty nations and helped care for or resettle 1.25 million Greek, 1 million Russian, 300,000 Armenian, and tens of thousands of Assyrian, Assyro-Chaldean, Bulgarian, and Turkish refugees.

BIBLIOGRAPHY:

A. *Armenia and the Near East* (London, 1928); *Farthest North*, 2 vols. (New York, 1897); *In Northern Mists.* 2 vols. (New York, 1911); *Russia and Peace* (London, 1923); *Through Siberia, the Land of the Future* (New York, 1914).

B. James A. Joyce, *Broken Star: The Story of the League of Nations (1919–1939)* (Swansea, England, 1978); Frederick Lynch, "Fridtjof Nansen," *World Unity Magazine* 5 (Oct 1929), 20–28; Arno J. Mayer, *Politics and Diplomacy of Peacemaking: Containment and Counterrevolution at Versailles, 1918–1919* (New York, 1967); Jon Sorensen, *The Saga of Fridtjof Nansen*, (New York, 1932).

C. The Nansen papers are in Univ. of Oslo Library.

A. LeRoy Bennett

NASH, Philip Curtis (28 August 1890, Hingham, MA—6 May 1947, Toledo, OH). *Education*: B.A., Harvard Coll., 1911, M.C.E., 1912. *Career*: assistant engineer, Boston Transit Commission, 1912–17; Army and director, Military Trade Schools, 1917–19; professor, Northeastern Univ., 1919–21; dean, Antioch Coll., 1921–29; executive director, League of Nations Association, 1929–33; president, Univ. of Toledo, 1933–47; moderator, American Unitarian Association, 1942–44.

As an association director and author, Nash was an advocate of the League of Nations between the world wars and a contributor to the debate on postwar world order in the United States, 1941–45. It was his unwavering conviction that the United States had no greater task or responsibility than to foster the growth of an international organization founded on reasoned discourse, impartial expertise, respect for law and the peaceful settlement of disputes, and collective opposition to aggression.

As an executive director of the League of Nations Association (1929–33), Nash supervised one of the most important pro-League agencies in the country. By the time he assumed his post, it was clear that the prevailing political climate would not permit immediate membership in the League. During his tenure as director, the Association upheld membership as its ultimate goal but confined its short-term objectives to education and a modest program of political action designed to convince the public, the Congress, and officials in Washington that the United States had to extend its ties with the League and accept greater responsibility for preserving peace. The Association's political program encompassed support for disarmament, the Kellogg–Briand Pact, membership in the World Court, and a resolution of the Senate to without hold governmental protection from American nationals who assisted foreign aggressors. During the Far Eastern crisis, the Association urged the closest cooperation between Washington and Geneva, including ad hoc representation of the United States on the Council of the League, participation in any economic boycott of Japan approved by the Assembly, and a consultative agreement to supplement the Kellogg–Briand Pact. The disturbing events in the Far East helped to persuade Nash to attempt to move the Association toward a more venturesome political strategy, but he met with only mixed success. He faced further difficulties because of a sharp decline in membership and revenue resulting from the Depression. Under fire from critics within the Association for alleged mismanagement and poor planning, he resigned as director in July 1933.

Not until the publication of *An Adventure in World Order* (1944) did Nash again reach out to a national audience with his views on international organization. He presented a timely amalgam of ideas under discussion among moderate internationalists for a new and improved body. Nash believed that the League had failed not so much because of intrinsic weakness as because of the willingness of peoples and nations to support it. *An Adventure in World Order* presented a draft constitution for a United Nations to preserve peace. It reflected the League Covenant, but Nash included such innovative features as an international police force, the absence of a big-power veto, and a collective security mechanism by which member nations pledged themselves to economic but not military sanctions. Following the publication of the Dumbarton Oaks proposals for the UN, Nash recommended additions and changes, but he found much more to admire than to criticize in the proposals and joined the internationalist chorus which called for U.S. participation in the UN.

BIBLIOGRAPHY:

A. *An Adventure in World Order* (Boston, 1944).

B. Charles DeBenedetti, *Origins of the Modern American Peace Movement, 1915-1929* (Millwood, NY, 1978); Robert A. Divine, *Second Chance: The Triumph of Internationalism in America During World War II* (New York, 1967); NYT 7 May 1947, 27; WWWA 2, 393.

Robert D. Accinelli

NASH, Walter (12 February 1882, Kidderminster, England—4 June 1968, Lower Hutt, New Zealand). *Education*: primary school, Kidderminster. *Career*: member of New Zealand Parliament, 1929-68; minister of finance, 1935-49; ambassador to United States, 1942-43; leader of opposition, 1951-57; prime minister, 1957-60.

Nash's first involvement in international affairs came when he attended the last meeting of the Second Socialist International in Geneva in 1920 as the representative of the New Zealand Labor party. There he met many of the best-known non-Bolshevik Socialists of his day. In 1926 he became a foundation member of the Institute of Pacific Relations, a study organization, and led the New Zealand delegation to its conference in Honolulu in 1927 and Banff in 1933. He was also active in the Institute of International Affairs, which was British in origin. Partly under Nash's influence, the first New Zealand Labor government, after 1935, adopted a pro-League of Nations and anti-appeasement policy and advocated collective security against Fascism, an idealistic policy supported by the Soviet Union but with little chance of success.

From this time onward, Nash became a determined activist in international affairs. In 1942-43 he was minister to Washington, New Zealand's first diplomatic representative, where he took part in many discussions of the Pacific War Council and elsewhere. He also became intensely involved in the series of conferences planning a peaceful and rational postwar world. In 1944 he was at the Bretton Woods Conference where the International Monetary Fund was created. He fought successfully for New Zealand's right to maintain its system of exchange controls. He also attended conferences at Geneva, Havana, and elsewhere when the General Agreement on Tariffs and Trade emerged, and he became involved in exploring the abortive International Trade Organization. The number of countries represented at these wartime conferences was not great, and more notice was taken of New Zealand views than might be expected.

Nash's final international efforts came as prime minister, 1957-60. He seemed almost constantly at conferences abroad. He called on Nehru, Khrushchev, Eisenhower, *John Foster Dulles, Harold Macmillan, and others to discuss world problems, but especially disarmament. In 1959 he was an influential voice opposing American or SEATO military intervention in Laos to assist the government against the Pathet Lao. He was extremely outspoken against U.S. policy. On this occasion the voices of peace prevailed.

It could not be expected that the government of a small nation like New Zealand could achieve a position of great importance in world affairs, but New Zealand did sometimes speak for other lesser powers to help modify the point of view of great ones. Nash thus received a measure of international recognition.

BIBLIOGRAPHY:

A. *New Zealand: A Working Democracy* (New York, 1943).

B. CB 1942, 630–31; LT 5 Jun 1968, 10, 12 Jun 1968, 12; Keith Sinclair, *Walter Nash* (Auckland, New Zealand, 1976).

C. The Nash papers are in the New Zealand National Archives.

Keith Sinclair

NASMYTH, George William (9 July 1882, Cleveland, OH—20 September 1920, Geneva). *Education*: B.A., Cornell Univ., 1906, M.A., 1908, Ph.D., 1909. *Career*: instructor, Cornell Univ., 1906–11; president, Corda Fratres, International Federation of Students, 1911–14; president, Federation of International Polity Clubs, 1914–17; secretary, Commission on Wheat Prices, 1917: head, Administrative Division, U.S. Fuel Administration, 1917–19; representative, World Alliance for Promoting International Friendship Through the Churches, 1920.

After a brief career as a physicist, Nasmyth devoted his attention and energies to constructing an international student movement. His interest had been aroused in 1906 during a European visit, and as a student he became involved in the Cosmopolitan Clubs that sprang up on American campuses in the years before World War I. He became a leader in the formation of Corda Fratres, the International Federation of Students, and of its successor, the Federation of International Polity Groups. At a meeting in Rome (1911) he was elected president of Corda Fratres and reelected two more times. In 1913 he organized a national rally at Cornell. Friendships across national boundaries among the leaders of the future world, he believed, eliminate "misunderstandings," that led to war.

Nasmyth spent the years 1910–13 in Germany as a postgraduate student in a nation notably resistant to his internationalist ideals, and the experience convinced him that a more "scientific" basis was needed for the peace movement than the vague good will on which the student groups had relied. He sought that scientific foundation first in the economic arguments of +Norman Angell, whose "new pacifism" found a forum in the student movement. Nasmyth also turned to biological evidence in his book *Social Progress and the Darwinian Theory* (1916), a work credited with helping to weaken the hold of social Darwinism on American thought. In it he argued that the militarists had misinterpreted Darwin's findings in identifying struggle within a species as the mechanism by which evolution occurred.

Although Nasmyth opposed the entrance of the United States into World War I, he served in various government administrative posts during America's participation in the conflict. A zealous supporter of the league idea after 1914, he was secretary to the Massachusetts branch of the League to Enforce Peace while a director of the World Peace Foundation. There, working with *Charles Levermore and supported by the Carnegie Endowment for International Peace, he also helped found International Polity Clubs on over forty campuses by 1917. He returned to Europe as a press representative at the Paris Peace Conference and stayed to build support for the League of Nations among religious groups. In the Balkans, working as an organizer for the World Alliance for Friendship Through the Churches, he contracted the typhoid fever that led to his premature death.

BIBLIOGRAPHY:

A. *Social Progress and the Darwinian Theory* (New York, 1916); *What I Saw in Germany* (London, [1914]).

B. Catherine Ann Cline, introduction to Nasmyth, *Social Progress and the Darwinian Theory* rpt. ed. (New York, 1973); NCAB 18, 246–47; NYT 22 Sept 1920, 15; David S. Patterson, *Toward a Warless World: The Travail of the American Peace Movement, 1887–1914* (Bloomington, IN, 1976).

C. The Nasmyth papers are in the Swarthmore Coll. Peace Collection.

Catherine Ann Cline

NEWFANG, Oscar [born Otto Neufang] (24 January 1875, Columbus, OH—14 February 1943, New York). *Education*: Capital Univ., 1890–93. *Career*: credit manager, New York banks, 1902–13; credit manager and assistant treasurer, woolen manufacturing firm, 1914–35; writer on credit and economics.

It is not clear when Newfang developed his interest in world federation, but his first writing on that subject appeared in a 1918 pamphlet, *A World Government Needed*. Three books on that theme followed in 1924, 1930, and 1939, and he wrote extensively for *World Unity* and *World Order* magazines in the interwar years. He capped his work with a 1942 volume, which showed some shift toward a more elaborate world government approach as a formula for peace.

Newfang saw the organization of the world as the task of the twentieth century. He foresaw that war was no longer logical but a distinct threat to civilization. People should abolish war, apply the rule of law, and adapt to the growing interdependence evident everywhere. The attainment of these ends, he declared, depended on how willing governments were to create machinery and respect it. The United States, in moving from the Articles of Confederation to the Constitution, provided a model for the world. In most of his writing, Newfang focused on problems the American system had faced, how it had resolved these, and how the League of Nations could learn from the United States experiences. Thus he called for extensive revisions in the Covenant to provide for more efficient executive leadership, additional powers within well-defined bounds, and a world police to enforce law, uphold the decisions of the Permanent Court of International Justice, and respond to aggressors. He totally rejected proposals like that of *Richard Coudenhove-Kalergi for regional federations. Only a general one would suffice.

For nearly two decades Newfang expounded on this theme without providing operational specifics. He assumed that negotiating processes would take care of details. The key lay in the willingness of people to accept the simple truth he sought to convey. In 1942, however, he did present a more detailed formula for the enlightenment of postwar planners in the form of a revised Covenant of the League. He suggested few operational changes but wanted the League to restrict the arms of members, possess the exclusive means to wage war, and enjoy the power to tax, to legislate, to prevent armed alliances, and to control all key garrisons, straits, and canals.

Newfang appears to have had but limited influence in his campaigns, reaching only a self-selected audience, and he never attained the prominence of contemporaries like *Ely Culbertson or *Carl Van Doren. He died during World War II without knowing that the world federation movement of the late 1940s would revive many of his ideas and the American system analogy he had sought to popularize.

BIBLIOGRAPHY:

A. *The Road to World Peace* (New York, 1924); *The United States of the World* (New York, 1930); *World Federation* (New York, 1939); *World Government* (New York, 1942); *A World Government Needed* (n.p., 1919).

B. NYT 15 Feb 1943, 15; WWWA 2, 396.

Warren F. Kuehl

NICHOLAS II. See *Biographical Dictionary of Modern Peace Leaders*.

NIEMEYER, Otto Ernst (23 November 1883, Streatham, England—6 February 1971, Lindfield, England). *Education*: B.A., Balliol Coll., Oxford Univ., 1906, M.A. *Career*: treasury official, 1906–27; Bank of England official, 1927–38, executive director, 1938–52; member, League of Nations Financial Committee, 1922–37; director, Bank for International Settlements, 1931–65.

Niemeyer is remembered in history as the official who in 1925 persuaded Winston Churchill, then chancellor of the exchequer, to return to the gold standard at the prewar parity of $4.86. It is generally believed that the economist *John Maynard Keynes was correct at the time in believing sterling would be overvalued at that rate and that the effect of Niemeyer's advice would be to inhibit British exports and to maintain high unemployment. Niemeyer, however, feared that without a fixed monetary standard there would be inflation and that only when instability in exchange rates ended would world trade and therefore employment be able to recover. As a member of the Financial Committee of the League of Nations he had gained an international perspective on currency and trade problems which many of his critics lacked. Although his university studies had been in classics, Niemeyer understood public finance. He had taken first place in the civil service examination in 1906 (when Keynes had been second) and had risen rapidly in the Treasury, becoming controller of finance in 1922. Niemeyer saw that any attempt by Britain to return to gold at a lower parity than what the world regarded as normal could only result in competitive devaluations and further exchange rate instability, as happened after sterling depreciated in 1931.

By then Niemeyer had been recruited to the Bank of England by its governor, *Montagu Norman, who required experienced lieutenants to deal with the Bank's expanding responsibilities. Much of Niemeyer's work concerned external finance, and such was his reputation for impartiality that he was invited by other governments, sometimes at the instigation of their London bankers, to advise on financial and economic policy. He went on missions to Australia (1930), Brazil (1931), Greece and Egypt (1932), Argentina (1933), India (1935), and China (1941). The scope varied, but in general Niemeyer promoted independent central banking and urged monetary stability and a reduction in tariff barriers. Niemeyer continued his membership on the Financial Committee of the League while becoming a director of the Bank for International Settlements (BIS), which had been set up to facilitate cooperation between central banks as well as to handle reparations and international debt payments. He was chairman of the board of the BIS from 1937 to 1940 and vice-chairman from 1961 until he was eighty, in 1963. He played a leading part in the Anglo–German negotiations which led to the International German Debt Agreement of 1952. Niemeyer was an internationalist in his approach to public finance in that he believed implicitly in the international division of labor and explicitly that governments should eschew "beggar-thy-neighbor" policies.

BIBLIOGRAPHY:

A. *Proceedings of the British Academy* 32 (1946), 401–5, an obituary on J. M. Keynes.

B. LT 8 Feb 1971, 12; Donald Moggridge, *British Monetary Policy, 1924–1931* (Cambridge, 1972).

C. The Niemeyer papers are in the Public Record Office in London.

George Peden

NIPPOLD, Otfried. See *Biographical Dictionary of Modern Peace Leaders.*

NISOT, Joseph (1894, Charleroi, Belgium—2 May 1978, Brussels). *Education*: Univs. of Ghent, Cambridge, Geneva, Freiburg, and Harvard; LL.D.

Career: assistant legal consultant, Ministry of Foreign Affairs, 1919–22; legal adviser, League of Nations, 1922–40; counselor, Belgian embassy in Washington, 1942–48; delegate, UN, 1948–59.

A legal background provided Nisot with an entry into the international community when in 1922 he entered the Legal Section of the Secretariat of the League of Nations. While there, he became involved in discussions to extend the principle of peace through the judicial settlement of disputes. He served on the Commission of Jurists to revise the statutes of the Permanent Court of International Justice, and he helped organize the conference in 1929 in Geneva which approved the changes. Nisot also became acquainted with *Manley Hudson when the latter worked in the Legal Section, and Nisot later (1940–42) became a member of Hudson's Harvard Research in International Law.

During World War II, Nisot served in the Belgian embassy in Washington and was a member of his country's delegation to the San Francisco Conference in 1945. Thereafter he became a regular figure at UN sessions, beginning with the Assembly of 1947. That year he sat on the Security Council, served as UN commissioner for conventional armaments, and later became involved in a wide-ranging variety of UN endeavors. He retired officially in 1959, but his interest in international affairs continued. He returned to Geneva, where from 1959 to 1974 he held title as honorary ambassador and served as assistant legal counsel with Belgium's delegation to the European office of the UN.

BIBLIOGRAPHY:
B. WB 1948, 3480.

Warren F. Kuehl

NITOBE Inazō (1 September 1862, Morioka, Japan—16 October 1933, Victoria, BC). *Education*: graduate, Sapporo Agricultural Coll., 1881; B.A., Johns Hopkins Univ., 1887; Ph.D., Univ. of Halle, 1890. *Career*: educator in agriculture, law, and international relations, Sapporo Agricultural Coll., Tokyo Univ., Tokyo First Higher School, and Tokyo Women's Coll., 1891–1919; under secretary-general, League of Nations, 1920–26; author and spokesman for internationalism; interpreter of Japanese–American relations.

Inspired by Quaker and Japanese emphasis upon self-discipline, bolstered by twenty years' residence abroad, fluent in English, an ardent Christian, and married to an American, this son of a samurai became one of Japan's best-known internationalists. Nitobe left his internationalist stamp on students and shaped the thinking of political, diplomatic, and educational leaders. A popular, articulate speaker, he frequently lectured at home and abroad on international cooperation, world peace, and Japanese-American relations. He actively participated in the League of Nations Association, the Japan Peace Society, the America-Japan Society, the

Fellowship of Reconciliation, and the Institute of Pacific Relations. In 1911 the Carnegie Endowment for International Peace made Nitobe its first Japanese exchange professor. As under secretary-general of the League of Nations he vigorously promoted internationalism and shaped the International Committee on Intellectual Co-operation. In his quest to interpret and improve international relations, Nitobe wrote thirteen books in English and twenty-nine in Japanese. His best-known work, *Bushido, the Soul of Japan*, was not a glorification of the warrior code but an expression of admiration for duty, discipline, and moral training.

A staunch spokesman for international peace, Nitobe was not an absolute pacifist but accepted war as an occasional necessity. He called it "an instrument of madness," and an act "incompatible with civilization" and urged people to prepare for peace rather than for war. A critic of military preparedness, Nitobe condemned excessive armaments as an invitation to conflict. Preparedness, he argued, should be in cooperation, not in armaments. Nitobe explained Japan's motives in Manchuria in apologetic terms—no territorial ambitions, protection of Japanese rights and honor, and the development of Manchuria—but grieved deeply over what happened in 1931. Much to the anger of the army leaders, he opposed their actions, criticized the government's policies, and pointed out the dangers of militarism.

In speeches and writings, Nitobe argued that internationalism and nationalism were complementary rather than conflicting forces. He exhorted his countrymen to be more internationalist while not abandoning the principles of nationhood. A staunch supporter of the League of Nations, Nitobe encouraged people to strengthen the League and to cultivate its spirit. After leaving his Geneva post, Nitobe lectured throughout Japan and the United States on world peace and internationalism. He strongly urged Japan not to withdraw from the League and proclaimed it an important instrument to maintain peace and promote world cooperation. Yet Nitobe criticized the League's misconceptions of the Far Eastern situation. In his final years, Nitobe emphasized that Japan must not isolate herself or abandon the principles of universal peace and international cooperation. He spent his last months explaining Japan, her people and culture, and her foreign policy to Americans. He died in Canada while representing Japan at a meeting of the Institute of Pacific Relations. The epitaph on his tombstone fittingly summarizes the life of Inazō Nitobe, as "A bridge across the Pacific."

BIBLIOGRAPHY:

A. *Nitobe Inazō zenshū*, 11 vols. (Tokyo, 1969); *The Works of Inazō Nitobe*, 5 vols. (Tokyo, 1972).

B. Ishii Mitsuru, *Nitobe Inazō den* (Tokyo, 1934); Sukeo Kitasawa, *The Life of Dr. Nitobe* (Tokyo, 1953); Tokyo Joshi Daigaku, *Nitobe Inazō kenkyū* (Tokyo, 1969).

C. Some Nitobe papers are in the Friends Historical Library, Swarthmore Coll.

William D. Hoover

NITTI, Francesco Saverio (20 July 1868, Melfi, Italy—20 February 1953, Rome). *Education*: jurisprudence degree, Univ. of Naples, 1904. *Career*: scholar, journalist, and professor, Univ. of Naples, after 1898; elected deputy, 1904; minister of agriculture, 1911–14; minister of treasury, 1917–19; president, Council of Ministers, 1919–20; exiled in 1924; held by Germans in France, 1943–45; member, Italian Constituent Assembly, 1946; elected to Senate, 1948.

This political economist and statesman, born in the Basilicata, commenced his career as a disciple of Giustino Fortunato, who championed the cause of the poverty-stricken Italian South. By the time Nitti joined the Giovanni Giolitti Cabinet in 1911, in which he served as minister of agriculture, commerce, and industry, he had produced a number of scholarly studies and had attained a European reputation. Following the beginning of World War I, he became an international figure.

At the outbreak of that conflict, Nitti had favored neutrality, but once Italy was drawn in, he considered it his duty to assist the government. During the summer of 1917, he visited the United States at the head of an economic and financial mission and in October 1917 entered the Orlando Cabinet as minister of the treasury. As such, he helped organize the country's economy for the war and played an important part in the restoration of the country's finances.

Nitti also sought a resurgence of the economic life of Europe, believing that trade barriers between states should be lowered if not eliminated. He therefore opposed what he considered to be Sidney Sonnino's excessive preoccupation with fulfillment of the terms of the Treaty of London, and he resigned from the Cabinet on the eve of the peace conference. He subsequently presided over the ministry from the time of Vittorio Orlando's fall in June 1919 to Giolitti's return in June 1920. As head of the government, he sought to solve the Fiume crisis by agreement with Yugoslavia.

Like many liberals, Nitti began to have doubts about decisions at the Paris Peace Conference. He had concurred with *Woodrow Wilson in favoring a "peace without victory," but he became one of the first critics of the Treaty of Versailles. He also opposed the League of Nations, considering it a union of victors against the vanquished and not in the best interest of the people of Europe. The parochialism and protectionism of the victors ignored the economic interdependence on which the Continent's prosperity rested. In a series of books, he predicted that the peace would be as detrimental to Europe as the war and that it would restore neither the Continent's economic life nor its tranquility. As an alternative to the League, he saw the need for an organized Europe. He revealed an interest in *Richard Coudenhove-Kalergi's ideas and served as honorary president of the First Congress of Pan-Europe, which met in Vienna in 1926. Nitti's prophecy proved accurate; he lived to see the rise of Fascism, World War II, and European unity movements after 1945.

BIBLIOGRAPHY:

A. *La Démocratie* (Paris, 1933); *Meditazioni dell' esilio* (Naples, 1947); *Peaceless Europe* (London, 1922); *Scritti sulla questione meridionale*, 6 vols. (Bari, Italy, 1958–68).

B. Frank J. Coppa, "Francesco Saverio Nitti: Early Critic of the Treaty of Versailles," *Risorgimento*, 2, no. 2 (1980), 211–19; Alberto Monticone, *Nitti e la Grande Guerra (1914–1918)* (Milan, 1961); Vincenzo Nitti, *L'Opera di Nitti* (Turin, 1924).

Frank J. Coppa

NKRUMAH, Kwame (21 September 1909 [official birthdate], Nkroful, Gold Coast—27 April 1972, Romania). *Education*: graduate, Anglican Achimota Coll., 1930; B.D., Lincoln Univ., 1939; M.S., Univ. of Pennsylvania, 1942, M.A., 1943. *Career*: teacher, 1930–35; president, African Students' Association in U.S., 1944; general secretary, United Gold Coast Convention, 1947–49; publisher, *Accra Evening News*, 1948–49; founder, Convention People's party, 1949; elected to Parliament, 1951–52; prime minister, 1952–66; president of Ghana, 1960–66.

With his ascendancy to the presidency of Ghana upon independence in 1957, Nkrumah capped a career termed at his death as one whose dreams could never catch reality. His frenetic political involvement raised to new heights of consciousness a sense of Pan Africanism along with a desire for self-government for his homeland, and the firm implantation of his Convention People's party as its dominant political force during thirteen years of increasingly tumultuous rule. Perhaps his most noteworthy contribution is symbolized by the inclusion in the first Ghanaian constitution of a provision for surrender of sovereignty to a future union of African states—a dream that has grown more distant with time.

Nkrumah thus stands tall in the search for political progress and stability at a time and place where lesser visions failed. Though Nkrumah was corrupted by power and ultimately driven from office in a military coup, the president of Sierra Leone could still remark at his death that, although Nkrumah was not perfect, his memory would live because of his role as a hero and pioneer in helping the African personality emerge.

Returning home in 1949 at the invitation of his mentor and later enemy, J. B. Danquah, to take up the secretaryship of the nationalist United Gold Coast Convention, he continued his shrewd, indefatigable devotion to independence for the Gold Coast and union for Africa. His radicalism resulted in his expulsion from the UGCC in 1949, and building upon his Committee on Youth Organization he then organized the vehicle which became his permanent power base, the Convention People's party, of which he was elected chairman for life in 1955. Agitation prior to independence led to his arrest. This was followed by his election to the National Assembly by an overwhelming majority, necessitating his release from jail and an invitation to be leader of government business. He then served as prime minister (1952–66) until deposed by the military while en route to Peking as a self-appointed mediator of the Vietnam conflict.

Seeing himself a leader of international stature he hosted the first conference of independent African states in Accra in 1958, led Ghana into an ill-fated union with Guinea in 1959 (later incorporating Mali), participated in the radical Casablanca group of African states, mediated the Algerian-Moroccan border dispute, and saw the election of Ghana's representative as first African president of the UN General Assembly. He became the third president of the Organization of African Unity in 1965, where he argued for a strong African union. He early visited the United States; later travels took him increasingly to Eastern bloc countries as hostility toward the West and the United States in particular developed.

In 1960 he supported Patrice Lumumba of the Congo and in 1961 the formation of the All-African Trade Union Federation to counter Western and Communist-dominated organizations. He received the Lenin Peace Prize in 1962, confirming his move into the Eastern bloc. At the time of his overthrow observers suggested that Ghana was only a few steps from becoming an African Cuba.

His problems mounted in the early 1960s—a failure not of imagination but of intellect. In addition to heightened opposition to Communist influence, unrest emerged as a result of his repression of opposition and the cult of Nkrumahism ("Osagyefo," he was termed, the Redeemer.). Serious economic problems appeared because of a drop in cocoa prices; finally, there was corruption, his as well as his associates. Having used Ghana as a sacrifice to Pan Africanism, he proclaimed his intentions to bring a new day, until the full extent of his misdeeds were publicized by the Army. Even in exile he remained adamant; in neighboring Guinea, he was proclaimed copresident by Sekou Toure. He died in 1972 while seeking medical treatment in Romania.

Nkrumah's legacy is mixed. Advocacy of an African union was an idea whose time had not come. His vision for Ghana was exaggerated and costly, though he did initiate the Volta River project, potentially the basis for a stable and strong economy. His "scientific Socialism"—often termed African Socialism—was not well articulated. His writings were more rhetorical than analytical. Yet when the record of African political development is compiled, Nkrumah will have a place—less than he would have liked, but more than his victims would acknowledge.

BIBLIOGRAPHY:

A. *Africa Must Unite* (London, 1963); *Autobiography of Kwame Nkrumah* (Edinburgh, 1957); *Axioms of Kwame Nkrumah* (London, 1967); *Challenge of the Congo* (London, 1967); *Class Struggle in Africa* (London, 1970); *Consciencism* (London, 1964); *Dark Days in Ghana* (London, 1968); *Handbook of Revolutionary Warfare* (New York, 1968); *Hands off Africa!* (Accra, 1960); *I Speak of Freedom* (London, 1961); *Neo-Colonialism: The Last Stage of Imperialism* (London, 1965);

Toward Colonial Freedom: Africa in the Struggle Against World Imperialism (London, 1962); *Towards Colonial Freedom* (London, 1947); *Voice from Conakry* (London, 1967).

B. Geoffrey Bing, *Reaping the Whirlwind* (London, 1968); Henry Bretton, *The Rise and Fall of Kwame Nkrumah* (New York, 1966); CB 1953, 458–60; *Dictionary of African Biography* 1 (New York, 1977), 272–79; Robert B. Fitch and Mary Oppenlander, *Ghanda: End of an Illusion* (New York, 1966); Samuel G. Ikoku, *Le Ghana de Nkrumah* (Paris, 1971); NYT *Magazine* 20 Jul 1958, 14–17, 14 Jan 1962, 13, 3 May 1964, 15, 27 Jun 1965, 20–21; Theodore H. Von Laue, "Reflections on Kwame Nkrumah," *Yale Review* 64 (Mar 1975), 321–33.

Richard A. Fredland

NOLDE, Otto Frederick (30 June, 1899, Philadelphia—17 June 1972, Philadelphia). *Education*: B.A., Muhlenberg Coll., 1920; B.D., Lutheran Theol. Sem., 1923; Ph.D., Univ. of Pennsylvania, 1928. *Career*: faculty, Lutheran Theol. Sem., 1923–68, dean, graduate school, 1943–62; faculty, Univ. of Pennsylvania, 1925–43; associate consultant to U.S. delegation, San Francisco Conference, 1945; director, Commission of the Churches on International Affairs, World Council of Churches, 1946–68; associate general secretary, World Council of Churches, 1948–68; member, Executive Committee, Trustees of Carnegie Endowment for International Peace, 1951–70.

Nolde was a leading diplomat and international affairs spokesman of the World Council of Churches for two decades following World War II. His involvement began in the 1930s with membership in the Department of International Justice and Goodwill of the Federal Council of Churches of Christ in America. In 1941 he became a member of the Commission on a Just and Durable Peace (CJDP) created by the Federal Council and several other interdenominational agencies to formulate proposals for a Christian peace settlement. Its report in 1943 reflected his influence in its call for a postwar international organization, for control of armaments, and for human rights and religious liberty. Nolde's concern for religious freedom grew during the years 1944–49, when he served as executive secretary of the Joint Committee on Religious Liberty, another agency of the Federal Council. In these posts he helped organize wartime conferences where church leaders from many countries gathered to discuss the peace settlement. At the San Francisco Conference (1945), Nolde representing the Federal Council is given substantial credit for the inclusion in the Charter of a Commission on Human Rights.

In 1946 the Provisional Committee of the World Council and the International Missionary Council asked the CJDP to plan a conference to discuss ways in which Christian churches could influence international affairs. Guided by memories of the inability of organized religion to sway events in the 1930s, the conference decided that a permanent agency backed by the emergent World Council would have the greatest influence. At a meeting in Cambridge, England, in 1946 the Commission of the Churches on International Affairs emerged. Nolde helped organize the sessions and was an obvious choice as director. When the World Council of Churches was formed in 1948, the CCIA became its official but nearly autonomous agency, and he became an associate general secretary with the portfolio on international affairs.

Nolde believed that Christians had a responsibility to make their views known on international issues, particularly those which safeguarded human rights or peace. They had an even greater responsibility to express their opinions in concrete and practical proposals. This philosophy guided his directorship. Religious liberty was an area in which the CCIA could be seen to have special competence. In 1948, after surveying Christian leaders, Nolde presented a precise plank on religious freedom to the UN General Assembly, then debating a declaration prepared by its Human Rights Commission. He is unofficially recognized as the father of the religious freedom clause in the Universal Declaration on Human Rights of 1948.

The CCIA's charter gave its officers a mandate to study deep-rooted social and economic problems and to assist world leaders in finding solutions to international crises. Although Nolde's reports and representations were varied in nature, he did adhere to certain basic principles. He always urged governments to seek mediation, to avoid violence, and to use the peacekeeping powers of the UN. In 1953 he helped persuade Syngman Rhee to agree to an armistice in Korea. The Hungarian revolt in 1956 and the United States-Soviet Union confrontation over Cuba in 1963 were only two of many crises which attracted Nolde's attention and intervention, and he early criticized U.S. military escalation in Vietnam. Concerned over the dangers of atomic war, he advocated policies ranging from UN control of atomic weapons to cessation of testing to nonproliferation treaties. Whatever the situation, he avoided moral condemnations and unequivocal demands, preferring conciliation and step-by-step improvement.

Although Nolde's behind-the-scenes activity makes it difficult to pinpoint the CCIA's influence on international events, it is clear that during his tenure the CCIA became a respected organization at the UN and in Christian countries. Nolde also helped the world's churches to develop a better understanding of international affairs and their own responsibility to lessen international tensions, thereby preserving peace.

BIBLIOGRAPHY:

A. *Christian Messages to the Peoples of the World* (New York, 1943); *Christian World Action* (Philadelphia, 1942); *The Churches and the Nations* (Philadelphia, 1970); *Free and Equal: Human Rights in Ecumenical Perspective* (Geneva, 1968); *Power for Peace* (Philadelphia, 1946); ed., *Toward World-Wide Christianity* (New York, 1946); *Yesterday, Today, and Tomorrow* (Philadelphia, 1933).

B. CB 1947, 34–36; Harold E. Fey, ed., *The Ecumenical Advance* (London,

1970); Darril Hudson, *The World Council of Churches in International Affairs* (London, 1977); NYT 19 Jun 1972, 36; Geraldine Sartain, "Church Diplomat," *National Council Outlook* 7 (Sep 1957), 7–8, 20.

G. F. Goodwin

NORMAN, Montagu Collet (6 September 1871, London—4 February 1950, London). *Education*: Eton; Kings Coll., Cambridge Univ., studied privately abroad. *Career*: joined Martin's Bank, 1892, Brown, Shipley and Co., 1894, chiefly as New York associate, 1895–99, partner, 1900–15; served in Boer War, 1900–02; elected to Court of Bank of England, 1907, on staff, 1915–18, deputy governor, 1918–20, governor, 1920–44; with Stanley Baldwin, negotiated war debt settlement with the United States, 1922–23; on Board of Directors, Bank for International Settlements, 1930–39.

Governor of the Bank of England for an unprecedented twenty-four years, Norman had more influence during the first half of his tenure on European financial diplomacy than any other non-American. In the 1920s he worked for European financial reconstruction, seeking stabilization on the prewar gold basis under British domination. His internationalism was founded on *Realpolitik*, not idealism. Although willing to use the League of Nations for emergency financial reconstruction of Central Europe as a vehicle to gain support and reduce political pressure, Norman preferred private contacts among financiers outside the political sphere. He maintained warm relations with his American and German counterparts, notably Benjamin Strong and Hjalmar Schacht, agreeing with them about the primacy of German revival, and he got on poorly with the French.

A secretive autocrat and an obsessive worker plagued by erratic health, Norman was both a traditionalist and an innovator. His battle to regain and maintain the prewar gold standard at $4.86 along with his dedication to deflation, payment of the American debt, and high interest rates, disregarded the effect on British industry, exports, and unemployment. The decision in 1931 to abandon the gold standard, taken while he was away ill, largely ended his influence outside the Bank, as Norman was increasingly overruled on policy matters.

An advocate of central banking free of governmental interference, Norman put the Bank of England on a professional basis, modernized it, and completed its transition from a commercial to a central bank, brooking no Treasury intervention in his heyday. He also sought an organization of central bankers, preferably under British auspices. Although the Bank for International Settlements created in 1930 disappointed him in the latter respect and in its connection to reparations, which meant political involvement, he worked hard to establish it and served on its Board from the outset, attending monthly meetings in Basel until World War II. He succeeded in turning it into a club of central bankers, as he had envisaged as a vehicle for international cooperation.

At home, the 1930s were spent fighting the Depression. Abroad, controversial talks about credits to Nazi Germany were terminated by Schacht's resignation. Norman's retirement was postponed by World War II, during which he worked on war finance. As he turned to postwar problems, his health broke in 1944, forcing retirement.

BIBLIOGRAPHY:

B. Andrew Boyle, *Montagu Norman, a Biography* (London, 1967); CB 1940, 619–20; Henry Clay, *Lord Norman* (London, 1952); DNB 1941–50, 633–36; LT 6 Feb 1950, 7, 8; D. E. Moggridge, *British Monetary Policy, 1924–1931: The Norman Conquest of $4.86* (Cambridge, 1972); NYT 5 Feb 1950, 85; R. L. Sayers, *The Bank of England, 1891–1944*, 3 vols. (Cambridge, 1976); Francis Williams, *A Pattern of Rulers* (London, 1965).

Sally Marks

NOVIKOW, Jacques. See *Biographical Dictionary of Modern Peace Leaders*.

O

OLDHAM, George Ashton (15 August 1877, Sunderland, England—7 April 1963, Litchfield, CT). *Education*: B.A., Cornell Univ., 1902; B.D., General Theo. Sem., 1905; special studies, Columbia and Oxford Univ. *Career*: minister, New York, 1905–22; bishop coadjutor of Albany, 1922–29; bishop of Albany, 1929–49.

Third bishop of Albany, Oldham had an eminent career as Episcopal churchman and advocate of world peace. During his tenure as bishop he was a member of the Episcopal Commission, World Conference on Faith and Order, Commission on Ecclesiastical Relations with European Churches, Commission to Confer with the Polish Catholic Church, and Board of Trustees of General Theological Seminary. He also chaired the General Convention.

Oldham was, moreover, a noted supporter of internationalism. Profoundly moved by the destructiveness of World War I, he wrote in *A Fighting Church* (1920) that the church was largely to blame for world troubles and called on it to become "an army and a fellowship" which would restore the church's primacy in the world. Addressing the Episcopal General Convention in 1928, he warned against thinking that the Kellogg-Briand Pact would end war, for it was only an act of faith which had to be followed by active preparation for peace. War was deeply rooted, for example, in nationalism, which he likened to a horse-and-buggy mentality in the automobile age. Like the need for traffic rules, nations needed to seek a "United States of the World." Oldham called on the church to lead the way. "The Christian church can never rest satisfied until all things are subdued unto him, that God may be all in all. We must accept the principle and seal its application to ever-widening circles." Peace would ultimately rest on "the peace of God." His widely reprinted poem, "America First," (1924), was a parody against nationalistic jingoism. Oldham was a delegate to the Lambeth Conference of 1930, a world assembly of Anglican leaders, and he subsequently was prominent in the World Alliance for International Friendship Through the Churches (president, 1943–45), the Church Peace Union, the Council on Foreign Relations, the Foreign Policy Association, and the English-Speaking Union. In 1944 he headed an American Episcopal Commission to the Church of England. The summit of his efforts was his appointment to the first Executive Committee of the World Council of Churches, created in 1948, following ecumenical conferences in the interwar years and in the belief that wartime destruction would lead to a theological renaissance. Oldham declared that while living with divinely provided superabundance, people still sought to kill each other in an ongoing struggle for inconsequential supremacies.

BIBLIOGRAPHY:

A. *The Catechism Today* (New York, 1929, 1954, rev. ed. 1961); *The Church's Responsibility for World Peace* (Washington, 1928); *A Fighting Church* (Milwaukee, WI 1920); *Lambeth Through American Eyes* (Milwaukee, WI,1930).

B. NYT 8 Apr 1963, 47; WWWA 4, 717-18.

Darrel E. Bigham

OLDHAM, Joseph Holdsworth (20 October 1874, Bombay—16 May 1969, St. Leonards, Sussex, England). *Education*: M.A., Trinity Coll.; Oxford Univ., 1895; D.D., New Coll., Edinburgh Univ., 1904; Univ. of Halle, 1905. *Career*: secretary, Student Christian Movement, 1896-97; missionary in Lahore, India, 1897-1900; mission study secretary, United Free Church of Scotland, 1906-10; secretary, World Missionary Conference, 1908-10, and its Continuation Committee, 1910-21; secretary, International Missionary Council, 1921-38; administrative director, International Institute for African Language and Culture, 1931-38; chair, Research Commission for Life and Work, 1934-38; senior officer, Christian Frontier Council, 1942-47; editor, *International Review of Missions*, 1912-27, *Christian Newsletter*, 1939-45.

Few persons in the twentieth-century ecumenical movement succeeded in activating and mobilizing people as did Oldham. A quiet, unassuming man who preferred to work behind the scenes, Oldham was one of the chief architects of the World Council of Churches. He spent practically his whole life in service to the international ecumenical movement. The Edinburgh Conference in 1910, often called the beginning of the effort, was successful largely because of Oldham's thorough preparation and organization as secretary. The International Missionary Council grew out of the Edinburgh meetings, and under Oldham's leadership it planned and coordinated Protestant mission work for many countries. In 1926 Oldham, turning to Africa, helped found the International Institute of African Languages and Culture in 1926.

Late in the 1920s, he immersed himself in a new problem, the Christian response to growing secularism. By 1934 this problem glared at the churches in the form of Fascism and totalitarianism. That year Oldham joined with the ecumenical Life and Work Movement and soon found himself chairman of the committee to prepare for the World Conference on Church, Community, and State held at Oxford in 1937. It was for Oldham and the ecumenical movement a second beginning. Out of the sessions came the proposal for uniting Life and Work with its sister movement, Faith and Order, to form a World Council of Churches.

Throughout his career, Oldham argued forcefully for an international league of churches. His background in mission work gave him an evangelistic vision of a future world, and the rabid nationalism of Italy and Nazi Germany in the 1930s made Oldham even more convinced of the need for internationalism. Oldham saw the Universal Church as the example of a good society, a prototype of what the world might be. The Church's mission was to bring *all* spheres of human life into a right relationship with God. Oldham's genius, however, was not in creative thinking but in organizing. Distrusting vague public resolutions by international groups, Oldham devoted his time to personal contacts with leading figures and the best minds of different countries. He was a master at bringing together people with different personalities and interests, at finding mutual grounds for discussion, and at directing their collaboration. His careful organization made Edinburgh, 1910, and Oxford, 1937, the turning points in the ecumenical movement.

BIBLIOGRAPHY:

A. *Christianity and the Race Problem* (London, 1924); *Church, Community, and State: A World Issue* (London, 1935); *A Devotional Diary* (London, 1925); *New Hope in Africa* (London, 1955); with B. D. Gibson, *The Remaking of Man in Africa* (London, 1931); *The Resurrection of Christendom* (London, 1940); *The World and the Gospel* (London, 1916).

B. John W. Cell, *By Kenya Possessed: The Correspondence of Norman Leys and J. H. Oldham 1918–1926* (Chicago, 1976); *Ecumenical Review* 21 (July 1969), 261–65; *International Review of Missions* 59 (Jan 1970), 8–22; NYT 19 May 1969, 47; *Oekumenische Gestalten* (Berlin, 1974), 47–54; *Oekumenische Profile* 1 (Stuttgart, Germany, 1961), 209–16.

C. There are Oldham papers at Edinburgh House, Sloane Square, London, and at the World Council of Churches Library.

Kenneth C. Barnes

OPPENHEIM, Lassa Francis Lawrence (30 March 1858, Windekken, Germany—7 October 1919, Cambridge). *Education*: doctor utriusque juris, Göttingen Univ., 1880. *Career*: taught law, Univ. of Freiburg, 1885–91, Univ. of Basel, 1891–95; lecturer, London School of Economics, 1898–1908; professor, Cambridge Univ., 1908–19.

Oppenheim's reputation as an internationalist is based primarily on his two-volume work, *International Law: A Treatise*, first published in 1905–6. It went through eight editions in fifty years of intense legal activity on the international scene, surviving two world wars. In the editor's preface to volume one of the eighth edition, *H. Lauterpacht refers to the ongoing demand for "Oppenheim," who continued to write on international law until his death.

In his teaching at Freiburg and Basel, he was primarily an expert in criminal law. At Basel he began lecturing on international law, and when his health demanded that he live in a milder climate, he gave up his position there and moved to London, where his newer interest in international law could command an audience. He began his British teaching career lecturing on international law at the London School of Economics, grounded himself in his new subject, published his treatise, and on the basis of its success was chosen to follow John Westlake in the Whewell chair at Cambridge.

Oppenheim believed that international affairs were governed by a body of law, approved and supported by the community of nations, and its enforcement was the responsibility of the states acting collectively. He took a positive view of the precedents set by the two Hague conferences even though World War I seemed to negate the efforts to advance peaceful solutions to international disputes. With the end of the war, he supported the idea of a league of nations and advocated a third Hague conference to implement it.

Oppenheim added to his distinction as an internationalist by cooperating with colleagues and government officials in Britain to bring new understanding to his chosen field. With James Edwards, he coauthored a manual for the War Office on international law as it applied to land warfare, and he assisted the Foreign Office in unraveling legal questions. With his Continental background, he was able to add breadth to the British view when called upon to advise the government before and during World War I.

He published a study of the Anglo–American dispute over the Panama Canal issue, and he edited the papers of John Westlake. His long list of publications provided evidence of the breadth of his meticulous scholarship, and he received wide acclaim as a leading authority on international law.

BIBLIOGRAPHY:

A. *International Law: A Treatise*, 2 vols. (London, 1905–6); *Land Warfare: An Exposition of the Laws and Usages of War on Land for the Guidance of Officers of His Majesty's Army* (London, 1912); *The League of Nations and Its Problems* (London, 1919); *The Panama Canal Conflict Between Great Britain and the United States of America* (Cambridge, 1913).

B. AJIL 14 (1919), 229–32; *British Year Book of International Law, 1920–1921*, 1–9; DNB 1912–21, 416–17; LT 9 Oct 1919, 13; R. F. Roxburgh, preface to Oppenheim, *International Law,* 3rd ed. (London, 1920–21).

Lyle A. McGeoch

O'RYAN, John Francis (21 August 1874, New York—29 January 1961, South Salem, NY). *Education*: City Coll. of New York; LL.B., New York Univ., 1898; graduate, Army War Coll., 1914. *Career*: attorney, 1898–1961; entered National Guard as private, 1897; major general, Allied Expeditionary Force, 1917–19; transit commissioner, New York State, 1921–26; police commissioner, New York City, 1934; director of civilian defense, New York State, 1941.

One of America's leading citizen-soldiers, O'Ryan first gained prominence in 1917 by leading New York's Twenty-seventh, or "Bulldog," Division to France. He was the youngest American division commander in Europe. His unit experienced heavy fighting, including the breaking of the Hindenburg Line, and its reputation propelled O'Ryan to fame. In the interwar period, he was New York transit commissioner, president of Colonial Airways, and a successful lawyer and real estate operator. In 1934 New York Mayor Fiorello LaGuardia appointed him police commissioner, but O'Ryan's authoritarian practices soon caused his removal. In 1941 he became the city's first director of civilian defense, and Secretary of War *Henry L. Stimson appointed him an adviser.

O'Ryan became one of the nation's leading advocates of collective security, and the *New York Times* always gave him much coverage. He often called for U.S. membership in the League of Nations, declaring in 1923 that it possessed effective machinery to eliminate war. He also sought American adherence to the World Court, asserting in 1925 that otherwise Europe would see American indifference as hostility and organize against the United States. O'Ryan always stressed that disarmament must come gradually, and in 1925 he proposed that each government reduce its land forces 25 percent. More radical arms reduction, he said, could result only when an international armed force capable of resisting aggression was created. Blaming Mussolini's invasion of Ethiopia upon America's refusal to join the League, he became treasurer in 1935 of the American Aid to Ethiopia Committee, a group that sent field hospital units and ambulances there.

World War II found O'Ryan a staunch interventionist. In February 1941 he announced the formation of Fighting Funds for Finland, Inc., an organization collecting money which Finland could use to buy and resist the Soviet invasion. Recruiting such prominent Americans as *Henry L. Stimson and Carrie Chapman Catt, Fighting Funds raised over $350,000 before a Soviet–Finnish truce was announced. From 1939 to 1941, O'Ryan often warned against a German invasion of the Americas, even going so far in April 1941 to declare that the Nazis had made the hemisphere a bullseye. Late in May, he called for entrance into the European war. America, he said, should immediately fly a thousand planes to Europe and send an equal number of trained pilots. He naturally testified in support of Lend Lease. O'Ryan, however, sought peace with Japan. In June 1940, he even traveled to the Far East as part of a Japanese-sponsored trade mission. Japan, he claimed on his return, was victimized by high tariffs and was experiencing "economic blockade."

Although O'Ryan was a strong believer in collective security, the international enforcement of peace, and an effective world organization to keep aggressors in check, he never developed clear plans for the use of force. His support of the League, the World Court, and intervention, however, clearly reveal his firm belief that the United States could not remain aloof to international responsibilities.

BIBLIOGRAPHY:

NYT 31 Jan 1961, 29; WWWA 4, 723.

Justus D. Doenecke

OTLET, Paul-Marie-Ghislain (23 August 1868, Brussels—10 December 1944, Brussels). *Education*: Coll. Saint-Michel, Univ. de Louvain; degree in law, Univ. Libre de Bruxelles, 1890. *Career*: bibliographer and author.

Otlet's activities covered many domains. Independently wealthy and free to pursue his intellectual propensities, he manifested a global vantage point by early adolescence, when he noted in his diary that he was "embracing the universal and the good for all."

Otlet was a pioneer in bibliography and documentation. With his lifelong collaborator +Henri La Fontaine, he founded the International Office of Bibliography in Brussels (1895). It was envisioned initially as a universal bibliographic repertory of catalog cards on all past and current publications contributed by libraries from all over the world. These were to be organized by the Universal Decimal Classification scheme which Otlet adapted and expanded, and the information pool created was to be shared for the advancement of human knowledge.

But the idea of a world bibliographic center soon expanded in the mind of this universalist visionary to include the collection of artifacts and documents. With the support of the Belgian government, Otlet and his companions proceeded to gather books, periodicals, pamphlets, pictures, and maps, the materials that embodied mankind's intellectual achievements in various fields. These were put on display in a World Museum, part of the World Palace in Brussels, where they symbolized the unity and universality of knowledge.

Recognizing the vital role that national and international scientific and professional associations play in the exchange and diffusion of knowledge, Otlet also convened in 1910 the first World Congress of International Associations, from which the present Union of International Associations emerged as a permanent world body. The Union's offices were installed in the World Palace, along with the International Office of Bibliography, the World Museum, and the World Library. This "Mundaneum," as it later became known, gradually expanded under Otlet's indefatigable work to become a veritable laboratory of "*mondialisme*" and was envisoned by its founder of one day becoming the world's intellectual center to include an international university as well.

All these efforts became only vehicles toward a broader political goal, the ultimate internationalization of mankind. The urgency of this task became all too evident to Otlet with the outbreak of World War I. He began increasingly to concentrate on the political dimension, working in Paris and Switzerland. In several influential publications he presented his ideas about the postwar order and formulated a charter of human rights upon which a supranational confederation of states would be built. Otlet intended these writings to serve as the guiding principles of a league under whose control he wished to place all intellectual and cultural institutions. In a plan submitted to the League of Nations in 1919, Otlet called for the establishment of an "Intellectual League of Nations," its seat in Brussels, The Hague, or Bern, consisting of an international academy of sciences, an international university, a network of scientific research institutes, bibliographical and documentation services, an information dissemination system, and a world congress addressing all varieties of intellectual activity. Only after years of efforts by Otlet, La Fontaine, and others did the League finally create a Commission on Intellectual Co-operation to deal exclusively with cultural and intellectual matters. Otlet prepared a plan for the Commission, but his secret hope that it would adopt his Mundaneum and settle in Brussels was dashed. It was more interested in a center in Paris with a French subsidy. Called the International Institute of Intellectual Co-operation, it was assigned a modest mandate and left Otlet out of its projects.

In subsequent years he suffered many adverse circumstances including the eviction of the Mundaneum from the World Palace and the loss of much of the collection. Otlet continued with his organizational and publishing work in Brussels, bringing out expanded editions of the Universal Decimal Classification and two major treatises, one devoted to the philosophy of internationalism, the other to documentation. Today, the Universal Decimal Classification, the International Federation for Documentation, a linear descendant of the Universal Office of Bibliography, and the Union of International Associations survive as witness to Otlet's farsightedness and his dedication to international cooperation in intellectual and cultural affairs. Moreover, the League's successor, the UN, with its mature system of international organization has actualized in its services and programs many of the ideas and plans originally conceived by Otlet's creative genius.

BIBLIOGRAPHY:

A. *Constitution mondiale de la société des nations; le nouveau droit des gens* (Geneva, 1917); *La Fin de la guerre: Traité de paix générale basé sur une charte mondiale les droits de l'humanité et organisant la confédération des états* (Brussels, 1914); *Les problèmes internationaux et la guerre* (Geneva, 1916); *Monde: Essai d'universalisme; connaissance du monde, sentiment du monde, action organisée et plan du monde* (Brussels, 1935); *Traité de documentation: Le livre sur le livre. Théorie et pratique* (Brussels, 1934).

B. *Biographie nationale* 32 (Brussels, 1964), 545–58; W. Boyd Rayward, *The Universe of Information: The Work of Paul Otlet for Documentation and International Organization* (Moscow, 1975).

C. The Otlet papers are in the Mundaneum.

Michael Keresztesi

OTTESEN-JENSEN, Elise (2 January 1886, Jaeren, Norway—4 September 1973, Stockholm). *Education*: dentistry training, Stavanger, 1904–5; Christiania Business Coll., 1906. *Career*: journalist, Trondheim, 1910–12, Bergen, 1912–15, Copenhagen, 1915–19, Stockholm, 1920s; founder-president, Swedish Association for Sexual Enlightenment, 1932–59; co-founder, International Planned Parenthood Federation, 1952, president, 1959–63.

Imbued with a sense of community responsibility from her Lutheran clerical family and critical of class differences, Ottesen veered politically

558   OTTESEN-JENSEN, ELISE

leftward by 1911 and became a Norwegian labor press journalist. From women industrial workers in Bergen, she learned their primary concern was sexual problems, particularly family limitation. By reading August Forel's *Die sexuelle frage*, she began to acquire an understanding of sexuality which would enable her to counsel workers. Five years after moving with her husband, Swedish syndicalist Albert Jensen, to Stockholm in 1919, she commenced a forty-year lecture career to all parts of Sweden to explain sexuality and give instruction in birth control techniques. She was unique among Swedish family planning pioneers in her tireless fieldwork and in her remarkable ability to convey her sympathetic interest to her audiences.

She attended World League for Sexual Reform conferences in Copenhagen (1928), London (1929), Vienna (1930), and Brünn (1932), and the Seventh International Birth Control Congress in Zurich (1930) hosted by Margaret Sanger, to update her knowledge of sexuality and contraceptive research from the doctors who comprised most of the membership. There was interest in her work among the poor, and she made several friends who survived the Nazi era to become a part of the group she convened in Stockholm in 1946 to restore the international movement.

Meanwhile, a Social Democratic government came to power (1932–66) in Sweden, which by 1942 had introduced sex education in the public schools. The major voluntary organization lobbying in behalf of this and other sexual reforms was the Swedish Association for Sexual Enlightenment (RFSU), of which Ottesen-Jensen was the founder-president (1932–59). With a membership approaching 100,000, extensive clinical services, and a record of political clout, it was the strongest national family planning organization in 1945. Thereupon, Ottesen-Jensen took the initiative to host an international conference in 1946 out of which evolved the International Planned Parenthood Federation by 1952, a development in which she, with Margaret Sanger of the United States and Lady Rama Rau of India, played the key roles. Until the UN agreed in the 1960s to support family planning through agencies like the World Health Organization, the IPPF was the major organization integrating efforts in the field. As vice-president, 1953–58, and president, 1959–63, her innovative efforts included visits to East Germany (1958) and Poland (1959) and the inclusion of abortion reform and sex education on the IPPF agenda. Her most persuasive and persistent themes with international as well as Swedish audiences were those emphasizing "the wanted child" and the obligation of each generation to provide a better future for its children.

BIBLIOGRAPHY:

A. *Livet skrev vidare* (Stockholm 1966); *Och livet skrev* (Stockholm, 1965); articles in *Ny Tid* (Trondheim), 1911–12, *Arbeidet* (Bergen), 1912–14, *Brand* and *Arbetaren* (Stockholm), 1922–37; editorials and articles in RFSU organs, *Populär tidskrift för sexuell upplysning* (1933–36), *Sexual frågan* (1936–49), *Populär tidskrift for psykologi och sexuell kunskap* (1950–59).

B. Elly Jannes, "Förbanna mörkret—tändett ljus!" *Vi* (6 Jan 1973), 10–13; LT 7

Sep 1973, 18; Beryl Suitters, *Be Brave and Angry: Chronicles of the International Planned Parenthood Federation* (London, 1973).

C. The Ottesen-Jensen papers are in the Labor Movement Archives, Stockholm; the IPPF papers are at the Univ. of Cardiff.

Doris H. Linder

OXNAM, Garfield Bromley (14 August 1891, Sonora, CA—12 March 1963, White Plains, NY). *Education*: B.A., Univ. of Southern California, 1913; S.T.B., Boston Univ. School of Theology, 1915; graduate work, Boston Univ., Harvard Univ., MIT. *Career*: minister, Poplar and Los Angeles, CA, 1916–27; prof., Univ. of Southern California, 1919–23, Boston Univ. Theological School, 1927–28; president, DePauw Univ., 1928–36; Methodist bishop 1936–39, Boston, 1939–44, New York, 1944–52, Washington, 1952–60; president, Federal Council of Churches of Christ, 1944–46.

One of the most prominent Protestant leaders of the twentieth century, Oxnam was from his youth a crusader for organized labor, minority groups, and international organizations. Son of an industrialist who encouraged his social awareness, Oxnam spent ten years in Los Angeles urban missions before becoming president of DePauw, where he was prominent for his abolition of ROTC and his admiration of the Marxist experiment in Soviet Russia, which he visited in 1926. A prolific author, he was especially noted for an address delivered in 1935, subsequently published as *Ethical Ideals of Jesus in a Changing World*, in which he used themes from the Social Gospel to insist that in religion, economics, and international affairs the world was moving from disunity, competition, and nationalism toward unity, cooperation, and internationalism. A tragic denial of the solidarity of the human family was war. The key to achieving these ideals was the formula that love rather than force provided the social bond. By 1941, however, Oxnam saw the defeat of Fascism as a needed but tragic act in the basic effort to rebuild a world community based on brotherhood and economic justice.

During and after the war, he became a prominent spokesman for ecumenism and international organization, which he perceived as inseparable. He served on the Federal Council of Church's (FCC) Commission to Study the Bases of a Just and Durable Peace and helped direct the Methodist church toward support of international organization. For example, in January 1944 he was one of four Methodist bishops who stated before a crowd of 2,000 in Brooklyn that the church had to be a force for postwar peace. While president of the FCC, he gained its endorsement for the Dumbarton Oaks proposals and UN membership. He went with two other delegates from the FCC to Germany in the winter of 1945–46 to restore ecclesiastical relations, and he was a presiding officer at the organization of the National Council of Churches in 1950.

Oxnam attended the 1937 international conferences to advance the idea of religious unity and was present at the formation of the World Council of Churches (WCC) in Amsterdam in 1948. He was named one of the six presidents of the organization from 1948–54. Bishop *Henry Knox Sherrill described him as "a dynamic leader" of both the Methodist church and ecumenicalism. No more apt selection for the WCC's presidency could have been made, given the organization's commitment as "a fellowship of churches which accept our Lord Jesus Christ as God and Savior." The WCC was an important channel for the theological renaissance of American and European churches after World War II. In his *The Church and Contemporary Change* (1950), Oxnam posited the WCC as the spiritual leader for a divided world and suggested that without it the United Nations would fail.

BIBLIOGRAPHY:

A. *The Church and Contemporary Change* (New York, 1950); *The Ethical Ideals of Jesus in a Changing World* (New York, 1941); *Facing the Future Unafraid* (New York, 1944); *I Protest* (New York, 1954); *Preaching and the Social Crisis* (New York, 1933); *Preaching in a Revolutionary Age* (New York, 1944); *Russian Impressions* (Los Angeles, 1927).

B. CB 1944, 41–43; DAB supp. 7, 596–98; NCAB G, 234–35; NYT 14 Mar 1963, 16; WWWA 4, 727.

C. Oxnam papers are in the Manuscript Division, Library of Congress, Wesley Theological Seminary, and Drew Univ.

Darrel E. Bigham

P

PADEREWSKI, Ignacy Jan (6 November 1860, Kuryłówka (Podolia), Russian Poland—29 June 1941, New York). *Education*: Warsaw Conservatory of Music, where he studied with Gustaw Roguski and Juliusz Janotha, 1872–78; studied composition with Friedrich Kiel in Berlin, 1882, orchestration with Heinrich Urban, 1883, piano with Theodor Leschetizky in Vienna, 1884–87. *Career*: taught piano, Warsaw Conservatory of Music, 1879–81, 1882–83; taught and performed, Strasbourg Conservatory of Music, 1885–86; concert pianist, 1891–1915; organizer and vice-president, Polish Victims Relief Committee (Vévey Committee), 1914–18; member of and official representative to U.S., Polish National Committee, 1917–18; prime minister and minister of foreign affairs, Poland, 1919; member of Sejm, 1919; delegate, Paris Peace Conference, 1919, Conference of Ambassadors, 1920, League of Nations, 1920–21; resumed concertizing and teaching, 1922–39; member, Front Morges, 1939; president, National Council of Polish government-in-exile, 1940.

World-renowned pianist and composer, Paderewski was dedicated to the resurrection of an independent, united Poland, which had been eliminated by the Partition of 1795. Friend of statesmen, politicians, and royalty, Paderewski's name was synonymous with Poland. A box office sensation, he concertized the world over. The outbreak of World War I, however, brought a temporary end to his music and catapulted him into the political arena. Concerned with the plight of his countrymen, Paderewski, with Henry Sienkiewicz and other Poles in Europe, organized the Vévey Committee headquartered in Switzerland. In April 1915 Paderewski arrived in the United States with a dual mission—to create a government-sponsored relief organization to assist Poles in occupied Polish territories and to unite Polonia in support of its war-devastated brethren. Realizing that the prewar political status quo would never be restored, Paderewski dedicated himself to the creation of a pro-Polish atmosphere and to gaining official recognition of the Polish cause by those who would decide the fate of Europe.

His acquaintance with *Edward M. House, *Woodrow Wilson, and other officials helped determine America's pro-Polish stand, as evidenced in Wilson's Thirteenth Point. The friendship with the president was solidified by Paderewski's concurrence with Wilson's vision of a postwar Europe. A great admirer of the American political system, Paderewski was a firm believer in the concept of a United States of Eastern Europe. He saw federalism as a solution to the conflicting territorial aspirations of the nationalities of the crumbling empires of Austro-Hungary and Russia and hoped to sway the Allies to support this concept. Along with other Eastern European representatives, he joined the Mid-European Democratic Union (1918). Jointly they hoped to develop, prior to the termination of the war, the basis of a peaceful settlement which would consider the emerging conflicting interests in Central Europe. Later as prime minister, he argued that federalism and not direct annexation would guaranty self-determination for those nations that were once part of prepartitioned Poland.

The Armistice ended Paderewski's usefulness in the United States, and he returned to Europe, where, with the support of the Allies, he hoped to reconcile and unify various Polish political groups. A compromise was reached between the two major factions with Józef Piłsudski as chief-of-state, Paderewski as prime minister and minister of foreign affairs, and Roman Dmowski, along with Paderewski, as delegates to the Paris Peace Conference. There Paderewski defended Poland's claims to her former territories while trying to persuade his countrymen to accept the decisions of the Allies. He realized the perturbing situation they faced in trying to sort out their interests in Central and Eastern Europe and the conflicting territorial claims of the emerging states in the area. He opposed the eastern military campaigns (1919) and during the Soviet–Polish war tried to facilitate a cease-fire and an acceptable solution.

While representing Poland at the Conference of Ambassadors and at the League of Nations, Paderewski worked to promote just and peaceful solutions of Poland's territorial boundaries. Criticized for his inability to bring about pro-Polish decisions, especially in the dispute over Lithuania, Paderewski resigned and resumed his musical career. A philanthropist and cosmopolitan humanitarian, he gave concerts for numerous causes, including the veteran organizations of the Allied countries, Jewish refugees from Hitler's Germany, the unemployed during the Depression, the actors' fund, the tuberculosis fund, and others. Paderewski remained on the fringe of politics till his death. With the outbreak of World War II, he resumed his efforts on behalf of occupied Poland and against Fascism. He supported the Polish government-in-exile and accepted the presidency of its National Council. His death and "temporary" burial in the National Cemetery at Arlington became a major American manifestation of opposition to Fascism and injustices committed against Poland.

BIBLIOGRAPHY:

A. *Archiwum Polityczne Ignacego Paderewskïego*, 4 vols., ed. Witold Stakiewicz (Warsaw, 1973–74). *Chopin: A Discourse* (New York, 1911); with Mary Lawton, *Paderewski Memoirs* (New York, 1938); "Poland's So-Called Corridor," *Foreign Affairs* 11 (Apr 1933), 420–33; numerous works for piano, violin, and orchestra.

B. CB 1941, 648–49; *Czy wiesz kto to jest?* (Warsaw, 1938), 548–49; Wladyslaw Doleba, *Paderewski* (Kracòw, 1979); Antoni Gronowicz, *Paderewski: Pianist and Patriot* (Edinburgh, 1943); Rom Landau, *Ignacy Paderewski: Musician and Statesman* (New York, 1934); NYT 23 Nov 1922, 26, 16 Feb 1941, VII-9, 3 Nov 1940, IV-11; *Polski Słownik Biograficzny* 24 (Kraców, 1979), 795–803; Aniela Strakacz, *Paderewski As I Knew Him* (New Brunswick, NJ, 1949); Zofia Sywak, "Paderewski in America," in *Poles in America: Bicentennial Essays* (Stevens Point, WI, 1978).

C. The Paderewski papers are in the Archiwum Akt Nowych Warsaw.

Zofia Sywak

PARANHOS, José Maria da Silva, Jr., the Baron of Rio-Branco (20 April 1845, Rio de Janeiro—10 February 1912, Rio de Janeiro). *Education*: degree, Law Faculty, Recife, 1866. *Career*: professor, Pedro II Coll., 1868; diplomatic mission in Platine region, 1869–70; deputy, Chamber of Deputies, 1869–75; consular service, Liverpool, 1876–91; director, Immigration Service of Brazil in Paris, 1891–93; chief, special arbitration mission to Washington, 1893–95, Bern, 1895–1900; minister to Germany, 1901–2; minister of foreign affairs, 1902–12.

A recent Brazilian president addressing the graduating class of the foreign service school, the Instituto Rio-Branco, observed that to represent Brazil worthily abroad, it was necesssary to have only the teachings of Rio-Branco. Brazilians of the twentieth century regard those teachings as profound. In fact, to understand the diplomacy of the largest Latin American nation during this century it is essential to know the statesman and his work. Born into a distinguished family, Rio-Branco received both the education and experience that destined him for an extraordinary diplomatic career. After service abroad, he assumed the portfolio of foreign affairs in 1902 and held it for a Latin American record of ten years during the administrations of four different presidents. In every respect his tenure was a period of transition, the pivotal point upon which modern foreign policy turned.

His first accomplishment was to settle the 400-year-old boundary disputes between Spanish-speaking and Portuguese-speaking South America by definitively delineating the frontiers. Always insisting on the principle of *uti possidetis*, Rio-Branco won a series of brilliant victories beginning with the arbitration award of the Mission territory made by Grover Cleveland in 1895 ending with the agreement with Peru in 1909. Arbitration settled the boundaries with Argentina and with the South American colonies of France and Great Britain. On a continent where almost all wars and border skirmishes erupted over boundary disputes, the "Golden Chancellor" patiently and peacefully delineated nearly 9000 miles of frontier and bloodlessly won for his country an area larger than France. In that way, he concluded more than four centuries of disputes. Through those settlements, Rio-Branco achieved stability in South America, ensured a greater degree of peace, and ended an era of South American diplomatic history. He declared, "The Brazilian Nation only wants to be known for its desire to work for peace."

The baron also set the course for a new Brazilian foreign policy. Under his direction, Brazil moved to play a new role on the international stage. Rio-Branco's policy here consisted of four related goals. First, he sought to increase national prestige abroad. Nothing revealed the new international interests better than the attitudes toward the two Hague Peace Conferences. Brazil declined an invitation to the first, claiming that no questions of national interest would be discussed. Later, clearly under the influence of Rio-Branco, Brazil not only eagerly accepted an invitation to the second conference but sent one of the largest delegations under the leadership of

*Ruy Barbosa, who spoke with the support of all of Latin America when he demanded the equality of all nations on the arbitration court.

Second, Rio-Branco wanted Brazil to exercise a leadership role in Latin America, especially in South America. Third, he placed a new emphasis on Pan Americanism. He hoped to see a "spirit of cooperation and good will" develop from the periodic conferences. He acted on that hope by settling the various frontiers with Spanish-speaking South America, by eliminating causes for disputes, and by opening the way for better understanding between Spanish and Portuguese America. He also arranged the highly successful Pan-American Conference in Rio de Janeiro in 1906. Debates had stultified the first two meetings. In contrast, the brief and well-planned third session consolidated and gave permanence to the Pan American movement. Rio-Branco also succeeded in harmonizing Spanish America and the United States, notably at the Rio Conference where, thanks largely to his diplomacy, the United States was accepted more by the Latin Americans and old suspicions and resentments were mitigated. Rio-Branco thus gave pragmatic form to the Brazilian sentiments favoring Pan Americanism.

At his fourth foreign policy goal, Rio-Branco closely aligned his country with the United States, thereby shifting Brazil's diplomatic axis from London to Washington because he foresaw that the emerging world power, if properly cultivated, could serve well Brazilian interests. The visit of *Elihu Root to Rio de Janeiro in 1906 climaxed the growing entente between the two giant republics. That foreign policy also constituted an important legacy of Rio-Branco.

BIBLIOGRAPHY:

A. *Obras do Barão de Rio-Branco*, 9 vols. (Rio de Janeiro, 1945–48).

B. E. Bradford Burns, *The Unwritten Alliance: Rio-Branco and Brazilian-American Relations* (New York, 1966); Luiz Viana Filho, *A Vida do Barão do Rio Branco* (Rio de Janeiro, 1959); Frederic W. Ganzert, "José Maria da Silva Paranhos, Baron of Rio-Branco," *Bulletin of the Pan American Union* 71 (Mar 1937), 231–38.

C. Papers related to Rio-Branco can be found in the Archives of the Ministry of Foreign Relations, Itamaratí Palace, Rio de Janeiro.

E. Bradford Burns

PARSONS, Herbert (28 October 1869, New York—16 September 1925, Pittsfield, MA). *Education*: B.A., Yale Univ., 1890; Univ. of Berlin, 1890–91; Harvard Law School, 1891–93. *Career*: attorney, New York, 1895–1925; alderman, 1900–1904; congressman, 1905–10; leader, New York Republican party, 1905–25; U.S. Army, 1917–19.

Parsons established a reputation in his legal and political activities as a man of personal integrity. His brief but prominent role as an internationalist related largely to his reputation as a person of conviction. Parsons supported the League to Enforce Peace (LEP) after 1915 and endorsed the idea in speeches, but his experiences in World War I convinced him of the soundness of the League of Nations. Even though a member of the Republican National Committee (1916–20), he did not allow partisanship to influence his thinking. This was unusual during the great debate over whether the United States should join the League, because internationalists like *William H. Taft and many signers of the Statement of the 31 did allow politics to affect their position.

Parsons' dominant role came during the election of 1920, when he refused to support the Republican presidential candidate, Warren G. Harding. He not only bolted his party over the League issue but also announced his position publicly. He did so by aligning with the Pro-League Independents created by *Irving Fisher and *Hamilton Holt to support *James M. Cox. Because Parsons was considered one of the most powerful and influential leaders of his party, his stand prompted widespread comment. Parsons did not hesitate to castigate his party as "cowardly" or to challenge those Republicans who argued that support for Harding would result in world cooperation. Harding's suggestion for an Association of Nations, said Parsons, was the "bunk," and his talk was "mush." He believed it to be the "highest duty" of citizens to work for membership in the League of Nations because it represented the "one practical opportunity" for peace and disarmament. Parsons continued to support the LEP in the early 1920s, continually striving to keep it loyal to League membership even as he condemned *Woodrow Wilson's intransigence for the failure of the Senate to approve the Treaty of Versailles. He refused to join the nonpartisan efforts to promote League membership because he believed the issue should be faced directly by the parties.

BIBLIOGRAPHY:
B. NCAB 32, 321–22; NYT 17 Sep 1925, 23.
C. The Parsons papers are in the Butler Library, Columbia Univ.

Warren F. Kuehl

PASSY, Frederic. See *Biographical Dictionary of Modern Peace Leaders.*

PASVOLSKY, Leo (28 April 1893, Pavlograd, Russia—5 May 1953, Washington). *Education*: B.A., Coll. of City of New York, 1916; Columbia Univ., 1916–25; Graduate Institute of International Studies, Geneva, 1932–33; Ph.D., Brookings Institution, 1937. *Career*: edited foreign-language publications, 1916–25; reporter, *Brooklyn Eagle, New York Tribune, Baltimore Sun*, 1919–22; staff member, Institute of Economics (later Brookings Institution), 1922–32; economist, U.S. Bureau of Foreign and Domestic Commerce, 1934–35; with State Department, 1935–46; director, International Studies Group, Brookings Institution, 1946–53.

As an economist, analyst of the Soviet Union, and State Department planner, Pasvolsky contributed in a variety of ways to international endeavors. He came with his family to the United States in 1905, but thereafter retained an interest in the land of his birth. He edited publications about Russia, translated books, and wrote studies of the Bolshevik Revolution, in which he recommended openness and flexibility. During his first tenure with the Brookings Institution, he prepared several books on war debts, reparations, and the impact of the Great Depression on the world. Pasvolsky attended the Monetary and Economic Conference in London in 1933 as an expert observer where he presented a paper on a stable international monetary standard. That concept, based on gold, did not materialize because of *Franklin Roosevelt's policies.

Throughout the 1930s Pasvolsky attended a variety of conferences, and he worked closely with *Cordell Hull, after joining the State Department in 1935, in developing Hull's reciprocity trade program. Then in 1939 Hull asked Pasvolsky to become his special assistant to consider "long-range problems bearing on the postwar future." Pasvolsky believed a formal process should be developed; and in 1940 he suggested the establishment of a Division of Special Research, which Hull created early in 1941. Pasvolsky seized the leadership, and his work led inevitably to planning for a new association of nations. In this effort no person played a more important role than Pasvolsky. He created outside advisory groups of political, private, and military leaders and included academics from many disciplines. He then coordinated the work, which resulted in the proposals presented at Dumbarton Oaks in August 1944.

When *Edward Stettinius became secretary of state late that year, he called on Pasvolsky to help prepare for the San Francisco Conference. Pasvolsky chaired the London Preparatory Commission, and at San Francisco, as chairman of a Coordinating Committee on wording, he helped draft the final version of the UN Charter. His most important task lay in reconciling provisions in the Charter with inter-American agreements incorporated into the Act of Chapultepec, which allowed for regional organizations and defense systems. He also contributed to formulating provisions for trusteeships. His "interpretation" of the veto clause also helped break a stalemate between the smaller states and the Big Five who would exercise it. His wording assured the former that the veto would not be used irresponsibly.

He left the State Department in 1946 because he thought his studies there could be assumed by the UN, but his interest continued. Ever involved in international concerns, he was engaged at his death in research on the UN's origin and history.

BIBLIOGRAPHY:

A. *Bulgaria's Economic Position, with Special Reference to the Reparation Problem and the Work of the League of Nations* (Washington, 1930); *Current Monetary Issues* (Washington, 1933); *War Debts and World Prosperity* (New York, 1932).

B. CB 1945, 447–50; DAB supp. 5, 537–38; Robert A Divine, *Second Chance: The Triumph of Internationalism in America During World War II* (New York, 1967); NYT 7 May 1953, 31: Dorothy B. Robins, *Experiment in Democracy: The Story of U.S. Citizen Organizations in Forging the Charter of the United Nations*

(New York, 1971); Ruth B. Russell and Jeanette E. Mather, *A History of the United Nations Charter: The Role of the United States, 1940–1945* (Washington, 1958); WWWA 3, 669.

C. Pasvolsky Office Files of the State Department in the National Archives contain vital material. Pasvolsky papers are in the Manuscript Division, Library of Congress.

Warren F. Kuehl

PAUL-BONCOUR, Joseph (4 August 1873, Saint-Aignan, Loire-et-Cher, France—28 March 1972, Paris). *Education*: Coll. de Pont-Levoy, Coll. Saint-Charles at Saint-Brieuc; doctor of law, Univ. of Paris. *Career*: lawyer, 1895–1960; private secretary to Premier René Waldeck-Rousseau, 1899–1902, Premier René Viviani, 1906–9; deputy from Loire-et-Cher, 1909–31; minister of labor, 1911; minister of war, 1932; premier, 1932–33; minister of foreign affairs, 1932–34, 1938; delegate, League of Nations, 1924–26, 1932–36; delegate, Consultative Assembly, 1944; head, French delegation to San Francisco Conference, 1945; *conseilleur* of the Republic, 1946–48.

Lawyer, orator, deputy, minister in several French cabinets between 1911 and 1938, Paul-Boncour reached the pinnacle of his political career as minister of foreign affairs from 1932 to 1934 and again in 1938. During his first stewardship of the Quai d'Orsay, Paul-Boncour was instrumental in attempting to revive an Anglo–Franco–Italian coalition against the Nazi threat, a strategy which eventually proved abortive. Fundamentally an independent within the complex party structure of the Third Republic, Paul-Boncour joined the Socialist party in 1919 and remained a member for twelve years. He resigned his affiliation in 1931 following disgruntlement at his service to bourgeois governments as France's delegate to the League of Nations.

His interest in the concept of a world organization for the regulation of international relations dates from the founding of the League of Nations. He was sent to Geneva as a member of the French delegation, a position he maintained throughout most of the interwar years. Subsequently, he made important contributions to the Dumbarton Oaks and San Francisco Conferences which inaugurated the United Nations. Throughout this period, Paul-Boncour's fundamental concern was to buttress collective security with a viable enforcement mechanism.

In 1924 he vigorously championed the Geneva Protocol, the spirit of which governed all of his subsequent crusades to establish a potent world organization. The Protocol stipulated that states would agree to submit disputes to arbitration. Aggression was defined as the refusal to accept arbitration or the verdict of it. If aggression should occur, a majority of two-thirds of the Council would agree upon sanctions against the aggressor, a decision binding on all League members. The formula received unanimous endorsement in the Assembly and was ratified by France and many other states. The failure to secure endorsement from England's Conservative government doomed the Protocol and ensured that the League would face the 1930s without effective enforcement procedures.

Paul-Boncour thus raised the issue of effective force early in planning for the League's successor in 1945. His critique of the Dumbarton Oaks proposals lamented the predominance assured the great powers by their veto prerogative, but he was realistic enough to accept its inevitability. At the San Francisco Conference, he advocated a permanent international armed force. His proposals, many of which were incorporated into the Charter, equip the UN with a military potential beyond that of the Geneva institution. Its effective use, however, requires the unanimous approval of the five permanent members of the Security Council.

BIBLIOGRAPHY:

A. *Entre deux guerres, souvenirs sur la IIIe république*, 3 vols. (Paris, 1945–46); *Lamennais, précurseur et martyr* (Paris, 1928); *Le Fédéralisme économique, étude sur le syndicat obligatoire* (Paris, 1900); *Les Syndicats de fonctionnaires* (Paris, 1906); *Trois plaidoiries* (Paris, 1934); *Un débat nouveau sur la République et la décentralisation* (Toulouse, France, 1904).

B. CB 1945, 453–57; LT 1 Apr 1972, 16; NYT 30 Mar 1972, 40.

C. The diplomatic papers of Paul-Boncour are at the Archives du Ministère des Affaires Étrangères.

William I. Shorrock

PEARSON, Lester Bowles (23 April 1897, Toronto—27 December 1972, Rockcliffe, ON). *Education*: graduate, Univ. of Toronto, 1919, Oxford Univ., 1924. *Career*: Canadian Army and Royal Flying Corps, 1915–19; lecturer and assistant professor, Univ. of Toronto, 1924–28; civil servant, Department of External Affairs, 1928–48; ambassador to United States, 1945–46; under secretary of state, 1946–48; secretary of state for external affairs, 1948–57; leader, Liberal party, 1958–68; leader of the opposition, 1958–63; prime minister, 1963–68; Nobel Peace Prize, 1957.

The product of a traditional and colonial upbringing in a Methodist manse in rural Ontario, Pearson might not have seemed destined to a career in international relations. But, uprooted by service in World War I, he found it difficult to reconcile himself to the more normal career that his background seemed to indicate. A more stimulating environment and higher salary lured him away from undergraduate teaching to a post in Canada's fledgling Department of External Affairs, largely preoccupied in the 1920s and 1930s with asserting Canada's international identity, particularly its right to be left on the sidelines of Britain's international quarrels. Pearson was by the 1930s a middle-ranking diplomat in London, bound by department policies but often distressed to see Canada standing aside when collective security was threatened and the League of Nations brought into disrepute. From his experiences, Pearson derived a deep conviction that only through international cooperation and a sense of collective responsibility could aggression be halted and peace be maintained. Though tempted by the easy nostrum of isolationism, Pearson eventually determined that Britain's approaching conflict with Germany would range the forces for decency against those of the new barbarism.

After Canada declared war on Germany in 1939, Pearson served in London for two years; then, after a brief stint in Ottawa, he was posted to the Canadian mission to Washington, first as minister-counselor and then as ambassador. With many of his American counterparts, he looked forward to a postwar world in which many of the evils of the 1930s would be expunged: "beggar-my-neighbor" trade and monetary policies, parochial isolationism, and the arms race. Pearson was convinced that Canada had much to contribute. He played a prominent role at the foundation of the UN Relief and Rehabilitation Administration in 1943, and while the great powers drew up the blueprints for the later UN he lingered outside, speaking against the great power veto. At the San Francisco Conference, 1945, Pearson played a prominent part in his country's efforts to protect the autonomy of smaller nations against the exigencies of the great powers in the Security Council.

In 1946 Pearson became under secretary of state for external affairs, the professional head of his department. Canada's policy had three principal foci: a close harmony of interests among the liberal democratic societies around the North Atlantic; the traditions and linkages of the British Commonwealth; and the newer, untried institutions of the UN. Though distressed by the divergence between the West and the Soviet Union, Pearson accepted it as inevitable and strongly supported measures for a strong collective defense to deter Soviet aggression. The West would simply have to outlast the Soviet Union in the hope that the Soviet dictatorship would disintegrate. Since the UN could not do the job, short of expelling the Soviet Union, Pearson urged the acceptance of NATO. Pearson's preference went beyond military security pure and simple. If NATO were to endure, its members should have common institutions (thus excluding a dictatorship like Portugal) and strive for cultural community and economic cooperation. Though Pearson's arguments were partially embodied in the North Atlantic Treaty's Article II, that clause remained a virtual dead letter.

As for the Commonwealth, Pearson attempted to use it as a forum for bringing together the newer nations of Asia and Africa with Canada and like-minded Western partners. The Canadian delegation to the UN received instructions to encourage as far as possible cooperation between the developing world and the Western powers. During the 1950s, however, Canadian policy also remained firmly anchored to Anglo–American accord. The Suez Crisis of 1956 gave Pearson a chance to bring all his policies into an effective alignment. Acting to preserve the Commonwealth, to sustain the rule of international law, to reconcile Britain and the United States, and to avoid a dangerous confrontation between former colonialists and their former colonial subjects, Pearson succeeded in piloting a proposal for an international peacekeeping force through the UN in November. For his achievement he was awarded the Nobel Peace Prize in 1957, but by the time he received that honor he was out of office, partly because the Canadian electorate failed to share his enthusiasm for international action when it was directed against the short-term interests of Britain and France, Canada's two mother countries.

In 1958 Pearson became leader of the Canadian Liberal party, and five years later he led it to victory in a general election. Now prime minister, Pearson attempted to pursue the same policies as earlier, and with some success. A peace force, with Canadian participation, was sent to Cyprus. Then, in 1967, the United Nations Emergency Force in the Sinai was ordered out of Egypt. Pearson protested that the UN authorities had capitulated to pressure and had acted hastily and wrongly; by their actions they had discredited the possibility of collective international actions in like situations in the future. Pearson also faced considerable difficulty in dealing with President Lyndon B. Johnson, whose Vietnamese policy he considered foolish and wasteful; Johnson contended that Pearson's proposals for mediation or a bombing halt were tantamount to surrender. Unsuccessful over Vietnam, Pearson had mounting political difficulties at home, where his domestic policies concentrated on ways and means of conceding enough to French Canadians to keep them happy inside Canada.

Retiring in 1968, Pearson performed one final international service, acting as chairman of a World Bank Commission on International Development. He had accepted the task "because I believe no problem to be more important to the future of the world." As for that future, Pearson by the end of his life was mildly pessimistic, confessing that "the dark" of humanity's "fears and hates" was matched only by "a declining public commitment to new international responsibilities."

BIBLIOGRAPHY:

A. *Mike: The Memoirs of the Rt. Hon. Lester B. Pearson*, 3 vols. (Toronto, 1972–75); *Peace in the Family of Man* (London, 1969); *Words and Occasions* (Toronto, 1970).

B. Robert Bothwell, *Pearson: His Life and World* (Toronto, 1978); Bruce Thordarson, *Lester Pearson: Diplomat and Politician* (Toronto, 1974).

C. Pearson papers are in the Public Archives of Canada.

Robert Bothwell

PEASLEE, Amos Jenkins (24 March 1887, Clarksboro, NJ—29 August 1969, Clarksboro). *Education*: B.A., Swarthmore Coll., 1907; Birmingham Univ., England, 1907–8; LL.B., Columbia Law School, 1911. *Career*: law practice in New York, 1911–17, 1919–41, 1945–53; wartime assignments, 1917–18, 1941–45; with American Peace Commission, Paris, 1919; ambassador to Australia, 1953–56; presidential assistant, Eisenhower administration, 1956–59; adviser, U.S. delegation to UN, 1957.

Like many internationalists, Peaslee's exposure to ideas came from study abroad and his assignment to the American Peace Commission in Paris, where he directed the diplomatic and courier service. He also took an interest in the drafting of the Covenant and made suggestions, following its initial draft, for a more elaborate judicial system. That became his particular focus during the interwar years in speeches, essays, and articles in both popular magazines and newspapers and law journals. Peaslee sought to advance general principles of international law. He served as president of the American Branch of the International Law Association (1922) and as the first secretary-general of the International Bar Association (1947–53).

During World War II, Peaslee became an enthusiastic supporter of the UN idea. He joined others in campaigning for its creation and wrote two books to promote not only the UN but the concept of international organization. His knowledge and commitment led Dwight Eisenhower to appoint him as a deputy special assistant to the president (1956–59) on international law and organization matters. While accepting service in both world wars, Peaslee also showed an interest in peace. While not a believer in nonviolent pacifism, he was a member of the Society of Friends because he saw the ideal of peace had to be advanced in an essentially conflict-oriented world. He thus served as president of the American Peace Society and represented the United States at London disarmament sessions in 1957. In his will, Peaslee provided for a foundation to continue those international efforts to which he had shown devotion.

BIBLIOGRAPHY:

A. *Constitutions of Nations*, 2nd ed., 3 vols. (Concord, NH, 1956); *A Permanent United Nations* (New York, 1942); *Proposed Amendments to Judiciary Articles of the League of Nations* (Paris, 1919); *United Nations Government* (New York, 1945).

B. NCAB E, 320–21; NYT 30 Aug 1969, 21; WWWA, 561.

Warren F. Kuehl

PECK, Lillie M. (28 December 1888, Gloversville, NY—21 February 1957, New York). *Education*: B.S., Simmons Coll., 1913. *Career*: assistant secretary and later secretary, Boston Social Union, 1913–24; fellow, National Federation of Settlements, 1924–26; secretary, Boston Social Union, 1926–28; assistant headworker, South End House, 1928–30; assistant to head, University Settlement, New York, 1930–34; executive secretary, National Federation of Settlements, 1934–47; secretary for international work, National Federation of Settlements, 1947–57.

Peck worked to strengthen the international ties among settlement workers and to develop settlement houses abroad and in the United States. Settlements met the needs of their neighborhoods through educational, recreational programs and support for reforms. U.S. houses also helped immigrants assimilate to American culture. Peck, the daughter of a German immigrant, was fluent in German.

Along with well-to-do Boston settlement worker Ellen Coolidge, Peck founded the International Federation of Settlements (1922). She devoted two years (1924–26) to helping European settlements form national federations for the Second International Conference of Settlements in Paris (1926). During the Great Depression and World War II, Peck concentrated on American work as executive secretary of the National Federation of Settlements. However, she managed to attend international conferences in 1927, 1932, and 1936.

In 1947, Peck resumed active involvement on the international level when she resigned as executive secretary of the National Federation of Settlements to concentrate on that organization's world work. She spent a year studying the English community center movement. The Nazis had suspended settlement houses, and Peck also worked to revive the activities there. During the 1949 Berlin Blockade, she served two months with the Civil Affairs Division of the Military Government studying settlement houses and working with German social welfare leaders. Then, during 1951–52, she established and directed a model settlement house in Bremen.

While abroad, Peck also resumed her activities with the International Federation of Settlements and became its president in 1947. Under her leadership, in 1952, it gained consultative status with the United Nations. From 1952 to 1957 she was its delegate to the UN Economic and Social Council and participated in many meetings which sought to raise living standards. Peck saw similarities between the settlement house efforts to improve their neighborhoods and the UN community development programs and thought that both could learn from each other's experiences.

More than any other American settlement house leader, Peck possessed an international outlook. As a resident at Henry Street Settlement, she welcomed numerous foreign visitors. Both the U.S. State Department and Atlantique, an organization devoted to American and French professional exchanges, had Peck plan settlement house itineraries for foreign visitors. Peck's great gift was her ability to get settlement house leaders to work together and to coordinate their efforts so that they might have greater impact on both the national and international scene.

BIBLIOGRAPHY:

A. With Helen Morton, "International Conference of Settlements," *Social Worker* 4 (Dec 1927), 15–17; "Robert A. Woods," *Die Eiche*, year 13, no. 2 (1925), 210; "The Soziale Arbeitsgemeinschaft," *Neighborhood* 1 (Jan and Apr 1928), 14–22, 57–65; "Thumbs in the Dyke: How Neighborhood Houses Aid in the Recovery of Holland," *Survey Graphic* 36 (Feb 1947), 156–58, 174.

B. DAB supp. 6, 499–500; Helen Hall, *Unfinished Business in Neighborhood and Nation* (New York, 1971); Judith Ann Trolander, *Settlement Houses and the Great Depression* (Detroit, MI, 1975).

Judith Ann Trolander

PEI, Mario Andrew (16 February 1901, Rome—2 March 1978, Glen Ridge, NJ). *Education*: B.A., City College of New York, 1925; Ph.D., Columbia Univ., 1932. *Career*: instructor, City Coll., 1923–37; assistant to full professor, Columbia Univ., 1937-70; consultant and lecturer, U.S. Army School, Monterey, CA, 1960; NATO lecturer, Univ. of Lisbon, 1961; visiting professor, Univ. of Pittsburgh, 1962-63, Seton Hall Univ., 1970-72.

The vast range of Pei's interests have gone far beyond the scope of philology, linguistics, and language in general, as reflected in his phenomenally rich production. His understanding of man and his universe gained through lifelong research into the nature of language, and his stimulating, pioneering, and valuable publications rank him among the foremost linguists of his day. His epoch-making study on *The Language of Eighth-Century Texts in Northern France* (1932), which noted the intimate relationship between the written and spoken language in Merovingian Gaul by underscoring that scribal errors in documents do not occur in a haphazard and illogical manner but tend in definite directions as manifestations of the new Romance tongue, is still widely cited.

As a true linguist, Pei was deeply interested in and concerned with the problem of an international language, for which he advanced eloquent arguments in his major publication on this issue, *One Language for the World* (1958). His point was not whether it would be better to have a constructed language or a national tongue for international use, or whether English would serve the purpose better than French, or Interlingua better than Esperanto. The question was whether it would be desirable to set aside a language, *any* language, for universal use by all inhabitants of the earth or, at a minimum, by those who have access to schooling. Pei was not guided by considerations of frequently advanced claims that an international language would lead to greater understanding, friendship, and peace among nations. History had shown this was not necessarily so; rather, he viewed the problem of an international language purely as a tool. Would we be able to communicate better with such a tool, and would it facilitate our international activities? These were the kinds of questions Pei raised. He was aware, however, of the enormous odds against the adoption of any international language under present political conditions. Despite all the lip service paid to the spirit of internationalism, few governments, Pei felt, truly favor such a spirit and, hence, an international language.

The record of Pei's many distinguished contributions would not be complete without mentioning his pioneering work in the field of geolinguistics, the study of the interplay of history, geography, and demography on languge, whose aims and methods he set down in his *Invitation to Linguisitics* (1965). He was also the founder of the American Society of Geolinguistics, a professional organization devoted to propagating the aims of this new branch of linguistic science.

BIBLIOGRAPHY:

A. *The Families of Words* (New York, 1962); *Glossary of Linguistic Terminology* (New York, 1966); *The Italian Language* (New York, 1941); *The Story of English*

(New York, 1952, 1967); *The Story of Language* (New York, 1949; rev. ed., 1965); *The Story of Latin and the Romance Languages* (New York, 1976); *Studies in Romance Philology and Literature* (Chapel Hill, NC, 1963); *The World's Chief Languages* (New York, 1947).

B. John Fisher and Paul A. Gaeng, eds., *Studies in Honor of Mario A. Pei* (Chapel Hill, NC, 1972), with a partial listing of Pei's many writings, 213–22; Gaeng, "In Memorium: Mario A. Pei," *Italica* 55 (Summer, 1978), 298–300; NYT 5 Mar 1978, 36.

C. The Pei papers are in the Department of Special Collections, Boston Univ.

Paul A. Gaeng

PESSÔA, Epitácio Lindolfo da Silva (23 May 1865, Umbuzeiro, Paraíba, Brazil—13 February 1942, Nova Betania, Rio de Janeiro). *Education*: graduate, Law Faculty, Recife, Pernambuco, 1888, Ph.D., 1891. *Career*: federal deputy from Paraíba, 1890–93; professor, Law Faculty, Recife, 1891–1902; federal minister of justice and interior, 1898–1901; federal senator from Paraíba, 1912–19, 1924–30; president, 1919–22; judge, Permanent Court of International Justice, 1923–30.

Pessôa's public career paralleled the Brazilian drive to secure international prestige and respectability that began with the Baron of Rio-Branco, *José Paranhos. Though he attained power and influence, he did not appear to seek it. It was said of him that he was a man who did not seek or avoid greatness. In 1912 he prepared at Rio-Branco's request Brazilian proposals for the Pan American code of law and served as president of the board that prepared the codes for the Pan American Union. This body of law would be discussed at the Santiago conference of 1923 and take final form under Pessôa's chairmanship in 1927. Representing Brazil at the Paris Peace Conference, he argued for the equality of nations and continental representation on each committee. Chosen president of Brazil in the midst of the Conference, he had the honor of leading Brazil into the League of Nations. The favorable impression of Brazilians that he, and *Ruy Barbosa before him, created among Europeans contributed to Brazil securing election to the League Council in 1920 and 1926. During his presidency, he sent representatives to the first International Conference on Labor and to various postal and weights and measures conferences, and he oversaw the demarcation of borders with Uruguay and Peru. His government also facilitated immigration into Brazil, especially from Japan and Germany. The contracting of military and naval missions from France and the United States signaled closer ties to those powers and their conceptions of world order.

In 1923 he was elected to succeed Barbosa on the World Court. His sensitivity to the Court's importance for the security of small countries was evident in his positions carefully written in French. His government so valued his role and that of the Court that, even when Brazil withdrew from the League in 1926, it rejected his suggestion that he resign. In Brazilian history, his name is permanently linked to Versailles, the League, and the World Court, symbolic of Brazil's commitment to peaceful arbitration of international disputes.

BIBLIOGRAPHY:

A. *Obras Completas* (Rio de Janeiro, 1965).

B. NYT 14 Feb 1942, 15; Laurita Pessôa Raja Gabáglia, *Epitácio Pessôa (1865-1942)*, 2 vols. (Rio de Janeiro, 1951); WWLA 1940, 392-93.

Frank D. McCann

PHELAN, Edward Joseph (25 July 1888, Tramore, Waterford, Ireland—15 September 1967, Creux-de-Genthod, Geneva). *Education*: B.A., M.Sc., Univ. of Liverpool, 1911. *Career*: British civil service, 1911–19; with mission to Russia, 1918; member, Labor Section, British delegation, Paris Peace Conference, 1919; helped organize and served as secretary, First Conference of the International Labor Organization (ILO), Washington, 1919; first official, ILO, 1919, head, Diplomatic Division, 1920–33, assistant director, 1933–38, deputy director, 1938–41, acting director, 1941–46, director-general, 1946–48, retroactive as from 1941.

While seeking to promote world peace by creating the League of Nations as a forum in which political issues between states could be discussed and, with luck, settled, the participants in the Paris Peace Conference realized there could be no lasting peace in the absence of social and economic justice, both within and between states. Phelan was one of the first to perceive how, in practice, such justice could be most effectively fostered through voluntary collaboration, on a worldwide basis, among governments, employers, and workers. His ideas largely inspired the British delegation's proposals which resulted in Chapter 8 of the Versailles Peace Treaty establishing the International Labor Organization. It was, therefore, only natural that *Albert Thomas, on becoming director of the newly created International Labor Office, should invite Phelan to become the first official of the ILO.

Phelan brought to the ILO a perceptive mind and a practical idealism, qualities which were to stand him in good stead when, upon the sudden departure of ILO director *John G. Winant in 1941 to become U.S. ambassador in Great Britain, Phelan found himself the senior official left to face unprecedented political, financial, and administrative problems brought on by the war. Throughout his period in charge of the Office, whether working from Montreal during the war years or later back at Geneva, he was active in preparing the ILO for the enhanced role which he foresaw it should fulfill to further social and economic justice. A ringing restatement by Phelan of the ILO's principles and aims forms the essence of the Declaration of Philadelphia, adopted by the International Labor Conference in 1944, and now part of the ILO Constitution. For the practical achievement of those aims, Phelan took action in numerous areas. First, he achieved financial autonomy for the ILO from the UN, something it had not possessed under the League of Nations. Second, by arranging for the ILO to become the first specialized agency of the UN, he won international recognition for the unique role it could play in coordinated action for a better world. Finally, he led in proclaiming and safeguarding basic human rights, saw to the setting up of tripartite committees to tackle the problems of the major world industries, and was active in creating new machinery to cope with the problems of different regions of the globe, ranging from the reconstruction of war-ravaged economies to the social and economic development of the poorer countries. When he retired, the ILO was able to face the tasks ahead with vigor and competence.

BIBLIOGRAPHY:

A. "After Pearl Harbour—ILO Problems," *Studies* 45 no. 182 (1957), 193–206; "The ILO Sets Up Its Wartime Centre in Canada," *Studies* 44, no. 174 (1955), 152–70; "The ILO Turns the Corner," *Studies* 45, no. 178 (1956), 160–86; "The International Labour Organisation, Its Ideals and Results," *Studies* 14, no. 56 (1925), 611–22; *The Necessity for International Labour Organisation* (London, 1923); "Some Reminiscences of the International Labour Organisation," *Studies* 44, no. 171 (1954), 241–70; "The United States and the International Labor Organization," *Political Science Quarterly* 1 (Mar 1935), 107–21; *Yes and Albert Thomas* (London, 1936).

B. CB 1947, 510–12; John Stearns Gillespie, "The Role of the Director in the Development of the International Labour Organisation," dissertation, Columbia Univ., 1956; LT 16 Sep 1967, 12.

C. Phelan's memoirs are in the ILO Library.

Michael O'Callaghan

PHILIP, André (28 June 1902, Pont-Saint-Esprit, France—6 July 1970, Paris). *Education*: doctor of laws, Univ. of Paris, 1924. *Career*: professor, Univ. of Lyon, 1928–42; member, Chamber of Deputies, 1936–40, 1946–51; member, First Constitutent Assembly of Fourth Republic, 1945–46; interior minister, Provisional Government, 1942–44; finance minister, 1946–47; chief, French delegation to U.N. Economic Commission for Europe, 1947–51; member, European Consultative Assembly, 1949–51; president, Socialist Movement for the United States of Europe, 1950–64; chief, French delegation to U.N. Conference on Trade and Development, 1964; president, Center for Development of the Organization for Economic Cooperation and Development, 1967–70; professor, Univ. of Paris, 1952–70.

Philip traveled widely in the 1920s and 1930s, becoming associated for a time with Gandhi and Tagore in India, lecturing in the United States for the World Alliance for International Friendship Through the Churches and the Institute of International Education, studying the labor movement in England, and producing significant works based on his experiences in each of these countries. Following France's defeat in 1940, he became actively involved in the Resistance until forced to flee abroad in 1942. As the end of the war approached, he shared the optimism on the Left that peace would bring both European unity and Socialism, and he met as early as 1945 with other European federalists to discuss plans.

Philip was, however, very much a pragmatist, and in 1948 he played a central role in transforming the strongly partisan committee for the Socialist United States of Europe into the Socialist Movement for the United States of Europe, which advocated working with non-Socialist groups to achieve European unity. Moreover, his stance, which was formally endorsed by the French Socialist Party (SFIO) in 1949, placed great emphasis upon the need for Europe to achieve economic unity in order to avoid becoming a satellite of the United States or the Soviet Union, a point of view echoed by many capitalist economists. Europeans could hope to secure sufficient autonomy to pursue independent social and economic policies, he argued, only within the context of a market of more than 200 million people.

Despite his fears of American domination, Philip endorsed the Marshall Plan as a means of modernizing the European economy and as a major step toward European unity. He was also convinced that progress toward a United States of Europe would help solve the problem posed by a revitalized and potentially aggressive Germany. He advanced a "functional" form of integration with a gradual extension of cooperation into all areas of life. He strongly supported the proposed European Defense Community, and its defeat in 1954 by the French National Assembly, in part by Socialist votes, was a major blow to his hopes. He was expelled from the SFIO in 1957 after bitterly criticizing the party and in particular the policies of the government of *Guy Mollet in Algeria and the Middle East. After briefly participating in the leadership of the small Socialist Unity party (1960–62), Philip withdrew from active involvement in partisan politics but continued to support the European idea in his writings, speeches, and organizational activities. Philip also blended his Christian and Socialist beliefs and from 1967 until his death showed a concern with conditions in developing countries. This led to his acceptance of the presidency in 1967 of the Center for Development of the Organization for Economic Cooperation and Development.

BIBLIOGRAPHY:

A. *Histoire des faits économiques et sociaux de 1800 à nos jours* (Paris, 1963); *Le Christianisme et la paix* (Paris, 1932); *Le Socialisme trahi* (Paris, 1957); *L'Europe unie et sa place dans l'économie international* (Paris, 1953).

B. CB 1943, 585–87; Byron Criddle, *Socialists and European Integration* (New York, 1969); *Dictionnaire biographique français contemporain* 2 (Paris, 1954), 528; IWW 1969–70, 1174; R. C. Mowat, *Creating the European Community* (London, 1973); NYT 7 Jul 1970, 39; WWF 1969–70, 1169.

Kenneth R. Calkins

PHILLIMORE, Walter George Frank (21 November 1845, London—13 March 1929, London). *Education*: Christ Church and All Souls Coll. Oxford Univ. *Career*: barrister; mayor of Kensington, 1909–11; lord justice of appeal, 1913–16; privy councilor, House of Lords, 1918–29.

Phillimore, a prominent British ecclesiastical lawyer, judge, and international jurist, in early 1918 was chosen by the British government to chair a committee charged with examining schemes for a league of nations currently before the public, and, if possible, recommending one of its own devising. Phillimore was selected for this task not only because of his reputation and experience in the field of international law but also because of the publication in 1917 of his *Three Centuries of Treaties of Peace and Their Teaching*, which presented a comparative analysis of modern European peace treaties with a view to determining which of their features had either contributed to enduring peace or sown the seeds of future conflict.

A principal feature, however, of Phillimore's book concerned clarification and extension of both international law on belligerent–neutral relations and humanitarian conventions on the conduct of warfare. Phillimore also addressed the crucial problem of preventing future wars. His principal recommendation was that standing tribunals of arbitration, mediation, or advice be established, with nations having the right to appeal for consideration of disputes and all states being required to submit disputes to attempted peaceful resolution before resorting to hostilities. Phillimore advanced beyond the prewar Hague system and arbitral agreements by recommending that participating states enforce international law and the peaceful settlement of disputes by a system of sanctions—diplomatic, economic, and military—against transgressors.

The question of guarantees, sanctions, and enforcement was central to the debate of the league of nations idea by 1917, and when the Phillimore Committee studied proposals in 1918, its report reflected the thinking of its chairman. In the scheme proposed by the committee an "alliance" of peaceful states would agree "collectively and separately" not to go to war with another allied state "(a) without previously submitting the matter in dispute to arbitration or to a Conference of the Allied States; and (b) until there had been an award or report by the Conference." Nor would participating states go to war with another member which had complied with the award or recommendations made by the conference. If any allied state should violate these commitments, "This State will become *ipso facto* at war with all the other Allied States, and the latter agree to take and to support each other in taking jointly and severally all such measure—military, naval, financial, and economic—as will best avail for restraining the breach of covenant." This reflected the thinking of groups in England and the United States, but Phillimore's hand in shaping the report can be seen in the provisions for handling judicial or legal disputes as distinct from political issues.

Although the Phillimore plan was never endorsed by the British government, its central features had a major impact in official circles in both Britain and the United States. While *Woodrow Wilson considered the Phillimore plan defective in certain respects, its principal recommendations were incorporated into American and British drafts at Paris, and much of its language as well as substance can be seen in the final Covenant of the League of Nations. In late 1918 Phillimore wrote the Foreign Office hand-book on peace schemes for purposes of briefing British representatives at the peace conference.

Phillimore also played an influential role in 1920 in designing the Pro-tocol of the Permanent Court of International Justice at The Hague. He would be a leading international jurist in the 1920s, and he served as presi-dent of the International Law Association, 1919–20.

BIBLIOGRAPHY:

A. *Schemes for Maintaining General Peace*, Foreign Office Handbook, no. 160 (London, 1920); *Three Centuries of Treaties of Peace and Their Teaching* (London, 1917).

B. DNB 1922–30, 677–79; George W. Egerton, *Great Britain and the Creation of the League of Nations* (Chapel Hill, NC, 1979); LT 14 Mar 1929, 21; NYT 14 Mar 1929, 27; WWW 1929–40, 1073.

George W. Egerton

PHRANGOULES, A. P. See *Frangulis, Antoine -F.*

PIECYŃSKI, Valerian Johannes. See Wanderwell, Walter.

PISTOCCHI, Mario (no records available regarding birth, death, or educa-tion). *Career*: A leader of the Italian Republican party in exile in France during Fascist dictatorship; writer on European federation.

Pistocchi was a leader of the Italian Republican party (PRI) at the time Premier Benito Mussolini outlawed non-Fascist Italian political parties and established his totalitarian dictatorship in 1925–26. Pistocchi escaped to France, where he joined several political refugees whom Mussolini deprived of Italian citizenship in 1926. Pistocchi helped such other émigrés as Eugenio Chiesa, Cipriano Facchinetti, Egidio Reale, Randolfo Pacciardi, and Giuseppe Chiostergi to reorganize their Mazzinian party abroad. He also contributed to the anti-Fascist Italian newspaper, *Corriere degli Italiani*, published in Paris in 1926–27.

Pistocchi also revealed an interest in European federation, which he presented in a 190-page book, *Le Destin de l'Europe*. It won second prize in a world competition sponsored by the *Revue des vivants*, and it was pub-lished in Paris in 1931 by Editions Eugène Figuière. Discussing it in his Paris newspaper, *La Liberté*, Claudio Treves, a democratic Socialist Italian exile, wrote on 29 October 1931, "We hope that the DESTINY of EUROPE will be as sensible and full of realistic idealism as that set forth in the book."

According to a well-informed historian of the anti-Fascist emigration,

Aldo Garosci, there is evidence that Pistocchi became an informer to the Italian Fascist police by World War II.

BIBLIOGRAPHY:

A. *Le Destin de l'Europe* (Paris, 1931).

B. Aldo Garosci, *Storia dei fuorusciti* (Bari, Italy, 1953).

Charles F. Delzell

PIVERT, Marceau. See *Biographical Dictionary of Modern Peace Leaders*.

PLANAS SUÁREZ, Simón (14 December 1879—2 March 1967, Caracas). *Education*: unknown. *Career*: diplomat, 1904–24; author.

Planas Suárez served his country as a diplomat and an authority on international law and international relations. Long a resident in Europe, his primary contributions are in his publications on international law. His particular interest focused on a general treatment of international public law and the question of diplomatic asylum. A member of a distinguished Venezuelan family from the state of Barquisimeto, his grandfather, Simón Planas, cosigned the law that liberated black slaves in Venezuela in 1854. Between 1904 and 1925, Planas Suárez served as the Venezuelan minister plenipotentiary before the governments of Austria, Italy, Greece, Holland, Hungary, Portugal, Romania, and Yugoslavia. In 1907 the government of Nicaragua recognized his diplomatic abilities by naming him that country's representative in Venezuela.

Perhaps his most important contributions in the area of scholarship include some twenty-four titles published between 1903 and 1961 covering a wide range of topics, mostly related to international law and international relations. These works earned Planas Suárez recognition from honorary and scholarly societies in America and Europe. He was a member of the Institute of International Law and professor of the Academy of International Law at The Hague.

BIBLIOGRAPHY:

A. *El asilo diplomático: Estudio jurídico y político internacional* (Buenos Aires, 1953); *La política europea y la Sociedad de las naciones: Una advertencia a la América* (Barcelona, 1935); *Les Principes americains de politique internationale et la doctrine de Monroe* (Basel, 1960); *Tratado de derecho internacional público*, 2 vols. (Madrid, 1916).

B. *Diccionario biográfico de Venezuela* (Madrid, 1953), 926; WWLA 1951, 141.

John V. Lombardi

POLITIS, Nicholas Socrate (1872, Greece—5 March 1942, Cannes, France). *Education*: doctor of laws and doctor of political science. *Career*: professor, Aix-en-Provence Univ., 1899–1903, Univ. of Poitiers, 1903–10, Univ. of Paris, 1910–14; permanent secretary-general, Ministry of Foreign Affairs of Greece, 1914–16; minister of foreign affairs, 1916–20, 1922,

1936; delegate to League of Nations, 1920–37, president of Assembly, 1932; minister to France, 1924–25, 1937–40.

Politis, a specialist in international law and arbitration, was appointed professor of international law at Aix-en-Provence University in 1899, and he moved to Poitiers in 1903 and to the University of Paris in 1910. With the outbreak of World War I, he returned to Greece, where he held key foreign affairs posts. When the victorious nations gathered in 1919, Politis was the Greek representative at the Conference.

After the establishment of the League of Nations, Politis served for many years as a Greek delegate, laboring constantly to keep peace. He became noted for his speeches on international arbitration, believing, as he often said, that it often succeeded when it involved matters of equity, but it usually failed when applied to questions of right and wrong. While serving the League, he was a representative of Greece in her noted dispute with Italy in 1923 over the island of Corfu, where he assumed a conciliatory position during discussions at Geneva. He apparently realized that the outcome could be important not only for Greece but also for the prestige of the League. Noted for his logic and brilliant mind, he was one of the framers of the Geneva Protocol, urged the admission of Germany as a full member of the League, worked diligently in an attempt to bring peace to the Sino-Japanese struggle in Manchuria, and then spent many months as a conciliator in the struggle between Italy and Ethiopia.

Politis expressed many times his deep and devoted interest in the League of Nations and firmly believed that it had a great future. He was convinced that the only hope for peace in Europe, and especially in the Balkans, lay with the League. In addition to his firm backing of the League, he was also noted for his support of the smaller nations of the world in their quest for justice and peace. While extolling the virtues of the League, indeed its necessity in the world, Politis constantly emphasized his belief that it would be a much greater force for peace if the United States joined. He also felt that the League should be empowered to consider all international conditions which were a threat to peace, as well as have the power to force reconsideration of all the treaties signed since World War I. Politis spent many months in the United States in the late 1920s giving speeches and conducting seminars on international law and arbitration. In 1929 he was president of the commission which prepared for the World Conference for Limitation of Armaments.

BIBLIOGRAPHY:

A. *Le grand problème du XXe siècle . . . la syntese de l'ordre et de la liberté* (Lisbon, 1942); *La justice internationale* (Paris, 1924); *La morale internationale* (Neuchâtel, Switzerland, 1943); *Neutrality and Peace* (Washington, 1935); *The New Aspects of International Law* (Washington, 1928); *The Problem of Disarmament* (Worcester, MA, 1934); *The Work of the Hague Court,* (Baltimore, MD, 1911).

B. James Barros, *The Corfu Incident of 1923* (Princeton, NJ, 1965); CB 1942,

669; *Ladies Home Journal*, 47 (Jan 1930), 25; NYT 5 Mar 1942, 23; Frank P. Walters, *A History of the League of Nations* (Oxford, 1952).

C. The Politis papers are in the League of Nations Archives.

David C. Riede

POLK, Frank Lyon (13 September 1871, New York—7 February 1943, New York). *Education*: B.A., Yale Univ., 1894; LL.B., Columbia Law School, 1897. *Career*: began law practice, 1897; captain, Quartermaster Corps, 1898; corporation counsel, New York, 1914–15; counselor, Department of State, 1915–19; under-secretary of state, 1919–20; acting secretary of state, 1918–19; head, American delegation to Paris Conference, June 1919.

When Polk entered the State Department he held clear ideas about foreign policy, though there is no indication that he had thought deeply or originally about the subject. He had accepted the concept of the United States as a major power with world responsibilities. Polk approved of intervening in Latin America to promote stability, although he believed the rights of the people there should be considered and he knew that investors exaggerated their claims. This interventionism was tempered by practical considerations, especially in Mexico. Though exasperated by Mexico's independent-mindedness and challenge to foreign property rights, Polk realized that undertaking a major military intervention would be costly, detract attention from the European situation, and effect the loss of Mexican oil. So generally he advocated negotiations and concessions to mitigate differences.

In World War I, Polk was pro-Ally. Committed to traditional neutral rights, he frequently grew angry over British infringements on the rights of the United States. Yet he worked hard to reconcile differences, he never seriously considered breaking relations, and he supported involvement in the war. Once in the conflict, the United States infringed on the rights of the remaining neutrals, but Polk, concerned with precedent, attempted to limit abuses.

Polk found it difficult to accept the Bolshevik revolution, which challenged *Woodrow Wilson's world view. Uncertain how to respond, Polk initially opposed armed intervention, believing it would make the United States appear reactionary and, because of the demands of the war, would be insufficiently supported. After intervention he recommended its continuation through most of 1919 and urged the recognition of Admiral Aleksandr Kolchak.

Polk's more direct internationalist involvement came in 1919, when Wilson returned to the United States from the Peace Conference and left Polk as head of the delegation charged with completing unfinished business. He generally followed a more conciliatory approach than Wilson. During the Senate debates over membership in the League of Nations, Polk agreed that altering Article X of the Covenant would change it significantly.

Nevertheless, he was willing to compromise to gain U.S. participation because he was eager for the United States to continue to cooperate with the Europeans in world affairs.

Though never again holding major office after leaving the State Department, Polk continued to be concerned about foreign affairs and in promoting a world outlook. He had clients with international business which required frequent contact with foreign policy officials. Polk was a charter member of the Council on Foreign Relations. He was active politically working in the 1920s to retain pro-League planks in Democratic platforms and managing *John W. Davis's campaign for the presidential nomination in 1924. Polk supported the Kellogg–Briand Pact, which he thought should be followed by disarmament, retained his faith in the League, participated in conferences of the Institute of Pacific Relations, and endorsed internationalist policies, 1939–41.

BIBLIOGRAPHY:

B. DAB supp. 3, 605–6. WWWA 2, 427.

C. Polk papers are at Yale Univ. and in the Manuscript Division, Library of Congress.

Kell Mitchell, Jr.

POMPIDOU, Georges Jean Raymond (5 July 1911, Montboudif, Cantal, France—2 April 1974, Paris). *Education*: Lycée d'Albi and Lycée Louis le Grand, Paris; graduate, Ecole Normale Supérieure; diploma, Ecole Libre des Sciences Politiques. *Career*: professor, Lycée, Marseilles, 1935–38; Lycée Henry IV, Paris, 1939–44, member, de Gaulle's staff, 1944–46; member, Council of State, 1946–54; deputy director of tourism, 1946–49; staff of Rothschild Frères bank, 1954, general director, 1956–62; director of de Gaulle Cabinet, June 1957–January 1958; member, Constitutional Council, 1959–62; prime minister, 1962–68; president, 1969–74.

Pompidou's internationalist role is primarily associated with European unification efforts following World War II. The British role was a problem from the beginning. When the European union began to take concrete form, British involvement became crucial. Although Britain agreed to join the Council of Europe, a loosely organized association of countries, it adamantly refused to participate in the supranational Coal and Steel Community or the European Common Market. However, it maintained contact with both communities and kept the hopes of the members high, especially when the Common Market appeared to be a viable, progressive union. In this way it effectively blocked several efforts by France to create a closer political collaboration among the six Community members and initiated much ill will between France and Britain. Georges Pompidou's place in the annals of internationalists was achieved through his role as president of France during the years when Britain was finally admitted into the Common Market.

A protégé of *Charles de Gaulle, Pompidou served as prime minister for most of the general's administration as president and shared his major concepts of a European unity based on strict adherence to the Treaty of Rome and a confederal rather than a supranational union. Economic ties and even a common currency were acceptable, but not a politically organized Europe. Cooperation should be developed, but not if it intruded on national interests. He also supported a French defense policy not tied to NATO. Pompidou, however, had remained in the background and thus was not publicly associated with the bitter and frustrating discussions over British membership. Moreover, his election to the French presidency coincided with several important changes in European affairs. By 1969 the provisions of the Treaty of Rome were well on their way to completion, and a strong, tightly knit Common Market of the six was in place. In addition, Great Britain, for the first time, appeared to recognize its need to be an integral part of the European complex. Thus the time was finally ripe for France to propose British membership and anticipate that the invitation would be accepted seriously. Unlike de Gaulle, Pompidou was a diplomat who knew how to exploit the fact that neither France nor Britain wanted a supranational organization of Europe. Under his leadership, the negotiations for British membership were conducted successfully, and for the first time since World War II it appeared that the two states might work together for European unity.

BIBLIOGRAPHY:

A. *Etudes sur Britannicus* (Paris, 1944).

B. CB 1962, 341–43; Pierre Bernard Couste, *Pompidou et l'Europe* (Paris, 1974); NYT 3 Apr 1974, 33; Stephen Rials, *Les idées politiques du President Georges Pompidou* (Paris, 1977); Paula Scalingi, *The European Parliament: The Three-Decade Search for a United Europe* (Westport, CT, 1980); WWF 1965–66, 2243.

Anne Tucker Moore

PONSONBY, Arthur Augustus. See *Biographical Dictionary of Modern Peace Leaders*.

POPE, James Pinckney (31 March 1884, near Jonesboro, Jackson Parish, LA—23 January 1966, Alexandria, VA). *Education*: graduate, Louisiana Polytechnic Inst., 1906; LL.B., Univ. of Chicago, 1909. *Career*: lawyer, Boise, ID, 1909–16, 1919–29; city attorney, Boise, 1916–17; assistant attorney general, Idaho, 1918–19; mayor of Boise, 1929–33; Democratic senator, 1933–39; director, Tennessee Valley Authority, 1939–51; lawyer, Knoxville, TN, 1951–63.

A tall, heavy-set individual, Pope was an outspoken advocate of Wilsonian internationalism and collective security from a predominantly isolationist state. Pope developed internationalist views in 1909, when he bicycled around the European continent. After becoming a lawyer in Boise, Idaho, he corresponded with numerous internationalists advocating cooperation between nations for world peace. During the 1920s, he often clashed over foreign policy issues with isolationist Republican Senator William E. Borah of Idaho. Borah strongly opposed the Treaty of Versailles and U.S. entrance into the League of Nations and the World Court. Pope was especially dismayed over the Senate rejection of the Treaty of Versailles because of "the present chaotic condition in the world." Besides making frequent visits to Europe, he supported the League of Nations Association, volunteered to crusade for U.S. entry into the League of Nations, and backed the World Court.

After his election to the Senate in 1932, Pope was that body's leading spokesman for internationalism. He argued that war could be prevented if the United States abandoned isolationism and stood behind the Western democracies against territorial expansion by totalitarian nations. Pope was the only member of the Nye Munitions Committee to support the idea of collective security. He actively participated in the early stages of the Committee's work probing the munitions trade and studying industrial mobilization. In 1935 he introduced a bill to establish a National Munitions Control Board to license all arms shipments and to publish annual export totals. An ardent admirer of *Woodrow Wilson, he protested the committee findings on U.S. entry into World War I.

In May 1935 Pope sponsored a resolution calling for U.S. participation in the League of Nations. Senate isolationists defeated the resolution despite Pope's fervent appeals for such involvement. Since the United States accepted in principle settling disputes by judicial means, he urged U.S. membership in the World Court. Pope constantly criticized neutrality legislation of the 1930s as encouraging a policy of "hiding" and "ducking." He denounced the acts as a rejection of America's moral commitment to maintain world peace through wider involvement in global affairs. "The destinies of the nations," Pope argued, "are too closely bound together for one to set itself aside and pretend that no other nation exists" (NYT 24 Jan 1966, 35).

The predominantly isolationist home constituents increasingly attacked Pope as the "Ambassador to Europe from Idaho" and as an "un-American meddler" with a "European complex." In 1938, two-term conservative Congressman D. Worth Clark, an isolationist, challenged Pope in the Democratic primaries. Clark, who urged the United States to stay out of both European affairs and the League of Nations, defeated Pope by 4,000 of 85,000 votes cast. Pope continued exhibiting interest in international affairs from 1939 to 1951 as a director of the Tennessee Valley Authority and for the next twelve years as a lawyer. By that time, Pope's internationalist philosophy and his steadfast support of collective security organizations to preserve world peace had seemingly been proven.

BIBLIOGRAPHY:

B. BDAC 1961, 1469–70; Robert A. Divine, *The Illusion of Neutrality* (Chicago, 1962); Michael P. Malone, *C. Ben Ross and the New Deal in Idaho* (Seattle, WA,

1970), "The New Deal in Idaho," *Pacific Historical Review* 38 (Aug 1969), 293-310; NYT 24 Jan 1966, 35; Robert C. Sims, "James P. Pope, Senator from Idaho," *Idaho Yesterdays* 15 (Fall 1971), 9-15; John E. Wiltz, *In Search of Peace: The Senate Munitions Inquiry, 1934-1936* (Baton Rouge, LA, 1963); "Who Is the Other Senator from Idaho?" *Literary Digest* 120 (7 Sep 1935), 27.

C. The Pope papers are at the Idaho Historical Society and the Univ. of Tennessee.

David L. Porter

PROCOPÉ, Hjalmar Johan Fredrik (8 August 1889, Helsinki—8 March 1954, Helsinki). *Education*: master in science of law, Univ. of Helsinki, 1913. *Career*: member of Parliament, 1919-22, 1924-26; minister of commerce and industry, 1920-21, 1924; minister of foreign affairs, 1924, 1927-31; ambassador to Warsaw, 1926-27; attended numerous meetings of League of Nations Council and Assembly, mainly in 1920s; ambassador to the United States, 1939-44; managing director, Finnish Papermills' Association, 1931-38.

Procopé was part of the generation that grew up at the time when Finland achieved its independence. In him, the successful resistance against Russification led to a strong belief in the victory of justice. When elected to Parliament in 1919, Procopé was one of its youngest members. Within a short time, he advanced to become one of the most notable experts on foreign policy of the Swedish People's party. During the first years of Finland's independence, he supported, without success, intervention in the Russian Civil War, and in 1922, when there was an acute threat of war with Russia, he unsuccessfully supported a military union between Finland and Estonia, Latvia, Lithuania, and Poland. As minister of foreign affairs, he tried to promote an orientation toward Scandinavia, particularly to Sweden. These attempts did not solve Finland's concern about the threat from Soviet Russia. Since the Western powers were unwilling to guarantee Finland's security, it could only withdrew to "splendid isolation," to use Procopé's own definition of his policy.

Yet like several Finnish, Scandinavia, and other representatives of mainly small countries, Procopé also placed hope in the League of Nations, at least through the 1920s. After Finland had been elected a member of the League's Council, he represented Finland in that body in 1927. As chairman he also opened the League's Ninth and Tenth General Assemblies in 1928 and 1929. The Kellogg-Briand Pact, obliging nations to solve their disagreements peacefully, had been signed in Paris on 27 August 1928. One week later, in his opening speech, Procopé greeted the new treaty as a peace triumph and a symbol for the League's future. Although Procopé's address consisted of a great deal of rhetoric, it nevertheless revealed his optimism, typical of that time.

Procopé's international way of thinking also appeared in economic matters. As a free trade ideologist, he played a significant role in developing the

Finnish foreign trade system. He represented Finland at the World Economic Conference (1933). In his work, *Trends in International and Nordic Trade Policy* (1935), he warned against a dangerous isolationism for individual nations and the civilized world. Unfortunately, by the time his book appeared in the mid-1930s, collective security and the international way of thinking appeared to have failed.

Procopé's ambassadorship to Washington was characterized by diverse political moods, from the very friendly one caused by the war between Finland and Soviet Russia, 1939–1940, to the crisis in the summer of 1944, when diplomatic relations were broken. A person familiar with international thinking, he did much to seek understanding in the face of tensions. On characterizing Procopé's thoughts and activities, one can join the affirmation of the ambassador of Germany to Helsinki in 1930, Martin Renner, who saw Procopé as a European-centered thinker with experience in his field.

BIBLIOGRAPHY:

A. *Oavhänghet eller fortsall förtrych* [Independence or continued oppression] (Helsinki, 1917); *Riktlinjer i internationell och nordisk handelspolitik* [Trends in international and Nordic trade policy] (Stockholm, 1935).

B. CB 1940, 663–65; NYT 9 Mar 1954, 27; WWWA 3, 702.

Magnus Lemberg

PUEYRREDÓN, Honorio (9 July 1876, San Pedro, Province of Buenos Aires—23 September 1945, Buenos Aires). *Education*: law degree, Univ. of Buenos Aires, 1896. *Career*: professor, Univ. of Buenos Aires, 1893–1916; minister of agriculture, 1916–17; minister of foreign affairs, 1917–22; ambassador to United States, 1923–30.

A distinguished member of the legal profession holding a chair of civil procedure at Buenos Aires University and known for his handling of highly important cases, Pueyrredón published several economic studies which launched him politically. He became an active member of the Unión Cívica Radical and represented his country at the Maritime Conference in Venice and at the International Expositions of Turin and Roubaix in 1911.

When Hipólite Yrigoyen became president in 1916, Pueyrredón served first as minister of agriculture and then as foreign minister, where his delicate negotiations enhanced both his personal and his country's prestige in the world. Pueyrredón became the steadfast and brilliant executer of Yrigoyen's foreign policy, maintaining neutrality during World War I and adhering to an idealist concept of world peace and cooperation in keeping with the Argentine president's *krausista* philosophy. It was in Geneva, as the representative of the first Latin American country to join the League of Nations, that Pueyrredón stated the Argentine thesis that "victory confers no rights," that war should not be waged for the collection of debts, and that all nations should be members of the League unless they specifically declined to join. He attacked the existing organization of the Council and wanted all the League's members to be elected by the Assembly. In line with his president's idealism, he asked for the establishment of a Permanent Court of International Justice and a continuing organization for economic cooperation. When the League took no action on his democratic proposals, Pueyrredón withdrew Argentina from further participation on 4 December 1920, and shortly thereafter from the League, the first country to do so.

In 1923 Pueyrredón became ambassador to the United States, also serving as Argentina's representative on the Board of Directors of the Pan American Union. He also represented Argentina at the Sixth Pan American Conference of American States in Havana, 1928. In these duties he became famous for his staunch defense of the concept of the sovereignty of all nations and of the principle of nonintervention. When his proposal for the abolition of customs barriers in order to facilitate free trade was not accepted, Pueyrredón withdrew Argentina from the 1928 conference. Pueyrredón remained active in Argentina for many years, becoming known as the party's most representative figure of the "Yrigoyenista" wing.

BIBLIOGRAPHY:

B. John Spencer Bassett, *The League of Nations: A Chapter in World Politics* (New York, 1928); *Conferencias internacionales Americanas, 1889–1936* (Washington, 1938); *Diccionario histórico Argentino* 5 (Buenos Aires, 1954), 904–5; *Enciclopedia universal ilustrada Europeo–Americana* 48 (Madrid, 1922), 398; *Gran enciclopedia Argentina* 6 (Buenos Aires, 1960) 571; Ricardo Levene, *A History of Argentina*, trans. and ed. William S. Robertson (Chapel Hill, NC, 1937); Harold F. Peterson, *Argentina and the United States, 1810–1960* (New York, 1962); NYT 24 Sep 1945, 19.

O. Carlos Stoetzer

PUGSLEY, Chester DeWitt (29 March 1887, Peekskill, NY—8 October 1973, Peekskill). *Education*: B.A., Harvard Coll., 1909; Harvard Graduate School of Business and Law School, 1910–13. *Career*: lawyer, New York, 1913–27; banker, Peekskill, NY, 1915–33; philanthropist.

Pugsley displayed a somewhat eccentric but committed interest in a variety of internationalist-oriented topics. His earliest concern appeared when he attended the 1907 Lake Mohonk Arbitration Conference. His enthusiasm led him to create a hundred-dollar prize in 1909 for the best essay on international arbitration by an undergraduate college student, an award he funded annually through 1914. He served as treasurer of the Mohonk Conferences of 1915 and 1916, and at that time joined the League to Enforce Peace, serving as chairman of its Membership Committee in 1916.

Pugsley believed firmly in education as a process for improving international understanding, and many of his gifts testify to that faith. He provided Harvard Law School with funds for research in international law and with a trust for scholarships in international law to foreign students; another large gift went to Yale for annual conferences on international relations; and lesser amounts were provided to Vassar, Rollins, and other colleges and high schools to promote interest in world studies. He helped fund the Institute of International Affairs at the College of William and Mary and provided gifts to foreign governments and institutions for essay prizes, lectures, and study programs. His checks, made out to the treasury of nations, often arrived unsolicited and without instruction regarding their application. In the 1930s he became interested in parks and provided modest sums to European nations to inaugurate park systems. While seldom in the mainstream of internationalist organizations or activities, Pugsley by his individual efforts sought to advance the ideal of internationalism through education.

BIBLIOGRAPHY:

B. NCAB 58, 664-65; WWWA 6, 333.

Warren F. Kuehl

Q

QUIDDE, Ludwig. See *Biographical Dictionary of Modern Peace Leaders.*

QUIÑONES DE LEÓN, José María (28 September 1873, Spain—21 November 1957, Paris). *Education*: Spain, France, and England. *Career*: deputy, Spanish Cortes, 1907–16; minister plenipotentiary, 1914, ambassador to France, 1918–31; member, League of Nations Council, 1919–31.

A warm friend and supporter of the League of Nations, Quiñones de León spent over a decade in Geneva involved in its principles and work. While some observers maintain that he subordinated the League to his diplomatic interests and career, there can still be little doubt that he applied himself diligently on its behalf. He participated in discussions in 1919 to draft the Covenant, sat on the Organizing Committee which planned the League's first sessions, and thereafter served on many commissions and groups, most of which sought to allay tensions stemming from rivalries and controversies. Although aristocratic in manner and tradition and not skilled as a politician, his good humor and polite demeanor led others to trust and like him. This, combined with a sharp mind, shrewdness, and a conciliatory spirit, gave him considerable influence as a modifying figure, a person who commanded respect. Given sufficient time and leeway, it was said he could achieve almost anything. So valued was his work by 1923 that the League decided that year to enlarge the Council, in part to keep Spain from rotating off and thus removing Quiñones de León from his position of prominence.

He was especially influential in resolving disputes that came before the Council. One of these involved the controversy between Poles and Lithuanians over the city of Vilna. In the Upper Silesia question, Quiñones de León submitted proposals which helped allay tensions there. He also played a prominent role in the Corfu confrontation between Greece and Italy over the island and charges that Italy had violated the Covenant in military action it had taken. Quiñones de León was assigned the task of drafting the recommended settlement when it came before the Council, and his conciliatory approach did much to resolve the problem.

He also became involved with proposals to admit Germany to the League and Council in 1926. That step would have removed Brazil from the Council. It threatened to withdraw, and Spain supported its position and also gave notice of its intent to leave. This caused consternation in League circles, some of which reflected concern over Spain's departure, but most observers worried more that they would lose the moderating voice of Quiñones de León. Spain did remain in the League, but its representative did not. He went into voluntary exile when the monarchy ended in 1931 and thus could no longer represent Spain at Geneva. Later, however, he supported Francisco Franco in the Spanish Civil War.

BIBLIOGRAPHY:

B. James Barros, *The Corfu Incident of 1923: Mussolini and the League of Nations* (Princeton, NJ, 1965); *Enciclopedia universal ilustrada europeo-americana*, supp. *1957–1958* (Madrid, 1961), 259; Salvador de Madariaga, *Morning Without Noon: Memoirs* (Westmead, England, 1974); Frank P. Walters, *A History of the League of Nations* (London, 1952).

Warren F. Kuehl

R

RAJCHMAN, Ludwik W. (1 November 1881, Warsaw—13 July 1965, Chenu, France). *Education*: M.D. Kraków Univ., 1905. *Career*: assistant bacteriologist, Pasteur Institute, Paris, 1906–8; lecturer, Kraków Univ., 1909–10; chief bacteriologist, Royal Institute of Public Health, London, 1910–13; research fellow, King's Coll., Cambridge, 1913–14; research fellow, Medical Research Council, London, 1914–19; organizer and general director, Polish National Institute of Health, Warsaw, 1919–31; Polish member, League of Nations Epidemics Commission, 1920–21; director, League of Nations Health Organization, 1921–39; League delegate for Republic of China, 1933–34; adviser, National Government of China, 1939–43; Polish member, UN Relief and Rehabilitation Administration, 1945; chief, Polish Supply Reconstruction Mission, Washington, 1945; organizer and chairman, Executive Board, UNICEF, 1946–50; organizer and deputy chair, International Children's Center, Paris, 1950–65.

Rajchman, bacteriologist and organizer of public health services, became involved in international health programs following World War I when he took charge of the medical struggle against typhus and cholera. He helped organize the National Institute of Health and acted as its general director. In 1920 he was appointed Polish member of the Epidemics Commission of the League of Nations. With the creation of the League's Health Organization to provide assistance to underdeveloped countries in the area of public health, nutrition, sanitation, and child care, Rajchman was appointed its director, a post he retained until the outbreak of World War II.

When China requested assistance from the League in 1925, Rajchman was appointed to head first the medical team and subsequently an entire development program. This appointment developed into a special relationship between the Pole and the Chinese. The Japanese objected to Rajchman's appointment and in 1934 succeeded in having him recalled. He is credited in persuading the Chinese to submit the Sino–Japanese dispute to the League for arbitration. In 1939 the League, in an effort to placate the Axis powers, dismissed Rajchman and other anti-Fascist members. Rajchman joined the Polish government-in-exile in London and in 1940 left for the United States, where he became an adviser to the Chinese National government.

Following the war, Rajchman affiliated with the Polish Communist government because he was convinced that only under Russian influence would Poland have a chance to rebuild. He was thus appointed Poland's representative to the UN Relief and Rehabilitation Administration, which had been created to provide assistance and help to war victims. His activities with the League enabled him to observe firsthand the need for special attention to children in the underdeveloped areas in the world, and Rajchman proposed the creation of a special agency to provide both long-term and short-term welfare programs to children. He lobbied for this among other UN delegates, especially at UNRRA sessions. In December 1946 UNICEF was created, and Rajchman was elected to chair the twenty-six-nation Executive Board. As a delegate, he could not act as executive director, a post offered to Maurice Pate. UNICEF worked through individual relief service programs set up in each country, and its budget consisted of voluntary contributions made by governments and individuals. Rajchman hoped that UNICEF would eventually become a permanent body of the UN. When the Soviet bloc countries boycotted the UN in 1950, Rajchman left UNICEF and retired to his home in Chenu, France.

Retirement did not last long. Dedicated to the field of public health, especially as it is applied to children, Rajchman organized the International Children's Center in Paris to provide technical information and assistance to underdeveloped countries. He acted as its deputy chair until his death. Rajchman also returned as part of the Polish delegation to the organization he founded when in 1957 Poland again became a member of the UNICEF Board.

Even though Rajchman advocated the use of world organizations, such as the UN and the League of Nations, to promote world cooperation and assistance, he faced a charge in 1957 by the U.S. Senate Judiciary Subcomittee on International Security that he had been a Soviet spy during World War II. Nothing came of these allegations, and Rajchman's services testify to his humanitarian rather than political approaches to world concerns.

BIBLIOGRAPHY:

A. League of Nations Reports: *Comtié d'hygiène* (Geneva, 1922); *Council Committee on Technical Co-Operation Between the League of Nations and China* (Geneva, 1934); *Health Committee* (Geneva, 1922); *Rapport du Dr. L. Rajchman, directeur médical de la Section d'Hygiène de la Société des Nations* (Geneva, 1922); *Report of the Technical Agent of the Council on His Mission in China* (Geneva, 1934); *Report on Technical Co-Operation Between the League of Nations and China* (Peiping, China, 1934).

B. *Encyklopedia Powszechna PWN* 3 (Warsaw, 1975), 687; IWW 1949, 755; "Japan Tries to Force League to Dismiss Dr. Rajchman," *China Weekly Review* 68 (19 May 1934), 466; "League's Technical Aid to China: Dr. Rajchman and T.V. Soong," *China Weekly Review* 66 (16 Sep 1933), 99–101; NYT 25 Jul 1965, 69; "The Real Significance of Dr. Rajchman's Mission to China," *China Weekly Review* 67 (16 Dec 1933), 126–27; *UN Weekly Bulletin* 2, no. 2 (1947), 52; *UNICEF Courier* 15, no. 9 (1965), 689–92; *The World's Destiny and The United States: A Conference of Experts in International Relations* (Chicago, 1941).

Zofia Sywak

RALSTON, Jackson Harvey (6 February 1857, Sacramento, CA—13 October 1945, Palo Alto, CA). *Education*: LL.B., Georgetown Univ., 1876. *Career*: attorney, 1876–1924; author.

Ralston had a distinguished career as an attorney who was an authority on constitutional labor law, taxation, and international arbitration. He did not become interested in international law until 1899, twenty-three years after beginning practice, when he became counsel for Felipe Agoncillo, the Philippine Republic's representative. In the 1902 *Pious Fund of the Californias* v. *Mexico*, the first case before the Permanent Court of Arbitration, Ralston served as U.S. agent and counsel. In that capacity, he helped the court develop the procedures later adopted by the Court of International Justice.

Thereafter, Ralston's professional and scholarly interest in arbitration grew. The United States appointed him umpire on the 1903 Italian-Venezuelan Commission, which adjudicated claims totaling $8 million. Even critics hailed Ralston's opinions as models of just disposition. Ralston's most important contribution, perhaps, came not from such work but from his scholarship. In 1902 and 1903 he edited the *Report of French-Venezuelan Mixed Claims Commission of 1902* (1906) and *Venezuelan Arbitration of 1903* (1904). The research gave Ralston an intimate knowledge of international arbitration, which enabled him later to publish *International Arbitral Law and Procedure* (1910). This book served as the basis for the useful *Law and Procedure of International Tribunals* (1926). He completed his best-known and most important study in 1929, *International Arbitration, from Athens to Locarno*, which described the historical and legal evolution of arbitration. His purpose was to establish support for the peaceful, just settlement of disputes. Ralston retired in 1924, devoting himself to civic affairs and lecturing on international law at Stanford University from 1928 to 1932.

A traditional pacifist, Ralston served as a vice-president of the American Peace Society, and he was a charter member of the American Society of International Law. He believed that arbitration was sound in theory and practice, and that arbitral agencies could operate effectively. Consistent with his pacifism, he downplayed the role of military force in international relations and remained convinced that a society of sovereign states only produced anarchy and war.

BIBLIOGRAPHY:

A. *Democracy's International Law* (Washington, 1922); *International Arbitral Law and Procedure* (Boston, 1910); *The Law and Procedure of International Tribunals* (Stanford, CA, 1926); *A Quest for International Order* (Washington, 1941).

B. AJIL 40 (1946), 182–84; Warren F. Kuehl, introduction to Ralston, *International Arbitration, from Athens to Locarno* (New York, 1972); NCAB 37, 501.

Daryl L. Revoldt

RAMADIER, Paul (17 March 1888, La Rochelle, France—14 October 1961, Decazeville, France). *Education*: Univs. of Toulouse and Paris; doctor of laws, Univ. of Paris, 1911. *Career*: attorney, Decazeville and Paris, 1912–36; member, Chamber of Deputies, 1928–40, 1946–51, 1956–58; member, Constituent Assemblies, 1945–46; under secretary, Ministry of Public Works, 1936–37; minister of labor, 1938; minister of food, 1944–45; minister of justice, 1946; prime minister, 1947; deputy prime minister, 1947–48; minister of national defense, 1948–49; minister of finances and economic affairs, 1956–57; chairman, Administrative Council, International Labor Office, 1952–55.

Although he had served in four cabinets during the Popular Front era of the 1930s, Ramadier did not gain prominence as an internationalist until after World War II. Having distinguished himself in the Resistance, Ramadier emerged during the postwar era as one of the most distinguished leaders of the moderate, European-oriented wing of the Socialist party (SFIO). Chosen as the first regular prime minister of the Fourth Republic in January 1947, he forced the resignation of the Communist members of his cabinet in May, when they refused to support him in a vote of confidence. Although the immediate cause of the Cabinet crisis was a conflict over domestic policy, Ramadier's handling of it opened the way for the emergence of an increasingly pro-Western French foreign policy involving European unity discussions. Later that year, Ramadier strongly endorsed French participation in the Marshall Plan. When the SFIO National Council met in July to consider withdrawing support from his government, Ramadier persuaded a majority to reject the proposal, arguing that the party should seize the opportunity to help direct the implementation of Marshall aid and emphasizing that the plan could be used to encourage European cooperation. Under his guidance, the French government played a leading role in the creation of the Committee of Economic Cooperation, which later evolved into the Organization for European Economic Cooperation.

Although the SFIO yielded to British Labor party pressure and refused to participate formally in the Hague Congress of Europe which met in May 1948, Ramadier attended and was named chairman of its Political Committee. It drafted the proposal which led in May 1949 to the establishment of the Council of Europe. Ramadier thus joined with *Jean Monnet, *Robert Schuman, and *Paul Reynaud to initiate the European integration movement.

BIBLIOGRAPHY:

A. *Les Socialistes et l'exercice du pouvoir* (Paris, 1961).

B. CB 1947, 530–32; *Dictionnaire biographique français contemporain* 2 (Paris, 1954), 560; IWW 1961–62, 797; NYT 15 Oct 1961, 88; WWF 1959–60, 2183.

Kenneth R. Calkins

RANDALL, John Herman (27 April 1871, St. Paul, MN—15 May 1946, New York). *Education*: B.A., Colgate Univ., 1892; Univ. of Chicago

Divinity School, 1893–96. *Career*: ordained as a Baptist minister, 1895; pastorates in Minneapolis, MN, Grand Rapids, MI, and New York; president and director, World Unity Foundation, 1927–35.

Randall attained prominence as an orator and as an author of philosophical works. In 1919 he joined John Haynes Holmes as the associate minister, and together they reorganized the Park Avenue, New York, Church of the Messiah as the Community Church, thereby pronouncing freedom from the limitations of a denominational church. Thereafter Randall proclaimed his stance for the "universal religion of human brotherhood."

Retiring from church work in 1927, he became president and director of the World Unity Foundation, editor of its magazine, *World Unity*, and a member of the World Unity Conference Committee. Opposed to political and economic nationalism, Randall worked to foster the spirit of a new age, one of cooperation and unity in diversity. To that end he edited *World Unity*, a monthly magazine, published from October 1927 to March 1935 with the stated purpose of interpreting and recording thought which examined the trend toward worldwide understanding and a humanized civilization. The editors aimed to create a medium wherein new and higher values could emerge in philosophy, science, religion, ethics, and the arts without prejudice of race, creed, class, or nationality.

In the first issue, "The Ideal of World Unity," Randall wrote of a new consciousness of world community, of the new forces making for unity and giving spirit to this new age. He saw modern science at work, increased economic links leading to interdependency, a developing global cultural life, the growing realization of the destructiveness of modern warfare, and the need for mankind to cooperate and cease conflict. His magazine presented an exceptional array of viewpoints reflecting this perspective. To further this goal, the Foundation also sponsored World Unity Conferences in the Eastern United States and Canada. These consisted of several consecutive meetings at which the leading speakers sought to promote the ideals of brotherhood, world peace, and understanding among religions, races, nations, and classes.

Although the Foundation fell in 1936, a casualty of finances and international strife, the conferences and the magazine helped foster a world outlook without prejudice and a faith in humanity which survived the horrors of World War II. *World Unity Magazine* gave young scholars a medium to which they could hone their insights toward global humanitarian values, thus broadening consciousness to recognize the moral and spiritual equality, "to realize that the interests of all men are mutual interests." One of his sons, John Herman Randall, Jr., professor at Columbia University, edited a book review section of *World Unity*, and together they wrote the influential *Religion and the Modern World* (1929).

BIBLIOGRAPHY:

A. *Culture of Personality* (New York, 1912); *Humanity at the Crossroads* (New York, 1915); *The Irrepressible Conflict in Religion* (New York, 1925); *Life of Reality* (New York, 1916); *The Mastery of Life* (New York, 1931); *A New Philosophy of Life* (New York, 1910); *The Philosophy of Power* (New York, 1917); *Religion and the Modern World* (New York, 1929); *The Spirit of the New Philosophy* (London, 1919).

B. NYT 17 May 1946, 22; WWWA 2, 437.

Anne L. Day

RAPACKI, Adam (24 December 1909, Lwów, Poland—10 October 1970, Warsaw). *Education*: Warsaw Univ.; France and Italy. *Career*: Institute for Social Research, Scientific Institute for the Study of Economic Cycles, 1932–39; member, Central Committee of the Polish Politburo, 1948–54, 1956–68; deputy member, Central Committee, 1954–56; minister of shipping, 1947–50; minister of higher education, 1950–56; foreign minister, 1956–68; member of Sejm, 1947–68.

The son of a well-known leader of the cooperative movement in prewar Poland, Rapacki studied economics and then worked for a number of cooperatives. When World War II began, Rapacki joined the Polish Army and was a German prisoner-of-war for five years. A Socialist from his university days, Rapacki joined the party following the war. With the merging of the Socialist and Communist parties in 1948, he became a member of the Central Committee of the newly formed Polish United Workers' party and started his political career in 1947 with his election to the Sejm. He held a number of ministerial posts and survived the Stalinist purge. During the de-Stalinization era in Poland, Rapacki emerged as foreign minister and retained this post until 1968, when he was forced to resign because he refused to back the government's anti-Semitic measures.

Rapacki is best known as the architect of the Rapacki Plan, which advocated the establishment of a nuclear-free zone in Central Europe. He took the initiative in the East-West deadlock over disarmament by proposing at the UN General Assembly session of 1957 the first of a number of such plans. Basically it provided that the two Germanies, Poland, and Czechoslovakia ban the production and stationing of nuclear weapons on their territories. In February 1958 Rapacki expanded his proposal by suggesting that both Germanies come forth with unilateral declarations and that an adequate system of inspection be developed. In November Rapacki presented his second or revised plan, which consisted of two stages. First, he suggested a ban on the production of nuclear arms in Central Europe and their distribution to armies there which as yet did not have them. In the second stage, a reduction of conventional forces would be carried out simultaneously with the removal of nuclear arms.

His proposals were rejected by the West for lack of adequate guarantees and on the ground that a nuclear shield in West Germany was essential against the Soviet bloc preponderance of conventional arms. Moscow supported the plan, which would break up NATO and prevent any further rearmament of West Germany, halt the possible reunification of the two Germanies, and provide for the eventual withdrawal of American forces in Europe, all of which would enable the Soviets to enjoy their superiority in conventional weapons. Warsaw had much to gain from such a plan. Even though a small power, Rapacki had given it some initiative in a major international situation, and strategically it offered Poland some advantages. Any lessening of tensions would also improve the atmosphere within the Soviet bloc.

Although it was rejected originally, Rapacki continued to refine his plan, and in March 1962 at the disarmament conference in Geneva he presented a third version, which included international control and inspection within the nuclear-free zone. In February 1964 he again urged a nuclear arms freeze in Central Europe. This proposal received serious consideration by the members of the Atlantic Alliance, and a year later Belgium suggested that the idea be reexamined. While Rapacki's plan did not materialize for Europe, the concept of nuclear-free zones emerged as a significant feature of international life elsewhere. Universal treaties established the Antarctic as the first such zone in 1959, the outer space accord of 1967 removed nuclear arms from that region, and the oceans were excluded in 1971. The Latin American nations agreed in 1967 to keep their area free of such devices. Rapacki's plan thus marks him as a unique type of internationalist.

BIBLIOGRAPHY:

A. "European Security," *Polish Perspective* 8, no. 4 (1965), 3–10; "Mr. Rapacki Speaks in Oslo," *Polish Perspectives* 1, no. 6 (1958), 3–10; "On Polish Foreign Policy," *Polish Perspective* 1, no. 5 (1959), 3–7; "The Polish Plan for a Nuclear-Free Zone Today," *International Affairs* 39, no. 1 (1963), 1–12.

B. *Britannica Micropaedia* (Chicago, 1981), 8, 420; *Britannica Book of the Year* (Chicago, 1971), 566; CB 1958, 350–52; Manfred Lachs, "Poland's Quest for European Security," *International Affairs* 35, no. 3 (1959), 305–9; *Newsweek* 76 (26 Oct 1970), 68; NYT 12 Oct 1970, 41; *Time* 96 (26 Oct 1970), 95; *UN Review* 4, no. 5 (1957), 84–85, 6, no. 5 (1959), 70–71; *Wielka encyklopedia powszechna PWN* 9 (Warsaw, 1967), 703–4.

Zofia Sywak

RAPPARD, William Emmanuel (22 April 1883, New York—29 April 1958, Geneva). *Education*: Univs. of Berlin, Munich, Harvard, Paris, and Vienna; LL.D., Univ. of Geneva, 1908. *Career*: professor, Univ. of Geneva, 1910–11, 1913–55; assistant professor, Harvard Univ. 1911–13; cofounder and director, Geneva Graduate Institute of International Studies, 1928–55; rector, Univ. of Geneva, 1926–28, 1936–38; Swiss representative on diplomatic missions to Washington, Paris, and London, 1917–20, 1944–46;

director, Mandates Section, League of Nations, 1920–24; member, Permanent Mandates Commission, League of Nations, 1925–39; member of Swiss delegation, League of Nations, 1928–39; member, Swiss National Council, 1941–43.

Rappard was one of the relatively few public figures in Switzerland during the first half of the twentieth century who had a special understanding for the Anglo-American world, and the Swiss government used Rappard's ties with Americans in a number of special missions. During World War I, he assisted the Swiss minister in Washington in negotiating for the purchase of much needed foodstuff and raw materials. He had access to *Woodrow Wilson and his advisers before and during the Paris Peace Conference, where he lobbied strenuously, though largely in vain, to have some of the Swiss ideas of a just and fair world organization incorporated into the League of Nations plan. During World War II, Rappard again was called upon to use his skills and connections in the protracted negotiations with the Anglo-Americans in London for the easing of the blockade; and at the end of the war he was a member of the Swiss team that had to wrestle with the victorious Allies for an understanding of the difficulties neutral Switzerland had faced and for the concessions that would enable the country to return to normal economic and financial conditions.

It was during the interwar years, however, that Rappard earned most of his reputation and renown as an internationalist. As the first director of the League of Nations Mandates Section and from 1925 on as a member of the Mandates Commission, he put his whole energy, enthusiasm, and expertise into the task of transforming this paper construct into a viable and effective organ of the new world organization. Without any means to enforce demands, through the sheer power of moral persuasion, the Mandates Commission was able to coerce most mandatory powers, except Japan, to carry out their duties toward the mandated territories and the League. Rappard pointed with considerable pride to the role of the mandates system in bringing former colonies closer to self-government and independence as one of the few success stories of the great League experiment.

As a member of the Swiss delegation to the League Assembly, Rappard did most of his work in the fourth committee, which was concerned with finances. The annual budget debates gave him a chance to present his ideas on the conditions and needs for a truly effective international organization. He watched with distress how the nations sacrificed their solidarity commitments to the misguided principles of national interest and sovereignty. The failure of the League was not due to theoretical, organizational, or administration weaknesses, but to the egotism and shortsightedness of its member states. Since the UN Charter did not solve the fundamental problem of how to harmonize national sovereignty with international security, he was not unhappy that Switzerland did not join the new world organization.

Throughout his life, Rappard was an effective and successful publicist. He had a facility with words, in speaking as well as in writing. The bibliography of 304 titles which forms part of *Varia Politica*, the seventieth-anniversary Festschrift, contains a goodly number of substantial books as well as scholarly articles in professional journals and occasional pieces in newspapers and magazines. They run the gamut from historical essays on Swiss and American topics to comparative political science subjects, and from fervent League propaganda to personal reminiscences.

A third career of Rappard, related closely to that of scholarly writer and publicist, was that of university professor. Having taught briefly as a junior professor at Harvard University, Rappard established himself permanently at the University of Geneva. His leadership qualities, recognized by his colleagues in his election to the rectorate of the university for two terms, found their most important and lasting outlet in the creation of the Graduate Institute of International Studies. Though accredited through the university, this institute assumed an identity of its own as a highly regarded school of professional and scholarly education in all areas of international affairs. There can be no doubt that the Institue is Rappard's most important and lasting contribution to the goal of achieving world peace through a better understanding among the peoples of this globe.

BIBLIOGRAPHY:

A. *Collective Security in the Swiss Experience, 1291-1948* (London, 1948); *The Crisis of Democracy* (Chicago, 1938); *The Geneva Experiment* (London, 1931); *International Relations as Viewed from Geneva* (New Haven, CT, 1925); *La Constitution fédérale de la Suisse, 1848-1948* (Neuchâtel, Switzerland, 1948); *La Politique de la Suisse dans la Société des Nations* (Geneva, 1925); *L'Avènement de la démocracie moderne à Genève, 1814-1847* (Geneva, 1942); *L'Individu et l'état dans l'évolution constitutionelle de la Suisse* (Zurich, 1936); *The Quest for Peace Since the World War* (Cambridge, MA, 1940); *Uniting Europe* (New Haven, CT, 1930); *Varia Politica* (Zurich, 1953).

B. CB 1951, 504-6; Heinz K. Meier, *Friendship Under Stress. U.S.-Swiss Relations 1900-1950* (Bern, 1970); NYT 30 Apr 1958, 33; Ania Peter, *William E. Rappard und der Völkerbund* (Bern, 1973); *William E. Rappard: In Memoriam* (Geneva, 1961).

C. The Rappard papers are in the Archives fédérales suisse.

Heinz K. Meier

RATHENAU, Walther (29 September 1867, Berlin—24 June 1922, Berlin). *Education*: Univs. of Berlin and Strasbourg, 1889. *Career*: industrialist; War Ministry, 1914; minister of reconstruction, 1921; foreign minister, 1922.

The son of Emil Rathenau, founder of the vast industrial combine, AEG, Rathenau was attracted to the Romantic age, which provided inspiration for the moral values he cherished. He was always painfully conscious of being Jewish and believed that he was condemned to being a second-class citizen; yet he was never attracted to Zionism. He strove to achieve recognition as an author, publishing several works, 1908–13. Rathenau attempted to develop a set of new spiritual values for German society, which he outlined in *Breviarium Mysticum*. The soul and its nature were at the center of his attention, with the powers of the soul being threefold: imagination, love, respect. In his social works he appealed for a *Volksstaat*, whereby hereditary wealth and class structure would be abolished. Industrial production would be used to improve the lot of the German worker and those of other countries.

Such an economic perspective molded his subsequent work both as nationalist and internationalist. At the beginning of World War I, he was appointed to direct the War Raw Materials Department in the War Ministry. There he effectively conserved and allocated Germany's resources in preparation for a long struggle. He also saw the expansion of state control of business which could be used to achieve Germany's domination and world leadership during a postwar era requiring international cooperation to recover from the war. Economic reorganization would also require social and political reorganization. Vast cartels would direct the economy, with the emphasis on efficient production. At the end of the war he predicted that a League of Nations could not succeed without some sort of accompanying Economic League.

Between 1920 and 1922, while Rathenau opposed German membership in the League as potentially restrictive, he particpated in League technical conferences, especially on economic and reparations matters. In 1920 he served on a Socialization Commission, and he was a technical adviser at the Spa Conference, where he launched the fulfillment policy of the Weimar government. In 1921 he became minister of reconstruction, with official assurance that foreign and financial policy would be linked through international reconciliation and the reorganizing of the German economy. He reluctantly accepted the post of foreign minister in the spring of 1922. Rathenau was interested in an international cooperative venture to help Soviet Russia recover, and the Treaty of Rapallo was the culmination of his *Realpolitik* and efforts to bring Russia and Germany together. The treaty devastated any hope that the Genoa Conference would have a fruitful conclusion. Nationalist opposition to his policies reached new heights of intensity culminating in his assassination by fanatics. Rathenau stands as a unique personality, torn by his idealistic social vision for mankind, his perceptions of an economically evolving world, and his national responsibilities.

BIBLIOGRAPHY:

A. *Briefe*, 3 vols. (Dresden, 1930); *Der neue Staat* (Berlin, 1922); *Die neue Gesellschaft* (Berlin, 1919); *Ein preussischer Europäer: Briefe* (Berlin, 1955); *Gesammelte Reden* (Berlin, 1924); *Gesammelte Schriften*, 5 vols. (Berlin, 1918); *Nachgelassene Schriften*, 2 vols. (Berlin, 1928); *Politische Briefe* (Dresden, 1929);

Reflexionen (Leipzig, Germany, 1908); *Schriften und Reden: Auswahl und Nachwort* (Frankfurt, Germany, 1964); *Tagebuch 1907-1922* (Berlin, 1930).

B. Helmuch M. Böttcher, *Walther Rathenau* (Bonn, 1958); David Felix, *Walther Rathenau and the Weimar Republic* (Baltimore, MD, 1971); James Joll, *Three Intellectuals in Politics* (New York, 1960); Harry Kessler, *Walther Rathenau: Sein Leben und sein Werk* (Berlin, 1928).

Stephen E. Fritz

REDLICH, Joseph (6 June 1869, Göding, Austria [now Hodonin, Czechoslovakia]—11 November 1936, Vienna). *Education*: doctor of laws Univ. of Vienna, 1891; *Career*: lecturer, Univ. of Vienna, 1901–5, professor, 1906–18; visiting professor, Harvard Univ., 1910, 1913; professor, Harvard Law School, 1926–31, director, Institute of Comparative Law, 1929–31; member, Diet of Moravia, 1906–7; member, Lower House of Austrian Parliament, 1907–18; minister of finance, 1918, 1931; member, Balkan Committee, Carnegie Endowment for International Peace (CEIP), 1913; member, European Center (Paris), CEIP, 1928–36; judge, Permanent Court of International Justice, 1930–36.

As legal scholar, teacher, historian, and liberal politician, Redlich devoted himself to promoting friendly and cooperative international relations. Before World War I, his efforts were directed chiefly toward reconciling Germans and Slavs in his native Austria. After the war, he worked for political reconciliation and international cooperation between the former warring powers through lectures, essays, support of the League of Nations, his association with the Carnegie Endowment for International Peace, and his close connection with influential circles in England and America.

Redlich's outlook was based on an idea of law rooted in the Enlightenment spirit of reason and tolerance. He did not, however, confound reason with reasoning. He viewed law as dynamic and social in its power and subjective and ethical in its forms. Law as well as education and art could transform moral and cultural values. This view lay behind his highly acclaimed study of English local government (1901), which noted the direct influence of political and social ideas of democracy on the organization and function of government. In a study of American legal education (1914), Redlich praised the case method but warned against its overuse to the detriment of the social and ethical sides of the law.

In accord with his view of the function of law, Redlich revealed a liberal tolerance in which he sought to transform the anachronistic Habsburg monarchy into a federation of free peoples through the creation of a legal and administrative system more adequate to ideas of liberty and equality. He failed, in part, because he focused on the dynastic supranational state itself, with its tradition of German-Austrian overlordship, as the object of reform, rather than offering an alternative which coordinated national autonomy with loyalty to a supranational organization. An additional reason for failure lay in his support of an active Austro-Hungarian foreign policy in the Balkan peninsula as a way of energizing the moribund Habsburg state. This policy, which climaxed with the annexation of Bosnia in 1908, only served to increase internal and international tensions, making reform more difficult.

The failure to resolve the nationalities conflict led Redlich to greet the war in 1914 as an opportunity to achieve empire reform. That proved a forlorn hope, and he shifted to opposition to the war. In December 1915 Redlich refused, along with *Heinrich Lammasch, to sign the prowar statement of German-Austrian university teachers. In 1916 he began openly to oppose the "chauvinist and imperialist" tendencies of the Central Powers. When Parliament reconvened in 1917, Redlich called for a federalist reconstruction of the empire. When his own German-Austrian Liberal party opposed this, he resigned. He aroused further antagonism when, in conjunction with Lammasch, he argued for a compromise peace rather than victory.

The war left Redlich thoroughly discouraged. He never accommodated himself to the disintegration of the Habsburg monarchy, with the exception of a few months as minister of finance, he withdrew from active politics. Despite his criticism of the Paris peace treaties and his pessimism about the future of European civilization, he devoted his energies to fostering something like a United States of Central Europe through an economic arrangement as preparatory to a political association in the future. Even the narrower economic association would fail, he warned, unless all of the governments of Central Europe first recognized the principle of full respect for minorities and the equality of all nations. His reputation earned him election as deputy judge of the Permanent Court of International Justice in 1930. There is no record of his having served on any panel to adjudicate a case. His last years were spent in declining health and deepening gloom over the rise of dictatorships in Central Europe.

BIBLIOGRAPHY:

A. *Austrian War Government* (New Haven, CT, 1929); *The Common Law and the Case Method in American University Law Schools* (New York, 1914); *Das Österreichischen Staats und Reichsproblem*, 2 vols. (Leipzig, 1920–26); *Emperor Francis Joseph of Austria* (New York, 1929); *Local Government in England* (London, 1903); "Reconstruction in the Danubian Countries," *Foreign Affairs* 1, no. 1 (1922), 73–85; *Schicksalsjahre Österreichs, 1908–1919: Das Politische Tagebuch Josef Redlichs*, ed. Fritz Fellner, 2 vols. (Graz, Austria, 1953–54); "Sovereignty, Democracy, and the Rights of Minorities," in *Harvard Legal Essays*, ed. Joseph H. Beale (Cambridge, MA, 1934), 377–97.

B. Fritz Fellner, "Der Plan einer Vortragsmission Redlich-Apponyi in den Vereinigten Staaten von Amerika . . . während des Ersten Weltkrieges," in H. Fichtenau and E. Zöller, eds., *Beiträge zur neueren Geschichte Österreichs* (Vienna, 1974), 469–88; "Josef Redlich: Leben und Werk," in *Schicksalsjahre Österreichs, 1908–1919: Das Politische Tagebuch Josef Redlichs*, ed. Fritz Fellner, 2 vols. (Graz,

Austria, 1953–54), 1: 9–19; *Harvard Law Review* 50 (Jan 1937), 389–91; *New Encyclopaedia Britannica: Micropaedia*, 15th ed., 8, 462; *New International Encyclopedia* (New York, 1936), 653; NYT 12 Nov 1936, 27.

Solomon Wank

REINSCH, Paul Samuel (10 June 1869, Milwaukee, WI—26 January 1923, Shanghai). *Education*: B.A., Univ. of Wisconsin, 1892, LL.B., 1894, Ph.D., 1898. *Career*: attorney, 1894–95; faculty, Univ. of Wisconsin, 1895–1913; exchange professor in Germany, 1911–12; delegate, Pan American Conferences, 1906, 1909, 1910; minister to China, 1913–19; law practice and counselor to the Chinese government, 1919–23.

Reinsch identified himself with the mainstream of American internationalism in the early twentieth century. As such, his approach was basically eclectic, cautious, gradualist, conservative, legalistic, and pragmatic, but also genuinely humanistic and idealistic. He would probably have labeled himself a practical idealist. A product of his time, Reinsch joined the peace movement partly to advance his academic career and candidacy for a diplomatic post and partly to enjoy contact with the professional, political, legal, and business elite. But other factors drew him to internationalism: a strong religious upbringing, broad classical and humanist education, legal training, and commitment to Wisconsin progressivism, with its emphasis on efficiency and administration and its idealism and spirit of commonwealth. Finally, there was his work as a political scientist specializing in international affairs and colonial studies. Reinsch was an avowed economic expansionist who believed that the United States had to assume its rightful place as a constructive world power. At the same time, he was a biting critic of formal imperialism and excessive nationalism, and he became well known for his condemnation of U.S. colonial policy in the Philippines.

Reinsch maintained that peaceful open door economic competition would promote progress and development as it reduced international tension and political confrontation. He also advocated the limitation of armaments and the elimination of secret diplomacy. But between 1900 and 1914, Reinsch devoted most of his energies to four approaches he believed would advance world peace: arbitration of disputes; expansion and codification of international law; analysis of the causes of war; and practical international cooperation. He was one of the early and original proponents of functionalism and the doctrine of "transferability," the belief that cooperation in technical and economic matters could be transferred to cooperation in the political sphere. In *Public International Unions* (1911), he argued that interdependence was a condition of modern science and invention which no government could end. While he hewed to a moderate course regarding national sovereignty, Reinsch looked forward to the day when a world consciousness would replace loyalty to the state and a comprehensive international law would govern a universal commonwealth.

Reinsch sought to advance the cause of internationalism through his prolific scholarly and popular writings, which publicized the work of different organizations, and by his active participation in a number of the peace movements. He was one of the few Midwesterners to join *Oscar Straus, *Elihu Root, and *Nicholas Murray Butler at the Lake Mohonk Conferences on International Arbitration. He collaborated with Root, *Robert Lansing, and *John Bassett Moore in founding the American Society for International Law. He also labored for the Carnegie Endowment for International Peace by soliciting and coordinating studies on the economic and historical causes of war. Reinsch was a delegate to the Endowment's Bern Conference (1911) and was on his way to the Lucerne Conference when World War I broke out.

Reinsch's appointment as U.S. minister to China cut him off from the activities of the peace groups. For six years he devoted himself to protecting the Open Door Policy for American trade and investment and China's integrity from Japanese duplicity and aggression. The outbreak of World War I complicated his mission. It also caused him much sorrow and deepened his commitment to international peace. Although he was suspected of harboring pro-German sympathies because of his ancestry and attachment to German culture, Reinsch favored the Allies and supported U.S. entry into the war. He was devoted to Wilsonian idealism and endorsed the League of Nations (he had sent his own plan for a league to *Woodrow Wilson in 1915), even though he broke with the president over the Shantung decision at the Paris Peace Conference. Thus, while Reinsch is remembered primarily for his diplomatic career in China, he made notable contributions to the internationalist cause and reflected many of its trends.

BIBLIOGRAPHY:

A. *An American Diplomat in China* (Garden City, NY, 1922); "The Carnegie Peace Fund," *North American Review* 193 (Feb 1911), 180–92; *Colonial Administration* (New York, 1905); "The Concept of Legality in International Arbitration," AJIL 5 (1911), 604–16; "International Administrative Law and National Sovereignty," AJIL 3 (1909), 1–45; "The New Internationalism," *Forum*, 42 (Jul 1909), 24–30; "Precedent and Codification in International Law," *Judicial Settlement of International Disputes* no. 12 (May 1913), 1–27; *Public International Unions* (Boston, 1911); *Secret Diplomacy: How Far Can It Be Eliminated?* (New York, 1922); *World Politics at the End of the Nineteenth Century as Influenced by the Oriental Situation* (New York, 1900).

B. DAB 15, 491–92; NYT 26 Jan 1923, 17; Noel H. Pugach, "Making the Open Door Work: Paul S. Reinsch in China, 1913–1919," *Pacific Historical Review* 38 (May, 1969), 157–75, *Paul S. Reinsch: Open Door Diplomat in Action* (Millwood, NY, 1979).

C. The Reinsch papers are at the State Historical Society of Wisconsin and in the Stanley Hornbeck Collection at the Hoover Institution on War, Revolution and Peace.

Noel H. Pugach

RETINGER, Joseph Hieronim (1888, Poland—12 June 1960, London). *Education*: unknown. *Career*: personal secretary to Polish Premier Wtadistaw Sikorski, 1939; general secretary, Joint International Committee of the Movements for European Unity, 1947–55; secretary, European League for Economic Cooperation, 1948.

Prior to World War II, Retinger was best known as a Polish politician and the author of a work on Joseph Conrad and contemporary Polish writers. During World War II, however, Retinger gained broader international recognition as the representative to the Soviet Union from the Polish government-in-exile in London. In August 1944, Retinger was dropped by parachute into German-occupied territory of Poland as a courier to Polish partisans. His secret mission succeeded, even though he contracted polio while in Poland and had to be evacuated on a stretcher from Poland to Egypt.

After the war, Retinger worked diligently toward the unification of Europe. As early as 1947, he had quickly won over leading European economists to the idea of eliminating national economic barriers in Europe. In June of that year he and eight other prominent statesmen wrote a concise memorandum urging that the nations of Europe accept U.S. Secretary of State George Marshall's offer of financial help. In late 1947, he became the general secretary of the Joint International Committee of the Movements for European Unity, later known as the European Movement. In 1948 he was also secretary-general of the European League for Economic Cooperation.

His major loyalty during the last fifteen years of his life was to the conception of a united Europe. He was called one of the outstanding creative political influences of the postwar period, although he always remained in the background of any organization, usually acting as secretary. He was a quiet, selfless, unassuming man who knew most of the major politicians of Europe. In working toward European unification he often invited a number of diverse personalities to a meeting, suggested a few ideas, then sat back to see what would evolve. Once an idea had been launched and taken root, he stayed on the sidelines urging it on, leaving the leadership to others. In this way, he contributed greatly to the formation of the European Payments Union, the Economic Cooperation Administration, the Council of Europe, and the European Community.

BIBLIOGRAPHY:

A. *All About Poland: Facts, Figures, Documents* (London, 1941); *Conrad and His Contemporaries* (London, 1941).

B. LT 13 Jun 1960, 12, 14 Jun 1950, 15, 20 Jun 1960, 16; NYT 18 Feb 1950, 14, 24 Jun 1960, 27.

David C. Riede

REYNAUD, Paul (15 October 1878, Barcelonnette, Basses-Alpes, France—21 September 1966, Paris). *Education*: LL.D., Univ. of Paris; Ecole des Hautes Etudes Commerciales. *Career*: lawyer, Court of Appeals of Paris; deputy from Basses-Alpes, 1919, from Paris, 1928–40; minister of finance, 1930, 1938–40; minister of colonies, 1931–32; vice-president, Council of Ministry of Justice, 1932; prime minister, 1940; minister of foreign affairs and national defense, 1940; interned by Vichy government and Germans, 1940–45; member, Second Constituent Assembly, 1946; deputy of the Nord, 1946–58; minister of finance, 1948; delegate, Council of Europe, 1949–55, Common Assembly of European Coal and Steel Community, 1952–55; chair, Constitutional Consultative Committee, 1958; deputy from the Nord, 1958–62; chair, Committee on Finances, National Assembly, 1958–62.

Thoroughly disillusioned by the failure of collective security from the national level in preventing World War II, Reynaud became one of the most vocal and tireless advocates of a united Europe in the postwar period. Joining the movement before it had official French support, Reynaud undertook to become its spokesman on an international level. His initial experience with the potential of supranational political cooperation came at the beginning of the war when, with *Jean Monnet, he presented Winston Churchill with a proposal for uniting France and Britain in the face of an overwhelming German attack. While this proposal had no impact on the conduct of the war, it did inspire those who initiated it, and for Reynaud it seemed to be the answer to Europe's future. As soon as the United States proposed the Marshall Plan, he urged that it be the occasion for rapid movement toward European unification, complete with political power.

When the Council of Europe was created in 1949, Reynaud became a delegate to its Consultative Assembly, where he spoke openly and vigorously for a much stronger organization. He also supported the Schuman Plan, the European Defense Community, and the political community that was expected to follow. As the major leader of the moderate conservative parties in the French National Assembly, he was especially effective in promoting ratification of the Schuman Plan and defended the Defense Community Treaty with passion until it was rejected in 1954. Like many of his colleagues, Reynaud initially saw Britain as France's natural ally in the European movement and feared Germany. However, when it became clear that Britain would not cooperate in creating a strong Europe, he accepted partnership with Germany wholeheartedly.

Reynaud was also very effective in selling the European idea in the United States. A strong proponent of French collaboration in NATO, he visited the United States many times to promote Franco-American collaboration and European integration. Although he supported de Gaulle's return to power in 1958, he did not agree with his concept of Europe because it excluded an Atlantic defense organization as the foundation of European security.

BIBLIOGRAPHY:

A. *Au coeur de la mêlée* (Paris, 1951); *Et après?* (Paris, 1964); *La Politique étrangère de gaullisme* (Paris, 1964); *Les Mémoires de P. Reynaud et la Belgique* (Brussels, 1946); *Mémoires*, 2 vols. (Paris, 1960); *S'unir ou perir* (Paris, 1951).

B. Michael Brandstadter, "Paul Reynaud and the Third French Republic, 1919–1939; French Political Conservatism in the Interwar Years," dissertation, Duke Univ., 1971; CB 1950, 485–88; Joseph Conners, "Paul Reynaud and French National Defense, 1933–39," dissertation, Loyola Univ., 1977; André Geraud, *Les Fossoyeurs, défaite militaire de la France* (New York, 1943); NYT 22 Sep 1966, 1; WWF 1965–66, 2245; Arnold J. Zurcher, *The Struggle to Unite Europe 1940–1958* (New York, 1958).

C. Reynaud papers are in the Archives Nationales and the Archives du Ministère des Affaires Étrangères.

Anne Tucker Moore

RHYS WILLIAMS, Juliet Evangeline (17 December 1898—18 September 1964, London). *Education*: The Links, Eastbourne. *Career*: private secretary to parliamentary secretary, minister of transport, 1919–20; honorable secretary, Joint Council of Midwifery, 1934–39; member, Interdepartmental Committee on Abortion, 1937–38; assistant commercial relations officer, Ministry of Information, 1939–40; assistant section officer, WAAF, 1940; Economic Section, Congress of Europe, 1948; United Europe Movement, 1947–58, chair, 1958–64; director, *Economic Digest*, 1954–64; governor, BBC, 1952–56.

Between the world wars, Rhys Williams worked in the field of medical welfare and became an expert on economics. After World War II, she was a major supporter of European unity. She attended the Congress of Europe that met at The Hague on 7–10 May 1948, and was elected an honorary secretary of the Congress. She also served in its economic section.

The Congress was a major step in the eventual creation of the European Community, and it served as a spur to proponents of a united Europe. Rhys Williams returned to England after the Congress to become the secretary (later chairman) and principal propagandist of the British branch of the European League for Economic Co-operation. The ELEC was intended to be a forum for the discussion of European monetary questions; it held public and private meetings and issued pamphlets on various issues. Rhys Williams assumed considerable responsibility for the British organization and vigorously appealed to leading British personages for support, without particular regard to their political ties. Because of a cautious outlook, the ELEC was not explicitly in favor of British participation in the European Economic Community (EEC), and some of its members were staunchly anti-EEC.

In 1962 Rhys Williams opposed Britain's entry into the Community on the terms proposed by the Continental nations. She was particularly concerned with deflationary tendencies and a seeming lack of concern for social welfare by some Community spokesmen. Nevertheless, she continued to hope for, and to support actively, Britain's eventual entry into the EEC.

BIBLIOGRAPHY:

A, *In Search of Reality* (n.p., 1925); *A New Look at Britain's Economic Policy* (Middlesex, England, 1965); *Something to Look Forward to* (London, 1943); *Taxation and Incentive* (London, 1952).

B. LT 19 Sep 1964, 10; WWW 1961–70, 1951.

Michael D. Smith

RICH, Raymond Thomas (13 May 1899, Hyde Park, MA—15 July 1959, New York). *Education*: B.A., Brown Univ., 1922. *Career*: secretary, German Student Department, European Student Relief, 1922–23, acting executive secretary, Geneva headquarters, 1923; Eastern director, American Student Friendship Fund, 1923–24; instructor, Canton (China) Christian Coll., 1924–25; national field secretary, Foreign Policy Association, 1925–27; director, World Peace Foundation, 1927–36; chairman, Raymond T. Rich and Associates, 1936–59.

Rich began his work for international understanding as an organizer and administrator of world student groups. In 1925 the Foreign Policy Association, hoping to expand its membership and influence, hired Rich as national field secretary, instructing him to travel throughout the country organizing local chapters of the Association and reporting to the board of directors on international thinking in the nation. Rich was not particularly successful, and on several occasions the board reprimanded him for spending too little time in organization. While Association membership grew during Rich's tenure, on the whole his activities produced limited results, and in 1927 the Association released him.

Rich then joined the World Peace Foundation, serving as executive director from 1927 to 1936. There he presided over the development of a *World Affairs* pamphlet series which aimed, along with similar publications by other internationalist organizations of the period, at raising public understanding of foreign policy issues and producing discussions of solutions to international problems. While not primarily a writer, Rich had gained experience as a Far Eastern specialist while with the Foreign Policy Association, when he produced one major report on extraterritoriality and China's political and economic integrity. As a member of the World Peace Foundation, he wrote a study of the Kellogg-Briand Pact and served as editor of the *World Affairs* pamphlets in 1936 and 1937.

In 1936 Rich quit the World Peace Foundation to establish a consulting firm. Thereafter, his association with the cause of internationalism was limited to consultations on fund-raising for a few organizations. He aided a number of humanitarian and educational bodies, including the American Council on Education and the English Speaking Union. He also established a communication network among the foundations and for several years published a survey of their assets and grant policies. During World War II, Rich left his company to serve the war effort, first as chief of the Division of

Organized Groups for the Office of Civilian Defense and then with *Nelson Rockefeller in the Office of Inter-American Affairs. While Rich's direct efforts on behalf of internationalism largely ended after 1937, he continued his interest in and support for world affairs through membership in the Council of Foreign Relations and his assistance to some groups. Despite his rather prominent role in two internationally minded bodies, Rich must be judged less significant than his contemporaries in advancing the causes of internationalism.

BIBLIOGRAPHY:

A. *American Foundations and Their Fields* (New York, 1931); *Extra-territoriality and Tariff Autonomy in China* (Shanghai, 1925); with Denys P. Myers, *Syllabus for the Implementation of the Pact of Paris* (Boston, 1931).

B. NYT 16 Jul 1959, 27; WWWA 3, 723–24.

C. Rich papers are in the New York Public Library.

Frank W. Abbott

RICHARDS, Henry. See *Biographical Dictionary of Modern Peace Leaders.*

RIDDELL, Walter Alexander (5 August 1881, Stratford, ON—27 July 1963, Algonquin Park, ON). *Education*: B.A., Univ. of Manitoba, 1907; M.A., Columbia Univ., 1908, Ph.D., 1916; B.D., Union Theological Sem., 1912. *Career*: social surveys for Protestant churches, 1913–16; superintendent of trades and labor, Ontario, 1916–19; deputy minister of labor, 1919; chief of section, International Labor Office (ILO), 1920–25; member, Canadian delegation to Assembly of League and ILO, 1925–37; Canadian adviser to League, 1925–37; member and chairman, governing body of ILO, 1935–37; counselor, Canadian legation, Washington, 1937–40; high commissioner to New Zealand, 1940–46; professor, Univ. of Toronto, 1946–52.

In the 1920s Riddell accepted a position with the International Labor Office of the League of Nations as a staff member and subsequently served on its governing body and represented Canada as a delegate to the League. The Canadian government in 1925 appointed Riddell its permanent representative in Geneva in addition to its delegate to the meetings of the ILO. Two major international incidents became central to Riddell's career: the Sino-Japanese dispute and the Italo-Ethiopian War. The rising power of Japan in the Far East threatened to upset the international situation fashioned by the Washington agreements of 1921–22. In September 1931, Japan manufactured the Mukden incident to invade three provinces of eastern China. The Canadian government wished an immediate armistice and a status quo in Asia; but a Conservative cabinet minister from Ottawa, C. H. Cahan, spoke to the Assembly on 8 December 1932, to urge sympathy with the Japanese effort to preserve "its rights and interests therein." Upset by this statement, the Canadian government could not repudiate one of its ministers. Instead Riddell was instructed to smooth things over by leaking information to the League that Cahan's view was not that of Canada. The Canadian minister in Washington gave similar assurances to the State Department.

The second major League development became known as the Riddell Incident. Italy invaded Ethiopia in October 1935, provoking discussion in the Assembly about possible sanctions against the aggressor and the appointment of the Committee of Eighteen to determine League action. The Canadian government favored the policy of Britain and France in supporting sanctions against Italy. As League momentum built for action and as Riddell recognized more clearly that sanctions were necessary to check Italy now and perhaps Germany later, the Conservative government lost the election and was replaced by Liberals, who leaned away from involvement in European affairs. In the confusion of policies, a Canadian press release stated that the government supported League sanctions but only under the most stringent conditions. Undeterred by this cable and other instructions and at a moment of crucial indecision in Geneva, Riddell pressed on firmly at the Committee of Eighteen for oil sanctions, giving voice to the so-called Canadian proposal. Discovering this Canadian initiative in the Ottawa morning newspaper, Prime Minister *MacKenzie King was furious and informed other governments that this response did not reflect Canadian policy but was the personal opinion of Riddell. King was dissuaded from dismissing him, and Riddell remained at Geneva two more years. He completed his career as counselor at the legation in Washington as high commissioner to New Zealand and as author of his internationalist belief in *World Security by Conference* (1947).

BIBLIOGRAPHY:

A. *Documents on Canadian External Relations* 5 (Ottawa), 377–93; ed., *Documents on Canadian Foreign Policy, 1917–1939* (Toronto, 1962); *World Security by Conference* (Toronto, 1947).

B. *Canadian Historical Association Reports* (1940), 74–84, (1972), 263–86; James Eayrs, *In Defence of Canada: Appeasement and Rearmament* (Toronto, 1965); *External Affairs* 21 (Oct 1969), 366–75; *Macmillan Dictionary of Canadian Biography* (Toronto, 1978), 703–4; C. P. Stacey, *Canada and the Age of Conflict: A History of Canadian External Policy, Volume II, 1921: The MacKenzie-King Era* (Buffalo, 1981); *University of Toronto Quarterly* 5 (Jul 1936), 482–98; Richard Veatch, *Canada and the League of Nations* (Toronto, 1975); WWC 1949–50, 848, 1958–59, 1312.

C. The Riddell papers are in York Univ. Archives.

Terence J. Fay

RIO-BRANCO, Baron of. See Paranhos, José Maria da Silva, Jr.

RITZEL, Heinrich Georg (1893, Offenbach a. Main, Germany—1971, Michelstadt, West Germany). *Education*: studied law, national economy, and philosophy. *Career*: professional municipal administrator, 1919–30; member of German Reichstag, 1920–33; general secretary, European Union, 1939–45; member, West German Bundestag, 1949–66; member, Council of Europe, 1951–66.

Ritzel was a lifelong fighter in the political arena, but he concentrated on two major areas—political tyranny and racial prejudice, and the unity of Europe. During the Weimar Republic he held many municipal and provincial offices and then was elected to the Reichstag. He was a member of the German Socialist party, and in 1933, after Hitler became chancellor, Ritzel voted against the Enabling Act, which gave Hitler dictatorial powers. As a result of his negative voice, Ritzel was arrested and imprisoned in a concentration camp, from which he escaped in June 1933, and made his way to Switzerland by way of the Saar and France. While in Switzerland he was a free-lance writer until 1939, when he became general secretary of the European Union in Basel. He served in this capacity during World War II and did much to further the concept of a united Europe. In 1947 he returned to Germany, where between 1949 and 1966 he was a member of the German Bundestag and the Council of Europe in Strasbourg.

While serving in the Bundestag he attempted to eliminate prejudice toward the Jews and was mainly responsible for the passage of the Restitution Law, which partially compensated Jews whom the Nazis had driven out. Because of his work, in 1962 at the age of sixty-nine Ritzel was made an honorary fellow of the Weizmann Institute of Science in Rehovot, Israel. Until his retirement from active political life in 1966, Ritzel showed continual interest in furthering the cause of European unification, primarily through his membership in the Council of Europe.

BIBLIOGRAPHY:

A. *Einer von Vierhundertundzwei* (Offenbach a. Main, 1953); *Europa und Deutschland, Deutschland und Europa* (Offenbach a. Main, 1947); *Kampf um Europa* (n.p., n.d.); with Hans Bauer, *Kampf um Europa von der Schweiz aus gesehen* (Zurich, 1945); with Hans Bauer, *Von der eidgenossischen zur Europaischen Federation* (Zurich, 1940).

B. Information from American Committee for the Weizmann Institute of Science and a son, Dr. Gerhard Ritzel; NYT 1 Nov 1962, 8.

David C. Riede

ROBERTS, Owen Josephus (2 May 1876, Philadelphia—17 May 1955, Chester Springs, PA). *Education*: B.A., Univ. of Pennsylvania, 1895, LL.B., 1898. *Career*: faculty member, Univ. of Pennsylvania, 1898–1918; special U.S. attorney general to investigate oil reserve scandals; associate justice, U.S. Supreme Court, 1930–45; on board of inquiry to investigate Pearl Harbor attack; dean, Univ. of Pennsylvania Law School, 1945–51; president, Atlantic Union Committee, 1949–55.

After a notable career as an associate justice of the U.S. Supreme Court,

Roberts retired in 1945. Vigorously opposed to isolation, he supported the Marshall Plan, UN, and NATO. He believed, however, that these approaches did not go far enough, that the world needed a federal union of free people. The vehicle for this ambition was the Atlantic Union Committee (AUC), which Roberts helped organize in 1949, and he served as its president until his death. The AUC was created as an independent political action counterpart of Federal Union, Inc., which Clarence Streit had formed in 1939 after publishing *Union Now* to educate the public on the need for a federal union of the Atlantic nations.

The AUC undertook a campaign to persuade Congress to pass a resolution calling a federal convention of the Atlantic democracies to explore the possibility of Atlantic unity. As structured, the Union would vest a common government with powers to conduct foreign policy and defense, regulate trade, currency, and communications, and establish a common citizenship, while other authority would remain with member nations. Initially, Roberts and his colleagues hoped to obtain as sponsors the Atlantic Pact nations—the United States, the Netherlands, Belgium, France, England, and Luxemburg. World events after 1949, however, forced the AUC to retreat gradually from its original view, and it came to accept NATO as the territorial and institutional basis for an Atlantic Union. Roberts and the Committee also modified its resolution from one which called for an Atlantic Union convention to an Atlantic exploratory meeting.

It was anticipated that the latter would study exhaustively the interrelated problems confronting the Atlantic nations (e.g., their separate policies) and recommend means of solving them which would be both practical and adequate. To advance this idea, Roberts cooperated with senators and representatives willing to introduce successive concurrent resolutions into both houses of Congress. Such connections as well as contacts with administrative leaders such as *George Marshall, James Forrestal, and Averell Harriman helped focus attention on Europe and the Atlantic Community concept.

During his six-year battle for a convention, Roberts's diligence and fine sense of timing nurtured the idea. The AUC and its work continued beyond Roberts's death in 1955, with a resolution passed in 1960 and an Atlantic Convention called in 1962. In Paris (8–20 January), the delegates did not conform to expectations. Instead of exploring the feasibility of Atlantic federal union, they considered techniques of extending greater cooperation among the NATO nations. A Declaration of Paris appealed to NATO governments to develop plans within two years for the creation of an Atlantic Community organized to meet challenges of the time. NATO members were also encouraged to appoint members to a special commission on Atlantic Union. An Atlantic Union was not created and never seriously considered by the United States or European governments.

Roberts's contributions to American and world safety and the judiciary were manifold, but, as Secretary of State George C. Marshall said, perhaps his most important act was his resignation from the Supreme Court to apply his talents to the cause of peace and Atlantic union.

BIBLIOGRAPHY:

A. "American Attitudes on World Organization," *Public Opinion Quarterly* 17 (Winter 1953–54), 405–42; "Atlantic Union: Shall It Be Created Now?" *Rotarian* 75 (Dec 1949), 14–15; "History Is Catching Up with 'Union Now,' " *Fortune* 39 (Apr 1949), 77–78; numerous articles in *Freedom and Union Magazine* and *Atlantic Union Now Bulletin*.

B. Articles, letters, and correspondence in *Atlantic Union Committee Papers*; DAB supp. 5, 571–77; NCAB A, 88–89; NYT 18 May 1955, 1; *Time* 52 (23 Aug 1948), 72.

Emmett E. Panzella

ROBINSON, Joseph Taylor (26 August 1872, near Lonoke, AR—14 July 1937, Washington). *Education*: Univ. of Arkansas, 1890–92; studied law, Univ. of Virginia, 1895, and in Lonoke. *Career*: state legislator, 1894–96; law practice, 1896–1902; congressman, 1903–13; governor of Arkansas, 1913; senator, 1913–37; Democratic vice-presidential candidate, 1928.

Robinson went to the House of Representatives in 1903 from a rural environment and while there displayed a nationalistic spirit in his big navy advocacy and in urging a strict policy on immigration. Yet his interest in internationalism appeared in 1910, when he introduced a resolution to allocate a peace fund of $10 million to be at the disposal of the secretary of state and the American delegation to the Inter-Parliamentary Union.

Robinson supported *Woodrow Wilson's war policy in 1917, and thereafter he became an enthusiastic exponent of Wilsonian internationalism. He approved the League Covenant, including Article X with its provision for collective security, because he did not think it would impair national sovereignty. The war power of Congress would protect it, and economic sanctions alone would keep the peace. He did much to rally Senate opposition to the Knox Resolution in 1919 to separate the Covenant from the Treaty of Versailles. Robinson stood stalwartly against approval with reservations during debates over membership and, as chairman of the Democratic National Convention in 1920, worked to commit the party to immediate entry into the League. Thereafter, Robinson as a senator revealed solid but not unqualified support for efforts to promote international cooperation and peace. He regularly attended meetings of the Inter-Parliamentary Union in Stockholm (1921), Copenhagen (1923), and Geneva (1934). In 1926 he voted for the World Court Protocol but opposed a renewed debate on the matter in 1927, feeling it was untimely. He approved the Washington Conference (1921–22) Five Power Treaty limiting naval construction and the Nine Power Treaty for Chinese territorial integrity, but he opposed the Four Power Treaty on Pacific territories, fearing commitments that favored Japan. He fought the high tariff Fordney-McCumber Bill of

1922, although he wanted rice protected. On war debts he succeeded in getting bipartisan membership of the Debt Funding Commission, and in 1923–26 he approved of several of the international debt settlements, balking at the Italian one, however, because Italy had not sufficiently limited armaments. He shared the parochialism of some Democratic colleagues in supporting the Emergency Immigration Act of 1921 and the Johnson Act of 1924, although he would have approved the entrance of Armenians hard-pressed by the Turks.

As the Democratic vice-presidential candidate in 1928, he criticized opponents of the League but did not press for U.S. entrance, a position consonant with his party's position. He supported the Kellogg-Briand Pact and the London Naval Treaty of 1930 further limiting naval forces, in part because he had helped draft it as a delegate. In 1935 he played a key role as majority leader in efforts to obtain Senate approval of membership in the World Court.

Robinson voted for the so-called Neutrality Acts of 1935, 1936, and 1937 with much reluctance because he doubted their efficacy in limiting war abroad and feared they would impair the true neutrality of the United States. Robinson left behind him the record of a respected lawmaker who reflected many of the internationalist currents of his time.

BIBLIOGRAPHY:

B. Harold T. Butler, "Partisan Positions of Isolationism vs. Internationalism (1918–1932)," dissertation, Syracuse Univ., 1963; DAB supp. 2, 566–68; Gilbert R. Grant, "Joseph Taylor Robinson in Foreign Affairs," *Arkansas Historical Quarterly* 9 (Autumn 1950), 133–71; Nevin E. Neal, "A Biography of Joseph T. Robinson," dissertation, Univ. of Oklahoma, 1957.

C. The Robinson papers are in the Univ. of Arkansas Library.

Harold T. Butler

ROCKEFELLER, John Davison, Jr. (29 January 1874, Cleveland, OH—11 May 1960, Tucson, AZ). *Education*: B.A., Brown Univ., 1897. *Career*: corporate executive, philanthropist, 1897–1960.

Rockefeller's international involvements were tied almost exclusively to his philanthropic interests. Early in the twentieth century he and his father saw a need to apply some of their rapidly increasing wealth toward public benefactions. To help them achieve this goal, they assembled aides and advisors, including *Abraham Flexner, Simon Flexner, Frederick T. Gates, and *Raymond B. Fosdick. Most of these men followed a scientific approach in applying research to resolve contemporary problems and to advance humanity. Family members and the Rockefeller Foundation, created in 1913, developed many international programs related to this public service concept.

While the most noted involved world health, the outreach encompassed many other global concerns. In all these efforts, Rockefeller played a predominant role. He insisted on careful study and analysis before commitment, and his approval of new programs requiring extensive fiscal involvement was always required. Activity in the human health field began in 1901 with the creation of the Rockefeller Institute for Medical Research to promote investigation into diseases to seek their prevention and cure and to disseminate the knowledge acquired. Among its major international achievements were the virtual eradication of yellow fever and the promotion of medical education. Rockefeller served as president of the Institute (1929–50) and contributed over $6 million toward its work. The Rockefeller Sanitary Commission, which began in 1909 and was absorbed into the Rockefeller Foundation in 1913, included international health activities directed toward the control and cure of tropical and semitropical diseases, especially malaria and typhus. It also sought to promote medical research and the training of nurses and doctors. Called the International Health Board of the Rockefeller Foundation and later the International Health Division, it contributed regularly to support programs of world agencies, especially those of the League of Nations. Rockefeller also became active in the Bureau of Social Hygiene, established in 1911. Its international outreach included studies of prostitution and police systems in Europe.

Under Rockefeller's leadership, the Foundation sought to fulfill its announced objective of bettering mankind everywhere. He served as the Foundation's president (1913–17) and as chairman of its board of trustees (1917–40). As such, he became involved in all important decisions related to allocation of its resources. Internationally, these included World War I relief to Belgium, sanitary work in the Balkans, and the restoration of historic buildings, including the Cathedral at Rheims and Versailles. Its medical work encompassed the China Medical Board and Peking (Peiping) Union Medical College and gifts to University College Hospital Medical School, London and to centers in Brussels, Belgium, Lyon, France, and New Delhi. Its agricultural programs led to research into new strains of plants to increase food production, especially in rice-growing areas of the world. It also engaged in a major attack upon anthrax strains.

Rockefeller also became extensively involved in international education. He created the International Education Board in 1923, with its work assumed after 1937 by the Foundation and another agency, the General Education Board. Rockefeller held no key positions, but his personal gifts exceeded $21 million. Scholarships, fellowships, exchange professorships, and grants to universities marked its work. He personally contributed $15 million to build International Houses in New York, Chicago, Berkeley, and Paris, which provided residence facilities for foreign students and thus encouraged them to attend U.S. colleges and universities. In return, they were to serve as good-will ambassadors while in the country.

Through contacts with Fosdick and *Arthur Sweetser, Rockefeller became concerned with League of Nations activities. Sweetser suggested many projects which the League's budget could not sustain, and he provided a steady flow of information, usually through Fosdick, to stimulate Rockefeller's interest. Rockefeller came to see the League as an agency which could pursue projec.s in science, health, social work, and economics, which had always been concerns of the family and the Foundation. This led to gifts by 1929 of $350,700 for Epidemiological Intelligence and Public Health Statistics, $500,800 for an exchange of public health personnel, $27,067 for the Center for Public Health Documentation, $155,000 to the Epidemiological Intelligence Bureau of the Far East, and nearly $724,000 to the League's Health Organization. The Foundation also assisted the Graduate Institute of International Studies in Geneva, and in 1930 it provided $90,000 for a League study on double taxation.

Rockefeller personally contributed by creating a Swiss corporation which held land surrounding the League's grounds to protect it from commercial intrusion, with the major area donated to the University of Geneva. He helped create and maintain an International School in Geneva, and he contributed $5,000 to the League's Disarmament Commission. Rockefeller's most significant impact appeared in 1927 with the announcement of a $2 million gift for a building and an endowment for a library for the League. That amount would build a structure so large that League administrators had to reconsider their plans for a new headquarters. Rather than build along the lakeshore, they acquired adjacent Ariana Park for the new office complex. In 1946 the announcement of Rockefeller's gift of land in Manhattan acquired at his personal cost of $8,515,000 provided a site for the United Nations. Thus, one man determined the headquarters location of the two major international institutions of the twentieth century. The latter gift proved to be a suitable capstone to Rockefeller's international philanthropy.

BIBLIOGRAPHY:

B. DAB supp. 6, 547–49; Raymond B. Fosdick, *John D. Rockefeller, Jr., A Portrait* (New York, 1956); NCAB 44, 1–7.

C. The Rockefeller papers are in the Rockefeller Foundation Archives and the family collection is in Tarrytown, NY.

Warren F. Kuehl

ROCKEFELLER, John Davison, 3rd (21 March 1906, New York—10 July 1978, Tarrytown, NY). *Education*: B.A., Princeton Univ., 1929. *Career*: philanthropist and foundation executive; founder, trustee, and chair, Asia Society, 1955–78; director, president, chair, Japan Society, 1952–78; founder, president, chair, Agricultural Development Council, 1953–73; director, president, chair, Lincoln Center for the Performing Arts, 1956–70; founder, trustee, chair, Population Council, 1953–78; trustee, and chair, Rockefeller Foundation, 1931–71.

The close of World War II brought the United States face to face with the unprecedented problem of rebuilding a world devastated by six years of total war. The problem of economic reconstruction was complicated by the outbreak of nationalist and Communist revolutions throughout Asia, the growing ideological and military confrontation between the United States and the Soviet Union, and the advent of the atomic age. The causes of this crisis and the proper responses to it were the subject of intense discussion during this period, a debate eventually resolved by the coupling of economic assistance to military aid, as in the model of NATO and the Marshall Plan.

John D. Rockefeller, 3rd contributed to the resolution of this debate by insisting that the vast material and intellectual resources of the United States should be brought to bear on the underlying causes of war, revolution, and social unrest. A strong anti-Communist and a staunch advocate of the liberal capitalist order as propounded by his father, *John D., Jr., Rockefeller believed that the problems of diseases, poverty, outmoded methods of agricultural production, and, most importantly, the new and alarming rates of population growth around the world were the seedbed of revolution. From the late 1940s until his death in 1978, he argued that the United States and its allies should pursue a policy of reform based on the elimination of these social inequities or face the consequences.

A liberal education at Princeton in economics and industrial relations was followed by a world tour in the company of *James G. McDonald, the director of the Foreign Policy Association (FPA). This trip brought young Rockefeller into contact with many national leaders of the day, including *Ramsay MacDonald of Great Britain, *Gustav Stresemann of Germany, and Kotaro Tanaka of Japan, and culminated with his attendance at the Institute of Pacific Relations (IPR) Conference in Kyoto in October 1929. This trip stimulated what would be a lifelong interest in the Pacific Basin, which was further strengthened by membership on the Council on Foreign Relations, FPA, and IPR, service as a trustee of the Rockefeller Foundation and the China Medical Board, and his work during World War II with the State-War-Navy Coordinating Committee. In the 1930s, Rockefeller also supported membership in the World Court and societies working to promote greater cooperation with the League of Nations.

Rockefeller's formal involvement with Asian problems began with his service as an adviser on cultural relations to *John Foster Dulles during negotiations for a Japanese peace treaty in 1951. In this report, Rockefeller urged that bilateral organizations be encouraged in both countries to foster greater understanding and cultural interchange. At the request of Dulles, Rockefeller initiated the development of the International House of Tokyo and the revival of the Japan Society in New York. In subsequent years, he also helped found the Asia Society, the India International Centre in New Delhi, and the JDR 3rd Fund, which supported the training and work of Asians in all artistic fields.

Concomitantly, Rockefeller supported basic research and training in the fields of agricultural economics and population studies, including the development of a safe, effective, and inexpensive contraceptive for use in the less developed world. Over time, these two activities became the central and interrelated elements of his approach to the problems of development and global interdependence. The work of both the Population Council and the Agricultural Development Council, as well as the efforts in scientific agriculture pioneered by the Rockefeller Foundation and leading to the so-called Green Revolution, was heavily influenced initially, by the neo-Malthusian doctrines of Fairfield Osborn, *Julian Huxley, Frank Notestein, and Wolf Ladejinsky. These organizations sought to impress upon the U.S. government, Asian, and later African and Latin American governments, as well as international organizations, the importance of family planning programs and rational land use and agricultural training schemes in the process of development.

In his later years, Rockefeller concentrated more and more on questions of "quality of Life," gradually fusing the concepts of population control and agricultural development into a theory which stressed the rights of the individual, the essentiality of voluntary efforts, and the importance of understanding the roles and status of women in the overall process of development.

Rockefeller occupied a unique position in American society because of his wealth and family name. He used both unstintingly to pursue a course of moderate reform aimed at eliminating the most overt abuses of the capitalist order and calling attention to the very great dangers which unchecked population growth posed to world civilization.

BIBLIOGRAPHY:

A. "Japan Tackles Her Problems," *Foreign Affairs* 33 (Jul 1954), 577–87; *The Second American Revolution* (New York, 1973).

B. Peter Collier and David Horowitz, *The Rockefellers: An American Dynasty* (New York, 1976); Geoffrey Hellman, "Profiles (John D. Rockefeller 3rd)," *New Yorker* 48 (4 Nov 1972), 56–58[+]; Alan Moscow, *The Rockefeller Inheritance* (New York, 1977); NYT 11 Jul 1978, 1.

Peter J. Johnson

ROCKEFELLER, Nelson Aldrich (8 July 1908, Bar Harbor, ME—26 January 1979, New York). *Education*: B.A., Dartmouth Coll., 1930. *Career*: family businesses, philanthropic interests, and art patron, 1930–40, 1945–53, 1956–58, 1977–79; coordinator, Office of Inter-American Affairs, 1940–44; assistant secretary of state for Latin American affairs, 1944–45; promoter of economic and social development in Latin America, 1945–53; under secretary of health, education, and welfare, 1953–54; special assistant to the president for foreign affairs, 1954–55; governor of New York, 1959–73; vice-president, 1974–77.

Born into a family of legendary wealth and advantage, Rockefeller developed an activist, charismatic personality. He learned to exercise the privileges that came with his fortune without flaunting them. His early education included European travel, and on his honeymoon he took a trip around the world. He trained briefly with the Chase National Bank, including posts in London and Paris, and he helped manage the Rockefeller Center. He developed a cosmopolitan taste in the arts, served as trustee for major museums, and developed his own collection.

Business and travel during the 1930s introduced Rockefeller to Latin America, an area that captured his interest. After investing heavily in the Venezuelan subsidiary of Standard Oil, he toured that country in 1937 and became convinced that U.S. firms had responsibilities to promote the economic and social advancement in their less-developed host nations. His efforts to work with the Latin Americans came just as *Franklin D. Roosevelt's administration was taking steps to prepare the Western Hemisphere for all contingencies, and Rockefeller easily gained access to the White House and helped create a special agency, the Office of the Coordinator of Inter-American Affairs (CIAA). Rockefeller accepted appointment as its head after consulting his family because he became the first Rockefeller to enter public service. It changed his life.

Rockefeller energetically led the CIAA's activities in a vast public relations operation to sell the United States and its war effort in Latin America. Unfortunately, the programs rarely included reciprocal coverage to educate the people of the United States about their neighbors. The CIAA almost became a second State Department in that region, and this precipitated bureaucratic clashes that were usually won by Secretary *Cordell Hull and his director of Latin American policy, *Sumner Welles. When Hull resigned, Roosevelt reorganized the State Department and elevated Rockefeller to a new assistant secretary post specifically for Latin American affairs.

Roosevelt believed absolutely in the Good Neighbor Policy, based on the principle of nonintervention, and he determined to end a deterioration in hemispheric relations stemming from divided viewpoints in the State Department. Rockefeller began to negotiate a face-saving rapprochement with Juan D. Perón, after major wartime misunderstandings with Argentina. He also succeeded in reconnecting hemispheric ties, sometimes merely by sympathetically acknowledging Latin American interests and needs, as in Mexico City in March 1945 at a special inter-American conference on regional matters of war and peace.

The positions Rockefeller took led to major battles at the San Francisco Conference to found the United Nations Organization. He supported the Latin American demands and votes for hemispheric solidarity that guaranteed Argentina's admission, which went against the Soviet Union's belief that Roosevelt had concurred at the Yalta Conference to bar such membership. Joining with Senator *Arthur H. Vandenburg, he also fought beside the Latin Americans for rights similar to the Soviets' in Eastern Europe for independent regional responses to aggression. The Latin

Americans saw this move as a way to bind the United States to them within the inter-American system. Over bitter opposition from the leading planners of the U.S. delegation, who feared regional diminution of the world organization's authority, provision was made for collective regional self-defense.

Rockefeller left his post in 1945 and was disappointed when the United States turned away from Latin America. For several years he tried to accomplish privately with Rockefeller resources what he had advocated publicly. He helped to secure the permanent home for the United Nations in New York City by convincing his father to purchase and donate the site. He funded philanthropic organizations to help Latin Americans learn how to develop businesses, and he founded joint venture companies to seek profits for his southern partners and his family. Some of the projects worked; others did not. Yet they illustrated his firm belief in capitalism and the system's viability for the advancement of Latin America, especially during the Cold War struggle against Communism. His governmental connections did allow his ideas to influence "Point 4," the well-conceived but underfunded aid program for technical developmental assistance to the Third World.

During the last quarter-century of his life, Rockefeller continued to devote major attention to foreign policy and defense matters while seeking and serving in high state and national posts. He was a foremost advocate of international positions for the United States promoting responsible capitalism, developmental aid, and a strong military defense.

BIBLIOGRAPHY:

A. *The Rockefeller Report on the Americas* (Chicago, 1969).

B. Robert H. Connery and Gerald Benjamin, *Rockefeller of New York: Executive Power in the Statehouse* (Ithaca, NY, 1979); James Desmond, *Nelson Rockefeller: A Political Biography* (New York, 1964); Michael Kramer and Sam Roberts, *"I Never Wanted to be Vice-President of Anything!" An Investigative Biography of Nelson Rockefeller* (New York, 1976); Joe A. Morris, *Nelson Rockefeller: A Biography* (New York, 1960).

C. Some Rockefeller papers are at Columbia Univ.

J. Tillapaugh

ROERICH, Nicholas K. (27 September 1874, St. Petersburg—12 December 1947, Punjab, India). *Education*: studied law, Univ. of St. Petersburg; graduate, Academy of Fine Arts, St. Petersburg.

As artist, archeologist, author, Asiatic explorer, orator, poet, and mystic philosopher, Roerich expended enormous energies fostering art as the unifying spirit of all humanity, as the indivisible element for the construction of future culture. In 1920, he came to the United States under the auspices of the Art Institute of Chicago, where he helped form the Cor Ardens, an international society of art workers. In New York he founded the Master

Institute of United Artists (1921) and the Corona Mundi (1922), an international art center for fostering and distributing art objects throughout the country, and in 1928, the Roerich Museum opened at 310 Riverside Drive. It contained a school of all the arts and was devoted to the exhibition of creative art from all parts of the world. Some 1,000 of Roerich's 3,000 paintings were exhibited here, while others were hung in galleries in twenty-five countries.

With the aid of fellow artists and friends of peace, the International Union for the Roerich Pact was formed and international conferences were held in 1931, 1932, and 1933. The Roerich Pact, drafted by Georges Chklaver of the University of Paris, sought international understanding through a common appreciation of culture and beauty. It also provided for the registration of all monuments, cultural institutions, and scientific and art collections. These sites, marked by a Banner of Peace, should be considered as neutral by all nations and thus protected from attack in time of war. Attributed to Roerich, the flag had three red dots inside one red circle on a white field, symbolic of the unity of the spiritual, artistic, and educational forces of humanity, which Roerich felt would protect the values of human genius and thus preserve the spiritual health of nations. International conferences to promote the idea were held in the 1920s and 1930s in Belgium and Washington, and Roerich Societies, twenty-two in the United States and over eleven in Latin America, sought to advance the concept. With Secretary of Agriculture *Henry A. Wallace representing the United States, delegates from twenty-one Pan American nations signed the Roerich Pact on 15 April 1935.

Roerich also created the Himalaya Research Institute at Naggar, India, where he brought together scientists from many lands to collect specimens and study biology, medicine, archaelogy, and astrochemistry. Followers of Roerich thought he was a genius and/or a god who could unify humanity through culture and that his paintings had divine healing qualities.

BIBLIOGRAPHY:

A. *Heart of Asia* (New York, 1930); *Himalaya* (New York, 1926); *Realm of Light* (New York, 1931).

B. Richard D. Burns and Charyl L. Smith, "Nicholas Roerich, Henry A. Wallace and the "Peace Banner," *Peace and Change* 1 (Spring 1973), 40–49; Frances R. Grant, "Nicholas Roerich's Plan for World Peace," *World Unity Magazine* 9 (Feb 1932), 307–13; Theodore Helene, *Voice of an Epoch: Nicholas Roerich* (New Age Press, 1948); NCAB C, 146–47; *Newsweek* 31 (22 Mar 1948), 27–29; NYT 16 Dec 1947, 33; *Bulletin of Pan American Union* 69 (May 1935), 359–69.

C. Roerich materials can be found in the Swarthmore Coll. Peace Collection and in the Univ. of Rochester Library.

Anne L. Day

ROLIN, Henri (3 May 1891, Ghent—20 April 1973, Paris). *Education*: LL.D., Univ. of Ghent, 1919. *Career*: Belgian Army, 1914–18, 1940; attaché, Paris Peace Conference, 1919; legal staff, Foreign Ministry, 1921, *chef de cabinet* to minister, 1925–27, legal adviser, 1927; expert or delegate to most League of Nations Assemblies, 1921–40, on Council, 1926; faculty, Free Univ. of Brussels, 1923, professor, 1932; professor, Hague Academy of International Law, 1926; member of Belgian Senate, 1932–68, president, 1947–50; vice-president, International Federation of League of Nations Societies, 1932, later president; under secretary of national defense, 1942; delegate, San Francisco Conference, 1945, UN General Assembly, 1946; judge, European Court of Human Rights, 1959, president, 1968–71; member, Permanent Court of Arbitration, 1939–51; chair, Legal Committee of Consultative Assembly, Council of Europe.

Rolin was a Belgian Socialist, jurist, and internationalist. Unlike most Belgians in positions of power after World War I, who continued the traditional orientation toward the historic guarantors, Britain and France, he committed himself wholeheartedly to international organization in 1919 and remained constant to it through his long career. As secretary to *Paul Hymans at the Paris Peace Conference, Rolin helped draft the League of Nations Covenant. In 1920 he served on the League's committee to prepare the statute of the Permanent Court of International Justice, before which he would plead in later years. In 1923, he and Hymans were outspoken at Geneva against Italy's seizure of Corfu and in trying to maintain the League's authority. Through his long career at the League, which extended into early United Nations sessions, Rolin championed the role of small nations in international organizations.

In 1925 as *chef de cabinet* to *Emile Vandervelde, Rolin largely conducted Belgium's diplomacy during the Locarno negotiations. In July and August, he tried unsuccessfully to resolve discrepancies between the proposed Rhineland pact and the League Covenant, broaden the League's role in the pact's operation, and extend its coverage to Luxemburg. Britain and France interpreted his moves as aimed at greater Belgian independence from France; British approval and French distrust thus increased. Rolin participated in the London jurists' conference to draft the pact and the jurists committee at Locarno. However, when *Gustav Stresemann promptly interpreted the pact as permitting German repurchase of Eupen and Malmédy from Belgium, he fought retrocession.

After 1936 Rolin deplored Belgium's reversion to neutrality. Upon Germany's invasion of Poland, he warned that Belgium's turn would come within a year. After wartime exile and the founding United Nations meetings, he returned to teaching and international law, also becoming the first Socialist president of the Belgian Senate. During the Cold War, he urged Western detente with the Soviet bloc, despite the unpopularity of this view. Primarily, the last phase of his career was again devoted to international organization as he contributed his legal talents toward construction of European union, notably in the Council of Europe and the European Court of Human Rights.

BIBLIOGRAPHY:

A. *La Belgique neutre?* (Brussels, 1937); *La Politique de la Belgique dans la Société des Nations* (Geneva, 1931).

B. *Documents diplomatiques belges, 1920–1940*, 5 vols. (Brussels, 1964–66); Paul Hymans, *Mémoires*, 2 vols. (Brussels, 1958); IWW 1971–72, 1364; LT 21 Apr 1973, 14, 28 Apr 1973, 16; NYT 21 Apr 1973, 30; WB 1948, 4062; WWBL 1962, 858.

Sally Marks

ROLIN-JAEQUEMYNS, Edouard (23 January 1863, Ghent—11 July 1936, Brussels). *Education*: Univs. of Ghent, Paris, and Brussels; LL.D., Univ. of Brussels, 1884. *Career*: lawyer, Brussels, 1884; editorial secretary, *Revue de droit international et de législation comparée*, 1887–89, member of editorial board, 1890–92, editor-in-chief, 1893–1914; associate member, Institut de Droit International, 1891–96, secretary-treasurer, 1891–94, member, 1896, president, 1922–23; delegate, First Hague Peace Conference, 1899; auditor, then member of Conseil Supérieur, Congo Free State; member of Conseil Colonial, 1908; founded Agency for the Assistance of Prisoners of War, 1914; secretary-general, Belgian delegation, Paris Peace Conference; secretary-general, Spa Conference, 1920; high commissioner, Inter-Allied Rhineland High Commission, 1920–25; minister of interior and of health, 1925–26; member, Permanent Court of Arbitration, 1928–30; delegate, League of Nations Assembly, 1928–30; judge, Permanent Court of International Justice, 1930–36; secretary-general, Academy of International Law, The Hague.

Rolin-Jaequemyns was born into a family of scholarly internationalists and continued the family tradition. As a youth, he joined the staff of the *Revue de droit international et de législation comparée*, founded primarily by his father, *Gustave. In 1893, he succeeded his father as editor-in-chief, continuing until World War I forced suspension of publication. He also participated in the First Hague Peace Conference, serving as rapporteur of the Second Committee, which established international regulations for land warfare. Meanwhile, he became a member of the Congo Free State's Conseil Supérieur, effectively its supreme court, and upon Belgian annexation in 1908 he joined the Conseil Colonial. In 1914, he established an agency, based upon the Hague regulations, to aid Belgian and French prisoners of war in Germany.

At war's end, *Paul Hymans appointed Rolin-Jaequemyns secretary-general of the Belgian delegation to the Paris Peace Conference. There he discovered a pronounced taste for practical involvement in international questions and an unusual talent as a diplomatist. He served on the committee to fix responsibility for the war, participated in the effort to revise Belgium's international status, ran the delegation during the final phase of the Conference, and signed the Treaty of Sèvres. He was also secretary-general of the 1920 Spa Conference, serving as intermediary between the German delegations.

Rolin-Jaequemyn's talent and energy at Paris earned him appointment late in 1920 as Belgium's first Rhineland high commissioner. At Coblenz, he pursued a moderate course between the extremes of British and French policy and was noted for his authoritative legal interpretations, integrity, serenity, and firmness. In October 1923, he moved decisively against Rhenish separatism, which soon collapsed in the Belgian zone.

In 1925 Rolin-Jaequemyns briefly joined the Belgian Cabinet. Thereafter he taught law at Ghent and became a member of the Permanent Court of Arbitration, serving on numerous arbitration and conciliation commissions. He also participated in League of Nations Assemblies, where he played an active role in commissions to study disarmament, arbitration, and security. In 1930, he was elected to the Permanent Court of International Justice, where his expertise, clear vision, lofty outlook, and even temperament were highly valued. Despite failing health, he brought his practical and scholarly experience to bear on the Court's work until his death ended a fifty-year career dedicated to international law, diplomacy, and organization.

BIBLIOGRAPHY:

A. Articles in *Revue de droit international et de législation comparée*.

B. Paul Hymans, *Mémoires*, 2 vols. (Brussels, 1958); IWW 1937, 935; New International Yearbook (New York, 1936), 527; *Seventh Annual Report of the Permanent Court of International Justice* (Leiden, Netherlands, 1931), 24–25; *Thirteenth Annual Report of The Permanent Court of International Justice* (Leiden, Netherlands, 1937), 20–21; Paul Tirar, *La France sur le Rhin* (Paris, 1930).

C. The Rolin-Jaequemyn papers are in the Archives Générales du Royaume, Brussels.

Sally Marks

ROLIN-JAEQUEMYNS, Gustave Henri Ange Hippolyte [took additional surname of wife, Emilie Jaequemyns, 1869] (31 January 1835, Ghent—9 January 1902, Brussels). *Education*: doctorate in law and political and administrative sciences, Univ. of Ghent, 1857. *Career*: lawyer, 1857–69; cofounder and editor, *Revue de droit international et de législation comparée*, 1869–78, 1884–91; active member of Liberal party; Chamber of Representatives, 1878–86; minister of interior, 1878–84; counselor, Conseil Supérieur, Congo Free State, 1889–92; general adviser to Crown of Siam, 1892–1902.

Son of a successful lawyer and politician, Rolin abandoned law to concentrate on political and international studies. His lectures and publications on the Belgian constitution, electoral reform, and political parties reflected and in part defined the position of the Liberal party. An opponent of universal suffrage, he was impressed by the German cooperative movement in economic affairs and introduced its principles to Ghent by means of the Gentsche Volksbank, which he founded in 1867. His interest in public welfare led to participation in the International Association for the Progress of Social Science. He was also instrumental in the creation of the Belgian

Institute of International Law (1873). Rolin's greatest interest was the *Revue de droit international,* which he founded in 1869 jointly with two other specialists in international law, *T. Asser and John Westlake. The journal acquired renown under his editorship, which he laid aside while minister of interior.

Defeated in the elections of 1886 and his fortune exhausted, he accepted appointment as adviser to the minister of the interior of Siam. There he helped bring about vast reforms, modernizing according to liberal precepts the Siamese municipal, penal, and civil law codes and various government departments. Rolin believed in international cooperation and supported the efforts of Leopold II in founding what Rolin considered a unique international colony in the Congo. In the journal which he edited and in his work as a government official in both Belgium and Siam, he drew attention to and borrowed from the legislative efforts of many countries. This led to certain assumptions revealed in his writings. Rolin held that international law is historically necessary and founded on public consciousness. He argued for the recognition of all states if their governments effectively control internal affairs and do not violate the laws of humanity. National sovereignty is not to be violated; the principle of nonintervention in the internal affairs of independent states should be upheld. He supported the concept of self-determination and saw no conflict between it and colonization. War should be only a defensive last resort, never used as a preventive measure.

BIBLIOGRAPHY:

A. *Armenia, the Armenians, and the Treaties* (London, 1891). Rolin's publications are listed in *Annuaire de l'Académie Royale de Belgique* (1910), 85–88; many of his articles in *Revue de droit international de royale de législation comparée* appear as reprints.

B. *Biographie nationale* 29 (Brussels, 1957), 803–9; E. Nys, "Notice sur Gustave Rolin-Jaequemyns," *Annuaire de l'Académie Royale de Belgique* (1910), 53–88; J.J.A. Salmon, "Gustave Rolin-Jaequemyns, (1835–1902)" in *Livre du centenaire 1873–1973,* (Basel, 1973), 103–21.

Jonathan E. Helmreich

ROOSEVELT, Anna Eleanor (11 October 1884, New York—7 November 1962, New York). *Education*: Allenswood School. *Career*: social reformer; columnist; delegate, UN General Assembly, 1946, 1949–52, 1961; chair, Commission on Human Rights, 1947–51.

Roosevelt occupied a unique position in American political and diplomatic life in the years after World War II. The former First Lady enjoyed access to Democratic policy makers because of her personal acquaintance with them. In addition, she represented U.S. foreign policy in the United Nations and interpreted policy through her daily newspaper column, her massive correspondence, her frequent public appearances, and her radio broadcasts. She also traveled abroad widely as an unofficial representative of the United States.

Her prominent postwar activity was, in many ways, an extension of an interest in peace which had appeared during the interwar years. She shared her husband's interest in the League of Nations in the early 1920s but unlike him did not have to subordinate her beliefs to political expediency. After becoming First Lady, she maintained close contacts with League and World Court advocates, and during the Senate debates over approval of Court membership early in 1935, she organized campaigns and presented national radio speeches. In the mid-1930s she also opened the White House door to a wide variety of peace workers. These included Clarence Pickett of the American Friends Service Committee. She also became involved in National Peace Conference programs, especially its Emergency Peace Campaign in 1936.

Her interest in peace stemmed from essentially humanitarian rather than theoretical or political concerns. Thus, when she became involved in the UN, she willingly served as a member of Committee 3, which dealt with humanitarian, social, and cultural matters, and she also chaired the Human Rights Commission. Although she resigned from the delegation after the 1952 election, she remained active in the American Association for the United Nations, even chairing its board of directors. John F. Kennedy then reappointed her a delegate to the 1961 UN session. Until her death, Roosevelt was an influential member of the Americans for Democratic Action and the Democratic party.

Roosevelt believed the lack of standards for human rights was a major cause of international conflict and that the recognition of human rights would be a cornerstone of peace. The Declaration of Human Rights produced by her committee was approved by the UN in 1948. Although not intended as a treaty, it has influenced a number of national constitutions and is now widely regarded as a binding convention. Roosevelt was nominated four times for the Nobel Peace Prize, primarily on the basis of her work for human rights.

On several occasions during her tenure on the UN delegation, Roosevelt disagreed with the Truman administration's foreign policies, especially when she believed the U.S. commitment to the international organization was being undermined by unilateral action. She disagreed with the decision to dismantle the UN Relief and Rehabilitation Agency in 1947 and with the Truman Doctrine of military aid to Greece and Turkey. Although she supported the Marshall Plan, she preferred to administer aid through a UN body. Roosevelt even offered her resignation as delegate over the administration's handling of the Palestine partition, which, she maintained, degraded the UN.

Convinced that wars frequently had economic causes, she emphasized in her speeches and writing the relationship between economic chaos and political extremism. She thus advocated aid programs as a primary means of ensuring peace and stability. Certain that misunderstanding often led to war, she urged frequent international dialog through summit diplomacy as well as through the UN. Even during the most dangerous years of the Cold War, she never accepted the premise that East-West conflict was inevitable.

BIBLIOGRAPHY:

A. *On My Own* (New York, 1958).

B. Mary Welek Atwell, "Eleanor Roosevelt and the Cold War Consensus," *Diplomatic History* 3 (Winter 1979) 99–113; Jason Berger, *A New Deal for the World: Eleanor Roosevelt and American Foreign Policy, 1920–62* (New York, 1981); Joseph P. Lash, *Eleanor and Franklin* (New York, 1971), *Eleanor: The Years Alone* (New York, 1972).

C. The Roosevelt papers are in the Franklin D. Roosevelt Library.

Mary Welek Atwell

ROOSEVELT, Franklin Delano (30 January 1882, Hyde Park, NY—12 April 1945, Warm Springs, GA). *Education*: B.A., Harvard Coll., 1903, special courses, 1903–4; Columbia Univ. Law School, 1904–7. *Career*: law clerk, New York, 1907–10; state senator, 1911–13; assistant secretary of navy, 1913–21; Democratic vice-presidential candidate, 1920; governor of New York, 1929–33; president, 1933–45.

Roosevelt was born in the latter part of that remarkable nineteenth century later noted for its long peace among the major powers and for its advances in settling disputes by peaceful means. Roosevelt expressed interest in international affairs in his early school days when he debated about them and read *Alfred Thayer Mahan's classic study of the influence of sea power on history. Roosevelt's country was gradually beginning to be viewed as a major power, especially after its quick victory in the Spanish-American War of 1898 and after *Theodore Roosevelt's assertion of American influence in international affairs.

In 1913 Roosevelt became assistant secretary of the navy in the *Woodrow Wilson administration. Long enamored of the sea, he appears to have been a "big navy man," something of a militarist and an imperialist, albeit a paternal and humanitarian imperialist very concerned about the welfare of dependent peoples. His militarism seems to have disappeared about 1919 in the wave of Wilsonian idealism, but his imperialism lasted another decade, during which he occasionally boasted about the good that U.S. imperialism had done.

The wave of Wilsonian internationalism converted Roosevelt into a champion of collective security. Yet there is no evidence that he ever engaged in a detached analysis of the principles of collective security; nor was he very interested in its details, machinery, or procedures. To him the important thing was the goal. The creation of an organization, even with defects, would start the world in a new direction for settling disputes. In hundreds of speeches during his vice-presidential campaign in 1920 he advocated membership in the League of Nations and insisted that whatever defects the League possessed could be corrected in time, just as the U.S. Constitution had been amended.

Despite the U.S. refusal to join and Roosevelt's gradual disillusionment with the League itself, he continued to support ideas of international organization and collective security even though the policy of isolationism officially predominated in the 1920s. In 1923–24, inspired by the Bok peace plan contest, he drafted a proposal for a new League he thought might be acceptable to the United States. In 1925 he again urged membership in the belief that, if the United States joined, the League might be made to work. By the time of his 1932 presidential election campaign, however, his disillusionment with the League was so great that it was not difficult for him to repudiate it almost totally. It was no longer the institution conceived by Wilson, he said; rather, it had become corrupted into a primarily European forum, and membership would no longer serve a useful purpose.

At his inauguration in 1933, Roosevelt announced his Good Neighbor Policy, an outgrowth of his optimistic view of the nature of man and his belief that most people had the ability to behave in accordance with enlightened self-interest and to recognize their interdependence with the world community. Roosevelt meant to apply the policy to the whole world; but it seemed to work only in the Western Hemisphere. Its most concrete result was that it ended the U.S. habit of intervening militarily in Latin American states, even in Cuba, where the United States had the right to do so by treaty. When in 1938 Mexico nationalized some American-owned properties and Roosevelt was urged to use military force, he stuck to his Good Neighbor Policy.

When first in office, Roosevelt was persuaded to take nationalistic positions on trade, financial and arms matters because of the distressed economy. But such positions were so contrary to Roosevelt's basic attitude that he held to them only a few months. He thus refused to commit the United States at the World Economic Conference (1932–33) or the Disarmament Conference (1932–34). As early as 1933, he caused the United States to join the International Institute of Agriculture and later the International Labor Organization. In 1935 he also attempted to get the United States into the World Court and was chagrined when the measure failed in the Senate.

In the late 1930s, when German, Italian, and Japanese aggressions could no longer be ignored, Roosevelt gave international affairs much more of his time. His inclination toward interventionism, visible since early in World War I, reasserted itself. In 1936 he attended a special Inter-American Conference at Buenos Aires in an effort to organize a defensive alliance against the dictators abroad and to begin the building of a collective security system within the hemisphere. In 1937 tentatively he suggested collective action against Japan and any other aggressor, probably by means of an economic blockade. He also cautiously urged the American people to abandon their isolationism and see that their interests were dependent on the welfare and security of all the people of the world.

By 1941 Roosevelt's internationalism was expressed in many ways. Most idealistically it came out in his call for "a world founded on the four freedoms—of speech, of religion, from want, and from fear." Freedom from fear could assure "a world-wide reduction of armaments to such a point and in such a thorough fashion that no nation will be in a position to commit an act of physical aggression against any neighbor—anywhere in the world" (*Public Papers and Addresses*, vol. 9, p. 672). His internationalism also appeared in his increasingly articulated global geopolitical theory, in which he assumed that the major struggles for power in his time were global, as revealed by world wars. He assumed also that security depended on the United States and its friends maintaining control of the seas to assure access to raw materials and to keep war from the Western Hemisphere, the "defense at a distance" he had been advocating for years.

His internationalism was expressed also in his commitment in the Atlantic Charter where, with Winston Churchill, he outlined postwar goals. These included access of all states to trade and the raw materials needed for their prosperity, the collaboration and promotion by all governments of better labor standards, economic advancement, social security, and another collective security system. As World War II progressed, so did Roosevelt's thinking about the kind of postwar world he wanted. First, he wished to eliminate Fascism. He wanted a world disarmed except for forces needed for domestic and international policing. He also hoped for the abolition of colonialism, including spheres of influence. He favored international trusteeships for peoples not ready for self-determination and for free ports and international waterways. He also envisaged a global New Deal to be achieved by U.S. exportation of the economic and social techniques used during the Great Depression by his administration. To promote this, he wanted a "workable kit of tools" in the form of international agencies, three of which he saw established before his death, the UN Food and Agricultural Organization, the International Monetary Fund, and the World Bank. From 1943 on, moreover, Roosevelt pushed for a new collective security system, and plans for the establishment of the UN were virtually completed before his death.

His long-term paternalism and perspective caused him to favor a UN under the control of the great powers, with the task of maintaining security and peace firmly in their hands. This solution, he believed, would relieve smaller states from spending money on armaments rather than on economic and social development. He was willing to accept a larger voice by the smaller powers in the economic and social activities of the UN, but even there he expected the great powers to lead the way.

There is no doubt that Roosevelt was an inspiring and influential leader in international affairs. Some of his domestic New Deal experiments and achievements inspired emulation, thereby promoting the welfare state as an almost universal institution. His Four Freedoms stimulated a wave of idealism reminiscent of the one Woodrow Wilson had aroused. His practical accomplishments such as making the United States the "arsenal of democracy" and acquiring unchallengeable control of the seas and much of the airspace caused him to be seen by some as a man of gargantuan talent and powers.

Yet Roosevelt had critics who challenged both his thinking and his actions. They noted that he was a superb player of power politics, who when he called for a world without power politics or spheres of influence must have been naive to think such a condition was possible or else had not thought through what he suggested. Moreover, his belief that a universal urge exists for individual liberty and democracy has also been questioned. Roosevelt's paternalistic attitude toward small states and colonial peoples has also been criticized, especially his plans for international trusteeships and his belief that small powers could be persuaded to disarm.

His demand for the "unconditional surrender" of Germany, Italy, and Japan has been declared by some critics to have lengthened World War II by promoting unity and determination in those states and creating power vacuums which handicapped his vision of the postwar world. Perhaps, however, the most vehement opposition arose from his analysis of the Soviet Union, in which he saw the Soviets as solely concerned with security and internal development and devoid of any ambition to expand. Conditions after 1945 again showed his faith in a cooperative system to have been somewhat naive. Whatever his faults and merits and the lack of a systematic world concept on his part, there is no doubt that Roosevelt early in life moved away from traditional isolationism for the United States, and, as he matured, his thinking and actions became more and more global.

BIBLIOGRAPHY:

A. *Franklin D. Roosevelt and Foreign Affairs*, Edgar B. Nixon and Donald B. Schewe, eds., 16 vols. (Cambridge, MA, 1969, New York, 1979). *The Public Papers and Addresses of Franklin D. Roosevelt*, ed., S. I. Rosenman, 13 vols. (New York, 1938–50).

B. James M. Burns, *Roosevelt*, 2 vols. (New York, 1956–70); Robert Dallek, *Franklin D. Roosevelt and American Foreign Policy 1932–1945* (New York, 1979); Robert A. Divine, *Roosevelt and World War II*, (Baltimore, MD, 1969); Frank B. Freidel, *Franklin D. Roosevelt*, 4 vols. (Boston, 1952–73); Willard Range, *Franklin D. Roosevelt's World Order* (Athens, GA, 1959); Robert E. Sherwood, *Roosevelt and Hopkins* (New York, 1948).

C. The Roosevelt papers are in the Franklin D. Roosevelt Library.

Willard Range

ROOSEVELT, Theodore (27 October 1858, New York—6 January 1919, Oyster Bay, NY). *Education*: B.A., Harvard Coll., 1880; Columbia Univ. Law School, 1880–81. *Career*: assemblyman, New York State, 1882–84; rancher, 1884–86; Republican candidate for mayor of New York City, 1886; free-lance writer, 1886–89; chair, U.S. Civil Service Commission,

1889–95; president, New York Board of Police Commissioners, 1895–97; assistant secretary of the navy, 1897–98; colonel, 1st U.S. Volunteer Cavalry Regiment, 1898; governor of New York, 1899–1900; vice-president, 1901; president, 1901–9; Progressive party presidential candidate, 1912; editorial writer, author, and columnist, 1910–19; Nobel Peace Prize, 1906.

Roosevelt's views on foreign policy lacked the surface consistency of his moderately progressive approach to domestic affairs. Pulled one way and another by the competing claims of ideals and realities in a world in flux, he appeared with almost rhythmic regularity as a warhawk and peacemaker, as an ultranationalist and an internationalist. Behind these contradictory postures, however, lay three convictions so firm as to constitute principles: (1) self-defense is the first imperative of the nation-state; (2) the interest of highly "civilized" peoples takes precedence over those of underdeveloped societies: and (3) advanced peoples are morally obligated to support the onward march of "civilization." Only in the light of these fixed assumptions can Roosevelt's glorification of the warrior, flirtation with imperialism, and qualified support of binding arbitration and international agreements be understood; and only in their light can his acquisition of the Panama Canal Zone in 1903 and his Nobel Prize-winning mediation of the Russo-Japanese War in 1905 be reconciled.

As president, Roosevelt's sense of responsibility frequently modified the application of his principles. His conception of the national interest became progressively more enlightened. He virtually abandoned the notion that a far-flung empire was the hallmark of greatness, even as he worked strenuously to strengthen the United States' position as a world power. He admitted an Oriental country, Japan, to that privileged circle of "superior" nations sanctioned to dominate the international polity. He even moved cautiously to advance international peacekeeping machinery. Yet he did so without illusion. As he wrote on the eve of the Second Hague Conference (1907), the U.S. Navy was a greater factor for peace than any and all peace societies. Always, moreover, his commitment to the national security circumscribed his internationalist impulses. His instructions to Secretary of State John Hay on the International Conference of American States in the fall of 1901 are revealing of this. Latin American aspirations should be encouraged, the president wrote, but only within the bounds of national interest.

Nonetheless, Roosevelt departed from past American practices, or expanded on them, on several fronts. He both interceded in and mediated disputes among sovereign powers. He experimented with compulsory arbitration. And he supported the strengthening or creation of international agencies. Partly because direct action promised immediate and concrete results and largely because of the direct linkages to the American national interest of certain disputes, he proved boldest in the first category. When, for example, Great Britain and Germany blockaded Venezuela in 1902–3 for nonpayments of debts, he persuaded the former and virtually forced the latter to end the blockade and submit their claims to the Permanent Court of International Arbitration. Two years later, having concluded that stabilization of the Far East was in both the American and world interest, he decided to mediate peace between Russia and Japan. Concurrently, he fostered the Algeciras Conference of 1906, though the dispute between Germany and France that prompted it had no direct bearing on the national interest of the United States. He did so, as Richard W. Leopold observed in *Growth of American Foreign Policy* (1962), because he had come to believe that "the republic had an obligation as a world power to exert its influence in behalf of peace whenever this could be done with safety."

Roosevelt's approach to compulsory arbitration was considerably more incrementalist. He did not regard the national interest as justiciable, but he did believe that binding arbitration of minor disputes was practicable and, more than that, desirable. He was so outraged in 1905 by the Senate's insistence that eleven bilateral agreements to arbitrate be recast into treaties (in order to assure that the arbitrator's decisions would be submitted to that body for approval) that he refused to complete the agreements. Persuaded subsequently by Secretary of State *Elihu Root that treaties should be viewed as a first step, he supported Root's negotiation of twenty-four new ones. He also encouraged Root's fruitless effort at the Second Hague Peace Conference (1907) to create a permanent, and true, international court empowered to pass judgment on cases of a limited nature. Finally, shortly before leaving office, Roosevelt agreed to submit the Newfoundland fisheries controversy to binding arbitration.

Between 1910 and late 1914, Roosevelt spoke intermittently about the need for a league with force to uphold treaties and the decision of its court, but World War I brought to the fore all Roosevelt's instinct for *Realpolitik*. He concluded that conflicts among the great powers could not be settled by a voluntary association of nations, and long before *Woodrow Wilson called for a League of Nations he refused to join *William Howard Taft in support of *Hamilton Holt's League to Enforce Peace. He proposed a universal arbitration treaty with the British, but he put his faith in a firm military alliance of the Western powers which had won the war. Only if such an alliance were made the keystone of American policy, he indicated shortly before his death in January 1919, would he countenance the League of Nations.

BIBLIOGRAPHY:

A. *An Autobiography* (New York, 1913); *The Letters of Theodore Roosevelt*, ed. Elting E. Morison and John Morton Blum, 8 vols. (Cambridge, MA, 1951–54); *The Works of Theodore Roosevelt*, ed. Hermann Hagedorn, 20 vols. (New York, 1926); *The Writings of Theodore Roosevelt*, ed. William H. Harbaugh (Indianapolis, IN, 1967).

B. Howard K. Beale, *Theodore Roosevelt and the Rise of America to World*

Power (Baltimore, MD, 1956); David H. Burton, *Theodore Roosevelt, Confident Imperialist* (Philadelphia, 1968); DAB 8, 135-44; William H. Harbaugh, *Power and Responsibility: The Life and Times of Theodore Roosevelt* (New York, 1961); Warren F. Kuehl, *Seeking World Order: The United States and International Organization to 1920* (Nashville, TN, 1969); Frederick W. Marks, III, *Velvet on Iron: The Diplomacy of Theodore Roosevelt* (Lincoln, NE, 1979); Edward C. Wagenknecht, *The Seven Worlds of Theodore Roosevelt* (New York, 1958).

C. The Theodore Roosevelt papers are in the Manuscript Division, Library of Congress.

William H. Harbaugh

ROOT, Elihu (15 February 1845, Clinton, NY—7 February 1937, New York). *Education*: B.A. Hamilton Coll., 1864; LL.B., New York Univ., 1867. *Career*: practiced law, 1867-99; U.S. district attorney for Southern District of New York, 1883-85; secretary of war, 1899-1904; secretary of state, 1905-9; U.S. senator, 1909-15; member, Alaskan Boundary Tribunal, 1903; U.S. counsel, North Atlantic Fisheries Arbitration, 1910; member, Permanent Court of Arbitration, 1910-37; president, American Society of International Law, 1907-24; president, Board of Trustees, Carnegie Endowment for International Peace, 1910-25; president, New York Constitutional Convention, 1915; ambassador extraordinary and head of mission to Russia, 1917; member, advisory committee to draft plan for Permanent Court of International Justice, 1920; commissioner plenipotentiary, Conference on Limitation of Armament, 1921-22; member, League of Nations committee to revise World Court Statute, 1929; Nobel Peace Prize, 1912.

Root's importance as an internationalist derived from his record as cabinet officer and, to a lesser extent, as member of the Senate Foreign Relations Committee; from his representing the United States at international conferences and on diplomatic missions; from his contribution as a private citizen to framing the Statute of the World Court and later revising it; and from his leadership of such organizations as the Carnegie Endowment for International Peace and the American Society of International Law. Although he was not an original thinker or learned writer, and although he was never in the mainstream of the peace movement, he commanded widespread respect for almost four decades because of his influence with presidents, congressmen, educators, and philanthropists and because of his receipt of the Nobel Peace Prize of 1912.

As secretary of war, Root concentrated on ending the revolt in the Philippines, governing the new colonies, limiting Cuban sovereignty, and reorganizing the Army, but he also advised presidents and helped draft the Open Door Notes of July 1900. As secretary of state, he worked harmoniously with *Theodore Roosevelt and the Senate, improved the consular and diplomatic service, and began to reorganize the State Department.

With Japan, he and the president divided the task of resolving the controversy over immigration and segregation in the San Francisco schools; in the Americas, he led in promoting hemispheric cordiality and conciliating Colombia. He attended the Third Inter-American Conference at Rio de Janeiro in 1906, sought New World participation in the Hague Conference of 1907, and cosponsored the Central American Peace Conference of 1907 that created the Central American Court of Justice. He wrote the instructions for the delegates to the Algeciras Conference of 1906, the Hague Conference of 1907, and the London Maritime Conference of 1908. He devised plans for a Court of Arbitral Justice that failed of adoption at The Hague in 1907 because of a single defect; he persuaded Roosevelt to propose twenty-four treaties requiring arbitration of certain types of disputes and in terms agreeable to the Senate. As senator, he accepted with reservations the more ambitious Taft-Knox arbitration treaties that Roosevelt rejected and *Henry Cabot Lodge sought to amend substantially. He endorsed the Declaration of London of 1909 and called for a third Hague Conference. He cooperated with *Woodrow Wilson in seeking repeal of the Panama Tolls Act of 1912 and, initially, on Mexico, but he later strongly criticized Wilson's course on Colombia, Mexico and the Ship Purchase Bill.

Out of office, Root was a belated interventionist during the Great War, a constructive critic of the Versailles Treaty, and an elder statesman on postwar diplomacy. Although the most logical Republican choice for the peace commission, he was excluded by Wilson as too reactionary. Root regarded Articles X and XVI of the League Covenant as dangerous; his efforts to commit the Republican leadership in the Senate to certain reservations, seemingly successful in June 1919, ultimately failed. Root was a principal author of the League plank in the Republican platform of 1920 and of the October statement by thirty-one moderate Republican notables urging Harding's election as the best way to ensure U.S. membership in an association of nations.

Root's course on the Versailles Treaty has been called devious by many internationalists; but although colored by personal and partisan considerations, it was consistent with his earlier stand on the Taft arbitration treaties. Wilson, he felt, had gone too far, committing the republic to obligations it would not fulfill in a crisis. A sounder approach, Root argued, was to codify international law, develop judicial machinery to settle international disputes, and educate the public through periodicals like *Foreign Affairs* or research supported by the Carnegie Endowment for International Peace.

In the postwar years he accepted an invitation from the League to join other jurists (1920) to frame a Statute for the World Court; served as a delegate to the Washington Conference in 1921–22, with particular responsibility for the Nine-Power Treaty on China and an abortive pact governing the use of submarines in future wars; supported the qualified membership on the World Court voted by the Senate in 1926; paid lip service to the

Kellogg–Briand Pact in 1928; and accepted (1929) another League invitation to attempt with other experts to remove the last American objection to joining the World Court. The resulting Root formula, in which others had a hand, was not voted on by the Senate until 1935, just before Root's ninetieth birthday, by which time world conditions had changed; and he lacked the strength to help goad *Franklin Roosevelt or stem the last-minute tide of opposition. Two years later Root died. His brand of internationalism was proving incapable of coping with the totalitarianism of Germany, Japan, and Italy.

BIBLIOGRAPHY:

A. Robert Bacon and James B. Scott, 8 vols. (edited eight volumes of Root's writings and speeches through 1923 under various titles, Cambridge, MA, 1916–25).

B. DAB supp. 2, 577–82; Sondra R. Herman, *Eleven Against War; Studies in American Internationalist Thought, 1898–1921* (Stanford, CA, 1969); Philip C. Jessup, *Elihu Root*, 2 vols. (New York, 1938); Warren F. Kuehl, *Seeking World Order: The United States and International Organization to 1920* (Nashville, TN, 1969); Richard W. Leopold, *Elihu Root and the Conservative Tradition* (Boston, 1954); Richard H. Werking, *The Master Architects: Building the United States Foreign Service, 1890–1913* (Lexington, KY, 1977).

C. The Root papers are in the Manuscript Division, Library of Congress.

Richard W. Leopold

ROOTH, Ivar (2 November 1888, Stockholm—28 February 1972, Lidingo, Sweden). *Education*: LL.B., Univ. of Uppsala, 1911; Univ. of Berlin, 1911–12. *Career*: law practice, Stockholm, 1912–14; banker, 1914–72; director, Bank of International Settlement, 1931–33, 1937–48; managing director, International Monetary Fund, 1951–56.

Rooth was an independently minded individual who believed in following international economic and banking policies, unrelated to political goals, which brought beneficial results to governments and people. His experiences in Swedish banking circles led to his appointment as governor of the regulatory Central Bank of Sweden, a post he held nearly twenty years (1929–48). That led to his increasing involvement in world financial circles, where he served as director of the Bank of International Settlement during the crucial depression and war years. While initially created to facilitate reparations payments under the Young Plan, it later operated as a clearinghouse for European banks.

Rooth resigned as head of the Central Bank of Sweden in 1948 because he objected to policies he believed would be inflationary. When he succeeded *Camille Gutt as managing director of the International Monetary Fund in 1951, he embarked on what he perceived as needed reforms. He sought modification or removal of discriminatory practices which restricted exchange and commerce, and the subsequent changes greatly broadened the role and work of the Fund in facilitating international development. Rooth retained an interest in world economic problems after he completed his term at the IMF in 1956. He headed the investment committee of the UN pension fund and the Kuwait currency board (1960–62).

BIBLIOGRAPHY:

A. *Planer för internationellt monetärt samarbete efter kriget* (Stockholm, 1944).
B. CB 1952, 501–3; IWW 1956, 805; NYT 29 Feb 1972, 38; WB 1948, 4074.

Warren F. Kuehl

ROSSELLI, Carlo (16 November 1899, Rome—9 June 1937, Bagnoles de l'Orne, France). *Education*: degree in social sciences, Univ. of Florence, 1921; law degree, Univ. of Siena, 1923. *Career*: writer, editor, publisher, 1925–26, 1929–37; political prisoner, 1927–29.

Rosselli came from a family of middle-class intellectuals whose ancestors on the side of both his father and mother were connected with leading figures of the Risorgimento. He fought as a lieutenant in World War I, then attended college. He became acquainted with leaders of right-wing Socialism, but the main influence on him was that of historian *Gaetano Salvemini, who directed his brother Nello's dissertation on the origins of Italian Socialism. This background and his dynamic temperament led him to clash with Fascism. He soon began to write for liberal and Socialist periodicals. After the Giacomo Matteotti murder, he joined the Socialist party. In January 1925, with Salvemini, *Ernesto Rossi, and his brother Nello, he launched the first clandestine paper *Non Mollare!* (Don't give in!). The next year, with Pietro Nenni, he published the political weekly, *Quarto Stato*, to continue *Rivoluzione liberale*, whose editor Piero Gobetti had just died in exile in Paris.

With Ferruccio Parri and Sandro Pertini, he then organized the escape to Corsica of old Socialist leader Filippo Turati, which led to his arrest. The lightness of his sentence showed that many judges had not yet become subservient to Fascist dictatorship. Rosselli spent his confinement on the penal island of Lipari, where he wrote *Socialismo liberale*. In that book, he criticized Marxism, Leninism, and Socialist "maximalism" as well as the piecemeal reformism of the Turati group. Rejecting revolutionary syndicalism of the Sorel school, he preferred trade unionism on the British model.

After a dramatic escape in July 1929, he went to Paris, where with others he founded a revolutionary movement to overthrow Fascism with its publication, *Quaderni di "Giustizia e Libertâ."* As editor (1932–35), he also used it as a forum to advance his ideas on a United States of Europe. He believed in a federation as the best solution to the diverse interests of European nationalities and even subgroups. After Hitler's rise to power, Rosselli realized that another world war was coming, and he became an advocate of collective security, even campaigning for a preventive war against Hitler and Mussolini. During the Spanish Civil War, he organized a column of

Italian volunteers to fight on the side of the Loyalists. His radio broadcasts from Barcelona to Italy aroused the wrath of Mussolini, and Galeazzo Ciano organized an assassination plot with French Fascists, the "Cagoulards." On 9 June 1937, they succeeded in killing both Roselli and his brother Nello.

In his last years, Rosselli, continued to argue that the future for Europe lay in its unity. "We must make Europe," he wrote. A constituent assembly, composed of delegates elected by the people, should draft the first European federal constitution. Rosselli's vision carried into the postwar era, when many Italians who had worked with him continued the quest for a united Europe.

BIBLIOGRAPHY:

A. *Oggi in Spagna, domani in Italia* (Turin, 1967); *Quaderni di Giustizia e Libertà* (Turin, 1959); *Socialismo liberale* (Turin, 1973).

B. Charles F. Delzell, "The European Federalist Movement in Italy: First Phase, 1918–1947," *Journal of Modern History* 32 (Sep 1960), 241–50; Aldo Garosci, *Vita di Carlo Rosselli*, 2nd ed. (Florence, 1973); Nicola Tranfaglia, *Carlo Rosselli dall'interventismo a Giustizia e Libertà* (Bari, Italy, 1968).

Enzo Tagliacozzo

ROSSI, Ernesto (23 August 1897, Caserta, Naples—9 February 1967, Rome). *Education*: degree in law, Univ. of Siena, 1923. *Career*: journalist, editor, publisher, public official.

Ever an idealist and often a visionary, Rossi when eighteen volunteered to fight in World War I for Mazzinian ideals of brotherhood and the self-determination of nations, and he was seriously wounded. During the postwar crisis, he opposed the demagogic positions of the left-wing Socialists and Communists and became editor of a weekly published by Tuscan landowners.

After the March on Rome, he became one of the founders of "Italia Libera," an organization of anti-Fascist veterans. A decisive influence on him had been a meeting in 1920 and a subsequent friendship with historian and professor *Gaetano Salvemini. In a protest against the suppression of a free press, Rossi joined with Salvemini and the Rosselli brothers, *Carlo and Nello, in publishing a clandestine paper, *Non mollare!* (Don't give in!). That initiative led to the imprisonment and trial of Salvemini and the escape of Rossi to Paris. He subsequently became involved in several efforts to overthrow Fascism, restore a democratic republic, and introduce political and social reforms. A spy caused his arrest 30 October 1930, and he spent nine years in jail until sent to the penal island of Ventotene, where he remained for over three years until Mussolini's fall.

While in Ventotene, together with Altiero Spinelli and *Eugenio Colorni, he drafted in 1940–41 the "Manifesto," which marked the birth of the Italian movement favoring the construction of a European federal state.

Such action could solve the problems of Germany's future, help Socialism develop, and lead in turn to a genuine international state. He emigrated in 1943 to Switzerland, where, with *Luigi Einaudi, he worked to promote the United States of Europe through an extensive publication campaign. One of Rossi's pamphlets, *L'Europe de demain* circulated underground in France. There he made contact with European federalists from other countries. He then returned to Italy, where as a member of the Action party he prepared for the anti-German insurrection of April 1945. Rossi served briefly as an under secretary in the Parri Cabinet (1945) and then became president of ARAR, a state agency for the disposal of leftover war materials. There he served until 1958, revealing surprising managerial capabilities.

A brilliant writer on topics of economic and financial policies, he denounced in the authoritative Rome weekly *Il Mondo* the financial abuses, scandals, and waste on the part of industrialists and politicians. After the death of Salvemini (1957) he organized the "Salvemini movement" and planned the publication of Salvemini's works in twenty volumes.

Devoid of political ambition, Rossi combined an ardent zeal for freedom and democracy with a deep sense of humor, adversion to rhetoric, and devotion to ideals of human tolerance and cooperation. While in jail, he elaborated on a state based on principles of freedom, democracy, and right-wing Socialism.

BIBLIOGRAPHY:

A. *Abolire la miseria* (Milan, 1946, 1979); *Critica del capitalismo* (Milan, 1945); *Elogio della galera, Lettere 1930-1943* (Bari, Italy, 1968); *Ernesto Rossi un democratico ribelle*, ed., Manlio Magini (Parma, Italy, 1975); with others, *Federazione europea* (Milan, 1948); *Gli Stati Uniti di Europa* (Capolago, Italy, 1946); *Guerra e dopoguerra. Lettere 1915/1921*, ed. Giuseppe Armani, 2 vols. (Florence, 1978); *I padroni del vapore* (Bari, Italy, 1955); *Il manganello e l'aspersorio* (Bari, Italy, 1958); *Settimo non rubare* (Bari, Italy, 1952).

B. Charles F. Delzell, "The European Federalist Movement in Italy: First Phase, 1918-1947," *Journal of Modern History* 32 (Sep, 1960), 241-50; Giampaolo Nitti, "Appunti biobibliografici su Ernesto Rossi," in *Movimento di liberazione in Italia* (Jan-Jun 1967), 86-87.

Enzo Tagliacozzo

ROSTWOROWSKI, Michał Cezary (27 August 1864, Dresden—24 March 1940, Tarnów, Poland). *Education*: St. Petersburg Univ.; graduate studies, Ecole des Sciences Politiques, Paris; Jagiellonian Univ., Kraków. *Career*: docent, later professor, Jagiellonian Univ., 1896-1930; cofounder and director, School of Political Science (Kraków), 1911-31; member, Codification Committee, Poland, 1920-35; member, Permanent Court of Arbitration, 1923; delegate, Hague Conferences for Codification of International Private Law, 1925, 1928; judge, Permanent Court of International Justice, 1930-40.

Rostworowski, scion of an old and distinguished Polish family, was interwar Poland's most eminent jurist. His long and productive career can be divided into two periods, separated by World War I. Before 1914 he devoted himself to teaching, research, and academic administration. Although he produced a number of significant works on the history of Polish administration, his main interest became international law and politics. This is reflected in a series of major publications concerning the legal position of the Vatican in international relations (1892), the regulation of maritime commerce (1895), the codification of international private law (1903), and the creation of a durable peace based on international covenants (1915-16).

In 1898 he joined the prestigious International Law Institute of the Jagiellonian University, where he established close ties with leading world internationalists. A dozen years later he was the *spiritus movens* behind the creation of the School of Political Science in Kraków to expand the Polish academic world's contact with the European intellectual community, especially the Paris internationalists at the Ecole des Sciences Politique.

When Poland regained its independence in 1918, Rostworowski became an active participant in many of the issues he had earlier addressed. One of the first members of the commission to codify reborn Poland's laws, Rostworowski's lengthy efforts regarding his country's domestic affairs culminated in coauthorship of the Polish Constitution (1935). Domestic affairs, however, were overshadowed by his involvement in international problems. In the 1920s he was an active participant in Poland's Commission for International Collaboration, serving as its delegate to the 1929 London Political Science Conference.

Rostworowski's background and interests made him the logical choice to represent Poland before the World Court. He did so repeatedly in the 1920s, establishing a reputation and helping define the still nebulous jurisdictional boundary between international bodies and sovereign states. In 1930 he was nominated by seven nations as their candidate for a seat on the Permanent Court of International Justice and elected on the first ballot. His tenure lasted until his death.

During his service on the World Court, Rostworowski demonstrated his independence and broad vision. Where he had once appeared before the Court as a partisan, representing Poland in its acrimonious debates with an increasingly aggressive Germany, he now conducted himself as an international jurist and not a champion of Poland. As a result he was severely criticized by his own government for not acting in accord with Polish policy. This criticism reflects the central concern of his long and multifarious career—to seek out and define the basis for the cooperation of nations.

BIBLIOGRAPHY:

A. *Diarjusz Sejmu z roku 1830-1831*, 6 vols. (Kraków, 1907-12); *Jurysdykcja karna na okrętach handlowych w portach zagranicznych* (Kraków, 1895);

Kodyfikacja prawa międzynarodowego prywatnego w Hadze (Kraków, 1903); *La Codification du droit international et interprovincial privé en Pologne* (Kraków, 1930); *La Situation internationale du St. Siège au point de vue juridique* (Paris, 1892); *Materiały do dziejów Komisyi Rządzącej z roku 1807* (Kraków, 1918); *Rada ministrów: Rada Stanu Księstwa Warszawskiego* (Kraków, 1912).

B. *Czy wiesz kto to jest?* (Warsaw, 1938), 629–30; *Diariusz i teki Jana Szembeka, 1935–1945* 2 (London, 1965), 279; *Dictionnaire diplomatique* 5 (Paris, n.d.), 939; *Encyklopedja powszechna ultima thule* 9 (Warsaw, 1938), 211; IWW 1938, 985; Edward Lindsey, *The International Court* (New York, 1931); LT 15 Aug 1929, 10, 26, Sep 1930, 12, 1 Dec 1938, 13; NYT 6 Aug 1923, 10, 17 Feb 1929, III-8, 17 Aug 1930, III-4, 25 Sep 1930, 4, 26 Sep 1930, 7, 24 Apr 1935, 9; S. Peretiakowicz and M. Sobieski, *Współczesna kultura polska* (Poznán, 1932); *Staty kultury polskiej, 1939–1945* 1 (Glasgow, 1945), 199–207.

M. B. Biskupski

ROWE, Leo Stanton (17 September 1871, McGregor, IA—5 December 1946, Washington). *Education*: Ph.B., Univ. of Pennsylvania, 1890; Ph.D., Univ. of Halle, 1892; LL.B., Univ. of Pennsylvania, 1896. *Career*: lecturer, professor, Univ. of Pennsylvania, 1894–1920; charter member, American Academy of Political and Social Science, 1889, secretary, 1899, president, 1902–30; member, Porto Rico Code Commission, 1900–1901, chair, 1901; delegate, Third, Fifth, and Sixth International Conferences of American States, 1906, 1923, 1928; charter member, American Society of International Law, 1906; delegate, First (chair), Second, and Third Pan American Scientific Congresses; chair, Pan American Committee, 1909; chair, United States–Panama Joint Claims Commission, 1913; secretary-general, Pan American Financial Conference, 1915; secretary, International High Commission, 1916; secretary, American–Mexican Joint Commission, 1916–17; assistant secretary of the treasury, 1917–19; chief, Division of Latin American Affairs, Department of State, 1919–20; director-general, Pan American Union, 1920–46; president, American Political Science Association, 1920–21; professor, Georgetown Univ., 1920–46; director, Latin American Round Table, Institute of Politics, Williams Coll., 1921–26; representative of the Pan American Union with special invitation at inter-American conferences, 1933–45; representative of the Pan American Union with special invitation, United Nations Conference, San Francisco, 1945.

Rowe came of age as powerful forces were reshaping the world. Economic dislocations and momentous changes in global relationships created the "psychic crisis" of the 1890s. Unbridled industrialism contributed to the deterioration of the cities, a major depression, and international tensions. Civil war engulfed Cuba, and it appeared that portions of Asia, Africa, and Latin America would become targets of the new imperialism. When Rowe completed his education, he undertook a career which these forces would shape.

The intellectually gifted son of a liberal Jewish inheritance, Rowe excelled as a student. Deeply influenced by German-trained economists at the Wharton School in the University of Pennsylvania and by Bismarckian reform while at Halle, his model became the progressive state. He specialized in municipal reform as a professor at Wharton, taking numerous leaves on public service assignments. It was the outcome of the Spanish-American War, however, which provided the opportunity for a career that would earn him a reputation as an internationalist.

Through the intercession of a university colleague who knew William McKinley, Rowe was appointed to the Porto Rico Code Commission in 1900. He demonstrated marked administrative ability, egalitarianism, and a natural affinity for working with the Latinos. When Secretary of State *Elihu Root began to promote Pan Americanism, Rowe became an obvious choice as a delegate to the Third International Conference of American States at Rio de Janeiro in 1906. Traveling extensively after that, he conducted research in Argentina and met many educators and officials interested in rapprochement. Through Rowe's personal influence, the first of a series of Pan American Scientific Conferences was initiated, creating considerable enthusiasm for the movement and leading to additional Latin American missions.

Rowe showed a broader world perspective when he joined with others in 1906 to form the American Society of International Law.

When World War I broke out, he became important to high-level policy makers holding posts in the Treasury and State departments. In 1920 he was appointed director-general of the Pan American Union, a post he had long coveted and which would fix his reputation as an internationalist. He finally resigned from Wharton but continued teaching part time at Georgetown University. He never entirely answered the criticism that as a scholar he was overly subservient to State Department policies, and he clashed on several occasions with *Samuel Guy Inman, the noted missionary and Latin Americanist, over intervention and the proper role of the Pan American Union.

At the helm of the Pan American bureaucracy Rowe threw himself into the work of fostering the hemispheric ideal. Through numerous publications, conferences, visits, and a prodigious personal effort, he promoted good will and cooperation. Although criticized as responding to political and economic interests, it is apparent that his values were professional, cultural, and scholarly.

The fruition of his work came with the promulgation of the Good Neighbor Policy in 1933. Rowe had firmly laid the foundation for a highly successful era of international accord. Because of an objection to his delegate status, he represented the PAU with "special invitation" at the celebrated inter-American conferences of the 1930s and 1940s. Acknowledged as a leader of hemispheric cooperation, he was honored in

1945 with a banquet in the Grand Ballroom of New York's Waldorf Astoria Hotel, hosted by the Pan American Society, to commemorate the twenty-fifth anniversary of his appointment as director-general.

Tragedy followed this signal honor. A year later Rowe died after a traffic accident, bequeathing a small fortune to the Education Fund of the institution he had perfected. By common consent he was now hailed, "citizen of the Americas." Due in part to his efforts the discord of the New Imperialism was deflected, and in its stead the tenuous tradition of hemispheric friendship greatly enhanced.

BIBLIOGRAPHY:

A. *The Federal System of the Argentine Republic* (Washington, 1921); *Problems of City Government* (New York, 1908); *The United States and Porto Rico, with Special Reference to the Problems Arising out of Our Contact with the Spanish-American Civilization* (New York, 1904); numerous articles, reports, and reviews, notably in professional journals and in the *Annals* of the American Academy of Political and Social Science.

B. AJIL 41 (1947), 132; *American Political Science Review* 41 (Feb 1947), 98–99; Lejeune Cummins, "The Origin and Development of Elihu Root's Latin American Diplomacy," dissertation, Univ. of California, Berkeley, 1964; DAB supp. 4, 705–6; *Hispanic American Historical Review* 27 (May 1947), 187–88; NCAB 18, 316–17; NYT 6 Dec 1946, 25; *Bulletin of Pan American Union* 81 (Apr 1947), 181–286; Gustav A. Sallas, "Leo S. Rowe, Citizen of the Americas," dissertation, George Washington Univ., 1956.

Lejeune Cummins

ROYCE, Josiah (20 November 1855, Grass Valley, CA—14 September 1916, Cambridge, MA). *Education*: graduate, Univ. of California, Berkeley, 1875; Univs. of Leipzig and Göttingen, 1875–76; Ph.D., Johns Hopkins Univ., 1878. *Career*: instructor, Univ. of California, Berkeley, 1878; instructor to professor, Harvard Univ., 1882–1916; visiting professor, Univ. of Aberdeen, 1899–1900, Univ. of California, Berkeley, 1911, 1916.

Defining the essentials of an international community which would engage the loyalty of patriots and express the deepest bonds among men was the task of Royce's last years as a philosopher. The leading post-Kantian idealist of the early twentieth century and a member of Harvard's famous Pantheon, he believed ardently in the scholar's obligation to function as an apolitical moral guide. While it is his brilliance as a logician which continues to impress academic philosophers, it was his ethical and religious works which reached the public, particularly *The Philosophy of Loyalty* (1908). In an age of blatant racism and imperialism, Royce cut through contemporary cant and stated boldly that true patriots should recognize devotees of other causes as their brothers. "Loyalty to loyalty" was the principle for resolving contradictions and conflicts. He viewed this goal as ideal but neither impossible nor static.

Every step in the development of Royce's essentially religious philosophy drew him closer to the definition of universal community. Reflecting childhood experiences in California as well as the conditions of American society at the turn of the century, Royce insisted that freedom was different from selfish individualism; that community denied mass conformity. By 1913 in his magnum opus, *The Problem of Christianity*, he had arrived at the triadic structure of community and its core function: interpretation. Spiritual and practical communities united free individuals, each of whom found the very meaning of life in relationship to the whole and to others. The process of interpretation was metaphysical, ethical, and psychological all at once. It forms the core of Royce's social philosophy.

Little wonder he felt deeply betrayed when his philosophical homeland, Germany, made war against the international community. Royce viewed the sinking of the *Lusitania* as a particularly heinous act of treachery. Immediately he sought practical applications of his theory of community to the war. In *War and Insurance* (1914) and *The Hope of the Great Community* (1916), Royce described the potential of a new kind of international relationship. Mutual antagonism was built into the present scheme of international relations because nations or alliances related to each other in "dangerous pairs." Dyadic relations risked conflict. However, when a third party, an agent or interpreter, representing the international community, made the relationship triadic, there was a chance of resolving conflicts and creating international loyalty. Specifically, Royce suggested creating an international insurance fund to protect individuals of all nations from the financial consequences of major natural disasters. Insurance tended to defuse business conflicts, and the international agents of the fund would, by their daily activities, enlarge national loyalties and make visible the community of mankind. While the scheme attracted little attention in Royce's day, and hardly any since, it faithfully reflected his mature insight into the psychological and economic roots of war. In a dawning age of insecurity, Royce understood the anxious nature of the citizen's attachment to his nation as well as its moral aspect. Devotion to a world community would have to develop through both practical and spiritual means. He anticipated the transnational loyalties of mediators and their dispassionate commitment. Nevertheless, Royce has received little recognition as an internationalist. His insurance scheme died aborning. The security provided by the welfare state has not generally outgrown national boundaries. In resolving international conflicts, however, mediators have often acted upon Roycean principles or religious transnationalism. Thus his community remains, as he foresaw, a "community of hope."

BIBLIOGRAPHY:

A. *California . . . a Study of American Character* (Boston, 1886); *The Hope of the Great Community* (New York, 1916); *The Letters of Josiah Royce*, ed. John Clendenning, (Chicago, 1970); *The Philosophy of Loyalty* (New York, 1908); *The Problem of Christianity*, 2 vols. (New York, 1913); *Race Questions, Provincialism, and Other American Problems* (New York, 1908); *The Religious Aspect of Philosophy* (Boston, 1885); *The Spirit of Modern Philosophy* (Boston, 1892); *War and Insurance* (New York, 1914); *The World and the Individual*, 2 vols. (New York, 1899–1901).

B. DAB 8, 205–11; *Encyclopedia of Philosophy* 7 (New York, 1967), 225–29; Sondra R. Herman, *Eleven Against War: Studies in American Internationalist Thought, 1898–1921* (Stanford, CA, 1969); Jacquelyn A. Kegley, Barbara Mackinnon, and Eugene Mayers, eds., *Theory of Community in the Philosophies of Royce and Hocking* (Hayward, CA, 1979); Bruce Kuklick, *Josiah Royce: An Intellectual Biography* (Indianapolis, IN, 1972); Thomas Powell, *Josiah Royce* (New York, 1967); John Edwin Smith, *Royce's Social Infinite: The Community of Interpretation* (New York, 1950).

C. The Royce papers are in the Harvard Univ. Archives and Houghton Library.

Sondra R. Herman

RUEFF, Jacques Léon (23 August 1896, Paris—23 April 1978, Paris). *Education*: Ecole Polytechnique, 1921; Ecole Libre des Sciences Politiques. *Career*: Inspector of Finance, 1923–26; in office of Premier Raymond Poincaré, 1926–27; Economic and Financial Section, League of Nations, 1927–30; French financial attaché, London, 1930–31; professor, Ecole Libre des Sciences Politiques, 1931–34; assistant director, then director, Mouvement Général des Fonds, French Treasury, 1934–37; vice-governor, Bank of France, 1939–41; delegate, Inter-Allied Reparations Agency, 1946–52; professor, Institut des Etudes Politiques, 1945–48; judge, Coal and Steel Community Court and European Court of Justice, 1952–62.

An economist with a special interest in financial and monetary affairs and a nineteenth-century liberal approach, Rueff quickly moved to the center of power, helping Premier Raymond Poincaré stabilize the franc in 1926–27. Rueff strongly believed in free enterprise and the gold standard, opposing the recipes of *John M. Keynes. He returned to the government in Paris in the Treasury and the Bank of France in the late 1930s. After the war, he became more involved in international activities as a delegate to the UN General Assembly, as a member of the Reparations Agency, and as a judge on the court of the Coal and Steel Community and then the European Court of Justice.

In 1958 he proposed a plan for financial reform to the de Gaulle government that included a balanced budget, elimination of most subsidies to producers and automatic wage escalations, liberalization of international trade by removing most quotas, and the creation of a new franc worth one hundred old francs. Most of Rueff's program was enacted, and the French economy prospered. In 1960 the "Armand-Rueff" report made further recommendations to free the French economy from restrictions. Less of it was adopted by the government.

In many books, articles, and speeches Rueff expressed his views on monetary affairs, as in his *Age of Inflation* (1964) and *Balance of Payments*

(1967). He argued that a fatal error was made in 1922 when monetary authorities decided to allow central banks to include as reserves not only gold but currencies exchangeable for gold—the gold exchange standard. This, he claimed, led to the explosion of currency and credit and brought endemic price inflation to the world. Rueff's solution was to return to a strict gold standard and so protect the world from the vacillating minds and feeble hand of men. Whatever the merits of his proposal, it did not find many supporters among economists or among government officials, for whom gold no longer was a credible alternative to the dollar as an international standard. Yet Rueff as a respected economist who focused most of his work on stabilizing world currencies nevertheless had some moderating influence difficult to measure.

BIBLIOGRAPHY:

A. *The Age of Inflation* (Chicago, 1964); *The Balance of Payments* (New York, 1967); *Combats pour l'ordre financier* (Paris, 1972); *De l'aube au crépuscule: Autobiographie* (Paris, 1977); *The Gods and the Kings* (New York, 1973); *L'Ordre social* (Paris, 1945); *The Monetary Sin of the West* (New York, 1972); *Théorie des phénomènes monetaires* (Paris, 1927).

B. CB 1969, 382–84; *Le Monde* 15 Apr 1978, 1; LT 25 Apr 1978, 18; R. Mundell, "The Monetary Consequences of Jacques Rueff," *Journal of Business* 46 (Jul 1973), 384–95; NYT 25 Apr 1978, 40; J. Saint-Ceours, "Le Meilleur Système monetaire internationale et les lancinantes thèses de M. Rueff," *Analyse et prévision* 8 (Dec 1969), 747–70.

James M. Laux

RUSSELL, Lindsay (18 November 1870, Wilmington, NC—8 October 1949, Wilmington). *Education*: read law in North Carolina. *Career*: attorney, New York and London, 1895–1937.

On a visit to England in the winter of 1901–2, Russell became appalled at British and American citizens' general ignorance of each other. Gathering with concerned persons in London, he organized the Pilgrim Society (1901–2) and a year later formed a branch in New York. These were the first of a large number of friendship societies to be established over the next two decades by Russell and his good friend *Hamilton Holt. In 1907 they created the Japan Society, and Russell, as its first president, nurtured it and saw it thrive. By entertaining visitors, publishing books, providing information on trade, encouraging travel, and organizing lectures, Russell saw a clear educational need being met by these bodies. At the end of World War I he organized a Committee on International Relations in New York City, where its select one hundred met for lunches to examine world problems. This forerunner of later groups, like the Council on Foreign Relations, proved the validity of Russell's original concept that people wanted to learn about the world. Russell also served as a director of the New York Peace Society.

BIBLIOGRAPHY:
B. NYT 4 Apr 1920, VII-7; 9 Oct 1949, 95.

Warren F. Kuehl

RUYSSEN, Théodore Eugène César (11 August 1868, Chinon, France—5 May 1967, Grenoble, France). *Education*: Ecole Normale Supérieure; agregé de philosophie and docteur ès lettres; Univs. of Berlin and Leipzig. *Career*: professor, lycées in La Rochelle, Limoges, Bordeaux, 1896–1904, Univs. of Aix-Marseille, 1904–6, Dijon, 1906–8, Bordeaux, 1908–21; chargé de cours, Univ. of Grenoble, 1939–45; secretary and president, Association de la Paix par le Droit, 1898–99; founding member, Congrès Nationaux des Sociétés de la Paix, 1902; Délégation Permanente des Sociétés Françaises de la Paix; president, Deuxieme Congrès National de la Paix, 1902, member, Institut International de la Paix (Monaco, Paris); secretary-general, International Union of Associations for the League of Nations, 1921–39.

Ruyssen joined the French and European peace movement as a young man after meeting +Ludwig Quidde during a trip through Germany in 1894–95. Ruyssen specifically affiliated with a relatively new French peace association, La Paix par le Droit instead of the older Paris-based groups. Most of its members were from southern France, associated with Radical and left republican parties, and interested in organizing peace societies among students in universities and high schools. Ruyssen was elected secretary of the organization in 1898 and a year later became its president and most important spokesman.

His reputation as a peace activist and as a philosopher, specializing in Kantian studies, grew rapidly in the years before World War I. Active in the movement to organize a national peace association, Ruyssen provided much of the energy to achieve that end as well as a good deal of the intellectual labor behind the reports and resolutions of the congresses. Under his careful eye, the journal, *La Paix par le Droit* became one of the best-edited and most thoughtful peace organs. It was the first French peace publication to crusade vigorously for the breakdown of cultural hostilities between Germans and French, to work for student exchanges, and to raise the issue of Alsace-Lorraine regularly. Ruyssen, unlike the old generation of French peace activists, was unafraid of discussing controversial issues in the journal and at conferences.

Essentially committed to the programs of arbitration and an evolving international organization typical of the pre-1914 peace movement, Ruyssen and his group did not condemn the government's declaration of war in 1914, sharing the view of most French that the country had been attacked. He was, however, one of the first peace activists to begin thinking and publicly addressing the question of what kind of peace should be developed after the war. As early as 1915, his proposals included recognition of the rights of nationalities, completion of the work begun by the Hague Peace

Conferences of 1899 and 1907, and creation of a society of nations committed to arbitration which would have an enforcement arm. These ideas were further developed during the war, despite police surveillance; and when *Woodrow Wilson articulated Allied war aims, Ruyssen believed he had found a leader. In 1917 he had a fully developed plan for a Society of Nations and was a spokesman both for La Paix par le Droit and the French Ligue des Droits de l'Homme.

Following the war, Ruyssen joined a French society for the League and eventually became secretary-general of the International Union of League of Nations Associations. His labors, lectures, and articles as well as books in service of the international ideal were numerous, winning for him recognition from governments, universities, and academies. Not till his seventieth birthday did he step down from his post at the International Union, and beyond his eightieth birthday he was still writing for *La Paix par le Droit*. Twice in his lifetime did his books achieve the coveted "crown" from the French Academy—the first in 1904 for *Kant* and the second in 1960 for *Itinéraire spirituel*. By his death, Ruyssen had spanned nearly three generations in the service of the cause of peace and internationalism while sustaining an honored academic career.

BIBLIOGRAPHY:

A. *De la guerre au droit: Etude de philosophie sociale* (Paris, 1920); *Kant*, 3rd ed. (Paris, 1929); *La Philosophie de la paix* (Paris, 1904); *La Société internationale* (Paris, 1950); *L'Alsace-Lorraine et la paix* (Bordeaux, 1913); *Le Problème des nationalités* (Paris, 1916); *Les minorités nationales d'Europe et la guerre mondiale* (Paris, 1923); *Les sources doctrinales de l'internationalisme*, 3 vols. (Paris, 1954–61); *Pacifisme et patriotisme* (Paris, 1908).

B. Alfred Fried, *Handbuch der Friedensbewegung* (Leipzig, Germany, 1910), 403–4; "Les 80 ans de Théod. Ruyssen," *La Paix par le droit* (1948), 197; Marie-Renée Mouton, 'L'Idée d'organisation internationale en France et en Italie pendant la première guerre mondiale," in *La France et l'Italie pendant la première guerre mondiale* (Grenoble, France, 1976), 100–21; Hans Wehberg, "Th. Ruyssens Abschied vom Weltverband der Völkerbundligen," *Friedenswarte* 37, no. 1 (1939), 63–64; WWF 1967–68, 1240.

Sandi E. Cooper and Bernerd C. Weber

S

SAAVEDRA LAMAS, Carlos. See *Biographical Dictionary of Modern Peace Leaders.*

SALTER, James Arthur (15 March 1881, Oxford—27 June 1975, London). *Education*: Brasenose Coll., Oxford, Univ., 1899-1904. *Career*: Admiralty Office, 1904-11, 1914-18; Home Office, 1911-14; League of Nations Secretariat, 1919-20, 1922-31; member of Parliament, 1937-53; Ministry of War Transport, 1940-43; minister of state for economic affairs, 1951-52; minister of materials, 1952-53.

Salter's career of sixty years was divided into two periods of nearly equal length, the first consisting of public employment in the British Civil Service and then in a broader arena mainly with the League of Nations. The second also involved a variety of public activities as professor, member of Parliament, minister, adviser to governments, and writer. His decision to enter the home service upon leaving Oxford set the tone for his life. After a seven-year apprenticeship in a small department of the Admiralty which chartered merchant ships, he moved to a new office created to administer *David Lloyd George's National Health Insurance Scheme embodying the basic features of the emerging welfare state. His position as private secretary to C.F.G. Masterman, the minister in charge, brought Salter into contact with many of the major figures in British public life and provided an outlet for his great gift of "contrivance"—improvisation to meet special situations. Back at the Admiralty during World War I, Salter participated in planning the voyages and allocating the tonnage of British and Allied shipping as well as keeping track of the world's ships. As director of ship requisitioning and chairman of the Inter-Allied Maritime Transport Executive, his work was instrumental in achieving maximum colloration in 1918.

So close to many problems of war planning and enthused by the social projects of Lloyd George, Salter was marked as one who could play a significant role in the League of Nations. Moreover he was, by his own description, imbued with the aspirations and idealism which found what seemed at the time to be the almost perfect expression in *Woodrow Wilson's creed. Thus he spent the next twelve years in League service, mainly as director of the Economic and Financial Section, with an intervening two-year stint as secretary-general of the Reparation Commission. Many challenging tasks came his way, including that of organizing the first World Economic Conference in 1927, and he later adjudged this the happiest period of work in his life—a time of laboring for a purpose which combined his most ardent hopes and deepest convictions. But he came to realize that the Secretariat was weakening in international character and status and that the League was lacking the powers it needed to function effectively. He resigned in 1931.

During the 1930s Salter devoted his energy to writing. Many of his books on economic and world political issues provide evidence of his continuing "international mind." He served a five-year term as chairman of the Railway Wage Tribunal, returned to academic life at Oxford in 1934, and represented Oxford in Parliament (1937–50). Early in World War II, Salter returned to government service. In 1941 he went to Washington as head of the British Shipping Mission and there administered perhaps the most effective British effort in America during the war, ensuring the passage of essential goods and participating in allocating tonnage for the Allied war effort.

Elected to Parliament in 1951, he accepted appointment as minister of state for economic affairs and later as minister of materials (1951–53). In his later years he continued to write. His interest in and support for internationalism remained strong, as evidenced by his active role in the United Europe campaign in Britain. The Suez Crisis of 1956, which found him in disagreement with government policy, initiated a gradual detachment from politics.

BIBLIOGRAPHY:

A. *Allied Shipping Control* (Oxford, 1922); *The Framework of an Ordered Society* (Cambridge, 1933); *Memoirs of a Public Servant* (London, 1961); *Personality in Politics* (London, 1947); *Recovery: The Second Effort* (London, 1932); *Security* (London, 1939); *Slave of the Lamp* (London, 1967); *The United States of Europe and Other Essays* (London, 1933).

B. LT 30 June 1975, 14.

William R. Rock

SALVEMINI, Gaetano (8 September 1873, Molfetta, Italy—6 September 1957, Sorrento, Italy). *Education*: Molfetta Sem.; liberal arts degree, Instituto di Studi Superiori, Florence Univ., 1896. *Career*: taught at Univs. of Messina, 1901–8, Pisa, 1910–16, Florence, 1917–25, 1949–54, Harvard, 1930, Yale, 1931; lecturer, Harvard Univ., 1937–48; member of Italian Parliament, 1919–21; in exile, 1926–49.

Salvemini encompassed within his life three careers: educator and scholar; political writer and activist against Fascism; and exponent of internationalism. The first covered his teaching posts in Italy, his exile after 1925 when he lectured in England and the United States, and the writing of several books. He also helped found in 1901 the Federation of High School Teachers and with Alfredo Galletti wrote a volume sketching urgent secondary school reforms (1908). Salvemini also became involved in politics and contributed to the Socialist magazine *La critica sociale*, writing essays on the problems of southern Italy and the needs of the local peasantry. He also campaigned for universal male suffrage, which was achieved in 1912. Abandoning the Socialist party, which in his opinion overlooked the needs of southern peasants, he edited (1911–20) the weekly, *L'Unità*, which opposed the Libyan War. After brief service in World War I, he used his journal to campaign for a peace based on Mazzinian and Wilsonian ideals, with respect for national self-determination and opposition to territorial expansion. He thus opposed Italian annexationist policy after the war, advocated friendship with Southern Slavs, and upheld enthusiastically the Wilsonian League of Nations.

Salvemini then reentered the Socialist party, experienced trial and imprisonment for publishing the first clandestine paper, *Non mollare!* (Don't give in!), and when granted amnesty in July 1925 went into exile. Thereafter he was a leader of Giustizia e Libertà, founded by *Carlo Rosselli to overthrow Fascism.

Between the wars, Salvemini supported the League of Nations and sternly criticized appeasement of dictators from the columns of American magazines. In 1940 in New York he founded the Mazzini Society to promote an Italian democratic republic after the fall of Fascism. He also wrote incessantly in favor of a just peace, not of revenge, and he proposed a postwar arrangement based on collective security and an internationally integrated military force.

As a vigorous writer, Salvemini was admired by numerous disciples and friends for his clarity of ideas and for his intellectual and moral integrity.

BIBLIOGRAPHY:

A. with others, *Europa federata* (Milan, 1947); *Fascist Dictatorship in Italy* (London, 1928); *Mussolini diplomate* (Paris, 1932); *Prelude to World War Two* (London, 1953); *Under the Axe of Fascism* (London, 1936); with G. La Piana, *What to Do with Italy* (New York, 1943); *Works*, 20 vols. (Milan, 1959–   ).

B. *Chi è?* (Rome, 1957), 490–91; Massimo L. Salvadori, *Gaetano Salvemini* (Turin, 1963); Ernesto Seston and others, *Gaetano Salvemini* (Bari, Italy, 1957); Enzo Tagliacozzo, *Gaetano Salvemini nel cinquantennio liberale* (Florence, 1959).

Enzo Tagliacozzo

SANTOS, Eduardo (28 August 1888, Bogotá—27 March 1974, Bogotá). *Education*: LL.D., National Univ. of Bolivia, 1908. *Career*: president, Municipal Council of Bogotá; member and president, Colombian House of Representatives, 1934, Colombian Senate, 1935–36; delegate, League of Nations, 1931–33, 1937; representative, Disarmament Conference in Geneva, 1932; founder, *El Tiempo*, 1912; president of Colombia, 1938–42.

Santos earned a reputation as one of Latin America's most famous journalists through his direction of and writings in the liberal newspaper *El Tiempo*. For six decades he spoke against dictatorships, social injustice, and other problems plaguing Colombia and Latin America. The newspaper was banned by several regimes for its open criticisms.

When he served as president of Colombia (1938–42), he was a moderate and conciliatory force in domestic politics and turned his efforts toward improvements in education, agriculture, and industry. Santos handled several international incidents involving Colombia in a manner which received worldwide attention. In 1942 he signed a pact with the Vatican ending church control of education and providing that bishops should be Colombian citizens, accepted by the government. In 1939, when World War II broke out, many of Santos's opponents called for strict neutrality, but he stood with the Allies and ordered a government takeover of German-owned airlines and airfields considered to be a threat to the Panama Canal. After Pearl Harbor he broke diplomatic relations with the Axis and increased ties with the United States. In 1941 he was credited with bringing a settlement to a longstanding border dispute with neighboring Venezuela. In these cases he drew upon his experience as an international statesman gained in the roles of chairman of the Colombia delegation to the League of Nations and of his nation's representative to the Disarmament Conference in Geneva in 1932. As a delegate he was a leading advocate of the peaceful settlement of disputes and human rights.

In 1944 he was assigned as a deputy general of the United Nations Relief and Rehabilitation Administration. He traveled extensively in the Western Hemisphere seeking support for the agency and could report pledges of over $42 million for refugees in the form of clothing, textiles, cotton, wheat, and other supplies. He was also instrumental in helping to settle displaced persons in various nations in Latin America. He continued to contribute commentaries on political and human rights issues to newspapers and has been widely quoted by writers in the fields of Latin American politics and world affairs.

BIBLIOGRAPHY:

A. Contributor to *El Tiempo*; *Las etapas de la vida colombiana, discursos y mensayes, 1938-1942* (Bogotá, 1946).

B. David S. Bushnell, *Eduardo Santos and the Good Neighbor, 1932-1942* (Gainesville, FL, 1967); NYT 28 Mar 1960, 29; *Quién es quién en Colombia* (Bogotá, 1961), 237; WWLA 3, 1951, 61.

Alan T. Leonhard

SAO-KE, (Alfred) Sze. See Shih Chao-chi.

SATŌ [born TANAKA] Naotake (30 October 1882, Osaka, Japan—18 December 1971, Tokyo). *Education*: graduate, Tokyo Higher Commercial School (Hitotsubashi Univ.), 1905. *Career*: began diplomatic career in St. Petersburg, 1906-14; consul-general, Harbin, Manchuria, 1914-18; minister to Poland, 1924-25; reopened Soviet Russia as chargé d'affaires, 1925; head, Japan Office, League of Nations, 1927-30; ambassador to Belgium and delegate to League, 1931-33; ambassador to France, 1933-36; foreign minister in Hayashi Cabinet, 1937; adviser to Foreign Office, 1938-42; ambassador to Soviet Union, 1942-45; member, House of Councillors, 1947-65, president, 1949-53; president, UN Association of Japan, 1948-70; Kajima Peace Prize, 1970.

Born a Tanaka of samurai lineage, Naotake was adopted into the family of diplomat Aimarō Satō, later ambassador to the United States (1916–18). He entered the Japan Foreign Office in 1905, serving until 1946, when he was released from internment in the Soviet Union. During this period Satō emerged as one of Japan's leading conference diplomats. He made a lasting impression in European diplomatic circles in an era when his own government's image became tarnished.

Satō was a vigorous supporter of international cooperation and conciliation. While associated with the League of Nations, he observed that the League recognized and utilized the unique talent of the Japanese for objectively handling disputes, especially among the European nations. The Japanese were very conscientious and worked hard to win international confidence. Satō served on many League committees, including those on mandates, minorities, narcotics, arms manufacture, and the protection of women and children. He also dealt with the difficult problems of disarmament and naval limitations. The Japanese delegates worked hard for parity with the Western powers but had to compromise to maintain international good will. The London Treaty in 1930 resulted in a series of incidents against the government in Japan and weakened the diplomats' efforts. Unfortunately, after the Manchurian Incident in 1931, Satō was faced with the unpleasant task of defending Japan against the weight of world opinion and condemnation. He had hoped Japan would be committed enough to ensure the success of the League experiment, but her withdrawal in 1933 isolated her and compounded world tensions.

Satō was again thrust into the forefront when he became foreign minister in 1937. Unaware of the domestic repercussions, he stated that Japan could avoid crises with the proper attitude. He also advocated dealing with China on an equal footing and reducing anxieties abroad by taking a conciliatory stance. His efforts to establish a "new deal" in Japanese diplomacy were continually attacked, as was his "orthodox" diplomacy. The Hayashi Cabinet folded after only three months in office, and war with China ensued the following month. Satō was disturbed by the movement toward the Axis and the miscalculations of Japan in expanding the war, particularly with the Americans. In his last diplomatic assignment, he had a difficult task of maintaining the tenuous Neutrality Pact while ambassador to the Soviet Union. In the final days of World War II, he strongly urged surrender and opposed his government's initiative to have the Soviet Union mediate the peace. After the war, Satō was a leading Diet member and a strong proponent of Japan's entrance into the world community, a dream realized in 1956 when Japan entered the UN with Satō as chief delegate.

BIBLIOGRAPHY:

A. *Futatsu no Roshia* [The two Russias] (Tokyo, 1948); "Japan Among the United Nations," *Contemporary Japan* 25 (Sep 1957), 1–5; *Kaiko hachijūnen* [Recollections of eighty years] (Tokyo, 1963); supervisory ed., *Kokusai Renmei ni okeru Nihon* [Japan in the League of Nations], vol. 14 in *Nihon gaikōshi* [Diplomatic history of Japan] (Tokyo, 1972); "The League and the U.N., *Japan Quarterly* 5 (Jan–Mar 1958), 15–20.

B. Greg Gubler, "The Diplomatic Career of Satō Naotake (1882–1971): A Samurai in Western Clothing," dissertation, Florida State Univ., 1975; *Japan Biographical Encyclopedia and Who's Who* (Tokyo, 1965), 1336–37; *Japan Times* 19 Dec 1971, 4; special commemorative issue on Satō, *Kokusai jihyō* [International affairs], no. 67 (Nov 1970); George A. Lensen, *The Strange Neutrality: Soviet-Japanese Relations During the Second War, 1941–1945* (Tallahassee, FL, 1972); Masatoshi Matsushita, *Japan in the League of Nations* (New York, 1929); NYT 19 Dec 1971, 61.

Greg Gubler

SCHÜCKING, Walther Adrian (6 January 1875, Münster, Germany—25 August 1935, The Hague). *Education*: Univs. of Munich, Bonn, Berlin; doctor of law, Univ. of Göttingen, 1897, habilitation, 1899. *Career*: professor, Univ. of Marburg, 1903–19, Handels Hochshule Berlin, 1919–26; professor and director, Institute for International Law, Kiel, 1932–36; member of the Reichstag (DDP), 1919–28; judge, Permanent Court of International Justice, 1930–35.

Schücking was the most outspoken and politically engaged international lawyer in Germany during the first third of the twentieth century. His background in a family dominated by a politically liberal father and the influence of his major professor, Ludwig von Bar, combined to make Schücking an advocate of a natural rights legal philosophy, which at the turn of the century was in discredit among German legal faculties dominated by legal positivism. Schücking's uncompromising devotion to the proposition that law proceeded from binding principles of justice resulted in his isolation from his professional colleagues in Marburg as well as in harassment from the Prussian government, whose policies he criticized in the light of his own legal and ethical principles.

Schücking's legal philosophy also informed his view of international politics. One of the founding members of the Verband für Internationale Verstandigung, he emerged before World War I as a leading proponent of international arbitration and the building of the judicial machinery established at The Hague into an international organization with obligatory arbitral and mediating powers in a broad range of international disputes.

The outbreak of war in 1914 brought a change of focus in Schücking's activities. He attempted, by means of communications with internationalists in enemy and neutral countries, to promote a compromise peace, as well as an effective international organization for the postwar period. The activities of Schücking and his contacts, which took place primarily under the aegis of the Central Organization for a Durable Peace, were frustrated by the uncompromising positions of the belligerent governments, although the German Foreign Office did recognize the value, if only for propaganda purposes, of Schücking's foreign connections.

By the war's end, these contacts and Schücking's reputation as an international lawyer and advocate of world organization brought him briefly into the diplomatic spotlight as a member of the German delegation to the Versailles Peace Conference. There Schücking protested that the League of Nations, which the victor powers were preparing to institute, made a travesty of the principles of international justice, but his view was ignored.

Schücking's activities in the 1920s were foreshadowed in these protestations. He devoted himself more centrally to politics, serving in the Reichstag as a member of the Democratic party from 1919 to 1928. His principal interest remained the cause of international organization, and he was a leading figure in the Deutsche Liga für Völkerbund, an organization dedicated to promoting popular understanding in Germany for the League of Nations. However, his uncompromising advocacy of international organization made him suspect both in Germany and abroad—in Germany because of the extent he seemed willing to sacrifice German sovereignty to an international body, and abroad because of his continued insistence that the Versailles Treaty was unjust and his professed desire to use the League of Nations as the agency to rectify Germany's grievances.

A man who found compromise difficult when he believed principle at stake, Schücking was never comfortable in politics. In 1926 he succeeded Theodor Niemeyer as director of the Institute for International Law in Kiel, and two years later he abandoned his seat in the Reichstag. The fulfillment of his career came in 1930 with his selection as a judge on the Permanent Court of International Justice, the only German to serve in that capacity. The Nazis had removed him from his position in Kiel in 1933, but he now remained beyond their reach at The Hague until his death in 1935.

BIBLIOGRAPHY:

A. *Der Staatenverband der Haager Konferenzen* (Munich, 1912); *Die Organisation der Welt* (Leipzig, Germany, 1909); *Garantiepakt und Rüstungsbeschränkung* (Berlin, 1924); *Internationale Rechtsgarantien: Ausbau und Sicherung der zwischenstaatlichen Beziehungen* (Hamburg, 1918).

B. Detlev Acker, *Walther Schücking (1875-1935)* (Münster, Germany, 1970); *Die Friedenswarte* 37 (1935), 162-234; NYT 27 Aug 1935, 19.

C. The Schücking papers can be found in the Bundesarchiv, Coblence, the Universitätsbibliothek, Münster, and the Landesmuseum für Kunst, Münster.

Roger Chickering

SCHUMAN, Robert (29 June 1886, Dutchy of Luxemburg—4 September 1963, near Metz, France). *Education*: Univs. of Bonn, Munich, Berlin; LL.D., Univ. of Strasbourg. *Career*: deputy, National Assembly, 1919-61; under secretary of state for refugees, 1940; minister of finance, 1946-47; premier, 1947-48; minister of foreign affairs, 1948-53; minister of justice, 1955-56.

Although born in Luxemburg, Schuman grew up in Metz, France, which he considered his permanent home. Schuman was bilingual and binational, a condition which was to stand him in good stead when the time came for a Franco-German reconciliation at the end of World War II. He was truly a "man of the border," to use the words of Dean Acheson. He practiced his profession in Metz for a short time only. Most of his life he spent in French politics. It was a third career, however, which constitutes his greatest legacy as the principal figure in the creation of the first institution of a united Europe—the European Coal and Steel Community, popularly called the Schuman Plan. Schuman more than any other European statesman realized shortly after the end of World War II the need for Europe to federate to survive and for Germany to be included in the arrangement. He also accepted the reality of its economic and political revival and the need to harness the power of a revived Germany. The solution was to place Germany's war-making capacity under the control of an international authority with supranational power. In April 1950 *Jean Monnet, long an advocate of such a scheme, hammered out a draft proposal. By 8 May, with the task completed, an emissary of Schuman took the proposal to *Konrad Adenauer, the German chancellor, who accepted it immediately. The next day, in the Salle d'Horloge at the French Foreign Office, Schuman publicly unveiled the plan and invited other European nations to join. The three Benelux countries and Italy accepted the offer, and on 11 April 1951, the six signed the treaty and the European Coal and Steel Community came into being. Under Schuman's guidance, the French National Assembly ratified the document on 13 December 1951, after one week of debate. A new Europe was born.

Schuman was less successful in his efforts to create an integrated European military force as another means of gathering Germany into Europe and of controlling her army. The proposal in November of 1950 was opposed by many French political figures, chiefly the Gaullists, and it was defeated in the Assembly. At the same time, Schuman left the Foreign Office. For two years he held no post save membership in the National Assembly. Then in 1955 he took over his last cabinet office, the Ministry of Justice, where he remained one year. The movement toward unity moved ahead, culminating in 1958 in the creation of the European Economic Community. It was fitting that Schuman was elected by acclamation first president of its new Parliament in March 1958, until March 1960. After that, and for three years until shortly before his death, he served as a member of the Parliament and its honorary president. He was buried in Metz, and a monument erected on his gravesite faces east across the Rhine, symbolizing his singular achievement of bringing Germany into the European federation. Towering in his achievements, he was physically a small man described as an ascetic, single, frugal, lonely, and even Spartan. Dressed always in black and carrying a black briefcase, he appeared even smaller than he really was. His habit of rubbing his nose added to his air of diffidence. His one great passion in life was his collection of books. In an otherwise blameless life, there was one blot of Schuman's career: he supported Marshal Pétain in 1940. As a member of the Assembly, he voted him full powers and served briefly in his Cabinet. He regretted his action and as if by atonement joined the Resistance.

BIBLIOGRAPHY:

A. *Le Plan Schuman: Ses mérites, ses risques. Lettre de Robert Schuman, ministre des affaires etrangères*, ed. J. F. Kövér (Paris, 1952); *Pour l'Europe* (Paris, 1963).

B. Lutz Hermann, *Robert Schuman: Ein Porträt* (Freudenstadt, Germany, 1965); René Hostiou, *Robert Schuman et l'Europe* (Paris, 1969); LT 5 Sep 1963, 14, 11 Sep 1963, 17; NYT 5 Sep 1963, 1; 8 Sep 1963, 86.

Armin Rappaport

SCHURMAN, Jacob Gould (22 May 1854, Freetown, PEI—12 August 1942, Bedford Hills, NY). *Education*: B.A., Univ. of London, 1877, M.A., 1878; D.Sc., Univ. of Edinburgh, 1878. *Career*: professor, Acadia Coll., Nova Scotia, 1880–82, Dalhousie Univ., Halifax, 1882–86, Cornell Univ., 1886–92; president, Cornell Univ., 1892–1920; president, First Philippine Commission, 1899–1900; minister to Greece and Montenegro, 1911–12, to China, 1921–25; ambassador to Germany, 1925–30.

Schurman had a remarkable career as an educator and, as such, knew the leading Republican leaders of his day. These contacts led to his public service activities during and after his tenure as president of Cornell. On the Philippine Commission, he urged self-government for the Filipinos as soon as they proved capable. As minister to Greece, he gained valuable knowledge of the Balkans and provided suggestions to *Edward M. House for use by the Inquiry prior to the Versailles settlement and establishment of the League of Nations after World War I. Schurman endorsed U.S. membership in the League of Nations in 1919 and during the election of 1920 helped draft the Statement of the 31, which argued that a vote for Warren Harding would best promote United States membership in an association of nations.

In China, Schurman was one of the first influential Western diplomats to urge an end to extraterritorialty. During his service in Germany, he pointed out the difficulties posed for the Germans and Europe by the harsh Versailles settlement. These experiences in Europe and Asia from 1910 to 1930 eventually led Schurman to endorse a more frequent use of the World Court. Although not one to suggest an end to national sovereignty, he clearly felt rational men could and should abandon some measure of national sovereignty to ensure that all had the benefit of international law and justice. After his diplomatic service ended in 1930, he continued to travel and lecture and by the late 1930s gradually came to suggest international cooperation to deal with the growing threat of Hitler in Germany.

BIBLIOGRAPHY:

A. *The Balkan Wars, 1912-1913* (Princeton, NJ, 1914); *Philippine Affairs: A Retrospect and Outlook* (New York, 1902).

B. DAB supp. 3, 696–99; Kenneth P. Davis, "The Diplomatic Career of Jacob Gould Schurman," dissertation, Univ. of Virginia, 1975; Maynard Moser, "Jacob Gould Schurman: Scholar, Political Activist, and Ambassador of Good Will," disseratation, Univ. of California, Santa Barbara, 1976; NYT 13 Aug 1942, 19; WWWA 2, 473.

C. The Schurman papers are in the Olin Library, Cornell Univ.

Kenneth Penn Davis

SCHWELB, Egon (18 December 1899, Prague—20 March 1979, New York). *Education*: graduate, Faculty of Law, Charles Univ., 1922; law degree, Univ. of London, 1942. *Career*: law practice, Prague, 1922–39; following German occupation of Czechoslovakia (1939) was imprisoned by Gestapo but escaped to England before outbreak of World War II; member, Legal Council, Czechoslovak government-in-exile, 1942; legal counsel, UN War Crimes Commission, which prepared trials of major Nazi war criminals, 1945; deputy director, Division of Human Rights, UN Secretariat, 1947–62; senior fellow and lecturer, School of Law, Yale Univ., 1962–68.

Schwelb's name as an internationalist is entwined with developing concepts of human rights. The idea of the universal protection of fundamental human rights was conceived during World War I and became prominent during the drafting of the UN Charter and the creation of the UN Organization. The task of implementing the generalities of the Charter by creating an instrument or instruments that would spell out the rights of man fell upon a group of dedicated men and women in the Human Rights Commission and the Secretariat of the UN. Schwelb, as one of these, played a major part in the drafting of the Universal Declaration of Human Rights adopted by the UN General Assembly in 1948 and in the preparation of the International Covenants on Human Rights which were opened for signature by the nations of the world in 1966.

Supreme scholar of international human rights, Schwelb charted in his writings the course of international action in regard to a more effective protection of individual rights. He held that procedural arrangements are of greater importance than a mere restatement of international human rights standards in treaty form and that, accordingly, the bill of rights must go beyond mere enunciation and provide for sufficient international guarantees. Schwelb thoroughly studied the general issues, notably the bearing of various Charter principles. One of his conclusions accepted by the Human Rights Commission was that the domestic jurisdiction of states, if rightly interpreted, only covered questions which had not become international in one way or another; once states agreed that such questions should form the subject of a declaration or convention they clearly placed them outside their exclusive jurisdiction and beyond the doctrine of noninterference with internal matters.

BIBLIOGRAPHY:

A. *Human Rights and the International Community: The Roots and Growth of the Universal Declaration of Human Rights* (Chicago, 1964); a catalog of extensive writings appears in a special issue of the *Human Rights Journal* 4, nos. 2 and 3 (1971), 198–205.

B. René Cassin, "Introduction," *Human Rights Journal* 4, nos. 2 and 3 (1971), 195–96; NYT 22 March 1979, B-13.

Vratislav Pechota

SCIALOJA, Vittorio (24 April 1856, Turin—19 November 1933, Rome). *Education*: law degree, Univ. of Rome, 1878. *Career*: professor, Univs. of Camerino, 1879–80, Siena, 1881–83, Rome, 1884–1933; senator, 1904–33; minister of justice, 1909–19; minister without portfolio, 1916–17; minister for foreign affairs, 1919–20; delegate, League of Nations, 1921–32, vice-president, Academia Nazionale dei Lincei, 1923–26, president, 1926–33.

Scialoja served as Italy's delegate to the League of Nations from 1921 to 1932, first in the Assembly (1921–24) and then in the Council (1925–32). He was well suited for association with the Geneva experiment. On the one hand, he had no direct role in the "old diplomacy," which came under increasing criticism after 1918 for its secrecy and its failure to avert World War I. Only in 1919 did Scialoja assume an important role in the formulation of Italian foreign policy. As foreign minister, he became identified with the policies initiated by the Nitti government: moderation toward the defeated powers, conciliation toward Yugoslavia regarding the question of Fiume, and concentration on the means to revive international commerce. He had attended the Paris Peace Conference, sat on the commission (1920) to draft the statutes for the Permanent Court of International Justice and the one (1929) to revise them, and signed the Treaty of Locarno (1925). He made his real mark as an internationalist, however, at Geneva.

Before his appointment there, Scialoja had established his reputation as a scholar in Roman law, a field which endowed him with a sense of the practical and an awareness of the limits of collective security. In a Council speech in the early 1920s, he warned that a supranational organization like the League would prove effective only to the extent that each member state would forfeit its national sovereignty. He considered this as only a remote possibility in his lifetime. Nonetheless, he considered the League to be a safeguard of peace because it provided a forum for discussion and allowed diplomats more time to resolve potential disputes. To those who pointed to the inherent weakness of the League, Scialoja retorted that its very creation represented a tremendous step forward.

Unlike some of his colleagues at Geneva, Scialoja placed little stock in efforts to define "aggression," "collective guarantees," and similar terms. Elaborate definitions were sterile and dangerously misleading because they failed to identify and ameliorate the deep-seated social and economic causes of war. Many of Scialoja's most important observations centered around economic issues, particularly the growing disparity between "producer" and "consumer" nations. Fearing the destabilizing effect that uneven socio-economic development among nations would have in world affairs, he succeeded in having the Economic Section of the League address the problem. Similarly, he urged that the League examine the question of combustibles and other raw materials from the viewpoint of pricing and accessibility.

For over a decade, Scialoja's keen insight, wit, and vision touched virtually every aspect of the League's activity. He took part in the organization of its machinery and helped to establish the perimeters of the League's jurisidiction. He fostered close ties between it and various cultural and intellectual organizations, such as the International Institute for the Codification of Law, founded under his presidency in 1928. The dream of peace, Scialoja once remarked, was as old as man himself. Few persons contributed more in working creatively to help the League become the means through which that timeless dream might become a reality.

BIBLIOGRAPHY:

A. *Alcuni testi e documenti giuridici* (Rome, 1898); *Discorsi alla Società delle nazioni* (Rome, 1932); *I problemi dello stato italiano dopo la guerra* (Bologna, Italy, 1918); *Influenza dell'Italia sul diritto all'estero* (Rome, 1922); *Studi giuridici,* 1 (Rome, 1933).

B. Vincenzo Arangio-Ruiz, "Vittorio Scialoja nel centenario della nascita (1856–1956)"; *Chi è?* (Rome, 1928), 685–86; NYT 20 Nov 1933, 15; *Problemi attuali di scienza e di cultura,* no. 39 (Rome, 1956), 3–13.

Louis A. Cretella

SCOTT, James Brown (7 June 1866, Kincardine, ON—25 June 1943, Annapolis, MD). *Education*: B.A., Harvard Coll., 1890, M.A., 1891; studied law, Harvard, Berlin, Heidelberg, Paris Univs.; J.U.D., Heidelberg Univ., 1894. *Career*: practiced law, Los Angeles, 1894–99; founder and first dean, Los Angeles Law School (now Law Department of the Univ. of Southern California), 1896–98; dean, College of Law, Univ. of Illinois, 1899–1903; professor, Columbia Univ., 1903–6; solicitor, Department of State, 1906–11; secretary and director, Division of International Law, Carnegie Endowment for International Peace, 1911–40.

As a scholar, educator, author, editor, government legal adviser, diplomat, founder, and leader of international legal societies and journals, Scott's life was dedicated to the cause of achieving peace through international law. His career as a diplomat and practitioner of international law began in 1906, when he accepted the post of State Department solicitor. This assignment also marked the beginning of Scott's long association with

*Elihu Root, then secretary of state. Root appointed Scott as a technical delegate to the Second Hague Peace Conference in 1907. Although Scott had hoped that the delegates would accomplish more toward establishing an international court of justice, he did feel that some progress had been achieved. He compiled two volumes on the conferences, partially to present evidence of the trend toward the creation of an international court. For the next dozen years, most of Scott's work was motivated by the goal of establishing such a body. As he tended to project America's traditions, democratic heritage, and institutions upon other nations, Scott's model of an international agency was based upon the U.S. Supreme Court.

Scott often accepted governmental assignments after he left the State Department in 1911 to join the Carnegie Endowment for International Peace. He served as a special adviser in matters of international law (1914). After the outbreak of World War I, Scott was chairman of the Joint State and Navy Neutrality Board (1914–17), a major in the Judge Advocate's corps, and a participant in the preparation for the Paris Peace Conference, which he attended as a legal adviser. Scott was frequently named as a delegate or technical adviser to other international conferences. He was proudest of his service with Root at the 1920 meeting at The Hague, where a panel of jurists drafted the protocol for the Permanent Court of International Justice. When the PCIJ formally opened in 1922, Scott wrote that an age-old dream had been realized. Although he did, not believe it would prevent all future wars, he hoped that it could adjudicate many disputes before they led to larger conflicts.

In addition to his public service, Scott worked for the accomplishment of his ideals through private organizations, many of which he founded or administered. He was a guiding force behind the group of lawyers who established the American Society of International Law. Root became its first president, and Scott its first secretary (1906–24). He later served as its vice-president (1924–29) and president (1929–39). Scott was also the first editor of the society's *American Journal of International Law* (1907–24) and even aided in financing early editions. In order to promote the concept of an international court, Scott helped in 1910 establish the American Society for the Judicial Settlement of International Disputes and became its first president. Scott was also actively involved in international societies. He was president of the European-based Institute of International Law (1925–27, 1928–29), and it provided the model upon which Scott helped create the American Institute of International Law. The latter reflected Scott's interest in Latin America by bringing together international lawyers from the Western Hemisphere interested in codification. Scott was named its first president in 1915 and remained active in it for the remainder of his career.

Scott achieved his greatest influence through the Carnegie Endowment for International Peace as secretary for nearly thirty years and also director of its Division of International Law. The Endowment allowed Scott to pursue his interests, ranging from scholarly research to promoting international legal education, from the rights of women to establishing the PCIJ and codifying international law. Under Scott's guidance, the Endowment published volumes of materials and financed new studies, programs, fellowships and institutes.

Scott stressed the importance of the individual to society and emphasized the value of education. Regardless of his other commitments, he remained an active teacher throughout his career, and he lectured at numerous universities and law schools around the world. He founded the Hague Academy of International Law, whose summer sessions attracted scholars, students, and diplomats.

An early advocate of the casebook method of teaching law, Scott prepared several. He also felt that students required easier access to historical texts. As a result he edited a series of "Classics of International Law," which reprinted the works of great international legal thinkers in their original languge and English translations. Scott's research for the series led him to conclude that the sixteenth-century Dominican theologian Francisco de Vitoria, rather than Hugo Grotius, was the "founder of international law." Scott's thinking was influenced by Vitoria's adherence to moral principles and the belief that justice was an attainable ideal in individual and international relations. It was this concept of justice which motivated Scott's life and career.

BIBLIOGRAPHY:

A. *The Hague Peace Conferences of 1899 and 1907*, 2 vols. (Baltimore, MD, 1909); *James Madison's Notes . . . and Their Relation to a More Perfect Society* (New York, 1918); *Peace Through Justice* (New York, 1917); *The Spanish Origin of International Law* (New York, 1934); *The United States of America: A Study in International Organization* (New York, 1920); many of Scott's writings are listed in *Publications of the Carnegie Endowment for International Peace, 1910–1967* (New York, 1971).

B. AJIL 44 (1944), 183–217; DAB supp. 3, 699–701; Warren F. Kuehl, introduction to *The Hague Peace Conferences of 1899 and 1907*, rpt. ed. (New York, 1972); Ralph D. Nurnberger, "James Brown Scott: Peace Through Justice," dissertation, Georgetown Univ., 1975.

C. The Scott papers are in the Georgetown Univ. Library.

Ralph D. Nurnberger

SERRARENS, Petrus Josephus Servatius (12 November 1888, Dordrecht, Netherlands—26 August 1963, De Bilt, Netherlands). *Education*: graduate, Rotterdam Teacher's Coll., 1907; Leiden Univ., 1915–16. *Career*: delegate and technical adviser, International Labor Conferences, 1919–51; secretary-general, International Federation of Christian Trade Unions, 1920–52; member of Netherlands Parliament, 1929–52; deputy member, International Labor Organization (ILO), governing body, 1934–51; member, Consultative Assembly, Council of Europe, 1949–52; judge, Court of Justice, European Coal and Steel Community, 1952–58.

Following World War I, Christian trade unions in Europe were involved in a general labor upheaval. War feelings, however, had caused deep cleavages in the Christian International between German and Allied members. Attempts by union leaders from neutral countries to rebuild the International succeeded after a declaration of guilt by the German contingent. A congress at The Hague (1920), presided over by Serrarens, established the International Federation of Christian Trade Unions (IFC-TU). Serrarens, who had been appointed secretary-general, presented a world economic program in 1922 which, in contrast to both laissez-faire capitalism and Socialism, was explicitly based on "Christian social principles," emphasizing the nonmaterial needs of workers, class cooperation, and, in particular, the ennoblement of the individual. To provide an alternative to the antireligious approach of Socialist and Communist organizations, Serrarens's main task was to make "the voice of Christian labour" heard on international issues, especially in the International Labor Organization (ILO). Relations with the larger Socialist International, the International Federation of Trade Unions, which exercised a controlling influence in the Workers' Groups of ILO bodies, were generally antagonistic. The monopolistic position of the IFTU was first challenged at the ILO Conference in 1921, when Christian labor organizations of the Netherlands combined to nominate Serrarens as delegation leader and "the most representative" of the Dutch workers. The objection of the IFTU to Serrarens's credentials occasioned an advisory opinion of the Permanent Court of International Justice, which ruled in his favor (1922). In the following years, Serrarens became a member of the Consultative Economic Committee of the League of Nations and a deputy member of the ILO governing body. As a result of his successful endeavors for adequate representation, the ILO Workers' Groups were governed in the 1930s by a coalition of Christian and Socialist trade unions.

Reconciliation between the two international federations was precipitated by the rise of Fascism in Europe. Consistently defending the right to freedom of association, Serrarens had objected to the admission of workers' delegates from Fascist countries since the mid-1920s. His position was formally adopted by the IFCTU Congress in Montreux (1934). The liquidation of their Italian, German, and Austrian affiliates deprived both the Christian and Socialist internationals of their largest member organizations. After World War II the Christian unions, unwilling to sacrifice their separate existence in the interests of labor unity, did not join the newly established World Federation of Trade Unions. Instead, they reconstructed the prewar IFCTU, extended its organizational resources to the developing countries, and gained consultative status in UN specialized agencies and other organizations. In the postwar period, Serrarens became involved in

European unity movements. He was active in Netherlands groups and served in the Assembly of the Council of Europe (1949–52). In 1952 he became a member of the Court of the European Coal and Steel Community. During his unusually long career as secretary-general, he had played a crucial role in the consolidation and universalization of the Christian International and, through his activities in the ILO, had made a substantial contribution to widening the scope of the international labor movement.

BIBLIOGRAPHY:

A. *The Problem of Austria* (Utrecht, Netherlands, 1934); *The Revolution of the Hooked Cross* (Utrecht, Netherlands, 1933); *Russia and the West* (Utrecht, Netherlands 1948); *Towards a Christian Social Order* (Utrecht, Netherlands, 1951).

B. A. Vanistendael, "P.J.S. Serrarens ten gedenken," *Labor* 36, no. 1 (1963), 235–40; *Wie is dat?* (1956), 549–50.

J.H.W. Thijssen

SEWALL, May Wright. See *Biographical Dictionary of Modern Peace Leaders.*

SEYMOUR, Charles (1 January 1885, New Haven, CT—11 August 1963, Chatham, MA). *Education*: B.A., Kings Coll., Cambridge Univ., 1904; B.A., Yale Coll., 1908; M.A., Cambridge Univ., 1909; Ph.D., Yale Univ., 1911. *Career*: faculty, Yale Univ., 1911–18; member, the Inquiry, 1917–18; special assistant, Department of State, 1918; chief, Austro-Hungarian Division, American Commission to Negotiate Peace, 1918–19; professor, Yale Univ., 1919–27, provost, 1928–37, president, 1937–50; curator, Edward M. House Collection, Yale Univ., 1950–63.

Seymour's internationalism was an outgrowth of his studies of pre-World War I European diplomacy. In 1917 he became a member of the Inquiry organized by *Edward M. House, and Seymour accompanied *Woodrow Wilson on the USS *George Washington* to attend the Paris Peace Conference. Seymour's memoranda provide a rare insight into Wilson's ideas for an international organization. Seymour supported the president's plan enthusiastically and welcomed the early formulation of the Covenant of the League of Nations. He anticipated that the League would facilitate a constructive reorganization of the world and provide the nations with necessary insurance against a recurrence of war.

In Paris Seymour served as chief of the Austro-Hungarian Division of the American Commission to Negotiate Peace. He recommended border settlements based on the Wilsonian promise of self-determination of the people, their ethnography, history, and economic condition. As the conference progressed, Seymour became increasingly depressed and frustrated about Wilson's failure to honor the principles he had enunciated. Seymour was convinced that significant deviations from principle would lessen prospects of achieving a just peace. Nevertheless, Seymour was not rigid. He recognized that some concessions were unavoidable and looked at the final peace treaty as a significant step forward. It contained the Covenant, which to him represented the hope of mankind for a better world.

Seymour condemned the Senate for attacks on Wilson and the League. He deplored its efforts to separate the League from the Treaty and frowned on maneuvers to prevent U.S. participation in the League. He also regretted Wilson's stubborn refusal to compromise with moderate senators and attributed his unyielding attitude to his illness. He considered the defeat of the Treaty in the Senate as a disaster for the United States and mankind. During the interwar period, Seymour remained a staunch defender of the League. When in the early 1940s an opportunity arose to form a new international organization, Seymour pointed to crucial shortcomings of the League and the manner of its origin to avoid a similar debacle in the Senate. The formation of the United Nations and its overwhelming acceptance by the Senate pleased him, but he was disappointed when it failed to live up to expectations.

Seymour's writings after his return from the Paris Peace Conference concentrated on U.S. diplomacy during World War I and the peace that followed. House made his diplomatic papers available to Seymour and to Yale University in 1923, and this material and House's personal accounts put Seymour in a unique position to examine events during the Wilson years. Seymour's subsequent writings were influenced by House's version of events. Even so, Seymour remains a prominent authority of the diplomatic history of World War I and its aftermath, in which he presented the League ideal in a favorable light.

BIBLIOGRAPHY:

A. *American Diplomacy During the World War* (Baltimore, MD, 1934); *American Neutrality, 1914–1917* (New Haven, CT, 1935); *The Diplomatic Background of the War, 1870–1914* (New Haven, CT, 1915); ed., *The Intimate Papers of Colonel House*, 4 vols. (Boston, 1926–28); Harold Whiteman, ed., *Letters from the Paris Peace Conference* (New Haven, CT, 1965); Edward M. House and Charles Seymour, eds., *What Really Happened at Paris: The Story of the Peace Conference* (New York, 1921); *Woodrow Wilson and the World War* (New Haven, CT, 1921).

B. CB 1941, 773–74; DAB supp. 7; "Guide to the Charles Seymour Papers," Yale Library, i–xiii; Reuben A. Holden, *Profiles and Portraits of Yale University Presidents* (Freeport, ME, 1968); NCAB F, 56; NYT 12 Aug 1963, 21; *Time* 82 (23 Aug 1963), 82; *Time* 53 (18 Apr 1949), 88–89.

C. The Seymour papers are at Yale Univ.

Kurt Wimer

SFORZA, Carlo (24 January 1872, Lucca, Italy—4 September 1952, Rome). *Education*: graduate in law, Univ. of Pisa, 1895. *Career*: adviser at Italian embassies in Cairo, Paris, Constantinople, and Peking, 1896–1904; chargé d'affaires, Bucharest, 1905, Constantinople, 1908–9; secretary,

Algeciras Conference, 1906; chief adviser, Foreign Ministry, 1910–11; high commissioner, Constantinople, 1918–19; under secretary of state, Foreign Ministry, 1919–20; minister for foreign affairs, 1920–21; in exile, 1927–43; high commissioner for sanctions against Fascism, 1944–45; minister for foreign affairs, 1947–51.

Few statesmen have done more for the cause of European federation than Carlo Sforza, who served as Italian foreign minister (1920–21, 1947–51). Sforza's realistic appraisal of Italy's post-World War I economic and diplomatic position relative to the other European powers is the key to understanding his internationalism. He rejected as dangerous and outmoded the post-1919 nationalist and Fascist worldview, which premised a world of political and economic struggle and advocated that Italy take unilateral action to advance its interests. Sforza realistically held that Italy, although a great power in name, could not compete politically, militarily, or economically with its former allies. To the contrary, Sforza felt that Italy needed allied diplomatic support, credit, raw materials, and the resumption of international trade. Italy's long-term interests thus lay in working for a peaceful world order where justice prevailed over might.

As foreign minister in 1920 and 1921, Sforza worked for the political and economic stablization of Europe. He urged moderation on the questions of war debts and reparations, feeling that a harsh policy would impede commerce and enhance international tension. Italy's deficiency in raw materials led him to oppose the Anglo-French San Remo Oil Accord of 1920, and he prophesied that monopolistic control over raw materials would widen the gulf between rich and poor nations and ultimately precipitate new conflicts.

Sforza's moderate foreign policy was subject to derision by Fascist critics, who ranked him among liberal Italy's *rinunciatarii*. Sforza reciprocated the antipathy and resigned as ambassador to France upon Mussolini's accession to power in October 1922 because he considered the future Duce's pronouncement on foreign affairs to be a collection of resentments and sentiments. Sforza's political courage made him persona non grata in Fascist Italy, and in 1927 he left to become one of the most important *fuorusciti*, or exiled opponents of Fascism. His long experience in government, his foreign diplomatic contacts, and his sustained attacks on the dictatorship made him a logical candidate to preside over the Conference on Free Italy held at Montevideo in August 1942. Acclaimed the spiritual leader of Italian anti-Fascists there, Sforza was charged to organize a National Council to coordinate political efforts to bring about the fall of Fascism.

The destruction caused by World War II served to reconfirm Sforza's belief that excessive political nationalism had to be curtailed. He feared that without European federation Europe would become a "poor, insignificant peninsula" of the Asian land mass. The architect of Italy's postwar foreign policy therefore announced his intention to examine Italian problems from a European viewpoint, thereby expressing his willingness to limit Italian sovereignty. Sforza welcomed the Marshall Plan as a catalyst toward permanent European economic collaboration. He favored, however, not a functional system but a true political and constitutional one that would include Germany and Britain. As foreign minister from 1947 to 1951, he sought to eliminate trade barriers, argued strenuously for the integration of Germany into the European mainstream, and played a key role in the negotiations that led in 1951 to the creation of the European Coal and Steel Community.

BIBLIOGRAPHY:

A. *Cinque anni a Palazzo Chigi: La politica estera italiana dal 1947 al 1951* (Rome, 1952); *Les Italiens tels qu'ils sont* (Montreal, 1941); *L'Italia alle soglie dell'Europa* (Milan, 1947); *L'Italia dal 1914 al 1944 quale io la vidi* (Rome, 1945); *Pensiero e azione di una politica estera italiana* (Bari, Italy, 1924); *Per una nuova democrazia* (Rome, 1924); *Problemi italiani* (Naples, 1942); *The Totalitarian War and After* (Chicago, 1941).

B. Charles F. Delzell, "The European Federalist Movement in Italy: First Phase," *Journal of Modern History* 32 (Sep 1960), 241–50; Maria Grazia Melchionni, "La politica estera di Carlo Sforza nel 1920–1921," *Rivista di studi politici internazionali* 36 (Oct–Dec 1969), 537–70; F. Roy Willis, *Italy Chooses Europe* (New York, 1971); Livio Zeno, *Ritratto di Carlo Sforza* (Florence, 1975).

Louis A. Cretella

SHEPARDSON, Whitney Hart (30 October 1890, Worcester, MA—29 May 1966, New York). *Education*: B.A., Colgate Univ., 1910; B.A., Balliol Coll., Oxford Univ., 1913; LL.B., Harvard Law School, 1917. *Career*: attorney, U.S. Shipping Board, 1917; U.S. Field Artillery, 1918; member, U.S. Peace Commission, 1919; with P. N. Gray and Co., New York, 1920–23; International Education Board, 1923–27; president, Bates International Bag Co., 1928–30; vice-president, International Railways of Central America, 1931–42; special assistant to U.S. ambassador, London, 1942; Office of Strategic Services, 1943–46; director, British Dominions and Colonies Fund, Carnegie Corp., 1946–53; president, Free Europe Committee, 1953–56.

While serving in Paris as secretary to the international commission that wrote the Covenant of the League of Nations, Shepardson helped form an Anglo-American community of individuals attending the peace conference who believed that a continuous study of international relations was desirable. In New York the group was known as the American Institute of International Affairs; its London counterpart was called the Royal Institute of International Affairs. In August 1921 Shepardson served as executive secretary of the committee which brought about the formation of the modern Council on Foreign Relations through a merger of the American Institute and an informal organization also known as the Council on Foreign

Relations. Its stated purpose was to study and evaluate objectively major political, economic, and financial issues in U.S. foreign policy. The Council sought to bring together international thinkers in order to foster a continuous conference on foreign affairs and to promote a better understanding of international problems. Shepardson was a director of the Council from 1921 until his death and also served as its treasurer. From 1934 through 1940 he was editor of the Council's annual review *The United States in World Affairs*.

Shepardson served briefly on the Secretariat of the League of Nations and thereafter worked closely with American internationalists promoting membership. He became treasurer of the *Woodrow Wilson Foundation and associated with groups friendly toward the League. As an unabashed Anglophile, perhaps dating from his years in England as a Rhodes scholar, Shepardson's friendships and activities reflected that persuasion. In 1939 he vehemently attacked Charles Lindbergh for suggesting that Canada had no right to draw the United States into the European conflict. Just prior to American entrance into World War II, Shepardson led the Council's War and Peace Studies Project, which tried to persuade President *Franklin D. Roosevelt to effect a Destroyer-Bases exchange with Britain. Shepardson left his mark on the Council, which manifested over the decades a decidedly conservative, pro-British stand and labored to influence American foreign policy accordingly. Its annual reviews, under Sherpardson's editorship, tended to interpret American foreign relations in a manner that reflected those preferences.

BIBLIOGRAPHY:

A. *Early History of the Council on Foreign Relations* (New York, 1960); *The Interests of the United States as a World Power* (Claremont, CA, 1942).

B. NYT 1 Jun 1966, 47; WWWA 1961–70, 1026.

Stephen D. Bodayla

SHERRILL, Henry Knox (6 November 1890, Brooklyn, NY—11 May 1980, Boxford, MA). *Education*: B.A., Yale Coll., 1911; B.D., Episcopal Theol. School, 1914. *Career*: minister, Boston, 1914–30; bishop, Episcopal Diocese of Massachusetts, 1930–47, presiding bishop, 1947–58; first president, National Council of Churches, 1950–52.

Sherrill was one of a few American churchmen responsible for providing Protestantism a more ecumenical perspective in this century. In an age in which Protestantism reigned as an American establishment, he thought the church lacked breadth, openness, and self-criticism. The key to renewal was unity, which in turn would guarantee that international organization would succeed. Progress, he declared in 1947, would come not through intermittent action by individual churches but only through a well-coordinated strategy backed by Christian conscience and church purpose.

Heavily influenced by Phillip Brooks, in whose former parish (Trinity,

Boston) he began his ministry, and by Bishop William Lawrence, who ordained him in 1915, Sherrill spent his life working toward church renewal and unification. By the mid-1920s he had become known as a liberal, "Low Church" minister who opposed intolerance and isolationism. As bishop he actively supported interdenominational cooperation, including reunion of the Episcopal and Presbyterian churches, and in World War II he chaired the interdenominational General Commission on Army and Navy Chaplains. Wartime destruction reinforced his support of ecumenism. In late 1945, the Federal Council of Churches appointed him to a three-member committee to restore relations with German churches. The dangers, he said, lay within people. Universal peace had to begin within the fellowship of Christians, where racism and nationalism had to be eliminated. Until people could agree with each other, international cooperation would be ineffective. Thus he worked to promote world as well as national church unity, and his proudest moment occurred in Amsterdam in September 1948, when the World Council of Churches was formed. Sherrill served on the presidential nominating committee and during the next decade participated in the WCC's Central and Executive Committees. At the second convention of the WCC in 1954, he was elected one of six presidents. The World Council was led by men of great vision and humanity, he recalled in 1962, with deep experience in their worship. Sherrill argued that differences in practices were understandable, because of diversities, but Christ's purposes could not embrace competing or contradictory views and ideas.

BIBLIOGRAPHY:

A. *Among Friends* (Boston, 1962); *The Church's Ministry in Our Time* (New York, 1942); *A Harvest of Happy Years* (Boston, 1933); *The Upward Way* (Boston, 1942); *William Lawrence: Later Years of a Happy Life* (Cambridge, MA, 1943).

B. CB 1947, 569–71; NYT 13 May 1980, IV-23, 15 May 1980, IV-27; WWA 1973–74, 2807.

C. Sherrill papers are in the Union Theological Seminary Library.

Darrel E. Bingham

SHIH Chao-chi [Sao-ke (Alfred) Sze] (10 April 1876, Chentsechen, Kiangsu, China—3 January 1958, Washington). *Education*: St. John's Acad. (later Univ.), Shanghai, 1887–90; B.A., Cornell Univ., 1901, M.A., 1902. *Career*: supervisor of Hupeh students in U.S., 1902–3; director-general, Peking-Hankow Railway, 1906; superintendent of customs at Harbin, 1908–10; acting commissioner of foreign affairs, Kirin, 1910; counselor, Board of Foreign Affairs, 1911; minister to Great Britain, 1914–21, 1929–32, to United States, 1921–29; 1933–35; ambassador to United States, 1935–37; director, Propaganda Section, International Relief Committee, 1937–41; vice-chair, China Defense Supplies Commission, 1941–45; senior adviser, Chinese delegation, UN Conference at San Francisco, 1945; Advisory Council, International Bank for Reconstruction and Development, 1947–50.

Sze was involved in diplomatic affairs during the Ching Dynasty and the Bei Yang and national governments. He attended many international conferences, including Paris in 1919, and he delivered impressive speeches, including ones at the Washington Conference, 1921–22, and at the League of Nations, 1931, which gave him some fame. Sze was also involved in international discussions related to China's independence and territorial integrity. He is credited with the principles embodied in the ten points at the Washington Conference in which the signatories "respect and observe the territorial integrity and political independence of the Republic of China." The fifth point called for the removal of "existing limitation upon China's political, jurisdictional, and administrative freedom of action." This would allow China self-determination regarding tariffs, the abolition of extraterritoriality, and the recovery of Shantung. China played an active role in the Conference, and the principles were included in the Nine Power Treaty.

Sze's role as a defender of China continued into the 1930s, but in his positions he also disclosed a commitment to international organization. When Japan invaded Manchuria in 1931, Sze was China's head representative at the League of Nations. On 30 September he suggested that a committee of neutral nations supervise a Japanese withdrawal. On 19 October he observed that the Covenant of the League of Nations and other nonmilitary treaties provided the central column for the world's peace building. If it were broken, the entire structure would collapse. He saw the aggression of Japan as a great and initial test.

In 1937, at age fifty-nine, Sze resigned his ambassadorship to the United States and left the diplomatic profession. That year the war between Japan and China began, and he sought to rally the international powers to support China. Thereafter he devoted considerable effort to obtaining American aid to China. Sze held the unusual distinction of attending the Hague Peace Conference of 1899, that of Paris in 1919, and the UN meeting in San Francisco in 1945.

BIBLIOGRAPHY:

A. *Addresses* (Baltimore, MD, 1926); *Sao-ke Alfred Sze: Reminiscences of His Early Years as Told to Anming Fu* (Washington, 1962).

B. *Biographical Dictionary of Republican China* 3 (New York, 1970), 123–26; *Eastern Magazine* 10 Jan 1922, 25 Jan 1922; *Geneva Opium Conferences* (Baltimore, MD, 1926); *Modern Chinese Characters: China Diplomatic Annual* (Shanghai, 1935), 167; NYT 5 Jan 1958; *Who's Who in China* (Shanghai, 1936), 206; WWWA 3, 839.

Shong Li-Ling

SHORT, William Harrison (4 December 1868, College Springs, IA—10 January 1935, Philadelphia). *Education*: B.A., Beloit Coll., 1894, M.A., 1897; B.D., Yale Theol. School, 1897. *Career*: Congregational minister in Massachusetts, Wisconsin, and Minnesota, 1897–1908; executive secretary,

New York Peace Society, 1908–17; secretary, League to Enforce Peace, 1915–23; secretary, Twentieth Century Fund, 1922–23; executive director, League of Nations Non-Partisan Association, 1923–25; editor, *League of Nations Herald*, 1923–25; director of development, Doane Coll., 1925; director of development, Rollins Coll., 1926–27; executive director, Motion Picture Research Council, 1927–35.

Short's interest in internationalism derived from his early commitment to social betterment. While still in college he wrote a prize-winning essay which emphasized that "humane education" could abolish social ills, including war. As a young minister he participated in the burgeoning social gospel movement. He preached sermons on peace and exhorted his congregations to support a wide range of reform causes.

Short was increasingly attracted to the cosmopolitan Northeast, where he believed his benevolently paternalistic ideas would gain a more receptive hearing. Thus in 1908 he left the ministry to become executive secretary of the New York Peace Society (NYPS) founded two years before by prominent academics, lawyers, clergymen, editors, and philanthropists. One of the founders, his Yale classmate, Reverend *Frederick Lynch, persuaded the Executive Committee of the Society to hire Short.

Despite occasional speaking and writing on peace questions, Short was noted more for his administrative and organizational talents than as an original thinker on questions of war and peace. Though liberal, he displayed a remarkable ability to cooperate with all nonradical peace workers. He believed that broad support of public causes by elite public opinion was a prerequisite for success, and he worked assiduously in cultivating business and professional establishments. His efforts nearly doubled the NYPS membership to more than one thousand and expanded its activities in support of various diplomatic initiatives, especially on behalf of arbitration treaties. He also promoted the Society's cooperation with numerous friendship groups interested in assimilating immigrants into the mainstream of the city, and he served as trustee of the American Scandinavian Foundation (1911–27). By 1914 the NYPS was the second largest peace group in the nation, rivaling the older American Peace Society in finances and influence.

In 1910 Short worked closely with his friend, journalist *Hamilton Holt, and other more adventuresome internationalists in forming the World-Federation League to promote a union with limited authority to maintain the peace. Though little then resulted from this initiative, his participation suggested his emerging interest in moving the peace movement beyond its current emphasis on international law and arbitration to a more advanced internationalist program.

When World War I erupted in 1914, Short consulted with *Elihu Root, a vice-president of the NYPS, and agreed with the latter that, while little could be done to stop the war, the Society could explore the formation of a league of peace to prevent future wars. With Holt and *Theodore Marburg, Short perceived the need for a wide-ranging and coordinated campaign to realize this ideal at the end of the war. In June 1915 they brought together prominent citizens to organize the League to Enforce Peace (LEP), which became a nationwide internationalist effort. Short served as its secretary throughout its eight-year existence. The leadership of the new group agreed that nations were not ready to create an international police force to preserve the peace but believed they might be willing collectively to use their economic and military forces against nations refusing to agree to a cooling-off period for consultation before going to war.

Throughout the war, Short played a central role in expanding the influence of the League to Enforce Peace. He helped attract well-known political figures, including *William H. Taft, who agreed to serve as its president. He and other leaders also used their influence with *Edward M. House, who in turn persuaded *Woodrow Wilson to speak to the LEP on 27 May 1916, where he committed the United States to a league of nations and outlined his conception of its basic principles.

Difficulties in sustaining a unified program arose, however, when Allied leaders at Paris developed the Covenant of the League of Nations with its specific functions and powers. It was evident the LEP had little influence in the drafting on Wilson, who had his own strong notions and had kept Short and his coworkers at arm's length. The inevitable debate on specific articles of the Covenant and the insistence of some senators for reservations to the Treaty of Versailles, which embodied the Covenant, resulted in divisions within the LEP. Thus, even though membership in the group swelled to more than 300,000 in the spring of 1919, a split developed between those who favored moderate reservations and Short, Holt, and others who preferred the treaty without change. Nevertheless, after the Senate failed to approve membership late in 1919, Short urged senators to forget their differences and begin anew with a set of acceptable reservations. He continued to promote U.S. membership in the League of Nations as executive director of the League of Nations Non-Partisan Association during the early 1920s, and as editor of its bi-weekly publication, *League of Nations Herald*, he publicized the constructive activities of the League and vigorously criticized its opponents. Short's consistent commitment to international cooperation and his organizational abilities firmly established him as a leading internationalist.

BIBLIOGRAPHY:

A. "The Genesis of the League," *Saturday Review of Literature* 9 (3 Dec 1932), 290–91; "A Positive International Program," *Proceedings of the Third American Peace Congress, Held in Baltimore, Maryland, May 3 to 6, 1911*, ed. Eugene A. Noble (Baltimore, MD, 1911), 219–22; ed., *Programs and Policies of the League to Enforce Peace: A Handbook for Officers, Speakers, and Editors . . . September 7–9, 1916* (New York, 1916); "World's Greatest War Is Called Peace's Greatest Victory," *New York Press* 30 Aug 1914, 1.

B. Ruhl J. Bartlett, *The League to Enforce Peace* (Chapel Hill, NC, 1944); NCAB 26, 462–63; NYT 11 Jan 1935, 23; David S. Patterson, *Toward a Warless World: The Travail of the American Peace Movement, 1887–1914* (Bloomington, IN, 1976); Frederick W. Short, *The Man Behind the League of Nations* (New York, 1978); WWWA 1, 1121.

C. The Short papers are at Rollins Coll.

David S. Patterson

SHOTWELL, James Thomson (6 August 1874, Strathroy, ON—15 July 1965, New York). *Education*: B.A., Univ. of Toronto, 1898; Ph.D., Columbia Univ., 1903. *Career*: professor, Columbia Univ., 1908–42; director, Division of Economics and History, Carnegie Endowment for International Peace, 1924–48, president, 1948–50.

By the time World War I broke out in Europe in 1914, Shotwell had established himself as one of America's leading historians. Although trained as a medievalist, he developed several innovative courses at Columbia University that emphasized the impact of science and technology on Western civilization. In both lectures and writings he proclaimed his faith in the ability of organized intelligence and scientific inquiry to solve even the most difficult social problems in a democratic context. The coming of war intensified these interests and forced him to broaden his focus to include an examination of international conflict and the possibility of its elimination. His basic assumption, however, remained the same. If scientific inquiry could enhance democracy in industrial America, it could also reform the international system and promote peace. He quickly became one of the leading exponents of *Woodrow Wilson's New Diplomacy and a firm believer in liberal-internationalist ideals. For the next fifty years, as a publicist, public activist, and private diplomat, Shotwell sought to advance the proposition that a rational, peaceful world order based on expert planning, free trade, and measured change could be brought about through multilateral action.

In 1917 Shotwell took a leave from Columbia University to aid the war effort. In April he helped organize the National Board for Historical Service and became its first chairman. This agency, involving some of the nation's leading historians, proposed to explain the war and its implications to the American people. Four months later he joined *Walter Lippmann and *Edward M. House in The Inquiry, a committee charged by Wilson with studying the major political, economic, legal, and historical questions likely to arise at a future peace conference. With other Inquiry members, he accompanied Wilson to Paris in 1919 as an adviser to the American Peace Commission. Although he played only a minor role at the Paris Peace Conference, he did assist in organizing the International Labor Organization.

Shotwell had concluded by then that future international conflicts could be avoided only through collective security and free trade. Always an activist, he worked in a variety of ways to promote peace and keep alive the

Wilsonian vision. In 1919 he initiated the massive *Economic and Social History of the World War* for the Carnegie Endowment for International Peace. The project, which took seventeen years to complete and consisted of 152 volumes, sought to determine the precise impact of modern war upon advanced societies. Shotwell edited all of the works and concluded that they fully documented the proposition that war was no longer a viable instrument of national policy.

In 1924 he became director of the Endowment's Division of Economics and History and used this position to promote American entry into the League of Nations, the World Court, and the International Labor Organization. In addition, he sought to unify the diverse American peace movement into a coherent political force. Throughout the 1920s he worked diligently to identify issues around which pacifists, advocates of collective security, promoters of the outlawry of war idea, international legalists, church groups, and women's organizations might rally. One such issue was the Kellogg-Briand Pact. The idea for the treaty originated with a suggestion made by Shotwell to French foreign minister *Aristide Briand in 1927. Hoping to find a way to align America more closely with the League of Nations, Shotwell proposed that the United States and France negotiate an agreement renouncing war between the two nations. After more than a year of negotiations, Secretary of State *Frank B. Kellogg and Briand worked out a multilateral pact, eventually signed by some sixty-four nations, that renounced war as an instrument of national policy.

Shotwell combined his public activism with scholarly concerns. He not only wrote extensively on international issues but also headed research committees for such organizations as the Institute of Pacific Relations and the Social Science Research Council. From 1935 to 1939 he served as president of the League of Nations Association and agitated continuously for a more active world role for the United States. As a publicist he wrote four books and more than one hundred articles during the interwar period. The theme was consistent. The United States should join the League of Nations, or, failing that, it should accept a position of responsibility and independently align its power with the League system. He repeatedly proposed that the United States should revise its neutrality policies so that it would not be an obstacle to those nations seeking to preserve peace through collective security. He also called for international agreements that would provide more equitable access for all industralized nations to overseas markets and sources of raw materials. A strong defender of the open door, he believed firmly in the idea that world peace could be promoted through trade.

During the late 1930s, faced with the realities of Nazi and Japanese aggression, Shotwell urged the American people to resist such threats to peace. Never a pacifist, he believed the United States should take a stand even if it ultimately led to war. The savagery of World War II neither surprised him nor destroyed his optimism. Having long predicted that science and technology would be utilized by the military unless they could be harnessed for peaceful purposes, he now argued that the conflict reaffirmed the need to develop a viable international system based on world organization and collective security.

Thus he joined his colleague *Clark Eichelberger, executive director of the League of Nations Association, in establishing the Commission to Study the Organization of Peace. Once again relying on the mobilization of experts to define a rational peace, he guided the Commission's activities and helped produce numerous reports designed to provide a "practical" blueprint for a new world order. During the war he also served on the Advisory Committee on Post-War Foreign Policy established by Secretary of State *Cordell Hull, and in 1945 he became chairman of a consultants group to the American delegation to the UN Conference in San Francisco. In 1948 he took over the presidency of the Carnegie Endowment and retired two years later to devote himself to research and writing. Until his death in 1965 he persisted in his belief that the creation of an international system based on free trade, collective security, and world organization was the surest way to world peace.

Shotwell contributed richly to the American diplomatic experience, not as a policy maker but as the most important and articulate advocate of a liberal approach to internationalism and the Wilsonian tradition in the United States. His work for the Carnegie Endowment and other organizations brought him into contact with both political leaders and molders of public opinion. In addition, his extensive writings which included over a dozen books and four hundred articles on international affairs, brought him to the attention of the general public as an indefatigable fighter for peace and internationalist principles.

His recommendations and policy prescriptions were sometimes superficial and misguided. His dream of a new world order based on collective security was doomed to failure in an age of rising nationalism. Like many other liberal internationalists, he too readily equated the needs of humanity with the interests of American business and never fully perceived that his desire to militarize American foreign policy as a way to avoid the disastrous consequences of the 1930s might lead to global interventionism. Still, he did much to keep before the American people the central problem of finding alternatives to war and creating institutions through which international problems might be resolved. He kept alive the vision that through organized political intelligence mankind might control the vastly destructive physical powers uncovered by science. Perhaps this was his greatest contribution, for in an age of nuclear weapons and intercontinental ballistic missiles such a vision needed an articulate spokesman.

BIBLIOGRAPHY:

A. *At the Paris Peace Conference* (New York, 1937); *The Autobiography of James T. Shotwell* (Indianapolis, IN, 1961); *The Great Decision* (New York, 1944);

On the Rim of the Abyss (New York, 1936); *War as an Instrument of National Policy and Its Renunciation in the Pact of Paris* (New York, 1929); *What Germany Forgot* (New York, 1940).

B. Charles DeBenedetti, "Peace Was His Profession: James T. Shotwell and American Internationalism," in *Makers of American Diplomacy*, ed. Frank J. Merli and Theodore A. Wilson, 2 (New York, 1974), 81–101; DAB supp. 7, 687–88; Harold Josephson, *James T. Shotwell and the Rise of Internationalism in America* (Rutherford, NJ, 1975); NYT 17 Jul 1965, 1.

C. The Shotwell papers are in the Butler Library, Columbia Univ.

Harold Josephson

SKRZYŃSKI, Aleksander (19 March 1882, Zagórzany, Poland—25 September 1931, Ostrów, Poland). *Education*: doctorate in law, Univ. of Vienna, 1906. *Career*: member, Austrian diplomatic service, secretary to ambassador to the Holy See, 1910–14; entered Polish service in 1919; minister to Romania, 1919–22; minister of foreign affairs, 1922–24; prime minister and minister of foreign affairs, 1925–26; signed Treaty of Locarno, 1924; several times a delegate to League of Nations; neutral member, Standing Committee to Arbitrate Between U.S. and Peru, 1928.

Skrzyński's career as a lawyer, diplomat, and politician was highlighted by his prime ministry of a bipartisan government at a time of deep financial crisis in Poland. The fall of his Cabinet in April 1926 paved the way for Piłsudski's *coup de'état*. In 1925 he visited the United States and lectured at the Institute of Politics at Williamstown, Massachusetts, where he presented his interpretation of the Monroe Doctrine as not only meaning "hands-off America" but also that the United States would have nothing to do with European absolutism and reactionism, the "Americanization of Europe." Following his resignation as prime minister, Skrzyński retired from politics.

During his political career, Skrzyński advocated a "pacific" policy not only for Poland but for all Europe based on the stability of frontiers. He placed Polish issues in the wider context of post-World War I Europe. Skrzyński tried to convince the Western powers that Poland was a factor of peace and stability in Europe, and any European security agreement that did not include Poland could not bring a lasting solution. He also believed that German expansion was inevitable. Deprived of her colonies, crowded into a comparatively small and relatively poor and unproductive territory, Germany would be attracted to the great vacuum to the east, Russia. Therefore, he reasoned, any containment of Germany in the West, as incorporated in the Locarno Treaty, had to be balanced in the East.

Skrzyński believed that the problems of postwar Europe were directly related to the economic and financial reconstruction efforts. Each nation should put its house in order by itself without outside interference, but that could come only in a secure and stable international atmosphere of mutual support and cooperation. He continued to advocate the "Americanization of Europe" and the creation of a united consciousness of Europe. He hoped for a "United States" of Europe where the spirit of "American democracy," which he defined as combining the elements of necessity and freedom, would dominate. The development of such a democratic mentality would act as a deterrent to the emerging ideologies of nationalism and Communism where the victory of either one would mean the ruin of Europe.

Skrzyński also suggested that war be outlawed, that it not be regarded as an accepted form of trial between nations. A successful "pacific" policy demanded a strong standing army which would ensure the nation's right to reject the use of force and thus actually lessen conflict. The foreign policy of any nation should aim at bringing its national interests into accord with the common interests not only of Europe but also of mankind. Skrzyński's European perspective also allowed him to consider the dangers of emerging national aspirations of minority groups. Authority in the hands of a minority group would be antidemocratic, and assimilation through persecution and violence was wrong. The only proper solution was a mutual evolution and cultural progress which could transform a group into an organic part of the state.

BIBLIOGRAPHY:

A. *American Policy Towards Europe* (Washington, 1925); *Liga Narodów* (Warsaw, 1925); *Poland and Peace* (London, 1923); *Poland's Problems and Progress* (Washington, 1925).

B. IWW 1937, 1006; NYT 26 Sep 1931, 19; *Prszeglad polityczny* 16 (1932), 129–45; Jerzy Tomaszewski, "Gabinet Aleksandra Skrzyńskiego," *Najnowsze dzieje polski* 11 (1967), 5–24; *Wielka encyklopedia powszechna PWN* (Warsaw, 1967), 10, 577.

Zofia Sywak

SMILEY, Albert Keith. See *Biographical Dictionary of Modern Peace Leaders.*

SMITH, Jeremiah, Jr. (14 January 1870, Dover, NH—12 March 1935, Cambridge, MA). *Education*: B.A., Harvard Coll., 1892, LL.B., 1895. *Career*: lawyer, 1896–1935; adviser to Treasury Department at Paris Peace Conference; League of Nations commissioner general for Hungary, 1924–26; League of Nations Financial Committee, 1927–30.

Dependent on U.S. capital for postwar reconstruction and development, Europeans in the 1920s often appointed influential Americans as financial advisers or controllers. The Europeans hoped such bankers and lawyers would bring with them the keys to Wall Street's money chests. Divided by intense national rivalries, Europeans also looked to Americans for disinterested, conciliatory leadership in various economic commissions and conferences.

Americans like Smith exercised influence in Europe precisely because of their largely internationalist or objective stance on Old World territorial and political issues. The Republican administrations of the 1920s, which sought a stable, prosperous, and peaceful Europe, approved of this key role played by private Americans and the private loans. While such activity fit with the desire to remain aloof from European entanglements and responsibilities, the United States was not totally uninterested or neutral toward European issues. It consistently opposed leftist revolution and any sudden departures from the peace treaties. Most American leaders favored slow and moderate revisions of the peace treaties that would appease the defeated nations and so integrate them into a more stable European order.

This background is essential to understanding the importance and context of Smith's service in Hungary from 1924 to 1926 and at the League of Nations Financial Committee from 1927 to 1930. In Hungary, Smith operated as a benign but firm "financial dictator." As part of the plan to stabilize Hungarian finances, the League floated an international loan of $56 million and appointed Smith commissioner general. Thus the Boston lawyer, who had previously worked with J. P. Morgan and Company on Chinese and Mexican loans, controlled the expenditures of the Hungarian government. In two years Smith balanced the budget, principally by slashing the number of governmental employees. That action earned him mixed reviews from Hungarians, but Smith softened criticism by living simply and refusing the large salary due him. Smith thus advanced the international hope that a prosperous, stable Hungary would be more moderate in its revisionist ambitions. In 1926 Smith left *Royall Tyler in charge of a Hungary with a balanced budget but a bleak economic future, with falling world raw material prices and a chronic balance-of-payments deficit.

Declining world prices particularly hurt the British economy with its overvalued pound and undercompetitive industries. To secure relief, British financiers, who dominated the League of Nations Financial Committee, tried to snare American cooperation for reform of the international gold standard. The British wanted the Financial Committee to regulate the flow of foreign loans and alleviate the alleged gold shortage. The British believed the inadequacy of world gold stocks was depressing world prices. Consequently the British asked the Federal Reserve Bank of New York to appoint a representative to the Financial Committee. In 1927 the FRBNY, with Washington's approval, asked Smith to serve on the international committee. However Smith's mission, as outlined by the FRBNY, was to block rather than to facilitate British financial revisionism. In this task Smith succeeded, and plans to revise the international gold standard foundered in the collapse of the foreign loan market and world economy after 1928. Thus Smith demonstrated both the importance and the limits of private American assistance in the economic stabilization of Europe.

BIBLIOGRAPHY:

B. NYT 13 Mar 1935, 20; 27 June 1926, VIII-12; Arthur Salter, "The Reconstruction of Hungary," *Foreign Affairs* 5 (Oct 1926), 91-102; WWWA 1, 1145.

Frank C. Costigliola

SMUTS, Jan Christiaan (24 May 1870, near Riebeck West, Cape Colony—11 September 1950, at Irene, near Pretoria). *Education*: Victoria Coll., Stellenbosch Univ., 1891, Christ Coll., Cambridge Univ., 1894. *Career*: state attorney, Transvaal, 1898; Boer general and assistant commandant general 1899; colonial secretary and minister of education, Transvaal, 1906; minister of mines, defense, and interior, Union of South Africa, 1910; Imperial War Cabinet, 1917; prime minister, South Africa, 1919-24, 1939-48; British field marshall, 1941.

From an early age Smuts was interested in the Pan African ideas expressed by Cecil Rhodes. After the Jameson Raid (1895), however, he regarded Rhodes as a betrayer of the Africaners. His reputation for academic brilliance gained the attention of Paul Kruger, who appointed him state attorney for the Transvaal (1898). While his loyalty was transferred from Rhodes to Kruger, he continued to dream of a larger, unified South Africa under the British flag. In keeping with his holistic ideas, he took a larger view of relations with Britain in his efforts to avert conflict. During the Boer War (1899-1902) he served as a general and assistant commandant general of the Transvaal and fought brilliantly for the Boer cause. His tact and diplomacy were instrumental in concluding the Treaty of Vereeniging (1902).

He and General Louis Botha formed the Het Volk political party (1905), with self-government as one of its aims. Full responsible government was granted to the Transvaal in 1906, with Smuts being named colonial secretary and minister of education. When South Africa became a self-governing dominion in 1910, as the Union of South Africa, Smuts became minister of mines, defense, and interior. As a minister he acted boldly and swiftly to deal head on with labor, economic, and racial problems. His quick action against strikes and the equally fast deportation of various undesirables alienated many people.

In 1917 he went to London to represent South Africa at the Imperial Conference and as a member of the Imperial War Cabinet, where he quickly emerged as a world statesman. *David Lloyd George was especially attracted by Smuts's ability and intellect, relying upon his advice on many critical issues. While in London he was able to refine his views on world peace and harmony, publishing a paper in December 1918, *The League of Nations: A Practical Suggestion*. At the Paris Peace Conference of 1919 Smuts pressed for a peace of moderation and conciliation. Lloyd George sought his advice when he drafted the important Fontainebleau Memorandum. Smuts believed that one could not defeat Germany without also destroying Europe.

Following the death of Botha, Smuts became premier of South Africa (1919–24). After the defeat of his government in 1924, Smuts spent much time developing his philosophical and scientific ideas and was in demand world wide as a lecturer. In 1926 he published *Holism and Evolution*, in which he defined his ideas on holism. He believed throughout his life that there was purpose to all life and the universe, with man striving to attain wholeness, fullness, blessedness. His philosophy of life and the universe clearly shaped his high optimism for both the League of Nations and the United Nations.

In 1934 he and James B. M. Hertzog founded a fusion group, the United South African National party. It collapsed in 1939 over the debate on whether South Africa should join the war against Germany. Smuts became prime minister in 1939, was promoted to field marshall (1941), and provided valuable advice to Winston Churchill. In 1945 he represented South Africa at San Francisco in the creation of the United Nations, where he influenced the drafting of the Charter. Peace would come through a system of justice which international agencies could provide. His belief in justice, however, applied to the interrelationship of states, not toward individual rights.

He was defeated in 1948 and in that same year was named chancellor of Cambridge University. During his lifetime he molded the history of South Africa and shaped the creation of the Commonwealth, which made possible the survival of the British Empire. As a statesman and philosopher he was a person of conciliation, moderation, and peace, and through his holistic view of the world and universe and his faith in human progress he believed that all things were moving toward an ultimate harmonious and good purpose.

BIBLIOGRAPHY:

A. *Holism and Evolution* (New York, 1926); *The League of Nations: A Practical Suggestion* (London, 1918); *Our Changing World View* (Johannesburg, 1932); *Selections From the Smuts Papers*, ed. W. K. Hancock and J. Van der Poel, 4 vols. (London, 1966); *War-Time Speeches* (New York, 1917).

B. Hamilton Fyfe, "Jan Smuts," *World Unity Magazine* 14 (May 1934), 78–84; W. K. Hancock, *Smuts: The Fields of Force, 1919–1950* (Cambridge, 1968), *Smuts: The Sanguine Years, 1870–1919* (Cambridge, 1962); L. M. Thompson, *The Unification of South Africa, 1902–1910* (Oxford, 1960); Basil Williams, *Botha, Smuts and South Africa* (New York, 1948).

C. The Smuts papers are in the South African Government Archives.

Stephen E. Fritz

SNOW, Alpheus Henry (8 November 1859, Claremont, NH—19 August 1920, New York). *Education*: A.B., Yale Univ., 1879; LL.B., Harvard Law School, 1883. *Career*: lawyer, Hartford, CT, 1883–87, Indianapolis, IN, 1887–95; writer on colonial administration and international law, Washington, 1899–1920; lecturer, George Washington Univ., 1908–9; U.S. delegate, International Conference on Social Insurance, The Hague, 1910; member, Executive Council, American Society of International Law, 1910–20.

Two questions regarding international affairs in the late nineteenth and early twentieth centuries are answered in the works of Snow. First, what reasons were offered by the educated and the conscientious to justify the European and American expansionism of the period? Second, why did some dedicated internationalists oppose the League of Nations?

The moral imperatives of imperialism were perfectly expressed by Snow, who believed unquestioningly in the responsibility of "civilized states" to administer the affairs of those areas viewed as incapable of self-government. So great was his interest in this burning question of his day that he retired from the active practice of law and moved to Washington to devote his time to study. He became a leading authority, called on by the State Department to supply background information for the discussion of dependencies at the Paris Peace Conference in 1919.

Snow's views were grounded in his political theories, and, in particular, in his central idea of the imperial state or federal empire as the highest form of political organization. Such a government acted as agent and trustee for *all* the governed, not just those in colonies or dependencies. Those capable of self-government delegated plenary powers to the imperial state to secure fundamental human rights for everyone, capable and incapable alike, in a cooperative and federative union.

Snow's opposition to the League was rooted in this same high concept of government and of human nature. He favored an international organization but thought the League had too much power. Any world organization would have to be based, as was the federal empire of the United States, on a union of cooperation, not coercion, and each member state would have to be free to act according to its own conscience. In this global competition of consciences, the American idea would, he thought, surely someday prevail.

Snow firmly believed that such a competition could be kept in the realm of ideas, just as he believed that empire meant the spread of enlightenment. Here was the faith that animated many internationalists of his day and underlay the founding of many international societies. That faith helps explain the frequent foundering of the League of Nations and the rapid downfall of empires in the years that followed the period that Snow devoted his life to understand.

BIBLIOGRAPHY:

A. *The Administration of Dependencies* (New York, 1902); *The American Philosophy of Government: Collected Essays* (New York, 1921); *Considerations in the Interest of the People of the Philippine Islands* (Washington, 1906); "Cooperative Union of Nations," *World Court* 4 (Apr 1918), 202–10; *The Question of Aborigines in the Law and Practice of Nations* (New York, 1921).
B. AJIL 14 (1920), 613–19; NYT 20 Aug 1920, 9; WWWA 1, 1154.

Dorothy V. Jones

SÖDERBLOM, Nathan (15 March 1866, Trönö, Hälsingland, Sweden—12 July 1931, Uppsala). *Education*: B.A., Uppsala Univ., 1886; doctorate, Sorbonne, 1901. *Career*: ordained priest, 1893; pastor in Paris and Calais, 1894–1901; professor, Uppsala Univ., 1901–14; archbishop of Uppsala, 1914–31; Nobel Peace Prize, 1931.

Söderblom played a critical role in the ecumenical movement from the latter part of the nineteenth century which culminated in the World Council of Churches in 1948. He contributed to the three distinct sources of ecumenism: an international mission enterprise; an emphasis on the church active in society; and a reexamination of hitherto divisive questions of faith and ecclesiology.

Reared in a clerical family, Söderblom became a candidate for the ministry at Uppsala University (1883) and joined a missionary group which shared with the international Student Christian Movement a world perspective and an emphasis on the history of religion and society. Active in the group, he attended student conferences in the United States (1890) and Amsterdam (1891), acquiring the global outlook and contact which subsequently he employed in the service of Christian unity.

His ensuing education and pastorates in France broadened him even more and stimulated his interest in the comparative history of religions. Under his leadership as archbishop, the Swedish church experienced a period of renewal, especially with regard to music and liturgy. Moreover and beyond Sweden, Söderblom promulgated the vision of a united church addressing the burning social issues of peace and justice on the basis of its testimony. World War I sharpened the urgency of this task, brought him into closer touch with other world religious leaders, and was followed by church relief work in Germany and Austria (1919–21) and a bishops' protest over the occupation of the Ruhr (1923). In 1915 he issued an invitation for a World Alliance Conference of churches, and in 1925 he organized a Universal Christian Conference on Life and Work in Stockholm. The creation of a continuation committee institutionalized the movement.

Life and Work was the second great source of twentieth-century ecumenism. It represented the application of the social gospel, an attempt to bring together many churches into one dynamic instrument of Christian world opinion and action. For Söderblom the ecumenical view included practical, cooperative service as a first step, but it should lead to church renewal and supranationalism and to world peace, which, as the revelation of God in history, is related to church unity. The Life and Work movement was paralleled by a third source of ecumenism, Faith and Order. Although Söderblom has been interpreted as eschewing ecumenical efforts with regard to theology and ecclesiology and, it is true, did not play a key role in their organization, he nonetheless contributed significantly to this thrust through his scholarship.

Söderblom's overarching contribution was his notion of revelation. He distinguished it from theology, which is to clarify revelation. He found the distinctive quality of Christian thought in its understanding of the historical and personal character of the revelation of eternal truth at certain relative times and situations. Accordingly, there are no static meanings, and there is a variety of authentic expression. This process view of revelation established an important ground for ecumenical dialog and therefore promoted modern world cooperation among the churches.

BIBLIOGRAPHY:

A. *Christian Fellowship; or the United Life and Work of Christendom* (New York, 1923); *The Death and Resurrection of Christ: Reflections on the Passion* (Minneapolis, MN, 1967); *The Living God* (London, 1933); *The Nature of Revelation* (New York, 1933).

B. Charles J. Curtis, *Nathan Söderblom: Theologian of Revelation* (Chicago, 1966), *Söderblom: Ecumenical Pioneer* (Minneapolis, MN, 1967); Bengt Sundkler, *Nathan Söderblom: His Life and Work* (Lund, Sweden, 1968).

Charles Chatfield

SOERGEL, Herman (2 April 1885, Regensburg, Germany—30 December 1952, Munich). *Education*: trained as architect in a technical university; diplom-ingenieur. *Career*: founder, Musterschulen fuer Bauhandwerker, Bavaria; founder, director, and proprietor, Atlantropa-Institut, Munich.

Although trained as an architect, Soergel became interested in geopolitics and devoted much energy to the study of international cooperation and the ways in which to establish transnational organizations to further such cooperation. Soon his ideas were influenced by the proposals of *Richard Coudenhove-Kalergi to establish a Pan-Europa and a Pan-America, and as well by Wladimir Woytinsky's plan to found a European customs union.

It was not long, however, before Soergel developed his own notions to facilitate international cooperation. In his scheme, the world was to be divided into three large autarchical landmasses—Panamerika, Panasien, and Atlantropa (a vast territory stretching from the North Sea to the Cape of Good Hope). Soergel conceived this idea in December 1927, and by the following May, after having explored the geopolitical aspects of the plan, he was outlining it in numerous articles for journals and newspapers. Within a few years' time Soergel won, at least in Germany, the support of an impressive number of academicians, civil servants, and businessmen.

The lynchpin of the scheme was Atlantropa. To achieve its creation, Soergel wanted first to establish a "Vereinigte Kraftwerke Europas" to be managed by a transnational consortium whose home was to be Central Europe. This consortium was to become the nucleus for a "Europa Union" that would include all European states. In view of its vast economic and political power, the Europa Union would eventually take over Africa as a mandate in order to cultivate the Sahara Desert and press forward the industrialization of Central Africa, especially the Congo Basin. This part of

Soergel's grand design, however, could be realized only within the framework of a "Grosskontinent," Atlantropa, which would come into existence by lowering the water levels of the Mediterranean Sea and by damming the Straits of Gibraltar and Gallipoli. The difference in water levels between the Atlantic Ocean and the Black Sea would be utilized through the installation of giant turbines for the generation of electricity to be used to help construct irrigation works for cultivating the Sahara and unlocking the mineral wealth of Central Africa. Of great importance, too, would be the fact that Atlantropa would enlarge the amount of living space in the Mediterranean area, for as a result of the lower water levels, additional land bordering the Mediterranean could be farmed and developed for urban use. In Africa, moreover, two large seas, the Congo and Chad, would be created by damming the Congo River, while the electricity generated would be used to industrialize Central Africa and develop a vast interior waterway system. As a result of these all-encompassing changes, Soergel argued, Africa would be able to support a much larger population, predominantly European, than had been the case.

Atlantropa, Soergel was convinced, would provide Europeans at once with both energy in limitless amounts—water was the *perpetuum mobile* for the development of energy—and living space. Europeans would finally have sufficient "Kraft und Raum." As the centrally located landmass of the world, moreover, Atlantropa would in time dominate the globe. Panamerika and Panasien, separated from one another by the Pacific Ocean, would after all be forced by their peripheral geopolitical locations to cooperate with Atlantropa. Rather than abuse its vast economic and political power, however, Atlantropa would be concerned with preserving peace, harmony, and order in the world. Finally the community of interest between Atlantropa, Panamerika, and Panasien would be more effective in furthering international cooperation than the League of Nations. To proselytize on behalf of this plan, Soergel established an Atlantropa Society, and this organization eventually had its institute at Munich with some 1,200 members.

BIBLIOGRAPHY:

A. *Amerika, Atlantropa, Asien, die drei grossen "A"* (Munich, 1938); *Atlantropa* (Munich, 1932); *Mittlemeer-Senkung—Sahara-Bewaesserung Panropa-Projekt* (Leipzig, Germany, 1929).

B. *Deutscher Buecherverzeichnis* 18 (New York, reprint, 1961), 1087; *Deutsches Literatur-Lexikon* 3 (Bern, 1956), 2748; *Kuerschners Deutscher Literatur-Kalendar Nekrolog 1936–70* (Berlin, 1973), 638; NYT 31 Dec 1952, 15; *Wer ist Wer* 11 (Berlin, 1948) 632.

Werner E. Braatz

SPAAK, Paul-Henri (25 January 1899, Schaerbeek, Belgium—31 July 1972, Brussels). *Education*: LL.D., Université Libre de Bruxelles, 1921. *Career*: Socialist deputy, 1932–56, 1961–66; minister of transport, posts and telegraphs, 1935–36; minister of foreign affairs and trade, 1936–38; prime minister, May 1938–February 1939, March 1946, 1947–50, 1954–57; minister of foreign affairs, 1930–45, 1946–50; deputy prime minister, 1945–46; president, UN General Assembly, 1946; president, Organization for European Economic Cooperation, 1948–50; chair, Council of European Recovery, 1948; president, Consultative Assembly of Council of Europe, 1949–51; chair, International Council of the European Movement, 1950–55; minister of state for Belgium, 1949; secretary-general to NATO, 1957–61; deputy prime minister, minister of foreign and African affairs, 1961–65; minister of foreign affairs and coordination of external policy, 1965–66; with ITT, Europe, 1966–72; chair, special NATO working group, 1967.

In an age of extreme nationalism reflected in the foreign policies of nation-states, Spaak emerged as one of the "great Europeans" and international statesmen of his century. Having become foreign secretary when only thirty-seven and the first Socialist prime minister at thirty-eight, Spaak helped write the Charter of the UN and served as the first president of the General Assembly in 1946; was first president of the Consultative Assembly of the Council of Europe; was the first to preside over the Organization for European Economic Cooperation; and was the moving spirit behind the European Coal and Steel Community, serving as president (1952–53) of its Assembly. He backed the plan for the European Defense Community, was one of the original signers of the North Atlantic Treaty Organization pact, and played a leading role in the negotiations which created the European Common Market and Euratom organization. From 1956 to 1961, Spaak served as secretary-general of NATO. Thus there is hardly an international organization in Europe that does not owe in part its birth and healthy existence to his tireless efforts. His support of these varied economic, political, and military efforts to preserve Western solidarity and independence in the critical years after World War II won for him the informal title of "Mr. Europe."

From Benelux in 1944, the Western European Union in 1948, the North Atlantic Treaty Organization in 1949, the European Coal and Steel Community in 1952, and the aborted European Defense Community in 1954, to the Common Market and Euratom in 1957, his inspiration, obstinacy, and political skill were felt. Remarkably, Spaak also found time to serve three times as Belgium's premier and six times as its foreign minister, in addition to numerous other cabinet and government posts.

Although not among the founding fathers of the New Europe who, in the 1920s, gathered at meetings and congresses around *Richard Coudenhove-Kalergi, Spaak more than anyone else will be remembered as the one responsible for the rebuilding operations set afoot when their overly ambitious structure collapsed. It was, above all, due to his constructive and patient execution that Spaak earned his honorific title. Thus his talents were those of a builder who, once the ground had been properly prepared, took charge of its construction, often finding it necessary to alter the original grandiose architectural design.

It was in London, where he spent four years in exile, that Spaak learned to think in global terms, where he became convinced that only collective security could assure peace. That led to his advocacy of the political, economic, and military organization of Western Europe, and he began his work when he signed the customs convention on behalf of Belgium with the Netherlands and Luxemburg to establish the Benelux common tariff. He also made new contacts in the world of international politics and saw to it that Belgium was among the victors at the peace conference. A constant champion of a unified and free Western world, Spaak thereafter served the world no less than his own country.

BIBLIOGRAPHY:

A. *Combats inachevés* (New York, 1969); "The Crisis of the Atlantic Alliance," *The Social Science Program of the Mershon Center for Education in National Security* (Columbus, OH, 1967); "The Integration of Europe: Dreams and Realities," *Foreign Affairs* 29 (Oct 1950), 94–100; "A New Effort to Build Europe," *Foreign Affairs* 43 (Jan 1965), 199–208; *Strasbourg: The Second Year* (Oxford, 1952); *Why NATO?* (Baltimore, MD, 1959).

B. *Biographie Nationale* supp. 11, 799–806; Paul-Henri Laurent, "Paul-Henri Spaak and the Diplomatic Origins of the Common Market, 1955–1956," *Political Science Quarterly* 85 (Sep 1970), 373–96; LT 1 Aug 1972, 15, 17; Carolyn J. Zinn, "Paul-Henri Spaak and the Political-Economic Integration of Europe," dissertation, West Viginia Univ., 1967.

Carolyn J. Zinn

STEAD, Francis Herbert (20 October 1857, Howdon-on-Tyne, England —14 January 1928, London). *Education*: Owens Coll. (Manchester); Airedale Coll. (Bradford); M.A. divinity degree, Glasgow Univ. 1881; advanced study, Univs. of Halle, Göttingen, Giessen, Berlin. *Career*: reporter, *Northern Echo* and *Northern Daily Express*, 1874–76; pastor, Leicester, 1884–90; editor, *Independent and Nonconformist*, 1892–94; warden, Browning Hall Mission and Settlement, London, 1894–1921; assistant and acting editor, *Review of Reviews*, 1893–1912.

As a Congregational minister and journalist, Stead was a Christian Socialist and internationalist. In 1890 he and his wife embraced Tolstoyan ideas on Christian social service, nonviolence, and passive resistance. During a brief visit to the Columbia Exposition in Chicago (1893), Stead was greatly impressed by the "Social Gospel" movement in the United States and sought to apply what he had learned in the United States as warden of the Browning Hall Settlement. Thus, from 1894 until his retirement in 1921, he participated in campaigns for slum clearance and public housing, unemployment insurance, industrial peace, old age pensions, and international disarmament and the abolition of war.

A lifelong pacifist, Stead's greatest concern during the last three decades of his life was the abolition of war through international arbitration, the limitation of armaments, and disarmament. In advancing these causes, he worked closely with his elder brother, the renowned journalist and peace advocate *William T. Stead, until the latter's death on the *Titanic* in 1912. They promoted an Anglo-American arbitration pact, the First and Second Hague Peace Conferences, and the improvement of Anglo-German relations during the decade before 1914. In 1909, with the assistance of British trade union friends, Stead organized a "peace tour" of a score of Labor party MPs in Germany and, a year later, joined his brother in bitterly condemning Italian aggression in North Africa.

Although Stead supported the Allied cause during the 1914–18 war, the horrors of the conflict strengthened his dedication to internationalism and especially to the concept of a postwar association of nations which would accomplish the end of war as an instrument of national policy. In 1916 he organized a conference at Browning Hall which culminated in the organization of a League to Abolish War, whose major objective was the establishment of an international organization with an international armed force to accomplish its peacekeeping mission. Even after retirement, Stead tirelessly labored for international peace and in 1927 lectured in Finland on behalf of the League of Nations. On the eve of his death he was organizing a series of meetings to mobilize public opinion on behalf of the outlawry of war movement. Stead died as he had lived, a staunch pacifist and internationalist.

BIBLIOGRAPHY:

A. "Herbert Stead on American Peace Plans," *Survey* 34 (Apr 1915), 1–2; "How to Unify the Peace Movement," *American Review of Reviews* 51 (Jun 1915), 736–37; *Independent and Nonconformist* (1892–94); "International Labour Week," *Survey* 34 (Jun 1915), 249–50; *No More War! Truth Embodied in a Tale* (London, 1917); "The Opening of the World's Fair," *Review of Reviews* 7 (Jun 1893), 656–59; *The Story of Social Christianity*, 2 vols. (London, 1924); *To Abolish War. At the Third Hague Conference. An Appeal to the Peoples* (Letchworth, 1916).

B. G. N. Barnes, *From Workshop to War Cabinet* (London, 1962); *Congregational Yearbook* (London, 1928), 231–33; DLB 4, 161–63; LT 16 Jan 1928, 14.

Joseph O. Baylen

STEAD, William Thomas (5 July 1849, Embleton, Northumberland, England—15 April 1912, *Titanic*). *Education*: private tutoring, 1849–61; Silcoates School, near Wakefield, 1861–63. *Career*: editor, Darlington *Northern Echo*, 1871–80; assistant editor, 1880–83, *Pall Mall Gazette*, editor, 1883–89; editor, *Review of Reviews*, 1890–1912, *War Against War! A Chronicle of the International Peace Crusade*, 1899, and *War Against War in South Africa*, 1899–1900.

The son of a Congregationalist parson, Stead was a staunch Radical whose life and career reflected his strong nonconformist conscience. In addition to his lifelong advocacy of equal rights for women, religious freedom, and morality in politics and his faith in the "destinies" of the English-speaking and Russian peoples, Stead was also an ardent advocate of international peace through limitation of armaments, international arbitration, and collective security. As editor of the *Northern Echo* he championed the arbitration of the *Alabama* claims in 1872, sparked the Bulgarian Horrors Agitation in 1876, combated Disraeli's jingoism against Russia during the Eastern Crisis of 1876–78, and denounced the Tory government's wars in Afghanistan and South Africa in 1879–80. Indeed, Stead made the *Northern Echo* the most outstanding voice of Gladstone's program of "Peace, Retrenchment, and Reform" in the English North Country throughout the 1870s.

As the editor of the *Pall Mall Gazette* in London during the 1880s, Stead continued his campaigns for social and political reform and the cause of world peace. The only exceptions were his advocacy of a strong British Navy and British overseas expansion, which he deemed essential for the maintenance of a Pax Britannica in the world. Thus he applauded William Gladstone's termination of the wars in Afghanistan and South Africa and personally worked to facilitate a peaceful settlement of the Anglo–Russian Penjdeh Crisis in Central Asia during 1884–85. In 1888 he journeyed to Russia and was the first journalist to interview a Russian tsar in his efforts to promote Anglo–Russian understanding and amity.

Viewing the revolution in military technology and the escalating arms race as a threat to the economies and peace of the European powers, Stead persistently advocated arms limitation and international arbitration in the monthly *Review of Reviews*, which he founded in 1890. In this journal he urged the settlement of the Anglo–American Venezuelan dispute (1895–96) by arbitration and publicized the virtues of international arbitration in obviating the dangers of devastating wars with the slogan, "Always Arbitrate Before You Fight." It was Stead's concern for the development of machinery for international arbitration and with the need for arms limitation which prompted him (following his audience with the +Tsar Nicholas II in late 1898) to enthusiastically endorse and publicize the tsar's "Peace Rescript," which culminated in the First Hague Peace Conference in 1899. During the winter of 1898–99, Stead proclaimed an "International Peace Crusade" and, in collaboration with such leading pacifists as the +Baroness Bertha von Suttner, +Felix Moscheles, +A. H. Fried, and +Ivan Bloch, attended the sessions. There Stead rendered valuable service to the delegates and pacifist lobbyists by publishing a regular chronicle of conference proceedings (often leaked to him by friendly delegates) in The Hague's leading newspaper, *Dagblad*. He also published his knowledgeable versions of conference developments in the *Review of Reviews* and (as special correspondent) in the *Manchester Guardian* and duly reported on the Conference to the tsar in a series of personal letters.

It was his commitment to the principle of arbitration and the concept of an international court of justice to resolve international conflicts which was (in addition to his opposition to the British government's aggressive South Africa policy) a major reason for Stead's bitter condemnation of the Anglo-Boer/South Africa War (1899–1902). At the risk of his personal safety and financial ruin, Stead tirelessly inveighed against the conflict in numerous pamphlets, the periodical *War Against War in South Africa*, and *The Review of Reviews*.

Following the war, Stead continued to work with pacifists and, during the Dogger Bank affair, which almost led to an Anglo–Russian breach in 1904, labored diligently to calm the excited British public. From 1906 onward, Stead viewed with increasing alarm Anglo–German estrangement and strove with British and German peace advocates to lessen tensions between the two powers by arranging friendly exchange visits of journalists and clergymen and by assailing the British Foreign Office for "inveterate" Germanophobia. In 1907 he welcomed the Second Hague Conference and enthusiastically publicized its prospects and proceedings. He again attended and worked with Continental comrades to ensure success, but he was keenly disappointed and blamed the British Foreign Office for the failure of the Conference to achieve its major objectives.

Finally, during the last two years of his life, Stead launched a campaign against Italian aggression in North Africa and the Mediteranean in the Italo-Turkish War of 1910–11. It was all in vain; British and European opinion were not interested in the war. Disillusioned but still an ardent advocate of world peace and especially of an Anglo–American arbitration treaty, Stead was on his way to the United States to plead the cause of peace at a conference in New York when he died in the sinking of the *Titanic*. Stead's contributions to the peace movement were massive even though his work was prejudiced by the inconsistency of his advocating both supremacy of the Royal Navy and the limitation and control of armaments. But all who knew him agreed that he was a steadfast partisan of world peace and a sincere internationalist.

BIBLIOGRAPHY:

A. *Always Arbitrate Before You Fight* (London, 1895); *The Hague Conference: What It Was, What It Did, and What We Have Done Since* (London, 1901); *The International Union: What It Is, What It Wants to Do* . . . (London, 1900); *La Chronique de la Haye* (The Hague, 1901); *La Parlement de l'humanité* (Amsterdam, 1907); *Modern Weapons and Modern War* . . . (London, 1900); *The Parliament of Peace and Its Members* (London, 1899); Preface to I. S. Bloch, *Is War Impossible* . . . (London, 1899), vii–lxii; *To the Picked Half Million: An Appeal to the University Students of the World* (Boston, 1913); *Tripoli and the Treaties or Britain's Duty in This War* (London, 1911); *The Truth About the (South African) War* (London, 1900); *The United States of Europe on the Eve of the Parliament of Peace* (London, 1899); *War Against War in South Africa*, 20 Oct 1899–26 Jan 1900; *The War in South Africa, 1899-19—? How Not to Make Peace* (London, 1900).

B. J.O. Baylen, "The 'New Journalism' in Victorian Britain," *Australian Journal of Politics and History* 18 no. 3 (1972), 367–85, *The Tsar's "Lecture-General":*

W. T. Stead and the Russian Revolution of 1905 (Atlanta, 1969), *W. T. Stead: A Life* (London, 1982), "W. T. Stead: Apologist for Imperial Russia, 1870–1880," *Gazette: International Journal of the Science of the Press* 24, no. 3 (1961), 281–97, "W. T. Stead as Publisher and Editor of *The Review of Reviews*," *Victorian Periodicals Review* 1, no. 2 (1979), 70–83; J. O. Baylen and P. G. Hogan, Jr., "Shaw, W. T. Stead, and the 'International Peace Crusade,' 1898–99," *Shaw Review* 6, no. 2 (1963), 60–61; J. W. Robertson Scott, *The Life and Death of a Newspaper* (London, 1952); Estelle W. W. Stead, *My Father: Personal and Spiritual Reminiscences* (London, 1913); Frederic Whyte, *Life of W. T. Stead*, 2 vols. (London, 1924).

C. A microfilm collection of Stead papers is in the possession of J. O. Baylen.

Joseph O. Baylen

STETTINIUS, Edward Reilly, Jr. (22 October 1900, Chicago—31 October 1949, Greenwich, CT). *Education*: Univ. of Virginia, 1920–24. *Career*: assistant to the president, General Motors, 1926–31; vice-president, GMC, 1931–32; vice-chair, Finance Committee, U.S. Steel Corp., 1933–36, chairman, Finance Committee, 1936–38, chairman of the board, 1938–40; chair, Industrial Materials Division, National Defense Advisory Commission, 1940; chairman, Priorities Division, Office of Production Management, 1941; lend-lease administrator, 1941–43; under secretary of state, 1943–44; secretary of state, 1944–45; chair, U.S. delegation to the UN, 1945–46; rector, Univ. of Virginia, 1946–49; chairman of the board, Liberia Corp., 1947–49.

After a meteoric career in the industrial world in the 1930s in which he was concerned with employee relations and guiding the modernization program of the U.S. Steel Corporation, Stettinius devoted himself to wartime service in Washington. For two years he headed the country's arsenal of democracy program as lend-lease administrator, a post in which he gained valuable experience in dealing with the British and Russians. As planning intensified for America's drive to establish a postwar international security organization, *Franklin Roosevelt tapped Stettinius to become under secretary of state with the idea that the popular Stettinius would help lead the anticipated battle for Senate approval of the United Nations Charter. *Cordell Hull's failing health unexpectedly opened the way for Stettinius's elevation to be secretary of state in December 1944. By this time Stettinius had already led the U.S. delegation through the Dumbarton Oaks talks, where proposals for the UN Charter had been drafted. In rapid succession, Stettinius played a vital part at the Yalta Conference, then journeyed to Mexico City for a meeting of hemisphere nations, where international organization issues held a prominent spot. He then chaired the American delegation at the San Francisco Conference, where representatives from fifty nations drafted the Charter. Here Stettinius encountered many battles on the issues of regionalism, the operation of the veto, and the right of free discussion in the General Assembly. His unswerving faith that a Charter could be devised against all odds was a vital part in the successful conclusion of the work. At *Harry Truman's request, Stettinius then served for a year as U.S. representative to the Security Council. He constantly felt that his powers were being usurped by Secretary of State James F. Byrnes, and he left government service in June 1946, embittered by his final experience.

Stettinius's important role as an internationalist was not primarily in his contribution to the ideas that went into shaping the UN. Rather, his forte lay in implementing policies which the experts developed. During the war years Stettinius was a confirmed champion of the necessity of giving *Woodrow Wilson's dreams fulfillment, being influenced in his thoughts by the avid support his father had given to the League. With an ability to grasp difficult matters quickly, Stettinius made an able spokesman for the United States in the tough negotiations leading to adoption of the Charter. Enjoying a reputation for candor and honesty, he was able to keep more doubtful leaders, such as *Arthur H. Vandenberg and *Henry L. Stimson, in support of the UN. One of Stettinius's important contributions was restoring the State Department to a place of influence and seeing that preparations for the UN were well coordinated with the military, other federal agencies, and Congress. Additionally, Stettinius masterminded the department's intense campaign to maintain public support for the UN, and he headed administration efforts to assure Senate approval of U.S. membership. He was a strong proponent of great power cooperation and believed friendship with Russia would endure, a hope of which he despaired toward the end of his life.

BIBLIOGRAPHY:

A. *Lend-Lease: Weapon for Victory* (New York, 1944); *Roosevelt and the Russians: The Yalta Conference,* ed. Walter Johnson (New York, 1949).

B. Thomas M. Campbell, *Masquerade Peace: America's UN Policy, 1944–1945* (Tallahassee, FL, 1973); Thomas M. Campbell and George C. Herring, eds., *The Diaries of Edward R. Stettinius, Jr., 1943–1946* (New York, 1975); DAB supp. 4, 776–78; NCAB 38, 62–65; Richard L. Walker, "Edward R. Stettinius, Jr. in *The American Secretaries of State and Their Diplomacy*, eds. Robert H. Ferrell and Samuel Flagg Bemis, 14 (New York, 1965), 1–83.

C. The Stettinius papers are at the Univ. of Virginia.

Thomas M. Campbell

STEVENSON, Adlai Ewing, II (5 February 1900, Los Angeles—14 July 1965, London). *Education*: B.A., Princeton Univ., 1922; J.D., Northwestern Univ., 1926. *Career*: law practice in Chicago, 1926–41; special assistant to secretary of the navy, 1941–44; special assistant to secretary of state, 1945; senior adviser, U.S. delegation to UN General Assembly, 1946, alternate member, 1946–47; governor of Illinois, 1948–52; Democratic presidential candidate, 1952, 1956; representative to UN, 1961–65.

Following World War II there was an upsurge of interest in the United States concerning the country's international role symbolized by the establishment of the United Nations on American soil. Stevenson became a prominent spokesman for postwar internationalism, especially in relation to the UN. Between 1945 and 1965 he insisted that, notwithstanding its imperfections, the UN was mankind's only and final shield against the disaster of war.

Stevenson's interest in and knowledge of international affairs was quickened during the 1930s, when he became active in the Chicago Council on Foreign Relations. Later, as a member of the Committee to Defend America by Aiding the Allies, he debated with isolationists in the Chicago area. During the war Stevenson traveled widely as a special assistant to the secretary of the navy and as a State Department adviser, witnessing at first hand the destruction caused by modern warfare. It was a sobering experience. He became convinced that civilization could not survive another world war in the nuclear age. Henceforth Stevenson was haunted by visions of Doomsday, which underlay his policy proposals on two occasions: in the presidential election of 1956, when he publicly advocated unilateral suspension of atmospheric nuclear testing by the United States, and in the Cuban Crisis of 1962, when he privately suggested removal of NATO warheads from Turkey as part of a formula to secure withdrawal of the Soviet missiles from Cuba. When the United States negotiated a test ban agreement with the Soviet Union in 1963, Stevenson felt it was a fulfillment of his 1956 proposal.

From 1953 to 1960 Stevenson vigorously criticized the foreign policies of the Eisenhower administration, especially its overreliance on military pacts and nuclear weapons, its bellicose rhetoric, its insensitivity to "underdeveloped" nations, and its failure to make progress in achieving arms control. Yet, because Stevenson shared the fundamental anti-Communist sentiments of the administration, his strictures lost much of its force. Too often he was reduced to criticizing means rather than basic assumptions in foreign affairs. For all his misgivings, he was hard pressed to offer the electorate specific alternatives to the Eisenhower policies, and this shortcoming contributed to his failure in the presidential election of 1956.

Enthusiastic about the prospects for fresh directions in foreign affairs following the election of John F. Kennedy in 1960, Stevenson wanted to be secretary of state. Instead he was offered the ambassadorship to the United Nations. Although he was promised an increased voice in policy formulation, he quickly learned he was consigned to the role of advocate. At the UN he was personally respected and perhaps thereby enhanced the prestige of the position, but he had no substantial part in making policy. After Kennedy's assassination, Stevenson anticipated a better relationship with Lyndon B. Johnson. Again his hopes were disappointed, and he grew increasingly restless. He may have been close to resigning his position when he died suddenly in London.

Stevenson's importance in the history of internationalism rests less on specific policy contributions than on a general turn of mind. He aspired to alert the American people to a broader view of the world. In his final public address, at Geneva in July 1965, he likened the peoples of the earth to passengers on a spaceship, dependent on its fragile resources for survival. Should a world system of governance ever develop, Stevenson will be remembered as one of its prophets, for he was convinced that the world could no longer afford to indulge in competitive nationalism. But he was equally convinced, as a patriot, that the United States had a unique role to play as the model for the growth of democratic institutions. He dreamed of an effective international organization, inspired by the principles of the American political system, that would lead the way toward a new international order. In this respect he resembled *Woodrow Wilson, one of his political idols. Yet, by nature skeptical and tolerant, he shared none of Wilson's dogmatism. In 1962 he told a Boston University audience that the world was striving to create a community of the free, the equal, and the tolerant. This was the vision that sustained Stevenson amid a political career that contained more than its share of disappointments and frustrations.

BIBLIOGRAPHY:

A. *The Papers of Adlai E. Stevenson*, ed. Walter Johnson, with Carol Evans and C. Eric Sears, 8 vols. (Boston, 1972–79).

B. DAB supp. 7, 719–24; John B. Martin, *Adlai Stevenson and the World* (Garden City, NY, 1977), *Adlai Stevenson of Illinois* (Garden City, NY, 1976); *Newsweek* 66 (26 Jul 1965), 24–29; NYT 15 Jul 1965, 10.

C. The Stevenson papers are at Princeton Univ. and at the Illionis State Historical Society.

Rodney M. Sievers

STIMSON, Henry Lewis (21 September 1867, New York—20 October 1950, Huntington, Long Island, NY). *Education*: B.A., Yale Univ., 1888; M.A., Harvard Univ., 1889; Harvard Law School, 1889–90. *Career*: attorney in New York City, 1893–1950; U.S. attorney, Southern District of New York, 1906–9; Republican candidate for governor of New York, 1910; secretary of war, 1911–12; U.S. Army, 1917–18; presidential representative to Nicaragua, 1927; governor general, Philippine Islands, 1927–29; secretary of state, 1929–33; secretary of war, 1940–45.

Stimson's public career reflected America's unsteady journey toward a form of collective security. He was a cautious internationalist, combining a Burkean respect for order and legal process with a Wilsonian commitment to international cooperation. He was an actor, not a theorist, a politician rather than an ideologue. As an author he aimed to teach lessons. As a Cabinet secretary for three presidents he helped define America's role in the modern world.

Stimson was a member of the Eastern Republican Establishment (the term had yet to be coined when he died). His ancestry extended back to Puritan Massachusetts, providing him easy acceptance to the world of the Ivy League and, later, Wall Street. There he began to practice law under the wing of future senator and Cabinet secretary *Elihu Root, a giant in the evolution of internationalism.

Root introduced Stimson to international law as well as to Republican politics. Service as a U.S. attorney gave Stimson a reputation as a progressive in the *Theodore Roosevelt mold, which led in turn to an unsuccessful race for governor of New York in 1910. Stimson's distaste for campaigning guaranteed that his remaining public service would be appointive, and it was in the area of foreign policy and defense that he made his mark. Named secretary of war by *William Howard Taft in 1911, his accomplishments were mainly administrative. He modernized the Army by improving training procedures and, more importantly, by elevating the authority of the General Staff over that of the politically sensitive bureaus. Stimson did not confine his interest in military affairs to desk duty, which ended in 1913. He admitted his hunger for combat experience, and he advocated preparedness long before *Woodrow Wilson drafted his war declaration in 1917. The war, in which he served a short combat tour that he remembered as wonderfully happy, reinforced his belief that peace was contingent on military readiness.

By 1920 he had come to believe that peace also depended on the success of the League of Nations. Although opposed to the automatic guarantee built into the Covenant's Article X, he signed, together with other prominent Republicans, the campaign Statement of the 31, calling Warren Harding's election the best way to guarantee American membership in a league. A disappointed Stimson later saw his partisan support for Harding as a form of self-delusion. The rejection of the Covenant, he wrote years later, was "the greatest mistake made by the United States in the twentieth century."

As the Republican party abandoned all political interest in the League during the 1920s, Stimson remained in a quandary. A confirmed internationalist, he nevertheless resigned himself to the Senate's rejection of the Covenant. Indifference replaced enthusiasm, and he turned to other matters. With Root he helped to organize the Council on Foreign Relations. He also supported American membership on the World Court, opposed the trend toward higher tariffs, and advocated continued arms limitations efforts.

Even after *Herbert Hoover appointed him secretary of state, Stimson remained cool to the League. He satisified his internationalist instincts by supporting naval limitation (though without a consultation agreement) at the London Conference in 1930, and by calling for an extended moratorium on debt repayment during the financial crisis of 1931. The League, he claimed, had become primarily an instrument to settle purely European problems.

Not until the Manchurian Crisis would Stimson begin to reassess this judgment. The Japanese occupation of Manchuria, which began in September 1931, was the first important violation of the Covenant as well as of postwar treaties signed by the United States. Stimson initially offered only token support for League efforts to resolve the dispute, hoping that Japanese moderates would reassert their control in Tokyo. But when they proved impotent, Stimson dramatically reversed course by authorizing *Prentiss B. Gilbert to sit with the League Council.

Nevertheless, Stimson's support for the League remained inconsistent. He often undercut deliberations there by acting unilaterally, as when announcing the Nonrecognition Doctrine in 1932; and he frequently viewed the League as a device to shield the United States from Japanese hostility. Moreover, he exaggerated public opposition to U.S.–League cooperation, and he refused to give the League necessary promises of American support if it were to invoke sanctions against Japan. Although Stimson would later blame American inaction on Hoover's pacifism, he never seriously considered economic or military pressure because of his own fear of war. His caution contributed to failure in the Far East.

The Great Depression, combined with the rise of Fascism, turned many Americans toward isolationism and economic nationalism. Not Stimson. Reflecting on the failure of his Manchurian policy and free from official responsibility after 1933, he soon became the leading American advocate of collective security. During the Ethiopian Crisis, he urged what he had not proposed in 1931: an export embargo against the aggressor to parallel League sanctions. Stimson became a leading critic of neutrality legislation between 1935 and 1939 and once World War II began stood well ahead of the Roosevelt administration in advocating aid to the Allies.

The collapse of France in 1940 prompted *Franklin Roosevelt to ask Stimson to join his Cabinet as secretary of war. Although the selection of a Republican served Roosevelt's political interest, the appointment signaled the administration's determination to aid the opponents of Fascism. Stimson's next five years were filled with the task of building and managing the armed forces, and he offered advice on foreign policy matters as the line between foreign and military affairs grew very thin. Long before Pearl Harbor he advocated an export embargo against Japan. He counseled cooperation with the Soviet Union, especially after 1943, when he favored opening a second front. Like Roosevelt, he distrusted *Charles de Gaulle, but he was much more willing to work with him than was the president.

As he looked to the postwar period, Stimson believed that stability would necessitate a healthy world economy, which, in turn, would depend on American trade and a reindustrialized Germany. He also argued that peace would require a vital collective security organization. But Stimson in 1945 had less faith in the machinery of international organization than he had in 1919. He insisted that great power disagreements be resolved *before* launching the United Nations. After Hiroshima, he was willing to risk sharing atomic secrets with Moscow. Only this course, he argued, could reduce Soviet suspicions about U.S. policy, thereby preventing a nuclear arms race.

Stimson was not a model politician. He was often moralistic, inconsistent, and mistaken. Indeed, his historical significance can be found as much in his failures as his successes. Yet he usually was ahead of his time, as on the League, opposition to so-called neutrality laws, aid to the Allies, and the atomic arms race. More than most of his contemporaries, he represented the transition in internationalism from a Wilsonian reliance on public opinion to a recognition that force lay at the heart of a collective security system. system.

BIBLIOGRAPHY:

A. *American Policy in Nicaragua* (New York, 1927); *Democracy and Nationalism in Europe* (Princeton, NJ, 1934); *The Far Eastern Crisis: Recollections and Observations* (New York, 1936); with McGeorge Bundy, *On Active Service in Peace and War* (New York, 1947).

B. Richard N. Current, *Secretary Stimson: A Study in Statecraft* (New Brunswick, NJ, 1954); DAB supp. 4, 784–88; Robert Dallek, *Franklin D. Roosevelt and American Foreign Policy, 1932–1945* (New York, 1979); Robert H. Ferrell, *American Diplomacy in the Great Depression: Hoover–Stimson Foreign Policy, 1929–1933* (New Haven, CT, 1957); Elting E. Morison, *Turmoil and Tradition: The Life and Times of Henry L. Stimson* (Boston, 1960); NCAB F, 20–22; NYT 21 Oct 1950, 1; Gary B. Ostrower, *Collective Insecurity: The United States and the League of Nations during the Early Thirties* (Lewisburg, PA, 1979), "Secretary of State Stimson and the League," *Historian* 41 (May 1979), 467–82; Kent G. Redmond, "Henry L. Stimson and the Question of League Membership," *Historian* 25 (Feb 1963), 200–12; Martin Sherwin, *A World Destroyed: The Atomic Bomb and the Grand Alliance* (New York, 1975); Christopher Thorne, *The Limits of Foreign Policy: The West, the League, and the Far Eastern Crisis of 1931–1933* (London, 1972).

C. The Stimson papers and diary are at Yale Univ.

Gary B. Ostrower

STOWELL, Ellery Cory (12 December 1875, Lynn, MA—1 January 1958, Berkeley, CA). *Education*: B.A., Harvard Univ., 1898; Univ. of Berlin, 1903–4; graduate, diplomatic section, Ecole Libre des Sciences Politiques, Paris, 1906; docteur en droit, Univ. of Paris, 1909. *Career*: chemist, 1898–99; clerk, 1900–1901; adjunct secretary and member, Panamanian delegation, Second Hague Peace Conference; secretary, U.S. delegation, London Naval Conference, 1908–9; instructor, George Washington Univ., 1908–10; assistant professor, Univ. of Pennsylvania, 1910–13; lecturer to professor, Columbia Univ., 1913–18; law practice, Washington, 1918–22; professor, American Univ., 1922–44; president, Better Government League, Washington, 1925–30; founder and chair, Department of International Affairs, American Univ., 1935–44; exchange professor, Univ. of Washington, 1942–43.

Stowell established a major reputation in the field of public international law, where he combined the role of occasional civil servant, periodic practitioner, and prolific scholar. He is best known for his pioneering study of humanitarian intervention, contained in his fourth book, *Intervention in*

International Law (1921). Stowell's definition of humanitarian intervention as a means of "vindicating the law of nations against outrage" is still the most succinct description of that controversial doctrine, and his historical treatment of humanitarian intervention in the nineteenth and early twentieth centuries continues to be the most comprehensive treatment. His doctoral thesis presented a pioneering study of the office of diplomatic consul, which was paralleled by a large compilation of the *Consular Cases and Opinions* in English and American courts. He also wrote on the diplomacy of World War I, authored a general treatise on international law, and was the first scholar to do a monograph on the role of the legal adviser in the Department of State. In 1916, after a review of world needs and conditions, he concluded that only through a spirit of internationalism could political and economic problems be solved.

Stowell contributed a number of editorial comments to the *American Journal of International Law* in the 1930s and 1940s which denounced neutrality, praised collective security, supported extradition and the protection of the individual through international law, and warned against military transgressions against innocent civilians in occupied territories. Throughout his career he mixed public service with scholarly pursuits. During World War I he helped organize the Patriotic Service League. Later he chaired the National Civil Service Reform League's Foreign Service Committee, which aided in the planning of the Rogers Act (1930). Stowell also helped found the Hall of Nations Program in 1938, by which foreign students, many of them Latin American, were given financial support to come to Washington for training in the social sciences.

BIBLIOGRAPHY:

A. *Consular Cases and Opinions* (Washington, 1909); *The Diplomacy of the War of 1914* (Boston, 1915); coauthor, *International Cases*, 2 vols. (Boston, 1916); *Intervention in International Law* (Washington, 1921); *Le Consul* (Paris, 1909); *The Legal Adviser of the Department of State* (Washington, 1936); "Plans for World Organization," *Columbia University Quarterly* 18 (Jun 1916), 226–40; *Principles of International Law* (New York, 1931).

B. NCAB 47, 435–36; NYT 3 Jan 1958, 23; WWWA 4, 827.

C. The Stowell papers are in the Manuscript Division, Library of Congress.

Robert A. Friedlander

STRAUS, Oscar Solomon (23 December 1850, Otterburg, Bavaria—3 May 1926, New York). *Education*: B.A., Columbia Coll., 1871, LL.B., 1873, M.A., 1874. *Career*: lawyer, merchant, statesman, Jewish communal leader; minister to Turkey, 1887–89, 1898–1900, ambassador, 1909–10; secretary of commerce and labor, 1906–9; member, Permanent Court of Arbitration, 1902–26; Progressive candidate for governor of New York, 1912.

Like other middle-class American peace crusaders, Straus equated internationalism with concerted efforts among the major powers to maintain world peace. In the spirit of the Enlightenment's teachings, he optimistically believed that rational men could devise machinery for making war obsolete and that America, whose mission was to spread the ideals of liberty and righteousness, had to lead the world to that goal. An ardent Reform Jew, Straus was also inspired to translate the prophetic ideal of universal peace into contemporary reality.

Involvement in the peace movement followed logically for Straus, who opposed the Spanish-American War, the annexation of the Philippines, and dollar diplomacy. Reflecting the reform spirit of the Progressive era, he saw the peace movement as a projection of his blueprint for a harmonious America—where morality and humanitarianism governed the relationships between capital and labor, corporation and consumer, politician and public—onto the world scene. His legal training convinced him of the need to ground international relations in law and to utilize techniques of arbitration and mediation for the resolution of disputes. Straus's appointment to the Permament Court of Arbitration at The Hague in 1902 won him great esteem. Ever eager to enhance the tribunal's stature, he urged its utilization toward the settlement of the Venezuela debt dispute (1902) and the Russo-Japanese War.

Straus aired his views on world peace through solicited and unsolicited communications to government officials, in speeches and writings, and in public office. While secretary of commerce and labor, he interwove the cause of international peace with his defense of unrestricted immigration, his interest in the expansion of overseas trade, and his antiprotectionist stand. In private capacity, as when he sided with England on the Panama Canal tolls dispute and when he labored in the fall of 1914 to bring about a mediated peace between Germany and the Entente, he lost no opportunity to spread his message on international morality and the importance of juridical devices for avoiding war.

Through organized peace groups, Straus pushed strongly for a world that ran according to international law. He served as president of the New York Peace Society in 1906, officer of numerous Lake Mohonk Arbitration Conferences, and delegate to several national peace congresses. His work for the American Society of International Law earned the tribute that but for his interest and encouragement the Society and its journal would have failed. One favorite idea advanced in his speeches later found acceptance with +William Jennings Bryan; it called for a ban on loans and the sale of arms from individual citizens of neutral states to belligerents.

The climax to Straus's peace efforts came in his support of *Woodrow Wilson's League of Nations. On the Executive Committee of the League to Enforce Peace, a bipartisan organization of distinguished Americans who advocated the settlement of international disputes through a league, Straus became chairman of a committee designated to cooperate with Wilson at Versailles. There the American delegation used him to help overcome French opposition to a league. Straus enthusiastically endorsed the League of Nations in public statements abroad and in the United States during the fight for ratification. Initially he rebutted Wilson's formidable Republican critics, but as opposition forces grew stronger he too supported approval with reservations and even the election of Harding as the surest way to achieve some form of association of nations. Until his death, Straus continued to press for American participation in the League and for any other viable forms of international cooperation.

BIBLIOGRAPHY:

A. *The American Spirit* (New York, 1913); *Origin of Republican Form of Government in the United States of America* (New York, 1885); *Under Four Administrations* (Boston, 1922).

B. Naomi W. Cohen, *A Dual Heritage: The Public Career of Oscar S. Straus* (Philadelphia, 1969); DAB 18, 130-32; *Universal Jewish Encyclopedia* 10, (New York, 1943), 77-79.

C. The Straus papers are in the Manuscript Division, Library of Congress.

Naomi W. Cohen

STRAWN, Silas Hardy (15 December 1866, Ottawa, IL—4 February 1946, Palm Beach, FL). *Education*: Ottawa High School. *Career*: lawyer, businessman, government service.

During the era of Calvin Coolidge and *Herbert Hoover, internationalism had few business spokesmen who exceeded Silas Strawn in prominence or stature. Lacking both a college and a law degree, Strawn nevertheless rose to become one of Chicago's most respected lawyers, an expert on international law and commerce, and a board member of several major corporations. In 1925 he drew national attention as an American commissioner to a Peking conference on revising Chinese tariffs. This appointment, and his simultaneous chairing of an international commission to investigate the subject of extraterritorial jurisdiction, kept him in China for a year. Upon his return, Strawn spoke on contemporary China in influential public and business forums across the Northeast. The *New York Times* believed that he did more than an other person to shape American perceptions of the situation in China.

Returning to private life, Strawn occupied a succession of elite posts in American business and professional circles: president of the Chicago Council of Foreign Relations, member of the Executive Council of the Society of International Law, trustee of the Carnegie Endowment for International Peace, president of the American Bar Association, honorary vice-president and then president of the Chamber of Commerce of the United States, and director of the International Chamber of Commerce. He was also a major donor to and officer of the League of Nations Association. Such roles were in keeping with the beliefs of a man convinced that progress resulted from cooperation efforts by private enterprise. Strawn used his positions to impress American businessmen with the importance of foreign commerce, the benefits to be derived therefrom, and the need to adjust government and business policies to reflect the modern economic situation.

Strawn's views well illustrate one form of progressive capitalist ideology as it applied to international affairs. Strawn was convinced both that foreign trade was already vital to American prosperity and that its importance was bound to grow. He also recognized that industrialization had led to increasing economic interdependence among nations. In such a world it was necessary and desirable for America to exercise leadership. Anglo-Saxon law and commercial practices rested on principles and provided models for procedures which could bring order and progress if adopted overseas. While government could support this process of advancement through such means as equitable tariff laws and membership in the World Court, the main responsibility rested with private business.

Strawn vigorously supported both the Dawes and Young Plans as examples of cooperative efforts to solve economic problems, and he opposed protective tariffs and inflexible rate structures. No hidebound conservative, Strawn accepted and encouraged change as long as conduct was orderly and events moved in directions compatible with his beliefs. On his China mission he supported in principle greater Chinese control over their customs revenues and an eventual end to extraterritoriality for foreigners. Yet Strawn opposed implementation of these reforms until turmoil in China subsided, and he rejected any suggestion that the unequal treaties had worsened the situation, thereby fueling Chinese nationalism, attributing such views to local agitators. He opposed efforts to limit outside sales of arms to China, insisting that the Chinese government alone bore responsibility for stopping arms imports. Strawn's thinking reveals little understanding of nationalist feelings among underdeveloped peoples or any sense that Western capitalism might be unpopular among them. While he believed that morality should govern business conduct and supported action against those who transgressed, he never doubted the essential benevolence of the capitalist system or the integrity of most of those who ran it.

The Depression undermined public regard for businessmen like Strawn and exacerbated the nationalism which undercut the type of international cooperation he advocated. He insisted that only international action could achieve a return to prosperity. Strawn helped to negotiate a private bilateral agreement with India on trade in silver and urged it as a model means to stimulate trade and restore economic health. This effort proved a forlorn, isolated success. He grew bitter and largely withdrew from public life after 1933. Strawn, like progressive capitalism, itself, fell victim to the Depression.

BIBLIOGRAPHY:

A. *Chicago Tribune* 5 Feb 1946, 1; DAB supp. 4, 779–80; NCAB 34, 16; NYT 5 Feb 1946, 23; James Grafton Rogers, *American Bar Leaders* (New York, 1933), 242–44.

C. Strawn materials are in the Minnesota State Historical Society Library.

James C. Schneider

STREET, Cyrus H. (7 September, 1843, near Bloomfield, IA—21 July 1913, Oakland, CA). *Education*: Iowa public schools. *Career*: realtor, land developer, peace advocate.

After studying law with his father, Street moved to Council Bluffs, where he entered the real estate business. There Street laid out several subdivisions, but because of poor health he settled in California. Arriving in San Francisco in 1876, he became the secretary and land officer of the Immigration Association of California. With a partner, Street used the Immigration Association as a base to build his own business, C. H. Street and Company. Supported by bankers, boosters, and the San Francisco Board of Trade, Street's company offered information about private and government land, climate, soil, timber, and items of general interest to prospective settlers of the Bay Area. Street also began a small printing establishment in his Oakland home. This endeavor gave Street's fertile mind an outlet to express the vision of a united world.

In November 1908, Street printed the first issue of *The United Nations*, a publication which advocated "the early establishment of an international government, for the purpose of securing universal peace, progress, prosperity, and happiness." Dedicating the last five years of his life to this goal, Street's platform was a reaction to General William Tecumseh Sherman's famous remark, that "war is hell." Street believed the statement to be literally true and felt war should be abolished forever.

Between 1908 and 1911, Street published various issues of *The United Nations*. These went to school boards throughout the United States where superintendents offered encouragement. "Peace Work for Children to Do" programs developed in many regions as some teachers hoped to remove the glamor of war. Businessmen were also the target of Street's attention. Income from oppressive war taxes levied by the U.S. government in a one-year period, wrote Street, could instead be used to build a grand boulevard, two hundred feet wide, from Washington to San Francisco. Unlike expenditures for war which become junk in a few years, the grand boulevard would increase the value of land and aid commerce for generations. Street wanted the billions of dollars annually spent by the nations of the world for warfare applied in more productive ways.

A United Nations government with legislative, judicial, and executive branches would, according to Street, ensure forever the creation of basic laws to guarantee universal peace. Street found this alternative to be comprehensive and more effective than the Permanent Court of Arbitration established at the Hague Conference in 1899. +Andrew Carnegie, *Hamilton Holt, and the Friends of Peace helped Street in his far-sighted plans. While many of these concepts were never fully utilized, thirty-two years after his death, in 1945, Street's United Nations became a partial reality.

BIBLIOGRAPHY:

B. *Berkeley Daily Gazette* 2 Sep 1960; *Builders of a Great City: San Francisco's Representative Men* (San Francisco, 1891); *Los Angeles Times* 26 Jun 1955.

C. Miscellaneous Street items are in the Archives of the Hoover Institution on War, Revolution and Peace.

Marshall R. Kuehl

STRESEMANN, Gustav (10 May 1878, Berlin—3 October 1929, Berlin). *Education*: Abitur, Andreas-Realgymnasium, 1897; doctorate, Leipzig Univ., 1900. *Career*: National Liberal party delegate to Reichstag, 1907–12, 1914–18; chair, National Liberal Reichstag delegation, 1917–18; founder and chair, German People's party (DVP), 1918; member, National Assembly and Reichstag, 1919, 1920–29; chair, Reichstag Foreign Affairs Committee, 1920–23; chancellor and foreign minister, 1923; foreign minister, 1923–29; Nobel Peace Prize, 1926.

Stresemann's status as an internationalist has been tarnished during the last two decades. At issue is the role he played as foreign minister of the Weimar Republic from 1923 until his premature death in 1929. His career during and before World War I has evoked little dispute. The son of a beer distributor, he quickly rose to prominence in the imperial Reichstag after notable success as an organizer of German light industry. During World War I he emerged as the heir apparent to leadership of the National Liberal party due to his keen intelligence, outgoing personality, and oratorical skills.

Like so many others who had endorsed the Bismarckian solution to German unification, Stresemann's liberalism was tempered by his nationalism. He supported the acquisition of colonies and William II's efforts to play the role of a world power. He thought this was necessary to overcome Germany's geopolitical encirclement and need for foreign markets, but possible without resorting to war. When war did come, he emerged as an ardent supporter of Germany's annexationist aims.

Germany's defeat and internal revolution shattered those dreams and forced him to come to terms with both a new internal political climate and external distribution of power. Reluctant at first to accept the Weimar Republic, he formed his own German People's party (DVP). By 1923, however, he had become reconciled to the new order, including the powerful Social Democratic party. Beginning with his brief tenure as chancellor in 1923, Stresemann was also a leading advocate for reconciliation with France. Together with *Aristide Briand and Austen Chamberlain, he received the Nobel Peace Prize for his role in negotiating the Locarno Treaties of 1925. In those, Germany acknowledged the permanence of the Franco–German border set at Versailles and renounced the use of force to resolve any dispute concerning its eastern borders. As a corollary, Germany also entered the League of Nations as a permanent member of the Council. Once in the League, Stresemann resisted his critics and maintained a policy of accommodation. Both in the formal League sessions and the private tea parties with Briand and Chamberlain he played a very circumspect role. The result was a series of small victories: the end of inter-Allied military control, early withdrawal from the Rhineland, and reduction of Germany's reparations debt. His hopes for major treaty revision, however, remained unfulfilled.

How do we explain the apparent conversion from ardent wartime annexationist to advocate of accommodation? The emerging consensus is that he never renounced his nationalistic faith in Germany as a great power that should regain its rightful status in the concert of Europe. This meant revision of the Versailles Treaty, including the regaining of land lost to the resurrected Polish state. What set Stresemann apart from many of his contemporaries as well as his successors was his renunciation of war as senseless and his advocacy of reconciliation through cooperation versus bluster and defiance. He agreed with his contemporaries that the shackles of Versailles should go, but he differed over the means and recognized that Germany's territorial ambitions during World War I were now a pipe dream. It was only by a policy of peaceful adjustment of competing national interests that Germany would reemerge as an important force in the postwar European state system. Whether or not Stresemann's ambitious program of peaceful revision could ever have been achieved is open to doubt. Until his death, however, Stresemann never altered the goal or the means, only the timetable.

BIBLIOGRAPHY:

A. League of Nations speech, *Journal Officiel*, special supp., 44 (1926), 51–52; *Reden und Schriften*, 2 vols. (Berlin, 1926); *Vermächtnis: Der Nachlass in drei Bänden*, ed. Henry Bernhard, 3 vols. (Berlin, 1932–33).

B. Hans W. Gatzke, "Gustav Stresemann: A Bibliographical Article," *Journal of Modern History* 36 (Mar 1964), 1–13; Robert Grathwol, "Gustav Stresemann: Reflections on His Foreign Policy," *Journal of Modern History* 45 (Mar 1973), 52–70; Christoph M. Kimmich, *Germany and the League of Nations* (Chicago, 1976); Michael-Olaf Maxelon, *Stresemann und Frankreich, 1914–1929: Deutsche Politik der Ost-West Balance* (Düsseldorf, Germany, 1972); Henry A. Turner, *Stresemann and the Politics of the Weimar Republic* (Princeton, NJ, 1963).

C. The Stresemann papers are in the Political Archiv des Auswätigen Amtes in Bonn.

Kenneth Paul Jones

STUCKENBERG, John Henry Wilburn (6 January 1835, Bramsche, Osnabrück, Germany—28 May 1903, London). *Education*: B.A., Wittenberg Coll., 1857; theology graduate, Wittenberg, Coll., 1858; graduate study, Halle Univ. 1859–61, Göttingen, Berlin, Tübingen 1865–66. *Career*:

Lutheran pastor, Davenport, IA, 1858–59, Erie, PA, 1861–62, 1863–65, Indianapolis, IN, 1867–68, Pittsburgh, PA, 1868–73; chaplain, 145th Pennsylvania Volunteers, 1862–63; professor, Wittenberg Coll., 1873–80; pastor, American Church, Berlin, 1880–93; European editor, *Homiletic Review*, 1888–93, sociology editor, 1895–1903.

A philosopher who interpreted Germany to fellow Americans, Stuckenberg can be compared to Lester Ward as a pioneer sociologist, because Stuckenberg was the first American to formulate a Christian sociology. As a student of international law, he opposed American annexation of Spanish colonies as imperialistic, and he condemned war except in "the utmost necessity." The reality of international relations made absolute sovereignty impossible, and the growing extranational links of capital, labor, church, education, and culture revealed an emerging international era in which the nation-state and war would continue. The need to solve common problems, however, would lead to regional and then world federation. He coined the word *supernationalism* in 1888 to describe what is common to humanity transcending state and international political bodies. Since people made war and egoistic politics possible, he believed education was the key to changing government attitudes in the altruistic direction he desired.

BIBLIOGRAPHY:

A. *Christian Sociology* (New York, 1880); *International Law and the Islands Ceded by Spain to the U.S.* (Boston, 1900); *Introduction to the Study of Sociology* (New York, 1898); *The Life of Immanuel Kant* (London, 1882); *The Social Problem* (York, PA, 1897); *Sociology: The Science of Human Society*, 2 vols. (New York, 1903); *Tendencies in German Thought* (Hartford, CT, 1896).

B. Harry Elmer Barnes, "The Social and Political Theories of J.H.W. Stuckenberg," *Lutheran Quarterly* 51 (Oct 1921), 389–404; DAB 9, 179–80; *Encyclopedia of the Lutheran Church* 3 (Minneapolis, MN, 1965), 2271; *Encyclopedia of the Social Sciences* 14 (New York, 1934), 428; John D. Evjen, *The Life of J.H.W. Stuckenberg: Friend of Humanity* (Minneapolis, MN, 1938); *Homiletic Review* 46 (Jul 1903), 78–79; *New Schaff-Herzog Religious Encyclopedia* 11 (New York, 1911), 117–18; NYT 31 May 1903, 7; Eldon J. Underdahl, "The Social Thought of J.H.W. Stuckenberg," M.T. thesis, Luther Sem., 1969; WWWA 1, 1202.

C. The Stuckenberg papers are at Wittenberg Univ.

James W. Gould

SUGIMURA Yōtarō (27 September 1884, Tokyo—24 March 1939, Tokyo). *Education*: graduate, Tokyo Univ., 1908; LL.D., Univ. of Lyon, 1912. *Career*: Japanese Foreign Ministry, 1908–27, 1934–39; League of Nations Secretariat, 1927–33.

A career diplomat with extensive service in Europe, Sugimura was unique as an openly internationalist and anti-Axis spokesman in the 1930s. He is comparable to *Kikujirō Ishii and *Naotake Satō in his European orientation and to *Inazō Nitobe as a devotee of the League of Nations.

As a consul in training in Lyon, Sugimura studied international law at the university. A prolific writer, he frequently published articles in Japanese magazines dealing with such problems of international law as the discrepancies between the Anglo–Japanese Alliance and the League of Nations Covenant. On this issue he maintained in 1920 that until the League solidified its authority the conflict between the two was political rather than legal. As a frequent author of booklets on the League for the Japan League of Nations Association he was instrumental in educating the Japanese public on the ideals and functions of the new international organization.

When the League of Nations was established, Sugimura was assigned to the League bureau within the Japanese Foreign Ministry. In 1923 he was transferred to Paris to handle League affairs and in 1927 replaced Nitobe in Geneva as under secretary-general and director of the Political Section in the Secretariat. In dealing with such problems as German–Polish relations, the Transylvania boundary, and disputes between Bolivia and Paraguay, he earned the respect and fondness of Secretary-General *Eric Drummond and the esteem of other delegates. Drummond once intimated that among the thousand persons under him in the Secretariat, the only one he could trust was Sugimura.

To Sugimura, the rift that developed between the League and Japan over Manchuria was "an indescribable disappointment." In 1933 Drummond and Sugimura drew up a compromise formula designed to honor the Lytton Report and also placate the Japanese. This plan, however, failed to win approval by the Japanese Foreign Ministry and was negatively viewed by the European press. Despite Sugimura's pleas, Japan vacated the Assembly. He viewed this development as a personal failure and a national tragedy for Japan. His hope that Japan would return to Geneva was never realized. Exhausted and heartbroken, he took a leave and spent several months in the Alps writing his memoirs.

In 1934 Sugimura returned to diplomatic service and was appointed Japan's ambassador to Rome. This was an uncomfortable post in view of his personal distaste for Fascism and the proposed anti-Comintern pact. He feared the consequences for Japan of close association with Italy, a renegade from the European fold. He also felt apprehensive about jeopardizing good relations with Britain and the United States. In July 1937 Sugimura was transferred to Paris in an attempt by moderate Foreign Minister *Satō Naotake to place an international in a major capital. But ill health forced his return to Japan just before his death.

BIBLIOGRAPHY:

A. *Kokusai gaikō roku* [Reflections on international diplomacy] (Tokyo, 1933); *Renmei jūnen* [Ten years of the League] (Tokyo, 1930).

B. Masatoshi Matsushita, *Japan in the League of Nations* (New York, 1929); Ian Nish, "A Japanese Diplomat Looks at Europe, 1920–1939," *European Studies on Japan*, ed. Ian Nish and Charles Dunn (Tenterden, England, 1979), 134–39; Yōichi

Sugimura, ed., *Sugimura Yōtarō no tsuioku* [Reminiscences of Sugimura Yōtarō] (Tokyo, 1940).

                                                                    Thomas W. Burkman

SUMNER, Charles. See *Biographical Dictionary of Modern Peace Leaders*.

SUTTNER, Bertha von. See *Biographical Dictionary of Modern Peace Leaders*.

SWEETSER, Arthur (16 July 1888, Boston—20 January 1968, Washington). *Education*: B.A., Harvard Coll., 1911, M.A., 1912. *Career*: reporter, *Springfield Republican*, 1912–13, United Press, 1914; free-lance journalist, 1914–16; Associated Press, 1916–17; U.S. Signal Corps., 1917–18; American Peace Commission, 1918–19; Secretariat of League of Nations, 1919–42; deputy director, Office of War Information, 1942–46; special adviser to UN, 1946; director, UN Information Office, Washington, 1946–53.

Sweetser contributed more than any other American to the work of the League of Nations and helped lead the campaign to win popular support for the United Nations in its early years. Inspired by *Woodrow Wilson at the Paris Peace Conference, he became one of the country's first major international civil servants. In the last decades of his long life, he also played a vital part in recording the history of the League experiment.

After an apprenticeship in journalism in Massachusetts, Sweetser went to Europe virtually as a free-lance shortly after the outbreak of the Great War. Sweetser executed the extraordinary feat of describing the First Battle of the Marne from both sides of the fast-shifting front. In 1916 he turned his adventures into *Roadside Glimpses of the Great War*, a book which ranks with the best journalism of the war. Returning to the United States, he covered the State Department for the Associated Press and then entered the Aviation Section of the Signal Corps as a captain. A product of his publicity work for the new arm was *The American Air Service*, a book describing the commercial as well as military future of air power.

Shortly after the Armistice, Sweetser returned to France, again virtually as a free-lance. He had written a few articles for *The New Republic* and a naval trade journal, when he was selected by *Ray Stannard Baker as his assistant director of the press section of the American Commission to Negotiate Peace. As the Paris Peace Conference wore on, Baker increasingly left Sweetser to handle routine relations with the American press corps in Paris and to prepare special briefings. His most successful project was his summary of the draft Treaty of Versailles in early May 1919. Later that month, he was nominated by *Edward House to join the Secretariat of the League of Nations. Sweetser began work in July 1919 with Secretary-General *Eric Drummond in London and helped organize the inaugural meeting of the International Labor Organization in Washington later that year. *Raymond Fosdick's withdrawal as League under secretary after the Senate's defeat of the Versailles Treaty left Sweetser as the most influential of the small number of Americans who served the Secretariat throughout the League's existence.

Sweetser was merely a member of the Secretariat's Information Section, not becoming "acting" director until 1933 and director "without section" until 1934. His annual salary of £ 2000 remained constant from 1919 until the League's demise. Fortunately, his wife provided the financial means to maintain an elaborate home near Geneva, where they entertained American visitors to the League and other dignitaries. Regardless of title, Sweetser became one of the prominent figures in Geneva's diplomatic world. He was exceptionally close to the reserved Drummond, and he was a natural liaison between Geneva and American officials, journalists, and philanthropists.

Despite long-lived personal relationships with such patricians as Joseph Grew, Sweetser's journalistic inclination to publicize any move by Washington in favor of the League and his generally buoyant and idealistic nature dismayed the more secretive and cynical members of the American diplomatic world. But Sweetser, for whom the cause of international peace-keeping organizations was a "religion," ignored rebuffs while smoothing the way in the 1920s for Washington–Geneva cooperation in a mounting number of nonpolitical activities. When the Manchurian Crisis of 1931 brought the United States briefly into the League Council's political negotiations, Sweetser worked to coordinate U.S. Consul *Prentiss Gilbert's appearances at the Council table in October and, more importantly, to handle reports and other liaison matters for Ambassador *Charles Gates Dawes in the November–December Council session at Paris. Sweetser's contacts with President *Herbert Hoover and Secretary of State *Henry Stimson following the Dawes Mission and, later, with the new *Franklin Roosevelt administration aroused in Sweetser and others short-lived expectations of formal American recognition of the League and the appointment of a high-ranking emissary.

Nothing came of the project, possibly because of premature disclosures in the press of Sweetser's own indiscreet discussions. Sweetser was characteristically open with the journalists from all over the United States who visited the League. Expanding his publicist's function imaginatively, he also encouraged the students, teachers, and civic organization leaders who flocked to Geneva's schools and meetings each summer to support the League back home. Many of the newsmen and other American visitors later became influential supporters of the United Nations. Sweetser also worked closely with American philanthropists who championed the League, most notably the Rockefeller family. With the backing of *John D. Rockefeller, Jr., Sweetser was able to coordinate a number of important League projects, ranging from property acquisition to scholarly research.

The Rockefeller–Sweetser combination came to the rescue of key League personnel and sensitive records after the outbreak of World War II inspired fears of a German invasion of Switzerland. Sweetser found wartime quarters for certain officials and files at Princeton, NJ, while he became a deputy director in the Office of War Information in May 1942. Sweetser was also involved in planning for the United Nations. Despite a jovial interview with Roosevelt, Sweetser was not welcomed into the State Department's own UN planning effort. But he did coordinate a nationwide publicity campaign for the UN, and he assisted the many exiled diplomatists, journalists, and officers he had known in Geneva. As president of the Woodrow Wilson Foundation from 1943 to 1945, Sweetser promoted such projects as the 1944 movie, *Wilson*. The film lost money, but public opinion polls showed support for the UN to be overwhelming.

Sweetser attended preliminary UN planning conferences at Atlantic City, Montreal, and Bretton Woods, and he went to the San Francisco Conference in 1945. He tried but failed to give the last League secretary general, *Seán Lester, a role in the San Francisco proceedings. He served as special adviser in 1946 to the first secretary general of the UN but was not given a post commensurate with his seniority. Nonetheless, as director of the UN's Washington Information Office until his retirement in 1953 and beyond, he worked tirelessly to publicize the UN.

After the war, Sweetser tried to perpetuate the memory of the League. He helped arrange financing for publication of *Frank P. Walters's history of the League and Paul Mantoux's notes of negotiations at Paris in 1919. He took part in a presidential commission observing the centennial of Wilson's birth in 1956 and was founder of the International Schools Foundation, started in 1954 for the education of American children abroad. In all these ways he continued to show his commitment to advance an organized world.

BIBLIOGRAPHY:

A. *The Approach to World Unity, 1914–1919, 1920–1930* (Geneva, 1929); "The First Ten Years of the League of Nations," *International Conciliation* 256 (Jan 1930), 1–60; *The League of Nations at Work* (New York, 1920); *Opportunities in Aviation* (New York, 1920); *Roadside Glimpses of the Great War* (New York, 1916); *What the League of Nations Has Accomplished* (New York, 1924).

B. NYT 1 Jan 1968, 77; *Washington Post*, 21 Jan 1968; WWWA 4, 1067.

C. The Sweetser papers are in the Manuscript Division, Library of Congress.

J. B. Donnelly

SWING, Raymond Edwards [Gram] (25 March 1887, Cortland, NY—2 December 1968, Washington). *Education*: Oberlin Coll., 1906–7. *Career*: foreign correspondent in Europe, 1913–34; editor, the *Nation*, 1935–36; Washington correspondent for *The Economist*, 1936–37; radio news commentator, CBS, 1935, Mutual Broadcasting System, 1936–42, NBC-Blue (ABC), 1942–48, Voice of America, 1951–53; 1959–63; writer for Edward R. Murrow broadcasts, 1953–59.

A self-styled "typical" liberal, Swing was known during the late 1930s, his period of greatest prominence, as Raymond Gram Swing. He officially changed his original middle name to the surname of his second wife; after their divorce he preferred to be known as Raymond Swing. His world perspective was influenced by his journalistic career. He went to Berlin in 1913 as foreign correspondent for the *Chicago Daily News*, and he worked abroad until 1934 for the *New York Herald*, the *Wall Street Journal* and the *Philadelphia Public Ledger*. He served briefly as an editor for *The Nation* and in 1935 published a somber warning about the prospects for democracy in America, *Forerunners of American Fascism*. He became a national radio figure when world events after the autumn of 1938 led millions of Americans to listen to his earnest, carefully prepared broadcasts over the Mutual Broadcasting System.

Swing was considered an unofficial spokesman for the Department of State in the late 1930s; he was such an ardent interventionist that in July 1940 he agreed to serve as chairman of the board for the Council for Democracy, a group intended to encourage U.S. intervention in the war. He broadcast over the BBC to a large English audience once every two weeks during this period and came to advocate virtually any policy promoting step-by-step progress toward a declaration of war. It is surprising that his serious fifteen-minute news analyses ever attracted an enormous audience, but they did. In January 1942 he formed another committee, Citizens for Victory, based on the membership of *William Allen White's Committee to Defend America. Swing claimed that the enemy should be "blasted out of their last foothold." He moved to NBC's Blue Network (renamed ABC) in June 1942, but his decision in the fall of 1945 to devote one broadcast a week to the dangers of atomic warfare caused many listeners to try someone less somber. But Swing had been profoundly affected by the atomic bomb, for which he felt a personal responsibility. Either the weapons had to be destroyed or war had to be eliminated. The UN lacked the power to do either; only a world government would be sufficient for the task. While Swing lent his name to several emerging groups after 1945, he became most involved in the United World Federalists, which he served as a vice-president and as chairman of the board. Cold War animosities by the late 1940s, however, convinced Swing that his hopes for a strong cooperative world would not materialize.

Swing spent a good part of his life in Europe. He believed intensely in getting to know persons from other cultures as a method for breaking down national barriers, though he accepted widespread fears about the Soviet Union after 1945. His lasting legacy is as a serious student of foreign affairs who for a time captured a national, even international, following on radio and acquainted his listeners with the need for world unity.

BIBLIOGRAPHY:

A. *Forerunners of American Fascism* (New York, 1935); *"Good Evening!": A Professional Memoir* (New York, 1964); *How War Came* (New York, 1939); *In the Name of Sanity* (New York, 1946); *Preview of History* (Garden City, NY, 1943).

B. David H. Culbert, *News for Everyman: Radio and Foreign Affairs in Thirties America* (Westport, CT, 1976); NYT 24 Dec 1968, 23; Lawrence S. Wittner, *Rebels Against War: The American Peace Movement, 1941–1960* (New York, 1969).

C. Swing papers are in the Manuscript Division, Library of Congress, the Michigan Historical Collections, Univ. of Michigan, and the State Historical Society of Wisconsin.

David Culbert

SZE (Sao-ke) Alfred. See Shih Chao-chi.

T

TAFT, William Howard (15 September 1857, Cincinnati, OH—8 March 1930, Washington). *Education*: B.A., Yale Univ., 1878; LL.B., Cincinnati Law School, 1880. *Career*: collector of internal revenue, Cincinnati, OH, 1882; legal practice, 1882–87; judge, Superior Court of Ohio, 1887–89; U.S. solicitor general, 1889–92; judge, Federal Circuit Court, 1892–1900; chair, Philippine Commission, 1900; governor general of Philippines, 1900–1904; secretary of war, 1904–9; president, 1909–13; professor, Yale Univ., 1913–21; chief justice, U.S. Supreme Court, 1921–30.

Prior to 1900, Taft's career was primarily that of a lawyer and a judge. When William McKinley chose him to head the Second Philippine Commission in March 1900, he brought no experience in foreign affairs to that office. Taft remained for four years in the Philippines, becoming the first governor general of the islands. Although not an advocate of American expansion, he opposed independence and worked to establish a stable civil government. Many observers concluded that largely through Taft's efforts the Filipinos were reconciled to American rule. Developing a deep affection for the Filipinos, Taft twice refused *Theodore Roosevelt's offer of appointment to the Supreme Court because he thought his work in the islands was unfinished.

In 1904 Taft became secretary of war. There he continued to devote much of his attention to the Philippines. Taft also undertook diplomatic troubleshooting missions to Latin America and East Asia. As president, Taft often deferred the initiative for shaping diplomatic policy to Secretary of State Philander Knox and officials in the Department of State, and his administration is associated with expanding American commercial interests abroad. "Dollar diplomacy" took the form of endeavoring to bolster the open door in China and limit Japanese influence, but it drove Japan and Russia together to strengthen their mutual interests in North China. In Latin America, Taft hoped American capital would promote economic development and eliminate political instability in those regions adjacent to the Panama Canal. A strong believer in the ability of international law to promote world peace, Taft unsuccessfully sought approval of arbitration treaties which would have advanced greatly the scope of previous accords. His attempt to exact a reciprocal trade agreement with Canada also ended in failure. Defeated for reelection in 1912, Taft became a professor of law at Yale. While generally critical of Wilson–Bryan foreign policies, he supported American neutrality toward the European War.

Taft's belief in the ability of nations to resolve their disputes judicially led him in 1914 into organized efforts to advance peace through international organization. While initially apathetic toward peace movements, believing their efforts were impractical, he became converted in 1915 to the proposals developed by the League to Enforce Peace and agreed to serve as its president. The LEP proposed to establish an international body which would employ military and economic force against those nations which used force before they made any effort to settle their disputes peacefully through arbitration, conciliation, or other courts. Through public speeches and written articles Taft devoted major attention to advancing the work of the LEP. Its efforts, benefiting from Taft's name, did much to develop discussions about international organization (1915-18).

When the United States entered the war in 1917, Taft became joint chairman of the War Labor Board. He also supported *Woodrow Wilson's plans for the League of Nations with the United States as a member. He proposed modifications to the first draft of the League Covenant, and Wilson largely incorporated these into the revised document. Subsequently Taft became increasingly critical of Wilson's leadership of the fight for the Versailles Treaty. Believing that qualified membership in the League was better than no treaty, he reluctantly accepted suggested reservations, including one that would restrict American obligations under Article X of the Covenant. Torn between his loyalty to international goals and his attachment to the Republican party, Taft supported Warren G. Harding in the presidential election of 1920. He apparently believed that internationalists in the party would be able to influence Harding's policies, a hope which did not materialize. After he became chief justice of the Supreme Court, Taft no longer took a public stand on foreign policy issues.

BIBLIOGRAPHY:

A. *The United States and Peace* (New York, 1914).

B. Ruhl J. Bartlett, *The League to Enforce Peace* (Chapel Hill, NC, 1944); Warren F. Kuehl, *Seeking World Order: The United States and International Organization to 1920* (Nashville, TN, 1969); Ralph E. Minger, *William Howard Taft and United States Foreign Policy: The Apprenticeship Years, 1900–1908* (Urbana, IL, 1975); Henry F. Pringle, *The Life and Times of William Howard Taft*, 2 vols. (New York, 1939); Walter V. Scholes and Marie V. Scholes, *The Foreign Policies of the Taft Administration* (Columbia, MO, 1970).

C. The Taft papers are in the Manuscript Division, Library of Congress.

James R. Roebuck, Jr.

TER MEULEN, Jacob (3 December 1884, The Hague—12 August 1962, The Hague). *Education*: Univ. of Amsterdam, 1906-9; doctor juris public, Univ., of Zurich, 1914. *Career*: library, Univ. of Utrecht, 1917-21; librarian, Economic Academy, Rotterdam, 1921-23; librarian, Peace Palace, The Hague, 1924-52.

Son of the well-known landscape painter, F. P. ter Meulen, ter Meulen studied municipal law, but his interest in pacifism drew him to Zurich, to the courses of *Max Huber, who had played an important role at the Second Hague Peace Conference in 1907. Ter Meulen finished his studies with his thesis, "Beitrag zur Geschichte der internationalen Organisationen

1300–1700," which he later enlarged and published as *Der Gedanke der internationalen Organisation in seiner Entwicklung*. His appointment as librarian of the Peace Palace at The Hague brought him into contact with the Permanent Court of Arbitration, the Permanent Court of International Justice, and the Academy of International Law, where he sought to enlarge the holdings relevant to their needs. During his term as librarian, the collections were greatly enlarged, with 96 percent of all publication on private and public international law being present.

Ter Meulen also devoted much time to gathering documents on pacifism and antimilitarism, acquiring great quantities of ephemeral publications difficult to find elsewhere in the world. This led to the compilation and publication of bibliographical lists, including the *Bibliographie du mouvement de la paix avant 1899 (listes provisoires) période 1776–1899* and *Bibliographie du mouvement de la paix avant 1899 (listes provisoires) période 1490–1776*.

Developing an interest in Hugo Grotius, ter Meulen decided to obtain for the library studies about and by Grotius, the noted Dutch scholar of international law. This led to ter Meulen's life work, the publication, with P.J.J. Diermanse, of a bibliography of Grotius. Ter Meulen was a member of the Mennonite brotherhood, which rejects violence. As such, he devoted much time to the support of conscientious objectors to military service and to promoting disarmament. His pioneer study of the history of international organization has remained an outstanding resource for other scholars.

BIBLIOGRAPHY:

A. with P.J.J. Diermanse, *Bibliographie des éscrits imprimés de Hugo Grotius* (The Hague, 1950); *Der Gedanke der internationalen Organisation in seiner Entwicklung*, 2 vols. (The Hague, 1917–40).

B. AJIL 57 (1963), 391–93; P.J.J. Diermanse, "Jacob ter Meulen," *Jaarboek van de Maatschappij der Nederlandse letterkunde te Leiden, 1962–63* (The Hague, 1963), 128–33; P.J.J. Diermanse and B. Landheer, "Dr. Jacob ter Meulen herdacht," *Bibliotheekleven* 47 (Oct 1962), 676–81; W. S. Russer, "Dr. Jacob ter Meulen," *Bibliotheekleven* 37 (Nov 1952), 313–15; *Wie is dat?* (The Hague, 1956), 412–13.

J. B. van Hall

TEVFIK Rüştü. See Aras, Tevfik Rüştü.

THOMAS, Albert (16 June 1878, Champigny-sur-Marne, France—7 May 1932, Paris). *Education*: Ecole Normale Supérieure, Paris, 1898; *agrégé* in history, Univ. of Paris, Sorbonne, 1902; fellowship, Univ. of Berlin, and traveling scholarship to Near East, 1902–3. *Career*: high school teaching; journalist, *L'Humanité*, founder and chief editor, *Revue syndicaliste et coopérative*, 1905–10, and *Revue socialiste*, 1910–14; contributor, *Sozialistische Monatshäfte*; Socialist municipal councillor, 1908–12; mayor of Champigny, 1912–29; member, Chamber of Deputies, 1910–20; under secretary of state for artillery and munitions, 1915–16; minister of munitions, 1916–17; ambassador to Russia (Provisional government), 1917; representative of French Socialist party at international meetings, 1917–19; director, International Labor Office, 1920–32.

Albert Thomas, born in suburban Paris, entered active politics as a member of the Socialist party. His training as a historian, his gifts as a speaker and writer, plus his insight and administrative abilities gave him prominence in politics. Yet he abandoned all at age forty-two to embark on a hazardous venture, the directorship of an international agency of an entirely new pattern. In this effort he succeeded, leaving a strong institution of universally recognized authority.

The International Labor Organization originated in 1919. Its establishment was decided by the Commission on International Labor Legislation of the Paris Peace Conference chaired by Samuel Gompers of the American Federation of Labor. The ILO's constitution, incorporated into the peace treaty as Part XIII, provided for an agency independent of the League of Nations, and it was marked by a unique feature. There would be direct participation, with full voting rights and at all levels, of representatives of employers' and workers' organizations with those of governments. An International Labor Conference was to be regularly convened, and a permanent secretariat, the International Labor Office, was to be created. Shortly after the first conference in Washington late in 1919, Thomas, who was not present, was called by the newly elected governing body to assume its directorship.

International action was not virgin territory for Thomas: as a politician he had worked for peace and shown interest in ways to preserve it. In the words of *E. J. Phelan, Thomas came to be totally identified with the ILO. As he directed it in masterly fashion, it became almost a part of him. It is to Thomas's credit that various conventions and recommendations adopted which embody standards and guidelines for action within member states are not a mere collection of legal texts but a living reality. Thomas inspired the specialists who worked for the ILO, and he coordinated their research in a manner which gave it both high scientific value and immediate practical significance. Moreover, Thomas was anxious to establish the universal character of the ILO. He successfully argued before the Permanent Court of International Justice, opposing the views of the French government, that the ILO's technical competence extended beyond the protection of industrial workers to include those engaged in agriculture. He also listened with sympathy to the claims to representation of "native" workers. Referring to himself as the "wandering Jew of social progress," he visited not only the countries of Europe and North America but also those of South America and the Far East.

For quite different reasons, neither the Soviet Union nor the United States joined the ILO until after Thomas's death. He often had to withstand violent accusations from the Soviet Union of "reformism" and of "socialtraitorship." Thomas, in response, merely tried with limited success to establish a working relationship with Moscow in the field of research. On the other hand, while knowing it was beyond his means to bring the United States into the ILO after it refused to join the League, he obtained in 1922 during a visit to Washington an agreement that representatives from the AFL and the U.S. Chamber of Commerce could attend as observers. This diplomatic achievement, according to Phelan, "sowed the seeds" for U.S. membership in 1934.

BIBLIOGRAPHY:

A. *Annual Reports of the Director of the International Labour Office*, contain speeches, as does *International Social Policy* (Geneva, 1948).

B. "Albert Thomas," *Official Bulletin of the International Labour Office* 27 (15 Jun 1932), 95–97; H. B. Butler, "Albert Thomas, the First Director," *International Labour Review* 26 (Jul 1932), 1–7" John S. Gillespie, "The Role of the Director in the Development of the International Labour Organisation," dissertation, Columbia Univ., 1956; Daniel P. Moynihan, "The United States and the International Labor Organization 1889–1934," dissertation, Fletcher School of Law and Diplomacy, 1960; E. J. Phelan, *Yes and Albert Thomas* (London, 1936); Ernest Poisson, *Le Coopérateur Albert Thomas* (Paris, 1933); Bertus W. Schaper, *Albert Thomas, Dertig jaar social reformisme* (Leiden, 1953); *Un Grand Citoyen du monde: Albert Thomas vivant* (Geneva, 1957).

Grégoire Koulischer

THOMAS, Elbert Duncan (17 June 1883, Salt Lake City, UT—11 February 1953, Honolulu). *Education*: graduate, Univ. of Utah, 1906; Ph.D., Univ. of California, Berkeley, 1924. *Career*: missionary, Latter Day Saints Church, Japan, 1907–12; instructor, Univ. of Utah, 1914–16, secretary-registrar, 1917–21; faculty, Univ. of California, Berkeley, 1924–33; Democratic U.S. senator, 1933–51; U.S. high commissioner, Trust Territory of the Pacific Islands, 1951–53.

Thomas was a devout internationalist missionary, scholar, author, politician, and statesman. An admirer of Oriental culture, he served as a Mormon missionary in Japan from 1907 to 1912, mastered the Japanese language, and translated a Mormon tract into Japanese. His doctoral dissertation, published as *Chinese Political Thought* (1927), analyzed prominent thinkers from the Chou dynasty. An international law advocate, he attended the Carnegie European Conference of American Professors (1926) and two Conferences of the Teachers of International Law (1926, 1928) and was a vice-president of the American Society of International Law.

Before World War II, Thomas was an outspoken interventionist in the U.S. Senate. As a member of the Foreign Relations Committee, he fought neutrality legislation which benefited aggressor nations and urged military aid to Great Britain, France, and China. In February 1939 he proposed granting *Franklin D. Roosevelt broad powers to embargo the export of all raw materials and armaments to belligerents and, with congressional consent, lift the embargo for victims of aggression. Besides favoring selective service and lend-lease, he urged the United States to cancel Great Britain's war debt. During World War II he made monthly broadcasts to the Japanese people explaining why their government could not win and preparing them for capitulation.

Yet Thomas was an eloquent spokesman and practitioner of world cooperation. In *World Unity as Recorded in History* (1934) and *Thomas Jefferson: World Citizen* (1942), he pictured human nature as benevolent and espoused world unity. Thomas advocated continued American cooperation with Russia in *The Four Fears* (1944). Twice delegate to the Inter-Parliamentary Union (1936–37) and five times to the International Labor Organization (1944–48), he vigorously supported the United Nations, the Marshall Plan, and world control of atomic energy. While he recognized the necessity for using the atomic bomb in 1945, he argued that the greatest challenge facing the human species was to find a way in which principles of law could prevail. He returned to his earlier thinking about world unity and argued that an effective, cooperative, international system had to be developed.

BIBLIOGRAPHY:

A. "Atomic Bombs in International Society," AJIL 39 (1945), 736–44; *The Four Fears* (Chicago, 1944); *Thomas Jefferson: World Citizen* (New York, 1942); "World Unity as Recorded in History," *International Conciliation*, no. 297 (Feb 1934), 35–53.

B. BDAC 1961, 1703–4; CB 1942, 830–31; DAB supp. 5, 680–82; Robert A. Divine, *The Illusion of Neutrality* (Chicago, 1962); Rulon R. Garfield, "An Approach to the Politics of Elbert D. Thomas," M.A. thesis, Univ. of Utah, 1956; Frank H. Jonas, "The 1950 Elections in Utah," *Western Political Quarterly* 4 (Mar 1951), 81–91; J. H. Libby, "Senators King and Thomas and the Coming War with Japan," *Utah Historical Quarterly* 42 (Fall 1974), 370–80; NCAB 41, 600–1; NYT 12 Feb 1953, 27.

C. The Thomas papers are in the Franklin D. Roosevelt Library.

David L. Porter

THOMPSON, Dorothy (9 July 1893, Lancaster, NY—30 January 1961, Lisbon). *Education*: graduate, Lewis Institute, Chicago, 1912, and Syracuse Univ., 1914. *Career*: suffrage speaker and publicist, New York, 1914–17; social worker and publicist for the Social Unit, Cincinnati and New York, 1917–20; freelance writer, Vienna foreign correspondent, Berlin bureau chief, *Philadelphia Public Ledger* and *New York Evening Post*, 1920–34; syndicated columnist, *New York Herald Tribune*, 1936–41, *New York Post*, 1941–47, Bell Syndicate and *Washington Star*, 1941–56; columnist, *Ladies Home Journal*, 1937–58; lecturer and radio broadcaster, 1934–46; president, Freedom House, 1941–51; president, American Friends of the Middle East, 1951–56.

During the 1930s and 1940s, Thompson's vivid writing and dramatic voice over radio interested millions of Americans in the dangerous world of international politics. Her career as a correspondent began in Vienna and

Berlin in the 1920s. Thereafter she combined with ease the idealism of her small-town Methodist upbringing and the worldly sophistication of the Weimar liberals with whom she associated. In 1934 her disrespect for the views and person of Adolf Hitler resulted in her expulsion from Germany. In March, 1936, she became a syndicated columnist for the *New York Herald Tribune*, the journal of Eastern internationalist Republicans.

Thompson's panache and old-fashioned moralism blended with her insightful analyses of modern totalitarianism, attracting the attention of the public and political elite alike. She often combined reporting with shrewd interpretations of the cultural and economic background of various leaders and regimes. In 1927, for example, visiting the Soviet Union ten years after the revolution, she reported that Leninism was becoming a state religion with the system becoming a form of state capitalism run by experts and bureaucrats.

Her love of liberal Germany and Weimar culture blinded her briefly to the real possibility of Hitler's success, but her dramatic 1938 broadcast about a despairing refugee who shot a German attaché in Paris alerted thousands to the meaning of Nazi anti-Semitism. She formulated plans for an international procedure for financing the rescue of the immediately threatened European Jews. In 1938 she supported Jewish migration to Palestine, among other areas, but not a Jewish homeland there.

In the mid-1930s Thompson's columns became tocsins to awaken readers to the dangers of Fascist expansionism. She usually posed the issue in realistic terms. The 1937 neutrality act, for example, hurt American trade interests and diplomatic flexibility. Germany threatened American economic interests in Latin America. Increasingly appalled at the docility of liberals in the face of Nazism, she became a moral crusader. Although her real effectiveness in undermining American isolationism is difficult to gauge, she doubtless encouraged a renewed moral passion in American public opinion about foreign affairs. By 1941 she joined the Committee to Defend America by Aiding the Allies but in October went further than that group in advocating American entry into the war. After Pearl Harbor, Thompson devoted as much attention to the search for some postwar equilibrium as to the Allied cause. A columnist now for the liberal Democratic *New York Post*, she founded Freedom House, a lobby for free enterprise, full employment, and social reform. CBS commissioned her to broadcast to Germany in German (Listen Hans), hoping to reach democratic Germans.

Her internationalist proposals reflected the advanced edge of American thinking. A European federation, preserving national cultural autonomy, was the keystone of a successful international organization which should have its own police force and banking system. Its members should guarantee individual liberty in their basic charter. Finally, the U.S. Consititution should be amended to allow ratification of treaties by a simple majority vote of both houses.

718   TITULESCU, NICOLAE

After the war she visited the sites of concentration camps and expressed her shock. Nevertheless she thought the Nuremberg trials too sweeping and insisted that Germany be neither dismembered nor punished. She became a strong supporter of a Jewish national homeland in Palestine, viewing it as a necessity, as simple justice, and as a benefit to all the peoples of the Middle East. However, as the years passed, she grew increasingly sensitive to the moral complexities of the Palestine issue, to the plight of Arab refugees, and to attacks by the Irgun. By 1947 she was forthrightly anti-Zionist. She helped found and became president of the American Friends of the Middle East (AFME) a pro-Arab lobby sponsored by the Arabian American Oil Company and, without her knowledge, the Central Intelligence Agency. While she regarded her work as one of reconciliation of the three religious groups in the Holy Land, her employers considered her a propagandist. She thus resigned from the presidency of AFME in 1956 to continue to write for the *Washington Star*. There can be little doubt that charges of her anti-Semitism embittered her greatly. She saw her own actions as a reflection of her youthful goals of personal independence and social justice. A friend remarked that in the 1950s Dorothy Thompson, who had so embodied the moral fervor of Americans in World War II, was like a great stranded ship on the shore after the tide had left.

BIBLIOGRAPHY:

A. America Demands a Single Loyalty," *Commentary* 9 (Mar 1950), 210–19; *I Saw Hitler* (New York, 1932); *Let the Promise Be Fulfilled: A Christian View of Palestine* pamphlet, 1946; *Let the Record Speak* (Boston, 1939); *Listen Hans* (Boston, 1942); *The New Russia* (New York, 1928); *A Program for America*, pamphlet, 1944; *Refugees, Anarchy or Organization?* (New York, 1938); *There Is Only One Answer*, pamphlet, 1944.

B. DAB supp. 7, 739–41; Robert A. Divine, *Second Chance: The Triumph of Internationalism in America During World War II* (New York, 1971); NAW 2, 683–86; Marion K. Sanders, *Dorothy Thompson: A Legend in Her Time* (Boston, 1973).

C. The Thompson papers are in the George Arendt Research Library, Syracuse Univ.

Sondra R. Herman

TITULESCU, Nicolae (17 March 1882, Craiova, Romania—17 March 1941, Cannes, France). *Education*: J.D., Univ. of Paris, 1904. *Career*: attorney and associate professor, Univs. of Bucharest and Jassy, from 1905; minister of finance, 1917–18, 1920–21; delegate, Paris Peace Conference, 1920; minister to London, 1922–27, 1928–32; permanent delegate, League of Nations, 1920–36, president of Assembly, 1930–31; foreign minister, 1927–28, 1932–36.

Titulescu, Romania's outstanding interwar statesman, was both a theorist and practitioner of internationalism. On the theoretical side, his most important contributions were his internationally acclaimed speeches, "The Dynamics of Peace" (Berlin, 1929), "The Progress of the Idea of

Peace" (Cambridge, 1930), and "Order in Thought" (Bratislava, 1937). He also presented his views in numerous contributions to the *Dictionnaire diplomatique* and other specialized publications. Titulescu posited the indivisibility of international peace, which he perceived as being more a psychological sense of security than the absence of physical violence. Without peace, social and economic progress on either the international or the national level was impossible.

Titulescu dedicated his life to building a legal-institutional edifice of peace. Its foundation was the League of Nations and the Geneva principles of collective security and sovereign equality. Its superstructure was international law in general and the League Covenant in particular. Peace was to be built floor by floor, with each corrective supplement to the initial blueprint and each creative addition an extension of the Covenant, as in the Geneva Protocol (1924), the Kellogg-Briand Pact (1928), the Definition of Aggression (1933), and, as provided in Article XXI of the Covenant, regional security arrangements. The architect's plans foresaw perpetual construction with further additions in the areas of binding arbitration, disarmament, and economic and cultural cooperation on regional, then continental, and eventually global scales. The mortar which held the structure together was the incremental legitimacy of international law. Nation-states, Titulescu concluded, could be induced to live within the confines of the edifice if they had faith in its steadfastness. That faith could only be elicited if the institution consistently proved to be efficacious for all its members regardless of their power.

Titulescu's optimistic institutionalism, inspired by French jurisprudence and Wilsonian internationalism, rejected the notions of a hierarchical responsibility for peace and of exemption from legal constraints based on political power or affinity. He was thus among the most vocal critics of Mussolini's proposal for a four-power European directorate (1933) and among the most active supporters of anti-Italian sanctions following the invasion of Ethiopia (1935–36). As a practioner of internationalism, Titulescu exercised preeminent influence over the drafting of the Pact of Organization of the Little Entente (1933) and the treaties establishing and organizing the Balkan Entente (1934). Although initiated as antirevisionist military alliances, Titulescu's organization scheme established permanent institutions for diplomatic and economic coordination. Despite their failure to be regionally inclusive, the ententes are frequently cited as precursors of later attempts at functional integration.

Titulescu's name is usually associated with the League of Nations, where his oratory brilliance and diplomatic skills complemented his commitment to the institution. He played a significant role in nearly every major debate from 1920 to 1936 and was the only president of the Assembly to be reelected (1930–31). As the credibility of the League as a guarantor of security waned in the mid-1930s, so did Titulescu's support in an increasingly nationalist Romanian political system. Titulescu's dismissal as Romanian foreign minister (1936) was in part the perception that his priorities were more often those of Geneva rather than those of Bucharest.

BIBLIOGRAPHY:

A. *Nicolae Titulescu: Discursui*, ed., Robert Deutsch (Bucharest, 1967); *Nicolae Titulescu: Documente Diplomatice*, ed., George Macovescu (Bucharest, 1967).

B. Jacques de Launey, *Titulescu et l'Europe* (Nyon, Switzerland, 1976); Ion Grecescu, *Nicolae Titulescu* (Bucharest, 1980); Vasile Netea, *Nicolae Titulescu* (Bucharest, 1969); Ion Opera, *Nicolae Titulescu* (Bucharest, 1966), *Nicolae Titulescu's Diplomatic Activity* (Bucharest, 1968).

C. A collection of Titulescu's papers is in the Archives of the Hoover Institution on War, Revolution and Peace.

Walter M. Bacon, Jr.

TOBAR, Carlos. See *Biographical Dictionary of Modern Peace Leaders*.

TORRES BODET, Jaime (17 April 1902, Mexico City—13 May 1974, Mexico City). *Education*: graduate, National Preparatory School, Mexico City, 1917; studied law and philosophy at the National Autonomous Univ. of Mexico (UNAM), 1918-20. *Career*: secretary and teacher at National Preparatory School and secretary to the chancellor of UNAM, 1921-22; head, Library Department, Ministry of Education, 1922-24; professor, UNAM, 1924-28; official, Ministry of Health, 1924-28; diplomatic posts in Spain, Belgium, and France, 1929-36; director, Diplomatic Department, Ministry of Foreign Affairs, 1936-37; chargé d'affaires, Brussels, 1937-40; under secretary for foreign affairs, 1940-43; secretary of education, 1943-46; minister of foreign affairs, 1946-48; director-general of UNESCO, 1948-52; ambassador to France, 1954-58; secretary of education, 1958-64.

One of the many ironies in the life of Torres Bodet was that such an eloquent spokesman for peace should die a suicide. That he stood for peace and internationalism in thought and action is abundantly documented in his career, which involved a dozen major positions, produced more than thirty volumes of poetry, prose, criticism, and addresses, and carried him into major international conferences.

As a schoolboy in the elite National Preparatory School during a crucial phase (1910-20) of the Mexican Revolution, Torres Bodet received a classical humanistic education and formed relationships which later proved valuable. Ironically for one who twice served as secretary of public education (SEP), his college studies did not lead to a degree. Instead, his talents were developed through internship and teaching.

He served as secretary to the flamboyant José Vasconcelos, the first postrevolutionary SEP and the man who would give some social content to the revolutionary movement through his programs of mass literacy and rural adult education. Vasconcelos modeled educational statesmanship for Torres Bodet and, in some ways, the pupil surpassed the master. As a teacher of French literature, he was criticized by some as un-Mexican, and certainly the techniques he used in his poetry and novels and the name of the magazine, *Contemporáneos*, in which he and his cohorts published, were intended to identify them with European and North American literary fashions. He felt his countrymen had become too absorbed in their own "Mexican realism," so he dealt with similar Mexican themes, but differently. It was his bold as well as creative stance that carried Torres Bodet naturally into a diplomatic career in the next decade. Posts in Europe and South America during the 1930s provided valuable experience and kept him from internecine political conflicts. Among Mexico's many problems was an acrimonious debate over Socialist education. When Manuel Avila Camacho became president (1940–46), he named Torres Bodet secretary of education.

Torres Bodet's achievements can be grouped under three headings: the professionalization of the bureaucracy; the extension of the system through new buildings, teacher training centers, a literacy campaign, and the publication of inexpensive classics; and, finally, the resolution of the ideological conflict over Socialist education. By basing the system on such universal principles of Western civilization as democracy, freedom, and social justice, he placated the Roman Catholic church, private school educators, and intellectuals. At the same time, the political significance of his work had two dimensions. That post cleared the way for a closer diplomatic association with the ideals of the Atlantic Charter and the Western allies. There can be no doubt that Torres Bodet's personal commitment to the ideals of peace and internationalism were profoundly based in his family and educational roots. Thus, it was not surprising that he became foreign minister in 1946.

The postwar period found Mexico more stable and aware that the only sure path to peace was through international cooperation and continuing efforts to elevate the masses. As Mexico's chief diplomat, Torres Bodet carried this message into international conferences. He not only expressed these ideals, but he also bargained hard to build institutional structures to support them, even if this meant opposing the United States. One can see the germ of what would later become "nonalignment," but it was a separation based on the universal ideals of peace and international collective security. His idealism and independence of thought and action were rewarded in 1948 with the director generalship of the United Nations Educational, Scientific and Cultural Organization (UNESCO).

At UNESCO he gave the organization a stable administrative system and designed a comprehensive program for "establishing the structure of peace in the minds of men." He used the Universal Declaration of the Rights of Man as a rationale for a broad attack on the political and economic as well as intellectual causes of war and misunderstandings among peoples. Frustrated at the lack of financial support for his program of worldwide teacher training centers, literacy, and mass adult education, he resigned and returned to Mexico in 1952, but UNESCO continued to grow on the basis he built.

In 1958 Torres Bodet again became secretary of education. The issues remained, with literacy campaigns, teacher training centers, and new schools now a familiar formula with more sophisticated methods of planning. Torres Bodet's internationalism was now limited to Latin America, but he was no less effective or active than before. After his retirement he published essays on literary criticism and took his life in the face of a painful cancer.

BIBLIOGRAPHY:

A. *Discursos, 1941-1964* (Mexico City, 1965); *Obras escogidas* (Mexico City, 1961); *Poesía de Jaime Torres Bodet* (Mexico City, 1965); "Promoting an International Civic Spirit," *United Nations Bulletin* 11 (1 Dec 1951), 427; *Selected Poems of Jaime Torres Bodet*, ed. Sonja Karsen (Bloomington, IN, 1964).

B. William Benton, *The Voice of Latin America* (New York, 1961); John S. Brushwood, *Mexico in Its Novel* (Austin, TX, 1966); Emmanuel Caraballo, *Jaime Torres Bodet y su obra* (Mexico City, 1968); CB 1948, 624-26; Billy F. Cowart, *La obra educativa de Torres Bodet en lo nacional y lo internacional* (Mexico City, 1966); IWW 1948, 939, 1970-71, 1615; Sonia Karsen, *A Poet in a Changing World* (Saratoga Springs, NY, 1963); Raymond T. Multerer, "The Socialist Education Movement and Its Impact on Mexico: 1930-1945," dissertation, SUNY Buffalo, 1974); NYT 14 May 1974, 40; WB 1948, 4728; WWA 1948-49, 2494; WWLA 1940, 508.

Raymond T. Multerer

TOYNBEE, Arnold J. (14 April 1889, London—22 October 1975, York, England). *Education*: graduate, Winchester Coll., 1910; British Archeological School, Athens, 1911-12; Balliol Coll., Oxford Univ., 1914-15. *Career*: Political Intelligence Department, British Foreign Office, 1915-19; Middle Eastern Section, British delegation to the Paris Peace Conference, 1918-19; professor, Kings Coll., Univ. of London, 1919-24; war correspondent, Greece, *Manchester Guardian*, 1921; drafted outline of *A Study of History* while traveling on Orient Express, 1921; director of studies and editor, *Survey of International Affairs*, and professor, Royal Institute of International Affairs, 1925-55; director, Research Department of Foreign Office, 1936-46; Princeton Institute for Advanced Studies, 1948-49; travel and lecturing, 1955-73.

Toynbee was a unique person as an internationalist, possessing an ability to see all of history in one sweep yet able to work on a day-to-day basis in coping with contemporary world problems. His *Study of History* was an attempt to view the past in universal rather than nationalistic terms. In his travels, especially in the Near East, the young Toynbee had gained a sense of the impermanence of civilizations. He identified twenty-six past civilizations, of which he traced the rise and fall of twenty-one from ancient times to the present. He asked the same questions of the Persian, Greek, Macedonian, Roman, and Byzantine civilizations. Why did they rise and fall? He explained their rise by his "challenge and response" theory based on effective response to external challenges. Creative leaders who guided such responses renewed themselves through a process of "withdrawl and return." Decline set in when responses to internal and external challenges became routine and when civilizations succumbed to war, class, or nationalism.

Toynbee's application of his theory of history to Western civilization stirred intense discussion. He found that his own civilization, which began in A.D. 700, was in an indeterminate stage of decline. In contrast to Spengler, who was pessimistic, Toynbee suspended judgment and saw hope for the West in the establishment of a world state, which might save it from atomic war, and in a new world religion, which might synthesize Christianity, Islam, Hinduism, and Buddhism. His description of Judaism as a "fossil" excluded from the great world religions and his indictment of nationalism aroused critics.

In other writings, such as *War and Civilization, Civilization on Trial*, and *The World and the West*, in the annual *Surveys of International Affairs*, and in his work for the Institute of International Affairs, Toynbee adopted a more pragmatic approach to world conflict and acknowledged the need for diplomacy and the balance of power. In his editing of the *Surveys*, Toynbee imposed his broader historical concerns linking the present with the past. He also directed the studies of scholars who continued his work on the theory of international relations. However, his great contribution was to force contemporaries to look beyond their parochial societies to recognize that history over the centuries was not a story of unending progress or immortal civilizations and to provide a universal perspective on societies that rise, fall, and pass from the scene.

BIBLIOGRAPHY:

A. *A Study of History*, 12 vols. (London, 1939–61); *The World and the West* (New York, 1955).

B. CB 1947, 644–46; LT 23 Oct 1975, 17, 19, 31; Kenneth W. Thompson, "The Philosophy of International Relations of Arnold J. Toynbee," dissertation, Univ. of Chicago, 1951.

Kenneth W. Thompson and Beverly C. Thompson

TREVELYAN, Charles Philips (28 October 1870, London—24 January 1958, Wallington, Northumberland, England). *Education*: B.A., Trinity Coll., Cambridge Univ., 1892. *Career*: Liberal member of Parliament, Elland Division, West Riding Yorkshire, 1899–1918; Labor member of Parliament, Central Newcastle, 1922–31; member, London School Board, 1896–97; parliamentary charity commissioner, 1906–8; parliamentary secretary, Board of Education, 1908–14; president, Board of Education, 1924, 1929–31.

Trevelyan began his political career as a Radical, on the left wing of the British Liberal party. Although he supported British intervention in South Africa during the Boer War, he declared that opponents of the conflict should be free to express their opinions. In 1906 he was appointed to a minor position in the Liberal government, and in 1908 he became parliamentary secretary to the Board of Education.

By this time he was an advocate of peace in international affairs. He had been a cofounder in 1904 of the National Peace Council, which developed into the most important of British peace organizations. He was critical of his country's diplomatic ties with Russia and France, and he opposed the tsarist government in Russia and its policy in Persia. While not a doctrinaire pacifist, he was nonetheless out of sympathy with his government's foreign policy for some years before 1914. Trevelyan regarded the Anglo-German naval rivalry as "terrible." He was opposed to conscription and armament increases. He considered that Foreign Secretary *Edward Grey was committed to the concept of a balance of power and did not judge issues on their merits. He did not believe, however, that Britain had made an ultimate commitment to France. When war threatened in July 1914, Trevelyan was the principal contributor to the British Neutrality Committee. When that group failed to prevent British entry into the war, he resigned from the government.

Trevelyan then began to work with +E. D. Morel and others to organize the Union of Democratic Control (UDC). It did not oppose the war directly but worked for a lasting peace based on four cardinal points: no territory should be transferred from one government to another without the consent of the population concerned; democratic control should prevail in British foreign policy; an "international council" should be created to prevent future conflicts; and arms should be drastically reduced. Trevelyan helped the Union's cause by raising funds and making public speeches. He aimed to create a public opinion which would make another war "impossible." Following other members of the UDC, he joined the Independent Labor party and lost his parliamentary seat in the general election of 1918. He explained after the war that Liberalism was "hopelessly destroyed" and that the Labor party, with its influx of UDC members, was generally "sound" on foreign policy. He was chosen to fill the post of president of the Board of Education, with a Cabinet seat, in the short-lived Labor government of 1924. For the remainder of his parliamentary career his attention was largely fixed upon educational issues rather than international affairs.

BIBLIOGRAPHY:

A. *The Union of Democratic Control: Its History and Policy* (London, 1919).

B. DNB 1951-60, 989-90; A.J.A. Morris, *C. P. Trevelyan, 1870-1958: Portrait of a Radical* (Belfast, 1977), "C. P. Trevelyan's Road to Resignation, 1906-14," in *Doves and Diplomats*, ed. Solomon Wank (Westport, CT, 1978), 85-108; Marvin Swartz, *The Union of Democratic Control in British Politics During the First World War* (Oxford, 1971).

C. The Trevelyan papers are in the Library of the Univ. of Newcastle.

Marvin Swartz

TRUEBLOOD, Benjamin F. See *Biographical Dictionary of Modern Peace Leaders*.

TRUMAN, Harry S (8 May 1884, Lamar, MO—26 December 1972, Independence, MO). *Education*: public schools, Independence, MO, 1892–1901. *Career*: judge, Jackson County Court, 1922–26, presiding judge, 1926–34; Democratic senator from Missouri, 1935–44; vice-president, 20 Jan–12 Apr 1945; president, 1945–53.

Truman played a crucial role both in the creation of the United Nations and in securing U.S. entry into this international body dedicated to the preservation of peace. In his first official act, Truman confirmed the holding of the San Francisco Conference in 1945. Throughout that spring he labored to ensure the success of this meeting charged with drafting the charter for a new world body. He supervised and fully supported Secretary of State *Edward Stettinius and the delegation *Franklin D. Roosevelt had appointed. He assisted in resolving differences within and outside the Conference over questions such as the admission of pro-Fascist Argentina as a founding member, Polish representation, and voting procedure in the Security Council. He took deliberate actions—such as speaking bluntly to Soviet Foreign Minister V. M. Molotov on the Polish question and dispatching Harry Hopkins to Moscow to talk with Stalin on Poland and Security Council voting procedure—all aimed at preventing a breakdown of the Conference. Fittingly, Truman appeared in San Francisco 26 July, when the Charter was signed. Without him the UN might have been aborted or still-born.

Truman embraced the Charter enthusiastically, presenting it in person to the Senate for approval. Once it acted, he influenced congressional deliberations on the United Nations Participation Act, the enabling legislation which implemented the relevant provisions of the Charter and placed the American UN representative under presidential directive. Truman had attained what the Senate had denied *Woodrow Wilson: U.S. entry into and leadership within a world organization committed to maintaining peace through collective security.

The basis of Truman's internationalist commitment lay in his analysis, developed fully during 1942, that the root cause of World War II lay in America's failure to join the League of Nations in 1919 and the League's consequent inability to prevent aggression during the 1930s. This perspective influenced his deliberations on prescriptions for the postwar world, convincing him that a new organization would be essential to maintain peace and that the United States must participate in it. The principal danger to such involvement was American isolationism. Eager to redeem the error of 1919, Truman as a senator in 1943 and 1944 promoted U.S. entry into an international organization. His support for endorsing membership placed him in the forefront of Senate internationalists, and he took his cause directly to the American people in speaking trips sponsored by the United Nations Association. After his nomination as the Democractic party's vice-presidential candidate in 1944, he toured the country hammering home an anti-isolationist message. His main intention as vice-president was to aid in gaining Senate approval of the administration's postwar world program. He desired to help Roosevelt avoid Wilson's failure, but the president's death moved this responsibility to him.

Truman's conception of the UN involved neither the surrender of any element of American sovereignty nor the assumption of any significant new responsibility. Rather, he saw the UN as an arena in which the United States should accept the world leadership it had declined in 1919. America would be the UN's "strongest link." In 1945–46 he attempted to work through the UN in this manner, particularly in an eventually unsuccessful endeavor to obtain international control of atomic energy. On this specific issue, the UN, whose success depended upon cooperation among the major powers, foundered upon the distrust and developing conflict between the Soviet Union and the United States. As the antagonism between the Americans and the Soviets deepened, the UN framework proved unable to resolve superpower differences, and it became largely irrelevant because of the Soviets' use of the veto on the Security Council and Western responses to the perceived threat of the Soviet Union.

Truman's predicament in the period 1947–49, was that to counter the Soviet challenge he had to abandon his commitment to collective security through the United Nations, although he never so conceded. The Truman Doctrine and the Marshall Plan were formulated and implemented outside the UN framework, even though obeisance was made to the UN to assuage public concern about bypassing the international organization. Even the acceptance of NATO, explicit acceptance of the continuing reality of the balance of power as the dominant force in international politics, was presented as compatible with the UN Charter. Truman needed to stress this fact to win public allegiance for his initiatives and policies and to satisfy himself of his own fidelity to the UN.

In Truman's 1949 inaugural address concentrating on foreign policy, he outlined four major points, the first of which was unfaltering support for the UN. In June 1950, the North Korean invasion of South Korea gave him the opportunity to demonstrate this support. He saw the attack as a clear violation of the Charter. To preserve the principle of national self-determination, he authorized his advisers to work through the UN to organize a collective response to what he believed was Soviet-inspired aggression. It is almost certain that Truman would have acted outside the UN if necessary, but the Soviet boycott of the Security Council allowed him to respond through the world body and to demonstrate, at least once, the reality of collective security, even though the United States bore the brunt of fighting and exercised the predominant role in collective decision making.

Some of Truman's actions, such as his de facto recognition of the state of Israel on 14 May 1948, while the UN General Assembly was attempting to find a political solution to the Palestine question or his refusal to endorse the peace proposals for Palestine of the UN mediator, *Folke Bernadotte, in September 1948, undercut the viability of the UN. That he blocked the admission of the People's Republic of China to the international body after 1949 also served to restrict its scope. Nonetheless, Truman's importance as an internationalist is assured by his role in the creation of the UN, in securing U.S. entry and involvement, and in working through the UN to respond to North Korean aggression.

BIBLIOGRAPHY:

A. *Memoirs*, 2 vols. (New York, 1955–56); *Off the Record: The Private Papers of Harry S Truman*, ed. Robert H. Ferrell (New York, 1980); *Public Papers of the Presidents of the United States: Harry S Truman, 1945–1953*, 8 vols. (Washington, 1961–66).

B. Robert J. Donovan, *Conflict and Crisis: The Presidency of Harry S Truman, 1945–1948* (New York, 1977), *Tumultuous Years: The Presidency of Harry S Truman, 1949–1953* (New York, 1982); Lawrence S. Kaplan, "Isolationism, The United Nations and the Cold War," in Morrell Heald and Lawrence S. Kaplan, *Culture and Diplomacy: The American Experience* (Westport, CT, 1977), 215–41; Wilson D. Miscamble, "The Evolution of an Internationalist: Harry S Truman and American Foreign Policy," *Australian Journal of Politics and History* 23 (Aug 1977), 268–83.

C. The Truman papers are in the Harry S Truman Library.

Wilson D. Miscamble

TUDELA Y VARELA, Francisco (24 December 1876, Paris—1962, Lima). *Education*: doctor of administrative and political science, Univ. of San Marcos, 1900. *Career*: secretary to President Manuel Candamo, 1903–4, to President José Pardo, 1904–8; member, Chamber of Deputies, 1907–19, president, 1915; mayor of Miraflores; diplomat, 1901–39.

The public life of Tudela touched both the domestic and international realm of Peruvian history. It is, however, his diplomatic life that is most remembered. Tudela's very first governmental appointment was as secretary of the legation in Bogotá in 1901. In 1913 and 1917–18 he was minister of foreign affairs. He represented Peru as ambassador to the United States, 1918–19, and to Spain, 1939–40. He was president of the Peruvian delegation to the League of Nations in 1935–36 and again in 1939. At Geneva Tudela gained a reputation for public spirit and moderation, and he accepted a frustrating assignment to a committee in 1939 to suggest reforms for the League structure. It rendered the noted Bruce Report, which came too late to be meaningful then but was important when the UN was organized.

Perhaps his most demanding post was as head of his country's delegation to the Ecuador–Peru boundary conference held in Washington in 1936–38.

There Tudela maintained a tough negotiating position, demanding that Peru's possession of the Amazon area be recognized as a political and geographical fact that could not be disputed by Ecuador. This boundary issue continued to interest Tudela throughout his life, culminating in a 1952 book in which he accused Ecuador of an aggressive attitude and of not negotiating in good faith. An accomplished scholar, Tudela taught administrative law and international law. His writings have been published throughout Latin America.

BIBLIOGRAPHY:

A. *El arbitraje permamente y las doctrinas de Chile* (Bogotá, 1901); *El derecho internacional americano* (Lima, 1900); *El movimiento emancipador de la América Latina* (Lima, 1943); *La posición jurídica internacional del Perú en el proceso de la determinación de su frontera con el Ecuador* (Lima, 1952); *Socialismo peruano: Estudio sobre las comunidades de indígenas* (Lima, 1908).

B. Alberto Tauro, ed., *Diccionario enciclopédico del Perú* (Lima, 1966), 269–70; Alberto Wagner De Reyna, *Historia diplomática del Perú, 1900–1945*, 2 vols. (Lima, 1964), 381; Frank P. Walters, *A History of the League of Nations* (London, 1952); David H. Zook, Jr., *Zarumilla-Marañón: The Ecuador–Peru Dispute* (New York, 1964).

Paul E. Masters, Jr.

TUTTLE, Florence Guertin (23 July 1869, Brooklyn, NY—16 April 1951, Northampton, MA). *Education*: Nassau Institute, Brooklyn. *Career*: author and reformer, 1889–1931.

Tuttle, a prominent feminist who became interested in international affairs after World War I, devoted her considerable energies to further the cause of world peace during the interwar years. She became active in the women's movement at the beginning of the century, was elected president of the Civitas Club, a Brooklyn-based pioneer civic club for women, and worked with Margaret Sanger by assisting Sanger in the publication of her *Birth Control Review* and by contributing to the publication. Tuttle became visible among leaders of the movement to promote international peace during the administration of Warren G. Harding (1921–23), and she was a pro-internationalist leader throughout the interwar years, strongly endorsing membership in the League of Nations and the World Court. In 1920 she chaired the Women's Pro-League Council, and after the League of Nations Non-Partisan Association was organized (1922) she headed the Executive Committee of the Greater New York branch. Writing and public speaking were tactics she employed fully; in addition she frequently expressed her views to national leaders.

Alternative to War (1931), her last book, was her most prominent statement on behalf of peace. Through its rather bland style flow some insightful perceptions of the world and America's role in it with three principal themes highlighted. First, the American policy of isolation arose because the United States had become a world power without a world point of view.

Second, the prevention of war should be a matter of international concern and joint responsibility with the League of Nations providing the means for political cooperation, and managing to serve quite adequately despite the great handicap of having to operate with the United States as an outsider rather than as an insider. Third, the two major states outside the League after Locarno were those destined for world leadership—Russia and the United States. The Russian revolution complicated the problem of their relationships because Russia believed that wars both among nations and classes were inevitable.

Drawing upon the two great interests of her long and energetic life, Tuttle suggested that the liberated twentieth-century woman should assume extensive responsibility for organizing public opinion and rallying the nations to internationalism. She continued to speak in favor of international organization throughout her life. She was one of three women delegates who attended the League disarmament conference; they called themselves representatives of the cause and cure of war and carried petitions for peace and disarmament signed by one million American women. As long as the League endured, Tuttle traveled regularly to Geneva to broadcast a sample of its proceedings to America.

BIBLIOGRAPHY:

A. *Alternatives to War* (New York, 1931); *Women and World Federation* (New York, 1919).

B. NCAB E, 407–8; NYT 17 Apr 1951, 29.

Barbara M. Shaver

TYLER, Royall (4 May 1884, Quincy, MA—2 March 1953, Paris). *Education*: New Coll., Oxford Univ., 1902–3; Univ. of Salamanca, 1903; École des Sciences Politiques, Paris. *Career*: interrogator, World War I; with U.S. delegation, Paris Peace Conference, 1919; delegate, U.S. Reparations Commission, 1919–23; Economic and Financial Committee and Financial Section, League of Nations, 1924–41; World Bank, 1946–49; scholar.

Tyler established a noteworthy reputation as an authority on Byzantine art and as an historian of European and Spanish history. Independently wealthy, he traveled extensively and lived most of his life in Europe, where he mastered several languages. As a cosmopolitan citizen, Tyler was thus an internationalist in his lifestyle, but he chose to become involved in concrete ways.

He was one of several young Army officers chosen for their intelligence and abilities to serve on the U.S. delegation to the Paris Peace Conference, where he participated in discussions on reparations. As a result, he spent four years as a U.S. delegate on the Reparations Commission (1919–23). His work there impressed *Arthur Salter, who recommended him as League of Nations deputy commissioner general to oversee the economic reconstruction of Hungary. There he assisted *Jeremiah Smith, Jr., in supervising currency, helping subscribe loans, negotiating with creditors, and successfully stabilizing finances. When Smith returned to the United States in 1926, Tyler remained to complete the work. This complex operation involved more than economics; dangerous irridentist conditions threatened the equilibrium. The work done in Hungary was copied in Austria and had an impact on the Dawes Plan's proposals for a general reduction in reparations. Between 1931 and 1937, Tyler returned to Hungary many times as a financial adviser.

Such work led to a regular association with the Economic and Financial Committee of the League, which sent Tyler on other missions to Greece (1927), and after 1938 he worked with the League's Financial Section. After World War II, he served on the staff of the World Bank (1946–49), then accepted a UN assignment to Beirut on an Economic Survey mission. After his retirement, he sat as a European representative on the National Committee for a Free Europe and worked to create the Free Europe College in Strasbourg.

BIBLIOGRAPHY:

B. DAB supp. 5, 699–701; *The United States and the League of Nations, 1920–1927* (Geneva, 1928); Frank P. Walters, *A History of the League of Nations* (London, 1952).

C. There are Tyler materials in the Helen Tyler Brown Collection, Vermont Historical Society and in the League of Nations Archives.

Warren F. Kuehl

U

U THANT (22 January 1909, Pantanaw, Burma—25 November 1974, New York). *Education*: Univ. Coll., Rangoon, 1926-28. *Career*: high school teacher, later headmaster, of high school in Pantanaw, 1929-46; appointed press director, Burma, 1947; secretary in Ministry of Education, 1948-53; secretary for projects, Office of Prime Minister, 1953-57; executive secretary, Economic and Social Board, 1955-57; permanent representative to UN, 1957-61, president, General Assembly, 1959, acting secretary-general to fill *Dag Hammarskjöld's unexpired term, 1961-62, secretary-general, 1962-71.

The United Nations faced a serious crisis in 1960-61, when the Soviet Union withdrew its support for Secretary-General Dag Hammarskjöld and demanded the substitution of a triumvirate for a single person, arguing that "while there are neutral countries, there are no neutral men." Then, after the tragic death of Hammarskjöld while on mission in the Congo, it appeared that the Soviet Union would veto his successor. Due greatly to the availability of U Thant, whose moral authority and total impartiality had been widely recognized, it proved possible to arrive at an interim solution with U Thant's appointment as acting secretary-general for the remainder of Hammarskjöld's term. As a Buddhist, U Thant was trained to be tolerant and to cherish moral and spiritual qualities, especially modesty, humility, and compassion, which helped attain emotional equilibrium. He firmly believed that in the UN nations learn to tolerate differences of opinion and to understand different points of view. He believed that the small states, rather than the great powers, needed the protection the UN could give. In his view, the lesser countries were to be part of a bridge between the big powers, especially on issues of global interest; at the same time, it was their duty to speak the truth as they saw it and to let the chips fall. He also held that the twentieth century was that of the common man and that in the UN aspirations of mankind found a voice and an expression. The task of the UN was to bring about a real international democracy so that the common man everywhere might live free from fear and want.

In the UN he saw an organ for pragmatic executive action on behalf of the world community. He held that, if the UN was to have a future, it must assume some of the attributes of a state: it must have the right, the power, and the means to keep the peace. He held that the issue facing mankind was not primarily the contest between Communism and representative democracy; the more essential problem was the division of the world into the prosperous and the poor, the strong and the weak, the ruler and the ruled.

U Thant was determined to keep the office of the secretary-general clear of political controversy. Yet he believed the secretary-general had a political role to play if he was to be of real assistance to member states in a dynamic and imaginative search for peaceful solutions to international problems. He saw his role in quiet diplomacy geared at preventing differences between states from developing into major crises and of achieving results on sensitive problems before they became insoluble. If a way out was to be found, it should be through mutual confidence, respect, and absolute discretion. U Thant held that any hint that credit might be claimed publicly on his behalf for this or that development would almost invariably render his efforts useless. In this spirit he played a part in the resolution of the Cuban Missile Crisis in 1962 and in the late 1960s made several personal initiatives to bring the parties involved in the Vietnam conflict to the negotiating table. However, his peace efforts were frustrated by the intransigence of the parties. Through his "good offices" he mediated and conciliated dozens of international disputes; perhaps his most remarkable success was the cease-fire in the 1965 war between India and Pakistan and the subsequent observation of the cease-fire through UN personnel.

U Thant held that the secretary-general must tread his way through the jungle of conflicting national policies with the UN Charter as his only compass and a general direction from one of the principal organs of the United Nations as his only guide. When U Thant was faced, in May 1967, with an Egyptian demand for the withdrawal of a UN Emergency Force which had policed for more than ten years the armistice lines between Israel and Egypt, he had no basis on which to refuse. His attempt to get Gamal Nasser to rescind the request and have Israel accept the stationing of UNEF on its territory failed, and U Thant then complied with the Egyptian demand. The decision was criticized, especially in the West, and U Thant became the scapegoat for the Six-Day Middle East War in 1967.

BIBLIOGRAPHY:

A. *Toward World Peace: Addresses and Public Statements* (New York, 1964); *View from the UN* (Garden City, NY, 1978).

B. June Bingham, *U Thant: The Search for Peace* (New York, 1966); Andrew W. Cordier and Max Harrelson, eds., *Public Papers of the Secretaries-General of the United Nations*, vols. 6–8 (New York, 1976–77); CB 1962, 414–16.

Vratislav Pechota

UNDÉN, Bo Östen (25 August 1886, Karlstad, Sweden—15 January 1974, Stockholm). *Education*: M.A., Univ. of Lund, 1905, LL.B., 1910, LL.D., 1912. *Career*: assistant professor, Univ. of Lund, 1912–17; professor, Univ. of Uppsala, 1917–56, rector, 1929–32; minister without portfolio, 1917–20, 1932–36; minister of justice, 1920; minister of foreign affairs, 1924–26, 1945–62; member, Permanent Court of Arbitration, 1930–42.

A noted expert on international law and a prime mover of social reform legislation domestically, Undén became involved with both the League of Nations and the UN. He attended sessions of the former as a Swedish delegate (1927–39) and served as a member of the Council (1924, 1926).

While at the League, Undén established a reputation as a man of principle, arguing stubbornly on behalf of what he believed was right. This appeared when Germany sought membership in 1926 and several governments protested against it assuming a permanent seat on the Council as had been promised. Undén insisted that the pledge be honored despite threats of an economic boycott against Sweden for his stand. Adherence to principle became evident during debates over Japan's attack against Manchuria and during the Mosul issue over the ending of Great Britain's mandate over Iraq. At the League, Undén also became involved in studies of the opium question, problems regarding Turkey, and the codification of international law.

Undén became a leading advocate during the interwar years for the extension of arbitration. When foreign minister in 1925, he proposed that Sweden accept open arbitral accords, and these appeared in a 1928 treaty. He served on tribunals in 1930 and 1933 and acted as arbitrator in 1932 in a dispute between Greece and Bulgaria. He saw the creation of the Permanent Court of International Justice as a significant forward step, and he regularly defended the League, especially in the 1930s. He perceived it as a major evolutionary step in international relations.

During World War II, Undén remained a vigorous critic of the Axis powers and called for the creation of a new and just international body. During discussions whether to create a Scandinavian bloc, Undén agreed only if it were part of a universal body. He had major reservations about the UN Charter, which he saw relying too much on great-power principles. Yet Undén headed Sweden's first delegation when it joined the UN in 1946. He fully endorsed commitments which imposed limitations upon Sweden, whether in aiding refugees, accepting the terms of the International Trade Organization, or pledging it to the military support of the UN.

Undén's firm beliefs prompted him to speak frankly on issues even when he was not a representative in international bodies. He persistently criticized nations which he thought violated the principles of the Charter. Thus he opposed U.S. intervention in Lebanon in 1948, favored the admission of the People's Republic of China, and castigated governments which stubbornly supported the Taiwanese Republic of China. He also spoke against Soviet intervention in Hungary in 1956.

Undén also gained a reputation as a peace advocate. He continued to suggest a broader use of international law to resolve problems, and he became an outspoken critic in the 1950s of the testing of nuclear weapons. He viewed with concern the growing network of military alliances after 1945 and argued strongly for Sweden's neutrality while endorsing its participation in international peacekeeping forces. Throughout his life he maintained that, while political systems were necessary, lasting peace would come only when coupled with principles of justice—social, economic, and legal.

BIBLIOGRAPHY:

A. *L'Affaire Martini, une sentence arbitrale internationale* (Uppsala, 1933); *L'Article 181 du traité de Neuilly, une sentence arbitrale internationale* (Uppsala,

1932); *Internationall Äktenskaparätt* [International family law] (Lund, Sweden, 1922); *Tankar om Utrikespolitik* (Stockholm, 1963).

B. CB 1947, 649–52; S. Shephard Jones, *The Scandinavian States and the League of Nations* (Princeton, NJ, 1939); Erik Lönnroth, "Sweden: The Diplomacy of Östen Undén," in *The Diplomats, 1919–1939*, ed. Gordon A. Craig and Felix Gilbert (Princeton, 1953) 86–99; Salvador de Madariaga, *Morning Without Noon: Memoirs* (Westmead, England, 1974); NYT 17 Jan 1974, 42.

C. The Undén papers are in the Royal Library, Stockholm.

Warren F. Kuehl

UPHAM, Thomas C. See *Biographical Dictionary of Modern Peace Leaders*.

URRUTIA, Francisco José (12 April 1870, Popayan, Colombia—6 August 1950, Bogotá). *Education*: doctor of law and political science, Univ. of Quito, 1893. *Career*: under secretary for foreign affairs, 1906; minister for foreign affairs, 1908, 1913; delegate, League of Nations, 1920–30; judge, Permanent Court of International Justice, 1931–42.

Urrutia acquired skill both as a diplomat and as a legislator from 1910 until 1918, holding positions of secretary of legation, under secretary for foreign affairs, minister to Brazil, Spain, and Switzerland, minister for foreign affairs, member of the Colombian Chamber of Representatives, and president of the Colombian Senate.

In 1920 he was appointed as the first Colombian delegate to the League of Nations Assembly, and from 1926 to 1928 he was a representative on the Council. Urrutia gained a reputation as a skilled negotiator and jurist in the area of the resolution of international disputes. He presided over the Council during the 1928 May–June session and participated in the Communications and Transit Conference (1923), the Conference on Trade and Ammunition (1925), the Conference on the Treatment of Foreigners (1929), and the Conference on the Codification of International Law (1930). During this period he also lectured at the Academy of International Law at The Hague and published works on international arbitration, diplomatic history, and the Pan American movement.

In the capacity of rapporteur of the League Council, Urrutia argued in favor of the expansion of the World Court's power to render advisory opinions on legal questions. His background as a distinguished international administrator and legal scholar led to his appointment to the Permanent Court of International Justice. During his tenure (1931–42), Urrutia led in drafting opinions on disputes between Germany and Poland over the territory of Upper Silesia and the Free City of Danzig. In these cases he advocated judicial settlement in an attempt to ease some of the tensions which eventually resulted in the outbreak of World War II.

Urrutia's major contributions toward fostering world peace are found in his diligent and scholarly approach to international tensions. Inasmuch as he devoted himself to detailed studies of legal questions, he was never accorded public prominence. Although his work is buried in the archives of the proceedings of the Council and the Court, he fully revealed leadership in promoting what was called "the Geneva spirit," or optimism about the League of Nations as an experiment in international organization.

BIBLIOGRAPHY:

A. *A Commentary on the Declaration of the Rights of Nations* (Washington, 1916); *El derecho internacional en América* (Paris, 1928); *La evolución del principio de arbitraje en América* (Bogotá, 1908); *Las conferencias pan-americanas* (Paris, 1923); *Le Continent américain et le droit international* (Paris, 1928).

B. IWW 1961–62, 989; WWLA 1951, 409–10.

Alan T. Leonhard

V

VALENSI, Georges (11 November 1889, Algiers—19 March 1980, Paris). *Education*: Ecole polytechnique (Paris) and Ecole nationale supérieure des télécommunications. *Career*: engineer in the French PTT (postal, telegraphic, and telephone service), 1912–24; secretary-general of the International Telephone Consultative Committee (CCIF), 1924–56.

In 1919 and 1920, Valensi set up the laboratory of the French administration's Technical Research Department, the nucleus of the present Centre national d'études des télécommunications. Between 1921 and 1923, he installed the first French national broadcasting station. Then, in 1924, he entered the international scene with his appointment, at 35, as secretary-general of what was to be known as the International Telephone Consultative Committee (CCIT). For over twenty years, until his retirement in 1956, Valensi guided the destiny of this highly productive international body until its amalgamation in 1956 with the CCIT to form the existing International Telegraph and Telephone Consultative Committee.

But the heavy responsibility of directing the CCIT did not absorb the whole of his intellectual energy and vision. In 1927, at the Conservatoire des arts et métiers in Paris, he set up a laboratory for the European Basic Telephone Transmission Reference System, and in the same year he created the first section of the International Joint Committee for Tests relating to the Protection of Telephone Lines. From 1920 to 1938, he was a lecturer at the Ecole supérieure des postes et télégraphes.

It is as an inventor, perhaps, that Valensi most clearly demonstrated his versatility and orginality. In 1927, he patented an ion relay. Fascinated by television from its infancy, he conducted experiments with reception on cathode ray oscillographs in the French PTT Research Department as early as 1923. Between 1938 and 1940, he took out a number of United States, British, and French patents, in which the principles of compatibility in color television—the basis of all color television today—were first announced.

After his retirement, he continued research, and at the 1961 Montreux Symposium, he presented two new methods for reception of color television pictures on large screens.

In 1979 the International Telecommunications Union's Administrative Council made the first award of the Union's Centenary Prize to Valensi for "his exceptional contribution to the development of international telecommunications."

BIBLIOGRAPHY:

C. Valensi's papers are in the ITU Archives, Geneva.

Gilberte Perotin

VAN DOREN, Carl (10 September 1885, Hope, IL—18 July 1950, Torrington, CT). *Education*: B.A., Univ., of Illinois, 1907; Ph.D. Columbia Univ., 1921. *Career*: lecturer, Columbia Univ., 1911–30; managing editor, *Cambridge History of American Literature*, 1911–21; editor, *The Nation*, 1919–22; editor, *Century Magazine*, 1922–25; Pulitzer Prize for biography of Benjamin Franklin, 1939; author and literary critic; expert on the American Revolution; World Federalist and peace advocate.

As a World Federalist, Van Doren lobbied for a redrafting of the United Nations Charter to create a world republic with power over armaments and military forces. He and others, notably Mildred Blake, Tom Griesemer, and Vernon Nash, initially endorsed Clarence Streit's Federal Union Plan, which envisaged a union of the Atlantic democracies, but they moved to embrace the broader federalist ideal that became popular late in the 1940s.

To help implement the creation of world federalism through the United Nations, Van Doren became chairman of the international editorial board of *World Government News*. While utilizing this and other publications to proselytize the need for a more secure world, he often compared the difficulties of strengthening the United Nations with those problems faced by American statesmen trying to write the Constitution in 1787.

These parallels between the interstate anarchy of 1787 and the international anarchy after World War II forced people to ask whether the obstacles to a world government outweighed those to the union of the thirteen states. Van Doren's last book, *The Great Rehearsal*, provided a detailed and positive answer in his account of the creation by a few statesmen of a federal constitution for a collection of thirteen feuding, jealous, and sovereign states.

Van Doren revealed other qualities which reflected an international perspective. Concern for world justice and humanity as well as federalism had manifested itself in 1938, when he rejected the offer of five Nazi publishers who wanted to publish his biography of Benjamin Franklin. Instead, he granted the book rights to a German publishing house "in exile" in the Netherlands. Moreover, he participated in diverse symposia dealing with human rights, including the United Nations Commission on Human Rights, always fervently proclaiming that the happiness of the people is the end of government.

Although vehemently opposed to dictatorship, Van Doren, while extolling American democracy, also viewed the Soviet Union hopefully rather than pessimistically. He did not view it as a monolith. Both countries, he believed, had something to learn from each other. For example, he felt that the Soviet Union might learn from the United States how to achieve its programs more efficiently. The United States might learn from the Soviets how to devise programs to provide more people with useful work so that no one would have to work to fill only others' pockets.

A fluent, practical, and concerned scholar until his death, Van Doren, espoused the cause of human rights, a world united under a federal form of government, and ultimately international peace.

BIBLIOGRAPHY:

A. *The Great Rehearsal* (New York, 1948); *Mutiny in January* (New York, 1943); *Secret History of the American Revolution* (New York, 1949).

B. DAB supp. 4, 846–48; Charles I. Glicksberg, "Carl Van Doren, Scholar and Skeptic," *Sewanee Review* 46 (Apr–Jun 1938), 223–34; NCAB 39, 587–88; NYT 19 Jul 1950, 31; "Proceedings," *American Antiquarian Society* 60 (18 Oct 1950), 183–85; WWWA, 3, 873.

C. Van Doren papers are at Princeton Univ.

Emmett E. Panzella

VAN KIRK, James W. (27 February 1858, Feed Springs, OH—14 June 1946, Youngstown, OH). *Education*: Mount Union Coll., Boston Univ. School of Theol., Harvard Coll., 1885–94. *Career*: pastorates in northeast Ohio, 1894–1905; crusader for brotherhood, peace, and world unity, 1905–46.

This eccentric minister had a vision of an interdependent world long before that concept became commonplace. It came on 22 June 1899, at 6 P.M., while walking on a street in Canton, Ohio, when he felt a "call" to go around the world on a friendship tour. He had left his job as a contract plasterer in 1885 to go to college and in 1905 abandoned his career as a minister and embarked on his first pilgrimage. By his death he had been around the world four times and covered over 100,000 miles in his peace tours. He visited Europe many other times where he developed ties with peace- and internationalist-minded leaders. He often worked at his trade as a plasterer while en route to obtain funds for his mission. By his trips in the 1920s, Van Kirk had lost one leg and relied on a 1920 Model T which, because of its extensive world travel and mileage, went to the Ford Museum. Dressed in a wide-brimmed hat, string tie, and black suit, he reached out to the people of the world.

Van Kirk saw a growing world consciousness through commerce, religious ecumenism, and an emerging sense of brotherhood and oneness. The two Hague Peace Conferences, to Van Kirk, represented the epitome of such developments which would in time lead to the world's political federation. The United States, because of its more advanced social and political systems, had a distinct responsibility to seize the initiative. On 9 September 1909, Van Kirk read before the Liberty Bell in Philadelphia his "Declaration of Interdependence," originally written in 1898, in which he saw not only a growing movement toward political unity but also a trend "from patriotism to humanitarianism." War should give way to a world organized under a system of law, and world citizenship would become "the norm of cosmopolitan society."

Van Kirk believed that such changes could be implemented more easily if people had a concrete symbol, and in 1911 he devised an international flag toward this end. It depicted the earth in a spectrum of the major colors, with this "rainbow" representing the races of the world and their struggle to advance. Stars could be added for every nation subscribing to world unity.

Thereafter, he sought to persuade people and organizations to adopt his flag. He was present in 1913 at the dedication of the Peace Palace at the Hague, was in Paris in 1920, and on 4 July 1929, he spoke in Ariana Park in Geneva, which was to become the headquarters grounds for the new League of Nations buildings. There he ceremonially set up his universal flag. He gave out tens of thousands of miniature flags and lapel buttons reproducing his seven-color symbol. Van Kirk never departed from his singular approach, although he eagerly endorsed all efforts, such as the League of Nations and the UN, which he saw as advances toward world unity. He also campaigned against U.S. entry into both World Wars, particularly in the late 1930s, when he worked with the National Peace Campaign and the Committee to Keep America out of War. This tireless apostle also spoke extensively in the United States. On one pilgrimage in the early 1920s he addressed audiences in 2,507 high schools, colleges, and universities and in over 700 clubs. He was seventy-nine when he embarked on his last world tour, and until his death he exhorted his fellow citizens of Youngstown, Ohio, to declare their town a world city.

BIBLIOGRAPHY:

A. *The Rainbow: A World Flag for Universal Peace* (Youngstown, OH, 1914); *A Real Life Story. A Life: Stranger than Fiction* (Youngstown, OH, 1938).

B. *Youngstown Vindicator* 8 Jan 1939, 27 Feb 1942, 14 Jun 1946.

Warren F. Kuehl

VAN KIRK, Walter W. See *Biographical Dictionary of Modern Peace Leaders*.

VAN ZEELAND, Paul. See Zeeland, Paul van.

VANDENBERG, Arthur Hendrick (22 March 1884, Grand Rapids, MI—18 April 1951, Grand Rapids). *Education*: Grand Rapids public schools; Univ. of Michigan, 1900–1901. *Career*: editor and publisher, *Grand Rapids Herald*, 1906–28; U.S. senator from Michigan, 1928–51.

As a young editor of the *Grand Rapids Herald* and supporter of an assertive foreign policy, Vandenberg first advocated international cooperation during the Senate fight over the League of Nations. While carrying on an extensive correspondence with *William Howard Taft and *Henry Cabot Lodge, Vandenberg editorially endorsed Senate approval of the Treaty of Versailles and the Covenant of the League of Nations with mild reservations. After the Treaty's defeat, Vandenberg called for a nationalist and generally isolationist foreign policy, a position he maintained as a senator, except for his affirmative vote to join the World Court in 1935, until the Japanese attack at Pearl Harbor. During World War II, he came to share the syndrome of guilt of most Americans that somehow participation in the League and greater presidential discretion in determining foreign policy might have prevented the war. He therefore gradually abandoned isolationism and espoused membership in a postwar international organization to keep the peace.

Within the Senate Committee on Foreign Relations Vandenberg worked closely with the State Department to formulate the United Nations Relief and Rehabilitation Administration. He also played a decisive role not only in writing the Connally Resolution, but also the Mackinac Declaration, which put the Republican party on record as favoring American participation in a postwar international peacekeeping organization. After lengthy consultations as a member of the committee of eight with the State Department during the formative stages of the Dumbarton Oaks proposals for a United Nations, Vandenberg on 10 January 1945, made a dramatic Senate speech calling for close cooperation between the administration and Congress to ensure American adherence to the proposed UNO. His speech drew worldwide attention and resulted in *Franklin D. Roosevelt appointing Vandenberg a delegate to the San Francisco Conference.

Deeply involved in most of the crucial decisions made there, Vandenberg helped draft articles LI–LIV of the Charter, which ensured the right, previously asserted under the Monroe Doctrine, to form regional defense pacts. Many persons felt this concesssion was a deviation from the concept of collective security. Vandenberg was instrumental in attaining the 89–2 Senate vote ensuring membership. He served as a delegate to the first and second sessions of the UN General Assembly as well as the Big Four Foreign Ministers Conferences in Paris and New York as an adviser. His overwhelming reelection in 1946 and the Republican control of the Senate resulted in Vandenberg becoming chairman of the Committee on Foreign Relations. Throughout this period Vandenberg, a leading spokesman for a bipartisan foreign policy, urged a strong anti-Soviet stance and supported policies which weakened international action through the UN.

He cooperated with the *Harry S Truman administration in blunting the supposed Communist threat. He led efforts in 1947 to win Senate approval of aid to Greece and Turkey consistent with the Truman Doctrine, which committed the United States to assist any nation resisting the threat of internal subversion or aggression by Communists or the Soviet Union. He gained Senate endorsement of the Marshall Plan and subsequent appropriations to rebuild a war-ravaged Europe. With the cooperation of Assistant Secretary of State Robert A. Lovett, he drafted the Vandenberg Resolution (S. 239), which paved the way for the formation of the North Atlantic Treaty Organization, a return to the balance-of-power concept of maintaining peace. During the 1948 election he persuaded Thomas E. Dewey, the

Republican candidate, and his foreign policy adviser, *John Foster Dulles, to refrain from making foreign policy a partisan issue. Although Vandenberg's influence began to wane after 1949 when the Democrats regained control of Congress, he continued to support administration policies, except on China, and strove for a bipartisan foreign policy until his death in 1951. Vandenberg had advocated international cooperation to achieve American objectives but never fully accepted or understood collective security and by the end of his career realized that the UN would not be able to preserve peace as he had hoped in 1945.

BIBLIOGRAPHY:

A. *The Private Papers of Senator Vandenberg*, ed. Arthur H. Vandenberg, Jr. (Boston, 1952); *The Trail of a Tradition* (New York, 1926).

B. DAB supp. 5, 702–5; Aurie Nichols Dunlap, "The Political Career of Arthur H. Vandenberg," dissertation, Columbia Univ., 1955; NYT 19 Apr 1951, 1; C. David Tompkins, *Arthur H. Vandenberg: The Evolution of a Modern Republican* (East Lansing, MI, 1970).

C. The Vandenberg papers are in the Michigan Historical Collections, Bentley Library, Univ. of Michigan.

C. David Tompkins

VANDERVELDE, Emile (25 January 1866, Ixelles, Belgium—27 December 1938, Brussels). *Education*: graduate, Univ. of Brussels, 1886. *Career*: member, War Committee, 1917–18; minister of justice, 1918; Socialist deputy minister for foreign affairs, 1925–27.

A Belgian statesman and international Socialist, Vandervelde entered public life at twenty and led a Socialist student delegation to an International Congress in Brussels (1888). By 1894 he had assumed the leadership of the Belgian Socialist party, which he retained till his death.

Before World War I, Vandervelde became a major figure in the Second International, particularly at the Amsterdam meeting in 1904. Along with Jean Jaurès and the new British Laborites, Vandervelde was a staunch defender of reformism and not revolution. He also became identified with the eight-hour day and other social and economic questions, including penal reform. He personified the prewar Socialist ideal of a cooperative world. His international stature was augmented when he advocated the transfer of the privately owned Congo Free State to the Belgian nation in 1906, and when he provided strong support for the newly created international courts at The Hague. After the Great War, Vandervelde was a delegate to the Paris Peace Conference and with *Paul Hymans signed the Treaty of Versailles for Belgium.

In the 1920s, Vandervelde became identified with the Charter of the International Labor Organization. He was a primary drafter of that document and one of the initial members of the Labor Commission, where he championed the idea of the standardization and amelioration of work conditions for all League member states. As minister of foreign affairs in 1925, he helped negotiate and signed the Locarno Treaty of Mutual Guarantee and the four accompanying arbitration coventions. In the 1930s, he was passionate in his struggle against Fascism and in defense of the Spanish Republic.

Vandervelde has often been criticized as a Socialist first and internationalist second, but it is clear that he saw the new international organizations as proper vehicles for the achievement of both working class goals *and* global peace among states.

BIBLIOGRAPHY:

A. *La Belgique envahie et le socialisme internationale* (Brussels, 1917); *Le Parti Ouvrier Belge, 1885–1925* (Brussels, 1925); *Souvenirs d'un militant socialiste* (Paris, 1939).

B. Barbara Emerson, *Leopold II of the Belgians* (New York, 1979); IWW 1937, 1095; LT 28 Dec 1938, 12; Jane K. Miller, *Belgian Foreign Policy Between the Two Wars, 1919–1940* (New York, 1951).

Pierre-Henri Laurent

VEBLEN, Thorstein Bunde (30 July 1857, Cato, WI—3 August 1929, Palo Alto, CA). *Education*: graduate, Carleton Coll., 1880; Johns Hopkins Univ., 1881; Ph.D., Yale Univ., 1884; postgraduate studies, Cornell Univ., 1891–92. *Career*: instructor to associate professor, Univ. of Chicago, 1892–1906; professor, Stanford Univ., 1906–9, Univ. of Missouri, 1911–18; teacher, New School for Social Research, 1919–26; U.S. Food Administration, 1918.

The twentieth-century debate about the origins of wars and the means of preventing them took an ironic twist in the anthropological economics of Veblen. While he postulated the peaceful and creative instincts of man, he remained deeply pessimistic about the prospects for peace, especially after 1919. From the turn of the century he had criticized Marxists for their excessive cheerfulness about man's rationality and the future. People rarely understood their self-interests. Instead, they tried to emulate the wealthy, whose power, possessions, and leisure reflected unearned past glories. This human capacity for self-deception, the linchpin of Veblenian psychology, perpetuated two useless institutions: the price system and the national state. Both reflected vestiges of barbarism which had in man's prehistory displaced the savage ethic of live-and-let-live. The first private possessions were female slaves captured in war. The peaceful savages had, as Veblen frequently remarked of others, the defects of their virtues. Feeling a benign but uncritical group solidarity, they allowed the most aggressive among them to use the community surplus to attack other tribes. The gains of the warriors appeared to the superstitious to be the gains of the entire tribe. Patriotism, in Veblen's schema, always retained the character of mythic advantages (prestige) won at the cost of real privations.

In modern society, Veblen detected three rival forces and their attendant viewpoints. First, industrial technology, growing out of cosmopolitan scientific knowledge, induced a dispassionate frame of reference. From this engineering mentality, which industrial workers might absorb, the logical conclusion was production for use, that is, an industrial republic. Second, the price system constituted the destructive opposition ("business sabotage"), aiming not at efficiency or usefulness but at narrow financial advantage. The result of this fundamental conflict was a series of depressions and monopolistic consolidations. However, by 1915 Veblen perceived in *Imperial Germany and the Industrial Revolution* that a third element, the garrison state, using the modern economy for war, might prove more powerful than either business or the machine process. Veblen saw that Britain was paying "the penalty of taking the lead" in industrialization. Prussianism, its cartels using the most advanced technology and a skilled but submissive population, might yet triumph. Veblen appears to have anticipated the contest among Fascism, traditional capitalism, and economic democracy. Despising wartime patriotism, he hoped the Allies could defeat Germany without themselves triumphing.

In *An Inquiry Into the Nature of Peace and the Terms of Its Perpetuation* (1917) Veblen's flickering hope for revolutionary common sense shines through. Real peace required a league of neutrals to lower trade barriers, dismantle armed establishments, free colonies, and let the rights of ownership fall into disrepair. By 1919 the Allied response to the Russian revolution indicated that these were hardly real possibilities. Yet Veblen played alternately with quirky proposals for a "soviet of engineers" to run the economy and gloomy pessimism over Americans' stubborn faith in the vested interests. Scholars have repeatedly questioned his seriousness. Perhaps his humorous barbs against "imbecile institutions" were designed to puncture his readers' faith in them and in the disserviceable elites whom they benefited. Certainly no one has ever fashioned sharper weapons or used them with less hope.

BIBLIOGRAPHY:

A. *Absentee Ownership and Business Enterprise in Recent Times* (New York, 1923); *The Engineers and the Price System* (New York, 1919); *The Higher Learning in America* (New York, 1918); *Imperial Germany and the Industrial Revolution* (New York, 1915); *An Inquiry Into the Nature of Peace and the Terms of Its Perpetuation* (New York, 1917); *The Place of Science in Modern Civilization and Other Essays* (New York, 1934); *The Theory of Business Enterprise* (New York, 1904); *The Theory of the Leisure Class* (New York, 1899); *The Vested Interests and the Common Man* (New York, 1919).

B. DAB 19, 241-44; John P. Diggins, *The Bard of Savagery: Thorstein Veblen and Modern Social Theory* (New York, 1978); Joseph Dorfman, *Thorstein Veblen and His America* (New York, 1934); Douglas Dowd, *Thorstein Veblen* (New York, 1966); Sondra R. Herman, *Eleven Against War: Studies in American Inter-*

natioanlist Thought 1898–1921 (Stanford, CA, 1969); Bernard Rosenberg, *The Values of Veblen: A Critical Appraisal* (Washington, 1956).

Sondra R. Herman

VISSCHER, Charles. See De Visscher, Charles.

VOLLENHOVEN, M. C. von. See *Biographical Dictionary of Modern Peace Leaders*.

W

WADSWORTH, Eliot (10 September 1876, Boston—29 May 1959, Washington). *Education*: B.A., Harvard Univ., 1898. *Career*: partner, Stone and Webster (electrical engineering firm), 1907–16; vice-chair, Central Committee of the American Red Cross, 1916–19, member, 1921–42, national treasurer, 1921–26; assistant secretary of treasury, 1921–25; member, Massachusetts State legislature, 1926–32; chair, Board of Commissioners Sinking Fund, Boston, 1926–29, 1934–40; vice-president and director, Franklin Savings Bank, 1908–43; president, Boston Chamber of Commerce, 1933–39; director, U.S. Chamber of Commerce, 1934–40; member, Loyalty Review Board, Civil Service Commission, 1950–53.

A Harvard-educated, wealthy, old-stock American, Wadsworth led an active life as financier, politician, and philanthropist. As was common during the first half of the twentieth century for many of America's Eastern seaboard elite, internationalism provided a practical, well-respected outlet for his public concerns. Wadsworth expressed his internationalism in three ways. The first began with his long association with the American Red Cross, dating from service during World War I in Eastern Europe and Russia while at the same time working for the European Relief Committee of the Rockefeller Foundation. Over the next forty years he held various executive positions within the ARC, and in 1929 he represented the United States at the Conference for Rewriting the Red Cross Convention. Second, Wadsworth expressed his internationalism through his official position within the U.S. government. In 1923, while serving as assistant secretary of treasury, he attended a conference in Paris on the costs of retaining U.S. forces in Germany. From 1923 to 1925, as secretary to the World War Foreign Debt Commission, he negotiated with the British about refunding their debt. Third, Wadsworth actively promoted American commerce and trade abroad through two important organizations, the International Chamber of Commerce (ICC) and the Carnegie Endowment for International Peace (CEIP).

While director of the Chamber of Commerce of the United States from 1934 to 1940, Wadsworth accepted the chairmanship of the American Section of the ICC in 1937, the same year he became a trustee of the CEIP. The CEIP, whose policies were dominated by *Nicholas Murray Butler, called for lowering barriers to world trade and stabilizing international currencies as a prescription for maintaining world order and thus ensuring peace. Wadsworth's own internationalism grew from these perceptions that American interests, political and economic, were best served when there was world stability. Until the outbreak of World War II, Wadsworth contributed to the work of a joint CEIP and ICC committee, established through the urging of Butler and under the leadership of *Thomas Watson, which sought to promote international economic cooperation. By the late 1930s, however, world order had already broken down. In 1941, following U.S. entrance into World War II, Wadsworth was able to criticize the Endowment's and his own cautious approach to the problem of maintaining world peace. He did not, however, challenge his assumption that internationalism promoted American interests. He ended his career as a member of the Loyalty Review Board of the Civil Service Commission.

BIBLIOGRAPHY:

B. DAB supp. 6, 659–60; NYT 30 May 1939, 17; WWWA 3, 881.

John Greco

WALLACE, Henry Agard (7 October 1888, Orient, IA—18 November 1965, Danbury, CT). *Education*: B.S., Iowa State Coll., 1910. *Career*: agricultural scientist, economist, and editor, Des Moines, IA, 1910–33; secretary of agriculture, 1933–40; vice-president, 1941–45; secretary of commerce, 1945–46; editor, *New Republic*, 1946–48; Progressive party presidential candidate, 1948.

Despite sharing a Midwestern agrarian background with many prominent isolationists, Wallace was a dedicated internationalist throughout most of his career. For a time during the 1920s, as editor of his family's farm newspaper, *Wallaces' Farmer*, he argued that economic nationalism was the best way to combat the agricultural depression. By 1930, however, he had concluded that international cooperation was necessary to meet the global economic crisis. Wallace's internationalism derived from both his economic views and his religious convictions. Persuaded that America's tariff and war debt policies during the 1920s had contributed significantly to the onset of world depression, he argued that measures to lower trade barriers and foster world economic cooperation were imperative to promote recovery. Wallace also believed that the universal fatherhood of God and brotherhood of man unified the world in a spiritual sense. Anyone who took Christianity seriously, he once wrote, had to incline toward the idea of international cooperation.

As *Franklin D. Roosevelt's secretary of agriculture, Wallace campaigned actively for internationalism. He published numerous books and articles urging the American public to recognize that world cooperation, both economic and spiritual, was necessary to combat the depression and foster peace. He staunchly supported *Cordell Hull's efforts to promote reciprocal trade agreements on an unconditional most-favored-nation basis, and he advised the State Department on its negotiations of the pacts. Wallace also implemented his views by directing the American delegation during the multilateral discussions that led to the International Wheat Agreement of 1933, and by playing an instrumental role in securing U.S. adherence to the Roerich Pact to protect cultural treasures and monuments, signed in 1935.

During World War II, Wallace then serving as vice-president, commanded wide attention as a prominent spokesman for internationalism. He called on Americans to abandon their isolationist traditions and to assume world leadership to bring about "a century of the common man." Unless the United States took action to improve living standards, encourage education, and promote industrialization throughout the world, he contended, it would face a new round of depression and war. Wallace emphasized the importance of establishing an effective international organization and maintaining harmonious relations between the United States and the Soviet Union because he believed that his vision of the postwar world would never materialize in their absence.

Wallace was profoundly disturbed by the course of postwar events. As *Harry S Truman's secretary of commerce, he advocated international control of atomic energy and efforts to ease the growing tensions with the Soviets. He became increasingly outspoken as the Truman administration gradually adopted a posture of firmness in dealing with the Soviet Union. In September 1946, Wallace's public appeal for a more accommodating position led to his dismissal from the Cabinet. After leaving the government, he denounced Truman's foreign policies in nationwide speaking tours and in columns he wrote as an editor of the *New Republic*. He accused the administration of undercutting the fledging United Nations, unnecessarily antagonizing the Soviet Union, dividing the world into hostile camps, and destroying hopes for a century of the common man.

Wallace's belief that Truman had betrayed the ideals for which the war had been fought impelled him to run for president in 1948 as an independent, campaigning for a stronger world order. He insisted that significant numbers of voters would rally behind him, but he made a dismal showing on election day. In the prevailing Cold War atmosphere, Wallace's vision of unity and his call for international cooperation to ensure global peace and prosperity seemed hopelessly naive and unrealistic to the overwhelming majority of Americans.

BIBLIOGRAPHY:

A. *America Must Choose* (New York, 1934); *The American Choice* (New York, 1940); *Democracy Reborn* (New York, 1944); *New Frontiers* (New York, 1934); *Statesmanship and Religion* (New York, 1934); *Toward World Peace* (New York, 1948).

B. John Morton Blum, ed., *The Price of Vision: The Diary of Henry A. Wallace, 1942–1946* (Boston, 1973); DAB supp. 7, 759–63; Russell Lord, *The Wallaces of Iowa* (Boston, 1947); Norman D. Markowitz, *The Rise and Fall of the People's Century: Henry A. Wallace and American Liberalism, 1941–1948* (New York, 1973); NYT 19 Sep 1965, 1; J. Samuel Walker, *Henry A. Wallace and American Foreign Policy* (Westport, CT, 1976); Richard J. Walton, *Henry Wallace, Harry Truman, and the Cold War* (New York, 1976).

C. Wallace papers are in the Manuscript Division, Library of Congress, the Franklin D. Roosevelt Library, and at the Univ. of Iowa. An Oral History is at Columbia Univ.

J. Samuel Walker

WALSH, Edmund A. (10 October 1885, Boston—31 October 1956, Washington). *Education*: B.A., Woodstock Coll., 1902, M.A., 1916; Ph.D., Georgetown Univ., 1920. *Career*: teacher, Georgetown Univ., 1909–18; founder and regent, Georgetown Univ. School of Foreign Service, 1919–55, Institute of Languages and Linguistics, 1949–55; vice-president, Georgetown Univ., 1924–56.

Walsh joined the Society of Jesus, a Jesuit religious order of the Roman Catholic church, in 1902, was ordained to the priesthood in 1916, and after philosophical and theological studies in his own country and at Dublin and London universities and Innsbruck, Austria, he became a member of the faculty of Georgetown University, where he spent most of his career as teacher and administrator. After World War I, he headed a papal relief mission to Russia, a humanitarian program for feeding the people during the Bolshevik revolution. From this contact with the totalitarian government of Stalin he derived his lifelong interest in and wariness toward Communism. The fruit of his preoccupations with the new tyranny appeared in his books, and he was consulted by *Franklin Roosevelt on problems with Russia and by a succession of popes on international matters affecting the Church. He was a fact-finding expert regarding Nazi crimes against religious freedom for Robert H. Jackson at the Nuremberg trials.

Walsh was a pioneer in the new study popularized by the German political theorist *Karl Haushofer, a description of the dynamic of the political and military expansion of nations as determined or at least permanently influenced by the realities of geography. Typical of Haushofer's outlook was his postulate that the European "heartland" of Central and Eastern Europe was the key to the outbreak and conduct of wars. For his students at Georgetown, Walsh wrote his *Syllabus for Two Courses of Study on the Political Economy of Total War Including an Essay on Geopolitics* (1942), which contains the clearest extant short account of what geopolitics is.

Experience in 1918–19 in the War Department convinced Walsh of the need for the study of international relations and languages. Thus, he established the Georgetown University School of Foreign Service (SFS) in 1919. Never before in the United States had there been a school devoted exclusively to the training of diplomats for the United States, and in Walsh's mind of equal importance was the instruction of young men and women in the art and science of international trade. The long-term purpose of the SFS was, as Walsh saw it, the forwarding of peace between nations by means of enlightened diplomacy and by drawing peoples together in more friendly bonds by commercial intercourse. Again, in the avowed interest of international accord, Walsh created his Institute of Languages and Linguistics in 1949. He believed that the more people of different cultures communicated through language, the more likely they would be to understand each other, thus increasing the possibilities for world harmony.

Walsh expressed the philosophy basic to his two educational establishments. "History has one clear lesson: that no nation can long endure which founds its habitual policy on contempt of fundamental human rights and disregard of human relationships" ("The Aims of the School of Foreign Service," Address, 25 Nov 1919, typescript, Georgetown Univ. Archives). It was to the defense of this belief that Walsh's numerous lectures were constantly directed. A keen appreciation of the utility of imaginative literature to education in political science was one of Walsh's chief pedagogical attributes. He realized that politics, since it dealt with the behavior collectivities of people, could be best understood and practiced in proportion to the extent of our knowledge about the way people acted; and nothing was more likely to impart this kind of knowledge than the great novel, poem, or drama. Imaginative literature is the most profound prober of human nature. For this reason, Walsh's two Georgetown University schools included core courses in belles-lettres.

BIBLIOGRAPHY:

A. *The Fall of the Russian Empire* (Boston, 1928); ed., *The History and Nature of International Relations* (New York, 1922); *The Last Stand* (Boston, 1931); *Total Empire: The Roots and Progress of World Communism* (Milwaukee, WI, 1951); *Total Power: A Footnote to History* (Garden City, NY, 1948).

B. DAB supp. 6, 661–62; Louis J. Gallagher, *Edmund A. Walsh, S.J.* (New York, 1962); NCAB 47, 640–41; NYT 1 Nov 1956, 39.

Joseph T. Durkin

WALSH, Thomas James (12 June 1859, Two Rivers, WI—2 March 1933, near Wilson, NC). *Education*: LL.B., Univ. of Wisconsin, 1884. *Career*: schoolteacher and principal in Wisconsin, 1877–83; practiced law, Redfield, Dakota Territory, 1884–90, Helena, MT, 1890–1913; Democratic senator from Montana, 1913–33.

Like *Woodrow Wilson and many other Americans, Walsh became an internationalist in the period of World War I. That event convinced him that it was in the national interest to cooperate with other countries to avert the threat of another great war. During the fight in the Senate in 1919 over the Versailles Treaty and membership in the League of Nations, he ably supported the president. In 1920, however, in the final ballot, he was a leader of those Democrats who favored acceptance of Republican reservations to the Covenant. Only in this way, he argued, could the necessary votes be obtained to pass the Treaty. Walsh also supported the president in his call for a special "security treaty" with France that would guarantee aid to her in the event of an unprovoked attack by Germany. Walsh believed fervently in the necessity of proceeding in new directions in the hope of achieving European stability.

The failure of pro-League forces and the return to power of Republican presidents in the 1920s left Walsh generally discouraged regarding the long-range prospects for international cooperation. He continued to do what he could, however, as a minority senator occupying seats on the powerful Judiciary and Foreign Relations committees. He supported attempts at naval limitation, such as those in Washington in 1921–22 and London in 1930, while believing at the same time that the United States should maintain a Navy as large as that of any country in the world. He supported the movement to renounce war that culminated with the Kellogg-Briand Pact of 1928. He gave his time and legal skills to a continuing fight for membership of the United States in the World Court. This body, he asserted, was important at least as a beginning in juridical cooperation. Though often cooperating with administration Republicans, such as *Frank Kellogg, in their foreign policy efforts, Walsh bitterly opposed the high tariffs of this era, regarding them as a nonsensical deterrent to world trade.

To explain Walsh's ideas and motives is seldom easy. He was an idealist and a moralist of democratic tendencies, and usually a party man as well, to whom Wilsonian principles strongly appealed. A dedicated lawyer, he believed in the possibility of gradually extending the rule of law. Economic and other considerations also affected his decisions. The state of Montana had quantities of copper and wheat to export, and he came to believe after 1914 that questions of international trade, together with other influences, made American involvement in a general war almost inevitable. Thus the need to prevent such wars by fostering orderly trade and the rational solution of disputes that arose. Not surprisingly, Walsh was in some respects a strong nationalist. He never escaped entirely from a degree of anti-British feeling, stemming in part from his Irish origins. He shared in the overwhelmingly critical view of Japanese immigration in the 1920s and supported the policy of exclusion. He could not reconcile himself to the cancelation of European debts owed to the United States, particularly when his Montana constituents were suffering economically and when the money surrendered might be put to mischievous use by Mussolini and other foreign leaders. Meanwhile, he continued through the 1920s to view the League of Nations favorably and to comment occasionally on its good work. Walsh showed a capacity, all in all, to assess foreign policy issues judiciously and to rise to a level of statesmanship that was unusual for his time.

BIBLIOGRAPHY:

A. "America's Aloofness from European Politics Unmodified," *Current History* 27 (Jan 1928), 458–60; "The Urge for Disarmament," *Annals of the American Academy of Political and Social Science* 96 (Jul 1921), 45–48; "We Approach the World Court," *Review of Reviews* 79 (May 1929), 43–46.

B. J. Leonard Bates, "T. J. Walsh: Foundations of a Senatorial Career," *Montana Magazine of History* 1 (Oct 1951), 23–34, "Senator Walsh of Montana, 1918–1924," dissertation, Univ. of North Carolina, 1952; *Christian Century* 50 (15 Mar 1933), 348; DAB 19, 393–95; NCAB 24, 10–11; NYT 3 Mar 1933, 16.

C. The Walsh papers are in the Manuscript Division, Library of Congress.

J. Leonard Bates

WALTERS, Francis Paul (4 June 1888, Castleton, Isle of Man—14 April 1976). *Education*: Univ. Coll., Oxford Univ. *Career*: fellow and tutor in Greek and Latin, Univ., Coll., Oxford Univ.; officer during war, 1914–18; private secretary to *Edward Grey, 1918, to *Robert Cecil during Paris Peace Conference, 1919; personal assistant and then chef de cabinet to League of Nations Secretary-General *Sir Eric Drummond, 1919–33; under secretary-general and director, Political Section, League of Nations, 1 July 1933–31 May 1939, deputy secretary-general, 1 June 1939–29 May 1940.

Walters was the archtypical international civil servant. His entire career was spent in the shadow of more significant figures, beginning with his service as private secretary to Edward Grey and Robert Cecil. At the Paris Peace Conference he assisted Cecil and then Eric Drummond in planning the League of Nations, and then joined the latter as a key behind-the-scenes official, first in London and then in Geneva. As Drummond's righthand man, he earned the reputation of being a highly competent and trusted official.

In 1930 Drummond proposed appointing Walters director of the League's Disarmament Section. The suggestion met with broad approval but ran into German opposition on the ground that such an important and sensitive post should not be held by a national of any of the great powers. Drummond reluctantly gave way before this objection, although he was criticized by knowledgeable observers for not appointing the best man regardless of his nationality.

During the Sino–Japanese conflict that started in September 1931, Walters played an important but unofficial role as Drummond's agent. He traveled to the Far East, visited both China and Japan, and advised the secretary-general to be cautious in proposing sanctions against Japan.

When Drummond retired in June 1933, his successor, *Joseph Avenol, who also had high regard for Walters, named him under secretary-general and director of the Political Section. Then the highest-ranking official of British nationality in the Secretariat, Walters worked closely with Avenol, serving as one of his main channels of communication with London.

After Munich, Walters became increasingly unhappy with the British policy of appeasement, and when after the fall of France to Hitler in May 1940 Avenol seemed to lean toward Vichy and the Axis, Walters resigned from the Secretariat. He would never forgive either the British government or Avenol for betraying the League's ideals.

Walters spent the war years in England, participating with Drummond and other League veterans in discussions at Chatham House on the future of international organization. After the war, with the aid of a Rockefeller Foundation grant, he wrote a masterful history of the League. It was marked by a considerable degree of candor but shed no light on his career as an international official.

While Walters does not seem to have had full-time employment after his retirement from the League, in 1952, following the publication of his book, he was engaged by United Nations Secretary-General *Trygve Lie to evaluate the qualifications for continued service of some four hundred members of the United Nations Secretariat. Walters's last years were spent in retirement in Southern France.

BIBLIOGRAPHY:

A. "Dumbarton Oaks and the League: Some Points of Comparison," *International Affairs* 21 (Apr 1945), 141–45; *A History of the League of Nations* (London, 1952); "San Francisco Conference," *Spectator* 174 (16 Mar 1945), 244; "Yalta Compromise," *Spectator* 174 (6 Apr 1945), 312.

B. LT 27 Apr 1976; NYT 21 Nov 1952, 2 Dec 1952; Christopher Thorne, *The Limits of Foreign Policy: The West, the League, and the Far Eastern Crisis of 1931–1933* (New York, 1973); "United Nations Diary," *United Nations World* 7 (Feb 1953), 40–41; WW 1962, 3186.

Martin David Dubin and Carole Fink

WAMBAUGH, Sarah (6 March 1882, Cincinnati, OH—12 November 1955, Cambridge, MA). *Education*: B.A., Radcliffe Coll., 1902, M.A., 1917. *Career*: assistant, Radcliffe Coll., 1903–6; executive secretary, Massachusetts Branch, Women's Peace Party, 1915–17; expert on mandates, 1919–55; professor, Academy of International Law, The Hague, 1927; lecturer, Institute for Advanced International Studies, Geneva, 1935.

The recognized world authority on the plebiscite, a technique widely used in contested territorial awards after World War I, Wambaugh was an important practitioner of the ideals of internationalism. In 1917, aided by a grant from the Carnegie Endowment for International Peace, she embarked on her pathbreaking investigation of plebiscites since the French Revolution. Her exhaustively researched *Monograph on Plebiscites* influenced the diplomats at Paris, London, and Geneva. Invited to replace the American member of the League of Nations Administrative Commission and Minorities Section of the Secretariat, Wambaugh followed the new organization to Geneva, where she witnessed its first Assembly and its fledgling efforts to establish procedures administered by an international civil service.

Following a one-semester position at Wellesley College (1921–22), Wambaugh returned to Europe. After reviewing the plebiscite in Upper Silesia, she undertook a three-month investigation of the plebiscite areas of Austria, Poland, Denmark, Belgium, and Germany and later published the results. Remaining in Geneva through 1924, she served as expert adviser for the Saar Basin and the Free City of Danzig. In a 1924 article, she maintained that the League of Nations had placed a "healing finger" on Europe's trouble spots. From the Åaland Islands to Corfu, from Upper Silesia to Albania, from the protection of minorities to the establishment of mandates, the League had prevented conflicts. Moreover, it had established the principle of impartial investigation, which she compared favorably with the more politically motivated practices of the victorious Allies.

In 1925–26 she and her lawyer-father aided the Peruvian government in conducting the Tacna-Arica plebiscite that settled the territorial claims between Peru and Chile, with John J. Pershing as the impartial arbitrator. In 1934 Wambaugh joined Italian and Dutch jurists in drafting under League auspices the regulations for the plebiscite held in the Saar in January 1935. As technical adviser and deputy member of the Saar Plebiscite Commission, Wambaugh lived in the volatile region for seven months. Afterwards she received widespread acclaim for its success and wrote the definitive study of the voting.

Wambaugh was a noted lecturer and popular writer. She stressed the achievements of the League, urged American participation, and called for peace and disarmament throughout the interwar years. In 1940 she joined the Commission to Study the Organization of Peace and worked for the establishment of the United Nations. The outbreak of World War II convinced her of the necessity of a world state and an international armed force. During World War II, Wambaugh served as consultant to the director of the Enemy Branch of the Foreign Economic Administration. After the war she was an observer of the Greek elections (1945–46) and advised the United Nations (1949) plebiscite commission in Jammu and Kashmir. She is remembered primarily for her work on plebiscites, a notable contribution to international pacification.

BIBLIOGRAPHY:

A. *La Pratique des plebiscites internationaux* (Paris, 1928); *Monograph on Plebiscites, With a Collection of Official Documents* (London, 1920); *Plebiscites Since the World War*, 2 vols. (Washington, 1933); *The Saar Plebiscite* (Cambridge, MA, 1940); "Why the League Succeeds," *Civic Pilot* 2 (Apr 1924), 9, 31.

B. CB 1946, 619–21; Harold B. Hinton, "She Specializes in Plebiscites," *New York Times Magazine* 17 Feb 1946, 24; NAW 3, 723–24; NYT 13 Nov 1955, 88; WWA 1946–47, 2469.

C. The Wambaugh papers are in the Schlesinger Library, Radcliffe Coll.

Carole Fink

WANDERWELL, Walter [born Valerian Johannes Piecyński] (1897, Poland—5 December 1932, Long Beach, CA). *Education*: unknown. *Career*: world touring promoter, lecturer, film producer.

A Polish-American, Wanderwell was a curious eccentric and enthusiast for the League of Nations and for world touring. He began his first trip around the world in 1919 and in 1923 traveled from Capetown to Cairo. In 1926 he embarked on an expedition consisting of six Ford automobiles and in 1930 drove from Buenos Aires to Panama. He appeared in Geneva in 1925 and was remembered by *Rachel Crowdy because he drove around the city in an armored car accompanied by a young woman dressed as a cowgirl. He also had a fear that the League of Nations was threatened, that a plot existed for its destruction, and that he had been commissioned to save it. Thus, he sought to organize a volunteer international police force for its protection.

On his world tours, especially the one from 1926 to 1928 when he went to Africa and India, Wanderwell lectured on the need for such a unit and its administrative aspects. He also sought a cadre of volunteers to his Wanderwell International Police Force. The League of Nations Archives contains lists of several hundred names of interested volunteers from Canada and Western Europe. He also wanted to design an ideal international flag, and "Law, not War" appeared as a slogan on his letterhead. His eccentricities proved to be embarrassing to League officials, who sought to dismiss him as crazy. He also hoped to create an international house in New York City, but that dream disappeared. In the early 1930s he moved to Hollywood, where he and his wife, Aloha, produced travelog movies designed to extend the world outlook of viewers. He was murdered aboard his yacht, the *Carma*, in Los Angeles Harbor just prior to a planned departure to Latin America and the South Seas. He claimed to have visited forty-three countries on four continents. His wife continued to promote his name and the ideal of world touring through the Walter Wanderwell and Work Around the World Educational Club for International Police.

BIBLIOGRAPHY:

B. Material in League of Nations Archives; NYT, 7 Dec 1932, 1.

C. Wanderwell materials are in the League of Nations Archives.

Warren F. Kuehl

WANG Ch'ung-hui (1881, Hong Kong—15 March 1958, Taiwan). *Education*: graduate, Law School, Peiyang Univ., Tientsin, 1900; LL.M., Yale Univ., 1903, D.C.L., 1905; advanced study in jurisprudence and international law, Germany and England, 1905–7. *Career*: teacher, Nanyang Coll., Shanghai, 1900; editor, *Kuo-min-pao* (newspaper), Tokyo, 1901–2; editor, *Journal of the American Bar Association*, 1904–5; vice-chancellor, Futan Univ., Shanghai, 1913. Offices held in Republic of China: minister of foreign affairs, 1912, 1937–41; minister of justice, 1912, 1921–22, 1927–28; chief justice, Supreme Court of China, 1920–22; premier, 1922; president of judicial yuan, 1928–31, 1948–58; secretary-general, Supreme National Defense Council, 1942–45; aide to head of Chinese delegation, Second Hague Conference, 1907; delegate for revision of the League of Nations Covenant, 1921; delegate, Washington Conference, 1921–22; deputy judge, Permanent Court of International Justice, 1922–25, judge, 1930–36; member, League Committee for the Progressive Codification of International Law, 1925; delegate, San Francisco Conference, 1945.

By the late nineteenth century, the once strong and respected Empire of China had reached its nadir. The many attempts made by Chinese leaders to reinvigorate imperial institutions and restore China's traditional world order came to naught. From the 1890s, a new generation of educated leaders emerged who looked toward establishing new and modern institutions in China and attaining equal status in the international community. Wang Ch'ung-hui was a part and a symbol of this new generation.

Wang was a nationalist, and he was active in trying to destroy the rule of the Ch'ing dynasty; he became a close associate of Sun Yat-sen. Simultaneously Wang became an internationalist, for he realized that the world had changed from the days of China's primacy in East Asia and that international organizations were important in keeping stability in the world. China in attempting to keep her old system came to be dominated by the power politics of imperialism; this, Wang believed could be ended in China and in all nations through strong international organizations. Even though Wang never lost his nationalism, he worked toward strengthening international organizations from his first exposure at the Second Hague Conference in 1907 to his attending the meeting to create the United Nations in San Francisco in 1945.

This gentleman, scholar, diplomat, politician, and internationalist was a man of the twentieth century. Early he realized that only through international organizations could the world community provide security for the nation-state. The high point of his career was when he served as a judge on the World Court from 1931 until 1936. From his training in Chinese law, in Western law, and in international law, and from being a delegate at many international conferences, Wang had gained a worldwide reputation as a legal scholar. He resigned from the World Court in 1936 to take on the onerous duties of foreign ministry in the Kuomintang government.

BIBLIOGRAPHY:

B. Howard L. Boorman, ed., *Biographical Dictionary of the Republic of China* 3 (New York, 1970), 376–78; IWW 1954, 1006; NYT 16 Mar 1958, 87; *Who's Who of Contemporary China: Biographies of Important Personalities of New China* (in Chinese) (Taipeh, n.d.).

Raymond M. Lorantas

WARBURG, James Paul (18 August 1896, Hamburg, Germany—4 June 1969, New York). *Education*: B.A., Harvard Coll., 1917. *Career*: vice-president, International Acceptance Bank of New York City, 1922–29; director, Bank of Manhattan, 1932–35; deputy director, Office of War Information, 1943–45; author, 1934–68; Gandhi Peace Prize, 1962.

As the peace accord signed at Versailles in 1919 unraveled in the 1930s, opinion in the United States split along isolationist/internationalist lines. Within the internationalist camp two more or less distant groupings emerged, the realists and the utopians. Both were interventionist, although for somewhat different reasons. The utopians, mostly former Wilsonians who supported variations of a collective security concept, wanted the United States to intervene in crises in Europe and elsewhere to shore up the failing League of Nations. Collective security could be made to work only if the United States cooperated with the League. They endorsed intervention in the name of principle. Realists, however, supported involvement solely because they believed that it was in the United States' interest to intervene. Largely because he supported the idea of world government after World

War II, Warburg may be thought of as a utopian internationalist. However, while undoubtedly idealistic, he was also a transitional figure who attempted to influence the leaders of both groups.

A financier, public servant, writer, and banker, Warburg at thirty-five was named president of the International Acceptance Bank. A year later he became a director of the Bank of Manhattan, and he subsequently served on the boards of several railroads. Nonetheless, in the early 1930s Warburg severed most of his business ties because he felt that big business had had an unfavorable effect on foreign policy. In 1933 he served as monetary adviser to the American delegation at the London Economic Conference; then he broke with *Franklin Roosevelt over differences on monetary policy and grew critical of the New Deal. As war loomed in Europe in the late 1930s, however, Warburg again offered to support Roosevelt's efforts to aid the Western democracies. He opposed the neutrality acts and urged that an attack on Western Europe should be viewed as an attack on the United States. When the United States entered the war, Warburg became deputy director of the Office of War Information. Warburg largely remained aloof from the public discussions over the role of the United States in a new international collective security after the war. However, once the war ended Warburg again left public service and began to speak for a continuation of foreign policies associated with Roosevelt.

Warburg especially focused on the weaknesses of the Four Power Agreement on Germany, characterizing it as unworkable and a threat to the newly won peace. Also, soon after *Harry Truman assumed office, Warburg criticized the administration's shift from Roosevelt's formula for peace, which focused on principles embodied in the Atlantic Alliance and, especially, cooperation with the Soviets. Thus Warburg emerged as one of the earliest and most vocal of the critics of the Truman Doctrine and the concept of a global policeman.

In 1947, although hardly doctrinaire, Warburg helped found and assumed directorship of the newly formed United World Federalists. The UN's failure to deal effectively with the first postwar crisis had convinced many UWF advocates that only a radically different and stronger international organization could guarantee peace. Total disarmament, the abolition of national armies, world law, universal membership, and a system of weighted representation were required. Permanent peace could not come without world government, and that goal could not be achieved piecemeal or through an evolutionary process.

Despite being critical of the administration's UN policy, most UWF leaders eschewed criticizing specific government actions. International tensions were viewed as a natural byproduct of international anarchy; thus, no one government could be blamed for tensions and disorder. Warburg opposed this "ivory tower" approach as he attempted to get the UWF to speak out on issues, but his efforts went for naught, and UWF stuck largely to its policy of making statements of principle only. After 1948 Warburg, although maintaining his membership in the UWF, decided to pursue his own course and wrote a series of books analyzing U.S. foreign policy. Throughout much of the late 1940s and early 1950s he constituted one of the few influential voices critical of the containment policies of Truman and his successors.

BIBLIOGRAPHY:

A. *Disarmament: The Challenge of the 1960's* (Garden City, NY, 1961); *Faith Purpose and Power* (New York, 1950); *Foreign Policy Begins at Home* (New York, 1944); *How to Co-exist* (Boston, 1952); *Last Call for Common Sense* (New York, 1949); *The Long Road Home: Autobiography of a Maverick* (Garden City, NY, 1964); *Peace in Our Time* (New York, 1940); *Turning Point Toward Peace* (New York, 1955); *The United States in a Changing World* (New York, 1954); *The United States in the Postwar World* (New York, 1966); *Victory Without War* (New York, 1951); *The West in Crisis* (Garden City, NY, 1959).

B. CA 21–22, 561–62; NCAB 56, 231–33; NYT 5 Jun 1969, 47; Thomas G. Paterson, ed., *Cold War Critics* (Chicago, 1971); WWWA 4, 1017.

C. The Warburg papers are in the John F. Kennedy Library.

John F. Bantell

WARD, Paul W. (9 October 1905, Lorain, OH—24 November 1976, Washington). *Education*: Univ. of Akron, 1921–22; West Virginia Univ., 1922–23; B.A., Middlebury Coll., 1925. *Career*: reporter and writer, *New Bedford Standard*, 1926–30, *Baltimore Sun*, 1930–70.

Ward joined the *Baltimore Sun* in 1930 as a business writer and for three decades (1940–70) was its diplomatic correspondent. His lengthy dispatches were in the grand tradition of his British and continental precursors and were treated as standard references by all concerned with foreign affairs in Washington during World War II and the Cold War. During the New Deal he specialized in the work of the emergency agencies. His debut in international affairs came after he was named head of the London Bureau of the *Sun* in 1937. He correctly predicted in detail the outcome of the Munich Conference of 1938, Hitler's subsequent seizure of Prague, and Mussolini's preparations for the Albanian invasion. He covered France until it fell and then served as a correspondent for a Free French publication until the liberation.

Formally named diplomatic correspondent in 1940, Ward established a reputation for covering international conferences, notably Dumbarton Oaks and San Francisco. His reports did much to educate Americans to changing conditions after 1945. While in Moscow in 1947 for the extended Foreign Minister's Conference, he wrote a series, "Life in the Soviet Union," for which he received the Pulitzer Prize in 1948. Published as a book, it was translated into several languages. Ward became a confidant of many notable international figures, including diplomats, secretaries of state, and presidents, and he was often consulted by officials and other correspondents because of his remarkable memory and linguistic ability. Ward continued for the last six years of his life as the *Sun's* Washington Bureau manager.

BIBLIOGRAPHY:

A. *Life in the Soviet Union* (Baltimore, MD, 1947).

B. *Baltimore Sun* 25 Nov 1976, A-1, A-18; NYT 25 Nov 1976, 32.

J. B. Donnelly

WARREN, Earl (19 March 1891, Los Angeles—9 July 1974, Washington). *Education*: B.L., Univ. of California, 1912, J.D., 1914. *Career*: law practice, 1914–17; U.S. Army, 1917–18, clerk, California legislature, 1919; city attorney, Oakland, 1920; deputy district attorney and chief deputy attorney, Alameda County, 1923–39; California attorney general, 1939–43; governor of California, 1943–53; chief justice, U.S. Supreme Court, 1953–69.

Warren is not usually thought of in the context of the United Nations; yet his contributions to the development of the UN Association of the United States were significant. His deep interest in young people and his commitment to the advancement of human welfare through the rule of law were the strong underpinnings of his strong support of the UN.

After his retirement as chief justice, he remained an officer of the Supreme Court and thus was extremely reluctant to assume outside activities not directly related to the interests of the Court. However, his friend, former Associate Justice Arthur Goldberg, persuaded him that the objectives of the UN and the values that he had fought for so courageously were in harmony. Once having made the decision to accept the chairmanship of the United Nations Association (UNA) in May 1970, he never stinted in his activity.

He welcomed opportunities to visit campuses and speak about the UN. His door at the Court was always open to the representatives of youth groups interested in international organization and peace. Although the officers of the UNA had told him, in deference to his position, that he would not be asked to participate in fund-raising activities, as soon as he learned the Association was seeking to create a scholarship fund in honor of *Ralph Bunche to attract minority young people into the field of international relations, he volunteered to fly to Chicago and speak at a major fund-raising event.

Meetings of international jurists and legal associations immediately went on his calendar. A speech he made in Nigeria on international communications and human rights remains a valuable contribution to policy formulation in this still-emerging field.

During his tenure as chair of the UNA, which lasted until his death, he inspired another imaginative contribution to the education of young people in international affairs. Each summer hundreds of college students serving as public service interns came to Washington. Warren realized that, while they were receiving a valuable experience in domestic affairs, little was being done to broaden their international outlook or their awareness of the UN. He thus assumed leadership of a series of Seminars on the United Nations for Congressional Interns, which reached out also to the executive and judicial branches. The opportunity to attend such sessions under the leadership of a former chief justice whose record in the Court was of particular interest to young people met with enthusiastic response. Each year, when asked if continuation of the activity imposed on his time, he responded that he gained more from the experience than the young people did.

None of his biographers pay special attention to Warren's international interest, and some ignore it entirely. This he would regret deeply.

BIBLIOGRAPHY:

A. *The Memoirs of Earl Warren* (Garden City, NY, 1977).

B. NCAB I, 24–27; NYT 10 Jul 1974, 1; Jack H. Pollack, *Earl Warren, the Judge Who Changed America* (Englewood Cliffs, NJ, 1979); John D. Weaver, *Warren: The Man, the Court, the Era* (Boston, 1967); G. Edward White, *Earl Warren: A Public Life* (New York, 1982).

Porter McKeever

WATSON, Thomas John, Sr. (17 February 1874, East Campbell, NY—19 June 1956, New York). *Education*: one-room schoolhouse and Addison Academy, Painted Post, NY; Miller School of Commerce, Elmira, NY, 1892. *Career*: salesman, W. F. Bronson Co., 1892–95, National Cash Register Co. (NCR), 1895–99; branch manager, Buffalo office of NCR, 1899–1904; special representative, NCR, 1904–8; general sales manager for NCR, Dayton, OH, 1908–14; president, Computing-Tabulating-Recording Co., 1914–24; president, International Business Machines Corp., 1924–49; chairman of the board and chief executive officer, IBM and IBM World Trade Corp., 1949–56.

A self-made businessman, Watson devoted much energy to public and civic activities intended to promote the exchange of goods both domestically and internationally. He adopted an internationalist perspective soon after embarking on his career as a salesman. Influenced by John Patterson, the strong-willed executive of the National Cash Register Company whose motto was "The World Is Our Field," Watson was one of those businessmen whose practical internationalism was fostered by his deeply rooted belief in the importance of promoting world trade.

During the 1930s, Watson supported the New Deal, championed *Cordell Hull's reciprocal trade agreements, and wished to strengthen the League of Nations. No nation, he believed, could become economically self-sufficient. Conditions created by the Depression and the rise of Fascism, however, would not be resolved by governments and politicians; they were economic problems and could be most effectively dealt with by businessmen and industrialists. Watson expressed his internationalist ideal that unfettered commerce could ensure world peace through his work as a trustee of the Carnegie Endowment for International Peace (CEIP). Its head, *Nicholas

Murray Butler, was a friend Watson admired second only to Patterson. To the International Chamber of Commerce, where he served as president (1937–39), Watson brought his missionary zeal because its program harmonized with his conception of the "basic laws of the universe." Through the ICC he strove to adjust international trade issues and promote agreements in such fields as limitation of armaments and stabilization of currencies. He assumed leadership in the cooperative efforts of the ICC and the CEIP to lower barriers to international trade. He coined the phrase, "World Peace Through World Trade," which became one of the slogans of IBM and the ICC. In 1937 Watson made a five-month tour of Europe to develop fuller exchange. He spoke with financial leaders as well as heads of state, including Hitler and Mussolini, and came back confirmed in his belief about the importance of moving goods and not armies across borders.

As a result of World War II and the Cold War, however, Watson modified his internationalism. He continued to seek increased trade but realized that it was not a panacea. He believed that America must not only be militarily prepared but also assume world leadership by its own example. He never doubted the moral superiority of the free enterprise system and viewed the Cold War in the same way that he looked at competition in business. Believing in the necessity of American economic aid abroad, he supported the Marshall Plan, seeing it as international rather than a national approach to economic problems. He strongly supported the United Nations and served as a director of the American Association for the United Nations. Indeed, the UN in Watson's mind replaced the ICC as the hope of the future. The changing world situation increased his confidence in the efficacy of governmental and political organizations and modified his earlier belief in the primacy of economics, especially the virtues of trade, for solving the world's problems. His ideas provide one example of a significant shift in internationalist thinking in America marked by World War II and the beginning of the Cold War.

BIBLIOGRAPHY:

A. *Men, Minutes and Money: A Collection of Excerpts from Talks and Messages Delivered and Written at Various Times* (New York, 1934).

B. Thomas G. and Marva R. Belden, *The Lengthening Shadow* (Boston, 1962); CB 1940, 845–46, 1950, 600–2; DAB supp. 6, 673–76; NCAB 47, 1–4; NYT 20 Jun 1956, 1; William H. Rodgers, *THINK: A Biography of the Watsons and IBM* (New York, 1969); WWWA 3, 895.

C. The IBM Corporation possesses the Watson papers.

John Greco

WEBSTER, Charles K. (25 April 1886, Freshfield, Liverpool, England—21 August 1961, London). *Education*: King's Coll., Cambridge Univ., 1904–9. *Career*: professor, Liverpool Univ., 1914, Aberystwyth Univ., 1922–23, Harvard Univ., 1923–32; Univ. of London, 1932–53.

Webster is best remembered as a noted scholar and teacher of international history, but he effectively combined scholarly interests with practical service, acknowledging that it is by action that one is made most keenly aware of the limitations which human nature imposes on the conduct of policy. Always fascinated by the mechanics of policy making, Webster insisted that how decisions are made is as important as the decisions themselves.

Having decided by the time of his election to a fellowship at King's College, Cambridge, in 1909, to devote himself to the study of British foreign policy in the nineteenth century, he emerged after World War I as a specialist in international affairs, then a new field of study. While working on the foreign policy of Castlereagh, he helped prepare material for the British delegation at Paris, and he there served as secretary of its Military Section. In the interwar years he popularized, by extensive speaking, the study of international affairs in the universities and the country at large. Many of his appearances were under the auspices of the League of Nations Union, and Webster played a considerable role in the formation of an opinion in Britain sympathetic toward international organization. He was also active in the Royal Institute of International Affairs from its foundation.

Traveling widely to lecture and teach, writing (including a book on *The League of Nations in Theory and Practice*, with Sidney Herbert, 1933), and making a strong impact on the University of London from his Stevenson Chair of International History, Webster was well along in a study of Palmerston's foreign policy when World War II began. He became deputy of the Chatham House Foreign Research Service and then was transferred (1943) to the Reconstruction Department, where he and Gladwyn Jebb contributed to the drafting of the UN Charter. He attended the Dumbarton Oaks Conference in July 1944 and the San Francisco meeting in 1945. There he presented the British position while on the committee responsible for the security sections of the Charter. Later (1945–46) he served as a special adviser to the minister of state on United Nations affairs and was involved in the UN Preparatory Commission and its Executive Committee.

Returning to academic life, he completed his two-volume work on Palmerston (1951), served for four years (1950–54) as president of the British Academy, and, after retirement, devoted much time to writing. Meanwhile, he continued to be active at international discussions and conferences. Especially noteworthy was his stalwart work for UNESCO. He sat as a member of United Kingdom delegations to UNESCO's General Conference, was a leading member of the UK's National Commission for UNESCO, and became involved in many volunteer societies and associations of scholars and scientists through which it worked.

BIBLIOGRAPHY:

A. *The Art and Practice of Diplomacy* (New York, 1962); *The Congress of Vienna, 1814–1815* (London, 1919); *The Foreign Policy of Castlereagh, 1815–1822*,

2 vols. (London, 1925, 1931); *The Foreign Policy of Palmerston, 1830–1841*, 2 vols. (London, 1951).

B. LT 23 Aug 1961, 10; NYT 23 Aug 1961, 33.

William R. Rock

WEHBERG, Hans (15 December 1885, Düsseldorf, Germany—May 1962, Geneva). *Education*: univ. studies in Jena, Bonn; doctor of law, Göttingen Univ., 1908. *Career*: *referendar* in Prussian civil service, 1909–16; editorial board, *Zeitschrift für Völkerrecht*, 1912–14; member, Institut für Weltwirtschaft und Seeverkehr, Kiel, 1917–19; editor, *Die Friedenswarte*, 1924–62; professor, Geneva Institute of International Studies, 1928–59; general secretary, Institut de Droit International, 1950–62.

Wehberg was one of the most influential international lawyers in Central Europe during his long career as academician and publicist. The son of a physician who was also a social activist, Wehberg became interested early in the field of international law, owing largely to the influence of Philipp Zorn, with whom he studied in Bonn, and to the Hague Conferences. After taking his doctorate, he entered the Prussian civil service but pursued the study of international law as an avocation. He came under the influence of ⁺Alfred Fried and *Walther Schücking, both of whom were arguing that the domain of international law should be extended to the point of creating an international organization empowered to resolve all international disputes by arbitration. Although not yet thirty years old when World War I began, Wehberg had become a prominent figure among a small group of progressive German international lawyers, he was a leading member of the Verband für internationale Verständigung, and he served, with Josef Kohler and Robert Oppenheim, on the editorial board of the *Zeitschrift für Völkerrecht*.

During the war, Wehberg's personal and philosophical association with Schücking became closer as they attempted both to promote a compromise peace and to help lay the foundation of an effective international organization at the war's end. In 1918–19 Wehberg served on the German commission drafting proposals for a society of nations. In the early 1920s, he devoted his efforts, both as a leader of the German Peace Society and in his capacity as chairman of the Legal Section of the Deutsche Liga für Völkerbund, to secure Germany's entry into the League of Nations and to rectify what he, like Schücking, held to be the grave injustices to Germany contained in the League Covenant.

Within the German peace movement Wehberg spoke for the tradition of Schücking, Fried, and ⁺Ludwig Quidde in insisting that the abolition of warfare could only come by means of the extension of international law and the creation of international legal and political institutions. He was opposed in this view by more radical sectors of the German peace movement, which contended that the end of warfare was contingent upon a massive refusal to bear arms or upon social revolution.

Wearied of the tensions within the peace movement, Wehberg eagerly accepted an academic position in 1928 at the Geneva Institute of International Studies which *William Rappard and Paul Mantoux had recently founded. Wehberg moved there, and his influence as an international lawyer grew. As an academician he lectured and supervised dissertations on specialized topics of longstanding interest to him, such as disarmament, international law in time of war, international mediation, and the concept of outlawing war. As successor to Fried as editor of *Die Friedenswarte*, he attempted to kindle popular interest in international law and organization beyond a circle of specialists. He also served, from 1950 to 1962, as general secretary of the Institute of International Law, an organization with which he had long been associated.

Wehberg never wavered in his belief that an international organization had to be empowered not only to mediate and adjudicate disputes but to enforce its decisions, if necessary, by military means. This was the only feasible alternative to international anarchy. Like his activity after World War I, his efforts after 1945 were directed at making the international organization established by the victor powers more capable of fulfilling what he held to be its potential.

BIBLIOGRAPHY:

A. *Der internationale Gerichtshof* (Offenbach, Germany, 1948); *Der Kampf um die Reform des Völkerbundes (1920-1934)* (Geneva, 1934); *Die internationale Beschränkung der Rüstungen* (Stuttgart, Germany, 1919); with Walther Schücking, *Die Satzung des Völkerbundes, kommentiert* (Berlin, 1921); *Internationale Schiedsgerichtsbarkeit* (Berlin, 1911).

B. *Die Friedenswarte* 56 (1961/66), 297–418; Peter K. Keiner, "Bürgerlicher Pazifismus und 'neues' Völkerrecht: Hans Wehberg (1885–1962)," dissertation, Freiburg Univ., 1976); Walter Schaetzel and Hans-Jürgen Schlochauer, eds., *Rechtsfragen der internationalen Organisation. Festschrift für Hans Wehberg zu seinem 70. Geburtstag* (Frankfurt, Germany, 1956); Solomon Wank, introduction to Wehberg, *Die internationale Beschränkung der Rüstungen*, rpt. ed. (New York, 1973).

C. The Wehberg papers are in the Bundesarchiv, Coblence.

Roger Chickering

WELLES, Sumner (14 October 1892, New York—24 September 1961, Bernardsville, NJ). *Education*: B.A., Harvard Univ., 1914. *Career*: secretary, Tokyo embassy, 1915–17, Buenos Aires, 1917–19; assistant chief, Latin American Affairs Division, 1919–20, chief, 1920–22; Commission to Dominican Republic, 1922; mediated the Honduran revolution in 1924; resigned from State Department in 1925; assistant secretary of state for Latin American affairs, 1933–37; ambassador to Cuba, 1933; under secretary of state, 1937–43; delegate, Buenos Aires Conference, 1936, Panama

Conference, 1939, Rio de Janeiro Conference, 1942, European peace mission, 1940.

Although Welles began his diplomatic career early in World War I, he did not seriously promote in *Woodrow Wilson's dream of an international organization until the outbreak of World War II. At that time Welles established and chaired a State Department committee to examine postwar problems. While that body's deliberations proceeded slowly, the under secretary started to speak publicly about a future world organization. In an address on 22 July 1941, he closely associated hemispheric (his special concern) and global peace under the same heading. Later in the year he warned an audience that the United States' failure to follow Wilson's crusade after World War I must not be repeated.

The under secretary broadened the scope of his postwar committee's planning activities once the United States entered the war. His public declarations on a future international organization also became more frequent and explicit. On 30 May 1942, he called for a worldwide police force and economic stability. Within his concept, Pan Americanism occupied a key position in achieving these goals. He wanted the inter-American system to form a cornerstone of the new world organization.

During his last years in office, Welles reiterated and refined several themes: the hope for a lasting peace, a major U.S. role in postwar international relations, and a functional world organization that made provision for wide-ranging regional initiatives. Using these ideas as his base, he discouraged calls for an American League of Nations because the world body would grant the Americas sufficient latitude to supervise their internal affairs.

Welles's resignation in 1943 abruptly changed the State Department's emphasis on Latin America in the world body. Secretary of State *Cordell Hull and his chief subordinates turned toward a more universal organization which would end spheres of influence. Welles aggravated the conflict within the State Department over the regional versus universal approach when he lobbied for his regional plan from a public forum. *Roosevelt, he argued, had to provide leadership in creating international stability by first negotiating an accord among the major Allies and then building a global structure with an executive committee where regional associations reported. Throughout 1944 he continued his press campaign. The State Department, he said, needed to solicit advice from nations like Brazil and Mexico. He refined his conceptualization of the world order. Using his rationale, hemispheric multilateralism formed the foundation for any world federation, and the region should therefore have autonomy to settle internal disputes. Welles's publications stimulated widespread discussion, but within the foreign service they only served to reinforce Hull's antipathy toward whatever Welles promoted.

Even though Welles did not attend the San Francisco Conference or directly participate in formulating the results, his views affected the outcome. The Latin American delegates had no intention of having the United Nations Organization destroy Pan Americanism. Thus, the inter-American delegates led in the fight for the passage of Article LI, which provided for collective self-defense without Security Council permission, and for Article LII, which allowed regional arrangements that would try to achieve peaceful settlements of local problems, and Article LIV, which reaffirmed the Security Council's interest in regional agencies and their role in the maintenance of world peace.

Welles never again participated in diplomatic affairs. He strongly supported the idea of the United Nations in private, and he did edit a book, *An Intelligent American's Guide to The Peace* (1945) to publicize the ideal of world cooperation, but did not take an active role in advancing the world organization's goals. In the early 1950s, he did lament that if Roosevelt had survived the war in good health the world would have been very different.

BIBLIOGRAPHY:

A. ed., *An Intelligent American's Guide to the Peace* (New York, 1945); *Naboth's Vineyard: The Dominican Republic, 1824–1924*, 2 vols. (New York, 1928); *Seven Decisions That Shaped History* (New York, 1950–51); *The Time for Decision* (New York, 1944); *We Need Not Fail* (New York, 1948); *Where Are We Heading?* (New York, 1946); *The World of the Four Freedoms* (New York, 1943).

B. DAB supp. 7, 776–78; Irwin F. Gellman, *Good Neighbor Diplomacy: United States Policies in Latin America, 1933–1945* (Baltimore, MD, 1979), *Roosevelt and Batista: Good Neighbor Diplomacy in Cuba, 1933–1945* (Albuquerque, NM, 1973); Frank Graff, "The Strategy of Involvement: A Diplomatic Biography of Sumner Welles, 1933–43," dissertation, Univ. of Michigan, 1971; Peter F. Krogh, "The United States, Cuba and Sumner Welles: 1933," dissertation, Fletcher School of Law and Diplomacy, 1966.

C. The Welles papers are in the Franklin D. Roosevelt Library.

Irwin F. Gellman

WELLS, Herbert George (21 September 1866, Bromley, Kent, England—13 August 1946, London). *Education*: Normal School of Science (later Royal Coll. of Science), London, 1884–87; B.S., London Univ., 1890. *Career*: teacher, Henley House School, London, 1889–90, Univ. Tutorial Coll., London, 1890–93; freelance writer, 1893–1946.

The founder of futurism as a science in its own right, a pioneer of science fiction, and the author of more than a hundred books, Wells was one of the most broadly popular writers in the English language during the first quarter of the twentieth century. He had the literary gifts to do almost anything he pleased. But the ruling passion of his professional life was to help achieve the integration of mankind as a single community governed by a meritocracy of men and women schooled in the world view of modern science. This *idée fixe* appears in some of his earliest essays and was first expounded systematically in 1902 in *Anticipations*. Wells returned to his vision of world order in many books, especially in the second half of his life. Of his fictional treatments of world order, the best is a novel, *The Shape of Things to Come*, converted by Wells into the screenplay for Alexander Korda's film, *Things to Come*. The novel foresees the outbreak of a second world war in 1940, the collapse of civilization, and its eventual recovery. A world movement of technocrats establishes a planetary state in 1978. The closing chapters trace the withering away of its governmental apparatus in the next century as an enlightened mankind outgrows the need for rulers.

In addition to his copious writing, Wells was a leader of important British initiatives to promote world order. In 1918 he helped launch the League of Free Nations Association. He also organized a committee of distinguished public figures who drafted a comprehensive Declaration of the Rights of Man in 1940. But Wells would have objected to being remembered as an "internationalist." His cause, all his life, was a scientifically planned unitary world state, not a federation of sovereign nations. He withdrew his support from the League of Nations as soon as he realized that it would not constitute a true world government. The word that sums up his point of view, in its original Greek sense, is *cosmopolitan*, a champion of world polity.

BIBLIOGRAPHY:

A. *Anticipations of the Reaction of Mechanical and Scientific Progress Upon Human Life and Thought* (London, 1902); *Experiment in Autobiography* (London, 1934); *The New World Order* (London, 1939); *The Open Conspiracy: Blue Prints for a World Revolution* (London, 1928); *The Rights of Man* (London, 1940); *The Shape of Things to Come* (London, 1933).

B. DNB 1941–40, 944–49; *Encyclopaedia Britannica* 19 (Chicago, 1974), 757–59; *Encyclopedia of World Literature in the 20th Century* 3, 499–501; Norman and Jeanne MacKenzie, *H. G. Wells: A Biography* (London, 1973); W. Warren Wagar, *H. G. Wells and the World State* (New Haven, CT, 1961); WWW 1941–50, 1219.

C. The Wells papers are in the Library of the Univ. of Illinois.

W. Warren Wagar

WHEATON, Henry (27 November 1785, Providence, RI—1 March 1848, Dorchester, MA). *Education*: graduate, Rhode Island Coll. (later Brown Univ.), 1802; private study and travel, 1802–5. *Career*: admitted to Rhode Island bar, 1805; lawyer, Providence, 1806–12; editor, *National Advocate*, 1812–15; divisional judge advocate, U.S. Army, 1814; chief justice, Marine Court, New York, NY, 1815–19; reporter, U.S. Supreme Court, 1816–27; member, New York State Assembly, 1824; U.S. chargé d'affaires, Denmark, 1827–35; chargé (later envoy), Prussia, 1837–45; corresponding member, Academy of Moral and Political Sciences, Institute of France, 1842.

Modern writing on international law begins with the publication of Wheaton's *Elements of International Law* in 1836. Lawyer, diplomat, editor, scholar, Wheaton was well qualified to write the book that went through many editions in English as well as in French, Spanish, Italian, Japanese, and Chinese.

The leisurely diplomacy of the early nineteenth century afforded time for Wheaton to discharge his duties and still pursue his studies. While on assignment in Denmark and Prussia, he wrote reviews and literary and scientific papers and published books in English and French, including a history of Scandinavia and a history of the law of nations. His major contribution to internationalism, however, is his work on international law.

Throughout his career, Wheaton was immersed in the specifics of the law. Like Edmund Burke, he believed that general principles take their distinguishing shape and effect from specific circumstances. In the *Elements*, the general abstractions of earlier writers are fleshed out and shown in action through Wheaton's incomparable command of relevant detail. As an example, in his discussion of agreements between nations, Wheaton set out the subject in general terms drawn from the classic treatments of Grotius, Vattel, and *Martens. Then he took the general principles into the field and applied them to the specific case of property titles in the United States and Great Britain. He brought into play the treaties of 1783 and 1794 to show how such accords could function to protect property against forfeiture for alienage, even through the renewed hostilities of 1812. Here Wheaton drew on decisions of the U.S. Supreme Court and the English Court of Chancery to enrich with contemporary examples his discussion of an old question in international law.

Wheaton wrote when European contacts with non-Europeans around the world had generated abundant litigation. Here, too, his book has a modern tone. He used examples from Turkey, Egypt, the Barbary States, China, the Philippines, and the Indian nations of North America. It was a time of stretching for the ethnocentricity of the law as it had come to Wheaton, and because he stretched his vision to match, his work provided a useful framework for those who came after him, when contacts and conflicts were still more frequent.

In one respect Wheaton stood firmly with earlier writers on international law. He insisted that human reason was one of its sources. Through reason, people could apprehend international law's higher sanction, the law of nature. That, in turn, was only another name for the law of God, the ultimate source of justice. Not for him the positivism of some later writers who limited the sources of law to the custom and convention of nations. The decision of one editor of Wheaton's *Elements* to omit the sections on ethics would have shocked the original author. For Wheaton, ethics was inseparable from the whole discussion, and in that, too, he revealed a distinctly modern tone.

BIBLIOGRAPHY:

A. *Digest of the Law of Maritime Captures and Prizes* (New York, 1815); *Elements of International Law* (London, 1836); *Enquiry into the Validity of the*

British Claim to a Right of Visitation and Search . . . in the African Slave Trade (London, 1842); *Histoire des progrès du droit des gens en Europe depuis la paix de Westphalie jusqu'au congres de Vienne* (Leipzig, 1841); *History of the Law of Nations in Europe and America*, enl. ed. (New York, 1845); *Reports of Cases . . . Supreme Court of the United States*, 12 vols. (Philadelphia, 1816–27).

B. Elizabeth F. Baker, *Henry Wheaton, 1785–1848* (Philadelphia, 1937); DAB 20, 39–42; *Encyclopedia Britannica* 28 (Chicago, 1968), 583, 23 (Chicago, 1973), 472–473; Warren F. Kuehl, introduction to Wheaton, *History of the Law of Nations in Europe and America*, rpt. ed. (New York, 1973); *La Grande Encyclopédie* 31 (Paris, 1971), 1211.

C. The Wheaton papers are in the Pierpont Morgan Library and at the Brown Univ. Library.

Dorothy V. Jones

WHEELER-BENNETT, John W. (13 October 1902, Keston, Kent, England—9 December 1975, London). *Education*: Malvern Coll. *Career*: independent intelligence gatherer and unofficial adviser to British officials on international relations, 1920s–1930s; professional historian, author, lecturer (after 1945) at Oxford and other leading universities; British editor-in-chief, German Foreign Ministry archives (1946–48).

Known primarily as a distinguished historian and authority on international affairs, Wheeler-Bennett was a committed internationalist both in his general outlook and in his wide-ranging contacts with notable persons in many countries. Growing to manhood during the World War and impressed by *Woodrow Wilson's struggle for sanity in diplomacy and ideals, he was, like others of his generation, indelibly influenced by the horror of the great conflict. His interest in international affairs, and in particular the role played by Germany in the postwar settlement of Europe, was awakened when he served with the British Military Mission in Berlin after the Armistice. In 1924 he created the Information Service on International Affairs. He went to Germany to live while traveling extensively and began issuing a fortnightly publication, *The Bulletin of International Affairs*, which lasted until 1955. He quickly gained a reputation as an astute observer of world politics whose views were widely sought. Writing books on the problems of security, disarmament, and reparations, he also worked in the publicity department of the League of Nations Union (1923–24) and was closely associated with the Royal Institute of International Affairs, at length merging his Information Service with it and becoming its director of information. His books on Hindenberg (1936) and Brest–Litovsk (1939) solidified his reputation in governmental, journalistic, and academic circles as an authority on Germany. He held no official post during these years but was frequently consulted by British officials on questions concerned with Germany.

With the outbreak of World War II, Wheeler-Bennett's international perspective became more detached and scholarly. He served in Washington, in

New York, and in the Political Intelligence Department of the Foreign Office and in the Political Adviser's Department in Supreme Headquarters of the Allied Expeditionary Forces (SHAEF). He was attached to the British prosecution team at the Nuremberg trials in 1946. Teaching appointments at Oxford and other leading universities in Britain and America followed, as did his selection as British editor-in-chief of the captured archives of the German Foreign Ministry. Notable books on Munich, the German Army, King George VI, Viscount Waverley, and the postwar settlement raised him to the first rank among historians.

Wheeler-Bennett's principal interest lay in the theory and practice of diplomacy. He was fascinated by the interplay of arresting personalities and by the parts played by audacity and espionage, by the fortuitous, the gallant, and the unforeseen in human affairs. Modest and diffident, but erudite and wise, he both chronicled the pageantry of international history through scrupulous and indefatigable research and writing and shared his understanding directly with others in positions of power and influence. He probably understood generals, diplomats, and politicians as well as any Englishman, and he sought to enlighten others in the interest of constructive international relationships. By all accounts a warm-hearted person, he sought to reduce the differences which divide men by underscoring a basic humanity which knows no artificial bounds.

BIBLIOGRAPHY:

A. *The Forgotten Peace: Brest-Litovsk, March 1918* (London, 1938); *The Wooden Titan: Hindenburg in Twenty Years of German History, 1914–1934* (New York, 1936); *Knaves, Fools and Heroes: In Europe Between the Wars* (New York, 1974); *Munich: Prologue to Tragedy* (London, 1948); *The Nemesis of Power: The German Army in Politics, 1918–1945* (New York, 1954); with Anthony Nicholls, *The Semblance of Peace: The Political Settlement After the Second World War* (London, 1972); *Special Relationships: America in Peace and War* (New York, 1975).

B. LT 10 Dec 1975, 19.

William R. Rock

WHITE, Andrew Dickson (7 November 1832, Homer, NY—4 November 1918, Ithaca, NY). *Education*: graduate, Yale Univ., 1853. *Career*: professor, Univ. of Michigan, 1857–63; New York State senator, 1864–66; president, Cornell Univ., 1865–85; minister to Germany, 1879–81, to Russia, 1892–94; Venezuela Boundary Commission, 1896; ambassador to Germany, 1897–1902; president, American delegation, to First Hague Peace Conference, 1899.

Although White is known primarily as a reformer of higher education, he was deeply interested in international relations throughout his long career. Shortly after his graduation from Yale, he served as an attaché to Thomas H. Seymour, minister to Russia. During the next year White traveled through much of Europe, forming impressions of national, political, and cultural styles. When he returned to the United States as an educator, he also retained his interest in a diplomatic career.

Several times mentioned as a possible secretary of state, White never quite reached the level of policy maker. His numerous diplomatic assignments probably resulted from his service to the Republican party and to the prestige his name carried in intellectual circles. As a commissioner to Santo Domingo in 1871, he recommended annexation, but the Senate rejected the treaty. As minister to Germany, he attempted without success to help avoid a tariff and monetary war between Germany and the United States, but the dispute was settled in a court of arbitration. Appalled by the treatment of Russian Jews, White wrote sympathetic dispatches that won him the praise of American Jews, but he saw no way to persuade the Russian autocracy to stop the persecution. Appointed by Grover Cleveland to a commission investigating the Venezuela boundary dispute, White began work only to find that the British had yielded and submitted the issue to arbitration.

White's deep respect for German culture made his appointment as ambassador a happy one, with contact with German intellectuals and excellent rapport with the foreign ministry. One incident, however, marred his tenure. White believed that the United States did not want to acquire any Spanish colonies in the Pacific during the Spanish-American War and therefore may have encouraged German aspirations for the Philippines. Rebuked by his government, White drew back in embarrassed confusion and exercised care thereafter.

Appointment as head of the American delegation to the First Hague Peace Conference was the capstone of White's diplomatic career. The conference was significant, he believed, less for its accomplishments than for its effect on public opinion. The signatories agreed to create a permanent panel for arbitration but made participation voluntary; White joined his colleagues in resisting any arrangement that might imperil the national interest or weaken the Monroe Doctrine. The Hague meeting, he concluded, had introduced rational discourse to international affairs; the outlook for peace was hopeful indeed. In the final decade of his life, White's optimism turned to despair when his beloved Germany attacked Belgium and World War I began. He died before it ended, but he probably shared the conviction that this would be "the war to end all wars."

BIBLIOGRAPHY:

A. *Autobiography of Andrew Dickson White*, 2 vols. (New York, 1905); *The Diplomatic Service of the United States with Some Hints Toward Its Reform* (Washington, 1905); *The First Hague Peace Conference* (Boston, 1912); *Seven Great Statesmen in the Warfare of Humanity with Unreason* (New York, 1910).

B. Glenn C. Altschuler, *Andrew D. White: Educator, Historian, Diplomat* (Ithaca, NY, 1979); Calvin D. Davis, *The United States and the First Hague Peace Conference* (Ithaca, NY, 1962); DAB 19, 88–93; Frederick Holls, *The Peace Conference at the Hague* (New York, 1900).

C. White papers are at Cornell Univ.

Glenn C. Altschuler

WHITE, William Allen (10 February 1868, Emporia, KS—29 January 1944, Emporia). *Education*: Coll. of Emporia, 1884–86; Univ. of Kansas, 1886–90. *Career*: journalist and editor, Kansas and Missouri, including *Kansas City Star*, 1884–95; editor-owner, *Emporia Gazette*, 1895–1944; author, fiction and nonfiction, 1893–1944; politician, 1896–1944.

White's early writings emphasized local and national affairs, disdaining most overseas issues; however, after 1913 he became interested in the world. White dismissed the Balkan Wars, 1912–13, as of little consequence to the United States, but he kept abreast of subsequent events, and his 1914–16 editorials supported neutrality because both sides were blameworthy. In 1915 White became an advocate, and vice-president, of the League to Enforce Peace because he understood the need for U.S. participation in international organizations devoted to peacekeeping.

White observed the Versailles Conference, 1919, and supported membership in the League of Nations, perhaps with Lodge-type reservations as a means to assure ratification. He spoke in favor of the League and signed the Statement of the 31 prominent Republicans that said that in 1920 a vote for Harding was the best way to bring the United States into an effective league. He should have known better. White urged U.S. aid to rebuild Europe after the war, and he later contended that self-centered, economic, nationalist maneuvering at Paris led to World War II.

The Midwestern editor participated from 1920 to 1940 in organizations advocating multinational cooperation, opposing the isolationist Republican factions and his own Midwest locale. He served on the board of the Woodrow Wilson Foundation and was a director of the League of Nations Association, a judge of the Bok Peace Prize, a friend of U.S. membership in the World Court, and a member of the Education Committee in the Interests of World Peace. Various other peace, disarmament, and neutrality movements claimed White's interest. He responded warmly to the Washington Conference, 1921–22, and believed the treaties would force more international participation by the United States. Favorable to the Kellogg-Briand pact to renounce war as an instrument of national policy, White nevertheless sensed its weaknesses. He wrote a biography in 1924 of *Woodrow Wilson which he described as "a vindication" of Wilson.

A critic of U.S. intervention in Latin America, White proposed respect for Latin America and withdrawal of American troops. *Herbert Hoover appointed him a commissioner to investigate the U.S. occupation of Haiti. White editorially supported the Good-Neighbor Policy and lauded the Reciprocal Trade Agreements Act (1934) because it countered economic nationalism. He earlier opposed protective tariffs, especially the Hawley-Smoot bill (1930). White also dissented from the widespread international boycott of the Bolshevik regime. After 1918, contrary to much national and international sentiment, he insisted upon the right of the Soviet peoples to form a government of their choosing.

As events unfolded leading to World War II, White urged international cooperation to halt "aggressor" nations, perhaps through boycotts. In 1932 he proposed U.S. joint effort to end the Japanese military action in Manchuria. Contrariwise, White endorsed neutrality legislation from 1935 to 1939, but after Germany's invasion of Poland he worked for U.S. aid to the Allies "short of war." He led a committee of influential persons determined to revise the neutrality laws to allow Britain and France to purchase arms on a "cash-and-carry" basis. White's influential editorials attacked isolationism. In May 1940 he united with *Clark Eichelberger of the League of Nations Association to found the Committee to Defend America by Aiding the Allies, sometimes called the White Committee. The CDAAA supported U.S. aid which might obviate U.S. military participation in the war. It mobilized public opinion for the destroyer bases agreement with Britain. White supported Roosevelt's lend-lease program. After the United States entered the war, White continued to write and speak favorably regarding international goals and organizations.

BIBLIOGRAPHY:

A. *The Autobiography of William Allen White* (New York, 1946); for an almost complete bibliography of White's writings, see *A Bibliography of William Allen White*, 2 vols. (Emporia, KS, 1969); ed., *Defense for America* (New York, 1940); *The Martial Adventures of Henry and Me* (New York, 1918); *The Old Order Changeth* (New York, 1910); *Woodrow Wilson, the Man, His Times, and His Task* (Boston, 1924).

B. DAB supp. 3, 815–18; David Hinshaw, *A Man from Kansas* (New York, 1945); Walter Johnson, *William Allen White's America* (New York, 1947); NCAB 11, 95; NYT 30 Jan 1944, 38; Everett Rich, *William Allen White: The Man from Emporia* (New York, 1941).

C. The White papers are in the Manuscript Division, Library of Congress.

William W. Cuthbertson

WICKERSHAM, George Woodward (19 September 1858, Philadelphia— 25 January 1936, New York). *Education*: Lehigh Univ., 1873–75; LL.B., Univ. of Pennsylvania, 1880. *Career*: legal practice, Philadelphia and New York, 1880–1909, 1914–36; U.S. attorney general, 1909–13.

Although Wickersham gained his greatest fame in the areas of domestic and business law, he maintained an active interest in international affairs throughout his life and remained a constant champion of internationalism. He supported the Allied cause during World War I, and he served the government as a special agent in trade negotiations during the conflict. Convinced of the necessity of using international law to promote world peace, Wickersham supported the activities of *Woodrow Wilson at Paris in attempting to create a just peace. He left his legal practice to act as a special correspondent for the *New York Tribune* in Paris, reporting on the activities of the conference.

In the debate over the League of Nations, Wickersham joined with other moderate Republicans in urging membership with minor reservations. Like his close friend *William Howard Taft, Wickersham supported the concept of the League, hoping that collective security could end war. He rejected the nationalistic concerns of *Henry Cabot Lodge and other strong reservationist Republicans as failing to recognize the new complexities of America's position as a world power. The debate over the League became confused by the existence of many groups urging support, each one with different suggestions. While most of the country expected the treaty to be approved by the Senate, internationalists such as Wickersham hoped to modify the treaty to produce maximum American flexibility within the overall framework of international law. Wilson's nonyielding posture complicated the struggle within the Senate, making the final vote on approval confusing.

Wickersham joined other internationalist-minded Republicans during the 1920 campaign urging the election of Warren G. Harding as president in order to bring the executive and legislative branches into a unity. Only in this way would it be possible to gain American entry into the League of Nations. He signed the Statement of the 31 in which prominent Republicans argued that a vote for Harding was the best way to ensure membership in an effective league. Harding's later rejection of this route disappointed Wickersham. Yet he remained loyal to internationalist causes during the 1920s. Late in 1922 he helped form the League of Nations Non-Partisan Association. He headed its Council until early in 1928, when he became its president. Wickersham did not hesitate to criticize Republican administrations for their narrow perspective toward the world, yet he would not support efforts to commit that party's platform to League membership. He believed that the wise course was to educate people about the constructive work of the League and hope for later results. Wickersham favored disarmament negotiations, urged the approval of the Five Power Treaty of the Washington Conference; endorsed adjustments in the difficult war debts/ reparations questions, and called for the cancelation of all war debts. He also served as president of the international arbitration tribunal under the Young Plan to modify German reparations payments. When the League of Nations established an international commission to codify international law, Wickersham became the American member.

Wickersham was one of that number of Americans in the early years of the twentieth century who saw law as the most efficacious remedy for the problems of the nation, both in domestic affairs and in international relations. He supported Taft's efforts as president to achieve international arbitration agreements as a means of forestalling war and settling disputes. He also saw the laws as the means of achieving a just social order. In later life he became embroiled in controversy as head of the National Commission of Law Observance and Enforcement, particularly on those sections dealing with the enforcement of the Eighteenth (Prohibition) Amendment. Wickersham represented that middle ground of American internationalism in the first three decades of the twentieth century in which leaders sought to apply their beliefs on domestic law to the world arena. As they struggled to create a sense of order at home, so too did they seek international order.

BIBLIOGRAPHY:

A. *The Changing Order* (New York, 1914); with others, *The Covenanter* (New York, 1919); *Thoughts Concerning the League of Nations* (New York, 1919?); *The World Court; How It Began; How It Works; What It Has Done* (New York, 1927).

B. DAB supp. 2, 713-15; WWWA 1, 1342.

C. Wickersham papers are in the Manuscript Division, Library of Congress.

Frank W. Abbott

WILBUR, Ray Lyman (13 April 1875, Boonesboro, IA—26 June 1949, Stanford, CA). *Education*: B.A., Stanford Univ., 1896, M.A., 1897; M.D., Cooper Medical Coll. (now Stanford Univ. Medical School), 1899. *Career*: lecturer, Cooper Medical Coll., 1898-1900; assistant professor, Stanford Univ., 1900-1903; private practice, 1904-9; professor, Stanford Univ., 1909-11; dean, Stanford Univ. Medical School, 1911-16; president, Stanford Univ., 1916-43, chancellor, 1943-49; chief, Conservation Division of Food Administration, 1917-18; secretary of the interior, 1929-33.

Wilbur attained fame as an educator and public servant, making real contributions in both areas. In various posts at Stanford (1909-49), he helped it develop into one of the nation's leading universities while remaining conscious of undergraduate needs. Friendship with *Herbert Hoover led naturally to public service, which he began as head of the Conservation Division of Hoover's Food Administration during World War I. There he coined the popular slogan, "Food Will Win the War." With Hoover's election to the presidency, Wilbur became secretary of the interior, where he devoted special attention to conservation. He reorganized the Bureau of Indian Affairs, increasing health and educational facilities available to the Indians and encouraging greater autonomy for the Indian reservations.

Wilbur also found time for participation in world affairs. His internationalist perspective was spurred by medical study in Frankfurt-am-Main, Vienna, and London (1903-4) and in Munich (1909-10). Given the location of California and the number of Japanese-Americans and Chinese-Americans living there, Wilbur became interested in the Far East and served as chairman of the Institute of Pacific Relations (1925-27), organized to reduce racial tensions between the people of East Asia and the United States and to increase understanding. This assignment led to extensive visits to Japan, China, and Korea. He was an American delegate to the Sixth Pan-American Congress in Havana in 1928, serving on Committees on Social Problems and Intellectual Cooperation. All of these activities, as well as America's participation in World War I, convinced him of the importance of developing international understanding. He thus viewed with sadness deteriorating relations between the United States and Japan in the 1930s.

He continued his connection with the Institute of Pacific Relations after World War II, even when it became the subject of criticism for being a "Communist front" organization. He defended the Institute and its activities as furthering world understanding.

Wilbur's views toward broader international involvement were more mixed. He endorsed Republican administration positions in the 1920s which opposed membership in the League of Nations while endorsing participation in the World Court. Then, in 1938, he joined *Anita McCormick Blaine's World Citizens Association (WCA), where he showed considerable commitment to advancing the ideal of community while doubting the need for elaborate political systems. He served as chairman of the WCA (1938–43) and presided over its noted Owentsia Conference in 1941. In all his international involvements, Wilbur emphasized that people had to move from national to world thinking, and as a concerned citizen he sought to advance that end.

BIBLIOGRAPHY:

A. *The Hoover Policies* (New York, 1937); *Human Hopes: Addresses and Papers on Education, Citizenship and Social Problems* (Stanford, CA, 1940); *The Memoirs of Ray Lyman Wilbur, 1875–1949* (Stanford, CA, 1960).

B. *Biographical Directory of the United States Executive Branch, 1774–1977* (Westport, CT, 1977), 358; DAB supp. 4, 891–95; A. Guerard, "Ray Lyman Wilbur," *Nation* 168 (30 Jun 1949), 111; *The Secretaries of the Department of the Interior* (Washington, 1975), 237–45; *The Vice Presidents and Cabinet Members* 2 (Dobbs Ferry, NY, 1975), 563–65.

C. The Wilbur papers are at Stanford Univ.

Eugene P. Trani

WILEY, Alexander (26 May 1884, Chippewa Falls, WI—26 October 1967, Philadelphia). *Education*: Augsburg Coll., 1902–4, Univ. of Michigan Law School, 1904–6; LL.B., Univ. of Wisconsin, 1907. *Career*: lawyer, 1907–38; district attorney, Chippewa Falls, 1909–15; Republican U.S. senator, 1939–63.

The gregarious son of Norwegian immigrants, Wiley changed from isolationist to internationalist as a freshman U.S. senator. Before Pearl Harbor, Wiley shared the noninterventionist sentiments of his Wisconsin constituents and most Republican legislators. Although advocating military preparedness, he opposed repeal of the arms embargo, peacetime selective service, and lend-lease. By 1943, however, Wiley had begun supporting *Franklin D. Roosevelt's foreign policies. Totalitarian expansionism, American economic and military power, awesome wartime technology, and vastly improved world transportation and communication convinced Wiley that the United States should take the lead in promoting peace. He even proposed a Cabinet-level Department of Peace to prevent global wars and promote international cooperation.

After becoming a member of the Foreign Relations Committee in 1945, Wiley increasingly backed a bipartisan foreign policy. He joined *Arthur H. Vandenberg and other Republicans in advocating an American political, economic, and social partnership with non-Communist nations. Besides desiring to safeguard his country's interests, he urged advancing those of other like-minded countries. In 1945 he vigorously endorsed the Bretton Woods monetary agreement and approval of the UN Charter. Seeing the UN as a significant new adventure and pathway to peace, Wiley encouraged the United States to fulfill its responsibilities to promote peace, justice, and prosperity. Yet as a staunch anti-Communist, Wiley insisted on American control of the atomic bomb, backed a controversial $3.7 billion loan to Great Britain in 1946, favored military and economic assistance to Greece and Turkey in 1947, defended the Marshall Plan in 1948, and supported NATO, SEATO, and other collective security organizations. In 1947 he urged that the United States favor the creation of a United Democratic State of Europe excluding Communist nations.

Wiley often represented the United States at international conferences. He attended the Inter-Parliamentary Union meetings in Oslo (1939), Bern (1952), Helsinki (1955), and London (1957), and the British Empire Parliamentary sessions in Bermuda (1946 and 1948). He also participated in the Japanese Peace Conference in San Francisco and the Council of Europe at Strasbourg, France (1951), the UN General Assembly (1952), and the Inter-American Economic Conference in Rio de Janeiro (1954). Bucking state and party sentiments, Wiley steadfastly promoted a bipartisan foreign policy and world cooperation, particularly with anti-Communist nations.

BIBLIOGRAPHY:

A. Robert A. Divine, *Second Chance: The Triumph of Internationalism in America During World War II* (New York, 1967); Justus D. Doenecke, *Not to the Swift: The Old Isolationsts in the Cold War Era* (Lewisburg, PA, 1979).

B. BDAC 1961, 1815; CB 1947, 679–81; Mary McGrory, "An Outsider Views Senator Wiley," *Milwaukee Journal* (26 Apr 1953), 1; NYT 27 Oct 1967, 45.

C. The Wiley papers are at the State Historical Society of Wisconsin.

David L. Porter

WILLKIE, Wendell Lewis (18 February 1882, Ellwood, IN—8 October 1944, New York). *Education*: B.A., Indiana Univ., 1913, LL.B., 1916; Oberlin Coll., 1916. *Career*: attorney, Ellwood, IN, 1916–19; U.S. Army, 1917–18; lawyer, Akron, OH, 1919–32; president, Commonwealth and Southern Corporation, 1933–40; Republican presidential candidate, 1940.

Almost until the moment of his nomination as Republican candidate for president in 1940, Willkie was primarily known as a liberal business leader, indeed a Democrat who opposed specific New Deal programs while endorsing the principle of government intervention in the economy. Although he had desired American membership in the League of Nations in the 1920s, he spoke out with force on foreign policy only after Denmark and Norway fell in April 1940. His endorsement of aid to Britain and France helped to catapult him to the presidential nomination and thereafter made him a leading spokesman for internationalism.

During the 1940 campaign, Willkie endorsed defense preparations, the destroyer bases agreement, and the draft, while claiming that *Franklin Roosevelt's general posture was too warlike. Although Willkie lost, he continued to call for aid to Britain. Once the United States entered the war, Willkie dedicated himself, with mixed success, to converting the Republican party to internationalism. He was unable to purge the party of isolationists in the 1942 congressional primaries but saw his party's National Committee in April of that year pledge itself to postwar international cooperation.

With Roosevelt's encouragement, Willkie embarked on a world tour. Boarding a converted bomber, the *Gulliver*, in August 1942, and accompanied by *Look* publisher Gardner Cowles and *New York Herald Tribune* correspondent Joseph Barnes, Willkie flew 31,000 miles in forty-nine days. In the Middle East he stressed the need for an orderly transition to self-government. In the Soviet Union he met with Stalin, called Soviet-American postwar cooperation essential, and publicly echoed the Soviet demand for a second front, an act which led to much criticism. His journey reached its climax in China, where he forged a friendship with Generalissimo and Madame Chiang Kai-shek and where he also learned that the communist leader Chou En-lai was leading "a national and agrarian awakening." In Chungking he demanded a "firm timetable" for the liberation of colonial peoples, a slap at the British that irritated Roosevelt. His initial report over the radio was heard by 36 million people.

Willkie also described his trip in his book *One World* (1943), a work that enjoyed a phenomenal distribution of more than 2 million copies. Over a hundred daily newspapers printed an abbreviated version. In this work he combined anecdotal description of his trip with a sermon on internationalism, one that proclaimed that America's destiny was intimately connected with the fate of other continents. Peace, he went on, must be planned on a world basis, with the United States launching the process by establishing a United Nations Council with representatives from all member states. He also stressed the inevitability of colonial liberation, a development that, if encouraged, would result in a global partnership based upon economic and political justice.

In the last two years of his life, Willkie grew more outspoken. He endorsed a proposal, spearheaded by Minnesota Senator Joseph H. Ball, calling for a postwar United Nations police force. His attempt to win the Republican nomination in the presidential primaries of 1944 failed despite considerable popular support. He had antagonized party wheelhorses and neglected to build an organization. Like *Woodrow Wilson in 1918, he made the campaign a vote of confidence in his internationalism. He won only six of eleven delegates in New Hampshire, a state he had hoped to sweep, and in Wisconsin he failed to win a single delegate. In the ensuing presidential race he refused to support either Roosevelt or Thomas E. Dewey, the standard-bearer of his own party, claiming that neither candidate was facing squarely the issue of international organization. Limiting the sovereign power of all nations to make war, he said, was necessary to create an effective world body. In a series of newspaper articles published posthumously, Willkie declared that the age of economic imperialism had ended. He called for international currency stabilization, long-term investment in underdeveloped areas, and a world organization in which small nations had a genuine voice.

Willkie was neither a profound nor a systematic student of international politics. Some of his observations, especially those concerning Russia and China, were superficial. Yet because of his ability to reach the people he brought a global consciousness to many Americans, capturing their imagination in a way that no other wartime leader could. He was thus able to neutralize much isolationism within the Republican party as he developed an awareness of and sympathy for Third World aspirations.

BIBLIOGRAPHY:

A. *An American Program* (New York, 1944); *One World* (New York, 1943).

B. Ellsworth Barnard, *Wendell Willkie: Fighter for Freedom* (Marquette, MI, 1966); DAB supp. 3, 828–30; Robert A. Divine, *Second Chance: The Triumph of Internationalism in America During World War II* (New York, 1967); Donald B. Johnson, *The Republican Party and Wendell Willkie* (Urbana, IL, 1960); WWWA 2, 582.

C. There are Willkie papers in the Franklin D. Roosevelt Library, at Indiana Univ. and in Rushville, IN.

Justus D. Doenecke

WILLOUGHBY, Westel Woodbury (20 July 1867, Alexandria, VA—26 March 1945, Washington). *Education*: B.A., Johns Hopkins Univ. 1888, Ph.D., 1891. *Career*: professor, Johns Hopkins Univ., 1895–1933; constitutional adviser to the Chinese government, 1916; technical expert to Chinese delegation to Washington Conference, 1921; counselor and adviser to Chinese delegations at International Opium Conference, 1924–25, to League of Nations Conference on Narcotic Drugs and legal adviser to Chinese representative on the Council of the League of Nations, 1931; for several years in the 1930s adviser to the Chinese legation in Washington.

The revolution in China in 1911 ended the long reign of the Manchus, followed in 1912 by the establishment of a republic under a provisional constitution. Republicanism, however, did not bring the order and prosperity its leaders cherished. Many decades of misgovernment, corruption, and, worst of all, foreign intervention had created a political, economic, and social climate that prevented an easy transition to republican government. Moreover, by 1913 two separate governments had emerged disputing for central authority, one at Peking and one at Canton.

Beginning in 1913 the Chinese employed eminent American political scientists as advisers as part of an effort to make China a constitutional republic on the Western model. Willoughby was the third academician to serve in that capacity. Out of his advisory experiences both in China and at various conferences came a number of publications, all well received by the academic community; some became standard works in their fields. In 1920 he published *Foreign Rights and Interests in China* (revised in 1927 and enlarged to two volumes), an authoritative book on extraterritorial rights, spheres of interest, special interests, war zones, leased territory, treaty ports, concessions, settlements, legation quarters, commercial concessions, and revenue services under foreign control in China. Willoughby looked at all these violations of China's sovereignty with misgiving.

His appointment as a technical expert to the Chinese delegation to the Washington Conference on Limitations of Armament and Pacific and Far Eastern Questions (1921–22) resulted in the publication of *China at the Conference*. Willoughby saw Japan as China's principal enemy and viewed the Conference's chief task as restraining an imperialistic Japan. He was largely responsible for drafting the ten points which China presented in an attempt to gain the respect of the major powers to the territorial integrity and the political and administrative independence of China.

At a League of Nations conference on the traffic in opium in 1924–25 Willoughby served as China's adviser. From this experience came his *Opium as an International Problem* (1925), which described the discussions from which both China and the United States withdrew when it became apparent that decisions would not be acceptable to the two countries. The discussions had sought to limit production of opium to no more than what was needed for medical and scientific purposes, to stop the legalized traffic in prepared opium, and to control the international movement of such drugs. None of these goals was reached, according to Willoughby, because of the economic interests of the colonial powers.

After his retirement in 1933, Willoughby published two books, both on international topics: *The Sino-Japanese Controversy and the League of Nations* (1935), and *Japan's Case Examined* (1940). Both are substantial contributions to the literature on the troubled Far East, revealing of an important international servant.

BIBLIOGRAPHY:

A. *China at the Conference* (Baltimore, MD, 1922); *Foreign Rights and Interests in China* (Baltimore, MD, 1927); *Japan's Case Examined* (Baltimore, MD, 1940); *Opium as an International Problem* (Baltimore, MD, 1925); *The Sino-Japanese Controversy and the League of Nations* (Baltimore, MD, 1935).

B. DAB 3, 830–31; William H. Hatcher, "The Political and Legal Theories of Westel Woodbury Willoughby," dissertation, Duke Univ., 1961; NCAB 13, 435.

C. Some Willoughby papers are in the Johns Hopkins Univ. Library.

William H. Hatcher

WILSON, George Grafton (1 April 1884, Plainfield, CT—30 April 1951, Cambridge, MA). *Education*: B.A., Brown Univ., 1886, M.A., 1888, Ph.D., 1891; Univs. of Heidelberg, Berlin, Paris, Oxford, 1890–91. *Career*: school principal, Groton, CT, 1886–87, Rutland, VT, 1889–90; associate to professor, Brown Univ., 1891–1910; professor, Harvard Univ., 1910–36; lecturer, U.S. Naval War Coll., 1900–1937, Fletcher School of Law and Diplomacy, 1933–36.

Although *Who Was Who in America* lists him as a "publicist," Wilson, a prolific writer, built his reputation as a professor of international law specializing in maritime and naval codes. He began his distinguished career in 1891 at Brown University teaching social and political science but in 1894 switched to international law. While at Brown, Wilson began lectures in international law at the Naval War College which he continued for thirty-seven years. This new interest coincided with a burst of pioneering scholarship. Wilson published *Insurgency* in 1900, which was followed a year later by *Submarine Telegraph Cables in Their International Relations*. That year also marked the appearance of a textbook, *International Law*, a product of Wilson's collaboration with George Fox Tucker, which ran through ten editions. In 1902 Wilson inaugurated one of his most auspicious projects when under the Naval War College imprint he began to publish an annual *International Law Situations*. These monographs, numbering 36 volumes and totaling 7,000 pages, applied precedents, regulations, and instructions to hypothetical maritime situations, thereby providing naval officers with precise answers to problems which might be encountered at sea. In his essays Wilson concealed his personal view, permitting the reader to interpret the basic information. Wilson left Brown in 1907 for Harvard, where he remained until retirement. He also helped establish Tufts University's Fletcher School of Law and Diplomacy. Wilson's reputation as an excellent teacher twice carried him overseas; he taught for a year at the University of Paris (1912–13) and at the Académie de Droit International at The Hague (1923).

While Wilson was interested in expanding the body and knowledge of international law, he avoided public and political activities aimed at promoting legislation or institutions. He did work, however, outside academia. From 1895 through 1916 he attended the Lake Mohonk Conferences on International Arbitration, and in 1906 he joined delegates such as *James Brown Scott, *David Jayne Hill, and *John Bassett Moore to organize the American Society of International Law. Active from the onset, Wilson edited and contributed to the society's *American Jounral of International*

Law. He was a plenipotentiary delegate to the 1908–09 London Naval Conference and in 1914 served as the American legation's counselor at The Hague. Following World War I, he advised the American delegation at the Washington Naval Conference and helped to settle Dutch claims for ships seized during the war. Wilson joined the U.S. Maritime Commission in 1941, and held that post until his death in 1951.

Throughout his long career, Wilson believed that nations had common interests which could be regulated by law, thereby reducing friction and the likelihood of war. International legal systems offered the best promise for order and peace. He thought courts and legislation would render better decisions and prove more enduring because justices, basing their opinions on established "fact" and legal precedent, were less prone than politicians to be swayed by popular passions or expediency. For those nations that would not respect international legal custom, he advocated nonrecognition. But for effective law continual revision was essential lest statutes become outdated.

At his death, Wilson was no doubt disappointed that international law had not produced enduring peace. Yet, despite two world wars, the body of international law had grown. This situation would have pleased him.

BIBLIOGRAPHY:

A. *The First Year of the League of Nations* (Boston, 1921); *The Hague Arbitration Cases* (Boston, 1915); *Insurgency* (Washington, 1900); *International Law* (New York, 1901); *International Law*, Hornbook series (Boston, 1910); *International Law Situations*, 36 vols. (Washington, 1902–37); *Submarine Telegraph Cables in Their International Relations* (Washington, 1901); ed., Wheaton's *Elements of International Law* (Oxford, 1936).

B. AJIL 45 (1951), 549–52; DAB supp. 5, 751–52; NCAB 47, 78–79; NYT 2 May 1951, 31; WWA 3, 926.

Daryl L. Revoldt

WILSON, Hugh Robert (29 January 1885, Evanston, IL—29 December 1946, Bennington, VT). *Education*: B.A., Yale Univ., 1906; Ecole Libre des Sciences Politiques, Paris. *Career*: private secretary to American minister, Lisbon, 1911; secretary of legation, Guatemala, 1912; posts in Buenos Aires, Berlin, Vienna, Washington, Bern, and Tokyo, 1913–24; chief, Division of Current Information, 1924–27; minister to Switzerland, 1927–37; secretary-general, Conference for Limitation of Naval Armaments, Geneva, 1927; adviser and delegate, Preparatory Commission and Disarmament Conference, Geneva, 1928–30, 1932–37; assistant secretary of state, 1937–38; ambassador to Germany, 1938–39; Office of Strategic Services, 1941–45.

For thirty-five years, 1911–46, Wilson was actively concerned with American foreign affairs as a diplomat or close observer of foreign policy. He entered the Foreign Service in 1912 as a diversion from business routine to travel and study. The years 1912–27 saw him occupying low-ranking posts in Latin America, Europe, and Japan.

In 1927 he became minister in Switzerland, where for ten years he reported on American relations with the League of Nations. Much work concerned such technical matters as prisoners of war, export–import prohibitions, and counterfeit currency suppression. Mainly his energies were directed toward disarmament conferences to which he was a delegate, although ordinarily he was outranked by specially appointed American emissaries, usually *Hugh Gibson or *Norman Davis.

Invariably limited by U.S. policy, Wilson's association with the League was restricted in matters like arms control, the Manchurian Crisis, the Italian–Ethiopian incident, and disarmament difficulties. His government considered many issues to be European-related, so officials chose not to become involved. Wilson developed an attachment to internationalist principles, as embodied in the League, which he had to subordinate to official policy. Sometimes he personally advocated American action only to see his suggestion overridden. Frankly, Wilson believed that only the highest-ranking world leaders could successfully resolve the major impediments to disarmament.

Wilson was a quiet but considerably competent diplomat. During the 1930s he gradually concluded that the United States should deal with its own interests and not be concerned with other nations' affairs. Yet he disliked a moralistic formulation and conduct of foreign relations. Despite a limited contribution to policy making, he represented the United States well at Geneva.

In January 1938 he became ambassador to Germany, hoping it would be the peak of his diplomatic career, but he was disappointed. Strained German–American relations, primarily over Nazi persecution of Jews, led to his recall in November and his resignation in August 1939. He left the Foreign Service in 1940. During World War II he served in the Office of Strategic Services, concentrating on the prospective postwar international environment. In 1945 and 1946, as a foreign affairs adviser to the Republican National Committee he advocated close Soviet–American cooperation to head off the separation of the world into two antagonistic persuasions and to further world peace.

BIBLIOGRAPHY:

A. *Diplomat Between Wars* (New York, 1941); *The Education of a Diplomat* (New York, 1938); *For Want of a Nail: The Failure of the League of Nations in Ethiopia* (New York, 1959).

B. CB 1941, 926–28; DAB supp. 4, 897–99; Marvin Downing, "Hugh R. Wilson and American Relations with the League of Nations, 1927–1937," dissertation, Univ. of Oklahoma, 1970; NYT 30 Dec 1946, 19.

C. The Wilson papers are in the Hoover Presidential Library.

Marvin L. Downing

WILSON, Mary Florence (29 January 1884, Lancaster, PA—4 January 1977, La tour de Peilz, Switzerland). *Education*: Drexel Inst., Univ. of Pennsylvania Extension; Columbia Univ. *Career*: librarian, Columbia Univ., 1909–17; librarian and researcher, the Inquiry, 1917–18, librarian, American Commission to Negotiate Peace, 1918–19, League of Nations, 1919–27; researcher, Carnegie Endowment for International Peace, 1927–29.

Although Wilson did not furnish any novel ideas to the body of internationalist thought, her efforts had an important impact upon two international organizations. She began her career in 1909 at Columbia University, offering classes in cataloguing and classification and organizing several departmental libraries. She developed a special interest in international relations, which prompted *Edward M. House's invitation in 1917 to establish a library for the Inquiry, then in need of data for its study of European issues. Her acceptance led in turn to an assignment with the American Commission to Negotiate Peace. Her excellent work at Paris caused *Raymond Fosdick, as League of Nations under secretary-general, to request in 1919 that she join the infant international agency as assistant librarian. Fosdick wished to bind the United States to the League by offering Americans positions, and he hoped that U.S. standardized methods of cataloguing would bring a high level of efficiency to the central League library then taking shape.

The League Secretariat soon elevated Wilson to the post of chief librarian, and in 1920 she was the only woman library director in Europe. Like Fosdick, Wilson envisaged a research library that would meet the needs of League delegates and staff and provide solutions to complex international problems. Wilson worked diligently to acquire materials, train a staff, catalog and classify acquisitions, and satisfy book and document demands. She also established an archives for League publications and a weekly index to journals. These efforts proved so successful that by 1922 the library had outgrown its quarters, leading Wilson to seek a new building from American library circles friendly toward the League. By 1926 Fosdick, then an adviser to *John D. Rockefeller, Jr., enlisted *Abraham Flexner to convince Rockefeller to fund construction and endow a magnificent library.

Wilson did not participate in the planning or serve in the new structure. In 1926 she fell victim of male chauvinism, and her contract was not renewed. Sexism, however, could not erase her contributions. The procedures she introduced remained in effect until the League's end and were later adopted by the UN library.

After leaving the League, Wilson briefly traveled through Europe and the Near East for the Carnegie Endowment for International Peace. She compiled bibliographies for the Endowment, lectured in Paris at the Ecole de Bibliothécaires, and published a documentary history of the League's Covenant. In the 1930s she abandoned these activities, devoting her energies to volunteer work in Europe.

BIBLIOGRAPHY:

A. "The Library of the League of Nations" *Library Journal* 47 (15 Dec 1922), 1057–61; *Near East Educational Survey* (London, 1928); *The Origins of the League Covenant: Documentary History of Its Drafting* (London, 1928).

B. Mildred Adams, "Librarian to the World," *Everybody's Magazine* 53 (Dec 1925), 141, 182; Doris Cruger Dale, "An American in Geneva: Florence Wilson and the League of Nations Library," *Journal of Library History* 7 (Oct 1972), 366–71; NCAB C, 420; WWA 1940–41, 2789; *Who's Who of American Women and World Notables* (Chicago, 1970–71), 1344–45.

Daryl L. Revoldt

WILSON, Thomas Woodrow (28 December 1856, Staunton, VA—3 February 1924, Washington). *Education*: Davidson Coll., 1874–75; B.A., Princeton Univ., 1879, M.A., 1882; LL.B., Univ. of Virginia, 1881; Ph.D., Johns Hopkins Univ., 1886. *Career*: practiced law, Atlanta, 1882–83; associate professor, Bryn Mawr Coll., 1885–88; professor, Wesleyan Univ., 1888–90; professor, Princeton Univ., 1890–1910, president, 1902–10; governor of New Jersey, 1911–13; president, 1913–21.

More than any other American, indeed any world leader, the name of Wilson is linked with the ideal of international organization and collective security. As president during World War I, Wilson forcefully articulated the need for a liberal peace program, including a postwar concert of nations to replace the balance-of-power system. At the Paris Peace Conference, he chaired the commission which drafted the Covenant for the League of Nations. Then he undertook a major campaign, including a dramatic speaking tour of the United States, to convince the people and the Senate to approve the Treaty of Versailles and thereby bring the nation into the League. That he failed in this attempt—and almost died as a result—only served to strengthen the association of the man with the ideal he had labored to bring to birth.

The sources of Wilson's ideas about the nature of international order are inevitably complex and deep-rooted. No doubt the most important single influence on him was his religion. It significantly shaped not only his political beliefs and moral values but also virtually all aspects of his personal relationships. As taught by his father, a distinguished Presbyterian, Calvinism viewed the world as an organic whole, its temporary disturbances at last made orderly by God's law. Individuals were required to take an active role in fulfilling divine purposes. When conflicts arose in the world, they were to be seen as confrontations between contending principles of right and wrong, not simply as struggles between ordinary mortals.

Along with his reading of English social theorists, Presbyterianism helped Wilson form a belief in human progress and the capacity of people for self-government. While individuals were capable of determining their own self-interest, they realized their full humanity only in service to others. Wilson accepted the view that individuals desired power and influence and that it was proper to seek positions of leadership; but leadership must always be exercised altruistically. Wilson would carry this set of assumptions into his foreign policy, and they would allow him to reconcile pursuit of national interests with professions of international disinterestedness.

Wilson had long believed that the most disinterested nation was the United States. First, Americans were unique in their diversity. They had been "compounded out of the peoples of the world," as he remarked at a Memorial Day address in 1916. Therefore, they were always wrestling with the problem of union, melding their individual selves into a stronger whole. Moreover, their successful experience with the federal system of government gave them great advantages in understanding the difficulties of effecting harmony among political units of differing size and resources. As early as 1887, Wilson wrote that nations were exhibiting a tendency, "as yet dim, but already steadily impulsive and clearly destined to prevail," toward federation into ever larger systems. Such would fail, he said, if it did not preserve the independence of individual nation-states while ensuring cooperation and interdependence of the nations united. Those who would solve this problem would "pilot the world."

That Wilson had seen himself from an early age as a "pilot" of sorts was manifested through his well-known penchant for writing constitutions. Perhaps the corollary to the structuring of the world by divine law was the human effort to achieve order through covenants or constitutions. From his first constitution that has survived, written when he was seventeen, to that of the League of Nations, evidence abounds of the impact of Scottish covenant theology on his view of leadership and power.

As the United States thrust outward in the late nineteenth century, leading to friction with a number of countries and to war with Spain, Wilson added his voice to those nationalists calling for expansion. In 1897 Wilson noted that the nation's history had been one of continuous and stupendous growth, bringing many problems. America's interests had to move forward, and other countries should stand back and not hinder the United States. Growth was important not only economically. It was vital as well for the nation's democratic ideals. Ideals at home could not be realized if allowed to be discredited in the eyes of people seeking liberty, order, peace, and progress.

Wilson's primary concerns before he became president were, like those of his contemporaries, largely domestic in nature. Yet his academic preparation in foreign affairs was far superior to most of his predecessors in the White House. Still, he had not been one of the leaders in that group of Americans in the early twentieth century who campaigned to strengthen international institutions or who saw the United States as the leader in that cause. Although he joined the American Peace Society in 1908, he was never a strict pacifist. Abhorring war as a means of settling disputes, he nevertheless accepted it as a nation's only alternative in certain situations.

As president, Wilson was forced to deal with issues of war and peace on an almost daily basis. His policies in the early years were mixed. Armed interventions in the Caribbean represented no real break with the past; on the other hand, repeal of the Panama Canal tolls exemption for American ships, support of mediation with Mexico, and conciliation treaties with some twenty-one nations suggested a more cooperative posture. It was, in fact, the deepening American intervention in the Mexican revolution that led Wilson in December 1914 to propose a Pan American union which foreshadowed the League of Nations. In his original draft of this pact, which never came to fruition, Wilson called for "mutual guarantees of political independence under republican form of government and mutual guarantees of territorial integrity," words strikingly similar to those later incorporated as Article X of the League Covenant.

Wilson's next significant steps toward collective security came in September 1915, when he privately pledged to *Edward Grey, the British foreign secretary, that the United States was prepared to support a postwar concert of nations as part of a mediated peace ending World War I. Then in May 1916 he endorsed the idea of a "universal association of nations to maintain the inviolate security of the highway of the seas . . . and to prevent any war begun either contrary to treaty covenants or without warning and full submission of the causes to the opinion of the world—a virtual guarantee of territorial integrity and political independence." Henceforth, the president was recognized as the preeminent leader for international organization.

In January 1917 Wilson announced the general terms of peace he thought worth defending by an American-supported league of nations. These included freedom of the seas, self-determination for all nations, arms limitation, and "equality of rights" for small as well as large nations. Wilson did not mean by equality a correspondence of power or wealth. There could never be equality of resources or territory or equality not stemming from the legitimate and peaceful development of the people. Few persons desired or expected more than equality of rights. Everyone wanted freedom of life, not balances of power. Such a view placed him within the liberal tradition of democratic capitalism, supportive of open door internationalism, critical of traditional European imperialism and revolutionary socialism alike.

In subsequent speeches following American entry into the war, Wilson added other points to his projected peace terms: open diplomacy, removal of trade barriers, an impartial settlement of colonial claims, and a system of mandates for former German colonies. He frequently explained that joining a league of nations would not mean forsaking the nation's tradition of no entangling alliances, since such did not exist in a concert of power. What he intended, he maintained, was an expansion of the Monroe Doctrine to the world.

As the war drew to a close in November 1918 and Wilson decided to represent the nation personally at the Paris Peace Conference, attention turned from general concepts to specific negotiations. Until that time he had purposefully avoided discussion of details. Wilson's efforts at Paris were successful in many areas, notably in committing the Allies to the League of Nations and in moderating some of the harsher features of the terms meted out to Germany. There were compromises, to be sure, but the Versailles Treaty was a more liberal document than if Wilson's ideas had received less credence.

Most Americans approved of the Treaty, which included the League in its first twenty-six articles, but critics were not wanting. They doubted, for example, that the Monroe Doctrine, whose express purpose was to protect U.S. interests, could or should be universalized. They worried that the League would attempt to regulate a nation's immigration or tariff policies. They argued that Article X assumed an advanced stage of cooperation that did not exist. By imposing obligations that its members would not uphold, the League would fail and thus weaken respect for international institutions generally. Other critics who favored legal and evolutionary steps toward union maintained that Wilson's version of collective security placed undue reliance upon handling crises after they had arisen rather than creating machinery to resolve disputes before they became acute.

As a result of the 1918 congressional elections, Republicans controlled both the House and the Senate. *Henry Cabot Lodge, the Massachusetts senator for whom Wilson had contempt, became majority leader in the Senate and chairman of the Foreign Relations Committee. Lodge's primary concern was to unite Republican senators behind a program of reservations that would qualify or reject those articles of the Treaty deemed unacceptable. In this he succeeded. The most important reservation disavowed any American obligation under Article X unless Congress should so authorize in each case.

Wilson's task was to persuade at least two thirds of the senators to approve the Treaty in a form he could accept. Convinced that the Lodge reservations nullified the essence of collective security, he refused to yield other than to agree to "interpretations" that clarified the League's articles without altering their substance. Such clarifications fell short of what most Republicans and a few Democrats considered adequate. Neither parliamentary maneuvering nor Wilson's "swing around the circle" could break the deadlock. On 19 March 1920, the Senate failed by seven votes to give the Treaty the necessary two-thirds approval.

Despite the enormity of his defeat, Wilson never relinquished his conviction that he had been right to spurn the Lodge reservations; nor did he waver in his faith that his ideals would ultimately triumph. In a limited way they did. While collective security failed to prevent World War II, the United States joined the UN; and American foreign policy after 1945 exhibited a Wilsonian coloration that combined hostility to leftist revolutions, distrust of European colonialism and of global capitalism, and hope for a world organization that might one day become the reality that Wilson had so eloquently envisioned.

Wilson remains a controversial figure in historical literature. Some scholars accept the essential validity of his ideas on world organization while faulting hs unwillingness to compromise on the Lodge reservations. Others question that he was well informed on the subject, being relatively ignorant about ideas, programs, and movements prior to 1918. Some question the practicality of collective security itself as formulated by Wilson given the state of the world after 1918. So-called realists have condemned Wilson as responsible for much of the idealistic–moralistic thinking they believe has plagued American diplomacy since World War I. Since the 1960s a number of historians have found in Wilson the source of America's Cold War anti-Communist and anti-Socialist policies. It seems certain such disagreements will continue as long as fundamental issues of war and peace remain unresolved.

BIBLIOGRAPHY:

A. Ray S. Baker and William E. Dodd, *The New Democracy: Presidential Messages, Addresses, and Public Papers, 1913–1917*, 2 vols. (New York, 1926), eds., *War and Peace: Presidential Messages, Addresses, and Public Papers, 1917–1924*, 2 vols. (New York, 1927); *Division and Reunion, 1829–1889* (New York, 1893); *Congressional Government* (Boston, 1885); *Constitutional Government in the United States* (New York, 1908); Arthur S. Link, with others, eds., *The Papers of Woodrow Wilson,* 40 vols. in progress (Princeton, NJ, 1966–82); *A History of the American People,* 5 vols. (New York, 1902); *The State* (Boston, 1889).

B. Ray S. Baker, *Woodrow Wilson: Life and Letters,* 8 vols. (New York, 1927–39); DAB 20, 351–68; Warren F. Kuehl, *Seeking World Order: The United States and International Organization to 1920* (Nashville, TN, 1969); N. Gordon Levin, *Woodrow Wilson and World Politics: America's Response to War and Revolution* (New York, 1968); Arthur S. Link, *Woodrow Wilson and a Revolutionary World, 1913–1921* (Chapel Hill, NC, 1982), *Woodrow Wilson: Revolution, War, and Peace* (Arlington Heights, IL, 1979), *Woodrow Wilson: The Road to the White House; The New Freedom; The Struggle for Neutrality, 1914–1915; Confusions and Crises, 1915–1916; Campaigns for Progressivism and Peace, 1916–1917* (Princeton, NJ, 1947, 1956, 1960, 1964, 1965); John M. Mulder, *Woodrow Wilson: The Years of Preparation* (Princeton, NJ, 1978); Edwin A. Weinstein, *Woodrow Wilson: A Medical and Psychological Biography* (Princeton, 1981).

C. The Wilson papers are in the Manuscript Division, Library of Congress and at Princeton Univ.

Ralph A. Stone

WINANT, John Gilbert (23 February 1889, New York—3 November 1947, Concord, NH). *Education*: Princeton Univ., 1909–12. *Career*: schoolmaster, St. Paul's School, 1912–17, vice-rector, 1919–21; New Hampshire state legislator, 1917–18, 1921–24; U.S. Air Force, 1917–19; governor of New Hampshire, 1925–26, 1931–34; deputy director, International Labor Organization 1935, 1937, director, 1938–41; chairman, Social Security Board, 1935–36; ambassador to Great Britain, 1941–46; U.S. representative to European Advisory Commission, 1944–45, to UN Economic and Social Council, 1946.

The product of middle-class conservative Republican parents, Winant nevertheless imbibed from the Christian Socialism of John Ruskin and the social welfare Republicanism of Theodore Roosevelt's 1912 presidential race. Unable to graduate from Princeton University, he returned to St. Paul's School in New Hampshire to teach American history and to inspire some students as a tall, quiet, yet caring Lincolnesque figure. Endlessly driven to serve the community, he won election in 1916 as a Republican state legislator. Thereafter he displayed a lifetime commitment to social welfare legislation and to the underprivileged.

After serving as a pilot and officer during World War I, and having attained momentary success developing oil wells in Texas, Winant returned to politics as state senator and then a three-term governor. For years he sustained defeats in a struggle for a 48-hour work law and the child labor amendment, but he did achieve a cooperative marketing law, acquired the Old Man of the Mountain for the state, and placed the University of New Hampshire on a firm basis. Responding to the Great Depression, he initiated state responsibilities akin to *Franklin D. Roosevelt's New Deal. Gaining national recognition as an enlightened Republican, Winant, at the behest of Roosevelt, ensured a face-saving settlement of a nationwide textile strike in 1934.

Committed to social justice and world peace, Winant accepted Roosevelt's recommendation in 1935 to become assistant director of the International Labor Organization (ILO) in Geneva. Within months, however, Roosevelt called him to become the first head of the Social Security system. Although Winant helped establish it on a firm foundation, Republican party attacks on the program in 1936 led Winant to resign his post and endorse Roosevelt for reelection. Thus he destroyed any future hopes for the presidency for himself.

In 1937 Winant returned to the ILO and soon became its director. Upon the outbreak of World War II, he converted the ILO into a fighting weapon for the embattled democracies, and after the downfall of France in 1940, he saved the organization almost singlehandedly for postwar endeavors by transferring its headquarters and a staff nucleus to Canada.

Appointed U.S. ambassador to Great Britain in 1941, Winant undid the harm of his appeasing predecessor, Joseph P. Kennedy. His aid was not material but a pervading spiritual support. He walked the burning streets of London, bringing confidence and courage to the embattled British. Although handcuffed by the absence of unified directives from Washington concerning plans for a defeated Germany and confronted with an intensely suspicious Soviet representative, Winant's integrity and unbending commitment to postwar planning helped avert utter disaster in the European Advisory Commission meetings in London. Winant resigned as ambassador in

1946 and assumed a post as U.S. member on the UN Economic and Social Council. Overwork combined with severe financial setbacks led to his suicide.

BIBLIOGRAPHY:

A. *Letter from Grosvenor Square: An Account of a Stewardship* (Boston, 1947); *Our Greatest Harvest: Selected Speeches of John C. Winant 1941–1946* (London, 1950).

B. Bernard Bellush, *He Walked Alone: A Biography of John Gilbert Winant* (The Hague, 1968); DAB supp. 4, 899–901; Ethel M. Johnson, "The Mr. Winant I Knew," *South Atlantic Quarterly* 48 (Winter 1949), 24–41; Alvin Knepper, "John Gilbert Winant and International Social Justice," dissertation, New York Univ., 1955; NCAB 38, 80–81; NYT 4 Nov 1947, 1.

C. The Winant papers are in the Franklin D. Roosevelt Library and at Dartmouth Coll.

Bernard Bellush

WINIARSKI, Bohdan Stefan (27 April 1884, Bohdanów, Poland—4 December 1969, Poznan, Poland). *Education*: studied law at Warsaw and Kraków; Ph.D., Paris, 1910. *Career*: lecturer, School of Political Science, Kraków, 1911–14; member, Polish National Committee in Paris, 1917–20; Polish delegation, Paris Peace Conference, 1919–20; professor of law, Univ. of Poznan, 1922–39, dean, 1936–39; professor, Academy of International Law, The Hague, 1933; professor of law, Oxford Univ., 1944–46; member of Polish delegation, League of Nations, 1920–22; member of various international commissions, 1921–46; judge, International Court of Justice, 1946–67, president, 1961–64.

Upon completing his doctorate, Winiarski lectured on French and Russian constitutional law in Kraków. During the war he served in the Russian Army and in 1917 found his way to the West, where he joined the Polish National Committee in Paris and acted as secretary to its Legal Section. At the Paris Peace Conference he was legal adviser to the Polish delegation.

Winiarski's legal expertise qualified him as a member of the Polish delegations to various international meetings, including the Barcelona Conference in 1921. He became involved in the work of the League of Nations and served as a member of the Polish delegation to the first three sessions (1920–22). He was appointed to the League's Permanent Commission on Communication and Transit (1921–27) and served as the commission's vice-president from 1924 to 1926. From 1925 to 1946 he was president of the League's Committee on River Law. Winiarski was an assessor of the Permanent Court of International Justice (PCIJ) for communication and transit questions which was created under the League. As a member of the international Oder River Commission (1921–30), he was the Polish agent before the PCIJ in the case concerning the Oder in 1929. In 1936 he became a member of the Academy of International Law's Permanent Conference on Higher International Studies.

Besides his academic career in Poland, Winiarski was active in Polish politics. He served on the government's Commissary for the Liquidation of German Property (1924–27) and sat as a deputy to the Polish Sejm from 1928 to 1935. During his tenure he opposed the existing Pilsudski regime.

With the outbreak of World War II, Winiarski was arrested by the Germans in September 1939 and held for two months. With his family he was deported from Poznan, which was incorporated into the Reich, to German-occupied Poland, and his property was confiscated. In January 1940 he managed to leave Poland and joined the Polish government-in-exile in London. While there he became president of the London-based Bank of Poland and taught international law at Oxford. He also served on an Inter-Allied Committee (1944–46) to discuss the future of the PCIJ.

The newly created International Court of Justice under the auspices of the United Nations saw Winiarski elected to a three-year term as one of the fifteen original judges (1946–49). He was reelected in 1949 to a nine-year term and again in 1957 to a third. In 1961 his fellow judges elected Winiarski president of the Court.

Winiarski's affiliation with international organizations spanned almost fifty years, which witnessed major political and governmental changes in Poland. His opinions and judgments were not influenced either by his government or the Soviet block. At times, as in the South West African Case (1966), his opinion was in opposition to both systems. Although he rarely made definitive official statements, he was influential behind the scenes and had the respect and admiration of his colleagues. Winiarski wrote nearly fifty works on various aspects of international law, including transportation, communication, disarmament, arbitration, as well as Polish and French constitutional law.

BIBLIOGRAPHY:

A. *Les Institutions politiques en Pologne au XIX-e siècle* (Paris, 192?); *Materyały do sprawy polski,* ed. Michael Radziwil and Bohdan Winiarski (Warsaw, 1915); *Obrona Konieczna prawio narodów* (Lwow, Poland, 1936); *Principes généraux de droit fluvial international* (Paris, 1934); *Rzeki polskie ze stanowiska prawo międzynarodowego* (Poznan, Poland, 1922); *Ustrój polityczny ziem polskich w XIX wieku* (Poznan, Poland, 1923); *Ustrój prawno-polityczny Galicyi* (Warsaw, 1915); *Wybor źródeł do nauki prawa miedzynarodowego* (Warsaw, 1938).

B. *Britannica Book of the Year* (Oxford, 1970), 591; CB 1962, 468–69; *Encyklopedia Powszechna PWN* 4 (Warsaw, 1976), 655; *ICJ Yearbook (1946–47),* 46–47, (1963–64), 5–6, (1966–67), 23–24; NYT 6 Apr 1961, 14; *Time* 77 (14 Apr 1961), 34; *United Nations Bulletin* 5, no. 10 (1948), 936–37; WWUN 1951, 471–72.

Zofia Sywak

WOLD, Emma (29 September 1871, Norway, SD—21 July 1950, Washington). *Education*: B.A., Western Coll., 1892; B.A., Univ. of Oregon, 1894, M.A., 1895; Sorbonne, Columbia Univ., Univ. of California, 1908–10; LL.B., Washington Coll. of Law, 1923. *Career*: taught in high schools,

Mills Coll., 1905, Univ. of Oregon, 1907; organized College Equal Suffrage League for Oregon, 1912; researcher, Woman's party, 1920s; lawyer, 1928–50; chair, Women's Committee for National Disarmament, 1921–22; technical adviser, Conference for Codification of International Law, 1930; rapporteur, Inter-American Commission of Women, 1930s; special attorney for Justice Department translating laws of European countries, 1933–34.

Wold gained recognition in international affairs through her work in peace and disarmament, nationality law, and women's legal rights in various nations, all of which were intimately related to her concern with the rights of women. Through work in the suffrage campaign, Wold became affiliated with the National Woman's party and in 1921 moved to Washington. Soon she and others, impatient with the Woman's party, founded the Woman's Committee for National Disarmament, of which she was national chair. Their objective was an international conference for disarmament as a step toward the abolition of war and reduced, fairer taxes. Wold quickly organized mass state meetings to urge a conference. She had support from the Woman's Joint Congressional Committee, a powerful lobbying force in Washington. Though never again a leader in the peace movement, Wold continued to work for the cause, including joining +Jeanette Rankin and others in 1932 on a speaking tour which culminated with various groups converging on Chicago for the Democratic Convention.

In most countries, women's marital status affected their nationality, but the United States, under feminist pressure, had removed most of its discrimination in 1922. Early in her legal career Wold became interested in nationality laws affecting women. The Pan American Union in 1928 created the Inter-American Commission of Women (IACW), which decided its first concern would be nationality, an issue on the agenda of the Conference on the Codification of International Law which was to meet at The Hague in 1930. Wold, who had conducted a study of nationality laws, worked with the Commission, and *Herbert Hoover appointed her as a technical adviser. That Conference adopted a convention on nationality which did not remove all discrimination, and the United States refused to sign. The delegates did adopt a proposal by the United States that countries study the possibility of equal treatment. The IACW, which had urged acceptance of an equality treaty on nationality, took its proposal to the seventh Pan-American Conference, where it was accepted. Subsequently the treaty was ratified by several American states, including the United States. Also in the early 1930s, the IACW began to investigate the political and civil rights of women within nations. Wold prepared the study on the United States and it became part of an unsuccessful effort to persuade various Pan American conferences to adopt an equal rights convention and later a women's suffrage treaty. After the late 1930s, through interested in cultural exchange, Wold was not again in the international limelight.

BIBLIOGRAPHY:

A. *A Comparison of the Political and Civil Rights of Men and Women in the United States*, Senate Doc. no. 270 (Washington, 1936); *A Compilation of the Nationality Laws of 72 Countries as Affected by Marriage*, House Hearing no. 70.1.8 (Washington, 1928).

B. *American Women: The Standard Biographical Dictionary of Notable Women* 3, 999–1000; NCAB 38, 606–7.

Kell Mitchell, Jr.

WOLL, Matthew (25 January 1880, Luxemburg—1 June 1956, New York). *Education*: graduate, Lake Forest Coll. of Law, 1904. *Career*: founder and first president, International Photo-Engravers' Union of North America, 1906–29; vice-president, American Federation of Labor, 1919–55; War Labor Board; chair, International Labor Relations Committee, AFL. 1943–55.

For fifty years Woll was an influential member of the conservative wing of the American labor movement with an intense concern with world conditions for workers. Along with Samuel Gompers, Woll believed that cooperation between labor and government during World War I strengthened labor's position in the economy. In the postwar era, Woll aligned himself with Secretary of Commerce *Herbert Hoover and the view that government should limit its interference in collective bargaining situations. Opposed to state economic control of labor, he was an intense anti-Communist. During the 1920s Woll stood in the forefront of the American Federation of Labor leaders who purged radicals from leadership positions within the Federation. In 1934 he became an AFL activist in international relations when he advocated a boycott of German foods as a protest to the persecution of trade unionists and Jews. At the International Federation of Trade Unions meeting of 1937, Woll opposed the invitation of representatives from the Soviet Union on the grounds that Soviet worker organizations were state-controlled.

Prior to U.S. entry in World War II, Woll expressed the fear that the postwar balance of power in Europe might lead to Communist domination. Along with David Dubinsky, Woll prevailed upon the AFL to work with the Jewish Labor Committee to rescue hundreds of Jewish labor leaders from Nazi Germany. In response to Nazi persecutions and at Woll's urging, the AFL created (1938) the Labor League for Human Rights. With Woll as chairman, it worked with emigrés during the war to build democratic trade unions in postwar Europe.

The planning led to the creation of the AFL Free Trade Union Committee (FTUC) in 1944. Headed by Woll and set up to support non-Communist unions in the postwar world, the committee also included George Meany and Dubinsky. The FTUC channeled AFL and, after 1947, U.S. government funds to unions in France, Italy, Austria, and Germany. Led by Woll, workers created the International Federation of Free Trade Unions in 1949. Woll persuaded General Lucius D. Clay, commander of the American occupation forces in Germany, to turn over confiscated union equipment and records to anti-Communist and anti-Fascist labor groups. In policy circles, Woll urged a revision of the agreement which allowed the Soviet Union to dismantle Germany industry in lieu of reparations. Woll also articulately advocated the restoration of a democratic Germany to full partnership in the community of nations.

Beginning in 1938 Woll worked with the Department of State to promote pro-U.S. labor unions in Latin America. The FTUC continued this effort, which culminated in the creation of the anti-Communist Inter-American Regional Organization of Workers (ORIT) in 1951. Woll's efforts often met with criticism from more activist elements of U.S. labor. One wag, James Carey, cynically observed, "The AFL considered Matty Woll an expert in foreign affairs because he was born in Luxemburg."

BIBLIOGRAPHY:

A. *Labor, Industry and Government* (New York, 1935).

B. DAB supp. 6, 706–7; Roy Godson, "The AFL Foreign Policy Making Process from the End of World War II to the Merger," *Labor History* 16 (Summer 1975), 325–37; NCAB 42, 14–15; NYT 2 Jan 1956, 19.

James E. Cebula

WOOLF, Leonard Sidney (25 November 1880, London—14 August 1969, Sussex, England). *Education*: B.A., Trinity Coll., Cambridge Univ., 1902. *Career*: Ceylon Civil Service, 1904–11; editor, *International Review*, 1919; editor, International Section, *Contemporary Review*, 1920–21: literary editor, *The Nation*, 1923–30; joint editor, *Political Quarterly*, 1931–59; founded Hogarth Press, 1917.

Cambridge was an important influence upon Woolf, shaping his values through his association with the philosopher G. E. Moore and an undergraduate society, the Apostles. His university friends remained close to him and formed the nucleus of the famous Bloomsbury Group. Woolf spent seven years in Ceylon, gradually turning from an unconscious imperialist to a fervent anti-imperialist. His experience there taught him that, whatever technological progress British rule brought to subject races, it was nullified by the immorality of the domination of a stronger over a weaker culture. He returned to London on home leave, married the writer Virginia Stephen, and resigned from the imperial service to spend the rest of his life working for peace and social justice.

Woolf recognized that his talents lay in the field of persuasion rather than political activism. He served for two decades on the Labor party's Advisory Committees on International and Imperial Questions, preparing position papers and reports. He wrote easily and well, turning out research pieces for the Fabian Society and various periodicals. His *International Government* in 1916 stimulated discussion and made an important contribution to the theoretical basis of the League of Nations. Woolf spent the decade of the 1920s chiefly on the issue of imperialism. *Empire and Commerce in Africa* was a cogent piece of economic and social analysis. His novel, *The Village in the Jungle*, retained its popularity in Sri Lanka.

The 1930s demonstrated to Woolf that international peace was the crucial issue. A strong supporter of the League of Nations and of the concept of collective security, he argued for revision of the Covenant to make the League more effective. The Japanese invasion of Manchuria alarmed him, and he pointed out the imminence of war as early as 1932. The Ethiopian and Rhineland crises seemed to confirm his warnings, and the tenor of his writing gradually took on a more strident tone.

In politics, Woolf was a moderate Socialist, but he was astringent on the failures of the Labor party to provide alternatives to Conservative policies in the interwar period. He was also strongly anti-Communist. *Barbarians at the Gate*, commissioned by Victor Gollancz for the Left Book Club, was originally rejected on the basis that it was too anti-Soviet. Woolf's fundamental belief in the values of civilization, by which he meant education, reason, and tolerance, as well as Mozart and Shakespeare, led him to reject all attacks on the liberty of the individual, whether from the left or the right.

Woolf once estimated that he had spent 150,000 hours in totally useless work, but his biographer rejects this claim. Woolf helped shape the Labor party's policies on imperial and international questions, and his political journalism educated a postwar generation to the need for international cooperation and social progress throughout the world.

BIBLIOGRAPHY:

A. *After the Deluge, Vol. 1* (London, 1931); *After the Deluge, Vol. 2* (London, 1939); *Autobiography*, 5 vols. (Oxford, 1960–69); *Barbarians at the Gate* (London, 1939); *Diaries in Ceylon* (London, 1963); *Economic Imperialism* (London, 1920); *Empire and Commerce in Africa* (London, 1919); *Fear and Politics: A Debate at the Zoo* (London, 1925); *International Government* (New York, 1916); *The League and Abyssinia* (London, 1936); *Mandates and Empire* (London, 1920); *Principia Politica* (London, 1953); *The Village in the Jungle* (New York, 1913).

B. CB 1965, 469–71; NYT 15 Aug 1969, 82; Stephen J. Stearns, introduction to Woolf, *The Framework of a Lasting Peace*, rpt. ed. (New York, 1971); Stephen J. Stearns, introduction to Woolf, *The War for Peace*, rpt. ed. (New York, 1972); Sylvia Strauss, introduction to Woolf, *Imperialism and Civilization* (New York, 1971); Duncan Wilson, *Leonard Woolf: A Political Biography (New York, 1978).*

Cynthia F. Behrman

WOOLLEY, Mary Emma (13 July 1863, South Norwalk, CT—5 September 1947, Westport, NY). *Education*: B.A, Brown Univ., 1894, M.A., 1895, Litt.D., 1900. *Career*: instructor, Wheaton Sem., 1886–91; instructor, Wellesley Coll., 1895–96, associate professor, 1896–99, professor and head,

Department of Biblical History and Literature, 1899–1900; president, Mount Holyoke Coll., 1900–1937.

One of the first two women to graduate from Brown University, Woolley was president of Mount Holyoke College for thirty-seven years. A minister's daughter and Biblical scholar, she was a religious humanitarian and internationalist devoted to world education. Before World War I she served as vice-president of the American Peace Society and the American School Peace League and served on the Committee on Educational Institutions of the Second National Peace Congress (1909). Unlike so many members of the nineteenth-century peace movement, she did not hasten to support World War I. For a while she promoted a Mount Holyoke chapter of the Woman's Peace Party, a feminist pacifist group formed to coordinate opposition to the conflict in Europe. Reluctantly, Woolley conceded to U.S. entrance into the war and allowed various resources of the college to be used in the service of patriotic work. During the war, as a member of the Church Peace Union and the League to Enforce Peace, she disseminated information on an international organization to promote disarmament and world order.

Although intense support for the League of Nations characterized most of her international activities during the interwar period, Woolley's internationalism was grounded in Christian ethics, not political and social issues. She directed the World Alliance for Promoting International Friendship Through the Churches, and as a member of the 1921 China Educational Commission, created by the Foreign Missions Conference of North America, she traveled in the Orient studying Christian missionary schools. Woolley served on the Executive Committee of the Institute of Pacific Relations, which attempted in a small area to achieve objectives similar to those of the League of Nations. The Institute, which had grown out of a YMCA Pacific Conference in 1920, did have political, economic, and social themes, but it was predominantly religious and educational. Of her many other organizational affiliations, most promoted international understanding through education, including the U.S. Peoples Mandate for Inter-American Peace and Co-operation and the American Association of University Women, where she served as president from 1927 to 1933 and subsequently headed the International Relations Committee (1933–39).

In 1932 Woolley was appointed by *Herbert Hoover to serve as the only woman U.S. delegate to the Geneva Conference for the Reduction and Limitation of Armaments. Although she enthusiastically attended, she did not believe that one conference could make significant gains. In publications and at public meetings she strove to define peace and disarmament as the final outcome of an ongoing daily process of world education. Nonetheless, a special urgency characterized her work for she believed that human beings would eventually develop technology to destroy the earth if the basic human capacity for evil were not countered. In the late 1930s she became involved in the Peoples Mandate to End War. Having suffered ridicule for her predictions of the coming manmade apocalypse, Woolley lived to see the detonation of atomic weapons in Japan.

BIBLIOGRAPHY:

A. *Internationalism and Disarmament* (New York, 1935).

B. CB 1942, 896–98; DAB supp. 4, 912–13; Jeanette Marks, *Life and Letters of Mary Emma Woolley* (Washington, 1955); NAW 3, 660–63; NYT 6 Sep 1947, 17; Anna Mary Wells, *Miss Marks and Miss Woolley* (Boston, 1978).

C. The Woolley papers are in the Mount Holyoke Coll. Library.

Rosemary Rainbolt

WOOLSEY, Theodore Salisbury (22 October 1852, New Haven, CT—24 April 1929, New Haven). *Education*: B.A., Yale Coll., LL.B., Yale Law School. *Career*: professor, Yale Law School, 1878–1911; author and businessman.

From the mid-1880s until 1920, Woolsey wrote and spoke widely on the subject of international relations, especially emphasizing the need for more effective means of resolving disputes among nations. In numerous articles in scholarly journals and mass-circulation magazines, he brought a keen understanding of history and diplomacy to his analysis of international developments.

Woolsey was neither a pacifist nor a committed anti-imperialist. Between the early 1890s and World War, he frequently warned that an aggressive American foreign policy risked war with Latin American neighbors and the European powers. A social conservative in the mugwump tradition, he also feared that increased military spending would engender further instability in American society by preventing needed domestic reforms. Yet he ultimately came to support American armed intervention in Cuba and later in Europe, as well as the suppression of the Aguinaldo insurrection and the establishment of colonial rule in the Philippines.

In the 1890s, Woolsey considered diplomacy, with its allowance for compromise and adjustment, to be superior to arbitration as a means of settling international disputes. He never went as far as many of his fellow legalists in the post-1900 peace movement in subordinating diplomacy to the judicial process in international relations. At the same time, however, he was a leading proponent of voluntary arbitration of questions of law, fact, or treaty interpretation but not of national honor or sovereignty. A professor of international law in Yale Law School he, with *John Bassett Moore, *Elihu Root, and other academicians and arbitration veterans, played an increasingly important role in the Lake Mohonk Conferences on Arbitration, which sought to promote the arbitration process. In 1906 these judicially oriented internationalists, who believed that the correct application of international law within the framework of a world court was vital to the maintenance of world peace, founded the American Society of International Law. For several years Woolsey served on its Board of Editors and Executive Committee.

The failure of the Second Hague Peace Conference to establish a world court convinced Woolsey that some form of compulsion was needed to compel governments to respect international law. His plan for a concert of powers in the Western Hemisphere, using the combined police powers of its member nations—as opposed to unilateral American action under the Monroe Doctrine—to maintain hemispheric stability and peace, was viewed by some internationalists during World War I as a model for a regional union upon which an international league might be constructed. An outspoken sanctionist during the war, he strongly supported the League to Enforce Peace. Both before and after the Armistice, he called for the establishment of an international league and world court with sufficient administrative and judicial, though not legislative, powers to punish aggressors and keep the peace. His argument that peace could be preserved only if all member nations in such a world body were disarmed was unacceptable even to many sanctionists after the war.

BIBLIOGRAPHY:

A. *America's Foreign Policy: Essays and Addresses* (New York, 1898); *Introduction to the Study of International Law* (New York, 1886).

B. NCAB 31, 122–23; NYT 25 Apr 1929, 29.

C. The Woolsey Family papers are in the Yale Univ. Archives.

Hugh H. Davis

WRENCH, Evelyn (29 October 1882, Killacoona, County Dublin, Ireland—11 November 1966, London). *Education*: Eton. *Career*: Northcliffe newspapers, 1904–12; Overseas League, from 1912; English-Speaking Union, from 1918; Royal Air Force, 1914–18; editor, *Spectator*, 1925–32; American relations officer in India, 1942–44; author.

Though he sought a diplomatic career, Wrench made his contribution to international affairs primarily through the founding and promoting of several agencies whose function was to create a better world through international understanding and cooperation. A man of intense energy, imagination, and charm, he devoted his life mainly to two objectives: developing understanding and fellowship among all sections of the British Empire (then Commonwealth), for which he organized the Overseas League; and increasing Anglo–American understanding and cooperation, for which he developed the English-Speaking Union (ESU). The All Peoples Association, which he founded in 1930 to do in the wider field what the two other organizations were doing in more limited spheres, proved difficult to cultivate. Forces were at work too powerful for any voluntary organization to overcome in the cause of universal, international amity, and particularly in developing Anglo–German understanding, where the organization tried to be helpful.

Upon leaving Eton, Wrench traveled on the Continent, ventured into the picture postcard business, and joined the publishing enterprises of Lord Northcliffe in 1904. In the next eight years he performed special tasks and held at different times the editorship of the *Overseas Daily Mail*, the *Weekly Despatch*, and a continental edition of the *Daily Mail*. Then pursuing a vision he acquired on a visit to Canada and the United States in 1906, Wrench left his newspaper posts for a round-the-world empire tour. On his return, he founded the Overseas League, an organization which prospered and undertook a variety of modest war-related activities.

After wartime service and inspired by the partnership of the English-speaking peoples during the conflict, Wrench in 1918 set about forming the English-Speaking Union, encouraged and assisted by Sir George Perley and American ambassador Walter Hines Page, as well as others on both sides of the Atlantic. The first American branches appeared in Philadelphia, New York, Baltimore, Boston, and Pittsburgh; and in 1920 *William H. Taft consented to be the first president of the ESU in the United States. Believing that Anglo–American friendship and cooperation were essential to world peace and to the benefit of humanity generally, Wrench tirelessly expounded that theme at countless receptions, banquets, and public meetings. Occasionally labeled a propagandist for British interests, he saw the Union as a brotherhood uninvolved in internal politics but concerned with making peoples better known to each other and with promoting comradeship. Serving the Overseas League as secretary and the ESU as chair and later honorary secretary, Wrench still found time to edit (1925–32) the *Spectator*, of which he remained chairman of the board for life.

On a world tour in 1940 and unable to proceed home from India, Wrench became involved in helping American soldiers in the area. That led to an appointment as American relations officer to the government of India, 1942–44. After the war, writing consumed much of his time. To volumes of personal memoirs and wartime books (including *I Loved Germany*), he added several biographies. To celebrate his eightieth birthday, the English-Speaking Union announced a fund bearing his name for travel grants. Deeply religious and sensitive to world conditions, Wrench was profoundly devoted to improving international friendship, as his efforts testify.

BIBLIOGRAPHY:

A. *Alfred Lord Milner: The Man of No Illusions* (London, 1958); *Francis Yeats-Brown: A Portrait* (London, 1949); *Geoffrey Dawson and Our Times* (London, 1955); *I Loved Germany* (London, 1940); *Immortal Years, 1937–1944* (London, 1946); *Struggle, 1914–1920* (London, 1935); *Transatlantic London: Three Centuries of Association Between England and America* (London, 1949); *Uphill: The First Stage in a Strenuous Life* (London, 1934).
B. LT 12 Nov 1966, 10; NYT 12 Nov 1966, 29.

William R. Rock

WRIGHT, Elizabeth Washburn (19 November 1874, Minneapolis, MN—11 February 1952, Washington). *Education*: private schools in the United States and Europe; Radcliffe Coll., 1897–98. *Career*: author of short stories and travel observations on the Orient and of essays on the opium trade, 1909–27; assessor, Opium Advisory Committee of League of Nations, 1921–25; U.S. delegate, Geneva Opium Conference, 1924–25; investigator of the opium problem in the Philippines, U.S. Bureau of Narcotics, 1930–31.

During the nineteenth century, following the conclusion of the Anglo-Chinese Opium War (1839–42), the United States concluded bilateral treaties with China, Japan, and Korea barring Americans from participation in the Far Eastern opium trade. Beginning in 1906, however, the United States became the prime mover in a campaign to rally the international community to the anti-opium cause, first in behalf of China and later in the interest of the West as well. After World War I, the League of Nations assumed control of the movement. Refusing to join the League, the United States vacillated between cooperating with that body and again relying mainly upon bilateral antinarcotics diplomacy.

The career of Wright symbolizes both the continuity and discontinuity between the pre- and post–World War I phases of America's narcotics diplomacy. From 1908 to 1915 Wright assisted her husband, *Hamilton, in studying the narcotics problem and in drafting both the domestic and foreign drug policy of the United States. A year after he died in 1917 she decided to continue his work. She was inspired in part by the tradition of public service set by her father, William Drew Washburn, and several of his brothers, who served as members of the U.S. Congress, governors of states, and American diplomats abroad. Feeling that she was a medium controlled by an outside force for some specific purpose, she subordinated her traditional role as a woman and mother to the demands of the anti-opium cause.

As a private citizen, Wright attended the peace conferences at Paris and Lausanne at the close of World War I to encourage incorporation of the Hague Opium Convention of 1912 into the peace treaties and to urge the United States to continue its leadership of the international drug control movement. In 1920 she returned to the Orient to study the revival of opium production and the increase in the narcotics traffic in China. Despite her widely acknowledged expertise, she failed to secure a permanent position similar to that of her late husband in the State Department. Nevertheless, as an assessor on the Opium Advisory Committee of the League of Nations, a member of the American delegation to the Geneva Opium Conference, and an interested private citizen with access to prominent periodicals and personages such as *Charles H. Brent and Secretary of Commerce *Herbert Hoover, she exerted considerable influence on American policy.

By 1922 Wright had become convinced that curtailing cultivation of the poppy would be the most effective means of bringing the problem under control. In 1923, following a study in Turkey and Persia, major opium-producing countries, she urged American businessmen to help develop the cultivation of silk as a substitute crop for the poppy. Through her initiative, a League of Nations Commission of Inquiry visited Persia in 1926, and in 1927 she again went to Turkey to explore possibilities of introducing substitute crops.

In 1924–25, at the Geneva Opium Conference, the U.S. government propounded Wright's thesis that the ultimate solution to the narcotics problem lay in restriction at "the source." The failure of the conferees to adopt the American position led both the U.S. government and Wright to question whether the League of Nations was sincerely interested in solving the problem. Nevertheless, she continued to urge the United States to take the initiative in working for limitation at the source, in cooperation with or independent of the League. In 1931 she attributed the failure of the U.S. policy of prohibition in the Philippines to the continued excessive cultivation of the poppy in opium-producing countries. Shortly thereafter she was employed by the Bureau of Narcotics to persuade state officials to enact the Uniform Narcotic Drug Control Act of 1930, which contained a provision restricting poppy cultivation in the United States.

Near the end of the 1930s, the United States cooperated with the Opium Advisory Committee of the League of Nations in preparing a draft convention to limit the growth of the poppy. The outbreak of World War II interrupted this movement. In 1953, a year after Wright's death, a UN conference on narcotic drugs adopted the Protocol for Limiting and Regulating the Cultivation of the Poppy Plant, the Production of, International and Wholesale Trade in, and Use of Opium. This protocol did not go into effect, however, until 1973.

BIBLIOGRAPHY:

A. *The Colour of the East* (New York, 1914); "The Opium Question," *Outlook* 92 (20 Mar 1909), 642–44; "Passing of the Opium Question," *Outlook* 106 (14 Feb 1914), 365–68; "Some Points in the Turkish Situation," *Outlook* 134 (20 Jun 1923), 213–14; "Trail of Opium," *Asia* 24 (Sep 1924), 667–71.

B. NYT 14 Feb 1952, 26; Arnold H. Taylor, *American Diplomacy and the Narcotics Traffic* (Durham, NC, 1969); *Washington Evening Star* 13 Feb 1952, A-14; WWWA 5, 800.

Arnold H. Taylor

WRIGHT, Hamilton Kemp (2 August 1867, Cleveland, OH—9 January 1917, Washington). *Education*: M.D., McGill Univ., 1895; Cambridge Univ., 1896, Heidelberg Univ., 1897–98, Johns Hopkins Univ., 1903–4. *Career*: Royal Victoral Hospital, Montreal, 1895–96; assistant director, London County Pathological Laboratory, 1897–99; director, Institute for Medical Research, Kuala Lumpur, 1900–1903; medical researcher, Europe and America, 1903–8; member, American delegation to Shanghai Opium Commission, 1908–9, to Hague Opium Conferences, 1911–12, 1913.

The tendency toward greater international cooperation on a host of social, economic, and technological, but politically significant, problems in the late nineteenth and early twentieth centuries inspired governments to turn increasingly to professional and technical experts for short-term service as diplomats. Like many of these authorities, Wright, prior to his appointment by Secretary of State *Elihu Root to the American delegation to the Shanghai Opium Commission, had neither diplomatic training nor experience. He had spent virtually all of his adult life in medical study and research in Canada, England, continental Europe, the Far East, and the United States. The post came unsolicited because of his work in tropical medicine. Shortly after graduating from McGill University he spent about a year in China, Japan, and other areas of the Orient observing such diseases as beriberi, malaria, and the plague. While continuing his study of these diseases in the Federated Malay States and the Straits Settlement from 1899 to 1903 under the auspices of the British Colonial Office, he founded and directed a research institute at Kuala Lumpur, which provided him with data that led to several publications.

During the six years he was officially involved with the opium problem, Wright became the chief drafter of both the foreign and domestic narcotics control policy of the United States. He prepared and helped formulate the proposals put forward by the United States at the Shanghai Commission and at the First and Second Hague Opium Conferences. In close collaboration with the Chinese delegation, he and his colleague, *Charles H. Brent, secured grudging international recognition of the principles that transactions in opium should be limited to medical and scientific purposes and that countries should prohibit or control the shipment of opium to countries that banned or restricted its entry.

In preparation for the meeting at Shanghai, convened by the United States mainly to help China, Wright undertook the first full-scale study of opium and cocaine trafficking and consumption in the United States. His estimate of some 200,000 opium smokers may have been an exaggeration, but his report provided a factual and conceptual basis for subsequent remedial legislation. But Wright's ambitions and interests went beyond opium and eventually embroiled him in controversy with the State Department. His unsuccessful quest in 1909 for the position of minister to China aroused the hostility of some of the department's career officers. His attempts at the Shanghai and Hague conferences to free China of treaty restrictions only marginally related to the opium question ran afoul of other interests of the United States. Finally, his insistence on becoming a permanent officer in the State Department brought him into conflict with Secretary of State *William Jennings Bryan, who, on the eve of the convening of the Third Hague Opium Conference in June 1914, unceremoniously dismissed him from the American delegation.

Unable to secure another desirable position in government, Wright went to France in 1915 where, while engaged in civilian relief work, he was severely injured in an automobile accident. For several decades following his premature death in early 1917 from pneumonia, his widow, *Elizabeth Washburn Wright, continued his antinarcotics work.

BIBLIOGRAPHY:

A. *The Malarial Fevers of British Malaya* (Singapore, 1901); *On the Classification and Pathology of Beri-beri* (London, 1903); *The Opium Problem* (Washington, 1910); *Second International Opium Conference* (Washington, 1913).

B. *British Medical Journal* (7 Apr 1917), 470–71; DAB 10, 552–53; *Dictionary of American Medical Biography* (New York, 1928, 1937); Arnold H. Taylor, *American Diplomacy and the Narcotics Traffic* (Durham, NC, 1969); *Washington Evening Star* 11 Jan 1917, 3.

Arnold H. Taylor

WRIGHT, Quincy (28 December 1890, Medford, MA—17 October 1970, Charlottesville, VA). *Education*: B.A., Lombard Coll., 1912; M.A., Univ. of Illinois, 1913, Ph.D., 1915. *Career*: research fellow, Univ. of Pennsylvania, 1915–16; assistant and instructor, Harvard Univ., 1916–19; assistant to professor, Univ. of Minnesota, 1919–23; professor, Univ. of Chicago, 1923–56; visiting research scholar, Carnegie Endowment for International Peace, 1956–57; professor, Univ. of Virginia, 1958–61; consultant to Foreign Economic Administration and Department of State, 1943–44, to UNESCO, 1949, to U.S. high commissioner for Germany, 1949–50.

At the center of Quincy Wright's contributions was his magisterial *A Study of War* (1942), which his wife Louise Leonard Wright abridged in 1964. In this work, to quote Karl W. Deutsch, Wright gathered "a larger body of relevant facts, insights, and far-ranging questions about war than any other man." He drew upon and integrated, with informed political judgment, a vast scholarship in numerous disciplines, including history, law, behavioral sciences, statistics, and mathematics. Wright carried forward his principal concerns of *A Study of War* in subsequent writings, particularly in his textbook on *The Study of International Relations* (1955). These efforts to contribute to peace through a multidisciplinary analysis of war fixed his place in history as a pioneer in modern peace research.

In 1931 Wright had founded at Chicago the Committee on International Relations, a pioneering, interdepartmental, degree-granting body, and thereby played a leading role in advocating the academic study of international relations. His teachings of international law and relations was perhaps as influential as his writings, for in fifty years of teaching he supervised over 200 graduate students who went into the world in academic, diplomatic, and other responsible positions.

Wright also advanced both the study of and respect for international law. He urged its observance as incorporated in the League of Nations Covenant, the Kellogg-Briand Pact, the London or Nuremberg Charter, and the UN Charter, all of which tended to limit national sovereignty. He demonstrated one perspective in 1945 when, as adviser on international law to the U.S. member of the International Military Tribunal for Germany, he prepared a memorandum embodying the principles implicit in the Nuremberg judgment. Wright considered the judgment important in the development of international criminal law and as a "clear pronouncement that aggression is an individual crime."

Wright participated in the 1940s in plans to create an effective world organization. He prepared several reports of the Commission to Study the Organization of Peace and served on the Central Committee of *Anita Blaine's World Citizens Association. By 1959 he could see that "the conditions of the world require a more effective international law and a more effective United Nations," but he recognized the difficulties of instituting change. Although the UN was designed to maintain peace and security, it was not intended to be a world government; however, Wright believed it should develop the concept of world citizenship as a means of preserving national citizenship. This could lead to a sense of world community, he said, which he saw as essential for effective international law.

Wright did not hesitate to oppose official U.S. actions and policies in international affairs when he considered them legally wrong. He criticized the 1962 quarantine of Cuba as a violation of the freedom of the seas, and he saw U.S. military operations in Vietnam as illegal intervention in a civil war. Wright also condemned policies which advanced the likelihood of nuclear war.

Wright published 21 books and about 1,000 essays, a vast array of scholarship which made him one of the most productive publicists of his or any generation. There was, however, more to Wright than the respected international legal scholar and social scientist, for he was at the same time a humanist and even a social reformer who sought to alter old patterns and move toward that peaceful world community under a humane jural order that he could visualize but not yet grasp.

BIBLIOGRAPHY:

A. *The Control of American Foreign Relations* (New York, 1922); *Mandates under the League of Nations* (Chicago, 1930); *The Study of International Relations* (New York, 1955); *A Study of War*, 2 vols. (Chicago, 1942; 2nd ed., 1 vol., Chicago, 1965).

B. *AAUP Bulletin* 56 (Dec 1970), 358–59; AJIL 65 (1971), 130–31; CB 1943, 845–47; Karl W. Deutsch, "Quincy Wright's Contribution to the Study of War," in Wright, *A Study of War*, 2nd ed. (Chicago, 1965); Clinton F. Fink and Christopher Wright, "Quincy Wright on War and Peace: A Statistical Overview and Selected Bibliography," *Journal of Conflict Resolution* 14 (1970), 543–54; Albert Lepawsky, Edward H. Buehrig, and Harold D. Lasswell, eds., *The Search for World Order: Studies by Students and Colleagues of Quincy Wright* (New York, 1971); NYT 18 Oct 1970, 92; Paul J. Scheips, "On the Study of War and Peace: Some Remarks in Memory of Quincy Wright, 1890–1970," *Maryland Historian* 2 (Fall, 1971), 105–16.

C. The Wright papers in the Univ. of Chicago Library.

Paul J. Scheips

WRONG, Humphrey Hume (10 September 1894, Toronto—24 January 1954, Ottawa). *Education*: B.Litt., Univ. of Toronto, 1915; M.A., Oxford Univ., 1921. *Career*: British Army, 1915–18; assistant professor, Univ. of Toronto, 1921–27; first secretary, Canadian legation, Washington, 1927–30, counselor of legation, 1930–37; permanent delegate, League of Nations, 1937–39; special economic adviser, London, 1939–41; minister-counselor, Canadian legation, Washington, 1941–42; assistant under secretary of state for external affairs, 1942–44; associate under secretary of state, 1944–46; ambassador to Washington, 1946–53; under secretary of state for external affairs, 1953–54.

From 1927 until his death in 1954, Wrong was one of three or four individuals who can accurately be described as architects of Canadian foreign policy. He was also an internationalist of a kind common to diplomats representing lesser powers. As such, he sought protection in international collaboration and collective security. He represented Canada at several sessions of the League Assembly and sat as a delegate at the final meeting in 1946. There, in assessing the League, he found its weakness not in machinery but in the inability of the members to act collectively. He brought insight to this evaluation, because he had served on a committee to revise the League in the late 1930s.

After World War II, Wrong participated actively in the formation of the North Atlantic Treaty Organization and sought the closest possible military collaboration between the United States and Canada. His efforts were crowned in 1950 by a military assistance pact with the United States. He worked unceasingly for the integration of the American and Canadian economies, arguing that if closeness had been good during the war the two nations should collaborate in peacetime. Among his achievements was the Niagara Power Treaty in 1950, which laid the foundation for the more ambitious St. Lawrence Seaway Project. He was also a strong believer in full-scale aid to Europe and liked to point out that Canada's contributions to European recovery were greater on a per capita basis than those of the United States.

Wrong was always a strong partisan of the United Nations. He was outspoken on his insistence on the maintenance of a UN command during the Korean War, and he continually advocated the revision of the Charter to eliminate the veto, or at least agreement by the powers to limit the areas in which the veto could be used.

BIBLIOGRAPHY:

A. *The Government of the West Indies* (Oxford, 1923); *Sir Alexander MacKenzie: Explorer and Fur Trader* (Toronto, 1927).

B. CB 1950, 630–32; NYT 25 Jun 1954, 19; Denis Stairs, *The Diplomacy of Constraint: Canada, the Korean War, and the United States* (Toronto, 1974); Richard Veatch, *Canada and the League of Nations* (Toronto, 1975); WWWA 3, 943.

C. The Wrong papers are in the Public Archives of Canada.

Douglas W. Houston

Y

YEPES, Jesús María (1892, Marinilla, Antioquia, Colombia—1962, Colombia). *Education*: graduate, Seminario Conciliar de Medellín; Universidad de Antioquia; Ecole Consulario, Antwerp; Université Catholique de Louvain. *Career*: consul general, Antwerp, 1912–16; professor, Universidad de Antioquia, 1917–23, 1926–30; first secretary, Colombian legation, Great Britain, 1923–26; Colombian senator, 1923–27, 1931–35; consul general, Switzerland, 1933–45; president, Colombian delegation, Inter-Parliamentary Union Conference, Washington, 1935; legal consultant, Ministry of Foreign Affairs, 1926–30; delegate, Inter-American Congress of Jurists, Rio de Janeiro, 1927; Sixth Pan American Conference, Havana, 1928; League of Nations, 1936–40; San Francisco Conference, 1945; UN General Assembly, 1946–47.

Yepes revealed his internationalist perspective as a long-term supporter of creating ways to resolve disputes and tensions between nations. At the Pan American Peace Conference in 1936, Yepes argued that the Pan American Union should have the power to examine and resolve political problems in the Americas and be able to gain respect for peace. He argued for various reforms in the institutions and treaties then part of the Inter-American System. The Governing Board of the Pan American Union should be converted into a supreme agency of hemispheric conciliation with the ability to safeguard peace, or restore it when broken. He recognized that the juridical nature of the Union would probably be modified through technical studies. Nevertheless, this process would probably transform the Pan American Union into a "league of American nations," with a Governing Board acting as a "great continental tribunal." He had argued for the creation of a Pan American court of international justice as a member of the Colombian delegation to the 1928 Havana Conference. This court would apply "American juridical principles" to resolve disputes. In a 1936 article in *World Affairs*, Yepes argued that the Conference that year should carefully consider modifying the 1929 Washington Conventions on Conciliation and Arbitration so that conciliation would become part of an obligatory set of interim measures ultimately leading to the arbitration of disputes not otherwise resolved. Nonjuridical as well as juridical matters would undergo arbitration. In addition, decisions should not require legislature approval, as in the case of the U.S. Senate, which insisted on the right to veto an arbitral *compromis* or treaty.

Yepes also argued that the hemisphere nations should abolish the reservations to the 1933 South American Anti-War Treaty whereby nations could declare themselves neutrals in case of wars of aggression in the Americas. These reforms, along with the acceptance of international law and diplomacy as means of resolving mistrust and tension between nations, would open the way to arms limitation and the elimination of the "germs of militarism." Yepes was also a strong supporter of the Kellogg-Briand Pact of 1928.

He may have made his most important contribution to international relations in his writing and personal interventions on behalf of the rights of territorial and political asylum. In his classic *El derecho de asilo*, he discussed the history of the concepts, their application in Latin America, and the classic case of Victor Raúl Haya de la Torre, the Peruvian Aprista political leader who sought refuge in the Colombian Embassy in Lima in 1948. In 1953 Yepes, no longer in the diplomatic service of his country, traveled privately to Lima to meet with President Manual Odria and his minister of foreign relations in an effort to resolve five years of fruitless negotiations over Haya. After further efforts by Yepes to resolve the case through the Inter-American Commission of Peace, Haya was "expelled" by Odria as an "undesirable person and without safe conduct." Nevertheless, he was allowed to travel to Colombia and several other Latin American nations until his return to Lima after the 1956 presidential elections, when President Pedro Beltran granted amnesty to all political exiles.

Yepes took up the border dispute between Ecuador and Peru over territories in the Marañon River basin in 1960–62. At a January 1942 meeting in Rio de Janeiro, Ecuador had been forced to give up territories it had considered part of its soil dating from Spanish rule because the United States and other nations wanted to show a united front against Japanese and German aggression. Subsequently, aerial surveys showed that old maps used in the negotiations did not include rivers and a mountain chain that would have affected the decision. Yepes argued that no nation could agree to a treaty as valid when it was signed under pressure.

BIBLIOGRAPHY:

A. with Pereira da Silva, *Commentaire théorique et practique du Pacte de la Société des nations et des statuts de l'Union panaméricaine*, 3 vols. (Paris, 1934–39); *Del Congreso de Panamá a la Conferencia de Caracas, 1826–1954*, 2nd ed. (Bogotá, 1970); *El derecho de asilo* (Bogotá, 1958); *El panamericanismo y el derecho internacional* (Bogotá, 1930); *Estudios internacionales* (Bogotá, 1929); *La codificatión del derecho internacional americano y la Conferencia de Rio de Janeiro* (Bogotá, 1927); "La Contribution de l'Amerique latine au dévéloppement du droit international publique et privé," *Recueil des cours* (Paris, 1930); *La Controversia fronteriza entre el Ecuador y el Perú* (Quinto, 1960); " 'Pax Americana,' The New Panamericanism and the Pan American Peace Conference," *World Affairs* 99 (Jun 1936), 80–88.

B. *Quién es quién en Colombia* (Bogota, 1944), 277–78; WWLA 1940, 549–50, 1951, 3, 72.

Neale J. Pearson

YOSHINO Sakuzō (29 January 1878, Miyagi-ken, Japan—18 March 1933, Tokyo). *Education*: graduate, Tokyo Univ., 1904. *Career*: taught in Tientsin, China, 1906–9; professor, Tokyo Univ., 1909–24; journalist, *Osaka Asahi* (newspaper), from 1924.

In the intellectual ferment of the World War I years, a liberal movement emerged in Japan known as Taisho democracy. Yoshino, a Tokyo University professor of political history and political theory, was the leading spokesman for that phenomenon and a formidable exponent of liberal and social democratic thought. A prolific writer and early convert to the Christian faith, Yoshino produced a torrent of articles in the journals *Chūō Kōron, Kaizō*, and *Reimei*, as well as a host of Christian publications. His complete works, published in 1948, fill eight volumes.

After assuming his post at Tokyo University in 1909, Yoshino spent four years in travel and study in the United States, France, England, Germany, and Belgium, an experience he considered the greatest influence on his life. In a 1916 article in *Chōō Kōron* he advanced his theory of *minpon shugi*, or government whose end is the people. Throughout his career he struggled to harmonize this notion with the orthodoxy of Japan's imperial institution. Beginning with his students, Yoshino organized such liberal societies as the Shinjinkai (New Man Society) and Reimeikai (Bright Dawn Society), which in turn published journals of radical thought. They promoted such changes as universal male suffrage and an end to oligarchic influences in government.

The stimulus of World War I evoked in Yoshino and his followers an intense interest in Japan's role in the world. Though Japan was a victorious Ally, it could not lead the world in democratization because, lamented Yoshino, Japan as a nation was controlled by ultraconservatives. "We must," he asserted, "clarify the basic character of our country in order to achieve the special mission of Japan on the world stage." Seeking a foreign policy concomitant of his liberal political theory, Yoshino early embraced Wilsonian idealism and became the first intellectual figure in Japan to urge affirmation of the League of Nations scheme. He warned in *Chūō Kōron* that Japan dare not risk isolation from the global diplomatic and economic systems of the future. He also advocated disarmament and racial equality. Though a League Covenant guarantee of racial nondiscrimination was rejected by the Paris Peace Conference, Yoshino remained committed to the organization. Yoshino's liberal political activities led to his forced resignation from his Tokyo University professorship in 1924. Thereafter he continued to promote his progressive views in the liberal and influential *Osaka Asahi* newspaper and as a part-time lecturer at Tokyo University.

BIBLIOGRAPHY:

A. *Minponshugiron: Yoshino Sakuzō Hakushi minshushugi ronshu* [Theory of minponshugi: The collected works of Dr. Yoshimo Sakuzō on democracy], 8 vols. (Tokyo, 1948).

B. Taichirō Mitani, ed., *Yoshino Sakuzō (Tokyo, 1972);* Tetsuo Najita, "Some Reflections on Idealism in the Political Thought of Yoshino Sakuzō," in *Japan in*

Crisis: Essays on Taishō Democracy, ed. Bernard S. Silberman and H. D. Harootunian, (Princeton, NJ, 1974), 29–66; Walter S. Perry, "Yoshino Sakuzō, 1878–1933: Exponent of Democratic Ideals in Japan," dissertation, Stanford, Univ., 1956; Bernard S. Silberman, "The Political Theory and Program of Yoshino Sakuzō," *Journal of Modern History* 31 (Dec 1959), 310–24; Kiyoko Takeda, "Yoshino Sakuzō," *Japan Quarterly* 12 (Oct–Dec 1965), 515–24; Sōgoro Tanaka, *Yoshino Sakuzō* (Tokyo, 1958).

Thomas W. Burkman

YOUNG, Owen D. (27 October 1874, Van Hornesville, NY—11 July 1962, Saint Augustine, FL). *Education*: B.A., Saint Lawrence Univ., 1894; LL.B., Boston Univ., 1896. *Career*: attorney, Boston, 1896–1912; vice-president, General Electric Co., 1913–22; chair, Radio Corporation of America, 1919–33; chair, General Electric, 1922–39; member, Expert Commission on Reparations, 1923–24; chair, American Section, International Chamber of Commerce, 1925, Second Expert Commission on Reparations, 1929; member, Committee on Foreign Aid, 1947; member, Hoover Commission, 1948.

Young served as a semi-official American financial expert on two reparation committees during the 1920s and attempted to resolve one of the most difficult economic problems of the postwar period. He had gained international prominence when he organized and became the first chairman of Radio Corporation of America (RCA) in 1919. He negotiated a series of agreements pooling existing and future technology among major American companies and divided up the radio equipment and transmission business. In subsequent years, Young engineered agreements with foreign companies which partitioned the world into radio zones and facilitated universal wireless communication. Young believed that international radio service and broadcasting were important forces for the advancement of civilization and world peace.

In 1923 the Allied Reparation Commission, with the advice and consent of Secretary of State *Charles E. Hughes, appointed Young to the Expert Committee to study the reparations question. Young helped construct a plan which would put Germany on a sound economic basis, restart the flow of reparations, and be acceptable to the Allies and Germany. He believed that many European controversies stemmed from international political indebtedness, because reparations and war debts served as a reminder of wartime rivalries and hatreds. Europe disharmony could be reduced only by resolving the reparations and war debts issue. To Young, the Dawes Plan, which the experts proposed, was a first step in that process because it would demonstrate Germany's ability and willingness to pay. Young played a leading role in formulating this temporary solution, which greatly reduced German yearly payments, provided for a sound transfer mechanism, and proposed an international loan for Germany to help stabilize its economy. The reparations experts unanimously accepted the Dawes report in April 1924.

That summer Young returned to Europe to help assure ratification by the interested governments. After the plan was adopted and bankers underwrote a sizable loan for Germany, Young was appointed agent general for reparations, ad interim, in charge of transferring payments. During his short tenure, Young put the complex machinery of the Dawes Plan in motion. It helped restore prosperity in Europe and created a climate for greater political cooperation among the major powers, but it was only a temporary solution to the problem. When conditions deteriorated, Young unsuccessfully appealed to Secretary of Commerce *Herbert Hoover to reduce the American tariff and cancel war debts to facilitate the payment of international political debts.

By late 1928, European and American leaders decided to propose a final reparations settlement. Young was appointed chairman of the Second Expert Commission in February 1929. Patiently he brought the opposing sides together, and the resulting Young Plan of June 1929 reduced yearly reparations payments, scheduled them to run for fifty-nine years, and unofficially linked the annuities to the Allied war debts owed the United States. It also provided for the withdrawal of all economic control agencies from Germany and paved the way for the termination of Allied military occupation of the Rhineland.

Perhaps the most creative feature of the Young Plan was the creation of the Bank for International Settlements (BIS). It was an instrument for central bankers under business control to remove the reparations problem from politics and allow decisions which would eventually eliminate indebtedness associated with the Great War. The Young Plan and the BIS went into operation in June 1930, but the effects of the Great Depression made the plan unworkable. Although the BIS survived the 1930s, it could not prevent the collapse of the international banking structure. Despite the failure of the reparations plan bearing his name, Young is remembered because of the venturesome action he took to ameliorate world problems.

BIBLIOGRAPHY:

B. John M. Carroll, "Owen D. Young: The Diplomacy of an Enlightened Businessman," in *U.S. Diplomats in Europe, 1919-1941*, ed. Kenneth Paul Jones (Santa Barbara, CA, 1981) 43–60; Josephine Y. and Everett N. Case, *A Purely Private Citizen, Owen D. Young: A Biography* (Boston, 1982); DAB supp. 7, 808–10; Ida M. Tarbell, *Owen D. Young: A New Type of Industrial Leader* (New York, 1932).

C. The Young papers are at the Van Hornesville Community Corporation.

John M. Carroll

Z

ZAHLE, Herluf (1873, Copenhagen—4 May 1941, Berlin). *Education*: Univ. of Copenhagen. *Career*: Danish foreign service, 1900–1904; first secretary, legation in Paris, 1904, Stockholm, 1905–8, and London, 1908–9; secretary, Ministry of Foreign Affairs, 1910–11; chamberlain to king of Denmark, 1911–41; minister to Sweden, 1919–24, to Berlin, 1924–41; delegate, League of Nations, 1920–28; member, Permanent Court of Arbitration, 1921–27.

Zahle established a reputation as a diplomat who became known in international circles through his extensive participation in world bodies. He presided in 1917 over a conference on prisoners of war held in Copenhagen, and in 1920 he headed the Danish delegation to the League. Thereafter, he served regularly, establishing a reputation as a working delegate, not a figurehead. He presided over the Assembly in 1928 and sat as president of the International Opium Conference in Geneva in 1925.

Zahle also became involved during the interwar years in efforts to resolve disputes peacefully. He encouraged the League to become more involved in allaying controversies, notably during the Corfu crisis, and he endorsed the Geneva Protocol and efforts to extend the principle of compulsory arbitration. He served on the Permanent Court of Arbitation at The Hague (1921–27), and he presented the case in 1932–33 for Denmark in a dispute over territory in Greenland. One of Zahle's last acts came as minister to Germany in June 1939, when he signed a nonaggression pact.

BIBLIOGRAPHY:

B. IWW 1937, 1159; NYT 6 May 1941, 21.

Warren F. Kuehl

ZAMENHOF, Ludwik Lazar (27 December 1859, Bialystok, Russian Poland—27 April 1917, Warsaw). *Education*: studied medicine, Univ. of Moscow, 1879–81; completed medical studies, Univ. of Warsaw, 1885. *Career*: general medical practice, later specializing as an oculist.

Zamenhof's fame stems not from his practice of medicine but from his accomplishments as a linguist and as the creator of Esperanto. That he was the son of a language teacher and was born in Bialystok largely explains Zamenhof's early interest in languages. The majority of Bialystok's population was Jewish, but groups of Russians, Poles, and Germans also dwelt in the city. Exposed to and distressed by the intense national and religious hostility among the inhabitants, he conceived the idea that this tension could be overcome if people understood each other better through use of a common language.

In 1873 the Zamenhof family moved to Warsaw. At the gymnasium Zamenhof added Greek, Latin, French, and German to the Yiddish,

Hebrew, Russian, and Polish he had acquired in Bialystok. During his last years as a gymnasium student, he became convinced that a common or universal language would bring the peoples of the world together. It was at this time that he devised the basic elements of a new, artificial language.

Zamenhof worked many years to perfect his ideas before he finally published in 1887 his *International Language*, a textbook of forty pages. Out of fear of compromising his medical career, he used the pseudonym Dr. Esperanto (one who hopes), and it was this name by which the new language became known.

An idealist who believed that peace and the brotherhood of man could be achieved by means of an international language, Zamenhof dedicated his life to propagating Esperanto. He published new editions of his grammar and compiled dictionaries, translated many classics of world literature into Esperanto, including the Old Testament, and composed poetry in the new language. He corresponded with Esperantists in many countries, assisted in organizing them on an international scale, and participated in their annual international congresses.

The outbreak of World War I struck a severe blow to Zamenhof's hopes and idealism, but he never abandoned his faith that Esperantism would contribute to peace, tolerance, and brotherhood. The Esperanto movement continues to exist, although its progress has been hampered by two world wars, dictatorships, and continuing national rivalries.

BIBLIOGRAPHY:

A. *Fundamenta krestomatio de la lingvo esperanto* (Paris, 1903); *Historio de esperanto, 1887–1912* (Warsaw, 1913); *International Language* (Warsaw, 1887); also translations of the Bible and literary classics from various languages.

B. Majorie Boulton, *Zamenhof: Creator of Esperanto* (London, 1960); Lidja Zamenhof, "Ludwik L. Zamenhof," *World Unity Magazine* 9 (Nov 1931), 84–88.

Charles Morley

ZEELAND, Paul van (11 November 1893, Soignies, Belgium—22 September 1973, Brussels). *Education*: LL.D. and doctorate in political and social science, Univ. of Louvain; M.A., Princeton Univ. *Career*: professor, Univ. of Louvain; economist and banker; vice-governor, National Bank, 1934–35; prime minister, 1935–37; president, League of Nations Assembly, 1936; foreign minister, 1935–36, 1949–54.

Belgium produced a number of statesmen working for European unity in the twentieth century, and of these van Zeeland was one of the more illustrious. Trained in law and economics, as much at home in the university atmosphere as in high banking circles, he emerged in the mid-1930s as a statesman of first rank. With almost no previous political experience, he was appointed prime minister of Belgium in 1935 to solve economic problems created by the Great Depression. Employing policies similar to those of the New Deal, he achieved a dramatic improvement in the economy and at the same time played no mean role in defeating the challenge of the Rexists, a Belgian Fascist movement. With his success and reputation, he was formally commissioned by the French and British governments in 1937 to make an inquiry into the possibility of removing obstacles to international trade. He had attended world economic conferences in 1922 and between 1929 and 1933, and in less than a year he issued the famous Van Zeeland Report. In this he outlined a realistic program designed to increase the flow of goods. The Report generated much discussion in Europe and further enhanced his stature. In the late 1930s he participated in League of Nations meetings and presided over the famous Assembly which debated the invasion of Ethiopia. Even by then, he was beginning to doubt whether the League could perform its functions, and these uncertainties may have focused his mind on European unity as an answer.

After World War II, Belgium played a leading role in Europe's quest for economic recovery and political unity. The country was involved in the negotiations which eventually led to the Benelux Union, the Marshall Plan, NATO, and the European Common Market. In these negotiations, van Zeeland was almost always present, usually working in close collaboration with his countryman, *Paul-Henri Spaak. Sometimes van Zeeland's presence was official; he served as foreign minister during the crucial period 1949–54. At other times his contributions were indirect, as in his work with academic institutes promoting Atlantic unity. Again, one of his guiding principles was the freeing of international trade.

Van Zeeland was a product of that rich tradition of postwar Christian Democracy which also produced *Konrad Adenauer of Germany, *A. De Gasperi of Italy, and *Robert Schuman of France. Christian Democracy represented the more progressive and enlightened side of European Catholicism which despite tradition could transcend national boundaries. While philosophically anti-Marxist and committed to the right of private property, Christian Democrats supported parliamentary institutions, social welfare legislation, and Pan European organizations. Van Zeeland was associated with the Catholic party (later the Christian Social party) and, although possessing a Cold War mentality and vigorously supporting NATO, he envisioned a United States of Europe which would not simply cooperate on economic issues, but would also achieve a substantial measure of political integration as well. He, with other Europeanists, deserves credit for initiating one of the boldest, most hopeful, and probably more successful ventures in European history.

BIBLIOGRAPHY:

A. *Economics or Politics?* (Cambridge, 1939); *International Economic Reconstruction* (New York, 1938); *La Réforme bancaire aux Etats-Unis d'Amérique de 1913 à 1921* (Brussels, 1922).

B. LT 24 Sep 1973, 16; NYT 23 Sep 1973, 65; Jean Albert Noville, *Paul van Zeeland au service de son temps* (Brussels, 1954); Frank P. Walters, *A History of the League of Nations* (London, 1952).

David C. Lukowitz

ZILLIACUS, Konni (13 September 1894, Kobe, Japan—6 July 1967, London). *Education*: Ph.B., Yale Univ., 1915. *Career*: British intelligence office, Siberia, 1917–19; Information Section, League of Nations Secretariat, 1919–39; Ministry of Information, London, 1939–45; member of Parliament, 1945–50, 1955–67.

Zilliacus won distinction as an official of the League, a prolific writer on international affairs, a leader in the British peace movement, and finally as a Laborite M.P. Throughout his career, he remained committed to a vision of Socialist internationalism which others had difficulty in categorizing. Often labeled a fellow traveler or crypto-Communist, he still criticized the Soviet Union and championed the case of Marshall Tito of Yugoslavia against it. As a member of the Labor party, he constantly ran afoul of party discipline.

Zilliacus's path to prominence in British left-wing politics was as unusual as his life. The son of an eminent Swedo-Finnish journalist and a Scottish-American mother, he was born in Japan and educated in the United States, Finland, Sweden, and Britain. His experience with the British military mission in Siberia gave him a knowledge of the Russian people which he drew on in later years. As a member of the Information Section of the League of Nations Secretariat he followed Soviet affairs. Noted for his command of languages, he attained some prominence in Geneva. During his two decades of service to the League, Zilliacus wrote a great deal, usually to promote collective security. He used many pen names—so many, in fact, that A.J.P. Taylor said in *The Troublemakers* (1957), "It is a safe rule which I present to future researchers that anyone writing in the nineteen thirties under a name other than his own was Konni Zilliacus." He advocated a Socialist foreign policy for Britain and criticized Conservatives and the government for failing to support the League. In 1935, as "Vigilantes," he published *Inquest on Peace*, which championed a policy of sanctions against Italy for its aggression against Ethiopia and cautioned the government not to deal with Mussolini.

During World War II, while in the Ministry of Information, he also became a leader of the League of Nations Union, Britain's largest internationalist society. As a member of its Executive Committee, he led the challenge to the policies of *Viscount Robert Cecil of Chelwood, the Union's longtime president, and he urged members to champion social change at home and oppose imperialism abroad. When Zilliacus won a seat in Parliament from Gateshead in 1945, his views did not seem too unusual for a Laborite. However, over the next few years, as the Labor government supported U.S. Cold War policies, he emerged as an annoying gadfly to his party leaders. In 1949 he was expelled, charged with being more sympathetic to Communism's aims than to Labor's. When he tried to contest the 1950 election as a "Labor Independent" candidate, he lost his seat. Many Laborites viewed Zilliacus as a well-meaning eccentric, and in 1952 he was allowed to rejoin the party. In 1955 he was returned to Parliament from Groton, and for a few years he moderated his criticism of Labor. By the end of 1960, Zilliacus was in trouble again because he had attacked Labor officials in a pamphlet entitled *The Anatomy of a Sacred Cow.* Suspension followed in 1961 but was lifted the following year. Zilliacus retained his seat in the 1964 and 1966 elections.

BIBLIOGRAPHY:

A. *Inquest on Peace* (London, 1935); *Mirror of the Past* (New York, 1946); *A New Birth of Freedom?* (New York, 1958).

B. LT 7 Jul 1967, 10.

Donald S. Birn

ZIMMERN, Alfred Eckhard (26 January 1879, Surbiton, England—24 November 1957, Avon, CT). *Education*: Winchester Coll., 1892–98; M.A., New Coll., Oxford Univ., 1905. *Career*: lecturer, New College, Oxford Univ., 1903, fellow and tutor, 1904–9; univ. secretary, Joint Committee on Oxford and Working-Class Education, 1907–8; staff inspector, Board of Education, 1912–15; Political Intelligence Department, British Foreign Office, 1918–19; Wilson professor of international politics, Univ. Coll. of Wales, 1919–21; acting professor, Cornell Univ., 1922–23; director, Geneva School of International Studies, 1925–29; deputy director, League of Nations Institute of Intellectual Co-operation in Paris, 1926–30; Montague Burton professor of international relations, Oxford Univ. 1930–44; deputy director, Research Department, British Foreign Office, 1943–45; adviser on information and external relations, Ministry of Education, 1945; secretary-general, Constitutent Conference, United Nations Educational, Scientific and Cultural Organization (UNESCO), 1945; executive secretary, later adviser, UNESCO Preparatory Commission, 1946; visiting professor, Trinity Coll., Hartford, CT, 1947–49; American International Coll., Springfield, MA.

Historian, foreign affairs specialist, and firm supporter of world government, Zimmern was one of the outstanding academic internationalists of the twentieth century. A brilliant Oxford lecturer and an articulate cosmopolitan commanding four languages, his first book, *The Greek Commonwealth,* won universal esteem. He then forsook the university community for government work. During World War I he served with a team of Foreign Office specialists that studied the boundaries of Eastern Europe and established the Minority Treaties. One of the founders of the Royal Institute of International Affairs, Zimmern was outspoken on Britain's obligations to restore and maintain peace in Europe.

During the next two decades, as teacher, administrator, writer, and lecturer, Zimmern pleaded the cause of the League of Nations, urged cooperation between Britain and France, and also advocated the transformation of the British Empire into a responsible self-governing commonwealth. His internationalism consisted neither of vague formulations of supranational loyalties nor of adherence to great power direction. He called for an enduring internationalist network based on the expansion of liberty, national freedom, and generous, vigorous contacts between those who had both freedom and a firm national identity. Though a spokesman for peace and disarmament in the 1920s, Zimmern perceived the Fascist menace and urged that the League lead the resistance in the 1930s. An important contributor to the founding of UNESCO, Zimmern settled after World War II in the United States, where he found a new and ready audience for his message of world leadership and responsibility.

BIBLIOGRAPHY:

A. *The American Road to World Peace* (New York, 1953); *Europe in Convalescence* (London, 1922); *Henry Grattan* (Oxford, 1902); *The League of Nations and the Rule of Law 1919–1935* (London, 1936); *Nationality and Government, with Other Wartime Essays* (London, 1918); *The Prospects of Democracy and Other Essays* (London, 1929); *Spiritual Values and World Affairs* (Oxford, 1939); *The Third British Empire* (London, 1926); with others, *The War and Democracy* (London, 1914).

B. DNB 1951–60, 1096–97; NYT 25 Nov 1957, 31; Arnold J. Toynbee, *Acquaintances* (London, 1967); WWA 1958–59, 3088; WWW 1951–60; WWWA 3, 950.

C. Zimmern papers are in the Bodleian Library, Oxford Univ.

Carole Fink

ZOOK, George Frederick (22 April 1885, Fort Scott, KS—17 August 1951, Arlington, VA). *Education*: B.A., Univ. of Kansas, 1906, M.A., 1907; Ph.D., Cornell Univ., 1913. *Career*: instructor to professor, Penn State Univ., 1909–16; president, Univ. of Akron, 1925–33; commissioner for education, 1933; president, American Council on Education; 1934–51.

Zook's teaching career was short-lived, interrupted in 1918 by service on the Committee on Public Information, for which he wrote the series *America at War*. In 1919 he was associate director of the U.S. Treasury Savings Division and in 1920 served as chief of the Division of Higher Education in the U.S. Bureau of Education. His plans as president of the University of Akron, 1925–33, for developing its graduate and research capacities were frustrated by the Depression. During those years he became a leader in organizing the accreditation work of the North Central Association of Schools and Colleges, and he was active in the National Advisory Committee on Education.

In 1933 Zook was appointed U.S. commissioner for education by President *Franklin Roosevelt. He left this post one year later to begin his long association with the American Council on Education. As its president, Zook became the premier lobbyist for higher education, helping to gear the educational establishment in support of the nation's World War II effort. In 1946–47 he was appointed chairman of the Commission on Higher Education. Its report had broad consequences for American education, including extension of vocational education programs, an expanded junior college program, and federal aid to education which resulted in large sums for construction and for programming. Zook also urged government subsidies for veterans and endorsed the establishment of the National Science Foundation.

Zook's formal involvement in international education stemmed from 1939, when he edited the report of proceedings of the League of Nations annual meeting on intellectual cooperation. In the post–World War II era few if any Americans were as involved in international educational matters. He was chairman of the 1946 U.S. Educational Mission to Germany, which recommended a restructuring of German educational institutions. He advocated and supported student and cultural exchange programs. When controversy arose as to whether such efforts should be handled by private institutions or by the federal government, Zook supported the interests of private institutions, perhaps because the American Council on Education was involved. He helped gain provisions on education in the Charter of the United Nations, and he became intimately involved with the United Nations Educational, Scientific and Cultural Organization. As U.S. national commissioner for UNESCO, he attended that group's conferences from 1946 to 1951. He was a founder (1950) in Nice, France, of the International Association of Universities.

His practical, resourceful organizational and management skills, coupled with his entree to powerful government and foundation resources, made Zook a most successful educational leader. He was not an ideologue; he sought to put useful programs into action. He has been called a consumate bureaucrat—politic, well-prepared, unflappable. He died about one month after returning from Paris where he had represented the United States at the sixth UNESCO conference.

BIBLIOGRAPHY:

A. *The Company of Royal Adventurers Trading Into Africa* (Lancaster, PA, 1919); with M. E. Haggerty, *Principles of Accrediting Higher Institutions* (Chicago, 1936); numerous reports for governmental and educational agencies.

B. CB 1946, 678–81; DAB supp. 5, 761–63; George W. Knepper, *New Lamps for Old: One Hundred Years of Urban Higher Education at the University of Akron* (Akron, OH, 1970); NCAB 38, 563–64; Frank A. Ninkovitch, *The Diplomacy of Ideas: United States Foreign Policy and Cultural Relations 1938–1950* (Cambridge, 1981); NYT 19 Aug 1951, 83; WWWA 3, 950–51.

George W. Knepper

Appendixes

CHRONOLOGY

This chronology provides a valuable perspective on internationalist trends and growth. While a few developments prior to 1800 were significant to the development of internationalism, the nineteenth century saw the first consistent pattern in the growth of an ideal. The era prior to 1914 is best described as one of disorganized growth. The European Concert system, while not designed to create an open cooperative world, nonetheless showed governments that they could organize collectively. An emerging sense of oneness impelled citizens and states toward accord in striving for a more cooperative arrangement. They made progress in nonpolitical areas and in advancing the dream of resolving disputes peacefully, especially through arbitration. The Hague Conferences of 1899 and 1907 seemed to document the growing conviction that nation-states could accept some limit on their absolute sovereignty.

World War I and the interwar years saw a second stage in the evolutionary movement. Many individuals came to believe that a better organized world could have averted the catastrophe of 1914–18. That led to the first universal international political organization, the League of Nations. A chronology shows the extent of planning and the continuing efforts to support the League. It also discloses the exceptional amount of energy expended in the interwar period to solve world problems cooperatively outside the League. These were primarily economic and political, reflecting the unsatisfactory peace settlement of 1919, but progress was also evident in the realm of social, humanitarian, and intellectual concerns. These were adventuresome years in which ideas were explored and tested.

The third era dates from 1939. It has been marked by a trend toward both universal and regional cooperation. Extensive alliance systems show that the nation-state has remained a powerful force at the same time governments and their leaders proclaim the virtues of interdependence, seek to advance human rights and a new economic order, and build a larger and larger international system. Outside the political sphere a vast network of nongovernmental organizations provide evidence of interrelated interests.

What is most remarkable about chronology is the documentation it provides of an impelling current. It took centuries from the Greek amphityonic councils to the League of Nations; yet since 1919 the changes have been dramatic. Most of the subjects in this biographical dictionary contributed toward this development and would be pleased to see the results of their labors.

1815	Congress of Vienna and Concert of Europe
1818	Aix-la-Chapelle Conference
1820–21	Troppeau and Laibach Conferences
1822	Verona Conference
1826	Panama Conference
1851	First International Health Conference, Paris

1856	Declaration of Paris
1864	Geneva (Red Cross) Convention
1865	International Telecommunications Union formed
1872	Geneva Arbitration Award, Alabama Claims
1873	Meteorological Organization formed
1873	Institut de Droit International created
1873	International Law Association created
1874	Universal Postal Union created
1874	Declaration of Brussels
1875	International Bureau of Weights and Measures formed
1878	Berlin Conference on Balkans
1884	Conference and Convention on Submarine Cables
1885	Berlin Conference on Congo
1889	Inter-Parliamentary Union created
1889–90	Pan American Conference, Washington
1890	Brussels Slave Trade Act
1890	International Bureau of the American Republics created
1892	Permanent International Peace Bureau created, Bern, Switzerland
1895	First Lake Mohonk Arbitration Conference
1896	National Arbitration Conference, Washington
1899	First Hague Peace Conference
1899	Permanent Court of Arbitration created
1901–2	Pan American Conference, Mexico City
1902	Pan American Sanitary Bureau
1904	Convention on White Slavery
1905	International Institute of Agriculture formed
1906	Pan American Conference, Rio de Janeiro
1906	Radiotelegraphic Union formed
1906	Association for International Conciliation established
1907	International Office of Public Hygiene created
1907	Second Hague Peace Conference
1908	Central American Court of Justice organized
1909	Shanghai Opium Conference
1910	Pan American Conference, Buenos Aires
1910	American Society for the Judicial Settlement of Disputes created
1910	World Peace Foundation created
1910	Carnegie Endowment for International Peace created
1912	American Institute of International Law formed
1913	Hague Peace Palace completed
1914	Church Peace Union created
1914	World Alliance for International Friendship through the Churches
1914	Constance World Conference of Church Leaders
1915	League of Nations Society (England) organized
1915	Central Organization for a Durable Peace created
1915	American Institute of International Law founded
1915	League to Enforce Peace organized
1919	Paris Peace Conference

1919	Covenant of League of Nations
1919	International Labor Organization created
1919	Federation of League of Nations Associations
1920	Statute of Permanent Court of International Justice drafted
1920	First Assembly of League of Nations, Geneva
1920	Brussels Financial Conference
1920	Permanent Court of International Justice created
1921	General Conference on Communications and Transit, Barcelona
1921–22	Washington Conference on the Limitation of Naval Armaments
1922	Committee on Intellectual Co-operation organized
1922	Permanent Court of International Justice opened
1922	Foreign Policy Association created
1922	League of Nations Non-Partisan Association formed
1923	Hague Academy of International Law begins
1923	Health Section of League of Nations organized
1923	Pan American Conference, Santiago
1924	Dawes Plan
1924	Geneva Protocol for Pacific Settlement of International Disputes
1924–25	Geneva Opium Conference
1925	International Conference on the Control of the Traffic in Arms
1925	International Bureau of Education formed
1925	International Institute of Intellectual Co-operation began
1925	World Council of Churches Conference, Stockholm
1925	Locarno Conference
1926	First Session, Preparatory Commission on Disarmament, Geneva
1927	World Conference on Faith and Order, Lausanne, Switzerland
1927	World Economic Conference, Geneva
1927	Conference on Reduction of Naval Armament, Geneva
1928	Pan American Conference, Havana
1928	Kellogg-Briand Pact [Pact of Paris]
1929	Young Plan
1930	London Naval Conference
1930	Bank for International Settlement created
1930	Hague Conference on Codification of International Law
1931	Manchurian Crisis
1932–34	General Disarmament Conference, Geneva
1933	Argentine Anti-War Pact
1933	Pan American Conference, Montevideo
1933	London Economic Conference
1935	Saar Plebiscite
1935	Ethiopian Crisis
1935–36	London Naval Conference
1936	Montreux Conference
1936	Pan American Conference, Buenos Aires
1937	Oxford Conference on Church, Community, and State
1938	World Council of Churches, Edinburgh
1938	Pan American Conference, Lima

1941	Atlantic Charter
1943	Food and Argriculture Organization planned
1943	United Nations Relief and Rehabilitation Administration (UNRRA) created
1944	Bretton Woods Conference
1944	International Monetary Fund created
1944	International Bank for Reconstruction and Development
1944	Dumbarton Oaks Conference
1945	International Court of Justice created
1945	Food and Agriculture Organization formed
1945	UN Educational, Scientific and Cultural Organization (UNESCO) formed
1945	Pan American Conference, Mexico City
1945	UN Conference on International Organization, San Francisco
1946	Benelux Customs Union created
1946	World Health Organization organized
1946	UN Children's Fund created
1946	Food and Agricultural Organization launched
1947	United Europe Committees created in Britain, France, and the United States
1947	United World Federalists organized, Ashville, NC
1947	General Agreement on Tariffs and Trade signed
1948	Congress of Europe convened
1948	Marshall Plan
1948	Brussels Treaty of Alliance and Cooperation
1948	General Agreement on Tariffs and Trade concluded
1948	World Council of Churches formed
1948	Organization of American States formed
1948	Universal Declaration of Human Rights
1949	North Atlantic Treaty Organization signed
1949	Council for Mutual Economic Assistance formed
1949	Council of Europe created
1950	Schuman Plan presented
1950	"Uniting for Peace" Resolution
1950	European Convention for the Protection of Human Rights and Fundamental Freedoms
1951	Conference of Six, Paris
1951	European Coal and Steel Community formed
1952	European Defense Community formed
1952	European Coal and Steel Community inaugurated
1953	European Union Charter approved
1954	Inter-American Conference, Caracas
1954	Geneva Conference on Southeast Asia
1955	Warsaw Pact
1955	Action Committee for the United States of Europe created
1957	International Atomic Energy Agency in force
1958	European Economic Community formed
1958	European Court of Human Rights created
1958	European Economic Community formed

1960	European Free Trade Association established
1960	Organization for Economic Co-Operation and Development formed
1962	Alliance for Progress
1962	Organization of African States planned
1968	Non-Proliferation Treaty signed in UN
1969	Strategic Arms Limitations Talks begin
1971	People's Republic of China admitted to UN
1972	SALT I signed
1973	Great Britain joined European Economic Community
1975	Helsinki Conference on Security and Human Rights
1979	First General Elections to European Parliament

Appendix I

Internationalists by Birthplace and Country with Which Identified

There is no satisfactory way to identify internationalists according to national status. First, many of them move across boundaries, while wars and treaties often move boundaries. Second, names of countries change. This listing is according to contemporary name, not what the place was called at their birth. Third, their natal land may not be representative of race or culture because many of the subjects were children of diplomats, missionaries, or business figures living abroad. It thus is not necessarily indicative of where they lived the bulk of their lives. For convenience and clarity, the names of persons whose careers and lives are identified with a country other than that of their birth are noted in brackets.

ALGIERS
Georges Valensi

ARGENTINA
José Antonio Arce
[Carlos Calvo]
Luís María Drago
Honorio Pueyrredón

AUSTRALIA
Carl August Berendsen
Stanley Melbourne Bruce
Ronald William Gordon Mackay
George Gilbert Aimé Murray

AUSTRIA
[Richard Coudenhove-Kalergi]
Alcide De Gasperi
[Friedrich von Gentz]
[Hans Kelsen]
Heinrich Lammasch

BELGIUM
August-Marie-François Beernaert
Charles de Visscher
Camille Adolphe Gutt
Paul Hymans
Théodore Joseph Albéric Lefèvre

[Joseph Nisot]
Paul-Marie-Ghislain Otlet
Henri Rolin
Edouard Rolin-Jaequemyns
Gustave Henri Ange Hippolyte Rolin-
    Jaequemyns
Paul-Henri Spaak
Emile Vandervelde
Paul van Zeeland

BRAZIL
[Oswaldo Euclides de Sousa Aranha]
José Philadelpho Azevedo
Ruy Barbosa
Raul Fernandes
José Carlos de Macedo Soares
Afranio de Mello Franco
José Maria da Silva Paranhos, Jr.
Epitacio Lindolfo da Silva Pessôa

BURMA
U Thant

CANADA
Herbert Brown Ames
Fannie Fern Phillips Andrews
Robert Laird Borden
Isaiah Bowman
Charles Henry Brent

George Brock Chisholm
John Wesley Dafoe
Raoul Dandurand
George Eulas Foster
William Lyon MacKenzie King
Lester Bowles Pearson
Walter Alexander Riddell
Jacob Gould Schurman
James Brown Scott
James Thomson Shotwell

CEYLON
Hamilton Shirley Amerasinghe
Humphrey Hume Wrong

CHILE
Alejandro Alvarez
Benjamin Alberto Cohen Gallerstein
Agustín Edwards Mac-Clure

CHINA
Cheng T'ien-hsi
Chou Ken-sheng
[Hoo Chi-Tsai]
Hsu Mo
Shih Chao-chi
[Wang Ch'ung-hui]

COLOMBIA
Eduardo Santos
Francisco José Urrutia
Jesús María Yepes

CUBA
Aristides de Agüero y Betancourt
Antonio Sanchez de Bustamante

CZECHOSLOVAKIA
Eduard Beneš
Hans Kelsen
Jan Masaryk
Joseph Redlich
Egon Schwelb

DENMARK
Per Haekkerup
Jens Otto Krag

EGYPT
Abd al-Hamid Badawi

EL SALVADOR
José Gustavo Guerrero

ENGLAND
[Charles Stewart Addis]
William Edward Arnold-Foster
Herbert Henry Asquith
Arthur James Balfour
Jeremy Bentham
Norman de Mattos Bentwich
Johann Heinrich von Bernstorff
Violet Bonham Carter
Bramwell Booth
Evangeline Booth
Henry Noel Brailsford
Robert Henry Brand
James Leslie Brierly
Harold Beresford Butler
Anthony Buxton
George Catlin
Edgar Algernon Robert Gascoyne Cecil
Rachel Eleanor Crowdy
[Eyre Alexander Crowe]
Goldsworthy Lowes Dickinson
Willoughby Hyett Dickinson
Eric Drummond
Albert Freiherr Dufour-Feronce
Herbert Albert Laurens Fisher
James Clerk Maxwell Garnett
Edward Grey
Selskar Michael Gunn
[Edmund Hall-Patch]
[Maurice Pascal Alers Hankey]
Henry Wilson Harris
Leonard Trelawney Hobhouse
John Atkinson Hobson
Thomas Erskine Holland
Cecil James Barrington Hurst
Julian Sorell Huxley
Herbert Ernest Hyde
Clarence Wilfred Jenks
Frank Noel Keen
John Maynard Keynes
Peter Michael Kirk
Cecil Hermann Kisch

[Hersch Lauterpacht]
Walter Thomas Layton
David Lloyd George
Alexander Loveday
[Ivison Macadam]
[Ronald William Gordon Mackay]
Geoffrey Le Mesurier Mander
Arnold Duncan McNair
[George Gilbert Aimé Murray]
Walter Nash
Otto Ernst Niemeyer
Montagu Collet Norman
George Ashton Oldham
[Joseph Holdsworth Oldham]
[Lassa Francis Lawrence Oppenheim]
Walter George Frank Phillimore
Juliet Evangeline Rhys Williams
James Arthur Salter
Francis Herbert Stead
William Thomas Stead
Arnold J. Toynbee
Charles Philips Trevelyan
Francis Paul Walters
Charles K. Webster
Herbert George Wells
John W. Wheeler-Bennett
Leonard Sidney Woolf
[Evelyn Wrench]
[Konni Zilliacus]
Alfred Eckhard Zimmern

FINLAND
Rafael Waldemar Erich
Hjalmar Johan Frederik Procopé

FRANCE
Louis Armand
Joseph Louis Anne Avenol
Louis Barthou
Jules Basdevant
Léon Blum
Henri Bonnet
Léon Victor Auguste Bourgeois
Aristede Pierre Henri Briand
René-Samuel Cassin
Pierre Comert
Charles A.J.M de Gaulle
[Christian Fouchet]
André François-Poncet
[Antoine -F. Frangulis]

Henri-Auguste Fromageot
Maurice Pascal Alers Hankey
Albert Auguste Gabriel Hanotaux
Edouard Herriot
Léon Jouhaux
Henry de Jouvenel
Harry Klemens Ulrich Kessler
René Mayer
Guy Mollet
Jean Omer Marie Gabriel Monnet
Joseph Paul-Boncour
André Philip
Georges Jean Raymond Pompidou
Paul Ramadier
Paul Reynaud
Jacques Léon Rueff
Théodore Eugène César Ruyssen
[Robert Schuman]
Albert Thomas
Francisco Tudela y Varela
[Georges Valensi]

GERMANY
Konrad Adenauer
Thomas Willing Balch
Richard Bartholdt
[Johann Heinrich von Bernstorff]
[Johann Casper Bluntschli]
Heinrich von Brentano
Eyre Alexander Crowe
[Albert Freiherr Dufour-Feronce]
Fritz Kurt Gustav Erler
Friedrich von Gentz
Karl Ernst Nikolaus Haushofer
Ernst Jaeckh
Francis Lieber
[Paul Gustav Emil Loebe]
Hans Joachim Morgenthau
Lassa Francis Lawrence Oppenheim
Walther Rathenau
Heinrich Georg Ritzel
Michał Cezary Rostworowski
Walther Adrian Schücking
Herman Soergel
Oscar Solomon Straus
Gustav Stresemann
John Henry Wilburn Stuckenberg
James Paul Warburg
Hans Wehberg

GHANA
Kwame Nkrumah

GREECE
Antoine -F. Frangulis
Nicholas Socrate Politis

HAITI
Dantès Bellegarde

HONG KONG
Wang Ch'ung-hui

INDIA
Atul Chandra Chatterjee
Ariot Ramaswami Mudalier
Joseph Holdsworth Oldham

IRELAND
James Bryce
Seán Lester
[Edward Joseph Phelan]
Evelyn Wrench

ITALY
Pompeo Aloisi
[Henrik Christian Andersen]
Bernardo Attolico
Giuseppe Antonio Borgese
Eugenio Colorni
[Alcide de Gaspari]
Luigi Einaudi
Ugo La Malfa
Pasquale Stanislao Mancini
Gaetano Martino
Francesco Saverio Nitti
Mario Andrew Pei
Mario Pistocchi
Carlo Rosselli
Ernesto Rossi
Gaetano Salvemini
Vittorio Scialoja
Carlo Sforza

JAPAN
Adachi Mineichiro
Richard Coudenhove-Kalergi
Jerome Davis Greene
[Sidney Lewis Gulick]
Hideyo Noguchi

Ishii Kikugirō
Makino Nobuaki
Nitobe Inazō
Satō Naotake
Sugimara Yōtarō
Yoshino Sakuzō
Konni Zilliacus

LEBANON
Jamil Murad Baroody

LUXEMBURG
Joseph Bech
Robert Schuman
Matthew Woll

MARSHALL ISLANDS
Sidney Lewis Gulick

MEXICO
Daniel Cosio Villegas
Isidro Fabela Alfaro
Jaime Torres Bodet

NETHERLANDS
Michael Carel Tobias Asser
Bernard Cornelis Johannes Loder
Philipp Christiaan Molhuysen
Petrus Josephus Servatius Serrarens
Jacob ter Meulen

NEW ZEALAND
[Carl August Berendsen]
[Peter Fraser]
Leslie Knox Munro
[Walter Nash]

NORWAY
Hendrik Christian Andersen
Erik Andreas Colban
Carl Joachim Hambro
Edvard Isak Hambro
Christian Lous Lange
Trygve Halvdan Lie
Johan Ludwig Mowinckel
Fridtjof Nansen
Elise Ottesen-Jensen

PANAMA
Ricardo Joaquín Alfaro

PERU
Víctor Andrés Belaúnde y Diéz Canceco
[Francisco Tudela y Varela]

POLAND
Adam Jerzy Czartoryski
Hersch Lauterpacht
Paul Gustav Emil Loebe
Ignacy Jan Paderewski
Ludwik W. Rajchman
Adam Rapacki
Joseph Hieronim Retinger
[Michał Rostworowski]
Aleksander Skrzyński
Walter Wanderwell
Bohdan Stefan Winiarski
Ludwik Lazar Zamenhof

PUERTO RICO
[Pablo Carlos Salvador Defillo de Casals]
Eugenio María de Hostos

ROMANIA
Ely Culbertson
Nicolae Titulescu

SCOTLAND
Charles Stewart Addis
John Boyd-Orr
Peter Fraser
David Maxwell Fyfe
Arthur Henderson
James Lorimer
Ivison Macadam
James Ramsay MacDonald
Andrew McFadyean

SOUTH AFRICA
Seymour Jacklin
[Albert John Mvumbi Luthuli]
Jan Christiaan Smuts

SOVIET UNION
Vera Micheles Dean
Edmund Hall-Patch
Lewis Levitzki Lorwin
Maksim Maksimovich Litvinov
Frederic Frommhold de Martens

Mikhail Nikolaevich Murav'ev
Leo Pasvolsky
Nicholas K. Roerich

SPAIN
Pablo de Azcárate y Flórez
Pablo Carlos Salvador Defillo de Casals
Salvador de Madariago y Rojo
Arturo de Marcoartú y Morales
José María Quiñones de Leon

SRI LANKA
Hamilton Shirley Amerasinghe

SWEDEN
Folke Bernadotte
Karl Hjalmar Branting
Dag Hjalmar Agne Carl Hammarskjöld
Per Jacobsson
[Elise Ottesen-Jensen]
Ivar Rooth
Nathan Söderblom
Bo Östen Undén

SWITZERLAND
Johann Caspar Bluntschli
Carl Jacob Burckhardt
Louis Curchod
Christian Fouchet
Max Huber
[Clarence Wilfred Jenks]
Giuseppe Motta
[Edward Joseph Phelan]
[William Emanuel Rappard]
[Hans Wehberg]

TURKEY
Tevfik Rüştü Aras

URUGUAY
Carlos Calvo
José Antonio Mora Otero

UNITED STATES OF AMERICA
Grace Abbott
Herbert Baxter Adams
Chandler Parsons Anderson
[Fannie Fern Phillips Andrews]

Hamilton Fish Armstrong
Frank Cooke Atherton
Henry Avery Atkinson
Warren Robinson Austin
Frank Aydelotte
Newton Diehl Baker
Ray Stannard Baker
[Thomas Willing Balch]
John Barrett
[Richard Bartholdt]
Charles Christian Bauer
Richard Reeve Baxter
George Louis Beer
Robert S. Benjamin
Anita Eugenie McCormick Blaine
George Hubbard Blakeslee
Tasker Howard Bliss
Rupert Lee Blue
William Hervey Blymer
Edwin Montefiore Borchard
[Isaiah Bowman]
[Charles Henry Brent]
Raymond Landon Bridgman
Arthur Judson Brown
Raymond Leslie Buell
Ralph Johnson Bunche
Nicholas Murray Butler
Robert J. Caldwell
James Cannon, Jr.
Edward Clark Carter
Samuel McCrea Cavert
Joseph Perkins Chamberlain
Ben Mark Cherrington
Grenville Clark
John Hessin Clarke
Bainbridge Colby
Everett Colby
Samuel Colcord
Archibald Cary Coolidge
Andrew Wellington Cordier
Frederic René Coudert
James Middleton Cox
Wilbur Fisk Crafts
Charles Richard Crane
Oscar Terry Crosby
[Ely Culbertson]
Hugh Smith Cumming
Edward Cummings

Hayne Davis
John William Davis
Malcolm Waters Davis
Norman Hezekiah Davis
Charles Gates Dawes
[Vera Micheles Dean]
Eberhard Paul Deutsch
Edwin DeWitt Dickinson
Norris Edward Dodd
Michael Francis Doyle
Laurence Duggan
Stephen P. Duggan
John Foster Dulles
Frederick Sherwood Dunn
Victor Hugo Duras
Samuel Train Dutton
Clyde Eagleton
Cyrus Stephen Eaton
Clark Mell Eichelberger
Charles William Eliot
Martha May Eliot
Brooks Emeny
Alona Elizabeth Evans
Herbert Feis
Abraham Howard Feller
Charles Ghequiere Fenwick
David Dudley Field
Edward A. Filene
George Augustus Finch
Thomas Knight Finletter
Irving Norton Fisher
Abraham Flexner
James Jackson Forstall
Raymond Blaine Fosdick
John Watson Foster
Leon Fraser
Harry Augustus Garfield
James Wilford Garner
O. Benjamin Gerig
Hugh Gibson
Prentiss Bailey Gilbert
S. Parker Gilbert
Huntington Gilchrist
Virginia Crocheron Gildersleeve
Edwin Ginn
Carter Lyman Goodrich
Caspar Frederick Goodrich
[Jerome Davis Greene]

Roger Sherman Greene
Theodore Ainsworth Greene
[Sidney Lewis Gulick]
[Selskar Michael Gunn]
Reuben G. Gustavson
Green Haywood Hackworth
John Hays Hammond
Richard Heathcote Heindel
Amos Shartle Hershey
David Jayne Hill
Gilbert Monell Hitchcock
Richmond Pearson Hobson
Paul Gray Hoffman
Arthur Norman Holcombe
George Kenneth Holland
George Chandler Holt
Hamilton Holt
Hoo Chi-Tsai
Herbert Clark Hoover
Ernest Martin Hopkins
Halford Lancaster Hoskins
Edward Mandell House
Herbert Sherman Houston
Manley Ottmer Hudson
Charles Evans Hughes
Cordell Hull
Robert Lee Humber
Howard Riggins Huston
Robert Maynard Hutchins
Charles Cheney Hyde
Samuel Guy Inman
William Henry Irwin
Frank Billings Kellogg
Frances Alice Kellor
Chase Kimball
Florence Cross Kitchelt
Arthur Kline Kuhn
Ellen Newbold La Motte
Harriet Burton Laidlaw
Thomas William Lamont
Robert Lansing
Henry Goddard Leach
Herbert Henry Lehman
Henry Smith Leiper
Charles Herbert Levermore
[Francis Lieber]
Walter Lippmann
Henry Cabot Lodge

James Addison Logan, Jr.
Breckinridge Long
[Lewis Levitzki Lorwin]
Abbott Lawrence Lowell
Frederick Henry Lynch
Charles Stedman Macfarland
Alfred Thayer Mahan
Theodore Marburg
George Catlett Marshall
Charles Emanuel Martin
Herbert Louis May
William Gibbs McAdoo
Vance Criswell McCormick
Porter James McCumber
James Grover McDonald
William Osborne McDowell
Edwin Doak Mead
Lucia True Ames Mead
Sidney E. Mezes
David Hunter Miller
Raleigh Colston Minor
Samuel Chiles Mitchell
Jay Pierrepont Moffat
John Bassett Moore
Laura Puffer Morgan
[Hans Joachim Morgenthau]
Henry Crittenden Morris
Dwight Whitney Morrow
Blanche Rosalie Slaughter Morton
John Raleigh Mott
Edgar Ansel Mowrer
Paul Scott Mowrer
Denys Peter Myers
Philip Curtis Nash
George William Nasmyth
Oscar Newfang
Otto Frederick Nolde
[George Ashton Oldham]
John Francis O'Ryan
Garfield Bromley Oxnam
Herbert Parsons
[Leo Pasvolsky]
Amos Jenkins Peaslee
Lillie M. Peck
[Mario Andrew Pei]
Frank Lyon Polk
James Pinckney Pope
Chester DeWitt Pugsley

Jackson Harvey Ralston
John Herman Randall
William Emmanuel Rappard
Paul Samuel Reinsch
Raymond Thomas Rich
Owen Josephus Roberts
Joseph Taylor Robinson
John Davison Rockefeller, Jr.
John Davison Rockefeller, 3d
Nelson Aldrich Rockefeller
[Nicholas K. Roerich]
Anna Eleanor Roosevelt
Franklin Delano Roosevelt
Theodore Roosevelt
Elihu Root
Leo Stanton Rowe
Josiah Royce
Lindsay Russell
[Jacob Gould Schurman]
[Egon Schwelb]
[James Brown Scott]
Charles Seymour
Whitney Hart Shepardson
Henry Knox Sherrill
William Harrison Short
[James Thomson Shotwell]
Jeremiah Smith, Jr.
Alpheus Henry Snow
Edward Reilly Stettinius, Jr.
Adlai Ewing Stevenson II
Henry Louis Stimson
Ellery Cory Stowell
[Oscar Solomon Straus]
Silas Hardy Strawn
Cyrus H. Street
[John Henry Wilburn Stuckenberg]
Arthur Sweetser
Raymond Edwards Swing
William Howard Taft
Elbert Duncan Thomas
Dorothy Thompson
Harry S Truman
Florence Guertin Tuttle
Royall Tyler
Carl Van Doren
James W. Van Kirk

Arthur Hendrick Vandenberg
Thorstein Bunde Veblen
Eliot Wadsworth
Henry Agard Wallace
Edmund A. Walsh
Thomas James Walsh
Sarah Wambaugh
[Walter Wanderwell]
[James Paul Warburg]
Paul W. Ward
Earl Warren
Thomas John Watson, Sr.
Sumner Welles
Henry Wheaton
Andrew Dickson White
William Allen White
George Woodward Wickersham
Ray Lyman Wilbur
Alexander Wiley
Wendell Lewis Willkie
Westel Woodbury Willoughby
George Grafton Wilson
Hugh Robert Wilson
Mary Florence Wilson
Thomas Woodrow Wilson
John Gilbert Winant
Emma Wold
[Matthew Woll]
Mary Emma Woolley
Theodore Salisbury Woolsey
Elizabeth Washburn Wright
Hamilton Kemp Wright
Quincy Wright
Owen D. Young
George Frederick Zook

VENEZUELA
Simón Bolívar
Simón Planas-Suárez

WALES
Clement Edward Davies
David Davies

ZIMBABWE (Rhodesia)
Albert John Mvumbi Luthuli

APPENDIX II

INTERNATIONALISTS BY CAREER

Internationalists often pursued careers in more than one field. Many were attorneys who practiced law briefly if at all because they found other interests. Those who became international civil servants usually had established careers before they accepted administrative positions with world agencies or bodies. This appendix thus has double listings, where appropriate, to show achievement or considerable involvement in two or more career activities.

ACADEMIC
Herbert Baxter Adams
Alejandro Alvarez
Tobias Michael Carel Asser
Frank Aydelotte
José Philadelpho Azevedo
Jules Basdevant
Richard Reeve Baxter
George Louis Beer
Norman de Mattos Bentwich
George Hubbard Blakeslee
Johann Caspar Bluntschli
Edwin Montefiore Borchard
Giuseppe Antonio Borgese
Isaiah Bowman
James Leslie Brierly
Raymond Leslie Buell
Carl Jacob Burckhardt
Antonio Sanchez de Bustamante
Nicholas Murray Butler
René-Samuel Cassin
George Catlin
Joseph Perkins Chamberlain
Ben Mark Cherrington
Chou Ken-sheng
Archibald Cary Coolidge
Andrew Wellington Cordier
Charles de Visscher
Edwin DeWitt Dickinson
Golsworthy Lowes Dickinson
Stephen P. Duggan
Frederick Sherwood Dunn
Samuel Train Dutton
Clyde Eagleton

Charles William Eliot
Alona Elizabeth Evans
Herbert Feis
Charles Ghequiere Fenwick
Herbert Albert Laurens Fisher
Irving Norton Fisher
Harry Augustus Garfield
James Wilford Garner
Virginia Crocheron Gildersleeve
Carter Lyman Goodrich
Reuben G. Gustavson
Richard Heathcote Heindel
Amos Shartle Hershey
David Jayne Hill
Leonard Trelawney Hobhouse
Arthur Norman Holcombe
Thomas Erskine Holland
Hamilton Holt
Ernest Martin Hopkins
Halford Lancaster Hoskins
Eugenio María de Hostos
Manley Ottmer Hudson
Robert Maynard Hutchins
Julian Sorell Huxley
Charles Cheney Hyde
Samuel Guy Inman
Hans Kelsen
Arthur Kline Kuhn
Heinrich Lammasch
Hersch Lauterpacht
Charles Herbert Levermore
Francis Lieber
James Lorimer
Abbott Lawrence Lowell

Salvador de Madariaga y Rojo
Frederic Frommhold de Martens
Charles Emanuel Martin
Gaetano Martino
Arnold Duncan McNair
Sidney E. Mezes
Raleigh Colston Minor
Samuel Chiles Mitchell
John Bassett Moore
Hans Joachim Morgenthau
George Gilbert Aimé Murray
Philip Curtis Nash
Otto Frederick Nolde
Lassa Francis Lawrence Oppenheim
Mario Andrew Pei
William Emmanuel Rappard
Joseph Redlich
Paul Simon Reinsch
Owen Josephus Roberts
Michał Cezary Rostworowski
Josiah Royce
Théodore Eugène César Ruyssen
Gaetano Salvemini
Walther Adrian Schücking
Jacob Gould Schurman
Charles Seymour
James Thomson Shotwell
Ellery Cory Stowell
Arnold J. Toynbee
Thorstein Bunde Veblen
Edmund A. Walsh
Charles K. Webster
Hans Wehberg
John W. Wheeler-Bennett
Andrew Dickson White
Ray Lyman Wilbur
Westel Woodbury Willoughby
George Grafton Wilson
Bohdan Stefan Winiarski
Mary Emma Woolley
Theodore Salisbury Woolsey
Quincy Wright
Yoshino Sakuzō
Alfred Eckhard Zimmern
George Frederick Zook

ADMINISTRATOR/DIRECTOR
John Barrett
Charles Christian Bauer

Norman de Mattos Bentwich
Folke Bernadotte
Henri Bonnet
Raymond Leslie Buell
Harold Beresford Butler
Nicholas Murray Butler
Edward Clark Carter
Malcolm Walters Davis
Charles de Visscher
Laurence Duggan
Stephen P. Duggan
Clark Mell Eichelberger
Brooks Emeny
Abraham Howard Feller
George Augustus Finch
Abraham Flexner
Raymond Blaine Fosdick
Antoine -F. Frangulis
James Clerk Maxwell Garnett
O. Benjamin Gerig
Huntington Gilchrist
Carter Lyman Goodrich
Jerome Davis Greene
Roger Sherman Greene
Sidney Lewis Gulick
Selskar Michael Gunn
Camille Adolphe Gutt
Edmund Hall-Patch
Edvard Isak Hambro
Richard Pearson Hobson
George Kenneth Holland
George Chandler Holt
Max Huber
Léon Jouhaux
Florence Cross Kitchelt
Christian Lous Lange
Henry Goddard Leach
Alexander Loveday
Frederick Henry Lynch
Ivison Macadam
Charles Stedman Macfarland
Salvador de Madariga y Rojo
Herbert Louis May
James Grover McDonald
José Antonio Mora Otero
John Raleigh Mott
Philip Curtis Nash
George William Nasmyth
Leo Pasvolsky

Joseph Hieronim Retinger
Raymond Thomas Rich
Walter Alexander Riddell
Ivar Rooth
Leo Stanton Rowe
James Brown Scott
Petrus Josephus Servatius Serrarens
William Harrison Short
James Thomson Shotwell
Arthur Sweetser
Arnold J. Toynbee
Sarah Wambaugh
Matthew Woll
See also Appendix II, International Civil
  Servant

ARCHITECT
Herman Soergel

ARTIST
Nicholas K. Roerich
See also Sculptor

ATTORNEY/BARRISTER
Newton Diehl Baker
Thomas Willing Balch
Robert S. Benjamin
William Hervey Blymer
Cheng T'ien-hsi
Grenville Clark
Bainbridge Colby
Everett Colby
Frederic René Coudert
Hayne Davis
John William Davis
Eberhard Paul Deutsch
Michael Francis Doyle
Luís María Drago
John Foster Dulles
Victor Hugo Duras
Abraham Howard Feller
Raul Fernandes
David Dudley Field
Thomas Knight Finletter
James Jackson Forstall
Raymond Blaine Fosdick
Christian Fouchet
Leon Fraser
Henri-Auguste Fromageot

David Maxwell Fyfe
Robert Lee Humber
Frank Noel Keen
Chase Kimball
Bernard Cornelis Johannes Loder
José Carlos de Macedo Soares
Ronald William Gordon Mackay
Herbert Louis May
William Gibbs McAdoo
David Hunter Miller
Henry Crittenden Morris
Leslie Knox Munro
John Francis O'Ryan
Herbert Parsons
Amos Jenkins Peaslee
Walter George Frank Phillimore
Jackson Harvey Ralston
Lindsay Russell
Jeremiah Smith, Jr.
Alpheus Henry Snow
Silas Hardy Strawn
Earl Warren
George Woodward Wickersham
Emma Wold
See also Appendix II, International
  Law/Legalists

BANKER/FINANCIER
Charles Stewart Addis
Charles Gates Dawes
Leon Fraser
S. Parker Gilbert
Per Jacobsson
Thomas William Lamont
James Addison Logan, Jr.
Dwight Whitney Morrow
Otto Ernst Niemeyer
Montagu Collet Norman
Chester DeWitt Pugsley
Ivar Rooth
James Paul Warburg

BRIDGE EXPERT
Ely Culbertson

BUSINESS FIGURE
Charles Christian Bauer
Robert S. Benjamin

Robert Henry Brand
Robert J. Caldwell
Samuel Colcord
Charles Richard Crane
Oscar Terry Crosby
David Davies
Norman Hezekiah Davis
Albert Freiherr Dufour-Feronce
Cyrus Stephen Eaton
Edward A. Filene
Huntington Gilchrist
Edwin Ginn
Paul Gray Hoffman
Howard Riggins Huston
Walter Thomas Layton
Geoffrey Le Mesurier Mander
William Gibbs McAdoo
Vance Criswell McCormick
William Osborne McDowell
Jean Omer Marie Gabriel Monnet
Oscar Newfang
Walther Rathenau
John Davison Rockefeller, Jr.
John Davison Rockefeller, 3d
Nelson Aldrich Rockefeller
Whitney Hart Shepardson
Edward Reilly Stettinius, Jr.
Oscar Solomon Straus
Cyrus H. Street
Eliot Wadsworth
Thomas John Watson, Sr.
Owen D. Young

DIPLOMATIC FIGURE
Adachi Mineichiro
Aristides de Agüero y Betancourt
Ricardo Joaquín Alfaro
Pompeo Aloisi
Alejandro Alvarez
Hamilton Shirley Amerasinghe
Oswaldo Euclides de Sousa Aranha
Tevfik Rüştü Aras
Pablo de Azcárate y Flórez
Jamil Murad Baroody
Dantès Bellegarde
Johann Heinrich von Bernstorff
Henri Bonnet
Aristede Pierre Henri Briand

Carlos Calvo
Atul Chandra Chatterjee
Benjamin Alberto Cohen Gallerstein
Erik Andreas Colban
Eyre Alexander Crowe
Laurence Duggan
John Foster Dulles
Agustín Edwards Mac-Clure
Rafael Waldemar Erich
John Watson Foster
André François-Poncet
Antoine -F. Frangulis
Friedrich von Gentz
O. Benjamin Gerig
Hugh Gibson
Prentiss Bailey Gilbert
Edward Grey
José Gustavo Guerrero
Green Haywood Hackworth
Albert Auguste Gabriel Hanotaux
David Jayne Hill
Hoo Chi-Tsai
Hsu Mo
Charles Evans Hughes
Cordell Hull
Cecil James Barrington Hurst
Paul Hymans
Ishii Kikujirō
Frank Billings Kellogg
Harry Klemens Ulrich Kessler
Cecil Hermann Kisch
Robert Lansing
Maksim Maksimovich Litvinov
Breckinridge Long
Makino Nobuaki
Afranio de Mello Franco
David Hunter Miller
Jay Pierrepont Moffat
John Bassett Moore
José Antonio Mora Otero
Mikhail Nikolaevich Murav'ev
Joseph Nisot
José Maria da Silva Paranhos, Jr.
Simón Planas-Suárez
Nicholas Socrate Politis
Frank Lyon Polk
Hjalmar Johan Fredrik Procopé
Honorio Pueyrredón

José María Quiñones de León
Elihu Root
Satō Naotake
Carlo Sforza
Shih Chao-chi
Aleksander Skrzyński
Edward Reilly Stettinius, Jr.
Sugimara Yōtarō
Nicolae Titulescu
Jaime Torres Bodet
Francisco Tudela y Varela
Bo Östen Undén
Francisco José Urrutia
Wang Ch'ung-hui
Sumner Welles
Henry Wheaton
Hugh Robert Wilson
Humphrey Hume Wrong
Jesús María Yepes
Herluf Zahle

ENGINEER
Louis Curchod
John Hays Hammond
Herbert Clark Hoover
Ivison Macadam
Arturo de Marcoartú Morales
George Macadam
Georges Valensi

FARMER
Norris Edward Dodd

INTERNATIONAL CIVIL SERVANT
Herbert Brown Ames
Joseph Louis Anne Avenol
Pablo de Azcárate y Flórez
Henri Bonnet
Ralph Johnson Bunche
Harold Beresford Butler
Anthony Buxton
Erik Andreas Colban
Pierre Comert
Andrew Wellington Cordier
Rachel Eleanor Crowdy
Norris Edward Dodd
Eric Drummond
Edvard Isak Hambro

Dag Hjalmar Agne Carl Hammarskjöld
Howard Riggins Huston
Julian Sorell Huxley
Seymour Jacklin
Clarence Wilfred Jenks
Herbert Henry Lehman
Seán Lester
Trygve Halvdan Lie
Jean Omer Marie Gabriel Monnet
Joseph Nisot
Nitobe Inazō
Edward Joseph Phelan
Ludwik W. Rajchman
William Emmanuel Rappard
Egon Schwelb
Arthur Sweetser
Albert Thomas
U Thant
Georges Valensi
Francis Paul Walters
John Gilbert Winant
Konni Zilliacus

JOURNALIST
Ray Stannard Baker
Henry Noel Brailsford
Raymond Landon Bridgman
John Hessin Clarke
Pierre Comert
Daniel Cosio Villegas
James Middleton Cox
John Wesley Dafoe
Malcolm Waters Davis
Luigi Einaudi
Henry Wilson Harris
Gilbert Monell Hitchcock
John Atkinson Hobson
Hamilton Holt
Herbert Sherman Houston
William Henry Irwin
Ernst Jaeckh
Peter Michael Kirk
Seán Lester
Walter Lippmann
Paul Gustav Emil Loebe
Edwin Doak Mead
Edgar Ansel Mowrer
Elise Ottesen-Jensen

Paul Scott Mowrer
Carlo Rosselli
Ernesto Rossi
Francis Herbert Stead
William Thomas Stead
Dorothy Thompson
Carl Van Doren
Paul W. Ward
Hans Wehberg
Herbert George Wells
William Allen White
Leonard Sidney Woolf
Evelyn Wrench
See also Publicist

LIBRARIAN/BIBLIOGRAPHER
Philipp Christiaan Molhuysen
Paul-Marie-Ghislain Otlet
Jacob ter Meulen
Mary Florence Wilson

MILITARY FIGURE
Tasker Howard Bliss
Caspar Frederick Goodrich
Karl Ernst Nikolaus Haushofer
Richmond Pearson Hobson
James Addison Logan, Jr.
Alfred Thayer Mahan
George Catlett Marshall

MINISTER/CLERIC
Bramwell Booth
Charles Henry Brent
Arthur Judson Brown
James Cannon, Jr.
Samuel McCrea Cavert
Wilbur Fisk Crafts
Edward Cummings
Theodore Ainsworth Greene
Sidney Lewis Gulick
Henry Smith Leiper
Frederick Henry Lynch
Charles Stedman Macfarland
Otto Frederick Nolde
George Ashton Oldham
Joseph Holdsworth Oldham
Garfield Bromley Oxnam
John Herman Randall
Henry Knox Sherrill

Nathan Söderblom
John Henry Wilburn Stuckenberg
James W. Van Kirk

MUSICIAN
Pablo Carlos Salvador Defillo de Casals
Ignacy Jan Paderewski

NURSE
Rachel Eleanor Crowdy
Ellen Newbold La Motte

PHILANTHROPIST
Anita Eugenie McCormick Blaine
John Davison Rockefeller, Jr.
John Davison Rockefeller, 3d

PHILOSOPHER
Jeremy Bentham

PHYSICIAN
Tevfik Rüştü Aras
José Antonio Arce
Rupert Lee Blue
George Brock Chisholm
Hugh Smith Cumming
Martha May Eliot
Hideyo Noguchi
Blanche Rosalie Slaughter Morton
Ludwik W. Rajchman
Hamilton Kemp Wright
Ludwik Lazar Zamenhof

POLITICAL FIGURE
Konrad Adenauer
Herbert Brown Ames
José Antonio Arce
Joseph Louis Anne Avenol
Abd al-Hamid Badawi
Newton Diehl Baker
Arthur James Balfour
Ruy Barbosa
Richard Bartholdt
Louis Barthou
Joseph Bech
Auguste-Marie-François Beernaert
Víctor Andrés Belaúnde y Diéz Canceco
Eduard Beneš

Carl August Berendsen
Folke Bernadotte
Léon Blum
Simón Bolívar
Violet Bonham Carter
Robert Laird Borden
Léon Victor Auguste Bourgeois
Karl Hjalmar Branting
Heinrich von Brentano
Aristede Pierre Henri Briand
Stanley Melbourne Bruce
James Bryce
Edgar Algernon Robert Gascoyne Cecil
Eugenio Colorni
Adam Jerzy Czartoryski
Raoul Dandurand
Clement Edward Davies
Alcide De Gasperi
Charles A.´J.M. de Gaulle
Luigi Einaudi
Fritz Kurt Gustav Erler
Isidro Fabela Alfaro
Thomas Knight Finletter
George Eulas Foster
Peter Fraser
Camille Adolphe Gutt
Per Haekkerup
Carl Joachim Hambro
Edvard Isak Hambro
Maurice Pascal Alers Hankey
Arthur Henderson
Edouard Herriot
Gilbert Monell Hitchcock
Herbert Clark Hoover
Edward Mandell House
Charles Evans Hughes
Henry de Jouvenel
William Lyon Mackenzie King
Jens Otto Krag
Ugo La Malfa
Heinrich Lammasch
Théodore Joseph Albéric Lefèvre
Herbert Henry Lehman
David Lloyd George
Henry Cabot Lodge
Paul Gustave Emil Loebe
Albert John Mvumbi Luthuli
James Ramsay MacDonald

Pasquale Stanislao Mancini
Gaetano Martino
Jan Masaryk
René Mayer
Porter James McCumber
Andrew McFadyean
Guy Mollet
Giuseppe Motta
Johan Ludwig Mowinckel
Ariot Ramaswami Mudalier
Walter Nash
Francesco Saverio Nitti
Kwame Nkrumah
Joseph Paul-Boncour
Lester Bowles Pearson
Epitacio Lindolfo da Silva Pessôa
André Philip
Mario Pistocchi
Georges Jean Raymond Pompidou
James Pinckney Pope
Paul Ramadier
Adam Rapacki
Paul Reynaud
Heinrich Georg Ritzel
Joseph Taylor Robinson
Henri Rolin
Edouard Rolin-Jaequemyns
Gustave Henri Ange Hippolyte Rolin-
    Jaequemyns
Franklin Delano Roosevelt
Theodore Roosevelt
James Arthur Salter
Eduardo Santos
Robert Schuman
Jan Christiaan Smuts
Paul-Henri Spaak
Adlai Ewing Stevenson II
Henry Lewis Stimson
Gustav Stresemann
William Howard Taft
Elbert Duncan Thomas
Charles Philips Trevelyan
Harry S Truman
Arthur Hendrick Vandenberg
Emile Vandervelde
Henry Agard Wallace
Thomas James Walsh
Earl Warren

Alexander Wiley
Wendell Lewis Willkie
Thomas Woodrow Wilson
Paul van Zeeland

PUBLICIST
William Edward Arnold-Foster
Richard Coudenhove-Kalergi
Vera Micheles Dean
Clark Mell Eichelberger
George Augustus Finch
James Clerk Maxwell Garnett
Herbert Ernest Hyde
John Maynard Keynes
Charles Herbert Levermore
Theodore Marburg
Lucia True Ames Mead
Laura Puffer Morgan
Denys Peter Myers
Walter Wanderwell
James Paul Warburg
See also Journalist

RADIO COMMENTATOR
Raymond Edwards Swing

REFORMER
James Cannon, Jr.
Florence Guertin Tuttle
See also Social Worker

SCIENTIST
John Boyd-Orr
Selskar Michael Gunn
See also Physician

SCULPTOR
Hendrik Christian Andersen

SOCIAL WORKER
Grace Abbott
Frances Alice Kellor
Harriet Burton Laidlaw
Elise Ottesen-Jensen
Lillie M. Peck
Juliet Evangeline Rhys Williams

Appendix III

Types of Internationalists

This listing attempts to classify the subjects according to the type of internationalist they were, either in the advocacy of a certain kind of organization or as exemplified in their work or writings. Duplicate listings appear for persons who believed in more than one approach. A discussion of the various types can be found in the preface.

AFRICAN UNITY
Albert John Mvumbi Luthuli
Kwame Nkrumah

ARBITRATION SYSTEM
Ricardo Joaquín Alfaro
Thomas Willing Balch
Richard Bartholdt
Léon Victor Auguste Bourgeois
Antonio Sanchez de Bustamante
Hayne Davis
Agustín Edwards Mac-Clure
Raul Fernandes
John Watson Foster
Henri-Auguste Fromageot
Frances Alice Kellor
Heinrich Lammasch
Robert Lansing
John Bassett Moore
Henry Crittenden Morris
José Maria da Silva Paranhos, Jr.
Jackson Harvey Ralston
Paul Simon Reinsch
Theodore Roosevelt
Théodore Eugène César Ruyssen
William Howard Taft
Francisco Tudela y Varela
Bo Östen Undén
Theodore Salisbury Woolsey
Jesús María Yepes
Herluf Zahle
See also Hague System

ATLANTIC UNION
George Catlin
Ely Culbertson
Samuel Chiles Mitchell
Owen Josephus Roberts
See also English-Speaking Union

COLLECTIVE SECURITY/ SANCTIONISTS
Louis Barthou
Folke Bernadotte
Aristede Pierre Henri Briand
Chou Ken-sheng
Oscar Terry Crosby
Ely Culbertson
John Wesley Dafoe
David Davies
Clyde Eagleton
Clark Mell Eichelberger
Charles William Eliot
Edwin Ginn
Caspar Frederick Goodrich
Ernest Jaeckh
Walter Lippmann
Maksim Maksimovich Litvinov
Geoffrey Le Mesurier Mander
Lucia True Ames Mead
Edgar Ansel Mowrer
John Francis O'Ryan
Joseph Paul-Boncour
Lester Bowles Pearson
Walter George Frank Phillimore
Henry Lewis Stimson

COMMUNITY

Grace Abbott
Hendrik Christian Andersen
Jeremy Bentham
Norman de Mattos Bentwich
Evangeline Booth
Pablo Carlos Salvador Defillo de Casals
George Brock Chisholm
Leonard Trelawney Hobhouse
Eugenio María de Hostos
Max Huber
Albert John Mvumbi Luthuli
George Catlett Marshall
Charles Emanuel Martin
Lillie M. Peck
John Herman Randall
Walther Rathenau
Paul Simon Reinsch
Nicholas K. Roerich
Josiah Royce
Jan Christiaan Smuts
John Henry Wilburn Stuckenberg
Elbert Duncan Thomas
Arnold J. Toynbee
James W. Van Kirk
Thorstein Bunde Veblen
Edmund A. Walsh
Walter Wanderwell
Herbert George Wells
Ray Lyman Wilbur
Wendell Lewis Willkie
Matthew Woll
See also Socialist; World Citizens

ECONOMIC/FINANCIAL ADVISER

Charles Stewart Addis
Robert Henry Brand
Daniel Cosio Villegas
Norman Hezekiah Davis
Charles Gates Dawes
Herbert Feis
Leon Fraser
S. Parker Gilbert
Camille Adolphe Gutt
Edmund Hall-Patch
Paul Gray Hoffman
Per Jacobsson

John Maynard Keynes
Cecil Hermann Kisch
Thomas William Lamont
Walter Thomas Layton
James Addison Logan, Jr.
Lewis Levitzki Lorwin
Andrew McFadyean
Dwight Whitney Morrow
Otto Ernst Niemeyer
Montagu Collet Norman
Ivar Rooth
Jacques Léon Rueff
Jeremiah Smith, Jr.
Royall Tyler
Eliot Wadsworth
Owen D. Young

ENGLISH-SPEAKING UNION

George Louis Beer
Caspar Frederick Goodrich
Ronald William Gordon Mackay
Theodore Marburg
Theodore Roosevelt
Evelyn Wrench
See also Atlantic Union

EUROPEAN UNITY

Konrad Adenaur
Joseph Bech
Jeremy Bentham
Violet Bonham Carter
Heinrich von Brentano
Aristede Pierre Henri Briand
Eugenio Colorni
Richard Coudenhove-Kalergi
Adam Jerzy Czartoryski
Alcide De Gasperi
Charles A.J.M. de Gaulle
Luigi Einaudi
Fritz Kurt Gustav Erler
Christian Fouchet
David Maxwell Fyfe
Friedrich von Gentz
Camille Adolphe Gutt
Per Haekkerup
Edouard Herriot
Léon Jouhaux
Peter Michael Kirk

Jens Otto Krag
Ugo La Malfa
Walter Thomas Layton
Théodore Joseph Albéric Lèfevre
Paul Gustav Emil Loebe
Ronald William Gordon Mackay
Gaetano Martino
Jan Masaryk
René Mayer
Andrew McFadyean
Guy Mollet
Jean Omer Marie Gabriel Monnet
Francesco Saverio Nitti
André Philip
Mario Pistocchi
Georges Jean Raymond Pompidou
Paul Ramadier
Joseph Hieronim Retinger
Paul Reynaud
Juliet Evangeline Rhys Williams
Heinrich Georg Ritzel
Carlo Rosselli
Ernesto Rossi
Jacques Léon Rueff
James Arthur Salter
Robert Schuman
Petrus Josephus Servatius Serrarens
Carlo Sforza
Aleksander Skrzyński
Herman Soergel
Paul-Henri Spaak
Dorothy Thompson
Paul van Zeeland

FRIENDSHIP SOCIETIES
Robert J. Caldwell
Hamilton Holt
Henry Goddard Leach
Lindsay Russell
See also Community

GEOPOLITICS
Isaiah Bowman
Karl Ernst Nikolaus Haushofer
Alfred Thayer Mahan
Herman Soergel
Edmund A. Walsh

HAGUE SYSTEM
Richard Bartholdt
August-Marie-François Beernaert
Léon Victor Auguste Bourgeois
Raymond Landon Bridgman
Eyre Alexander Crowe
Hayne Davis
Samuel Train Dutton
Edwin Ginn
John Hays Hammond
Amos Shartle Hershey
David Jayne Hill
Christian Lous Lange
Henry Cabot Lodge
Frederic Frommhold de Martens
Lucia True Ames Mead
Edwin Doak Mead
Mikhail Nikolaevich Murav'ev
Théodore Eugène César Ruyssen
Walther Adrian Schücking
Francis Herbert Stead
William Thomas Stead
Oscar Solomon Straus
Andrew Dickson White
See also Arbitration System

HEALTH/FOOD
Rupert Lee Blue
John Boyd-Orr
Charles Henry Brent
Stanley Melbourne Bruce
George Brock Chisholm
Wilbur Fisk Crafts
Hugh Smith Cumming
Norris Edward Dodd
Martha May Eliot
Abraham Flexner
Roger Sherman Greene
Selskar Michael Gunn
Hideyo Noguchi
Ellen Newbold La Motte
Herbert Louis May
Blanche Rosalie Slaughter Morton
Elise Ottesen-Jensen
Ludwik W. Rajchman
John Davison Rockefeller, Jr.
John Davison Rockefeller, 3d

Elizabeth Washburn Wright
Hamilton Kemp Wright

HUMANITARIAN
Bramwell Booth
Evangeline Booth
Carl Jacob Burckhardt
Pablo Carlos Salvador Defillo de Casals
René-Samuel Cassin
Wilbur Fisk Crafts
Rachel Eleanor Crowdy
Edward Cummings
Norman Hezekiah Davis
Willoughby Hyett Dickinson
Samuel Train Dutton
Abraham Flexner
André François-Poncet
Theodore Ainsworth Greene
Jerome Davis Greene
Richmond Pearson Hobson
Herbert Clark Hoover
Fridtjof Nansen
Ignacy Jan Paderewski
Egon Schwelb
Anna Eleanor Roosevelt
Eliot Wadsworth
See also Health/Food

INTELLECTUAL
COOPERATION
Dantès Bellegarde
Henri Bonnet
Ben Mark Cherrington
Malcolm Waters Davis
Stephen P. Duggan
George Kenneth Holland
Paul Hymans
Paul-Marie-Ghislain Otlet
Alfred Eckhard Zimmern
George Frederick Zook

INTER-AMERICAN/
PAN AMERICAN UNITY
John Barrett
Dantès Bellegarde
Simón Bolívar
Daniel Cosio Villegas

Charles Ghequiere Fenwick
José Gustavo Guerrero
Cordell Hull
Samuel Guy Inman
José Antonio Mora Otero
José Maria da Silva Paranhos, Jr.
Nelson Aldrich Rockefeller
Leo Stanton Rowe
Sumner Welles
Jesús María Yepes

INTERDEPENDENCE
Cyrus Stephen Eaton
Walther Rathenau
Paul Samuel Reinsch
Silas Hardy Strawn
James W. Van Kirk
Thomas John Watson, Sr.

INTERNATIONAL EDUCATION
Frank Aydelotte
George Hubbard Blakeslee
Isaiah Bowman
Raymond Leslie Buell
Nicholas Murray Butler
Edward Clark Carter
Ben Mark Cherrington
Archibald Cary Coolidge
Malcolm Waters Davis
Vera Micheles Dean
Laurence Duggan
Stephen P. Duggan
Frederick Sherwood Dunn
Clyde Eagleton
Brooks Emeny
Harry Augustus Garfield
James Wilford Garner
Edwin Ginn
Carter Lyman Goodrich
Jerome Davis Greene
Richard Heathcote Heindel
George Kenneth Holland
Ernest Martin Hopkins
Halford Lancaster Hoskins
Ivison Macadam
Charles Emanuel Martin
James Grover McDonald

Philipp Christiaan Molhuysen
Hans Joachim Morganthau
Paul Scott Mowrer
George William Nasmyth
Chester DeWitt Pugsley
William Emmanuel Rappard
Raymond Thomas Rich
Vittorio Scialoja
Whitney Hart Shepardson
Ellery Cory Stowell
Jacob ter Meulen
Edmund A. Walsh
Paul W. Ward
John W. Wheeler-Bennett
Mary Emma Woolley
Quincy Wright
Alfred Eckhard Zimmern
George Frederick Zook

INTERNATIONAL LABOR
Harold Beresford Butler
Atul Chandra Chattejee
Isidro Fabela Alfaro
Carter Lyman Goodrich
Clarence Wilfred Jenks
Léon Jouhaux
Edward Joseph Phelan
Paul Ramadier
Walter Alexander Riddell
Petrus Josephus Servatius Serrarens
James Thomson Shotwell
Albert Thomas
Emile Vandervelde
John Gilbert Winant
Matthew Woll

INTERNATIONAL LANGUAGE
Mario Andrew Pei
Ludwik Lazar Zamenhof

INTERNATIONAL LAW/ LEGALISTS
Adachi Mineichiro
Ricardo Joaquín Alfaro
Alejandro Alvarez
Tobias Michael Carel Asser
José Philadelpho Azevedo
Abd al-Hamid Badawi

Ruy Barbosa
Jules Basdevant
Richard Reeve Baxter
Johann Caspar Bluntschli
Edwin Montefiore Borchard
James Leslie Brierly
Antonio Sanchez de Bustamante
Carlos Calvo
Joseph Perkins Chamberlain
Cheng T'ien-hsi
Frederic René Coudert
Charles de Visscher
Eberhard Paul Deutsch
Edwin DeWitt Dickinson
Luís María Drago
Samuel Train Dutton
Clyde Eagleton
Alona Elizabeth Evans
Isidro Fabela Alfaro
Charles Ghequiere Fenwick
Raul Fernandes
David Dudley Field
George Augustus Finch
John Watson Foster
Henri-Auguste Fromageot
James Wilford Garner
José Gustavo Guerrero
Green Haywood Hackworth
Carl Joachim Hambro
Edvard Isak Hambro
John Hays Hammond
Amos Shartle Hershey
David Jayne Hill
Thomas Erskine Holland
Hsu Mo
Max Huber
Manley Ottmer Hudson
Charles Evans Hughes
Cecil James Barrington Hurst
Charles Cheney Hyde
Clarence Wilfred Jenks
Frank Billings Kellogg
Hans Kelsen
Arthur Kline Kuhn
Heinrich Lammasch
Robert Lansing
Hersch Lauterpacht
Francis Lieber

Bernard Cornelis Loder
James Lorimer
Pasquale Stanislao Mancini
David Hunter Miller
Arturo de Marcoartú y Morales
Frederic Frommhold de Martens
Arnold Duncan McNair
Alfranio de Mello Franco
John Bassett Moore
Lassa Francis Lawrence Oppenheim
Amos Jenkins Peaslee
Epitacio Lindolfo da Silva Pessôa
Simón Planas-Suárez
Joseph Redlich
Paul Simon Reinsch
Henri Rolin
Edouard Rolin-Jaequemyns
Gustave Henri Ange Hippolyte Rolin-
   Jaequemyns
Elihu Root
Michał Cezary Rostworowski
Walther Adrian Schücking
Jacob Gould Schurman
Egon Schwelb
Vittorio Scialoja
James Brown Scott
Alpheus Henry Snow
Ellery Cory Stowell
William Howard Taft
Jacob ter Meulen
Elbert Duncan Thomas
Francisco José Urrutia
Thomas James Walsh
Wang Ch'ung-hui
Hans Wehberg
Henry Wheaton
George Grafton Wilson
Bohdan Stefan Winiarski
Emma Wold
Theodore Salisbury Woolsey
Quincy Wright
Jesús María Yepes
See also Appendix II, Attorney/Bar-
   rister

LEAGUE OF NATIONS
Adachi Mineichiro
Aristides de Agüero y Betancourt

Pompeo Aloisi
Alejandro Alvarez
Herbert Brown Ames
Tevfik Rüştü Aras
William Edward Arnold-Foster
Pablo de Azcárate y Flórez
Newton Diehl Baker
Ray Stannard Baker
Arthur James Balfour
Louis Barthou
George Louis Beer
Víctor Andrés Belaúnde y Diéz Canceco
Dantès Bellegarde
Eduard Beneš
Norman de Mattos Bentwich
Johann Heinrich von Bernstorff
Anita Eugenie McCormick Blaine
Tasker Howard Bliss
Violet Bonham Carter
Henri Bonnet
Robert Laird Borden
Léon Victor Auguste Bourgeois
Henry Noel Brailsford
Karl Hjalmar Branting
Aristede Pierre Henri Briand
Stanley Melbourne Bruce
James Bryce
Carl Jacob Burckhardt
Anthony Buxton
Robert J. Caldwell
Atul Chandra Chaterjee
Edgar Algernon Robert Gascoyne Cecil
John Hessin Clarke
Erik Andreas Colban
Bainbridge Colby
Everett Colby
Samuel Colcord
Pierre Comert
Frederic René Coudert
James Middleton Cox
Rachel Eleanor Crowdy
John Wesley Dafoe
Raoul Dandurand
David Davies
John William Davis
Norman Hezekiah Davis
Goldsworthy Lowes Dickinson
Willoughby Hyett Dickinson

Michael Francis Doyle
Eric Drummond
Albert Freiherr Dufour-Feronce
Agustín Edwards Mac-Clure
Clark Mell Eichelberger
Charles William Eliot
Rafael Waldemar Erich
Herbert Feis
Edward A. Filene
Herbert Albert Laurens Fisher
Irving Norton Fisher
Abraham Flexner
James Jackson Forstall
Raymond Blaine Fosdick
George Eulas Foster
Antoine -F. Frangulis
James Clerk Maxwell Garnett
O. Benjamin Gerig
Hugh Gibson
Prentiss Bailey Gilbert
Huntington Gilchrist
Virginia Crocheron Gildersleeve
Edward Grey
Carl Joachim Hambro
Edvard Isak Hambro
John Hays Hammond
Maurice Paścal Alers Hankey
Albert Auguste Gabriel Hanotaux
Henry Wilson Harris
Arthur Henderson
Edouard Herriot
Gilbert Monell Hitchcock
John Atkinson Hobson
Richmond Pearson Hobson
Hamilton Holt
Hoo Chi-Tsai
Herbert Clark Hoover
Edward Mandell House
Herbert Sherman Houston
Manley Ottmer Hudson
Charles Evans Hughes
Cecil James Barrington Hurst
Howard Riggins Huston
Herbert Ernest Hyde
Paul Hymans
William Henry Irwin
Ishii Kikujirō
Seymour Jacklin

Henry de Jouvenel
Frank Noel Keen
Harry Klemens Ulrich Kessler
Chase Kimball
William Lyon Mackenzie King
Florence Cross Kitchelt
Ellen Newbold La Motte
Harriet Burton Laidlaw
Christian Lous Lange
Seán Lester
Charles Herbert Levermore
Walter Lippmann
Maksim Maksimovich Litvinov
David Lloyd George
Henry Cabot Lodge
Breckinridge Long
Alexander Loveday
Abbott Lawrence Lowell
Frederick Henry Lynch
James Ramsay MacDonald
José Carlos de Macedo Soares
Salvador de Madariaga y Rojo
Makino Nobuaki
Geoffrey Le Mesurier Mander
Theodore Marburg
Herbert Louis May
William Gibbs McAdoo
Vance Criswell McCormick
Porter James McCumber
James Grover McDonald
Lucia True Ames Mead
Afranio de Mello Franco
Sidney E. Mezes
David Hunter Miller
Samuel Chiles Mitchell
Jay Pierrepont Moffat
Jean Omer Marie Gabriel Monnet
Dwight Whitney Morrow
Giuseppe Motta
Johan Ludwig Mowinckel
George Gilbert Aimé Murray
Denys Peter Myers
Fridtjof Nansen
Philip Curtis Nash
Walter Nash
Joseph Nisot
Nitobe Inazō
Herbert Parsons

Joseph Paul-Boncour
Epitacio Lindolfo da Silva Pessôa
Walter George Frank Phillimore
Nicholas Socrate Politis
Frank Lyon Polk
James Pinckney Pope
Hjalmar Johan Fredrik Procopé
Honorio Pueyrredón
José María Quinoñes de León
Ludwik W. Rajchman
William Emmanuel Rappard
Walter Alexander Riddell
Joseph Taylor Robinson
John Davison Rockefeller, Jr.
John Davison Rockefeller, 3d
Henri Rolin
Edouard Rolin-Jaequemyns
Franklin Delano Roosevelt
Jacques Léon Rueff
James Arthur Salter
Gaetano Salvemini
Eduardo Santos
Satō Naotake
Walther Adrian Schücking
Jacob Gould Schurman
Vittorio Scialoja
Charles Seymour
Whitney Hart Shepardson
Shih Chao-chi
William Harrison Short
James Thomson Shotwell
Jan Christiaan Smuts
Francis Herbert Stead
Henry Lewis Stimson
Oscar Solomon Straus
Silas Hardy Strawn
Gustav Stresemann
Arthur Sweetser
William Howard Taft
Nicolae Titulescu
Charles Philips Trevelyan
Francisco Tudela y Varela
Florence Guertin Tuttle
Bo Östen Undén
Francisco José Urrutia
Thomas James Walsh
Francis Paul Walters
Sarah Wambaugh

Walter Wanderwell
Charles K. Webster
George Woodward Wickersham
Mary Florence Wilson
Hugh Robert Wilson
Thomas Woodrow Wilson
Leonard Sidney Woolf
Mary Emma Woolley
Humphrey Hume Wrong
Yoshino Sakuzō
Herluf Zahle
Paul van Zeeland
Konni Zilliacus
Alfred Eckhard Zimmern

RELIGIOUS ECUMENISM
Norman de Mattos Bentwich
Charles Henry Brent
Arthur Judson Brown
James Cannon, Jr.
Samuel McCrea Cavert
Willoughby Hyett Dickinson
John Foster Dulles
Theodore Ainsworth Greene
Henry Smith Leiper
Charles Stedman Macfarland
John Raleigh Mott
Otto Frederick Nolde
George Ashton Oldham
Joseph Holdsworth Oldham
Garfield Bromley Oxnam
Henry Knox Sherrill
Nathan Söderblom

SOCIALISTS
Léon Blum
Henry Noel Brailsford
Emile Vandervelde
See also Community; World Citizens

**TECHNICAL ANALYST/
EXPERT**
Louis Curchod
Laura Puffer Morgan
Georges Valensi
Westel Woodbury Willoughby
Elizabeth Washburn Wright

THEORISTS
William Hervey Blymer
George Catlin
Arthur Norman Holcombe
Hans Kelsen
John Maynard Keynes
Lewis Levitzki Lorwin
Hans Joachim Morganthau
Arnold J. Toynbee
Thorstein Bunde Veblen
Quincy Wright

UNITED NATIONS
José Antonio Arce
Hamilton Shirley Amerasinghe
Oswaldo Euclides de Sousa Aranha
Warren Robinson Austin
Pablo de Azcárate y Flórez
Jamil Murad Baroody
Víctor Andrés Belaúnde y Diéz Canceco
Dantès Bellegard
Robert S. Benjamin
Carl August Berendsen
Folke Bernadotte
Ralph Johnson Bunche
René-Samuel Cassin
Benjamin Alberto Cohen Gallerstein
Andrew Wellington Cordier
Daniel Cosio Villegas
Ely Culbertson
John William Davis
John Foster Dulles
Clyde Eagleton
Clark Mell Eichelberger
Abraham Howard Feller
Thomas Knight Finletter
Peter Fraser
O. Benjamin Gerig
Huntington Gilchrist
Virginia Crocheron Gildersleeve
Carter Lyman Goodrich
Reuben G. Gustavson
Edvard Isak Hambro
Dag Hjalmar Agne Carl Hammarskjöld
Paul Gray Hoffman
Arthur Norman Holcombe
Hoo Chi-Tsai
Ernest Martin Hopkins
Cordell Hull

Julian Sorell Huxley
Seymour Jacklin
Herbert Henry Lehman
Trygve Halvdan Lie
Ariot Ramaswami Mudalier
Leslie Knox Munro
Philip Curtis Nash
Joseph Nisot
Leo Pasvolsky
Joseph Paul-Boncour
Lester Bowles Pearson
Amos Jenkins Peaslee
Ludwik W. Rajchman
Adam Rapacki
John Davison Rockefeller, Jr.
Anna Eleanor Roosevelt
Franklin Delano Roosevelt
Eduardo Santos
Egon Schwelb
James Thomson Shotwell
Edward Reilly Stettinius, Jr.
Adlai Ewing Stevenson II
Arthur Sweetser
Dorothy Thompson
Jaime Torres Bodet
Harry S Truman
U Thant
Bo Östen Undén
Arthur Hendrick Vandenberg
Henry Agard Wallace
Earl Warren
Thomas John Watson, Sr.
Charles K. Webster
Alexander Wiley
Wendell Lewis Willkie
Humphrey Hume Wrong
George Frederick Zook

WORLD CITIZENS
Henri Bonnet
Edgar Ansel Mowrer
Henry Agard Wallace
Ray Lyman Wilbur
Quincy Wright

WORLD FEDERATION
John Boyd-Orr
Grenville Clark
Oscar Terry Crosby

Ely Culbertson
Thomas Knight Finletter
George Chandler Holt
Hamilton Holt
Robert Lee Humber
Arturo de Marcoartú y Morales
Edwin Doak Mead
Oscar Newfang
Alpheus Henry Snow
Raymond Edwards Swing
Carl Van Doren
James Paul Warburg

WORLD GOVERNMENT
Anita Eugenie McCormick Blaine
Giuseppe Antonio Borgese

Raymond Landon Bridgman
Clement Edward Davies
Hayne Davis
Victor Hugo Duras
Clyde Eagleton
Hamilton Holt
Robert Maynard Hutchins
Herbert Ernest Hyde
William Osborne McDowell
Raleigh Colston Minor
Oscar Newfang
Cyrus H. Street
Sarah Wambaugh
Herbert George Wells

INDEX

Note: The location of main entries in the dictionary is indicated in the index by *italic* page numbers.

American School Peace League, 20, 295, 796

American Society for the Judicial Settlement of International Disputes, 320, 471, 661

American Society of Geolinguistics, 573

American Society of International Law (ASIL): bequests to, 517; creation of, 19, 61, 174, 211, 248, 257, 374, 420, 661, 780, 797–98; members of, 408, 533, 699; presidents of, 61, 211; work of, 175, 231, 281, 363, 478, 698, 715

American Teacher, 514

American Union for Concerted Peace Efforts, 237

American University School of International Service, 353

American Women's Hospitals, 519

Americana, 227

American-Israel Cultural Foundation, 70

Americans United, 352

Americans United for World Organization, 259

Ames, Herbert B., *16–17*

Amsterdam Conference (1948), 669

Anatomy of a Sacred Cow (K. Zilliacus), 815

Andersen, Hendrik C., *17–18*

Anderson, Chandler P., *18–19*

Anderson, Frank M., 330

Andreotti, Giulio, 410

Andrews, Fannie F., *19–21*

Angell, Norman, 29, 250, 538

Anglo-American: code of law, 254; cooperation, 297, 416; hegemony, 466; relations, 119–20. *See also* Anglo-Saxonism, ideal of; English-speaking people; English-Speaking Union; Federal Union

Anglo-American Committee of Inquiry on Palestine, 489

Anglo-Chinese Opium War, 800

Anglo-German Association, 146

Anglo-German rapprochement, 214, 220, 798

Anglo-Japanese Alliance, 705

Anglo-Norwegian fisheries case, 58

Anglo-Russian Trade Agreement (1921), 440

Anglo-Saxonism, ideal of, 6, 261

Anglo-U.S. internationalists, 302–3

Annual Digest of Public International Law Cases, 422

Annual Register of World Events, 458

Annual Review of United Nations Affairs, 231

Annunzio, Gabriele d', 97

Anticipations (H. G. Wells), 765

Anti-imperialism, 411, 794

Anti-Saloon League, 137

Appeasement, 118, 149, 399, 470, 751

Arabian American Oil Company, 718

Arab-Israeli war, UN armistice, 125

Aranha, Oswaldo E., *21–22*

Aras, Tevfik Rüştü, *22–24*

Arbitration: advocates of, 6, 28, 49, 87–88, 107, 421; compulsory, 49, 52, 60, 87, 254, 270, 303, 329, 370, 388, 414, 459, 466, 473, 578, 719, 797, 811; development of, 12, 395; gains of, 128, 476; and international law, 762; and Inter-Parliamentary Union, 444; limits to, 120, 441, 466, 797; as peace pillar, 193; pre-1914 movement, 180, 197, 361, 476, 530, 647, 654, 671, 687, 688–89; process of, 578; settlements, 94, 120, 269–70, 277–78, 419, 563, 733, 770; theory of, 413; treaties of, 55–56, 179, 414, 516, 711, 733, 806; use of, 19; and world organization, 114, 197, 495. *See also* Locarno Treaties; Permanent Court of Arbitration

Arbitration in International Controversy (A. Kellor), 394

Arce, José A., *24–25*

Arena, 114

Argentina, 24, 541, 725

Ariana Park, 739

Armaments: control of, 82–83, 479; danger of, 104; traffic in, 464

Armand, Louis, *25–26*

Armand-Rueff Committee, 26

Armed International Tribunal Association, 180

Armenia-America Society, 135

Armenian relief, 179, 229

Armstrong, Hamilton F., *26–28*

tional Education

International Emergency Food Council, 103

International exchange programs, 274, 297, 425, 697. *See also* Cultural exchange programs

International Experiment (A. L. Fisher), 261

International Federation for Documentation, 557

International Federation of Christian Trade Unions, 663

International Federation of League of Nations Societies, 214, 471

International Federation of Settlements, 571, 572

International Federation of Trade Unions, 663, 793, 794

International Federation of University Women, 294

International finance: importance of, 201, 416; and planning, 404; and stabilization programs, 383

International flag, 739

International Fur Seal Conference (1911), 420

International German Debt Agreement (1952), 541

International government, advocacy of, 231, 337, 375, 448. *See also* World federation, ideas and movements

International Government (C. Eagleton), 231

International Government (L. S. Woolf), 794–95

International Health Committee, Rockefeller Foundation, 298

International Health Conference (1946), 243

International Health Division, Rockefeller Foundation, 307

International High Commission (Pan-American), 484

International Institute for the Codification of Law, 660

International Institute of African Languages and Culture, 552

International Institute of Human Rights, 144

International Institute of Intellectual Co-operation, 91, 556

International Joint Commission, (Canadian-U.S. boundaries), 487

International Joint Committee for Tests (telephone), 536

International labor, study of, 450, 451

International Labor Office (ILO), 16, 450; advisers to, 250; and British Dominions, 96; and Brazil, 460; Chemical Industry Committee of, 371; Committee of Experts, 527; Conference (1919), 3, 129, 574, 706–7, 714; Conference (1921), 663; Conference (1922), 10; Conference (1932), 348; Conference (1940), 249; constitution of, 369, 575; creation of, 388, 575, 673, 714; governing board of, 151; information sources of, 514; and Mexico, 259; relations of, with labor unions, 663, 664; support for, 188, 257, 789; and UN, 527; U.S. participation in, 136, 296, 674, 716, 789; work of, 129–30, 150, 196, 386–87, 388, 575–76, 714. *See also* India, and ILO; Paris Peace Conference (1919): and ILO

International Language (L. L. Zamenhof), 812

International languages, 573, 811–12

International law: advocates of, 400; and antipositivists, 493, 767; codification of, 14, 32, 43, 87, 94, 115, 127–28, 136, 254–55, 278, 282, 304, 311, 312, 361, 363, 434–44, 473, 476, 493, 510–11, 574, 660, 661, 734, 773; and collection of debts, 217; decline of, 374; defined, 136; development of, 19, 52, 60, 62, 254–55, 304, 391, 803; ethics of, 767; evolutionary nature of, 414; exponents of, 497; foundation of, 435; and human rights, 493, 658–59; and Latin America, 719; and League of Nations, 343, 363, 719; natural law school of, 115, 415, 448; nature of, 343; need for, 175, 496, 571, 773; and neutrality, 94–95, 578; and

Masaryk, Thomas, 68, 179, 480
Mass Education Movement (China), 307
Massachusetts, internationalist interests in, 114, 539
Massachusetts Peace Society, 494
Massawa, 469
Master Idea (R. L. Bridgman), 114
Masterman, C.F.G., 649
Maxwell Fyfe, David. *See* Fyfe, David Maxwell
May, Herbert L., *481–83*
Mayer, René, *483–84*
Mazzini Society, 651
McAdams, Thomas B., 501
McAdoo, William G., *484–85*
McCarthyism, 318, 371, 379
McCloy, John J., 157
McClure's, 47
McCormick, Cyrus, 521
McCormick, Nettie, 79
McCormick, Vance C., 224, *485–86*
McCoy, Frank, 81
McCumber, Porter J., *486–87*
McCurdy, Charles, 196
McDonald, James G., *488–90*
McDowell, William O., *490–91*
McFadyean, Andrew, *491–92*
McKinley, William, 270, 354, 711
McNair, Arnold D., 422, *492–93*
McNary, Charles, 37
Mead, Edwin D., 295, *493–95*
Mead, Lucia Ames, 20, 494, *495–96*
Meany, George, 793
Mediation, 170, 235, 355–56, 433, 456
Medical Education in Europe (A. Flexner), 263
Medical Education in the U.S. and Canada (A. Flexner), 263
Medical Women's National Association, 519
Mediterranean Sea, 684
Meili, Friedrich, 408
Mein Kampf (A. Hitler), 324
Mello Franco, Afranio de, *496–97*
Mellon, Andrew, 290
Memel, 13, 201
Memorandum for Peace Through the

United Nations, 434
Mendes France, Pierre, 271, 505
Mercurio de Valparaiso, El, 234
Mesopotamia Note, 162
Methodist Church, and internationalism, 559–60
Metternich, Klemens, 188, 284
Meulen, Jacob ter. *See* Ter Meulen, Jacob
Mexican American Claims Commission (1943–44), 211
Mexican Italian Claims Commission (1929–33), 249
Mexican Revolution, 19, 226, 786
Mexico, 19, 226, 249, 416, 417, 488, 518, 721
Meyer, Cord, Jr., 80, 157, 259
Mezes, Sidney, E., *497–98*
Middle East, 570. *See also* Palestine question
Mid-European Democratic Union, 561
Militarism, 494
Military Board of Allied Supply, 203
Mill, James, 71
Mill, John Stuart, 71
Miller, David Hunter, 83, 369, 498, *499–500*
Milner mission, 424
Miner's Freedom (C. L. Goodrich), 296
Ministry of Information, 182
Minor, Raleigh C., *500–501*
Minorities, 43, 116–17, 161, 193, 292, 677, 815
Missing Persons' Bureau, 93
Mission territory, 563
Missouri Peace Society, 361
Mitchell, Samuel Chiles, *501–2*
Mixed Claims Commission (Mexico), 226
Moch, Jules, 483
Moffat, Jay P., *502–4*
Molhuysen, Philipp C., *504–5*
Mollet, Guy, *505–6*, 577
Molotov, V. M., 725
Monnet, Jean, 36, 38, 91, 206, 224, 376, 427, 483, 505, *506–8*, 656

About The Contributors

Fredrick Aandahl was the editor of the official documentary series, *Foreign Relations of the United States*, and then deputy director of the Historical Office, U.S. Department of State, until his retirement in 1979. Earlier he was an associate editor of two other series, *Documents on German Foreign Policy, 1918–1945* and *The Papers of Thomas Jefferson*. He is now an associate editor of *The Papers of Woodrow Wilson* at Princeton University.

Frank W. Abbott is associate professor of history and chairs the Department of Social Sciences at the University of Houston Downtown College. He holds a M.A. and a Ph.D. from Texas Tech University. His interest is internationalist organizations in the twentieth-century. He has written several articles on areas of internationalism in the United States and is currently working on aspects of the problem of American vulnerability in an interdependent world.

Paul P. Abrahams holds a Ph.D. from the University of Wisconsin. His research interests have been in American foreign policy and economic history. To these he has added quantitative history. He is currently an associate professor at the University of Wisconsin-Green Bay.

Robert D. Accinelli teaches at the University of Toronto where he is the associate chairman of the Department of History. A specialist in American diplomatic history, he holds his M.A. and Ph.D. from the University of California, Berkeley. He has published articles on the American peace movement and internationalism in the interwar period.

Aamir Ali, a native of India, has been an official of the International Labor Office for over thirty-five years. He is at present chief of personnel. He is a graduate of Bombay University and has published several books, including novels.

Glenn C. Altschuler is assistant dean of the College of Arts and Sciences, Cornell University. He received a B.A., Magna Cum Laude from Brooklyn College and a M.A. and a Ph.D. in American history from Cornell. He is the author of several articles, as well as *Andrew D. White—Educator, Historian, Diplomat* (1979), *Race, Ethnicity and Class in American Social Thought, 1865–1919* (1982) and *On Whose Side Was God? Abolition, Temperance and Women's Rights on Trial* (forthcoming).

Effie Ambler is on the faculty of Wayne State University. She holds a M.A. and a Ph.D. in history and Soviet area studies from Indiana University. She has published *Russian Journalism and Politics, 1861–1888* (1972) and has a special interest in the problem of cultural survivals in revolutionary societies.

Joseph L. Arnold is associate professor of history at the University of Maryland Baltimore County. He has his B.A. degree from Denison University and the M.A. and Ph.D. from Ohio State University. Dr. Arnold has published works on the history of city planning, urban social and political structure, and the history of poverty. He is currently completing a study of Baltimore, MD, in the 1880s and 1890s.

Mary Welek Atwell is associate professor of History at Hollins College in Virginia.

She holds a Ph.D. from St. Louis University. She has published several articles dealing with Eleanor Roosevelt and with the Cold War.

Walter M. Bacon, Jr., a native of New York City, received degrees in history and international relations from Colorado College and the University of Denver. A member of the political science faculty at the University of Nebraska at Omaha since 1976, Dr. Bacon is the author of a book on Soviet-Romanian relations, as well as numerous journal articles and chapters on aspects of contemporary Romanian politics.

Robert C. Bannister is professor of history and department chairman at Swarthmore College. He holds a B.A. and a Ph.D. in American studies from Yale, and a B.A. in philosophy, politics, and economics from Oxford. His books include a biography of Ray Stannard Baker and a revisionist study of social Darwinism in Anglo-American thought. He is currently completing a book on the quest for objectivity in American sociology through the 1930s. In 1977–78 he served as bicentennial professor at the University of Helsinki.

John F. Bantell received his doctorate in political science in 1979 from the University of Connecticut. His major area of interest is recent U.S. foreign policy. Included among his publications are articles dealing with U.S. rearmament after World War II and the American world government movement during the same period. Dr. Bantell has taught at a number of colleges in Connecticut and is currently employed by the State of Connecticut as a senior policy analyst.

Kenneth C. Barnes is assistant professor of History at Concordia College, River Forest, IL. He holds a M.A. from the University of East Anglia and is currently completing work for the Ph.D. at Duke University. His area of research is the ecumenical movement and social problems in the 1920s and 1930s.

Ruhl J. Bartlett, now retired, holds the Ph.D. degree from Ohio State University and the LL.D. degree from Tufts University. He was professor of American history and dean of the Graduate School at Tufts and professor of American diplomatic history in the Fletcher School of Law and Diplomacy. He was visiting professor at various universities in the United States and Europe. Among his publications are books on Latin America and on American foreign relations.

Suzanne Bastid has been president of the Administrative Council of the UN, 1952–1968, 1979–1981, and secretary-general of the Institute of Law, 1963–1969. She has represented France at the UN and published extensively on international administrations, courts, and law.

J. Leonard Bates is a professor of history at the University of Illinois, Urbana. He received his M.A. and Ph.D. in history from the University of North Carolina. His principal area of research and publication is the early twentieth century, and he is currently writing a biography of Senator Thomas J. Walsh of Montana. Dr. Bates spent the spring of 1981 in the Soviet Union as a Fulbright-Hays lecturer in American history.

Joseph O. Baylen is Regents' professor of history at Georgia State University. Dr. Baylen has published extensively on British social and political history of the Late Victorian and Edwardian eras and on Anglo-Russian relations during the 1870–1914 era. He has been a Guggenheim, American Council of Learned Societies, and Institute for Advanced Study (Princeton) Fellow and twice Fulbright-Hays Senior Lecturer in the United Kingdom.

David P. Beatty is an associate professor and former head of the Department of

History at Mount Allison University, Sackville, NB. He holds a M.A. and a Ph.D. in history of international relations from Michigan State University. Dr. Beatty's special interests are in Canadian-American defense.

Cynthia F. Behrman is professor of history at Wittenberg University. Educated at Barnard College, University of California (Berkeley), and Boston University, she has held fellowships from the American Council of Learned Societies, the American Philosophical Society, and the National Endowment for the Humanities. She has published articles on modern British social and intellectual history and is the author of *Victorian Myths of the Sea* (1977).

Patrick Bellegarde-Smith is an assistant professor at Bradley University. He holds a Ph.D. in international studies from American University and teaches in the fields of Caribbean, Latin American, African, and Afro-American history and politics. His research has focused in the areas of social thought and ideology, international development, and political economy.

Bernard Bellush is resident professor at the City College of New York. He holds the M.A. and Ph.D. degrees in American history from Columbia University. His earlier works have dealt with Franklin D. Roosevelt, John G. Winant, and the New Deal period. His present interests include public employee unionism in New York City and American radical political movements.

A. LeRoy Bennett has been professor of political science and coordinator of the interdisciplinary major in international relations at the University of Delaware since 1962. He holds M.A. and Ph.D. degrees from the University of Illinois. In 1951–52, he was at the United Nations headquarters on a Ford Foundation fellowship and in the spring of 1980 spent a sabbatical semester in Geneva. In addition to many articles, he is the author of *International Organizations: Principles and Issues*, 2nd ed. (1980).

Clarence A. Berdahl is professor of political science, emeritus, at the University of Illinois, where he received the Ph.D. He has the B.A. from St. Olaf College, M.A. from the University of South Dakota, and the honorary LL.D. from each. During summers and after retirement, he taught at several other leading universities, specializing in political parties and international organization. Among other experiences were close association with the League of Nations in Geneva, war service with the U.S. State Department, with the OSS in London, and with the UN Conference in San Francisco.

Darrel E. Bigham is professor of history at Indiana State University Evansville, where he has been since 1970. He holds the B.A. in history from Messiah College and the Ph.D. in American social and intellectual history from the University of Kansas. He was a Rockefeller Fellow at Harvard Divinity School, 1964–65. His research interests include American religious history, urbanization, ethnic and racial minorities, and urban elites. His most recent publication is a history of Evansville blacks.

Donald S. Birn has taught history at the State University of New York at Albany since 1966. He holds a M.A. and the Ph.D. in modern European history from Columbia University. His book, *The League of Nations Union, 1918–1945* (1981), reflects his interest in peace and internationalism in interwar Britain.

Louis R. Bisceglia is a professor of English history at San Jose State University. He is author of several articles on pacifism and internationalism and a book entitled *Norman Angell and Liberal Internationalism in Britain, 1931–1935* (1982).

M. B. Biskupski, a specialist in modern Polish and Russian history, earned his doctorate at Yale University. The recipient of Fulbright-Hays, IREX, and International Studies Association fellowships, Professor Biskupski taught at Yale before joining the history department of Millersville State College in Pennsylvania. He has published articles and reviews in a number of scholarly journals and recently coedited a collaborative work on Polish politics in Europe and America. He serves as Polish history editor of the journal, *East Central Europe*.

Kenneth John Blume teaches at the State University of New York-Binghamton, where he is also a doctoral candidate in American diplomatic history. He holds a B.A. from Hamilton College and an M.A. from St. John's University. He is book review editor for the Steamship Historical Society and is currently completing a dissertation on the relations between the United States and the British West Indies during the Civil War.

Stephen D. Bodayla received his Ph.D. from New York University and is head of the Department of History and pre-law coordinator at Marycrest College, Davenport, IA. His special interest is United States relations with Latin America in the twentieth century. He is completing a biography of Dwight Whitney Morrow.

Ernest C. Bolt, Jr., is a professor of history at the University of Richmond. He received his Ph.D. from the University of Georgia and is the author of *Ballots before Bullets: The War Referendum Approach to Peace in America, 1914–1941* (1977). His essays on American foreign policy between World War I and World War II and Louis Ludlow have recently appeared in *American Foreign Relations: A Historiographical Review* (1981) and *Their Infinite Variety: Essays on Indiana Politicians* (1981). He is working on a biography of Louis Ludlow.

Leon E. Boothe is currently vice-president for academic affairs and provost at Illinois State University. Previously he was dean of the College of Arts and Sciences, 1970–80, at George Mason University. He holds the B.S. and M.A. from the University of Missouri-Columbia and his Ph.D. in American history from the University of Illinois-Urbana. His teaching field is American diplomatic history, and his primary research and publishing field has been in the Woodrow Wilson and Franklin D. Roosevelt presidential administrations.

Robert Bothwell is a professor of history at the University of Toronto. He holds a doctorate from Harvard University and was for some years editor of the *Canadian Historical Review*. He has published widely on recent Canadian history, including a biography, *Pearson: His Life and World* (1978), and is currently working on aspects of Canadian nuclear history.

Werner Braatz is on the faculty of the University of Wisconsin-Oshkosh where he is the coordinator of European Studies. He holds the Ph.D. in history from the University of Wisconsin-Madison. His most recent publications are in modern European economic and social history. He is a frequent contributor to professional journals and has for some years helped as well with the editing of *Societas: A Review of Social History*.

John J. Broesamle is professor of history and former associate dean of the School of Social and Behavioral Sciences at California State University, Northridge. A graduate of the University of the Pacific, he holds the M.A. and Ph.D. from Columbia University. He is the author of *William Gibbs McAdoo: A Passion for Change, 1863–1917* (1973). Professor Broesamle is working on an interpretive study of twentieth-century American politics, focusing on the relationship between reform and reaction.

Robert Craig Brown is professor of history and associate dean for the Humanities Division, School of Graduate Studies, University of Toronto. He is a former editor of the *Canadian Historical Review* and a former president of the Canadian Historical Association. His books include *Canada's National Policy, 1883–1900* (1964), *Canada, 1896–1921, A Nation Transformed* (1974), and *Robert Laird Borden, A Biography, 1854–1937*, 2 vols. (1975 and 1980). He is currently preparing a study of Canadian society during the Great War.

Ian Brownlie is Chichele professor of public international law in the University of Oxford and fellow of All Souls College, Oxford. He is also editor of the *British Year Book of International Law*; a member of the English Bar (Queen's Counsel, 1979); and a fellow of the British Academy.

Kathleen Burk was born in California but now lives in England. She took a B.A. in diplomatic history and political science at the University of California-Berkeley, and a M.A. and a D.Phil. in modern history at Oxford University, where she was a Rhodes fellow. She is currently lecturer in history and politics at Imperial College, London University. Dr. Burk has published widely in the fields of twentieth-century British politics and diplomacy, Anglo-American relations, and economic diplomacy.

Thomas W. Burkman is an associate professor of history at Old Dominion University where he has taught Japanese history since 1976. He holds a Ph.D. in history from the University of Michigan. He has been a Fulbright fellow and visiting research scholar at the University of Tokyo (1978) and a visiting lecturer at the University of California-Davis (1981–82). He has edited *The Occupation of Japan: Educational and Social Reform* (1982). His major research is on Japan and the League of Nations and problems of world order between the world wars.

E. Bradford Burns, professor of history and dean of the Division of Honors, University of California-Los Angeles, has published eight books on Latin American history. His study of the diplomacy of the Baron of Rio-Branco, *The Unwritten Alliance. Rio-Branco and Brazilian-American Relations* (1966), won the Bolton Prize and prompted his election to the Instituto Histórico e Geográfico Brasileiro.

June K. Burton is associate professor of history at the University of Akron. She holds a B.A. and M.A. from Stetson University and a Ph.D. from the University of Georgia. A Europeanist by training, Dr. Burton's specialties are Napoleonic France, on which she has published, and international human rights.

Harold T. Butler studied history and political science and received his B.A. and M.A. from the University of Rochester and his Ph.D. from Syracuse University. He has taught at Rochester Collegiate Center for low-income students, the Associate Colleges of Upper New York for veterans, Rensselaer Polytechnic Institute, and Hudson Valley Community College, Troy, NY. His courses included ones on European history, international relations, U.S. government, and comparative government.

Kenneth R. Calkins is professor of history at Kent State University. He holds the M.A. and Ph.D. in history from the University of Chicago. He has produced a number of publications in the field of modern German history including a biography of Hugo Haase, a leading figure in the German Social Democratic opposition to World War I.

Thomas M. Campbell holds his M.A. and Ph.D. degrees from the University of Virginia. He is a professor of history at Florida State University and has published extensively on planning for peace during and after World War II. Among his major works is the volume *Masquerade Peace: America's UN Policy, 1944–1945* (1973).

Elisa Carrillo is academic dean at Marymount College, Tarrytown, NY, where she is also professor of history. Her research and publications have been primarily in the field of twentieth-century Italian history. She is the author of a biography of Alcide De Gasperi. Her Ph.D. is from Fordham University.

John M. Carroll is associate professor of history at Lamar University. He received his B.A. from Brown University and the Ph.D. from the University of Kentucky. Dr. Carroll has published extensively on a variety of subjects in twentieth century American history. His special area of interest is diplomacy in the 1920s and 1930s. He has recently coedited a book, *Sports in Modern America* (1981).

Ian Casselman is a graduate of Oxford University. He is currently studying at the University of Toronto.

Alan Cassels was born in England and educated at Oxford University. He received his doctorate from the University of Michigan and now resides in Canada where he is professor of history at McMaster University. He has served as president of the Society for Italian Historical Studies. Fascism and European international affairs comprise the subject matter of his four books and several articles.

James E. Cebula is an associate professor of history at Raymond Walters College of the University of Cincinnati. He holds a Ph.D. in history from the University of Cincinnati. Currently working on a biography of James M. Cox, Dr. Cebula also has a number of publications in the field of labor history.

John Whiteclay Chambers II is assistant professor of history at Rutgers University-New Brunswick. He received his Ph.D. in history from Columbia University, then taught at Barnard College, Columbia University, where he received the Outstanding Teacher Award in 1975. He is author of *The Tyranny of Change: America in the Progressive Era, 1900–1917* (1980) and editor of anthologies on the draft, the officer corps, and the peace movement and U.S. foreign policy. In 1981, he was a Rockefeller Humanities fellow and in 1982, he was a Fulbright scholar in Italy.

Charles Chatfield is professor of history and director of international education at Wittenberg University. He holds the M.A. and Ph.D. from Vanderbilt University. He has contributed to the history of pacifism and peace movements in the United States with some original writing, a good deal of editing of books and journals, and he has served as president of the Conference on Peace Research in History.

Roger Chickering is professor of history at the University of Oregon. He received his Ph.D. from Stanford University. His publications include a study of the German peace movement, *Imperial Germany and a World Without War* (1975), and a book on the Pan-German League, *We Men Who Feel Most German* (1983). He has held research fellowships from the Fulbright Commission and the Guggenheim Foundations.

J. Garry Clifford is associate professor of political science at the University of Connecticut. He is a graduate of Williams College and received his Ph.D. from Indiana University. He has published *The Citizen Soldiers* (1972) and *American Foreign Policy: A History* (1977). He is currently researching a book about the great debate over American intervention in World War II.

Catherine Ann Cline received her B.A. degree from Smith College, her M.A. from Columbia University, and her Ph.D. from Bryn Mawr College. She is professor of history at Catholic University of America and the author of *Recruits to Labour: The British Labour Party, 1914–1931* (1963) and *E. D. Morel, (1873–1924): The Strategies of Protest* (1981).

Ruth Clinefelter is humanities research librarian and associate professor of bibliography at the University of Akron. She holds a M.A. in history from the University of Akron and an MALS from Kent State University. She is past president of the Association for the Bibliography of History. She has had varied experience as a librarian. Her special interests are history and classics.

Naomi W. Cohen is professor of history at Hunter College and the Graduate Center of the City University of New York. She holds graduate degrees in history from Columbia University and has served on the boards of various academic organizations. Her special interest is American Jewish history, and she has published several books, including a biography of Oscar S. Straus, and numerous articles in that field. She also teaches courses in twentieth-century American history and the history of immigration.

Warren I. Cohen is professor of history and director of the Asian Studies Center at Michigan State University. He has written widely on American-East Asian relations including *The Chinese Connection: Roger S. Greene, Thomas W. Lamont, George E. Sokolsky and American-East Asian Relations* (1978). His most recent book was *Dean Rusk* (1980) in the American Secretaries of State series.

Joel Colton, professor of history and formerly chairman of the department of history at Duke University, served from 1974 to 1981 with the Rockefeller Foundation as director for humanities. The author of *Léon Blum: Humanist in Politics* (1966, French translation, 1968), he has also written other books and articles on modern and contemporary European history. He has received Guggenheim, Rockefeller, and National Endowment for the Humanities fellowship awards.

Sandi E. Cooper, professor of history at the College of Staten Island, CUNY, received a Ph.D. from New York University. She has worked extensively on European peace movements and ideas, served as coeditor of the Garland Library of War/Peace, and published several articles on liberal internationalism and peace ideologies. Dr. Cooper was editor for Western Europe for the *Biographical Dictionary of Modern Peace Leaders* (1984). She has been president of the Berkshire Conference of Women Historians, national chair of the Coordinating Committee on Women in the Historical Profession, vice-president of the Conference on Peace Research in History, and on the editorial board of *Peace and Change*.

Frank J. Coppa is professor of history and chairman of the Department of History at St. John's University. A prominent historian of modern Italy, he has published monographs on Giovanni Giolitti, Camillo de Cavour, and Pope Pius IX and has edited a half dozen other volumes and contributed to numerous others. His articles have appeared in the *Journal of Modern History*, the *Journal of Economic History*, and the *Rassegna Storica del Risorgimento*. Currently, he is editing a *Dictionary of Modern Italian History* for Greenwood Press.

Richard A. Cosgrove is an associate professor of history at the University of Arizona. He holds the M.A. and Ph.D. degrees from the University of California, Riverside. His research interests are Victorian legal and diplomatic history. His major work is *The Rule of Law: Albert Venn Dicey, Victorian Jurist* (1980).

Frank C. Costigliola is an associate professor of history at the University of Rhode Island. He attended Hamilton College and the Universität München and holds a Ph.D. from Cornell University. His special interest is American diplomatic, economic, and cultural relations with Europe.

Louis A. Cretella holds a M.A. from Southern Illinois University, Carbondale, and a Ph.D. from the University of Connecticut. In 1976, he was awarded a

Fulbright fellowship for doctoral research in Italy. His main interest is European history in the twentieth century. He has contributed articles in the areas of European diplomatic relations in the interwar years and contemporary Italian politics.

Robert D. Cuff is a professor of history at York University in Toronto. He holds a M.A. and a Ph.D. from Princeton University. His research interests include business-government relations in the United States and Canadian-American relations. His publications include, *The War Industries Board: Business-Government Relations during World War I* (1973) and *American Dollars/Canadian Prosperity: Canadian-American Economic Relations 1945–1950* (1978).

David Culbert is associate professor of history, Louisiana State University, Baton Rouge. He holds his Ph.D. from Northwestern University. He is the author of *News for Everyman: Radio and Foreign Affairs in Thirties America* (1976) and *Mission to Moscow* (1980). He has recently completed a 150-minute documentary film, *Television's Vietnam: The Impact of Visual Images* (1982).

Lejeune Cummins is professor of history at California State University, Hayward. He holds a M.A. and the Ph.D. in history from the University of California, Berkeley, and specializes in inter-American relations. He is a student of intervention in the Caribbean and is currently working on a study of the diplomatic holdings of the Costa Rican National Archives. He has published a series of reviews and articles in historical journals.

Raymond J. Cunningham is an associate professor of history at Fordham University in the Bronx, New York. He holds his Ph.D. from Johns Hopkins University. His work and publications have been chiefly in the areas of American intellectual history and historiography.

William W. Cuthbertson has a B.D. from Southern Baptist Theological Seminary and a Ph.D. from the University of Rochester. He is professor of history and head of the department at William Jewell College. He is interested in American progressivism, religious history, and diplomatic relations.

Calvin D. Davis is professor of history at Duke University. His first book, *The United States and the First Hague Peace Conference* (1962), received the Albert J. Beveridge Award. *The United States and the Second Hague Peace Conference: American Diplomacy and International Organization, 1899–1914* (1976) continued his study of the era, and he is currently completing research for a book about the making of peace after World War I. He holds a Ph.D. from Indiana University.

Harold Eugene Davis is university professor emeritus of history and international service at American University. He holds a B.A. degree from Hiram College, a M.A. in history from the University of Chicago, and a Ph.D. in history from Case-Western Reserve University. The author of numerous books and journal articles on Latin America, he has specialized in the intellectual and diplomatic history of the area. Under a joint appointment he has taught graduate courses on Latin America in the history department, the School of Government, and the School of International Service in the University.

Hugh H. Davis is professor of history at Southern Connecticut State College where he specializes in nineteenth-century American history. He holds a Ph.D. from Ohio State University and has written widely on nineteenth-century reform movements.

Kenneth Penn Davis holds a B.A. from Oglethorpe University, a M.A. from Georgia State University, and a Ph.D. in American diplomatic history from the University of Virginia. He worked four years for the National Archives and currently serves as senior management analyst performing quantitative and organizational studies in the Office of Management Improvement, General Services Administration, in Washington.

Anne L. Day is professor of history and coordinator of the Secondary Education Social Studies Program at Clarion State College, Clarion. She holds the Ph.D. in history from St. Louis University, concentrating in the field of U.S. diplomacy. She has published in the areas of competency-based teacher education and peace research. Her special research and teaching interests are in the humanistic aspects of global economics and science, technology, and peace.

Roberta Allbert Dayer currently is writing a biography of Sir Charles S. Addis in which she continues her investigation of the influence of private finance on foreign policy, first begun as doctoral research at the State University of New York at Buffalo. She is the author of *Bankers and Diplomats in China, 1917–1925: The Anglo-American Relationship* (1981). She has taught American foreign policy and Sino-American relations at the State University of New York at Buffalo and Fredonia.

Charles DeBenedetti is a professor of history at the University of Toledo. He received a B.S. degree from Loyola University (Chicago) and a M.A. and the Ph.D. from the University of Illinois-Urbana. He has published articles and books on peace activism in American history including *The Peace Reform in American History* (1980). He is especially interested in the work of the Conference on Peace Research in History and has served as its president.

Terry L. Deibel is professor of national security policy at the National War College, National Defense University, Washington, D.C. He is an international affairs specialist who has taught at the School of Foreign Service, Georgetown University, and worked at the Office of Management and Budget and the Department of State. His doctoral dissertation on "The League of Nations and American Internationalism, 1919–1929" was written under Professor Ruhl J. Bartlett of the Fletcher School of Law and Diplomacy, Tufts University.

Charles F. Delzell is professor of modern European history at Vanderbilt University. He received the Ph.D. in history at Stanford University. He is coauthor of *The Meaning of Yalta* (1956); author of *Mussolini's Enemies: The Italian Anti-Fascist Resistance* (1961); *Mediterranean Fascism, 1919–1945* (1970); *Italy in the Twentieth Century* (1980); and others. He has been president of the Society for Italian Historical Studies and the American Committee on the History of the Second World War.

Justus D. Doenecke is professor of history at New College of the University of South Florida. He received his B.A. from Colgate University and his M.A. and Ph.D. from Princeton University. He has written widely in the field of American diplomatic history. Among his books are *Not to the Swift: The Old Isolationists in the Cold War Era* (1979), *The Presidencies of James A. Garfield and Chester A. Arthur* (1981), and a forthcoming study of American public opinion and the Manchurian crisis of 1931–33.

J. B. Donnelly is professor of history at Washington & Jefferson College. He has a B.A. in English literature from Johns Hopkins University, a M.A. in political science from Georgetown University, and a Ph.D. in history from the University of Virginia. A former military intelligence officer, reporter for the *Baltimore Sun*, and government aide, he has published essays in the fields of early twentieth-century diplomatic and cultural history.

Murray Donnelly is a professor of political science at the University of Manitoba. He is the author of *Dafoe of the Free Press* (1968).

Marvin L. Downing is professor of history at the University of Tennessee at Martin. He received his M.A. from Texas Christian University and the Ph.D. from the University of Oklahoma where his dissertation was "Hugh R. Wilson and American Relations with the League of Nations, 1927–1937."

Martin David Dubin, an associate professor of political science and coordinator of the international relations minor at Northern Illinois University, holds a B.A. from the City College of New York and a M.A. and the Ph.D. from Indiana University. He has published several articles in the area of his special interest, the history of the peace movement and the evolution of international institutions.

Juanita Montague Duffer is a part-time history instructor at Southside Virginia Community College in Alberta, VA. She holds a M.A. in history from the University of Richmond. Her area of specialization is nineteenth-century Europe.

Joseph T. Durkin, S.J., born in Philadelphia, PA, 1903, is professor emeritus, American history department, Georgetown University. He holds the Ph.D. in history from Fordham University. His publications include a biography of *Stephen R. Mallory: Confederate Navy Chief* (1954), *General Sherman's Son* (1959), and eight other books. He is director of the American Studies Collection and former director of the Alexis Carrel Archives at Georgetown University.

Lawrence O. Ealy held the Ernest J. King chair, U.S. Naval War College; was provost and dean, Hobart and William Smith Colleges; vice president and dean, Rider College; and professor of history, Temple University. He received LL.B., M.A., and Ph.D. degrees at the University of Pennsylvania. His fields of interest are international law, diplomacy, and Latin American studies. Dr. Ealy has published many books and articles and is a recognized authority on Panama and the Panama Canal.

George W. Egerton is associate professor of history at the University of British Columbia. A graduate of the University of Toronto, he has published works on the League of Nations and British and American foreign policy in the period after World War I. His most recent work addresses the ideological and cultural dynamics of the interwar peace movement.

John D. Fair is professor of history at Auburn University at Montgomery. He holds a Ph.D. in history from Duke University. His publications, including *British Interparty Conferences* (1980), have dealt chiefly with British political and constitutional issues in the late nineteenth and early twentieth centuries. He has been working recently on diplomatic and historiographical topics in the interwar period.

Terence J. Fay is an assistant professor at the University of Manitoba and teaches Canadian and American foreign relations. He publishes on Canadian-United States diplomatic relations and on Minneapolis and Winnipeg cross-border urban comparisons. He is a member of many Canadian and American scholarly organizations and holds several M.A. degrees and a Ph.D. in diplomatic history from Georgetown University.

John Finan is director of Latin American Studies and professor of Latin American history in the School of International Service, American University. He is co-author of *Latin American Diplomatic History: An Introduction* (1977) and of *Latin America, International Relations: A Guide to Information Sources* (1981). He received his Ph.D. in Latin American History from Harvard University.

Seymour Maxwell Finger is professor of political science at the College of Staten

Island and the Graduate Center, City University of New York, and director of CUNY's Ralph Bunche Institute on the United Nations. From 1946 to 1971 he was a career diplomat, serving the last four years at the United States Mission to the UN as ambassador and senior adviser to the permanent representative. He is the author of *Your Man at the UN: People, Politics and Bureaucracy in the Making of American Foreign Policy* (1980) and editor of several other volumes. His numerous essays on foreign policy, terrorism, and the UN have appeared in books and scholarly journals.

Carole Fink is an associate professor of history at the University of North Carolina at Wilmington. She received the M.A. and Ph.D. degrees from Yale University, has published several books and articles on twentieth-century international history, and in 1982–83 was awarded a research fellowship by the American Association of University Women to write the first biography of Marc Bloch.

Clinton F. Fink is a research associate of the Peace Museum (Chicago). A graduate of Swarthmore College, he holds a Ph.D. in social psychology from the University of Michigan. He is former editor of the *Journal of Conflict Resolution* (1969–1972) and co-author of *Peace and War: A Guide to Bibliographies* (1983). His current research deals with the history of peace education and with the role of music in the struggle for peace.

Richard A. Fredland is professor of political science and department chairman at Indiana University-Purdue University at Indianapolis. His advanced degrees in international relations are from American University. His writings include *Africa Faces the World* (1980), and he co-edited *Integration and Disintegration in East Africa* (1981). He has recently been a consultant to the Zairean government.

Frank Freidel is Bullitt professor of American history at the University of Washington and Charles Warren professor emeritus of American history, Harvard University. He is author of a number of books, including a biography of Francis Lieber and a multivolumed biography of Franklin D. Roosevelt. He is past president of the Organization of American Historians.

Robert A. Friedlander is professor of international and criminal law at the Pettit College of Law, Ohio Northern University. He has a B.A., M.A., and Ph.D. in history from Northwestern University and a J.D. from the DePaul University College of Law. He is a member of the advisory board of the *Denver Journal of International Law and Policy* and a member of the editorial board of the T.V.I. [Terrorism/Violence/Insurgency] Journal. He has coedited a treatise on self-determination and is the author of a three-volume documentary analysis of terrorism.

James Friguglietti is professor of history at Eastern Montana College, Billings, Montana. A specialist in modern French history, he received his doctorate from Harvard University in 1966. Among his publications are *The Shaping of Modern France* (1969) and *Albert Mathiez (1874–1932): Historien Révolutionnaire* (1974). He is preparing a history of French pacifism between the two world wars.

Stephen E. Fritz is vice president for academic affairs and professor of history at Pikeville College. He holds a M.A. from Southern Illinois University and the Ph.D. from the University of Kentucky. His principal research interests are the life and career of David Lloyd George and British foreign policy during the 1920s.

Paul A. Gaeng is professor of French and head, Department of French, University of Illinois at Urbana-Champaign. He held appointments at Hofstra and Queens Colleges and the Universities of Cincinnati, Virginia, and Columbia. He earned a Ph.D. in Romance Philology at Columbia. His research is focused on "Vulgar" Latin and early Romance. His latest book, *A Study of Nominal Inflection in Latin Inscriptions* (1977), is an attempt to determine the extent to which Latin inscriptions, specifically Christian, reveal the survival of the classical nominal system and trends in the direction of its collapse. Gaeng collaborated with Mario Pei on *The Story of Latin and the Romance Languages* (1976). In 1976 he was named a *chevalier* in the Order of Academic Palms by the French government.

Lawrence E. Gelfand is professor of history, University of Iowa. A native of Cleveland, Ohio, he is a graduate of Western Reserve University and holds the Ph.D. in history from the University of Washington. His principal interest, reflected in books and articles, lies in American foreign policy during the era of Woodrow Wilson. He has also served as president of the Society for Historians of American Foreign Relations.

Irwin F. Gellman lives in Newport Beach, California. He received his B.A. and M.A. from the University of Maryland and his Ph.D. from Indiana University. His special area of interest centers on United States-Latin American relations in the twentieth century, and his most recent book is *Good Neighbor Diplomacy: United States Policies in Latin America, 1933–1945* (1979). Dr. Gellman also serves on the editorial board of *Diplomatic History*.

Roy E. Goodman is reference librarian at the American Philosophical Society in Philadelphia. He holds a M.A. in American civilization from the University of Pennsylvania and an M.S. in Library and Information Science from Drexel University. He has written articles on Philadelphia and its international context and in scholarly journals on the history and technology of science internationally.

G. F. Goodwin is an associate professor of history at Carleton University in Ottawa. He holds the Ph.D. in history from Princeton University. His research interests are United States politics and foreign relations from 1919 to 1941.

Colin Gordon is senior lecturer in international relations at the University of Salford, England. He graduated from University College, Oxford, in 1953 and spent six years in industry before joining Salford. He took a Master's degree at that University in 1967, is a member of the International Institute for Strategic Studies, and has published widely and lectured extensively on European defense on both sides of the Atlantic.

James W. Gould is professor of international relations at Scripps College and Claremont Graduate School, teaching international organization and Asian foreign policy. Educated at the Sorbonne and Fletcher School of Law and Diplomacy, he was an interpreter and U.S. foreign service officer in the Netherlands Indies, Hong Kong, and Indonesia, and Fulbright lecturer at Munich. Active in state associations for the UN and human rights, he writes and lectures on altruism in international organization.

H. Roger Grant is professor of history at the University of Akron. A specialist in the Populist-Progressive era and American transportation history, he is the author of numerous articles and four books, the most recent of which is *Self-help in the 1890's Depression* (1983).

John Greco is director of education at the College for Human Services in New York City and teaches a variety of interdisciplinary courses there. He holds a Ph.D.

in history from Syracuse University and spent a year doing postdoctoral study as a visiting scholar at Teachers College, Columbia University. He is interested in ideas within the peace movement in the United States.

Greg Gubler is an assistant professor of history and Asian studies at the Brigham Young University, Hawaii Campus. He holds a Ph.D. in history from Florida State University, was a Fulbright scholar to Singapore, formerly taught at the University of Florida, and until recently was the research specialist for East Asia at the Genealogical Society (1976–82). His publications and interests are in Asian genealogy and Japanese diplomatic history.

Marcel Hamelin is professor at the University of Ottawa where he is dean of the Faculty of Arts. He specializes in the history of Québec since 1850.

Wolfram F. Hanrieder is professor of political science at the University of California, Santa Barbara. He has published extensively in the area of West German foreign policy, trans-Atlantic relations, and the theory of international relations.

William H. Harbaugh is Langbourne M. Williams professor of American history at the University of Virginia. His books include *Power and Responsibility: The Life and Times of Theodore Roosevelt* (1961) and *Lawyer's Lawyer: The Life of John W. Davis* (1973). He is presently working on a volume on 1900–1932 for the Oxford History of the United States. He holds a Ph.D. from Northwestern University.

Victoria A. Harden is a pre-doctoral research fellow at Smithsonian Institution's National Museum of American History. She will receive her Ph.D. in American history from Emory University and is completing her dissertation on the early history of the National Institutes of Health. Her special interest is in the social context of biomedical research in the twentieth century.

James W. Harper is currently an associate professor of history at Texas Tech University. He holds a B.A. and M.A. from Marshall University and a Ph.D. from the University of Virginia. He has published articles and reviews in U.S. diplomatic and military history as well as the history of sports.

Benjamin T. Harrison is an associate professor of liberal studies at the University of Louisville. He holds a M.A. in history from California State College in Los Angeles and a Ph.D. in history from the University of California, Los Angeles. He has published articles in various journals concerning a wide range of topics and is writing a monograph on the influence of economic pressures on U.S. foreign policy in Latin America around the turn of the century.

William H. Hatcher is chairman of the political science department at the University of Southern Mississippi. He received his B.A. and M.A. from the University of Arkansas and the Ph.D. from Duke University. He has written for the *Dictionary of American Biography* and is the former editor (1965–74) of *The Southern Quarterly*.

Morrell Heald is Samuel B. and Virginia C. Knight professor of humanities at Case Western Reserve University and chairman of its American studies program. He holds the Ph.D. degree from Yale University and is the author of *The Social Responsibilities of Business: Company and Community, 1900–1960* (1970) and *Culture and Diplomacy: The American Experience* with Lawrence S. Kaplan (1977). In 1966–67, he served as visiting professor and consultant to the Indian Institute of Technology, Kanpur, India.

Jonathan E. Helmreich is professor of history at Allegheny College. He recently completed fifteen years as dean of instruction there. Professor Helmreich holds the

M.A. and Ph.D. degrees from Princeton University and has been a Fulbright grantee in Belgium. His interests include small power diplomacy; he has written a book and articles focusing on Belgium's performance in this area.

Sondra R. Herman is a professor of history at De Anza College, where she teaches recent American history and woman's history. She is the author of *Eleven Against War: Studies in American Internationalist Thought 1898–1921* (1969) and articles in American and Swedish women's history. Her doctorate in American intellectual history is from Rutgers University.

David W. Hirst is senior research historian, department of history, Princeton University, and senior associate editor, *The Papers of Woodrow Wilson*. He holds the M.A. and Ph.D. in history from Northwestern University. Forty volumes of the Wilson Papers are now in print; twenty more are projected to complete the series. Dr. Hirst is also editor of *Woodrow Wilson: Reform Governor* (1965) and has an additional interest in twentieth century diplomacy and biography.

Paul F. Hooper is an associate professor of American studies at the University of Hawaii where he specializes in Hawaiian studies and Pacific Basin international relations. He has traveled widely in Asia and the Pacific and has published on numerous topics relative to the area. His most recent publication is *Building A Pacific Community* (1982) which concerns current efforts to form a Pacific-wide regional organization.

William D. Hoover is an associate professor and chairs the History Department at the University of Toledo. Having earned his Ph.D. at the University of Michigan, he has published articles on several nineteenth-century Japanese economic modernizers and is presently researching internationalism and pacifism in Japan during the early twentieth century. In 1977–78, he was a research scholar in Japan under the Fulbright-Hays program.

Douglas W. Houston is an associate professor of history at Fordham University. He holds the Ph.D. degree from the University of Pennsylvania.

Robert V. Hudson, professor at Michigan State University, is the author of *The Writing Game: A Biography of Will Irwin* (1982). A mass media historian, he has published many articles and papers. He holds a B.S. in business from Indiana University, a M.S. in journalism from the University of Oregon, and a Ph.D. in mass communication from the University of Minnesota. He has been a wire service and newspaper reporter, magazine writer, and public relations executive.

Robert P. Ingalls is an associate professor of history at the University of South Florida, where he also serves as department chairperson. He holds a Ph.D. in history from Columbia University and is the author of *Herbert H. Lehman and New York's Little New Deal* (1975).

Akira Iriye is a professor and chairs the History Department at the University of Chicago. He holds a B.A. from Haverford College and Ph.D. from Harvard University. His publications, mainly dealing with American-Asian relations, include *After Imperialism* (1965), *Across the Pacific* (1967), *Pacific Estrangement* (1972), and *Power and Culture* (1981). He has been president of the Society for Historians of American Foreign Relations.

Fred L. Israel holds a Ph.D. degree from Columbia University. He is professor of history at the City College of New York, the author of *Nevada's Key Pittman* (1963), and the editor of *The War Diary of Breckinridge Long* (1966), and of *Major Peace*

Treaties of Modern History (1967–80) in 5 volumes. He is coeditor of *Justices of the Supreme Court* (1969–80) in 4 volumes and of *History of American Presidential Elections* (1971) in 4 volumes.

H. B. Jacobini is professor of political science at Southern Illinois University at Carbondale and holds a M.S. degree from Fort Hays Kansas State College and a Ph.D. from the University of Kansas. He has written on international law (including Latin American theory), public comparative law, and Southeast Asian politics and administration.

Herbert Janick is a professor of history and the director of the Center for Urban Studies at Western Connecticut State College. He holds a Ph.D. in history from Fordham University. A specialist in Connecticut history he is the author of *A Diverse People: Connecticut, 1914 to the Present* (1975). He is a former president of the Association for the Study of Connecticut History.

Sabine Jessner is an associate professor of history at the Indiana University School of Liberal Arts in Indianapolis. She holds a M.A. and a Ph.D. from Columbia University. Her research interests are French, Swiss, and women's history, and she has written a biography of *Edouard Herriot* (1974).

Peter J. Johnson is an associate with Rockefeller Family and Associates. He holds advanced degrees from the Maxwell School of Citizenship and Public Affairs at Syracuse University. He is currently completing a biography of John D. Rockefeller 3rd and his influence on the modern population field.

Dorothy V. Jones is a fellow of the Newberry Library, Chicago, where she is working on a study of the functioning of treaty systems in a colonial situation. She holds the Ph.D. in diplomatic history from the University of Chicago. Her most recent publication is a study of diplomacy in early America, *License for Empire* (1982).

Kenneth Paul Jones is a professor of history at the University of Tennessee at Martin. He has served as a Fulbright junior lecturer at Mainz University in Germany. He is the editor and contributing author to *U.S. Diplomats in Europe, 1919–1941* (1981). He has published articles about the Ruhr crisis of 1923–24 and is preparing a book-length diplomatic history of the crisis.

Mary Van Hulle Jones is a registered nurse whose work experience includes orthopedic and psychiatric nursing as well as the home care of emotionally disturbed children. She holds a B.S. in nursing and a M.A. in the history of science from the University of Wisconsin-Madison, where she is a doctoral candidate in the history of medicine. She is currently a project assistant for the University of Wisconsin-Extension, Health and Human Services.

Robert S. Jordan is professor of political science at the University of New Orleans. He has doctorates from Princeton and Oxford Universities, where he studied international law, politics, and organization. He served for several years as director of research at the United Nations Institute for Training and Research (UNITAR) and has taught at Columbia, Princeton, George Washington, Pittsburgh, and South Carolina Universities (as the Dag Hammarskjöld visiting professor). He has written or edited thirteen books and many articles and monographs.

Harold Josephson is professor of history at the University of North Carolina at Charlotte. He holds a M.A. and a Ph.D. in history from the University of Wisconsin-Madison. He is editor of the *Biographical Dictionary of Modern Peace Leaders* (1984) and has written on various subjects dealing with U.S. foreign policy.

He is currently writing a book on the role played by ex-Communist witnesses during the Cold War.

Thomas A. Julian is associate manager, command, control, and communications systems requirements analyst of the BDM Corporation, McLean, Virginia. He holds a Ph.D. from Syracuse University and has taught at the U.S. Air Force Academy and served as chief, Nuclear Policy Section, Supreme Headquarters Allied Powers, Europe, 1974–76.

Sugwon Kang is a professor of political science at Hartwick College, where he teaches political theory and American constitutional law. He holds a Ph.D. from Columbia University and is a frequent contributor to academic journals. A native-born Korean and a naturalized American citizen, Dr. Kang is a student of U.S. foreign policy and is a member of the American Committee on East-West Accord.

Lawrence S. Kaplan is director of the Lyman L. Lemnitzer Center for NATO Studies and university professor of history at Kent State University. His doctorate is in American diplomatic history from Yale University. He has served as Fulbright lecturer in Germany, France, and Belgium and as visiting professor at the European University Institute in Florence. His recent publications include *Culture and Diplomacy: the American Experience*, with Morrell Heald (1977), and *NATO After Thirty Years* (1981). He has served as president of the Society for Historians of American Foreign Relations.

Albert N. Keim is dean of Eastern Mennonite College and professor of history. His M.A. is from the University of Virginia and his Ph.D. from Ohio State University. His field of interest is in twentieth century church-state relations. His publications include work on John Foster Dulles, public-private education issues, and the politics of conscientious objection to war during World Wars I and II.

James T. Kenny is assistant to the president at the University of Maine at Presque Isle where he serves as an adjunct faculty member in political science. He holds a M.A. in political science from Kent State University and a Ph.D. in international studies from the University of Denver. He is a frequent contributor to professional and educational journals whose special interests include the politics of developing nations and international law.

Michael Keresztesi is associate professor of library science at Wayne State University. He holds a Ph.D. in library science and an advanced degree in history. Dr. Keresztesi specializes in international organizations and has written extensively on UNESCO. Lately, he has been concentrating on the theoretical aspects of bibliography, which he explored in a chapter that appeared in *Theories of Bibliographic Education* (1982).

Majid Khadduri is professor emeritus at Johns Hopkins University School of Advanced International Studies. He is the founder and former director of the Center for Middle East Studies at that institution. He is the president of the Shaybani Society of International Law in Washington, D.C. and is an authority on Islamic law. He has published many books and articles on legal and political problems on Islam and the modern Middle East.

Christine C. Kleinegger is a Ph.D. candidate in the history of women and the family at SUNY Binghamton, where she also earned a M.A. in history. She teaches courses on women and the family and rural America at SUNY Binghamton. Her current research is on the role of farm women in American agriculture between 1880 and

1960, and she has written a bibliography on rural women for the Organization of American Historians.

Stephen J. Kneeshaw is a professor of history and coordinator of faculty development at the School of the Ozarks in Missouri. He also serves as editor of *Teaching History: A Journal of Methods*. He holds the B.A. from the University of Puget Sound and the M.A. and Ph.D. in American diplomatic history from the University of Colorado at Boulder. His teaching and research interests include twentieth-century American diplomatic history and teaching methodologies, and he has published articles on the Kellogg-Briand Pact.

George W. Knepper is professor of history and university historian at the University of Akron. His special field of interest is state and local history. He has been active in many professional organizations and has published widely. His most recent book is *Akron: City at the Summit* (1981).

William A. Koelsch is professor of history and geography at Clark University. He holds a M.A. in geography from Clark and the Ph.D. in American history from the University of Chicago. A principal research interest has been the institutionalization of geography and related disciplines in the late nineteenth and early twentieth centuries in American universities. He has served as Clark's first university archivist and was recently named university historian.

Grégoire Koulischer is a retired official of the International Labour Office, having served for twenty years in Geneva, Latin America, and Africa. Prior to joining the ILO, he was foreign editor of the Belgian Socialist daily *Le Peuple* and associated with various other newspapers, namely with the *New York Times* staff correspondent for Belgium. He holds a doctor's degree in political science from the Free Brussels University.

Marshall R. Kuehl received a B.A. and M.A. from the University of Akron and is presently a Ph.D. candidate at Kent State University in history, where he serves as a teaching fellow. He is working on a biography of Philip C. Jessup.

Olga Llano Kuehl holds a B.M. from Rollins College, a M.M. from Northwestern University, and the D.M.A. from the College-Conservatory of Music of the University of Cincinnati. Her articles have appeared in professional journals and encyclopedias. As a concert pianist she has four recordings and has performed in the United States, Europe, and Latin America. She has a special interest in Spanish music and musicians.

Warren F. Kuehl is professor of history and director of the Center for Peace Studies at the University of Akron. He is the biographer of internationalist, Hamilton Holt, and has published *Seeking World Order: The United States and International Organization to 1920* (1969). He is writing the companion volume for the interwar years. He is the editor of the Library of World Peace Studies, a microform series which reproduces peace and internationalist journals and bibliographical materials (now over 3000 fiche).

Bruce R. Kuniholm is director of undergraduate studies and an assistant professor of public policy studies and history at Duke University, where he received an M.A. in public policy studies, and a M.A. and Ph.D. in history. He taught at Robert College in Istanbul, Turkey, was a member of the Department of State's Policy Planning Staff, and writes on both the history and current problems of United States policy in the Middle East.

Lester D. Langley is professor of history at the University of Georgia. He has a

Ph.D. from the University of Kansas. His teaching fields are American diplomatic and Caribbean history. He has published several works on United States-Latin American relations, including *The United States and the Caribbean, 1900–1970* (1980).

Richard R. Laurence is professor of humanities at Michigan State University. He received his Ph.D. in History and Humanities at Stanford University. His scholarly interests center on the history of the Habsburg monarchy and on the problems of war and peace, topics on which he has published a variety of articles. He has held research and study grants from the Fulbright-Hays program, the Austrian government, and the National Endowment for the Humanities.

Pierre-Henri Laurent is professor of history, Tufts University, and adjunct professor of diplomatic history at the Fletcher School of Law and Diplomacy. His interests are twentieth-century European relations, especially France and the Benelux states. Recent publications appeared in British, French, Swiss, Belgian, Dutch, Canadian and American journals and reviews.

James M. Laux has been a member of the history faculty at the University of Cincinnati since 1957. He has published widely in economic history, with special emphasis on France and on the automobile and aircraft industries.

Marshall M. Lee is an associate professor and chairs the department of history at Pacific University. He holds a Ph.D. in modern European history from the University of Wisconsin-Madison. A diplomatic historian, Lee has published on Weimar Germany's foreign policy, Gustav Stresemann, and the League of Nations. In addition, he is an archives consultant to private business and industry.

Magnus Lemberg is employed by the State Alcohol Monopoly of Finland. He passed his M.B.A. in the Swedish School of Economics in Helsinki in 1965. In 1982 he gained a licentiate-degree of political history at the University of Helsinki. The subject of his research has been the political activities of Hjalmar J. Procopé.

Alan T. Leonhard is an associate professor of political science at the University of New Orleans, where he specializes in the fields of international law and Latin American politics. In these fields he has published articles in the *Inter-American Economic Review, Inter-American Law Review* and other journals. He is coeditor of the *The Enduring Questions of Politics* (1969, rev. ed. 1974) and contributed an essay to David Deener (ed.), *De lege Pactorum* (1970). Dr. Leonhard holds a Ph.D. degree from Duke University.

Richard W. Leopold is the William Smith Mason professor of American history emeritus at Northwestern University. A graduate of Princeton University, he received his doctorate from Harvard University and taught at Harvard from 1937 until he moved to Northwestern in 1948. A specialist in American foreign policy, he is past president of the Organization of American Historians and of the Society for Historians of American Foreign Relations and is a fellow of the Society of American Archivists.

Shong Li-Ling is a professor in the department of history at Shanghai Teachers College. His studies focus on the modern history of China and the Chinese-United States relations. He has published six books and about ninety articles. He has a special interest in Sino-American relations.

Doris H. Linder of the history department, College of San Mateo, holds the Ph.D. in history and Scandinavian studies from the University of Minnesota. Her most recent work has been in modern Scandinavian history and women's history.

John V. Lombardi is a professor of history at Indiana University specializing in the study of Venezuela. He has written a number of books and articles on Venezuelan history and currently is the dean of international programs at Indiana University.

A. William Loos is the former president of the Council on Religion and International Affairs, an organization founded by Andrew Carnegie in 1914 to work for the establishment of international peace. Dr. Loos holds a B.D. degree from Andover Newton Theological School and a Ph.D. in theology from the University of Edinburgh.

Raymond M. Lorantas is an associate professor of history at Drexel University. He has taught twentieth-century world history for over a decade in the United States and in Asia. His writings and lectures have concentrated on symbolic individuals of the twentieth century.

David C. Lukowitz is a professor of modern European history at Hamline University. He holds a M.A. from Michigan State University and the Ph.D. from the University of Iowa. His research interests deal primarily with British pacificism during the interwar period. He travels frequently to Europe and has published a number of articles on British peace societies in the twentieth century.

Michael A. Lutzker is an associate professor of history, as well as director of the Program in Archival Management and Historical Editing at New York University. He received his Ph.D. from Rutgers University and served as a post-doctoral fellow with the Woodrow Wilson Papers, Princeton University. His research interests include war and peace studies, and he has published several articles in these fields. He has served as president of the Conference on Peace Research in History.

James Ross Macdonald is an attorney with the law firm of Roberts & Holland in New York City. He holds M.A., M.A.L.D., and Ph.D. degrees from the Fletcher School of Law and Diplomacy and a J.D. degree from the University of Pennsylvania Law School. He is a frequent contributor to professional journals in the areas of international law and organization and international taxation.

Paul D. Mageli is a freelance writer, translator, and editorial and research assistant. He received a Ph.D. from the University of Chicago in history, having written a dissertation on "The French Radical Party and the Problem of French Relations with Russia, 1917–1939." He has written historical essays for the *Great Events from History* series published by Salem Press and is a regular contributor of book reviews to *Magill's Literary Annual*.

Christian J. Maisch was born in Peru and holds a M.A. and a Ph.D. from the American University. He is currently working on a study of the Inter-American Development Bank, Office of External Relations.

Raymond Manning is a former career official of the International Labour Office and was for some years its archivist. He was a co-author of the UNESCO guide to the archives of organizations in the United Nations system and rapporteur of the Section of Archivists of International Organizations of the International Council on Archives. He has organized the archives of the Inter-Parliamentary Union and of the smallpox eradication program of the World Health Organization and served as archives consultant to the World Intellectual Property Organization.

Sally Marks, who received her doctorate from the University of London, is professor of history at Rhode Island College. In addition to numerous articles about the international history of the post-World War I era, she has published *The Illusion of*

Peace: International Relations in Europe, 1918-1933 (1976) and *Innocent Abroad: Belgium at the Paris Peace Conference of 1919* (1981), which was awarded the George Louis Beer Prize in international history in 1981.

Paul E. Masters, Jr. is an associate professor of political science at West Georgia College. He received the Ph.D. from St. Louis University. His teaching interests include international relations and comparative politics. In addition to contributing articles on international education to such professional journals as *International Studies Notes* and *Southeastern Latin Americanist*, Dr. Masters is currently managing editor of the *Southeastern Political Review*.

William J. Maxwell is president and professor of history at Jersey City State College, where he previously chaired the department of history and served as dean of the School of Arts and Sciences. He holds master's and doctoral degrees in history from Columbia University. He has been a contributor to the *American Quarterly* and the *Pan-African Journal* and has written on the subjects of race relations, higher education, and international arbitration.

George T. Mazuzan is chief historian at the United States Nuclear Regulatory Commission. He holds a M.A. from the University of Vermont and a Ph.D. from Kent State University. He has had varied experience as a teacher, administrator, and archivist and has contributed widely to the scholarly literature in recent American history.

Frank D. McCann is professor of history at the University of New Hampshire. A specialist on Latin America, his principal research and publications have dealt with United States relations with the region, Brazilian diplomacy, and the Brazilian army. His *Brazilian-American Alliance, 1937-1945* (1973) won the 1975 Stuart L. Bernath Prize. He is past president of the New England Council on Latin American Studies and the international Committee on Brazilian Studies.

Lyle A. McGeoch was born in Tanta, Egypt. He is an associate professor of history at Ohio University where he specializes in nineteenth-century European diplomatic history. His Ph.D. is from the University of Pennsylvania. He has contributed to the professional literature on British foreign policy and political biography.

Ian C. McGibbon is senior historian in the Historical Publications Branch of the New Zealand Department of Internal Affairs. The holder of an M.A. from Victoria University of Wellington, he has specialized in the history of New Zealand's international relations and is currently writing the official history of New Zealand's involvement in the Korean War. He is also managing editor of the New Zealand Institute of International Affairs' publication, *New Zealand International Review*.

Porter McKeever has served as director of information of the United States Mission to the UN, 1947-1952, and as an executive officer, Chicago Council on Foreign Relations, the Ford Foundation, and the Committee for Economic Development. He was president of the UN Association of the United States, 1965-1975.

John P. McSweeney is a professor of education at Old Dominion University. He holds a M.A. in School Administration and a Ph.D. in history and philosophy of education from the University of Nebraska. He is a frequent contributor to professional journals. His special interests are in the history of American education, middle school education, and school communications.

Richard Megargee is a professor of policy and strategy at the United States Naval War College.

Heinz K. Meier, a native of Zurich, Switzerland, is dean of the School of Arts and Letters and professor of history at Old Dominion University. He has published two books on U.S.-Swiss relations. A former president of the Swiss American Historical Society and editor of its *Newsletter*, Dr. Meier has been active in many ways in furthering the cause of Swiss history and culture in the United States.

Joyce Laverty Miller currently develops corporate historical resources for use by management in a high technology firm. She holds the Ph.D. in history from Bryn Mawr College and has previously used her historical training as a university instructor, a news analyst, and a communications specialist. Her most recent scholarly article, "The Syrian Revolt of 1925," appeared in the *International Journal of Middle East Studies* (1977). At the present time, she is primarily interested in corporate history as a valuable decision-making resource.

Marion S. Miller is an assistant professor of history at the University of Illinois, Chicago. She is an author of various articles on nineteenth-century Italian social and political history in *The Historical Journal, Eighteenth Century Studies, Canadian Review of Studies in Nationalism, Proceedings of the Consortium on Revolutionary Europe* (1975, 1977). She is also a contributor to the *Dictionary of Italian History*, edited by Frank Coppa, which is being published by Greenwood Press.

Virginia N. Mills is professor emeritus of political science, Frostburg State College. She earned her Ph.D. in international organization and administration at American University. For nearly nine years she worked in Brazil in educational social work. She served some nine years on the staff of the National Education Association in Washington, D.C., mostly writing and editing. She has taught international law, international organization, and comparative government courses and now resides in Roanoke, Virginia.

Wilson D. Miscamble is a native of Brisbane, Australia, and until recently was North American analyst in the Office of National Assessments, Canberra, Australia. He has published a number of essays on the foreign policy of the Truman administration. Dr. Miscamble holds a Ph.D. degree from the University of Notre Dame.

Kell Mitchell, Jr. is associate professor of history at Memphis State University where he teaches the diplomatic history of the United States and the history of women in America. Dr. Mitchell received his Ph.D. from the University of Georgia.

D. E. Moggridge is professor of economics at the University of Toronto. He holds a Ph.D. from the University of Cambridge where he taught from 1967 to 1975. He is joint managing editor of the Royal Economic Society's thirty-volume edition of *The Collected Writings of John Maynard Keynes* now nearing completion. He has also published *British Monetary Policy, 1924–1931* (1972).

Anne Tucker Moore is a professor of history at Campbell University. She holds the M.A. and Ph.D. from the University of North Carolina, Chapel Hill. Her specialty is modern European history, and she wrote her dissertation on the French role in the formulation of the Schuman Plan, the forerunner of the European Economic Community. She has spent several summers in Europe researching this topic and has read papers on it at meetings of the Southern Historical Association. She is currently working in Cape Fear Valley history and is a member of the North Carolina China Council.

Jamie W. Moore is professor of history at The Citadel. He holds a Ph.D. from the University of North Carolina, Chapel Hill. His interests are diplomatic and public history and national security policy. His most recent publications have been in the areas of the origins of national security thought, deterrence theory, and policy development in public agencies.

Charles Morley is professor emeritus of history at Ohio State University, where he taught Russian and Polish history from 1944 to 1981. He received his B.A. from Ohio State, his M.A. and Ph.D. from Wisconsin, and studied one year at the University of Warsaw. A frequent traveler and researcher in Eastern Europe, his books and articles reflect his interest in this area and especially Russo-Polish relations in the early part of the nineteenth century.

Raymond T. Multerer is part of the faculty of the Colegio de los Montañas, (College of the Mountains) of the University of Puerto Rico having held several teaching and administrative positions in the United States and Puerto Rico. In addition to an Ed.M in curriculum and instruction, a M.A. and a Ph.D. in Latin American and Modern European History, all from SUNY at Buffalo, and an M.P.A. in personnel from the University of Puerto Rico, he has done post-doctoral studies in higher education. His work has involved innovation in the preparation of educational materials and programs and consultation as well as research in Mexican and Puerto Rican social history.

Charles E. Neu is professor of history at Brown University. He received his B.A. from Northwestern University and his Ph.D. from Harvard University. A specialist in twentieth-century American foreign policy, he is the author of two books and many essays. He has received fellowships from Harvard University's Charles Warren Center, the American Council of Learned Societies, and the Guggenheim Foundation. He is currently writing a biography of Colonel Edward M. House, Woodrow Wilson's intimate political adviser.

Frank A. Ninkovich is an assistant professor of history at St. John's University. His published work has focused on the cultural and ideological aspects of American foreign policy, notably his book *The Diplomacy of Ideas* (1981).

Ruth V. Noble holds degrees from Wellesley College and Columbia University. She has had a varied career as teacher, librarian, writer, editor, and publisher. She is joint author of *Preliminary Memoranda for Conference on International Cultural, Educational and Scientific Exchanges* (1947). She founded Bershire Publishing Company and was president and editor-in-chief. She is represented in several Who's Who's, including *Who's Who of American Women, Dictionary of International Biography*, and *Foremost Women in Communications*.

Emiliana P. Noether, a native of Italy, holds M.A. and Ph.D. degrees from Columbia University and is professor of history at the University of Connecticut. A specialist in modern Italian history, she was a fellow of the Bunting Institute, Radcliffe College, in 1961–62 and senior research scholar in Italy under the Fulbright-Hays program in 1965–66 and 1982. She has published widely and has been active in the American Historical Association, the Society for Italian Historical Studies, and the New England Historical Association.

Ralph D. Nurnberger is a legislative liaison officer for the American Israel Public Affairs Committee (AIPAC) and a lecturer in diplomatic history and international relations at Georgetown University. He previously served as foreign policy adviser to Senator James B. Pearson, professional staff member of the Senate Foreign Relations Committee, and as a senior fellow at the Georgetown Center for Strategic and

International Studies (CSIS). He is the coauthor of *Congressional Leadership* (1981) and coeditor of *The Growing Power of Congress* (1981). His Ph.D. in diplomatic history is from Georgetown University.

Michael O'Callaghan, writer and lecturer, studied in his native Ireland, in Austria, and at the Sorbonne, and he holds a degree in civil engineering from the National University of Ireland. As industrial specialist with the ILO and as consultant to the UN on the environment and human settlements, he has been active in promoting international collaboration. Now in consultancy practice in Geneva, he is particularly interested in the historical background to current affairs.

Gary B. Ostrower is the author of *Collective Insecurity: The United States and the League of Nations During the Early Thirties* (1979). He has also written a number of articles on internationalism and international organization. Having received his Ph.D. from the University of Rochester, he has taught at Vassar College and has been a visting lecturer at the University of Pennsylvania. He currently teaches at Alfred University.

Emmett E. Panzella is a professor of history at Point Park College. His Ph.D. in history is from Kent State University. Dr. Panzella has done extensive work in computer science, electronics, library science, and educational communications technology to provide the foundation for his special interest: the development of multidisciplined academic education, linking the technical and the liberal arts.

Aubrey L. Parkman is a professor of history at Tufts University. He holds the Ph.D. in history from the University of Rochester. His special interests include American diplomatic and political history. In addition to his biography, *David Jayne Hill* (1975), Dr. Parkman has published *Army Engineers in New England, 1775-1975* (1978).

Edward B. Parsons is professor of history at Miami University. He received his Ph.D. from SUNY at Buffalo. Topics explored in his publications include the skill and subtlety of Theodore Roosevelt's diplomacy as a peacemaker and the effects of Allied-American economic and naval rivalry on the conduct of World War I and the Paris Peace Conference of 1919.

David S. Patterson is a historian in the Department of State. He holds M.A. and Ph.D. degrees in history from the University of California, Berkeley. He has taught diplomatic history and war/peace subjects at several universities and currently teaches part-time at the University of Maryland. His research interests are national security policy, arms control, peace movements, and international organizations. He is author of *Toward a Warless World: The Travail of the American Peace Movement, 1887-1914* (1976) and has contributed many articles to professional journals.

Neale J. Pearson is an associate professor of political science at Texas Tech University. He is the author of many articles on agrarian reform, Marxist groups, political parties, peasant and trade union pressure groups in Brazil, Costa Rica, Guatemala, Honduras, Nicaragua, Panama and Peru. He contributed articles on Chile, Peru, and Venezuela during the past five years to the *Annual Yearbook* of the *Encyclopedia Americana*.

Vratislav Pechota holds the LL.D and Ph.D. from Charles University, Prague. He has taught and practiced international law and published books and articles on the United Nations and other subjects. He teaches international law at the New York University School of Law.

George Peden is a lecturer in economic and social history at Bristol University. He holds an M.A. from Dundee University and a D.Phil. from Oxford University. Dr. Peden's most recent work has been on J. M. Keynes and the British Treasury, and his publications include *British Rearmament and the Treasury 1932-1939* (1979).

Monty N. Penkower is professor and chairperson of the Department of History at Touro College. A Columbia University Ph.D., his numerous publications include *The Federal Writers' Project* (1977) and *The Jews Were Expendable: Free World Diplomacy During the Holocaust* (1983). Professor Penkower is also a consultant to the U.S. Holocaust Memorial Council, the National Jewish Resource Center, and the Holocaust Survivors' Memorial Foundation.

Gilberte Perotin, following studies at the Paris Ecole des Chartes and varied library and museum installation experience, is the archivist of the International Telecommunication Union, Geneva, and was first president of the Section of Archivists of International Organizations of the International Council on Archives, co-author of the UNESCO guide to the archives of organizations in the United Nations system, and has carried out various archives and records management consultancy missions in other organizations, including the Council of Europe.

Nikolaj Petersen is an associate professor of political science at the University of Aarhus, Denmark. He has written books and numerous contributions to professional journals on strategic affairs, foreign policy, political attitudes, and Scandinavian foreign and defense policy.

Sara Pienaar was born in England and has lived in South Africa for the last eighteen years. She holds a M.A. degree in international relations and a Ph.D. in history from the University of Witwatersrand, Johannesburg. She is at present teaching high school history and preparing a book on South Africa's involvement with the League of Nations.

Walter E. Pittman, Jr. is a professor of history at Mississippi University for Women. He has three degrees in history and one in chemistry and works primarily in the history of science and technology. He has published a biography of *Richmond P. Hobson* (1981). He is particularly interested in changing military technology and its effects upon society and upon society and upon international relations, Dr. Pittman also serves as a consultant in mining technology for the U.S. Bureau of Mines.

Forrest C. Pogue is director of the Dwight D. Eisenhower Institute for Historical Research, National Museum of American History, Smithsonian Institution. For eighteen years, he headed the George C. Marshall Research Center (after 1964 the Marshall Library). He is completing the last book of a four-volume biography of General George C. Marshall. His Ph.D. is from Clark University. He was an American exchange fellow in international relations at the University of Paris, 1937-38.

David L. Porter, professor of history and political science at William Penn College, holds an M.A. from Ohio University and the Ph.D. from Pennsylvania State University. The recipient of grants from the National Science Foundation, National Endowment of the Humanities, and Eleanor Roosevelt Institute, he has published two books on the U.S. Congress and numerous articles on diplomatic, political, and sports history in popular and academic journals.

Russell Porter, professor emeritus of theatre of the University of Denver, went there in 1946 to organize the department of radio, but in 1950-51 he took leave to become executive director of the World Affairs Institute sponsored by the Social Science Foundation. He continued for some time as the Foundation's media director. Again, in 1962–64 he was appointed executive director of the year-long symposium marking the centennial celebration of the University of Denver.

John P. Posey is professor of history and he chairs the international studies department at Saint Joseph's College. He holds a M.A. and a Ph.D. in history from the University of Georgia. He has published articles in American diplomatic and Russian history. As director of a required course in Afro-Asian culture, he has participated in post-doctoral study in Egypt and India. He also administers study abroad programs and has directed ones in Western Europe, the Soviet Union, and the People's Republic of China.

Salvatore Prisco, III is an associate professor of humanities at Stevens Institute of Technology where he specializes in diplomatic history and international relations. He holds a Ph.D. in history from Rutgers University. Dr. Prisco's most recent book is *An Introduction to Psychohistory* (1980). He also teaches courses in American social history, urban affairs, and psychohistory.

Noel H. Pugach is an associate professor of history at the University of New Mexico, where he specializes in United States diplomatic history. Dr. Pugach, who received his Ph.D. from the University of Wisconsin, is the author of *Paul S. Reinsch: Open Door Diplomat in Action* (1979). He has also published numerous scholarly articles and book reviews in leading historical journals.

Rosemary Rainbolt holds a M.A. degree from Antioch University and has taught at Carnegie-Mellon University. She has a special interest in the history of peace movements.

Willard Range is professor emeritus of political science at the University of Georgia. He holds a M.A. from the University of Georgia and a Ph.D. from the University of North Carolina at Chapel Hill. During his academic career he specialized in international politics and organization and was especially interested in the basic views on foreign affairs of such managers as F. D. Roosevelt, Nehru, Nasser, and Sukarno.

Armin Rappaport is a professor of history at the University of California, San Diego. His field of research is twentieth-century American foreign policy and diplomatic history. He is a past president of the Society for Historians of American Foreign Policy and a past editor of the Society's journal, *Diplomatic History*. He has written *A History of American Diplomacy* (1975) and other works.

Alan Raucher is an associate professor of history at Wayne State University. He holds a Ph.D. in history from the University of Pennsylvania and has taught at several American universities and at the American Studies Research Centre in Hyderabad, India. He has published work on business history, intellectual history, and foreign relations.

Daryl L. Revoldt received his B.A. and M.A. from Miami University and his Ph.D. from the University of Akron. He has taught at the University of Akron and Hiram College. He devotes his energies to business interests and community activities.

David C. Riede is a professor of history and head of the Department of General Studies at the University of Akron. He received his B.A., M.A. and Ph.D. degrees from the University of Iowa. His major fields of interest are twentieth-century Europe, Modern Europe since 1500, nineteenth- and twentieth-century history of the Catholic Church, and National Socialism.

Marc Riga, a native of Belgium, is a Licentiate in Political and Social Sciences from the Catholic University at Leuven. He has been a collaborator at the Belgian Prime Ministers' Services and is now an associate researcher at the Department of Political Sciences, Division of International Relations, of the Catholic University at Leuven.

Thomas W. Robinson is Sun Yat-sen professor of China studies at the School of Foreign Service, Georgetown University. After receiving the Ph.D. in international relations and Soviet studies at Columbia University, he was a member of the Soviet Science department of the Rand Corporation, fellow at the Council on Foreign Relations, and professor at the National War College. He has taught at American universities on the East and West coasts. He is a leading student of Chinese and Soviet politics and foreign policies, Asian and general international relations, forcasting and national security studies, and has published widely in all these fields.

William R. Rock, whose doctorate is from Duke University and whose research and publications are primarily in British appeasement and the origins of World War I, is professor of history at Bowling Green State University. He has written *Neville Chamberlain* (1969).

James R. Roebuck, Jr. is an assistant professor of history at Drexel University. He is a native of Philadelphia and holds a B.A. with honors from Virginia Union University and a M.A. and a Ph.D. from the University of Virginia.

Nancy A. Rosenblatt (deceased) was a lecturer in the department of history at the Pennsylvania State University from 1965 to 1981. She received her Ph.D. and M.A. degrees in European history from the University of California, Berkeley, and her B.A. from Swarthmore College. In her research she focused on nineteenth century Spain, with a special interest on political, church, and woman's issues.

Malcolm Saunders is a tutor in Australian history at the James Cook University of North Queensland. He holds a Ph.D. in Australian history from the Flinders University of South Australia. He has published several articles in professional journals on the peace movement in Australia in general and the anti-Vietnam War movement in particular. His most recent research has been in the area of the Australian colonies' participation in imperial wars during the late nineteenth century.

Paula Scalingi, author of *The European Parliament: The Three-Decade Search for a United Europe* (1980) and articles on the European Economic Community, resides in McLean, Virginia. She holds a Ph.D. in recent European history from Florida State University.

Paul J. Scheips is a senior historian in the U.S. Army Center of Military History in Washington, D.C. He holds an M.A. from the University of Chicago, where he had courses under Quincy Wright, and a Ph.D. from American University. He is a generalist in American history, with special interests in civil-military relations. He is currently collaborating on a comprehensive history of the U.S. federal military role in civil disturbances.

William J. Schmidt is professor of theology at Saint Peter's College, Jersey City, the first ordained Protestant scholar to hold the post at this Jesuit school. With a Ph.D. from Columbia University, he specializes in American church history as well as the theology and history of the ecumenical movement. He has a particular interest in ecumenical biography.

Hans A. Schmitt received his graduate training at the University of Chicago. His relevant work includes *The Path to European Union* (1962), *European Union from Hitler to DeGaulle* (1969), and "French Politicians and the European Community," in Sidney N. Fisher (ed.), *France and the European Community* (1964). Since 1971 he has been professor of history at the University of Virginia.

James C. Schneider is an assistant professor of history with the Division of Behavioral and Cultural Sciences at the University of Texas at San Antonio. He holds both a M.A. and a Ph.D. in history from the University of Wisconsin. His interests include the role of public opinion in the political process, modern American history, and American foreign relations.

Franklin D. Scott is professor of history emeritus, Northwestern University, and curator of the Nordic Collections in the Honnold Library of the Claremont Colleges. He has written a number of books especially in the fields of Scandinavian history and immigration, including *Scandinavia* (1975), and *Sweden: The Nation's History* (1977).

Roy V. Scott is professor of history at Mississippi State University. He is a graduate of the University of Illinois, Urbana, where he studied under the late Fred A. Shannon. He is the author or editor of four books and some thirty articles on agricultural and railroad history. In 1978–1979 he served as president of the Agricultural History Society.

Barbara M. Shaver is acting associate dean, San Diego State University, Calexico, California, where she also teaches. Her Ph.D. in United States diplomatic history is from the University of Colorado, her M.A. from the University of New Mexico. She has worked in Mexico and been a faculty member at the Catholic University and the University of Chile, Valparaiso. Her research interests and publications are in Latin America, diplomatic history, and women's scholarship.

William I. Shorrock is a professor and he chairs the department of history at Cleveland State University, where he specializes in European and diplomatic history. He holds the M.A. and Ph.D. from the University of Wisconsin, Madison. His most recent work has been in French imperial history and Franco-Italian diplomacy between the two world wars.

Robert C. R. Siekmann is research officer in the public international law department of the T.M.C. Asser Institute for International Law, The Hague. He holds a M.A. in Slavonic languages and a M.A. in law, both from the University of Leiden. His main interests include the documentation of Netherlands state practice on international law and the study of UN peacekeeping operations.

Rodney M. Sievers is associate professor of history at Humboldt State University. He holds a Ph.D. from the University of Virginia. In 1975 he was a National Endowment for the Humanities fellow at the University of Michigan.

Keith Sinclair is professor of history at the University of Auckland. He has published two biographies, one on *Walter Nash* (1976), and several other works of history, including the *Pelican History of New Zealand* (1959, rev. ed., 1980). He has also published several volumes of verse and a children's book. He is at present researching the origins of a New Zealand sense of national identity.

Harold L. Smith received his Ph.D. from the University of Iowa and is currently an associate professor of history at the University of Houston, Victoria Campus. His primary interests are in the social and intellectual history of modern Britain. He has published extensively in professional journals in both areas. He has made frequent research trips to England supported by grants from several sources, including the American Philosophical Society.

Michael D. Smith holds a Ph.D. in Russian and modern European history from Florida State University. He is the author of *Poets and Poems of the First World War: The English* (1978).

John Stevens is lecturer and Aikido instructor at Tohoku College of Social Welfare in Sendai, Japan. He has published numerous books and articles on various aspects of oriental culture and the harmonization of Eastern and Western thought.

O. Carlos Stoetzer is a native of Argentina and holds a Dr. iur. degree from the University of Freiburg (Germany) and a Ph.D. in international relations from Georgetown University. He was a civil servant of the Organization of American States (1950–1961), including acting secretary of the Inter-American Institute of Agricultural Sciences. As professor of Latin American and African history at Fordham University, he specializes on Latin American thought.

Ralph A. Stone is professor of history at Sangamon State University, where he teaches courses on recent American history, U.S. foreign policy, and social movements. He has written *The Irreconcilables and the Fight Against the League of Nations* (1970) and has edited *Woodrow Wilson and the League of Nations: Why America's Rejection?* (1967).

Ralph Summy lectures in political science at the University of Queensland, Australia. A graduate of Harvard University, he also holds a M.A. from Sydney University. His publications are mainly in the areas of nonviolent politics and contemporary American political thought. He edits the quarterly, *Social Alternatives.* Currently he is engaged in jointly writing a history of the Australian peace movements.

Marvin Swartz is an associate professor of history at the University of Massachusetts/Amherst. He holds a Ph.D. from Yale University. Among his publications is a book on *The Union of Democratic Control in British Politics during the First World War* (1971). His special interest is modern British politics and foreign policy.

Ronald E. Swerczek is assistant chief for diplomatic records in the Legislative and Diplomatic Branch of the National Archives. He holds the Ph.D. from the University of Iowa.

Richard N. Swift holds the B.A., M.A., and Ph.D. degrees from Harvard University. He is professor of politics at New York University, where he has been a member of the faculty since 1949. He has been a visiting lecturer at both Harvard and Yale Universities, is the author of *World Affairs and the College Curriculum* (1969) and *International Law: Current and Classic*, (1959), and edited the first 15 volumes of the *Annual Review of United Nations Affairs.*

Zofia Sywak is the director of Rhode Island Historical Records. Dr. Sywak holds the Ph.D. degree from St. Johns University, has edited *Paderewski* (1980), is co-author of *Poles in America: Bicentennial Essays* (1978), and has published articles and reviews.

Enzo Tagliacozzo was born in Naples, Italy. He is presently professor [f.z. ob] of the history of parties in the department of political science of the University of Florence. He has published several historical books and essays, principally on nineteenth- and twentieth-century Italy. He contributed essays and articles to several historical magazines.

Arnold H. Taylor is professor of history and chairs the department of history at Howard University. He holds a M.A. in history from Howard and the Ph.D. from

Catholic University. Among his publications are *American Diplomacy and the Narcotics Traffic* (1969) and *Travail and Triumph: Black Life and Culture in the South Since 1865* (1976).

Sandra C. Taylor is an associate professor of history at the University of Utah. Her Ph.D. is from the University of Colorado, where she worked in American diplomatic history, emphasizing American-East Asian relations. Her research interests include American Protestant missionaries in Japan and the relocation of Japanese-Americans during World War II. She has just completed a biography of Sidney Lewis Gulick.

Philip Terzian is assistant editor of the editorial pages at the *Los Angeles Times*. A native of the Washington, D.C. area, he studied at Villanova and Oxford, and has served as assistant editor of *The New Republic* and associate editor of *The Lexington Herald*. During 1978–79, he was a member of the Policy Planning Staff at the Department of State.

J.W.H. Thijssen is a research associate in the department of public international law of the T.M.C. Asser Institute at The Hague. He holds a M.A. in public law and international relations from the University of Utrecht.

Jack Ray Thomas is professor and vice-chair of the history department at Bowling Green State University. His Ph.D. is in Latin American history from Ohio State University. He has published two books and twelve articles on Latin American history, focusing upon nineteenth- and twentieth-century Chile, Latin American socialism, and Latin American historiography. His latest book, a *Biographical Dictionary of Latin American History* will be published by Greenwood Press.

Beverly C. Thompson is an educator and consultant with a M.A. in English from the University of Missouri and a Ph.D. in higher educational administration from Arizona State University. She has directed North Central Association accreditation studies, assisted in the evaluation of the Institute of Technology and Advanced Studies, Monterrey, Mexico, and directed a Center for Institutional Research and Development in Phoenix, Arizona.

J. A. Thompson chairs the department of history at the University of Kentucky. He holds a Ph.D. from Stanford University. The editor of *The Collapse of the British Liberal Party* (1969) and the author of *The Modern British Monarchy* (1971), he is now preparing a new history of the famous peace ballot of 1934–35.

Kenneth W. Thompson is director of the Miller Center of Public Affairs at the University of Virginia. He holds the M.A. and Ph.D. in political science from the University of Chicago and has received nine honorary doctorates. He was formerly vice-president of the Rockefeller Foundation. He is the author of twenty books and a contributor to fifty others.

J. Tillapaugh is associate professor of history and chairs the faculty of history and government at the University of Texas of the Permian Basin. He holds bachelor and master's degrees from the University of Oregon and a Ph.D. in history from Northwestern University. A specialist in twentieth-century United States foreign and domestic affairs, his interests include relations with Latin America and historic preservation.

C. David Tompkins, professor of history at Northeastern Illinois University and a native of Battle Creek, MI, studied at Northwestern, Wisconsin, and Michigan with Richard W. Leopold, Alexander DeConde, and Bradford Perkins. A biographer of Arthur H. Vandenberg, he is working on Vandenberg and bi-partisan foreign policy and Franklin D. Roosevelt and the origins of the United Nations and teaches courses in diplomacy, biography, and recent American history.

Eugene P. Trani is vice-chancellor for academic affairs and professor of history at the University of Missouri-Kansas City. He holds a M.A. and Ph.D. in American history from Indiana University. A student of diplomatic and political history, Dr. Trani has contributed significantly to the field of American history and to the understanding of diplomatic relationships with the USSR. In 1981, he served as a senior Fulbright lecturer at Moscow State University.

David F. Trask is the chief historian, U.S. Army Center of Military History in Washington. His M.A. and Ph.D. are from Harvard University. Formerly director of the Office of the Historian, U.S. Department of State, and professor at several universities, he has published a number of books and articles on the relations between force and diplomacy in American history, the most recent being *The War with Spain in 1898* (1981).

Judith Ann Trolander is an associate professor of history at the University of Minnesota, Duluth. She holds M.S.L.S., M.A. and Ph.D. degrees from Case Western Reserve University. Her publications include *Settlement Houses and the Great Depression* (1975) and articles relating to social welfare history in social work and history publications. She is currently working on a history of settlement houses, tentatively titled, *Permanence Amidst Social Change: From Settlement Houses to Neighborhood Centers, 1939–1970*.

Brian Urquhart is under secretary-general for Special Political Affairs, United Nations. The biographer of Dag Hammarskjöld, he holds a doctor of laws from Yale University.

Daun van Ee is executive editor of *The Papers of Dwight David Eisenhower*. He is a Viet Nam combat veteran and holds a M.A. and a Ph.D. in history from Johns Hopkins University. His interests are in the fields of American military and legal history.

J. B. van Hall was born in Amsterdam. He studied law at the University of Amsterdam and was director of the library of the Royal Tropical Institute in Amsterdam and of the library of the Peace Palace in The Hague. He retired in 1980.

Richard Veatch is professor of political science at the University of Winnipeg. He holds master's degrees in history and political science from Indiana University and the University of California, Berkeley, and a doctorate in political science from the University of Geneva. His principal research interests are in international relations and international organization in the 1920s and 1930s.

W. Warren Wagar is professor of history at the State University of New York at Binghamton, where he teaches the intellectual history of modern Europe and future studies. Holder of a Ph.D. from Yale University, he has published thirteen books, including a study of the thought of H. G. Wells and an anthology of Wells's journalism and prophetic writings.

J. Samuel Walker is associate historian of the U.S. Nuclear Regulatory Commission in Washington. He received his Ph.D. from the University of Maryland. He is the author of *Henry A. Wallace and American Foreign Policy* (1976) and coeditor of *American Foreign Relations: A Historiographical Review* (1981).

Solomon Wank is professor of history at Franklin and Marshall College where he teaches nineteenth- and twentieth-century European history. He received his Ph.D. from Columbia University and has published numerous articles on Austro-

Hungarian and European diplomacy as well as *Doves and Diplomats: Foreign Offices and Peace Movements in Europe and America in the Twentieth Century* (1978).

H. Landon Warner is professor emeritus of history at Kenyon College. He holds a M.A. and Ph.D. from Harvard University. He is the biographer of John H. Clarke and has published books on the progressive era. The peace movement in the United States in the 1920s has been one of the areas of his special interest and research.

Bernerd C. Weber is professor of history at the University of Alabama. He received his M.A. and his Ph.D. degrees from the University of California, Berkeley. In 1956–57 he served as senior Fulbright scholar at the Royal University of Malta. His most recent work has been in the political history of Europe during the sixteenth and seventeenth centuries.

Robert H. Whealey is associate professor of history at Ohio University and took advanced degrees at the University of Michigan, with additional study at Oxford University. He has written articles and reviews and has a special interest in the Spanish Civil War and the diplomatic history of the Nazi era. In 1977–78 Dr. Whealey held a research fellowship in Madrid from the Joint U.S.-Spanish Committee for Educational and Cultural Affairs. Peace questions have been a special interest for twenty years.

Harold B. Whiteman, Jr. is president and professor of history at Sweet Briar College. He holds the B.A. and Ph.D. degrees from Yale University, where he wrote a political biography of Norman H. Davis for his dissertation. He also edited a volume of Charles Seymour's *Letters from the Paris Peace Conference* (1965) and teaches in the field of American diplomatic history.

Donald R. Whitnah is professor and chairs the department of history, University of Northern Iowa. He earned the Ph.D. degree from the University of Illinois and teaches courses in U.S. diplomatic, constitutional, and administrative history. Author of *A History of the United States Weather Bureau* (1961), *Safer Skyways: Federal Control of Aviation, 1926–1966* (1967), he is editor of a forthcoming book, *Government Agencies*, for Greenwood Press and has completed a book manuscript on U.S.-Austrian relations since 1945.

William C. Widenor is associate professor of history at the University of Illinois, Urbana-Champaign. He spent eight years as a foreign service officer before continuing his education in diplomatic history at the University of California at Berkeley, where he received both his M.A. and a Ph.D. degree. Dr. Widenor's first book, *Henry Cabot Lodge and the Search for an American Foreign Policy* (1980) received the Organization of American Historians' Frederick Jackson Turner award.

J. Patrick Wildenberg is an archivist at the Herbert Hoover Presidential Library. He holds a M.A. degree in history from the University of Maryland. He has held offices in both state and regional archival organizations.

F. Roy Willis is professor of history at the University of California, Davis. He holds a B.A. from King's College, Cambridge, and a Ph.D. from Stanford University, and has been awarded fellowships by the Rockefeller and Guggenheim Foundations. He has published several books on European integration, with special emphasis on France, Germany, and Italy, and is currently working on regional economic development in France.

Kurt Wimer is professor emeritus of Pennsylvania State College at East Stroudsburg. He chaired the department of political science at that college and holds M.A.

and Ph.D. degrees from New York University. He is an expert on Woodrow Wilson and has written widely on Wilson's struggle over the League of Nations. His most recent contribution is in *Woodrow Wilson and a Revolutionary World* ed., A. S. Link (1982).

Roger Wines is associate professor of modern European history at Fordham University. He holds an M.A. and a Ph.D. from Columbia University and has been a Fulbright scholar at the University of Wuerzburg. His publications in learned journals and books have dealt with topics in modern history, most recently an edition and translation of Leopold von Ranke's ideas on the nature of historical study.

Alan M. Winkler is an associate professor of history at the University of Oregon. He holds a Ph.D. in history from Yale University and has taught at Yale and at Helsinki University in Finland. He is author of *The Politics of Propaganda: The Office of War Information, 1942–1945* (1978) and is currently working on a number of projects dealing with the recent American past.

Willem G. Zeylstra is a former ambassador of The Netherlands, having as such represented his country in Ecuador, Zaire, Australia, and Nigeria. He holds a LL.M. from Amsterdam University and a Ph.D. in economics from the Free University in Amsterdam. Since 1978, Dr. Zeylstra has been active in affairs of foreign trade, development cooperation, and international law, serving as an adviser to academic and other interests.

Martha Moore Ziegler is assistant dean of the School of Arts and Letters and an assistant professor of history at Old Dominion University. She holds the Ph.D. from the University of Virginia.

Carolyn J. Zinn is academic dean and professor of political science at Shepherd College. For the previous ten years, she has chaired the department of political science at Arkansas State University. She holds a Ph.D. in political science from West Virginia University and studied as a Fulbright scholar at the Free University of Brussels.

ABOUT THE EDITOR

WARREN F. KUEHL is Professor of History and Director of the Center for Peace Studies at the University of Akron. He has studied the evolution of internationalist ideas and efforts for over thirty years. Kuehl is the author of *Hamilton Holt: Journalist, Internationalist, Educator; Seeking World Order: The United States and International Organization to 1920; Dissertations in History: An Index of Dissertations Completed in History Departments of the United States and Canadian Universities, 1873–1960* and *1961–June 1970*; introductions to several books; and articles which have appeared in *World Affairs Quarterly*, the *AHA Newsletter*, and *Diplomatic History*.